DATE			

TO RENEW THIS BOOK
CALL 275-5367.

● THE BAKER & TAYLOR CO.

Kissinger
ON THE COUCH

PHYLLIS SCHLAFLY
AND
CHESTER WARD
Rear Admiral, U.S. Navy (Ret.)

ARLINGTON HOUSE·PUBLISHERS
NEW ROCHELLE, N. Y.

MANUFACTURED IN THE UNITED STATES OF AMERICA

Library of Congress Cataloging in Publication Data

Schlafly, Phyllis.
    Kissinger on the couch.

    1.   Kissinger, Henry Alfred.   2.   United States--
Foreign relations--1969-1974.   I.   Ward, Chester Charles,
joint author.   II.   Title.

E840.8.K58S34   973.924'092'4 [B]   74-20963

ISBN 0-87000-216-3

Contents

No, it is not any difficulties of perception that the West is suffering, but a desire not to know, an emotional preference for the pleasant over the unpleasant.

—Aleksandr Solzhenitsyn, 1973

Throughout this book, all emphasis is added by the authors unless otherwise indicated. The reader will find a glossary of military, diplomatic, and technical terms at the back of this book.

Kissinger

ON THE COUCH

1

Look beneath all his brilliance and sophistication. Look through his many-splendored media-projected public images. By sheer numbers and variety, they seem to be trying to tell us something. The Henry Kissinger everybody knows is the superstar-salesman of shuttle-diplomacy, the Nobel Peace Prize winner, the "Prince Metternich of the West Wing," the theoretician of the "Pentagonal Equilibrium of Power," "our hero," the "man most admired by most Americans," the former escort of world-publicized jet-set glamour girls. And, finally after five years in power, *Time* bestowed upon him the accolade of "the world's indispensable man" and the cover of *Newsweek* endowed him with the flying attributes of Superman.

Henry Kissinger and the media were partners in the creation, crafting, and proliferation of all these images. But as to one special concept, he himself was the sole creator: Henry Kissinger, "the Lone Cowboy." "This romantic, surprising character suits me, because being alone has always been part of my style, of my technique," he said.

Does this cumulation of images effectively conceal a secret substance? Could the concealed reality of Kissinger be a Kissinger who has lost touch with reality? Suppose that Henry Kissinger is, in the common parlance, "some kind of a nut or something." That so-often-burlesqued phrase is uniquely expressive of two distinct possibilities. In Kissinger's case, these approach uncomfortably close to being, respectively, a fair probability and a high probability.

The undesirability of having a "nut" exercise so much power over the destiny of a great nation, and even over the world, is obvious. But

11

far worse has happened, even in our own century. Consider Adolf Hitler or Josif Vissarionovich Dzhugashvili Stalin. Their aberrations involved macabre and malevolent aspects far beyond the customary connotation of "nut," which is usually more good-naturedly derisory than condemnatory.

The changes which Henry Kissinger has wrought in the world have been generally accepted as "good." He brought the world from an era of confrontation into an era of negotiation. He terminated the Cold War and substituted the detente he negotiated with the Kremlin along with the SALT I Agreements at the Moscow Summit in May 1972.

But SALT I enshrined and publicized to all the world the strategic inferiority of the United States to the Soviet Union, and this "new relationship of forces" soon revolutionized the pre-Kissinger world. The prestigious International Institute for Strategic Studies in London evaluated the Arabs' use of the "oil weapon" in October 1973 as bestowing "the greatest shock, the most potent sense of a new era, of any event in recent years." It was Kissinger's SALTed detente which generated that new era by destroying the credibility of the U.S. nuclear umbrella to protect the great industrial nations of the Free World, and by establishing the credibility of a Soviet nuclear umbrella to protect the militarily weak Arabs from retaliation.

The huge increase in oil prices caused economic repercussions which spawned governmental upheavals in all major NATO nations. Within months, 1974 became known as "The Year Europe Lost Its Head." The heads of all major European nations were replaced. Before Kissinger and his detente, the Free World nations had a Cold War, but hard currencies. They had some inflation, but only in the controllable degree which accompanies increases in Gross National Product. Subsequent to Kissinger and SALT, every great Western industrial nation slid into double-digit inflation, the disappearance of governmental stability, and a loss of confidence in national security.

The only beneficiaries, other than the oil-rich Arabs, are the Soviets themselves. Their currency has not been devalued, they suffer no inflation, and their governmental stability is more assured than ever. They have reaped huge windfall profits from the increase in the value of their gold hoard and from the real wealth they can get from the West at favorable exchange rates and on credit. Everything Dr. Kissinger touches turns out very much like his great wheat deal.

If Kissinger is indeed a "nut"—even of a type that would be relatively harmless in a position of less power—would not the United States, and especially the new President, be better off to face it now rather than too late? Already Henry Kissinger and Leonid Brezhnev are working in close concert to render their version of detente irreversible.

The possibility certainly merits consideration—even if only because Dr. Kissinger has himself toyed with this diagnosis over a period of many years. He has often coyly referred to his "megalomania" and his "paranoia." Such self-psychoanalysis may be significant; the Doctor knows himself very well and is deeply impressed. Even the most rabidly enthusiastic members of the Kissinger cult accept this potential, and do not too drastically damn Kissinger's critics for exploiting it. For example, Max Lerner, in his short but perceptive biographical sketch of Dr. Kissinger, concedes:

> He may not be the "psychotic egomaniac" that John Mitchell once called him but he himself confesses that his ego is massive.[1]

Dr. Kissinger's compulsion to discuss his "megalomania" may possibly grow out of the precision with which that term describes the highly stylized Kissinger techniques of conducting diplomacy. Both definitions of megalomania in the Merriam-Webster desk dictionary are so apt that perhaps he could not resist their relevance:

1. a mania for great or grandiose performance.
2. infantile feelings of omnipotence especially when retained in later life.[2]

Any character who asks us to take seriously his supposedly serious beliefs that his 1972 "season of Summits" really has "changed the world" necessarily opens himself up to a suspicion of meeting both dictionary definitions. This is especially so when the planet upon which he asserts that he has imposed a "new world order" includes the nation with the most massive military power the world has ever known—both conventional and strategic nuclear—as well as the nation with the greatest population the world has ever known, whose strategic nuclear capability is rapidly expanding; and when both of these unprecedentedly powerful nations are under the total dictatorial control of cadre Communists.

Evidence suggesting megalomania will be submitted later in this book, but first we must open the additional question of whether Dr. Kissinger may also be some *other* kind of "nut." He has in the past demonstrated a desire to escape reality and seek scholarly refuge in artificially created worlds. When he divorces himself from contact with objective facts, he compounds his vulnerabilities by plunging into unfounded defeatist attitudes about the capabilities of the United States.

These symptoms initially appeared at least 15 years ago. Unfortunately, they have now reappeared in more acute manifestations. In critical issues concerning the grand strategy of the United States vis-a-vis the Soviet Union, he exhibits the syndrome of surrender.

Here is Dr. Kissinger's own description, excerpted from a book he published in 1961, of what he then believed was the strategic environment of the world. Set off against it in a parallel column—again in his own words, but written in 1970—is an accurate description of the world in the 1960s.

It is generally admitted that from 1961 until at least the end of 1964, the Soviet Union will possess more missiles than the United States. . . .

There is no dispute that the "missile gap" will materialize in the period 1960-64. . . .

The missile gap in the period of 1961-1965 is now unavoidable.[3]

In as late as 1962, during the Cuban missile crisis, the Soviet Union had around 40 ICBMs. We had over 1,000 bombers and over 200 missiles that could reach the Soviet Union.[4]

Dr. Kissinger's 1970 figures are, of course, the correct ones. In 1968 Richard Nixon put the ratio of our 1962 strategic superiority over the Soviets as 8-to-1. It is worth noting that the year 1962, which Dr. Kissinger used as the basis for his 1970 figures, is midterm in the period covered in the first column; and that, by the end of 1964, the United States had 1,398 missiles capable of reaching the Soviet Union (934 ICBMs and 464 SLBMs), whereas the Soviets had only 331 missiles capable of reaching the United States (224 ICBMs and 107 SLBMs).

The difference in the strategic significance that Dr. Kissinger attributed, respectively, to the two estimates for the same timeframe is also interesting:

The only controversy concerns its [his predicted "missile gap" as described above] significance. It may mean that we could lose if the Soviet Union struck first. In that case, we would be fortunate if we escaped a surprise attack.[5]

In short, our strategic superiority was overwhelming [in 1962, as described in the right-hand column, above].[6]

Thus, in Dr. Kissinger's artificial out-of-touch-with-reality world, he imagined the threat of a Soviet strategic force substantially more powerful than ours; he vested this nonexistent Soviet missile force with such a margin of superiority over us that it was possible, or even probable, that they had a first-strike capability against us; and he attributed to the Kremlin dictators the will to use this missile force so that we would be "fortunate" if they did not launch a surprise attack against us.

The fact is, as Dr. Kissinger officially conceded in 1970, that U.S. strategic superiority was "overwhelming" in the 1961-1964 timeframe. Therefore, his 1961 vision of the United States "losing" to the

Soviets was not only defeatism, but sick defeatism. At the time of his early writings, there not only never was any basis for this fear, but instead there was every possible reason for *absolute* confidence that, in a strategic confrontation, the Soviets would lose. The strategic military balance at the time of the Cuban missile crisis provided pragmatic proof that this was so.

Just suppose that Henry Kissinger had held in 1961 the power over U.S. strategy and military policy that he began to build in January 1969. Would he have negotiated some sort of clandestine delayed-action surrender on the theory that it was necessary to avert that massive nuclear "surprise attack" that he considered probable because of the margin of superiority he *imagined* the Soviets then had?

Perhaps not. He might not have done so *if* he had faith that the United States could build up strategic power in time to close the imagined "missile gap" before the Soviets could exploit their advantage. But Dr. Kissinger did not have that faith in America. He actually suffered another and more serious manifestation of defeatism, which appears in its tersest form in the sentence immediately following one of those quoted above from his 1961 book:

> The missile gap in the period 1961-1965 is now unavoidable. Lead times of modern equipment are so long that even should we change course immediately, *we could not close it.*

It is difficult to escape a chilling sense of *déjà vu* when evaluating Dr. Kissinger's rationalizations of the imbalances he allowed the Soviet Union in the SALT I pacts. His defeatism is now in a much more advanced stage. Whereas the imaginary "missile gap" shook his faith in the United States, the present very real and massive gap—which he deliberately allowed to open and then to widen after he took office—has utterly destroyed his faith in America's strength and resources. He fell into a state of panic as to our chances against the Soviet Union: sophisticated panic, but hopeless panic nevertheless.

When dealing with the imaginary gap before his faith was totally destroyed, Dr. Kissinger conceded that, although we could not close the gap, we could at least narrow it. Now, when faced with the real gap, he contends that this great United States of America cannot, within five years, produce a single additional missile launcher, either land-based or submarine-based, or a single additional strategic bomber. Thus, in the central document of the many briefings providing his rationalizations of the SALT I pacts, he presented these contentions:

> For various reasons during the 1960s, the United States had, as you know, made the strategic decision to terminate its building programs in major offensive systems. . . . By 1969, therefore, we had no active or

planned programs for deploying additional ICBMs, submarine-launched ballistic missiles, or bombers. The Soviet Union, on the other hand, had dynamic and accelerated programs in both land-based and sea-based missiles. You know, too, that the interval between conception and deployment of strategic weapons systems is generally five to ten years. . . .

The U.S. completed deployment of Minuteman and the Polaris submarines in 1967. . . . We were, and are, developing a new submarine system, although it cannot be deployed until 1978 or until after the end of the freeze.

In other words, as a result of decisions made in the 1960s, and *not reversible within the timeframe of the projected agreement,* there would be a numerical gap against us in the two categories of land-based and sea-based missile systems whether or not there was an agreement. *Without an agreement, the gap would steadily widen.*[7]

We are not exaggerating Dr. Kissinger's defeatism nor are we presenting out of context some single statement he made extemporaneously or without careful consideration. Here is another example—and there are at least five more—stating the same substance. This one adds the interesting admission that the present *real* missile gap began after he took office. Here is how he put it at a press conference in Moscow during the 1972 Summit:

On any day you would have picked over the last year, over the last two years, and on any day you are going to pick in the future, you will be able to demonstrate *a Soviet numerical advantage.* Moreover, it was a numerical advantage that was growing, because in the ICBM field we have, as you know, no ongoing program.

In the submarine field . . . we also have no program for missiles which will be operational. . . . We have no submarine under construction. The first submarine that we have that would become operational would do so early in 1979 or late in 1978.

Therefore, any time over the next five years we were confronting a numerical margin that was growing, and *a margin, moreover, that we could do nothing to reverse in that five-year period.* Therefore, the question of whether the freeze perpetuates a Soviet numerical superiority is beside the point.[8]

As is demonstrated in the quotation cited just prior to this last one, Dr. Kissinger slickly lays the blame for our present alleged helplessness to reverse the gap on a strategic decision made "in the 1960s" to terminate U.S. building programs in major offensive systems; and he implies that by 1969, when he took over, it was too late to do anything to cure our helplessness.

This was not so. If he and President Nixon had permitted Secretary of Defense Melvin Laird to tell the American people the truth about Soviet capabilities *and intentions* in early 1969, and had instituted strategic building programs early in 1969, we could have produced hundreds of additional missile launchers by 1972. We could then have produced not only hundreds but thousands of additional strategic weapons by 1974, three years within the five-year period within which Dr. Kissinger claimed we "could do nothing." This U.S. capability will be documented later in this book; but, of course, it means nothing if those in control of America's destiny have no faith in the United States but unlimited faith in the power of the Soviet Union.

Dr. Kissinger even asserted that a *crash* program to build missile submarines of a type "similar to our current fleet, and without many of the features most needed for the 1980s and beyond," could "not produce results before 1976."

This is the Kissinger surrender syndrome in full display. He wants to default the greatest industrial power in all history to a less-than-half-size competitor—and he wants to do this in a *production* race in which the very survival of the United States is at stake. He wants to default America in a competition with a government so snarled up in Communist ideology that it cannot come within a thousand million dollars worth of grain a year of feeding its own people; a nation whose farmers are so fouled up in bureaucratic restrictions that, whereas each American farmer feeds himself and 58 other people on a high-protein diet, each Russian farmer is falling short of his government-prescribed quota to feed himself and seven other people on a starchy diet.

Dr. Kissinger wants to default America with our Gross National Product measured in trillions of real-wealth dollars ($1.3 trillion estimated for 1974), whereas the Soviet GNP for the same period is less than $600 billion. In capability of inventing, developing, and deploying strategic systems, America deployed its full fleet of 41 Polaris submarines some 10 years ahead of the Soviets' frantic efforts to compete, even aided by the Polaris designs that the Gordon Lonsdale espionage ring stole from the Portland (England) Naval Base.

This make-believe world Henry Kissinger is trying to drag us all into is one in which the United States is not merely a pitiful helpless giant, but a tragic fool of a giant—a giant with great capabilities for creating power, but without the common sense or courage or will to use its potentials: scientific, technological, industrial, or spiritual.

In the real world from which Dr. Kissinger compulsively seeks to escape, the United States has ample capability to produce within five years not merely a few additional strategic missile launchers, but quite literally thousands if we needed them. But we don't. An additional 496 SLBMs and 1,500 mobile Minuteman missiles, all with the improved guidance and greater explosive power that are within our technological capability, would be adequate. They would provide us with an invulnerable deterrent within the relevant timeframe.

We cannot, of course, rebuild the strategic deterrent that is essential to our national survival so long as we have a surrender-prone defeatist sitting astride the formulation of U.S. grand strategy. Nor can we hope to survive if he can continue to deceive the President and the people into believing that we do not *need* additional strategic power, and could not produce any in time even if we did. Fortunately, however, Henry Kissinger and his policies can be evicted from power by exposing to the public what he really is up to, and how he is going about it.

It will be argued that Dr. Kissinger was not alone in being suckered into the great 1960 missile-gap-that-never-was; that many others fell into the same "gap"-trap. That is true. But all those who did were vulnerable to the Soviet trap because they were mentally crippled by the ideological preconception that freedom cannot, over the long run, compete successfully against communism; that the United States could not win, or even sustain a draw, in a strategic arms competition against the U.S.S.R.

There are two points in answer to this argument that are pertinent to discuss here. First, although Henry Kissinger and others were suckered into the nonexistent "missile gap" by the fantasia orchestrated by Soviet psychological warfare experts, to paralyze U.S. official leadership with the fear of *even attempting* to compete with the Soviet Union in nuclear weapons, there were many others who did not fall into that trap. Secondly, there are many additional instances in which Henry Kissinger succumbed to his compulsion to abandon the real world (in which U.S. strategic power was superior to that of the Soviets) in favor of an artificially created world (in which we could not successfully compete with the Soviets).

Every once in a while, despite the fact that America will for years continue to stagger under the cruel burden of having suffered a McNamara and a Kissinger in the same generation, there still seems to be a not-irreverent residual in the flip quip of the late Justice Felix Frankfurter: "God takes care of little children, drunks, and the United States of America." It happens that the same material will serve to make the two points mentioned just above; namely, to introduce one of the responsible and respected authorities who did not fall for the Soviet hoax called the "missile gap"; and he, in turn, will present evidence of other manifestations of Kissinger's surrender syndrome. A short preface will be helpful, however, before letting this experienced authority speak for himself concerning the nature of the strategy advocated by Dr. Kissinger and those who share his ideology.

"Fool me once, shame on you; fool me twice, shame on me," resentfully quoted young President Kennedy in the heat of his reaction to the Soviet betrayal of the first nuclear test ban in 1961. All too soon, however, his palace guard turned off his resentment against the Kremlin's cheating. His Camelot courtiers turned him around so effectively, indeed, that he ordered the court-martial of one of the authors of this book for quoting that Kennedy quip in a full-page advertisement that appeared in the *Washington Post* opposing the Moscow Test Ban Treaty of 1963.

The Kennedy comment is relevant here because, when the Soviets suckered the unilateral-disarmament intellectuals into the illusory "missile gap" of 1960-64, it was not a case of fool-me-once. This was the *second* time they had been played for fools—and by exactly the same techniques. In 1954 and 1955, in their then-huge May Day parades that were always attended by foreign military and air attaches, the Soviets simply *displayed* two new types of heavy bombers: the Tu-20 Bear and the Mya-4 Bison. By a carefully engineered psychological campaign conducted by both military and political leaders, they conned U.S. intelligence into believing that these types had actually been produced in large numbers.

Thus was born the nonexistent "bomber gap" of the middle 1950s, which was exploited for the substantial benefit of the Russians for several years before the trick was penetrated. The advantages that the Soviets gained from having deceived the unilateral-disarmers far outlived the actual duration of the deception itself. It was the stratagem by which the Soviets "covered" themselves while they leapfrogged from heavy intercontinental bombers to intercontinental missile programs—and did so some five years ahead of us. They started their ICBM program no later than 1949, whereas we did not begin serious work on ours until mid-1954. This explains how the Soviets beat us to the first earth satellite, Sputnik I, and the first ICBM in 1957.

Also, the Soviets needed resources for their massive and protracted clandestine preparations for their surprise abrogation of the nuclear test ban in 1961. They simply did not have the money for a large force of heavy bombers, but politically they needed to create an *immediate* image of strategic superiority. Here is the explanation by a British strategic expert of how the Soviets accomplished their "bomber gap" spoof:

> . . . The *simulated* intercontinental capability of 1955 [large numbers of Bison and Bear heavy strategic bombers which the Soviets successfully bluffed U. S. intelligence and unilateral-disarmament intellectuals into believing they had, but which the Soviets never actually built] was enough to bring about a transformation in the perceived balance of strategic power toward the implicit parity of the "balance of terror."

Enunciated in Churchill's elegant prose, this phrase conveyed a compelling image of two equilibrated forces. This was enough to undermine the credibility of Massive Retaliation [the prevailing Dulles-Eisenhower nuclear strategy] (at least to *Western* observers) even though the actualities of the rival strategic force deployments were such that America had a vast—and growing—superiority by every numerical index. (The latter most probably implied a capacity to disarm the Soviet Union in a surprise attack.)

The Russians thus secured their half of the "balance of terror" *without having to invest major resources in their heavy bomber force,* which never exceeded 200 units as against more than 600 U.S. B-52s.[9]

When Melvin R. Laird took office as Secretary of Defense of the United States in January 1969, conservatives and anti-Communists on the one hand, and power-elite internationalists and Soviet-accommodating unilateral disarmers on the other hand, acting from opposite motives, adopted an identical tactic: neither side would mention or quote from Laird's book, *A House Divided—America's Strategy Gap,* which had been published in 1962.

Although *any* new Secretary of Defense, possibly including a member of the Kremlin's Politburo, would have been better for U.S. national security than Robert Strange McNamara, Mel Laird had exceptional qualifications. These included 15 years' experience in the most relevant Congressional Subcommittee, Defense Appropriations, plus nearly eight years of outstanding and effectively articulate opposition to Secretary McNamara's policies.

To conservatives, however, his most exciting qualifications were his convictions concerning the essential grand strategy of the United States, strategic doctrine, and Communist strategy and long-term objectives, all of which had been declared with apparent sincerity in his book. But conservatives were motivated not to quote Laird's book, or even to mention that he had written one, because they did not want to embarrass him with the President or cause unnecessary confrontations between Laird's former hard line and the soft line that was rapidly surfacing as the Kissinger-Nixon policy.

The elite internationalists and accommodationists were motivated not to mention Laird's book because of the inherent power of many of the truths enunciated in it. Such truths might have appealed to the intuition, if not the intelligence, of the American people. They might even have shocked us out of the euphoria and apathy essential to the Kissinger-Nixon success in changing America's global stance from anti-Communist to be-friends-with-the-Communists, and in reducing our strategic power to a very weak Number Two.

In any event, and for varying motives, the be-silent-about-Laird's-book tactic was operative for the full four years of his term as Secretary of Defense. The silence by conservatives, however, failed in their objective: Henry Kissinger had read the book anyway. With the long memory of megalomania, he had not forgotten the challenge to his omniscience—the slur on the Great Book on which his reputation had been built, which was contained in the quotations from *A House Divided* set forth below. Here is how Congressman Melvin Laird, in early 1962, described the way Dr. Kissinger was twice taken in by Communist deceit—on the imagined "bomber gap" and on the phony "missile gap":

> Beginning in 1958, many persons were saying that the Soviets already possessed nuclear parity. In a Senate speech on August 14, 1958, then Senator Kennedy expressed his alarm about the missile gap, and called upon the United States to follow an "underdog strategy." Similarly, in June 1960, Governor Rockefeller released a statement in which he indicated his alarm over Soviet missile superiority.
>
> The very able writer-professor, Henry Kissinger, likewise based many of his observations in his excellent book, *Nuclear Weapons and Foreign Policy*, on the assumption that we were caught in a missile gap.
>
> Each of these observers mistakenly assumed that we had moved into the fourth strategic stage, that our nuclear preponderance was lost, and that deterrence by nuclear power was only a frail hope. These considerations led then Senator Kennedy to advocate his "underdog" strategy. It was thus that we entered the full swing of our extremely damaging "underdog" strategy . . . .
>
> Actually, the Soviet Union is unwilling to take a real risk of war as long as we hold our nuclear lead. But they maintain the advantage when, in Phase Three, although we still hold an edge in nuclear power, we succumb to an underdog strategy, and behave as if we were in Phase Four, when the Soviets are assumed to have parity, or even—*as some hysterical statements held in 1960-61*—an actual superiority.
>
> The so-called "underdog strategy" was not only false, but *everything stemming from it has tended to national suicide.* While there is still time to correct the tragic error, the underdog strategy must give way to a strategy of initiative.[10]

Not lost on Henry Kissinger for an instant was the criticism of his Great Book by name, and the branding of it as having helped to lead to a strategy tending to "national suicide." Perhaps an even more serious act of lese majesty against the "admittedly massive ego" was Congressman Laird's characterization of statements made in 1960-61, which credited the Soviets with actual strategic superiority, as "hysterical statements." Henry Kissinger's book *The Necessity for Choice* was published in 1961 and makes *exactly* such assertions of Soviet superiority, as illustrated by the several excerpts cited earlier.

What revenge would Dr. Kissinger take against a man who had dared to charge him with hysteria in a field in which he professed to exercise supreme expertise? The fact that Laird's book was accurate, and Kissinger's 1961 book demonstrably foolish (as illustrated by the quotations set forth above), made the Laird book all the more intolerable to Kissinger.

It did not take long for evidence of the Kissinger vendetta versus Laird to surface. Dr. Kissinger set out to convince President Nixon that his new Secretary of Defense was a political liability, an obstacle in the path of Nixon's grandiose quest for a "generation of peace."

Laird played into Kissinger's crafty hands almost with his first official public statement. Testifying before a congressional committee in February 1969, within weeks of taking office, Secretary Laird was asked *why* the Soviets were engaged in such a massive buildup of strategic weapons, especially the huge 25-megaton SS-9 supermissiles. He responded with the only rational and completely commonsense explanation:

> The Soviets are going for a first-strike capability. There is no question about that.

That did it. If there were anything that could block acceptance by the American people of the Kissinger-Nixon vision of utopia via a partnership with the Kremlin in a new world order, having a Secretary of Defense who would tell the truth about Soviet intentions would indeed be it. They could not afford to fire him—then. It would have provided Laird with a national forum and publicity that could not be suppressed. So Laird was continued as Secretary of Defense, but in name only—and muzzled from telling the truth. The next time he was asked the same question, he meekly replied that it was not his function to interpret Soviet intentions.

Not the function of the U.S. Secretary of Defense to interpret the meaning of a huge buildup by the Soviets of nuclear weapons that are good for two things only—the destruction of so much of the U.S. retaliatory force that we could not retaliate, and the nuclear incineration of so many scores of millions of Americans that it would be irrational even to attempt retaliation?

If *not* the Secretary of Defense, who-the-hell's function *is it* to answer such questions of national life or death? The President's? Henry Kissinger's? Those two have said it is beyond them, that they are unable to answer. Henry Kissinger, writing the 1972 annual *State of the World Report* for himself and the President, using the royal first-person-plural pronoun, for once "made it perfectly clear" with an unambiguous assertion: "We cannot know the intentions of Soviet leadership." Not even after having declared, in the preceding paragraph, that the Soviet Union was continuing to build its capability "in virtually every category of strategic offensive and defensive weapons." Not even after listing six major areas of strategic weaponry in which the Soviets were continuing to generate momentum in their buildup. Not even after concluding that:

> The Soviet Union is continuing to create strategic capabilities beyond a level which by any reasonable standard already seems sufficient.

Both President Nixon and Dr. Kissinger knew that the Soviet Union had invested quite literally scores of billions of dollars of scarce resources in building weapons far beyond any reasonable sufficiency. But for the life of them—and for the lives of 210 million Americans— they simply could not think of any reason *why* the Soviet leadership would do such a thing.

Henry Kissinger had an additional reason to seek revenge against Mel Laird. In his book *A House Divided,* Laird not only enunciated a key doctrine concerning communism, but supported it with conclusive historical evidence and convincing logic. If this truth gained any currency it would expose the fact that the assumptions on which Kissinger proposed to build a new "structure of world peace" were as false as his earlier "hysterical" assumption of Soviet strategic superiority in the 1960-64 timeframe. A man who, like Mel Laird, would state such a shattering doctrine once, just might do it again. So he must be discredited and shorn of power over administration defense and foreign policies—even if he carried the title "Secretary of Defense."

By coincidence, a particular Laird quotation is also relevant to the question raised at the beginning of this preliminary consideration of the complexities of Dr. Kissinger: suppose he really is "some kind of a nut, or something." It just happens that this excerpt defines a kind of "madness." Here is the way former Congressman (post-Watergate White House Chief Domestic Adviser) Melvin Laird, in his book *A House Divided,* reviewed history following World War II:

> The postwar era found the Soviet Union the strongest nation on the continent and the second strongest in the world. The first step of postwar Soviet strategy was to weld Hungary, Bulgaria, Albania, Czechoslovakia, and Rumania into a solid bloc under complete control of Soviet autocracy. With this accomplished, Communist strategy turned to the Middle East and Southeast Asia. . . .
>
> The United States and the Western powers have not been entirely idle: they moved into Korea and fought a "police action," executed the Berlin airlift, moved naval forces into Lebanon. . . .
>
> In addition, repeated attempts were made to "negotiate" with the Com-

munists and convince them of the West's sincere desire for peace. The unvarying failure of these endeavors is now a matter of historical record.

Does communism necessarily have to remain true to its core of irrational dogma? . . .

The hard fact is that communism will always remain true to its core because it has no choice. If the basic tenets of communism were altered or even modified, the whole Communist Empire would collapse. The hard core of Communist doctrine is the foundation of every government, every institution, and every system of rule in the Soviet Empire.

Remove any part of this foundation and chaos would result. If the Communists ceased to view the West irrationally, as a warmonger, what justification would the Communist masters have for maintaining their autocratic privileges in the garrison state in Russia? Or in China?

Communism can abandon no part of its basic attitudes. Without the dialectic of historical necessity promising the inevitability of Communist victory, the heart would go out of the overburdened peoples; the thirst for human rights would become unquenchable.

Without the ruthless doctrine of ends and means, the Communist rulers could not pursue the strategy which brings them victories. Without the maintenance of atheism, they could not enforce the sacrifices which maintain their own power in the deified state.

Communism cannot change; and to believe in the possibility of change is a madness almost as far from the true ordering of reason as the ideology itself. Communism, while it exists, must remain what it is. It is caught up in the most vicious circle in human history.

That's it: madness. Madness. Madness!

Is Melvin Laird, with his 15 years of practical experience on the House Defense Appropriations Subcommittee, with wide access to classified as well as unclassified information on Communist strategy, tactics, and objectives, the only authority who contends that to believe in the possibility of communism changing is "madness"? Perhaps as to the explicit use of the term "madness"; but he is only one of hundreds who have concluded that communism *cannot* change and still remain communism. Among those who believe this are all the dictators of the U.S.S.R.: Lenin, Stalin, Khrushchev, Brezhnev, and all the Politburo's long line of chief theoreticians, including the incumbent Suslov. Khrushchev probably put it the most authoritatively in the fewest words in a speech at the Academy of Social Sciences and the Institute of Marxism-Leninism:

The Communist Party of the Soviet Union has been, is, and ever will be loyal to the doctrine of Marxism-Leninism, to proletarian internationalism and friendship among the peoples. It will always fight for world peace, for the victory of communism, as the great Lenin taught us.[11]

That quotation is from the speech President John F. Kennedy characterized as a "Red blueprint for eventual world domination." The speech itself repeated the doctrine adopted by the World Communist Declaration of 1960, which in turn was reaffirmed by Leonid Brezhnev at the formal state banquet he gave for Fidel Castro a month *after* the SALT I Agreements were signed. It is still operative and is *not* out of date. It is the basic and therefore unchanging doctrine of communism that there can be no world peace until communism is victorious over the entire world; and, as Khrushchev pledged, in equating the two, the Communist Party of the Soviet Union will always fight for the worldwide victory of communism. It is noteworthy that the SALT I Agreements and related documents of the 1972 Moscow Summit were signed, not by any official of the U.S.S.R., but by Leonid Brezhnev as General Secretary of the Communist Party of the Soviet Union.

Not only do all Communist leaders and theoreticians agree with Melvin Laird that communism cannot change; so do all objective and knowledgeable Western authorities on communism. Gerhart Niemeyer, Professor of Political Science at Notre Dame University and principal lecturer on Communist philosophy at the U.S. National War College, considers this absolutely basic, and has documented it in many books, articles, and lectures. So do all the others who have applied realistic analysis to the Communist system. Another authoritative statement is presented in *A Forward Strategy for America* by Robert Strausz-Hupe, William R. Kintner, and Stefan T. Possony.[12] Although their book was published in 1961, it represented a watershed in enunciation of an enlightened strategy for the United States in the nuclear-space age, and it has stood the test of time triumphantly. It embodied as much faith in America as Dr. Kissinger's 1957 and 1961 books displayed defeatism; it is as truly learned as Dr. Kissinger's books are pretentious. Here is their considered and documented conclusion on the question of whether communism *can* change:

> Of the many factors which account for the failure of the West to pursue a Forward Strategy, the more important will be briefly enumerated here.
>
> The first and major factor is the *defensive* psychology of the West and the moral aversion of the free nations to employ force for purposes other than defense against physical aggression.
>
> The second factor is the strange reluctance of the West to face the plain fact that *the goals of the enemy are as fixed as his methods are flexible.* At times, the understanding of this basic fact is forced upon the West by Communist action. Then again Communist legerdemain raises unrealistic hopes of change in heart in the Communist camp.

The second paragraph above, which states that "the first and major factor" in the failure of the United States to develop an effective strategy versus the Soviet Union is our "defensive psychology," should be compared to Dr. Kissinger's admission (it is almost a boast!) in the President's annual *State of the World Reports* (e.g., February 25, 1971) that his vaunted doctrine of "strategic sufficiency" (which he substituted for the "strategic superiority" that the pre-Kissinger Nixon had pledged) is "defensive in essence." Any strategy that is "defensive in essence" is necessarily defeatist in essence and results, as those three distinguished and realistic strategic experts recognized a decade before Dr. Kissinger began attempting to pretend that defeatism is a virtue.

Can communism change? The answer is no, and primarily for the reasons explained by Melvin Laird, although this book presents many other authorities and much other evidence.

Laird's assertion that belief in the changeability of communism "is a madness" puts it perhaps brutally. It does seem, however, to suggest some sort of irrationality—a loss of touch with reality—to assert that communism *has* changed, when there is such overwhelming evidence to the contrary. To establish the proposition that it is necessary to consider whether Dr. Kissinger is "some kind of a nut" because he has staked the lives and freedom of 210 million Americans on his belief that communism *has* changed, it is not at all necessary to prove that communism *cannot* change. If it can be proved merely that communism *has not* changed, and that the evidence is so convincing that no rational man would disbelieve it, then we have established the point.

The evidence submitted in this book will include testimony by Leonid Brezhnev and other ruling members of the Politburo. This testimony is not old stuff, although necessarily much of it will affirm or reaffirm earlier material for the very reason that basic Communist doctrine does not change, and has not changed in more than half a century. All the testimony presented speaks as of the time of the 1972 Moscow Summit or later—*after* the signing of the SALT I pacts that Dr. Kissinger contends have changed the old approaches and developed a "new style of international relations," and have established "for the first time" a "new foundation of restraint, cooperation, and steadily evolving confidence" with the Soviet Union.

Does Henry Kissinger really believe that the Communists, either the Russians or the Red Chinese have changed? If so, how much? And if so, who changed them?

This book will detail how and how much Dr. Kissinger would have us believe that he believes the Soviet Communists have changed. Here is an example of the type of test Dr. Kissinger applies to determine whether the Soviet leadership is truly sincere in its "changed" attitudes toward the "capitalistic, imperialistic warmongers" and "atomic maniacs" (terms that have been applied to us within the last several years by the Politburo's chief theoretician).

Dr. Kissinger was discussing the *Joint Declaration of Principles* that President Nixon was conned into signing at the 1972 Moscow Summit, thereby committing the United States to abide by the dictates of "peaceful coexistence" in the Soviet meaning of that term— that is, a strategy designed to bring about the liquidation of capitalism and the worldwide victory of communism. But it was larded with soothing phrases and was regarded by U.S. newsmen as a "nonaggression pact." So they questioned Dr. Kissinger about it:

> Q: Henry, three months ago the President said in the *State of the World* that he regarded the use of tensions as a permanent feature of Soviet foreign policy. Is this signing of this statement a recognition that this was a wrong judgment?
>
> Dr. Kissinger: . . . I think it is a correct judgment to say that in the period covered by the *Report* and, indeed, in most of the postwar period, it is difficult to point to any extended length of time in which tension was not a feature of the foreign policy or which did not result from the foreign policy that was conducted by the Soviet Union.
>
> On the other hand we do not consider this document as characterizing the past foreign policies. We consider this document as indicating a direction for the future. . . . So don't consider this document inconsistent with the retroactive judgments expressed in the *World Report*.
>
> Now, again, I don't want to give the impression here that we have suddenly gone soft-minded. We do not exclude that one could return to this previous period. This reflects our goal.
>
> We assume that the Soviet leaders are *serious people and that they would not sign such a document in a rather solemn ceremony unless they had some serious intention.*[13]

In evaluating this new criterion invented by Dr. Kissinger for testing the sincerity of Soviet promises, one wonders if the learned Doctor could recall offhand many instances in which such formal documents were *not* signed in rather solemn ceremonies. One wonders also if he remembers that the signing by the Soviets of a nonaggression pact or an agreement of friendship and peace with a smaller nation—with appropriate solemn ceremonies—was routinely the prelude to an invasion by the Red Army to crush the independence of the weaker party.

President Dwight Eisenhower, for one, reached a conclusion different from Dr. Kissinger's concerning the effect on Soviet leadership of having entered into an international agreement in a "solemn" ceremony:

> We have learned the bitter lesson that international agreements, historically considered by us as sacred, are regarded in Communist doctrine and in practice to be mere scraps of paper.

The most recent proof of their disdain of international obligations, *solemnly undertaken,* is their announced intention to abandon their responsibilities respecting Berlin.

As a consequence, *we can have no confidence in any treaty to which Communists are a party except where such a treaty provides within itself for self-enforcing mechanisms.* Indeed, the demonstrated disregard of the Communists of their own pledges is one of the greatest obstacles to success in substituting the rule of law for rule by force.[14]

To determine whether President Eisenhower or Dr. Kissinger was wrong, a look at the record is helpful. The documents to be considered should include Soviet pledges of peaceful coexistence, of alliance, of mutual assistance, or of nonaggression. Here is the list, stretching back to 1920, of the Soviets' treaty partners, together with a summary statement of how "seriously" Soviet leadership looked upon treaty obligations undertaken in solemn ceremonies:

Georgia: Independence recognized, diplomatic relations established, May 7, 1920. Red Army attacked and took over, February 11, 1921.

Ukraine: Treaty of Alliance, December 28, 1920; absorbed into the Soviet Union, December 30, 1922.

Lithuania: Nonaggression pact, 1926; invasion by Red Army, August 1940.

Estonia: Nonaggression pact, 1932; invasion by Red Army, August 1940.

Latvia: Nonaggression pact, 1932; invasion by Red Army, August 1940.

Poland: Nonaggression pact renewed May 1934 for 10 years; invasion by Red Army, September 1939 (jointly with Nazi Army).

Finland: Nonaggression pact, January 21, 1932; invasion by Red Army, November 1939.

Czechoslovakia: Treaty guaranteeing independence of Czechoslovakia, August 3, 1968; invasion by Red Army, August 20, 1968 (also in violation of 16 additional international agreements signed under solemn circumstances).

In the light of this historical evidence, it might be concluded that "whom the Soviets would destroy, they first offer peaceful coexistence, then join in signing a nonaggression agreement." Also, in the light of this and much other evidence known to Dr. Kissinger, it might be argued that his enunciation of the signed-in-a-rather-solemn-ceremony test of the sincerity of Soviet intentions was not the result of a considered judgment by him, but an impromptu invention that should not be held against his great intellect.

Not so, however. In his carefully prepared rationalization of SALT before the five congressional committees at the White House on June 15, 1972, of which copies were printed and distributed in advance, Dr. Kissinger reaffirmed his trust that the Soviet leaders would hold inviolate not only the SALT I Agreements, but all the other Moscow Summit agreements, on the basis of his judgment that:

> The Soviet leaders are *serious men*, and we are confident that they *will not lightly abandon the course* that has led to the Summit meeting and to these initial agreements.

Dr. Kissinger is, of course, totally correct in his estimate that the Soviet leaders are "serious men." No one has risen to dictatorial power in the Politburo of the U.S.S.R. by laughing and joking on the way up (although Khrushchev displayed some earthy peasant-type humor from time to time *after* he reached the top, and Brezhnev was quite jovial on his 1972 visit). It is a reasonable assumption that they did not "lightly abandon" a single one of the solemnly signed treaties listed above. But, after "serious" consideration, they *did* abandon each and every one of them. This is because it is basic Communist doctrine that, immediately upon an international agreement's losing its "revolutionary significance"—that is, once it is no longer to the advantage of the Soviet Union to abide by its obligations—it is no longer binding upon the Soviet Union, and not only may, but must, be broken.

It is incredible that Henry Kissinger truly believes in the validity of his newly enunciated criterion for testing whether the Soviets sincerely intend to honor the obligations of an international agreement. Any researcher can uncover masses of evidence refuting the Kissinger assertion that Soviet signature of a document "in a rather solemn ceremony" constituted assurance that they had serious intentions of keeping their written promises. There is so much authoritative evidence that it is impracticable to summarize or even cite the principal documents in this book.

Even the brief summary given above proves conclusively that Kissinger's proposition is so totally misleading that he is insulting our intelligence in expecting us to swallow it. It presents a picture in which the reader can see for himself that it is a *moral certainty* that a distinguished Doctor of Political Science from Harvard, with years of special study in international relations, *must* know about that evidence. But although our evidence demonstrates that Kissinger's proposition is invalid, it is *not* direct evidence that Kissinger himself could not believe in his own proposition.

The point is critical. If we could present direct evidence that Dr. Kissinger himself *knew* that his proposition was misleading, that it was contrary to the mass of evidence, contrary to history, and contradicted by Communist doctrine, Communist traditions, and Communist practice, we would have a strong case that Dr. Kissinger was deliberately attempting to deceive the American people, Congress, and probably also the incumbent President. Such motivation would be helpful in reaching a determination as to whether Kissinger really is "some kind of a nut or something." When deception in the control of national security and foreign relations is demonstrated to be deliberate, we have Watergate-type arrogance and cynical dishonesty operating in the two areas critical to national survival.

In this case, the evidence of the motivation to deceive did not readily surface. Diligent research finally unearthed it in this colloquy from the Kissinger "Background Briefing" for the press on September 16, 1970:

> *Question by Mr. Black, Cincinnati Inquirer:* How much confidence does it give you in the Russians' willingness to keep an agreement, in view of their violations or complicity in violations in the Middle East, if some accord were reached at SALT?

> *Dr. Kissinger:* This is a very important question. One of the things I find so puzzling in the Soviet performance on the cease-fire in the Middle East is to try to figure out a motive for it. . . .But why the Egyptians and the Russians violated the cease-fire literally practically from the first day onward in a way that was so flagrant, I have really found it very hard to explain to myself. . . .

> With respect to SALT and commenting generally about the Soviet performance, this Administration has never believed that the Soviets will keep an agreement just because they like to keep their word.

> We have always assumed that as Marxists they would believe that they will keep an agreement only so long as it serves their interests. *As Marxists, they have almost no mechanism by which they would keep an agreement that is against their interests.* . . .

> If the Russians ever get the idea in a SALT Agreement that they could get a free ride, that they could construct hundreds of missiles and then we would do nothing, then we would be in terrible shape. *Then they will do it.*

So, Henry Kissinger does know not only the Soviet practice of violating agreements, but that their inexorable doctrine *requires* that they *not* keep an agreement once it becomes against their interests to do so—regardless of the degree of solemnity with which they may have signed the document.

It may be, of course, that Dr. Kissinger thinks there is something very special about a "rather solemn ceremony" conducted in connection with an East-West Summit meeting. Such an illusion could be held only by someone unwilling to read the staff study made by the Senate Judiciary Committee of the Soviet record in 25 summit agreements. The result: of the 25 summit agreements, the Soviets have honored one and broken 24. The study covered summits from the one at Teheran in 1943 through the Geneva summit of 1955. This study was published in *U.S. News & World Report* for May 29, 1972, and it revealed many violations of other agreements with the United States, as well as with many other nations.

In view of the mass of evidence supporting the Eisenhower analysis of Soviet treaty relationships, perhaps it would not have been too much to ask that Dr. Kissinger give some consideration to the critical and specific point that President Eisenhower asserted had been established by extensive experience:

> We can have no confidence in any treaty to which Communists are a party except where such a treaty provides within itself for self-enforcing mechanisms.

Neither the SALT I Anti-Defense Treaty nor the SALT I Interim Agreement provides any self-enforcing mechanisms, or any enforcement provisions at all. Furthermore, not only is there no provision for on-site inspection to determine violations, but the only inspection provisions included are completely illusory, as will be demonstrated in this book.

Why should we expect Dr. Kissinger to give consideration to enforcement and inspection provisions in the SALT I pacts? Because all our lives, our freedom, and the survival of the United States depend upon them. As he himself has emphasized: in the SALT I pacts "national survival is at stake," because in them the parties "have agreed to restrain the very armaments on which their national survival depends."[15] And especially because—if the Soviets do violate the SALT I Agreements, or even if they merely take advantage of the technicalities or loopholes or advantages Dr. Kissinger has allowed them, and we then activate the six-month escape clause—there is *no way at all* in which we can recover the lead time that we will have thrown away in reliance on the reassurance Dr. Kissinger has given us about the "seriousness" of the Soviet leaders in signing the Agreements in a "rather solemn ceremony."

Herman Kahn diagnoses an influential group of U.S. self-styled intellectuals (whom he refers to by a code-name: "the upper middle class") as "manic." Faulting their judgment in a specific manner, he explains:

> The basic thing is you have to be smart in a *reasoned* way. *If you are smart in an illusioned way, you are smart and crazy.* That's today's American upper middle class.[16]

It is clear that Dr. Kissinger has rejected the mass of evidence that communism has not changed, and that communism cannot change; that his rejection of reality on these crucial points is generated by his illusions as to the sincerity and reliability of Communist leaders; and that, therefore, he qualifies within the Kahn formula as being "smart and crazy." Or, within the terminology we have been using, as "some kind of a nut."

The Kissinger quotation presented above for its enunciation of his "solemn ceremony" test of Soviet sincerity, which illustrates his illusions about the Politburo leaders, also demonstrates several other important illusions he holds about his own world-shaking accomplishments.

The first two paragraphs of the quotation from Dr. Kissinger's May 29, 1972, Moscow news conference (quoted above on page 27) constitute his admission that the use of tensions was a permanent fixture of Soviet foreign policy up until at least three months before the Kissinger Moscow Summit of '72. Thus, he admitted that the Soviets were still conducting the Cold War (under the code term "peaceful coexistence") until that time.

He makes it clear also that he contends that his Summit negotiations marked the great watershed dividing past Soviet foreign policies, which involved permanent use of tensions against the United States, and the new "direction for the future" of Soviet foreign policies, which is a sharp departure from "this previous period." So, Dr. Kissinger not only believes (or would have us believe) that the Soviet Communists have changed, but that *he* changed them; and that this change was not a process of evolution or gradual mellowing, but a change that he brought about substantially overnight by his negotiations with them at the Moscow Summit of '72.

If that doesn't demonstrate a mania for grandiose performance and a feeling of omnipotence in exact accordance with the dictionary definition of megalomania, what could?

The particular agreement that Dr. Kissinger relies on as demonstrating that (1) the Soviet Communists *can* change, (2) the Soviet Communists *have* changed, and (3) the Moscow Summit negotiations *changed* them, actually demonstrates the exact contrary on all three points. The specific document he referred to was the so-called "Joint U.S.-Soviet Declaration of Principles of Relations," in which the Soviets conned Kissinger, and he in turn conned President Nixon, into agreeing to conduct "mutual relations on the basis of peaceful coexistence."

That means—as Dr. Kissinger well knows, or should know—that we have agreed to participate in and support a Soviet strategy designed to bring about the liquidation of "imperialism" (which means the United States) and the worldwide victory of communism. More specifically, in this connection, the concept of "peaceful coexistence" includes the Brezhnev Doctrine.

Although Dr. Kissinger may have missed this point—or pretended to miss it—our NATO allies did not. They were stunned and shocked that Dr. Kissinger had, behind their backs, capitulated to the Brezhnev Doctrine, which they had been trying to resist.

The Brezhnev Doctrine has a dual meaning: (1) that *Soviet communism will never be allowed to deviate from the established doctrines* of Marxism-Leninism as interpreted by the Politburo in the Kremlin—that is, that *Soviet communism will never "change"*; and (2) that not only will the Soviets not change, but *they will not permit any of the Soviet satellite states to change*—even if blocking the change requires an all-out invasion by Soviet armed forces. The Brezhnev Doctrine originated in the 1968 invasion of Czechoslovakia, in violation of 17 solemn Soviet agreements. The "serious" Soviet leaders did not do this "lightly"; they had planned and prepared for it for six months.

On July 4, 1973, the Soviet spokesman at the European Security Conference in Helsinki announced to the world that the U.S.S.R. specifically reserves its "future" right to other Czechoslovak-type invasions of Eastern European satellite nations.

If Dr. Kissinger's estimate of the magnitude of the "change" he had wrought in Soviet foreign policy was colossal, words simply are not adequate to convey his estimation of the change he thinks he accomplished in the policies and attitudes of the rulers of the People's Republic of China. Grandiose would be a pallid understatement. Dr. Kissinger's opinion of his own accomplishment is so dramatic that parallel-column treatment is again indicated. The left-hand column sets forth his view of the character of the Red Chinese leaders and the nature of the Red Chinese nuclear threat against the United States, as of the timeframe of his 1961 book, *The Necessity for Choice*. The right-hand column sets forth his estimates of exactly the same Red Chinese leaders after his move toward China, that is, after the Peking Summit of 1972 that he and President Nixon referred to as "the week that changed the world."[17]

KISSINGER ON RED CHINA, 1961	KISSINGER ON RED CHINA, 1972
The prospect that China by 1975 might have the nuclear capability of the Soviet Union in 1960 is terrifying. Many of the notions of nuclear deterrence may not apply with respect to a country which has shown so callous a disregard of human life. What has come to be called the bal-	Congressman Lucien N. Nedzi: Has anything happened to that threat [the Red Chinese nuclear threat, used by the President from 1969 through February 1972 as a principal justification of the Safeguard ABM program)? . . . Dr. Kissinger: Our estimate of the

33

ance of terror may seem less frightful to fanatics leading a country with a population of 600 million. Even a war directed explicitly against centers of population may seem to it tolerable and perhaps the best means of dominating the world.

Chou En-lai is reported to have told a Yugoslav diplomat that an all-out nuclear war would leave 10 million Americans, 20 million Russians, and 350 million Chinese. The question then becomes whether we can stand idly by while this peril develops, simply trusting that a more humane group of leaders will replace the incumbents. Can we afford to permit China to develop the power to destroy humanity without control?

likelihood of our being involved in any nuclear conflict with the People's Republic of China is considerably less . . . because of the political developments that have happened since then, specifically the opening toward China. . . .

We accept now . . . in the light . . . of improvement in relations with the People's Republic of China, that we could pay this price of foregoing the additional protection that the President requested in his original statement.

We could do this all the more so because if our estimates turn out to be incorrect, we have such an overwhelming retaliatory capability vis-a-vis any other country than the Soviet Union, that the idea of a third nuclear country attacking the United States is a rather remote possibility.

So here again we see the Kissinger symptoms of illusions of omnipotence and of a belief in his own grandiose performance. It is true that there was a substantial lapse of time between his two estimates, but he does not attribute the change in Red Chinese leadership to the 12 years between 1960 and 1972, but *to one week in 1972* (February 21-28)—"the week that changed the world," the Kissinger "opening toward China." As he himself once described it:

What we are doing now with China is so great, so historic, that the word "Vietnam" will be only a footnote when it is written in history.

Obviously, a no-win war that cost the United States 50,000 lives and $140 billion—money diverted away from strategic weapons while the Soviets were building a nuclear first-strike capability—cannot compare in historic importance with a Kissinger diplomatic gambit. Not, that is, in Dr. Kissinger's estimation.

The contrast of Kissinger's estimates of the character, reliability, and humanity of the Red Chinese leaders, who then and now were the same, reveals more about his competence and character than it does about Mao Tse-tung and Chou En-lai. Either Dr. Kissinger was wildly irresponsible in smearing them then, or he is even more wildly irresponsible now in his estimate of how radically he has changed them, and in staking all our lives on his recent estimate.

Consider what he is really accusing the Red Chinese leaders of in his early estimate; not expressly, to be sure, but by inescapable inference and simple computation. The "fanatic" Red Chinese leaders—

especially his friend, Chou En-lai—would be capable of launching a counterpopulation all-out nuclear war, recognizing in advance that it would kill 170 million Americans, 200 million Russians, and 250 million Chinese; and they would do this because they see such a nuclear war as "perhaps the best means of dominating the world."

It is significant that Dr. Kissinger did not see this Chinese-motivated nuclear war as a mere remote possibility; he saw it instead as such a real threat that it posed the vital question of "whether we can stand idly by *while this peril develops.*" It is also significant that he then saw no possibility of the then-leaders of Red China *changing* from their atomic insanity (which regarded the nuclear incineration of some 620 million people, including some 200 million of their own, as "tolerable"). The only hope he then entertained was for replacement of the then-leaders by a "more humane group."

Of prime interest to all Americans should be Kissinger's concluding and climactic question: "Can we afford to permit China to develop the power to destroy humanity without control?"

This question is vital to us now because (and this is an ironic point) to appease the men in the Kremlin and to bribe them into signing his bundle of agreements that would create a new "broad political relationship" with the United States, Dr. Kissinger deliberately deprived the entire population of the United States of all defense against nuclear incineration in a Red Chinese nuclear attack. He was so eager to give the Soviet missiles a "free ride" into the United States, with the capability of incinerating our population, that he extended the free-ride benefits also to the Red Chinese.

Whereas Dr. Kissinger once questioned whether we could afford to *permit* China to develop the capability to destroy humanity, he has now *given* China the unlimited opportunity to destroy scores of millions of Americans.

The strategic significance of what he has done is simply staggering. First, it must be recognized that there is no question but that we were capable of building—within the relevant timeframe—an almost totally effective antimissile defense against any capability which the Chinese might develop in the 1970s. Even McNamara estimated officially that, without any ABM system, the Red Chinese might kill between 25 and 30 million Americans, but that even a light ABM system would save nearly all those lives, and might save them all. President Nixon, on March 14, 1969, in urging Congress to fund the Safeguard ABM system, declared that it was necessary to fulfill three objectives:

1. Protection of our land-based retaliatory forces against a direct attack by the Soviet Union.
2. Defense of the American people against the kind of nuclear attack that Communist China is likely to be able to mount within the decade.
3. Protection against accidental attacks from any source.

There is no question but that an effective defense *would have been possible.* Kissinger, however, in his anxiety to secure the SALT I Agreements with the Soviets, bound the United States to forswear *all three objectives* "for a period of unlimited duration."

The American people do not yet understand that the Kissinger-Moscow Summit SALT I ABM Treaty amended the Constitution of the United States to prohibit the U.S. Government from providing for the common defense of the people against nuclear missile attack by the Soviet Union. This is why it can be accurately called the SALT I Anti-Defense Treaty. It also prohibits our government from defending us against nuclear missile attacks by the Red Chinese—an additional result that Dr. Kissinger has effectively concealed from the American people. On this point alone he has forfeited any right to the confidence of the nation.

Take, for example, his coverup in this colloquy with Senator William Fulbright during the question-and-answer period after the White House briefing of June 15, 1972, for the five congressional committees:

> *Senator Fulbright:* Can I ask you to comment on one aspect, on the significance of ABM . . . ?
>
> How do you evaluate what appears to me to be a renunciation of the effort to create a defense? What you have left in the ABM is surely nothing more than a token? . . .
>
> *Dr. Kissinger:* I believe, Mr. Chairman, this is a very good point. The limit on ABMs or effective ABMs of *both sides,* really creates a situation, as I said in my statement, in one sentence, in which the offensive weapons of *both sides* really have a *free ride* into the country of the other.
>
> So that, therefore, the difference in numbers is somewhat less significant than you would assess otherwise. There is still a danger that one side will get such an enormous numerical advantage in warheads that it can completely obliterate the force of the other.
>
> *But in the absence of significant defenses, even relatively small forces can do an enormous amount of damage.*

Thus Dr. Kissinger himself has admitted that, in the absence of "significant defenses" (such as are prohibited by the SALT I ABM Treaty), even "small" forces (such as the Red Chinese will soon possess) will be able to "do an enormous amount of damage." Yet he makes no mention of the fact that our entire population is being offered up as hostages not only to the Soviet Union, but to Red China as well; he speaks only of "*both* sides," indicating only the United States and the Soviet Union.

The only time in his briefings on SALT I in which he even mentioned the Red Chinese nuclear threat was when Congressman Lucien N. Nedzi asked him a direct, specific question, and Dr. Kissinger could not avoid answering. Here is Dr. Kissinger's full reply, revealing one of his most devious and deliberately deceptive techniques:

> *Congressman Nedzi:* Dr. Kissinger, on March 14 [1969] the President gave as a rationale for the broad Safeguard system, part of his rationale, was the defense of the American people against the kind of nuclear attack which the People's Republic of China is likely to be able to mount within the decade.
>
> Has anything happened to that threat?
>
> *Dr. Kissinger:* Our estimate of the Chinese nuclear capability is still approximately what it was at the time that Safeguard was developed. (Dr. Kissinger then continued with the material quoted in the right-hand column on pages 33-34.)

This cannot be interpreted, in context, in any way other than that Dr. Kissinger was deliberately trying to make the American people, and the five key congressional committees, believe that the Red Chinese had made no substantial progress in the development of their nuclear capability in more than three years: from March 1969 to June 15, 1972.

U.S. intelligence estimates of the development of the Red Chinese nuclear threat have been shockingly bad in their consistent underestimation. Senator James L. Buckley, for example, in his testimony on SALT I before the Senate Foreign Relations Committee, emphasized these critical points:

> I would point out that these intelligence analysts are the ones who have consistently underestimated Soviet nuclear force objectives. It is these same intelligence analysts who advised Secretary of Defense Robert S. McNamara in the mid-1960s that the Soviet Union had permanently accepted the status of strategic inferiority.
>
> It is these same intelligence analysts who concluded in 1964 that the Chinese Communists would detonate a primitive nuclear device made of plutonium rather than the uranium device actually detonated which required a huge gaseous diffusion plant for the manufacture of nuclear material.[18]

But during the three years in question, 1969 through June 1972, our intelligence estimates had actually demonstrated that the Red Chinese threat was far more advanced than Kissinger would have us believe. In this period, in which he would have us think that the Chinese were "approximately" standing still, they had made the final and climactic step toward development of a long-range nuclear missile capability that would actually threaten the United States.

The Red Chinese launched an orbiting space satellite on April 24, 1970. This satellite capability was proof positive that ICBM capability is within the realized state of their technology. U.S. intelligence reported this major development in Chinese strategic nuclear delivery capability, but Dr. Kissinger ignored it. More accurately, he suppressed it at a time when he was trying to justify the SALT Anti-Defense Treaty and the way it prohibited any effective defense by the American people against the Chinese ICBM threat. As late as February 25, 1971, he had admitted in the Kissinger-Nixon *State of the World Report* that "before this decade is over, the Chinese will have the capability to threaten some of our major population centers." Even in the 1972 *State of the World Report*, delivered on February 9, only three months prior to the SALT signing, the fact that "the Chinese are continuing to develop a strategic offensive capability" was presented as one of the factors that "confirm the wisdom of the decision to begin Safeguard ABM deployment."

As might be expected, the only *accurate* information as to U.S. intelligence reports on Red Chinese nuclear threat developments was revealed by Secretary of Defense Melvin Laird—and it all squarely contradicted the misinformation put out by Dr. Kissinger—who had implied an "approximate" standstill from 1969 through 1972. In his report to Congress dated February 20, 1970, Secretary Laird said:

> We know that the Chinese have the capability of testing an ICBM in the immediate future and that they are likely to have an operational capability in the next several years.

In his report dated March 9, 1971, he added:

> The Chinese have continued to make progress toward the development of an ICBM system. Estimated earliest possible initial ICBM capability is 1973 with the more likely time being in the mid-1970s.

By February 17, 1972, his language was stronger:

> The growth of Chinese nuclear strike capability has been remarkable, given the short time it has been in existence and the formidable obstacles that had to be overcome. . . . China is now focusing on development of liquid-fueled ICBM/IRBM systems. There is some evidence that the Chinese are engaged in the *deployment* of solid fuel missiles. . . .
>
> The two Chinese space satellites launched during the last year and a half, and the approximately one dozen nuclear tests since 1964, indicate a fairly high degree of sophistication in both missile and warhead development. The two space satellites . . . should be considered as part of China's progressive development of an ICBM . . . a reduced-range testing of an ICBM system may have already occurred.

In his Final Report dated January 8, 1973, which covered 1972 (the last year of the three-year period which Dr. Kissinger asserted was a standstill period of China's nuclear strike development), Secretary Laird revealed:

> The remarkable growth of the People's Republic of China's nuclear strike

capability in both missiles and bombers has been maintained during 1972. The Chinese are moving forward rapidly with their program to deploy liquid-fueled MR/IRBM missiles and to develop an ICBM.

Richard A. Helms, in his last official briefing prior to being ousted to make room for Henry Kissinger's first nominee for CIA Director, told the Senate Armed Services Committee in a closed session that China was on the verge of becoming a nuclear superpower, and that actual deployment of ICBMs was imminent. Senator Stuart Symington, who has a penchant for getting the strategic significance of such developments backwards, declared he was shocked, and that "this to me reduced the practical effects of the SALT talks." As a matter of hard fact, it has doubled, in nuclear spades, the vulnerability of the United States under the SALT I Anti-Defense Treaty. To phrase it more accurately in terms of an attempted play on game-words, we became *vulnerable* upon the signing of SALT; and we were *doubled* when the Red Chinese began deployment of their ICBM force.

In contrast to Symington, Henry Kissinger knows very well the way that SALT I guarantees the Red Chinese a free ride for their nuclear missiles to incinerate American cities. He attempts to justify paying "this price of foregoing the additional protection" which President Nixon had requested in proposing the original Safeguard program. Dr. Kissinger contends that we can safely rely entirely on our retaliatory capability, even though we have abandoned all defense. This means that he has staked all our lives on the validity of his assumption that:

> We have such an overwhelming retaliatory capability vis-a-vis any country other than the Soviet Union, that the idea of a third nuclear country attacking the United States is a rather remote possibility.

Just how "remote" is remote enough? If you examine the countervailing strategic analysis, it becomes clear that abandoning defense and relying solely upon our retaliatory capability, regardless of how relatively "overwhelming" it may be vis-a-vis Red China, is a wildly irresponsible gamble. Here again, the pseudosophistication of a Kissinger theory is exposed by a contrary and commonsense evaluation by Defense Secretary Melvin Laird to the Senate Armed Services and Appropriations Committees on February 20, 1970:

> Some have contended that a relatively small number of warheads detonated over China's 50 largest cities could destroy half of their urban population and more than half of their industry, as well as most of their key government officials and a large majority of their scientific, technical and skilled workers. This amount of destruction, they maintain, should be a sufficient deterrent to an attack by Communist China on the U.S.
>
> However, there are other ways the Chinese Communists might use their nuclear capability—as a threat to the U.S. or our friends in Asia—and

while the fact that we can destroy a sizable proportion of the Chinese urban population and industrial capacity is important, it may not necessarily be decisive in this latter case.

China is a predominantly rural society where the great majority of people live off the land and are dependent only to a limited extent on urban industry for their survival. The key government officials and even the skilled workers can be evacuated from the cities in time of crisis. The Chinese are taking steps to decentralize their industry.

In contrast to China, our population is heavily concentrated in a relatively few large cities—25 percent in the 10 largest cities of the U.S., compared with 11 percent in the 1,000 largest Chinese cities. Consequently, they could inflict on us a proportionately greater number of fatalities in a smaller attack than we could inflict on them in a very large attack. Finally, in any nuclear confrontation, we would still have to maintain a sufficient deterrent against the Soviet Union. . . .

. . . in view of the nature of the developing Chinese nuclear threat, *it would seem foolhardy on our part to rely on our deterrent forces only—* if a better alternative is available.

A flexible Safeguard defense would serve a future President far better than a rigid offensive capability. As President Nixon said: "No president with the responsibility for the lives and security of the American people could fail to provide this protection." It is crucial that we provide a more complete counter to this Chinese threat, and, with Safeguard, we have the option to do so.[19]

Tragically, Richard Nixon has demonstrated that a President who has been completely turned around by a Henry Kissinger can indeed— despite his responsibility for the lives and security of the American people—fail to provide such protection. Even worse, under such influence he could and did deprive the American people of *all* effective protection against nuclear missiles launched by *any* enemy, for a "period of unlimited duration" into the future. "Foolhardy" seems an understatement. Any successor President who continued Kissinger in power would be similarly influenced.

All this paints a bleak picture of the threat from Red China. There has been, however, a resounding new development that makes the potential of the Red Chinese nuclear threat vastly more dramatic—so dramatic, indeed, that a presentation of it must take the form of a scenario.

2

Time: September 1976.
Place: Secure Conference Room, Imperial Palace, Peking.
Premier Chou En-lai (or his successor) is conducting a Top Secret conference with Dr. Henry Kissinger. No staff members are present. Chou and Kissinger are alone. Chou is doing all the talking:

"I summoned you to Peking, Dr. Kissinger, to discuss with you the most serious, the most momentous emergency in the history of the world. Some of the circumstances creating this emergency are already known to you, through information supplied for your eyes only by U.S. intelligence. I happen to know, however, that through your total control of the U.S. intelligence community you have suppressed this information and not permitted the President to hear about it.

"I refer, of course, to the Top Secret Soviet war plans. You have had the information that six members of the Politburo and three highly trusted members of the General Staff are even now working out the final details for a strategic nuclear attack against the United States, and that the attack will be launched within six months. You realized that, if this intelligence were allowed to reach the President, it would discredit you. It would reveal to him that all your advice about relations with the Soviet Union has been disastrously wrong; and that your new strategy and foreign policies have put the President in a position in which his only alternatives are to await the total destruction of the United States, or to interpose a preemptive surrender to the Kremlin in the hope that they would accept it.

"What your intelligence did not discover, however, is that those nuclear-power-mad atomic maniacs of the Soviet Politburo and the Red Army Chiefs plan to launch a strategic attack against the People's Republic of China concurrently with their strike at America. This will make us—whether we like it or not—cobelligerents with you. But we can survive only if we become allies, also.

"Ever since 1960 we have known of the Soviet plans to attack the United States. Khrushchev revealed the *political* version of these plans in his speech of January 6, 1961, in language not easily penetrable to the West, but readily understood by all Communists. We also obtained the Top Secret *military* version of these plans—which the Soviets had withheld from us even though at that time we were supposed to be close allies in the great Communist cause. Their highly knowledgeable defector, Colonel Oleg Penkovskiy, had passed those plans to the British, and we obtained them through our contacts in London. We know that, ever since 1960, the Soviet Union has been run on a wartime basis to give top priority for all resources to the buildup of a first-strike capability against the United States. Now they have attained their full force levels.

"Back then, they considered that destruction of the military power of the United States would remove the last obstacle to their control of the entire world. They thought that the leadership of the People's Republic of China would submit to domination by the Kremlin. When we surprised them by refusing to accept their crude revisionism and distortion of true Communist doctrine, they turned against us. Now they know that the United States is no longer the sole obstacle to Soviet rule of the world, so they plan on wreaking enough nuclear devastation on us at the same time that they will be able to oust Chairman Mao and all of us who are true to pure Communist doctrine.

"This is why we must be allies. I will be frank with you: I do not like being allied with the leader of the capitalist-imperialistic camp. But we have no choice if we are to avert the destruction of the People's Republic of China and save 800 million Chinese people from nuclear incineration or slavery to the Soviet deviationists.

"In any nuclear confrontation, the effective strategic power of a nation is the capability of its strategic forces *multiplied* by the credibility of the leadership's will to use that force if necessary. You have prattled so long about nuclear power being 'unusable,' that no one, least of all the ruling members of the Kremlin's Politburo, would ever believe in your *will* to attempt to use it. Thus, no matter how great the actual strategic power of the United States, when multiplied by the zero representing your credibility, the product would be zero.

"Unfortunately, in an actual nuclear strategic conflict, as distinguished from a psychological confrontation, your actual will, as distinguished from your credibility, is a factor in the product. Your eloquence and your brilliance in dealing with theories have so long enabled you to rationalize failure of will that you have never needed to develop willpower, either for yourself or for the leadership of the nation that you unofficially, but so effectively, control.

"Therefore, U.S. strategic power *times* Kissinger *equals* zero.

"We have studied your career and analyzed your character. You have always been surrender-prone. We have no question that, if the Soviets delivered an ultimatum demanding unconditional surrender of the United States under threat of an all-out nuclear attack, you would tender the surrender. We are also convinced that, if you have sufficiently convincing intelligence estimates that the Soviets are planning a surprise attack, you will volunteer a preemptive surrender.

"With you in charge of U.S. strategy and policies, therefore, all the strategic forces of the United States would be wasted. An even higher probability exists that you would meekly surrender them intact to the men in the Kremlin, and they could add them to their own vast power to threaten or destroy the People's Republic of China.

"This we will not tolerate. You are probably at this moment turning over in that world-famous mind of yours the question, how could those Red Chinese fanatics (we recall your early characterization of us by that term) possibly control your actions?

"The answer is that you yourself made it possible for us to do so. Back in 1972, in your eagerness to appease the men in the Kremlin and build your own reputation as a peacemaker, you sold the SALT I ABM Treaty to your too-trusting countrymen. By doing so, you destroyed and left in a shambles a truly splendid antimissile defense program that was just attaining momentum. You bound the United States never to provide a defense for its people against incineration by nuclear missiles. For a 'period of unlimited duration' you rendered them powerless to defend against even the smallest and least sophisticated force of missiles, regardless of which nation in the world might launch them, and even regardless of whether they were launched intentionally or accidentally.

"Without your destruction of the U.S. Safeguard ABM program, there would have been no use for China to attempt to build substantial numbers of ICBMs before 1977, which is the date we estimated the Soviets would launch a strategic nuclear attack. Even the light point-defense plus area-defense proposed in the Nixon program, when netted together, could have provided substantially a total defense against the numbers and sophistication of the missile force that we could produce. We demonstrated our ICBM capability in April 1970, but it would have required 10 years for us to produce an offensive force of ICBMs in sufficient numbers and with adequate penetration aids and multiple warheads to penetrate and saturate the ABM defense that you could have had by 1976.

"In 1971, your then Secretary of Defense Melvin Laird estimated that our Chinese ICBM program would produce only 20 missiles for deployment by mid-1976.[1] But he could not foresee—and you, Dr. Kissinger, have not recognized even yet—that, when you bound the United States to the SALT I ABM Treaty in May 1972, you provided the incentive for China to produce the maximum number of ICBMs in the least possible time. SALT I guaranteed us that each and every missile we could launch against the U.S. *population* would have what you described as a 'free ride,' because none could be shot down by ABMs. You gave us assurance that we would not be wasting our limited technological and industrial resources on a strategic weapons program that U.S. ABM defenses would doom to failure. We knew from then on that we could count on success. So we marshaled our resources to double and then redouble our missile production.

"I would not have you think that we were so easily fooled—as the Americans were—into believing that, because the General Secretary of the Communist Party of the Soviet Union had solemnly signed a treaty with the United States binding the Soviets also not to deploy more than 100 ABM launchers to defend people, that they would actually deprive the peoples of the Soviet Union of all effective defenses against nuclear missiles. Not even renegade Communists would do such an immoral and shocking thing. Only surrender-prone U.S. liberals would do that.

"Even that most evil of deviationists Nikita Khrushchev, for all his apparent adventurism in clandestinely deploying missiles to Cuba against a United States then eight times stronger strategically, bowed to Lenin's doctrine that the *first* priority must be given to saving the people. True, in his speech of January 6, 1961, Khrushchev declared a longterm policy of building a first-strike capability against the United States so as to launch a preventive nuclear war against the United States with a massive surprise attack. But he made it clear that, in this buildup of strategic forces, *defense* of the population would be given equal priority with *offensive* mobilization. Thus he quoted Lenin:

> If we can save the working man, save the main productive force of society — the worker—we shall get everything back, but, should we fail to save him, we are lost.

"Thus, Dr. Kissinger, we here in the People's Republic of China were under no such illusions as you believed—or led the American people to believe you believed. We did not think for one minute that, if we had a substantial ICBM force deployed before 1977, we could count on launching it against a Soviet Union that would be stripped of all active missile defenses (except for the SALT I nominal allowances). We knew they were already cheating on the 1972 SALT I ABM Treaty before they signed it, and that they had planned even more massive cheating later—or, as they prefer to call it, utilizing 'technical interpretations.'

"So we recognized that it would be useless and a waste of our resources to build an ICBM force *unless we could suppress the extensive Soviet missile-defense networks.* But the *capability* of suppressing them was far beyond the realized state of our technology, and even further beyond our industrial capability.

"The *solution* to the problem of suppressing the Soviet ABMs was not, however, beyond Chinese ingenuity.

"Our great leader, Chairman Mao Tse-tung, conceived the most brilliant stratagem of the nuclear age. His solution was so splendid that it solved not only our preliminary problem of suppressing Soviet ABM defenses (obviously, not an end in itself), but also our primary problem: providing for the launch of a sufficient number of missiles and warheads against the Soviets to insure that, in their retaliatory strike against us, they would not be able to devastate China beyond prompt recuperation. Hopefully, as you American liberals would say, perhaps the attack against the Russians could be made so massive that really effective retaliation would be impossible or, at least, irrational.

"Communist leadership—even revisionist leadership—tends to comprise men of common sense with the courage to face facts, including the macabre facts of nuclear war. The basis of our nuclear strategy, therefore, is similar to that of the Soviet Communists; first and most important is: *never permit your nation to be hit by the undamaged nuclear forces of the enemy.*

"That is why, for all these years, the Soviets have been building their first-strike force against the United States: they plan 'to strike first, at any costs,' as Colonel Penkovskiy accurately reported to British and U.S. intelligence. In this way, they calculated, they would never be hit by more than the badly damaged remnants of the enemy's peacetime inventory of strategic weapons. Against such a *preventive war* strategy, as you well know, the theory of minimum deterrence cannot possibly work. Minimum deterrence is an old Pugwash fallacy which you gave new window dressing under the label of 'nuclear sufficiency.' But even your sophisticated verbiage can't make it work. If they have to be hit at all, the Soviets plan to be hit by no more than a decimated deterrent, instead of by a full undamaged force.

"That same determination *not* to be hit by an undamaged enemy strategic force is what has compelled us to decide on a *preemptive strike* against the Soviet Union. We must preempt the Kremlin strategists' plan to strike the United States and China by surprise, simultaneously. Although they plan to target most of their strategic weapons against Americans, against your missiles and your bombers, the number and power of the weapons targeted against us would still be enough to kill nearly 100 million of our people by blast or fallout, to bring on the death of millions more by starvation, and to destroy 90 percent of our rapidly growing industry. This we will not accept.

"I am briefing you carefully on these points, Dr. Kissinger, because I want you to realize fully that Chairman Mao and I have reached a firm and final decision to accept serious risks in order to avert being hit by the surprise first-strike of an undamaged Soviet strategic force.

"You realize, of course, that there is only one strategic force in the world that can accomplish enough damage to Soviet strategic weapons, defensive and offensive, to serve our purpose. We do not have such a force, nor do we have the capability of building such a force in the relevant timeframe. But the genius of Chairman Mao has conceived a method by which we can obtain control of that one-and-only strategic force that is essential to our survival.

"We are going to *compel* the United States to deliver an all-out preemptive disarming surprise attack against the Soviet Union. I use the term 'compel' advisedly and precisely. Logic, common sense, and hard evidence should persuade you that doing so will be the best and, indeed, the only rational course of action for the United States. Your only other alternatives are nuclear incineration or abject surrender. Even those stark courses are not really at your option. If you should attempt to surrender, the Kremlin may not accept it; or, they may accept and then destroy you anyway by nuclear means.

"We are convinced that neither logic nor common sense nor any amount of hard evidence could prevail against the ideological preconceptions that you expressed in both words and actions in your SALT I negotiations in 1972. Nor would we trust you to go through with it if you assured us you were persuaded. We have sized you up, Dr. Kissinger, as the total embodiment of the American type that old Nikita Khrushchev appraised as 'too liberal to fight—even in defense of your own vital interests.' Although he was a reckless deviationist, he certainly understood the character of U.S. liberals. 'A country's leader's fear of a nuclear war can paralyze that country's defenses,' he warned, 'and if a country's defenses are paralyzed, then war really is inevitable: the enemy is sure to sense your fright and take advantage of it.' The members of the Kremlin's Politburo have sensed your fright, and they are taking advantage of it.

"So we can't trust you, and we can't rely on persuading you. We are left with no alternative except to *threaten* you. We recognize that the threat must be completely credible: we cannot afford to leave you with any doubts about our determination to act.

"The second essential of our threat is equally vital: the consequences with which we threaten you, if you fail to launch a disarming strike against the Soviet Union in accordance with our instructions, must be so terrible and so certain as to override your fear of what will happen to you if you do deliver the disarming strike against the Soviets.

"With the relatively meager resources at our command in China, only the genius of Chairman Mao could have contrived the imaginative blend of strategy and supporting programs to bring into being—in time—a threat both sufficiently credible and sufficiently massive.

"The strategic concept of a 'catalytic' nuclear war is not new; it dates from the time that the potential of nuclear weapons was first analyzed. It is well, but briefly, described in Herman Kahn's great treatise *On Thermonuclear War* (to which we and the Soviet strategists have given much understanding attention). Unlike some other so-called strategists, however, Dr. Kahn gives credit where credit is due, and he credits Amron Katz with originating the name of this fascinating type of nuclear strategy.

"Two types of catalytic nuclear war are recognized. The first is one touched off by the catalytic action of an 'ambitious' third nation. If China were 10 years more advanced in the buildup of strategic nuclear forces, we might have considered this strategy, although we are not ambitious in the sense the Soviet Union is. By hypothesis, the third nation is less powerful than either of the others, but is able to create a situation best described in colloquial American terms as 'let's you and him fight.' They do, and either they accomplish mutual destruction or, before the conflict can be terminated, so weaken each other that the third nation achieves its ambition of becoming the world's sole nuclear superpower.

"It is the second type of catalytic nuclear war in which we are interested. It just so happens that China was chosen as a hypothetical example by Herman Kahn in explaining the catalytic motivation:

> There is another type of catalytic war which may be more plausible—
> where a *desperate* third nation has a problem which can be solved if it
> touches off the right type of catalytic war. Imagine, for example, a war
> between India and China, which the Indians were losing. The hard-
> pressed Indians might feel that the United States was morally obligated
> to come to their aid, and that any way of obtaining this aid was as good
> as any other.
>
> Or imagine a situation in which China felt hard-pressed by the United
> States—possibly over Formosa. The Chinese might tell the Soviets, "We

are going to strike the imperialists at 5 A.M. tomorrow and you might as well come along and help us do a thorough job, for they will undoubtedly strike you even if you don't."

"Even though Herman Kahn's hypothetical war game is now outdated by changed political circumstances, you can see the possibilities Chairman Mao studied before adapting this strategy to our desperate need to degrade or avert the Soviet attack against us, which we knew would be timed no later than 1977. In the Kahn examples, however, the catalytic trigger employed was *actual use*—the firing or launching—of nuclear weapons. Resorting instead to the *threat* of use, rather than actual use, is sometimes far more intelligent and effective. In this case, Chairman Mao immediately recognized that bringing in the United States by a credible and effective threat would serve our purpose brilliantly, whereas the actual use of nuclear weapons would not.

"In planning how to make our threat against the United States both sufficiently credible and terrible to serve as the catalyst, Chairman Mao's principal tool was a short table presenting the urbanization and industrial dispersal of the three great powers. It is taken from the report of the then U.S. Secretary of Defense Melvin R. Laird, entitled *Fiscal Year 1971 Defense Program and Budget*. It was presented by him to a Joint Session of the Senate Armed Services and Appropriations Committees on February 20, 1970.

"Fortunately for our purposes, it deals in percentages rather than finite numbers. We have checked it out and found it still sufficiently accurate as of 1976. This is the verbatim text, Dr. Kissinger, and I want you to study it on your long plane trip back to Washington. When we add to it the results of the two Chinese strategic programs which Chairman Mao has linked to it, it will explain our position better than 10 times 10,000 words:

Cumulative Percentage Distribution
Population and Industrial Capacity

No. of Cities	United States		Soviet Union		Communist China	
	Pop.	Ind. Cap.	Pop.	Ind. Cap.	Pop.	Ind. Cap.
10	25.1	33.1	8.3	25.0	3.7	30-35
50	42.0	55.0	20.0	40.0	6.8	50-60
100	48.0	65.0	25.0	50.0	8.6	65-75
200	55.0	75.0	34.0	62.0	9.0	80-90
400	60.0	82.0	40.0	72.0	10.0	85-90
1000	63.0	86.0	47.0	82.0	11.0	

"I cannot resist pointing out, parenthetically, that the 'fanatic'

Chou En-lai you quoted in your 1961 book was very accurate in estimating that an all-out nuclear war would leave '10 million Americans, 20 million Russians, and 350 million Chinese.' This table shows why. Low urbanization is the key to nuclear war survival.

"Even a glance at the table shows that, if we developed the capability to destroy only the 10 largest U.S. cities, we could directly threaten the death of some 53 million Americans—that is, 25 percent of your 1976 population of roughly 215 million.

"The threat of 50 megadeaths should be—to a Westerner, anyway—a terrible threat, especially on an absolute basis. But we were also up against a requirement for what might be called *relative* terror when compared to the Soviet threat against the U.S. population. So we decided to build up to a strategic nuclear force level that would enable us to have high confidence in our capability to destroy the 100 largest American cities, thus enabling us to threaten directly more than 103 million Americans with nuclear death.

"Starting with our total peacetime inventory, we can apply crude rule-of-thumb degradation factors as follows: launchers available = 95 percent of inventory; launchers ready = 95 percent of launchers available; launch reliability = 90 percent of those ready; so the subtotal that an attacker can count on as reliable is 81 percent of inventory. Early flight failures subtract another 5 percent, late flight failures an additional 5 percent, and failures at target a final one percent. Thus, it is calculated that we require a reserve of about 40 missiles, or a total inventory of 140 ICBM launchers with a capability of hitting targets throughout the entire United States.

"As a practical matter, we hope and plan not to launch *any* ICBMs against our unwilling and unwanted, but badly needed, ally, the United States. We really plan to launch against the Soviets, who have built to the capability of destroying both China and America and plan to use that capability.

"Our next computation is whether the total number of ICBM launchers needed to establish a sufficiently terrible threat against the United States is sufficient also for our targeting purposes against the Soviets. Fortunately, although we could well use more, we will have just barely enough missiles to target the Soviet Union when our force is supplemented by the U.S. strategic arsenal. I say this is fortunate because this number of 140 is also the absolute upper limit that we could produce and deploy within the Soviet-fixed deadline.

"A check back at the Urbanization Table shows that we would probably take out somewhat less than 70 million of the Soviet people directly in their 100 largest cities, out of a 1976 population of 275 million. Actually, we could probably take out only something more than 90 of the 100 cities we target, because our reprogramming facilities can take care only of preflight and very-early-flight failures. But we do have an extra segment of reserves calculated in case we get 'real-time' intelligence as to late-flight and target-kill failures. We would get at least 50 percent of Soviet industry with our missiles.

"Added to the Soviet targets *we* would destroy would be those assigned by us to the American missiles and effectively hit by them. In making the assignment, we took the 100 largest cities as our targets for a reason you might not guess. *Our missiles are far superior to U.S. missiles.* By superior I mean in destructive power resulting from greater accuracy of guidance and vastly more explosive power in the warheads. We have not been handicapped in our missile development (as has the United States) by any disarmament-oriented theoreticians. Whereas you deliberately blocked improvements in accuracy of guidance and increase in warhead power, both of which were well within your technology, our scientists worked for the most accurate and powerful missiles we could produce.

"Chairman Mao ordered the acceleration of our ICBM program in 1972, immediately after we obtained the text of the SALT I ABM Treaty and recognized the opportunity it created for a Chinese ICBM force that was small in relation to either the Soviet or the American missile force. At that time the Soviets had completed the development of their SS-17, SS-19, and SS-18 ICBMs and were nearing completion of their testing prior to deployment. The SS-17 and SS-19 are updates of their most numerous previous missile, the SS-11. The SS-18 updates their SS-9s. They have more powerful and more accurate warheads—and, even though they are somewhat larger, they can be retrofitted—because of the Soviets' cold-launch technique—into SS-11 and SS-9 silos, respectively. They are more accurate than U.S. missiles, because there were no handicaps imposed by any artificial policy brakes on improvement in guidance accuracy.

"Of course, we obtained our improvements in guidance largely through information from U.S. sources, some unclassified, and some through Pugwash contacts. In fact, the origin of the improvements was in the guidance systems developed by the Americans in their Apollo moon program. Pugwash conferees from the U.S.S.R. had access to the theory and drawings of all elements of the Apollo inertial guidance system, and such refinements as stellar-assisted inertial guidance. For the first time, the Soviets were able to incorporate an on-board computer in their missile-guidance package.

"The effects of the Soviet improvements in the SS-11, which changed it into the SS-17 and SS-19, were to make them very effective silo-destroying, missile-killing counterforce weapons. Although the SS-11 has always been several times more powerful than the U.S. Minuteman as to warhead, the U.S. public has always been deceived into regarding them as equals. Our experts estimate the explosive power of the SS-17 and SS-19 single warheads at more than 12 megatons, but probably less than 18; or they can be fitted with six MIRVs of one to two megatons each.

"This brings me to the capability of our own small-in-numbers, but very effective, missile force, and to why we have assigned the priority counterpopulation targets to our own ICBMs instead of to U.S. weapons. By a combination of hard work and good luck, by superb coordination and cooperation between our teams of scientists and intelligence experts, we have been able to develop and produce a missile even better than any of the Soviet SS-17s, SS-19s, and SS-18s for our purposes. We have no need for either MRVs or MIRVs, and we cannot afford the waste of nuclear explosive materials that results from mounting multiple warheads on single missiles. In your Poseidon MIRVed warheads, you replace 3½ megatons of explosive power with 1/2 megaton divided among 10 miniature MIRV warheads. That is, a single Poseidon warhead would yield four megatons, whereas your 10 Poseidon MIRVs yield only a total of one-half of one megaton.

"Soviet burning techniques—that is, the methods of developing maximum explosive power per unit of weight—have been vastly superior to those of the United States ever since the Soviet ban-breaking tests of 1961-62. But, like the United States, the Soviets have not been able to do any atmospheric testing for more than 10 years. This has been no disadvantage to them vis-a-vis the United States, of course, and was an inconsequential price for them to pay for the Moscow Test Ban Treaty of 1963 that froze U.S. technological inferiority in high-yield warheads.

"By our intelligence and scientific teams' brilliant accomplishments, we were able to acquire Soviet burning techniques that they developed in their last atmospheric tests in 1962, but which they have been able to refine only through the limited means of underground tests. Extrapolation never equals the real thing. We have passed them in yield/weight ratios, especially in the weapons of 10+-megaton range. This is why all our 140 ICBMs are in the 10+-megaton range—all more powerful than their SS-17, SS-19, and SS-18 Soviet prototypes—and our guidance package is just as accurate as that of the Soviets. You know this is not mere bluff. I remember that back in 1974 the Chairman of your Joint Chiefs of Staff rated our Chinese ICBM as in the SS-9 class, that is, 25+ megatons.[2]

"Thus, we have high confidence that no city in either the United States or the Soviet Union can survive a hit by one of our ICBMs, nor will any life survive even in the suburbs of the targeted areas. Like the Soviets (but unlike you Americans), we have 'dirtied up' our missiles somewhat.

"So much for the destructive capability of our ICBM force to create a sufficiently terrible *threat* against your American people and nation, and an effective strategic capability against the U.S.S.R.

"Now, let us consider the *credibility* of our threat against the United States—the degree of credibility necessary to compel you to join us in our disarming-counterpopulation strike against the Soviet deviationists, those atomic maniacs who would, if we give them the opportunity, destroy both our nations.

"When you, Dr. Kissinger, sold the United States on the suicidal theory that your country needs no missile defense against China because of the great retaliatory capability of the U.S. strategic missile force, you reversed the pre-SALT I commonsense decision of both President Johnson and President Nixon—that a *defense* was needed, as well as a deterrent. The slick and deceptive arguments of the Pugwash unilateral-disarmament advocates, so well indoctrinated by Moscow, served us very well indeed. These arguments try to make it appear that, in a city-swapping exchange of nuclear weapons, the United States would be better off than China because your weapons are more numerous.

"They speciously contend that missiles targeted on our 50 largest cities would destroy 'more than half' of China's urban population, as well as more than half of our industrial capacity. However, they suppress the fact that the impressive-sounding 'more than half' of our *urban* population is but a tiny fraction of our *total* population. After such a strike, we would still have left a population on the order of 697.5 million—3 times more people than the United States and nearly 2½ times more people than the Soviet Union. That is quite enough for a viable nation destined to be the greatest power in the world.

"The credibility of a threat, however, is a psychological matter. It must be evaluated from the standpoint of the one threatened. Thus, we were concerned that the ruling elitists in the United States—led by yourself, Dr. Kissinger—might continue to believe in the effectiveness of the deterrence against us, based on your asserted capability of killing millions of Chinese by destroying our 50 largest cities and half our industrial capacity at the same time.

"Again, Chairman Mao's genius solved our problem. Ever since 1969, when the Soviet threat against the People's Republic became unmistakable, he has inspired the masses of our people to tremendous volunteer efforts in digging deep fallout and blast shelters, both for our people and our industries. After the U.S.-Soviet signing of the SALT I ABM Treaty, from which he evolved his brilliant catalytic strategy that will enable us to survive in triumph, he realized that this great passive defense against nuclear attack, which he had already

52

initiated, would be doubly valuable. It would not only protect our people and our new industries from *actual Soviet attack,* but it would make entirely credible—even to U.S. liberals paralyzed by fear of nuclear war—the fact that China would have nothing to fear from a U.S. retaliatory attack against Chinese cities.

"At the same time that he ordered the acceleration of our ICBM program, he inspired our very loyal masses of people to work even harder and for longer hours on the missile shelter programs. Studies by Soviet experts—confirmed by U.S. analysis—demonstrate that the Soviet passive defense program can limit fatalities in an all-out U.S. attack to a mere six percent of the Soviet population—fewer than they lost in World War II. In our case, we are building even more and more extensive shelters against nuclear attack. Furthermore, we are far less vulnerable to attack than the Soviet Union because the intensity of their urbanization is three times greater than ours. Their 50 largest cities contain 20 percent of the total Soviet population, as against only 6.8 percent of ours.

"The unequalled stature of Chairman Mao as a leader has been demonstrated by the near-unanimous response of almost 800 million of our people, who realized that his appeal was based on his concern for them. 'Dig your tunnels deep,' he enjoined them, 'and store grain everywhere.' The underground factories and shelters they have created in a few short years are among the wonders of the world! Some go seven stories underground. How far would you get with such an appeal in the United States to add "regular" extra working hours without any extra pay?

"The result is such an extensive network that more than 500 of our cities have adequate shelter-protection against missile attack. The United States has *no* missiles of sufficient explosive power to kill any substantial number of our people in these shelters or to destroy the new, modern segments of our growing industry, most of which is now safely underground.

"The wisdom of Chairman Mao, however, is so great that he recognized immediately that it is not enough that we *have* this effective protection against U.S. retaliatory attacks. The American people and their intelligence sources must *know* about it. We are completely aware of how your administrations keep your people from access to information on which their lives depend. Chairman Mao wanted to transmit the facts about our massive shelter and passive defense program through channels that the American people and their leaders would trust. He conceived the idea of inviting for a personal survey a nationally prominent American columnist who had an established reputation of being *against* the Chinese Communists.

"So Chairman Mao invited Joseph Alsop. We wanted him not only to see for himself our great passive defenses against nuclear attack, but also our new and efficient and swiftly growing industries and agricultural system. In the late 1950s and early 1960s, Alsop had described our agricultural communes as 'fearful,' 'hideous,' and 'ruthless.' He had concluded that the Chinese policy of 'forced labor' demonstrated that we Chinese leaders had 'chosen to out-Stalin Stalin.'

"Yet, in late 1972 he wrote from China upon the completion of his unrestricted tour:

> Everything in China has changed, in truth, except the endlessly resilient, hard-working, and clever Chinese people. The quality of life has changed, vastly for the worse for the ancient ruling class, but for the better for everyone else.[3]

"Even more in point for our present purposes, he spoke of the evolution of

> a strong community of interests between the United States and China from the moment the Soviet threat began to be serious, . . . [and] given the consequences of a successful Soviet attack against China, I'm convinced that if the danger becomes much more serious, we ought to do everything in our power, which is limited, to go to China's aid.

"Our prime purpose in arranging for Joseph Alsop to have free access all over China was to have him describe to the American people, through his 250 newspaper outlets in the United States, the fundamentals of our extensive shelter system.

"Dr. Kissinger, I want to impress you especially with one short but fair sample of his writings about our passive defense system. You are constantly misleading the American people by outrageously false statements pertaining to their very survival. For example, in the first week of February 1973, in a nationwide CBS television interview conducted by Marvin Kalb, you made the assertion that 'this Administration' (meaning, of course, yourself and President Nixon) will

> try to deal with the root fact of the contemporary situation, that we and the Soviet Union and the Chinese are ideological adversaries; that we are bound together by one basic fact: *none of us can survive a nuclear war.*

"This is the most cruel deception of a great people ever perpetrated by their purported leaders. You would have them believe that all three of the great powers are in the same nuclear-destruction boat. This is not true, as you very well know. Ever since the early 1950s, the Soviet Union has put massive effort into passive defense systems, and they even began to deploy *active* systems of ABMs as early as 1964. They have more than 10,000 SAM launchers for air and probably missile defense. Their shelter and passive defense systems alone could insure their surviving a nuclear war as a viable nation. As for us, although we have no *active* defenses, we have our new passive defenses, which are briefly described in an Alsop column.

"Of the three great powers, *only the United States has deliberately exposed its people to unlimited nuclear incineration.* You, Dr. Kissinger, are now primarily responsible for their present defenseless situation. Even your pussyfooting, Soviet-fearing Lyndon Johnson proposed and secured congressional support for a missile defense system to protect the people—a far more effective system than Nixon supported; but even the pre-Kissinger Nixon did support a limited missile defense system for the American people.

"To refresh your memory, I will quote the American writer Joseph Alsop on what we had accomplished four years ago to insure that *our* people *would* survive a nuclear war:

This busy city, Ta Sha La, has a secret. I learned of it in a bustling store where they sell the padded coats Peking people wear against the cold. Ta Sha La's Gloria Steinem, fair but formidable, dramatically revealed the secret by stepping on a hidden spring.

Whereupon a section of the store's flooring slid back. A concrete staircase appeared, steeply descending into the earth. And so our party went down to inspect one section of Peking's all but incredible system of air-raid shelters.

Ta Sha La is only one of the countless districts into which Peking is divided. The shelters are tunnels, the main ones eight meters (26 feet) below street level, all brick and concrete built, and all wide and high enough for three tall men to walk abreast. Ta Sha La alone has a couple of kilometers of these tunnels all connecting, in turn, with similar tunnels in other districts.

All of this was begun in 1969 when the Soviets came so close to launching a preventive nuclear attack on China. Under a fulltime staff of four, the Ta Sha La tunnels were entirely built by the employees of the street's enterprises, "like me," proudly said the local Ms. Steinem, who is a shop assistant.

Nowadays, in fact, there are two complete cities of Peking, one above the ground and another underground. The theory of the shelter system is that of the Soviet civil-defense system—not to provide permanent hiding holes but to move the people safely out of the city into the countryside in case of threatened attack.

Fallout travels with the wind. Peking's winds are all but invariably from the north. Peking has this enormous network of underground tunnels, while Moscow depends solely on early warning for timely evacuation. In sum, the Peking civil-defense system is 10 times better than that of Moscow—as well as 100 times, even 1,000 times more costly in human and material investment.

All this is pretty awesome, if you reflect upon it. To begin with, every other major city in China today, and almost all of the smaller ones, too, have close to identical shelter systems, all proportionately costly. . . . For the investment put into the underground city, every family in Peking could surely have been provided with one more room of precious living space.

In all Peking districts, the people gave their work without pay for the construction of the shelter system. Until a year ago, too, work went on as late as 11 at night, after the long ordinary working days.

Weigh these astonishing facts. No government in its senses could have ordered such enormous sacrifices and burdensome investments without a grimly serious, grimly urgent motive. There is no doubt at all about the motive, either. It was the fear of Soviet surprise attack, which became acute when the Soviet Government vainly asked for U.S. support for such an attack in 1969.[4]

"I also direct your attention, Dr. Kissinger, to a major article in the *New York Times Magazine* of March 11, 1973, by Joseph Alsop. It elaborates on the reality and imminence of the Soviet threat against China, on how seriously we take it, and on the effectiveness of our passive defense efforts. Also, we noted that, in your Administration's off-the-record background briefings to selected media representatives in 1973, the official estimate of the probability of a Soviet attack against China was 50 percent.

"In his *Times* article, Joseph Alsop described the Soviet buildup on the border of China in this manner:

By now the Soviets have many hundreds of thousands of soldiers along the frontier, they have great numbers of aircraft on newly constructed jet airfields there; great quantities of armor, mechanized equipment, and artillery of all types; huge supply dumps to sustain prolonged operations; and large numbers of heavy but mobile "Scaleboard" nuclear missiles, which have the range and power to take out any target connected with the Chinese nuclear program, except for missiles in well hardened sites.

"As a matter of fact, as of the time Alsop wrote that, the Soviets had well over one million troops on our border, in more than 50 divisions. The Soviet SS-12 Scaleboard missile, to which Alsop referred, is a very modern type, first introduced in 1969. It is the *only* tactical missile, *anywhere*, in the megaton range, and is by far the most powerful tactical offensive weapon in the world.

"I am giving you this information to impress on you that we Chinese believe we are seriously threatened with strategic nuclear attack, and we fully realize the reality of that threat. We *must* avert it. To do so, we require control of the entire U.S. strategic nuclear arsenal. The United States has no alternative—no *rational* alternative, that is— to joining forces with us, and doing so immediately.

"The next point I will explain is why we have made you an offer you cannot refuse; or, to look at it another way, an offer you *dare* not turn down; an offer that, after you consider it carefully, you will see you *would not want to refuse,* and that will accord you great stature in history as a hero and savior of your adopted country, instead of as a betrayer of the nation that has been so generous to you, a poor immigrant. This part will be intensely personal to you.

"Your own intelligence—and you are the only American who has full access to all U.S. strategic intelligence—has convinced you that the Soviets are planning a massive surprise attack against the United States. You have withheld this from the President, the Joint Chiefs of Staff, and the National Security Council. You have kept the underlings of your own staff, and the few intelligence experts who had access to vital bits of information, from speaking out by convincing them that the evidence was not 'conclusive' and that the Soviet plans they had uncovered were contingency plans only and not purposive plans. You yourself knew better, but you did not know how to extricate yourself from the predicament, let alone the United States.

"We have a way out for you personally—and the *only* way for the United States to avoid suffering both a nuclear attack and either total destruction or surrender to the Soviets.

"First, we must point out to you why your own theories designed to avert a Soviet nuclear attack on the United States did not work, and could not work. This is just in case you are really so stupid that you did not yourself realize this, which we doubt. There is always the possibility that your objective was to gain influence with the side you were *sure*—because of your surrender-prone ideology—would ultimately win. More probably, you just went along with your associates in the Council on Foreign Relations, led by Paul Nitze, in their plan to avert a Soviet strike by interposing a voluntary preemptive surrender. That is, you planned to say to the Kremlin: don't strike—you don't need to—we surrender; take the goose intact which can lay so many golden eggs.

"But the vehicles you used to con the President and the American people were your theories of the new 'pentagonal balance of power,' and your fusion of a policy of bribing the Kremlin *not* to employ its strategic nuclear power against the United States with a policy of offering yearly installments of nuclear blackmail in the form of U.S. trade with bountiful credits at the expense of the U.S. taxpayers, together with the U.S. technology the Soviets so desperately needed.

"To get through to you why *our* plans will work, whereas *yours* could not, we must point out the false assumptions in your 'new world order.' You recognized that Soviet strategic nuclear power was so vast that to balance it in similar power would require five Americas and 30 Chinas. So you deviously threw into your hypothetical 'balance of power' the *economic* power of Western Europe and Japan. This made your so-called 'equilibrium' five-sided instead of merely three-sided, as it would be with military power only. But, as you know, *economic* power requires five to ten years to produce *strategic* nuclear power. So, that part of your 'new world order' was merely window dressing to fool the naive.

"For those who were sufficiently knowledgeable to recognize this, you attempted to make the 'equilibrium' appear realistic by contending that your brilliant diplomacy had brought China to the side of the United States, and that our great population of 800 million, and our conventional military power and incipient nuclear power, together with the strategic nuclear power of the United States, could 'balance' that of the U.S.S.R.

"Strategic nuclear weapons *can* easily be made 100 million times more powerful, per weapon, than conventional weapons. However, let us take a more modest in-being example: the Soviets have about 3,000 deliverable strategic nuclear weapons, which now average about 10 megatons each. Let us compare the explosive power of that force with a force comprising an *equal number* of conventional weapons of about the largest practical explosive power: the 2,000-pound bomb. Here is what the 'balance' would look like with the same number of weapons on each side:

NUCLEAR	CONVENTIONAL
30,000,000,000 tons **of TNT explosive power**	**3,000 tons** **of TNT explosive power**

"Although your purported theory of a 'balance' or 'equilibrium' of conventional versus nuclear power was absurd when analyzed by knowledgeable objective people, you got away with it. Your President probably believes it. Most of the American people believe it. They will awaken only when blasted by actual Soviet nuclear missiles, or shocked by your surrender to the Kremlin.

"But we have always known better. We realize that, although our vastly greater population gives us a potential conventional military advantage over the Russians, neither our actual nor our potential conventional military power can realistically be weighed in the balance against Soviet strategic nuclear power.

"There is only one thing that can balance offensive strategic nuclear power in-being, and that is *offensive strategic nuclear power in-being.*

"That is exactly what we propose to do. We would, of course, prefer for China to have massive nuclear superiority, but we are realists, and we recognize that that is impossible.

"To establish a strategic nuclear balance or equilibrium that will terminate the Soviet Union's present capability substantially to destroy the cities of China, and the cities, industry, and population of the United States, there are only two *obvious* methods. It must be recognized that the Soviets have a missile throw-weight capability more than six times greater than the United States, and on the order of 30 times greater than China's; and the Soviet deliverable mega-tonnage capability is 10 to 19 times that of the United States.

"To establish a balance, therefore, we must either: (1) build up U.S. and Chinese forces to overtake the U.S.S.R. in time, or (2) by a disarming strike, destroy enough Soviet missiles to bring them down to our force level.

"Method #1 is impossible. Neither of us could overtake the Soviet headstart in five or even 10 years if they continued to build, which they would do (unlike you Americans after the Cuban missile crisis in 1962). Also, if the Soviets recognized that either of us was attempting to overtake them, they would launch a preemptive strike. As to us, they have that capability at any time. As to the United States, they will reach and pass the preemption point sometime in this year of 1976.

"Method #2 is also impossible. By definition, if the United States had sufficient counterforce weapons to accomplish this, the United States would have a first-strike capability against the Soviets. This is a capability that McNamara devoted eight years to blocking, and you, Dr. Kissinger, continued his policies for the next eight years. One or the other of you was continuously able, for 16 years, to make sure that the United States never developed sufficiently accurate guidance or sufficiently powerful warheads, or a sufficient number of missiles, to do any substantial disarming of the Soviets. And you assured them of this every year, in the annual *State of the World Report*. We Chinese simply do not have enough in numbers of missiles to attempt to employ them in a counterforce attack.

"Lesser men—even lesser geniuses—than Chairman Mao would have given up the plan for establishing a balance when it became apparent through analysis that neither of the two obvious methods, nor even a combination of them, could possibly succeed. But our Chairman never gives up—not when the survival and growth of the People's Republic of China is at stake. So here is his solution—the third answer, and the only one that can work:

A combined disarming attack by U.S. and Chinese strategic forces could not *destroy* enough Soviet weapons. The Soviets would still have a massive reserve of surviving weapons providing them with decisive superiority over whatever reserve weapons the U.S. and China might have retained.

But if Chinese-U.S. strategy is planned and timed so that the Soviets *expend* a major portion of their strategic offensive missiles in an attempt to disarm the U.S. of its land-based missiles, but the U.S. missiles are launched in time and are targeted on the remaining Soviet offensive missiles, the remaining Soviet missiles will not overbalance the joint reserves of strategic missiles retained by the U.S. and China.

"Chairman Mao's strategy is neither obvious nor simple; if it were, it could not work. It is the only way in which a large but insufficient U.S. strategic force, combined with a much smaller but powerful Chinese strategic force, can be employed to overcome the massive superiority of the Soviet strategic forces. In a few moments, I will present the intriguing ramifications of Chairman Mao's masterpiece by means of a scenario. First, however, we will make it perfectly clear to you why we know you will obey our directions on this project, and will carry your President and National Security Council along with you.

"If such an effective strategic balance as we propose is not established, the Soviets will attack or deliver an ultimatum for the surrender of the United States within six months. You will then be exposed as either history's most tragic fool and incompetent megalomaniac, or else as the most evil traitor in history.

"If, however, we do not secure your commitment to join with us, together with complete assurances that you are in fact cooperating, we will expose you and the Soviet plans to your President and Congress, as well as to the American people. We have intelligence agents who will monitor your every move. If you attempt to sell us out to the men in the Kremlin, we will know about that, too, because we have some very highly placed agents even at the Politburo level. They are dedicated, true Communists who hate the deviationist doctrines pursued by Khrushchev, Brezhnev, and Suslov, and who, on a personal basis, hate their more successful rivals for power in the Politburo.

"If you doubt our capability of exposing you in Washington, remember that you have powerful enemies, and we know who they are. They would enjoy helping us to bring you down while, at the same time, giving the United States a chance against the Soviets. Also, I can personally, in extremis, reach your President directly and secretly.

"We have methods of insuring your compliance up to the very last mini-second during the nuclear exchange. You have everything to gain and nothing to lose by going along with us. As a student of history, we are sure you remember that the surrender-prone leaders of ancient Carthage disarmed their people under promises of detente with Rome, and guaranteed their peaceful intentions by sending the sons of their leading families as hostages to Rome. When the Carthaginians discovered too late that their leaders had sold them out and left them helpless to be slaughtered by the Romans, they tore those peace-through-appeasement leaders apart, limb by limb. We know you don't want even the mildest version of that to happen to you. Your choice is to go along with us and be a living hero, or refuse and become a dead traitor. By going along with us, you will preserve your power, which may be even more important to you than your life.

"So you can fully understand our exciting scenario, we will reveal to you the substance of the Soviet objectives in launching a strategic attack on the United States. For many years they had planned to target your population as well as your retaliatory weapons. They calculated that they had the capability of destroying more than 95 percent of your land-based missiles and more than 90 percent of your people, including a free-ride mop-up of remaining pockets of population by using their strategic bombing force. This would make it irrational for the United States to launch a retaliatory attack with remnants of their land-based missiles or their surviving submarine-based missiles. The genocidal attack would have the additional benefit of relieving the Kremlin of the near-impossible problem of long-time administration of a stubborn and hostile population some 5,000 miles and an ocean away from Moscow.

"But a series of bad harvests, beginning in 1971, required the Soviets to change their plans. They still plan to launch a strategic nuclear attack against the United States, but will target only weapons, primarily Minuteman missiles and the aging B-52 bombers. They need to preserve the United States as a going concern for at least three additional years to serve as the breadbasket of the Soviet World Empire. After the U.S. surrender, which they confidently expect following their counterforce attack, they will impose at first only a skeleton occupation that will not strain their manpower, or their managerial, military, or transportation resources.

"After they secure their control of Western Europe, which they plan to take over at the time of their counterforce attack against the United States, they will begin to intensify their occupation of the United States, and impose selective genocide to thin out the American leaders who do not fit into Soviet plans. Later they plan to eliminate all but the most docile and valuable segments of the population. In the interim, they will have skimmed the cream of U.S. technology and industrial plant and production.

"But now to the scenario. It it, you will see that the men in the Kremlin are in for the surprise of their lives. They calculate that they are opposed only by Americans so liberal that, in Khrushchev's words that I have quoted to you before, they will not fight even in defense of their vital interests. They are so certain that command and control of U.S. strategic forces will be held by theoreticians such as yourself (who have so often declared that, if deterrence fails, it would be irrational to retaliate against a Soviet attack) that the Soviets do not anticipate any actual attempt at retaliation, although they will have taken precautions against it. Absolutely the last thing they will expect is that, by remote control exercised through Henry Kissinger, they are being countered by the genius and determination of Chairman Mao.

"But now to the scenario."

3

Time: Sunday, December 4, 1976, 1000 hours, Moscow time.
Place: The War Room in the Kremlin.
Present are Chairman Leonid Brezhnev (or his successor), the other
15 full members of the Politburo, the seven candidate members,
the chief of the Soviet General Staff and his top level assistants. They
are surrounded with display boards. Brezhnev is addressing the
assembly:

"Comrades, we are about to unleash the greatest destructive power
ever controlled by man. We are directing this unprecedented force
with the careful precision to bring to reality the 60-year ambition of
the Communist Party of the Soviet Union: a permanent world peace.
As you know, Lenin warned us time and time again that, so long as
capitalist imperialism continues to exist, the danger of aggressive
wars will continue.

"Within a few minutes, however, we will destroy utterly and forever
not only the power of imperialism to wage wars, but the totality of the
capitalist-imperialist system.

"We are not about to launch a nuclear *war*. We are, however, about
to use the vast strategic nuclear power of the Union of Soviet Socialist
Republics to accomplish the unilateral destruction of the entire American force of land-based nuclear missiles. This move is, of course, in
self-defense and to save the peoples of the entire world from incineration in the nuclear war that the U.S. imperialists have long planned
against the Soviet Union and our fraternal Communist allies. The mis-

siles we will destroy have long been targeted against the great cities and industries of the Soviet Union. The U.S. Secretaries of Defense and their Joint Chiefs of Staff have bragged for years that this missile force, which we will now eliminate, is capable of killing one-third of our people and destroying one-half of our industrial capacity; and that their missiles are so well protected, so highly survivable, that they could wreak this terrible destruction even after a Soviet disarming attack aimed at their weapons. The Americans will soon learn differently.

"Here are our plans, boiled down to essentials. Today, Sunday, we will launch at 1030 hours, Moscow time. In Moscow we are eight hours ahead of Washington, D.C., time. Our missiles will arrive over their U.S. targets at about 0300 or 3:00 A.M. Sunday morning.

"For a number of reasons, which most of you understand thoroughly, we plan to attack only counterforce or strategic military targets. Our prime targets will be the 1,054 Minuteman missiles. The odd 54 on the end of the thousand result from the Americans having replaced their 54 old Titan II liquid-fueled missiles with Minuteman III missiles, as allowed under SALT I. We know that these targets are hardened to withstand an overpressure of 300 pounds per square inch, and that 1,054 warheads of our two-megaton missiles with a CEP of 1,000 feet, delivered reliably on target, should destroy 99 percent of their total Minuteman force.

"To deliver those 1,054 warheads on target will require a reserve of 263 warheads. This is because, even though we have the advantage of setting our own timing for the attack and can thus 'peak' our force, we can count on only about 80 to 81 percent of our total peacetime inventory being at once available, ready, and reliable. Immediately after launch we have to accept the probability of another five percent loss in early flight failures. There will be late flight failures of another five percent, and terminal target-kill failures of one percent. These last two subtractions cannot be taken care of even by our most advanced Command Data Buffer reprogramming system.

"Out of the 1,054 Minuteman missiles, therefore, some 63 U.S. missiles may survive (according to our computations, which should be very reliable). But, Comrades, as you know so well, we are never adventuristic. We take no chances on serious damage to Motherland Russia, and especially to our power-base for world communism. We will launch a second wave of missiles carrying the same number of warheads, and identically targeted. If we fail to destroy 63 missiles on our first strike, we will kill all but three or four of these on the second wave. Here is the vital point: even if our first strike fails to destroy as many as 100 Minuteman missiles, we would get all except six on the second wave. The second wave will be launched six minutes after the first launch and will be backed up with the same reserve of 263 warheads plus reprogramming.

"These warheads will come primarily from our SS-9 and SS-18 force, with a few SS-19s added. We need twice a total of 1,317 warheads. U.S. intelligence, when SALT I was signed in May 1972, estimated our deployed SS-9 force at 288. U.S. intelligence figures are always on the low side. They had missed 12; our actual total was 300 SS-9s. Then, they estimated that we had begun construction of 91 additional silos and, judging by the dimensions they saw, they assumed that only 25 of these would be for SS-9s or SS-18s. Actually, we had started digging the holes for 100 additional silos; the nine they did not identify had not been dug very deep and were rather well concealed from satellite reconnaissance. For various reasons, one of which should now be obvious, we decided to make all these new holes into silos for the heaviest of our 'heavies,' the SS-18s, which carry either a single 50- to 100-megaton warhead or twelve 3-megaton MIRVs.

"The Americans no doubt assumed that it would be a violation of SALT I to enlarge the 75 smaller holes they had thought would become silos for light missiles such as SS-11s. As usual, their naive trust and sloppy thinking blinded them to the fact that it was perfectly legal and proper—and even in keeping with the so-called spirit of SALT— to enlarge the holes we had already started. There are two provisions of the Agreed Interpretations that apply:

I.

The Parties understand that fixed land-based ICBM launchers under active *construction* as of the date of the signature of the Interim Agreement may be completed.

J.

The Parties understand that in the process of *modernization* and *replacement* the dimensions of land-based ICBM silo launchers will not be significantly increased.

"Our 100 holes represented missile launchers under 'construction' —not 'in the process of *modernization* and *replacement*.' Use of the different specific terms in the two Agreed Interpretations demonstrates beyond legal question that they were intended to mean different things. Presumably, such important agreements, on which the survival of nations depends, are carefully drawn (at least by all other countries, if not by Americans).

"The point here is that we need a total of 2,634 warheads for our two waves against the Minuteman force, and that we have five 2-

65

megaton warheads on each of our 300 SS-9s, for a subtotal of 1,500; and twelve 3-megaton warheads on each of our 100 SS-18s, for a subtotal of 1,200; thus giving us a grand total of 2,700 warheads, or 66 more than we need to do the job *twice* in order to doubly assure our success.

"We still have the problem of suppressing or saturating the 100 SALT I ABM Treaty defensive missile launchers at the Grand Forks Minuteman site. For that, we will use those 66 extra SS-9 multiple warheads, plus 20 of our SS-17s or SS-19s equipped with five 1-megaton warheads. We need a few to destroy the ABM radars, as well as to saturate or destroy the ABM missile launchers or cause them to expend their missiles.

"One additional type of attack is required against the Minuteman force. For more than 15 years the U.S. scientists and unilateral disarmers who comprise our Pugwash penetration of U.S. policy-making elites have brainwashed successive U.S. Presidents and their advisers into a strategy based upon *not* launching retaliatory missiles until *after* attacking missiles have impacted against U.S. targets. Despite the common sense of launching on receipt of warning that enemy missiles are on the way, or at least on confirmation of such a warning, U.S. policy is set-in-concrete against this. Their ideology has been exploited by our psychological campaigns so that they would rather have all their multi-billion-dollar missiles destroyed in their silos, than launch them against the enemy that has *already* launched at them.

"Obviously, this destroys the credibility of the U.S. deterrent, and gives away the fact that their so-called retaliatory force is really only a bluff, not designed ever to be used. The Americans have been hypnotized into believing that a policy *against* launch-on-warning is necessary to prevent accidental nuclear war and to provide what they call 'crisis stability.' This means, in plain words, that the U.S. Government will give us the chance to confront them with a *fait accompli,* while they do nothing but wait for the nuclear dust to settle.

"The present incumbent in absolute charge of U.S. strategy and defense policies, Dr. Henry Kissinger, is totally committed to *prevent* a launch of U.S. missiles on warning or confirmation of warning. He has had the President repeat this declaration time after time in his *State of the World Reports,* beginning in 1971 and 1972. Since Kissinger controls the National Security Council and the entire U.S. intelligence community, and plays Svengali to the President, there is little real chance that the U.S. Minuteman missiles will be fired when they obtain their first satellite warning, or OTH radar warning, or BMEWS warning of our launch. They will not believe we would actually attack—until our warheads are destroying their missiles. Dr. Kissinger thinks he has bought our good will with the fruits of the so-called free enterprise system.

"In the Cuban missile crisis, Khrushchev made one miscalculation. He correctly estimated the fanatic compulsion-to-surrender of the civilian leadership surrounding the President; but he did not realize that the U.S. military, without any intention of mutiny, could start a chain of events that the White House palace guard, plus even the Secretary of Defense, could not stop without exposing their own treachery. Although those civilians were able to turn an otherwise certain U.S. victory in that crisis into a covered, delayed capitulation to the Soviets, it was a very close squeak. We cannot take such a chance again.

"We have taken precautions against any Americans—either civilian or military, who might think they are acting from 'courage' or 'common sense' or 'patriotism'—getting control of Minuteman launching procedures. That is one of the prime functions of our great fleet of modern missile-launching submarines. Our Y-class submarine missiles are neither powerful enough nor accurate enough to destroy the Minuteman missiles in their silos, but they can effectively pin down the U.S. missiles in the critical time interval between the time the Americans receive warning that we have launched and the time they must decide whether to act on that warning. By a series of nuclear explosions close by and slightly above the Minuteman missiles, we will prevent their launch.

"We are the only ones who have experimented with the pin-down technique, and although we understand some of the elements that make it work, such as electromagnetic pulse, radiation, and shock waves, we still do not understand the entire phenomenon. But we are so convinced it will work that we have invested many billions of rubles in our missile submarine fleet, which now consists of the full 62 allowed under SALT I. (This is, of course, the full number we had in our plans prior to the SALT negotiations. Dr. Kissinger justified that 33 percent Soviet advantage over the United States by arguing that, if we exercised our full building capacity, we could have 90 at the end of the five-year period. That was very helpful of him, because we have no use for 90—not even for the pin-down mission.)

"We will synchronize the launching of the first waves of our SLBMs against the Minuteman sites so that they will begin to arrive just before the Americans could receive and confirm the warnings of our launch of our SS-9 force from Soviet bases.

"We have assigned 30 missile submarines to that task. They will be assisted by IRBMs we have concealed in Cuban caves and can rapidly move into firing positions.

"There is one more related mission for our submarine-launched missiles: destruction of the aging U.S. strategic bomber force before it can take off. We estimate that 100 warheads would accomplish this mission, but we have assigned 160 to make sure. If any escape, we will have 10,000 air and space defense SAMs waiting to welcome them, plus some 3,000 interceptor or fighter-type aircraft, many of which are at least one mach faster than any the Americans have.

"The final segment of our attack is directed against the U.S. Polaris-Poseidon fleet of missile submarines. No more than 25 of these will be on station and ready, and we have assigned two, or in most cases three, of our fast nuclear-propelled attack submarines to track and destroy each one.

"So much for the physical elements of our strategic attack against the citadel of imperialism-capitalism and the prime breeder of aggressive wars.

"The psychological aspects—or what is termed 'post-strike nuclear blackmail'—will prove fairly simple. The Americans will have been utterly defeated, and this they cannot fail to understand. Their land-based missile force, the largest and only relatively powerful element of their strategic deterrent and retaliatory force, will be nearly totally destroyed: only four to six missiles will remain out of their preexisting 1,054. Some 80 to 90 percent of their strategic bomber force will have been destroyed prior to launch. Of the survivors, it will be doubtful that any could penetrate our massive air defenses, even if they attempted it. When the United States used to have more than 1,600 strategic bombers, and we were ringed in by their air bases, they could have saturated any air defenses we could have built. Thanks to McNamara, they no longer have either enough or effective strategic aircraft. All the Americans have operational now are some 200 B-52s of the G and H versions, plus 80 B-52 Ds which have been patched up to keep them in inventory. The other 170 which they had in 1972 were older and simply wore out.

"Of their once-proud Polaris-Poseidon fleet, eight are still out of action undergoing conversion to Poseidon configuration. We will destroy about 40 to 50 percent of those that are on station and ready. The largest number that could survive would be 15 Poseidons. True, they carry 16 missile launchers each, and each missile may have 10 MIRV warheads. But they are so relatively weak in explosive power that they could do no substantial harm to our population even if they impact on their targets. They have only 50 kilotons of explosive power —just 1/20th of a megaton. Furthermore, they are not reliable. They are not as accurate as land-based missiles. Against our nation, with its extensive passive defenses, they would be of negligible effect. In addition to our passive defenses, we have netted in several systems of SAMs to build a fairly heavy area missile defense. This was in violation of the 'spirit' of SALT, but we needed these defenses against the Chinese as well as the Americans. Our radars available for such defenses outnumber those of the Americans by a factor of 25.

"Realistically, however, we will not have to contend with the surviving American SLBMs. The United States cannot possibly fail to accept our ultimatum.

"About 10 minutes after the launch of our first wave of SS-9s from our Soviet bases, we will come up on the Hot Line to Washington with this ultimatum:

'Mr. President, 10 minutes ago, we launched a strategic nuclear attack against land-based U.S. nuclear missiles and bombers. The missiles which will destroy your missiles will impact in the most sparsely populated areas of the United States. Our counterforce weapons are very clean, and fallout will not be severe, although you should immediately warn your people that shelter—even improvised shelter—is desirable.

'We have deliberately and carefully spared your cities, your industries, your transportation, your agriculture, and your people.

'You have already received warning from your own intelligence that Soviet missiles in large numbers are speeding through space to impact on U.S. targets. I will add to that warning that we have launched two waves of missiles, each one powerful enough to destroy your entire Minuteman force. We are making doubly sure that your entire force will be totally destroyed.

'We are simultaneously launching an equally redundant attack against your aging bomber force. Substantially all of them will be destroyed, too. The small remnant, if any, certainly could not penetrate our massive air defense systems.

'You are probably now thinking about your Polaris-Poseidon force of missile submarines. Some of them will probably survive, although we have them shadowed and each one is now targeted by two or three of our fast, silent, nuclear-propelled attack submarines. Not many of your total of 25 on station and ready can hope to escape our attack.

'So this is your situation: We Soviets have left in our strategic arsenal more than 1,200 very powerful, highly accurate intercontinental ballistic missiles. They average more than five megatons in explosive power, and a substantial number are MIRVed.

'Our entire bomber force is intact and, as you know, it includes several hundred of our new Backfire supersonic strategic bombers, as well as 190 older heavy bombers. All these will have a free ride to whatever targets we assign them after our missile attack is completed.

'Our modern missile-launching submarine force is intact in its full number of 62, although 30 or 40 of them will need to reload their missile tubes. Many of these can be speedily serviced at our base in Cienfuegos, Cuba.

'Against all this, you could employ only 10 to 15 Poseidon submarines. Their missiles are not powerful enough to destroy any of our weapons.

With our passive defenses, they would be almost useless against our population (none of whom, incidentally, had anything to do with our counterforce attack against you). Add to that our ABM and allied SAM batteries which have both air defense and missile defense capabilities, and there is really nothing you can do in the way of effective retaliation.

'Even if your forces are stronger than I have outlined them, it would be irrational for you to attempt retaliation. Your cities are now our hostages, entirely helpless and defenseless against our scores of thousands of millions of tons of explosive power that we can deliver by missiles within a matter of minutes.

'If you attempt to launch missiles or bombs at any of our cities, you can do us no substantial harm. On the other hand, we can and will destroy all your cities and kill some 200 million of your people, if you attack us.

'So, Mr. President, we demand the unconditional surrender of the United States. We will not require your answer until the results of our missile attacks have been assessed by your military and intelligence, so that you can be totally convinced that you have no alternative, and that you must act to save the lives of more than 200 million Americans. We require your answer within six hours.' "

4

Time: *Still September 1976.*
Place: *Still Secure Conference Room, Imperial Palace, Peking.*
Premier Chou En-lai (or his successor) continues his briefing of Dr.
Henry A. Kissinger:

"At this point, Dr. Kissinger, we interrupt the scenario laid in the War Room in the Kremlin on Sunday, December 4, 1976.

"In your American television, you might describe this as a pause for a commercial by the producer. I, of course, am the producer of this apocryphal pre-attack lecture by the General Secretary of the Communist Party (so-called) of the Soviet Union, delivered to other members of the Politburo and the highest-ranking members of the General Staff of the Soviet Union.

"In my scenario I put the words in deviationist Brezhnev's mouth exactly as our intelligence has discovered them to be. We have also checked and rechecked all his statistics on the Soviet strategic order of battle, and all the computations as to the operational results he will obtain with the explosive power of Soviet missile warheads and their present CEP. We have even compared them with our U.S. contacts. They prove out.

"My purpose in presenting this to you is to let you figure it out for yourself. What will happen to the United States and to Henry Kissinger if you attempt to handle this Soviet strategic threat *your* way? We know that the way I have presented the Soviet Politburo's plan is substantially the way your own intelligence community has already reported it to you. We know that, thus far, you have taken no affirmative steps to meet the threat. All you have done so far is to conceal the information from the President and the National Security Council, and, of course, from the JCS.

"We know that, the way you have analyzed the situation, the United States will have no rational alternative to unconditional surrender *after the Soviets have delivered their disarming attack* against your strategic forces. We know your character is so surrender-prone that you will ultimately decide that, 'since we will have no alternative to surrender *after the Soviet attack*, why not surrender in advance and avert the attack by making it unnecessary for the Soviets to launch it?' You can square this preemptive surrender with your conscience (if such a sophisticated intellectual as you has a conscience) by rationalizing that the American people will be better off *not* having suffered a nuclear attack, even if the attack is targeted only against strategic military targets.

"We even know that giant brain of yours has churned out a method of forcing your decision on the President. Through your total control over all intelligence estimates, and because you alone have access to the President on such matters, you plan to withhold from him the fact that the Soviets plan to restrict their attack to strategic counterforce targets, and leave your cities, industries, agriculture, and people as hostages to blackmail you into making no attempt to retaliate with your submarine-based missiles. This deception will be easy because all Soviet war plans against the United States, prior to this final version, called for the counterforce attack to be combined with a genocidal targeting of the total population. The only thing that saved you from this plan—which would have rendered us helpless too—was the succession of disastrous harvests and other agricultural failures in the U.S.S.R., combined with a slower development in certain areas of technology than they anticipated. The Soviets need to preserve the United States as a going concern in order to supply the Soviet Union with food and technology and its fruits.

"So you plan on convincing the President that his only choice is between interposing in time a preemptive unconditional surrender to the Kremlin, or sacrificing the lives of 210 million Americans. We know you can convince him to do it your way.

"But doing it your way would be the worst possible thing for the United States and the American people, as well as for Henry Kissinger's present power and historic reputation. It would also be the worst thing for the People's Republic of China, and we do not intend to permit this to happen.

"Now I will reveal to you the brilliant gist of Chairman Mao's strategy. Only his genius would have reached the exact opposite result from your own analysis. He saw immediately that the United States would be far *better off by undergoing the Soviet nuclear attack.* He recognized that attack as the *sine qua non* of the American people's escaping the agony of total submission to the Soviet Commissars—an agony that would end only on the date when the Russians would have no further need for the slave services of the American people; at which time, of course, the entire population would be liquidated. Incidentally, Dr. Kissinger, have you ever read the book by that honest British reporter Robert Conquest called *The Great Terror?* If so, you would know what I am talking about because he asserts that the several Soviet dictators since Lenin have liquidated 22 to 30 million people. Your government should have made it required reading for every American, as well as Aleksandr Solzhenitsyn's *The Gulag Arch-ipelago;* he uses the figure 66 million people murdered in the U.S.S.R.

"We in China know from our own sources that Stalin, Beria, and Khrushchev liquidated 12 to 20 million of their own people—millions of them loyal Communists—in order to establish terror, discipline, and their own political system. We estimate that—in their initial program—the Russians would carry out a selective genocide in America that would kill about 10 percent of your population, or 20 million, in the first three years of their occupation, and another 10 percent in the next two years.

"In addition to those millions liquidated by the Soviets, *the Americans would kill each other* in equal or larger numbers. The French did this to each other during the German occupation, which was mild compared to any Soviet occupation. It will be a terrible conflict between the classes in America—between the majority whom your great strategist Herman Kahn calls the 'middle class,' and those like yourself, the pseudointellectuals, the internationalists, the Soviet accommodationists, and the others whom Kahn calls the 'upper middle class.' It will be Carthage all over again, with the people turning in desperation and madness against those who betrayed their country by unilateral disarmament that made them prey to the slaughter and slavery imposed by the Soviets.

"From the standpoint of the American people, surrender is *not* desirable. From our standpoint, which is the prime consideration, we do not want the deviationists of the Soviet Politburo to acquire the industrial and agricultural skills of the American people in order to tighten their rule over the peoples of the U.S.S.R., Europe, and Japan. So, we are not going to permit it. We demand that you follow our commands, Dr. Kissinger.

"The men in the Kremlin plan on expending their entire force of heavy missiles, the SS-9s and SS-18s, to destroy the U.S. Minuteman force. They will launch some 2,700 warheads carrying a megatonnage of 5,400 in this counterforce attack.

"We do not have the strategic offensive weapons to destroy such a force; you do not have them either. But when the Soviets launch them against the U.S. Minuteman force, they will, in effect, be destroyed. Expended missiles no longer represent strategic power in-being.

"The beauty of Chairman Mao's plan is that, although the Soviet missiles will be *expended* against U.S. missiles, they will *not destroy* any of the U.S. strategic power in-being—because we won't let you permit this. *This will be the first step* toward establishing that 'strategic equilibrium' that, until now, has been merely a phony figment of a megalomanic dream.

"*The second step is equally essential.* Chairman Mao and I have planned it with exquisite precision, and we demand your equally precise execution. Our concept is totally decisive, our objectives so extensive in scope and massive in character, that they boggle the mind, stagger the imagination, or call for the application of whatever other cliches you Americans use to describe the unthinkable.

"We have six tasks in our second step toward establishing what might be called the 'real Kissinger balance of power':

"1. Destroy the unexpended balance of Soviet land-based strategic missiles.

"2. Destroy Soviet capability of taking over Western Europe by either nuclear blackmail or actual invasion. This requires destruction of some 800 MR/IRBMs targeted on NATO and France, and 700 medium nuclear-capable bombers.

"3. Destroy Soviet active strategic defenses, especially all Henhouse, Doghouse, and other radar installations capable of netting SAMs that purport to be for air defense, but which have ABM capability; destroy all known ABM sites plus SA-5 missile launcher sites.

"4. With the vulnerability of Soviet cities accomplished by execution of #3, hold Soviet cities hostage to deter Soviet attacks on Chinese or U.S. cities, industries, and population. This will block their employing the reserve units of their 62-submarine missile fleet whose missiles have not already been expended against the United States.

"5. Destroy Soviet Army concentrations and installations that would support invasion of either NATO nations on the Western Front or China on the East.

"6. Destroy railroad yards, junction points, rolling stock, bus and truck depots, oil pipelines and all POL installations.

"In short, our objectives are those that a joint committee of American and Chinese targeting experts and strategic planners would include if you and we were voluntarily planning a joint surprise disarming strike against the Soviet Union.

"Our concern for destroying Soviet capability to take over Western Europe by nuclear threats or actual invasion is based on the same reason we are so concerned that they not take over as a going situation the U.S. industrial, agricultural, and technological capacity and the U.S. labor force. With either the United States or Western Europe as slaves, the Soviets could soon upset the new balance that we are going to create by effective employment of U.S. strategic power with Chinese brains and determination.

"I will now describe the tasks we are assigning you, and the forces you in turn will assign to accomplish those tasks.

"1. After the Soviets launch their two waves of SS-9 and SS-18 missiles in their attempt to destroy the U.S. land-based missile force, they will have some 1,200 strategic land-based missiles in reserve. Almost immediately, however, they will launch 400 of them at targets in China. They have intelligence that we have 150 ICBMs in silos and 200 MR/IRBMs also in silos. They have assigned first a sufficiency, and then a redundancy, of warheads to destroy that number of siloed missiles—and they know our silos are in hard rock.

"But don't feel too sorry for us or for our budding strategic nuclear capability. Our late start in developing ICBMs enabled us to leapfrog the silo-type launchers and go directly into land-mobile types, and yet do so at a time when it was still credible to the Soviets that we would build only silo-protected launchers.

"It must be remembered that in 1972, when we were beginning to go into production of ICBMs, both the superpowers were getting CEPs of more than 1,500 feet. The United States could have improved its accuracy years earlier to something like 1,000 feet, but was blocked by unilateral-disarmament policymakers such as Secretary McNamara and yourself. In any event, it is clear that by 1976, our present timeframe, the United States could have attained CEPs of 500 feet for land-based missiles. By 1980, if your country had been willing to spend the money on it, you could have attained the famous '30-meter miss,' or a CEP of 90 feet. Actually, there is no point in attaining accuracy better than a 200-foot CEP, because that will give even the lowest-yield missile warhead, the 50-kiloton Poseidon MIRV, a single-shot kill probability of 99 percent against a 300 psi silo missile launcher.

"The CEP which the United States should have had this very year of 1976 is 500 feet, because it would give the 3 MIRVed warheads of the Minuteman III (technically known as LGM-30G) each a single-shot kill probability of 98 percent with their 200 kilotons of explosive power.

"Obviously, we would have been insane to invest our scarce industrial resources and nuclear trigger and explosive materials to build 150 siloed missiles that could have been killed by 50 Minuteman missiles from the United States, or by 50 SS-17s or SS-19s from the U.S.S.R. So we didn't.

"But we did carefully prepare 150 silos and equip them with dummy ICBMs, salted with a few real ones which we equally carefully allowed Soviet spies to examine through apparent gaps in our security. Meanwhile, we patterned our land-mobile ICBMs and IRBMs on the Soviet self-propelled mobile version of their SS-11s of variable ranges and their newer SS-16s. We permitted no security gaps about these. They have been garaged in hiding places that will never be penetrated by their spies. We would not have had the technology and resources to build these mobile launchers for our missiles if you, Dr. Kissinger, had not arranged for David Rockefeller to handle the credits (with substantial profits for the Chase Manhattan Bank), and his CFR industrial associates to supply everything we needed under the guise of what you Americans call trade.

"You will be thankful that you helped us. For once, your actions also helped the American people. Our ICBMs and IRBMs are the only force that —when added to yours—can establish your fond illusion of a 'strategic equilibrium.'

"Now, I will describe the targets I am assigning to U.S. missiles under Task#1. Some 800 Soviet SS-11s, SS-17s, and SS-19s will remain in their silos. We estimate that some 200 of the original SS-11 silos have been retrofitted with the updated SS-17 version and another 200 with the SS-19; but the silos are still hardened only to 300 psi. We are assigning 540 of your Minuteman III 3-MIRVed missiles to destroy these Soviet weapons in their silos—an average of a little more than two 200-kiloton warheads each. If we assume a 1,000-foot CEP, the kill percentage would be only 65 percent, but we discovered that some smart and patriotic U.S. scientists and technicians have clandestinely designed your latest guidance packages so that several minor adjustments can reduce the CEP well below 1,000 feet. These men knew that, if you discovered this, you would have had them discharged; but they took a chance for their country. Now, their foresight will help both of us. With this secretly improvable CEP, we calculate a single-shot kill probability of about 80 to 83 percent.

"I realize, of course, that your active mind is already asking how I can be assigning destruction tasks to the U.S. Minuteman force when, according to the Brezhnev scenario I outlined, the Soviets will have launched against this Minuteman force two complete waves of SS-9 and SS-18 missiles, with 1,350 two-or-more-megaton warheads in each wave, plus 20 SS-19s to help absorb the 100 U.S. ABM missiles at Grand Forks. I am sure that you agree with our computations that each wave will have a kill capability of 94 percent, so that the second wave will result mostly in redestruction of silos already killed; but they will, however, certainly have the capability of killing all but four or five of the perhaps 60 Minuteman missiles that might have survived the first wave.

"The answer to this question is the basis of the entire strategic plan that Chairman Mao has so brilliantly conceived. By the time *the first wave of Soviet warheads begins to impact* against Minuteman silos, *the birds will have flown.* The huge explosions will destroy only empty launcher tubes in their silos—'empty holes,' as they have been termed. Not only will the Minuteman missiles have been safely launched before the Soviet heavy ICBMs arrive, they will have been safely launched even before the Soviet submarine-launched missiles can pin them down.

"To do this will require abandoment of the suicidal policy so dear to the heart of every U.S. Pugwash participant: the policy of *not* launching any U.S. missiles until *after impact* of Soviet weapons in force. Your new strategy will be to launch instantaneously upon first warning of Soviet launch. This commonsense policy of national self-defense has been denounced by every Pugwash-influenced intellectual ever since both nuclear superpowers developed substantial numbers of ICBMs. Hysterical campaigns against it have been conducted over the years.

"It is noteworthy that the Director of the U.S. Arms Control and Disarmament Agency appointed in April 1973 did not get his bid until after he had published an article in *Foreign Affairs* for January 1973 denouncing 'the launch-on-warning aberration' as one that aggravates the risk of accidental war through many less visible practices as well as its grand design.' Mr. Fred C. Iklé also made himself popular with the unilateral disarmers and Soviet accommodationists by coming out against 'swift' or 'prompt' retaliation against a Soviet strike, against a 'massive' retaliatory strike, and against designing retaliation to kill a 'major fraction of the Soviet population.'

"I am sure that Mr. Iklé's highly sophisticated smear of those U.S. advisers who advocate a launch-on-warning policy must have appealed strongly to you. Very subtly, but by inescapable implication, he characterizes them as insane, or at least with loss of rationality:

> The very fact that well-informed and well-intentioned advisers now recommend, in essence, that the balance of terror should rest on hair-triggered doomsday machines offers a chilling reminder that we cannot rely upon unswerving rationality among those who might affect critical strategic decisions.

"A launch-on-warning strategy may possibly increase the danger of accidental war in highly improbable exotic situations, but even that is minimal with the increasing perfection, reliability, and instantaneous warning of your new-capability satellite warning systems. But the mere possibility that such a changeover might take place in U.S. strategic policy is the *only* factor that has retained your Minuteman force as an effective deterrent in the critical years since 1969, since the Soviets realized they had a surrender-prone appeaser in total command of U.S. strategy and strategic forces.

"The launch-on-warning strategy—the mere possibility of which deterred the Soviets from attacking the United States until they had produced and deployed a sufficient number of missile-launching submarines to pin down your Minuteman force—will now be applied to *save* the United States from the stark alternatives of nuclear incineration or unconditional surrender.

"Immediately upon your return to Washington, Dr. Kissinger, you will take the necessary steps to shift over to the new strategy. Chairman Mao and I will require that the entire Minuteman force be launched by computer, without further human command, upon receipt of warning of a Soviet launch, whether the launch is from Russian bases or from their submarines. We believe that the Soviet ICBM launch will precede their submarine launch by four or five minutes, because they are convinced that, even in the highly improbable event that Henry Kissinger would permit a launch-on-warning policy, or that the military might circumvent his wait-until - the - nuclear - dust - settles - and - all - our - weapons - are - destroyed policy, it would take at least 12 to 15 minutes for the warning to reach the President and for his decision to be made and processed.

"We are also ordering an equally revolutionary change in your Minuteman targeting. We know that, heretofore, it has been limited to cities and industrial installations, with special emphasis on counterpopulation effects. Robert McNamara first stated this targeting philosophy in official testimony to the Senate Armed Services Committee in 1967, and the United States has adhered to it ever since under cover of euphemistic terminology. As Mr. Iklé, in the *Foreign Affairs* article I quoted earlier, observes, the McNamara strategy of "assured destruction" fails to indicate what is to be destroyed; but then "assured genocide" would reveal the truth too starkly.

"I have already assigned targets for 540 Minuteman missiles, which leaves 514 missiles with 1,542 warheads available for assignment to Tasks #2, 3, 4, 5, and 6. In addition to these land-based missiles, we will require you to assign 16 Poseidon submarines with their 2,560 warheads to be divided among these missions. That will provide a total of some 4,102 warheads or, roughly, more than 800 each for each of these five tasks. Targeting experts will supply the specific details, and we will furnish them to you later, but in ample time for stationing the Poseidons.

"Because the Soviets are targeting all U.S. strategic bomber bases and known dispersal facilities with their first-wave SLBMs, we want you to hold these bombers at a high state of alert, once we give you notice. We hope that they will be able to get safely into the air by virtue of the increased efficiency of your new satellite warning systems and phased array anti-SLBM radars, and will be able to mop up the military targets we have assigned initially to your Minuteman force. With luck, the U.S. missiles ought to be able to take out most of the Soviet interceptor and fighter aircraft bases and facilities, and suppress most of their 10,000 SAM air defense system. If they do, even your old B-52s may be able to penetrate effectively to their assigned targets or, hopefully, to the broken-backed remnants of the targets. Most of your FB-111s should make it. We expect that missiles will have taken care of the Soviet force of Backfire bombers. It's too bad that McNamara blocked the development of two generations of U.S. strategic bombers. We could have made good use of them.

"Of absolutely crucial importance in the success of the Mao strategy is effective communication by you on behalf of your President to the Politburo in Moscow, via the Hot Line. This will be in implementation of Task#4. You must make absolutely—'perfectly' used to be the more accustomed word—clear to the Soviets that the attack they are undergoing is exclusively targeted at military objectives; and that no attack is directed at cities or even industries. You must make sure that they recognize any near misses at cities as aimed at radar installations or other parts of ABM or air-defense systems, or at military transportation and supply dumps.

"It is even more important to make it perfectly clear to them that *we actually do* hold their cities and industry as hostages. At this point, you can reveal to them that we, the People's Republic of China, have (and you can be a little vague on the higher force level) between 140 and 200 land-mobile ICBMs with 10- to 100-megaton single warheads and CEPs of less than 1,000 feet. Because you will already have knocked out their ABMs and related radars, as well as many of their ABM and SAM launchers, our heavy missiles will have a free ride to their cities. If the Soviets have kept the SALT Treaty—which is not at all probable—our missiles would have been guaranteed a free ride to all Soviet cities other than Moscow, anyway.

"Meanwhile, we Chinese will have launched our entire force of land-mobile IRBMs at Soviet military installations and facilities threatening our borders. We will especially target supply depots. The only railroad the Soviets can use to move supplies for their million-man invasion is thin and vulnerable. We have quite a few MRBMs, which we will use to try to take out their so-called tactical nuclear weapons. If there really were a 'Kissinger strategic equilibrium' in the world, we wouldn't mind their trying an invasion at all!

"You might be thinking that, if the United States can really carry out all that destruction on the Soviet Union, you must have another alternative open to you; or, put another way, if you can do all that damage by launching your Minuteman force immediately upon warning that the Soviets have launched their attack, why shouldn't you deliver a surprise disarming attack a week earlier, or even a month before their attack is scheduled?

"There are several answers to this. In the first place, even if the United States had what is variously designated as a 'preclusive' or 'full' or 'credible' or 'splendid' first-strike capability against the Soviets, neither you nor any other civilian in authority in the United States—including the President—would have the *will* to use it. You would not use it even in the face of hard and conclusive evidence that the Soviets are preparing to launch a strike against your country. You see, we have studied your character very carefully. We know that you personally would be blocked emotionally, as well as intellectually, from giving the command to launch. Your ideology has destroyed your will. I have quoted this to you before, but it is critical in our plans. I agree with that evil but shrewd deviationist Nikita Khrushchev, who concluded that you are 'too liberal to fight, even in defense of your own vital interests.' You would not fight for the survival of the United States, for the freedom of the American people, or even for their lives.

"The hard fact is that Secretary McNamara and you, Dr. Kissinger, have together liquidated the first-strike capability that the United States held at the time of the Cuban missile crisis in 1962. You two insured that America would never build such a capability again. You both took all the required steps, sold your respective Presidents on the 'necessity' of not 'provoking' the Soviets, of not running an arms race; and, although you never said it openly, you initiated programs to bring the United States down to a very weak second place, strategically, to the Soviet Union.

"To put this situation into operational terms, which is the only practical way to evaluate such a situation, any attempt by the United States to launch a disarming strike against the Soviet Union would be a disaster without equal in history. It would be a cataclysmic disaster, that is, *if* it were launched *before* the Soviets launched their entire heavy ICBM force at U.S. missiles and another 400 ICBMs at Chinese missiles.

"You have not permitted the United States to build missiles in sufficient numbers, or with sufficiently powerful warheads, or with sufficiently accurate guidance, to disarm the Soviet Union in a surprise first-strike, even assuming that they have no more land-based ICBMs than the 1,618 you estimated they had at the time of SALT I. Your Dr. James Schlesinger estimated that, if you launched your entire Minuteman force against Soviet ICBMs, only 280 would survive. But he makes that claim only if you could get the same guidance accuracy in operational silo launches as is attained in test silo launches.

"'If you strike at a king, strike to kill,' was a familiar aphorism in the bygone days of royalty. An assassin might find favor with the successor of a suddenly deceased ruler, having helped him to premature power; but he would be vulnerable to the revenge of a wounded king still holding the prerogatives of the sovereign. So also today as regards a disarming strike at a superpower having overwhelming strategic supremacy, particularly when its absolute dictators have the *will* to use that power; if the strike does not kill the substance of the defender's offensive power, the retaliatory strike will incinerate the cities of the striking nation.

"The most probable result of a U.S. attempt at a surprise disarming strike against the Soviet Union would be (1) no substantial damage to the Soviets' strategic weaponry, and (2) absolute annihilation of the United States and the American people.

"Make no mistake. The Soviets consider a surprise disarming attack by the United States what might be called a high-confidence improbability. However, they are thorough planners and common-sense strategists. They must have a launch-on-warning strategy that can activate in case of any such threat.

"Indeed, Soviet strategists are obsessed with the concept of what they euphemistically call 'preemption.' This means striking an enemy before he starts his attack, if possible, but even in the worst situation, striking him before he can complete his attack. The uncensored open-language version of Soviet doctrine for strategic war from the military standpoint was contained in the Top Secret 'Special Collection of Articles' on nuclear war that Colonel Oleg Penkovskiy delivered to the West at the cost of his life. His sacrifice was in vain, because your predecessor Robert McNamara successfully suppressed it in the United States. Khrushchev gave the political version of the same strategic war doctrine, in Aesopian language, in his speech of January 6, 1961. The sanitized, and therefore publishable, military version is entitled *Soviet Military Strategy* by Marshal V.D. Sokolovskii and nine other Soviet generals.

"All of these three versions of Soviet doctrine for conducting nuclear war stress one point: the preferred method of initiating a nuclear war is by a massive surprise attack, and the U.S.S.R. must 'strike first, at any costs.' If, for some unplanned reason that is impossible, resort must then be to *immediate* retaliation, in a matter of seconds. Thus, the most recent edition of *Soviet Military Strategy,* published in 1968, treats of newly developed surveillance systems that permit detecting the adversary's 'immediate preparations for a nuclear attack' as well as his actual missile launch. This, the book asserts, now makes it possible to bar an aggressor's surprise attack and deliver prompt nuclear strikes against him. Even more current, Defense Minister Grechko—significantly now a member of the Politburo—demands a policy of such nearly instantaneous response as to be capable of

> frustrating an aggressor's surprise blow and successfully carrying out those military tasks, especially by the rocket troops . . . which *must be fulfilled in a matter of seconds.*

"So we cannot expect the Soviets to follow your stupid strategy, Dr. Kissinger, of waiting until actual impact and explosion of enemy missiles launched against them in a surprise first-strike.

"We *know* that the Soviets would launch on warning, in response to an attempted American disarming first-strike. But exactly *what* would they launch and—this is the vital question—*at what* would they launch?

"By launching your entire land-based missile force at the Soviet missile force in an attempt to destroy it, you would have eliminated all counterforce targets in the United States of immediate strategic significance. You would have left them only empty holes—silos whose missiles had been expended. You would have, in effect, *forced* them to target their entire land-based missile force at countervalue targets, that is, at cities, industries, transportation, communications, and—most vital of all—people.

"Here is how it would happen. Normally, Soviet land-based missiles are divided into four echelons for the preprogramming of their targeting: the first and most powerful echelon, the SS-9 and SS-18 heavies, are programmed for U.S. counterforce targets, that is, the Minuteman missiles. The second segment is targeted against U.S. countervalue targets. The third echelon (ever since 1972) is programmed against Chinese counterforce targets. And the fourth echelon is to be held in reserve, with the programming changed from time to time to follow current Soviet foreign and military policy developments.

"Consider how the situation will look to Brezhnev, Grechko, and the current chief of the General Staff when they receive warning that there has been a massive launch of U.S. missiles at the Soviet Union. What will they deduce will be the objectives of your strike?

"First, they will make the easy decision. Unless the Americans have gone wildy insane, they will have targeted Soviet offensive weapons, not cities. The Soviets know quite well that the United States does not have enough missiles to target both counterforce and countervalue targets in the Soviet Union. Indeed, they are sure that the United States does not have sufficient numbers, warhead explosive power, and accuracy of aim to attempt to destroy the entire Soviet land-based missile force, but they will conclude that either Soviet intelligence was inaccurate and underestimated one of those elements, or that the Americans have overestimated their strength.

"Regardless of their doubts as to U.S. capability of *destroying* the entire Soviet offensive force, however, the Soviets will have no doubts that the attempt is *directed at the entire force*. They will credit the Americans with at least enough common sense to be familiar with the rule about 'striking at a king.'

"So the Soviets will deduce that their entire missile force is under an attack that will arrive on target in about 20 minutes. Those missiles represent to the Politburo an investment of something like 250 billion rubles and 20 years of development. They would not want them to be destroyed without serving any useful purpose. Also, they would desire as much revenge as possible against the American atomic maniacs who had disrupted their planned results from a similiar disarming strike against the United States in order to turn that disàrmed nation into the breadbasket and technological and industrial supply source for the Soviet empire.

"So the Soviets would order an immediate launch of the echelon already targeted on U.S. cities and industry. At crash speed they would reprogram the missiles preset against the U.S. Minuteman force, and target them, too, on U.S. cities and population. Unlike McNamara, they have no desire to waste their expensive missiles on empty holes. The echelon targeted against Chinese offensive weapons and military targets will be launched. The Politburo has to figure that, if the U.S. disarming attempt had any substantial success, they cannot afford to permit the People's Republic of China to take advantage of it. This same motivation will probably lead the Soviets to reprogram their reserve segment of offensive land-based missiles against China too, because they will already have massively redundant coverage of all worthwhile targets in the United States. We estimate that nearly 200 million Americans would die during the attack or within 48 hours, and nearly all the remainder within another two weeks.

"The Soviets would rely for a reserve on their large force of more than 62 missile-launching submarines, plus their old and new cruise missile submarines that were built after they had completed construction of the SALT quota of missile-launching submarines.

"We do not wish the United States to go to Armageddon in such a useless fashion. For another few years, we will need you as our 'objective ally,' to establish that realistic type of 'strategic equilibrium' that you dreamed of during your 'season of Summits.'

"Also, we have a nagging suspicion that the entire reserve of Soviet missiles would be targeted on the great cities of China. In and under those cities, we are rapidly developing the technological and industrial resources for our 'take-off' as an industrial superpower. As your columnist Joseph Alsop had described it, China will soon become a 'Japan the size of China.' We would long ago already have achieved this if we had not had to commit such enormous resources in labor and materials to building our incomparable passive defense system, 1o times better than the Soviets'.

"Why then, you may ask, do we calculate that the Mao disarming strategy will work successfully, whereas a U.S. attempt to preempt the planned Soviet disarming strike would bring down an all-consuming nuclear holocaust on America?

"The short answer is that the Mao strategy alone can substitute brainpower for the large and potentially fatal gaps in U.S. strategic weapons power. In the first place, as I have just explained, a disarming strike, even if sufficiently powerful otherwise, could not prevail against a determined launch-on-warning strategy. You have a fatal gap in not having enough submarine-launched ballistic missiles or other short-warning offensive weapons to pin down the Soviet missile force. That is why the Soviets insisted in SALT I on a quota of 62 modern missile-launching submarines to the U.S. number of 41 (plus three that could not be built in time under your policies, minus seven or eight in this timeframe under conversion to Poseidon). The Soviets were taking no chances on not having a pindown capability.

"But, you may ask, why—in Chairman Mao's scenario—would not the same considerations hold for the balance of the Soviet land-based missile force not already launched against the U.S. Minuteman forces, or against Chinese ICBM silos?

"The answer to that question reveals one of the most brilliant aspects of Chairman Mao's superb stratagem. He developed this answer because he is masterful enough to recognize the common human tendency to 'think in a box.' In Soviet so-called Communist, but nevertheless generally competent, strategic leadership, such confined thinking is probably their most serious vulnerability.

"I'm sure you understand, Dr. Kissinger, what I mean by the expression 'thinking in a box.' You yourself are accustomed to thinking in 'boxes' built by the Pugwash group that, in turn, were designed by psychological war experts in the Kremlin. Probably the best-known illustration in the literature of the West is in the short story called *The Purloined Letter*. In that story, the 'think box' is the assumption that the letter, having been cleverly stolen, must be hidden in an equally clever hiding place. Instead, it was deliberately left in the most obvious place, exposed on the top of the desk.

"All the way back to the early 1960s, the Soviets have done their strategic planning about nuclear attack, retaliation, and targeting, in two entirely *separate* 'think boxes.' In one, they do their thinking about what happens and should happen *when they themselves launch the attack*. In the other, they think about the remote possibility that *the United States might launch an attack* against them.

"For many years, the Soviets planned that their massive nuclear surprise attack would be targeted against *both* U.S. weapons and U.S. population. It was to be a counterforce-counterpopulation, disarming-genocidal attack. To assure success and render retaliation nearly impossible and surely irrational, they planned to launch substantially their entire offensive force of land-based ICBMs in the shortest possible time.

"Thus they assumed that the targeting of a U.S. *retaliatory* attack would inevitably be limited to cities and industry, especially population. McNamara's goals of 'assured destruction' were repeated year after year: 'one-third of the population of the U.S.S.R. and one-half of Soviet industry.' Even in unprepared, unrehearsed testimony before congressional committees, he admitted again and again that Soviet *cities* would be the target of our retaliatory attack, and that *this* was what provided the United States with a reliable deterrent. He called it a threat of 'unacceptable damage' to Soviet values. In the 'think box' constructed of assumptions about a nuclear exchange initiated by a Soviet first-strike, therefore, the Soviet strategists immediately think that 'Soviet cities' will be the exclusive target of U.S. missiles.

"Only in the second and separate box do they think of targeting by the Americans in case *the U.S. launches* the first-strike. Then, as I have mentioned, the Soviets would assume that U.S. leaders are at least rational enough to target Soviet missiles. In their second 'think box,' the Soviet strategists assume that a U.S. first-strike *must* be a counterforce strike. Thus the immediate and overriding thought of the Soviet strategists would be to save their missiles from useless destruction. In order to get some dividend on their huge investment, they *must* launch on warning.

"In the Mao scenario, we are dealing with how the Soviets think in the *first* box. They think they are *sure* that the Americans will target cities in retaliation; and, therefore, their overriding and immediate concern will be to activate their passive and active defenses of cities and industries. They will not consider it immediately urgent to reprogram their unexpended missiles. Obviously, the Soviets will not consider it necessary to launch-on-warning in order to save their missiles when they are sure that U.S. retaliatory missiles are targeted on cities, population, and industrial capacity. The Soviet 'think box' will psychologically inhibit a launch-on-warning. No early warning can disclose the *destination* of the U.S. missiles.

"That, then, is the explanation of the Mao-planned disarming strike launched by U.S. weapons under the guise of a retaliatory countervalue strike. Because the United States does not have the required types and numbers of strategic weapons to pin down the Soviet missiles so they can be destroyed by ICBMs, Mao brainpower produces the equivalent pin-down result.

"A second outstandingly brilliant point in the Mao strategy is the employment of brainpower to bridge the gap in the sufficiency of U.S. strategic weapons to destroy the substance of the Soviet land-based missile force. You simply do not have, as I have pointed out before, the number of missiles, number of warheads, power of warheads, or accuracy of guidance, to kill enough Soviet missiles to make the *attempt* anything but an exercise in national suicide for the United States.

"If you will remember my figures, the Soviets in my scenario had launched their entire SS-9 and SS-18 force of 400 at the U.S. Minuteman force, and had launched another 400 land-based missiles with fewer warheads and less megatonnage at what they *thought* were silos housing several hundred Chinese ICBMs and IRBMs. Since the U.S. silos would be merely 'empty holes' when the SS-9s and SS-18s arrived on target, and the Chinese silos were mostly decoys, we obtain the same result as if all those Soviet missiles had been destroyed.

"But the critical result of the Soviet expenditure of those 400 heavy and 400 medium ICBMs will be to reduce by 800 the additional hardened targets in the Soviet Union that would have had to be covered by the U.S. Minuteman force. The 800-some Soviet missiles that would survive if the U.S. Minuteman force were spread so thin represents the differential between a sensational success and a totally disastrous failure for the joint Chinese-U.S. strategy.

"You may object that, after targeting 540 Minuteman missiles to destroy 800 Soviet missiles remaining after their launches at the United States and China, the remaining 514 Minuteman IIIs could have been targeted to destroy those additional 800 Soviet missiles *if they had not been launched* at the United States and China. There are, of course, two answers to that. First, as I have shown, if the

Soviets had not launched *first* in the scenario, the Soviets would have launched their entire missile force on warning, and we could not have destroyed any of them; instead, they would have utterly destroyed the United States and badly damaged the vital nucleus of Chinese modern industry. Second, those 514 Minuteman missiles assigned to the other tasks are essential to (1) the total Mao strategy, and (2) the killing by the 540 Minuteman missiles of the 800 remaining Soviet ICBMs.

"The 540 U.S. Minuteman missiles assigned to kill the balance of 800 Soviet missiles *could not do so* without preliminary or contemporaneous destruction of the Soviet ABMs and SAMs and associated radars defending the Soviet missile silos. The Poseidon mini-MIRV warheads have only 50 kilotons of explosive power each—1/20th of a megaton. The Minuteman III 200-kiloton MIRVed warheads, however, have a 98 percent single-shot kill probability, even as to ICBMs in hardened silos, and are equally effective against all types of targets, such as ABM launchers and radars.

"Also, for the totality of the Mao strategy to work, the ABM and ABM-capable SAM forces protecting Soviet cities and industry simply must be suppressed. China and the United States must hold those Soviet cities and industries as completely vulnerable hostages, or the Soviets will employ the reserve of their missile submarine fleet to destroy U.S. and Chinese cities. Of course, you should be even more interested in this than we; our population has our tremendously expensive and effective passive defense systems, whereas you and other American liberals, while pretending to be 'humanitarians,' have left the entire population of the United States totally vulnerable to nuclear incineration.

"So, Dr. Kissinger, you must do it Chairman Mao's way. If you do not give us your solemn commitment to do so, we will tell the President of the United States what you have done to him, and expose to the Congress and the people of America what you have done to them.

"We are sure you can handle the President. You handled Richard Nixon so well for so many years. If you have trouble, explain this to him. We have a fleet of Concorde supersonic reconnaissance aircraft that we bought between 1974 and 1976 when your Western friends and the United States rejected them. Although they are supposed to be Chinese commercial airliners, we have loaded them with electronic gear of all sorts. We expect to obtain through them and our brand-new satellite systems, plus some OTH radars, what is called 'real-time' surveillance of targets and missile launch sites.

"If the U.S. Minuteman force is not launched immediately after the Soviet launch against the United States—immediately on first warning, that is—we Chinese will launch 100 of our 17-megaton mobile ICBMs at your totally vulnerable cities that you, Dr. Kissinger, deprived of all defense (despite the highly advanced ABM technology within U.S. capabilities). This may kill up to 100 million of the American people; but it will be your fault, not ours.

"We have provided you with the only strategy by which the United States and the American people can survive free from Soviet rule. If you go along with us, few people will be killed. If you don't, hundreds of millions will die, mostly Americans, plus a few million Chinese and perhaps a few million Russians, because we are not going to use our reserve of 40 ICBMs to reprogram against the United States; we figure 100 megadeaths should be enough of a threat. We will target our remaining 40 at Soviet cities. We hope they will think these missiles have come from the United States, especially because they will believe that they have destroyed all of ours.

"In short, we will adopt the catalytic strategy that is set out in Herman Kahn's model that I previously called to your attention. We hope it will be a classic 'let's you and him fight' situation that will work.

"Thus it is, Dr. Kissinger, that we now offer you a chance to choose the only course that will save the United States and the American people: a chance to make your fable of a 'strategic equilibrium' come true in the real world, a chance for you to become an international hero and to save scores of millions of lives, a chance to make this a livable world for another generation, despite the ambitions of the Soviet deviationists.

"If you refuse to join us, we will have to be against you. We need you, but you need us even more desperately.

"We think we know your character well enough to predict your course of action. Your first temptation will be to try to work out an equivocal alternative. After more thought, however, you will realize that your present power, the continuance of that power, and ultimately your place in history, will be determined by your choice; and that, for once, you cannot afford to risk equivocation or your usual hypersophistication."

5

There are other and more easily believable consequences of Dr. Kissinger's no-defense mania.

In Defense Secretary Melvin Laird's official *Defense Program and Budget, Fiscal Year 1971*, which he delivered to the Senate committees on February 20, 1970, he made the point that, in view of the speedily developing Chinese nuclear threat, it would be "foolhardy," stupid, and suicidal to "rely on our deterrent forces only," when a far better alternative was available, namely, the Safeguard antiballistic missile defense program. He personally declared that this Safeguard defense was a "crucial" need for the United States, and he quoted President Nixon's unequivocal statement:

> No President with the responsibility for the lives and the security of the American people could fail to provide this protection.

No President, that is, as we have seen, except one completely turned around by Henry Kissinger. Kissinger's abject compulsion to secure Soviet signatures on some sort of SALT Agreements, in time for the conclusion of the Moscow Summit in May 1972, led him to trap the United States into a no-defense treaty with the Soviets that not only guaranteed Soviet missiles a free ride against U.S. cities and our entire population, but also guaranteed a free ride to the missiles of Red China or any other enemy.

The Chou En-lai scenario presents a practical illustration—from the operational point of view—of how Dr. Kissinger, in a perverted passion to appease the Soviets, has rendered the United States totally vulnerable to a Red Chinese missile attack, or to nuclear blackmail backed by a highly credible threat of such an attack. In an exchange of cities with Red China, the population losses would run 10-to-1 against us. The Chou scenario specifically illustrates how the treaty-guaranteed absence of all active U.S. defenses could be exploited by the Chinese to trigger a catalytic nuclear war between the U.S. and the U.S.S.R.

Although that scenario was highly realistic in postulating the threat of a Soviet strike against both China and the United States, it is a situation very difficult for Americans to contemplate as real. Most Americans simply do not believe that the Soviets will actually use their nuclear weapons—even though they have invested hundreds of billions of rubles in acquiring their huge arsenal and in building a first-strike capability against the United States, and even though this investment has given the Soviets a vastly greater first-strike capability against the Red Chinese.

Even though Americans don't believe this threat exists, the Chinese Communist leaders do. They believe in it so firmly that they have committed scores of millions of dollars worth of terribly scarce resources from industrial and agricultural programs in order to build their great passive-defense programs to save their people and their newly developed industries from nuclear missile attack.

Yet, most Americans remain unconvinced. Some can perceive it intellectually, but deep down inside they don't really believe it. Perhaps their faith that it can't happen here can be fractured by our scenario of a desperate China exploiting the national suicidal folly of the SALT I Treaty by which we abandoned all right to defend ourselves against incoming nuclear missiles. If not, then consider how Dr. Kissinger's ill-considered actions will—without any nation actually firing a missile at anyone—force the United States into a desperate and irreversible predicament.

Instead of China, let us consider Japan—an industrial superpower but a strategic nothing-power—as the principal protagonist in another forecast of the future. For realism, we will use many of Dr. Kissinger's own words.

The subject is really triple-headed: (1) the present and potential global importance of Japan, (2) the relative threats to Japan posed by the Soviet Union on the one hand and Red China on the other, and (3) the importance to the United States of Japan's not losing faith in the U.S. nuclear umbrella as a defense against nuclear blackmail by either of the two Communist giants.

The "Nixon Doctrine" was enunciated by the President in an address on Guam in July 1969. Dr. Kissinger was still trying to explain what it really means in September 1970 when he conducted a White House background briefing for the press, television, and radio. Under the ground rules announced, reporters were not permitted to make direct quotations or to name Dr. Kissinger; even paraphrased or non-quoted materials could be attributed only to "Administration officials."

We, however, were not invited; and the ground rules have long since been broken by those who were. We feel free, therefore, to give direct quotations and to name the brain in charge. The quotations are doubly intriguing because they provide a rather frank picture of how much more secure we and our allies were under the old JCS-Eisenhower-pre-Kissinger military posture of "strategic superiority" than we are under "strategic sufficiency." In effect, Kissinger conceded the superiority of the doctrine of "strategic superiority" over the doctrine of "strategic sufficiency."

At this September 1970 background briefing, Dr. Kissinger spoke of what the Joint Chiefs of Staff refer to with nostalgia as the "Cuba environment." Referring back to 1962, Dr. Kissinger stated:

> . . .our strategic superiority was overwhelming. The Soviet Union could not respond to our pressure on Cuba by bringing pressure on areas where we were vulnerable such as Berlin, because they had to be worried that we might do to them what later the Israelis did to the Arabs, namely, launch a preemptive strike.
>
> Therefore, *our strategic superiority defended not only us but our allies* and even those countries that were not our allies but that were thought to be likely to trigger an American response.
>
> There were many people, including myself, who criticized John Foster Dulles' massive-retaliation doctrine in the 1950s. But in historical retrospect, it was correct for the conditions of that period.
>
> But today [1970] the Soviet Union has over 1,400 long-range missiles. In other words, they have increased the number of their missiles 30-fold since 1962. Indeed, they have more long-range missiles than we do today. . . .
>
> It is a different decision for the President of the United States to risk a general nuclear war when the strategic equation is this than it was throughout most of the postwar period.
>
> Therefore the possibility of defending other countries with strategic American power alone has fundamentally changed, and no amount of reassurance on our part can change these facts.
>
> It is for all these reasons that the President. . .enunciated. . .the "Nixon Doctrine.". . .
>
> It says, first, we will, of course, meet our commitments. It says, secondly, *in the case of an attack by a nuclear country on a nonnuclear country, we recognize that we have a specific responsibility for the defense of that nonnuclear country,* because if we did not we would really be opening the door to the acquisition by every country around the world of nuclear weapons. . .

. . .Looking at the world through Peking's eyes, they see the eerie phenomenon that the Russians are building up their forces in the Far East to a point where now the Russians have already more forces facing China than they have facing Europe and have them deployed in a very aggressive posture towards the Chinese. *Believe me, the Russians do not believe in negotiating on the basis of good will.*

When the Russians negotiate, they put some tangible chips into the pot. And these Russian forces are growing by every month. So when the Chinese look at this they are facing a reality. . . .

One final point: Many people say, "After Mao dies maybe the Russians and the Chinese will get together again." This is not impossible for a short period of time, but if you are sitting in the Kremlin, you have to say to yourself, "If Mao is possible once, he's possible again." And you see 800 million Chinese developing nuclear weapons on your doorstep with this growth and this developing of missiles that will be able to reach Moscow long before they can reach Washington, with disputes with Moscow.

We don't really have any conflicts with China.

We don't have anything they want, except a capitalist system, which they would like to overthrow. . . .

Question by James Hoge, Chicago Sun-Times: Dr. Kissinger, on the other side of those 800 million Chinese sits Japan. We have successfully negotiated a security treaty with them. Still, they must be aware of the change in the strategic balance between us and the Soviet Union. They might well read more into the Nixon doctrine than we intended for them to do. They might well see the need for their own strength in military resources as part of their foreign policy growing in Asia.

With this insight, what is your prognosis for Japan and for our relations with it and what are some of the pitfalls we have to watch out for?

Dr. Kissinger: Actually, your question stated the issue extremely well. Japan's GNP with 100 million people is larger than that of China's with 800 million people. The industrial capacity of Japan has grown enormously. It has the fastest rate of growth of any industrial country. They have managed to establish a substantial degree of economic influence in many parts of Asia.

It has been our policy to recognize that Japan is to be a principal and maybe the principal country to determine the future of East Asia over the next decade or two. . . .

You have correctly pointed out the dangers we may face. They may misread the Nixon Doctrine, not as a way of remaining committed to Asia, but as a way of getting out of Asia, if not of the world.

They may watch what happens in Vietnam, and judge the degree of our capacity to influence events in Asia, whatever we may have intended to do. They have the option of either throwing in their lot by working with China, or by going on an independent course backed by us. They undoubtedly have to look at the security balance as I have described it earlier.

With respect to the security situation, that obtains, of course, primarily in our relationship with the Soviet Union, *and what that says is that U.S. strategic power is no longer exactly the same deterrent as it was before vis-a-vis the Soviet Union,* and, therefore, local power is more important.

On the other hand, the Soviet Union has no means of attacking Japan directly, except across the sea. And, therefore, the Soviet Union is not able to physically establish a fait accompli in Japan except through an operation of such a massive scale which would, of course, have a much higher probability of generating a general war.

China, on the other hand, which has a capability of encroaching on Japanese geographical interests, *is for the foreseeable future still deterred by American strategic power, because Chinese nuclear strength is still pitiful compared to that of the United States.*

So the strategic balance has not yet affected Japanese considerations. But we have to be extremely careful that the Japanese do not misread what we are doing as a retreat from Asia, that they do not get the idea that either we are too weak to protect our allies or too divided at home to use our strength.

If they do, we might see again one of these sudden shifts of Japanese policy since it is one of the aspects of Japan that they believe, and I think believe correctly, that their culture is so particular to them that they can adapt to many conditions and still preserve their national essence. This is what they have done through a long and, on the whole, very successful history.

But Japan, in many respects, is the key, and is one of the countries which we watch with the greatest of care.[1]

This is a typical Henry Kissinger performance. He shows that he understands some of our country's most vital, critical national security interests; and then he swings the United States, through his control over the President, on a course of action so potentially disastrous to those U.S. interests as to be explainable only by the appalling alternatives that he must be either "some kind of a nut," or the far more sinister "or something."

In this statement Dr. Kissinger shows that he recognizes that our former "strategic *superiority* defended not only us but our allies"; that the Soviets, having "increased the number of their missiles 30-fold since 1962" and thereby having "more long-range missiles than we do today (1970)" have deprived us of our former strategic superiority, so that "the possibility of defending other countries with strategic American power alone has fundamentally changed, and no amount of reassurance on our part can change these facts."

He recognizes also that "Japan is the key," that "Japan is to be a principal and maybe the principal country to determine the future of East Asia over the next decade or two," that Japan *has to* look at the strategic balance as he has described it, and that we must be "extremely careful" that the Japanese "do not get the idea that we are too weak to protect our allies."

Dr. Kissinger contrasts the Soviet and Red Chinese threats against Japan, and concludes that the Chinese threat is more imminent.

Then that most equivocal of men, Henry Kissinger, makes a positive prediction with no hedges or qualifications: a prediction that, when analyzed, is so wildly irresponsible that it would not have been made by any reasonably knowledgeable or prudent nuclear strategist:

> China. . .is for the foreseeable future still deterred by American strate-
> gic power, because Chinese nuclear strength is still pitiful compared to
> that of the United States.
>
> So the strategic balance has not yet affected Japanese considerations.

It should be remembered that Henry Kissinger was speaking in September 1970, almost exactly seven months *after* Secretary of Defense Melvin Laird had detailed to the Senate committees on Armed Services and Appropriations exactly why it would be "foolhardy" to rely upon *deterring* the Chinese even in the very easily "foreseeable future." He pointed out that U.S. population is heavily concentrated: "25 percent in the 10 largest U.S. cities compared with 11 percent in the 1,000 largest Chinese cities." Consequently, Secretary Laird explained, "they could inflict on us a proportionately greater number of fatalities in a small attack than we could inflict on them in a very large attack."

For that reason, Secretary Laird said we needed the type of anti-missile defense that Safeguard could provide for our population against the Chinese missiles. Dr. Kissinger's prediction regarding China's development of strategic power was, therefore, wildly irresponsible even at the time it was made; and his subsequent actions have destroyed it utterly.

Whatever it was then, Dr. Kissinger's Moscow-Summit SALT I Anti-Defense Treaty, plus the Chinese passive defense program, have made it almost infinitely worse. Although most of the considerations set out in the Chou En-lai scenario are relevant, focus here should be on the line of the Population Distribution Table showing the 100 cities. Destruction of the 100 largest cities would wipe out some 48 percent of our population, but only 8.6 percent of the Chinese population.

That was *before* the Chinese invested four years and incalculable resources in passive defense systems.

The Chinese have developed a realistic capability of strategic evacuation of their large cities and even many smaller ones. This capability, plus the shelters, could easily cut their potential population losses by 90 percent. Each year, as more industrial facilities go underground, their 65-75 percent potential loss of industrial capacity is reduced.

That raises another disproportion between the vulnerability of the American people as contrasted with the Chinese. Calculations based on the "cookie cutter" theory assume that the explosion of nuclear weapons takes out segments of the population in a neat circle, just as cookies are cut out of rolled-out dough. It does not include the huge numbers—especially in the United States—who would be killed by radiation or starvation.

If an enemy took out any substantial number of large U.S. cities, our entire complex system of transportation would be destroyed, frozen, or crippled. Even if food supplies were stored, there would be no effective way of distributing them nationwide. Millions of people would soon die of starvation. This would not happen in China. More than 90 percent of their people could live on local food supplies that require no elaborate transportation, whereas only about 7 percent of ours could survive on locally produced food.

How effective, then, will the U.S. strategic deterrent be in protecting Japan against a nuclear attack or nuclear blackmail conducted by Red China?

Look at the problem from the eyes of an intelligent and nuclear-knowledgeable Japanese. Japan is at once the richest prize and the most vulnerable target of the two Communist giants. Her future is inexorably a medley of imponderables. With her industrial production predicted to be the greatest in the world before the year 2000, Japan is the one nation a world-conquering superpower would most like to take intact as a going concern. On the other hand, she is the one nation that an ambitious and expanding superpower can least afford to let slip into the rival camp with her magnificent and modern industrial plant and skilled and disciplined labor force intact.

Suppose Japan were politically integrated with China, and her technological resources and industrial facilities were applied to the rapid industrialization of China. Within a decade, the result would be a combined industrial capacity potentially 20 times Japan's present capacity, plus agricultural production massive enough to make the China-Japan condominium independent of foreign sources of food.

All that, of course, would depend on the Soviet Union's not resorting to strategic nuclear weapons. Just five Soviet supermissiles could utterly destroy Japan—her industrial plant, agriculture, and the entire population, including her tremendously productive labor force. The 110 million Japanese live and farm and manufacture in a total area of less than 145,000 square miles. They are even more vulnerable than the United States, because our population of twice that size has some 3,000,000 square miles of land to spread out in—an area roughly 20 times greater.

On the other hand, if Japan were politically integrated with the Soviet Union, the resulting combination would be at once the greatest industrial superpower and the greatest military superpower the world has ever known—not in 10 years, but *now*. Overnight, the U.S.S.R. would gain resources of technology and industrial plant that she could not develop in more than 10 years—even with the U.S. help that Dr. Kissinger has pledged to the Politburo for those purposes.

The Russo-Japanese combination would be so massively powerful—economically, financially, industrially, and militarily—that all the states of Western Europe would rush to join the new world order established by the Kremlin. Nor would it be a "Finlandization" process. It would be total integration and subjugation. There would be no chance for any NATO nations to resist the new colossus.

Resistance would be impossible even for the United States—on a longterm or even medium-term basis. The Kremlin would not even need to *suggest* the use of strategic military power against us. A few peaceful measures would suffice: cut off our oil supplies from abroad, cut off our imports of other essential minerals, and make the dollar unacceptable in international trade. The Soviet Union already substantially influences the Persian Gulf states from whence most of our imported oil must come: Iran, Saudi Arabia, Iraq, and Kuwait, Abu Dhabi, and other small sheikdoms. These states would go willingly into the new world order, together with Western Europe and Japan—their essential customers for oil. Like it or not, however, they would have no realistic choice against the Soviets' new combination of military, industrial, and financial power.

Not only could the Soviets shut off our foreign supplies of oil and essential strategic materials, but they would also control the nations who own or control more than 90 percent of the world's shipping. Japan alone is the world's powerhouse in this vital area. Her shipyards lead the world in numbers and size of ships built, especially supertankers and bulk carriers of more than 300,000 tons. She builds 70 percent of the world's new construction, and her own merchant fleet includes more than 2,500 ships of more than 1,000 gross tons. There would be no ocean transportation available to carry the foreign trade of the last remaining relic of "capitalist imperialism."

Without resort to actual use of their strategic nuclear power, the Soviets can anytime close the sea lanes to any ships they want blocked. The U.S. Chief of Naval Operations, Elmo Zumwalt, in an interview a few weeks before his retirement, made this public statement:

> The Soviet Union's capability to deny us the sea lines, which is their job, is greater than our capability to keep the sea lines open, which is our job.[2]

This illustrates the value of having a strategic nuclear first-strike capability. Because of their naval supremacy in conventional power, the Soviets can shut off the United States not only from imported *oil*, but also from other essential raw materials. Our industrial plant would be crippled and our economy would shrink and collapse. Our conventional power would not be sufficient to break the Soviets' worldwide blockade against our shipping. If we had substantial nuclear supremacy, we could credibly threaten limited nuclear attacks against Soviet industrial facilities unless they withdrew the blockade; and they would not dare to launch even a limited retaliatory strategic nuclear attack against us because we would have the capability to destroy them.

A merger of Japan with the Soviet Union, which would trigger the rush of Western Europe and ultimately all the nations of the world into the Soviets' new world order, will be the most probable result of Dr. Kissinger's trapping the United States into the Moscow Summit SALT I Anti-Defense Treaty. The most probable *peaceful* result, that is, *if* neither the Soviets nor the Red Chinese decide to cash in on the free ride that the treaty guarantees for their nuclear missiles. Here is how this peaceful result might come about.

Let us look through the eyes of the intelligent and nuclear-knowledgeable Japanese statesman. He recognizes the unique and truly terrible vulnerability of Japan's cities, industries, and people to nuclear warheads. More than any other nation in the world, the Japanese know that strategic military nuclear power is, indeed, usable. They remember very well that they were once on the receiving end.

Japan is the bone of contention, the prize that would give either of the contending Communist giants near-immediate control of the entire world, or medium-term potential for such control. Japan is expending all its resources on production and substantially none for military power, either conventional or nuclear. Japan has, therefore, quite literally a desperate need for the protection of a nuclear umbrella in order to render the strategic nuclear power of the two Communist giants *unusable* against Japan—either for an actual attack or as backup for nuclear blackmail. In short, Japan's survival absolutely requires the protection of a strategic nuclear deterrent *that works*.

For the first quarter-century of the nuclear age the U.S. deterrent served Japan very well indeed. It enabled the Japanese to enjoy the best of two worlds: to expend zero percent of their Gross National Product on strategic defense, and yet to enjoy the security provided by the greatest strategic nuclear force in the world.

In 1969, however, the great change began to surface: the U.S.S.R. surged past parity with the United States, began to swing the strategic balance heavily against the United States, and then continued to increase the momentum of its nuclear buildup.

In that year also, the Soviets came close to launching their pre-emptive surgical strike to excise the developing nuclear power of Red China. They came so close to it, indeed, that Mao and Chou En-lai decreed an overriding national priority on all labor and resources for building passive strategic defense systems. They are convinced that the Soviet nuclear attack has not been canceled, but merely postponed.

The next revelation of the revolutionary shift in strategic nuclear power—which alone is sufficient to control the world—was the publication of the SALT I Agreements following the Moscow Summit of 1972. As objective strategic experts agreed, the SALT I "figures spell out a simple and compelling message of American strategic inferiority."[3] Even worse, Henry Kissinger, in his negotiations and his public rationale of the SALT I pacts, displayed an abject eagerness to freeze the United States in a position of treaty-perpetuated inferiority. He, in effect, heaped fulsome thanks at the feet of Soviet leaders for having given us an agreement "without which the [missile] gap would steadily widen" and which "makes a major contribution for our [U.S.] security."

The climactic factor emerging from SALT in 1972, however, was the Kissinger abjuration of all defense of U.S. cities and population, and his guaranteeing to the missiles of *any* enemy a free ride on a mission to destroy the American people, their cities, and their industries. Prior to that time, the U.S. ABM programs, even the one Nixon watered down from the Lyndon Johnson proposal, would have rendered U.S. cities substantially invulnerable to Red Chinese ICBM attack.

Most significant, this defense system would have been ready *before* the Red Chinese would have had the missiles in-being to launch or threaten such an attack. Such a missile defense program would have relieved the United States of the humanly unbearable disadvantage of a "cities-exchange" between our 76-percent-urbanized nation and an enemy only 7 percent urbanized.

In short, it would have *extended the credibility* of the U.S. strategic deterrent as an effective protection for Japan against Red Chinese nuclear threats. The deterrent would be automatically credible unless and until—but *only* unless and until—the Chinese developed a threat against U.S. cities. When they did develop an ICBM force capable of destroying even a few of our cities, our ABM system would have been ready to cancel out the threat.

But Dr. Kissinger's forswearing all effective and active protection against any enemy's ICBMs—now, and for a period of "unlimited duration" in the future—handed the Red Chinese a counterdeterrent on, so to speak, a uranium platter. It re-created their fantastic advantage of holding 50 million Americans as hostages by threatening merely 10 of our cities, whereas we would have to establish a threat against their 1,000 largest cities to gain only 11 percent of their population as hostages to our nuclear power.

That was the situation *after* the SALT I Anti-Defense Treaty, but *before* completion of the Chinese passive defense systems. To understate it, the U.S. strategic deterrent, for the purpose of providing a nuclear umbrella for the Japanese, lost its credibility with Nixon's signature on the SALT I Treaty. Now, with completion of those new Chinese passive defense systems, the U.S. strategic deterrent is not only incredible, it would be ridiculous were it not so tragic.

· The knowledgeable Japanese statesman, whose eyes we are borrowing, could have faith in the U.S. deterrent's capability of protecting Japan if—but only if—the U.S. President could say, in the words Jack Kennedy used in his famous "I am a Berliner" speech to the West Germans, "We will risk our cities to save your cities," and if—but only if—the Japanese statesman would believe him. But could he?

If the Red Chinese targeted our 100 largest cities, we would have more than 100 million people totally vulnerable to nuclear destruction. We have no capability for strategic evacuation of our cities. We don't even have plans for it. Our blast-shelter program is near zero; even our fallout-shelter program is a joke. Our people have had no instruction in civil defense against a nuclear attack. Even warning systems are inadequate, and there has been no attempt to program response. The best test we have had was a false alarm that should have sent millions of people scurrying to shelter. What happened? Nothing. The radio stations—except for one or two—simply did not believe the warning, even though it had all the indicia of an actual warning. Could we evacuate any substantial number of people by automobiles, buses and our highway system? Have you ever seen what a single flat tire on a single car can do to rush-hour traffic? Or a snowfall?

The absolute and stupid refusal of the American nation—leaders and people—to develop effective passive defenses is one overriding factor in our desperate need for the active defenses that Henry Kissinger has forsworn on our behalf. In evaluating the "risk to our cities" within a Kennedy-type offer to the Japanese, we would have to include the risk of nuclear incineration or destruction of more than 100 million Americans.

So what threat can we make against the Red Chinese to deter them from attacking or even threatening to attack Japanese cities, and to deter them also from striking at U.S. cities?

If we could target the 1,000 largest cities in China, we could hold hostage 11 percent of their total population of around 800 million, or

88 million. *But that would be true only if they had no effective passive defenses, and we know that they do have them.*

They have especially planned to take advantage of the 93-percent-agricultural orientation of their country to make strategic evacuation of their cities realistic. In addition, their entire shelter system is dual purpose: it provides both blast and fallout shelter, and at the same time provides safe evacuation routes for the urban population.

The Soviet Government has asserted that its civil defense system could limit fatalities to 6 percent of the population, even in an all-out U.S. nuclear attack. The Chinese system is reputed to be even better. Certainly it is more modern, all of it having been constructed since 1969. If it is 90-percent effective, the number of our Chinese hostages would drop to 8.8 million. If it were only 70-percent effective—and this is a low figure indeed—our hostages would number only 26.4 million.

Thus, in a U.S. planned attack against 1,000 Chinese cities, we could optimistically assume that we would hold 26.4 million Chinese as hostages. The Chinese, in their 100-city planned attack, would hold 100 million Americans hostages. What would the respective nations have left if such an attack were launched? The United States would have, say, 110 million people left, with transportation, communication, distribution and storage terribly damaged. It is questionable whether the United States, with its 100 largest cities in heaps of smoldering rubble, could mobilize the forces and facilities essential to the survival of the remaining 110 million people.

China, on the other hand, would have a surviving population of 773.6 million—and they could get along without their 1,000 cities very well. *More than 712 million Chinese do not live in any cities,* even when all the cities are in good shape. They will have food available without the transportation and distribution problems that arise out of our efficient, but incredibly complex, systems. Chairman Mao not only commanded his people to "dig deep their tunnels," but also "to store grain everywhere."

Thus, it would appear to be clear that the risk to U.S. cities in attempting to deter a Red Chinese attack on Japanese cities—even assuming that we could mount an attack against 1,000 Chinese cities—would be relatively so horrendous, while the threat to Chinese cities and population relatively so noncritical, that any U.S. President would be insane to make such a promise to the Japanese. The Japanese would be even more insane to believe it, if we did.

But that is not the worst of it. The assumption that we could mount an attack against 1,000 Chinese cities is totally false.

If we expended the number of strategic missiles required to target those Chinese cities effectively, we would concurrently in effect have tendered the strategic surrender of the United States to the Soviet Union. As Secretary of Defense Laird warned back in February 1970:

> In any nuclear confrontation with Communist China, we would still have to maintain a sufficient deterrent against the Soviet Union.

If that problem were serious then, when the Soviet Union had only 1,109 ICBMs and 240 SLBMs, it is ultracritical now, when the Soviets have *added* more than 500 ICBMs and an equal number of SLBMs to their offensive missile force capable of reaching U.S. targets.

The problem of targeting those 1,000 Chinese cities exposes part of the deliberately deceitful character of the "numbers game" put over on the American people by Robert McNamara. His clandestine program for the unilateral disarmament of the United States so cut down the *number* of U.S. strategic missiles relative to the *number* of Soviet missiles that it was becoming clear, even to non-experts, that the Soviets were gaining nuclear superiority, and that McNamara had thrown ours away.

McNamara, however, was never at a loss to cover himself with a slick, deceptive gambit. He committed the United States to a MIRV program, and then publicly declared that the important factor was no longer which side had the larger *number* of missiles, or even which side had the greater megatonnage delivery capability, but was which side had the greater number of *warheads*. He equated a Poseidon individual MIRV warhead of 50 kilotons of explosive power with a Soviet SS-9 single warhead of 25 megatons of explosive power, thus concealing a 24,950,000-ton-explosive-power advantage to the Soviets in each such comparison. This is what the seven members of President Nixon's own Blue Ribbon Defense Panel labeled the "numbers game," that is, "the mere counting of warheads without analysis of megatonnage, range, accuracy, survivability, and reliability of delivery."[4]

The continued relevance of the "numbers game" deception is that Dr. Henry Kissinger played it up to the hilt in selling SALT I to the nation. With the obvious and massive advantages he had conceded to the Soviets in ICBM launcher and SLBM launcher *numbers*, the only way he could even talk about missiles without admitting that we were frozen in inferiority depended on MIRVs:

> With our MIRVs we have a 2-to-1 lead today in numbers of warheads and this lead will be maintained during the period of the agreement, even if the Soviets develop and deploy MIRVs of their own.[5]

Dr. Kissinger seems to delight in making fools of Middle Americans by combining in a single sentence a highly misleading irrelevancy with a totally false prediction and a misleading assurance. The boast of a "2-to-1 lead today in numbers of warheads" is irrelevant because it treats all warheads as fungibles, and ignores all aspects of the questions "what good are they?" and "what can they *do?*" It dresses up the "2-to-1 lead" in warhead numbers as if having it were something that substantially contributes to U.S. security. He even asserts that our MIRVing gives us "a big advantage on warheads."

If you were in a dugout being hunted down by a lightly armored tank, and you were armed with one .50-caliber machine gun and plenty of armor-piercing and explosive shells, would you swap it for 100 rapid-firing .22-caliber guns? The shots from the .22s would rattle off the light armor like hailstones, whereas the .50-caliber bullets would penetrate, explode, and destroy the tank. Mere numbers never destroyed anything: 1,000 .22s would be as useless against a tank as 100 .22s.

The totally false prediction is that the 2-to-1 lead "will be maintained during the period of the Agreement even if the Soviets develop and deploy MIRVs of their own." Given MIRV technology— which Kissinger (in his press briefings) conceded the Soviets would have during the five-year period of the SALT I Interim Agreement (and which they demonstrated within one year)—the number of MIRV or MRV warheads that each side's missile force is capable of delivering is governed by the throw-weight of the missile force. There are no informed estimates that put the Soviet advantage in throw-weight at less than 4-to-1 over the United States; many authorities placed it at more than 5-to-1 at the time of the SALT I Agreements.

Thus, Dr. Kissinger's solemnly promised immutable 2-to-1 lead in numbers of warheads could easily be reversed, and the Soviets could lead us by 5-to-1. If they wanted to run a MIRV race with us, they could soon have 25,000 warheads, whereas the most we could have would be fewer than 10,000. And theirs could be vastly more powerful per warhead.

But the Soviets will *not* run us a MIRV race. They want warheads which will *do* something: which will serve some *operational* purpose, which will implement a rational strategy. Mini-MIRVs, such as our Poseidon 50-kiloton MIRVs, can serve only very limited purposes, as we will see in discussing the problem of the United States' planning an attack on 1,000 Red Chinese cities to deter a Chinese attack against us or against Japan.

If we could assume—as McNamara and his minions before, and Dr. Kissinger now, would have us believe—that *a warhead is a warhead is a warhead*, and that all we need do is to target 1,000 warheads (plus a small allowance for degradation) on 1,000 cities, it would be simple. We could assign seven Poseidon submarines to the task.

That would give a total of 7 x 16 missiles = 112 missiles, x 10 MIRV warheads per missile = 1,120 warheads available, or more than one warhead per city.

Could those 50 kiloton warheads do the job of holding the populations of the cities hostage by a capability of threatening their destruction? Not even if the Chinese had not built their massive and extensive passive defense system.

Let's first look at the situation without passive defense. *A 50-kiloton warhead is not a city-killer.* McNamara's estimates circa 1967 conceded that it would take three 50-kiloton warheads to destroy a city of 100,000 population; and that even 10 such warheads would not totally destroy a city of 500,000. China has six cities with a population of more than two million each; a total of 15 cities with more than a million; 25 with more than 700,000. In 1973 Shanghai was reported to have the largest population of any city in the world, even more than Tokyo. A very rough estimate, therefore, would suggest that to target those 1,000 largest Chinese cities effectively with 50-kiloton weapons would require an average of three Poseidon warheads each. This would require the assignment of 19 Poseidon submarines, which, in turn, is impossible. And remember that those 1,000 cities contain only 11 percent of the more than 800 million estimated total population.

Our Polaris force originally totaled 41; 10 of these will not be converted to Poseidons. As of 1974 only 20 had been converted to Poseidons. A minimum of two years is required for each conversion. Because of the number undergoing conversion at any time, the operational force of Polaris-Poseidons is estimated at between 29 and 33. Only slightly more than half this total number are at sea on station at any given time. If we attempted to assign anything like 19 Poseidons to a China mission, we would have depleted our deterrent against the Soviet Union to the point of uselessness. Considering the counterforce capability of their offensive missiles, especially the SS-9 and SS-18 force, plus their new SS-17s and SS-19s, our Minuteman force of land-based ICBMs cannot be regarded as survivable. This leaves our SLBMs as our only deterrent force with survivability.

We need not, however, worry too much about the problem of assigning Poseidons to the China mission in sufficient numbers. Once the Red Chinese completed their extensive passive defense systems, Poseidon 50-kiloton warheads were deprived of their capability to hold the populations of those 1,000 largest cities as hostages. Our Poseidons hold no substantial threat to the large percentage of the population that can be evacuated through the shelter systems, or to those remaining in the shelters. The extensive Soviet system of shelters is estimated to be protected to 25 psi—that is, capable of withstanding overpressure of 25 pounds per square inch. The Chinese system is reputed to be far better. The Chinese main shelter tunnels are reported to be 26 feet below street level, all made of concrete and brick structure. Some go seven stories underground.

Even the Soviet-type 25-psi shelters change the targeting picture radically. Against a population with that protection, it would require a 20-megaton warhead to do as much damage as a one-megaton warhead could accomplish against an unsheltered population.

Thus, it would be ridiculous to attempt to create a deterrent to a Red Chinese threat against Japanese cities—or even against U.S. cities—by employment of Poseidon warheads only. Unlike the situation that exists in targeting against weapons, an increase in the guidance accuracy of the warheads would not help. Cut the CEP of a Poseidon warhead to 500 feet, and it will have about an 80-percent single-shot chance of destroying a silo-protected ICBM; but a 500-foot CEP would not destroy any more shelter-protected people than a 1,000-foot CEP would. Like firing .22-caliber lead pellets at an armored tank, 50-kiloton warheads would be ineffective against people protected by extensive passive defense programs. We would just be wasting our Poseidons.

What do we have left, then, with which to create a deterrent against Red China? Our 1,054 Minuteman III missiles—as of 1976 —each with three 200-kiloton warheads. Each city would require a minimum of one warhead. To put one warhead on each city would require 1,000 warheads, or 333 missiles (with no allowance for degradation). But the 400 largest of the 1,000 cities would require an average of two warheads each—even if we assume, as before, that no extensive passive defense exists, and that the population is as vulnerable as in an American city. This would require another 400 warheads, or 133 additional missiles.

Therefore, we would have to plan on expending 466 missiles—or nearly half our entire Minuteman force—on Chinese targets. This would obviously cut down the number of missiles in the U.S. system that the Soviets would have to target for a disarming first strike. They would then have the *pin-down capability* with SLBMs (mostly flat trajectory), and the *destruction capability* with ICBMs, sufficient to provide a first-strike capability against the United States and still have a huge reserve of missiles remaining.

Actually, a *mix* of Poseidons with the Minutemen would be our most practicable strike against the 1,000-city Chinese target system. We could assign only one Poseidon warhead to each of the 600 second-ranking cities, which would require only five Poseidon submarines. But we would still have to assign an average of two of the five-times-more-powerful Minuteman warheads to each of the 400

104

largest cities. This would require 267 of our entire force of 1,054 ICBMs. Even five Poseidons is a substantial percentage of the total Poseidons we could expect to have operational and on station. Again, we would have reduced our strategic deterrent versus the Soviet Union to a point that would guarantee them a first-strike capability against us.

We are up against the harsh reality that Henry Kissinger never considered when he trapped us into the no-defense treaty with the Soviets. *There will never again be a chance to target Chinese cities as if their people were as vulnerable as ours.* Their passive defense systems are in place, and the populace has been drilled in strategic evacuation and in taking shelter.

There is also very substantial doubt that we could effectively hold hostage a decisively greater number of people with the 200-kiloton warheads of Minuteman MIRVs than with the 50-kiloton Poseidon MIRVs. The millions evacuated would be nontargetable by such small warheads, fallout would be minimal, and those in the main concrete and brick tunnels, 26 feet below street level, would be protected against any missile that did not impact in their immediate area.

This analysis, demonstrating how helpless we are to build confidence in our capability of accomplishing the "assured destruction" of more than one to three percent of the people in China, serves a dual purpose.

First, it demonstrates that the U.S. strategic deterrent is incredible and useless for the protection of Japan against a Red Chinese nuclear threat. *Second*, it illustrates what a cruel farce and deliberate deception has been perpetrated upon the people of the United States, who have been repeatedly and continuously assured that we have "overkill" capability and that our nuclear arsenal is capable of destroying the entire population of the world.

Henry Kissinger exploited this deceptive concept in selling SALT to the United States. He introduced his grand rationale of the SALT I Agreements with two superficially impressive assertions that are demonstrable lies. Speaking about the United States and the Soviet Union, he made these two statements to the members of the five congressional committees at the White House briefing of June 15, 1972:

> We each possess an awesome nuclear force *created and designed to meet* the threat implicit in the other's strength and aims.
> Each of us thus has come into possession of power singlehandedly capable of exterminating the human race.

The first assertion assumes the "action-reaction" theory of the "arms race"—that is, that the Soviets built their huge first-strike-oriented nuclear arsenal only in reaction to a U.S. buildup. No intelligent and objective nuclear strategist has made this statement since 1969, when the Soviets continued their buildup past both parity and sufficiency. Not even stupid but objective strategic analysts made such an assertion after 1971. In the 1971 and 1972 *State of the World Reports* prepared by Henry Kissinger and presented by President Nixon, it was revealed that the Soviets had continued their "creation of strategic capabilities beyond a level which by any reasonable standard already seems sufficient." Then, in the SALT I negotiations, the Soviets insisted on and gained from Dr. Kissinger massive additional imbalances carrying them beyond the U.S. "strength" that, in his SALT I rationale quoted above, he had the gall to assert was responsible for the *creation and design* of the Soviets' awesome nuclear force. Here again we have Henry Kissinger demonstrating that Dr. Kissinger is a liar.

Even liberal strategic analysts recognize that the "action-reaction" fable of the origin of the "arms race" has been conclusively repudiated by the evidence of history. Writing in *The Washington Papers* under the auspices of the Center for Strategic and International Studies, Georgetown University, Edward Luttwak summarized the evidence in this manner:

> If the Russians were indeed acting out the "reaction" part of the mechanistic arms race model prospected by McNamara, it is strange indeed that they went on "reacting" even after, (a) the number of American missiles was stabilized (1967 at the latest), (b) when the number of their ICBMs exceeded the number deployed by the United States (1969), and (c) at the SALT I, when they insisted on further increments in both ICBM silos (91 units) and SLBM tubes (210 units).
>
> As a matter of fact, *studies of Russian strategic deployments since the Second World War show quite conclusively that "action-reaction" phenomena can explain only some of their motives.* More important is the question of incentives.[6]

Dr. Kissinger compounds the fraud in his assertion of this action-reaction fable by asserting that the Soviet Union's "awesome nuclear force" was "created and designed to meet the threat implicit" in U.S. "strength and *aims.*"

It is not only historically untrue, but a particularly vicious calumny against the United States to assert that, at any time in the nuclear age, the United States has ever "aimed" to "threaten" the Soviet Union with our "awesome nuclear force." The proof of this is fivefold.

First, when we had a total monopoly of atomic weapons, we never threatened the Soviet Union, despite the fact that, in the face of the rapid demobilization of U.S. conventional power, the Soviets did not demobilize, but continued their buildup and employed their six-million-man army to coerce the nations of Eastern Europe into the Soviet camp.

Second, after the Soviets broke our atomic monopoly, we had a monopoly of the only effective strategic delivery system for H-bombs: the heavy, long-range bomber; and still we did not threaten the Soviets.

Third, at the time of the Cuban missile crisis in 1962, we possessed —in Dr. Kissinger's own words—"overwhelming nuclear superiority," and yet we did not even threaten to use our strategic nuclear power against the Soviets—except in retaliation if they actually launched a strike at the Western Hemisphere. In fact we did not even actually use our *conventional* power to cancel out the Soviet threat from Cuba.

Fourth, we defaulted ourselves out of the so-called "nuclear arms race" immediately after the Cuban missile crisis in 1962 by *stopping all input into the ongoing production lines of our strategic weapons systems,* canceling development of new strategic systems, and scrapping 1,400 strategic bombers, as well as holding down our strategic power developments, as summarized in the Luttwak quotation above.

Fifth, we entered into agreements with the Soviets guaranteeing them, initially, technological superiority in high-yield nuclear warheads in the Moscow Test Ban Treaty of 1963, and then operational superiority in ICBMs and SLBMs in the SALT I Agreements.

Even more clearly abjuring any U.S. threat to the Soviet Union was our refusal over the years since 1962 to develop any strategic forces with a substantial *counterforce* capability against the Soviet Union. We did this by deliberately holding down the *numbers* of our missiles, the *explosive power* of our warheads, and the *accuracy* of our guidance. So, Dr. Kissinger's explanation for the motivation of the Soviet buildup of their "awesome nuclear force" is not merely a lie, but a lie that libels the United States and whitewashes the Soviet motives for their buildup of the strategic power to destroy us.

This lie is basic to the fabric of Dr. Kissinger's deceit because it provides the rationalization for giving the Soviets the decisive strategic advantages and imbalances embodied in the SALT I pacts. This is because, according to that lie, the *purpose* of the Soviet buildup of first-strike capability against us is *not to destroy* or even injure us, but *merely to deter* us from executing a "threat" ("implicit" in U.S. "strength and aims") to destroy *them.*

The first sentence in the Kissingerism quoted on page 105 was designed to deceive us into accepting the potentially fatal strategic disadvantages imposed on us by the SALT I Agreements. The second Kissinger sentence was designed to terrorize us into accepting the SALT I Agreements *at any price,* so as to avert the "extermination of the human race."

If you strip his assertions of their high-flown verbiage and translate them into plain words, he is threatening us with his theory that our survival and the survival of the entire human race depend on our securing an agreement—his agreement, of course—with the Soviets. His terrorizing of us depends on our accepting his basic assertion as the truth. However it is a bald-faced lie, and furthermore must be *known to him* as a lie. He not only contends, but positively and unequivocally declares, that "each of us," the U.S. and the U.S.S.R., have "possession of power *singlehandedly* capable of exterminating the human race."

Why, then would we have an impossible task in attempting to hold hostage merely eight to 27 million Chinese, while still holding in reserve strategic weapons to threaten an equal number of Russians? Even if we could accomplish this impossible mission, that would leave some 773 million Chinese, 223 million Russians, and 2,446 million others, *not* exterminated. Those figures assume a world population of 3.5 billion. Kissinger's terroristic assertion that we have the capability "singlehandedly" of exterminating the human race appears to be an exaggeration by a factor of 64. That is an indication of what he thinks of the intelligence of the American people.

It should also be remembered that these estimates are based on the probable maximum kill *if the United States should launch a first-strike targeted on population,* not on weapons, and not on population-plus-weapons. Such a strike would be an act of insanity. In a first-strike (other than one such as the Chinese in their special situation might threaten to launch against us to trigger a catalytic war), the targeting *must* be against retaliatory weapons *first*; population can rationally be targeted *only* if enough weapons are available *after* the weapons have been massively attacked.

The Soviets could "exterminate" a vastly greater number of people, say, 200 million Americans and up to 100 million Chinese. This is because of their greater number of weapons, their five-times-greater throw-weight, and their 10-to-19-times-greater megatonnage delivery capability. Even that would still have Kissinger exaggerating by a factor of 11-2/3.

Actually, his figures are much farther off than they appear to be in this oversimplified computation. After nuclear weapons have killed the first few hundred million of the world's population, the number and megatonnage required to kill additional increments rise at an astronomical rate.

Back in 1962, when the United States had a delivery capability of 40,000 to 50,000 megatons, and the Soviets were estimated (or rather, overestimated) to have a delivery capability of 5,000 to 10,000 megatons, it was judged that, in an *exchange*—that is, with both sides delivering their entire capability without (miraculously) destroying any of the other side's capability—they could accomplish 1/10 of the then-so-called "Death of Earth," cheerfully referred to as DOE or "one beach." The term "beach" was derived from the unilateral-disarmament propaganda novel entitled *On the Beach*, by Neville Shute. This pseudoscientific fraud of a book was long ago exposed by Herman Kahn, in terms of generous understatement, as an "interesting but badly researched book."

One of the more authoritative estimates of the number of megatons required to constitute a "beach" or "Death of Earth" that leaked into unclassified discussion came from the "Summer Study on Arms Control," conducted under the auspices of the American Academy of Arts and Sciences in 1960 in Dedham, Massachusetts. Participants included unilateral-disarmers, scientists, political scientists, and weapons specialists. Among those who took part were Donald G. Brennan, Hans A. Bethe, Morton H. Halperin, Herman Kahn, Thomas C. Schelling, Louis B. Sohn, Leo Szilard, Victor F. Weisskopf, and Jerome Wiesner. The summer seminar was so heavily loaded with members of the Pugwash movement that there would have been a tendency to understate rather than overstate the magnitude of nuclear weapons detonations required for (in Dr. Kissinger's delicate expression) "extermination of the human race."

Throughout the discussion, the figure of 500 KMT (kilomegatons), that is, 500 *thousand* megatons, was referred to as "roughly one-half of a beach." How many megatons can the United States deliver "singlehandedly" in this timeframe? As will be shown later, our missile delivery capability is most optimistically estimated at about 808 megatons (and this does not allow for degradation or losses to ABM defenses). Our strategic bomber force in 1976 will be no more than 200 G and H model B-52s, 80 old B-52Ds, plus 72 FB-111 "light" bombers. No more than 20 percent of them could be expected to survive Soviet attacks by SLBMs and ICBMs. Even assuming that 20 percent survive, they will also have to survive 3,000 Soviet fighter-interceptor aircraft and 10,000 Soviet SAMs before they can reach Soviet targets. Let's say that our bombers could possibly deliver 200 megatons. Added to the approximately 800 megatons deliverable by missile, we have a round figure of 1,000 megatons, or one kilomegaton.

Applying estimates based on these figures, it would appear that Dr. Kissinger is exaggerating by a factor of about 1,000 in order to terrorize the American people about "singlehanded" capability of "exterminating the human race." From these two estimates, therefore, it appears that he is lying by a factor of something between 64 and 1,000. Such a discrepancy is highly unprofessional, as well as dishonest. The far more intriguing question remains, and will haunt us throughout this book: *why* does Kissinger lie?

It must be conceded, however, that estimates of how many megatons will be required to exterminate the human race involve many imponderables. Those figures from the American Academy of Arts and Sciences Summer Seminar of 1960 are the latest authoritative figures available in unclassified material. They apparently were based on extrapolation of fallout statistics from both U.S. and Soviet nuclear tests. As there have been no more atmospheric tests by either nuclear superpower since 1962, and as French and Chinese testing has been relatively limited, there is little reason to think that there is any significant information more recent than the Summer Seminar experts had in 1960. And they dealt only with one-half of a beach.

Computations based on the "cookie cutter" technique, however, also support charges of gross exaggeration by Dr. Kissinger in his terroristic claims. The method of computation excludes the imponderables of deaths caused by fallout, fires, and famine.

A quick look back at the Cumulative Percentage Distribution of Population table, presented as part of the Chou En-lai scenario, illustrates how steeply the ratio of weapons required to kill additional people rises. Take the United States for example. If the Soviets, on the "cookie cutter" technique, effectively took out our 400 largest cities, they would get 60 percent of our population. But to add another mere three percent to their kill, they would have to take out 600 more cities. And so it is, relatively, worldwide.

In passing, it is worth noting that killing people by the hundreds of millions requires large numbers of missiles of massive explosive power—something that McNamara and Kissinger have ensured that the United States does not have and will not have.

Just compare our 1962 megatonnage delivery capability with our present strength: roughly 50,000 megatons *then* versus the 1,008 megatons the U.S. can deliver *now*. One thing that accounts for the magnitude of the reduction is McNamara's feigned mania for mini-MIRVs, which Kissinger has perpetuated as U.S. policy. We have already seen that one Poseidon missile with a single warhead could have a yield of 4 megatons. But equip that same missile with 10 MIRVed warheads at 50-kilotons each, and all 10 have a total explosive power of only ½ of one megaton. That is, in order to get ½ of one megaton of explosive power in 10 MIRVs, we have thrown away 3½ megatons of explosive power. But the MIRVs provide "numbers" with which McNamara, and now Kissinger, could play the "numbers game" to deceive the American public. It was not until John Newhouse's book *Cold Dawn: The Story of SALT*[7] was published in mid-1973, detailing Top Secret security leaks, that we had authoritative evidence that McNamara insisted on 10 MIRVs to each missile in order to render them as harmless as possible to the Soviets because of their low explosive power.

It will, of course, be asked, who wants to kill hundreds of millions of people? The answer is simple. If we want to have an effective deterrent *against the Soviets' killing* 200 million Americans, or *against Red China's killing* 100 million Americans, we need to have that kind of kill-power too. Certainly, it would be what we need to be able to protect Japan from nuclear blackmail by the Red Chinese. This brings us back to the potentially disastrous consequences—even if none of the nuclear powers fires a single missile—of Kissinger's having guaranteed a free ride to *all* enemy missiles to kill American cities, regardless of whether the enemy turns out to be the Soviet Union, Red China, or any third nation.

We were perfectly capable—technologically, financially, and even politically—of deploying, in plenty of time, an ABM defense that could protect substantially our *entire* population from a Red Chinese missile attack in the 1970s. Such an ABM defense would have protected both our cities and our industrial plants from destruction.

Despite the new Chinese passive defense system, we could have extended the protection of our strategic deterrent to Japan by an implicit policy along these lines:

> Mao and Chou and/or your successors in power: if you launch a nuclear attack against Japan, or even threaten to do so, we will take out 100 of your largest cities. We thus hold as hostages up to 68.8 million of your people. We realize that your passive defenses may save up to 90 percent of the populations of those cities, but still you would stand to lose nearly 7 million people *and* your 100 largest cities, together with the industrial plant capacity above ground in those cities.
>
> Because of our *active* defense—our ABM system—you could not hope in an exchange to take out even one of our cities, or any substantial number of our people. So, don't even think of threatening our Japanese allies.

Contrast that with the situation into which Dr. Kissinger's SALT I Agreements have plunged us. If we attempt to extend our strategic deterrent to provide a nuclear umbrella for Japan, the Red Chinese leaders could simply say:

> Perhaps your self-styled intelligentsia still believe in fables, but we do not. We simply do not believe you will risk your 100 largest cities, their population and their industries—all of which are totally vulnerable to our missiles because of your SALT I Anti-Defense Treaty with Moscow—in an attempt to save Japanese cities and people, an attempt doomed to failure in any event.

111

We know that you cannot attempt to target more than 100 of our cities, because to do so would strip your retaliatory force down so low as to be tantamount to a strategic surrender to the Soviet Union. Because of our extensive passive defense system, you could not reasonably expect to kill more than about 7 million of our people; that would still leave us with 793 million. You, on the other hand, are risking 100 million American lives. Such an exchange would be too stupid even for an American who was willing to trap his nation into the SALT I Agreements with Moscow.

The need for the United States to have the capability to offer Japan a credible strategic deterrent, against both the Soviet Union and Red China, is not merely academic. For some time, the Japanese have been asking two questions: Can they believe us? Will the Red Chinese believe us?

In late November 1972 a seminar of 10 Japanese and 15 American newspaper editors was held in San Diego to discuss trade and security relationships between the two nations. A leading Japanese editor asked the outstanding question:

> If Japan is attacked by a nuclear power, will the United States be willing to sacrifice New York, Washington, or San Diego to help Japan?

Unfortunately, the answer to that question is clear from the strategic analyses presented above. Fortunately, however, there has been a lag in Japanese understanding of how swiftly and decisively the strategic balance has shifted against the United States under the Kissinger policies. For example, Yasuo Takeyama, editor-in-chief of Japan's economic journal, *Nihon Keizai Shimbun,* and a former correspondent in New York and Washington, made the statement at the seminar that he was fearful that nuclear superiority will tilt from the United States to the Soviet Union by 1978 or soon thereafter. If that happens, he asserted, the U.S. nuclear umbrella "cannot be taken at par value." We cannot expect the Japanese lag in understanding the true meaning of the SALT I Agreement to last much longer.

The Red Chinese leaders fully understand that the Japanese have a vital need for a third-power nuclear umbrella. Even more vitally relevant, they fear that the Japanese may seek it from the Soviet Union if and when the Japanese recognize that the U.S. strategic deterrent has lost its credibility. In a shrewd and subtle attempt to shore up Japanese confidence in the American nuclear connection, Chou En-lai even swallowed the bitter (for a Communist) ideological pill of approving continuance of the U.S.-Japan Security Treaty. He commented that, while it would eventually be abolished, at present it seemed necessary for Japan because of the "shadow over all of Asia cast by the Soviet Union." Thus, in a January 1973 conversation in Peking with Takeo Kimura, right-hand man of Prime Minister Kakuei Tanaka, Chou frankly suggested that Japan "needs the American nuclear umbrella for the time being." He added that it would be impossible for Japan to exchange the U.S. nuclear umbrella for a Chinese one, since China's weapons were not for offensive purposes.[8]

The wily Chou would rather have the Japanese depend upon the U.S. nuclear umbrella, which he knows cannot work against China and therefore would not interfere with China's nuclear blackmail, than to have them swap for the Soviet connection, which could very well work.

This analysis shows that Henry Kissinger, by his negotiation of the SALT I Anti-Defense Treaty with Moscow in 1972, has brought about all the consequences with respect to Japan that he conceded in his September 16, 1970, briefing we should be "extremely careful to avoid."

As Dr. Kissinger recognized, Japan has less to fear from the Soviet Union than from China, if only for geographical and demographical reasons. Most of the population of the Soviet Union—say, about 220 million out of the total of 250 million—are almost as far away from Japan as Russia is from the East Coast of the United States. Not so the 800 million Chinese.

When it comes to *occupation*, which would occur regardless of which Communist giant "merges" with Japan, the occupation would be far more intense by China than by the Soviet Union. The Soviet population—at least that part the Politburo considers sufficiently reliable for occupation purposes—will be spread pretty thin when it comes to administering the world. They could not spare much personnel to administer Japan. Thus, as even Kissinger has pointed out, the Japanese would feel that they could preserve much more of their "national essence" under Russian occupation than under Chinese occupation.

Accordingly, we can expect to see again "one of these sudden shifts of Japanese policy" against which Dr. Kissinger warned in September 1970—before he was completely overcome by SALT sickness. That change may ally the potentially greatest industrial superpower with the greatest in-being military superpower. Together, these two powers will combine the best of two worlds: economic and strategic. Japan has been investing only 0.7 percent of her GNP in conventional military power, and none in strategic power. The latest and by far the most reliable estimate of the U.S.S.R. expenditure on military power is more than 40 percent of its GNP. *Because economic power cannot resist military power-in-being*, the Kremlin will be in charge.

Because of the added resources from the Japanese industrial plant and labor force, the combination will be irresistible. All Western

Europe and the Middle East will have no alternative to begging a place from the Soviets in the new world order. The United States will then come in as a slave state or, as we saw above, will die of isolation and perpetual depression, starved for energy sources and essential raw materials even for our own domestic requirements, and cut off from any trade with the rest of the world.

All this will be thanks to Henry Kissinger—to his diplomacy, to his incredible strategic theories, and to his accomplishments in depriving the United States and 210 million Americans of all defense in the nuclear age.

One more result of the SALT I ABM Treaty requires consideration. Writing in the Council on Foreign Relation's prestigious quarterly journal *Foreign Affairs*, the new guru of U.S. disarmament, Fred Charles Iklé, made this observation:

> In the 1950s, prior to the missile age and Russia's massive buildup of her nuclear forces, one heard a great deal about the risk of accidental war. Now, when American and Soviet missiles by the thousand are poised in instant readiness, this concern has curiously diminished.[9]

To explain this relaxation, he cites the fact that no unauthorized detonation has ever occurred. He points to the U.S.-Soviet agreements for improvement of the Hot Line, and he recalls the elaborate safeguards with which the military "seem" to protect nuclear weapons.

Mr. Ikle does not, however, give the real reason why the term "accidental war" was so suddenly dropped from the lexicon of the unilateral-disarmers and was replaced by total silence on the whole subject. This was because it embodies a convincing and highly reasonable argument in favor of the United States' investing in a missile defense system. Since May 1972, even *thinking* about accidental war reveals too much of what Henry Kissinger was doing to the United States by the Moscow SALT I ABM Treaty.

U.S. unilateral-disarmament intellectuals and scientists as a group, especially those who follow the doctrines decreed by the Pugwash group, have *always*, since the dawn of the nuclear age, been committed *against* permitting the American people to have *any* defense—active or passive—against nuclear incineration by Soviet weapons. Their opposition to a missile defense began in 1957 when the Soviets developed the world's first ICBM. Before 1957, they were against bomber defenses. They then hysterically opposed programs to dig or build fallout or blast shelters. Back then, they were somewhat more frank in revealing their reasons: they declared that, if the American people felt the population could survive a nuclear attack by reason of such defenses, the people would not pressure the government to exhaust "all possibilities" of "settling" a nuclear confrontation "by negotiation." The Pugwash group always included the surrender of the United States as one of the possibilities of negotiation.

Any effective in-being defense, active or passive, at the last crucial minute might derail the Paul Nitze-enunciated, McNamara-Kissinger-implemented plan to interpose a preemptive surrender rather than risk a Soviet nuclear strike.

The argument for an ABM defense, based upon the possibility of an accidental launch of missiles against us, has one ideological feature so difficult for the Pugwash elite to counter that they would rather just suppress any discussion of the matter. They just pretend that it isn't there. Here is how it goes, and you can imagine yourself in the argument.

Suppose you are making the unsophisticated argument that it is immoral, insane, and stupid deliberately to expose the American people—totally without defense—to nuclear incineration by enemy missiles to which Henry Kissinger has guaranteed (in his own words) a "free ride." You argue that we have within our technology the capability for a defense system that has been proved to be so reliable, so effective, that even back in 1969 President Nixon made this solemn declaration:

> No President with the responsibility for the lives and security of the American people could fail to provide this protection.

You point out that, because of our urbanization and lack of passive defenses, by taking out our 100 largest cities, the Red Chinese could destroy 100 million Americans, and the Soviets could destroy 180 million of us. At this point, however, you are met by the Pugwash response:

> You are assuming that the Soviets or the Chinese would *deliberately* launch a nuclear strike at our population. This they would never do for at least two reasons: *first*, they would be deterred because of fear of the damage our surviving retaliatory forces could inflict; and *second*, no man, let alone the "serious" leaders of those two great Communist nations, could be so inhuman as deliberately to seek to kill 100 million people!

The first point of this argument brings up the entire subject of deterrence, together with a first-strike capability designed to destroy the deterrent. This subject is discussed later in this book. It is not necessary to engage it here except to mention that, in the prevailing Pugwash view, the possibility of even a *very small remnant* of our retaliatory force surviving a first-strike would be sufficient to deter the enemy's launching a deliberate strike. They define as "politically significant" not the absolute amount of damage one country can inflict on another, but the difference between the damage a country can cause to its opponent and the damage it would suffer from its opponent in return.

Yet *this "damage differential"*—no matter how favorable— *is irrelevant, for it is politically unacceptable if the damage suffered is not close to zero.*[10]

That is, of course, an extreme statement of the theory of minimum deterrence. The Pugwash group has always been extreme in pursuit of this theory of deterrence, because upon its acceptance depends the selling of unilateral strategic disarmament to the nation's elite power groups. Even McNamara conceded it would be necessary credibly to threaten the "assured destruction" of one-fourth of the Soviet population and one-half of their industry in order to establish a reliable deterrent.

The second point of the Pugwash argument is primarily relevant here: only a madman would deliberately seek to kill 100 million people. To many people, this is a most convincing argument. The average American would not do such a thing, and so the average American cannot believe that anyone else would.

There are many answers to this contention. Khrushchev explained in his important speech of January 6, 1961, how a Soviet dictator feels as to personal responsibility or guilt for such an action: *Nothing!* In the Kremlin's view, it is not Soviet leadership, but "history" that has "doomed" the forces of capitalist imperialism. The Soviet Communists, therefore, are merely assisting "history" in carrying out the predetermined doom. It is a matter of history that Stalin, aided by many still in power in the Politburo today, liquidated some 20 million people in the U.S.S.R.—not because they were in rebellion or were counterrevolutionaries, but merely to establish Communist discipline and collective agriculture. Abundant proof is provided in *The Great Terror* by Robert Conquest. Aleksandr Solzhenitsyn states in *The Gulag Archipelago* that Stalin, during only the two years 1937 and 1938, shot half a million political prisoners, and that other estimates place the number at 1.7 million persons shot in those two years alone.

The antidefense elitist groups cannot use either of these two arguments to deny the need of a missile defense system to protect our population against the *accidental* launch of missiles. Neither the concept of deterrence nor the unbelievability of a monster willing to kill 100 million people is relevant. They cannot argue that neither the Soviets or the Red Chinese would *do* such a thing because, by definition, an *accidental* launch is not deliberate.

The question is *can it happen?* Since, obviously, it is possible, the more precise question is, is the probability of its happening so great as to be unacceptable?

Let us consider the testimony of Fred Charles Iklé, the new Director of the U.S. Arms Control and Disarmament Agency, who replaced Ambassador Gerard C. Smith. Remarking upon the strange unconcern within the United States of the dangers of "accidental war," Iklé noted, in early 1973, that "American and Soviet missiles by the thousands are poised in constant readiness," and that

> nobody can predict that the fatal accident or unauthorized act will never happen. The hazard is too elusive. It is inherent not only in the ineradicable possibility of technical defects, but also in the inevitable vulnerability to human error of all command and operational procedures—during periods of high alert as well as during the many years of quiet waiting. So exceedingly complex are modern weapons systems, both in their internal mechanisms and in their intricate interactions, that it seems doubtful whether any group of experts could ever ferret out every intended ramification, discover every lurking danger. Indeed, the very word "system" misleads in that it suggests a clearly bounded combination of parts, their interactions all designed to serve the intended purpose.
>
> The deadly danger is deepened by the fact that latent dangers can be corrected only if they are sought out. To look, day in and day out, for some hidden risk of accident is not a task, however, that captures the attention of top decision-makers. It is far from unusual in military operations for serious oversights or occasional incompetence to go undetected or uncorrected until after a major disaster. . . .

Mr. Iklé then cites the inability of the *U.S.S. Pueblo* to destroy all cryptographic material before capture in 1968; the communications fiasco when JCS attempted to order the *Liberty* to safer waters during the Six-Day War in 1967; and the difficulties of communications with Polaris and Poseidon submarines "so serious that 'some of the messages never get delivered,' as a senior naval officer put it." Iklé then continues:

> The peril may well be greater on the Soviet side. Since the American military establishment is relatively open to outside scrutiny, pressures to ferret out safety hazards or to institute perhaps costly remedies can come from civilians in the executive branch, congressional committees, and even the public. Under the compartmentalized, pervasive secrecy of the Soviet military, however, past accidents and present hazards can be kept not only from the public but from senior civilian authorities as well.
>
> Given that occasional incompetence or malfeasance is predictable in large institutions—whether military or civilian—the safety of nuclear armaments remains a constantly pressing uncertainty. Given the huge and farflung missile forces, ready to be launched from land and sea on both sides, *the scope for disaster by accident is immense.*
>
> Given that our strategic dogmas demand the targeting of populations and *denial of defensive measures, the carnage would be without restraint.*[11]

Although the Pugwash group has for many years been promoting the "MAD" formula demanding a denial of defensive measures, it was not sufficiently powerful to impose it on the nation until Henry Kissinger gained his influence over President Nixon, sold him the SALT I Anti-Defense Treaty, and turned him around from what in 1969 appeared to be and probably was a sincere statement that no responsible President could fail to provide the American people with a defense against missiles. It is clear that, because of Dr. Kissinger's actions in denying us this defense, in Mr. Iklé's expression, "the carnage would be without restraint."

If such tragic and macabre aspects did not overshadow the entire situation, it would be ironic indeed that Kissinger's theory demands that we be totally vulnerable, so that as hostages we could be killed in the most massive numbers with the least effort by an enemy acting *deliberately and malevolently.*

Yet, it is possible that a few million of us could be killed without either of our chief enemies even wishing us dead. Mr. Iklé's exposition of the immensity of the scope for accidental disaster is reasonably accurate. As he indicated, accidental nuclear war used to be a well-worn subject of analysis—even in the days before ICBMs, when strategic bombers could be programmed to "fail safe." Bombers could be *recalled* if their dispatch had been due either to mistake or accident or unauthorized act. The probability was not so high when the Soviets had only 200-300 ICBMs and 40-60 SLBMs, but, as of 1974, they have a total of something like 3,000 ICBMs and SLBMs. The sheer increase in numbers of missiles has vastly increased the probability of the occurrence of the fatal accident, the unauthorized act, the negligent act, the act of malfeasance, or a sudden and unpredictable mental aberration of someone in the chain of command or control.

Not only has the proliferation of *numbers* of missiles increased the probability of an unauthorized launch, but the *consequences* of such a launch have also intensified. The dual developments in the character of the Soviet offensive missile force brought about by tremendously more powerful warheads in singles, and by multiple warheads on individual missiles, has magnified horrendously the consequences that could result from an unauthorized or accidental launch. We are not talking here about the consequences of a "war" accidentally started by reason of a retaliatory launch against the accidental launch. Over-the-horizon radar, and especially the new satellite warning system, are so tremendously discriminating that they eliminate the substance of that possibility.

We are talking about the situation that might be introduced by a call on the Hot Line from Leonid Brezhnev or his successor. He regrets to inform us that a major in the Soviet Rocket Troops suddenly

118

went berserk and launched three SS-18 missiles, respectively, at New York, Chicago, and Los Angeles; or that, because of a malfunction in the control system, three such missiles had been launched. He apologizes, but says the missiles are en route, and there is no way he can make them self-destruct in five seconds, because they got too much of a head start.

If it were not for the SALT I Anti-Defense Treaty, a few Spartan ABMs, backed up by a few Sprint ABMs, could insure that the incoming missiles would be destroyed without ever detonating their nuclear charges. As it is, all we could do—all the President, or even Henry Kissinger, could do—would be to pray that those missiles were duds and that a malfunction would deprive them of completing their mission of taking out the 24 million Americans in those metropolitan areas.

Actually, the *probabilities* are vastly against such powerful missiles being the ones accidentally launched, or against their being targeted against population centers. But even if only 1/10 of one percent of the Soviet missile force were involved in an accidental launch, there would indeed be three missiles on their way toward U.S. targets. Prior to 1970, three missiles would have meant three warheads. In 1974, three missiles might mean 30 warheads. Also, prior to 1970 the Soviets had few missiles carrying warheads of more than five megatons. As of 1974 they have something on the order of 400 ICBMs capable of carrying single warheads of 25 to 50+ megatons each. Even more significant on a statistical basis, their present force of more than 1,000 SS-11s, SS-17s, and SS-19s could now be carrying five or six multiple warheads each or, in single-warhead versions, more than 12 megatons each. This entire echelon of their ICBM force has been updated in the last few years.

The United States has more than 150 million people living in urban areas. We have 36 Standard Metropolitan Statistical Areas (SMSAs) ranging between one million and 12 million in population. Even a single Soviet missile, accidentally launched, realistically threatens more than a million of us. With bad luck, it could hit an "average" SMSA and take out four or five million Americans. The Politburo spokesman might say, "Sorry about that," but the Pugwash theories, as implemented by Henry Kissinger, would be the real murderers.

Merely pointing out how many of us could be liquidated by an accidental launch, if bad luck should beset us, emphasizes the factor of common sense—even the factor of morality—in the deliberate decision to render so many millions of our people *totally* vulnerable to *unintended* nuclear incineration. We could even obtain almost total protection against such a massive tragedy as a cost-free fringe benefit of an ABM system designed to protect our people against a Soviet attack, or even of a thin ABM system designed to protect our people against a Red Chinese attack.

If we do build an ABM system capable of defending us against the Soviets, we will get two bonuses: total defense against Red Chinese nuclear threats, and total protection against accidental nuclear launches by any nuclear nation.

Obviously, however, so long as Dr. Henry Kissinger holds his influence over our President and our policies, we will not be permitted to build a defense for our *people* against incineration by Soviet missiles, by Red Chinese missiles, or by any country's accidentally launched missiles.

It is important to recognize that it is Henry Kissinger, *not* the SALT I ABM Treaty, that prevents us from developing any defense against a genocidal attack. We can escape from the treaty with six-months' notice and go immediately into mass production of ABM launchers, radars, and interceptor missiles. Immediately upon getting rid of Kissinger and his policies, that is. It is true that the SALT I Treaty would require our withdrawal to be supported by a statement of "extraordinary events related to the subject matter of the treaty" that we regard as having "jeopardized our supreme national interests." But the construction and completion by the Red Chinese of such an elaborate and extensive passive defense system against nuclear missile attack would certainly constitute such a threat or jeopardy to our supreme national interests.

Because of that "extraordinary event," the United States is now left as the only one of the three great nuclear powers with *no* defenses— no *active* defenses and no *passive* defenses—against nuclear missile attack. Our supreme national interests are certainly jeopardized if we are left as the *one* great power that could not survive a missile attack, that could not even stand up to nuclear blackmail by either the Soviets *or* Red China. So we *can*—legally and morally—rid ourselves of the disadvantage of the SALT I Anti-Defense Treaty.

But can we rid ourselves of the fatal disadvantage of Henry Kissinger's policies, which are depriving us of both an effective defense and a credible deterrent? Yes. How?

By publishing the truth about what Henry Kissinger has done to the defenses of the United States—by making it known and understandable to the American people how he has rendered all 210 million of us helpless hostages to the Soviet Union; how he has rendered 100 million of us vulnerable to destruction by Red Chinese nuclear missiles; and how he has rendered millions of us vulnerable to nuclear incineration by sheer accident.

Making this truth available to our people must include the means that Henry Kissinger has employed to bring the United States to the brink of strategic surrender: his sophisticated deceit, his slick lies, and his out-of-touch-with-reality theories. Evidence will be presented in this book that will enable the American people—and our leaders—to determine whether he really is "some kind of a nut, or something."

The Kissinger affair should so far overshadow the Watergate scandal as to render it as remote as the tempest of Teapot Dome. The Watergate affair, however, proved that there is hope for freeing the American people from the clutches of even the most autocratic and powerful of the top-level White House palace guard.

There is this difference, however. The United States could have survived, somehow, if the Watergate masters had continued in power. But there is no way the United States can survive in freedom if Henry Kissinger and his policies continue in power. The truth can end his power.

6

Seldom in the history of Western civilization since Jesus has so much depended upon one man's personality. It is important to study it in depth.[1]

These words are accurate as to Adolf Hitler, about whom they were written. They would, however, be an understatement in relation to Henry A. Kissinger: the word "seldom" would have to be changed to "never," and Hitler himself would have to be included in the comparison.

In World War II, which Hitler started, battle deaths on both sides totaled about 15 million; deaths from all causes were estimated to be on the order of 40 million. Kissinger is risking more than 200 megadeaths. He has bet your life—and the lives and freedom of 210 million Americans—on an exotic parlay of Kissinger theories. Not merely one, but all, of the theories and the assumptions on which they are based must win out in the real world, or the American pawns in the Kissinger global game-plan will lose.

What are these theories on which he has staked our expendable lives, our devalued dollars, and our once-sacred honor? It would be naive to expect that the most sophisticated person of our century would do anything so simplistic as to reveal his key *action* theories to nonintellectuals. If he did, we might rebel and block the biggest gamble in history. However we cannot complain that he discriminates only against the public in concealing his modus operandi; on this score he treats us at least as well—and in some respects better—than he treats the President of the United States.

Dr. Kissinger does talk and write a great deal about his theories—but the ones he enunciates publicly and for the President are an ancillary set of "cover theories" that he selects with meticulous care. Although they come close to explaining what Kissinger is really up to, they never quite reveal it; and thus they serve as an effective diversion to protect his operational theories. It is a tribute to his rhetorical skill that these "cover" theories are at the same time simple enough for public consumption and highbrow enough to convince his several elitist constituencies that he is still working for them. He probably is: they were his sole pre-White House power bases, and their continuing support is vital to the achievement of his personal ambitions.

The Kissinger theory of a new world order—the "structure of peace" he is planning for generations to come—is a prime example of meeting the specifications of both these elitist groups. Known to his admirers as "Henry's triad," his theory postulates: (1) a pentagonal "equilibrium of power" involving the military and industrial power of the Soviet Union and the United States, the military and industrial potentials of the People's Republic of China, and the industrial power of Japan and Western Europe; (2) recognition by the two Communist giants and the United States that their differences are "nonessential" and are overshadowed by common vital national interests, and by what he asserts is "the basic fact" that "none of us can survive a nuclear war"; and (3) recognition that these common national interests can be "linked" together in a process for which all make concessions, but all gain and none loses.

The disingenuous verisimilitude inherent in this design for a coalition government for planet Earth demonstrates that Dr. Kissinger is a demiurge of exquisite craftsmanship and imagination. He fully realizes that both Moscow and Peking will play along with his new world order, at least on a temporary basis, while they respectively skim off all the goodies of trade and credits, of science and technology, and of prestige and power, that he is holding out to them as bribes for moving from confrontation to negotiation. Their temporary participation in the charade is all he needs to provide a facade of reality impressive enough to convince current skeptics that Henry Kissinger has, indeed, changed the world.

The whole purpose of the illusory world of detente, spun out of the theory of the triad-balance of the great powers' own national interests, is to provide essential concealment of the all-too-real changes he is wreaking in the real world.

Evidence of what Henry Kissinger was really up to did not surface in unclassified and documentable quantities until the Moscow Summit of May 1972 and his virtuosic performance in selling the SALT I Agreements to the President, Congress, and the American people. The learned professor had, of course, anticipated that such evidence would ultimately emerge; but this did not worry him because he had concealed his true objectives behind a curtain of impenetrable incredibility. Both his private, secret plan for changing the world, and the methods he proposed to go about it, are so shocking, so amoral, so revolutionary, and so theatrical, as to be incredible to most Americans.

As the old but still wistfully echoing question used to phrase it, *would you believe:*

•Dr. Kissinger has set up you and your family—and all 210 million Americans—as helpless hostages to the men in the Kremlin for a period of "unlimited duration"?

•that he has guaranteed to the Soviets (in Kissinger's own language) a "free ride" for their missiles over the entire United States, thus rendering us totally vulnerable to mass murder by nuclear incineration?

•that (because the "free ride" is also available to the Red Chinese) he has enabled the Chinese Reds to threaten, within three years, the destruction of half the U.S. population, whereas we will be able to threaten—as a deterrent—only 1/20 of their population?

•that he gave such massive advantages to the Russians in the SALT I Agreements that they can, without violating the agreements, complete the buildup of a first-strike capability against the United States, thus destroying the effectiveness of our strategic deterrent?

•that he has suppressed warnings by the former Secretary of Defense, by President Nixon's Blue Ribbon Defense Panel, by members of the Joint Chiefs of Staff, and by committees of civilian experts, that the Soviets are building a nuclear first-strike capability against the United States?

•that he has turned U.S. foreign policy from pro-NATO and anti-Communist, to anti-NATO, pro-Communist, anti-Japan, and pro-Red China?

•that he plans to establish a new world order by reducing U.S. strategic military power vis-a-vis the Soviets to a very weak second-rate, thus making the Soviet Union the world's only nuclear superpower?

And, *could* you believe:

•that Henry Kissinger has schematized a way to control *in advance* decisions by the President of the United States on matters of national life or death—and that his system will work against *any* incumbent President?

•that the Kissinger scheme for manipulating the President's decisions on national security and foreign policy is so brashly imaginative and far out that it overruns the frontiers of science fiction, and that it is so unprecedented that no one has penetrated its cover until now?

Of course you would not believe such strange and shocking things—probably not even after the Watergate scandal demonstrated that a

President can become the captive of cunning, arrogant, or stupid zealots who have lost touch with reality. The big-name culprits of Watergate held their influence *only* in the domestic areas of White House power. If Richard Nixon could become the captive of advisers in the political area in which he had 25 years of personal experience and has demonstrated exceptional expertise, then consider how much more effectively he could be controlled in the esoteric realms of Dr. Kissinger's mystiques of nuclear strategy and foreign policy.

If Kissinger has usurped *de facto* national-life-or-death powers of the President of the United States, what power sources of his own did he exploit to accomplish this feat? What possible motives could he have for what he is doing? Kissinger's power divides neatly into two segments: overt and covert, revealed and secret.

If Henry Kissinger's power bases merely enabled him to *control* our national destiny in the areas of defense and foreign policy, he would not have lasted a year in the Nixon Administration. His sources of power are unique in American government in that they enable him also to *conceal* the fact that he is exercising vast control. He is not only an unelected ruler but also an invisible ruler in the most critical policy areas. His powers in their totality—seen and unseen—are not only far more extensive than Hitler ever attained, but they are more complex and more intriguingly mysterious.

Kissinger's personality is the first of his four principal power bases. In an out-of-character emotional appeal to Congress on June 15, 1972, to approve the SALT I Agreements, Dr. Kissinger inadvertently exposed the *fact* that he had reversed the grand strategy of the United States by abandoning military strength as the primary support for our national security, and substituting for it total trust in the good will of the Politburo of the Communist Party of the Soviet Union. He stated:

> We are now at such a juncture where peace and progress depend upon our faith and our fortitude.

He should have added that they depend also upon the capability of Henry Kissinger to interpret accurately the intentions of the men in the Kremlin and to control their future conduct.

The personality of Henry Kissinger requires a vastly more important study than was made of Adolf Hitler, even in 1943 when his power was unshaken. In 1943 the U.S. Office of Strategic Services (predecessor to CIA) commissioned psychoanalyst Walter C. Langer to prepare an in-depth psychological profile of Hitler for OSS Chief William J. ("Wild Bill") Donovan. The catalogue of Hitler's apparent strengths of personality detailed in that study included will power, self-discipline, courage, energy, ability to manipulate crowds, and rhetorical power.

Kissinger's personality assets include those qualities and many more. His sense of humor, including irony and sometimes hilarious understatement, is alone a priceless asset. His fine intellect and sophistication cannot be denied. His generally unrecognized ruthlessness and amorality are assets in building personal power.

Probably his most significant superiority over Hitler in acquiring influence lies in the greater scope and versatility of Kissinger's power to manipulate audiences. Hitler's tremendous power over crowds had important emotional elements (he considered them feminine in nature), and depended essentially on the sound and reach of his voice. The magic empathy he evoked grew out of oral communication and dynamic personal presence. Some distant observers in the early years of his rise tended to denigrate him as a clown, but no one who had personally attended one of his speeches ever made that mistake.

Henry Kissinger can never inspire in huge crowds the emotional pitch of personal enthusiasm and loyalty that Hitler could. But then Kissinger does not need to. His forte is his power of hypnotic persuasion over select and highly critical audiences, such as the National Security Council and the Washington press corps. The versatility of his verbal appeal is exceptional. It extends from that all-important audience of one—the President of the United States—to the Congress, to the mass media, and, only through them, to the American people who voted him in the 1973 year-end Gallup Poll as the most admired person in the United States. By mid-1974 the Harris Poll reported that 75 percent of Americans feel that "no matter who is President, he should stay on as Secretary of State." His appeal reaches even to improbable groups in foreign lands; e.g., readers of the conservative Paris newspaper *L'Aurore* picked him as their man of the year, ranking him above all French politicians, above Willy Brandt (before spy scandals deposed him), and even above Olympic swimming champion Mark Spitz.

Kissinger's intense powers of persuasion are not limited to the spoken word. He is a gifted, effective, professional writer. His expertise with words, written or oral, coupled with his tremendous store of information and his lifelong skill in playing both sides of the street, enable him to communicate and obfuscate at the same time. That is, his audiences hesitate to criticize the segments they don't understand because they don't want to be publicly embarrassed by admitting they failed to follow the labyrinths of his sophisticated mind. He enjoys this tactic: it titillates his vanity.

Women seemed irresistibly attracted to him. And why? Just as he tells the President, the Congress, and the American people what they, respectively, most want to hear, he told each woman what she most enjoyed hearing. Thus, Mamie Van Doren was quoted in 1973 as saying that he remembered her nude pictures in *Playboy* eight years earlier and told her "they were wonderful."

Kissinger had an additional and more alluring stimulant for his partners in romance. Gossip columnists and folksy magazine writers seem to agree with Kissinger that "*Power* is the ultimate aphrodisiac." It is not surprising that one of his former girl friends, writing a book on his sex life, was reportedly considering the title *Much Talk—Little Action*. All that ended on March 30, 1974, when he took a Saturday afternoon off and married Nancy Maginnes, a former member of Nelson Rockefeller's personal staff, and the current director of international studies for Rockefeller's Commission on Critical Choices for America.

The second of Kissinger's above-the-surface power bases derived quite legitimately first from his position as Assistant to the President for National Security Affairs, later from the added dignity of the title of Secretary of State, and from the apparent quality of his performance in both positions. His official duties have apparently been carried out with consummate skill. What is more important, however, is that all his official public actions have advanced the ideological objectives of the most articulate and influential leaders of the liberal establishment. The unanimous acclaim that has resounded throughout the mass media has served both to increase his influence with the President and to conceal his hidden sources of power. For example, Joseph Kraft (heir apparent to Walter Lippmann) intoned that he hoped there would always be a "central place for the deep seriousness, the far-sighted vision and a sense of global structure concentrated in the person of Henry Kissinger." (Of course, that was before Kraft discovered that his telephones had been bugged on request of Dr. Kissinger.)

Even such divergent writers as George Ball and the Alsop brothers independently concluded, a year in advance of its happening, that Nixon should make Kissinger Secretary of State. C. L. Sulzberger set him up as outstandingly shrewd and unusually astute. Max Lerner exultingly pictured him as not merely brilliant, but with "an exact feel for history" and a sense of "detachment about power"; as "neither hawk nor dove, but a skillful, imaginative realist"; as blessed with "an ironic sense of history's contradictions and life's absurdities"; as skilled in "political theater and the tactic of surprise"; and as having "the kind of craftsman's skill and feel for power" that makes him "regard statecraft as a work of art."

This type of idolatrous praise was pervasive throughout the mass media during the years 1969 through early 1973. After the long-delayed signature of the Vietnam "peace" agreement, all criticism from the Left ceased, at least for a while. They were mollified by the slick manner in which he provided for the retention of some 300,000 North Vietnamese troops in South Vietnam, and they were struck with admiration for his verbal dexterity in labeling the proposed $2.5 billion payment to North Vietnam not as war reparations, blackmail, a handout, or a ransom, but as a "longterm investment in a structure of peace."

The potential of such euphemistic rationalization boggles the mind. Payment of a prostitute's fee could translate into "an investment in short-term love." Bribing a public official would sound so much better as "an investment in expediting and orienting the bureaucracy's decision-making process." The payer in any kidnapping or blackmail situation could always save face by calling his payment a "private investment in a structure of peace—hopefully longterm."

Such wordsmanship is a typical exemplar of Kissinger's skill with language. The objective of "peace at any price" lost popularity after Munich. But add just two words, "structure of," and he is selling an "investment" that is not immediately identified with Munich-type gullibility. The word "structure" evokes a mental impression of something with a firm foundation, built to endure.

One gets the nagging worry, however, that a man with such a skill for hypnotic employment of words might also be smart enough to realize that, in building a "structure of *world* peace," the firmest foundation would be just *one* nuclear superpower, not two competing powers. What "longterm investment" would he be willing to commit our nation for, what price would he ask us to pay to achieve that ideal? Might an answer be the surrender of such an outmoded concept as national sovereignty?

It was essential that the Nixon-Kissinger partnership be portrayed as one in which Nixon made his own foreign policy, designed his own national strategy and military posture, and set the objectives and limits on strategic agreements. This was necessary to enable Kissinger to pursue his covert ulterior objectives, and to exercise effectively the massive but unsuspected power that he derives from secret sources.

Most of the media went along with the fiction that Kissinger's role was only that of an astute implementer, while President Nixon not only had the overriding power of decision-making but actively and extensively exercised it. James Reston of the *New York Times* presented a typical example of the prevailing view:

> But how Kissinger goes on at this pace is a mystery, and, intelligent and tough as he is, may be even a danger.
>
> We have a government now of men, not really of laws and accepted procedures. We have an alliance with Chou En-lai but not yet with China. But if this is the way it is to be, it is not Kissinger's fault, and he is a man.
>
> *He is an instrument of the President*, but he has played his role with astonishing courage, patience and skill.

This is the key distinction between Dr. Kissinger's overt and covert powers. Power from the two sources which are known—his personal and personality capabilities, and the influence that flows from his official and powerful U.S. Government position—is exercised by him purportedly as "an instrument of the President." His covert powers, however, are exercised with calculated precision for a contrary and overriding purpose: to make any President of the United States *Henry Kissinger's instrument.*

Dr. Kissinger's third, and largely concealed, power base is his constituencies in powerful elitist groups, particularly the Council on Foreign Relations (CFR) and the Pugwash Conferences (the series of disarmament conferences that began in 1957 at Pugwash, Nova Scotia). "Elitist" is used here in complete harmony with its dictionary definitions, especially the third: "the choice part; a socially superior group; a powerful minority group."

The most powerful cliques in these elitist groups have one objective in common: they want to bring about the surrender of the sovereignty and national independence of the United States. They differ only as to the entity into which our sovereignty should be merged. Some dream of taking the United States into a one-world all-powerful global government—possibly a vastly strengthened United Nations, or possibly limited to the Atlantic community. They consider that this objective is at once so idealistic (the brotherhood of peoples or Parliament of Man concept) and so urgent (a lasting world peace can be secured only by disarming all nations down to internal police levels), that their end justifies *any* means. They have the same single-minded passion for achievement of *their* objectives that President Nixon's lawyer, Charles Colson, had for his objective—so aptly described in an August 28,1972, memorandum to the White House staff:

> Think to yourself at the beginning of each day, "What am I going to do to help the President's reelection today?" And then at the end of each day, think what you did in fact do to help the President's reelection. . . . Just so you understand me, let me point out that the statement in last week's UPI story that I was once reported to have said that "I would walk over my grandmother if necessary" [for President Nixon] is absolutely accurate.

Just as *any* means to reelect Richard Nixon included wiretapping, burglary, perjury, and coverup, *any* means to achieve global government includes the unilateral strategic disarmament of the United States down to the point at which we would be helpless against the Soviet Union. The elitist cliques calculate that such a posture would provide an irresistible incentive for us to join a global government before we were forced to surrender to the Soviets.

129

Most of the members of these elitist groups are one-world-global-government ideologists whose longterm goal was neatly and officially summed up in the September 1961 State Department Document 7277. Despite its age, it is not outdated. It was adopted and affirmed by the Nixon Administration. In August 1970 the U.S. Arms Control and Disarmament Agency declared the goal still to be "the total elimination of all armed forces and armaments except those needed to maintain internal order within states and to furnish the United Nations with peace forces . . . by the time it [the UN global government] would be so strong no nation could challenge it."

When it comes to the means to bring about this general disarmament, many of the elitist groups recognize that they are powerless to disarm the Soviet Union, and so they dedicate their influence to do this to the United States. This would, of necessity, set the stage for the U.S.S.R. to take over control of the world long before any "democratic" type of supranational government could be set up in the United Nations framework. Thus, there would surely be one world, one global government, and universal peace. But there would no longer be any need for a Berlin Wall or an Iron Curtain. There would be no place left for freedom, and no sanctuary for those who wanted to escape from Communist tyranny.

Smaller cliques in the elitist groups are more realistic. They concluded 10 to 15 years ago that, because of our democratic form of government and the freedom-loving economy-minded character of our people, we could *not* win out over the Soviet Union in a protracted strategic nuclear arms race. Because they were convinced that we could not come out a decisively stronger Number One, they believed it would be disastrous to allow ourselves to be a strong Number Two.

They calculated that the Soviets could and would build strategic nuclear power sufficient to destroy the United States so completely that we could not deter them from attacking us by threatening to retaliate. They figured that the *only* way to avert nuclear incineration was to reduce U.S. strategic power so *far below* the Soviets that our only rational alternative would be surrender. These elitist groups also considered *their* objective—saving 210 million Americans (including themselves) from nuclear incineration—vital enough to justify *any* means.

The means they chose was, by fraud and deception, to destroy or scrap 9/10 of U.S. strategic power in-being, and to block the production and deployment of additional advanced strategic systems. Without these elitist programs of self-fulfilling prophecy, the Soviets could not possibly have moved so close to completion of a first-strike capability against the United States as was revealed by the SALT I statistics in 1972.

The *Gaither Report*, which was completed on November 7, 1957, was a Top Secret study on the potential nuclear arms race between the U.S. and the U.S.S.R. It is a fascinating exemplar of the decisive influence that the Council on Foreign Relations and related elitist groups exerted on U.S. national security policies, even during the Eisenhower Administration. H. Rowan Gaither, CFR member and chairman of the board of the Ford Foundation, was director of the study panel. When he fell ill, CFR member Robert C. Sprague became panel director. The most influential and aggressive member was Jerome B. Wiesner, MIT, CFR, Pugwash conferee. Before the panel was formally convened, the Science Advisory Committee, dominated by members of the Harvard-MIT Axis, had given Wiesner the important assignment of drawing up the slate of members. Not surprisingly, the Gaither panel was loaded with like-minded men. The associations Wiesner developed on this project, coupled with his previous elite-group relationships, started him on a climb to power as Science Adviser to Presidents Kennedy and Johnson. During that period he built up influence over U.S. strategy that has been exceeded only by McNamara and Kissinger.

The greatest tribute to the power potential of the position of Science Adviser to the President was paid by Henry Kissinger in January 1973: he abolished the position, as well as the Science Advisory Committee. Wiesner had so successfully exploited the direct and unlimited access to the President provided by that position that Kissinger was taking no chances on a repeat performance by anyone else. The greatest single asset Kissinger has in controlling a President on matters of national security and foreign relations is his absolute monopoly of access to *all* matters relating to these critical areas.

Access to the *Gaither Report* was limited in a unique way. It was made available to nearly all civilians in the elite groups, but highly restricted for the military. A two-star general or admiral had no realistic chance of access, and even a three-star general probably would have had to prove a specific need-to-know. The American people were kept in a highly selective blackout about it for more than 15 years until January 1973, when the new Interagency Classification Review Committee, headed by John S. D. Eisenhower, son of the former President, declassified it.

During the 15 years of protracted Top Secret classification, a very selective type of deception was practiced against the American people. Parts of the *Gaither Report* were deliberately leaked to the press almost immediately after its presentation to the President. But the only portions leaked were carefully selected to create the impression that it had been prepared by a panel of highly patriotic Americans whose deep concern for the future of America led them to recommend to the President a great and terribly expensive buildup in U.S. military power and defenses.

The parts that were not revealed included those that forecast the horrendous specter of a rising threat from a nuclear-armed Soviet Union—"a threat which may become critical in 1959 or early 1960."

Warning of such a threat can be a good thing—but to follow such a warning with a picture of black despair of our ability to build the strength necessary to meet that threat can create a fatal defeatism. That is exactly what the *Gaither Report* was designed to do.

The parts of the *Gaither Report* that were held back from the public for 15 years, but which were made widely available to elite groups such as the CFR, the Pugwash scientists, and the Harvard-MIT Axis, scared hell out of them. It convinced them that the Russians were not only 10 feet tall, but would soon be 50,000-deliverable-megatons strong. It convinced them that, in a long-run arms race, the United States could not successfully compete with the highly disciplined, dedicated Soviets, who had the advantage of a dictatorial system of government. It convinced the elitist groups—then an easy thing, since the timing was so soon after Sputnik—that the Soviets had such a tremendous headstart over us in the nuclear arms race that we could not hope to hold our own.

It convinced them that we should spend thousands of millions of dollars in a crash program to dig fallout and blast shelters to save our soon-to-be miserable lives in the great Soviet attack that might come as early as "1959 or early 1960."

The *Gaither Report* shook the members of the CFR, the Pugwash group and the Harvard-MIT Axis. It injected them with nuclear paralysis, with atomic ague, with the dread of death by incineration. Those who already were on the Red side of the rather-Red-than-dead argument, became fanatic. They concluded that preemptive surrender was the *only* way to avoid death by incineration, and they would never permit the nonelite American people to thwart their plan. Those who had previously been willing to take *some* risk, rather than accept a sure future as Red slaves, were convinced by the *Gaither Report* that we *could not* match the Soviets in longterm arms competition, and that therefore it was too great a risk to try.

Paul Hilken Nitze was and is the outstanding example of this latter type. He had formerly been "a strong preparedness man," and had favored actively seeking a Class A nuclear capability for the United States. Following the *Gaither Report*, however, he turned around to lead the pragmatic preemptive-surrender faction within the CFR. The *Gaither Report* convinced him that we could not come out Number One in a strategic arms competition with the Soviets. Upon this assumption which, like the *Gaither Report* itself, was based upon disastrously false intelligence, he erected his theory that, if we tried to become Number One, we would fail, but end up as a strong Number Two; and this would be terribly dangerous because we would be tempted *not* to surrender soon enough, and we would therefore be "clobbered." This is how the maxim "it's safer to be weak than strong" originated as to strategic nuclear power. Nitze contended that the safest course for the United States was not to be Number One or a strong Number Two, but instead to make sure that we came out no stronger than a decisively weak Number Two.

Having publicly declared his safety-in-weakness credo before some 500 leading nuclear strategists and unilateral-disarmers at the Asilomar National Strategy Seminar in April 1960, he was appointed in January 1961 as McNamara's Assistant Secretary of the Navy, and finally as McNamara's Deputy Secretary of Defense. Nitze is intellectually superior to McNamara, but McNamara's slick and deceptive salesmanship was essential to put across Nitze's make-the-U.S.-a-weak-second-to-the-Soviets strategy.

Nitze's total success in working with McNamara to bring down the eight-to-one U.S. strategic superiority to actual inferiority within eight years made him a perfect candidate for appointment as a member of the U.S. SALT delegation. His unique qualifications were not overlooked by Kissinger, who had been on a CFR nuclear weapons lecturing team with him as early as 1957. Kissinger was in full control of "preparing and conducting the SALT negotiations" because he had preempted the position of chairman of the President's "Verification Panel," which was created in early 1969 and entrusted with overall control of all SALT matters.

Nitze turned against Kissinger in early 1974 because of Kissinger's failure to stand up to Barry Goldwater's resistance to the proposed appointment of Nitze to the important position of Assistant Secretary of Defense for International Security Affairs. To vent a little of his spleen, Nitze pretended to change his coat once again, and went to Senator Henry Jackson to "expose" how Kissinger was making secret deals with the Soviets.

7

Henry Kissinger's relationships with the elitist groups must be examined if we are to understand his motivation and the sources of his power bases. The power, influence, and interlocking memberships of these groups have been well documented elsewhere. The mission of this book, however, is to present only the evidence relevant to understanding what Dr. Kissinger is doing to the United States, why he is doing it, and how he came by his power.

None of the several books about the Council on Foreign Relations has been written by anyone with the advantage of longtime membership in the CFR. Nor is there any which recognizes that the CFR long ago changed from a monolithic force to a polycentrism of leadership that has fostered a vicious no-holds-barred internecine conflict; nor that out of that conflict developed *The Pentagon Papers* case and the Watergate scandal.

Kissinger has long recognized how much he owes to the Council on Foreign Relations. Writing in 1961, in the Preface to *The Necessity for Choice*, he said:

> Five years ago, the Council on Foreign Relations gave me my first opportunity to work systematically on problems of foreign relations. My relations with it have remained close and my admiration for it has, if anything, increased.[1]

More than any other man living today, Kissinger is a creation of the CFR. He is the only man alive who is accepted by and used by, and who in turn uses, the separate cliques of powerful individual CFR members who operate within the organization and control its long-range objectives. In language associated usually with the Mafia or the organized crime Syndicate, Henry Kissinger "owes" two of CFR's four ruling cliques. A quick look at his early life will suggest how much and why he owes them.

Heinz Kissinger was born in Fuerth, Germany, in 1923 to Louis, a teacher, and his wife, Paula. They moved to New York in 1938. Louis became a bookkeeper, Paula a cook, and Heinz-now-Henry entered public high school and took a part-time job in a plant manufacturing bristles for shaving brushes. After high school he went into the U.S. Army as a private and by 1943 was serving in Europe. His life-plan for the postwar world showed little ambition and less imagination: he hoped to rise one step higher than his father and become an accountant.

While he was still 19, however, he met a benefactor who changed his career: Private (later Colonel) Fritz Kraemer, who in 1943 was lecturing to Army audiences on U.S. objectives in the war against the Nazis. Private Kraemer was a German from a distinguished family who had already acquired two doctor's degrees and had been fighting the Nazis since the early 1920s. Although Kraemer was 16 years older than Kissinger, they became friends as soon as Henry heard one of the Kraemer lectures. From him, Kissinger acquired an interest in philosophy, in political theories, and in international relations.

As the war progressed, Dr. Fritz Kraemer attained some of the promotions his abilities merited. In turn he was able to bring his protege to the attention of his superiors. Kissinger became translator for his commanding general, and later administrator of an occupied German district.

After the war, because of his Kraemer-changed interests, young Kissinger went to Harvard on a government scholarship instead of attending accounting school. Meanwhile, Kraemer became a civilian adviser to the Secretary of the Army on military and political strategy. He is still there. How he survived McNamara's seven-year dictatorship of the Pentagon is a mystery because, just as Kraemer had been a courageous and informed anti-Nazi, he became an equally courageous and informed anti-Communist when that threat emerged. His son Sven Kraemer has survived more than five years on Kissinger's staff. Sven had written his honors thesis at Harvard under Kissinger's auspices, but went to work for the pre-Kissinger National Security Council during the Johnson Administration.

In Kissinger's undergraduate years at Harvard he had also been singled out by another distinguished anti-Communist, Dr. William Yandell Elliot. The combination of such a mentor with Kissinger's intellect resulted in graduation summa cum laude in 1950. He received his master's degree in 1952 and his doctorate in 1954. Professor Elliot was the last anti-Communist who influenced Kissinger's life or career (except for Dr. Edward Teller's influence on certain scientific matters that was soon erased by Kissinger's Pugwash connections). As the saying goes, Kissinger went to Harvard and then turned left.

The first CFR influence appeared while Kissinger was still an obscure instructor at Harvard. He was "discovered" by Hamilton Fish Armstrong, founder and longtime editor of *Foreign Affairs,* the most influential journal of its type in the world. Although its circulation is only 70,000, it carries the "CFR party line" set by the ruling cliques within the CFR. This prestigious quarterly starts to mold U.S. official foreign and defense policies some five to ten years in advance of the changes it finally brings about.

In this sense, *Foreign Affairs* has long operated as a revolutionary force in America, focusing scholarly scorn on traditions of nationalism and patriotism, and blazing the path toward the lofty ideals of supranationalism. The term "revolutionary" may sound shocking in relation to so revered a publication, but one of the Camelot historians, Arthur Schlesinger, Jr., gave this remarkably frank description in the July 1973 issue:

> I first met Hamilton Fish Armstrong 20 or so years ago when he was about 60 years old. I remember my surprise that the editor of what I had regarded as a rather stuffy magazine was so conspicuously lacking in pomposity and self-regard and so filled with charm and spirit.
>
> Later I also discovered that Ham was a far more cunning editor than I had realized. *His was an ideal way to communicate dangerous thoughts to the American establishment.* Among all those "Bulgaria at the Crossroads" pieces and those pronouncements by forgotten foreign ministers on forgotten problems, one encountered a surprising liveliness and ecumenicity of contribution—John Dewey, W. E. B. DuBois, John Gunther, Harold Nicolson, Isaiah Berlin, Harold Laski, not to mention Lenin, Radek and Bukharin.

The most far-out of these "dangerous thoughts" are, of course, masked under a light cover of Aesopian language; but some are quite open.

Thus, under the guise of "fighting isolationism," *Foreign Affairs* quite obviously advocates internationalism and an end to national sovereignty, including U.S. sovereignty. As policy director as well as the editor of *Foreign Affairs,* Hamilton Fish Armstrong was for half a century one of the most influential, and certainly one of the most articulate, of the largest clique within the CFR. Nonmember observers usually think this clique is the CFR. It can be accurately, if awkwardly, described as the group dedicated primarily to the ideology of one-world-under-an-all-powerful-global-government, a dedication openly reaffirmed in 1972.

Back in the 1950s Hamilton Fish Armstrong was struck by the potential of Instructor Kissinger's writings, and spent some time improving his style, which was then too cumbersome, abstract, and abstruse even for *Foreign Affairs*. In this tutelage "Ham" Armstrong was very successful. Despite his ideological impedimenta, he had always been one of the most highly civilized men of the era and one of the most gifted and perceptive editors, as well as a competent writer on his favorite subjects. It takes a true professional to turn out 13 books and 49 articles of high standards (in everything except ideology). He served an additional function for CFR as an undercover recruiter for the State Department, providing a continuing flow of CFR selectees for policy positions in that 12,000-man empire that his protege, Kissinger, was destined to take over.

Upon his retirement following publication of the 50th Anniversary Edition of *Foreign Affairs* in October 1972, Armstrong was deluged with encomia by the CFR powers that be. For this historic moment, they almost lowered their elitism to plunge into the Babbittry of bestowing on Armstrong the title of Mister CFR. CFR Chairman of the Board David Rockefeller came very close to this when he said: "To many in this country and abroad, Hamilton Fish Armstrong has personified the organization."

The highest accolade, however, considering the opinion he holds of himself, was conferred by Henry A. Kissinger. Said Henry to Ham: "You invented me."[2]

Perhaps Ham Armstrong did not really carry the burden of invention as distinguished from discovery on his conscience, but he did in a very significant way create the Kissinger career. First, he published several articles by the young instructor. A single article in *Foreign Affairs* will not make a career—but three or four will launch one off to a good start. That was just the beginning of what the ideological faction of CFR had in mind for Kissinger.

This CFR faction conferred upon him in 1956 the title—and the living and the prestige that went with it—of "Director of Nuclear Weapons and Foreign Policy Studies for the Council on Foreign Relations." By no coincidence, the book that CFR published for him in 1957 was entitled *Nuclear Weapons and Foreign Policy.*[3] It brought him fame and fortune, influence and prestige, and ultimately entree into the White House. His entire reputation as an authority on nuclear strategy and foreign relations was based on and grew out of that single book. He had published his dissertation on Prince Metternich earlier, and several books on nuclear strategy later, but they were merely makeweights compared to *Nuclear Weapons and Foreign Policy.*

Without his position as CFR Director of Studies on a project of the same name, he could not have written the book. He had at his command the entire CFR staff—research, technical, and secretarial facilities. More important, once the book was published, the pervasive influence of CFR in the media went into action to promote the book; the CFR prestige in universities and tax-free foundations multiplied the promotion campaign.

It worked. The upward spiral to fame was under way. The acclaim generated for his book brought Kissinger highly profitable and prestigious employment as an expert consultant to powerful government agencies. Thus he was introduced into the mystique of the National Security Council, gaining inside knowledge that enabled him to gather its powers quickly into his own hands 10 years later when he was appointed by President Nixon. Kissinger was also, prophetically, a consultant to the U.S. Arms Control and Disarmament Agency and to the Weapons System Evaluation Group of the Joint Chiefs of Staff.

Professor Stephen R. Graubard's 1973 book, *Kissinger: Portrait of a Mind*,[4] provides abundant friendly confirmation and documentation of how Kissinger "owes" CFR. Graubard reminds his readers of "how modest were Kissinger's educational accomplishments when the war liberated him from his New York refugee ghetto and launched him into a wider world." Graubard vividly describes how the CFR took Kissinger "out of his academic shell and brought him into contact with all sorts of people" and gave "confidence and encouragement to an awkward and lonely individual who knew how much he needed to feel something other than the dreary competitiveness of Cambridge, Massachusetts." Graubard tells how the invitation to be a CFR Study Director was "the most important event in Kissinger's adult life, second only to his decision to enroll at Harvard."

In spelling out more specifically how much Kissinger owes to the CFR, Graubard says that the book *Nuclear Weapons and Foreign Policy* "would not have been written in the way it was, or have achieved the renown that it did, but for the Council's sponsorship. . . . A more advantageous position for a young man, little known at the time, could scarcely have been invented. . . ." From his vantage point as Kissinger's "friend and colleague since they pursued their graduate studies at Harvard in the early 1950s," and as a fellow member of the CFR, after 278 pages of sympathetic portraiture of Kissinger's mind, Professor Graubard reserves the highest accolade for the climactic point in his book, the last sentence:

> Kissinger was not looking for heroes but for principles that would make it possible for states in the 20th century to avoid the terrors of nuclear war.

Kissinger did find that principle, and he enshrined it in SALT I: the strategic surrender of one of the world's two superpowers.

Meanwhile, a second clique of influential members in the CFR also made its contribution to the Kissinger career. A much smaller group but more powerful, with a low profile but controlling billions of dollars in the United States and elsewhere, this faction comprises the Wall Street international bankers and their key agents. Primarily, they want the world banking monopoly from whatever power ends up in control of the global government. They would probably prefer that this be an all-powerful United Nations organization; but they are also prepared to deal with and for a one-world government controlled by the Soviet Communists if U.S. sovereignty is ever surrendered to them.

This CFR faction is headed by the Rockefeller brothers. David is Chairman of the Board of CFR, but John D. III and Nelson Aldrich are also resident members. Out of the total CFR resident and nonresident membership of 1,551, there are 189 bankers or financiers from the Wall Street international finance groups. In addition, the Rockefeller clique includes the most influential of the 82 CFR foundation-administrator types and the 174 CFR academic-administration types who have disproportionate influence on what is taught in our universities and over professorial and department appointments.

Even before the Kissinger-CFR opus *Nuclear Weapons and Foreign Policy* was published, David and Nelson Rockefeller caught on to the potential of the then-obscure instructor at Harvard. They appointed him Director of the Special Studies Project for the Rockefeller Brothers Fund in 1956, and he continued in this position for several years. It may be assumed that this association with the Wall Street-international bankers clique within CFR initiated his belief that money power in human relations could balance megatonnage in international relations—or at least could be used to buy off or bribe those who control strategic nuclear power.

That formal assignment with the Rockefeller Brothers Fund was the beginning of a close association, the most obvious fruit of which was his employment as military and foreign policy adviser to Nelson Rockefeller in his campaigns for the Republican presidential nomination. It was probably also this close relationship with Nelson Rockefeller that brought him into the White House with Richard Nixon, even though Kissinger was quoted as saying, when Rockefeller lost to Nixon in Miami Beach in 1968: "That man Nixon is not fit to be President." Perhaps that is why Kissinger felt he should personally take over, in everything but name, U.S. defense and foreign policy.

The promotions that these two CFR cliques—the one-world ideologists and the money-power people—supplied to Kissinger were the *sine qua non* of his rise to White House power. This is why he "owes" those factions within CFR. Granting his own claim to having "a first-rate mind," there is little evidence in his early career, or even contemporaneously, that he has a *great* mind. But even a great mind would not have assured such a steep upward spiral of power.

Take, for example, the case of Kissinger's one rival in the field of the exposition of strategic nuclear power, Herman Kahn. Kahn has far more on the ball in every significant area. His education and experience were superior. When Kissinger was still an undergraduate, Kahn had already received degrees from UCLA and Cal Tech, and had joined the Physics Division of the Rand Corporation. By the time Kissinger had completed his academic study of Prince Metternich and was recruited as a novice into the CFR, Kahn had had seven years of active study of the intricate and critical relationships between nuclear weapons and strategy. Kahn also had practical experience dealing with the hard facts of nuclear weapons and strategy as a consultant to the Atomic Energy Commission and the Office of Civil and Defense Mobilization. Kahn, however, did not join the CFR until 10 years after Kissinger did.

Why did they choose Kissinger over Herman Kahn who, on the basis of objective criteria, was far better qualified to become the nation's foremost authority on nuclear strategy and national security in the nuclear-space age? Kissinger was chosen because most of his theories were internationalist and disarmament-oriented and could be used to advance the ideological objectives of the CFR. They knew also that Kissinger was sufficiently flexible, and appreciative of their assistance to his career, so that any of his theories that did not fit the CFR pattern would be appropriately reoriented. They were correct. Kissinger, the invention of the CFR kingmaker elites, became their prime agent. They used all their resources to build up Kissinger as the most influential nuclear strategist in America. Because Kissinger had CFR backing, he advanced swiftly in prestige and power, in fame, and in national and international influence.

Herman Kahn's mind is creative as well as cognitive, in the highest meaning and connotation of both terms: creative in the sense of capable of production through imaginative skill, and also capable of producing something original rather than imitated. Kissinger's mind is far more cognitive than creative, and not even cognitive in the full sense of the term that includes "knowing" through both awareness *and judgment.*

Herman Kahn creates and evolves theories, then follows them to their logical conclusions and makes sound judgments as to their validity. Kissinger does not create theories. He pirates theories enunciated by others. His only original contribution is that he instills these borrowed theories with added verisimilitude by dressing them in raiment fashioned of the language of erudition and employed for the purpose of circumlocution (e.g., ". . . as power has grown more awesome, it has also turned abstract, intangible, elusive.")

It must be conceded that, in advancing an amalgam of many theories, such as Kissinger has done in radically recasting the entire grand strategy of the United States, coincidence or necessity might explain inclusion of several theories of non-Kissinger origin. Not so, however, when *every single theory involved* can be traced back to a single source.

This contrast between the so-called Kissinger theories and those of Herman Kahn is not based on any personal preference, either philosophical, ideological, or operational. As Richard Nixon put it in a remarkable essay in *U.S. News* of June 26, 1972, which bears the undeniable indicia of self-authorship: "The final test of a foreign policy is whether it works." This is true, doubled in nuclear spades, of strategic theories. In this case, "whether it works" means: would it strengthen the national defense of the United States? The essential Kissinger theories, albeit with different labels and personnel, were the national policy of the United States for seven years under McNamara, for one year under interim Defense Secretary Clark Clifford, under Kissinger himself for an additional four years up to the signing of SALT I, and after.

The "final test" of the Kissinger theories of national strategy should be: what was the strategic balance before the theories were put into operation, and how did it stand at the time of SALT I? (A later date would be more enlightening, but since the forced departure of Melvin Laird, who had opposed some of the Kissinger policies, and his replacement as Secretary of Defense by a more pliable CFR member, Elliot L. Richardson, and Richardson's replacement by James R. Schlesinger, a Kissinger protege, Kissinger has been able to tighten his hold on the entire U.S. intelligence community. Now he can deny to Congress and the American people any updated authoritative information on the upward spiral of Soviet strategic superiority.)

To avoid even the appearance of selecting strategic statistics that might be unfair to the Kissinger-Nixon team, let us consider *their own figures* as to the strategic balance before and after. Here is Nixon's own estimate delivered at La Crosse, Wisconsin, on February 21, 1968:

> In 1962 at the time of the Cuban confrontation this nation had an 8-to-1 strategic advantage over the same Soviet Union which is approaching strategic equality today.

This was not merely a figure of speech pulled out of a hat for the purpose of a political address. It was abundantly confirmed both by official estimates and by the expert estimates of the American Security Council in the study prepared for the House Armed Services Committee in 1967 entitled *The Changing Strategic Military Balance: U.S.A.*

vs. *U.S.S.R.* This analysis estimated the U.S. advantage over the Soviets in 1962 to have been between 5-to-1 and 10-to-1, with the highest probability in the area of 8-to-1.

The Kissinger-U.S. intelligence statistics officially released for SALT I purposes revealed that, in the decisive area of strategic missiles, the Soviets held a 50 percent advantage in numbers, a 4-to-1 or 5-to-1 advantage in throw-weight, and a 10-to-1 to 19-to-1 advantage in missile-deliverable megatonnage. These official statistics also revealed an incalculable advantage to the Soviets in counterforce, or enemy-weapons-kill capability. They then had counterforce weapons (SS-9s) capable of delivering 8,950 megatons of explosive power, while the United States has no such weapons. Now, of course, the Soviets have added to their counterforce echelons an unknown number of SS-17s, SS-18s, and SS-19s, and probably scores of land-mobile SS-16s.

Time after time in his rationalization of the imbalances allowed to the Soviets under SALT I, Dr. Kissinger admitted the existence of "a numerical gap against us in the two categories of land- and sea-based missile systems." He emphasized that this gap "was not reversible within the timeframe of SALT I." Repetition of this concession of U.S. inferiority impressed even nonauthorities on nuclear strategy. For example, William Buckley, author, columnist, and television host, picked up a point nearly everyone else missed:

> *New York, Sept. 22, 1972*—When on accepting the renomination of his party at Miami Beach a few weeks ago, Richard Nixon said that he would never negotiate an arms limitation agreement from a position of inferiority, he ran a terrible risk.
>
> The risk was that someone would read out to him from the transcript of the various press conferences in Moscow in which Henry Kissinger gave out details of the SALT Treaty. I counted *seven* times that Mr. Kissinger defended lapidary relegation of the United States to inferiority on the grounds that after all we were talking not about an ideal situation but about the current situation.
>
> Mr. Kissinger's point was that the Soviet Union had been going hell-bent for strategic armament for three years while we have been coasting, and that we are better off more or less freezing the situation than waking up a year or two from now to find the Soviet lead drastically lengthened.
>
> In other words, we negotiated from inferiority.

The Nixon statement on our 8-to-1 strategic advantage over the Soviets in 1962, and the Kissinger statements and SALT I statistics admitting substantial inferiority to the Soviets in mid-1972, demonstrate that the Kissinger-McNamara policies have wrought tremendous damage to U.S. national security interests. Thus the strategic theories on which U.S. defense policies have been based have resulted in *weak-*

ening U.S. strategic defenses, perhaps disastrously.

This fact lays an objective foundation for a question, which, although controversial, must be answered on the basis of hard evidence if the United States is to have any substantial chance of surviving in freedom through the late 1970s. The question is: can such a massive shift in the strategic military balance be explained on the basis of accident or coincidence? Certainly the Soviets engaged in a deliberate strategic weapons buildup of huge proportions. But the shift in the balance did not merely involve *adding* about 30,000 megatons of explosive power to the Soviet side of the balance. It also involved *subtracting* about 30,000 megatons of deliverable strategic explosive power from the American side of the balance.

Did the U.S. cut-down and hold-down of strategic weapons "just happen"—or was it deliberately planned? McNamara destroyed more operational U.S. strategic weapons—with 10 to 20 years of effective life remaining—*than the Soviets could have destroyed in the same timeframe by a full-scale nuclear surprise attack* targeted on our weapons! By permitting no additional strategic weapons to go into the production lines after 1962, McNamara made sure that no additional weapons would emerge after 1967 (the gestation period for weapons is five years).

By blocking the development of any advanced new weapons systems after 1961, he deprived U.S. strategic power of two generations of weapons. These deliberately aborted systems included Skybolt, the air-to-surface long-range inertially guided missile that had been successfully tested; the B-70 strategic bomber, after it successfully proved out in 1964—10 years ahead of the world—at speeds of more than mach 3 (a full mach faster than the proposed B-1 will fly in the 1980s, if it is ever permitted to fly at all); the Advanced Manned Strategic Aircraft, a new-generation bomber designed to penetrate the massed Soviet air defenses; the Improved Capability Missile, a land-based strategic missile far more powerful and accurate than the Minuteman; and *all* orbital and space weapons systems.

Every operational strategic weapon that McNamara destroyed, every new or additional strategic weapon that he prevented from coming into being, was the equivalent of adding that much to the Soviet side of the strategic balance. McNamara's policies, and the strategic theories on which they were based, were therefore worth thousands of deliverable megatons to the Soviets. Ever since January 1969, when Kissinger came to power with Nixon, the Kissinger theories have blocked the rebuilding of any of the strategic power McNamara destroyed. Kissinger has not only blocked bringing into being any additional weapons to prevent the Soviets from attaining a first-strike capability, but *he has prevented the initiation of any programs that*

could produce additional strategic power within the next five years.
This is the meaning of the Kissinger statement on the missile gap of
the 1970s—the gap that he asserts with apparent pride "is not reversible within the timeframe" of the SALT I five-year Interim Agreement.

How much—in thousands of deliverable megatons—are Henry Kissinger's theories worth to the Kremlin?

The answer to that will depend in large part on whether Kissinger
really believes what he says, or merely wants us to believe that he believes it. He probably has the brainpower to recognize that the theories
on which he has staked our lives and the survival of the United States
have been tried—sometimes under different names—for more than 12
years, and have proved invalid in actual practice. Perhaps his ideology
has blocked his brain from recognizing reality; or perhaps he is
blocked because of his personal need to retain the active support of
the influential factions in the Council on Foreign Relations.

If Kissinger has not recognized that these theories will inexorably
plunge the United States into disaster, he has thereby demonstrated
that he is incompetent to hold either the position of Assistant to the
President for National Security Affairs or of Secretary of State. If
however, he does know that these theories are inviting disaster, and
he still palms them off on the President, suppresses all intelligence
that would expose their failures, and destroys the political careers
of all who warn against those theories, then his motivation must
be far more sinister—and his value to the Kremlin far greater. A fool
does not work in conscious cooperation with the enemy.

What's wrong with Henry Kissinger's being CFR's man in the White
House? His two predecessors in office as Assistant to the President
for National Security Affairs, McGeorge Bundy and Walt W. Rostow,
were also CFR members, as well as part of the Harvard-MIT Axis.

The objective of the influential majority of members of CFR has
not changed since its founding in 1922, more than 50 years ago. In
the 50th anniversary issue of *Foreign Affairs*, the first and leading
article was written by CFR member Kingman Brewster, Jr., entitled
"Reflections on Our National Purpose." He did not back away from defining it: *our national purpose should be to abolish our nationality.*
Indeed, he pulled out all the emotional stops in a hard-sell for global
government. He described our "Vietnam-seared generation" as being
"far from America Firsters"—an expression meant as a patronizing
sop to our young people. In the entire CFR lexicon, there is no term
of revulsion carrying a meaning so deep as "America First." Dr.
Brewster continued:

> It is hard to see how we will engage the young, and stand any chance
> of competing for the respect of mankind generally, if we continue to be

144

hold-outs, more concerned with the sovereignty of nations than with the ultimate sovereignty of peoples. . . .

Our new situation of mutual, national dependence is inescapable. If we would face it in a creative mood, we will have to take some risks in order to invite others to pool their sovereignty with ours on matters which none of us can control alone.

We shall have to abide by lawfully achieved results even when we might have wished or voted otherwise. Some day some President must convince all the American people that this is a proud and exciting call to be faced with zest rather than reluctance.

As we approach the bicentennial of the Republic, perhaps what we need most for 1976 is a resounding Declaration of International Interdependence. Maybe by 1987 we could then celebrate the 200th year of the Constitution of the United States with at least the beginning of global arrangements and institutions to safeguard the common defense and the general welfare of humanity everywhere.

Then we would rediscover the sense of purpose, and once more know the satisfaction, of those who saved the peoples of the colonies by making them into a nation. We, in our turn, might save the peoples of nations by making them into a world community capable of survival.

Most Middle Americans would dismiss this as the quintessence of utopian slobbering. But these excerpts are from the credo of the policy spokesman for the majority of members of the most powerful private organization in the world. Over the years we have seen substantially every one of their America-Last programs become the official policy of the United States Government.

Read the Brewster-CFR credo again. It is important not to miss the slightly concealed but intense hate of the terms "nation" and "sovereignty of nations." Note the holier-than-thou contempt and resentment of those who would serve America first, of those who would be loyal to the sovereignty of the United States, rather than to the "world community" or to the "ultimate sovereignty of peoples." Notice that we are implored to accept "some risks" in pooling our sovereignty with others. These risks include disarming down to the point where we would be completely helpless against the "peace-keeping" forces of the global government; if the plan goes sour, it would be too late to rebuild U.S. military strength.

Note also that we are admonished by Mr. Brewster to abjure the outdated and selfish concept of a United States Constitution that is concerned with the common defense and general welfare of the American people. That obsolete document must be scrapped so that we can enter "global arrangements and institutions to safeguard the common defense and general welfare of humanity everywhere."

One of the chilling aspects of this 50th-anniversary appeal is the frank exposure of the CFR lust to surrender, and a demand that "all Americans" not only share that lust but be thrilled by it. We are

145

admonished not only to surrender our national sovereignty to the "world community" and submerge it in the pool of the "sovereignty of peoples," but also to look forward "with zest" to the "proud and exciting call" to surrender American interests to the dictates of the global government. True CFR-one-worlders, such as Kingman Brewster, Jr., evince a shrill impatience for the time when they will have a chance to diminish American power to a single vote in the global government—ruled by the Communist bloc manipulating the votes of the newly emerging mini-nations. It is said that some men look forward with "pride and excitement" and "zest" to being raped, but this ilk is known to normal people as perverts.

Although, from the inside, CFR is certainly not the monolith that some members and most nonmembers consider it, this lust to surrender the sovereignty and independence of the United States is pervasive throughout most of the membership, and particularly in the leadership of the several divergent cliques that make up what is actually a polycentric organization.

Although the surrender syndrome is common to all influential segments of CFR, CFR members are magnanimously allowed diversity in preference and priorities as to whom they want to surrender. The majority visualize the utopian submergence of the United States as a subsidiary administrative unit of a global government; a majority of this majority probably have never sought to penetrate the facade of this "government" to see what was behind it and who would be in control. This obeisant group pays facile lip-service to "the rule of law" without ever thinking to inquire "whose law?" Such an inquiry is never attempted because even the brightest utopians could find no answers that would not shock or alienate most Americans.

Sharp divergence as to whom to surrender—and as to the timing of the surrender—exists between two of the cliques. One is the unilateral-disarmament intellectuals, a group of powerful pragmatists led by Paul Nitze, Robert McNamara, Jerome Wiesner, Roswell Gilpatric, Paul Warnke, and Henry Kissinger. The other clique consists of the articulate antiwarmongers, such as Daniel Ellsberg and Morton Halperin. This latter group comprises the several types included in CFR's select membership of 1,551 whom the "powers that be" consider too limited in intelligence to be cut in on the secrets of the CFR "intellectuals."

Most well-informed persons understand some aspects of the scope and intensity of the power exercised by key members of the Council on Foreign Relations. The year 1971 marked the 50th anniversary of its founding. For the last 40 years its most influential leaders have almost totally controlled the foreign and defense policies of the United States. In the 44-year time-span from 1928 through 1972, nine out of

12 Republican presidential nominees were members of CFR. In the 20-year time-span from 1952 through 1972, the presidential election resulted in victory for a CFR member four out of six times (the two exceptions being John F. Kennedy, whose entire palace guard was CFR-dominated, and Lyndon Johnson, who made it via the unplanned vice presidential route). During that same 20-year period, in three out of six presidential campaigns, both Republican and Democratic nominees were or had been CFR members.

Every Secretary of State from 1934 through Henry Kissinger, except James Byrnes, has been a member of CFR. All Secretaries of Defense and all Deputy Secretaries of Defense from 1958 through Elliot Richardson were members except Melvin Laird. CFR members included Thomas L. Gates, Robert McNamara, Clark Clifford, Roswell Gilpatric, and Paul Nitze. Even the position of Chairman of the Joint Chiefs of Staff is sometimes passed from one CFR member to another, as when General L. L. Lemnitzer was succeeded by General Maxwell Taylor. The CIA, during most of the years since its creation, has been under successive CFR control, including Allen Dulles and John McCone. Although the 1973 short-term director, James R. Schlesinger, was not a CFR member, he was a protege of CFR member Daniel Ellsberg, and his appointment to that position was totally manipulated by CFR-member Kissinger, as was the case also with Schlesinger's replacement, William E. Colby.

In the Kennedy-Johnson administrations, more than 60 CFR members held top policy-making positions. The buildup under Nixon to more than 100 is highly significant. It not only reached up to both his Secretaries of State, but down to little-publicized but highly influential positions. Thus, in February 1973, the year that Kissinger had officially designated as the "Year of Europe," it leaked out that Kissinger's then-Deputy for European Affairs, Helmut Sonnenfeldt, a CFR member long distinguished by his fawning attitude toward the Soviet Union, was threatening our NATO allies that, if they did not help more with the balance of payments problem, they could not expect continued U.S. assistance in the defense of Europe. Within that same week, the West German Government lost $600 million loyally trying to support the dollar.

Equally important is CFR's influence in the mass media. Out of its 1,551 members, 60 were listed in official CFR reports as engaged in "journalism." An additional 61 were listed in "communications management," a highly descriptive title, because CFR members do indeed "manage" mass communications media, especially the influential segments. They control or own major newspapers, magazines, radio and television networks, and they control the most powerful companies in the book publishing business.

The late Arthur Hays Sulzberger, chairman of the board of the *New York Times*, was a member, and presently there are at least nine CFR members active on the newspaper or in the *New York Times* Service. Katharine Graham, publisher of the *Washington Post* and a director of *Newsweek*, is one of the 18 women members admitted since membership was opened to them in 1970. Henry Luce, who founded and was editor-in-chief of *Time, Life,* and *Fortune* was a member. *Time's* present editor-in-chief Hedley Donovan and chairman of the executive committee James A. Linen are members, as are editorial director Louis Banks and Barry Zorthian, president of *Time-Life* Broadcasts, Inc.

And so it goes. John W. Cowles, Jr., who has the *Minneapolis Star,* the *Des Moines Register,* and Harper & Row Publishers, is CFR. So is Winthrop Knowlton, president of Harper & Row. So was *Encyclopaedia Britannica* chairman William Benton, and so is Kingman Brewster, Jr., president of Yale University Press. Then there are Axel G. Rosin, president of the Book of the Month Club; Gerard Piel, publisher of *Scientific American;* Alexander Trowbridge, director of Gannett Co., Inc.; and William P. Hobby, editor of the *Houston Post.* Columnists who are CFR members include Joseph Kraft, Bill Moyers, Joseph C. Harsch, Roscoe Drummond, Marquis Childs, James Reston, John P. Roche, and C. L. Sulzberger.

Not generally noticed is the fact that the Council on Foreign Relations has 174 members engaged in "academic administration" and 268 members engaged as "scholars." They extend CFR's influence on the ideology of university faculties—especially when coupled with the interlock of 82 key members in top positions in "nonprofit and foundation administration."

Previous attempts to document CFR's influence have been ignored or smeared by the liberal press as "exaggerated." This is to be expected, considering the beachheads that key CFR members hold in all parts of the media, and especially because any attempt to tell the truth about the power and activities of CFR members is bound to sound exaggerated. Actually, however, all the published accounts thus far have understated CFR's influence, just as all previous accounts of Henry Kissinger's power vastly underestimate him.

The reason this is so is that, in a world in which *political* control depends upon strategic *nuclear weapons,* it is impossible to understand the operations of a man or an organization which seeks to influence global destiny without a fundamental understanding of a few basic principles of nuclear strategy. This doesn't mean that you have to devote your life to it, or go into technical complexities. All you really need to know—and this is what the unilateral disarmers have been afraid the American people might find out—is in this book.

Strategic nuclear power is so fantastically massive that even an *understanding* of its use generates power. Henry Kissinger's career demonstrates this conclusively. As we have seen, he was nobody until the publication of his book *Nuclear Weapons and Foreign Policy* in 1957. In it he made a great show of understanding the revolutionary changes that nuclear weapons would bring about in the grand strategies of the great powers and in their international relationships. This single display of his understanding of the power of strategic nuclear weapons started him on his rise to a personal power so great that its limits are not yet defined.

It takes power to beget power. To exploit the power potential Kissinger gained from his reputation of understanding the nature and uses of strategic nuclear power, he needed the active influence of the ruling members of the CFR. He needed their pervasive influence over the government, over the mass media, and over the establishment as a whole. And he got it.

The first influential CFR clique, as we have seen, is composed of the one-world-global-government ideologists—more respectfully referred to as the organized internationalists. They are the ones who carry on the tradition of the founders. They act as if strategic nuclear power were merely another type of military force. Their ideology is the only one stated in any official accounts of CFR's history. For example, the President's Report dated August 31, 1972, recites:

> The origins of the°Council on Foreign Relations lay in the concern of the founders at what they regarded as the disappointing conduct of the Versailles negotiations (in which most of the founders had been participants), and at the short-sighted, as they saw it, rejection by the United States of membership in the League of Nations. In 1921 they founded the Council as a privately funded, nonprofit and nonpartisan organization of individual members.

Both sentences are significant. To cure their "disappointment" that we had stayed out of the League of Nations, they started to build a power base strong enough to insure that they could eventually merge the United States into a one-world organization even stronger. Thus they were ready with the influence and the personnel to move into the U.S. organization for the United Nations in irresistible force. More than 40 CFR members were included in the U.S. delegation at the first UN conference in San Francisco, including Alger Hiss, Nelson Rockefeller, Adlai Stevenson, Ralph Bunche, John Foster Dulles, and Secretary of State Edward Stettinius.

The immensity of the influence wielded by or through CFR members at once cries out for congressional investigation, and effectively precludes it. Only one such investigation even touched it. In 1954, long before CFR power crested in the Kennedy-Johnson-Nixon administrations, the Special House Committee to Investigate Tax-Exempt Foundations (the Reece Committee) concluded that CFR's "productions are not objective but are directed overwhelmingly at promoting the globalistic concept," and that it had become "in essence an agency of the United States Government . . . carrying its internationalist bias with it."

With 16 years' experience as a member, one of the authors of this book has concluded that this purpose of promoting disarmament and submergence of U.S. sovereignty and national independence into an all-powerful one-world government is the *only* objective revealed to about 95 percent of 1,551 members. There are two other—ulterior— purposes that CFR *influence* is being used to promote; but it is improbable that they are known to more than about 75 members, or that these purposes ever have even been identified in writing.

This does not mean that only 75 CFR members are important or influential. At least 500 represent very great influence. Another 500 are fully qualified as VIPs in their respective areas in the U.S. economy or government. Even the last 500 have some substantial raison d'etre; about 400 of them are of moderate reputation or influence, selected by the Membership Committee because of their established reputations or ideological enthusiasm for one-world or global government, and the remaining members are for window dressing or balance. Because of several spates of undesirable publicity resulting from the revelation from time to time of prominent CFR members having close connections with Communist agents or Communist causes (e.g., Alger Hiss, J. Robert Oppenheimer, Philip C. Jessup, Owen Lattimore), a few selected prominent and dedicated anti-Communists are included in the CFR membership list. Most of the 41 military members would fall in this group—but there are some who are politically ambitious, and some who simply recognize that access to CFR "confidential" sources can provide more significant intelligence information than can be secured from the reports made available to them from our $6 billion-a-year intelligence community.

This truncated estimate of the constituency of CFR *membership* is warranted by the little-recognized fact that the vast influence attributed to CFR is *not exercised* through or by the Council on Foreign Relations as an organization. As accurately stated in the excerpt from the 1972 President's Report quoted above, CFR is an "organization of *individual members*." This point has been missed by most of those who have attempted to picture CFR's power. CFR, *as such*, does not write the platforms of both political parties or select their respective presidential candidates, or control U.S. defense and foreign policies.

150

But CFR members, as individuals, acting in concert with other individual CFR members, do.

Thus, David Rockefeller does not exercise such vast powers because he is chairman of the board of directors of CFR, but because he is chairman of the board of one of the two most powerful banks in the world and a member of one of the world's wealthiest families. In this country his influence extends into finance, business, industry, transportation, communications, the press, television, universities, foundations, international organizations, and government. He has similar influence throughout the Free World, and is now rapidly expanding into the Communist world.

When he, or any other influential member of CFR, decides to take a hand in a policy or program within the cognizance of CFR, he will not act through the organization, but as leader of a sort of floating ad hoc coalition with other influential members having similar objectives. The policy-making members use CFR as an *instrument* rather than as an organization. It has proved to be a tool of great value, especially for propagandizing.

Once the ruling members of CFR have decided that the U.S. Government should adopt a particular policy, the very substantial research facilities of CFR are put to work to develop arguments, intellectual and emotional, to support the new policy, and to confound and discredit, intellectually and politically, any opposition. The most articulate theoreticians and ideologists prepare related articles, aided by the research, to sell the new policy and to make it appear inevitable and irresistible. By following the evolution of this propaganda in the most prestigious scholarly journal in the world, *Foreign Affairs,* anyone can determine years in advance what the future defense and foreign policies of the United States will be. If a certain proposition is repeated often enough in that journal, then the U.S. Administration in power—be it Republican or Democratic—begins to *act as if* that proposition or assumption were an established fact.

Soon after the Cuban missile crisis, the recurrent theme in *Foreign Affairs* became: the Cold War is over, international communism is no longer a monolith, multicentrism has set in, the threat to the Free World no longer exists, or at least has diminished so that the building of bridges should replace the maintenance of defenses in the West. Detente would be the order of the new era that was dawning for the one-world of peoples. President Johnson swallowed it hook, line, and sinker. On October 7, 1967, he delivered his famous "bridge-building" speech, offering all sorts of accommodations to the Communists.

When the CFR rulers decide to fashion a new political environment out of a blend of ideology, theory, and propaganda, their influence is usually sufficient to prevent the intrusion of reality. Thus, in 1968, when the Soviet invasion of Czechoslovakia broke 17 Soviet treaties, this raw event was not allowed to break the spell of CFR's newly created myth. CFR still continued the snow job that political and military power over the satellites in Eastern Europe was no longer a Moscow monopoly, but that there were many centers of power in the various capitals of the Warsaw Pact nations.

Then came the enunciation of the Brezhnev Doctrine. The General Secretary of the Central Committee of the Communist Party of the Soviet Union declared that the Soviet invasion of Czechoslovakia was no mere aberration; the Soviets would do it again and again, if necessary, whenever they suspected any deviation from the CPSU line. The CFR powers, however, did not let that brutal Soviet-Communist realism break in on their theory of multicentrism, detente, and the interment of the Cold War.

Foreign Affairs took the line that the invasion "showed that the Soviet leaders are no longer sure they can live with competitive coexistence themselves"; and that it was merely "the latest and most dramatic spasm in the nervous decomposition of the 'socialist commonwealth' and the attempt by its bosses to arrest the rot by repression." The "passive but remarkable resistance of the Czechs" was applauded (under CFR guidelines, passive resistance to Communist aggression is the *only* type *ever* applauded). Applauded also was the ultimate and only NATO reaction to the Soviet surprise overnight movement of an invasion force of more than 1/3 of a million men, with thousands of tanks and aircraft. Falling in with CFR-generated pressures, the NATO allies declared that "the only political goal consistent with Western values is that of secure, peaceful, and mutually beneficial relations between East and West."

8

For several years prior to the final Kissinger "peace" negotiations with the North Vietnamese Communists in Paris, it had become clear to astute observers that he had no aversion to selling out the South Vietnamese Government in a surrender to the Communists, but he kept dragging out the war and postponing the settlement. Most realistic analysts—left, right, and center—concurred in what became known as the "fig leaf" rationale. Such diverse commentators as James Burnham of *National Review* and Stewart Alsop of *Newsweek* agreed that what was delaying conclusion of the agreement was that Kissinger—at Nixon's insistence—was demanding a cover, a fig leaf, to give an appearance of decency to the surrender to the Communists after the expenditure of so much American blood, tears, and money.

What was more important to Kissinger, however, was that a brave-appearing stand against the North Vietnamese Communists was also the essential fig leaf he needed to assure the acceptance by the American people of his accommodation with the Chinese and Soviet Communists. The conservative, anti-Communist segment of Nixon's political constituency, although they had meekly tolerated many betrayals, would never have stood for the Kissinger-arranged "turn to Peking" or "move to Moscow" if they had not been misled by what appeared to be the Administration's "strong" concurrent stand against communism in Vietnam. Republicans could rationalize their continued faith in Nixon by arguing that the Kissinger deals with Mao and Brezhnev couldn't possibly amount to a surrender, or even to important unilateral concessions, because Nixon refused to surrender in Vietnam despite virulent political pressures.

Thus, Kissinger could not afford to permit Nixon to bend to political pressures to surrender in Vietnam *until* he had culminated his deals with Peking and Moscow.

The unsuspicious acceptance by the nation and the Congress of the potentially disastrous concessions to the Soviets in the SALT I Agreements is explained largely by public confidence in the courage of the Kissinger-Nixon partnership engendered by the mining of Haiphong Harbor and the so-called "wall-to-wall carpet" bombing of North Vietnam ordered by Nixon prior to his Moscow Summit. This theatrical display could easily have been arranged and discounted in advance by Kissinger on his preliminary visit to the Kremlin. There is much evidence suggesting a typical Kissinger deal in this matter. In essence, his proposition to Brezhnev could have been: Please let us look good in the short term for the sake of the American voters; we will repay you generously with the extra concessions in the SALT Agreements, in grain, credits, and technology.

Impressive circumstantial evidence of this is found in the otherwise shocking failure of the President to order a worldwide strategic alert of U.S. forces prior to announcing the mining and bombing orders. The only excuse for this otherwise inexplicable failure to alert our forces—which *in itself* could have tempted the Kremlin to order a nuclear attack—was the possession of advance assurance that the Soviets would ignore the U.S. "aggressive" action in Vietnam. Some five years earlier, when the Soviets had less than one-fourth of their 1972 strategic offensive power relative to the United States, Lyndon Johnson had feared that his order to bomb oil storage tanks in the Haiphong area (under the most restricted circumstances insuring no threat to Soviet shipping) would trigger a Soviet nuclear attack against the United States.

Kissinger needed the continuance of the war in Vietnam as much as McNamara had needed it years earlier. McNamara escalated it and continued it in order to divert some $140 billion into that bottomless pit so that there would be no defense dollars left over to build strategic weapons systems to stay ahead of the Soviets. After 1968 the Soviet momentum in arms buildup, coupled with the McNamara freeze on U.S. strategic weapons, was such that the gigantic diversion was no longer so urgently needed. The Russians were well on their way to strategic supremacy and a first-strike capability against the United States.

When Kissinger took over in January 1969, the dragging out of the Vietnam War became essential to his plans. He needed a backdrop to impress people with his "brilliant and effective employment of power" while he negotiated with Peking and the Moscow Politburo. He needed a record to support the Nixon myth that he would never surrender to communism. Above all, he needed a demonstration of courage and ability to "stand up to the Communists" at home and abroad in order to impress Nixon's anti-Communist and conservative supporters and keep them safely in the Nixon political corral.

The hypothesis that Kissinger had arranged for Soviet advance approval of Nixon's mining and bombing operations just prior to the Moscow Summit of 1972 cannot be proved by direct objective evidence. However, that kind of a deal certainly would have been the smart and slick thing to do, and it would have been in character for Henry Kissinger. In his view it would have been foolhardy and stupid to have given the Soviets such "provocation" without a prior deal guaranteeing their "restraint." Without such a deal, he would have risked initiating World War III because the Soviets might have been irresistibly tempted to strike our *unalerted* U.S. strategic forces.

Furthermore, of immediate and decisive additional importance to Kissinger's grandiose plans would have been the near certainty that the Soviets would cancel the Moscow Summit of May 1972. It was reasonable to assume that Soviet reaction to such "aggressive" action by the "U.S. imperialistic warmongers" against the "fraternal Communist client state" of North Vietnam would take the form of a refusal to extend Nixon and Kissinger honored-guest red-carpet hospitality in Moscow. Indeed, among many informed government personnel, the betting was 2-to-1 that the Kremlin would cancel the Summit—just as Khrushchev did in May 1960, when provoked by a much less "aggressive" U.S. action.

It would not have been in keeping with Kissinger's modus operandi to risk losing that Moscow meeting upon which he had pinned so many of his plans for a new world order. It is now known that he had been working with Soviet Ambassador Anatoly F. Dobrynin and Minister-Counselor Yuri M. Vorontsov on SALT and the 1972 SALT Summit for more than two years prior to the actual meeting. The fate of his planned "triangular strategy" and "pentagonal equilibrium" depended on that Summit. What Henry Kissinger has worked on so long, he would not unnecessarily risk. The risk could have been averted entirely by an advance deal in which the Politburo could be guaranteed massive benefits—such as the grain "trade"—with so many U.S.-subsidized advantages to the Russians that congressional committees are still trying to discover how U.S. representatives could have been so stupid.

The American people now partially understand how badly we were shortchanged in the grain deal because they see the effects in the skyrocketing prices of bread and meat. The 1972 Soviet grain deal cost us several billion dollars in credits, subsidies, shipping costs, and an inflationary spiral of prices of wheat products and meat. The Kissinger concessions in SALT, however, coupled with his policies in implementing his bargain with the Politburo, probably will ultimately cost us our country, including the annual loss of our $1.3 trillion GNP. Kissinger is fond of pontificating that Americans must learn that there is no guarantee against tragedy.

The desperate efforts of the Nixon Administration to prevent the publication of *The Pentagon Papers* in 1971 by recourse to the courts provided an exciting element of suspense, and generally whetted public interest in an otherwise essentially dull affair. Two years later, in June 1973, spurred by Watergate developments, the pundits were still puzzling for the reason why the administration pressed the panic button. *Washington Post* reporter David S. Broder on June 1, 1973, asked the still-relevant question:

> [What] can possibly explain the political anomaly of a Republican Administration trying desperately, in the case of *The Pentagon Papers,* to prevent publication of historical documents damaging to its Democratic predecessors?

The "only" answer Mr. Broder found is the "fanatic institutional commitment to secrecy" by the bureaucracy and a "fixation with national security."

An explanation that relies on a general bureaucratic mystique simply will not wash. When the Republican administration in June 1971 resorted to the federal courts, including the Supreme Court, in an attempt to suppress publication of *The Pentagon Papers,* the decision-makers were not merely accepting a risk that might or might not culminate in actual harm to the administration (as they did in Watergate, where they did not expect to be caught or to be blocked in a coverup). In *The Pentagon Papers* case, the minute they sought the first court injunction to muzzle the press, they knowingly accepted the consequences of actual and massive harm.

The administration knew it was furnishing ammunition for attacks based on their attempts to "censor" the "free press," and that this would provide incontrovertible evidence for accusations that they were attempting to limit or destroy the constitutional guarantees of freedom of speech and press. In addition to this actual political harm, they took the risk of further harm, not only in the political arena but also in the areas of credibility, morality, and intelligence. That is, they risked an unfavorable ruling by the Supreme Court that would state that their attempt to muzzle the press was in excess of the authority of government, as limited by the Constitution. That is, of course, exactly what happened. The Supreme Court decision gave judicial backing to the press for assertions that the administration was attempting to usurp totalitarian powers and take steps toward the establishment of a police state.

The Nixon Administration was then predictably lambasted by the press for being the first in American history to attempt to secure from the courts "prior restraint" of material to be published. The newspapers that published the stolen documents were the recipients of high praise by the members of the Supreme Court. As Justice Hugo L. Black put it in his concurring opinion:

> Only a free and unrestrained press can effectively expose deception in government. The . . . newspapers should be commended for serving the purpose that the Founding Fathers saw so clearly. In revealing the workings of the government that led to the Vietnam War, the newspapers nobly did precisely what the founders hoped and trusted they would do.

Thus, the Nixon Administration knowingly played into the hands of what they considered their longtime and vindictive enemy, the liberal press. By seeking to silence the press through the injunctive process in the federal courts, they built up the image of the press as patriotic, courageous, honest, and, in Justice Black's words, even "noble."

The Nixon Administration took office in January 1969. The last of the mountainous volume of *The Pentagon Papers* is dated April 1968. No Republicans were connected with the initiation of the Vietnam War nor with its continuance throughout the Johnson years. *The Pentagon Papers* presented the anomaly of a Republican administration deliberately opening itself to smears of attempting to restrict constitutional freedom of the press in order to protect Democratic predecessors.

The inherent improbability of Nixon Republican politicians embarking on such a self-sacrificial course of action out of altruistic motivation to save the reputations of Democratic predecessors approaches absurdity. There is, however, one explanation that is both logical and convincing: *self*-preservation. Those in the new administration, who apparently were attempting to suppress *The Pentagon Papers* to protect their predecessors in office, must in reality have been *protecting themselves* and their own priority objectives. Only such a powerful motivation of self-interest can explain their committing the Nixon Administration, through the Justice Department, to fight the mass media in such desperate fashion, with so much to lose.

We are forced to deduce that the power elite controlling the Nixon Administration *feared* something very important would be exposed by publication of *The Pentagon Papers*. The far-reaching significance of these fears is suggested by the intensity of Dr. Kissinger's reaction. One authoritatively leaked story, which has its own inherent plausibility, attributes the absolute origin of the organization that perpetrated the Watergate activities to Kissinger's fears of the consequences of *The Pentagon Papers* exposure. This authoritative story appeared in a Jack Anderson column, and we offer no apology for labeling it authoritative and authentic. Anderson had previously demonstrated his access to secret government and National Security Council materials, by which he proved conclusively that Kissinger had deliberately lied to the media about the administration's attitude toward the India-Pakistan conflict.

According to the Jack Anderson column of June 14, 1973, Kissinger led President Nixon to form the "plumbers" squad that burglarized the offices of Daniel Ellsberg's psychiatrist and engaged in other extralegal activities. Anderson identified former White House lawyer Charles Colson as the source of this authentic report. According to Anderson, "Colson described Kissinger as approaching 'near hysteria' over the leak of *The Pentagon Papers*," and then "got the President so 'psyched up' over security leaks that he authorized the plumbers to plug the leaks." Other sources close to Kissinger confirmed that he had been alarmed over the *Pentagon Papers* leak, "which he feared could have disastrous consequences."

What could have been exposed in *The Pentagon Papers* to drive Dr. Kissinger to "near-hysteria" and chill him with the dread of "disastrous consequences"? Certainly there were no new facts about the Vietnam War that the public learned from publication of *The Pentagon Papers*.

What we did learn from the publication of *The Pentagon Papers*— and obviously what Kissinger so feared we would learn—was the existence of a powerful governmental conspiracy, going back to the earliest Kennedy years, and the identity of the principal conspirators, of whom all the most influential were CFR members. What Kissinger really feared was the exposure of the *purpose* of the conspiracy, and the *continuity* of the conspiratorial campaign to effect the clandestine unilateral strategic disarmament of the United States *by means of the prolongation of the Vietnam War*.

A man in Dr. Kissinger's position simply is not seized with "near-hysteria" and fear of "disastrous consequences" by the threatened publication of secret papers that establish a conspiracy carried on solely by his predecessors—unless he himself is carrying on the *same* conspiracy, for the *same* purposes.

A secret continuum—an interlocking relationship of control—had to exist between those who had controlled the two preceding

Democratic administrations and the Nixon Republican administration. The power elite exercising invisible but unchallengeable control over the national administrations of both political parties must have a continuing identity of interest—concealed from the public—that bridged the nominal changeover from Kennedy-Johnson to Nixon.

This diversion of U.S. funds away from strategic into tactical military weapons was the essential link in the Nitze-McNamara-Gilpatric plan to insure that the United States would have no rational alternative to surrender to a Soviet nuclear ultimatum. These men could then fulfill their ambition to become the greatest peacemakers in history: those who saved the world from nuclear war and successfully averted the ultimate horror of a nuclear exchange. Such a noble end, they are convinced, justifies any means—including "only" 50,000 American servicemen killed and hundreds of thousands wounded in "McNamara's war." They could hope (although not necessarily expect) that the members of the Soviet Politburo would remember them with gratitude for making an impossible task possible.

The Daniel Ellsberg group, however, was zeroing in on a completely different wave length. Because every step up the ladder of "escalation" in Vietnam involved the application of *more* U.S. military power against the Communists, the Ellsberg-Halberstam-Hoopes clique and much of the media jumped to the conclusion that the purpose was to *defeat* the Communists. The Ellsberg group, knowing nothing of how wars are fought and won, did not understand that McNamara's "escalation" applied additional power in such small doses that the enemy had the time and resources to build up its own power to counter each U.S. increment. McNamara's purpose was *not* to *win* the war, but to squander so much in military funds and resources in the Vietnam stalemate that the U.S. would rapidly fall behind the Soviets in strategic nuclear power. The greater our involvement in the tactical rathole in Vietnam, the greater the diversion of funds away from our strategic deterrent.

The Ellsbergs and the other antiwarmongers persisted in their naive belief that *The Pentagon Papers* showed that the escalation of the War meant that the McNamara "conspirators" wanted to achieve victory over the North Vietnamese Communists—despite the fact that McNamara had tried time and time again to tell these articulate CFR antiwar agitators that victory over communism was *not* the U.S. objective in Vietnam. He officially declared to the Congress of the United States that the Vietnam War "was not a crusade against communism." He officially repeated several times that we had no purpose whatever of overthrowing the Communist government of North Vietnam.

The way McNamara conducted the war was, indeed, immoral. In a phony strategy patterned after the operation of cutting off a dog's tail by inches in order to "minimize the pain," he held down U.S. escalation to a creeping pace that would drag out the stalemate and result in the maximum number of casualties. He ordered the napalming of North Vietnamese peasants drafted into the Communist army, but would permit no action that might endanger the Communist bosses in Hanoi who were guilty of the aggression. Furthermore, he would permit no action by the U.S. or South Vietnamese military that might destroy the capability of North Vietnam to continue making aggressive war, or that would impose sufficient hardship on the civilian population (such as a food shortage by destroying the dikes) to cause unrest that might result in a counterrevolution against the Communist masters.

Despite McNamara's explicit denials of any intent to win the war against the North Vietnamese Communists, despite his actions that amply supported his words, such as his strategies of "no-win" and "creeping escalation," the Ellsberg clique never understood the true objective of the Nitze-McNamara-Gilpatric plan for the unilateral strategic disarmament of the United States.

Just as they did not understand what the McNamara conspirators were really up to, the Ellsberg CFR clique did not see that Kissinger had successfully led the Nixon Administration into continuing McNamara's purpose and strategy of clandestine unilateral strategic disarmament. If the Ellsberg clique had been savvy to these machinations by their more sophisticated brother-CFR members, they would not have unleashed against the Nixon Administration their all-out antiwar efforts by legal and illegal means—which was what incited the Nixon Administration into resistance by Watergate tactics.

Thus, it was the failure of the non-clued-in clique within the CFR to comprehend the more daring and cunning motivation and machinations of the CFR unilateral-disarmament intellectuals that precipitated *The Pentagon Papers* case.

Ellsberg did not originate the absurd theory that the purpose of the McNamara-Nitze-Gilpatric conspiracy to escalate the war in Vietnam was to *win* that war against the North Vietnam Communists, but he magnified it, fleshed it out with ideologically colored assertions of his own, and, more important, sold this aberrant theory to the liberal press in the course of acting out his role of antiwar folk hero. This bizarre delusion was so repetitively injected into the public's subconscious that it totally diverted attention from speculation as to the more plausible purpose designed by the plotters.

The "conspiracy" which Ellsberg thought he had discovered in *The Pentagon Papers* appeared to him to be a plot to "escalate" the war in Vietnam. What worked *him* up to a point of near-hysteria, and to a state of mind in which he determined to break the law, was what he conceived to be the *purpose* of this escalation. He thought that the "conspirators" were attempting to *win* the war against the North Vietnamese Communists! He visualized each step up the ladder of escalation as a further move intended to bring the United States to that most "immoral" of all objectives: a military victory over any segment of the armed forces of communism. One of history's bizarre jests is that the antiwar movement, which began to mushroom in late 1969 and early 1970, was triggered by this monstrously erroneous misconception.

To determine the true purpose of the U.S. escalation in the Vietnam War, we need to ask, first, who were these conspiratorial architects of "escalation," and, second, what does the record show motivates them?

To get the answer the hard way, you may read "The Senator Gravel Edition" of *The Pentagon Papers* (Boston: Beacon Press, 1971, 4 volumes, 2,899 pages, $45). Somewhat less of an intellectual burden would be to pore through *The Pentagon Papers* as published by the *New York Times* (New York: Quadrangle, 810 pages, $15). The least financial burden, if your eyes can stand the small print, is the same title as published by Bantam Books in 677 pages at $2.25.

The *New York Times*, in order to superimpose some human interest in its 677-page fine-print paperback of *The Pentagon Papers*, entitled the book "The Secret History of the Vietnam War," and spread over the entire back cover a glossy picture of Lyndon Johnson. Encircling him are the three principal actors in that "secret history" or "conspiracy": Robert McNamara, McGeorge G. Bundy, and Dean Rusk. These three are treated in the book as the prime conspirators in engineering the escalation of U.S. involvement in Vietnam. These three are CFR members, as also were the policymakers in the next echelon of the "conspiracy": Paul Nitze and Roswell Gilpatric, Cyrus Vance and John T. McNaughton. Under Rusk was "the other Bundy," William P., and, of course, Walt W. and Eugene V. Rostow.

The best summary of what can be learned from the nearly 3,000 deadly-dull pages was given by Nicholas von Hoffman in a column carried by the *Washington Post Service* on June 17, 1971:

> Not that the thousands and thousands of pages from the Pentagon archives reveal any secrets. That Johnson is a liar, that McNamara is a liar, that Rusk, McGeorge Bundy, Rostow, Taylor, are all liars is scarcely news to anyone free from hypnotic loyalty to what's official, authoritative, and governmental. The *Times'* exposé proves the case against this knavish lot with their own papers and their own words . . . . It provides us with an exact and textured knowledge of these men's mendacity, their stupidity, their presumption.

And so they were liars, all liars. They would lie to Congress as well as to the public. In a Watergate Senate subcommittee hearing on May 15, 1973, Ellsberg testified that he personally had documents on his desk during the 1965 debate on Vietnam "which would have shown that two Cabinet Secretaries (Dean Rusk and Robert McNamara) were lying directly to Senate Committees in executive session." Instead of speaking up, Ellsberg said, "I kept my mouth shut." That must have been the last time; it has been flapping ever since.

But the "case" that von Hoffman asserts has been proved against the knavish lot, "with their own papers and their own words," was the escalation of the Vietnam War; and the means was a "conspiracy." They participated in a plot; they were all plotters. So, *The Pentagon Papers* proved that powerful conspiracies can and do exist, and that such a conspiracy did in fact exist within the government at least during the Kennedy and Johnson administrations.

Who were these "conspirators"? What they all have in common is that all were CFR members except President Johnson, and all were architects-in-chief of plans for the unilateral disarmament of the United States and appeasement of the Soviet Communists. The Bundy brothers are famous for changing the U.S. national objective from trying to assist the captive nations to win freedom, to accommodating the Soviets. McGeorge Bundy was famous for his theory that the U.S. and the U.S.S.R. would "converge." Rostow was well known for his plea for "an end to nationhood" as we now know it, so that we could all join under a global government. McNamara was famous for his repeated official testimony to Congress that the Soviet Union has neither the capability nor the intention of seeking parity with the United States in strategic power, let alone superiority.

These are the men whom Ellsberg and his associates expect us to believe plotted the escalation of the Vietnam War because they secretly desired to secure the "unconditional surrender" of the North Vietnamese Communists! Not one of these men has ever in his life even suggested, under any circumstances, that we should *defeat* communism anywhere in the world. *The Pentagon Papers* shows that the then Joint Chiefs of Staff had practicable and reliable plans to secure an early end to the war by effective bombing of North Vietnamese targets; but these targets were scissored out of recommendations to President Johnson before he saw them.

These "conspirators" did *not* want to win the war. They wanted to drag it out, to escalate it slowly, to bleed us to near-death, and to give the Soviets the time to attain decisive strategic supremacy over us. These "conspirators" had no compunction about sacrificing the lives of 50,000 American fighting men and about $140 billion to advance their plan to reduce the United States to strategic impotence vis-a-vis Soviet Russia. Daniel Ellsberg, David Halberstam, Townsend W. Hoopes, et al., displayed only their own limited perception when they failed to fathom the true purpose of McNamara's creeping escalation.

If you want to win, at the lowest cost in men and money, you go for sudden, massive escalation as recommended by the Joint Chiefs, and do not give the enemy the chance to match your additional increments of military power. If you want to prolong the war and constantly increase its cost to the United States, you go for creeping escalation: you bomb, but not vital targets; you refuse to mine the harbor; you never cut off the enemy's source of supplies.

However, commentators with widely divergent views, over a wide ideological spread from right to far left, all missed the reality of what had happened and was happening to our country as a result of the Vietnam War. The Middle Americans and the conservatives closed ranks to support the "regular" government against the attacks of the antigovernment antiwarmongers, represented by the Ellsbergs and the McGoverns, because they believed that the "regular" government still functions as the legitimate instrument of the U.S. Constitution. The solid citizens are far too trusting to understand that, for years, the "regular" government has been only a shell of the republican form of government created by the Constitution—that, over the past 40 years, members of elitist groups and cabals, primarily members of CFR, first infiltrated and then took control of all the influential policy-making positions in the government; at least those dealing with military posture, national security, international relations, and finance.

Middle Americans simply cannot believe that other Americans, elevated by the nation to positions of the highest trust, could be plotting the unilateral disarmament of the United States that would put us in a position where we would have no alternative but surrender to the Soviet Union in the face of an ultimatum threatening nuclear attack.

On the other hand, the chic left as well as the hysterical left now profess to see a terrible danger to our constitutional system in "one man-rule," in "an outright presidential rule," in the "monolithic presidential system," and in "awesome power proceeding to one man." Of course, back during the administrations of Franklin Roosevelt and John F. Kennedy, these same types of liberal ideologues were stridently campaigning for exactly what they now deplore—a "strong presidency," unhampered by a "horse and buggy" Constitution and an "unenlightened" Congress. Senator William Fulbright is an outstanding example of these double-standard liberals.

The important point they are missing, however, is that what they think is one-man rule is actually one man being ruled. Instead of the

President having captured monolithic or totalitarian power, Richard Nixon himself had been captured. John Kennedy and Lyndon Johnson were captives just as much as Richard Nixon. While small, highly selected cliques of elitists were dominant in the Kennedy and Johnson administrations, the tremendous executive power of the Nixon-Ford Administration in the areas of national security and foreign relations is controlled almost totally by one man, Henry Kissinger, who has concentrated in himself a coalition of the powers of the elitist cliques.

Why did the unilateral disarmers in the CFR (who were continuing in precise detail the McNamara-Nitze-Kissinger tactic of using the Vietnam War as a diversion to accomplish their overriding objective) permit the Ellsberg-CFR group to continue their "war" to bring down the Nixon Administration over the Vietnam War issue? Because, if the unilateral disarmers explained their Vietnam-diversion stratagem, they would risk upsetting the strategic-surrender strategy they had been implementing since 1960. The more knowledgeable and discreet "intellectuals" in CFR felt it would be unsafe to clue in the Ellsberg group. Ellsberg was a blabbermouth and might tell all, possibly on one of his visits to a psychiatrist's couch, and most probably to the press. The Nitze-McNamara-Gilpatric-Bundy-Rusk clique in the CFR could not afford to let their plan for a preemptive surrender to the Soviet Communists be interfered with by a quickie and abject surrender to the North Vietnamese Communists, or exposed too soon in the press.

Ellsberg was considered unreliable for other reasons, too. His group had had the intoxicating success of bringing Lyndon Johnson down with their antiwar activities and, since nothing succeeds like success, they were encouraged to "go for another" with Nixon. They hoped to be kingbreakers again by generating sufficient political pressure against Nixon to topple him, as well as trigger immediate and unconditional surrender to the North Vietnamese Communists.

The Pentagon Papers case thus clarified the existence of two separate and distinct cliques within the CFR. It explains how there could be a "war" between administration officials and the antiwar groups, with CFR members as the influential leaders on both sides. It demonstrates that, while the CFR is not a monolithic organization whose members are under some kind of party discipline, all CFR factions lead ultimately to some kind of surrender to the Communists somewhere in the world.

Although the Ellsberg clique never discovered the true purpose of McNamara's creeping escalation, many others did. Back in 1964 and 1965 the coauthors of this book identified the McNamara-Nitze-Gilpatric-Rostow-Bundy cabal as liars, knaves, plotters, betrayers, and conspirators. The few other critics of McNamara at that time accused him only of bungling, of making mistakes, and of arrogance in substituting his judgment for that of the Joint Chiefs and military experts. McNamara was not stupid, but brilliant; he never made mistakes, despite appearances. When he "wasted" some $11 billion on the TFX/F-111, it proved not his stupidity but his skill at deception. He was actually insuring that this $11 billion would never add a single missile to U.S. strategic power, and would deprive the United States of three generations of fighter aircraft and two generations of strategic bombers. But the $11-billion-TFX/F-111 diversion was only a good start on his master plan; the $140 billion spent on creeping escalation in Vietnam was the crowning achievement of his diversion of defense moneys into a bottomless pit so that they could not be spent on nuclear weapons to defend the United States of America against Soviet Russia.

The conclusive proof of this is provided in the answer to the question: *who* has been the principal beneficiary of U.S. participation in McNamara's war in Vietnam? By virtue of U.S. funds being diverted from strategic military power to tactical throwaways, the Soviet Union has become the greatest military power in the world. Not until the signing of the SALT I Agreements in May 1972, however, did official government statements, released by Kissinger himself, confirm the fact of Soviet strategic superiority.

Even though the fact of our military inferiority to the Soviet Union could no longer be challenged, the trusting American people and Congress refused to believe that this result had been deliberately plotted by the McNamara clique. They prefer to assume that, somehow, it "just happened." That is impossible. When McNamara took power, we had an 8-to-1 margin of strategic superiority over the Soviets, and an industrial capacity 2½ times as great—not to mention superior technology. How then, could the McNamara clique have turned over to the Soviets a sufficient margin of nuclear superiority so that our only alternatives would be nuclear destruction or abject surrender?

The Pentagon Papers did, indeed, give the answer as to their methods. Not only did the plotters impose the no-win-creeping-escalation policies on the United States, but they conspired to prevent an end to the war by a negotiated settlement. When they feared that Diem would negotiate a settlement with the Communists, his assassination was set up. They not only went to extreme lengths to keep all highest-level military plans and proposals for winning the war from the U.S. President, but they intimidated the President so that he would not approve a war-winning strategy. They effectively played upon his fears that the Soviet Union would unleash a nuclear strike against the United States if we dared to abandon the McNamara no-win policy. *The Pentagon Papers* establishes the literal truth that the Vietnam War was indeed "McNamara's War," as he once said he was proud to have it called.

Some may argue that *The Pentagon Papers* shows that, in late 1966 and 1967, McNamara began to turn "dovish" and took a position somewhat against further escalation. There are two answers to this. First, it then began to appear that if our efforts were increased, even *creeping* escalation might bring so much U.S. military power against the North Vietnamese Communists that, despite McNamara, we would end the war by a military victory. Second, by late 1966 it had become clear that the Soviet Union's buildup of strategic nuclear weapons had attained such massive momentum that they would pass the United States in 1967 and nearly double their strategic power each succeeding year, while the United States would be producing no additional strategic weapons because McNamara had choked off the input into U.S. strategic weapons pipelines back in 1962.

The great Vietnam diversion was no longer needed to hold down U.S. strategic power while the Soviets built up to decisive superiority. McNamara's ultimate purpose was to avert a nuclear exchange with the Soviets; and he planned to accomplish this by leaving us no rational alternative to surrender to the Soviets, either on demand or preemptively. Having succeeded in condemning us to strategic inferiority, he could best promote his ultimate objective by contributing to the divisive efforts of the Ellsberg hate-America-the-Communists-are-always-right campaign.

This is why McNamara ordered a study to produce *The Pentagon Papers.* The pro-Soviet liberals whom he appointed to the project could be counted on to slant the report so the United States would look as evil and arrogant as possible, and to provide ammunition for the hate-America program. The second reason McNamara ordered *The Pentagon Papers* study was to produce material that could be used for the political blackmail of Lyndon Johnson. At the time McNamara ordered the study, Johnson appeared certain to run for and win another term as President. McNamara wanted to be able to inhibit the President if and when he should decide to block McNamara from continuing the unilateral strategic disarmament of the United States —which is exactly what LBJ finally attempted by overruling McNamara and ordering the production and deployment of the Sentinel ABM for the protection of the American people.

This is why McNamara would not let his *Pentagon Papers* research staff conduct any interviews with top echelon people at either the State Department or the White House. He didn't want President Johnson personally to discover that the material was being collected, and he didn't want Dean Rusk to find out and tell him.

9

The chilling consistency of the results of every single one of the major policies Henry Kissinger has developed as czar of U.S. national security matters and foreign policy raises a question that must be answered in his own complex personality. Without exception, Kissinger's strategic defense policies have fostered and speeded Soviet attainment of a "full" or "preclusive" nuclear first-strike capability against the United States.

When Soviet strategic forces do reach this level, Henry Kissinger will have surrendered to the Kremlin not only our defenses against nuclear attack, but also our deterrent against it. We will no longer be able to restrain the Soviets from launching a nuclear strike against us, or threatening to do so, by assuring them that, if they do strike at us, we will strike back and destroy them. A full Soviet first-strike would have destroyed so many of our own retaliatory weapons that we would no longer have the capability of accomplishing even a fourth of the damage they survived so successfully in World War II—or killing half as many Russians as Stalin did. So many scores of millions of Americans would have been killed that even to attempt to use our few surviving weapons against the Soviets would be irrational as well as ineffective.

This means that the unelected ruler of the strategic destiny of the United States would have handed over to the men in the Kremlin the option to render the American people and their government Red or dead.

Why should Henry Kissinger hold this power of life or death over our nation? How did he acquire this power?

Most Americans—even the well informed, and even after Watergate —believe that only their constitutionally elected President holds this power. Theoretically, the incumbent President still does have the ultimate power of decision. Realistically, however, any President can make decisions only on the basis of intelligence estimates of the strategic situation—and the only intelligence estimates he is allowed to see are those prepared under the personal direction of, and carefully censored by, Henry Kissinger.

Thus, although the President officially *makes* the decisions—and probably *thinks* they are his own decisions—what he "decides" has been comprehensively shaped for him in advance by Dr. Kissinger.

Without exception, all the nominally-Nixon-but-realistically-Kissinger negotiations and agreements with the Kremlin have built up the prestige, the political power, and the influence of the Soviets throughout Europe. Many of the specifics in these agreements have been reached behind the backs of our NATO allies and in violation of informal commitments and promises to them. He threatens our friends and appeases our adversaries.[1] As a result, we are losing friendship, respect, and trust in NATO. This helps set up Western Europe for easy "Finlandization" by the Kremlin. Kissinger bails the Soviets out of domestic crises resulting from agricultural failures, and thus helps perpetuate and tighten the hold that the 14-million-member Soviet Communist Party has over the 250 million people of the U.S.S.R.

In the area of U.S. defense policy, Kissinger completely turned Richard Nixon around from the solemn campaign promises on which he rode into the White House. On October 24, 1968, candidate Nixon charged in a nationwide radio speech that, since 1961, when McNamara took over the Defense Department, a "gravely serious security gap" had developed that could grow to a "survival gap." Blasting what he called the "peculiar, unprecedented doctrine called 'parity,'" he promised that, if elected, he intended to "restore our objective of clearcut military superiority" and "do away with wishful thinking either as to the capability or the intent of potential enemies."

Within weeks of his appointment, Kissinger beat a retreat not only from "superiority," but even from "parity," and he coined the term "strategic sufficiency" to replace both. It soon became clear that "sufficiency" did not mean equality, or even near-equality, but was a flexible term to cover a level that is substantially inferior to the Soviet Union.

In enunciating his theory of "sufficiency," Kissinger vehemently declared that "below that level is one vast undifferentiated area of no security at all, for it serves no purpose in conflicts between nations to have been almost strong enough." Yet, in bribing the Kremlin to sign the SALT I Agreements in time for the staged television spectacular at the Moscow Summit, and in selling SALT to Congress and the American people, Kissinger abandoned every one of his own four major criteria for "strategic sufficiency." Actually, he had been at work ever since he entered office in 1969 to hold down the level of U.S. strategic power. Although Secretary of Defense Melvin Laird gave official warning to Congress in February 1969 that the Soviets "are going for a first-strike capability—there is no question about that," Kissinger influenced the President to silence the Secretary of Defense on this vital point, and to overrule his recommendation that the U.S. respond to the massive Soviet arms buildup by adding to our own strategic forces.

Instead, Dr. Kissinger persuaded the President to continue the McNamara policy of unilateral disarmament, including a freeze on the development, production, or deployment of additional U.S. missile launchers, either land-based or submarine-based. The purported purpose of extending the McNamara freeze was to create a favorable climate for negotiation of a strategic arms limitation agreement with the Soviets.

In the face of America's generous and potentially suicidal weapons restraint, the Soviets exploited the opportunity by stalling the start of negotiations for a year, and then stalling for an additional 2½ years after the formal talks began. This gave them time to multiply their strategic power by a factor of five, adding more than 1,000 strategic missile launchers to their force. This was the time period in which the Soviets built up their greatest momentum toward a first-strike capability against the United States—thanks, of course, to Dr. Kissinger's policies.

Kissinger also sold the President on an additional hold-down of U.S. strategic power that is even more clearly a betrayal of the confidence and trust of the American people, as well as cheating them on their investment in national defense. He blocked all programs and efforts— in Congress, in the Administration, and in the military—to improve either the accuracy of guidance or the explosive power of U.S. missiles. His officially declared excuse was that such improvements might appear to the Soviets to be an attempt by us to develop a first-strike capability against them.

During the years he was thus degrading U.S. strategic power, the Soviets were openly deploying hundreds of SS-9s and developing and testing their even more monstrous SS-18s. These have no purpose other than to create a first-strike capability against the United States. During this same period the Soviets also expended huge resources to improve the guidance of their missiles and increase the destructive power of their warheads. The evidence that they were doing this is that they are already experimenting with onboard celestial object sighting mechanisms, to add stellar assistance to their already advanced inertial guidance devices in their new missiles (e.g., the 5,000+-mile-range SS-N-8 missiles carried by their new Delta-class submarines). Stellar assistance will probably be added to the guidance systems of their up-graded SS-9 missiles, their new SS-18s, and their SS-17s and SS-19s. All these types will more effectively destroy U.S. missiles when aided by this greater accuracy. Development and perfection of the stellar-assistance system must have required three to five years.

During all this time the men in the Kremlin gave no indication that they were worried about what Americans would think of their obvious moves to acquire a first-strike capability against us. They knew they could count on Dr. Kissinger's doctored intelligence estimates to prevent the President from becoming concerned.

Having plunged the United States into this substantially inferior strategic position, Kissinger enshrined it for an additional five years in the SALT I Agreements. Both the SALT I Anti-Defense Treaty and the Interim Agreement, purportedly limiting some types of some offensive strategic weapon launchers, are shot through with loopholes, ambiguities, technicalities, and gross imbalances, all favoring the Soviet Union. Any or all of them can be exploited by the Soviets to complete their buildup to a first-strike capability.

Many of the most critical provisions of the SALT I Agreements were concessions made by Dr. Kissinger himself in the last climactic 20 days before they were signed—over the head and against the objections of chief U.S. arms negotiator Gerard Smith. Ambassador Smith felt so strongly that the Kissinger concessions involved potential disaster for the United States that—speaking for the entire U.S. delegation—he insisted on including in the official record a warning to Congress and the American people. Thus, in Noteworthy Unilateral Statement A, it declares that the Interim Agreement is so strongly tilted against the United States that

> If an agreement providing for more complete strategic offensive arms limitations were not achieved within 5 years, U.S. supreme interests could be jeopardized. Should that occur, it would constitute a basis for withdrawal from the ABM Treaty.

That is rather strong language for six long-term-career disarmament-at-nearly-any-price buffs. Their warning went on to recite that an objective of the SALT II negotiations "should be to constrain and reduce on a long-term basis threats to the survivability of our respective strategic retaliatory forces."

Since—thanks to the Kissinger policies—we have absolutely no offensive weapons similar to the SS-9 and SS-18 25-to-50+-megaton missiles with which to threaten Soviet retaliatory forces, nor sufficient accuracy, explosive power, or numbers of other types of missiles to threaten them, the U.S. retaliatory forces are the only forces really threatened. Ambassador Smith's expression is diplomatic jargon which, at the same time, expresses and conceals the fact that the SALT I Interim Agreement did *not* constrain the threat to the survivability of *our* retaliatory force. That is to say, the SALT I Agreement left the way open for the Soviets to complete their buildup to a first-strike capability against us—again at Kissinger's insistence and on his sole authority.

Unfortunately, Congress, totally deceived by Kissinger's false statements about the alleged advantages of the SALT I Agreements, and under the hypnotic spell of his sophisticated eloquence, failed to heed the warning. Even though the ambassador's warning fell short of its purpose, such lese majesty against Kissinger's authority was a crime to be punished as severely as possible without exposing the true facts. Ambassador Smith was quietly fired, not only as chief of the U.S. SALT delegation, but even from his post as head of the U.S. Arms Control and Disarmament Agency. The public was told merely that his "resignation" had been accepted, and the nearest the press came to divulging the truth was the "speculation" that "Smith was unhappy at some of the intrusions of Presidential Assistant Henry A. Kissinger in the negotiations on the first strategic arms agreement."[2]

The supreme irony of the Smith affair culminated in a presidential statement revealing how far out of touch with reality Richard Nixon was:

> President Nixon believes that Ambassador Smith should take great personal pride and satisfaction that he played so critical a part in *one of the most important diplomatic achievements of all times.*

Thus, Smith's sacrifice of his career, influence, and prestige was not only denigrated, but his vindictive dismissal was exploited as a vehicle for extolling the very national suicide-trap he attempted to warn against.

Henry M. Jackson, one of the Senators best qualified to evaluate the SALT I negotiations, also characterized the U.S. SALT I position as "one of unimpeded deterioration." Explaining to our NATO allies, in November 1972, how it happened that we gave away so much, he revealed that we negotiated not in terms of an overall U. S. strategic objective, but rather in terms of what we believed would be acceptable to the Soviet Union!

> Negotiability became the central criterion by which much of what we thought and proposed and planned was evaluated. This is foolishness.
>
> To discard in advance propositions that are meritorious but believed to be unacceptable to the other side is to abandon the effort to persuade the adversary of the wisdom of one's position—to say nothing of abandoning the effort to influence.[3]

No concerned American, however, should take anyone else's

opinion about the magnitude and imminence of the danger to our national survival posed by the SALT I Agreements and the Kissinger policies related to them. What trapped us in our present highly vulnerable position is that too many people who were under obligation to form their own opinions on the basis of hard evidence (e.g., the President, Congress, the Joint Chiefs of Staff, and the media) accepted Kissinger's slick sales pitch without checking the true facts.

This book presents the facts, the documentation, and the evidence that should have been examined by responsible Americans. They are ultimately intertwined with the personality and influence of Henry Kissinger, and they have the suspense of a whodunit—except that the mystery is not *who* did it, but *why* he did it.

In search of an answer to that question, we have considered Kissinger's relationship with the Council on Foreign Relations and its most influential elite groups. Certainly CFR has been one of Kissinger's most important power bases and has shaped his ideology and his loyalties, personal and intellectual. But he has also been associated with another elitist group that is far more mysterious to Americans, even to some of its American members. Just as Kissinger "owes" CFR and its influential cliques, he is equally indebted to this other elite.

He owes to this other group all his major theories on nuclear strategy and the nature and significance of strategic military power. We are not talking here about the window-dressing type of theories in which he clothes his negotiations with Peking and Moscow, such as the "pentagonal equilibrium" or the "subtle triangular relationship." We are talking about his *action* policies—his actual grandiose strategy that he has substituted for the former national security policies of the United States—that have reversed the basic defense policies of the United States.

The Pugwash penetration is the Soviet Politburo's most brilliant creation in psychological warfare. Not since the Trojan horse has there been such an imaginative, yet practical, instrument for conquest by trickery and subversion, as well as for essential espionage on a legal and respectable mass-production basis.

The Pugwash movement derives its cover of respectability from the fact that it appears to be the spontaneous creation of scientists from several nations—but primarily from the United States and the U.S.S.R.—who were inspired to promote international cooperation and exchange of information, and who were primarily concerned with discussing "the nuclear menace and means for avoiding it." The leading organizer was the late Bertrand Russell. There is much evidence that his truncated and tricky credo, "rather Red than dead," has served as the motto of the movement. That is the text of the slogan as it is popularly known; actually, the Pugwashers behave as if their slogan were "rather Red than take *any risk* of becoming dead," which is not the same thing at all and is vastly more likely to be fatal to freedom.

The first Pugwash Conference was hosted and bankrolled in 1957 by Cyrus Eaton at his home in Pugwash, Nova Scotia, whence the name of the group originated. More than 20 principal conferences have been held since then, most of them outside the United States. Most of the proceedings have been conducted in secret and kept secret—although full reports are always submitted to the Soviet Government. The Sixth Conference, held in Moscow in 1960, was critical in charting the course for future activities of the scientist members.

Nikita Khrushchev, then at the peak of his dictatorial power, personally addressed that meeting. Only two months later, in his most famous speech on the Communist movement, he laid out in Aesopian language the political version of long-range Soviet strategic war plans for development of a capability to destroy the United States without incurring unacceptable retaliatory damage, and for ultimate use of that capability. To achieve Soviet goals, he explained, the United States would have to be substantially disarmed, and this was to be accomplished by mobilizing "the people" to apply "growing *pressure* on the imperialist governments."

Khrushchev then provided a veiled description of the scientific pressure with which the Politburo had established contact, or more accurately, that it had molded for the purpose:

> Lenin pointed to the need of establishing contacts with those circles of the bourgeoisie which gravitate toward pacifism, "be it even of the palest hue." In the struggle for peace, he said, we should not overlook the saner representatives of the bourgeoisie.
>
> The soundness of these words is confirmed by current events . . . There are . . . among the *ruling circles* of these countries those who know the danger to capitalism of a new war. . . . The Socialist countries . . . promote *personal contact* between statesmen of the socialist and capitalist countries.

Small wonder that the then President John Kennedy described this Khrushchev landmark speech as "a Red blueprint for eventual world domination." The U.S. Pugwash conferees meet all of Khrushchev's specifications for the most effective segment of the people to apply growing pressure on the U.S. ["capitalist"] Government: most of them not only "gravitate toward pacifism" but are pacifists of the most virulent type: nuclear pacifists. They certainly would qualify as being among U.S. "ruling circles."

President Eisenhower warned the nation, in his Farewell Address on January 17, 1961, of the *"danger that public policy could itself become the captive of a scientific-technological elite."* At the time his warning was sounded it could not be proved that the Pugwash movement would attempt any such grandiose program, or that it could possibly usurp the power required to accomplish it. Now we have more than 12 years of conclusive proof. During that critical period, every major change in U.S. strategic doctrine, in U.S. strategic posture, in weapons development and deployment, in nuclear testing, and in the nature and power of the U.S. strategic deterrent, originated with or was actively supported by U.S. Pugwash conferees.

This scientific and technological elite has indeed made a captive of U.S. public policy governing national security and nuclear defenses. The chief jailer of the captive is Pugwash conferee Henry Kissinger. Under his direction of U.S. defense programs a major Pugwash objective can be enshrined into official national defense policy within a matter of weeks—instead of the five to 10 years formerly required for implementation.

There would be nothing wrong with U.S. defense policies originating with a conference of scientists, or in the scientists lobbying the Government, *if* their policies favored the United States, or even, perhaps, if they were neutral, or promoted *bilateral* disarmament. Unfortunately, all their major programs have disadvantaged the United States vis-a-vis the Soviet Union in all areas of strategic nuclear power. Sometimes they are even nationally suicidal in nature, such as their most recent *cause célèbre*: a drive to block the United States from adopting a strategy of launch-on-confirmation-of-warning that a Soviet missile attack is actually underway. This is the *only* method of preventing the destruction of our Minuteman missile force by the Soviet SS-9/SS-18 force designed exclusively for that purpose. Adoption of such a strategy would prevent the Soviets from attaining a preclusive first-strike capability against the United States at least until their half-again-larger-than-ours nuclear missile submarine force, permitted them by the SALT I Interim Agreement, attains a pin-down capability against our Minuteman missile force.

The Pugwash conferees are against this strategy because it would buy the United States time to rebuild our deterrent against the Soviet threat. Their "cover" argument is that such a strategy would degrade "crisis stability." The practical meaning of the crisis-stability doctrine is that, when subjected to actual nuclear attack, the United States should practice "restraint"; that is, do nothing until it is too late to do anything. They ignore the fact that failure to adopt the launch-on-confirmation-of-warning strategy may well shorten the life span of the United States and the American people by, say, three years: three years that, if used intelligently and courageously, could give us a new lease on national life and freedom past the year 2000.

A staff study of the first six Pugwash conferences was issued by the U.S. Senate Internal Security Subcommittee in 1961. Looking back, it is fascinating to see that this study pinpointed precisely the purpose of the conferences. Here, for example, are excerpts from several of the study's many similar findings:

> . . . The Soviet delegation to the Pugwash conferences sought to impose on the American scientist-delegates a form of international discipline superior to the obligations of the American scientists to their own government . . .
>
> The Soviet delegation sought to exercise ideological leadership at the Pugwash conferences.
>
> From the viewpoint of Soviet interests, the Pugwash conferences served as an organic part of their cold war design to discredit American nuclear policy and accredit Soviet nuclear policy within the United States and throughout the world.

Looking back, it is now perfectly clear that the Pugwash influence, reinforced by the leverage of interlocking membership with the most influential cliques of the CFR, not only successfully discredited the preexisting American nuclear policy of superiority, but actually destroyed it. With the advent to White House power of Henry Kissinger, Pugwash conferee and member of the Pugwash-sponsored "Joint U.S.-U.S.S.R. Study Group on Disarmament," the former policy of insuring peace *and* freedom through U.S. military strength was replaced by the policy of so-called "nuclear sufficiency." This fulfilled at last the long-range objective that the Pugwash movement had pursued for 15 years: a U.S. nuclear strategy based not on the survival needs of the United States, but upon what would best "accommodate" (that is, appease) the Soviets.

This point is expressly admitted in the Kissinger-prepared Nixon-delivered *State of the World Report* of February 25, 1971, in which the "Doctrine of Strategic Sufficiency" is defined as "defensive in essence" and as permitting the United States only such "numbers, characteristics, and deployments of our forces which the Soviet Union cannot reasonably interpret as being intended to threaten a disarming attack." Within two pages of this abject appeasement, the same *State of the World Report* admitted that there was strong evidence that the Soviets were building strategic weapons systems far past "the level needed for deterrence" in *numbers*, and that the *nature* of the forces "could be uniquely suitable for a first-strike against our land-based deterrent forces."

With such serious and timely warnings, why didn't somebody do something to protect our country from this Soviet-designed, Soviet-oriented penetration at the highest levels of our government? The answer to this question is that the Pugwash penetration is a classic, if tragic, example of the famous quotation from the now-four-centuries-old but still true indictment of the pusillanimity of human nature:

Treason doth never prosper, what's the reason?
For if it prosper, none dare call it treason.[4]

The Pugwash penetration has indeed prospered and proliferated in the United States. Although the first five conferences were totally divorced from any official sanction by the U.S. Government, the Sixth, in 1960, had informal approval, and the Pugwash conferences subsequent to the Sixth have had express official approval and endorsement. As far back as 1964 a series of subconferences was instituted to expand the reach of the movement; these proceedings, like those of the principal conferences, were largely held secret. In 1967, an additional expansion was undertaken with the institution of a series of "International Pugwash Symposia." By 1971, 10 of these symposia had been held with the declared purpose of "bringing into the Pugwash 'movement' a much larger representation of the younger generation of scientists."

In contrast to the secrecy enshrouding most Pugwash activities, the proceedings of the symposia are published in order to extend their propaganda effect. Publication is by the MIT Press, and financial support now comes from tax-free foundations instead of primarily from Cyrus Eaton. Here is an example of the slush published in the proceedings of the Tenth Symposium:

War propaganda and calls for aggression are formal pretexts for developing work on armaments and block talks on disarmament.

Aggression and war propaganda are alien to the Soviet people. From the very first days of its existence, the Soviet state has fought for peace and establishment of neighborly relations with all states and for the adoption by all states of a policy of coexistence of states with different social orders. In our country, war propaganda is prohibited by law. In our country there are no people or groups of people whose welfare and prosperity depend upon the manufacture of armaments, on the activities of war industries. That is why our government can so easily make such decisions—it is not under pressure of those who are keenly interested in manufacturing armaments.

At the same time, in a number of countries in the capitalist world, especially in highly developed countries, there have emerged powerful groups of manufacturers of arms that are particularly interested in their production.

That little gem of dishonesty was part of a highly emotional conclusion of a presentation by Vasily S. Emelyanov, chairman of the Disarmament Commission of the U.S.S.R. Academy of Sciences. It illustrates how "objective" an attitude the Soviet delegates take at Pugwash conferences. This is the kind of "scholarship" and interchange of information that U.S. tax-free foundations are delighted to finance and the MIT Press publishes. It is too bad, however, that the six distinguished U.S. scientists who edited the proceedings for the MIT Press did not append a list of the states with which the Soviet Union has been so "neighborly" during the last few years, such as Poland, East Germany, Hungary, and Czechoslovakia. It is too bad that, during the course of the symposium, they did not put on the record a single good word for the United States.

The subject of the Tenth International Pugwash Symposium was "Impact of New Technologies on the Arms Race." Included in the oral presentations and recorded in the "Pugwash Monograph" of the proceedings was a lecture by D. G. Hoag, entitled "Ballistic-Missile Guidance." Did he say anything that was classified Top Secret? We don't know, and it would take a technical expert in a highly specialized scientific area to tell. But he certainly *could* have, because he is the director of the Apollo Guidance and Navigation Program.

The total Apollo program is estimated to have cost the United States something like $25 billion. A very substantial part of that must have been invested in research and development of guidance and navigational equipment. Even figuring out the course the Apollo spacecraft should take is impressively complex—let alone the equipment necessary to guide and navigate the craft on course. Take the adventurous case of the aborted moon mission of Apollo 13. It took the NASA computer 84 minutes to determine the correct trajectory for the return to earth. It would have taken the 220 people in the NASA Planning and Analysis Division about 47 centuries to compute it manually. That type of computer equipment is what we are now giving to the Soviets under Dr. Kissinger's trade and technology agreements.

In his speech, Dr. Hoag asserted that existing weapons are at least as accurate as 1,000 meters and,

> I further estimate that present technology is easily capable of achieving far better accuracy. Miss at the target of 30 meters or less CEP at ICBM ranges can be developed.

His paper devotes 80 tightly written pages to explaining exactly how to go about this and estimates that it would take until 1980 to reach such incredible accuracy. But the Soviets do not need to attain anything like that to be able to demand our surrender. If they could do only 1/15 that well—that is, reduce their former 1,000-meter CEP to 500 meters—it would give the 5-megaton multiple warheads of their SS-9 missile force a single-shot kill probability of 99 percent against our Minuteman missiles in their silos. Without adding a single launcher to the force they had at the time of the signing of SALT I in May 1972, they would have the capability of killing 95 percent of our total Minuteman missile force.

Perhaps the Soviets already knew everything Dr. Hoag related in his paper, including our experience in locating the causes of guidance error and the steps to correct such errors, but since they had no program equivalent to our Apollo, and since they then were still lagging notoriously behind us in computer technology, the chances are against it. In 1970, when Dr. Hoag delivered his paper in the presence of five Soviet representatives holding official positions subject to the Politburo, the Soviets did not have any missiles with stellar-assisted inertial guidance and had not even tested any such guidance. Dr. Hoag's dissertation included a section entitled "In-Flight Star Tracking To Improve Accuracy" in which he lays out the entire theory involved, what errors can be corrected, what errors should be avoided, whether to use two stars or only one, and which stars to select to improve a missile's CEP. That was in June 1970. In January 1973 it was reliably reported that the Soviets had tested missiles with inertial guidance, and most probably with stellar assistance.

Probably a coincidence. There is no proof that Dr. Hoag disclosed any classified material to the Soviets. There was no official representative of the U.S. Government at the Pugwash Symposium to check on security matters, but the Hoag paper may possibly have been cleared prior to its presentation. However, the point is that most of the proceedings of the more than 20 principal Pugwash conferences have been kept secret, and even the limited publication that is permitted for public consumption is always carefully edited by Pugwashers. Usually more than half the 20 or so American scientists attending have held Top Secret clearances and have had access to the most sensitive nuclear and strategic secrets existing in our government.

In addition to the formal Pugwash proceedings, there have always been the social activities connected with them that afford special opportunities. Khrushchev stressed the value of "personal contact" with groups from U.S. "ruling circles" that were to be used to "pressure" the U.S. imperialist government toward disarmament. This tactic has worked very well, indeed, even with the most influential U.S. Pugwash conferees. Conference participants have given us a few enlightening fragments, such as Walt Rostow's statement in his address to the Sixth Conference in Moscow in 1960:

> Trust is easy to develop between individual men who can talk and eat and drink together and look into each other's eyes.

Can you imagine some of the U.S. Pugwash participants looking deep into the eyes of the Soviet delegates—and telling all? Or, at least, all they knew that the Soviets needed to know? After a few drinks—and in private quarters? Suppose one or two of the U.S. conferees secretly wanted to surrender to the Soviet Union? Or suppose a member or two happened to have "gay" tendencies such as have surfaced—from time to time—up to the Under Secretarial level in the State Department? Such a possibility cannot be discounted. Supreme Court Justices William O. Douglas and Abe Fortas wrote in a Supreme Court opinion on May 22, 1967:

> It is common knowledge that in this century homosexuals have risen high in our own public service—both in Congress and in the Executive Branch.

The revolutionary advantages in espionage and subversion afforded by the Pugwash penetration over previous traditional methods is best appreciated by a comparison. An espionage agent formerly had to resort to involved circumlocutory procedures to get a microdot of information from his contact. He had to resort to a variety of evasive tactics on his way to a "dead drop." Most of all, the penetration and espionage agents had to face enormous risks and personal penalties if caught and prosecuted.

There are numerous authoritatively backgrounded spy novels available, but the best of the past few years is the one by a former U.S. agent who was nearly top echelon for 15 years. His publishers claim that the CIA obtained a court injunction to stop him from publishing "what he hopes and fears about the Agency," but that this action came too late to block publication in 1971 of his novel, The Rope Dancer. As described by the Saturday Review, this book is

> A novel of espionage as intricate in the plotting as a chess match between two grand masters. Victor Marchetti is a former CIA operative, and his facts are convincing enough to make one hope this story is fiction.

The reason for the Saturday Review's pious hope that Marchetti's book is fiction, is his revelation that the Agency has been penetrated by Soviet agents up to the very highest level. The story in the book is indeed fiction, the motivation of the principal character is incredible, and the plot is stupid. But the book, overall, is exciting because it rings true with the author's personal convictions about the CIA, its inner workings, its vulnerability to Soviet penetration, and his realistic description of the peculiar character of many individuals who have long filled the higher echelons of the Agency.

In addition to basing his conclusions on what he knows personally about CIA personnel, policies, and infighting, Marchetti is impressed with the mass of circumstantial evidence that every major estimate and recommendation about pivotal national policy made by, or originating in, the very highest levels of the CIA, ever since its creation, has fostered action that has advantaged the Soviet Union and disadvantaged the United States. Thus, this cloak-and-dagger intelligence expert's longtime observations coincide with those of objective students of nuclear strategy.

For the last decade or so, every estimate emanating from the U.S. intelligence community, especially from the CIA, has understated by large margins the strategic posture and overall force levels of the Soviet Union. For every year from 1962 through 1973, these intelligence estimates served to justify the cutting down and holding down of U.S. strategic force levels, and to preserve the serene overconfidence and apathy of the American people. They have also deceived four successive U.S. Presidents.

But these false and deceptive intelligence estimates have not always been *underestimates* of Soviet strategic forces. From 1956 through 1962 the Soviets were relatively so weak that they needed to create an image of vastly greater power than they actually possessed or even could attain for many years. The "bomber gap," which allegedly stretched from the mid-50s to the late 50s, was a fictional creation of U.S. intelligence. So also was the great missile-gap-that-never-was that supposedly yawned open from 1960 through 1964, and that Dr. Kissinger declared we would be helpless to close even if we resorted to a crash program. Whatever fabrication might be needed in U.S. intelligence estimates to advance Soviet interests and disadvantage U.S. interests has always been supplied—year after year after year. By their facile creation of fictitious "gaps" in the early years, they built up a "cry wolf too often" immunity in the American people toward the real gap that now threatens our survival.

What is especially relevant here is a discussion of some of the many ways in which the Pugwash penetration excels the traditional cloak-and-dagger methods. Soviet clandestine penetration of the CIA would have to have started before there was any CIA as such, back in the days of the World War II OSS, in order to climb to the highest echelons. Cover would have to be preserved year after dangerous year. Counterespionage efforts would have to be blunted and smeared, year after year. Then there are always the imponderables, such as a single unpredictable piece of bad luck blowing a near-perfect cover. The sheer task of contacting "control" or other communications carriers over the years is always a source of endless and risky rigmarole.

Most important, the procedures possible under the Pugwash penetration style of espionage and subversion *obviate all risk* to the individuals. The transmission belts provided by Pugwash procedures eliminate all need for circuitous and clandestine methods of conveying information. Neither the formal nor informal social contacts of the U.S. conferees with Iron Curtain representatives have ever been subjected to U.S. security precautions. Also, there have been so many individuals involved from time to time on both sides—more than 100 from the United States and about half that number from the Soviet Union—that, even if it were discovered that certain specific U.S. secrets had come into possession of the Soviets, it would be impossible to trace them to their source. Pugwash conferees have insulated themselves very well from any danger of prosecution for espionage or violation of U.S. security laws or regulations.

Pugwash conferees are particularly adept at logrolling to advance their own careers, influence, and job security. They hire and promote each other in governmental, university, foundation, and scientific organizations. Their Pugwash credentials identify them as like-minded with the most influential cliques in the scientific and intellectual elites that have long controlled U.S. defense and foreign policy.

Who are these influential U.S. scientists who over the years have participated in the Pugwash movement? The list reads like a "who's who" in American science. Some are patriotic Americans as well as distinguished scientists. The most influential and most numerous members, however, are those who have supported nuclear disarmament movements [unilateral, if necessary], accommodation with the Soviet Union, and surrender of national sovereignty to an all-powerful supranational one-world government. Thus, Walt Whitman Rostow, in summarizing the conclusions of the Moscow Pugwash Conference of 1960, expressed the objective agreed upon by the U.S. conferees:

> The maximum objective is a new system of relations among states based on general and complete disarmament with strict international control.

What they mean, although they seldom express it overtly, is that the authority exercising the "international control" would have overwhelming strategic and military supremacy, so that its "enforcement" powers could not be challenged by any state.

The danger to the survival of the United States from the activities of the U.S. Pugwashers is that all their specific programs allegedly designed to promote the ideal of "general and complete disarmament" have resulted in disarming only the United States, while promoting the Soviet Union's buildup of the massive strategic nuclear power that will soon enable it to become the "control" authority over the entire world.

Thus, proposals made in the Pugwash conferences as far back as 1960 by that most influential of all U.S. scientists in the 1960-1968 timeframe, Jerome B. Wiesner, Science Adviser to Presidents Kennedy and Johnson, anticipate some of Henry Kissinger's programs by as much as 12 years. At a time when the United States possessed an 8-to-1 strategic nuclear superiority over the Soviet Union, he proposed that we should seek to establish parity as a system of mutual deterrence. The United States had attained a huge superiority in strategic bombers, but he asserted that bombers were obsolete, and that missiles should be made "the favorite weapon for planning deterrent systems." He also asserted that there was no need for further nuclear testing. After the Soviets had betrayed the nuclear test ban in 1961, he persuaded President Kennedy to abide by this Pugwash objective and not carry out additional comprehensive test programs to regain the lead the Soviets had stolen from us by their surprise abrogation of the ban. Most important, at the Moscow Pugwash Conference in 1960 he proposed the measure that Henry Kissinger finally put over on an unsuspecting President and American people in the Moscow SALT I Anti-Defense Treaty of 1972:

> If it appears possible to develop one [a highly effective anti-missile defense system], the agreements [to be made with the Soviets] should explicitly prohibit the development and deployment of such systems.

The achievement of that objective took 12 years, but persistent Pugwashers never give up.

Sometimes, however, they put across a program in a few weeks. At the Eleventh Conference, in Dubrovnik, Yugoslavia in September 1963, Working Group #5 recommended "a declaration by the heads of state of the United States, the Soviet Union, and other nations that they will not place nuclear weapons in orbiting satellites." This was almost immediately picked up and included in the United Nations Outer Space Treaty in a form that enabled the Soviet Union to establish a monopoly in space weapons systems capabilities. Even the Pugwash language was followed: only the actual orbiting of weapons of mass destruction was prohibited by the UN Treaty. This permitted the Soviets to go ahead with developing and testing orbital and fractional orbital bombardment systems, as well as producing and stockpiling them. As they explained triumphantly, the treaty in no way banned these activities, but only the actual placing in orbit of weapons with nuclear warheads mounted.

The same wording, on the other hand, enabled McNamara to block all U.S. development, testing, and production of such systems on the ground that we were complying with the "spirit" of the UN treaty. At the same time, however, in his usual role as apologist for the Soviet Union, he approved and declared that the Soviet activities in violating the "spirit" of the treaty were perfectly legal.

The Space Treaty is a perfect illustration of the Pugwash technique: pressure on the U.S. Government to adopt a Pugwash-initiated proposal that, in theory, provides no advantage to either side—but that all Pugwashers and their intellectual and scientific confreres realize will, in practice, benefit the Soviets vis-a-vis the United States.

In addition to the Pugwashers already mentioned who have been decisively influential presidential advisers (Kissinger, Wiesner, and Rostow), George B. Kistiakowski, the Science Adviser to President Eisenhower, began participation in the movement in 1963 and was still a leading spirit in expanding its activities in 1971. Fondly known to members of the unilateral disarmament cliques as "Kisti," he earned his spurs with the Pugwashers by joining with Eisenhower's first Science Adviser, CFR member James Killian, Jr., in selling the President on plunging into the Soviet-promoted test-ban arrangement in 1958.

Pugwash conferees also hold other types of pivotally influential positions from which U.S. strategic posture and military strength can effectively be sabotaged. For example, among the remarks of John B. Phelps at the Sixth Conference was this gem:

> I happen to believe that the ultimate goal toward which we must work is the substantial elimination of *national* armaments.

Not surprisingly, Phelps attained a key postion to work on the elimination of U.S. national armaments: by the time of the Tenth Conference in September 1962, he had been appointed to the staff of the Institute for Defense Analysis. Known as IDA, this "private" organization was and still is engaged in conducting "studies" of U.S. defense policies and weapons systems. Two of IDA's most notorious publications, both written in 1963, were the *Phoenix Study* and *Study Fair*, the recommendations of which were so fantastically suicidal for the United States that few serious people could believe they were not hoaxes.

Professor J. P. Ruina participated in the Tenth Pugwash Conference in 1962 and, by the time of the Twelfth Conference in 1964, in which he also participated, he had been appointed president of IDA. At that time, IDA was holding $5 to $10 million a year in contracts for defense "studies." The so-called "private" nature of IDA was a corporate fiction designed to evade Civil Service ceilings on the pay and classification of disarmament advocates. Because IDA operated on a government "contract," its employees were not limited by the U.S. Civil Service pay scale. Professor Ruina was still an active participant in Pugwash projects as late as the Tenth International Pugwash Symposium in 1970.

Mention any agency in the U.S. Government that has the power to accelerate the unilateral disarmament of the United States, and influential Pugwash alumni will be found therein. For example, F. A. Long, who was Assistant Director for Science for the U.S. Arms Control and Disarmament Agency prior to mid-1963, presented two papers at the Eleventh Conference in September of that year that were touted as representing "one of the glories of the Pugwash concept" because of his "fresh government involvement" in the disarmament field. He is one of the numerous Pugwash conferees who is also a CFR member. Henry Kissinger and Jerome Wiesner, who also have overlapping memberships, are the most influential dual-members.

In addition to the massive influence attained by the Pugwash movement through placing its devotees in official U.S. Government agencies with policymaking power over defense and foreign relations matters, incalculable amounts of pressure are exerted through their appointment as "consultants" to such agencies. The more sensitive agencies keep their consultant lists confidential, but some information becomes available from private sources. Take, for example, the blurb on the dust cover of Henry Kissinger's 1965 CFR-published book, *The Troubled Partnership*. It states that "he has been a consultant to several governmental agencies including the National Security Council, the United States Arms Control and Disarmament Agency, the Weapons Systems Evaluation Group of the Joint Chiefs of Staff, and others."

An additional source of influence and pressure on the U.S. Government to disarm unilaterally comes from participation of the Pugwash members in projects sponsored and bankrolled by the large tax-free foundations. One outstanding example that surfaced briefly for public view, but was soon again covered in secrecy, was the so-called "Joint U.S.-U.S.S.R. Study Group on Disarmament." The Ford Foundation put up $325,000 to get it started in June 1964, and—for the convenience of the Harvard-MIT Axis—the first meeting was held in Boston. The meetings were to be informal, unofficial, and conducted in a "relaxed but serious working atmosphere."

Every single member of the U.S. discussion team had participated in one or more Pugwash conferences, all of which, prior to 1964, had been held outside the United States. Members included Paul Doty, Harvard (who is still active in the movement); Marshal Shulman, CFR; Donald Brennan, CFR; Louis Sohn, Harvard; David Frisch, MIT; and Henry A. Kissinger. Those were the names listed in contemporaneous newspaper accounts. The Pugwash movement's own newsletter, however, added four additional famous names, which perhaps were not released to the press because they had already actually held, or were slated for, policy-making positions in the U.S. Government: George Kistiakowski, F. A. Long, J. P. Ruina, and Jerome Wiesner.

Mere membership in the Pugwash movement, attendance at formal

185

Pugwash conferences, or participation in informal Pugwash study groups (as described above) or in International Pugwash Symposia, is certainly not evidence of having betrayed U.S. national security interests. Participation by Henry Kissinger and other influential U.S. scientists and intellectuals in secret and informal disarmament discussions with the Soviets back in 1964 is, for example, no evidence that they were planning to sell out U.S. interests.

Nor could it be *conclusively* proved, down through the years from the call issued in 1955 by "The Parliamentary Association for World Government" for the "Conferences on Science and World Affairs" (COSWA), which led to the formation of the Pugwash movement in 1957, that it is primarily a Kremlin instrument for influencing U.S. defense and foreign policy. There is, however, much circumstantial evidence of pervasive Soviet and pro-Soviet control of Pugwash programs and objectives.

The U.S. Senate Internal Security Subcommittee's staff analysis published in 1961 does a comprehensive and persuasive job of documenting both Soviet *official* influence overtly exerted on the Pugwash movement, and the influence exerted on it through pro-Soviet Americans. Entitled *The Pugwash Conferences*, this analysis required 139 tightly written pages of fine print and is still for sale by the U.S. Government Printing Office for 40¢. An equivalent job cannot be done in fewer pages. The study states *and proves* that Soviet participation in the Pugwash movement was totally controlled by the Soviet Academy of Sciences, and that the academy in turn is totally an arm of the Soviet Government. The study tells us that Dr. Aleksandr V. Topchiev, Vice President of the Soviet Academy of Sciences, was the leading Soviet representative in the formation of the Pugwash movement and the Soviet keynoter for the first 10 conferences. More important, the study documents the fact that, in the thin guise of a scientist, he was really the Communist Commissar of Soviet Scientists. He owed his success and position in the ruling Soviet circles to his ability to make Soviet scientists into willing, effective, and even enthusiastic tools of the Soviet Politburo. Under his stern administration, every Soviet scientist became first of all a "soldier of the Soviet Union," and a scientist only after that—never an independent individual.

The more enthusiastic U.S. Pugwash conferees affectionately and deliberately called him Dr. Top Chief and, indeed, that was his relation to them: he set the ideological parameters of the conferences and imposed discipline. The researchers for the Senate staff study took the trouble to dig into the Top Chief's record, and it was revealing. When he was chosen as First Secretary of the U.S.S.R. Academy of Sciences, he made one thing perfectly clear: he detested the scientists and intellectuals of the reactionary imperialist nations, especially the United States. He demanded that the scientists of the Soviet Union become ideological and political activists:

> Our scientists cannot and must not stand aside from the ideological struggle between communism and capitalism. Some scientific workers try mechanically to extend to the field of ideology the slogan of peaceful coexistence of states with different social and economic systems. . . . This is what our ideological adversaries want; namely, the ideological disarming of Soviet science. . . . Any indefiniteness, neutrality, or an apolitical stand, which V. I. Lenin constantly opposed, is now more than ever intolerable in our midst. It is our duty to be active fighters for our Marxist-Leninist ideology.

The intellectually soft, naive and egocentric scientists from the United States were no match for the professional propagandists, politicos, and conspirators of Soviet scientific circles under Topchiev's able and determined leadership. Many of them even seemed to find a perverted satisfaction in the bullying methods and pressuring to which they were subjected by their Soviet confreres—or, more accurately, comrades.

The Senate Internal Security Subcommittee's staff study also gives a detailed picture of the Americans who enthusiastically contributed to establishing Pugwash influence in this country. It details how Cyrus Eaton donated some $100,000 to finance the first five Pugwash conferences—until the movement gained enough momentum to attract financing by the big tax-free foundations. It documents comprehensively his anti-U.S., pro-U.S.S.R. bias, and how he earned the Lenin Peace Prize. It is difficult to overemphasize Eaton's importance in developing the Pugwash movement.

The other most enthusiastic promoter of more power for Pugwash, Dr. Linus Carl Pauling, added greatly to the scientific and academic prestige of the movement. His list of honorary degrees and honors, including the Nobel Prize in chemistry, is surpassed in length only by the list of Communist fronts that he has belonged to or supported. He is a full member of the U.S.S.R. Academy of Sciences. In 1958 he circulated a petition against nuclear testing to be signed by the "scientists of the world" and somehow obtained the signatures of 216 prominent Soviet scientists. This added greatly to the Pugwash effort in pressuring President Eisenhower into the first nuclear-test-ban trap into which the Soviets tricked us in 1958, and which they betrayed in 1961 (in President Kennedy's words) by "protracted preparations and a surprise abrogation."

Commissar Topchiev was always lecturing the American conferees on their guilt in the creation of the terrible nuclear weapons, and their corresponding moral obligation to bring about the destruction of the evil weapons—or at least the destruction of U.S. weapons and delivery systems. One method to meet this obligation, described and documented by the Internal Security Subcommittee study, was the formation of offshoot organizations from the Pugwash movement. The Tenth Conference laid down guidelines for "educating politicians" through creation of propaganda and political lobbying organizations.

Thus, in 1962, the late Dr. Leo Szilard, a brilliant scientist and a charming and imaginative writer, but totally captivated by Pugwash ideology, founded the Council for a Livable World. Other U.S. Pugwashers joined him on the board of directors: Jerome Frank of Johns Hopkins, Mathew Meselson of Harvard, and B. T. Feld of MIT (the American with the best attendance record at conferences and symposia).

The very name of this unilateral nuclear disarmament lobbying organization reveals one of the most effective propaganda devices: build a "good" reaction into the name. Who, for example, could declare himself against a group working for "a livable world"? Some of its specific action programs, however, reveal its real objectives: e.g., "press the United States Government to maintain its position against deploying an antimissile defense system and urge the Soviet Union not to deploy one" (this sounds fair enough on a bilateral basis, but the Livable Worlders have a lobbying office in Washington from which they very effectively "press" the U.S. Government, but no Moscow office from whence to "urge" the Soviet Government); "press for the abolition of U.S. legislative restrictions on peaceful East-West trade" (exactly as Secretary of State Kissinger was to do in late 1973); "press for treaty commitments to stop underground nuclear tests" (no safeguards or inspections required); "press the U.S. Government to offer the Soviet Union a package agreement which goes beyond the presently proposed freeze on the production of long-range missiles and bombers . . . "

The Livable World Council asks its supporters for two percent of their income to spend on political campaigns. An interesting sidelight is that the council, in effect, claimed credit for George McGovern's victory in the South Dakota Senate race in 1962. They liked him because he had introduced legislation to establish a commission charged with converting military spending to civilian spending. Since McGovern won by a cliff-hanging margin of only 600 votes, the council may deserve the credit for keeping him in the national political picture to meet his dramatic fate 10 years later.

The point of interest here is the contrast in what could be proved about the power of the Pugwash movement, and the purposes for which that power was employed, at any time prior to May 1972—

and what can be proved now. Henry Kissinger has been the Pugwash penetration's Man-in-the-White-House since January 1969, but exactly what he was doing to U.S. strategic defenses could not be proved until after publication of the text of the SALT I Agreements and the Kissinger rationale defending them. Because of the secrecy covering so much of the Pugwash movement, we could identify its role only by isolated segments of an incomplete jigsaw puzzle.

We could see, of course, as early as the late 1950s, that individual Pugwash objectives, when adopted by the United States as official policy, each provided an ad hoc advantage to the Soviets and deprived us of vital elements of strategic power. The Pugwash dictum that U.S. bombers must be scrapped because they made the Soviets nervous, and thus "heightened tensions," resulted in the scrapping of some 1,400 strategic bombers and the closing down of U.S. bomber bases in Europe and North Africa.

Those bombers are important because there were enough of them to saturate all Soviet air defenses, *then and now*, and deliver on target in the Soviet Union some 30 billion tons of explosive power. The same Pugwash pressures helped McNamara block for eight years, and helped Kissinger block for five more years, the development and production of an advanced strategic bomber. The same thing was true in regard to Pugwash programs to secure a treaty banning the "orbiting" of weapons of mass destruction; and to block production and deployment of a missile defense system, either to promote the survivability of our strategic deterrent against Soviet nuclear attack, or to protect the American people against nuclear incineration by either the Soviets or the Red Chinese.

When Henry Kissinger unfolded his SALT I Agreements, negotiations, and sales tactics, one thing became perfectly clear: when *all the individual* Pugwash strategic objectives were assembled and cemented in place by Pugwash ideology, the big picture revealed the strategic surrender of the United States to the Soviet Union.

Dr. Kissinger put it all together. Every theory on which he based his "new world order," the "pentagonal equilibrium" of power, the "broad new political relationship" with the Soviet Union, originated not in the Kissinger mind but in the Pugwash conferences. These theories have all been promoted in Pugwash circles for at least 10 years. These theories all have two additional features in common: (1) they constitute a rationalization for the United States' accepting strategic inferiority to the Soviets in all types of weapons systems, and for not rebuilding the power of the U.S. strategic deterrent, and (2) they are contradicted by the strategic posture and practices of the Soviet Union and the nature and volume of Soviet investment in strategic weapons systems.

In other words, Politburo planners, through Soviet political, psychological, and ideological dominance of the Pugwash movement, indoctrinated the U.S. conferees with theories of nuclear strategy loaded with suicidal fallacies, but designed to be plausible and attractive to nuclear pacifists and internationalists. The task of the U.S. members was to plant the theories as the new foundations of U.S. grand strategy and national security policy. So far as the Soviets were concerned, however, these theories were planted on the basis of "do as I say—not as I do."

Proof of the Pugwashian origin of the "Kissinger" theories on which he has rationalized both the SALT I Agreements and the "new world order" is simple and easy, and can be understood as clearly by the intelligent layman as by the expert in nuclear strategy.

> Two nuclear nations, each of which has the power to destroy humanity, have no alternative but to coexist peacefully because in a nuclear war, there could be no winners, only losers.[5]

In those lines prepared for presidential delivery, Dr. Kissinger managed to pack three Pugwash shibboleths: the myth of mutual and reciprocal "overkill," the plug for "peaceful coexistence" in the Soviet code-meaning of that expression, and the myth that no one can win a nuclear war because both sides will inevitably be losers.

In his own sophisticated rationale for the SALT I Agreements and the related spectrum of agreements establishing his "broad political relationship" with the Soviet Union, Dr. Kissinger took a more circumlocutory approach:

> We each possess an awesome nuclear force created and designed to meet the threat implicit in the other's strength and aims.
>
> Each of us has thus come into possession of power singlehandedly capable of exterminating the human race. Paradoxically, this very fact and the global interests of both sides, create a certain commonality of outlook, a sort of interdependence for survival between the two of us.
>
> Although we compete, the conflict will not admit of victory in the classical sense. We are compelled to coexist. We have an inescapable obligation to build jointly a structure for peace. . . .
>
> . . . the determination of national power has changed fundamentally in the nuclear age. . . . Now both we and the Soviet Union have begun to find that each increment of power does not necessarily represent an increment of *usable* political strength. . . .
>
> In other words, marginal additions of power cannot be decisive.[6]

In his first two lines, Dr. Kissinger introduces the additional Pugwash myth of the "arms race" being the result of "an action-reaction spiral." This happens to be a myth he himself has officially blasted at least nine times (in SALT press conferences, briefings, and *State of the World Reports*), primarily in explaining why he gave the Soviets such great advantages in strategic power in SALT negotiations. He pointed out that we were "not in the most brilliant bargaining position I would recommend people to find themselves in," precisely because we had *not* been racing, because we had not added a single missile launcher, land- or submarine-based, since 1967, and because—as he asserted—we had no ongoing programs for the production of any strategic weapons, whereas the Soviets had tremendous momentum in such production.

What he did *not* point out was that our strategic weapons could not have stopped *coming out* of the production pipeline in 1967 unless we had *stopped the input* into that pipeline about five years earlier, say in 1962. That, of course, is exactly what Robert McNamara did immediately after the Cuban missile crisis. The Soviets knew this very well, and nevertheless had been "racing" with ever-increasing momentum since then. They could not in any way have been creating nuclear forces to meet the "threat" of our buildup because such was nonexistent. The Soviets passed "sufficiency" in 1967, passed "parity" in 1968, and none of their buildup after passing parity can be explained as a "reaction" to our nuclear forces.

The remainder of that excerpt from Dr. Kissinger's rationale states his version of the theories that no one can win a nuclear war, that both sides would lose, that nuclear power is not usable power, and that nuclear superiority (which he labels "marginal additions") cannot be decisive, so that, as he added in his conclusion, an arms race is an "endless, wasteful, and *purposeless* competition." Also, his theory of the U.S.-U.S.S.R. "interdependence for survival" and the "inescapable obligation to build jointly a structure for peace" is a basis for his assertion that the nuclear superpowers have to share a common overriding national interest in survival—that is, of averting a nuclear war.

These theories had been enunciated in and accepted by the Pugwash movement at least as early as the Moscow Conference of 1960, but the most succinct statement demonstrating the origin of three of the "Kissinger" theories was presented during a reported discussion at the Tenth Conference in London in 1962 by Professor Jerome D. Frank, then of the Department of Psychiatry at Johns Hopkins Medical School:

> Our colleagues in the physical sciences seem to contradict themselves. On the one hand they have amply convinced us that *no one can win a nuclear war*. This can only mean that even the *possession of considerable superiority in nuclear weaponry cannot win victory*, otherwise the side that possessed such superiority *could* win a nuclear war. And yet disarmament discussions, both between governments and at Pugwash conferences, are bogged down by fears lest one side or the other achieve a temporary superiority in weaponry. *If the superior side can't win anyway, why all the concern?*

This paragraph was the genesis of both theories of nuclear strategy that Dr. Kissinger planted on Nixon ("in a nuclear war, there can be

191

no winners, only losers"; and also, in a nuclear arms race, "there can be no winners, only losers"), and of the three justifications he advances in his rationale for giving away so many massive advantages to the Soviets in the SALT I Agreements. That one paragraph confirms that, by 1962, it was established Pugwash doctrine, from which there was no dissent in the group, that "no one can win a nuclear war," and that "nuclear superiority" does not change that and is, therefore, meaningless.

Thus, Kissinger reasons—or at least would have us believe he reasons—that (1) we need not worry that the Soviets will launch a nuclear war against us because they know they could not win it and would be damaged in it; (2) that their having nuclear superiority still would not enable them to win a nuclear war ("marginal additions of power cannot be decisive"); and (3) if superiority will not enable them to win anyway, why all the concern that the SALT I Agreements allow them to retain their mid-1972 superiority and even add massively to it, while U.S. strategic forces remain frozen?

It is absolutely critical to note that these Pugwash theories about the nonusability of strategic nuclear power, *as Kissinger has employed them, cannot* justify the advantages accorded the Soviets in the SALT I Agreements *unless coupled with and based upon two assumptions*: (1) that the elements of nuclear superiority that the Soviets possessed as of May 29, 1972, considered either separately or in their totality, are no more than "marginal" as Kissinger employs that term; and (2) that the SALT I Agreements will effectively restrain the Soviets from creating additional elements of strategic power that, in themselves or even added to pre-SALT-existing elements of superiority, could be more than "marginal."

Why? Because when additions to one side's strategic forces attain sufficient magnitude, they exceed the definition of "marginal" and become—to use Dr. Kissinger's expression—"potentially decisive."

Dr. Kissinger very carefully refrains from telling what he means by "decisive," but he does not miss the opportunity to instruct us that it would be very, very dangerous to attempt to attain it:

> With modern weapons a potentially decisive advantage requires a change of such magnitude that the mere effort to obtain it can produce disaster. The simple tit-for-tat reaction to each other's programs of a decade ago is in danger of being overtaken by a more or less simultaneous and continuous process of technical advance, which opens more and more temptations for seeking decisive advantage.
>
> A premium is put on striking first and creating a defense to blunt the other side's retaliatory capability. In other words, marginal additions of power cannot be decisive. [Only Kissinger could get away with this non sequitur.] Potentially decisive additions are extremely dangerous, and the quest for them very destabilizing. The argument that arms races produce

war has often been exaggerated. The nuclear age is overshadowed by its peril.

All of this was in the President's mind as he mapped the new directions of American policy at the outset of this administration. There was reason to believe that the Soviets might be thinking along similar lines as the repeated failure of their attempts to gain marginal advantage in local crises or in military competition underlined the limitation of old policy approaches.[7]

The last sentence in the above quotation is not a pivotal point in his testimony, but it illustrates how much a slick and sophisticated speaker can get away with when he is not subject to cross-examination. President Nixon had introduced Kissinger for the briefing with a statement that he would not be allowed to testify as a witness on the SALT Agreements before any congressional committees, although there had been requests for his appearance, and although Dr. Kissinger's briefing indicated that he was vastly more familiar with the SALT negotiations than anyone else.

There simply was no one in the White House briefing who had the incentive to ask: "Just what was your reason, Henry, for believing that the Soviets might be thinking along similar lines. *And what were all those repeated failures you mention which the Soviets suffered in attempting to gain marginal advantages in local crises or military competition? Please name a few.*" This book fully documents the variety of advantages that the Soviets have gained over us in all significant strategic areas, and proves that they are not marginal, but massive, advantages.

Which side has failed, and which side has succeeded in attaining advantages, in the military competition based on conventional power? Since Kissinger came to power, the armed services of the United States have been reduced by a million and a quarter in military manpower, and another quarter of a million in civilian personnel. The admitted military personnel on active duty in the Soviet armed services is between 3.675 and 4 million—but that doesn't begin to tell the magnitude of their advantage in conventional power. They have 3 million trained and ready reserves who could be mobilized in 60 days—more than 2 million more than we have. They have 165 army divisions—to our 13, only nine of which are combat-ready—and theirs are more modern and far better equipped as to mechanization and airlift than ours. They have 102 motorized rifle divisions, 51 tank divisions, and seven airborne divisions. Their army totals more than 2.5 million men; ours is less than 800,000. This 3-to-1 ratio in favor of Soviet superior strength obtains across the board; tanks, large helicopters, aircraft. Their air defenses would make ours look ridiculous if it were not so tragic; they have more than 9,000 combat aircraft, including 3,200 fighter-interceptors, most of which are more modern than ours. Their most recent fighter, known as the Foxbat, is by far the fastest in the world, a full mach faster than our fastest. In surface-to-air defense missiles, they have 10,000 to our zero; and, by a Kissinger-imposed cut announced in October 1973, our 600 old-type aircraft-interceptor force will be reduced to 300.

One of the most dramatic contrasts is in main battle tanks: the crucial and decisive element in conventional warfare in the last quarter of the 20th century, if there is any more conventional warfare. More importantly, they are the key element in combined tactical-nuclear and conventional warfare. The sensational character of the superiority the Soviets have achieved in this area is equalled only by the tragic failure of the United States. Our last model main battle tank, the M-60, was deployed in 1960. It was recognized even then that we needed a new and improved MBT to compete with the Soviets. We spent 13 years and hundreds of millions of dollars attempting to design and develop a new model, the M-70. Then, in 1971, we gave up—the great "can do" America that started the Apollo program from scratch, researched completely new fields of science and technology, designed the hardware, produced it, trained the astronauts and ground-control personnel, and put six missions safely on the moon and brought seven missions safely back. We did all this in less time than was expended in trying to build a main battle tank. It took us two more years, until 1973, to decide to try again with the "cheap" substitute XM-1.

The Polaris missile-submarine system—a magnificent, imaginative creation that outdistanced the Soviets by some 10 years—was developed from scratch, from conception through deployment, involving entire new areas of science and technology, in less than half the time wasted on a new MBT. It even cost us some $20 million in 1972 just to terminate the M-70 project.

Was the MBT program planned to fail—or did it just happen? The eight years of "development" of the M-70 were, of course, under McNamara, and all the guidelines were imposed under his administration. Its failure has many of the indicia of the TFX pattern.

To sum up, in the military competition for supremacy in tanks, the Soviets now probably have some 15,000 to 20,000 more than the United States. More important, theirs are newer than ours and outgun us. Their T-62 model is at least five years newer than our standard tank and is in continuing mass production. They have attained an era of tank "plenty" that has permitted them to add, in the last months of 1972 and early 1973, more than 3,000 new T-62s to their already massive tank forces in East Germany and Czechoslovakia. These Soviet

T-62 tanks were the main force of the Arab surprise attack against Israel in October 1973.

We must also include seapower when discussing the "military competition" that Dr. Kissinger claims is marked by "repeated failures" of the Soviets to "gain marginal advantage." In the important strategic area of modern nuclear-propelled missile-launching submarines, they have overcome our 10-year headstart and passed us in numbers and more than doubled the range of their missiles. In all classes of combatant vessels, they are outbuilding us by the impressive ratio of 8-to-1.

In some categories the Soviet advantage is shameful. In torpedo and missile boats, including the potent types that sank the Israeli destroyer with one conventional missile, the United States has two, the Soviets have 560. In cruisers, we have nine and they have 25. More important, in addition to surface-to-air missiles, theirs carry large surface-to-surface missiles with a range of 150 to 300 miles, entirely capable of destroying our ships even with conventional warheads; and these Soviet missiles are all dual-purpose, nuclear-capable. Our so-called "missile" cruisers actually have—as of 1974—only surface-to-air missiles and could be sunk by enemy missiles that outrange our guns by 20 to more than 100 miles. We are now in the process of installing a makeshift-type "interim" missile, while we await development of an effective operational type.

In total nuclear-powered submarines, including attack submarines and cruise missile submarines, we have about 98 and they have 110. They are building at the rate of 10 to 12 a year, to our two. In other submarines, we have 42 and they have 260.

The *only* area in which the U.S. Navy has retained most of a long-preexisting headstart is aircraft carriers. The Soviets have even started to compete in this critical class of seapower. They have two helicopter carriers operational, and they have completed and deployed one 45,000-ton aircraft carrier that can handle vertical takeoff aircraft and relatively short-takeoff jets. Another similar but more capable carrier is under construction and nearing completion.

One vital factor that should be remembered in comparing the Soviet Navy to ours is that their ships are faster and much newer than ours. Their average age is eight years, ours is 18. With every passing year, the number of their combatant ships increases, whereas ours decreases and will continue to do so. Ours is aptly characterized as the "dwindling fleet." In 1971, 62 of our ships were retired; 84 were retired in 1972. Our pre-Kissinger total of 434 major combatant ships was cut to 253 by mid-1973, will drop to slightly more than 200 by the end of 1974, and will continue to drop until about 1978 when replacements are finally expected to equal the number being retired.

It remained for a British naval expert to console us. "Cheer up," he said, "you still have the second greatest navy in the world."

Put the whole picture together for an overview of our shrinking land and air forces and our dwindling seapower: the triad of our conventional military power. The contrast between what we have left now, after five years of Kissinger's policies, and what we had in the major areas of conventional military weapons before he attained power in January 1969 is shocking. Here are the official statistics on the major indicators of our posture, then and now, as revealed in the 1974 Defense Budget Report. This Report[8] was presented to the House Armed Services Committee on April 10, 1973, by then-Secretary of Defense Elliot Richardson, just before he was so suddenly summoned by President Nixon to put his finger into the Watergate dike:

End of Fiscal Years:	1968	1974
Ground Divisions (incl. Marines)	22 1/3	16*
Tactical Fighter/Attack Squadrons	210	163
Major Combatant Ships (incl. attack subs)	434	253
Air Lift Squadrons	63	34
Military and Civil Service Manpower	4.8 million	3.2 million
Total Defense Outlays in constant purchasing power (FY 1974)	$113.4 billion	$79 billion
Defense Related Employment in Industry	3.2 million	1.9 million

*Of the 16 ground divisions, 13 are Army and 3 Marine. Of the 13 Army divisions, only 9 could be considered combat-ready, as the Army Chief of Staff admitted in mid-1973.

Thus, the absolute cuts in U.S. conventional military power over which Henry Kissinger has presided are massive. Make no mistake: he did in fact "preside" over them; it was his influence over President Nixon that was decisive, not Secretary of Defense Melvin Laird's.

Much more vital, however, is the significance of the Kissinger cuts in U.S. conventional power *in relation to the buildup of all types of Soviet conventional military power* that was going on *at exactly the same time.* Kissinger continued his cuts despite the existing factors of Soviet superiority in conventional military power that range from 2-to-1 in their favor to more than 20-to-1 in their favor, as we have already seen.

The third, and truly staggering, aspect of the Kissinger performance is that he has been able to sell these massive cuts in U.S. conventional military power relative to the Soviet Union at exactly the same time that he is pontificating the Pugwash theory that strategic *nuclear* power is *unusable*.

By SALT I, and by his defeatist policy of declaring the United States helpless to add a single additional ICBM or SLBM launcher, Dr. Kissinger conceded to the Soviets massive imbalances of strategic nuclear power so great that they will soon enable the Soviets to demand the unconditional surrender of the United States. But they can successfully make that demand only if strategic nuclear power is *usable*.

In strict accordance with Pugwash dogma, Kissinger has imposed on U.S. grand strategy the theory that strategic nuclear power is *not* usable. This book presents copious evidence that the Soviets have staked hundreds of billions of dollars of value in scarce resources on their conviction that *they can make strategic nuclear power usable.* That is what their massive buildup of strategic power is all about.

However, let us assume for a few pages that Kissinger and the Pugwashers are, for once, right. Just suppose that nuclear power is *not* usable and that, therefore, strategic nuclear superiority would not provide the power to control the world.

What power is left to control the world? Obviously, conventional military power. That is the type of military power that the United States built up to defeat Hitler's Germany and Japan in World War II. By the end of that war the United States had ample conventional military power to control the world. We, however, had no ambition to conquer the world. Encouraged by Soviet agents and their "bring the boys home" campaign, we immediately and irresponsibly demobilized and scrapped our power. The Soviets never similarly demobilized their conventional power. Since 1964, when they so accelerated their buildup of strategic nuclear weapons systems, they have also stepped up the pace of both modernization and multiplication of the instruments of conventional power. Why do they need the best and the most of both types of power?

Quite obviously for offensive, not defensive, purposes. The nations of Western Europe are pygmies compared to the great U.S.S.R. The population of the Soviet Union is roughly 250 million. The population of France is roughly 51 million, Italy 54 million, and West Germany 61 million. These Western nations are peace-loving, friendly, politically fragmented, with very large Communist parties in France and Italy, and a governing Socialist Party in Germany. They are status quo powers and affluent societies of undisciplined people relative to the Communist nations.

All the Western European countries want from the Soviet Union, other than minor trade opportunities, is to be let alone. The Politburo members in Moscow know this. The so-called Chinese threat exists solely on the border areas of the Soviet Union—not at all to industrial regions. The Chinese are 15 years behind the Soviets in mechanization and mobility of their conventional forces. They are also, according to that 1974 U.S. Defense Report quoted above, "about 10 to 15 years behind the Soviets in applied aircraft technology."

A Soviet invasion of China by conventional forces would be a substantial undertaking, even with the more than 50 army divisions the Soviets already have on the border, with their armored, mobile, and mechanized equipment, and their scores of thousands of tanks and thousands of aircraft. But, on the other hand, a successful Chinese invasion of the Soviet Union, other than overrunning border areas, would be an impossibility.

Thus the Soviet Union's huge conventional military establishment in-being, which is being enlarged each month, cannot be explained as defensive. There is no offensive threat at all from the West, and no threat from the East that could not be overwhelmed by the 50 Soviet divisions already in place on the border with nearly 500,000 fighting men—with or without their tactical nuclear weapons and equipment that is the most advanced and powerful in the world. Some types of Soviet mobile *tactical* nuclear weapons are even in the megaton range, the only such weapons possessed by any nation.

Why do the Soviets need to invest such huge sums out of a scarce economy to buy the best and most of both worlds of weaponry—nuclear and conventional?

Conquest of the world is no modest task—and *administration* of the world after conquest is at least an equal challenge to the Politburo planners. The most obvious and logical explanation for their acquiring the best and the most of both types of military power is that they have assigned specific missions to each type of weapon. Their *nuclear* power has the task of (1) neutralizing or destroying U.S. strategic nuclear power, because that is the only power in the world capable of blocking their conquest of the remainder of the world, and (2) securing the preemptive surrender of Western Europe and Japan through the mere *threat* of employing that strategic nuclear power. The huge Soviet conventional forces are assigned the task of occupying and administering the nations of Western Europe and all the others that will follow them into the Soviet camp.

At this point, however, we are concerned solely with what the Soviets could do with their conventional power if strategic nuclear weapons actually are—as the Pugwash-Kissinger theory holds—un-usable.

If nuclear weapons actually are *unusable*, as the Pugwash-Kissinger

198

theory holds, what can the Soviets do with their conventional power? They can conquer all of Western Europe with it, that's what. Among Western strategists, there is no dissent from the fact that the Soviets could conquer all of Western Europe with their present conventional forces. The only debate is as to how long it would take. The optimists say 90 to 120 days. The realists say 30 to 60 days. Soviet forces can reach the suburbs of Vienna in 15 minutes. They could be in Frankfurt with thousands of tanks within two hours.

In the NATO Central Region (West Germany, Belgium, and the Netherlands), the Soviet Union and Warsaw Pact nations are believed to have about 800,000 combat and direct-support troops and 15,000 tanks, against 540,000 troops and 5,200 tanks for the NATO forces (including U.S. NATO forces in Europe). The Soviets would control the timing of any attack and would, therefore, have added at least another 500,000 troops and 5,000 tanks as reinforcements. If they do this job as well as they did in their Czechoslovakian preparatory exercise in 1968, NATO intelligence will not believe what is happening in time to reinforce.

How about reinforcements from the United States? Theoretically we have, of our nine supposedly combat-ready Army divisions, 2-1/3 "specifically earmarked" for European tasks; and we are supposed to have a strategic reserve that allegedly contains the equivalent of 3-1/3 divisions. This is supposed to amount to a total of about 160,000 men.

But these are in the continental United States. U.S. airlift forces are cut each year. Theoretically, we could airlift one division to Europe in one week. But this would apply *only* for the one division for which the heavy equipment is prepositioned in Europe. For units that had no prepositioned equipment in Europe, sea lift would be required, and we have less of that every year, too. Nor can we count on keeping the sea lanes open if the Soviets decide to block them with their superior navy. On NBC's *Meet the Press* on June 30, 1974, the then-retiring Chief of Naval Operations, Admiral Elmo Zumwalt, conceded that the United States has "lost control of the seas." Unfortunately, the evidence conclusively supports this shocking result of 5½ years of Kissinger's policies.

One thing that is quietly but totally suppressed in official presentations of plans for U.S. reinforcement of NATO forces, is that even this one division could be moved into Europe *only if the Soviets did not effectively oppose it.* With their more than 9,000 combat aircraft and more than 3,200 fighter-interceptor types, many of which are a full mach faster than any NATO or U.S. aircraft, our subsonic C-5s would have quite a task landing anywhere in Europe. Any landing at all, of course, must assume that the airports and landing fields had not yet been occupied by Soviet or Warsaw Pact ground forces.

But even *if* the United States could rapidly move to Europe all the forces we have in this country earmarked for NATO, they would still be peanuts compared to the Soviet and Warsaw Pact combat-ready divisions. The same 1974 U.S. Defense Report that claims a total of 16 divisions for the United States, including Marines, concedes to the Soviet side a total of "about 220 divisions," some 160 of which are Soviet. U.S. defense officials claim that these Soviet divisions are "understrength" in peacetime. As a realistic matter, if the Soviets planned a move in Western Europe, they could have the necessary divisions built up to full strength just prior to their move.

Consider the matter of tank forces alone. In 1973 the United States was still buying M-60 main battle tanks. These MBTs were first deployed in 1960, and probably designed some five years earlier than that. When we do buy them, we buy by the hundred (e.g., 360 for the entire Army in a year], whereas the Soviets build them by the thousand.[9] In February 1973 Western intelligence suddenly discovered that the Soviets had deployed an additional 2,000 T-62 MBTs opposite the NATO forces in the Central Region where they already had 12,500 deployed against the 5,200 NATO tanks, all older and with less firepower.[10]

Even more macabre than the specifics of conventional military power that we have already considered is the overall balance of military manpower on active duty plus trained and ready reserves. This balance is swinging more nearly decisively and swiftly to the Soviets every year. The United States has abandoned the draft and any realistic semblance of universal military service. The draft provided the incentive for men to join the reserves, as well as incentive for remaining in the ready reserve after active duty tours that were shorter for those committed to reserve service. The mass movement of men through active duty tours provided the United States with large numbers of men who had been trained and also had actual experience. This is all over now. The so-called "professional army" will result in the flow of trained and ready reserves being cut substantially to zero. Our less than one million present reserves will be a rapidly aging group.

The Soviet Union presently has on active duty some 4 million men, all highly trained and with the most modern equipment and arms, compared with the present U.S. Army of fewer than 800,000 men. Within 60 days, the Soviets could mobilize an additional 3 million men, all under the age of 27 and with two to three years of active-duty experience. Their total reserve for ground forces alone is 20 million.[11]

The critical point is that the Soviets *will continue* to train additional millions of soldiers, rocket troops, sailors, and airmen *each* year. They have an all-inclusive draft, with no loopholes for conscientious objectors or antiwar militants and activists. Universal military service is a pervasive fact of life in Russia. Conscription starts at age 18. An elaborate preinduction training starts at age 16 that facilitates selection of potential specialists with technical skills above the average. They receive hundreds of hours of extra preinduction schooling and provide the Soviet armed services with 150,000 to 200,000 new apprentice specialists each year.

Summarizing, therefore: by 1977 the Soviets could have an active-duty *plus* combat-ready and highly trained reserve manpower pool of more than 11 million with a back-up reserve of 20 million—against a U.S. active-duty force of 2.25 million, plus an aging reserve of less than 0.95 million. The result is the usual McNamara-Kissinger-era factor in the balance of military power: a Soviet superiority over us of between 3-to-1 and 4-to-1.

Can we shrug off the magnitude of the Soviet advantage by contending that our superior technology, mobility, equipment, and armament will offset the massive Soviet superiority in numbers of men? No. Only in a few limited areas can we claim technologically superior equipment. Across the board, the Soviets are ahead both qualitatively and, by a great margin, quantitatively.[12] One of the areas in which we have truly advanced developments is that of "smart" bombs and "smart" conventional air-to-surface missiles. These are fitted with "far-out" laser, infrared, and electro-optical devices. Furthermore, some of these types are not particularly expensive. A standard aerial bomb in the 3,000-pound class costs about $1,800, and a laser guidance system can be added for only $3,100.

The bad news is that, in the current political climate, some would consider such inexpensive bombs too costly for the survival of a nation with an annual GNP of $1.3 trillion. The U.S. Maverick missile, designed for air-to-surface employment, has a television-type guidance system that makes it very accurate, but the price tag is on the order of $27,000 per missile. "Stupid" missiles of the same class cost only about $5,000 each.

In their present state of development, television-guided missiles and bombs can be employed effectively only in good daylight conditions. Eventually, they may be given night capability when substantial additional progress is made in low-light-level television. This lack of night capability is a serious weakness in the present timeframe.

The hardworking Russians have been engaged for years developing night capabilities and night tactics for their tens of thousands of tanks. Their tank troops train and exercise by day; they train and exercise by night; and their night capabilities could be a potentially decisive stratagem in conventional warfare. There is a high probability that, if launched on a sufficiently massive scale, the night tank attack could confound and frustrate NATO defending forces that are vastly out-gunned, outnumbered, and outtanked in any event. In the dark all these disadvantages will seem worse.

One small personal incident made this very real. We were talking with a U.S. infantryman who had recently returned from duty in West Germany. He was describing Soviet exercises, such as were used to provide advance cover for the invasion of Czechoslovakia:

> Directly opposite us were the Russian tanks. Twenty miles of them, lined up abreast, tread-to-tread. *Twenty miles of them.* And do you know what we had to oppose them? Machine guns.

The estimate by objective strategists that the Soviets, using con-ventional power only, could sweep across Europe to the English Channel in 30 days is actually highly academic. The problem faced by the NATO nations, led by West Germany, France, and Italy (even including the ultimate assistance the United States could add in a crisis), would be like that of the king whose strategy is so eloquently described in St. Luke 14:31-32:

> Or what king, going to make war against another king, sitteth not down first, and consulteth whether he be able with 10,000 to meet him that cometh against him with 20,000?
> Or else, while the other is yet a great way off, he sendeth an ambassage, and desireth conditions of peace.

Requesting information as to the "conditions of peace" is now known as seeking the terms of a preemptive surrender. A pre-emptive surrender is the only rational course open to the NATO nations that face the overwhelming conventional military power of the Soviet Union. If they chose to resist, their defense would be futile, their countries would be devastated, and hundreds of thou-sands—perhaps millions—of the people would be killed. Surrender would—at some point—be inevitable. So, why undergo such devasta-tion *before* tendering the surrender?

A surrender to the Soviets of the nations of Western Europe would trip the dominoes against each other worldwide. The countries and sheikdoms of the Middle East; Japan; the Latin American nations; most probably Canada, all would race to enter into the Soviets' camp while they still had hope of retaining some national characteristics. The United States could be "frozen" to a national death: oil, other energy supplies, and essential raw materials would be denied us, as well as the use of ships and even the use of the oceans.

This is what *must* happen if Henry Kissinger's theory that nuclear power is "unusable" is valid. He has joined his administration with McNamara's to insure that the Soviets have overwhelming supe-riority in conventional military power, as well as overwhelming superiority in strategic nuclear power. Any way Henry Kissinger's theories and policies can be analyzed, they have all promoted the national suicide of the United States and the destruction of freedom in the world.

The only power that could have saved Western Europe—and, after that, the world—from surrender to or conquest by the Soviet Union was U.S. strategic *nuclear superiority* over the Soviet Union. The history of the 30 years since the end of World War II demonstrates this fact. Winston Churchill was perhaps the first, and certainly the most eloquent, world statesman to recognize this basic fact of life for nations in the post-World War II era. There would not be a single free man left in Europe, he declared, were it not for the United States nuclear deterrent. It was our nuclear deterrent, and only that, which has prevented the massive and never-demobilized Soviet conventional forces from overrunning Western Europe.

Even Dr. Kissinger himself has admitted specifically that, when the United States possessed strategic nuclear superiority, we had the capability of protecting our allies from the Soviet conventional military threat as well as from the Soviet nuclear threat. His explanation in his September 17, 1970, nonattributable background briefing was quoted earlier, but this time we add a key paragraph that is more critically relevant here. In tracing the history of the U.S. strategic deterrent from the time of the Cuban missile crisis in 1962, Dr. Kissinger said:

> In short, our strategic superiority was overwhelming. The Soviet Union could not respond to our pressure . . . because they had to be worried that we might do to them what later the Israelis did to the Arabs: namely, launch a *preemptive strike.*
>
> *Therefore our strategic superiority defended not only us but all our allies* and even those countries which were not our allies, but that were thought likely to trigger an American response.
>
> *There were many people, including myself, who criticized John Foster Dulles' massive retaliation doctrine in the 1950s. But in historical retrospect, it was correct for the conditions of the period.*
>
> But today the Soviet Union . . . has increased the number of their missiles 30-fold since 1962. Indeed, they have more long-range missiles than we do today.
>
> In these circumstances . . . it is a different decision for the President of the United States to risk general nuclear war when the strategic equation is this than it was throughout most of the postwar period.
>
> Therefore, the possibility of defending other countries with strategic American power alone has fundamentally changed, and no amount of reassurance on our part can change these facts.

What we have, therefore, is an admission by Henry Kissinger that the strategic nuclear power of the United States *used to be usable* when we held overwhelming superiority over the Soviets. It could and did "protect *all* our allies." Yet, the first thing he did when he came to power in 1969 was to *refuse* to rebuild our overwhelming superiority (which the Nixon Administration could then have done without any danger of a Soviet preemptive strike, and which would have been supported by Congress and the American people if they had been given the truth about the Soviet drive to attain a first-strike capability against the United States). Instead, Kissinger immediately abandoned the concept of *any* strategic superiority for the United States, let alone overwhelming superiority. He conned Richard Nixon with the concept of "nuclear sufficiency" that Kissinger admits is not sufficient to protect our allies.

Dr. Kissinger's pontification that strategic nuclear power is not "usable" is half right—that is, he is right in regard to the United States, but not the Soviet Union. He is half right only because of the policies he has imposed on the President and, through him, on the United States. Kissinger has made United States nuclear power "unusable," even as a deterrent, by continuing, extending, and exacerbating the McNamara programs of unilateral disarmament. The margin of overwhelming superiority that these two subtracted from the U.S. side of the strategic balance, while it was being added to the Soviet side, now renders U.S. nuclear power "unusable" to defend *either* our allies or ourselves. At the same time, it makes Soviet strategic nuclear power "usable" for nuclear blackmail against us or our allies.

Kissinger has handed the Soviets three distinct alternatives for compelling the surrender of the NATO nations: (1) the threat of strategic nuclear power being used against them, (2) the threat of an attack by combined conventional military power plus tactical nuclear power, and (3) the threat of an attack by conventional military power.

There is one way—and only one way—with which this threat can be met: the rebuilding of the U.S. strategic nuclear deterrent. This is *not* impossible for the United States. We have the capability—and we have, just barely, the time. *But only if we buy it* by abandoning the Kissinger strategy of permitting the Soviets to destroy our Minutemen in their silos, and changing over to a launch-on-confirmation-of-warning strategy.

Before discussing the necessary buildup of strategic power, let us consider why the conventional threat to Western Europe could not be met by a buildup of conventional military power, either by the United States or by the NATO nations, or in combination.

There is no question that the United States could (in the absence of a Soviet nuclear preemption) build conventional military power superior to even the present massive Soviet conventional military power. This is not guesswork. We did it once. By the end of World War II we had built a military force far greater than the Soviets have now. But it took us four years of near-total industrial mobilization and up to 43 to 48 percent of our GNP. Even 43 percent of our present GNP would be more than $550 billion a year, which would be more than enough money to pay for that quantum of military power. However, it would take several years to build a base of industrial mobilization that would enable us to spend even half that much per year on military hardware.

Even if we could do this, however, it would be useless. Even if we could produce and deploy to Europe two or three times the conventional military power the Soviets already have in being there, we could not use it against the Soviets. The Soviet Union's overwhelming superiority of strategic nuclear power would make our conventional military power—regardless of its magnitude or its superiority over their conventional power—"unusable" against the Soviets.

This was explained long ago, near the beginning of the nuclear age in the 1950s, by Dr. Edward Teller, the world's supreme nuclear physicist and inventor of hydrogen explosive power. He consoled us:

> Nuclear power does not mean the end of the world, but it does mean the end of nonnuclear power.

What he meant, specifically, was that nonnuclear military power could not be used against, or even against the wishes of, a superior nuclear power. It could not be used even against the wishes of an inferior nuclear power if it had a credible will to use it. This was clearly demonstrated in Vietnam. Although President Johnson, for political reasons, would have preferred to win that war, he was afraid to use our superior nuclear power to defeat a client state of the Soviet Union—even though, at the time, the Soviets had not attained strategic nuclear superiority over us. He was so much afraid, indeed, that he sacrificed his political career because he couldn't bring himself to give the order to win the war.

We have the wily Khrushchev's word for it in his memoirs: fear of nuclear war can paralyze a nation's leadership. The Lyndon Johnson-Dean Rusk team presented the outstanding example of such fear. Even during the Cuban missile crisis of 1962, Lyndon Johnson had shrunk back in fright at the mere idea of a blockade or quarantine that might stop Soviet missile-delivering ships. It would be "an act of war," he intoned.

When Johnson actually had the responsibility of the presidency, his paralysis of fear restrained him from permitting U.S. forces to fight to win. This fear even restrained him from permitting any action or program that might suggest to the Soviets that we had the resolution and courage to fight to win. Thus when, on June 28, 1966, he finally and reluctantly gave permission to attack the oil storage facilities at Haiphong, he couldn't sleep that night because of fear. He told his daughter Luci:

> Your daddy may go down in history as having started World War III. You may not wake up tomorrow.

So Luci, to quiet his fears, suggested that, although it was late on a rainy night, they go to pray at St. Dominic's Church in southwest Washington, which was run by an order of brothers Luci called her "Little Monks." Johnson, recalling that a business partner once had told him that, in times of trouble, heavy thinking and deep prayer were a comfort, agreed. After their return to the White House the reports of the bombing raid came in. There had been no miscalculation; no Soviet ships had been hit; no missile attack had been launched against the United States.

Lyndon Johnson told this story to personal friends many times during the following year, but it did not surface publicly until after he recounted it at a White House party for the Supreme Court Justices on May 11, 1967. A woman reporter leaked the story because she felt she had been discriminated against. The point here, however, is that both the story of "Luci's Little Monks," as it was known, and President Johnson's telling of it, reveal the wild fears and wildly irresponsible ignorance of U.S. Presidents of the most fundamental considerations of nuclear strategy. The United States has paid a terrible price in blood and treasure because of this ignorance.

The story demonstrates that Lyndon Johnson felt that, by permitting the bombing of a single military target in North Vietnam, he was risking the triggering of a Soviet strategic strike against the United States, including our cities and population. At that time—mid-1966—the Soviets' strategic buildup had not yet brought them even to parity with the United States. We had 1,054 ICBMs to their 224, and we had 544 advanced SLBMs to their 107 primitive SLBMs. If the Soviets had ordered a strategic strike at the United States, they could not have destroyed a fraction of our ICBMs. Since McNamara had by then been able to scrap only about half our 1962 force of strategic bombers, we could still have delivered on Soviet targets about 30 to 35 million tons of TNT explosive equivalent. That would have been enough to destroy all the large cities in the Soviet Union, more than half the entire population, and substantially all its industrial capacity.

In taking the very moderate step of bombing a military target in North Vietnam with conventional bombs, we were merely incurring a small risk of a Soviet strategic strike at the United States;

whereas, in that timeframe, if the Soviets actually launched a strike at us, they would be *ensuring* the retaliatory destruction of the Soviet Union.

President Johnson should have looked at the situation by asking the question: how great was our *risk* that the Kremlin would ensure the destruction of its own country, and of the power base of international communism, to retaliate against a single nondecisive military move with conventional bombs by the United States against North Vietnam? The answer would, of course, have been—for all practical purposes—zero. The answer would have been the same if he had mined Haiphong Harbor, or bombed out all the war-making potential of the North Vietnamese, or destroyed the dikes to cut off their food supplies for invading forces. Even if we had employed tactical nuclear weapons to destroy the war-making potential of North Vietnam, the answer would have had to be the same: the Soviet Union would not commit national suicide, and thus permit the power base of international communism to be destroyed, because of anything we might do in Vietnam. *Anything at all.*

The wildly irresponsible fear that paralyzed Lyndon Johnson was exactly what Melvin Laird warned of in his 1962 book *A House Divided*. He repeated time after time that the United States then had unchallengeable, massive strategic nuclear superiority, but that our leadership was *acting as if* the Soviet Union had reached a stage of parity, or even superiority. Thus, Mr. Laird exhorted the nation to remember that:

> Present deterrence is not a balance of terror, that favorite ringing phrase of status quorators.
> Present deterrence rests squarely on present American superiority.[13]

On this basis, he urged upon the United States a strategy of initiatives:

> Since we have superiority and have not incorporated it into our diplomacy, we are losing an essential advantage in our contest with communism.
> The Soviet Union is currently waging a war throughout the entire spectrum of power. An essential key to their strategy is nuclear blackmail. The only way we can defeat its effectiveness is by incorporating in our diplomacy our superior nuclear capability.
> In other words, *their nuclear blackmail is a bluff.* We must call their bluff, now, while we can—or deterrence will indeed fail, and so will the West....
> Actually, the Soviet Union is unwilling to take a real risk of war, as long as we hold our nuclear lead.[14]

Melvin Laird was exactly right, not only as of the time he wrote, but also of Lyndon Johnson's 1966 nuclear funk. Any supposed or expressed Soviet threat to launch a nuclear strike at the United States in retaliation for anything we might do in Vietnam was purely and simply a bluff.

The cost of not having the intelligence, the courage, and the common sense to face up to that bluff, cost the life's blood of 50,000 U.S. fighting men, $140 billion in treasure, and the abdication of presidential power by Lyndon Johnson—one of the most consummate politicians in modern times. Secretary McNamara planned it that way with his deliberate policy of no-win creeping escalation, so that he could divert that $140 billion away from U.S. investment in strategic defense. It was this McNamara planning that enabled the Soviet Union to surpass us in strategic power in exactly that timeframe so that, whereas the Soviet nuclear threat was merely a bluff in mid-1966, it had become a deadly peril by May 1972 when Richard Nixon gave the orders for the mining of Haiphong Harbor (with 16 Soviet ships in it) and unleashed U.S. airpower to hit hundreds of vital military targets that were off limits before.

This does not mean that the Soviets *would* launch a nuclear strike at the United States because of anything we might do in Vietnam, even in 1972. They will launch their strike when, and only when, they figure it is most advantageous to do and the risk of retaliation is the least. But if they *had* happened to be ready, it would have provided a handy excuse for "world opinion" and have set them up as global champions of small Communist states under "aggressive attack" by the "warmongering" U.S. "capitalist imperialists."

At the time when Johnson had been too paralyzed by nuclear fear to act, we still had a 4-to-1 numerical superiority over the Soviets in numbers of long-range missiles, and neither side had any missile defenses. At the time Nixon acted in May 1972, the Soviets—as revealed in the official SALT I statistics—had attained a 3-to-2 advantage over us in number of long-range missiles, and a from 4-to-1 to 5-to-1 advantage over us in missile throw-weight.

The greatest news story of the century should have been: *why* did the United States needlessly sacrifice 50,000 lives and $140 billion dollars when the whole thing could have been ended in 1966? But few people asked this life-and-death question. The media probably devoted less than 1/10,000 the space to this question of the century than it did to *The Pentagon Papers* theft by Daniel Ellsberg—or 1/100,000,000 the space given to the Watergate bugging and burglaries. Joseph Alsop was one of the very few newsmen who gave serious attention to this question of the century. In a brilliant column dated May 16, 1972, he wrote:

> The Soviet response to the mining of Haiphong Harbor was about as tough and stiff as a length of sadly overcooked spaghetti. Since 1965, horrifying consequences have been predicted whenever anyone advocated

the kind of action President Nixon has taken. So it is time for a little salutary self-examination.

The clever young men in Robert S. McNamara's Pentagon were all too persuasive. Blocking Haiphong Harbor was made to seem too unwise by their smooth arguments. . . .

Even the wickedest old warmongers cannot claim 20-20 foresight, in short. But what has happened suggests, nonetheless, that there is something dreadfully wrong, even shockingly wrong, in the way the U.S. Government weighs the risk of positive action to safeguard U.S. interests.

The heart of the trouble is in the U.S. government itself. Thence it spreads into the people in the newspaper and television business. Most of the media leaders positively long for seemingly sound arguments against any kind of active, tough policy. As for the wider academic and intellectual communities, they had better be passed over in silence.

In the present instance, once again, it is impossible not to charge the government experts and analysts with gross errors. . . .

But that is not the end of the story by any means. Any informed person can point to a dozen very high officials, past and present, formally charged with making such judgments. In varying degrees, all these men were (A) wrong about the Soviets' brutal action in Hungary in 1956; (B) dead wrong about the Soviet emplacement of nuclear missiles in 1962; and (C) just as wrong about the reinvasion of Czechoslovakia in 1968.

In sum, a particular kind of bias persistently produces a particular kind of error. In the case of the Vietnamese war the bias has prevailed in the government, in the media and elsewhere as well. And it has been remarkably expensive.

The grim Vietnamese story ought to have ended five years ago, for example. *If President Johnson had merely done the same thing in 1966 that President Nixon has now done, with apparent impunity, in 1972.*

If you consider the treasure and the blood poured out in the interval, it is all but unbearable to think about. But because of those smooth, persuasive young men, this reporter was against it along with most everyone else.

To excuse this demonstrated, really monstrous error, everyone implicated will now say that the Soviet response was only like overboiled spaghetti this time because their relations with the Chinese have worsened in the interval. That is sickly nonsense, however.

The Chinese factor is somewhat more important in Soviet policy precisely because of President Nixon's journey to Peking.

But by a course of flaccid folly, this country has also permitted a grave deterioration of the strategic balance in favor of the Soviets. *And the strategic balance is what they really care about in Moscow.*

If we could say the same for the United States—that the strategic balance is what we really care about—we could look forward to the survival of the United States as an independent nation, and to the survival of the American people as a free people, as well as to the successful deterrence of a Soviet takeover of Western Europe.

Unless and until we reconstitute the strategic balance and rebuild the credibility of our deterrent, it would be totally useless to build up our conventional power to two or three times that of the Soviet Union. We were terrorized out of employing our overwhelming superior conventional power to win a war against the Communist North Vietnamese for fear of Soviet nuclear action at a time when the nuclear odds were 4-to-1 in our favor. We shouldn't have been terrorized, but we were. The *in terrorem* effect of strategic nuclear military power is one of its very real assets, even though it is psychological. Our leaders did not have the brains or the fortitude to use this pyschological asset. The Soviets did, even when they were a pitifully poor Number Two in nuclear power. There is no question that they will use it now, with pride and full assurance, with their Kissinger-SALT-perpetuated superiority.

This review of history in the nuclear era proves that what Henry Kissinger and his Pugwash confreres claim about strategic nuclear power being "unusable" is completely wrong. Decisive nuclear superiority is not only usable to counter a *nuclear* threat, but it is also usable to deter an adversary from using *conventional* military power. Nuclear power may even render conventional military power "unusable."

We have also demonstrated that *if*—by some magic of a demiurge more powerful than Henry Kissinger—nuclear power should really become unusable, the Kissinger continuation of the McNamara-initiated policy of keeping the United States inferior to the Soviets in *all* areas of military power, together with Kissinger's own acceleration of the dismemberment of U.S. conventional forces, would still leave Western Europe—and ultimately the world—vulnerable to the Soviets' massive and modern conventional military might.

We have also demonstrated that, even if Henry Kissinger's Pugwash-oriented theories of nuclear strategy were valid—and we have seen that they are not—his policies would still seal the doom of the United States and of freedom in the world because of what he has done to our conventional military power. To be that far out of touch with reality, a chief theoretician must indeed be "some kind of a nut, or something."

10

Hubert H. Humphrey's promises in the campaign of 1968 sounded like an amalgam of the policies espoused by the Council on Foreign Relations and the Americans for Democratic Action. This, of course, was not too surprising because he had been a long-time member of each, and a leader in the ADA in which the competition in power and intellect was less keen. Richard Nixon talked a different game. Domestically, he attacked the Welfare State, deficit financing, and forced integration. As to national defense and foreign policy, he talked pro-American and anti-Communist. As to strategic military power, he heaped a realistic contempt on a national strategy based on the "peculiar concept of parity" with the Soviet Union. He displayed deep concern because prior administrations had abandoned the concept of American superiority and had "frittered away superior military capabilities," thus "enabling the Soviets . . . to move to cancel our lead entirely by the early seventies," a lead that he measured at "an 8-to-1 strategic advantage over the Soviet Union" in 1962. He warned of the "significant danger" to the United States arising out of the Soviet development of a "first-strike capability." He solemnly pledged to "give first priority" to restoring "the strength of the United States."

That was Candidate Nixon speaking. He promised all those things, and "more, much more," as the advertisements say when they run out of space for explicit additional claims.

In January 1969 Henry Kissinger moved into the White House with Richard Nixon. Within a matter of weeks a character who might appropriately have been tagged as Prince Metternich-Svengali of the West Wing had accomplished a complete turnaround of Richard Nixon. Just one specific can illustrate the 180 degree totality of his change of course in national security policy under the pervasive Kissinger influence. Candidate Nixon had run on a Nixon-dictated GOP platform reciting:

Grave errors, many now irretrievable, have characterized the direction of our nation's defense.

A singular notion—that salvation for America lies in standing still—has pervaded the entire effort. Not retention of American superiority, but parity with the Soviet Union has been made the controlling doctrine in many critical areas.

Yet, as President, Nixon perpetuated exactly that same freeze in production and deployment of U.S. strategic weapons that he had inveighed against in his 1968 speeches and platform. He enshrined as national policy that same singular notion that "salvation for America lies in standing still." The proof of the Nixon turnabout emerged in the Kissinger rationale for the SALT I Agreements in 1972: the United States, he disclosed, had not added a single missile launcher, either land-based or submarine-launched, since 1967—and, under his defense policies, would not have the capability of adding any additional strategic missile launchers until 1977. The so-sophisticated Dr. Kissinger admitted that a missile gap in favor of the Soviet Union had opened in the first year of his administration, and would continue to grow, and he claimed that we are helpless to prevent the gap from widening each year.

Governor George Wallace had warned in 1968 that "there's not a dime's worth of difference" between Nixon and Humphrey. That was a personal judgment based on common sense and intuition; the evidence was far from conclusive. Time demonstrated, however, that George Wallace had been right, especially on unilateral disarmament. During the presidential election campaign of 1972, he must have been sorely tempted to utter a rancorous "I told you so." Instead, he quipped: "Richard Nixon ran on my platform; but after election, he adopted Hubert Humphrey's." Nixon did, indeed, run and win on foreign policy and defense planks remarkably similar to those of the Wallace platform; but the ones Nixon shifted to after election were to the left of those espoused by Humphrey. They had, in fact, been fashioned with loving care in advance of the 1968 Republican Convention by Henry Kissinger for Nelson Rockefeller in his belated bid for the nomination.

The totality of Kissinger's turnaround of Nixon on the grand strategy of the United States and our foreign policy, the details of which are

212

merely sketched above, has been conclusively established. The great mystery is, how did Kissinger bring about such a dramatic and revolutionary change?

A President's "first responsibility" to the people of the United States is, as Lyndon Johnson defined it in his 1967 State of the Union Message,

> to assure that no nation can ever find it rational to launch a nuclear attack or to use its nuclear power as a credible threat against us or our allies.

Richard Nixon, during his election campaign, had pledged to the American people that he would meet that first obligation as President by never accepting strategic nuclear parity with the Soviet Union, and by rebuilding U.S. strength to unequivocal superiority.

How was Dr. Kissinger able to change Richard Nixon to the extent that he would betray his explicit promise to fulfill his most solemn responsibility to the nation? How do you go about changing a man so that he will do things he promised he never in the world would do?

The answer is embodied in that last question: you create for him a different world, an artificial world so designed that its perceived circumstances will compel him to do exactly what you want him to do.

This technique represents, of course, devious deception on a highly sophisticated level. Henry Kissinger's objective was quite as far from the ordinary as were his means for accomplishing it. In the real world, the policies he sought to impose on Richard Nixon would expose some 210 million trusting Americans to mass murder by nuclear incineration. Those policies would render our population totally vulnerable—and do it deliberately. They would deprive us of all defenses; they would vitiate the effectiveness of our strategic deterrent.

This sounds shocking beyond belief. The brutal fact, however, is that no knowledgeable authority on strategic nuclear power contests the fact that the Kissinger SALT I ABM Treaty makes the entire population of the United States hostages to the Kremlin. No one contests Dr. Kissinger's own admission that the treaty guarantees Soviet and Red Chinese nuclear missiles a free ride to destroy us by the scores of millions. No objective expert can deny that, if the SALT I Agreements and Kissinger defense policies permit the Soviets to complete the buildup of a preclusive first-strike capability against the United States, the continuation of our national existence and all our lives will depend totally on the good will of the men in Moscow's Politburo. We will have been set up for mass murder on a scale never before witnessed in the history of the world.

No elected President would knowingly do such a thing to his trusting people. Not so, however, as to an unelected ruler who exercises unlimited power without the restraint of responsibility. Dr. Kissinger has bet our lives on the sincerity of the Kremlin's gestures of detente. Perhaps he finds justification in a scholarly theory he enunciated before departing from Harvard's intellectually cloistered, ivy-covered halls for action-central in the White House:

> It is no accident that most great statesmen were opposed by their "experts" in their foreign offices, for the very greatness of the statesman's conception tends to make it inaccessible to those whose primary concern is with safety and minimum risk.

So we may take it that Richard Nixon was successfully deceived by his sophisticated assistant. Then the nagging question arises, how could an intelligent man, with access to all the information available to the President, be so totally taken in by mummery that should be penetrable by a bright high school student?

One compelling reason, of course, is that Dr. Kissinger told Richard Nixon what he, Nixon, would most like to believe—things that enabled him, without straining his conscience, to take political action that he believed would be popular and would win him worldwide acclaim. Most people have a compulsion to believe what they want to believe. In this respect any President of the United States is far more vulnerable than the rest of us humans, and it is especially so in this case. One of the most perceptive comments ever applied to Richard Nixon was this: "Only those who attain the heights of power can reach the heights of self-delusion."

The second reason is more intriguing. Most people already know the dramatic technique for accomplishing a major deception. They are completely familiar with it; that is, if they are among the some 40 million Americans who have viewed at least several episodes of the television series called *Mission Impossible*; or if they are among the some 20 million who (up through 1973) used to wait each week to see the recorder tape assign the impossible mission and then self-destruct in five seconds. The creators of the series hit on a format having much of the appeal of science fiction, but credible to and appealing to a much larger audience. *Star Trek*, for example, is time-framed in the 21st century and staged to be quite literally "out of this world." By contrast, MI, as it is familiarly termed by its fans, stages all its action on planet Earth, and its timeframe is the present. How, then, do the scriptwriters fulfill the desire of the audience for escapism from the dreary routine of day-to-day existence on this troubled planet? Imaginatively. They employ the near-miraculous scientific equipment actually available today and, when necessary for an especially dramatic effect, borrow some (such as minitelevision cameras) from just beyond the frontiers of the presently realized state of our technology. This scientific and pseudoscientific equipment is used to create highly specialized *artificial worlds* within this world. The audience is in on the trick, but the "targets" of the impossible missions are not.

The title is shrewdly chosen because the missions would be impossible in the real world. The set piece—a recurrent theme—is that of a bad guy who has hidden something of tremendous value. Only this man, the target of the mission, knows the hiding place, and he will not reveal it for love or money, or for immunity, or from torture. So, he must be tricked into going for it and thereby revealing the top-secret location. If the trick is obviously centered on the hidden object of value, the target person will become suspicious and never reveal its whereabouts.

The modus operandi adopted, therefore, is highly sophisticated. The plots are deliberately complex and elaborate. As presented on television, the *Mission Impossible* staff is briefed on the plan. Parts are assigned and scientific equipment distributed. Then they set about creating the specialized *artificial world* into which the particular target person is to be shanghaied or hijacked. It will be a world in which meticulously orchestrated developments, none of which has any apparent relation to the hidden thing of great value, leads the target person to conclude that a new use for the hidden item has developed for him, and that he must go to the hiding place immediately. *Mission Impossible* staff members then shadow him by scientific and spectacular means. The truly impossible mission, which thus becomes possible in the artificial world of specially created effects, is accomplished.

For many years, in many too-similar episodes, the hidden "thing" of tremendous value was computer tapes belonging to the crime syndicate or the "family." These are pictured as so vital to keep the operation going, and to keep the leaders out of jail, that the syndicate would willingly ransom them for five to 10 million dollars. Sometimes a rival crime gang wants the tapes for leads as to how to raid the established syndicate's territory. Or, the "thing" may be a top secret formula for the critical element of a new and revolutionarily accurate missile guidance system, which the MI force must regain before the traitor who stole and hid it can transmit it to the enemy.

The variety and adventure that kept the series so popular so long is in the type of *artificial world* created so that a sequence of developments can be staged to lead the target person to home in on his hidden treasure. The scriptwriters are not above using electronically evoked ghosts or chemically created hallucinations to shatter the nerves of the target to drive him to seek out his secret hiding place. By theatrical effects he may be convinced that he is about to die and must find his treasure and pass it on before it is too late; or that his fellow gangsters are plotting against him and will torture him to death if he doesn't get the evidence to the police in time for them to arrest the plotters.

Sometimes the appearance of reality is stretched a little thin. A syndicate man who had hidden the computer tapes was victimized by an MI-staged airplane crash in the remote and desolate mountain regions of Mexico. When he recovered consciousness he stumbled his way into a mysterious monastery, headquarters of the Brotherhood of the Golden Circle. The brothers and sisters all appear young, but the syndicate man is allowed to discover—by photographs and other documentary evidence he thinks they don't know he has found—that they are all really a couple of hundred years old, and the fountain of youth is right there in the monastery garden. In gangster fashion he deprives one of the sisters of her daily dosage of the magic water, and before his very eyes she ages 150 years and dies. Convinced that the fountain is the real thing, he decides to monopolize the water and market it. To get his distribution system going, he decides to make a deal with the syndicate, using the stolen tapes to get the crime group to furnish the organization he needs. So, he leads the MI staffers to the secret hiding place. The MI people had thus created an *artificial world* for him—a world in which he found it entirely credible that a fountain of youth could actually exist.

In contrast to such a naive and outdated plot, the MI series has produced some highly imaginative and elaborate scenarios—worthy patterns of the ones we will consider soon. One thing of tremendous value was a flask of a unique type of uranium. The target person was a formerly highly trusted scientist who had stolen and hidden the flask of uranium because he disapproved of its proposed use in a new type of nuclear weapon.

The MI staff did a real job on him. They knocked him out with an injection administered through a Lucrezia Borgia-type ring, and put him through an aging process that made him appear temporarily— even to himself, or rather, especially to himself—to be 20 years older than when he was last conscious. The made-to-order special-effects world created around him was oriented in a timeframe 20 years in the future. This future world was one that had been subjected to nuclear war *for 20 years*. The stage settings were elaborately designed to let the target scientist see for himself local samples of the presumably universal devastation by nuclear weapons. So also were the dramatic episodes played out before him, so that he could deduce for himself his own predicament in the wrecked but still ongoing world in which he believed he found himself after 20 years of amnesia. He is a member of a labor gang composed of old men of his own apparent age, and he discovers that he and they are scheduled for liquidation the following week because they are too old to justify continued allotments from the restricted food supply of the devastated country.

While seeking a way to avert his apparently imminent liquidation, the scientist makes a discovery: although the war is still going on, the antagonists are no longer exchanging nuclear attacks because both sides have run out of uranium. The first side to obtain additional uranium would win. The scientist recognizes that he is still in the area where he secreted the uranium flask more than 20 years before (he thinks). He secures an audience with the officer in charge of the area and makes his deal: he will lead them to a supply of uranium of unique potency if they spare his life. His offer is accepted; and he leads them to his treasure before discovering that the whole world in which he *thinks* he is living—including his apparent advanced age and the timeframe—is totally artificial and created especially for him.

That MI episode marked the high-water line in television creation of artificial worlds. Substantial resources were required to create the elaborate illusion: many thousands of dollars were expended on stage settings and special effects, and the imaginative approach to the whole problem has not been surpassed in current fictional presentations.

But nothing in the most far-out television story or movie plot, nothing in fiction, nothing recorded in the history of man, has attained the imaginative proportions in any way comparable with the fantastically elaborate scheme Henry Kissinger devised for turning the President of the United States into Kissinger's policy instrument. Its sheer incredibility is the prime cover used to make it invisible to and impenetrable by the American people, Congress, and the media. The Kissinger gambit is so totally unprecedented that it is incredible. It is so enormously shocking that it is incredible. It is so brilliant that it is incredible. It is so highly incredible, that is, that Dr. Henry Kissinger has gotten away with it.

In the past, emperors and kings have often been captured by the sheer military power of their palace guards, or by the superior intellects of their trusted advisers. Even religion has sometimes fronted for the transfer of political power from the nominal ruler to a "holy man." In 17th-century France royal power was exercised by Armand Cardinal de Richelieu; in the 19th century imperial Russia was subjected to the strange power of Grigori Efimovich Rasputin. In the United States substantial national influence has been exercised by presidential advisers such as Colonel House, Harry Hopkins, Sherman Adams, McGeorge Bundy, Walt W. Rostow, H. R. Haldeman, and John Ehrlichman.

Henry Kissinger, however, has surpassed them all. He has done so by creating a very special *artificial world* for the President. It is not, of course, a complete world; it does not relate to the nitty-gritty of domestic politics. It does include the more glamorous areas of presidential power and responsibility: the grand strategy of the United States, national security affairs of all types, strategic posture, international relations, and, especially, relations with the Soviet Union and Red China. Within these vital areas, Richard Nixon became the prisoner of the illusory world Dr. Kissinger designed especially for him. Kissinger played on Nixon's driving, irresistible ambition to accomplish grandiose, impossible missions; and—just as in the phony world of television—such missions can be accomplished only in an artificial world fashioned especially to make their accomplishment possible. Tragically, President Ford is similarly vulnerable.

It may all seem wildly improbable that Henry Kissinger created an artificial out-of-this-world environment for Richard Nixon and made him a prisoner of grandiose illusions in the realms of national security and foreign policy. You can believe this only if you are willing to consider the evidence. Some of this evidence is general, but other items are highly specific and susceptible of concrete, objective proof.

Significant fragments of Watergate evidence have established that, on the domestic side of the White House staff, H. R. Haldeman and John D. Ehrlichman paralleled the brilliant, sophisticated accomplishments of Henry Kissinger in the foreign policy field. They, too, in a crude but effective way, had created an artifical world for their boss. Their creation lacked the science fiction, deliberately obscurantic complexity, and many-splendored things of Kissinger's masterpiece. It operated more along the lines of a physical prison than an intellectual one. But it worked, as the Watergate revelations about the Nixon role in the affair demonstrated.

The basic ingredient for the creation of an isolation ward for the President—either domestic or foreign—was the same: monopoly of control of access to Richard Nixon. Many astute commentators recognized that this element of access-control was the sine qua non of decisive, as well as pervasive, influence over presidential policy decisions. Thus, Garnett D. Horner, columnist for the *Washington Star-News*, observed on May 1, 1973, that:

> For four years President Nixon has relied more and more on Haldeman and Ehrlichman to make his powers function.
> Steadily, their place at the very core of the White House has added to their authority, *not only to shape policy, but even to control what the President read or what he did with his time*. . . .

Some degree of their kind of unpopularity goes with the kind of power they wielded. This is particularly true of Haldeman's job as chief of staff and *guardian of any access to the President, either in person or by telephone.* . . .

Haldeman's job may be the toughest to fill. He has been the man closest to the President, the staff member who has seen him most often during each day. He has been the main channel for transmitting presidential instructions to most other members of the staff.

Until about three weeks ago, Haldeman presided at daily 8:15 a.m. meetings of senior staff members when the day's problems were discussed and the work laid out.

He was also the chief administrator at the White House, functioning much as a military chief of staff. Papers concerning presidential appointments throughout the bureaucracy normally crossed Haldeman's desk on the way to the President's.

Out of the entire vast flood of millions of words unleashed by Watergate, only those of columnist Joseph Alsop derived from intuition deep enough, and perception brilliant enough, to discover the uncharted *artificial world* that was created for Richard Nixon by his domestic advisers. Alsop introduced his explanation of what he calls "the Watergate horror" by a parable, an old New England story "which might have been invented by Eugene O'Neill," but was not, as Alsop assures us it is true.

Some forty years ago, according to Joseph Alsop in his syndicated column of May 7, 1973, the remnant of a formerly grand family lived in near-poverty behind the closed shutters of a once-pretentious house. The characters in residence were a brother and sister, middle-aged, and a mother past 80 who had been blind for decades.

The brother and sister, since early in life, had been incestuously in love. Their sense of guilt made them hate the light of day, and their blind mother had no means of knowing the time of day. Year after year, therefore, the brother and sister gradually changed the times of rising and going to bed. Finally, their mother was being wakened and breakfasted after sundown, and all other activities were timed in relation. The interiors of the house were shrouded, and the few callers were invited only for "morning coffee"—at 10 in the evening.

The aged blind mother had no idea that she was not leading a blind person's normal life, lovingly attended by her son and daughter. Sometimes, however, she did wonder why most of the traffic sounds were during the night instead of the day.

The significance of the parable, Alsop explains, is that, instead of incest, the passion of Watergate is love of power. Richard Nixon is abnormally reclusive and exceptionally intelligent. Unlike previous Presidents, he did not like the Oval Office because it is too open and airy. He liked to keep human contact to a minimum. He wanted to get the facts, to brood upon them, and then reach his decision. His custom, therefore, was to seclude himself in his hideaway in the Executive Office Building. Other than the special case of foreign policy advisers, no more than four persons had easy access to Nixon during his presidency.

Unlike the situation in the parable, there were not even traffic noises at apparently strange hours to raise questions in the President's mind. He never believed what he read or heard because he always believed that the press and television were unfair to Richard Nixon.

Among the four who had access to the President, moreover, the power to control the access of others was in the hands of one or two who were jealous of their prerogatives. Old friends sometimes attempted to use the President's longtime personal secretary, Rose Mary Woods, as a private channel to Richard Nixon, so that even she was made to suffer.

All of the four who had easy access to the President had three shared traits of character: none had any sweaty, practical, political experience; all suffered from a special kind of political tunnel vision; and all enjoyed the exercise of power.

In these circumstances, Joseph Alsop concludes, "the Watergate horror" becomes comprehensible. In his lifetime, he recounts, no President has ever failed to bend the law when there was a lot to be gained by doing so. Probably the ones who bent it most were Franklin Roosevelt and John Kennedy. But in Watergate the law was bent like a pretzel, and with inconceivable imprudence and no real prospect of gain for the President.

An intelligent President would not knowingly have permitted this sort of situation. Think, however, of Richard Nixon's passionate reclusiveness and the restrictions of access to him. Then think of the blind old lady. Then you can see how it all could have happened.

Washington reporter Aldo Beckman elaborated on Haldeman's success in erecting a barrier even between Nixon and his most faithful longtime associate, Rose Mary Woods, actually beginning before Nixon moved into the White House:

> She wanted an office adjacent to the Oval Office, where, during past administrations, personal secretaries had been quartered. Haldeman, however, concerned about controlling access to the President, insisted that she be installed in an office down the hall, larger than the one she wanted, but one that would not give her immediate access to the Oval Office.
>
> After a bitter battle, Miss Woods was assigned the office down the hall.[1]

It is clear that, by manipulating recluse Richard Nixon and

exercising selective exclusion over all domestic affairs, and by "controlling what the President read and what he did with his time," Haldeman and Ehrlichman were able to shut out the real world very effectively. Even *within* that artificial world, however, there may have been additional unsuspected restrictions on Nixon's cognitive opportunities. These relate to what might be tagged as internal communications. Stewart Alsop, in his column in *Newsweek* dated July 16, 1973, observed that Haldeman, Ehrlichman, Magruder, and Dean all shared a style, a way of speaking, and a point of view:

> They share a way of speaking—an oddly convoluted diction that sounds often like a difficult translation, and pat phrases like "signing on (off)," "brought up to speed," "in that timeframe," "at this point in time," "inoperative."

The Washington editor of *National Review*, George F. Will, in his column in the magazine dated June 22, 1973, offered a somewhat more intriguing possibility concerning internal communications in the Ehrlichman-dominated area of the White House:

> Mr. Ehrlichman was never more a child of this dreary time than when he stepped out of a closed meeting with a Senate subcommittee and told reporters that the burglarizing of Daniel Ellsberg's psychiatrist "was at that time oppressed [sic] with a very sensitive national security characteristic as far as we were concerned and as well as the investigating authorities were concerned and continued to be oppressed with that characteristic until very recently."
>
> . . . Mr. Ehrlichman talks as he does naturally, and he is not alone. All governments are chock-full of people who talk that way. So we return to the short-term significance of Mr. Ehrlichman's statement: perhaps he is just afraid to talk sense. But you cannot infer from the fact that he talks nonsense. . . .
>
> Perhaps the most interesting possibility (and it is *not* a probability) is that the White House often talks worse than it acts. For more than 5 years men around Mr. Nixon's White House have been talking to one another and to the rest of us in Ehrlichmanese about "protective reaction strikes" (that's bombing, friend) and Cambodian "incursions" (as in the verb, "to incurse"). The bombings and the incursions were good policy cloaked in language that made them seem embarrassing.
>
> Be that as it may, the *possibility* exists that Mr. Nixon really did not know what his assistants were saying to him when they talked—or hinted, or obfuscated—about the Watergate coverup they were administering.

The point that Nixon may not have understood, or may at least have been confused, by Ehrlichmanese is certainly not susceptible of proof, and Will emphasizes the fact that he offers it as a mere *possibility*. Whether or not Richard Nixon was restricted in his opportunities for knowledge by the language used in his artificial world is mere speculation. But the fact that Haldeman and Ehrlichman had, indeed, created such a private world—for all practical purposes, that is—appears to be reasonably well established.

There is immeasurably more evidence—and more specific evidence—that Henry Kissinger was successful in creating an artificial world in which to imprison Richard Nixon for the purpose of controlling his decision-making in foreign and military policy matters. Henry Kissinger has a vastly greater intellect than Haldeman or Ehrlichman, and his imagination has an incalculably longer reach. Furthermore, in the area of domestic politics, Nixon is the lifelong professional and Ehrlichman and Haldeman were the amateurs; whereas, in the fields of both nuclear strategy and international relations, Kissinger is the expert and the learned authority, while Nixon is the credulous novice.

If you believe that Haldeman and Ehrlichman were able to isolate the President from most congressional contacts, from contacts with Republican Party officials, and from nearly all individuals, and thus to create an insulated world for him in domestic matters, then this will help you to accept the evidence that Kissinger did the same in his esoteric areas. Even if you don't accept the facts of the Haldeman-Ehrlichman power, the abundant evidence as to Kissinger's masterpiece of imagination and brashness should be sufficient. Certainly, if Nixon could ever possibly be confused by Ehrlichmanese, there is a tremendously greater possibility that he could be entirely snowed by Kissinger's highly sophisticated and complex jargon.

In addition, there is the point of the fantastic resources available to Kissinger for the creation of his fabulous world of foreign relations: resources of science and technology, human resources, military resources, and money, money, money. Never in history has so much been available to one man for such a project.

To create the artificial worlds presented in the *Mission Impossible* television programs required special effects, theatrical props, and technical equipment costing thousands of dollars for a single episode. But for every thousand dollars expended for such a television program, Kissinger has quite literally had the use and control of resources costing *thousands* of millions of dollars; that is, billions of dollars.

The intelligence community of the United States costs the taxpayers an estimated $6 billion each year. Henry Kissinger has quietly, but inexorably, gained absolute dictatorial power over all segments of this tremendous apparatus. Only a longterm student of nuclear strategy can possibly appreciate the power potential of complete control of the totality of the intelligence organizations and facilities of a nuclear superpower. Fortunately for the impenetrability of Kissinger's plans, almost all students of nuclear strategy are "kept" men. That is, they are employed directly by the government, or by think-tanks whose principal source of income is the government. Even the few not so influenced may have hopes that, if they do not rock any Kissinger boat, they may be appointed as ambassadors or to direct some government agency.

That leaves very few qualified nuclear strategists for Kissinger to worry about. Even here there is an ironic twist. Regardless of how familiar one may be with the U.S. intelligence community, the tendency is to "think in a box" about it. Those concerned are so accustomed to thinking of its legitimate functions, and there is so much room for improvement in those areas, that they never get around to evaluating or imagining its potential value to a would-be dictator, or even to a would-be foreign-policy national-grand-strategy czar.

Consider the resources involved. With some 16 major agencies in the conglomerate, a total of something like 200,000 employees are included in the U.S. intelligence community. The pieces of the federal budget involved in this operation add up to a yearly expenditure of some $6 billion, not including what should be considered as capital investment in facilities and equipment. It surely has the most massive banks of the most complex and technologically advanced computers in the world. One segment alone, the National Security Agency headquarters at Fort Meade, Maryland, has more than a billion dollars worth of code-breaking and data-storage computerized equipment.

Billions of dollars have been invested in space and aerospace equipment to provide electronic and photographic eyes and electronic ears for U.S. intelligence. We have a fleet of SR-71 spy planes, and hundreds of multipurpose Project 647 surveillance satellites. These latter orbit at 22,000 miles altitude, scanning, sniffing, and listening over all important areas of the earth's surface. There is also a newly developed force of "Big Bird" satellites, weighing 10 tons each and loaded with the most intricate, complex, unbelievable scientific instrumentation man has ever dreamed of and produced. These were first flown in 1970. Under development since 1971 has been the most far-out satellite project ever conceived: the Air Force project code-numbered 1010. It is officially tagged as a "crisis-spotter" satellite. Whereas several days are frequently required with present equipment to process pictures taken on the other side of the world for transmission to Washington, these new satellites will translate their pictures into electronic signals that can then be transmitted to communications satellites, and then relayed to Washington almost instantaneously. The cost is more than a billion dollars, and worth it.

As always, however, when a development will advantage the

United States against the U.S.S.R., this brilliant project is being deliberately slowed down. It is not scheduled for operational employment until 1978. That date may have been carefully chosen. Under the Kissinger programs for the freeze of U.S. developments and the Brezhnev programs for continued Soviet buildup of strategic weapons systems, the Soviets should attain a preclusive first-strike capability against the United States before that time. *If we had an adequate force of such satellites deployed,* neither Pugwash scientists nor Henry Kissinger could contend that a launch-on-confirmation-of-warning strategy would risk triggering a mistaken or accidental war. The credibility of our Minuteman missile force as a deterrent would be extended a matter of years, *if,* that is, the Soviets do not advance unpredictably in pin-down techniques.

Just this thumbnail sketch of a mere fraction of the equipment and facilities developed for the U.S. intelligence community is convincing that we have not only exceeded any intelligence capabilities in history, but that our potential is quite literally fantastic. We owe this tremendous defense asset to American science, American technology, American industrial plant, and to American labor and taxpayers. It *could* save all of us from nuclear incineration.

To balance this vast potential, however, we have an equally great vulnerability: one-man absolute control over the entire U.S. intelligence community. Henry Kissinger, like a pudgy spider at the center of a web, has for more than five years preempted pervasive powers over our entire intelligence network, spinning out hardly noticed but ever-stronger, ever more far-reaching, lines of control over all segments of the intelligence community. Concurrently with his efficiency-masked reorganizations of structure to support his total control, he has achieved a clean-sweep ouster of all top-level officials who formerly exercised power over key agencies in the overall intelligence organization. That is, he not only drew up the organization charts that establish the lines of communication, command, and control in the bureaucracy, but he either selected, or exercised veto power over, the names of the men who were to fill the command boxes in the charts.

Dr. Kissinger's takeover of the U.S. intelligence community, his fourth power base, demonstrates that he has an intuitive understanding of power, a feeling for it, and exquisite skill in exercising it, just as the admiring articles in the media have so long told us. His performance has been marked by brilliance and brutality, by bold strokes and subtle maneuvering, by flashes of inspired imagination and by the sustained patience of a determination to achieve his objective. In short, he has displayed all the traits of character, all the capabilities, the momentous mental power, the understanding of nuances, and the skill in administration that America has so long and so desperately needed in our number-one statesman. He actually proved that he can get things done *now*, as well as plan for the future; that he *could* have fulfilled the hope of so many Americans in negotiations with foreign nations, namely, that one of ours would prove smarter than any of theirs.

Tragically, however, in a pitifully few years, the lament of Americans who finally find out what has happened to the United States may sound as an imperfect paraphrase of a Shakespearean character in the throes of remorse:

> Had Henry Kissinger but served his country with half the zeal
> He served himself, America would not at the end of her second century
> Be left naked to her enemies.

His handling of power is what reveals the decisive split in Henry Kissinger's personality—a sort of muted schizophrenia that can be fatal to us. When Kissinger exercises power to create or consolidate new power sources for his own personal aggrandizement, when he exercises power to orchestrate actions of his long-existing power bases to gather in control of their influence, he acts with courage and confidence.

When acting on behalf of the United States, however, he never acts to extend or intensify our national power. He never uses our power in-being to build more power in-being, whether strategic, political, or economic. He never employs our massive and unmatched power potential to create power to fill in potentially fatal gaps. Working for himself, when he has power, he exerts it with a facility matched only by his brutality. His personnel policy in regard to his own staff has been described by a surviving member—speaking figuratively, no doubt—as "rule or castrate." Waves of resignations suggest that excisions in intellectual and ideological areas have been vindictive as well as cruel. His memory for slights is as long as his mind is reputed to be great. Consider the protracted vendetta he conducted for so long against Melvin Laird; or his many humiliations of Ambassador Gerard C. Smith, culminating in the final discharge both as head of the U.S. SALT delegation and as director of the U.S. Arms Control and Disarmament Agency.

When Kissinger is negotiating with a NATO ally or with the Japanese, all the arrogance that marks the conduct of his personal drive for power is manifest. He confronts them with faits accomplis—unnecessarily, and for no apparent purpose other than the humiliation of the lesser power.

But Henry Kissinger dealing with the rulers in Moscow and Peking is entirely different from Henry Kissinger building up his personal

225

power or dealing with U.S.-allied nations of inferior power. Protected by a shroud of secrecy from having his attitude or actions exposed to the American people, to Congress, or even to his President, whenever he deals with the Communist dictators, he becomes servile, ingratiating, and unctuous. Although our most sophisticated negotiator, he volunteers concessions before they are asked, beyond any the Soviets would have dared to demand, beyond the most extravagant ambitions of the Red Chinese—at least during this century.

It matters not what cards he holds, what "bargaining chips" he has with which to demand fair play for U.S. vital interests. If the United States has enough millions of tons of grain to stave off an imminent famine in Russia, if the United States is the *only* country that can supply the human food and cattle food essential to avert chain-reaction food crises in the Soviet Union, does Dr. Kissinger secure a quid pro quo from the masters of the Kremlin? Did he secure a single concession for our side, for freedom inside Russia, or in the slave states, or even for communication with the Western world? No, he didn't, even though the cost to the American taxpayer of the Kissinger wheat-deal gift to the Kremlin was nearly a billion dollars in direct costs, subsidies, and credits; hundreds of millions in profits lost to the U.S. farmers, from whom the magnitude of the deal was concealed until too late, and in increased shipping charges; and at least $3 billion in increased prices of wheat products and meat paid by the American consumers already burdened with inflation.

If Kissinger's compulsion to appease the Soviets was so strong as to make him risk this great grocery giveaway gimmick—the one-sidedness and high cost of which every American who eats and reads (including every American housewife) could understand—how much would he give away in the SALT I Agreements? Especially when not 1/100 of one percent of the U.S. population could be expected to understand the purposes of the agreements, their terms, their imbalances, their assumptions, their loopholes, their psychological effect, and their operational implications. Sections of this book on the decisive fundamentals of nuclear strategy will expose the inexorable results of the Kissinger policies of no-defense and inferior-offense in the military posture of the United States; and analysis of the terms of the SALT I Agreements will demonstrate the totally national-suicidal nature of Kissinger's concealed concessions to the Kremlin.

One explanation of this sensationally split personality of Henry Kissinger is Khrushchev's formula that liberal leaders are subject to a paralysis of fear of nuclear war. This fear is so corrosive as to destroy all sense of national pride and patriotism, as well as national and personal honor. The SALT I Agreements, as we observe and demonstrate elsewhere in this book, spell out a simple and compelling message of American strategic inferiority.

The tragic character of the Kissinger concessions in the SALT I Agreements is that they constitute a sellout of the United States to the Communist Party of the Soviet Union. They constitute a betrayal of the American people. They demonstrate that this sellout of America, this betrayal of our people, has been accomplished by the conspiratorial machinations of Henry Kissinger. Although there is much other evidence of both Dr. Kissinger's conspiratorial actions and his betrayal of vital national security interests of the United States, the conspiracy is amply proved by the fraudulent nature of the 2½ years of the SALT I negotiations; and the sellout to the Soviets is demonstrated by the fact that the Kissinger concessions not only will enable the Soviets to attain a preclusive nuclear first-strike capability against the United States, but that Kissinger concealed the true results of the SALT I Agreements by resorting to direct and demonstrable lies calculated to deceive the President, the Congress, and the American people.

The point here is that, to deceive the Congress and the American people required only the false front of the Vienna-Helsinki years of negotiations, plus a crash effort when the SALT I Agreements were submitted to Congress in the summer of 1972 while the euphoria generated by the Kissinger-Nixon TV spectaculars during the Moscow visit was still strong. But to deceive the President of the United States is an entirely different problem—especially when it involves the survival of the United States, its free and independent government, and the American people, in the nuclear-space age.

The President's greatest responsibility is to ensure us against nuclear attack and nuclear blackmail. The latter could seal the national doom of America just as surely as the first, although it would be on an installment process. To protect us against these supreme threats, the President has—so far as all relevant intelligence is concerned—an all-embracing need to know, and an overriding right to know. No President could in conscience delegate to any other person, regardless of apparent competence and trustworthiness, any essential element of his personal responsibility for national survival. The ultimate evaluation of the threat must be his alone, and the critical decisions as to meeting the threat must be his alone.

Unfortunately for our chances for survival in freedom, the side of Henry Kissinger's split personality that serves his personal power-building was operating at full capacity when he sought to solve the problem of a continuing deception of the President on all matters relating to the grand nuclear strategy of the nation and on relations with the Politburo in Moscow and the powers in Peking.

Kissinger surely did *not* derive his "artificial world" solution from any clue or inspiration in the television series *Mission Impossible*. A dedicated megalomaniac makes a poor audience for any performances other than his own. He is driven to *be* the principal character: the great intellectual, the great lover, the lone cowboy, or Kissinger at one of his self-dramatized "battle stations." While *Mission Impossible's* set pieces can assist the reader to understand how a scenario artist can devise a bold and imaginative artifically created environment in order to reach a brash and brilliant solution to his plot, Kissinger had no need for such a stimulus. He has actually *lived* in such an imaginary, artificially created world. He was thoroughly familiar with the means for creating an artificial world and endowing it with a strategic environment that differed drastically from that of the real world, but that could be convincing enough to make fools of the experts.

Kissinger was one of the principal architects of the artificial world of the "missile-gap-that-never-was" that existed in the macabre imaginations of several cliques of U.S. unilateral-disarmament intellectuals *circa* 1957-63. In the real world then, the strategic environment was shaped and dominated by (1) a decisive U.S. superiority over the Soviets in strategic weapons plus effective delivery systems; and by (2) U.S. possession of a near-total counterforce capability (and, without this type of capability, strategic nuclear power is not rationally usable).

In what the Joint Chiefs of Staff sometimes refer to as the "Cuban environment," *the Soviets had no substantial counterforce capability against the United States.* As we have seen, Henry Kissinger, in an off-the-record briefing for newsmen in September 1967, admitted that in 1962 "the Soviets had around 40 ICBMs; we had over 1,000 bombers and over 200 missiles that could reach the Soviet Union."

But in the artificial world of which he was cocreator, Kissinger asserted flatly in 1960 that a massive missile gap in favor of the Soviets had become "unavoidable" for the period 1961-65, and that the Soviets might have a win/strike-first capability against us. ("It may mean that we could lose if the Soviets struck first. In that case, we would be fortunate if we escaped a surprise attack.")

The great missile-gap-that-never-was, which spanned the years 1958 until 1962 when its predicted life span was cut short by the Cuban missile crisis, taught the unilateral-disarmament intellectuals a number of lasting lessons:

(1) An artificial world, featuring a totally imaginary strategic environment diametrically opposite to that of the real world, *can* be created by erroneous intelligence.

(2) Such intelligence can be innocently, naively or negligently in error; or it can be deliberately distorted and intentionally false.

(3) Regardless of its origin or motivation, the cause which effectively creates the artificial world is intelligence which does not represent reality.

(4) A "department of misinformation"—such as the Soviets operate along with their KGB and GRU—or its equivalent is a valuable instrument in the effective dissemination of intelligence which is contrary to objective reality.

(5) Just as an artificial world featuring imaginary strategic postures and relationships between the superpowers can be created by misleading intelligence, it can be destroyed by accurate and authoritative intelligence. Regardless of how much the structure cost in time, money, and boldly imaginative creative efforts, it will be continuously vulnerable to destruction if reality is allowed to intrude. (Perhaps this is the nuclear-space age application of the ancient aphorism, "Nothing is so powerful as the truth.")

Most people remember most vividly those segments of history that they personally lived through. Those who struggled through the great depression of the 1930s will never forget it; it was, in the liberal lexicon, a "meaningful" experience. Henry Kissinger lived through the imaginary-missile-gap period of history and learned its lessons well. He learned that, to accomplish his Mission Incredible—the protracted deception of the President of the United States on matters of strategic military posture and balance, and about Soviet and Chinese intentions — he would have to obtain and maintain total control of the entire U.S. intelligence community. Kissinger could see, when he looked back with the 20/20 vision of hindsight, that the phony missile gap of the 1960 period had been created by the slick and sinister design of the Soviets' misinformation service from within their foreign intelligence organizations, with a big assist from (1) Soviet agents or accommodationists within U.S. intelligence, or State, or Defense, plus (2) the defeatist nuclear-terror-paralyzed minds of the U.S. unilateral-disarmament intellectuals.

What stuck in Kissinger's mind is that it had worked. It had endured for some four or five years. It had been a durable illusion because U.S. intelligence—in both meanings of that word—was incredibly poor. Ironically, the accurate, authoritative intelligence that finally destroyed this artificial world came not at all from U.S. sources but from the great Soviet defector Colonel Oleg Penkovskiy. The wildly irresponsible, staggeringly wrong U.S. intelligence of that period has been accepted ever since as innocent—as just a good-faith mistake. But suppose that the highest levels had in fact been penetrated by Soviet agents; that is, that they had a stage manager in U.S. intelligence who had presided over the creation and maintenance of the phony missile gap. The only thing he *could not have foreseen*, and thereby averted, was an accident such as Colonel Penkovskiy. Because the Penkovskiy information came through British contacts and went directly to President Kennedy during the Cuban missile crisis, Defense Secretary Robert McNamara had no opportunity to suppress it at that critical time. There is no way of telling what might have happened to the United States in October 1962 if Colonel Penkovskiy had not stayed on the job and furnished up-to-the-minute and accurate information to President Kennedy on Soviet strategic capabilities and even the geography of the Soviet missile sites.

The manner in which the Penkovskiy information actually reached President Kennedy demonstrated the danger to national survival of an intelligence organization without competing agencies, each of which has direct access to the President. This version, which we have checked out as substantially correct, was used by *Newsweek*, November 22, 1971, as an introduction to that magazine's comprehensive writeup of Kissinger's drastic reorganization of U.S. intelligence:

One day in the fall of 1962, President John F. Kennedy summoned his top intelligence advisers to the White House for an urgent conference. Russian missiles had been discovered in Cuba, and in planning the U.S. response that was shortly to unfold as the Cuban missile crisis, it was essential to have the most accurate possible estimate of the Soviet capacity for nuclear war.

The chiefs of military intelligence arrived from the Pentagon with elaborate tables showing the latest projections of Russian rocket power: if the U.S.S.R. had produced all the missiles it was capable of producing, they indicated, the American advantage in a show-down would be perilously slight.

The man from the Central Intelligence Agency, on the other hand, brought a single piece of paper. This spare document revealed that the Soviet arsenal was in fact much weaker than had been feared—and thus John Kennedy discovered that he had the muscle to twist Nikita Khrushchev's arm in the confrontation that lay ahead.

The source of this crucial information was Oleg Penkovskiy, a Colonel in Soviet military intelligence who had been passing vital Russian secrets to the West for 16 months, only to be caught in November 1962 and executed 6 months later.

Newsweek continued with this comment: "He was a brave but not particularly admirable character . . ." This is typical of the continuing efforts made through elitist sources to smear Penkovskiy and degrade the valuable intelligence he gave us, critical material that has been suppressed as tightly under Kissinger as under Mc-

Namara. Certain members of the intelligence community have never given up trying to discredit Colonel Penkovskiy's great and unique contribution to the security of the United States. Seeking to take advantage of the public's lack of knowledge in such a specialized field, they risk even stupid lies in their attempts. Thus, the following article was planted in *U.S. News & World Report* on August 12, 1973:

JFK's ACE. Satellite operations have come a long way since the late 1950s when the first experiments were conducted by the Air Force under the code name "SAMOS," which stands for "satellite and missile observation system."

The first real test of the system came during the 1962 Cuban missile crisis when it appeared that the United States and the Soviet Union were headed toward a nuclear confrontation over the latter's placement of 1,500-mile range rockets in Cuba.

President Kennedy needed to know the size of Moscow's intercontinental missile arsenal in order to assess the risks to the U.S. from a possible Soviet attack. The intelligence community had projected as many as 400 long-range missiles scattered throughout the Soviet Union. A reconnaissance satellite counted only about a dozen. Armed with this knowledge, President Kennedy stood firm on his demand that the Russians remove their missiles from Cuba—and they did.

A stupid lie is one that can be convincingly exposed as such. Let's look at this one. Whatever else President Kennedy may have been, he was not stupid. He would not in the timeframe of his administration rely on a satellite count of missiles because the lives of scores of millions of Americans were at stake. As President, he had access to all intelligence information. Khrushchev, by the device of throwing a public tantrum over the May 1, 1960, U-2 flight over the Soviet Union, had effectively shot down all subsequent U-2 flights over Russia. The Eisenhower Administration would not have taken such risks to dispatch U-2 flights in mid-1960 if satellite photography were sufficiently advanced to provide reliable intelligence. The first U.S. satellite in 1958 weighed 18.13 pounds, and the second one 3.24 pounds—not much room for high-resolution camera or communications equipment. The first satellite we developed capable of carrying a man in orbit was the Mercury spacecraft that carried John H. Glenn, Jr., on February 20, 1962. The only reconnaissance satellites we had in 1962 were experimental. We did not have really sophisticated satellites with high-resolution cameras operational until 1963-64 at the earliest.

The reconnaissance gap between the last U-2 flight in May 1960 and the first operational reconnaissance satellites in 1962 gave the Soviets the opportunity in that timeframe to deploy *and conceal* scores of hundreds of missiles, and these would not have been revealed by the 1962 reconnaissance satellites with their primitive capabilities of resolution.

Furthermore, if the satellites that photographed the "only about a dozen" Soviet ICBMs in 1962 were so reliable, why did they not detect the shipment of the missiles to Cuba? As James Daniel and John G. Hubbell put it in *Strike in the West:*

> The missiles themselves were probably manufactured behind the Urals, moved by land and sea half way around the world, unloaded in ports only a few miles from Florida, transported across Cuban highways, and then put in place.[2]

Satellite photography did not reveal the digging of the missile sites in Cuba, or the installation of radar equipment, buildings, and vehicles included in the deployment of the Soviet missiles. If they did not reveal missile sites in Cuba, how could the President have responsibly relied on a satellite count of missiles in the U.S.S.R.? And satellite photography of the Soviet Union is far more difficult: cloud cover prevails 80 percent of the time there, and our cameras still cannot cope with it.

Finally, the alleged reconnaissance satellite count of "only about a dozen" Soviet ICBMs in October 1962, which is given in the *U.S. News* article cited above, is erroneous by more than 200 percent. We know from Henry Kissinger's own figures, quoted earlier, that the Soviets "had around 40 ICBMs" in October 1962. In other words, our satellites counted fewer than 1/3 of the Soviet ICBMs actually deployed. President Kennedy would not have staked the fate of millions of Americans on the then-unreliable satellite information; but he could and did rely on the intelligence furnished by Colonel Penkovskiy.

Oleg Penkovskiy loved his Russian people. He felt that they had been betrayed and enslaved by the Communist Party of the Soviet Union, by its Politburo, and by the police-state government it had imposed on the people. He defected not from his country, but from the illegitimate government oppressing his country. *Newsweek* understated it when characterizing Penkovskiy as "brave." He was one of the most courageous men of the 20th century. He was also one of the most perceptive and brilliant intelligence analysts and an accurate prophet. The accuracy of his psychoanalysis of Nikita Khrushchev has been demonstrated as absolute. Penkovskiy's concept of nuclear strategy was common sense, as distinguished from theoretical.

The Paul Nitze-Robert McNamara elitist school reasoned that a nation that was a *strong* second-best in strategic nuclear power would be the one most likely to get "clobbered"—an elitist euphemism meaning scores of millions of people incinerated. Penkovskiy, had it figured out that, with a leader such as Khrushchev in absolute power, it was the *weak* second-best nation which would get clobbered the worst. Penkovskiy did not want that to happen to the Russian people. His greatest fear was that Khrushchev would start a nuclear war despite the fatal relative weakness of the Soviets against the enormous U.S. strategic power. He recognized that Khrushchev was on the brink of this horrendous adventure when Khrushchev, Brezhnev, and Kosygin kept secret from the others in the Politburo their scheme to sneak missiles into Cuba, and he knew that Khrushchev relied on the advantage of surprise to make up for Soviet weakness in nuclear weapons systems. Penkovskiy correctly reasoned that, if deprived of the advantage of surprise, Khrushchev would not dare to initiate the war in which Penkovskiy believed scores of millions of Russian people would be killed in the inexorable U.S. retaliation. That was what brought Colonel Penkovskiy to defect to the West: love of and loyalty to his own people and his country, and his desire for peace and freedom throughout the world.

Henry Kissinger fully realized that, to make and create an artificial world with an imaginary strategic environment invulnerable to surprise destruction by intrusion of the truth, he would have to establish a control over the entire U.S. intelligence organization so absolutely total that there could never again be another Penkovskiy-type development. There was no way to guarantee full insurance against a Russian patriot defecting and seeking to give information to the West; but sufficiently tight control within the U.S. Government could prevent any such information from *actually reaching* the President.

Both the planning and execution of total Kissinger control over the U.S. intelligence community have been exquisitely thorough. Kissinger has virtually encircled the entire organization; more accurately, he has boxed it in with a quadrilateral structure. He has left nothing to chance: organization, personnel, operating procedure, even standards of proof. All have been restructured, purged, or altered to meet the requirements of Kissinger's grand design.

Is it not possible that Kissinger's intensive and extensive reorganization has been simply to promote efficiency and effectiveness? Yes; but the evidence is overwhelmingly to the contrary. Not since the days of President Franklin Roosevelt, when weird characters and Communist accommodationists penetrated the embryo U.S. intelligence organizations, has our intelligence been either efficient or effective—or reliable. But to change that required the elimination of the ideological blocks and emotional blinders that are pervasive in all echelons of most U.S. intelligence agencies. These are what prevented belief in the evidence at the time of the Cuban missile crisis, and to this day they stand in the way of what might redundantly be characterized as an intelligent intelligence estimate of the Soviet capabilities involved in their enormously expensive "heavy" missile program of SS-9s and SS-18s. But nothing Kissinger did in his reorganizations and personnel purges in any way weakened the ideological and emotional bias that has customarily dictated faulty interpretations of Communist intentions.

The best evidence of Kissinger's purpose in his extensive reorganization is the concrete result he accomplished. It would defy the percentages of probability to conduct an intensive reshuffle of such a heterogeneous conglomerate of agencies and inadvertently come up with leak-tight one-man control over all phases of the operation. It would be especially difficult to accomplish this and, at the same time, create the illusion that the reorganization still permitted entire entities within the intelligence community to compete with each other for the attention of the President.

It was essential to Kissinger to ensure against the *appearance* of monopolistic control of the entire intelligence organization, a flaw widely recognized as one of the chief perils of any intelligence system. All nations strive to avert this special danger. This effort in the Soviet Union explains the incredibly extensive and expensive overlap between the KGB and the GRU. Henry Kissinger, when scheming for himself, never falls into the trap of permitting his ulterior purpose to become obvious. Thus, in his reorganization of U.S. intelligence, he resisted the temptation to justify centralization on the ground of eliminating-extravagant-overlaps-and-welding-intelligence-gatherers-into-a-single-streamlined-mechanism.

Instead, he indulged in a chain of typical Kissinger subtleties. He invoked economy as a driving force, while paying elaborate obeisance to the preservation of diversity. In *Newsweek's* November 22, 1971, account of the Kissinger reorganization, a self-serving rationale appears as a sincere interview:

Modern spying does not come cheap, the administration is quite prepared to admit, but neither does it require the extravagant overlaps between different intelligence agencies or the excesses of trivia amassed in the name of thoroughness. Hence [CIA director Richard McGarrah] Helms' reinforced powers as intelligence superchief, with authority to oversee other agencies' budgets and reorder their priorities.

Neither Richard Helms nor Richard Nixon wants to weld the intelligence gatherers into a single streamlined mechanism. The President, according to one of his aides, "has given careful thought to what degree of diversity in the intelligence community is an essential luxury in a democratic society." If there were only one single agency and if on some crucial point its information were wrong, this staffer warns, "by God, it would be all over." Having some diverse views coming to the White

House as they do now means one intelligence service is effectively acting as a check on another.

First, the unnamed White House "staffer" must be Kissinger himself, or someone speaking for him, because he long ago established a monopoly on intelligence functions within the White House, probably immediately in January 1969. Second, he uses a statement that is technically true in order to imply something that is not true, namely, that under the reorganization it is still possible to have "some diverse views coming to the White House"; in fact, he has ensured against any views uncensored by him getting into the hands of the President. Third, the reorganization was timed while Richard Helms was still Director of CIA, although Kissinger had already decided to purge him and replace him with Daniel Ellsberg's protege, James R. Schlesinger.

Kissinger's timing was perfect. It enabled him, without arousing suspicion that he was working a personal power play, to "reorganize" vastly greater and more centralized power into the hands of the director of the Central Intelligence Agency, and make him also director of Central Intelligence (boss of the whole intelligence show), head of the U.S. Intelligence Board (which is the board of directors of the intelligence community), and head of the Intelligence Resources Advisory Committee (which has potent budget-reduction powers over all intelligence agencies). This move did not arouse suspicion because the then-incumbent was not a Kissinger stooge. Helms' secretly selected prospective replacement, however, had already made his brownie points with Kissinger. The grand strategy underlying the reorganization of U.S. intelligence was Kissinger's, but the details of the plan were the work of James R. Schlesinger. Schlesinger had had no experience in intelligence work, but he holds three degrees from Harvard, had been professor at the University of Virginia, and, on Daniel Ellsberg's recommendation, had been hired by the Rand Corporation as an "expert" on strategic matters. Here is how *U.S. News & World Report* tells how Kissinger had Helms fired and replaced:

> Knowledgeable sources say that Richard Helms, now Ambassador to Iran, was replaced by Mr. Schlesinger as CIA Director because he failed to carry out the overhaul mandate to Mr. Nixon's satisfaction.
>
> A top man in the intelligence network put it this way: "The President and his national security adviser, Henry Kissinger, just didn't think they were getting their money's worth."
>
> The reorganization plan, in fact, is Mr. Schlesinger's own handiwork. He drafted it while serving as Assistant Director of the Office of Management and Budget. Later he was named Chairman of the Atomic Energy Commission—the job from which he was transferred to his present post as America's "superspy."[3]

Having drafted the intelligence reorganization plan for Kissinger,

James Schlesinger knew exactly how to implement it with speed and effectiveness. He took charge on February 2, 1973. By April 16, 1973, Keyes Beech, writing for the *Chicago Daily News,* reported that morale of the CIA "has sunk to an all-time low under the impact of a drastic reorganization under the new director." Even more significantly, he added that the "greatest fear" about the reorganization expressed by most CIA field men

> is that in the process, and under an administration that seems to insist on absolute loyalty to the President, the CIA will lose its most precious assets—its integrity and independence of judgment, regardless of who is in power.

In the area of intelligence, sadly, "absolute loyalty to the President" really means "absolute loyalty to Dr. Kissinger." In executing the Kissinger-desired purges, Schlesinger fired three experienced deputy directors and more than 1,000 employees, cutting some divisions 18 percent. With a significance that would emerge only when he himself left the CIA after less than six months as director, Schlesinger replaced the deputy director for Plans with William E. Colby, who had served with the exotic Office of Strategic Services during World War II. Thus, the loyalty lines were kept intact: Schlesinger was beholden to Kissinger; Colby was beholden to Schlesinger. After Watergate propelled Elliot Richardson from Defense to Justice, and Schlesinger from CIA to Defense, Colby advanced to director of CIA.

The Kissinger technique is nothing if not thorough. After he had instituted the reorganization, but before he had placed the skids under Helms, Kissinger tackled the problem of the Number Two man in the CIA: the Deputy Director, Lieutenant General Robert E. Cushman, Jr., of the United States Marines. Marines are notoriously inflexible, especially in areas in which unilateral-disarmament intellectuals regard flexibility as highly desirable. The entire plan for the creation and maintenance of an artificial world with an imaginary strategic environment might be upset by a stubborn Marine demanding access to the President to convey some emergency intelligence. General Cushman had a record of some three years of highly effective service as the Deputy Director. Being only second in command, he was not vulnerable to a fabricated charge of failing to carry out a Kissinger reorganization plan swiftly enough. Not being a political creature, he could not be ousted as a political gambit.

When a plan to build personal power is concerned, Kissinger displays remarkable resources. After all, he had been brash enough to secure the promotion of his own military deputy, Alexander Haig, from colonel to four-star general in four years. When the post of Commandant of the Marine Corps became vacant, Kissinger seized on this as the solution to his problem. General Cushman had been considered ineligible by reason of the Marine tradition that an officer who voluntarily departs from the chain of command in the Corps has made his choice forever, so far as becoming Commandant of the Marines is concerned. Furthermore, at the time the vacancy occurred, the General was too portly to fit the trim Marine image. But Kissinger is not one to permit a military tradition to stand in his way. Lieutenant General Cushman became General Cushman and moved from Number Two Spy to Number One Marine.

Kissinger's slick and brash purges of key officials in the intelligence community were exceeded only by the brilliance of his charts for the grand reorganization. The more experienced one is in the ways of bureaucracy, the more one can appreciate its ingenious character. In the organization chart, all the lines indicating flow of information, and especially all the lines of authority, run up to and through Henry Kissinger. To make trebly sure of his total control, both information and authority must flow up through him sitting in three different capacities and exercising ultimate authority, plus a monopoly of access to the President. The following chart shows the power Kissinger had gathered into his own hands even before he became Secretary of State and thereby senior statutory member of the National Security Council (with the power to cast two votes in NSC meetings).

The most brilliant innovations, so far as achieving the overriding purpose of the reorganization, are the National Security Council's Intelligence Committee, an entirely new type of unit, and the Net Assessment Group. The former has the unprecedented authority to assign projects, problems, and all types of work to the entire intelligence community. Equally without precedent, it has the authority to "review" all the results; that is, to suppress, alter, or veto any reports. That new unit is, of course, headed by Henry Kissinger.

The Net Assessment Group segregates from all other intelligence information the one area most vital to the President of the United States: the strategic military balance. The "net assessment" authority of this group endows it with exclusive power to interpret the present and prospective state of such balances—primarily, of course, the state of the strategic military balance between the United States and the Soviet Union. Nothing could shock a President out of the euphoria of a temporary vision of detente faster than an expert, objective assessment of the strategic balance—now, and what it will be like at the end of 1976.

Dr. Kissinger exercises total personal control over this Net Assessment Group. He is in charge, and its few members were handpicked by him. The information it collects is the most closely held in the entire government. It comes in segments to be put together only by this select group. In this way, Kissinger has established a monopoly of

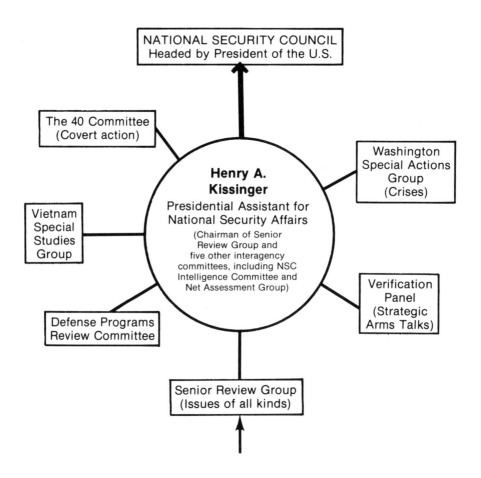

NATIONAL SECURITY COUNCIL
Headed by President of the U.S.

The 40 Committee
(Covert action)

Washington
Special Actions
Group
(Crises)

Henry A.
Kissinger
Presidential Assistant for
National Security Affairs
(Chairman of Senior
Review Group and
five other interagency
committees, including NSC
Intelligence Committee and
Net Assessment Group)

Vietnam
Special
Studies
Group

Verification
Panel
(Strategic
Arms Talks)

Defense Programs
Review Committee

Senior Review Group
(Issues of all kinds)

Interdepartmental Group

Middle East   Africa
Far East   Europe
Latin America Political-Military Affairs

information crucial to estimates of the strategic balance. This is the way he controls the most authoritative and comprehensive information about Soviet strategic capabilities—that is, what they *can do* to us with the weapons systems they have in-being or that will soon become operational.

Kissinger needs, however, to put a leash too on what the intelligence community can put together as to Soviet *intentions:* that is, what they *plan to do to us* with their massively superior strategic systems; or more specifically, what they plan to do with their first-strike capability against us when they complete it. As so often happens when Kissinger is working for himself, his solution is deceptively simple; but it works.

Suppose the U.S. Supreme Court were to rule as a matter of U.S. constitutional law that, to support a conviction for a criminal offense, it was no longer sufficient to meet the old standard of "proof beyond any reasonable doubt"; that instead, due process of law required "absolute proof, by scientific evidence." Eyewitnesses to a murder would not be adequate to get a conviction; eyewitnesses are often proved to have been mistaken, or to disagree as to what they saw. The clincher would be providing proof of "criminal intent," or in legal Latin, the *mens rea.* Conviction for crime requires, in effect, proof of what the defendant was thinking, of what he intended. If the legal standard of "proof beyond any reasonable doubt" were ditched in favor of a new standard of "absolute proof, by scientific evidence," there would be—as a practical matter—no more convictions. If the new rule were given retroactive effect, prisons would be required to turn their convicts loose on a helpless society.

In mid-1972 all levels of the U.S. intelligence community having cognizance over evidence concerning Soviet "intentions" in their massive buildup of offensive strategic weapons suffered severe symptoms of frustration because a new standard of proof of intentions was decreed from The Top: only "scientific proof" would henceforth be considered sufficient as a basis for an evaluation. By a rare coincidence, this new and preposterous standard of proof was imposed just in time to block within the intelligence community any development of evaluations that might challenge the sincerity and good will of the Soviets in relation to the SALT I Agreements. Kissinger had acted just in time because, within six months after the signing of those agreements, there was substantial evidence about new strategic weapons developments to support an evaluation that SALT had *not* slowed the dynamism of the Soviet buildup. By the end of the first year of SALT I, cumulating evidence would have supported a finding "beyond any reasonable doubt" that the Soviets—talking much of detente and seeking scores of millions more bushels of U.S. grain—were even accelerating a program to increase their already massive counterforce capability against the United States.

This evidence is presented in this book so that you can make your own evaluation—by whatever standards you yourself prefer—of Soviet intentions and Kissinger's motivations. But we cannot offer "scientific proof" of either. Furthermore, we are convinced that, to apply any of the standards of proof normally employed in legal actions—all of which are far less strict than those imposed by Kissinger on the U.S. intelligence community—is potential national suicide. The minimum such standard decides a civil case upon "a fair preponderance of the evidence," which means that one side may win by showing that his version of the disputed facts is just a little more probable than his opponent's. The evidence has to be just a little his side of equipoise: 51 out of 100 is the least that will get action for a plaintiff from a civil court.

It would be suicidal insanity to do nothing to shore up our strategic deterrent until the odds were 51 out of 100 that the Soviets were planning to launch a nuclear strike against us or to subject us to nuclear blackmail. If the odds were "only" 10 out of 100 that the Soviets were going to strike, it would be common sense to go to the highest state of strategic alert with what we have, and to declare an unlimited national emergency to start crash programs to build more strategic power before it becomes too late.

Intelligence cannot control the odds, but—with Kissinger's brash and brilliant capture of the entire U.S. intelligence community—it can control how the odds will appear. Just as Kissinger discovered, circa 1960, that misleading intelligence could create an artificial world with a strategic environment totally contrary to reality, and vividly picture a massive Soviet superiority that did not exist, he has now demonstrated that, by exquisite orchestration of his fingers of control over intelligence, he can create—first for the President, and then for all of us—a picture of "sufficiency" of our strategic deterrent. By manipulating the President's perception of the strategic balance, of Soviet capabilities, and of Soviet intentions, Kissinger can hypnotize him into the absolute conviction that the United States is in no danger from the men in the Kremlin; that, as for a nuclear strike against us, they couldn't if they would, and they wouldn't if they could.

The artificial world that Dr. Kissinger so successfully created for Richard Nixon was all the more convincing because of the majestic role assigned to him as U.S. President. Nixon is a compulsive, if sincere, hyperbolist. It was perfectly natural for him to think to himself in naive, extravagant exaggerations. When he spoke publicly in such terms as our "two weeks that changed the world," "my historic decisions for peace," or "my time on the great world stage," he was not posing or engaging in verbal posturing. Those are the terms in which he really and truly thought of himself. He saw himself as the first statesman in history great enough to change formerly implacable and malevolent enemies into warm friends and eager partners. No wonder Mr. Nixon preferred the soft and rosy hues of Kissinger's artificial world to harsh reality. Kissinger had him hooked.

The reader may question whether it is not impossible for one man to seize such total control of the entire U.S. intelligence community; or, if not quite impossible, than is it not at least so wildly improbable as not to merit serious consideration?

To answer this question, consider the case of Melvin Laird: a dedicated Secretary of Defense, so loyal to Richard Nixon as President and Commander-in-Chief that he suffered public humiliations when Nixon repeatedly supported Kissinger and overruled Laird; so loyal that, after all this, he returned to a thankless, politically unpopular, hopeless job in the post-Watergate White House. Laird would not give a serious warning to the nation unless it was both possible and chillingly probable.

In several ways Laird may be an equivocal man. In his confrontations with Kissinger, however, Laird while Secretary of Defense was always on the side of building up the desperately dwindling strategic power of the United States, and facing up to the threat of the momentum of the Soviet buildup of nuclear weapons to the point of a preclusive first-strike capability against the United States. However, in his entire four-year term as Secretary of Defense, he demonstrated durable loyalty to Nixon not only by uttering no reproach for his treatment, but (and this must have been even harder) by never publicly criticizing Henry Kissinger.

In leaving his position as Secretary of Defense, Melvin Laird must have felt he owed it to the American people to give them a warning, worded as clearly as it could be while he was still officially on the Cabinet team of his President. So thus it was that, in his precedent-making "Final Report to the Congress," he resorted to circumlocutory phraseology rather similar to Kissinger's own. Upon analysis, Laird's message becomes perfectly clear. Here it is:

> In the field of intelligence, we have gone a long way in solving the problems which Congress has cited, but *this progress will be lost if efforts are made to cut back on intelligence resources or to put a straitjacket on*

the independence of our intelligence outputs.

All duplication has not been eliminated, nor should it be. Unlike many of our activities, there is a need in intelligence for some duplication of effort, and it should continue. . . .

For the future, the requirements of quality intelligence will be increasingly critical to our national security. Not only will it be necessary to maintain adequate funding and to continue to increase productivity, but also to continue to upgrade the quality of the intelligence product.

*The intelligence product must continue to be independent and objective, dominated by no one—*not the Secretary of Defense, not the Director of Central Intelligence, not the Chairman of the Joint Chiefs of Staff, *nor by anyone else.*[4]

First, there is the cryptic warning to watch out for efforts to straitjacket the independence of our intelligence outputs. Now, why would the Secretary of Defense suspect anyone in the U.S. Government, with the power to do so, of wanting to do a thing like that? Because someone had just done it, that's why. Laird made his report in early January of 1973; the drastic reorganization of the U.S. intelligence community had been imposed in the late fall of 1971. So the identity of the planner, his modus operandi and his purpose, plus an entire year of frustration in attempting to break out of the intelligence bind, were still freshly rankling the departing Secretary of Defense. The drastic reorganization had been prescribed in and carried out under the inexorable authority of a Top-Secret NSDM (National Security Decision Memorandum), one of the series of executive orders theoretically representing the will of the President, but which only Henry Kissinger had authority to draft.

Then Mr. Laird uses the term "no one" in his explicit warning against "domination" of the intelligence product. Failure to say "no one *agency*," or something of that type, indicates that he had a *person* in mind. This interpretation is reinforced by analysis of the three straw men he sets up as possible potential "dominators" of the intelligence product; each one is a person. Their true character as straw men employed in his warning to avoid naming Henry Kissinger, or directly identifying him as the "dominator" of intelligence, is demonstrated by the fact that none of these three persons identified by their titles could possibly dominate the intelligence product. The JCS Chairman does not even appear in the organization chart of the intelligence community and has no official authority over our intelligence product. The Secretary of Defense has authority only over the Department of Defense branches of the intelligence community. He has no influence whatever over the intelligence products of the Central Intelligence Agency, the State Department Intelligence and Research Bureau, the secret "Forty Committee" or "303 Group," or the Atomic

Energy Commission's nuclear intelligence group. The third straw man, the Director of Central Intelligence, would be a possible potential "dominator"—except that he cannot reach the President with any intelligence outputs without going through Henry Kissinger in at least two, and in important matters three, of Kissinger's capacities in the top-center of the organization chart, as Kissinger reorganized it.

This brings us to the last words of the key last sentence of Secretary Laird's warning. Who is the "anyone else" whose authority over our intelligence product is sufficiently extensive, and sufficiently exclusive or monopolistic, as to enable him to "dominate" the product and destroy its independent and objective character? There is no answer to this question except Henry Kissinger.

The Kissinger-directed reorganization of U.S. intelligence, imposed through a Kissinger-drafted NSDM, was so bald-faced in imposing a straitjacket on otherwise independent intelligence outputs that reputable news sources could not avoid comment. In order to stem the spread of any criticism of the intelligence reorganization, Kissinger allowed a member of his staff to be "interviewed" by *Newsweek* to explain the "real" reasons for the change. *Newsweek* then drew this conclusion and presented it as its own:

> And the new Kissinger review panels are not designed, as some critics suggested last week. to screen out views contrary to the Administration's policy, but to draw in more information in a form that is useful.[5]

Here again is evidence of the slick schemer at work. This planted answer to critics of the Kissinger reorganization did not attempt to deny that the new Kissinger review panels provide the *power* to screen out views contrary to the Administration's policy, because that was a *fact* that could not rationally be disputed. Instead, the planted answer raised the question of the *purpose* of creating such elaborate and redundant screen-out or veto powers in one man. This could not be treated as a provable fact. At the time the reorganization went into effect, it was merely Kissinger's word as to his intentions against that of his critics. The only decisive test would be how the screen-out powers were actually used over a period of time.

Thus it was that, after a year's bitter personal experience, Melvin Laird concluded that the demonstrated purpose for the newly created powers over the entire intelligence community was such as to require an urgent public warning to Congress against the domination of formerly independent and objective intelligence outputs by one unnamed person: a person who could be identified no more specifically than someone *other* than the Secretary of Defense, the Director of Central Intelligence, or the Chairman of the Joint Chiefs of Staff.

Before leaving Melvin Laird's warning about one-man domination of intelligence outputs, we must credit him also with another highly perceptive warning in his Final Report:

> For the future, the requirements of quality intelligence will be increasingly critical to our national security.

His swan song on national defense speaks as of January 1973. Why should the quality of our intelligence become—in the future, measured from then—increasingly critical to our survival? Because the SALT I Agreements had been signed in Moscow some seven months earlier. Because Kissinger and Nixon were assuring the American people and the world that their newly created structure of peace would ensure a "generation of peace." Because the members of the Politburo in Moscow, led by Leonid Brezhnev, were making carefully qualified, but warm and friendly sounding, noises touting the Kissinger-Nixon detente. Because certain segments of the mass media were hypnotizing the public into a national orgy-of-peace euphoria. Because the anti-defense lobby in Congress, more potent with each passing month, was planning and pushing to cut still further our investment in national defense. And especially because a CFR group, led by Paul W. Warnke, who was one of Robert McNamara's chief coconspirators in going secretly to the Soviets to initiate the SALT negotiations to block the JCS-Congressional drive for strategic defense, was exploiting the SALT-inspired euphoria as a basis for cutting an additional $14 billion each year from the defense budget.

Nothing other than accurate objective intelligence information could possibly alert Congress and the American people to the snowballing momentum of the Soviet drive to achieve what Laird had defined four years earlier: a first-strike capability against the United States. Laird himself had been the first to pass to the nation any of the critical information concerning the actual operation of SALT I. Six months after the Moscow agreements were signed, he released a statement that told all those knowledgeable in the strategic balance that, so far as the United States was concerned, the SALT I Agreements had failed to fulfill their major purpose in relation to our security, namely, stopping the momentum of the Soviet buildup of offensive strategic weapons systems, especially first-strike-capable systems.

During a news conference at the Pentagon on November 28, 1972, Laird announced that this Soviet momentum in arms development "today is just as dynamic as it ever was."[6] Taking his last chance to support this conclusion with specific evidence, he included in his Final Report nine "significant developments" in the Soviet strategic buildup, among them the dramatic upgrading of the Soviet SS-11 missile, of which they have (to our knowledge) nearly 1,000; the testing of the more powerful SS-18, already by far the world's most powerful counterforce weapon; development of multiple warheads; upgrading of the nuclear-powered missile-launching submarine fleet, the deployment of the new 4,000-mile-range submarine-launched missile, and the development of the Delta-class missile submarine; test-flying of the new strategic swing-wing supersonic bomber, announcement of the bomber's serial production, and the probable assignment of a number of them to strategic and naval air units; continued development of the Galosh ABM system around Moscow, plus addition of new radar and other facilities at two more complexes; development of a "follow-on ABM system"; and massive developments in naval capability, including construction of a new aircraft carrier.

Your first thought in reading these intelligence reports made public by the Secretary of Defense may well be: well, that proves that Kissinger has not established complete domination of the intelligence community. Unfortunately, it does not prove that. What Kissinger has accomplished is a monopolistic control of all strategic intelligence information *which can reach the President of the United States.* Under his reorganization he had no way of preventing intelligence outputs from the Defense Intelligence Agency from reaching the Secretary of Defense; and although the Secretary could officially report such matters to Congress, he could not reach the President with them because of Kissinger's monopoly of access on all matters of national security and foreign relations.

Although Kissinger was primarily concerned with controlling the President's perception of the strategic balance, and of Soviet compliance with the spirit of SALT and the "broad new relationship" with the United States, it was nevertheless threatening to his plans to have a Secretary of Defense reporting to Congress items that might raise questions about the success of Kissinger's new world order. He had handled Nixon's first-term Secretary of Defense by controlling the President's intelligence so that he would always overrule Laird and sustain Kissinger. The answer to the problem for the second term was to control the nomination of the new man. Thus it was that Nixon's original nomination for SECDEF for his second term was Elliot L. Richardson, CFR and member of the Ripon Society, a longtime SALT-seller. As Under Secretary of State he had exerted substantial influence in support of SALT. He was recognized as having a persuasive voice in the White House, thanks, as John Newhouse puts it in his book on SALT, "to an excellent working relationship with Henry Kissinger." So, with Richardson as Secretary of Defense, Kissinger would no longer have to contend with the annoyance of objective intelligence reaching Congress and the public through the Department of Defense.

For a while, it appeared as if Kissinger's so-well-laid plan to cut off intelligence unfavorable to SALT and the broad new relationship with the Soviet Union might be blocked by Watergate developments, which caused the shift of Richardson from Defense to Justice. But Kissinger had a fall-back nominee ready for SECDEF: Daniel Ellsberg's protege and Kissinger's own tool in reorganizing the intelligence community to Kissinger's specifications. In a number of ways this enhanced Kissinger's control: Richardson had some stature of his own; but James R. Schlesinger had none, and he "owed" Kissinger because of the ouster of Richard Helms as Director of Central Intelligence Agency to make that key post available for Schlesinger's appointment.

Would such influence as Henry Kissinger might wield for those reasons really be sufficient to control what Schlesinger might say as Secretary of Defense? Being willing to lie for one's sponsor is, indeed, a test of loyalty; but the acid test is being willing not only to tell an official lie, but to tell a lie so stupid as to be downright ridiculous. Here is an inconspicuous item from *U.S. News & World Report*, dated July 9, 1973:

> A speech by James R. Schlesinger, newly appointed Defense Secretary, occasioned surprise at a closed-door meeting of the North Atlantic Treaty Organization Defense Ministers. Contrary to earlier intelligence that NATO conventional forces needed beefing up, Mr. Schlesinger maintained that present strength was adequate for defense of Western Europe against any nonatomic Soviet invasion. Some U.S. analysts are suggesting that, in the light of the Nixon-Brezhnev summit, the speech was prepared by the White House with political rather than military considerations uppermost in mind.

11

Having examined Henry Kissinger's creation of a monopoly of power over the entire structure of U.S. intelligence, and previewed the fact that controlling this extensive organization provides him with an instrument unprecedented in history for creating an artificial world with a strategic environment squarely contrary to reality, we move on to consideration of an adjacent segment in his scheme. It is not as theatrical as the intelligence stratagem, but is one that produced the most breathtakingly brilliant power-grab in the history of the presidency. Kissinger's planning is as complex as his personality. Each segment is inextricably interwoven with the other parts, under orchestration of the maestro.

Leverage was Kissinger's goal in grasping control of U.S. intelligence. Leverage is used here in the sense that it is employed by canny investors in the securities and commodities markets: small amounts of money-power are applied via a fulcrum to gain control of disproportionately huge amounts of money-power. To shift the analogy, while one doubts that Kissinger ever spent much time at the horse races, he is nevertheless a past master of the parlay.

When he was Secretary of Defense, Robert McNamara exercised more power than any man who had ever lived. If, that is, destroying power can be considered exercising it, because he scrapped U.S. strategic-delivery vehicles capable of delivering 40 billion tons of explosive power on enemy targets. Much of his power derived from his exploitation of the *spending* power of the then $50-billion-per-year defense budget. Much of Kissinger's power derives from Kissinger's skill at using leverage through control of *intelligence*, of parlaying that increment of power into placing his stooge in the same job that McNamara had. Under Kissinger's program, the Secretary of Defense's spending power is nominal only: the real power resides in the one man who makes the *policy* that controls the spending. One of the six operating committees of the National Security Council chaired by Henry Kissinger is the Defense Program Review Committee. Also, he has two votes in the National Security Council—enough to kill any program.

Creation of such a complex and extensive plan to control the President as that worked out by Kissinger through intelligence control would not be warranted in the case of just *any* President of the United States. Normally, the powers personally exercised by a President in the areas of national security and foreign relations would not have been worth the bold and imaginative character of Kissinger's program.

As Kissinger himself had brilliantly analyzed the power equation, there was ample power in the executive branch of the federal government to put across his plans, but only if it could be concentrated in one man. Under previous Presidents, there were too many separate power centers. Suppose he had been confronted with a situation such as existed in Dwight Eisenhower's time. Even if a potential Svengali had a sure-fire method of "capturing" Ike, what good would that have done when presidential power in the key areas was distributed among such strong personalities as JCS Chairman Arthur W. Radford in the national security area, Secretary of State John Foster Dulles in foreign relations, Allen W. Dulles in intelligence, James Killian and George Kistiakowski in science, and such a straightforward character as "Engine Charley" Wilson in the Defense Department? Each of these men dominated policy in his own area.

Similarly, neither John F. Kennedy nor Lyndon Johnson was a personally strong President in dominating policies in the areas of national security and international relations. The most influential man in both these Administrations was Robert Strange McNamara, but there were other diffusions of power. To the general public, one of the least known was Jerome Wiesner, CFR and Pugwash, who had parlayed his position as Science Adviser to such an intensity that insiders knew him as one of the most influential men in the world. His access to the President had been so nearly unlimited that Kissinger abolished the *position* in order to insure maintenance of his own monopoly and prevent a Wiesner-successor from working the same approach.

The massive inertia of the bureaucracy likewise stood in the way of a one-man concentration of executive powers that Kissinger's plans required. Eisenhower, Kennedy, and Johnson all confessed that they were unable to change the habits or scrap the bureaucratic prerogatives of the State Department. In Defense, an eight-year buildup by McNamara elites had so solidified that his departure hardly changed a thing, despite a few initial efforts by Melvin Laird. Civil service tenure and traditions render individuals near-invulnerable to dismissal for nonperformance, resistance, or disloyalty to new policymakers. Even specialized agencies, such as the Arms Control and Disarmament Agency, had preempted bureaucratic powers in their own area.

The ancient aphorism, "when you strike at a king, strike to kill" could be amended like this to fit the Kissinger plan: "When you capture a king, promote his power." The captor's power is derivative only; it can rise no higher than its source. What made Kissinger so different from his predecessors in the office of Assistant to the President for National Security Affairs was his drive to exercise more power. Not just more power than any previous presidential assistant had ever exercised, but more power than any President of the United States—or any of the 55 previous Secretaries of State—had ever exercised in the areas of national security and foreign policy.

Abolishing the traditional polycentric power system within the executive branch, and concentrating all power in the person of the President, is hardly a revolutionary or even an original concept. Kissinger's contribution was that he devised a method to accomplish this. Where previous Presidents had tried and failed, Kissinger succeeded. Kissinger surgically removed the capabilities of the competing power-centers, the Cabinet positions, to create policy; after the emasculation, one-man rule was both practicable and inevitable.

In imposing a leash on the bureaucracy, it was critical to invoke the precise formula of words. Having lived through a term as a consultant to the National Security Council, Kissinger remembered one phenomenon very well: a presidential order is *least* subject to challenge—either politically or juridically—when he acts in the name of national security. A second reason for resorting to the national-security formula was the secrecy which could be achieved by Top Secret classification. A President and his assistant could hardly be the subject of public criticism for a reorganization of the executive branch designed to establish monolithic dictatorial power *if* the whole thing were a closely guarded national security secret. People generally and, more important, unfriendly influences in the media not only would have no access to the specifics of the reorganization; they wouldn't even know that there had been a reorganization.

After Kissinger was appointed Secretary of State on August 22, 1973, Herblock published a cartoon that showed Kissinger applying for a marriage license with his bride-to-be, "Miss Secretary of State." She was wheeling a baby carriage with a four-year-old child who was a miniature Henry. This cartoon expressed the consensus of political observers that the Kissinger appointment was the mere solemnizing of a 4½-year-old living arrangement. The generally accepted explanation of *how* Kissinger had been able to function for 4½ years as the *de facto* Secretary of State was that he had a stronger personality, a more brilliant mind, and a more creative imagination than the titular Secretary of State, William P. Rogers. Actually, Kissinger and Rogers could have reversed positions, and, if William Rogers had operated within the White House with the advantage of Kissinger's secret reorganization directives, Rogers would have appeared as the stronger and more innovative personality.

To make a particular presidency the most powerful in the nation's history in the foreign policy and national security areas, the theoretician-designer of the reorganization must have the cooperation of the incumbent. Presidential backing, on a highly personal basis, is required to fend off the counterattacks that inexorably result from status-quo power centers seeking to "get" the new power aspirant before he gets them. Richard Nixon possessed the inner personal drive for power that gave Kissinger full active cooperation in his buildup of presidential power into a monolith. As many commentators have observed, Nixon was not merely conscious of history, he was downright self-conscious about it. He spoke publicly of himself in grandiose terms appropriate to the central and pivotal character of a great epoch. In his first inaugural address, for example, he declaimed: "The greatest honor history can bestow is the title of peacemaker."

Throughout the ages, "peace" has always been a charmed-magic, talismanic word. This has been especially true in the United States since World War I and the formation of the Council on Foreign Relations with its spawning of elitist organizations seeking to trade in American independence for a world government. "Peace" is forever held out as the irresistible bait. To the American people who have patiently endured the sacrifices and the costs of three wars within 30 years, the mere mention of that magic word "peace" in a political speech can generate power, and signal a drive for power.

"Peace is wonderful." Those were the words of a freshman Congressman named William Fulbright in a speech in the early 1940s. That's just about all he said. But the potency of that verbal talisman was such as to move him rapidly to the U.S. Senate, where he leapfrogged the anonymity of freshman members of the club and was immediately touted by the media as a great statesman. His particular pursuit of "peace" propelled him to the chairmanship of the

Senate Foreign Relations Committee to expand his advocacy of warmer relationships with the Soviet Union, with no questions asked.

By no coincidence, on the very same day that Richard Nixon announced his goal of pursuing history's greatest honor, the title of peacemaker, Henry Kissinger activated the system that would concentrate in Nixon an amalgam of powers and resources vastly greater than had ever been available to any earlier U.S. President. Nixon had staked out the objectives; Kissinger provided the means.

An entirely new national-security foreign-policy structure for the entire executive branch was initiated on the first day of the new President's first term, January 20, 1969. It stemmed, however, from a comprehensive Kissinger memorandum approved by Nixon several weeks earlier. Its most brilliant feature was an apparently innocuous device that appeared to be predominantly procedural in nature. In operation, however, it served as the surgeon's scalpel to emasculate all former centers of executive power involved in foreign relations, national security affairs, or the grand strategy of the United States.

Kissinger's innovatory mechanism was based on two systems of memorandums that operate in tandem and are known simply as NSDMs and NSSMs. When a piece of paper is called a "memorandum," it does not sound like a document potent enough to effect a revolution. But the NSDM series did. The innocent-sounding initials stand for National Security Decision Memorandum. Actually, it is a highly specialized form of Executive Order and, like many types of executive orders, has the force and effect of law in the areas it controls. These memorandums bind, as if by law, executive agencies such as the State Department, the Defense Department, the Joint Chiefs of Staff, intelligence agencies, and specialized agencies such as the U.S. Arms Control and Disarmament Agency.

The NSDMs tell these formerly powerful agencies what they can and cannot do, what they must do, how they must do it, and by when. They draw jurisdictional lines and assign operational procedures. For one example, Kissinger accomplished his drastic reorganization of the entire structure and procedures of the U.S. intelligence community by means of a Top Secret NSDM. It is a tribute to the tight security imposed on NSDM actions that this one did not surface publicly until three years after it had been put in effect.

The NSDM series is rigorous in intensively controlling the *actions* of executive agencies in national security and foreign policy areas, but the NSSM series constitutes an even more revolutionary concept. It tells the bureaucracy, and even the heads of departments, what to *think* about. Called National Security Study Memorandums, this series tells the agencies what they must study and prepare reports on. NSSM is Kissinger's thought-control system. It is highly ingenious and innovative, and it operates from the top down. This system of thought control is a practice long ago perfected—on an informal level—by the cogs in the bureaucracy against the big wheels. In the State Department, once there was an Under Secretary who had not been selected by or from the Council on Foreign Relations. He was a sincere, courageous, informed anti-Communist and patriot. But the various "desks" and staffs were able to handle him and to control his thoughts. They would pile his desk each day with huge stacks of papers to be read, and approved and signed, or disapproved and returned. When he complained of this burden on his time, and that he did not have any time left to think about important matters, he was assured that every paper imposed upon him was serious and urgent. The bureaucrats were professionals with years of experience; he had no reason to suspect them of misleading him. But they did. By controlling the way he spent his time, they were able to exclude vital matters from his consideration—that is, from his thoughts.

This is one way in which Kissinger's NSSM series imposes thought control on formerly important, quasi-independent agencies. He keeps them so busy with assigned "studies"—usually of intricate and illusory "options"—that they have no time to attempt to innovate on their own behalf or to think independently. They are required to give first and monopolistic priority to NSSM assignments and their reports. They are afraid not to expend their best efforts on them; after all, Kissinger might even read some of them.

One of the most obvious reorganizational results of the NSDM series was the revival of the National Security Council to the influence and prestige it had enjoyed in the era of its creation a quarter of a century earlier. John Kennedy and Lyndon Johnson had cut most of the guts out of its jurisdiction at the prodding of their respective palace guards. They preferred the counsel of, say, an Adlai Stevenson at the UN, to a dynamic, functioning National Security Council in Washington.

Kissinger's use of the resurrected National Security Council as the set piece for his reorganization served brilliantly to cover both its ulterior purposes. It lent a touch of verisimilitude to the declared purpose of increasing efficiency and adding effectiveness to the preexisting setup within the executive branch for dealing with matters of national security and foreign policy. It diverted attention away from the fact that it concentrated all such matters *within the exclusive jurisdiction of the President*. This first ulterior purpose served both Nixon and Kissinger, while the second served Kissinger alone and has not been understood by the President. By loading the President with exclusive jurisdiction over so many vitally important matters—a jurisdiction that Kissinger took care could not be delegated outside the White House staff—he made the President totally dependent on Kissinger for getting anything done in these key areas.

No one man could possibly attend to so many complex matters, especially a President whose time was burdened by crisis after crisis in domestic and political matters. Kissinger had his own staff for exactly this purpose. Nixon had only Kissinger to act for him in these areas. The whole thing was exquisitely slick. Nixon thought Kissinger was doing it all for Nixon by concentrating in the President all defense and international-relations jurisdiction and power to act. Nixon was touched by this act of such apparent personal loyalty to the boss. Pragmatically, however, it made the President a captive in Kissinger's artificial world. Nixon could perceive the environment and even climactic developments only as Kissinger staged them through his control of intelligence; and once Nixon's policy thinking had been shaped by Kissinger's theatrical effects, Nixon would act to implement the decisions that he believed were his own, but that actually were Kissinger's.

For Kissinger, the newly reconstituted National Security Council served as far more than a cover and a diversion. He shaped it into his principal instrument for dominating State, Defense, JCS, and the entire intelligence community. It would have been too crude and obvious to have these formerly powerful and largely independent agencies and individuals subservient to and reporting to the President only through an individual whose official status was merely that of a presidential assistant. So Kissinger needed what might be called a corporate personality. Few things in this world are absolutely perfect, but the National Security Council was indeed the perfect organizational alias or corporate alter ego for Kissinger. Each of the three words in the title augment the aura of authority, integrity, and overriding importance of this agency. For the 4½ years while Kissinger's title was merely Presidential Assistant, the then-incumbent titular Secretary of State would have lost face too obviously—and thousands of bureaucrats who constitute State and Foreign Service would have shared in his humiliation—if he had access to the President only through Henry Kissinger. Not so, however, if he were given the appearance of reporting through the National Security Council, a prestigious corporate body. The same was true of the Secretary of Defense, the Chairman of the Joint Chiefs of Staff, and the Director of Central Intelligence.

Thus, because the reconstituted NSC was, for all practical purposes, Henry Kissinger, his reorganization did far more for it than just restoring its Eisenhower-era powers and the functions assigned to it by law. Even the names of the two revolutionary systems of White House directives, the National Security Decision Memorandums and the National Security Study Memorandums, tied them in with the NSC itself and its (or Kissinger's) powers. The first two NSDMs were promulgated on January 20, 1969, the day the newly inaugurated President proclaimed his crusade to become history's great peacemaker. They preempted—for the President nominally, for Kissinger in actuality—a monolithic control of initiatives and innovations in the defense and foreign policy areas.

The NSSMs could be drafted only in the White House—and they constituted the exclusive official means of assigning the problems to be studied and reports to be prepared by State, Defense, and Intelligence. They were equally handy for Kissinger in giving the bureaucrats something to do to keep them out of mischief (such mischief, that is, as innovating or developing options for the President contrary to, or not in complete conformity with, Kissinger's own plans), or in assigning serious studies in areas in which Kissinger had no special ax to grind. He kept the bureaucracy very busy from the earliest days of the administration. The most numerous and authoritative leaks on these Top Secret documents tell us that as many as 12 in the NSSM series were issued within the first 10 days after Nixon's inauguration, and that the number grew to 55 within the administration's first 100 days; by mid-1973 the total NSSMs had spiraled to more than 200.

For Kissinger, this massive assignment of studies to be prepared on a highest-priority basis served two purposes: it kept the bureaucrats too busy to have time to buck the new system of total White House control; and it provided him with the raw material he could use in his creation of an entire artificial world for Nixon's crusade to become the Number One peacemaker of history. Of course, some of this raw material would have to be colored to suit the needs of the artificial strategic and foreign relations environments that Kissinger had in mind; but much of it could be used as it had been produced because of the Kissinger-compatible ideological slant of most of the bureaucrats involved. The Kissinger secret reorganization by means of NSDM and NSSM directives has provided the nation with an entirely different national security system from any we had in the past.

The system introduced by Kissinger in 1969 is autocratic. Like all autocratic systems, it would be the "best" system if it could include a provision that the despot-in-charge would be the most brilliant, balanced, knowledgeable, patriotic, dedicated, selfless, commonsense American in the world; as well as experienced, mature and courageous. Does Kissinger qualify for the position? Tragically, the answer is very late in developing. It can be found in what he has done to the United States in the exercise of his powers; especially in the effects of the SALT I Agreements, their accompanying broad new relationships established with the Communist Party of the Soviet Union at the Moscow Summit in May 1972, together with the strategic military posture developed by Kissinger to accompany the SALT I Agreements.

One of the prime and potentially fatal weaknesses of the new system is that a Kissinger proposal or policy springs full-grown from his massive forehead and makes its first appearance in the guise of a *presidential* directive—an NSDM. This provides it with an impenetrable armor against criticism by members of the defense or foreign policy communities. They are reluctant enough to make any criticism of a document attributed to Henry Kissinger alone, because of his widely known vanity and vindictiveness; but no federal employee who values his career, his reputation, or his retirement, is going to speak up in a critical vein against both Kissinger and the name of the President. Kissinger's overwhelmingly academic and theoretician's career experience simply does not qualify him for such total responsibility as a nonchallengeable military expert with the fate of the nation hanging in the balance. He has been wrong too often in the past.

Secondly, the system is potentially fatally weak in blocking out the development of options for the President by anyone other than Kissinger himself or members of his staff. Strike that word "potentially." We have an actual example: a case in which all 210 million Americans who have been exposed without defense to nuclear incineration by free-riding Soviet or Red Chinese missiles may have been *needlessly* so exposed. The Kissinger SALT I ABM Treaty is based on the MAD (Mutual Assured Destruction) theory of arms control. As we have seen, *if* the SALT I Agreements, either defensive or offensive, do not in fact assure "mutuality," and if the aggressor takes advantage of the openings, the MAD arrangements set up our entire population as helpless victims for mass murder. The MAD arrangement appeals to theoreticians such as Kissinger *because* it sets up the highest possible number of hostages, and guarantees that the hostages will be defenseless.

Objections to the MAD theory include the fact that there is absolutely no evidence that it will *decrease* the risk of the outbreak of nuclear war; that it ensures that the outcome of such a war would be a disaster of maximum dimensions; and that it deliberately creates a system in which scores of millions of innocent civilians would be exterminated if the system fails. Experts have denounced the MAD assumptions as not worthy of the name of a theory, saying that they merely represent a bizarre "fashion" in arms control. The MAD theory represents such a horrendous gamble with so many millions of lives, that even the most zealous advocates of disarmament agreements should, if not wildly irresponsible, have sought out and given serious consideration to *alternative* bases for arms control agreements.

There *are* other alternatives to the "high-level-hostage" arrangement. These alternatives are considered by some of the most prestigious experts to offer a better chance of reducing the risk of outbreak of nuclear war and, with absolute certainty, minimizing instead of maximizing the disaster and number of megadeaths which would result if such a war were actually to break out. What alternative to the MAD posture is available? Dr. Donald Brennan, a career-long dedicated devotee of disarmament agreements, with wide experience in both the government and in private think-tanks, and a former adviser to Henry Kissinger on arms control, has capsuled it this way:

> The answer is to put increasing emphasis on defense, with a corresponding reduction in the effort devoted to strategic offensive forces . . . . There is very little controversy over the fact that defense can be made quite effective if the opposing offense is suitably reduced, while the allowed defense is built up.
>
> This is precisely the direction that the Strategic Arms Limitation Talks should have taken, but did not.[1]

In addition to massively reducing the potential casualties of a nuclear war, this "emphasis-on-defense, cut-down-the-offense" approach to an arms control agreement would also minimize the nuclear-blackmail opportunities of an aggressor and his chances to gain politically even from implied threats.

With these unchallengeable advantages, we might have expected comprehensive consideration of the alternatives before adopting the MAD theory that condemns us as defenseless hostages. Surely we humans were entitled to that. But did we get it? Here is the tragic answer from Dr. Brennan's testimony before the Senate Foreign Relations Committee on June 28, 1972:

> In consequence of both my work with the Hudson Institute and my occasional consulting work for the government, I have been close enough to the analyses of the American positions for the SALT to know what major alternatives and avenues have been considered and examined within the government. *I should like to state flatly for the record that no serious consideration has been given to possible alternatives to a MAD posture.*[2]

Doesn't it sound as if everyone charged with the security of the United States and the survival of the American people must have been at least temporarily insane? Why *didn't* they consider alternatives to offering us all up as guaranteed-helpless nuclear-vulnerable burnt offerings to Moscow and Peking?

The answer is, because of Henry Kissinger's total domination of U.S. defense and foreign relations policies. And especially because our national security system, as reorganized by him, blocks the development and serious consideration of any options other than those instituted and approved by him. This is just one example of how Dr. Kissinger and his system block out consideration of even the most vital options and opportunities for national survival in freedom. There must be many others; God only knows how many. Even Kissinger doesn't know because he has arranged it so that he does not have to listen and because his thought-control procedures choke off everyone else from even thinking about alternatives to the Kissinger programs and policies.

An amusing measure of the sophistication and success of the pressentations Kissinger made to the President in selling his proposed new national security system is found in the fact that he claimed that it would *prevent* the blocking out or reduction of the number of options open to the President. The entrenched bureaucracy was pictured as the culprit. In a tacit you-scratch-my-back-and-I'll-scratch-yours arrangement, the several major agencies allegedly had established a practice of presenting "agreed positions" designed to avert undermining any one of the agencies' special concerns. To provide for the development of positions upon which agreement could be reached, a system of interagency committees had grown up, a number of them working (at least theoretically) with or for the National Security Council; in any event, much of the shaping of the most vital national policies took place in these committees. Some of these interagency committees operated at such high levels that, if they had developed an "agreed position" representing the concurrence of State and Defense on a question of major policy, they might have had the prestige and influence to make an end run around the tight Kissinger organization, and thus have broken his monopoly of direct access to the President in the areas of national security and foreign policy.

Although Kissinger operates in a subtle manner when it serves his purpose, he will resort to a bold frontal attack when necessary to establish or maintain his personal power in his special areas. So he met the interagency-committee challenge head-on. He simply abolished or dissolved the most influential of the committees, including the most prestigious, the Senior Interdepartmental Group. It had been largely influenced by the State Department and was chaired, on an ex-officio basis, by the Under Secretary of State, and (a feature that Kissinger found intolerable prior to his appointment as Secretary) its decisions were required to be cleared by the office of the Secretary of State before being transmitted to the White House. Kissinger replaced the Senior Interdepartmental Group with a newly created committee he designated as the Senior Review Group. It had many of the same members but a different chairman—guess who. This worked out so well that he created five additional top-level committees, each with himself as chairman, and assigned them cognizance over the entire range of issues vital to national security matters and related international affairs. This committee structure provided an in-depth defense against possible end runs around other Kissinger strong points, and set a network of traps to sidetrack unsolicited options before they could possibly reach the President.

Much of the near-instant and almost-100-percent success of Kissinger's complex scheme to concentrate the functions and powers of all executive branch agencies operating in national security and foreign policy derived from his exceptionally adroit, sophisticated saturation of his reorganization program with invocations of the magic formula of those two talismanic words: "national security." Until clouded by what the media has labeled "the obscenities of Watergate," national security meant the difference between the national life or death of our nation, and other things not valued by Watergate extremists, such as the preservation of freedom in the world and the splendid continuum of Western civilization.

A colloquy between Senator Stuart Symington and Henry Kissinger during the hearings on his confirmation as Secretary of State gives a good insight into the powers he has gathered into his own hands:[3]

> Senator Symington. We have also discussed the structure of the intelligence apparatus, in which, in effect, you keep two jobs. In effect, also, you will be the most powerful person in the intelligence field except, of course, the President. . . .

Dr. Kissinger did not contest this assertion, which, of course, is an understatement. The questioning continued:

> Senator Symington. I have a list of the National Security Council subcommittees. There are 7 of them; first, the Washington Special Actions Group. I understand you chair that; correct?
> Dr. Kissinger. That is correct, Senator.
> Senator Symington. And then the Senior Review Group. I understand you chair that.
> Dr. Kissinger. That is correct, Senator.
> Senator Symington. Then, a Verification Panel, National Security Council, I understand you chair that. [This is the control group for SALT.]
> Dr. Kissinger. That is correct.

Senator Symington. And the Defense Program Review Committee, I understand you chair that.

Dr. Kissinger. That is correct, Senator.

Senator Symington. The Under Secretaries Committee, you could not chair; that is chaired by Under Secretary Rush, correct? [The Under Secretary of State, ex officio, chairs this Committee, and he is Kissinger's subordinate.]

Dr. Kissinger. That is correct.

Senator Symington. The Intelligence Committee, you also chair? [This is the most powerful policy-making committee in intelligence.]

Dr. Kissinger. That is correct.

Senator Symington. And the Forty Committee, you also chair? [This Committee deals exclusively with covert operations.]

Dr. Kissinger. That is correct.

Survival, or self-defense, is the first law of nature. It is recognized in criminal law as a defense against liability even for the deliberate killing of another human. National self-defense is the first law of international law; it has through the centuries been the basis of most of the law of the sea, including such diverse doctrines as freedom of the seas on the one hand, and the rules of blockade and declaration of contraband on the other. The specific inclusion in the Constitution of the power to declare war, as well as other broad powers given the federal government to provide for the common defense, is recognition of the high priority that our Founding Fathers accorded to national survival and the concomitant right of national self-defense. These powers have survived for nearly two centuries and have enabled Americans to enjoy those centuries in freedom. The words "national security" were good words, and they still represent a concept essential to preserving both the independence of the United States and the freedom and survival of the American people.

But even the best and most basic concepts can be exploited. Also, the more potent the concept, the more it can justify exploitation, and consequently the greater the temptation to exploit it for ulterior purposes. Kissinger did, indeed, exploit the concept of "national security" to cover and support his sophisticated scheming—just as Nixon's domestic and political lieutenants exploited a pretense of "national security" by bugging and burglary in order to secure the reelection of the President.

Dr. Kissinger's programs for the subjugation of U.S. strategic power to that of the Soviets, which carried on the similar programs of the predecessor elitist cliques headed by McNamara, Nitze, and Gilpatric, have finally gotten us into that dread situation prophetically described by Allen Drury's inspired writing:

The United States had gotten herself into a position vis-a-vis the Russians

259

in which the issue was more and more rapidly narrowing down to a choice between fight and die now, or compromise and die later. And out of that fearful peril only the most iron-willed and nobly dedicated and supremely unafraid men could lead the nation.[4]

If the Power that hath made and preserved us a nation should ever free us from the crisis of leadership that has been the curse of these United States for the last half-century, our new President would need some of those same powers over the grand strategy of the nation, over our strategic posture, and over our foreign relations, that Kissinger has made available to the President but appropriated unto himself. No leader, regardless of how nobly dedicated and unafraid, can save America from the Kissinger-created posture of strategic surrender if he is blocked by the pragmatic vetoes of a State Department invincibly controlled by CFR elitists, and by a Defense Department pervasively penetrated at all levels by McNamara plants and holdovers.

12

By establishing total dominance over all U.S. intelligence agencies, and by reorganizing the national security system so as to centralize in himself the realistic control of all major policy decisions in the areas of grand strategy, strategic posture, and foreign relations, Dr. Henry Kissinger has fashioned instruments of power sufficient to manipulate the President.

But, specifically, how did he go about manipulating Richard Nixon? More important, as a practical matter, how did Kissinger get away with it without Nixon's realizing what had been done to him? And what is the proof that Kissinger operated as Richard Nixon's Svengali as well as his Prince Metternich of the West Wing?

A fascinating picture of the Kissinger modus operandi was authored by the syndicated columnist Joseph Kraft, an ex-friend of Kissinger who became "ex" in the summer of 1973 upon learning that Kissinger had requested a tap on Kraft's telephone. However, his column on the Kissinger technique in handling Nixon was published long before that, on January 10, 1973. It not only exposes Kissinger's technique and motivation, but it reeks with admiration for them:

> For the most of the past four years, Kissinger has been an undoubted force for good.
>
> A supreme example is the accord with Russia in the Strategic Arms Limitation Talks, or SALT. Nixon entered office hostile to an agreement limiting defensive missiles, or ABMs, which had been projected by the Johnson Administration.

As late as January 1970, Nixon was moving toward full development of an American ABM—a step that would have precluded any limit on either offensive or defensive missiles.

But Kissinger organized within the Administration a process of analysis which showed that an effective ABM could not be built. By the same means, he demonstrated that it would be possible to monitor any secret Soviet moves to develop a full-scale ABM system.

The upshot was not that Kissinger changed the President's mind. What he did was to build a track along which the President was able to move toward what eventually became the Moscow agreements on arms limitation.

Kraft makes the Kissinger technique sound honest, loyal and helpful to the President—nothing so crude as "changing" the President's mind. Looking at the Kraft description objectively, however, reveals that Kissinger engaged in a calculated, cunning, elaborate, and deliberate deception of Richard Nixon; and that this deliberate deception dealt with a measure critical to the survival of the United States.

Kraft reveals that Kissinger set up an "analysis" to show "that an ABM could not be built." Any analysis which purports to show *that* is necessarily fraudulent because that is a lie. The United States does not yet have the capability to build a perfect ABM system, that is, one that would provide *total* protection for our lives, our cities, our industry, our transportation, and our agriculture. We do, however, have the capability and the technology right now to build a very "effective" ABM system: a system so effective that it could save scores of millions of us from being incinerated in a massive Soviet attack; so effective that, in a Red Chinese attack in this decade, it could save all (or at least almost all) of the up to 100 million Americans who otherwise would be incinerated or starved; a system that could protect our retaliatory missiles from destruction in a Soviet surprise attack, thus ensuring survival of a deterrent force "sufficient" (at least theoretically) to prevent the Moscow planners from ever actually launching a nuclear attack.

The Safeguard system, which Nixon actively supported until Kissinger turned him around, would not do all that, but it would have been a good start toward the more comprehensive Sentinel system supported by Lyndon Johnson that, "thickened" a little more, could have served even better. Scores of millions of lives better.

The way Kissinger turned Nixon around, from campaigning to save the American people from mass nuclear incineration to deliberately making them totally vulnerable to it, is accurately expressed in Joseph Kraft's analogy. He explains that what Kissinger did was "to build a track along which the President was able to move toward what eventually became the Moscow agreements." The term "track," as he used it, is an effective figure of speech: any vehicle confined to a track is a prisoner of that track, so far as ultimate destination and the route in reaching it are concerned. Both are inexorably predetermined by the builder of the track. The familiar expression "one-track mind" reminds us that it is part of our folk knowledge that the human mind can be so captivated and conditioned.

The Kraft figure of speech fails, however, on a critical point. It is hard to convince a locomotive engineer, who can see the track stretching endlessly ahead, that he is making the decisons as to where he is going and how to get there, or that he is free to decide to turn right when the single track turns left. Yet the supreme success of the Kissinger mystique in manipulating Richard Nixon depended on Nixon's not even suspecting that the historic decisions he prided himself on making had in fact been predetermined by one who was supposed to be his "instrument." The only development that could have been disastrous to Kissinger's entire campaign, and that would have destroyed him as a national, international, and historic figure, would have been if Richard Nixon had discovered that he had been duped into making decisions that would ultimately close off from the United States all except two options: nuclear destruction or abject surrender.

The Kraft report accurately presents the technique used by the White House demiurge-in-residence to create the totally-divorced-from-reality strategic environment through which he accomplished his sophisticated deception of the President. Kraft confirms that Kissinger had organized "a process of analysis" within the administration. In the specific case of turning Nixon around so he would sign away to the Soviets for a term of umlimited duration the right of the American people to any defense against incineration by nuclear missiles, this process of analysis purportedly "demonstrated" two propositions: (1) "an effective ABM could not be built," and (2) "it would be possible to monitor any secret Soviet moves to develop a full-scale ABM system."

We will pass over the obvious inconsistencies implicit in these two propositions such as why would the U.S.S.R. be so anxious for a treaty binding the United States not to build an ABM system that would cost us billions of dollars but that could not be "effective"; and why should we be so happy that it is possible to monitor any secret Soviet moves to develop a full-scale ABM system when, if they actually did build one, all they would be doing would be wasting billions of rubles on a system that Kissinger's analysis had concluded could not be effective.

For the present, let us focus on Kraft's leak that Kissinger had "organized within the administration" his "process of analysis" that was capable of demonstrating those two specific propositions. A process of analysis designed to develop the *truth* on such controversial subjects must be tremendously complex, studded with the complications of scientific apparatus and fettered by the fallibility of the human cogs. But the Kissinger "process" must have all the capabilities of an honest system, plus superadded secret capabilities for distorting the objective results of *each phase* in the process, to Kissinger's order. These phases include the collection of raw intelligence; the selection, marshaling, and evaluation of the raw intelligence; the construction of an estimate of the situation based on the evaluation of the "finished" intelligence; a new evaluation of the state of the strategic military balance in the light of the new intelligence and estimate of the situation; the preparation of a set of options for the President's consideration; and the presentation of the whole package to the President. At each stage, the results are vulnerable to slanting, so that together they will present the President not reality, but an artificial situation: a situation so fabricated that a man of the character and ambitions of Richard Nixon would conclude that there was no rational alternative to making the precise policy decision that Kissinger had predetermined.

Such a process for capturing the mind and shaping the conclusions of an audience is not at all unusual. In less protracted and complex forms, it is sometimes used in news stories, editorials, columns, and television documentaries. We are most familiar with it in books. An author is usually not guilty of planned distortion; he may merely want his readers to believe what he himself sincerely believes; and he may try hard to make sure that his readers' conclusions are not substantially different from his own. Regardless of how admirable or usually honest a scholarly writer may be, if he starts out with a thesis, he is up against a continuous sequence of temptations to pick and choose among items of raw intelligence, and then to marshal, evaluate, and present estimates that fit and support his thesis.

The most relevant instance here, of course, is Professor Stephen R. Graubard's *Kissinger: Portrait of a Mind.* The professor had a thesis. Reviewer Frances FitzGerald accurately identified Graubard's thesis and quoted from two pointed passages:

"There is a link between what Kissinger wrote in the 1950s and 1960s and what he has been doing since January 20th, 1969."

He argues that journalists and others have . . . neglected *the published works of Kissinger, a more intimate knowledge of which would have* "made it easier . . . to anticipate the foreign policy developments of recent years." Graubard does not prove this thesis either explicitly—by relating the works to the foreign policy developments—or implicitly. Graubard's digest shows that while Kissinger has had a fairly consistent outlook, he has changed his mind a number of times, and the world has changed in ways he never predicted.[1]

Actually, Graubard does, indeed, prove this thesis—and brilliantly, too, if somewhat tediously because of redundancy. But the "foreign policy developments" that he proves were not only latent but comprehensively explicit in Dr. Kissinger's published works, are only the "foreign policy developments" that have been *publicly* declared or acted out by Kissinger and Nixon and that have been *perceived* (and applauded) by most of the news media worldwide. But the Kissinger "structure for world peace" is not a monolith, but a triad.

Professor Graubard's own perception is myopic because he lacks awareness (possibly because of a solely academic background) of the potential for drastic character change under the acquisition of power. "Power tends to corrupt," as Lord Acton stated; but not always. It often constructs: a man is said to "grow into his job" when he is suddenly thrown into great responsibility and concomitant power. This frequently happens providentially in the case of military commanders and statesmen. Bankrupt-haberdasher-Pendergast-machine-ward-heeler Harry Truman turned out, in many areas, far better than his background might have foretold. The late Arthur Radford, once excoriated by General Dwight Eisenhower during Radford's command of naval aviation, grew overnight into the stature of the most impartial triservice commander and greatest military strategist of the post-World War II era. He commanded magnificently the greatest military power the world has ever known.

The second part of the Lord Acton aphorism is proving more prophetic in the case of Henry Kissinger. Accession to near-absolute power has wrought a near-total change in the Kissinger character—at least from his character insofar as it was observable prior to January 20, 1969. Only when all the evidence is in will it be discovered whether such near-absolute power did indeed corrupt near-absolutely. Certainly nothing revealed in the copious analyses and documentation of the Graubard tome suggests the lust for *personal* power demonstrated by Kissinger's amalgam of covered actions since he has risen to the White House.

It was clearly evident that Kissinger, like most academic theoreticians, wanted to see his pet theories put into practice. But this human ambition does not evince a megalomanic drive to become one of the Big Three ruling the world, or to reduce the President of the United States to a puppet in order to crash his way in. Between the day Nelson Rockefeller belatedly entered the race for the 1968 Republican nomination—following George Romney's fatal faltering and Lyndon Johnson's forced abdication at the hands of the antiwar activists—and the day Nixon won the nomination at Miami Beach,

Kissinger completely prefabricated an across-the-board, around-the-world foreign policy. He had intended it for instant installation if his CFR sponsor and employer, the New York Governor, actually made it to the White House.

This prefab plan for a "creative world order" was really a remarkably imaginative and sweeping achievement. Neither Kissinger nor anyone else could have put it together in three months without a backlog of some 10 years of writings on foreign policy to draw from, update, and shape as planks for a platform for a prospective presidential candidate. Most of Nixon's support at Miami Beach in 1968 came from conservative, anti-Communist Republicans who opposed Nelson Rockefeller and his foreign policy. Yet once Nixon won the election, he adopted, verbatim and in toto, the Nelson Rockefeller foreign policy platforms designed by Henry Kissinger. When Kissinger was recruited for the Nixon staff in mid-November 1968, he came on board with every one of his prefabricated policies. Graubard demonstrates this beyond any reasonable doubt and documents it beyond any rational challenge.

One of the first of the older-generation liberals to turn against Kissinger was Emmet John Hughes. Writing about Kissinger's policy in Vietnam, Hughes said:

> I happened to have had a long chat with Dean Acheson a few weeks before his death, and his talk turned to the rationale for the slow pace of withdrawal from Vietnam that Kissinger had long been privately propagating throughout the Washington community.
>
> The essence of this rationale argued that the nation's reactionary right would rise in wrath against a hasty retreat, and the disengagement therefore had to be artfully "staged" to blur the truth and avoid the backlash. Ever the sardonic observer, Acheson rather savored this as the most cunning charade in town, adding: "Kissinger's eyes almost fill with tears when he talks of the President's brave resistance to expediency . . . ."
>
> And which "cover-up" will seem more "gross" before the bar of history: the hush-money paid by agents of the Nixon Administration to seven Watergate burglars—or the hush-lives of thousands of Americans killed during four years of a military withdrawal "staged" to appease militant patriots and to protect the President's political right flank?[2]

Hughes makes a planned postponement of American withdrawal from Vietnam sound not merely immoral but sadistic.

Kenneth O'Donnell, an aide to President John Kennedy, purports to report an explanation of the Vietnam situation as Kennedy saw it, and Jack Valenti, former adviser to Lyndon Johnson, has given it much play to support his campaign for a single six-year term for U.S. Presidents. Here is the O'Donnell quote in a *Washington Post* Service column of July 9, 1973, written by George Will:

> O'Donnell claims that by 1963 Kennedy had decided upon complete military withdrawal from Vietnam. "But," President Kennedy is supposed to have said, "I can't do that until after 1965, after I'm reelected." O'Donnell says President Kennedy feared "a wild conservative outcry."

We have not been able to confirm elsewhere this purported Kennedy quotation. Our own research, however, is convincing that it is more rather than less probable that President Kennedy did make such a statement. Certainly he made no move in 1963 to prepare for a U.S. withdrawal. We can dream of how different the world—controlled as it must be by the strategic military balance—would have been in 1973, if President Kennedy had carried out his 1963 decision for a U.S. withdrawal. His Secretary of Defense would not have had an ongoing conflict to magnify by "creeping escalation" into "McNamara's war"; thereby diverting $140 billion into a tactical rathole instead of into investment in U.S. strategic power; thus inviting the men in the Kremlin to build a first-strike capability against us. In 1972 Kissinger would not have had a theatrical backdrop against which to stage spectacular displays of "bold" Kissinger-Nixon resistance to communism, such as the mining of Haiphong Harbor and the "carpet bombing" of the Hanoi area.

Kissinger did, as the Acheson and Hughes quotations expose, go far in conceding that the refusal of the Administration to negotiate an immediate and unconditional surrender to the North Vietnamese Communists was indeed "staged" to impress the nation's right wing. But the reason he gave for *needing to impress* the so-called reactionary right had to provide at least a thin cover for the real reason: he reportedly attributed this need to the necessity of avoiding an "orgy of recrimination" for having surrendered in Vietnam. The true reason, however, was his need to impress scores of millions of Middle Americans that the Nixon Administration was resolved never to surrender to communism. Thus, Kissinger put Vietnam to work to win support for his grand design, which depended on popular support of his deals with Moscow and Peking. With articulate liberals and much of the mass media screaming for surrender-now in Vietnam, and with Kissinger-Nixon apparently standing firm against all that pressure, the average Middle American simply could not bring himself to believe that the "peace-but-only-with-honor" stalwarts in the White House would turn around and abjectly negotiate a preemptive strategic surrender to the men in the Kremlin—or sell out all our Asian allies to the men in Peking. The fanatics of the New Left and those segments of the older Liberal Establishment who go along with them, by their extremist opposition and irresponsible smears, provided Richard Nixon with his broadest base of support. A typically Middle American reaction has been: "If they hate him that much, he must be on *our* side." This is why, in 1972, he won 49 out of 50 states.

This ultimate and overriding Kissinger objective in the Vietnam stall, and the "cunningly" staged withdrawal, was and still is impenetrable to the antiwar activists such as Emmet John Hughes and to at least 11 former members of Kissinger's own staff who resigned because of what they called the "immorality" of the policies he supported in Vietnam. They are out to get Kissinger for all the wrong reasons. What is relevant here is that they really know a great deal about his mainspring and what makes him tick. However, they do not understand his *objectives* because they are blocked ideologically and emotionally. They are totally obsessed with hate for any influential liberal who did not support their drive for immediate surrender in Vietnam.

We can learn a great deal about Kissinger's character, motivation, and modus operandi from his erstwhile friends. Emmet John Hughes puts a key question to himself:

> Since Watergate manifests above all *a state of mind pervading the whole White House*—a unique mixture of moral density, intellectual arrogance, and political ruthlessness—must not such a mentality have poisoned the conduct of world affairs as well as national affairs?[3]

Once you go along with his unsupported assumption that Watergate manifests a state of mind "pervading the *whole* White House," you are projected automatically to an affirmative answer to his question. Since you have conceded that the Watergate mentality pervades the "whole White House," it must necessarily have "poisoned the conduct of world affairs."

After such a preface, there are, in the Hughes column, some high-pitched vilifications of both Nixon and Kissinger, but there are also some highly perceptive illustrations of what Hughes calls "strikingly specific linkages between this White House's conduct of domestic affairs and foreign affairs." Here is one of Hughes' comments:

> Beyond all such details, what gravely matters is that the *consequences* have been so akin in national and global affairs. The passion of H.R. Haldeman and John Ehrlichman to suck all domestic power into the White House has been wholly shared by Henry Kissinger's like appetite for foreign power; the Haldeman-Ehrlichman contempt for Congress found a perfect parallel in the Kissinger contempt for the Foreign Service; and all that the former *tried* to do to the Congress the latter *succeeded* in doing to the State Department. [All emphasis in the original.]

Hughes follows this realistic and intelligent analysis with an emotionally charged indictment of Kissinger for a half-dozen legitimate activities in the conduct of foreign affairs. These include "tilting" in favor of Pakistan over India against the opposition of "almost every competent diplomatic officer in the government"; "invading" Cambodia in 1970; and "trying to turn the tide in the Vietnam truce negotiations by the Yuletide carpet-bombing of Hanoi and Haiphong." Then Hughes soars to a height of understanding inconsistent with his ideology:

> Daily headlines notwithstanding, the greatest menace of presidential power still hides and haunts in the realm of foreign policy. What John Kennedy said of his own administration applies no less to the very life of the Republic: "*Domestic policy . . . can only defeat us. Foreign policy can kill us.*"
>
> And in the life of the White House, an occasional felony can corrupt less grievously than a systematic fakery.[4]

Emmet John Hughes, the writer who summed up the 1952 presidential campaign with the five electric words he ghost-wrote for Eisenhower ("I will go to Korea"), has thus recalled for us another equally powerful five-word statement from President Kennedy: "Foreign policy can kill us." The evidence is inescapable that foreign policy *can* kill us. As Henry Kissinger is shaping it through his "systematic fakery," it inexorably will kill us. Only one of the two can survive: the Kissinger policy or the United States of America.

In summary, here is what we have learned about Kissinger from Emmet John Hughes:

(1) Kissinger operates "the most cunning charade" in Washington.

(2) His appetite for foreign power is wholly like that displayed by Haldeman and Ehrlichman in their passion to suck all domestic power into the White House; but, where they failed, he "succeeded."

(3) Kissinger had emasculated the State Department and taken over all its significant powers while he was working in the White House, long before taking over the residuals as Secretary of State; and he has "contempt for the Foreign Service."

(4) His domination of U.S. defense and foreign policy was so nearly total as to permit his stalling the Vietnam settlement for more than four years *so that* he could artfully stage diversions for political purposes and "blur the truth and avoid the backlash."

(5) He fancies himself as a dramatic actor to the extent that his "eyes almost fill with tears when he talks of the President's brave resistance to expediency."

Additional insight is added by Frances FitzGerald, whose *New York Times* review of Professor Graubard's book we cited above.[5]

(6) Kissinger's turning Nixon toward Moscow and Peking was not motivated by the high-flown sophisticated theories he invoked to rationalize them, such as "in a subtle triangle of relations with Washington, Peking, and Moscow, we improve the possibilities of accommodations with each as we increase our options toward both;" no, he was actually motivated by the down-to-earth (or, more accurately, down-to-one-world) consideration that such accommodations were the priority objectives of his predominant power base: "the prestigious academics, civil servants and Wall Street bankers of the Council on Foreign Relations."

Those six items, extracted from a sampling of writings about Kissinger published in the late summer of 1973 by anti-Vietnam liberals, demonstrate how well they know some facets of his remarkable character. They did not, however, decipher his ultimate motivations and priority objectives. They unanimously regarded him as a rigid "cold warrior"; as, for example, Frances FitzGerald wrote:

> In his published works, Kissinger always took the position that a stable balance of power between the nation-states was the most desirable form of international organization. Whether he came to this conclusion before or during his early work on Metternich and the Congress of Vienna is a debatable, but perhaps uninteresting question. Balance of power— or balance of terror—was just as commonplace an idea in the mid-20th century as it was at the beginning of the 19th.
>
> Kissinger's insistence that the overriding concern for the United States was not the attainment of peace but the attainment of a stable international order was *in essence the doctrine of the cold war*—as I. F. Stone wrote, "our old friend '*better dead than red*' in glossier wrappings."[6]

One of fate's ironies is that, of all national figures in the 1970s, Kissinger has been the most active, the most incredibly effective, in swinging weight to the *Red* side of that balance. What McNamara, Nitze, Gilpatric, *et al.*, did in the 1960s, Kissinger did more than ever in the first five years of the Nixon administrations. Whereas McNamara quite literally decimated the strategic power in-being of the United States, and blocked development and production of all new, advanced strategic weapons systems, he at least was covered by an inherited-from-Eisenhower U.S. strategic superiority as he brought it down from 8-to-1 in our favor at the beginning of his term to, say, 1.001-to-1 at the time Lyndon Johnson caught him in his doublecross over the Sentinel ABM and fired him. In continuing the McNamara freeze on strategic weapons, Kissinger has had the greater psychological burden of operation in an era in which the Soviet strategic advantage over us has climbed to as much as 19-to-1 in missile-deliverable megatonnage.

The motivation for these unilateral-disarmers is still the same. Paul Nitze gave the sophisticated version back in April 1960 at the U.S. Army-Stanford Research Institute-RAND National Strategy Seminar at Asilomar, California. Nitze explained that, in the longterm competition with the Soviet Union, the United States could not win and come out Number One; and that, if we ended up a strong Number Two, we might "stay in the bidding and get clobbered," so we had better plan on coming out no better than a very weak second. His underlying thesis was that, not only is it safer to be weak than strong, but it is better to be Red than take any substantial risk of becoming dead.

We do not fault Kissinger or Nitze or McNamara or any of the other defeatists for not choosing to be "dead rather than Red." That was never *our* alternative. Where they fail in their loyalty to America is in refusing to assume even very small *risks* of becoming dead, rather than embracing a *certainty* of becoming Red or dead at the option of the Kremlin. At the time the Nitze group made its choice, we had an 8-to-1 strategic superiority, and probably a 3-to-1 advantage in GNP and industrial capacity—not to mention tremendous technological superiorities in substantially all areas except rocket thrust for huge missiles. Accurate intelligence would have shown that the Soviets were exploiting 40 percent of their GNP for a military power buildup, and still were falling behind. With determined and dedicated leadership—or even with average-but-loyal leadership—the United States could have maintained for a term of unlimited duration the war-winning capability of overwhelming strategic superiority, which is the only absolutely reliable deterrent to nuclear war. But the unilateral-disarmament intellectuals would not take even the slightest risks for freedom, for America, for Western civilization, or for their own children and grandchildren. To them, no value could ever be worth dying for.

By the time Kissinger came to power, the risks to America were increasing each year with a momentum equivalent to that of the Soviet buildup past "parity," and on toward the overwhelming superiority that will give first-strike capability. As we have seen, Kissinger has always been a defeatist so far as concerns the capability of the United States to compete with the Soviets in the strategic area. To the same man who saw our position as hopeless in the 1960-64 era when we had an actual strategic advantage of 8-to-1, and who saw the continuance of that gap for at least four years as inevitable even if we started crash programs, the all-too-real missile gap of the 1970s must appear terrorizing indeed. This explains why every actual program Dr. Kissinger has initiated in the areas of grand strategy, of strategic nuclear posture, and of relationships with the

Soviet Communists—and why every one of his "cunning charades," his elaborate "systematic fakeries," and the sophisticated rationales with which he covers his programs—has been part of his grand design to make us all Red rather than risk being made dead.

The anti-Vietnam War activists hate Kissinger because they mistake his motive as a decision to oppose Communist expansion. This is a majestic irony, because Kissinger is just as much a pro-surrender activist as they are—only on a worldwide scale, instead of containing that surrender in Southeast Asia. It is a misnomer to label these people "antiwar." They were anti-*Vietnam* War only because it appeared to be resistance to Communist expansion. They, or their predecessors in ideology, were enthusiastic supporters of the United States' aid to the Soviet Union during World War II; before that, they had supported the war waged by the "loyalist" Communists in the Spanish Civil War. But, like Lyndon Johnson, they continually feared that our conduct of McNamara's war in Vietnam might "provoke" the Soviets into launching a nuclear war. Kissinger, McNamara, Paul Nitze, and Roswell Gilpatric are all brothers in nuclear pacifism. Exactly as Khrushchev predicted, they are paralyzed with fear of nuclear war and, as a consequence, seek to paralyze our nation's defenses. Perhaps because the antiwar liberals are such soul brothers with Kissinger and the nuclear pacifists, they have been able at least partially to penetrate Kissinger's "cunning charades" and elaborate "systematic fakeries" so much better than the conservatives who have formed Nixon's primary base of popular support.

The comments quoted from the liberal writers confirm our own conclusions that Henry Kissinger, despite his intellectual attainments and unctuous attitude, is, to say the least, tricky. But there are degrees of trickiness. Some people, as the saying has it, simply cannot be smart without being slick, even when no ulterior motive is involved. There are, however, also tricks that are merely dirty, and tricks that are monstrously evil. Burglarizing the Democratic headquarters at Watergate was a dirty trick; but there were hundreds of thousands of other burglaries committed nationwide in that same year. The Watergate motivation could hardly be classified as monstrously evil.

It would seem that betrayal would have to be an essential element for a dirty trick to qualify for the classification of "evil"—for example, if someone had entrusted you with great power, and with his own reputation and his place in history, and you exploited his trust in a manner that would make him appear as an incompetent and ridiculous, even if tragic, fool. To make a trick "monstrously evil," some sort of an extension of the effects of the evil would appear to be required, such as having the betrayal extend to an entire population so that it will be totally vulnerable to being rendered Red or dead, *at the sole option* of the Politburo of the Communist Party of the Soviet Union.

It would be difficult for anyone who has studied how Henry Kissinger's actions line up, or do not line up, with his sophisticated words to deny that he is compulsively tricky. Without looking further, his methodology in securing the ouster of two Cabinet officers (Melvin Laird and William P. Rogers), one director of the Central Intelligence Agency (Richard Helms), and at least one ambassador (Gerard C. Smith), plus what we have quoted from liberal sources, seem to establish that he would indulge from time-to-time in dirty tricks. But what about the "monstrously evil" category? That would involve not only highly deliberate deception but, in old legal terminology, lots of "aforethought."

To probe this aspect of Dr. Kissinger's personality, the best approach is through a return to the explanation by Joseph Kraft of how Kissinger, without "changing the President's mind," was able to "build a track along which the President was able to move toward" the Moscow Summit-SALT I Agreements of May 1972. We set forth this quotation at the beginning of this chapter, but postponed analyzing it until after the presentation of comments by other liberals. It should be remembered that Kissinger's pre-Watergate friend Joseph Kraft reported that Kissinger had organized within the administration a "process of analysis which showed that an effective ABM could not be built ∴ . . . [and] demonstrated that it would be possible to monitor any secret Soviet moves to develop a full-scale ABM system."

These twin propositions are, as we have seen, both false, and demonstrably so. To evaluate the Kissinger motivation in persuading the President that they are valid, it is necessary to ascertain whether Kissinger knew at the time he created them that they were false. Did he know before he persuaded the President to sign the SALT I ABM Treaty that the United States then had the capability of building an "effective" ABM system; that is, that it was within the then-realized state of our technology to build and deploy such a defense against enemy missiles?

Certainly he knew. He had all the U.S. information and intelligence on the subject, plus some very persuasive additional evidence from the Russians. He knew that the capability of our ABM system was no longer an academic matter, that it no longer involved imponderables. This was fairly well established by the time the first SALT negotiations were held in late 1969, but the rate of progress in the development and testing of all elements of the ABM system was far greater than had been anticipated. From that time and continuing during the 2½ years of purported negotiations in Vienna and Helsinki, progress was dramatic. Not only had all components been tested and proved-out, time after time, but the accuracy and reliability of the intercepts greatly exceeded expectations. This applied both to our endoatmospheric defensive missile, the Sprint, that intercepts the offensive missile *after* it reenters the earth's atmosphere in the terminal phase of its flight, and to our exoatmospheric defensive missile, the Spartan, that intercepts while the offensive missile is still in outer space sometime toward the end of the midcourse. Our radar systems demonstrated the capability of reliably detecting and tracking enemy missiles. Just as important, the long-anticipated difficulties in distinguishing between real warheads and decoys and other penetration aids were met and overcome.

Dr. Kissinger also knew that the Russians knew that our system, if deployed, would be effective. Thus, several times in his congressional briefings, he repeated a reference to the Soviets' "desire of stopping the deployment of the [U.S.] ABM system." He also testified that

> What drove these [SALT] negotiations for the first year was their desire to limit our ABM deployment. And it was not until we insisted that we could not agree to an ABM treaty without offensive limitations that they reluctantly included offensive limitations.

In addition, he conceded that:

> . . . it is perhaps true that in the ABM field we had the more dynamic program which is being arrested as a result of these developments.[7]

It would appear to be a logical deduction that the Soviets would simply not be all that interested in blocking a U.S. program that would not, could not, be "effective." Rather, if they did not expect it to be effective, they would be happy to see us waste a few billion dollars on a worthless weapon. So when Dr. Kissinger turned his "process of analysis" into a cunning charade to convince the President that the United States could not build an effective ABM system, he was engaging in deliberate deceit.

Turning to the second theatrical effect created by the Kissinger "process of analysis," namely, that it "would be possible to monitor any secret Soviet moves to develop a full-scale ABM system," it is even easier to demonstrate that the illusion created to "move" the President toward the Moscow Agreements was not only fraudulent, but was deliberately so.

There is simply no way—no way at all—in which we could possibly reliably monitor their secret moves to develop a full-scale ABM system. The Soviets may even right now have a system "thick" enough and extensive enough to protect all the vital target areas in the U.S.S.R. If they do, it is probably not yet operational, at least as a large-scale area defense system. But they might well have such a system set up and ready to go operational as soon as a few underground connections are made to establish the required radar nets.

It is remarkable, even with his brashness and contempt for the American people's lack of understanding of the problems of nuclear strategy, that Kissinger would dare to assure the President that we could have high confidence—or any reasonable confidence at all—in monitoring Soviet secret moves toward development of a full-scale ABM system. And he must have convinced the President, or the President could not in conscience have bound the American people to expose themselves totally to nuclear incineration "for a term of unlimited duration."

The reason that this contention is such a shocking surprise is that, from the beginning of its construction in 1964 through at least 1970, the U.S. intelligence community was locked in interminable debate as to whether the Soviets' so-called Tallinn system of surface-to-air missiles (SAMs) and associated radar nets were merely a defense against aircraft, or had the dual capability of defending also against ballistic missiles. The primary capability of this system against missiles would be in its more than 1,000 SA-5 missile launchers, which undeniably have substantial ABM capability; but the Soviets have also some 10,000 additional SA-2 launchers, many of which have been retrofitted to handle nuclear-warheaded missiles, and these also have some, although less, ABM capability.

No one could ever give a reason why, in 1964, the Soviets should launch construction of such an elaborate additional surface-to-air missile system to defend against *aircraft,* especially when they already had 10,000 antiaircraft missiles and 3,000 interceptors. The last U.S. B-52 had been completed in October 1962, when McNamara shut down production. He never again permitted the production of a single additional large strategic bomber for the United States. By the time the Soviets were deploying the first segments of the Tallinn defensive missile launchers, McNamara had killed Skybolt, the great air-to-surface missile that would have kept our obsolescent subsonic bombers effective until the early 1980s, and he also killed the great B-70 strategic bomber. Our strategic bomber force in-being was being cut back from more than 1,500 to fewer than 500—all of which, such as McNamara's TFX/FB-111, were obsolescent or inadequate for their strategic mission. The British had had an impressive potential in strategic bombers; however it was dependent on Skybolt, which we had promised to share with them, but canceled unilaterally after its successful testing. Other NATO bomber forces were inconsequential.

At the time the Soviets were building it, there was simply *no bomber threat anywhere in the world* to justify such a massive national effort and expenditure of resources on an extensive system of SAMs and radars *unless* they had antimissile as well as antiaircraft capability. The Soviets did have in hand the technology required for producing and deploying an ABM system. They were already deploying their Galosh system around Moscow. Thus it was that the U.S. intelligence estimates of that era credited the Tallinn system with ABM capability. The best objective expert opinion was that "either the Russians were incredibly stupid," or else more than 1,000 SA-5s in the Tallinn systems either already had ABM capability or could swiftly be upgraded to provide it.

A clinching item of evidence of the high probability of the Tallinn system's having ABM capability was that the U.S. deployment of MIRVs in the late 1960s was justified on the basis that it was necessary to saturate the missile defense capability then attributed by U.S. experts to the Tallinn system. Adrian S. Fisher, Deputy Director of the U.S. Arms Control and Disarmament Agency, so testified in 1970, and Paul Warnke, McNamara's most influential assistant secretary of Defense, so testified in 1971, before the Senate Foreign Relations Subcommittee on Arms Control.

Securing strategic arms control agreement with the Soviets was a personal and political imperative for Henry Kissinger. He recognized that, if the United States did not agree to an ABM treaty that would destroy the momentum of our program and permit actual deployment of no more than a nominal number of launchers, the Soviets would not touch an agreement even purporting to limit their offensive missile buildup. So, by a rare coincidence, *after* Kissinger had assumed active control both of U.S. intelligence and of the SALT negotiations, a surprising consensus developed in the U.S. intelligence community that the Tallinn system (1) did not originally have an ABM capability, (2) had not been upgraded to an ABM capability, and (3) could not be upgraded, either overtly or secretly, without the upgrading's being exposed by U.S. monitoring.

Without all three of those purported evaluations of the Tallinn system, entry by the United States into the SALT I ABM Treaty would have been exposed as a crude and obvious move—beyond the point of no-return—toward strategic surrender to the Soviet Union. No President could possibly have justified it to himself, let alone to the Senate and the nation. It would immediately give the Soviets 1,000 *more* known ABM launchers than the U.S. was allowed. More important, these 1,000 additional defensive missile launchers, and their extensive radar systems, could be tied into the new 100 missiles and the high-capability long-range Henhouse radars allowed to the Soviets under the ABM Treaty, giving them an "area defense"—that is, the capability of defending *people* by the scores of millions, and cities and industry, as well as large numbers of offensive missiles. The strategic result would be to give the Soviets a preclusive first-strike capability against the United States. Their offensive missiles of the SS-9, SS-18, SS-17, and SS-19 classes could easily destroy the U.S. Minuteman land-based retaliatory missile force, and they would have an ABM system capable of effectively defending against the relatively small force of submarine-launched missiles the United States would retain as a last resort.

If we could not determine during all the years of intensive intelligence surveillance of the installation and deployment of the more than 1,000 SA-5 missiles and radars of the Tallinn system whether the system had ABM capability, how could we hope to monitor successfully "any secret Soviet moves to develop a full-scale ABM system"?

If we couldn't get the answer in some six years in the case of the Tallinn system, how long would it take with a *new* system? After actual deployment of such a system, even six months could well be a fatal lead-time advantage. The upgrading of the Tallinn system itself always presents a current and massive danger. The missiles themselves have an undeniable ABM capability. In the case of the 1,000 SA-5s, this capability is very substantial, indeed; and even the 10,000 SA-2s are known to have a 100,000-foot reach-up, and a 30-mile range on the slant—and these ranges may well have been secretly extended by new techniques, perhaps similar to the pop-up-launch retrofits that make the old SS-11s into the new SS-17s and SS-19s.

The only element needed to provide the Soviets with a relatively heavy area-defense system is the actual connection of these surface-to-air missiles to appropriate radar networks. The Soviets have a highly suspicious number of radars capable of being interconnected into nets. The Soviets have, already deployed and operational—according to recent testimony by General Bruce Holloway, former Commander of the U.S. Strategic Air Command—some "25 times as many radars as the United States."

In addition to their vast numbers, Soviet radars have fantastic capabilities. Their Henhouse radars range up to half a mile in length, and are nearly 100 feet high. Dr. John Foster, Director of Research and Engineering for the Defense Department, has testified that six Soviet Henhouse radars "can in the near term provide the same radar coverage we will have eight years from now [from 1972] if all the Safeguard program is completed." This, of course, can't be, because Dr. Kissinger's SALT I Anti-Defense Treaty binds us against building the Safeguard system or any other similar ABM system for a "term of unlimited duration."

Dr. Foster also commented, prior to the SALT I Agreements, that "the vast network of Soviet radars and defense sites, whether anti-aircraft or antimissiles, has already complicated the problem of effective arms control of ABM to where it may not be practical." That was before anyone thought that the U.S. representatives would be stupid enough or sufficiently appeasement-minded to agree to arms control agreements without any on-site inspection.

What must be considered a conclusive item of evidence that U.S. "national means of verification" are unable to monitor any secret upgrading by the Soviets of so-called air defense systems and their components into full-scale ABM systems is found in a naive admission by the U.S. delegation. Our SALT delegates included in the official record of the SALT I Agreements the following "Noteworthy Unilateral Statement":

> G. No Increase in Defense of Early Warning Radars
> ... Since Henhouse radars [Soviet ballistic early warning radars] can detect and track ballistic missile warheads at great distances, they have a significant ABM potential. Accordingly, the U.S. would regard any increase in the defenses of such radars by surface-to-air missiles as inconsistent with an agreement.

The practical meaning of this is that U.S. delegates recognized the impossibility of reliably detecting a clandestine move by the Soviets to tie early warning radars into a network with surface-to-air missiles having an ABM capability when so connected. Being helpless to monitor such Soviet moves, the U.S. delegates sought, by this feeble unilateral declaration, to restrain the Soviets from adding additional defenses for such radar installations to make them invulnerable to attack by U.S. bombs or missiles. In this poor-substitute attempt, however, all they succeeded in doing was to make another appeal to Soviet good faith and good will. A U.S. "unilateral" declaration has no binding effect in limiting Soviet rights under the ABM Treaty. In making this official unilateral declaration, however, our own delegation certainly clinched the case against our ability to inspect for the true purpose of Soviet radars.

Thus the "demonstration" Dr. Kissinger arranged for the President must also have been fraudulent as to the reliability of our "monitoring" the upgrading of existing so-called air-defense systems to an ABM role, or even discovering whether such systems already have it. Even more obviously and deliberately false, however, would be any staged "demonstration" that purported to "prove" that it is possible for us to "monitor any secret moves to develop a full-scale ABM system" by *violation of the prohibitions of Article V of the ABM Treaty.* By this provision, each party agrees

> not to develop, test, or deploy ABM systems which are sea-based, air-based, space-based or *mobile land-based*

and not to

develop, test, or deploy ABM launchers for launching more than one ABM interceptor missile at a time from each launcher, nor to modify deployed launchers to provide them with such a capability, nor to develop, test, or deploy automatic or semi-automatic or other similar systems for rapid reload of ABM launchers.

The development of such advanced ABM system components has to take place in laboratories and production facilities that are under cover—so any of these could be developed without any chance of our "monitoring" the process. Then they could be produced in quantities (the ABM Treaty contains no prohibition against production) and stored under cover, and thus kept secret and ready for rapid surprise deployment.

In addition, the Soviets may already have "developed" some of these improved prohibited types—such as land-mobile ABM launchers—and may even have tested them. If so, they can—without any violation whatsoever of the Treaty's Article V—produce them in numbers and store them secretly to stand by for speedy deployment. As to a rapid reload capability, for example, Senator James Buckley testified before the Senate Foreign Relations Committee on June 29, 1972, that the "nature of the Soviet ABM missile launcher makes it relatively simple for the Soviet Union to covertly develop for later deployment, a rapid reload capability." Or, if they have already developed the reloading element, they can produce it and store it for standby for speedy attachment to all deployed launchers.

Another massive and possible critical capability the Soviets possess for making secret preparations for deployment of "a full-scale ABM system" revolves around their land-mobile ABM launchers. They already have had substantial experience in producing mobile surface-to-air missile launchers. The admitted ABMs in the Moscow system are mobile; the SA-2s they sent to Vietnam to shoot down our aircraft are mobile; and they have a very modern (first deployed in 1967) SA-4-type (Ganef) with a range of 50 miles on the slant that, if given added altitude, would have ABM capability. Their SA-6s are highly mobile and ultrasophisticated—far beyond anything we even knew about until the Israelis captured one in October 1973. We know also that they have the capability of producing surface-to-air launchers by the thousands.

Thus, if the Soviets have already "developed" a land-mobile ABM launcher, or a dual purpose air-defense antimissile launcher, they could produce them by the thousands, garage them under cover, and keep them ready for near-instantaneous deployment and tie-in with existing radar nets. This would not be in violation of the ABM Treaty unless and until actual deployment, and they may already have done exactly this.

A solid-fuel missile was displayed for the first time in the annual Revolution Day parade in Red Square, Moscow, on November 7, 1973. Western military experts first classified it as an ABM, but "closer analysis showed it to be a rocket that might be used against targets in Western Europe or the United States," and that it "could be transported and fired from temporary sites instead of fixed positions."[8] Later, the Kissinger-dominated U.S. intelligence community evaluated this new missile, now identified as the SS-16, as an ICBM. It was so described in both the FY 1975 Department of Defense Report by the Secretary of Defense and in the FY 1975 Posture Report by the Chairman of the Joint Chiefs of Staff. Both reports conceded that the SS-16 was capable of being deployed in the land-mobile mode. Our prediction is that further analysis will show that it probably can be adapted as either a mobile ICBM or a mobile ABM. If, as appears probable, the SS-17s, SS-19s, and SS-18s provide all the offensive weapon power the Soviets need, the SS-16s could provide the last needed element for a preclusive first-strike capability.

If they produce hundreds of the ABM version, they could then give us six months' notice to terminate the treaty and thus make the entire procedure legal. By doing this they could gain a five- to six-year advantage over us in attaining a thick ABM defense in-being. No part of the process short of the actual deployment could be monitored by the means permitted us by the treaty.

As one expert summed up our possibilities of monitoring Soviet compliance with Article V of the ABM Treaty:

> Neither satellite photography nor any other known means of surveillance can verify compliance with the terms of this article fully and unambiguously (certainly not with respect to development activities). It follows that this segment of the agreement, like the recent convention on biological warfare, is *an expression of trust and good will* rather than a reliable control measure.[9]

Here, then, as in all other critical segments of both SALT I Agreements, we have no provision for realistic control of the Soviets' massive strategic arms buildup; no constraints on their sustaining their momentum toward completion of a first-strike capability against the United States. All that we do have is another example of Henry Kissinger's incomprehensible compulsion to stake the lives of all 210 million Americans on his trust in the good will of the men in the Kremlin.

Summing up, then, the two Kissinger-"demonstrated" propositions in question are: (1) an effective ABM cannot be built, and (2) we can monitor any secret Soviet move to develop a full-scale ABM system. If it can be so easily established by a brief objective analysis that both propositions are false, then was Richard Nixon *really* taken in by Dr. Kissinger's fraudulent analysis and demonstrations purporting to prove that they are true?

The best evidence that he really was deceived is found in his actions. Shortly after January 1970, he withdrew his support of "a full deployment of an American ABM," which was the preliminary objective of the Kissinger "demonstrations." The convincing proof of Nixon's belief, however, is found in his going along with Kissinger's Moscow SALT I Anti-Defense Treaty. As we have seen, no authority anywhere contests the fact that the treaty makes the entire U.S. population hostages to the Kremlin, and a substantial segment hostages also to Peking. No one contests Dr. Kissinger's admission that the Treaty ensures Soviet and any other enemy missiles a free ride to destroy both the American people and our strategic deterrent against nuclear attack. No objective expert could contest the fact that, if the SALT I Interim Agreement fails to prevent the Soviets from attaining completion of their first-strike capability against us, entry into the SALT I Anti-Defense Treaty will have set us up for mass murder by nuclear incineration.

No President could knowingly do such a thing to his trusting people. By their votes, they place him under an obligation of loyalty. The unelected Dr. Kissinger, however, apparently has no care about our safety or the magnitude of the risks to which he has subjected us. He is willing to bet our lives on the sincerity of any gesture of detente by members of Moscow's Politburo. Perhaps he finds self-justification in the fact that he has, at times, given us both general and specific warnings that we are involved in a gamble. Thus, he has affirmed: "I believe in the tragic element in history." And: "Nothing is more difficult for Americans to understand than the possibility of tragedy."

With respect to specific warnings, it is well at this point again to recall one from a "backgrounder" presented for the press in Chicago on September 16, 1970:

Dr. Kissinger: With respect to SALT and commenting generally about the Soviet performance, this Administration has never believed that the Soviets will keep an agreement just because they like to keep their word.

We have always assumed that as Marxists they would believe that they will keep an agreement only so long as it serves their interests.

As Marxists, they have almost no mechanism by which they would keep an agreement that is against their interests.

13

Professor William R. Van Cleave, now of the Department of Strategic and Defense Studies at the University of Southern California, and formerly a special assistant in the Office of the Secretary of Defense and adviser to the U.S. delegation to the SALT conferences, testified sadly before the Senate Armed Services Committee in June 1972 that the agreements were

> a light year removed from the outcomes contemplated in the studies and planning for SALT . . . . There has since the start of SALT been a constant erosion of U.S. SALT positions and expectations.

Why was there a constant erosion of U.S. positions and expectations? Why were the finalized agreements astronomically removed from the comprehensively and meticulously planned objectives?

Although Kissinger conceded at the time that "national survival is at stake" in the SALT negotiations, not a single U.S. senator asked the simple question "why?" When Charles Murphy, former editor of *Fortune*, quoted that same excerpt in the introduction to his article in that magazine entitled "What We Gave Away in the Moscow Arms Agreements,"[1] *Fortune's* elite and affluent subscribers were not enough interested to ask why. As a group, they have much to lose: their fortunes, of course, but also their lives and the lives of their families. All their assets have been preserved, thus far, by the U.S. strategic deterrent that will be destroyed if, to use Charles Murphy's words, "what we gave away" in SALT turns out to have been decisively too much.

Because no one else asked it, we will put the question ourselves:

Why were the outcomes embodied in the SALT I Agreements 5,878,000,-000,000 miles removed from the outcomes contemplated in the studies and planning for SALT?

The 2½ years of negotiations conducted with solemnity and fanfare in Helsinki and Vienna were, so far as the U.S. delegation knew, based upon protracted, extensive, and intensive studies and planning. These pre-SALT studies were formally initiated a year before the negotiations commenced and were of stunning magnitude and depth. At times, more than 1,000 experts from the National Security Council, the Departments of Defense and State, JCS, CIA, and ACDA were engaged in preparing analyses for SALT planning.

The negotiations were based upon these studies and planning. *But the negotiations had nothing to do with the substance of the SALT Agreements.* The 2½ years of negotiations were a deliberate fraud on the American people and the Congress of the United States.

Members of the U.S. negotiating delegation were mere puppets created by Henry Kissinger to stage his most cunning charade. The whole thing was a slick trick, a theatrical effect, cynically conceived to deceive us into believing that the SALT I Agreements were the products of some 2½ years of good-faith bargaining at conference tables in Helsinki and Vienna. Window dressing was provided by planted stories describing the SALT I Agreements as having been "hammered out" in a process of "give-and-take" that involved "concessions" on both sides.

This was not true—not even a partial truth. It was a satanic trick. The U.S. SALT delegation never negotiated a single provision of any substantial importance in either the ABM Treaty or the Interim Agreement. The Soviet delegation was likewise composed of puppets, but at least the Russian delegation knew they possessed neither the responsibility nor the authority. The one exception was Colonel-General Nikolai Ogarkov, First Deputy Chief of the General Staff, who was elected a full member of the Soviet Communist Central Committee, and thereupon was relieved from wasting time on the SALT charade.

If the SALT I Agreements were not the product of 2½ years of negotiations by the U.S. and U.S.S.R. delegations, and were not hammered out at the conference table, how were they actually drafted?

Every single key provision of both SALT Agreements originated with Soviet strategic experts and planners in the Kremlin, was approved by Leonid Brezhnev and his closest associates in the Politburo, and was passed—usually by Soviet Ambassador Anatoly F. Dobrynin—to Henry Kissinger, who then provided the rationalization for it and "sold" it to President Nixon.

This, then, is the shockingly incredible answer to the question, how could the SALT Agreements be so astronomically distant in substance from the U.S. studies, planning, positions, and expectations that preceded and accompanied the negotiations. Although some of the "inputs" were American, the "outcomes" were exclusively Russian. The pragmatic managers for the Politburo knew in advance that the multiplex "options" and many-splendored "alternative solutions" submitted month after month by the U.S. delegation did, indeed, represent months of preparation by the Kissinger-controlled bureaucracy; but they also knew that none of it meant a damn thing to Henry Kissinger.

Kissinger's direct source of power, Richard Nixon, faced an election in the fall of 1972. For that purpose, Nixon needed Soviet agreement to an arms control arrangement. To insure the continuance of his own power and its enhancement through increased influence with Nixon, Kissinger needed to secure an arms control agreement for Nixon. So the Kissinger secret deal was this: Nixon would get the *agreement* from the Kremlin, but the Kremlin would get what it wanted *into* the agreement.

The SALT I Agreements revealed that Henry Kissinger had revolutionized the grand strategy of the United States, and that he had done so without the President, the National Security Council, the Secretary of Defense, or the Joint Chiefs of Staff even suspecting that he had done so.

Our original intuition that the SALT I Agreements had been written by the Soviets seemed a ridiculous idea. Everyone knew that the U.S. delegation had been negotiating intensely with the Soviet delegation over every provision of the SALT Agreements, for more than two years, before the President finally signed for the United States and the General Secretary of the Communist Party signed for the Soviet Union. President Nixon himself, in introducing Kissinger at the White House briefing on June 15, 1972, assured the members of five congressional committees:

This is an agreement which was very toughly negotiated on both sides.

The evidence indicates that Richard Nixon believed in the truth of that statement.

It was easy to accept the universal assumption that the SALT I ABM Treaty and Interim Agreement had been hammered out at the negotiating tables in Helsinki and Vienna over a period of some 2½ years by negotiating teams representing the two sides. It was natural to assume that the two teams had been given the responsibilities and authority customarily accorded high-level diplomatic delegations. After all, the chairman of the U.S. delegation, Gerard C. Smith, held the rank of Ambassador. The other delegates were similarly prestigious: another Ambassador, Llewellyn E. Thompson; former Deputy Secretary of Defense Paul Nitze; Lieutenant General Royal B. Allison, purportedly representing the Joint Chiefs; Cal Tech President Dr. Harold Brown, a former Secretary of the Air Force; and Raymond L. Garthoff, the delegation's senior adviser. The most influential four of the six delegates were CFR members.

In addition, there were 18 top-level advisers attached to the U.S. team, all of whom had staffs of a sort, so that some 88 Americans were involved at the SALT meetings. They were supported by up to 1,000 specialists in various U.S. departments and agencies in Washington. Our SALT team certainly had all the indicia of authority backed up by tremendous resources.

Starting with the assumption that the SALT I Agreements were actually "toughly negotiated" as President Nixon had assured us, and that they had been produced by give-and-take between the delegations over 2½ years, the tendency of any objective analyst would be to accept Kissinger's own explanation for the imbalances and one-sidedness of SALT I. He conceded a substantial missile gap, a U.S. position of inferiority, and asserted that the Soviets had "dynamic and accelerated deployment programs in both land-based and sea-based missiles" that were ongoing, and that we had no such programs. In short, he claimed he got the best bargain he could because we were bargaining from weakness. His most quoted statement on the subject is phrased in typical Kissingerese:

> The United States was in a rather complex position to recommend a submarine deal since we were not building any and the Soviets were building 8 or 9 a year, which isn't the most brilliant bargaining position I would recommend people to find themselves in.[2]

William F. Buckley Jr, who covered those Kissinger press conferences in Moscow for his own columns as well as for *National Review*, states that he counted seven times that Kissinger defended U.S. relegation to inferiority on the ground that we had to deal with the existing current situation rather than an ideal situation. His brother, Senator James L. Buckley, one of the three or four reasonably well-informed members of the Senate on the SALT I Agreements and consequently one of their severe critics, also accepted the Kissinger we-did-the-best-we-could-and-actually-cut-our-risks argument. The Kissinger version, briefly, is:

> The Interim Agreement perpetuates nothing which did not already exist in fact, and which could only have gotten worse without an agreement.

The Senator Buckley version is this:

I am quite prepared to accept the proposition that given the rate at which the Soviet Union has been overtaking us in its deployment of ICBMs and nuclear powered submarines, the risks which we are most assuredly assuming under the Interim Agreement are nonetheless *far smaller than we would be assuming if current trends were allowed to continue.*[3]

This Senator Buckley excerpt provides an enlightening introduction to probing to a second depth in the analysis of the SALT I Agreements and Kissinger's motivation. Kissinger is claiming, in a backhanded but inescapable manner, that the agreement will prevent the U.S. situation from getting worse; as he says in another place, "without an agreement, the gap would steadily widen." Senator Buckley, accepting the Kissinger premise, bases his argument that the risks will be smaller under the agreement on the assumption that the Agreement will block the "current trends," *i.e.*, not permit those current trends to continue.

But the SALT I Agreement did *not* block those "current trends" (to use Senator Buckley's language), nor (to use Dr. Kissinger's) did the agreement prevent the gap from "getting worse." As a matter of fact, the gap got worse with each passing month. The agreement permitted the Soviets (in the *Wall Street Journal*'s colorful expression) "to go on turning out submarines like sausages." It permitted them to emplace new and immensely more powerful missile launchers in the 91 new holes they had dug prior to the SALT cutoff date. (U.S. intelligence conceded 91 holes; more credible estimates set the number at 100.) Thus, SALT I permitted the Soviets to complete their total planned force level of fixed land-based missiles. They developed new and more powerful ICBMs to replace their 1,000 SS-11s, which already were far more powerful than U.S. Minuteman missiles. Designated the SS-17 and the SS-19, each can be fitted with a single warhead or up to six MIRVed warheads, and these can be retrofitted into all existing SS-11 silos without violating the SALT I Interim Agreement (although this does "violate" a U.S. Noteworthy Unilateral Declaration defining a "heavy" missile).

In addition, the Soviets revealed a new very heavy missile, now known as the SS-18. It is so named appropriately because it is between 20 and 100+ percent more powerful than their SS-9 model that U.S. intelligence acknowledges can carry 25 megatons of explosive power in a single warhead, or three 5-megaton MIRV warheads. In August 1973 Kissinger's new Secretary of Defense, James R. Schlesinger, officially admitted that the Soviets had successfully conducted an open test of MIRVed warheads for the SS-17, SS-18, and SS-19. Actually, the Soviets had been testing multiple warheads for some five years, but in continuing to play McNamara's old "numbers game," and to conceal from the American people the vast imbalances of the SALT I Agreements, Kissinger had them categorized merely as tests of highly sophisticated MRVs. They were highly sophisticated, indeed—too sophisticated to have lacked individual targeting capabilities. With their openly demonstrated capability of MIRVing their ICBMs, the Soviets can, if they wish, add to their SALT-enshrined numerical superiority in missile launchers a 6-to-1 superiority in numbers of deliverable warheads capable of individual targeting, and at least a 19-to-1 superiority in missile-deliverable megatonnage—all by exploiting their 6-to-1 superiority in throw-weight.

So, the Kissinger explanation that the SALT I Interim Agreement was the best bargain he could get, bargaining as he was from inferiority, will not wash. The United States did not get any bargain at all. Kissinger did *not* get an agreement that would prevent the missile gap from "getting worse." He did *not* secure, in Senator Buckley's words, an agreement that would block the "current trends" of the momentum of the Soviet strategic weapons buildup toward decisive superiority. The reason why the Interim Agreement did not stop the momentum of the Soviet buildup is that the Soviets wrote it. They drafted it with the overriding purpose of *not* blocking the momentum of their drive toward strategic supremacy.

If Kissinger did not accept the Soviet-written agreement because of the reason he stated, then why did he accept it? Seeking the answer to this question drove us to a still-deeper level of analysis. At this point, it appeared that Dr. Kissinger *simply did not care* that the SALT I Agreement enshrined Soviet strategic superiority and provides for their continued buildup to supremacy. He did not care that, by persuading the President to sign, he had abandoned every one of his own criteria for strategic "sufficiency" that the Nixon-Kissinger team had conceded were necessary to maintain the credibility of the U.S. strategic deterrent.

That, it appeared, was the key to his motivation in accepting all the imbalances and the 14 major loopholes benefiting the Soviets. He appeared really to believe that there was no longer a *need* for a U.S. strategic military deterrent. It appeared that he really believed that he had established a new type of deterrent that would effectively substitute for strategic military power: his very own goose-that-laid-the-golden-eggs type of deterrent, under which he was buying off the Soviets from using their strategic supremacy against us. He prefers explaining it on the basis of creating an economic interdependence that will provide the Soviets with a continuing incentive toward self-restraint from the use of their military power. So it appeared that he didn't *care* what the SALT Agreement actually provided as to strategic weapons systems; and, if the Kremlin insisted on drafting all the key provisions as its price for signing at all, then Kissinger was willing to let them do it.

The theory that Kissinger simply didn't care whether the SALT Agreements enshrined Soviet superiority and would allow its further increase, and that he therefore accepted Soviet domination of all key provisions of the agreements, is attractive in that it imputes no betrayal by him of the United States in the worst sense of that term. In making this judgment, he might have been merely naive and irresponsible. A wrong judgment to accept decisive Soviet strategic supremacy as a fact, and to rationalize that acceptance on the ground that it is not dangerous to U.S. survival because he had effectively bought the Soviets off from actually using their strategic power against us, carries with it none of the traitorous taint of acting affirmatively and deliberately to bring the United States down to a position of helpless strategic inferiority to the U.S.S.R.

Unfortunately, the deeper an analyst digs, the more facts turn up that destroy the theory that Dr. Kissinger didn't care whether SALT enshrined Soviet superiority, even to the point of a preclusive first-strike capability. These additional facts make a highly persuasive case that Kissinger *did* care about strategic supremacy—and that *he urgently wanted the Soviets to have it.* Most of these facts revolve around the point that all the Kissinger policies as to strategic power and the military posture of the United States actively hold down U.S. capabilities, and increase our relative inferiority to the Soviets as they continue their accelerated momentum in adding more and more increments of strategic power, both quantitatively and qualitatively.

A short way of summarizing this is that *SALT cannot kill us, but Kissinger can.*

Later we will consider some of the more interesting facets of these Kissinger policies and some of the evidence that they all were designed to degrade U.S. strategic power while the Soviet buildup continued under the protection of the SALT I Agreements. Now, from even deeper probing, we have the answer to the question of why Kissinger would accept and sell to the American people and their President the arms control agreements that were not only *signed* in Moscow, but *made* in Moscow. He and the Kremlin were working toward the same goal: a preclusive first-strike capability for the Soviet Union over the United States. So it was that the Soviet-drafted SALT I Agreements became one more instrument to be used by Dr. Kissinger in shaping his new world order.

This analysis provides the answer to the question that opened this chapter: why should the outcomes of the SALT I Agreements have been "a light year removed" from the outcomes contemplated in the

U.S. studies and planning for SALT? The answer is that the Kremlin's strategic planners had little to do with the U.S. studies and planning for SALT, but they had everything to do with what came out in the finalized agreements.

To look at SALT from another point of view, the studies and planning for SALT in all the concerned agencies of the U.S. Government were, at least officially, based on an objective of obtaining agreements that would *stop* the momentum of the ongoing Soviet strategic buildup in time to prevent their attaining a preclusive first-strike capability against the United States. On the other hand, the objective of the strategic planners for the Kremlin was to obtain agreements that would *accelerate* the U.S.S.R. momentum but *degrade* U.S. strategic power. Two lines of evidence establish the fact that the Kremlin planners attained their objective: the express terms of the SALT I Agreements themselves, with their 14 major loopholes and overt imbalances favoring the Soviets, and the actual operation of the agreements since the signing. The agreements themselves, and the post-SALT governmental actions implementing them, represent reality, while the 2½ years of staged "negotiations" at Helsinki and Vienna are exposed as elaborate and protracted charades, designed to divert attention from the reality of the SALT Agreements.

> For the kingdom of heaven is as a man travelling into a far country, who called his own servants, and delivered unto them his goods. And unto one he gave five talents, to another two, and to another one; to every man according to his several ability; and straightway took his journey.
>
> Then he that had received the five talents went and traded with the same, and made them other five talents. And likewise he that had received two, he also gained other two. But he that had received one went and digged in the earth, and hid his lord's money.
>
> After a long time the lord of those servants cometh, and reckoneth with them. And so he that had received five talents came and brought other five talents, saying, Lord, thou deliveredst unto me five talents; behold, I have gained beside them five talents more. His lord said unto him, Well done, thou good and faithful servant; thou hast been faithful over a few things, I will make thee ruler over many things: enter thou into the joy of thy lord. . . .
>
> Then he which had received the one talent came and said, Lord, I knew thee that thou art a hard man, reaping where thou hast not sown, and gathering where thou hast not strewed: and I was afraid, and went and hid thy talent in the earth: lo, there thou hast that is thine.
>
> His lord answered and said unto him, Thou wicked and slothful servant, . . . thou oughtest therefore to have put my money to the exchangers, and then at my coming I should have received mine own with usury. Take therefore the talent from him, and give it unto him which

hath ten talents .... And cast ye the unprofitable servant into outer darkness: there shall be weeping and gnashing of teeth.[4]

If Henry Kissinger's policies are not reversed in time, the destruction of freedom and religion, of peace and Western civilization, will have resulted because a great nation failed to heed the lesson of "the one talent which is death to hide," as John Milton so beautifully paraphrased it in the sonnet on his blindness.

A footnote in the English translation of the massive French *La Bible de Jerusalem* explains the parable of the talents:

Christians are servants expected by Jesus, their Master, to make full use of any gifts he has given them so that His kingdom may grow on earth; they must give an account of their administration.

It is more to the point here, however, to understand that the one talent represented *power.* A footnote in an old King James edition says that a talent was worth about 935 dollars—but that was before inflation set in, and the dollar thrice devalued. So a talent did represent substantial monetary power. The servants who were motivated by faith, not fear, used the power with which they had been entrusted in order to earn more power; so their Master called them to enter into his joy. But the one motivated by fear, who lacked the courage to put to use the power entrusted to him, had everything taken from him and was cast into outer darkness.

God entrusted to the United States the incomparably greatest power He has ever permitted to man—the only power since creation sufficient to control the entire planet Earth. And what have we done with it? President John F. Kennedy's palace guard laced his speeches with such exhortations as "we must get the nuclear genie back in the bottle," and we must "destroy these evil weapons before they destroy us." This attitude is unfortunately not outdated, even now. Kissinger echoed this "nuclear genie" fear as late as September 11, 1973, in testimony before the Senate Foreign Relations Committee relating to his confirmation as Secretary of State.

Contrast the cowardly, faithless attitude of U.S. leaders with that of the Soviet rulers. Stalin refused the Bernard Baruch plan of sharing the U.S. atomic monopoly with the U.S.S.R. Why? Because Stalin was a dedicated cadre Communist, and the Baruch plan would have subjected atomic military power to international control. Stalin was planning to steal or develop that power himself, and he had no intention of burying that talent in the ground, or putting the nuclear genie back in the bottle. He planned to put that power to work to gain more power.

Stalin and his successors and all the Politburo rulers seriously and sincerely believe that it is their "historic mission" to control the world. Strategic nuclear military power is the only type of military power that could possibly allow them to attain this objective. Conventional military power alone is simply not adequate; even the most highly mechanized and armored weapons would require a personnel force of tens of millions of men.

Of the total population of nearly 250 million in the U.S.S.R., only 14 million are even members of the Communist Party. No doubt many of them are dedicated, and most will fight to the last ditch to save Motherland Russia from invaders; but how many could be counted on to fight and risk death to spread the blessings of communism worldwide?

Strategic nuclear military power is the made-to-prescription instrument to accomplish that historic Communist mission. It eliminates any need for a massive propaganda effort to stir up the populace to crusade against the non-Communist world. The General Secretary of the Communist Party of the Soviet Union can stand alone in front of his console and press the buttons that will set aflame any part of the world that resists or obstructs the "historic mission." After he has done so, he can have his controlled press explain that the Soviet strike, "delivered in good time," has thwarted a plot by the "imperialist warmongers" to destroy the people of the Soviet Union and Europe.

Is strategic nuclear power really *usable* for such a purpose?

Giving Henry Kissinger full credit for sincerity in motivation, the most favorable interpretation that can be placed on his policies, his international deals, and his overt agreements is that he has gambled the survival of the United States and the lives and freedom of all Americans on the theory that strategic nuclear power is *not usable* by the Soviet Union against the United States; not usable either for purposes of actual attack or nuclear blackmail, or even for "political pressure."

The Soviet Communist leadership, with never-failing consistency and continuity through three successive dictators—Stalin, Khrushchev, and Brezhnev—has invested scores of billions of dollar equivalents *each year* to back up their judgment that strategic nuclear power *is* usable.

This, then, is the most momentous question in the history of man. Is the answer too complex, too technical, too esoteric, too awesome, for the understanding of ordinary Americans? Can only career-long specialists in nuclear strategy comprehend the decisive considerations? The elitist groups that have controlled the nuclear destiny of the United States since 1961 would like us to think so. If we give up and say that it is beyond us, we will have surrendered to those elitists the decision over our life or death, and they in turn will surrender us to the masters of Kissinger's new world order.

Our assertion that such a new world order is Henry Kissinger's planned objective is not a figment of a fevered imagination. In his initial appearance at the Senate Foreign Relations Committee hearings on his confirmation as Secretary of State, on September 7, 1973, he pontifically invited Congress to share his demiurgical mission:

> Our task is to define—together—the contours of a *new world*, and to shape America's contribution to it.
> . . . with good will on all sides I deeply believe we can reach this goal. . . .
> Our foreign policy cannot be effective if it reflects only the sporadic and esoteric initiatives of a small group of specialists.

If *that* quote seems to harbor nuances of megalomania, consider *this* one, excerpted from an address about a month earlier to the International Platform Association in Washington, D.C.:

> Our influence for good or ill will be measured by the world's judgment of our constancy and self-confidence. Our foreign policy will mean little if other nations see our actions as sporadic initiatives of a small group reflecting no coherent national purpose or consensus.
> No foreign policy—*no matter how ingenious*—has any chance of success if it is born in the minds of a few and carried in the *hearts of none*.

Kissinger is often fascinated by the sound of his own words and seldom abandons a resounding concept before elaborating it. Thus, in early August 1973, he deplored reliance on the "sporadic initiatives of a small group," but by September he had embroidered the concept to the "sporadic and esoteric initiatives of a small group of specialists."

The first excerpt above proves by his own words that Kissinger is quite serious about designing a "new world." Never mind where he acquired a mandate to design a new world, or from whom; and never mind about his magnanimity in inviting Congress to be a codesigner of his new world. In no way can that legitimize his *ultra vires* enterprise, because Congress doesn't have a mandate to create a new world, either; nor does it have such authority under our Constitution, which gives to the federal government only limited and enumerated powers. The U.S. Constitution does not enumerate a "new world" project. It does, however, enumerate the duty to provide for the "common defense" of the states of the United States. Influential CFR members have worked half a century to change this.

In the second Kissinger excerpt quoted above, there is a necessary implication in the second paragraph that he considers his foreign policy highly "ingenious." He also implies that we must not only go along with his project for the creation of a one-world new world, but we must learn to love it and carry it in our hearts.

One does not have to use Kissinger-type jargon in order to discuss the fundamentals of nuclear strategy. The most famous statesman of the 20th century spoke in language that is at one and the same time both eloquent and clearly communicable to the average person. One statement by Winston Churchill revealed the most brilliant perception, and conveyed the most down-to-earth warning uttered by any Western leader in the entire nuclear age. If our leaders could understand this one statement, they could cut through the Pugwashian ideological impedimenta that has brought us to the brink of disaster.

The revolutionary character of strategic nuclear power is highly dramatic. Suppose a biochemist came up with a pill that would extend the human life span by a factor of 30 million. Instead of looking forward to the traditional three score and 10 years of life, we would face a life span of 2,100,000,000 years. Think of the population explosion! One thing is reasonably sure: each of us would do some serious thinking about the new aspect of life thrust on us by such a fantastic factor of increase. We would not abdicate our interest in it to a small group of specialists who fancied themselves as "life-span intellectuals."

Or suppose another gifted chemist invented an additive for gasoline that would increase its power by a factor of 30 million. Instead of our hoped-for 20 miles per gallon, efficient use of the newly-pepped-up fuel would give us 600 million miles per gallon. Very few automobiles would last long enough to run out of gas. With that much mileage, it would take only some 9,797 gallons to drive the 5 trillion, 878 billion miles that Professor William Van Cleave estimates separates the Kissinger NSSM studies and plans for SALT, and the outcomes he accepted in the final SALT I Agreements.

The longevity pill and the gasoline additive may appear to be incredible flights of fancy—but the factor of 30 million is not fantasy. It is not even science fiction when applied to the increase of power of nuclear explosives over conventional explosives such as TNT (tri-nitro-toluene).

The most powerful strategic warhead practicable for conventional explosives was designed for the 2,000-pound bomb; that is, it had the explosive power of one ton of TNT. As long ago as 1962, the Soviets tested hydrogen devices that Secretary McNamara testified would "weaponize at 100 megatons." In 1972 Senator Henry Jackson revealed that the then-new Soviet update of the 25-megaton SS-9 ICBM would carry a single warhead of "50-plus" megatons. There is little question that, if the Soviets so desire, their new heavy missile, known now as the SS-18, could carry a single warhead of 100 megatons. That establishes the fantastic factor: whereas a conventional warhead has the power of one ton of TNT, a Soviet strategic nuclear warhead *could* carry the equivalent of 100 million tons of TNT. But since the U.S. Department of Defense admits only that the SS-18 can carry 30 megatons, we made our computations on the ultraconservative factor of 30 million, instead of on the more realistic factor of 100 million.

One of Mao Tse-tung's much-quoted sayings is that political power grows out of the barrel of a gun. Now political power is delivered, multiplied by that factor of 30 million, in the warhead of a strategic nuclear missile. The very existence of such an expanding type of power inexorably creates the potential of a revolution in internal power-politics relationships and in the entire field of foreign relations.

We pointed out earlier that merely having theorized about the magnitude of this thermonuclear revolutionary effect on foreign relations was enough to start Henry Kissinger on the road to fame, to the West Wing of the White House, and to the seventh floor of the State Department. *Thinking* about it got him where he is. *Not thinking* about it has gotten the rest of us Americans where we are; and we will be far worse if enough Americans do not soon out-think Henry Kissinger.

Some people tend to think that, because the 30- or 100-megaton missile has not *yet* shaken the organization of the world, it cannot; or, just as wishfully, it will not, even if it can. But think back to the fantastic additive that would magically multiply the power of gasoline from 20 miles a gallon to a potential of 600 million miles a gallon. A premature attempt to employ such fantastic power would no doubt result in an explosion that would destroy the driver who was over-anxious to exploit it. But the power base for the revolution would be there, waiting for the development of an engine that could exploit the available power.

That has been the situation as to employment of strategic nuclear power to bring the entire world under Moscow's political control. The development of thermonuclear strategic power created the potential for bringing about a revolution in international relations. The men in the Kremlin invested more than a quarter of a century and about 40 percent of the Soviet GNP over those years in translating that potential of power into weapons systems in-being. For the first 30 years of the nuclear age, which started in 1945, they were more or less in the position of the owner of a gallon of that 600-million-miles-per-gallon gasoline. If the Soviets had actually attempted to use their great power in-being, they would have been destroyed in the attempt. The "engine" for harnessing the horrendous power of thermonuclear explosives for military purposes is known as a "first-strike capability," and they had not yet attained it.

This situation is not immutable. Robert McNamara and the Pugwash movement, however, managed a propaganda program that convinced substantially all Americans who would read, or would view and hear television, that strategic nuclear power is, as Henry Kissinger has bet our lives it is, "unusable." The average otherwise-well-informed American businessman, professional man or woman, teacher, worker, mother or Ms., if forced to think about it at all, usually cuts short his or her thinking process with this passionate declaration:

> I don't care if the Soviets *do* have *twice* as many missiles as we do; or that they can carry 5 times the payload, or deliver 19 times the explosive power. They are just wasting their money building those awful weapons because they will never be used. The Soviets know that, if they struck at us, *we would strike back and destroy them.*

If anyone mildly suggests that we may not have enough left to "strike back and destroy the Russians," they have a preprepared Pugwashian response for that too:

> Oh, yes we will. We will always have enough left to strike back and destroy them because we have *overkill.* We have enough nuclear weapons to kill every person in the Soviet Union 10 times over.

Or 30 times over, depending upon which of the cynical liars has been sounding off recently.

Unless and until that edifice of deliberate genocidal deceit can be shaken loose from its false foundations in sophisticated distortions of strategic reality, the United States has no chance of surviving as an independent nation even to 1980. We have no chance of surviving in freedom, that is, *unless* the Soviets abandon the doctrine they have cherished for more than half a century, the doctrine that makes them Communists: the doctrine that there can never be a lasting world peace unless and until the capitalistic-imperialistic warmongers have been liquidated. This doctrine has been reaffirmed in each and every year of each Soviet dictator's rule, including Brezhnev's.

Furthermore, we cannot survive in freedom even until 1980 unless the Soviets (in addition to abandoning their most fundamental doctrine) also make an informed and considered decision to abandon all the substantial benefits that the investment of more than a quarter of a century of time and hundreds of billions of rubles in strategic military power, backed by conventional military power, can now bring them.

How would you like to be in Leonid Brezhnev's shoes if he had to explain to the other 15 members of the Politburo, and then to the Central Committee, why it was that he had commandeered 40 percent of the resources of the Soviet Union each year for some eight years of his own reign in order to buy thousands of land-based missiles and 62 modern nuclear-propelled missile-launching submarines, plus about the equivalent of $30 billion on Research and Development *annually*, when none of it was actually to be used—not even used as a basis for nuclear blackmail?

Thus, unless *we* are willing to stake our lives on the good will of the Soviet Politburo, we will have to find some way of persuading the average well-informed American to break out of the Pugwash-McNamara-Kissinger fable that "nuclear weapons can never be used against us, because the Soviets know that if they do strike at us, we will strike back and destroy them." What is now a fable under Kissinger, we must make reality under a new pro-American strategy.

The man who can do that for America will have done more for Americans than the Royal Air Force fighter pilots did for the British in the Battle of Britain, about whom it was said, "Never have so many owed so much to so few." The same British statesman who said that also left us a legacy that may save Western civilization.

The legacy that Winston Churchill left to warn and inform us dates from 1963. Earlier, Robert McNamara had persuaded the British to abandon their own development of the Bluestreak strategic nuclear missile, and to rely on the U.S. development of the Skybolt. The U.S. Skybolt was a 1,000-mile air-to-surface missile that would have kept the U.S. B-52 bombers as effective strategic delivery vehicles until 1985, and that would have done the same for the British bomber force of Vulcan IIs. In December 1962, shortly after the Cuban missile crisis, McNamara abruptly announced cancellation of the entire Skybolt program. The missile had successfully passed its most difficult tests, but McNamara claimed it was a failure. Actually, it was the most advanced missile design in the world, with the type of inertial guidance that later made the most advanced U.S. ICBMs so accurate.

The cancellation of the Skybolt was an unprecedented shock to the British. McNamara's action (approved by the Kennedy palace guard) was known in London as "the greatest double-cross since the Last Supper." It crippled Britain's chances of maintaining an independent strategic nuclear deterrent.

Actually, McNamara was not discriminating against the British. Cancellation of Skybolt hurt the United States even more because we had six times as many heavy strategic bombers to carry them. So far as we were concerned, it was the second step in a two-step maneuver by McNamara. First, he canceled the B-70 heavy bomber, despite full funding for its development by Congress and its spectacular successes in flight tests at mach 3. The explanation he gave was that we did not need the B-70 because the B-52s equipped with Skybolt missiles would do the same job more "cost-effectively." Then, after a few months, he canceled Skybolt.

Despite the fact that Winston Churchill was in retirement, in a once-so-valiant Britain that was then heading down the slide to welfare statism and Soviet accommodation, he had strong feelings on what should be done. He spoke out forcefully on May 3, 1963, in a speech to the Primrose League, a patriotic and Conservative organization of which he had been the Grand Master:

> Sometimes in the past we have committed the folly of throwing away our arms. Under the mercy of Providence, and at great cost and sacrifice, we have been able to recreate them when the need arose.
>
> But if we abandon our *nuclear deterrent*, there will be *no second chance*. To abandon it now would be to abandon it forever.

Everything you ever needed to know about strategy in the nuclear-space age, but were afraid you didn't know how to ask, is included either expressly or by necessary implication in those lines. Churchill said it all without resort to jargon, affectation, or an attempt to create a mystique. When Churchill used the term "nuclear deterrent," he referred to exactly the same arsenal of nuclear weapons that the average American envisions is necessary "to strike back and destroy them" if the Soviets should ever dare to launch a strike against us. Churchill recognized that it is the threat of this retaliatory strike that will convince the Soviets not to strike at us.

Churchill presented his statement about "no second chance" against the background of history: when we *had* thrown away our conventional weapons (as in the classic example of British/American disarmament prior to World War II), we had been given a "second chance" to recreate our weapons. In the case of the nuclear deterrent, there will be no second chance because the *enemy will gain a "first-strike" capability against us immediately upon our abandoning our nuclear deterrent.* When and if we are no longer able to deter the enemy from striking against us with his nuclear weapons, he could and would prevent us from recreating our nuclear deterrent by *threatening* to launch his strike against us if we attempted to do so. Thus, he would have the power to destroy us and we could not strike back at him and destroy him because we would have abandoned our capability of doing so.

This brings us to the pivotal point in all controversies over nuclear strategy: what, exactly and objectively, does the term "first-strike" capability mean? And why should you care? The reason you should care is that Kissinger and Nixon, following the nuclear theology of the Pugwash movement, insist that attaining a "first-strike" capability is an impossibility—and they have staked your life on their being right about it. For example, take a recent assertion on this subject by Defense Secretary James R. Schlesinger:

A first-strike capability . . . if properly understood in terms of a disarming capability, is obtainable by neither side—neither the Soviets nor . . . ourselves.[5]

This same assertion, in various words, has been made for years. At first it appeared to be merely a deliberate lie created to justify the unilateral strategic disarmament of the United States. The formula works so effectively: if the enemy cannot obtain a "first-strike" capability against us, it does not matter how far we go in disarming; by definition, the enemy dare not launch a strike against us and, therefore, we have him effectively deterred.

There is, however, a *partial* truth in this fable. It could truthfully read like this:

A "first-strike" capability is obtainable by neither side *unless the other side is being betrayed by its leadership.*

Returning to the matter of the definition of "first-strike," the term is massively misleading. If taken literally, all it would mean would be the capability of launching missiles at the enemy *before* he launched at you. Thus, even if we had only one 1-megaton ICBM, and the enemy had 1,000 100-megaton missiles, we might literally be said to have a "first-strike" capability; that is, we could press our launch button before the enemy turned his own electronic launch-key. There are reasonable grounds for suspecting that the elitist groups, which for so many years have controlled not only U.S. nuclear policies but even the language used in discussing them, deliberately chose an expression so truncated as to mislead those who are not specialists in nuclear strategy. At least one prominent defector from the Pugwash movement has suggested cynical motivation in the deliberate creation of the jargon of nuclear strategy, some of which he himself admitted to having invented, or, to use his more sophisticated term, "articulated."

The term "first-strike" probably originated as an abbreviated version of the earlier expression "win/first-strike." In the early days of strategic discourse, prior to the influence of the unilateral disarmers who flooded into office with the Kennedy Administration in 1961, practical considerations had crowded out sophisticated fantasies. The assumption was that no aggressor would start a war if our strategic power was so great that we would *win* the war. The entire grand strategy of the United States was based on a maxim officially adhered to by the Joint Chiefs of Staff through 1960: "Forces that cannot win will not deter."

So, nuclear force levels were evaluated as to the sufficiency for *winning* a nuclear war. One capability was described as enabling us to "win/strike-first"; a second and higher classification involved sufficiency of survivability as well as power to "win/strike-second"; and the third was the capability to "win/strike-first or second." This concept of winning is the only key to what was later cut to "first-strike capability"; the word "win," which was the critical part, was eliminated. We cannot "win" against an enemy unless we can disarm him in the strategic levels, and do it so comprehensively that he would not have enough nuclear weapons remaining operational to destroy our own population.

At any time during the period 1963 through 1967 the Soviets had the capability of launching a surprise strike against us and killing from 25 to 140 million Americans—despite the fact that we held a strategic nuclear superiority over them ranging from 8-to-1 downwards to 1+-to-1, as the McNamara unilateral disarmament programs progressed. The Soviets *could* fire their missiles first—but they did not have a "first-strike" capability within the proper definition of that expression because they did not have the capability to destroy enough of our retaliatory nuclear weapons to prevent our striking back and destroying their cities and industries. This is the strategic environment of the past, in which the typical American businessman still lives. His perception of a new and harsher strategic reality is totally obscured by a combination of his own reluctance and deliberate deception by the entire Kissinger-Pugwash structure of thought-control in national security.

If the Soviet capability of launching first and killing, say, 140 million Americans, did not give them a "win/first-strike" capability or—in the confusing truncated version, a "first-strike" capability—what *would* it take to do so? It would take a *disarming capability*; that is, sufficient strategic nuclear weapons to destroy or disable enough U.S. weapons *so that we could not strike back and "destroy" the Soviet Union.*

But would our survivable retaliatory force really have to be sufficiently powerful to strike back and "destroy" the Soviet Union? Would they not be reliably deterred if we could count on "destroying" only 1/2 the Soviet Union with our surviving weapons? or only 1/4? Or maybe even 1/10? Some of the Pugwash group purport to believe something like 1/100, and others of that group profess to believe that all we would need would be something just a little more than "close to zero."

Rather than discuss fractions that perhaps could be computed, the elitist propagators of the "finite," or "minimum deterrent," concept resort to the term "unacceptable damage"—a term that will permit only assumptions, not statistics. "Unacceptable damage" is a highly unscientific concept; to use it, you simply guess how much damage would be "unacceptable" to the Soviets; then you compute how many weapons would have to survive in order to inflict that quantum of damage. Then you figure that 10 times that many weapons will survive because you do not credit the Soviet missiles with accurate guidance.

This concept of "unacceptable damage" became the cornerstone of the so-called Mutual Assured Destruction theory of "stable deterrence," and thus of arms control. If both powers have survivable strategic weapons sufficient to ride out an enemy's disarming "first-strike" and still wreak on the attacker a degree of damage that will be "unacceptable" to the attacker, then there will be a situation of "Mutual Assured Destruction." Once this MAD theory is accepted, the disarmament theoreticians claim it is obvious that the most effective means of accomplishing this will be to have the populations of both nations exposed as helpless hostages to the potential attacker. This is what Henry Kissinger accomplished in the SALT I ABM Treaty—but, of course, only insofar as the population of the United States is concerned.

The point is that, by limiting active defenses (ABM systems) to a nominal minimum so that the population is exposed to maximum mass murder by even a few strategic nuclear weapons, a "win/first-strike" capability demands a near-total capacity for *disarming* the nation that is to be subjected to attack. The aggressor must build a huge arsenal of weapons with characteristics that make them highly effective "weapon killers," technically described as "counterforce weapons."

This is exactly what identifies a weapons-buildup program designed for a "first-strike": a force tailored to support the most dread strategy of the nuclear age, *i.e.*, the strategy of a "calculated win." If the potential aggressor's strategic posture is capable of destroying substantially all the attacked nation's retaliatory weapons, the aggressor is recognized as having acquired a "preclusive first-strike" capability; that is, he has enough counterforce weapons to destroy so many of the defender nation's weapons that the defender is "precluded" from accomplishing substantial damage in a retaliatory strike. Earlier terms that mean the same thing are a "splendid first-strike" capability and a "full first-strike" capability. The more effective an aggressor's defenses (civil defense plus ABMs) are, the less he needs to destroy *all* the defending nation's retaliatory weapons.

The practical strategic meaning of the enemy's possessing a preclusive first-strike capability is that, *by permitting him to build such a capability,* we would have, in the resounding words of Winston Churchill, "abandoned" our "nuclear deterrent."

Following the Churchill reasoning, once we have abandoned our deterrent we can no longer deter the enemy from striking, and therefore he can prevent us from attempting to reconstitute our deterrent. All he need say is: if you try it, we will launch; and if we do, the United States will cease to exist.

Also, if the enemy's threat to strike-if-we-attempt-to-rearm is credible enough to restrain us from that action, it is credible also to back a demand that we surrender; or that we destroy all the nuclear weapons we possess, and all our conventional weapons as well; or that we turn over to him, say, 45 percent of our Gross National Product, or roughly $600 billion per year. Not to mention making a few changes in our political, economic, and social systems, which would be administered by the commissars in charge of occupation.

All those things *can* happen to us if we abandon our deterrent. There can be no rational challenge to the Churchill assertion that "to abandon it now would be to abandon it forever."

The question of the survival in freedom of the United States depends on the state of our nuclear deterrent. Have we already abandoned it? If not, how far have we been led down the road toward abandonment?

At this point, a critic of this analysis might interpose, "But you are assuming that the Soviets *are trying* to attain a preclusive first-strike capability against the United States; what proof do you have of that?" A second critic might add, "And besides, attaining a preclusive first-strike capability is an impossibility, at least as between nuclear superpowers."

The same evidence will answer both these questions. It will also answer a third question: whether the Brezhnev policy of detente is a sincere, longterm movement toward closer and genuinely friendly relations with the United States and the Free World, or a short-term expedient designed to exploit U.S. trade, technology, and credits, and evoke an orgy of euphoria in America that will paralyze efforts to preserve some credibility for our nuclear deterrent?

The MADvocates (as Donald Brennan calls them) seek to justify setting up hundreds of millions of innocents for mass incineration by propounding the perverted aphorism: Weapons that kill people are good; weapons that kill weapons are bad. If you torture this twisted principle back into rationality, it has truth in it: strategic nuclear weapons that are effective only for killing people can never rationally be employed in a first-strike, and hence are "good" weapons; whereas weapons having the capability of killing weapons are first-strike weapons and therefore are "bad" weapons.

The answer to these three questions so crucial to the survival of the

United States can be found by examining the capabilities of the strategic weapons deployed by the Soviet Union. Because Kissinger could claim that everything prior to SALT I and the Moscow Joint Declaration of Principles makes pre-SALT I developments in nuclear armament irrelevant, we will focus on Soviet weapons developments and deployments after the signing of the SALT I Agreements in Moscow in May 1972.

Since then, there have been momentous developments in all major Soviet strategic programs. How do we know whether these new developments relate to counterweapons capability? Telltale elements are *numbers of missiles, accuracy of guidance, numbers of warheads,* and *explosive power* of warheads. It should be kept in mind that *all* counterforce weapons have "bonus" *people*-killing capabilities, but should be identified primarily as *weapons* killers *if* the Soviets went to the substantial extra expense to build in anti-weapon capabilities. Weapons designed primarily for counterpopulation use, however, seldom have significant bonus capabilities against weapons. For example, the oldest still-operational Soviet ICBMs, the SS-7s and SS-8s, are still effective city-busters because they carry five megatons of explosive power in their single warheads; but because they were designed and built before 1964, the accuracy of their guidance is simply not good enough to make them effective weapon-killers, notwithstanding their relatively powerful warheads.

Proof positive of the counterforce-preclusive first-strike pattern of the Soviet strategic weapons program, across the board, began to surface within six months after the signing of the SALT I Agreements in May 1972. Toward the end of November of that year, *after* Nixon had exploited his "generation of peace" accomplishments in the Kissinger-Moscow agreements purportedly "restraining" the Soviets' rush to first-strike capability, the then-Secretary of Defense Melvin Laird exposed the actual fact. The Soviet momentum in the production, deployment, and improvement of strategic arms *"today is just as dynamic as it ever was."* Thus, *SALT I did not achieve even a partial slowdown in the Soviet weapons drive.* So far as the prime purpose of the United States was concerned, SALT I was already a failure.

In his "Final Report to Congress" delivered on January 8, 1973, Secretary Laird provided some of the specifics on the dynamism of the Soviet arms buildup after SALT I. Even a summary listing of their developments required two pages. Here is a highly compressed summary of his summary:

A new version of the . . . SS-11 has been tested repeatedly and appears ready for deployment. *This new missile is more accurate than earlier versions* of the SS-11 *and probably will be deployed with a MRV capability.*

A new SS-9 type, large, liquid-fueled ICBM is being tested.

Construction of approximately 100 new ICBM silos continues. Some 60 of these are small silos capable of launching SS-11-size missiles and could be completed in a matter of months. The larger silos can handle SS-9 missiles and may be destined to hold the new large missile.

The Soviet SLBM force has been methodically upgraded. The SS-N-8 missile, which has a range of some 4,000 nautical miles, is expected to become operational in the next few months. [Later versions of the SS-N-8 have demonstrated a range of more than 5,000 nautical miles.]

The Soviets have continued test flying Backfire, their new supersonic swing-wing bomber, which may now be in series production. I expect a significant number of these bombers to be assigned to strategic and naval air units.

The Soviets have continued to develop their Galosh ABM system around Moscow. . . .

A follow-on ABM system is under development.

Soviet naval capability has expanded at a rapid rate. . . .

The capability of Soviet land forces has been increased by the production of two new tanks and improved conventional artillery shells, bombs, and missile and rocket warheads.

All these developments were reconfirmed in the "Annual Defense Department Report, FY 1974" presented by Defense Secretary Elliot L. Richardson to the House Armed Services Committee on April 10, 1973, a few days before he was shifted by Watergate developments to the Justice Department. He added that the Soviets not only had an improved version of the SS-11 missile (of which they have more than 1,000 deployed), but "a new SS-11 follow-on ICBM," a "new SS-13 follow-on ICBM," and a "new SS-9 follow-on ICBM." He added the usual underestimate of Soviet technological capabilities:

Although Soviet ICBMs with multiple reentry (MRV) payloads may now be ready for deployment, we do not expect the Soviets to achieve the more sophisticated MIRV capability before the mid-1970s.

This particular false prediction only lasted four months. On August 17, 1973, his successor, James R. Schlesinger, was forced to admit that "in recent weeks the Soviets have successfully demonstrated in inflight tests the MIRV capability for at least two of their missiles." He identified the two missiles on which he said there is "hard evidence" of MIRV capability as the SSX-17 (one of the two follow-on ICBMs for the SS-11) and the SSX-18 (the new SS-9 follow-on ICBM, rated at 50+ megatons).

Such a short-lived prediction by the $6-billion-a-year U.S. intelligence community may be regarded as evidence of incompetence—partially. But it also illustrates how the impossible standard of proof imposed upon our intelligence by Henry Kissinger has emasculated its potential for making reasonably accurate predictions. The clue is found in testimony by the chairman of the Joint Chiefs of Staff, Admiral Thomas H. Moorer, before congressional committees on March 27, 1973. He said there was still "no *conclusive* evidence" that the Soviets had actually developed an operational MIRV. His statement means, of course, that there could have been overwhelming evidence that the Soviets had succeeded—but still not enough to meet the arbitrary Kissinger standard of "conclusive" evidence.

Admiral Moorer's admission of the existence of this impossible "standard of proof" provides us with conclusive evidence of a critical development in the Soviet weapons buildup program. In the same statement, the chairman of the Joint Chiefs of Staff reported that there was then "sufficient" evidence that the Russians were trying hard to improve the *accuracy* of their intercontinental missile force. We know from the standard applied to the Soviet MIRV program that, in this connection, the word "sufficient" means that it was sufficient to meet the Kissinger requirement, that is, "conclusive." When Admiral Moorer said the Soviets are *trying hard,* he clearly means that the Soviets have accorded their ICBM-guidance-upgrade program high priority in the allocation of scientific, industrial, and technological resources—in other words, a "crash program."

Are the Soviets just "trying" to upgrade the accuracy of their missiles—or are they succeeding? As a general rule, R&D efforts pay off in proportion to the national effort concentrated in the particular area. Also, the accuracy of missiles depends on the amount of money that the political leadership is willing to allocate to a particular class of missiles. Soviet leadership has made unlimited funds available. For example, the Soviets are estimated now to be some five years ahead of us in accuracy of guidance of submarine-launched ballistic missiles because they have added inertial guidance with on-board computers to theirs, whereas we have not and apparently have no plans to do so, at least until the proposed Trident missile becomes operational *circa* 1980, if at all.

Unfortunately, this assertion of the revolutionary improvements in Soviet SLBMs is not a mere estimate. It is based on so much hard and conclusive evidence that Henry Kissinger can no longer silence the official witnesses; or at least not silence those witnesses determined to warn the American people, although there are fewer of them around with every passing month of the Kissinger double incumbency. On June 21, 1972, Secretary of Defense Melvin Laird, testifying before the Senate Foreign Relations Committee, was standing up with dogged determination to one of Chairman J. William Fulbright's supercilious attacks. Laird did not back down on this question as to Soviet SLBMs:

> *The Chairman:* Are you saying that the extended Y-class submarine is going to be superior to our existing Poseidon in range?
>
> *Secretary Laird:* What I am saying is that it will have a longer range and a larger missile; *it will have a missile system that has an inertial guidance system which we do not have.* It will have certain improvements.

As to the improvement in the guidance of missiles that the Soviets have already achieved, a quick look back at our excerpt from Secretary Laird's "Final Report" will recall his testimony that "the new version" of the SS-11 "is more accurate than earlier versions" and "probably will be deployed with a MRV capability."

Evidence derived from the characteristics of strategic weapons is far more reliable than any other type of evidence. It cannot be falsified or distorted. The cost of embodying special capabilities in these weapons is so tremendous that it cannot rationally be resorted to in order to create a hoax or a diversion. An analysis of the post-SALT I Soviet programs exposes an undeniable orchestration bringing all segments together, to create a preclusive first-strike capability against the United States of America. The terrible triad of characteristics of weapons systems specially designed to kill a defending nation's protected retaliatory weapons comprises redundant numbers, accurate guidance, and massive explosive power. These special capabilities of Soviet weapons are so obvious that they can no longer be successfully concealed even by the most duplicitous of the U.S. apologists for the Kremlin.

May God give these United States one Senator who will ask the right questions. For example, when a Kissinger-coached Secretary of Defense asserts that it is impossible for the Soviet Union to attain a first-strike capability against the United States, one courageous Senator could ask:

> *Senator Strong:* Isn't it true, Mr. Secretary, that President Nixon in his *State of the World Report* on February 25, 1971, made this statement:
>
> "By any standard, we believe that the *number of Soviet strategic forces now exceeds* the level needed for deterrence. Even more important than the growth in numbers has been the change in the nature of the forces the U.S.S.R. chose to develop and deploy. These forces include systems—particularly the SS-9 ICBM with large multiple warheads—which, if further improved and deployed in sufficient numbers, could be *uniquely suitable for a first-strike* against our land-based deterrent forces."

And isn't it true, Mr. Secretary, that, although they had in February 1971 more than enough nuclear missiles for reliable deterrence against the United States, they continued to add both ICBMs and SLBMs to their forces each year, by the hundreds, at what Dr. Kissinger testified was an average annual rate of 200 ICBMs and 100 SLBMs, but which some years reached as many as 375 of the two types?

Mr. Secretary, you have stated as a fact that a first-strike capability is not "obtainable" by the Soviet Union against the United States. Why, then, have the Soviets continued to spend scores of billions of rubles by adding, each year, hundreds of ICBMs and SLBMs to a force which was already in excess, "by any standard," of the numbers required for an effective deterrent?

Do you consider the Soviet leaders insane, or wildly irresponsible fools, to throw away so many billions on unneeded weapons, at the same time that their farm system cannot come within millions of bushels of the grain necessary to feed their own people?

And why, Mr. Secretary, if it is impossible for the Soviets to obtain a first-strike capability against the United States, should President Nixon have been concerned—back in early 1971—with the *nature* of the forces the Soviets were developing and deploying, which he emphasized "could be uniquely suitable for a first-strike against our land-based deterrent forces"?

Was our President—like the Soviet leaders—also insane in believing that it is possible for the Soviet Union to attain a first-strike capability against the United States?

Also, Mr. Secretary, are you familiar with this testimony by the Secretary of Defense in the Nixon Administration who also had many years of experience in national security matters as a member of the Defense Appropriations Subcommittee of the House Appropriations Committee? He made this statement while testifying on the "Strategic and Foreign Policy Implications of the ABM Systems" before the Disarmament Affairs Subcommittee of the Senate Foreign Relations Committee:

"*Secretary Laird.* Well, we were and still are going for a second-strike capability, as you know.

"With the large tonnage the Soviets have, they are *going for our missiles* and they are *going for a first-strike capability. There is no question about that.*"

Would you say, then, Secretary Schlesinger, that the then-Secretary Laird was grossly incompetent, wildly irresponsible, or even insane, to give solemn, considered testimony before a Senate committee, that the the Soviets "are going for a first-strike capability"—which you declare is impossible of attainment?

And here is another question, Mr. Secretary, that will bring up to date the evidence apparent in the Soviets' onrushing drive for more weapons, more powerful weapons, more warheads, and more accurate guidance. As of early 1971, the President reported that the Soviets already had weapons in excess, by any standard, of the force required for reliable deterrence. As of that time, they had deployed and operational, three primary systems of ICBMs: the SS-9s, the SS-11s, and the SS-13s. They not only added hundreds of these to those they already had, but, *after the signing of the SALT I Agreements of May 1972*, they invested billions of additional rubles in dramatically upgrading each of these types of ICBMs.

Now, Mr. Secretary, perhaps you can tell us *why* the Soviets did all that. We all recognize—and this includes, as we have seen, President Nixon and Dr. Kissinger—that the SS-9 has only one rational purpose: the destruction of U.S. retaliatory weapons. The Soviets have now increased the payload capability and the single warhead explosive power of the SS-9. Although you admit only a 20-percent increase in explosive power, they have multiplied it by a factor of up to 4. Once they enter the very high-yield range—the tens of megatons range—their warhead technology is so superior to ours that we do not really understand w̧hat they are doing. Their new SS-9 and SS-18 warheads may well be the operational version of the capability they demonstrated in 1961 of a hydrogen device which could weaponize at 100 megatons. I realize that all this dates back beyond your own experience, Mr. Secretary, while you were a law professor, or perhaps even a student; but you will find all the specifics in the testimony of the Joint Chiefs of Staff and then Secretary of Defense McNamara in the Senate Hearings on the Moscow Test Ban Treaty of 1963, the agreement that froze the Soviets' ill-gained superiority in the technology of high-yield warheads.

According to your own statement to the press on August 17, 1973, Mr. Secretary, the Soviets now not only have multiple warheads for their SS-9 upgrades and SS-18s, but have flight-tested multiple *independently targeted* warheads for those most powerful weapons the world has ever known.

Incidentally, Mr. Secretary, we noted with sadness some of your other statements in relation to your announcement of the open flight-testing of Soviet MIRVs. For example, you asserted that the Russians could have "a very formidable force structure" by the early or mid-1980s.

That statement, Mr. Secretary, is so disingenuous that some may consider it downright deceptive. Does it mean that you consider that the Soviets do *not* have a "very formidable force structure" right *now*?

The President and Dr. Kissinger, to judge from their unequivocal statements in their *State of the World Report,* considered that the Russians had gone way beyond force levels required by "any standard" for deterrence by the end of 1970. Since then, as we have seen, they added many hundreds of ICBMs and SLBMs. That was up to the time of the signing of the SALT I Agreements in 1972. Since then, they have, as the President feared in early 1971, and you stated in August 1973, fitted the SS-9 missiles "with large multiple warheads" and "further improved them" so that, in the words supplied by Dr. Kissinger for President Nixon, they now are "uniquely suited for a first-strike against our land-based deterrent forces." Now, they are deploying the huge new SS-18s in the 91 so-called empty holes that they dug (by fortuitous timing) just in time to beat the SALT I deadline on digging holes. Later intelligence indicates that there were really "about 100" such holes, and that they may deploy as many as 40 of the 30- to 50+-megaton SS-18s in them.

Mr. Secretary, the only rational implication of your statement that the Soviets *could have* a "very formidable force" by the early or mid-1980s is that they do not have a "very formidable" force right now. Therefore, what would you say about the force *we* have right now: a force that is only 2/3 as formidable as theirs in numbers of missiles, only 1/5 as formidable as theirs in throw-weight, and less than 1/10 as formidable as theirs in missile-megatonnage delivery capability?

Perhaps I shouldn't have asked that question, Mr. Secretary. I'm sure that, as a Rand graduate, you can produce a highly sophisticated term of nuclear jargon that, when spoken with a scholarly and superior air, would make present U.S. forces sound impressive, indeed. Perhaps you might claim that "even now, the United States possesses a strategic force that is *fractionally formidable.*" The media might let you get by with this doubletalk.

But, Mr. Secretary, we were examining specifically your assertion that "a first-strike capability . . . if properly understood in terms of a disarming capability" is not "obtainable," either by "the Soviets or ourselves." We have seen that, in post-SALT I developments, the Soviets, in relation to their SS-9 and SS-18 series ICBMs, have already accomplished what Dr. Kissinger and President Nixon consider to be necessary to attain a force "uniquely suited for a first-strike capability against our land-based deterrent forces."

What I am especially interested in having you answer, Mr. Secretary, is *why* the Soviets have also made such dramatic improvements in their SS-11 and SS-13 series ICBMs. These were entirely adequate, even in the lesser numbers in which they were deployed at the end of 1970, for the deterrent function of destroying cities and industry and incinerating Americans by the scores of millions. Furthermore, the Kissinger-Moscow Anti-Defense Treaty of 1972 guaranteed that all 210 million Americans would be totally defenseless against incineration by those Soviet missiles.

Please tell us, Mr. Secretary, why it is that with 210 million guaranteed hostages to those Soviet ICBMs—that is, with their ensured capability to *kill people* by the scores of millions during the treaty's term of unlimited duration—the Soviets invested additional scores of millions of rubles in increasing the destructive capability of these two types of ICBMs?

We know, Mr. Secretary, that even the single version of the older SS-11 carried a warhead of up to three megatons. We know from your own Department of Defense reports that the Soviets have made substantial improvements in both the accuracy of guidance and the payload of the SS-11 series—and that the improvements have been so dramatic that you have designated them as two new series of missiles, the SS-17 and SS-19.

We know also, Mr. Secretary, that since the warhead of the SS-11 was originally designed, the Soviets have been experimenting with improvements in the yield/weight ratio of their warheads for nearly 10 years; and we know that some of these tests have involved explosions of the range of 6+ megatons. Is it not probable, Mr. Secretary, with increases in both throw-weight and yield, that each SS-17 may carry five 2-megaton MIRVs? And each SS-19 may carry six 2-megaton warheads?

Isn't it true also, Mr. Secretary, that even if we assume that the SS-17s carry only four 2-megaton MIRVs and the SS-19, five—and this is a highly conservative estimate, as you know—that 400 of them would be enough, theoretically, to destroy 99 percent of our Minuteman force? This is assuming a 1,100-foot CEP, a guidance accuracy now well within Soviet technology. Is it not true that, with a reserve of, say 20 percent, or 100 more missiles, theoretical destruction capability would be reality?

Mr. Secretary, do not the Soviets have more than 1,000 SS-11s, all of which could be upgraded to SS-17 and SS-19 capabilities?

As to the SS-9 and SS-18 heavy missile force, I'm sure you would concede, Mr. Secretary, that the 1,300 warheads sufficient to destroy 99 percent of the U.S. Minuteman force could be furnished by the expedient (fully within the presently realized state of Soviet technology) of mounting five warheads each on only 263 of the SS-9 force, or 10 warheads on half that many SS-9s after upgrading to SS-18 capabilities.

Thus, it cannot be denied that the Soviets have an "either/or" choice of separate and independent missile capabilities for near-total destruction of the land-based U.S. deterrent force. Either way they choose, by use of SS-9s and SS-18s, or by SS-17s and SS-19s, they will have expended only a relatively small fraction of their long-range missile force.

Suppose then, Mr. Secretary, that the Soviets' Tallinn system of so-called "air defenses" has in fact been upgraded to ABM capabilities, or that, in some way, they have enough active antimissile defenses so that, combined with the extensive passive civil defense systems they established long ago, the U.S. Poseidon-Polaris potential for damage could be limited to a highly acceptable risk—would you not say, Mr. Secretary, that, in that case, the Soviets would have obtained what you have characterized as "unattainable": a "first-strike capability" in terms of a disarming capability?

About the capability of containing the U.S. SLBM retaliation through a combination of active and passive defenses, is it not true that, at any given time, not more that half the U.S. missile-submarine force is on station—because five or six are always under conversion to Poseidons or in the yard for major overhaul, or in training or transit; and that, of those on station, unless a great improvement has been attained in Poseidon reliability since 1973, only 42 percent of the missiles they attempt to fire can be counted on to reach target areas?

Also, consider this, Mr. Secretary. If you were the sole survivor of a Soviet missile attack with command authority to order our submarines to launch a retaliatory attack, and if they had launched a counterforce attack targeting only U.S. missiles and the National Command Center in Washington, D.C., and had destroyed 99 percent of our Minuteman missiles, and retained 2/3 of the Soviet ICBMs and nearly 1,000 SLBMs in reserve to attack our cities and population in case we *did* attempt to retaliate—would you, Mr. Secretary, order our submarines to launch their missiles at the Russian people who had had nothing to do with the Soviet counterforce attack? Would you give the order, Mr. Secretary, knowing that, if you did, you would be condemning some 200 million fellow Americans to death through Soviet retaliation?

Finally, Mr. Secretary, if you were one of those Americans who had trusted you as Secretary of Defense, and Dr. Kissinger as the builder of a structure of lasting peace, how would you feel about a Secretary of Defense who had led the American people, as late as mid-1973, to believe that the Soviets would not attain a "very formidable" strategic force until the early or mid-1980s, and that it was impossible for them ever to attain a first-strike capability against the United States?

These are my questions, Mr. Secretary. After we hear your replies, perhaps the American people will have some additional questions.

14

George Washington was not only the Father of His Country; he was the father of the concept of deterrence in his country. His famous prescription for peace was not merely that, to preserve the peace, we must always be prepared for war. He put it precisely, as might be expected from a great strategist: "it must be known that we are at all times ready for war." When someone is contemplating doing you great harm, it is usually far better to deter him from acting—than to let him act and punish him later.

This is, incidentally, why the concept of a "secret weapon" does not work in the nuclear age. When Henry Kissinger and Richard Nixon gave away so much in the SALT I Agreements, some trusting Americans convinced themselves that we must have a secret weapon— probably a type of laser weapon—so powerful that we did not have to worry about advantaging the Soviets with ICBMs and SLBMs.

Suppose we did have an incredibly powerful and destructive secret weapon while our known weapons were so greatly outclassed in number and power that they no longer impressed a potential aggressor. So the aggressor launches a counterweapon counterpopulation strike and kills 200 million Americans. Then the sole U.S. survivor, deep in a blast shelter, says triumphantly: "Ha! We certainly fooled them! They didn't even suspect that we have our secret weapon that I will now launch and use to liquidate them, too." So he launches it and destroys the enemy population; but it does not bring back to life a single one of the 200 million dead Americans. A "secret weapon" operates under the concept of punishment—not deterrence.

Our uncomfortably convincing parallel to the history of Carthage has been duly noted by many strategists. Year after year, Rome threatened destruction, yet year after year Carthaginian leaders tried, step after fatal step, to appease the Romans and buy peace. All the Carthaginians wanted, peaceful and prosperous people that they were, was peaceful coexistence with the Romans in the sense that Americans understand that term. What they got was "peaceful coexistence" in the sense that Leonid Brezhnev and his predecessors use that code term. The Carthaginians disarmed unilaterally, under the policies of their own McNamaras and Kissingers. At each succeeding summit conference, Rome demanded more. The Carthaginian leaders even persuaded the people to send the sons and daughters of their leading families as hostages to Rome. Now, of course, we are more democratic: the Moscow SALT ABM Treaty sets up *all* 210 million Americans as helpless hostages to Soviet missiles.

Appeasement and unilateral disarmament did not work in ancient times. Rome was an expansionist state, not a status quo power. The Carthaginian leaders assumed that Rome had the same objective as Carthage: stability. But no. What Rome wanted was enough unilateral disarmament by Carthage so Rome could proceed with absolute and total destruction of Carthage. That is what Rome got. When the Carthaginians saw that it was too late to rearm effectively and that the fall of their city was inevitable, they turned on their stupid aggressor-trusting leaders and literally tore them limb from limb. Such revenge may have been satisfying, but it did not prevent the Romans from killing all the men of Carthage, pressing their wives and daughters into slavery, burning their buildings, and ploughing the fields with salt.

Salt served then both as an instrument and as a symbol: an instrument to insure that Carthage could never rebuild and sustain itself, and a symbol that the disarmed city was doomed forever. SALT may do the same for us.

The men of Carthage wreaked their vengeance on their leader-betrayers, but would it not have been better instead to have at least tried deterrence on them? When their leaders said it was safe to disarm because Carthage had a broad new trade relationship with the Romans and they had promised peaceful coexistence, the intelligent citizenry should have replied: "We will follow your orders. But remember, *our* lives and *our* freedom are at stake. If your advice turns out disastrously wrong, either through stupidity or treachery, you will be the first to die; and it will not be a pleasant death. We will feel obliged to make your fate worse than what the Romans will do to us. If disaster does result from our unilateral disarmament policies, we will tear you limb from limb." After such a warning, the leaders

312

might have reconsidered and replied: "Well, perhaps we *are* going too fast. Perhaps it would be better to have the Romans prove their peaceful intentions by actions over the course of a few years and, meanwhile, to keep our military deterrent credible; that is, keep our ships of war in full strength and visible readiness, and encourage each citizen to keep his sword and shield at hand."

That might have saved Carthage. But how can America be saved? Obviously, we cannot expect such brutal tactics to be tolerated in our country. One thing, however, is becoming increasingly clear as the Soviet Communists approach closer and closer to a preclusive first-strike capability against us: *we simply cannot hope to survive if we reward the betrayers of our nation instead of punishing them.* Take the case of Robert Strange McNamara's *specific* acts of betrayal— quite apart from the really heinous things he did, such as to rig "Mc-Namara's war" in Vietnam with a no-win strategy of creeping escalation that cost the United States the lives of some 50,000 fighting Americans and $140 billion; or such as destroying 9/10 of U.S. strategic power in-being and blocking the creation of modern weapons systems, thus doing us more military damage than a full-scale Soviet nuclear attack could have done in any year prior to 1967; or such as guaranteeing Soviet technological superiority in the Moscow Test Ban Treaty of 1963; or such as bringing us down from an 8-to-1 strategic superiority to parity, so that the Soviet momentum in arms buildup would carry them to a first-strike capability.

One of McNamara's *specific* acts of betrayal involved the antiballis-tic missile system. President Johnson had overridden McNamara on the issue of providing the American people with a defense against nuclear incineration. McNamara did not like this, and double-crossed his boss by announcing the proposed deployment of an ABM system in a long speech in which he gave every trumped-up argument against ABM systems, but none in favor. But that wasn't all McNamara did to sabotage the ABM that President Johnson insisted on. As parentheti-cally described by Dr. Donald Brennan in his great article in *National Review* of June 23, 1972, entitled "When SALT Hit the Fan":

> At McNamara's instruction the Sentinel system design also had some specific weaknesses introduced to make the system more easily pene-trable by the Soviets.

Thus, the Secretary of Defense, entrusted with the defense of the United States and the life of every American, entrusted with invest-ing some $40 billion a year in taxpayers' funds to provide defense, deliberately ordered "weaknesses" in our ABM defense system so the Soviets could penetrate it more easily. And for what purpose would they penetrate our ABM defenses? To kill more Americans.

The life of every American incinerated would be on the conscience of the architect of the "weaknesses."

For betraying the nation and double-crossing the President, who on every issue had always supported him, McNamara was rewarded by being appointed President of the World Bank.

Another interesting example of McNamara's specific sabotage of U.S. strategic power is related in John Newhouse's *Cold Dawn: The Story of SALT*. This provides a typical example of McNamara's exploiting the public's inability to understand such concepts as MIRVs:

> McNamara also struck a blow for stability by deciding to outfit Poseidon with 10 to 14 small MIRVs; in doing so, he chose to reject another version of the system that, using just three much bigger ones, would have packed a wallop so enormous as to inspire Soviet fears of a first-strike weapon.[1]

Note that he "struck a great blow" for the Soviets as well as for an alleged "stability" by this decision. He effectively and drastically weakened the U.S. strategic deterrent in order to appease the Soviets. With the Soviets' first-strike SS-9s, SS-18s, SS-17s, and SS-19s threatening total destruction of the U.S. land-based deterrent, the Poseidon force is our last hope to retain some credibility in our deterrence. By deliberately ordering MIRV warheads too weak to threaten important Soviet targets, McNamara has done much to strip us of this last hope. When he ordered 10 to 14 warheads, he reduced the power of Poseidon missiles from 4-megaton single warheads *or* three 333-kiloton MIRVs *to* either 50 or 17 kilotons—an explosive power that is simply no good for "killing people" in a country with extensive civil defense systems and a strategic evacuation capability. These Poseidon MIRVed warheads are 1/5,000 the explosive power of a Soviet SS-18. Another point McNamara scored for the Soviets on this issue was to make the Poseidon warhead so complex and so excessively miniaturized (in order to handle so many MIRVs) that, as of the summer of 1973, 58 percent of all Poseidon MIRVs had failed in their operational tests. The "Poseidon Modification Program" which is required to repair this McNamara sabotage is only costing us an estimated $126 million in money, but it has imposed on our nation an incalculable added risk of a Soviet attack or ultimatum for the five years it has degraded the reliability of the one "survivable" element of our deterrent triad. This program will not be completed until 1977. Robert McNamara's reach thus stretches that far into the future.

McNamara's extreme miniaturization of the Poseidon MIRVs also enabled him to deceive the American public about our strategic power compared with that of the Soviets. Playing the "numbers game," McNamara compared his MIRVs on a 1-to-1 basis with the Soviet SS-9 individual warheads that were 2,500 times more powerful (in the pre-SS-18 timeframe). John Newhouse, in his book on the SALT negotiations, confirmed this McNamara tactic:

> Even with the Russians trying to catch up, MIRV would permit him [McNamara] both to continue claiming the advantage and to hold out against pressure, coming from the services and elsewhere, to expand the strategic inventory.[2]

Newhouse also recounts another illuminating incident showing McNamara's interest in the Soviet side and his active hate of the very idea of the American people having any defense against incineration by Soviet missiles. The Newhouse narrative reveals a sample of McNamara's arrogance and hypocrisy. Both Congress and the Joint Chiefs of Staff were supporting deployment of an ABM system to protect the American people. In late spring and summer of 1966 both the House and the Senate approved funds ($167.9 million) for procurement of ABM hardware. This so enraged McNamara, who had not requested the money, that he went behind the backs of Congress and the JCS to plot with the Russians to get strategic arms control talks in time to head off U.S. deployment of an ABM. According to Newhouse, McNamara telephoned one committee chairman to protest angrily against the action, "making clear in the bluntest possible language that he had no intention of spending one dime of the appropriated funds."[3] Newhouse's narrative tells what happened:

> The autumn of 1966 seemed to be the moment for deciding whether to request funds for ABM deployment. McNamara was to do all he could to avoid, or delay, deployment; at the same time, he began the process that would lead to talks with the Russians. . . .
>
> The die was cast in the form of a tenuous and perishable compromise worked out by McNamara and Vance in the meeting with Johnson in Austin on December 6. All the Joint Chiefs were also present, and they unanimously urged on the President an anti-Russian defense of American cities, a system larger than the anti-Chinese alternative and one with a sturdy growth potential. The ground on which McNamara's hard position rested was crumbling. He had already cut from the budget for the next year funds for initial ABM procurement that had been requested by the Joint Chiefs. At this meeting, it was decided to restore the money. . . .
>
> On returning to the Pentagon, McNamara immediately called the State Department. . . . Rusk was out of town. McNamara told . . . Llewellyn E. 'Tommy' Thompson, who was returning to Moscow in January for a second tour as Ambassador, he was authorized to contact the Russians, and, if possible, to get negotiations started. . . .

For closely involved figures, like Garthoff and the late Tommy Thompson, the days and weeks that followed marked the precise beginning of SALT. . . .

On arriving in Moscow, Thompson proposed to the Soviet leadership that talks be carried on secretly in the two capitals. . . .

While Thompson was making contact with the Russians, Garthoff and a few colleagues from State and Defense began working up a U.S. position for the talks. . . .

Most of this activity, especially the work of Garthoff's group, was very closely held. Whole agencies, like ACDA, were kept entirely in the dark. *So, initially, were the Joint Chiefs. McNamara, according to one of his very senior colleagues, feared that something like this would trigger a lot of conflict with the Chiefs, so he insisted that it be kept small and private.* Probably no more than a dozen or so people in the State and Defense Departments were fully aware of what was happening.[4]

Another incident recounted by Newhouse suggests that he obtained much of his information on this subject from McNamara himself:

McNamara presented his posture statement [to Congress, early 1967], and even now remembers precisely what he said about ABM deployment; he can almost recall appropriate page numbers of the hearings. "The language," he says in a rather understated way, "was very carefully chosen. I wanted to leave open the loophole that even a failure to start negotiations would not necessarily mean that a decision to deploy would be taken."[5]

That's the way McNamara was: always slick and duplicitous in dealing with the U.S. Congress, always leaving that loophole open to defeat any proposed strengthening of U.S. defenses, especially the defense of people. His contempt for the American people was obvious over the years he played the numbers game of mini-MIRVs versus SS-9s. His passionate determination never to permit us to have any defense against nuclear incineration by the Soviets surfaced again in the next installment of the Newhouse account:

The subcommittee found his aversion to city defense against Russian missiles to be complete and unshakeable. The split between McNamara and the Joint Chiefs on this point also emerged and entered public record. When the subcommittee chairman, the late Senator Richard Russell, asked specifically for the views of the Joint Chiefs, General Wheeler replied:

"We believe, sir, that we should go ahead now and start to deploy a light defense as a first step. . . . You will recall that last year the Joint Chiefs of Staff recommended deployment [of] an area defense of much of the country, with defense also of (deleted) the highest density populated areas.

"We made this recommendation for two reasons. First, we had continued to watch the growing Soviet ability to destroy our population and our industry, and second, the research and development program on Nike-X had reached a point where we felt that the Nike-X was ready for deployment."

Meanwhile, McNamara continued maneuvering against the anti-Russian system. In late January, he sent to the President a DPM [draft presidential memorandum] restating his position, but noting the possible utility of ABM defense against China. . . .

To counter the Joint Chiefs and their congressional allies, McNamara tried to confront Johnson with other viewpoints compatible with his own.[6]

By no coincidence, six out of seven of the scientists McNamara lined up to convince Lyndon Johnson were dedicated advocates of U.S. unilateral disarmament. These included Jerome B. Wiesner, the most influential of the Pugwash conferees; George B. Kistiakowski, another Pugwash member who had had earlier experience in trapping a U.S. President into an arrangement to advantage the Russians (the first nuclear-test-ban unilateral-reciprocal agreement in 1958, through which the Soviets overtook our preexisting 2-to-1 technological advantage in high-yield nuclear warheads); and two additional CFR members. President Johnson didn't have a chance against that crew. McNamara took no chances on President Johnson's getting a balanced view. According to Newhouse's narrative: "The Joint Chiefs were also present, but McNamara controlled the meeting."[7]

Not surprisingly, McNamara prevailed and President Johnson approved his scheme for seeking negotiations with the Soviets. An interesting point was that the Russians made a public announcement at that time, February 1967, of their deployment of an ABM system around Moscow, a system on which they had been working clandestinely since 1964. At a news conference early that month, Soviet Premier Kosygin, when asked what he thought of McNamara's proposed ABM moratorium, responded with the official Soviet line: the defensive system "is not a cause of the arms race but designed instead to prevent the death of people." Taking note of this, Newhouse states that "inhibiting offense, not defense, was to be a hard Russian position for the next 2½ years." This statement should be compared with Henry Kissinger's argument in defense of the massive imbalances that he conceded to the Soviets in the SALT I Interim Agreement:

Neither the freeze of ICBMs nor the freeze of submarine-launched missiles was a Soviet idea, and hence, it is not an American concession.[8]

Here are three very short excerpts from John Newhouse's Cold Dawn that present the atmosphere of the McNamara drive to head off Congress and the Joint Chiefs of Staff and go behind their backs to prevent the deployment of an ABM defense for the American people:

> The United States proposed holding the talks in Moscow, as this seemed the best way for the McNamara/Rusk group, working through Thompson, to maintain tight control. . . .
>
> The momentum apparently gathering behind the talks was deceptive; it was generated in Washington, not Moscow. Kosygin's responses committed the Soviet Union to nothing specific, and Washington's optimism was self-induced. *McNamara and those allied with him needed the talks.* Less-involved skeptics in the Pentagon and State Department saw that the pressure to deploy an ABM would be hard to sidetrack, talks or no talks. . . .[9]
>
> In April, Soviet Ambassador Dobrynin sent word to McNamara through an intermediary suggesting a talk. *McNamara responded to this singular initiative by offering to meet in his office or home. Dobrynin came alone to McNamara's home and they talked for three hours. Dobrynin* then flew to Moscow for consultation. . . .[10]

The talks, however, did not then materialize. The Soviets seemed evasive. When Secretary McNamara was required to state the dimensions of the Soviet strategic threat as part of his 1968 Posture Statement, he had to admit that the *Soviets had more than doubled their ICBM force, from 340 to 720, in 12 months.* Thus it appeared that the Soviets had been stalling the start of the negotiations, while they built momentum in their drive toward decisive nuclear superiority— a stall that was to be repeated and extended during the actual SALT negotiations from 1969 through May 1972, at which time Nixon was forced to take what the Soviets prescribed because his election year deadline was approaching.

The Soviets had agreed that talks would commence on September 30, 1968. However, they staged their invasion of Czechoslovakia on August 20. Without a decent interval to ease the sting, Lyndon Johnson could hardly plunge into highly publicized disarmament negotiations with so notorious, brutal, and recent an aggressor. It would have been difficult even for McNamara to justify seeking an agreement with the Kremlin masters when they had just—with high arrogance— broken 17 agreements. He did not give up, however, in his determination to prevent the American people from ever attaining a defense against nuclear incineration. Although he had left the Pentagon in February of that year, he had passed the anti-ABM torch to Paul C. Warnke, Assistant Secretary of Defense for International Security Affairs. Warnke, in turn, enlisted a Kissinger protege from Harvard, Morton H. Halperin,[11] who was such a far-out advocate of unilateral disarmament that later, when working on SALT negotiations, Kissinger approved one of the famous phone taps on him.

318

To make up for the loss of McNamara, whom Newhouse character-izes and documents as "the apostle of SALT, and, moreover, the man with the best record for managing the Chiefs," Halperin and his elite disarmament clique resorted to "operating clandestinely." Their ob-jective was to finesse the Joint Chiefs; that is, to prepare some sort of U.S. position paper with which the Chiefs could go along. In that way, the United States could be drawn into negotiations that would ultimately enable the Soviets to take over. Halperin and his group tricked the Chiefs into believing that there would be no important changes in the document to which they finally agreed. Newhouse described it this way:

> The first sentence of the proposal was directed not to the Russians but to reassuring the Joint Chiefs. It said:
> "This proposal should be viewed as an entity, since that is the basis on which it has been evaluated."
> Narrowly interpreted, this language meant that any alteration of the proposal during negotiations might nullify the whole.[12]

As it turned out, by the time the Kremlin had finished dictating its last-hour demands in May 1972, there was nothing left of the original JCS-evaluated proposal—or of the Halperin group's pledge to the Joint Chiefs. Donald Brennan, in his *National Review* article on SALT, ex-pressed wonder at the Joint Chiefs' having gone along with both SALT I Agreements. He assumed that they probably "faced a set of unpleasant alternatives, and judged these [SALT] Agreements to be the least unpleasant." That was part of the explanation, but there was more. The JCS were led to believe that, if they went along with SALT, they would get the Trident and the B-1, but without SALT they would get nothing. Dr. Brennan did not know at the time he wrote that the Joint Chiefs *had not been allowed to see a copy of the final drafts of the SALT I Agreements after* the last-hour Kissinger-approved changes were made and *before* the President signed—a circumstance that drew shocked and incredulous comment from the chairman of the Senate Armed Services Committee. Nor did Dr. Brennan know that the Paul Warnke-Morton Halperin team had played games to finesse the Chiefs; nor that this team conducted its campaign in such a clandestine and far-out manner that even Newhouse (who exudes fulsome admiration for the results) described it by such terms as "bizarre" and "cabalistic, almost conspiratorial."[13]

"Conspiratorial" is the precise term to describe the nature of the entire process involving SALT. It was initiated in a conspiracy de-signed by McNamara, and secretly carried on through Soviet Ambas-sador Dobrynin. Its undenied purpose was to abort the U.S. anti-missile program that for years had had the unanimous support of the Joint Chiefs of Staff and the near-unanimous support of both houses of Congress. The anti-ABM zealots were so eager in their desire to deprive the American people of any defense against incineration by Soviet missiles that they allowed the public only two months to forget the Soviet perfidy in Czechoslovakia. Dean Rusk admitted that in November 1968 he "took the initiative" in reopening with the Soviets our request for negotiations to limit ABMs.

The Kremlin masters were receptive. Their worldwide image had been somewhat tarnished by their bald-faced barbarism in the invasion of Czechoslovakia. Entry into nuclear disarmament negotiations would polish up that image.

The Kremlin also had continuing American contacts that enabled it to recognize *who* was still *the conspirator in charge of SALT* so far as the U.S. Government was concerned—even though his desk was no longer in the Pentagon and his job had been changed to a supranational organization engaged in handing out billions of U.S. dollars. So, a funny thing happened to Robert McNamara on his way to Kabul on business for the World Bank. He had scheduled a short stopover in Moscow. As the story-teller explains it, this was so that "he and his wife could look around a city they had never seen." John Newhouse then provides the conclusion of the so-well-covered cloak-and-dagger episode:

> Kosygin sent word that he would like to chat. The subject was SALT. That was November 11. The following day, Moscow's UN ambassador announced that his government was ready "without delay to undertake a serious exchange of views on this question."[14]

Thus it was that Robert McNamara, after his single-handed success in decimating the strategic power of the United States, was able to deliver America into the negotiations that would perpetuate and accelerate our strategic military inferiority. He served up SALT, ready and waiting, for further exploitation by Henry Kissinger when the latter assumed similar power over U.S. defenses in January 1969.

At this point it may appear that we have been pirating material from *Cold Dawn: The Story of SALT*—and you may be wondering why we have done it and how we got away with it. Fortunately, the basic facts of history cannot be copyrighted. As to the facts of the SALT negotiations, *Cold Dawn* represents what has accurately been characterized as "the monopolistic control of history." The Senate Foreign Relations Committee submitted to Henry Kissinger for his comment an excerpt from *The New Republic* of June 30, 1973, commenting on *Cold Dawn*. This was the vehicle used by Dr. Kissinger to discuss the book and to express his opinion of the author.[15] Here is the *New Republic's* comment on *Cold Dawn*, as reprinted by the Senate Foreign Relations Committee:

> This is the only publicly available account of the two-and-a-half years of negotiations that led to the 1972 Moscow Agreements. The United

States and the U.S.S.R. have agreed that the Strategic Arms Limitation Talks—SALT—would be conducted in secrecy, in order to encourage candor and flexibility. On the whole the rule of privacy was carefully observed, except for occasional brief reports that appeared in the American press. (The Russians were irritated by these leaks, but seemed to understand such American eccentricities are to be expected.) What makes *Cold Dawn* important are the detailed revelations of discussions that took place behind closed doors in Helsinki and Vienna, and the equally tough negotiations between the various satrapies of the American bureaucracy in Washington. (Will we ever learn of the parallel conflicts within the Kremlin?) *Mr. Newhouse has been the chosen instrument for the publication of a vast array of official data still very closely held—indeed some of it is unknown even to members of the delegation staff. He names, summarizes, and dates National Security Council studies and decisions.* He has access to notes of private tete-a-tetes, telegrams, and telephone conversations. *For the next 50 years his book will be a primary source for historians.*

It is difficult to criticize Newhouse's accuracy or judgment, since he is dealing with arcane material not available to other scholars. But the reader can get his bearings rather quickly; he is seeing the procession from the viewpoint of Henry Kissinger at the White House rather than that of Gerard Smith at the SALT delegation; he notes that the important talks are in the "back channel." The conference is less important. Coming at a time when all documents remain highly classified and the participants are under a pledge of silence, when the government has yet to issue basic descriptions of the negotiations, the agreements, or their verification procedures, save for the few pages of turgid bureaucratese that appear in annual reports and collections of documents, *the publication of Cold Dawn demonstrates that monopolistic control of history is a considerable executive privilege.*[16]

15

John Newhouse's book *Cold Dawn: The Story of SALT* appeared in serial form in *The New Yorker* from May 5 through June 7, 1973, and as a hardcover book in June 1973.[1] Despite its title, this book deals not at all with the actual SALT Agreements but is, in the author's words,

> . . . an account of the background and conduct of the talks between the United States and the Soviet Union on limiting strategic arms. The story is, of course, contemporary, *culminating* in the historic agreements reached in Moscow on May 26, 1972.

The best summary of the significance of the Newhouse book was written by *Washington Post* columnist Nicholas von Hoffman. He was not exaggerating when he discussed the security leaks in the book. Indeed, he may have been making an understatement when he said:

> Newhouse didn't write—by collating newspaper clippings. With all the Administration's yowling about *The Pentagon Papers* and Jack Anderson, it appears that *Cold Dawn* is the recipient of leaks on the scale of a crack in the Grand Coulee Dam.
>
> Although the author cannot discuss his sources, it's apparent from his text that he has secured something like near complete access to the files of the National Security Council. The only information he may not have been able to get his mitts on is notes of the conversations between Nixon and Kissinger and their Russian counterparts.[2]

The incredible revelations of Newhouse's book, coupled with a specific knowledge of what Kissinger put across for the Kremlin in the SALT I Agreements themselves, provide a potential for changing history. Kissinger himself has certainly changed history; and this combination of revelations will change Henry Kissinger, his status, and his power. The Newhouse revelations and the SALT I Agreements are two parts that, when put together, make a vastly greater whole. It is as if we had two batches of a new type of explosive material; if detonated separately, each would produce power equal to a conventional explosive such as TNT, but, if combined, they would produce explosive power on the order of a hydrogen warhead, namely, a million times greater than TNT.

The Top Secret leaks involved in the publication of the Newhouse book represent one of the most devastating security breaches ever perpetrated. Yet Newhouse gives the impression that he hasn't the vaguest idea of what he has done. If this book were perceptively analyzed by strategic experts in West Germany, France, England, Belgium, Holland, Spain, Japan, and other important nations not yet beyond the Iron Curtain, each of those nations would race all the others to negotiate a separate peace with the Kremlin in the hope it could still get favorable terms. Analysis of *Cold Dawn* would absolutely and finally kill NATO. It would reduce all future European conferences on security or reduction of forces to farces. Why?

First, the Newhouse book reveals that the U.S. foreign and defense policies have been under total control of fatuous fools or brilliant evil traitors, or a combination of the two; and that, therefore, no country seeking national self-preservation could, with common sense, rely on us as an ally against the Soviet Union, unless the new administration ousts them.

Second, the book reveals that, instead of using our great bargaining power in food, trade, and technology to promote our interests and those of our allies, and to secure a relaxation of police-state restriction of freedom behind the Iron Curtain, we gave away these great assets in advance, with no strings attached, asserting that we will promote a vague and generalized concept of detente with the Soviets. No nation wants a fool for a partner.

Third, it reveals that every single substantive provision of both SALT I Agreements was dictated secretly to Kissinger by the Kremlin (without the knowledge of our puppet "negotiating team"), was accepted by Kissinger, and was finally rationalized by Kissinger and "sold" by him to the President, the Congress, and the American people.

Fourth, it exposes the fact that the claimed U.S. advantages in weapons technology—the so-called "qualitative" matters—that Kissinger had advanced to "prove" that SALT established parity between the two parties, and that he asserted offset the massive imbalances favoring the Soviets in numbers of strategic missile launchers, in throw-weight of missiles, and in missile-delivered megatonnage are, in fact, frauds. Further, the book exposes the fact that these frauds were designed for the dual purposes of permitting Kissinger to play numbers games with the American people and to reduce rather than reinforce the strategic power of the United States.

As an example of this, the book reveals that the alleged U.S. superiority in *number of warheads*—the only specific claim that could be offered to justify what the United States gave away—had been manipulated by Robert McNamara so that it would constitute no threat to the Soviets. He accomplished this by excessive miniaturization designed to reduce the explosive power of each MIRV warhead so that, coupled with deliberate dilution of the accuracy of guidance, it would be incapable of destroying any important Soviet targets. The supposed U.S. advantage in number of warheads was the primary reason NATO governments retained any confidence in the United States as an ally after the SALT I statistics and concessions were made public.

Fifth, the Newhouse book reveals that the entire SALT negotiation originated in a conspiracy hatched by McNamara *with the Soviets* to circumvent the U.S. Joint Chiefs of Staff and Congress at a time when Congress was vigorously insisting on deployment of an ABM system to protect the American people from nuclear incineration. (How much confidence would you have in a nation whose Secretary of Defense secretly conspires with a foreign government to reduce the people of the nation to helpless hostages of an enemy? Remember that Donald Brennan, in his *National Review* article of June 23, 1972, exposed the fact that McNamara deliberately "had some specific weaknesses introduced to make the system more easily penetrable by the Soviets.")

Sixth, the Newhouse book reveals that Kissinger had established such an extensive, intensive, and totally comprehensive control over all phases of the SALT negotiations that he was personally and solely responsible for the giveaways to the Soviets that surfaced in the terms of the SALT I Agreements themselves.

Seventh, the book exposes the fact that Kissinger, negotiating secretly (through Soviet Ambassador to Washington Anatoly Dobrynin) with the Kremlin Politburo members in charge of SALT, often made agreements and proposals that he kept secret from the entire U.S. delegation, including Ambassador Gerard C. Smith, the nominal head of it, and that the Soviet delegates (who knew little about Soviet positions) frequently knew far more about final U.S. positions, and knew farther in advance, than the U.S. delegates.

Eighth (to summarize a large additional number of individual exposés), the Newhouse book reveals that the entire organization for, and course of, the SALT I negotiations constituted a slick fraud cynically conceived by Henry Kissinger to deceive the U.S. Congress and the American people; that the purpose of this elaborate and cunning charade was to make the Congress and the public believe that the SALT I Agreements were the product of some 2½ years of give-and-take good-faith bargaining "hammered out" at the conference table, while, in fact, this was not so at all. The evidence is in the Newhouse book that all this window dressing was a satanic trick and that, actually, the U.S. delegation never negotiated a single provision of any importance.

The reason why the sensational exposés in the Newhouse book have not attracted the publicity they deserve (say, 10 times the publicity given to *The Pentagon Papers* plus Watergate) is that *Cold Dawn* must be combined with the SALT I Agreements themselves in order to produce the explosion. If your analysis of the SALT I Agreements is superficial, so also will be the information you glean from *Cold Dawn*. The sensational revelations are buried deep, but they are there.

The primary concern of all honest and expert U.S. officials concerned with SALT was to obtain a restraint on the Soviet buildup and improvement of their SS-9 force of heavy counterforce missiles that was rapidly approaching the capability of destroying the entire U.S. land-based deterrent, our 1,000 Minuteman missiles. No official statement of this was available to the public because the negotiations were shrouded in secrecy. But in the Newhouse book it is repeated time after time. For example:

> SALT would hopefully offer a means of achieving a limit on the single weapon system that most bothered Washington, the giant SS-9 ICBM. Indeed, negotiating a hold on the SS-9 program was not only basic to the U.S. position, but an excellent reason to press SALT vigorously. . . .[3]

> In return for indulging Moscow's preference on ABM, Washington hoped to gain what it wanted most; a ceiling on the Soviet offensive missile program and, beneath that ceiling a so-called sublimit on the number of SS-9s. The Soviets had about 300 of these monster missiles either deployed or under construction. Washington sought a sublimit of 250, but would have settled happily for an agreement on 300.[4]

You may ask, "What's so important about revealing the primary objectives of the United States in the SALT negotiations?" Well, set that information from the Newhouse book up for comparison with the actual provisions of the SALT I Interim Agreement, and you will discover that *the United States did not attain a single major objective that it had sought in the negotiations.* Henry Kissinger deliberately lied about this special objective. In his briefing at the White House to the five congressional committees on June 15, 1972, he made this assertion:

> In essence this agreement will freeze the number of strategic offensive missiles on both sides at approximately the levels currently oper-

ational or under construction. For ICBMs, this is 1,054 for the United States and 1,618 for the Soviet Union.

Within this overall limitation, *the Soviet Union has accepted a freeze of its heavy ICBM launchers*, the weapon most threatening to our strategic forces.

The truth is that the Soviet Union absolutely did *not* accept any such limitation. The Soviets expressly, specifically, repeatedly, and finally refused to agree to a limitation on their heavy ICBM launchers. They even refused to define a "heavy" missile, or a "light" missile. They refused to disclose how many they had, or how many they were going to have. The U.S. delegation wept, figuratively, bitter tears over the Soviet refusal; but these tears were in vain because the Soviets were adamant. So the U.S. delegation, in an official "Noteworthy Unilateral Statement" numbered "D," appended to the text of the Interim Agreement, expressed official "regret" at this refusal. As we show elsewhere, there are no less than four loopholes that will permit the Soviets to add from 100 to an unlimited number of missile launchers capable of handling SS-9 missiles or their upgraded version, the SS-18.

But Kissinger was so confidently and aggressively persuasive that he convinced everyone, including the President, that the Soviets *had agreed* to limit their heavy missiles. Indeed, Kissinger had Secretary of State William P. Rogers so thoroughly confused that Rogers officially reported to Congress that Article II of the SALT Interim Agreement prohibits the conversion of launchers for light ICBMs into launchers "for modern heavy ICBMs, *such as the Soviet SS-9.*" Poor Secretary Rogers was thus left out on the end of the long limb of a positive assertion that can be positively disproved; he simply did not have Dr. Kissinger's consummate skill in the crafty wordmanship of lies.

While the exposés of the Newhouse book are sufficient to cause NATO to self-destruct and our allies to race to make their separate deals with the Kremlin, the book must be set up for contrast with what the SALT I Agreements themselves actually provide, in order to get the explosive effect. How could we expect the heads of state of the NATO nations to attempt such a complex job on matters of nuclear strategy?

When Henry Kissinger began attracting so much international attention back in 1969, it became a matter of national prestige for each nation's prime minister or premier to have his own version of a "Henry Kissinger." If they were lucky, these states acquired one without Kissinger's peculiarly personal shortcomings; but no head of state could afford to lose face by not having his own distinguished adviser who could be identified with the image of President Nixon's adviser. So, West Germany acquired Egon Bahr as Willy Brandt's "Kissinger."

Brandt referred to him as his "ambassador at large"; according to some reports, others called him "the fox in the chancery." For French President Pompidou, the Secretary General of the Elysee Palace, Michel Jobert, served in a Kissinger-like capacity. The English equivalent was said to be Sir Burke St. John Trend, Secretary of the Cabinet. Israel was reported to have one in the person of General Ahron Yariv, former chief of intelligence, who gained international attention in the Middle East war of October 1973.

Each one of these advisers can, of course, call upon the entire resources of the intelligence organizations of his respective nation. Each one had to be rather intelligent to attain his position of influence without formal political support. So they are respectively qualified to match up the Newhouse book and the SALT I Agreements themselves, and come up with the correct answers. To show how this would work, let's take a composite Adviser to a chief of state, and a composite chief of state as his Boss, and project the scenario of a secret conference between them:

Adviser: Boss, I have just completed, with the help of your intelligence chiefs and military advisers, an in-depth analysis of a book that was recently published in the United States by a John Newhouse, entitled *Cold Dawn: The Story of SALT.* It is reliably reported to be based almost totally upon leaks of Top Secret material. It certainly contains a mass of material that our intelligence has not been able to get its hands on. In my opinion, it is the equivalent of a major intelligence coup—the greatest since Colonel Oleg Penkovskiy delivered to the West the entire Top Secret Soviet long-range war plans.

I have summarized most of the principal revelations contained in the book. By themselves, they don't mean much. But I have put them together with the actual provisions of the SALT I Agreements; they fit like the interlocking pieces of a jigsaw puzzle. In my opinion, the eight exposés I have listed require your personal consideration. I most respectfully recommend that you take this summary and study it overnight, and then allow me another conference to secure your ideas on it.

(The Adviser presents his Boss with the eight-point summary given above. The scenario continues the next day with only the two composite characters present.)

Boss: I have been over your summary. These eight exposés will certainly justify an agonizing reappraisal of our relationships with both the United States and the Soviet Union; and also, of course, with the other NATO nations. It appears that we must abandon our reliance on U.S. support against the U.S.S.R., that the Kremlin can take over Europe without effective opposition whenever it considers it opportune to move, and that our only rational course is to seek negotiations and tender a preemptive accommodation while we can still hope to secure some recognition of our national identity.

It appears that we must no longer resist "Finlandization," but embrace it. It will be our last chance to head off full integration and a treat-

ment of our people the way Stalin treated the Ukrainians: eight million starved to death to establish collective farming, and hundreds of thousands of party members liquidated to establish discipline by terror.

But I have one reservation, and it is a vital one. These leaks of Top Secret U.S. documents *appear* to be genuine; they have been so reported, and Newhouse gives the numbers of specific descriptions of individual documents. I note that the press in the United States considers the leaked material to be genuine. The *Washington Post,* I remember, described the book as "disclosing some of the most tightly held secrets of the Strategic Arms Limitation Talks."

What we may have to do, however, will change the course of history for perhaps a century or more. Certainly it will break up the NATO alliance, and thus open up all Western Europe, and soon the whole world, to Soviet domination.

In my duty to our country, to freedom in the world, and to the future of Western civilization, I feel that I simply cannot act on the basis of this book and your analysis of the SALT Agreements with it, unless and until it is totally verified and authenticated. So I am asking you, as my chief adviser, can this be done, and how can it be done?

Adviser: I have considered this problem. Actually, I have consulted with the most brilliant of our intelligence experts and our political and strategic analysts. They tell me that anywhere near total verification or authentication of the book *Cold Dawn* would require unlimited access *to the most secure, tightly held, Top Secret files over a five-year period* of the U.S. National Security Council, as well as access to many Top Secret files in the U.S. departments of Defense and State. Not only that, but they tell me that we would have to have access to many of the principal officials involved, on a personal and highly confidential basis. Much of John Newhouse's background material had to be secured from high officials whose leaks should make them liable to prosecution by the United States as security violators and dismissal as security risks.

Our people assure me that, until publication of the Newhouse book, it was universally accepted that no one in the United States or the world knew that much about the preparations for the SALT negotiations, the U.S.-prepared positions, objectives, and intragovernmental manipulations, except Henry Kissinger himself.

To give you a short answer, Boss, I simply don't think there is any way this Newhouse material can be authenticated or verified by our intelligence services, regardless of how much effort and expense we were to invest in it. I fully realize that such verification is essential either to get the best possible conditions for our country from the Kremlin on the one hand, or, on the other, to avoid the premature destruction of the NATO alliance.

I have, therefore, made informal and highly confidential approaches to intelligence contacts we have in other NATO nations. They are in the same position we find ourselves in. But we have all agreed to consider it further, to see if by joint efforts, we can either verify or discredit *Cold Dawn.* I assure you that I have not given away anything to our NATO associates unnecessarily. They have all been studying the Newhouse book, too; and they all have their own analyses of the actual provisions of the SALT Agreements. As you know, these analyses have been worrying us for some time; but our worries could not be decisive without the revelations of this book.

If the Newhouse book is accurate, the sooner we cut all ties with the United States, the better will be our chance of survival with some retention of our identity.

I suggest, Sir, that we hold the matter under consideration for a short period. Within two days, I will report to you the final conclusion of our intelligence services and contacts as to the possibility of verifying or authenticating the leaks of classified material in the Newhouse book.

(Two days later, the Adviser reports to his Boss at another secret conference.)

Adviser: Boss, we have concluded our intelligence estimate of the probabilities of securing authoritative confirmation of the secret material leaked on such a sensational and wholesale basis in the Newhouse book.

I have mentioned before, in this connection, that the consensus in several NATO intelligence communities was that only Henry Kissinger knew as much about the U.S. side of the SALT negotiations as is exposed in the Newhouse book. Checking further along these lines, we discovered that a number of officials in Washington, both Americans and non-Americans, believe that Henry Kissinger himself must have been the source of the massive leaks set out in the book.

For example, a book review of *Cold Dawn* in *National Review* for September 14, 1973, by J. L. Johnson is a fine demonstration that even a supposed expert on strategy can miss the entire point of the book if his analysis of the SALT Agreements themselves is superficial. If you don't *understand what it is that Kissinger accomplished in his SALT give-*aways to the Kremlin, then you can't understand what Newhouse is revealing in his book. But the Johnson review is somehow accurate on the most probable source of the leaks and on the identity of the single person who knows it all. Johnson is overcoy in his refusal to name the great and obvious name, but what he is getting at is clear in these excerpts:

> It is the most comprehensive account of SALT I we are ever likely to get and the most accurate until the major players themselves tell all. Newhouse, you see, had settled upon him the unique benefice of substantial and sustained access to much inside material. Which of the major players was most responsible for this philanthropy is doubted by few in Washington. . . .
>
> On balance, the book is well worth reading (with appropriate grains of salt) [parenthetical humor in the original], but *to get to the real inside skinny we shall have to wait until you-know-who's memoirs* tell us what the butler really saw.

Our final intelligence consensus as to the possibilities of obtaining authoritative verification of the secret material in the book is somewhat along the same lines. We are convinced that only Henry Kissinger could supply it. We are convinced also that he will not supply such verification until publication of his memoirs—and probably not even then (unless they are written in Russian). Under the American constitutional process, a Secretary of State can be impeached. Kissinger would be inviting dismissal if he verified the *Cold Dawn* material. Of course, *he would be inviting dismissal or impeachment by doing so only if* (1) some high U.S. official or influential public person has an expert, accurate analysis of the SALT I Agreements, and (2) is sufficiently diligent and courageous to put it together with the major exposés of the Newhouse book, and then publicize the results. But we do not think Henry Kissinger would risk his power and his power bases even if such a contingency were unlikely, since he would appear to have everything to lose and very little to gain by doing so, insofar as his own career is concerned. We have noticed that his own career is his first priority concern.

So, Boss, my very best and deeply considered advice to you is that we not at this time make any changes in our policies toward the United States or the Soviet Union, and that we continue to adhere to the NATO alliance. Granted that "Finlandization" is a national fate less terrible than being reduced to a totally slave state, we might be able to avert both calamities for a few more years. If we can delay tendering a preemptive accommodation long enough, there is always a possibility that the Americans will solve their crisis of leadership, or that something will happen in or to the Soviet Union that might change the course of history.

Boss: Very well. I have been thinking along these same lines myself. We will stay in NATO and continue to work with our allies to resist even "Finlandization" and try not to be either seduced or overwhelmed by the Kremlin's latest version of detente. But we must accept the fact that, if the revelations and exposés of the Newhouse book, as read together with an accurate analysis of the SALT I Agreements themselves, are verified, we will have to move from our present position—and move fast. There will be little time left to us or to any of our allies.

(*Boss and Adviser drop the discussion of the Newhouse book and its exposés. A month elapses before the subject is raised again.*)

Adviser (out of breath, having rushed into his Boss' office without awaiting the formality of an appointment): Boss, you won't believe it. I can't believe it, but it has happened.

Boss: What's happened? What can't I believe?

Adviser: It's Kissinger. Henry Kissinger has done it.

Boss: Done what, for God's sake?

Adviser: He has come out in official testimony and confirmed and, in effect, verified the book *Cold Dawn: The Story of SALT.* Furthermore, he has given unqualified endorsement of the author, John Newhouse. He has had Newhouse appointed as counsellor to the U.S. Arms Control and Disarmament Agency where he will now have official access to secret documents.

Boss: How do we know all this?

Adviser: Well, we got it first from a dispatch from the *Washington*

Post dated September 14, 1973. Because of its importance, I telephoned our embassy and had them confirm it from an advance copy of the official record of the Senate committee hearings. But the news story sums it up very well. Here it is:

> *Washington*—John Newhouse, the author of a book disclosing some of the most tightly held secrets of the Strategic Arms Limitation Talks, has been offered a top post with the Arms Control and Disarmament Agency [ACDA].
>
> Fred C. Iklé, the director of the Agency, said yesterday that he had talked with Newhouse about taking a long-range policy-planning job that would permit him to do studies in the general field of disarmament and troop reductions. It is expected that Newhouse will accept the post and is expected shortly to be named counsellor.
>
> *Newhouse's most recent book "Cold Dawn: The Story of SALT" won high praise earlier this week from Secretary of State-designate Henry A. Kissinger.* During his hearings before the Senate Foreign Relations Committee,. *Kissinger denied a report he had been "leaking" information* or authorizing his staff to leak information *to Newhouse.*
>
> *Kissinger, however, went out of his way to say that the book is "outstanding"* and that *"I have the highest regard for John Newhouse,"* who had written some outstanding treatises on NATO and on other matters.

You may be interested in the story that was planted to explain and cover such a totally unprecedented step as to reward a major security violator with a high-level sensitive governmental position. According to this rather thin rationalization reported by the *Washington Post*:

> Newhouse, it was understood, was sought out because he is believed to have a broad view of the entire range of issues that go under the rubric of disarmament, including strategic arms, conventional armament, and troop deployment.

That's about it, Sir, except a couple of personal items we have picked up about John Newhouse. First, he gave the principal paper at a highly secret international meeting on May 10-13, 1973, at Saltsjöbaden, Sweden. And now he has been named to membership in the most powerful elite organization in the United States, the Council on Foreign Relations.

Boss: Adviser, summon our Minister of Foreign Affairs. I want to give him some Top Secret instructions immediately. Tell him before he comes, to phone the Soviet Embassy and request an appointment on a most urgent basis to discuss a matter of paramount importance to both of our governments.

For your own personal information, so that you can start things rolling, I will instruct him to seek an appointment for me in Moscow with Leonid Brezhnev as soon as possible. Please get for me our emergency contingency plans listing the offers we can make to the Politburo in return for a treaty of nonaggression and friendship. And get me the contingency material for setting in motion our withdrawal from NATO.

What had Henry Kissinger done?

The common law of England is perhaps America's greatest heritage. Down through the ages it has protected human rights as well as property rights. Either directly growing out of it, or closely associated with it, are nearly all our most treasured safeguards for life, liberty, and the pursuit of happiness, and especially of justice. These include the right to trial by jury, the writ of habeas corpus, the presumption of innocence, and the standards of proof required. They are characteristic features of our life as an independent nation that we will sorely miss under the new world order being shaped by Henry Kissinger, by "Members of Congress for Peace Through Law," and by Leonid Brezhnev, who continues to predict "the inevitable triumph of socialism" throughout the entire world.[5]

The common law is the distillation through the centuries of what might be called educated folk-wisdom. It is pragmatic rather than sophisticated, commonsense rather than theoretical. Its outstanding feature, proved by generation after generation, is that it works. It works to accomplish justice as best as human beings can accomplish it. One of the most significant areas in which folk-wisdom and intuition shine through apparently needlessly complex rules is in the law of evidence governing the exceptions to the hearsay rule. Common sense and human experience have taught us that a witness should not be allowed to testify before a jury as to something he has merely heard someone else say. The fact that someone had said it is no proof of the truth of what was said, or even that the overheard speaker himself believed what he had said. The usual safeguards developed by common law to aid the jury in determining the truth of direct evidence, that is, when a witness is himself testifying that something is a fact, could not be applied in instances of hearsay. These safeguards include cross-examination of the witness by opposing counsel, and an opportunity for the jurors to observe the witness and form their own opinions as to his veracity. So, the general rules of evidence exclude hearsay.

Human experience has also established, however, that, under certain circumstances, there could be reasonable assurances that hearsay is, in fact, truthful. One example is the deathbed statement or "dying declaration." If the one who had originally spoken the words was about to die, and fully realized he had but a few hours or minutes before leaving this world, this is considered assurance that, since he had nothing on earth to gain by lying or by bearing false witness, the jury might consider what the dying man had said, as testified to by the witness.

Another exception is an "admission against interest." If the statement that had been heard by the witness was obviously and substantially against the interests of the person who originally spoke it, it is presumed that he would not have said it unless it was probably true. So, admissions against interest constitute another recognized exception to the rule against hearsay: the probability of their truth coincides with the experience of the Anglo-American system of justice over the centuries.

This is what Henry Kissinger did when he solemnly testified before the Senate Foreign Relations Committee that John Newhouse's book *Cold Dawn: The Story of Salt* is an "outstanding book," and that he has "the highest regard for John Newhouse." Kissinger reinforced this testimony by having Newhouse appointed to a high-level sensitive position in the Arms Control and Disarmament Agency.

What did the Newhouse book represent *before* the Kissinger endorsement? It was loaded, of course, with sensational exposés, some of which we have summarized; and it listed scores of Top Secret NSSMs and NSDMs by number. But what guarantee was there that the sensational material was, in fact, genuine? Any writer ambitious to make a name for himself and sell thousands of books could draw on his imagination to make the "story of SALT" very spicy indeed. He could count on the fact that the only way his fictional version of Top Secret memorandums could authoritatively be contradicted would be if the originals were declassified and publicized. Even in that remote contingency, the sensation would have been accomplished. Such an ambitious sensationalist could also have talked with a few low-level staff assistants and have received material from them that might or might not be authentic.

Without authoritative verification, the Newhouse book could not have been a basis for important official action by the U.S. Government or any other nation. But, much more important to Henry Kissinger, not even a handful of people in America would have believed that he had set up the elaborate hoax and fraud on the American people that can be traced through *Cold Dawn;* nor that he had personally supervised the sellout of U.S. strategic power in the SALT I Agreement and enshrined Soviet strategic superiority.

The Kissinger interests were all *against* providing verification of the Newhouse book. Kissinger's interests lay in maintaining his reputation as a competent and loyal Secretary of State and Assistant to the President of the United States for National Security Affairs. Kissinger's interest lay in *not* risking his personal power and power bases.

Thus, when he did endorse both the Newhouse book *and* its author, he made "admissions against interest" in a bundle of historic size and importance. In practical effect, he endorsed the "story of SALT" as Newhouse had narrated it. Kissinger verified the Newhouse version of what was in all those Top Secret NSSMs and NSDMs that are pervasive throughout the book. In essence, the Newhouse story of SALT became the Kissinger story of SALT. What was previously just a book by an unknown author became, eo instante, a historic document.

It must be assumed that a person of Henry Kissinger's tremendous official responsibilities and importance would not endorse a book as "outstanding" without reading it, especially so when the subject of the book is that of the supreme Kissinger accomplishment: the negotiations with the Soviets concerning which he twice attested that "the national survival is at stake."[6] In that same briefing, the President himself had said that "the very survival of a nation" was involved.

Also, it must be assumed that Henry Kissinger would not publicly and officially volunteer that he had "the highest regard for John Newhouse" unless he did, indeed, desire to present Newhouse to the public and the Congress as a man of high integrity, loyalty, and ability, a man who would neither intentionally falsify nor irresponsibly distort or exaggerate in writing about the vital specifics of the negotiation of an agreement with the Soviet Union in which the survival of the United States was at stake. In short, Kissinger built up, without reservation, the reputation for veracity and expertise of a potentially damning witness against himself.

Most of the potentially incriminating exposés of Henry Kissinger in Cold Dawn do not translate into reality until they are matched together with the actual provisions of the SALT Agreements themselves. But there are some that any casual reader, without the benefit of an analysis of SALT, could hardly miss. For example, there are disclosures in the Newhouse book that—once the validity of the book and the authenticity of the author are authoritatively endorsed—tend to destroy the carefully cultivated image that Henry Kissinger has created for himself among the elite press corps. It is inconceivable that his appointment as Secretary of State would have received such a resounding 78 to 7 approval if even half the Senators who have so vehemently attacked concentrations of power in the executive branch had read the book's exposure of Kissinger's obsession with accomplishing exactly that. In describing the speed with which Kissinger took over in the first few days of the Nixon Administration in January 1969, Newhouse observes:

It rapidly became clear that Kissinger and his staff had seized control of national security policy and that Kissinger dominated his staff. He alone dealt with the President. He assigned staff members their tasks, but told them no more than they needed to know. . . .[7]

The Nixon-Kissinger design went far beyond merely restoring the statutory role of the NSC. *Their system would be invincibly White House controlled.* Other agencies and institutions—the Departments of State and Defense, the Joint Chiefs of Staff—would be held strictly subordinate to the President and his senior adviser.

A number of new devices would clip bureaucracy's wings, not least the NSSM-NSDM innovation. Both are written in the White House and signed by the President, which means that only he (and his staff) can assign the issues to be studied and frame the questions to which bureaucracy must respond. Thus *the NSSM allows him to monopolize initiative,* while the NSDM, the decision memorandum, becomes a kind of executive order.[8]

Another thing that many Senators deplore is secrecy. Yet a passion for exactly that, according to Newhouse, characterized Kissinger's entire term as Presidential Assistant. A few Senators should have cared enough to read what the Newhouse book had to say along that line. Here is just one of scores of examples:

> *The current leadership conceals many of its activities and attitudes, not only from the public, but to the degree possible, from the bureaucracy as well.* Not only are the State Department and other agencies often kept in the dark, but the expert staff toiling under Henry Kissinger's direction in the Executive Office Building next door to the White House is sometimes no better informed.
>
> *This celebrated bureaucracy, erected by Nixon and Kissinger to strengthen their hold on national security matters,* works at an exhausting pace to prepare and hold open options for presidential decision. But it is often not consulted on what the President and his chief adviser ultimately decide to do. *It has no access to the President* himself and must rely for guidance on what Kissinger tells it, which may be much, little, or nothing—depending on the issue and the moment.[9]

Newhouse is enlightening also as to the total control that Kissinger has exercised over all phases and parts of the SALT negotiations. "Kissinger, it bears repeating," he says, "keeps the SALT bureaucracy on a short leash." Newhouse does keep repeating this, and also documenting it. One of the many really vital Top Secret documents that the Newhouse book totally compromises is NSSM 28, which contained detailed expositions of the five options agreed upon by concerned agencies for consideration as the official U.S. negotiating approaches to the Soviet Union. He not only tells *what* they were, but *who* supported each option. He even reveals the date it was presented to the National Security Council—June 25, 1969—and that General Wheeler, JCS Chairman, "made an usually harsh statement in which he expressed 'serious doubt' about the quality of the study's treatment of the verification problems," and also that "nobody, including Kissinger, could ignore so hostile a line on a central issue from the President's senior military adviser. Everyone realized that something had to be done."[10]

Then Newhouse reveals that "the White House lost no time in exploiting this golden opportunity" to seize total control of SALT and all preparations for the upcoming negotiations. Kissinger established that overall control would be exercised by the Verification Panel that he himself chaired, and a SALT Working Group that was chaired by one of Kissinger's assistants. The new group immediately took charge of all analytical work on SALT, "a function it has never relinquished."

The Newhouse book also reveals the magnitude of the Kissinger buildup for the charade he staged for the SALT negotiations. In the autumn of 1969, "a gaggle of task forces had been organized" to prepare options and studies on SALT positions. Newhouse exposes all the details, including their official designations and other secrets. Kissinger described the nine options as "building blocks." His idea was that "the elements of each could be shuffled into various combinations and packages, giving greater flexibility to the U.S. negotiating position." And "the building blocks were, moreover, yet another device by which White House control of SALT would be assured."[11]

In short, the "story of SALT" as told by John Newhouse pictures Henry Kissinger as continuously scheming to grasp more power and more control over both positions and personnel. It shows him as not merely the chief U.S. architect of SALT, but as substantially the *sole* architect having the power of decision. Furthermore, the book not only pictures Kissinger as playing all the key parts, but it documents its assertions. Henry Kissinger is revealed as power-obsessed, secrecy-obsessed, and suspicious even of his own staff members.

Thus the Newhouse book establishes that if the SALT I Agreements are shown by analysis to constitute a sellout of U.S. strategic power to the Kremlin—as, in effect, the essential prelude to a strategic surrender of the United States to the Communist Party of the Soviet Union—then Henry Kissinger is the architect of that U.S. surrender. At the high point of his apparent invulnerability, Kissinger in effect "signed" a "constructive confession."

Why did Henry Kissinger do such a thing? The very multiplicity and importance of his interests that are adversely affected by those endorsements, plus the magnitude of the risks he assumed in authenticating the Top Secret material that could not otherwise have been substantiated, tell us that his reasons for doing so must have been of overriding importance.

We can dispose summarily of the more obvious personal reasons. First, he clearly "owes" John Newhouse. The writer of a book about such a technical and complex subject as the SALT negotiations has an urgent need for sensational material that can be understood by the nonexpert reader. The most sensational development in the entire negotiations on behalf of the United States was the rebellion of Ambassador Gerard C. Smith against the eleventh-hour concessions to the Soviet Union that Kissinger imposed on the U.S. delegation. Despite all the pressure Kissinger could bring to bear, including that by the President of the United States, Gerard Smith, as head of the delegation, insisted on including an official, explicit, and (for a diplomat) vigorously worded warning that the Kissinger concessions to the Soviets imperil the supreme interests of the United States.

Kissinger took a well-calculated risk at the time by permitting Smith to include his warning in the official "Noteworthy Unilateral Statements" appended by the United States to the SALT I Agreements. Kissinger also went along with the Smith demand that his warning be brought officially to the attention of Congress. Kissinger did this rather than risk a public showdown with the head of the U.S. delegation.

Congress ignored the Smith warning; and, as we have described, Kissinger took full measure of revenge, firing Smith from his position as ACDA director as well as from head of the U.S. SALT delegation. Kissinger also fired most of Smith's senior staff, some of whom had been in disarmament work for 20 years—but they had supported Smith, or might do so in the future. Of course, the example Kissinger made of Smith was not lost on Smith's successor, Fred Iklé. This is one reason why it is clear that Newhouse would not have been appointed to ACDA unless Kissinger had arranged it.

Ambassador Smith's exit from SALT could have been related by Newhouse in dramatic narrative form that would have provided insight into a facet of the Kissinger character that has been well concealed from the public and is therefore newsworthy. But Newhouse did not mention a single word about it.

Newhouse also went so far as to exclude from the appendix to his book the absolutely essential addenda to the official text of the SALT I Agreements, namely, the "Agreed Interpretations" and the "Unilateral Statements." It was insulting to his readers to exclude this material, without which no authoritative or even intelligent interpretations of the SALT I Agreements could be undertaken. By doing so, he was able to exclude the Gerard Smith warning. So, Kissinger "owes" Newhouse for that.

Are we making too much about the importance of what was included in and excluded from the Newhouse book? Not really. His was the first serious treatment of SALT that the general public might be expected to buy and read. The texts of the SALT I Agreements received very little—indeed, suspiciously little—publicity even from publications that usually carry the full text of important international agreements.

Have you, the reader, ever read the full text of the SALT I Agreements, together with the "Agreed Interpretations" and "Unilateral Statements"? Ask your friends the same question.

By not mentioning the Smith episode in his narrative, and by excluding the text of Smith's "noteworthy" warning to the Congress and the nation, Newhouse accomplished two important tasks for Kissinger: he averted the damage to the carefully crafted Kissinger image of a brilliant but not dangerous or malevolent figure, and he suppressed from availability to the largest SALT audience the substance of a highly authoritative criticism on the SALT I Interim Agreement.

Richard J. Whalen, in his *National Review* book review of Graubard's *Kissinger: Portrait of a Mind*,[12] remarks that when Kissinger

> opened his heart to the bitchy Italian journalist Oriana Fallaci and likened himself to a solitary cowboy hero ("Americans admire that enormously") he revealed the derivative nature of his national identity in almost pathetic fashion.
>
> He cuts a dashing figure in chic drawing rooms; ordinary Americans would never mistake him for John Wayne.

Mr. Whalen is so right. But perhaps Kissinger nevertheless accomplished a more subtle psychological ploy. Ordinary Americans identify the lone cowboy as the prototype of a "good guy," and it is significant information to us that a character who looks so little like John Wayne *thinks* of himself as a cowboy. But it is more probable that we have reached another level of the Kissinger sophistication where he is just trying to make *us* think that *he* thinks of himself as a good guy. It is somewhat shocking to consider that he has seized so much power that the fate of our sometimes too-trusting America depends on whether he is really a good guy, or a very evil one.

Even if Kissinger does not present the proper image for the fastest gun in the West, he has brought down some very big game. Notches in the butt of his gun could appropriately represent the bringing down of one Secretary of State, one Secretary of Defense (from actual power to in-name only), one Director of CIA, and one career Ambassador. Not a bad score for a man who started as a poor immigrant boy. But whether or not Kissinger matches the image of the fastest gun in the West, he is certainly the slickest bribe in the West.

Why did Kissinger endorse John Newhouse's book when it was greatly against his paramount personal interests to do so? Why did he have him appointed to an important position in the Arms Control and Disarmament Agency? If Newhouse knew so much Top Secret material, perhaps he knew much more—and did not reveal it publicly. He did reveal, in descriptions exuding awe and admiration, the Kissinger technique of "back channel" operations in the negotiation of the SALT I Agreements. Kissinger may have had the fearful thought that, if Newhouse knew so much about the operations of the second or "back channel" on SALT, he might just possibly know about a third channel, which no one ever mentions but which logical analysis demonstrates must exist. It might be called the "subterranean channel" because, in the United States, only Henry Kissinger has access to it—not even the President.

As much as Newhouse's book shows that he knows about Kissinger's domination of the actual context of the SALT I Agreements through back channel operations, Newhouse does not see—or pretends that he does not see—that Kissinger's technique in operating through the back channel was both so secret and so decisive as to reduce the U.S. SALT delegates to the status of puppets on a set stage. Thus he explains:

> Kissinger's initial contacts with China are a good example of back channel activity. So, too, is the White House initiative taken in January 1971; five months later, it produced the first, perhaps the major, breakthrough on SALT. *Nearly all this activity was carried on in the back channel by Henry Kissinger, who kept fully informed only his constituency of one.*
> It began with a meeting on January 9 between Kissinger and Soviet Ambassador Dobrynin. . . . The security on this correspondence was, and is, remarkable. Even after the breakthrough in May, senior members of the Administration were not allowed to see it unless they had absolute need, as in the case of Ambassador Smith. The same restriction applied, for the most part, to the Kissinger staff.[13]

Cold Dawn is replete with similar material. But when Newhouse discusses what should have been to him a pivotal tip-off that the delegates purportedly representing both parties at the "bargaining conferences" were merely puppets on a set stage, he appears to miss the significance completely:

> The Soviet military bureaucracy, as Washington discovered, was then playing a more-critical role in SALT than its American counterpart. And Soviet leaders, at this stage, seemed to agree only that they wanted to limit ABMs; the rest they played by ear.
> Vienna pointed up the stylistic differences, although these may have been more disconcerting than instructive to the parties.
> *The Americans, it bears repeating, were struck by the lack of precision in Soviet statements and, indeed by their reluctance, or lack of authority, to talk about most issues in detail.*
> *The Americans were also struck by the ignorance of the Soviet civilian delegates about their own weapons; even Semenov, heading the delegation, knew little about the numbers and characteristics of Soviet strategic weapons. . . .*[14]
> The Soviets would neither confirm nor deny deploying the kinds and numbers of weapons that U.S. intelligence ascribed to them. Moscow's position had hardened . . . their immediate position would combine in-

flexibility, generality, and an unwillingness to negotiate on issues on which they were still uncertain or divided.

The effect was to reinforce a suspicion among the Americans that it was they who were negotiating with themselves.[15]

When Newhouse says "it bears repeating," he definitely does that in describing how often the American delegation was surprised by the Soviet delegation's lack of knowledge of their own weaponry, and their lack of authority. Yet this never raised his suspicions that the Soviet delegates were merely puppets, whose primary purpose was to prolong the negotiations year after year, so that the Soviets could exploit their massive momentum in producing and deploying strategic weapons.

Another point that John Newhouse *apparently* missed from his own account is that, although the Soviet delegates were merely puppets whose primary mission was to stall for years while going through the motions of negotiating, they did have another function. They played a game with our delegates, and through it obtained much intelligence about U.S. strategic weapons systems and policies. Consider this gem from the Newhouse book:

> A vexed American official unburdened himself in these words:
> "We have tabled three proposals in minute detail. They complain bitterly about the degree of detail, yet they have learned a great deal about our programs. They've told us nothing. All we've gotten in return is general statements. And whatever they want in the way of agreement is supposed to be based upon our acceptance of these general statements.
> "The bulk of this negotiation is not bilateral but internal. We make presentations. They complain, because by objecting to the wealth of detail, they get more of it. They'll say, for example, 'we do not understand the following points.' That obliges us to go into even more detail. Let's face it. They are learning a lot, but nothing else is happening."[16]

That is a striking summary of how negotiations with the Soviets are carried out on behalf of the United States, under the personal direction of Henry Kissinger even when, as he has repeatedly asserted, "national survival is at stake" in the negotiations.

One of the Soviet delegates was assigned to supervise the intelligence operation at the SALT negotiations and advise the Politburo on what more could be gained from the naive Americans. Apparently, by the end of the third session of the SALT I conferences, the Soviets decided they had learned all the American delegates knew about strategic systems, problems, and policies. Although the delegations and their staffs had changed very little at that time, Newhouse explained the significance of one change:

> On the Soviet side, there was only one change, but it was an important one. Colonel-General Nikolai Ogarkov, First Deputy Chief of General Staff, was clearly the most important figure on the Soviet delegation,

even though Semenov was the nominal leader. Ogarkov failed to turn up at SALT IV, and was replaced by a considerably less-powerful officer, Konstantin Trusov. A partial explanation emerged during the Party Congress [The Twenty-Fourth, convened on March 30, 1971], when Ogarkov was promoted from candidate member to full membership in the Central Committee. He was also known to be in the running for the job of Chief of Staff, soon to be vacant. *Ogarkov, it seems, had become too important for SALT.* Semenov, another candidate member, was not promoted.[17]

It seems far more probable that he had always been too important to be a SALT puppet "negotiator," but was included in the delegation because of his intelligence mission, which he had accomplished by the end of the third session.

Kissinger's sudden, shocking endorsement of the Newhouse book, and his appointment of Newhouse to a sensitive and prestigious position with ACDA, might have been in the way of a carrot. If there were to be a sequel to *Cold Dawn*, it might reveal too much of the real story of SALT. As we have shown, all the book needs to give it megatons of political explosive power is to combine it with an objective, comprehensive analysis of the provisions of the two SALT I Agreements.

Although Kissinger placed Newhouse in an excellent position in which his future conduct could be massively influenced, it does not appear that Newhouse is sufficiently important to justify Kissinger's taking such risks of exposure by endorsing both the book and the author. So, why did he do it?

Kissinger was signaling. Let us refer back to our NATO scenario, in which a composite of a NATO-nation premier or prime minister is being advised by a composite of the "Henry Kissinger" that it has become fashionable for all European governments to have. As a result of several in-depth analyses—intelligence and political—it was considered that the exposés that could be derived from the Newhouse book, when combined with a strategic analysis of the SALT I Agreements themselves, would require the breakup of NATO and the "Finlandization" of Western Europe. They did not want to do so, but to have even a slim chance of maintaining national identity under Soviet rule, each NATO nation would have to negotiate its own "preventive accommodation" with the Kremlin. In the scenario, the NATO nations had decided against taking that action until they were totally certain that they were really *in extremis*; they could not be certain until they obtained authoritative verification of the accuracy of the Newhouse book; and the only man in the world who could do so, publicly and officially, did exactly that.

By doing so, Henry Kissinger signaled all the governments of the NATO nations, and all knowledgeable governments throughout the

341

world, that the United States would no longer assist in opposing Soviet Communist expansion, in Western Europe or anywhere else. He also signaled that it would be just a question of time before the already established and fast-growing Soviet strategic supremacy would become decisive as to the credibility of the U.S. strategic deterrent to protect us from a Soviet ultimatum for surrender; and that we were already subject to nuclear blackmail whenever the Soviets should care to apply more pressure.

Why would Dr. Kissinger go about sending such signals in this particular manner? It is required by the exigencies of domestic politics. He wanted the NATO governments to understand, but not the American people or even the U.S. Congress. NATO officials would be saddened that the U.S. foreign and defense policies were so totally controlled by fatuous fools or brilliant traitors; but they could do nothing effective about it so far as ousting them or even alerting the American people to what had happened. Then, he would achieve the ultimate in abandoning allies without apparently pushing them over. All the U.S. public would see would be the NATO nations rushing to negotiate their separate accommodations with the Kremlin, or, as in the case of the October 1973 War, with the Arabs. We would not know why they were being forced to do so, so we would be outraged at them as faithless allies who had (as he made it appear to us) deserted the forces of freedom. And the American people would not be outraged at Henry Kissinger, as they were not outraged when he made the deal to oust Free China from the United Nations.

One reason he could rely on his signal's being understood by foreigners but not by Americans is that we have an emotional block that they don't. As a people, Americans simply cannot believe that any high government official is going to sell out the United States to the Soviet Communists. It doesn't matter what the evidence is, or how persuasive, or even that it may be conclusive. The American people simply will not believe it. Government officials in the NATO nations, however, will believe the evidence. They are under a duty to their countries, so they cannot shut their eyes to reality.

Would the U.S. Secretary of State deliberately attempt to destroy the NATO alliance? There is a precedent. We had a seven-year Secretary of Defense who made repeated efforts to break up NATO and, indeed, was partially successful.

When President John Kennedy, in his famous "I am a Berliner" speech in 1963, assured the NATO nations that "we will risk our cities to save your cities," Robert McNamara attempted to cancel out any confidence this might have aroused in our allies by a warning that "we are not prepared to destroy our nation in the process."[18] To repeat this warning and drive it home to our European friends, year after year in his annual military Posture Statements to Congress, he would exhibit his famous computer-calculated tables showing that, in any nuclear exchange with the Soviets, scores of millions of lives would be lost. His 1966 figure, for example, gave a range of from 90 to 160 million Americans dead. This was an attempt to remove from NATO the primary guarantee of security: the U.S. strategic umbrella.

But the NATO nations still had hope, based on use of U.S. *tactical* nuclear weapons, to deter the Soviets from invading Western Europe with their massively superior conventional forces. McNamara found a way to kill that hope, too. It was a bit weird, but he got away with it. He adopted as the U.S. strategy the disastrous doctrine of the "pause." That is, he informed NATO that, if the Soviets attack Western Europe, we will do nothing until we first "pause" and permit the Soviets to reflect on the seriousness of their action. It sounds incredible, and it is, that our strategy would assume that the compulsive planners in the Kremlin would launch an invasion without first considering what they were doing, and how serious it was. To make doubly sure that our allies understood his signals, McNamara embellished the "pause" doctrine with an additional restriction: he would not allow U.S. tactical nuclear weapons to be employed— even after the "pause"—unless the NATO armies were already being overwhelmed by the Soviet invasion. This warned Western Europe that no nuclear weapons would be employed until after the Soviets had penetrated so far into NATO territory that Western use of nuclear weapons would destroy their own cities, industry, and people—and *not* damage anything beyond the Iron Curtain. In short, McNamara signaled that it would be better to surrender to the Soviets than to resist, and that NATO could not count on any assistance from the United States that would be effective against the Soviets.

The tragedy of this strategy was that, to deter the Soviets effectively at that time, we did not even need to assume serious risks. Our margin of strategic superiority was at least, as Nixon himself has attested, 8-to-1. All we had to do was to make a threat or a promise, and the Kremlin could not afford to chance that we might be bluffing. But McNamara took care of that for the Soviets. After watching his actions, which were reducing U.S. military power as the Soviets built theirs, de Gaulle declared in January 1963:

> No one in the world, particularly no one in America, can say whether or where or when or how or to what extent U.S. nuclear weapons will be used to defend Europe.

By the next year, McNamara's signals were coming through so loud and clear that de Gaulle had the annual French war games run on the assumption that "a Communist seizure of West Berlin would be met only by conventional, and hardly more than a token, U.S.-West German resistance."[19] In 1965, recognizing that McNamara had carried the United States further down the road to ultimate accommodation with the Kremlin, de Gaulle refused French participation in the planned 1966 NATO war games for the very good reason that "its strategy is not directed toward immediate nuclear retaliation against any Soviet attack on the West."[20] Three months later, former West German Chancellor Adenauer put it still more bluntly: U.S. nuclear policies would "hand Europe over to the Russians."

Why didn't McNamara succeed in destroying NATO? First, it must be remembered that he did succeed in tearing out the vital center: de Gaulle was too much of a realist to fail to recognize the fact that McNamara was cutting down U.S. strategic power, and imposing on the Americans ridiculous and suicidal strategies that stripped the still physically powerful U.S. strategic deterrent of essential credibility. That is, de Gaulle assessed the character of the McNamara-Kennedy palace-guard leadership exactly the same as had Nikita Khrushchev: "too liberal to fight, even in defense of their own vital interests." So McNamara, although he did not destroy NATO, split it in half. The reason he did not succeed in destroying it completely— why it was still alive for Henry Kissinger to deliver the coup de grace— is that the rest of the NATO powers still had faith in the strength and will of the American nation.

At the time McNamara made his attempt at NATOcide, he had destroyed thousands of U.S. strategic weapons, but we still had massive nuclear power and retained a margin of superiority over the Soviets. That is, we still could defend Western Europe with our strategic deterrent and our tactical nuclear deterrent. The only question was, would we? The West Germans, especially, have clung to their faith that so long as we could, we would. Just as we Americans have an emotional block that prevents us from believing that our high officials would make surrender-type deals with the Communists behind our backs, the Germans have an emotional block against believing that Americans would willingly betray them to the Communists.

That is why Kissinger can now succeed in destroying NATO utterly, whereas McNamara could not. Kissinger has the far easier task of convincing the remaining NATO nations that the U.S. will not assist them against Soviet aggression because we cannot. This, of course, was one of the prime purposes of the SALT I Agreements, so far as both the Soviets and Kissinger were concerned. As no honest and objective student of strategy can fail to understand, but too few have enunciated, this is one effect of SALT I:

> Nontechnical observers can hardly be faulted for thinking that allowable SALT I Russian force levels of 1,618 ICBMs and 950 SLBMs imply more power than the visibly smaller options allowed to the United States.

In nontechnical terms, the only ones whose validity are general, *the SALT I figures spell out a simple and compelling message of American strategic inferiority. . . .*

Ministers in New Delhi or Rome . . . may simply reflect that the Americans are showing great anxiety over a thing known as the SS-9, while the Russians, as always, boast of their power.[21]

One of the few props left to hold up NATO after SALT I was the Kissinger rationalization of Soviet superiorities in all other areas, on the basis of U.S. superiority in *numbers of warheads,* in turn based upon our claimed *monopoly* of MIRV technology. Having no other hope to cling to, our allies clung to this MIRV myth as representing the last shred of credibility of the U.S. strategic deterrent as a nuclear umbrella that could shelter them against Soviet strategic supremacy. This Kissinger claim of a U.S. monopoly of MIRV technology was false when it was made in June 1972 in his SALT briefings at the White House. The Newhouse book reveals that in 1969 we knew that the Soviets had tested multiple warheads in 1968 that our intelligence insisted were MRVs, but which were "for practical purposes, already a MIRV"; and that President Nixon himself had said that, despite the split in the intelligence community as to whether the Soviet SS-9 "triplet" has an independent guidance system "as ours will have" (we did not have any MIRVs ourselves until 1969-70),

there isn't any question that it is a multiple weapon, *and that its footprints* indicate that it just happens to fall in somewhat the precise area in which our Minuteman silos are located. [He meant "precise *pattern*" in which our Minuteman silos are laid out.][22]

So thus it was that the announcement by Secretary of Defense Schlesinger on August 17, 1973, softened the resistance of our NATO allies and rendered them highly vulnerable for the totally unexpected blow of the Kissinger endorsement of the John Newhouse book on SALT and its exposés of Kissinger's modus operandi.

Is there any proof that the body blows in the area of strategic power that Kissinger has dealt NATO in the SALT negotiations and in the SALT I Agreements themselves were *intended* to injure NATO, and that he would deliberately signal the NATO ministers of the preemptive strategic surrender of the United States, which is foreshadowed by SALT and exposed in the Newhouse book?

The proof became crudely obvious during the Yom Kippur War in the Middle East in October 1973. On October 24 a strategic alert was ordered for all U.S. forces around the world. It was only the second in the entire nuclear age, and it was enmeshed in mystery—the reason for it, if any; and precisely who ordered it and when. It was ordered without consultation with any of our NATO allies. Worse, no NATO nation was given notice that the alert had been ordered until hours afterwards. Not even the great myth-maker himself could think up a reason for this delay. But it produced results so predictable that they must be considered to have been intended—or else the alert was planned and executed by an idiot. It split off the European members of NATO from the United States. The rift was exacerbated by most undiplomatic criticism of the manner in which the NATO nations had reacted during the crisis, by Secretary of State Kissinger, by a spokesman for the State Department, and by Defense Secretary James R. Schlesinger. Dr. Kissinger publicly accused them of being "more interested in gaining marginal individual advantages than in cooperating on united actions," and of acting "as though the alliance didn't even exist."

Media in the United States focused public attention on the harsh and undeniable fact that, during our efforts to resupply Israel to offset the massive Soviet resupply of the Arabs, Washington was deserted by every ally except Portugal. Little publicity was given to Kissinger's provocations that long ago had initiated the rift. Summing up, *Newsweek* conceded:

> It was hard to quarrel with the West European contention that on the Mideast, Washington had negotiated with a Communist rival over the heads of its friends.[23]

As to the totally unnecessary and undiplomatic public criticism of NATO by the U.S. Secretary of State, the *New York Times* reported what Kissinger had been heard to say in an aside after testifying in private before the House Foreign Affairs Committee on October 29: "I don't care what happens to NATO, I'm so disgusted." The spokesman for the State Department promptly issued a sophisticated denial that Dr. Kissinger had "made a specific remark of disgust with NATO"— which, of course, was not what the *Times* had quoted him as saying.

But the Mideast alert gambit and his harsh criticism of NATO were merely late steps in a campaign Dr. Kissinger had been conducting for years. In the Moscow Summit Agreements of May 1972, which Kissinger negotiated with the Kremlin to set up his "broad new relationship" between the United States and the U.S.S.R., he cut the throats of our allies behind their backs, as the twisted metaphor so vividly puts it, with his usual expertise. He abandoned the preconditions that the United States as well as the European members of NATO had preserved for painful years as insurance against a Soviet walkaway with the European Security Conference that they had sought for so long.

The John Newhouse book is primarily a vehicle for all the Pugwash-MAD theories, but it does have some valuable material in it in addition to all the Top Secret security leaks. He picked up one terse quotation that sums up the NATO attitude toward the SALT negotiations and Kissinger's conduct in particular:

> "If Nixon is diddled and has to negotiate himself in Moscow, it would be

terrible," observed one Washington-based diplomat. "Nixon is running a great risk." And Henry Kissinger, he complained bitterly, "is consumed by *folie de grandeur.*"[24]

Time has proved this diplomat to be an accurate prophet: Nixon was indeed diddled in the negotiations—as much by Henry Kissinger as by the Kremlin. He was caught in Moscow at the eleventh hour with both SALT I Agreements still open as to their most critical terms—so he *did* have to negotiate himself, or rather, accept anything that Kissinger, at Soviet dictation, told him to accept. What Nixon accepted was, indeed, in the diplomat's words, "terrible." And Henry Kissinger's *folie de grandeur* may haunt us to the end of our nationhood—and monstrously accelerate it.

16

At stake in SALT are the lives of some 210 million Americans, our thousand-billion-dollar-a-year economy, the continued existence of the United States and of Western civilization, and the future of freedom in the world. The issue may be decided forever within the five-year term established by the SALT I Interim Agreement.

This is the inevitable conclusion of a comprehensive strategic analysis of the SALT I ABM Treaty and of the Interim Agreement that imposes *some* limits on *some* components of *some* types of offensive missile systems. The unprecedented importance of the 1972 twin SALT pacts is confirmed by the most authoritative official sources. Former Secretary of State Rogers officially reported to Congress that they "constitute the most important step in arms limitation ever undertaken by this country." Dr. Henry A. Kissinger, Assistant to the President for National Security Affairs, Secretary of State, and chief theoretician for both the negotiations and the SALT Agreements themselves, has expressly conceded that "national security is at stake" in SALT, and that "the agreements restrain the very armaments on which . . . the national security depends."

Unfortunately, the SALT I Agreements are not only the most important in history, they are the most mysterious. The sheer magnitude of the human and material values at stake in these agreements would seem to demand that their provisions be drafted with supreme expertise and caution—as if the lives of the drafters and the signers depended upon them (which they do, as well as the lives of all Americans).

The U.S. delegation conducting the SALT negotiations had 2½ years of time, a large staff of experts, and all the facilities of the National Security Council, the Defense Department, the State Department, and the U.S. Disarmament Agency. They were under the overall supervision of the President's "Verification Panel," chaired by Dr. Kissinger, who was very much in charge of the entire SALT project. It is an intriguing mystery, therefore, how they could have done such a shockingly bad job of protecting the national security interests of the United States. This conclusion applies both to the substance and to the mechanics of the drafting. It applies also to the calculated weakness of the inspection provisions and enforceability.

Some senators expressed concern over what they euphemistically characterized as the "loose wording" of SALT. From a professional legal standpoint, or even from that of an informed layman, a more realistic description would be that the drafting is imprecise, ambiguous, irresponsible, and confusing. This appraisal is confirmed by the fact that, within hours of the signing of the agreements, it was found necessary to issue four different types of official interpretations, and major conflicts about the meaning of the language had developed between the United States and the U.S.S.R., and between the U.S. departments of State and Defense. The defects in draftsmanship tremendously increase the risks already imposed upon the United States by the substance. In sharp contrast, no incompetence or negligence is apparent in the drafting of provisions protecting the interests of the Soviet Union.

Several stalwart U.S. senators rather speedily discovered that nothing was to be gained by telling the documented truth about the risks of SALT. *Congress and the American people simply refused to believe it.* When the lopsidedness of the SALT pacts was set forth in shocking detail, and when the horrendous risks were accurately defined, an emotional blocking came into play and generated this reaction:

> It can't be *that* lopsided—or President Nixon wouldn't have signed it. If SALT is as detrimental to the United States as you say, then you are saying, in effect, that Richard Nixon sold out to the Soviets at the Moscow Summit—and I know he wouldn't do that. Therefore, what you say about SALT cannot be true; and I don't care what impressive-sounding statistics you quote, because they can't be true, either.

Senator Barry Goldwater, who supported the Nixon Summit trips to Peking and Moscow despite his career-long reputation as an anti-Communist, joined with Senator James Buckley and others in this short summary of SALT:

> The Moscow Agreements freeze the U.S. to a 4-to-1 disadvantage comparing our overall missile payload to that of the Soviet Union;
> The Soviet Union has three missiles for every two of ours, theirs are

substantially larger, and the agreements guarantee that this gap will remain and probably widen;

Soviet missiles carry payloads several times larger than those of the U.S. missiles, an advantage which the agreements not only protect, but allow to be enhanced;

The agreements forbid the U.S. to increase the number of its nuclear submarines while authorizing the Soviets to continue building them until they equal and then surpass the United States.

Similarly, Senator Henry Jackson, one of the most knowledgeable senators on national defense, gave one of the shortest but sharpest summaries of SALT on June 16, 1972:

Simply put, the agreements give the Soviets more of everything: more light ICBMs, more heavy ICBMs, more submarine-launched missiles, more submarines, more payload, even more ABM radars. In no area covered by the agreement is the United States permitted to maintain parity with the Soviet Union.

The closest any prominent Congressman of the same party as the President has come to questioning motivation of the administration was when John M. Ashbrook knocked down the claim that SALT would maintain a U.S. advantage in numbers of individual warheads achieved by MIRVing. He pointed out that, because of the massive Soviet advantage in missile payload or throw-weight, the Soviets could wipe out the U.S. present advantage and build up to a 5-to-1 lead in such numbers, merely by developing the same technology the United States has possessed for years. Referring to the "very poor record" of administration officials in "forecasting Soviet capabilities," and their consistency in underrating what the Soviets can do, Congressman Ashbrook concluded:

In the opinion of nongovernmental defense experts with somewhat better records of prediction, these improvements are well within Soviet capacities in the next five years.

What this means is that the administration is *consciously* entering into an agreement that insures our inferiority if the Soviets do what they have asked and have been given the legal right to do.

Yet, none of these statements showing the SALT I odds in favor of the Soviet Union and against the United States made any substantial impression on Congress or on the public. These statements simply did not convince the public that SALT seriously endangers U.S. survival—because of the public's trust that, if such a terrible danger really did exist, the President would *know* about it, and he would not knowingly plunge the nation into it, and, therefore, the asserted danger could not exist.

A strategic analysis serves no useful purpose unless it can be believed. Its purpose is to present the facts, develop the possibilities and probabilities by logic and demonstration, and thereby enable the reader to reach his own informed opinion. No amount of documentation and evidence, however persuasive or conclusive, can avail unless we can remove the emotional block and open the minds of well-informed Americans to *consider* whether SALT I subjects the United States to massive risks that are immediate (within five years) rather than in the vague and distant future.

"National survival is at stake," as Dr. Kissinger said, in SALT. But national survival is just as surely at stake in whether a sufficient number of dedicated Americans can be enabled—before time runs out for our country—to understand exactly *how* our survival is at stake in SALT; and to understand also what the real-life consequences will be to all of us, as individuals. We must face the question of whether the *theories* and *assumptions* of SALT have set us up as sure losers in the greatest gamble in history. The risks in SALT are quite literally catastrophic, and they threaten every man, woman, and child in the nation. Can these risks be made believable?

The greatest mystery about SALT is *why* both Dr. Kissinger and President Nixon showed so little concern about the specific contents of the SALT Treaty and Interim Agreement; *why* they remained so unflappable in the face of the lopsidedness of substance and the irresponsibly loose drafting; *why* they did not bother with precautions against obvious gaps or concealed loopholes; and *why* they remain so unconcerned about the demonstrable inadequacy of the inspection provisions.

The very existence of such massive inequities and imbalances in the SALT pacts is strong circumstantial evidence that Dr. Kissinger was either very careless or simply didn't care about these matters, and that the President relied on him completely. Such evidence does not, however, answer the question "why?" Dr. Kissinger himself answered this question. In the White House briefing on SALT on June 15, 1972, for members of five congressional committees having official concern with the matter, the President requested and authorized Dr. Kissinger to present "the White House perspective on these agreements." Dr. Kissinger then read and distributed a formal typed statement, showing that his remarks were not impromptu but had been considered and prepared in advance. Here is the key paragraph of his introduction:

> Let me start, therefore, with a sketch of the broad design of what the President has been trying to achieve in this country's relations with the Soviet Union, since *at each important turning point in the SALT negotiations we were guided not so much by the tactical solution that seemed most equitable or prudent, important as it was, but by an underlying philosophy and a specific perception of international reality.*

The above quotation clearly and positively explains why Dr. Kissinger, and on his recommendation the President, could negotiate and accept the SALT I Agreements that any honest and accurate analysis must reveal as grossly inequitable and wildly imprudent. The *overriding priority,* in Dr. Kissinger's own words, was given to "underlying philosophy and a specific perception of international reality." The giving away of such great military advantages, the accepting of a poor second place in strategic power, and a formal acknowledgement of the Soviet Union as the preeminent superpower, did not, therefore, make the SALT I Agreements necessarily a deliberate "sellout."

They did, however, constitute a deliberate decision to abandon the reliance on U.S. military power as the primary guarantee of our national survival and, instead, to stake the life or death of the United States and the American people on an "underlying philosophy"—that is, on Henry Kissinger's theories—and on a "specific perception of international reality"—that is, on President Nixon's assumptions, based on the Kissinger theories, as to what international reality is.

The SALT I Agreements, together with the arguments by which they were sold to Congress and the American people, are based entirely on *three theories* adopted by Dr. Kissinger. These theories were then accepted by President Nixon as warranting the *assumptions* on which he has totally committed the United States through the SALT negotiations and agreements.

The evidence supports Dr. Kissinger's statement that he and the President were more concerned with theories than with either the equity or the prudence of the SALT I provisions themselves. This conclusion is supported by the Senatorial criticism quoted earlier, *e.g.,* Senator Henry Jackson's comment that the agreements give the Soviets "more of everything" and do not permit the United States to approach parity with the Soviet Union in any area; and the Goldwater-Buckley summary stressing inequitable and imprudent advantages for the Soviet Union ("a 4-to-1 disadvantage comparing our overall missile payload," the fact that the Soviet Union is assured "three missiles for every two of ours, theirs are substantially larger, and the agreements guarantee that this gap will remain and probably widen"). Also, Senator James Buckley, in his testimony on SALT before the Senate Foreign Relations Committee on June 29, 1972, presented irrefutable evidence of three major gaps or loopholes in the treaty and six in the Interim Agreement, *all of which favor the Soviet Union,* thus demonstrating major elements of inequity and imprudence.

The crux of SALT I is this: *if* the Kissinger theories are totally valid, and *if* the Nixon assumptions based on those theories are therefore justified, *then* it doesn't really matter *what* specific provisions are in the treaty and agreement, or how lopsided they may be, or how shot through with loopholes, or how inadequate the inspection provisions. As Dr. Kissinger himself said in his Moscow news conference on May 29, 1972:

> . . . we do believe that to put the central armaments of both sides for the first time under agreed restraint is an event that transcends in importance the technical significance of the individual restrictions that were placed on various weapons systems.

This is a good illustration of how a sophisticated spokesman can score with different audiences at the same time. He made an emotional appeal to all those vast and influential forces that support any disarmament agreement as a "good" thing (including much of the media), without at the same time raising any question in the minds of the commonsense elements that believe that disarmament should be fair, equal, and prudent. Suppose he had said, instead:

> We were so anxious to get a disarmament agreement with the Soviets that we really did not care what was in the agreement.

That is exactly the way he acted.

The Kissinger theories and assumptions do not by any means constitute *strategic doctrine*. And when we question his theories and assumptions, we do not by any means question the importance of strategic doctrine *per se*. Many times, in history, sound and brilliant strategic doctrine has proved to be a more decisive element in effective employment of military power than the military hardware that is the mechanical instrument of that power. One striking example in the recent past was the German blitzkrieg doctrine and the flanking of the Maginot Line.

Even as to strategic *nuclear* power—which is a hundred million times more powerful than conventional power—strategic doctrine can be pivotal. A simple order by the President changing the U.S. present deterrent strategy, which he could make effective within 24 hours, could neutralize—at least for the next several years, which are critical to our national life or death—the capability of the Soviet SS-9, SS-18, SS-17, and SS-19 first-strike missiles to destroy the majority of our Minuteman retaliatory force. This would not mean shifting from a second-strike-only to a first-strike strategy. This we cannot do because we do not have any effective first-strike weapons. But we can and must take advantage of a technological breakthrough in early warning of a missile attack in order to save our 1,000 Minutemen from destruction.

Strategic doctrine is, by nature, affirmative. It deals with how to apply military power most effectively to secure national objectives. The Kissinger *theories*—as distinguished from strategic *doctrine*—are predominantly negative as to strategic nuclear power: they question whether such power can be either necessary or useful. That they are the creation of a theoretician rather than a strategist is conclusively demonstrated by the strange structure of SALT I.

Before turning to a brief survey of the three Kissinger theories upon which all our lives are staked, it is interesting to note that the Kissinger admission that abstract theory was given priority over operational strategic weapons systems, "at each important turning point in the SALT negotiations," clears up another mystery: why the administration did not advance a single argument in support of SALT I that can stand up under objective analysis.

Because the SALT pacts were negotiated by the U.S. delegation with "an underlying philosophy" being decisive in all conflicts with military requirements, it is not surprising that even the most sophisticated strategy-based argument that the SALT I supporters could muster collapses under close scrutiny. Their most apparently persuasive argument was presented in many versions, but the gist of it is: *whatever price we had to pay* in the ABM Treaty, or in accepting inferiority and imbalance in the Interim Agreement, was worth it because we nevertheless made a great gain. This great gain was identified as the claimed interruption of the Soviets' massive momentum in ongoing programs by which they are building up increasingly superior offensive missile forces. As Dr. Kissinger phrased it, "the Interim Agreement perpetuates nothing which did not already exist in fact and *which could only have gotten worse without the agreement.*"

This "momentum-interruption" argument, especially in its slightly twisted version that "it has great arms control significance because it actually stops weapons from coming into being," has deceived a number of otherwise knowledgeable critics of SALT. Upon analysis, however, it becomes clear that the Interim Agreement does *not* stop weapons from coming into being, and that the *only* momentum it interrupts is the momentum of digging holes.

Even President Nixon apparently did not understand what the Interim Agreement actually provides on this subject. In his official letter to the House of Representatives transmitting the ABM Treaty and the Interim Agreement, he gave this explanation:

> The Interim Agreement limits the overall level of strategic offensive missile forces.

Members of Congress believed this and they were seriously misled. It simply is not true. It is not even anywhere near true. The Interim Agreement does not prohibit, or even control in any way, the continued *production of missiles* (either land-based or sea-based) or their associated electronic equipment. Yet it is the momentum relating to the *production* of missiles that it would have been to the advantage of the U.S. to "interrupt." Soviet production lines were turning out new and more powerful missiles and their electronics at the rate of 350 or more per year, and they can continue to do so under the agreement. Leonid I. Brezhnev gave President Nixon official warning "that they are going forward with defense programs in the offensive area which are not limited by these agreements." The production of missiles—even vastly more powerful and accurate missiles— is *not* limited by these agreements.

There are only two limitations in the Interim Agreement that apply to land-based ICBM systems at all, and these apply only to "fixed land-based launchers." The first prohibition is against starting "construction of additional fixed land-based ICBM launchers"—that is, digging more holes; and the second prohibits converting launchers for two undefined types of ICBMs into launchers for a third unidentified type of ICBM. At least four major loopholes were crammed into the four short lines of this "conversion" article. The U.S. purpose was to limit conversion of "light" ICBMs into SS-9s or missiles heavier than existing "light" ICBMs; but we certainly did not achieve this limitation.

SALT-at-any-price supporters contend that the Interim Agreement really does interrupt Soviet momentum in the production of missiles for all practical purposes because it would be a waste of money and irrational to continue producing additional missiles without being able to launch them. Contrary to this assumption, there are at least five very practical uses for the continued production of missiles. First, and most obvious, the Soviets can make them *mobile* land-based missiles. The U.S. delegation recognized the massive extent of this gap in the agreement and tried, at least partially, to close it; but the Soviets expressly and firmly refused. So, "in the interest of concluding the Interim Agreement" (probably in time for signature before President Nixon left Moscow), our side caved in. The U.S. delegation, in a fit of frustration, then made a "Unilateral Statement" that piously deplores the thought of deploying any mobile land-based missiles—but leaves the Soviets totally free to do so.

Since 1969 the Soviets have been producing an excellent hard-fuel mobile ICBM on a tracked self-propelled carrier, and they claim that the entire "complexes" of these systems "have high maneuverability, can be well camouflaged, and therefore cannot be spotted by the enemy's aerial or space reconnaissance."[1] They can also mount mobile missiles on railroad cars or even on extra-large heavy-duty trucks, such as those that will be produced at the world's largest heavy-truck manufacturing plant on the Kama River, which the United States is helping to build.

The suggestion that the Soviets will actually use their *right* under the Interim Agreement to produce and deploy mobile missiles—a right that they insisted on retaining—is certainly not a far-out theory. They have already deployed at least 100 intermediate-range SS-11-type self-propelled tracked-vehicle mobile missiles, thus demonstrating practicability and strategic desirability. These missiles can be given ICBM range merely by adding one additional propulsion stage that this missile is already designed to accept. In 1973 the Soviets displayed a new solid-fuel missile which can be launched either from silos or from land-mobile launchers, and which may have ABM as well as ICBM capability.

The United States considered mobile ICBMs so desirable and practicable that we invested scores of millions of dollars in research and development of a mobile Minuteman type. Just prior to production the project looked so valuable as a strategic system that Robert McNamara canceled it—as he did all other programs that would have retained U.S. nuclear superiority over the accelerating Soviet buildup.

With their three years' experience in deployment of these modern self-propelled mobile ICBMs, and with the momentum of their production lines for both the missile and its launcher expressly not interrupted by the Interim Agreement, and with already far more than a "sufficiency" of numbers of secure survivable missiles in hardened concrete and steel silos, the Soviets have no need to dig more holes in the ground. Missile holes are expensive, take from a year to a year and a half to construct, and are more easily detected by satellite reconnaissance than any other survivable launchers.

By 1973 Soviet developments in missile technology made it clear that the Soviets had already completed their hole-digging program before 1972, and therefore gave up nothing in the Interim Agreement in regard to land-based launchers. Even if they had not completed their hole-digging, the mobile-launching program has benefits of added survivability, better concealment, and economy of time and money in building up their "splendid" first-strike capability.

The other four major methods of employing the continued missile production permitted by the Interim Agreement include producing upgraded models to replace old models in existing silo launchers; storing them at missile launch sites for reloads; stockpiling them in warehouses for rapid surprise deployment on prefabricated pads; and substituting them for IRBMs in existing silos, or for use in newly constructed silos that purport to be for launching IRBMs but that are fully adequate to accommodate the variable-range SS-11 that can be intercontinental range. The ongoing production line, which has already turned out more than a thousand versatile offensive SS-11s, could be shifted to produce the new SS-17 and SS-19 upgrades of the SS-11, and also continue in operation for the production of missiles to be used in an additional method of circumventing the Interim Agreement, in order to build an essential segment of a massive surprise strategy. All these methods of exploiting the loopholes in the Interim Agreement are discussed in Chapter 19.

The other half of the SALT supporters' argument that the United States will gain great and essential benefits because the Interim Agreement "interrupts" ongoing Soviet offensive programs relates to their momentum in the production of modern nuclear submarines and submarine-launched ballistic missiles. Unfortunately, the agreement leaves open to the Soviet Union almost as many practical methods of circumvention pertaining to missile submarines as are available to them in regard to land-based weapons.

First, it must be remembered that the Soviet Union may have no use whatsoever—from either a strategic or a cost-effectiveness viewpoint—for more missile submarines than the incredibly large and superior number allowed under the Interim Agreement and Protocol. This includes the expansion of the Soviet fleet of modern Y-class, Delta class, and Extended-Delta class nuclear submarines to 62 and the retention of 22 diesel-powered G-class submarines, for a total of 84 missile-launching submarines. The United States, on the other hand, is allowed 44, but we do not plan to add to the 41 we now possess, even if the proposed Trident is produced. The Soviets can have up to 950 ballistic missile launchers on their modern submarines, whereas we are limited to 710.

The Kissinger claim that this massive superiority allowed to the Soviets is really an advantage for the United States is based on his theory that, without the Interim Agreement, the Soviets could, during the five-year term, build up to 90 or more modern missile-launching submarines. But Dr. Kissinger has no explanation of *why* the Soviets might *want* that many. It would be both logical and in accord with traditional Kremlin bargaining techniques to sign no agreement unless it allowed them their *maximum planned number* of modern missile-launching submarines and launchers—just as they refused to accept any limit whatsoever in the case of mobile land-based missile launchers. If this is the case—that is, if they did not plan on more than 62 modern missile submarines—*the Soviets are not giving up anything* in regard to their ongoing production program in modern missile-launching submarines or submarine-launched ballistic missile launchers.

But even assuming that the Kissinger estimate that they *might* want 90 submarines is correct, the momentum of their production program is still not necessarily interrupted. He estimated that they have 43 or 44 operational or under construction, and that they have the capability of producing nine a year. Of Kissinger's total of 44, not more than 35 are estimated operational as of the July 1, 1972, effective date of the Interim Agreement. This leaves 27 to be completed. This is enough to prevent any interruption in the momentum of their submarine production lines for at least three years. This is hardly a sudden or drastic interruption of momentum during the most critical 3/5 of the timeframe of the agreement. Furthermore, much can be done to continue the momentum at the end of that period and to maintain the input momentum.

In the first place, as in the case of the land-based missile systems, no limit is put on the *production* of the *missiles* themselves. This momentum can continue uninterrupted to provide missiles for the 27 submarines under construction. After that need is filled, there are other additional uses for continued production. One is the production of the new Soviet 2,500-nautical-mile-range submarine-launched missile to replace the earlier 1,500-mile-range models on some of the 35 ballistic missile-firing submarines operational when SALT I was signed. After all those requirements are met, all production can be shifted to their 5,000-nautical-mile-range SS-N-8, and the missiles stockpiled for other uses suggested below.

What about the submarines themselves and the launching tubes to mount on them? Here again there is a convenient ambiguity or loophole in both the SALT I Interim Agreement and Protocol provisions: neither prohibits the *manufacture* of submarines or ballistic missile launchers to mount on submarines. The language used in Article III of the Interim Agreement is "limit . . . to," and the limitation defined in the protocol is that the Soviet Union "may *have* no more than 950 ballistic missile launchers *on* submarines and no more than 62 modern ballistic missile submarines."

Thus, the Soviets could continue the momentum of their production lines for launchers and stockpile them ready for swift installation on submarines—because the prohibition is not against having them, but against having them "on" submarines. The submarines themselves could continue to be produced as before, but without installing the launchers "on" them. Extra torpedo tubes could be installed and, in the remaining two-year period covered by the Interim Agreement, they could be employed, together with the growing force of fast nuclear-powered attack submarines, in trailing U.S. Polaris or Poseidon submarines, ready to destroy them on signal; or, they could be modified to carry cruise missiles temporarily, or even permanently. Cruise missiles would be very useful in pinning down U.S. strategic forces for a Soviet first-strike, and the Soviets already have a model which can be launched from a submerged submarine.

A third, and highly probable, method would be to continue producing the hull sections, but to postpone their final assembly and mating with the launchers. This can be done either openly, because it is entirely permissible under the agreement and protocol, or clandestinely, because the hull sections are produced in shops and manufacturing plants that are not as visible to satellite reconnaissance as are the sheds in which final assembly of the hull sections takes place.

These stockpiling techniques may sound devious, but actually they represent a highly realistic preparation by the Kremlin for either of two possible and not improbable contingencies. (1) The Soviet schedule may now call for, or be modified later to call for, a "surprise abrogation after protracted preparations." This is the way President Kennedy described this favorite Soviet technique by which the Soviets abrogated the 1958 unilateral-reciprocal nuclear test ban in September 1961 after nearly three years of massive preparations to resume testing. (2) If the United States should give notice of termination under the six-months provision, and propose a crash program to rebuild to parity because a developing Soviet first-strike capability is becoming increasingly obvious, the Soviets could reveal the existence of their stockpile, point out that it would enable them to augment their strategic forces years faster than we could increase ours, and threaten to preempt if we terminated the Interim Agreement and Treaty.

The SALT-at-any-price advocates, of course, contend that the Soviet Union "would never do such a thing" as to take advantage of technical gaps or loopholes in treaties or agreements. Without opening here the question of whether the Soviet Union would *violate* international agreements, the point here is that the Soviets have indeed taken advantage of every major technicality or loophole provision in agreements or arrangements limiting the development of strategic nuclear power. The surprise abrogation of the first nuclear test ban was one outstanding example.

Another example is the UN Outer Space Treaty prohibiting the orbiting of weapons of mass destruction. The ink was hardly dry on the ratification of the treaty when, in 1967, the Soviets boasted of their development of a Fractional Orbital Bombardment System (FOBS). Since then, they have conducted more than a dozen tests of their FOBS or Multiple Orbital Bombardment System (MOBS), which we have identified. They have thus exploited two technicalities of the UN Outer Space Treaty to acquire a monopoly of powerful space weapons systems that can be rationally employed only in the no-warning spearhead of a massive surprise attack.

It cannot be logically contended that the Soviets will not take advantage of technicalities open to them in treaties. They always have. They always will, unless they break completely with Communist ideology, Communist political doctrine, and Soviet strategic doctrine. All three of these most powerful factors that control Soviet policy impose irresistible compulsions on the Kremlin leaders to secure the maximum advantages for completion of the task that they believe history has delegated to the Soviet Union as the vanguard of international communism. The attitude of the Kremlin rulers toward taking advantage of historic opportunities was best summed up by their first practicing nuclear strategist, Nikita S. Khrushchev, in explaining why they so suddenly abrogated the first nuclear test ban after spending years and money on antitest propaganda: "If we did not conduct the nuclear tests, we would be slobbering idiots."

Kremlin leadership is not comprised of slobbering idiots, but of coldly calculating compulsive planners. They are impelled to take advantage of major opportunities, and they do not give away major advantages.

This leads to one more reason to reject the contention that the Interim Agreement so seriously interrupts the momentum of ongoing Soviet offensive-missile buildup programs that it delivers a great advantage to the United States. Dr. Kissinger's own claims for such an advantage are so glowing as to suggest that they are altogether too good to be true. Here are two typical statements, taken from his prepared text in briefing the five congressional committees at the White House on June 15, 1972:

> The agreement would not create the gap. It would prevent its enlargement to our disadvantage. In short, *a freeze of ICBMs and sea-based systems would be overwhelmingly in the United States' interest. . . .*
>
> What is disadvantageous to us, though, is the trend of the new weapons deployment by the Soviet Union, and the projected imbalance five years hence based on that trend. The relevant question to ask, therefore, is what the freeze prevents; where would we be by 1977 without a freeze?
>
> Considering the current momentum by the Soviet Union in both ICBMs and submarine-launched ballistic missiles, the ceiling set in the Interim Agreement can only be interpreted as a sound arrangement that makes a *major contribution to our national security.*

In an additional highly optimistic claim about the Kremlin's contribution to U.S. national security through SALT, Dr. Kissinger explained *how* we got into the predicament whereby we desperately needed an interruption in Soviet missile-buildup momentum, and *why* only an agreement with the Soviets could save us:

> As a result of decisions made in the 1960s, and not reversible within the timeframe of the projected agreement, there would be a numerical gap against us in the two categories of land and sea-based missile systems whether or not there was an agreement.
>
> *Without an agreement, the gap would steadily widen.*

Thus, Dr. Kissinger is saying that Robert Strange McNamara (who made the "decisions . . . in the 1960s") plunged us into a missile gap from which we are helpless to extricate ourselves, but that the "serious" gentlemen in the Kremlin have bailed us out of our predicament by entering into a SALT Agreement that will "make a major contribution to our national security" and that is "overwhelmingly in the United States' interest."

Dr. Kissinger knows that the Soviet Communist leadership has invested 15 years of time (since they produced the world's first ICBM in 1957) and some $300 billion of resources (wrung out of an economy less than half the magnitude of ours) in creating the present missile gap and in building the momentum to widen it to decisive proportions. How, then, can he believe that they would decide to bail the "capitalist imperialists" out of a potentially fatal predicament, make a major contribution to U.S. national security, and actually "freeze" the momentum of their nuclear arms buildup just several years short of attaining the decisive power to defeat the United States and gain control of the world?

Dr. Kissinger cannot believe that "good will" would motivate the men in the Kremlin to accept an agreement when the key provisions are "overwhelmingly in the United States' interest." Such a belief would be naive in the extreme, and certainly Dr. Kissinger is one of the most sophisticated theoreticians in the Western world. More specifically, he cannot believe in "good will" as the Soviet motivation because he has held a completely contradictory conviction at least since 1961 when, in his book *The Necessity for Choice*, he described the psychology of Communist leaders like this:

> Since everything depends on a correct understanding of these "objective factors" and the relation of forces they imply, "good will" and "good faith" are meaningless abstractions.[2]

Explaining further, he added:

> No member of the Soviet hierarchy—whatever his convictions—can advocate a program to his colleagues with the argument that he is promoting good will in the abstract.[3]

Dr. Kissinger was still holding fast to his realistic convictions about Soviet negotiations as late as his 1965 book, *The Troubled Partnership*, in which he wrote:

> No Soviet leader could make an agreement based on the proposition that he has been impressed by the personal qualities of a capitalist statesman.[4]

Of course, there is always the possibility that Kissinger does not consider himself a capitalist; and the additional possibility that the Politburo considers him neither a capitalist nor a statesman.

What Dr. Kissinger wants us to believe that he believes about Soviet motivation is this: a radically new relationship with the U.S.S.R. has been built up during the Nixon Administration that was brought to fruition in a "spectrum of agreements" at the Moscow Summit conferences in 1972. In this new relationship, the United States has conferred upon the Soviet Union a "vested interest" in sharing the wealth generated by U.S. industry, agriculture, technology, science, trade, and credits. In addition, Dr. Kissinger has thrown in a sophisticated sales pitch to the Kremlin leaders to convince them that they have far more to gain by choosing tremendous economic bird-in-the-hand benefits *with no risk* than by gambling for speculative gains by *assuming the catastrophic risks* of attempting the actual *use* of their nuclear superiority to attack or blackmail us.

What Dr. Kissinger has accomplished is the creation of a new and drastically different theory of deterrence against nuclear war, and the committal of U.S. security to this new theory. What he *hopes* he has accomplished is the acceptance of this theory by the Soviet Union. U.S. survival (and the lives of all Americans) are now staked primarily upon this theory instead of on our retaliatory strategic weapons.

For more than a decade, from the advent of the Kennedy Administration in January 1961 through June 1972, the U.S. strategic deterrent consisted of strategic nuclear weapons that were assumed to be capable of riding out even a massive enemy nuclear surprise attack and then striking back to wreak unacceptable damage against the aggressor's population, cities, industry, and agriculture. The theory was that the potential aggressor would be deterred from launching a nuclear war because of the defender's threat of retaliation with weapons capable of accomplishing "assured damage" or massive destruction. In the words of Henry Kissinger in *The Necessity for Choice,* the defending nation must possess enough invulnerable weapons, and a sufficiently credible will to use them in retaliation, so that:

> In weighing his self-interest, the potential aggressor must reach the conclusion the "deterrer" is seeking to induce.
> In other words, the penalties of aggression must outweigh its benefits.[5]

The pre-SALT I U.S. strategic deterrent was all "stick" and no "carrot." The new Kissinger "deterrent" substitutes a huge carrot for the big stick, retaining only a small stick. The carrot is the activating element of the deterrent, and the small stick is retained merely as a precaution to provide some element of risk to make the guaranteed no-risk carrot more appealing to Soviet decisionmakers.

This new theory changes the last eight words in the 1961 Kissinger theory of deterrence quoted above. Instead of saying, "the *penalties* of aggression must outweigh its benefits," Kissinger's new theory could be summed up like this: *The rewards of restraint* must outweigh the *gains by aggression.*

The decisive factor as to whether the deterrent will work, however, is still the same: how the potential aggressor "weighs his self-interest." Kissinger considers that he has taken care of this adequately by offering the Soviets very substantial "rewards of restraint"—not just one "carrot" on a one-shot basis, but an initially impressive and progressively abundant annual crop of "carrots."

Dr. Kissinger relies heavily upon having sweetened the "wide spectrum of agreements" with "enlightened self-interest" that should be valued by the Soviet leadership. His grand rationale of the SALT I Agreements and of the other relationships involved in creating a new era of mutual trust with the Soviet Union is replete with references to the "self interests" of the two superpowers, such as:

> We have . . . sought to move forward across a *broad range of issues* so

that progress in one area would add momentum to the progress in other areas.

We hoped the Soviet Union would acquire a stake in a wide spectrum of negotiations and that it would become convinced that *its best interests* would be served *if the entire process unfolded.* We have sought, in short, to create *a vested interest in mutual restraint.* . . .

We advocate these agreements not on the basis of trust, but on the basis of the *enlightened self-interests* of both sides.[6]

It is also significant that, in question-and-answer periods in all his SALT briefings, when asked about either the weakness of inspection provisions or the possibility of the Soviets violating the provisions, either openly or clandestinely, he invariably replied that our assurance lies in the fact that the Soviets recognize that abiding by the agreements is in their own "enlightened self-interest," and the fact that the Soviets entered into the agreements voluntarily attests to their recognition of their self-interest.

This is the answer to how Dr. Kissinger may have sincerely convinced himself, and then persuaded President Nixon, that—despite the massive and protracted investment the Soviets have made in developing strategic nuclear superiority—the Soviets were acting in their own self-interest when they signed the SALT I Agreements that (1) bail the United States out of our widening missile-gap predicament, (2) interrupt Soviet momentum in ongoing missile programs, and (3) are, in general, "overwhelmingly in the United States' interest."

This is also the answer to why neither Dr. Kissinger nor President Nixon is worried about weak inspection provisions, or possibilities that the Soviets might exploit loopholes or violate the agreements. These same answers show *why* Dr. Kissinger and President Nixon are *not* concerned about such things as the Soviet 4-to-1 missile throw-weight advantage (which so suddenly expanded to a 6-to-1 advantage within two years), or the wide-open gap permitting the Soviets to mass-produce and *deploy* additional hundreds or even thousands of modern mobile ICBMs (such as the SS-16).

Dr. Kissinger and Richard Nixon apparently convinced themselves that the new and revolutionary Kissinger theory of deterrence, i.e., making "the rewards of restraint" outweigh the gains of aggression, has persuaded Soviet rulers that their self-interest will be best served by *not using* against the United States whatever margin of strategic superiority they enjoy now or in the future.

Dr. Kissinger purported to believe that he has convinced the Soviet policymakers and planners that the fastest and surest road by which the U.S.S.R. can attain the status of the outstanding economic superpower is *only* by an active partnership with the United States, that is, by accepting a "vested interest" in sharing all our "economic growth" resources, especially our industrial, agricultural, electronic, fuel-production, and space technologies. This type of tangible assistance can be skimmed off *only* from a "going-concern" partner-nation—not from a nation of nuclear rubble or from a nation disrupted by military occupation.

Similarly, Dr. Kissinger and Richard Nixon purported to believe that—by an amalgam of the Kissinger theories on nuclear strategy *plus Dr. Kissinger's sales pitch*—they have persuaded the Kremlin bosses that their enlightened self-interest would not be served by accelerating the strategic arms race (as they legally can do and are doing under the SALT I Agreements). This particular belief, however, was blasted within six months of the SALT I signing, at least so far as Henry Kissinger was concerned. Of course, he may never have passed on to Richard Nixon the intelligence confirming the Soviet buildup in ICBMs which Defense Secretary James Schlesinger characterized in early 1974 as "staggering in size and depth."

These theories were accepted in their totality by Richard Nixon, and they became major determinants in the formulation of the grand strategy and national security policies of the United States. A short review of them is necessary, therefore, as a basis for making two critical estimates: (1) has the Kremlin seriously accepted them as a basis for Soviet strategic doctrine? and (2) can the survival of the United States and the lives of the American people safely be staked on the validity of the Kissinger theories by the Ford administration?

When we refer to the "Kissinger theories," we do not imply that he *originated* them. Most of the theories he advocates were originated by others and date back to the debates on strategy by the unilateral-disarmers in the 1957-1961 period. Several of these theories were basic to the defense policies of the McNamara era. They are relevant now because Henry Kissinger has made them the basis for the new U.S. national strategy that culminated in the 1972 summits in Moscow and Peking, and which he has carried over into the Ford administration.

The two crucial theories were more simply stated in the Nixon echo than in the Kissinger originals. In President Nixon's June 1, 1972, report explaining the Moscow agreements to the joint session of Congress, he asserted that the "landmark" Joint Declaration entitled "Basic Principles of Mutual Relations Between the United States and the U.S.S.R." provides a solid framework for the future development of better American-Soviet relations, and he presented this theory as the cornerstone of the "Basic Principles":

> They begin with the recognition that two nuclear nations, each of which has the power to destroy humanity, have no alternative but to coexist peacefully—because *in a nuclear war there would be no winners, only losers.*

The more sophisticated genesis of this theory is stated in Henry

Kissinger's 1965 book entitled *The Troubled Partnership,* in which he offered this statement of what he characterized as "the basic paradox of the nuclear age":

Power has never been greater; it has also never been less useful.[7]

In theorizing that strategic nuclear power is not *useful* power, Dr. Kissinger in one way goes somewhat further than Mr. Nixon's hyperbolic statement. Whereas Mr. Nixon asserted, in effect, that, if a nation tries to use nuclear power by starting a nuclear war, it cannot win and will end up a "loser," Dr. Kissinger questions whether nuclear power can even be "useful" in *threatening* a war, adding:

Though states have an unprecedented capacity to devastate their opponent, their threats to do so have only a limited credibility.

This is because the ability to destroy is not related to the ability to disarm—so that using one's nuclear arsenal indiscriminately against a major opponent guarantees only self destruction.[8]

The aphorism that, in nuclear war, "there can be no winners, only losers," is one of the oldest and most widely and least intelligently quoted of the nuclear age. The second basic Kissinger-Nixon theory has been less widely quoted, but it is now advanced to negate the critical effect of substantial imbalance in arms control agreements in general and the SALT I Agreements in particular. Mr. Nixon enunciated it repeatedly. In his "Address to the People of the Soviet Union" on Moscow television, he stated:

In an unchecked arms race between two great nations, there would be no winners, only losers.

Again, in his essay called "The Real Road to Peace," which was published in *U.S. News & World Report* on June 16, 1972, President Nixon explained his theory more fully:

The choice for both sides has really been whether to limit arms, or to have a runaway nuclear arms race—and in such a race, there would be no winners, only losers.

Neither the United States nor the Soviet Union would, over the long run, allow a situation to develop in which either would confront the other with the sort of overwhelming nuclear advantage which the United States held at the time of the 1962 Cuban missile crisis. To continue the nuclear arms spiral unchecked would set up a contest in which neither side could win, because neither would feel it could afford to let the other win.

Dr. Kissinger, in his rationale of the SALT pacts, uses both these theories. In effect, he asserts that the Kremlin bosses have come around to accepting his theory that nuclear power is not usable power. Here are the relevant excerpts from his June 15, 1972, briefing for the five congressional committees:

It would have seemed inconceivable even a generation ago that such power once gained could not be translated directly into advantage over one's opponent. But now both we and the Soviet Union have begun to find that *each increment of power does not necessarily represent an increment of usable political strength.*

With modern weapons, a potentially decisive advantage requires a change of such magnitude that the mere effort to obtain it can produce disaster. The simple tit-for-tat reaction to each other's programs of a decade ago is in danger of being overtaken by a more or less simultaneous and continuous process of technological advance, which opens more and more temptations for seeking decisive advantage.

A premium is put on striking first and creating a defense to blunt the other side's retaliatory capability. In other words marginal additions of power cannot be decisive. Potentially decisive additions are extremely dangerous, and the quest for them very destabilizing. . . .

All of this was in the President's mind as he mapped the new directions of American policy at the outset of this Administration. There was reason to believe that *the Soviet leadership might also be thinking along similar lines* as the repeated failure of their attempts to gain marginal advantage in local crises or in military competition underlined the limitation of the old policy approaches. . . .

Taking the longer perspective, what can we say has been accomplished?

First, it is clear that the agreement will enhance the security of both sides. No agreement which fails to do so could have been signed in the first place or stood any chance of lasting after it was signed. An attempt to gain a unilateral advantage in the strategic field must be self-defeating.

Thus Dr. Kissinger's twin theories are: (1) there are no winners, only losers, in a nuclear war, and (2) one side cannot even gain a decisive advantage in a nuclear arms race. These twin theories are the pivotal strategic concepts of the "underlying philosophy and specific perception of international reality" that he concedes were given priority over attaining "equitable or prudent" tactical solutions—that is, priority over specific provisions—in the SALT pacts "at each important turning point."

These two theories are employed by Dr. Kissinger not only as the philosophical underpinning of both SALT and his "carrot" theory of deterrence, but also to support his third theory: a unique concept of a classic balance of conventional military power in the pattern of the 19th century. If the nuclear genie can be lured back into the bottle and reliably imprisoned therein by nonusability theories, then what power is left to control the world? What else is there but conventional weapons? And how can peace be restored and maintained in a world in which conventional weapons are again the ultimate strategic power?

Dr. Kissinger's book entitled *A World Restored: Castlereagh, Metternich and Restoration of Peace, 1812-1822*[9] was published in 1957 but written, of course, before that crucial year in which the Soviets produced the first intercontinental ballistic missile, thus giving global range, and hence the potential of global control, to strategic nuclear weapons. Nevertheless, Dr. Kissinger's fascination with the "structure of peace" set up by the Congress of Vienna provided the model of a proposed somewhat similar structure tentatively presented in President Nixon's *State of the World Report* in February 1972.

Under the heading "The Philosophy of a New American Foreign Policy," the President's 1972 message, prepared of course by Dr. Kissinger, proclaimed:

> The end of the bipolar postwar world opens to this generation a unique opportunity to create a new and lasting structure of peace.

Various descriptions of this proposed new structure are dispersed throughout the 236 pages of the report, which is appropriately entitled "The Emerging Structure of Peace." President Nixon's own truncated and simpler statement of his concept of the new structure was stated informally and quoted in *Time* magazine on January 3, 1972:

> We must remember that the only time in the history of the world that we have had any extended period of peace is when there has been a balance of power. It is when one nation becomes infinitely more powerful in relation to its potential competitor that the danger of war arises.
>
> So I believe in a world in which the United States is powerful. I think it will be a safer world and a better world if we have a strong, healthy United States, Europe, Soviet Union, China, Japan, each balancing the other, not playing one against the other, an even balance.

Commenting on this in the July 1972 issue of *Foreign Affairs,* Alastair Buchan, Oxford University Professor of International Relations and Director of the International Institute for Strategic Studies in London, retorted that Nixon's statement about periods of peace "is historically untrue," and that a "pentagonal balance of power" produced only two periods of peace of about 40 years each between the battles of Waterloo and the Marne. As for the applicability of such a balance to present conditions, he commented:

> It assumes that, as in the 18th century, the five powers concerned have broadly the same range of resources at their disposal. This simply is not true today. The Soviet Union and the United States possess a degree of strategic, military, and economic resources which the other three partners do not.

Actually, the only relevance of the concept of the "pentagonal balance of power" at the present time is that this balance is urged by some as a countervailing power that, in some not-explained manner, might be able to offset massive Soviet advantages in strategic nuclear power that may be developed vis-a-vis the United States under the SALT I Agreements. It must be noted that the creator of the "pentagonal" concept (whom Alastair Buchan, C.B.E., refers to as "Mr. Nixon's Prince Metternich of the West Wing") does not himself make this argument. Unfortunately, however, many intelligent people have been taken in by it—especially by the attractive myth that President Nixon's Peking Summit resulted in at least a tacit assurance by Red China that, in a crisis, her growing nuclear power would be thrown into the strategic balance on our side and against the Soviet Union.

Even if we could afford to gamble our survival on the aging Mao-Chou regime (1) surviving in power and (2) abiding by such a verbal agreement—despite the fact that this would make them targets of Soviet supermissiles—the Chinese contribution would be negligible (unless they themselves initiated its use as a catalyst or against the United States).

Within the five-year timeframe of the SALT I Interim Agreement, the Red Chinese may be able to develop an intercontinental ballistic missile delivery capability of about 100-150 missiles ranging from 15 to 30 megatons in single warheads. Few of these missiles would be in hardened silos, however; so all those that were not mobile would be vulnerable to a preventive or a preemptive strike by the Soviet Union unless they develop an advanced satellite early warning system and a launch-on-warning strategy.

If the Red Chinese opted to be on the U.S. side, they would be tied down to our no-first-strike-retaliation-only strategy, which we cannot change because we have no missiles with effective counterforce capability. Thus, although they might have 100-150 ICBMs in their peacetime inventory available for a first-strike, they could not count on having any missiles survive a strike by the Soviet Union, unless they are mobile or protected by satellite early warning. Therefore, they could contribute nothing in this timeframe to the credibility of the U.S. strategic deterrent.

Using their newly developed ICBMs as a first-strike threat against the United States, however, they would have an all-too-probable capability of killing up to 50 to 100 million Americans. The full 12-site Safeguard ABM system could have saved substantially all those hostages, but the SALT I Treaty blocks us from defending any city except Washington, D.C., and guarantees Red Chinese as well as Soviet missiles a free ride to destroy all other U.S. metropolitan areas. Because 73 percent of the U.S. population is urban as against only 15 percent for the Chinese, and because of their extensive civil defense system, our vastly greater missile capability is not reliably effective as a strategic deterrent against them.

The relevant point here, however, is simply that the Kissinger-Nixon "pentagonal balance of power" theory can in no effective way diminish the Soviet strategic nuclear threat against the United States that can be built up through SALT I gaps and loopholes. Just as Chinese strategic nuclear power can add nothing in the relevant timeframe to our side of the equation, neither can the other two nations of the "pentagonal balance." Japan is not a nuclear power, nor is Western Europe, as such. The nuclear capability of England and France is negligible compared to the United States or the U.S.S.R., and will be less even than Red China's by the end of the five-year timeframe. In any event, England and France could not credibly threaten the use of nuclear power against the Soviet Union because the Soviets have 800 to 1,000 intermediate- and medium-range strategic missiles operational and zeroed in on NATO and French targets—plus 700 strategic medium bombers available to saturate the NATO area.

Can conventional military power balance nuclear power? Not even in the highest flights of the fantasies of the unilateral-disarmament intellectuals. This single scenario illustrates the unbridgeable chasm between nuclear and nonnuclear power:

> The highly placed but anonymous assigner of Impossible Missions tapes this instruction (which will self-destruct five seconds after play-back):
>
> "One of our B-52 bombers is capable of delivering in a single flight, on a single day, two 24-megaton hydrogen bombs—a total of 48 megatons—on Nation X.
>
> "The same bomber aircraft is normally capable of delivering in a single flight, on a single day, 27½ tons of conventional bombs; but we will bring this bomb-delivery capability up to 48 tons for this mission.
>
> "Your mission is to pilot a B-52 on one bombing trip per day, including Sundays, against Nation X. You will carry a full load of conventional bombs—and keep flying until you have dropped explosive power equivalent to what you could deliver in just one mission *if* you carried hydrogen bombs with 48 megatons of explosive power."

How long would it take for completion of this truly Impossible Mission? How long would you guess? The average answer given by non-experts varies from one to five years. The actual answer is 2,739 years. If the MI pilot had started flying his daily bombing run at the time of Christ, he would still have more than 700 years to go.

Of course, this scenario is based on an oversimplification. Mega-tonnage is a measure of nuclear explosive power based on the equivalent explosive force of millions of tons of tri-nitro-toluene (TNT). Explosive power is not the equivalent of destructive power, which involves computation with a complex of variables such as type of target, accuracy of delivery (CEP), and even weather conditions. But megatonnage is the most convenient and meaningful measure of fire-power in the nuclear-space age. *Tactical* nuclear power, measured in kilotons, is *thousands* of times greater than conventional weapons power; *strategic* nuclear power is *millions* of times greater.

This disposes of the argument—naive, but widely accepted—that having Red China on our side of the military balance (if we ever do) is a brilliant accomplishment that enables us to "play off" the Communist giants against each other, and that the 800 million Chinese, with potentially the largest number of fighting men, can swing the balance back from its sharp tilt in favor of the Soviet Union. Soviet strategic doctrine calls for winning a war against the Chinese without ever engaging the armies in combat. A small fraction of the Soviet strategic forces could destroy the total effective military capability of the People's Republic, both conventional and nuclear, in a matter of hours.

This is also true as to the military capabilities of Western Europe and Japan, the other two members of the Kissinger-Nixon five-sided "balance of power." It is clear that the "pentagonal balance of power" concept, therefore, does not provide any strategic support either for SALT or for the Kissinger doctrine of deterrence by "carrots" instead of by retaliatory weapons.

Thus, only the first two of the three Kissinger-Nixon theories advanced as the philosophical basis for SALT remain as relevant. Unless the theories of nonusability of nuclear power and nonwinnability of a nuclear arms race are both (1) strategically valid, and (2) accepted as such by the Soviet Union, exploitation by the Soviets of the open gaps and concealed loopholes of the SALT I Agreements can be potentially fatal to the survival of the United States. The most meaningful practical analysis of these two aspects of the SALT I Agreements requires a combination of evaluation of the substance and specifics of the agreements, together with a *testing* of the theories in the context of the diametrically opposite alternatives open to the Soviets: (1) exploiting SALT I, or (2) accepting the benefits of the Kissinger "carrot" doctrine of deterrence on a permanent rather than an interim basis.

On this point of testing, Richard Nixon cogently concluded his essay entitled "The Real Road to Peace": "The final test of a foreign policy is whether it works." Unfortunately, however, and probably even tragically, when the foreign policy amounts to putting into actual and irrevocable practice a novel and totally untried doctrine of deterrence against nuclear attack, the "final test" can come too late to save the 210 million Americans whose lives are staked on "whether it works." Before risking our lives on this "final test," the untried doctrine should be subjected to the most hard-nosed, objective, nonpolitical, expert analysis possible, in order to make an advance judgment about two vital questions: "Can it work?" and, if the answer to that is affirmative, "How good are the chances that it *will* work?"

These are not theoretical questions. It will not do to say merely that the theory *can* work as a theory; the question is whether it *can* work *in practice*. For example, if the Soviets have already made a firm decision to adopt a course of action that will circumvent SALT I and *prevent* the Kissinger carrot-type deterrent from working successfully, the answer is that it *cannot* work. There is much evidence that the Kremlin leaders have in fact made such a decision. There is a very substantial indication that this evidence has been identified by U.S. intelligence; but there is also evidence that Dr. Kissinger and other administration officials are (1) covering for the Soviets and (2) withholding from the American people the dimensions and imminence of the new Soviet threat. In each month since the signing of SALT I, the *balance of probabilities* has been swinging more heavily against the success of the new "carrot" deterrent. It is essential to analyze this evidence.

17

Upon ratification by the United States Senate on August 3, 1972, the SALT I Treaty banning defense against ballistic missiles became "the supreme law of the land." As such, it is more authoritative than any law passed by Congress and signed by the President. *Laws* must conform to the Constitution, but *treaties* are not so limited. Not even the United States Supreme Court can challenge the legality or validity of the SALT I Treaty. By virtue of the supremacy accorded treaties by the Constitution, the provisions of the SALT I Treaty will reverse the most fundamental function and duty entrusted to the government of the United States by that same Constitution.

For nearly two centuries the federal government's greatest power and highest responsibility to the nation, the states, and the people has been to "provide for the common defense." The new function of the government will be to execute the SALT I Treaty's guarantee that this nation will *refrain from providing for the common defense.* Explicitly and specifically the treaty prohibits our defending against the most massive and imminent threat of total destruction ever faced by any nation in past world history, and one of far greater magnitude than any possible threat facing the Soviet Union today.

The only defense permitted us will be uncommon, indeed, and highly discriminatory. The original SALT I Treaty limited us to two missile defense sites of 100 ABM launchers each. The 1974 Moscow Summit Protocol cut this in half, to one site with no more than 100 ABM launchers. We are given the "option" of moving this one site with its 100 launchers from Grand Forks, North Dakota, where it gives limited protection to 150 U.S. Minuteman ICBMs, to Washington, D.C., where it would give limited protection to perhaps one million people in that area, but leave the other 209 million Americans (or 99½ percent of our population) totally unprotected by any active defenses against nuclear incineration. But this 1974 Protocol "option" is illusory because it would require the scrapping of a brand new billion-dollar installation and the expenditure of additional hundreds of millions of dollars in the Washington, D.C., area; and the defense which would result from either option is also illusory because 100 ABM launchers could be saturated by the multiple warheads of fewer than 15 Soviet missiles.

The Moscow Treaty's prohibition against defense thus ensures enemy offensive missiles a "free ride" into our country. To exploit this "free ride"—a highly descriptive term used repeatedly by Dr. Henry Kissinger—the Soviets have a delivery capability of 2,359 offensive missiles that we know of; they may have even more. These missiles can rain upon our undefended nation explosive power equivalent to more than 12 thousand *million* tons of TNT. Naive babblers of the "overkill" theory would neatly assign about 57 tons of explosive power to each of the unprotected 210 million Americans. Actually, explosive power cannot be that equally distributed by missiles, but that really doesn't matter because hydrogen warheads do not kill by explosion alone. With so many of them exploding, there would be more than enough radioactive fallout to kill most of those who survive the explosions.

Statistics, however, cannot possibly convey an understanding of the human risks imposed by the SALT Treaty's prohibition of defense against missiles. As Joseph Stalin once explained to Winston Churchill about the way he "wiped out" some seven million *kulaks* (peasant farmers) in the 1930s, "the death of a man can be a tragedy, but the death of a million is merely a statistic."

To introduce the human and personal factor, just imagine that you and your family have been selected by the government to be turned over to the Kremlin to be held as hostages. How would you take the news that the Politburo bosses would hold the unchallengeable power of life or death over you? Since the Senate ratified the SALT I ABM Treaty, 210 million Americans have become helpless hostages to the Kremlin for a period of "unlimited duration," as expressly provided in the treaty.

Even Senator William Fulbright, chairman of the Senate Foreign Relations Committee, conceded the accuracy of the term "hostage" to describe our status under the SALT I Treaty, but he tried to make it sound more palatable by assuming that there will be effective mutuality:

> The anti-ballistic missile treaty before us has in it the central fact that the United States and the Soviet Union are indeed each other's hostage for reasonable behavior in the nuclear era.

Is Senator Fulbright's assumption valid that *both* sides are hostage to the other? There is no question—considering the present massive tilt of the strategic military balance in favor of the Soviet Union, and the opportunities under SALT I that the Soviets are already exploiting to continue their strategic buildup—that the SALT I Treaty and Interim Agreement make the United States and our entire population hostages of the Soviet Union. The question of national life or death, however, is: do *we* have "sufficient" strategic nuclear power under SALT I to hold the Soviet Union and its population as *our* hostages?

To reach a reliable answer, we must consider the theory on which the SALT I Anti-Defense Treaty is based. This theory is known as the "Mutual Assured Destruction" concept.

Dr. Donald G. Brennan, Hudson Institute arms control specialist, consultant to the U.S. Arms Control and Disarmament Agency, and former adviser to Dr. Henry Kissinger on arms control matters, has given an accurate description of this theory:

> The concept of mutual assured destruction provides one of the few instances in which the obvious acronym for something yields at once the appropriate description; for it, that is, a Mutual Assured Destruction posture as a goal is, almost literally, mad. MAD.[1]

Even if the SALT I Agreements themselves were near-perfect in draftsmanship and substance, and in inspection and enforcement provisions, they could attain no greater merit or validity than the concept on which they are based.

The MAD assumption is incredibly dangerous and highly immoral, even under postulated ideal conditions. It becomes suicidal, however, if the hypothetical element of "mutuality" is absent initially or subject to erosion later. The theoretical basis of the concept is that mutual deterrence against the launching of a strategic nuclear attack is best accomplished by making the entire population of both sides completely vulnerable to nuclear blast and incineration. The theoretical objective is to hand the entire population over as helpless hostages in order to guarantee against the launching of an attack. The hundreds of millions of hostages are made deliberately vulnerable by each side's binding itself to the other by the provision that it will provide no active defense for its own people (other than an agreed optional token defense for that small fraction of the population living in the area of the two capital cities).

This guaranteed absence of active defense assures—or is supposed to assure—a "free ride" for each side's missiles, in order to maximize both sides' ability to incinerate human beings by the hundreds of millions.

The mutuality element is supposed to cover *both* the assured vulnerability of the respective populations *and* the attack-survivable capability of striking back and accomplishing the destruction of an attacking side's population. In reality, the capability to strike back after attack, and destroy the attacker's population, depends upon not one but both of two factors in combination: (1) the aggressor's having actually abandoned defending its population, that is, not having circumvented either the letter or the spirit of the ABM Treaty; and (2) the defender's possession of a retaliatory missile force capable of surviving the most massive surprise attack that the attacking side could launch.

To make the MAD concept work—even in theory—each side should be capable of accomplishing "unacceptable" and *something like equal damage* on the other, regardless of which strikes first.

Mutuality disappears, therefore, if either side has a striking force more-than-marginally more powerful than the other, or if either side has a powerful counterforce capability sufficient to give credibility to a full or preclusive first-strike capability, or if either side circumvents the ABM Treaty. If mutuality disappears, then the leadership of the defender nation is in the position of having set up its own people as undefended and helpless victims of calculated mass-murder. Of course, no leadership would do such a thing *intentionally* or even *knowingly;* but to the 210 million hostages, it is important this not be done at all.

Even if the SALT I Agreements worked perfectly in setting up the postulated conditions for the MAD theory, the theory itself contains three built-in self-defeating dangers of shocking magnitude.

1. No theory of deterrence is 100-percent reliable. If deterrence should fail for *any* reason, MAD assures the absolute maximum of civilian casualties—not merely in the millions, but in the hundreds of millions.

2. MAD assures that such a large proportion of the defender's population will be destroyed (far more than half) that *no rational purpose* could be served by the defender-nation's surviving leadership (if any) *even attempting* to launch a retaliatory strike. It is highly incredible that a surviving U.S. leadership would order such a wildly irrational act as the killing of millions of innocent Russian civilians (who bore no responsibility for the attack) with no purpose other than revenge. As the deterrent value of a retaliatory force depends upon *both* its surviving-destruction-capability *and* the credibility of its actually being launched, MAD in practical operation will probably fatally degrade the deterrence it was supposed to strengthen.

3. The MAD-established vulnerability of the population does thereby promote the theoretical purpose of assuring that a retaliatory strike, even by a missile force that had been massively damaged by the aggressor's first strike, would kill an "unacceptable" percentage of the attacker's population. Conversely, however, it also inevitably assures that the defender's retaliatory force will be vulnerable to massive destruction, thereby reducing its power to inflict destruction on the

aggressor, and consequently degrading its advance value as a deterrent.

To be sure of not becoming accessories-before-the-fact to the mass murder of its own people, the leadership of a nation with no effective counterforce capability (and hence no credible or preclusive first-strike capability), can reasonably enter into a MAD-type arrangement *only* if it secures reliable protection against the other side's having or developing a credible first-strike capability during the term of the arrangement. This can be done reliably only by including in the agreements adequate provision for comprehensive and unhampered on-site inspection. Even inspection provisions would be of no avail unless the agreements themselves are iron-clad—in substance and mechanics and draftsmanship—against development by any potential aggressor of a first-strike capability. Analysis of the SALT I Agreements must be made on the basis of these requirements.

From the strategic point of view, our national survival and the lives of our 210 million hostages depend on whether the two SALT I Agreements do in fact contain provisions fully insuring the existence and preservation of mutuality. Without actual mutuality, we must recognize that, whereas the MAD arrangement commits us to having *no defense* for our 210 million hostages, it would *also* subject us to having *no effective deterrent* either. In this case, the United States would have no rational alternative to surrender, and we would be totally dependent upon the mercy of the Kremlin for the opportunity to do so.

As it turned out, the Soviet Communist negotiators were not the most generous and fair-minded in the world, and the U.S. negotiators were not the most prudent, prescient, and competent. Even if they had been, however, the drafting of an anti-ABM treaty that would give reasonable protection to the 210 million American hostages would be a near-impossible task. Two major elements of the absolutely essential mutuality of a MAD arrangement simply cannot be controlled by agreement.

The first factor is that of geography. The Soviets have a national area of nearly 8½ million square miles in which to disperse population, cities, industries, and weapons. The United States has only 3½ million square miles. The strategic result is, as summarized by Defense Secretary Melvin Laird in testimony before the Senate Foreign Relations Committee in April 1969, that the United States needs to be able to deliver six times as many warheads as the Russians in order to have destruction "parity" with them. It would take, he reported, some 1,200 one-megaton warheads to destroy 45 percent of Russia's population, while the Soviets would need only 200 warheads of identical size to wipe out 55 percent of our population.

The second factor that militates against the effective "mutuality" of a MAD arrangement is the Soviets' splendid passive defense in-being. The most recent authoritative comparison of U.S. versus U.S.S.R. passive defense, the primary element of which is known as civil defense (CD), was set forth by Donald G. Brennan in his landmark article in *National Review,* June 23, 1972, entitled "When SALT Hit the Fan." Here is the relevant excerpt:

> There is probably another sense in which the ABM Treaty is a strategic non sequitur. It is intended by its American proponents to institutionalize a permanent MAD posture, but it is actually doubtful that, as matters now stand, the United States has an assured destruction capability (measured by standard criteria) against the Soviets, in view of their civil defense program.
>
> The Soviet Government has declared that their CD program could limit Soviet fatalities in an all-out war with the United States to perhaps 6 percent of their population, which would be substantially less than the fatalities they suffered in World War II. American students of the Soviet CD program agree that this estimate is reasonable. In contrast, current Soviet forces could probably destroy 60 percent of the American population with high confidence, given our lack of CD preparations. Thus it appears that the current assured destruction capabilities are not exactly mutual.

The Soviet civil defense capability of strategic evacuation of cities is itself a pivotal and staggering advantage. They have spent more than 10 years in training and practice, and millions of rubles on instruction books and education of the populace. With a first-strike capability and strategy, they are in control of the timing of an attack. As a result, it is authoritatively calculated that, if they executed their strategic evacuation plans, we could inflict a total of only a few million fatalities; moreover, we could accomplish this much *only if* (1) our entire strategic retaliatory force survived the Soviet attack or were fired on warning, (2) all our missiles were launched against Soviet population targets, and (3) none of our weapons were intercepted by Soviet ABM systems.

Even without resorting to strategic evacuation, the Soviets have enormous advantages in their shelter program. Dr. William Kintner, Director of the University of Pennsylvania Foreign Policy Research Institute, estimates that they can protect fully half their urban population in shelters that will withstand an overpressure of 25 pounds per square inch (psi). The Moscow subway system was especially designed to serve as a combination fallout and blast shelter. This means that we would need a 20-megaton warhead to do as much damage to their

25-psi-sheltered population as they could do to our substantially un-sheltered population with 1-megaton warheads. We do not happen to have any deliverable 20-megaton warheads.

Our Poseidon MIRVed individual warheads, on which many are blithely relying for deterrence, are rated at between 40 and 50 kilotons. That is, they have about 1/400 the explosive power of a 20-megaton warhead. They can hardly be considered effective "city-busters." The Department of Defense estimate has been that it would require three 50-kiloton warheads to destroy a small city of 100,000 population. A dozen would be required for a city of half a million people; if that city had the protection of 25-psi shelters, only a small fraction of the people would be killed.

On April 13, 1972, nuclear scientist Dr. Edward Teller was asked the question on television, "If the Soviets launch a surprise nuclear attack against the United States, what would be the result?" He replied:

> The question is when. Right now, they could do terrible damage. In a few years, if present trends continue, it is practically certain that it will be the end of the United States. The United States will not exist—not as a state, not as a power, not as an idea. I think that more than 50 percent of our people would be killed. I believe that the Soviets could so behave that there would be very few casualties in Russia because we would not have forces enough left to retaliate. They have excellent defenses: air defenses, missile defenses, civil defenses. It is possible that, in a few years, we shall be at the mercy of the Soviet Union, unless present trends change.

These difficulties—or near-impossibilities—in drafting an antidefense treaty that would give fair and rational protection to the U.S. population, and not set us up as helpless hostages to the Kremlin while the Soviet population is substantially home free, do not mean that we should not enter into any type of arms control agreement with the Soviets. It merely means that our policymakers and SALT planners took the worst possible route for us. The effort should have been to build up defense and reduce expenditures on offensive weapons. As the advocates of rational, rather than MAD, arms control put it, U.S. representatives should be more interested in living Americans than dead Russians. Nobel prizewinner Dr. Eugene P. Wigner said it tersely on June 10, 1972: "It would have been better if each nation was assured that the other could not destroy it."

But here is what they did. The substance of the SALT I Treaty is stated in Article I, Section 2:

> 2. Each party undertakes not to deploy ABM systems for a defense of the territory of its country and not to provide a base for such a defense, and not to deploy ABM systems for defense of an individual region except as provided in Article III of this treaty.

Article III allows for a limited defense of not more than 100 ABM launchers and 100 interceptor missiles for each of the capital cities, Moscow and Washington, and a second limited defense of the same numbers of "one ABM system deployment area" in each country. The 1974 Moscow Summit Protocol amends Article III to permit only one of these two defense objectives.

Other provisions attempt to limit the deployment or conversion of radars for ABM, to prevent the conversion of air-defense missiles (SAMs) to ABM capability, and to define ABM radars and ABM interceptor missiles. A highly significant provision (especially because it has no parallel in the *offensive* missile provisions in the Interim Agreement) prohibits each party from transferring to other states or "deploying outside its national territory, ABM systems or their components limited by this treaty."

Then there are the inspection—or, more exactly, the "no-inspection"—provisions of Article XII. No on-site inspection is permitted. Under Section 1, each party is generously allowed to "use national technical means of verification at its disposal in a manner consistent with generally recognized principles of international law." This relegates us primarily and almost exclusively to satellite and electronic reconnaissance.

In an attempt to prop up this sole means of "verification," each side in Section 2 agrees not to interfere with the other's "national technical means." In Section 3 each side agrees not to use "deliberate concealment methods which impede verification" by such means. But the sentence immediately following this in Section 3 is the most intriguing: "This obligation shall not require changes in current construction, assembly, conversion, or overhaul practices." This can mean nothing other than, if one side (guess which) is "currently" engaged in practices of deliberate concealment of construction, assembly, conversion, or overhaul, it need not change its concealment "practices."

Because the arithmetic of the SALT I ABM Treaty (in contrast to that of the Interim Agreement) does not on its face give the Soviets superiority over the United States, it has escaped much of the criticism and scrutiny focused on the offensive missile limitations. It was accorded the unanimous approval of Senator Fulbright's disarmament-minded Senate Foreign Relations Committee. Not surprisingly, Chairman Fulbright's only expressed concern about the SALT I Agreements was that—because of the administration's proposal for development of the B-1 strategic bomber and the Trident submarine (although actual deployment is scheduled for years after the initial five-year period of the Interim Agreement)—the men in the Kremlin might be suspicious of the "sincerity" of the United States in signing the agreements. Although "puzzled" and "worried" about U.S. actions, Senator Fulbright never expressed worry over the motives or actions of the Soviets.

No one should question the "sincerity" or, more accurately, the acute eagerness, of the Kremlin in seeking the anti-ABM Treaty. Senator Henry Jackson predicted, as far back as 1968, that the Soviets would never sit down to strategic arms limitation negotiations unless and until the United States actually started work on an ABM system. His analysis was completely confirmed by this admission made by Dr. Kissinger in the question-and-answer period of his June 15, 1972, White House briefing for the members of five congressional committees:

> I would think it probable . . . that we could not have negotiated the limitations on offensive weapons if it had not been linked to the limitations on defensive weapons and to their desire of stopping the deployment of the ABM system.
>
> So, what drove these negotiations for the first year was their desire to limit our ABM deployment. And it was not until we insisted that we would not agree to an ABM treaty without offensive limitations that they reluctantly included the offensive limitations.

Unfortunately and somewhat mysteriously, no one on the U.S. side expressed any worry over just *why* the Kremlin had developed such an overriding "desire to limit our ABM deployment." It is no answer to say that they wanted to avert—as the disarmament lobby delights in phrasing it—"another upward spiral in the deadly nuclear arms race." The Kremlin staged its ABM warhead and weapons-effect tests way back in 1961 and 1962. They began deploying their first generation ABM systems in 1963, and are now working on their fourth generation (that we know of). By the time of the SALT I ABM Treaty, they were ahead of us by some six years in actual deployment experience, and it will be eight years by the time our first site is operational at Grand Forks. If the Soviets did not want an ABM race, they needed to restrain only themselves.

What, then, was the realistic motivation of the Soviets in their burning "desire" to stop U.S. ABM deployment? Prior to the 1972 Moscow Summit, the U.S. Safeguard ABM system was specifically designed *not* to protect any of our people, but *only* our Minuteman retaliatory missile force. There is one logical answer: the Soviets have an investment of the equivalent of some $30 billion in the research, development, production, silo digging and hardening, and deployment of their force of SS-9 missiles and their new SS-18s.

This force has only one rational use: to destroy the U.S. Minuteman retaliatory missiles. With their huge warhead explosive power of some 25 to 50 or more megatons each, or the equivalent in multiple warheads, the Soviets have a tailormade capability of digging out and wiping out our Minuteman missiles—*if*, that is, the Soviet missiles are not intercepted and destroyed by ABM interceptor missiles. With an investment of such magnitude—and with a strategic doctrine based on this counterforce capability—the Soviets did not want us to have enough ABMs to frustrate the purpose of the SS-9s and SS-18s.

Without keeping this overriding Soviet purpose in mind, the realistic effect of the SALT I ABM Treaty simply cannot be deduced from its provisions. This purpose was decisive of the character of the loopholes. In the Interim Agreement restricting some elements of some types of offensive missiles, ordinary common-contract-variety loopholes met the Soviet purpose. In the ABM area, however, the United States was beginning a production and deployment momentum. Thus the Soviet loopholes had to take on a new sophistication: they had to be fabricated to stop the U.S. momentum dead in its tracks *without* blocking the Soviets' own expanding program. The loopholes, therefore, had to open only on one-way streets, going the Soviets' way. This is exactly what happened.

1. *Asymmetric advantages.* The operating area of the in-being Moscow ABM system encompasses the sites of 300 or more Soviet ICBM launchers. The population of Moscow is more than seven million. A great proportion of the Soviet industrial and scientific complex is in the Moscow region. The Kremlin is in Moscow, and hence so are the members of the Politburo of the CPSU and the Central Committee.

Thus, whereas the single U.S. ABM site at Grand Forks, North Dakota, protects only 150 ICBMs, the Soviet Moscow ABM site protects: (1) at least twice as many ICBMs; (2) more than seven million people (the U.S. site protects almost zero people); (3) vital and massive industrial and scientific installations and facilities (the U.S. site protects no such installations); (4) the Soviet National Command Authority; and (5) the members of the political high command of the USSR—the Politburo and Central Committee. The latter is especially significant because, if a massive nuclear strike were delivered on the United States, these men, rather than the Russian people, would be the rational targets for U.S. retaliation.

2. *Reload Capability.* The characteristics of presently operational ABM systems, plus the Soviets' traditional compulsion to circumvent the spirit while scrupulously adhering to the letter of an agreement, plus their superior skill in draftsmanship, have opened substantial and inviting one-way loopholes through the reload potential.

The ABM systems that the treaty and the 1974 Protocol permit to each side are each limited to "no more than 100 ABM launchers and no more than 100 ABM interceptor missiles *at launch sites.*" In addition, Article V, Section 2 is generally understood to prohibit development of reload capability. This is crucial to mutuality in "assured vulnerability."

What Article V actually provides is simply this:

2. Each party undertakes not to develop, test, or deploy ABM launchers for launching more than one ABM interceptor missile at a time from each launcher, nor to modify deployed launchers to provide them with such a capability, nor to develop, test or deploy *automatic or semiautomatic or other similar systems for rapid reload of ABM launchers.*

Note that what is prohibited is not "reload" capability, but "rapid reload" capability *that is similar to automatic or semiautomatic systems.* It would be an entirely legitimate interpretation for the Soviets to contend that the treaty did *not* prohibit any reload capability less "rapid" than semiautomatic.

By no coincidence, the presently deployed ABM launchers in the Moscow system have exactly that type of permissible reload capability. The only other restriction against reloads is the restriction to 100 interceptor missiles at "launch sites." The limits of "launch sites" are nowhere defined. An "ABM deployment area," however, is expressly defined as "having a radius of 150 kilometers," but the express and specific use of the different term "launch site" when setting a limit on the number of reload missiles, indicates that something other than "ABM deployment area" was meant. The term "launch site" could reasonably be related to the immediate area around individual launchers—say a radius of 50 to 100 yards—and the reload missiles could legally be stored just outside that limit. Fast mechanical means of moving the stored reload missiles to the launcher could legally be provided. The only requirement for legality would be that the operation be slower than "semiautomatic"—and semiautomatic is very fast, indeed.

If the Soviets should choose to take the clandestine route instead of the technical-interpretation route, they could "develop" the necessary mechanical equipment for automatic or semiautomatic reload, store them in warehouses, and have them available for speedy installation on the already deployed launchers. Or, without a violation of the treaty, if they have already "developed" a prototype rapid-reload system, they could manufacture the reload systems in large numbers and store them, ready for fast, surprise deployment. The prohibitions expressly relate only to development, test, or deployment—not production. Neither of these programs could be detected by U.S. satellite reconnaissance.

3. *Upgrading of SAMs.* By the time of the 1972 SALT Treaty, the Soviet Union already had operational the most extensive integrated air defense network the world has ever known. They have 25 times

as many operational radars as the United States, so that they can detect enemy aircraft or missiles coming in from any direction. They have deployed a force of more than 10,000 surface-to-air missiles (SAMs), whereas the United States cut back to 500 in 1972 and to zero in 1974.

More important, between 1,000 and 2,000 of their 10,000 SAMs are SA-5s, which can reach to a 100,000-foot altitude and whose range is estimated to be more than 100 miles. The entire SA-5 force, therefore, has the capability of intercepting and shooting down missiles, as well as aircraft. All they need in order to become an effective anti-ballistic-missile system is to be connected into an appropriate radar network.

In a *Washington Report* of November 5, 1971, Dr. Stefan T. Possony of the Hoover Institution stated:

> . . . the SA-5 has the high altitude required for missile interception. And as soon as about six additional Henhouse radars are completed—by 1973 or 1974—the Tallinn line could be used for antimissile defense. Hence, by the mid-1970s, the U.S.S.R. could have about 2,000 ABM launchers.

There is no disagreement among experts that the SA-5 missiles *could* be given ABM capability. Dr. William Schneider, former military analyst at the Hudson Institute, is one of those who believe that the far more numerous Soviet SA-2 SAMs also have an ABM potential. In a study entitled "A Program for American Survival, 1973-1978" published in 1971 by the American Conservative Union, he gave this chilling report:

> A new antiaircraft missile, the SA-5 Griffon, is widely deployed along the so-called Tallinn line in the northwestern part of the Soviet Union. Particular emphasis is focused on the SA-5 and the SA-2 because their "footprint" [their area of effective attack] could, with appropriate radar support, pose a threat to U.S. ICBMs; *i.e.,* the SA-5 and SA-2 appear to be "upgradeable" to the ABM role.
>
> There are about 8,000 SA-2, and 1,000 SA-5 launchers, all with a reload capability. If it became feasible for the Soviets to employ Henhouse and Doghouse ABM radars, they would have a very formidable ABM capability indeed.

It therefore appears that, if the Soviets have operational or under construction enough radars with ABM capability, and have made or can make the necessary "net" connections and interconnections, instead of having an ABM capability of 100 interceptor missiles, they can have a force of missiles capable of intercepting and shooting down many hundreds of U.S. ICBMs or SLBMs. The United States has no SAMs with ABM capabilities, and only 1/25 of the number of radars that the Soviets have operational.

Unfortunately, it is a near-certainty that the Soviets have or will have amply sufficient numbers of high performance radars of all types to do the job. Henhouse, their longest-range phased-array ABM tracking-system radar, has an unambiguous missile search-and-track range of 3,200 nautical miles. Most of them are between 50 and 90 feet tall and at least 1,000 feet long. An official report, however, confirms that one may be a half-mile long and another is reported to be 6,000 feet long. They have track-while-scan capabilities that enable them to track a number of targets while searching for others, all of which they can hand off later to the Doghouse network that has a range of 1,500 nautical miles, and which in turn can hand off to the site radars for discrimination and launch control.

The disposition and operation of the extensive Soviet radar network controlling the SA-7 Galosh ABM system deployed around Moscow, which President Lyndon Johnson revealed to the U.S. public in 1967, is now being upgraded with a new generation of ABM interceptor missiles with increased capability.[2] From the scope and range of this radar system, the potential for connection with the ICBM defense site allowed by the SALT Treaty, and for interconnection with the Tallinn line SA-5 system, is obvious.

In a purported attempt to prevent circumvention of the original limit of a total of 200 antimissile missiles for each party, the treaty itself (as distinguished from the four addenda of "interpretations") provides:

Article VI

To enhance assurance of the effectiveness of the limitations on ABM systems and their components provided by the treaty, each party undertakes:

(a) not to give missiles, launchers, or radars, other than ABM interceptor missiles, ABM launchers, or ABM radars, capabilities to counter strategic ballistic missiles or their elements in flight trajectory, and not to test them in an ABM mode; and

(b) not to deploy in the future radars for early warning of strategic ballistic missile attack except at locations along the periphery of its national territory and oriented outward.

Article VII

Subject to the provisions of this treaty, modernization and replacement of ABM systems or their components may be carried out.

Article VIII

ABM systems or their components in excess of the numbers or outside the areas specified in this treaty, as well as ABM systems or their components prohibited by this treaty, shall be destroyed or dismantled under agreed procedures within the shortest possible agreed period of time.

These provisions purportedly intending to prevent "upgrading" or conversion, and to provide for the destruction of ABM systems or components in excess of or prohibited by the treaty, must be read in relation to the complex provisions regarding radars.

Article III

Each party undertakes not to deploy ABM systems or their components except that:

(a) . . . on the party's national capital, a party may deploy: . . . (2) ABM radars within no more than six ABM complexes, the area of each complex being circular and having a diameter of no more than three kilometers; and

(b) . . . [at each party's ICBM-defense deployment area], a party may deploy: . . . (2) two large phased-array ABM radars comparable in potential to corresponding ABM radars operational or under construction on the date of the signature of the treaty in an ABM system deployment area containing ICBM silo launchers, and (3) no more than 18 ABM radars each having a potential less than the potential of the smaller of the above-mentioned two large phased-array ABM radars.

As would be expected in dealing with such a highly complex attempt to control evasion, the above-quoted articles of the treaty were the subject of numerous attempts at "Agreed Interpretations" and "Common Understandings," as well as of additional "Unilateral Statements." The first of the Agreed Interpretations negated important restrictions on radars by granting to the Soviets—in addition to all radars permitted by the treaty—retention of all non-phased-array ABM radars operational on the date of signature of the treaty within their Moscow ABM system deployment area.

Then, a prohibition was added against deploying phased-array radars having a potential "(the product of mean emitted power in watts and antenna area in square meters)" exceeding three million, except as provided in Articles III, IV, and VI of the treaty. However, in the same sentence, an exception was provided "for the purposes of tracking objects in outer space or for use as national technical means of verification."

Although the treaty—as amended by the 1974 Moscow Summit Protocol—appears to limit each side to a total of 100 missile launchers and interceptor missiles, the entire elaborate and complex attempt at preventing circumvention of the attempted limitation will work perfectly against the United States. It will not work at all against the Soviet Union, except possibly on a basis of 100-percent trust and good will. It is history's outstanding example of a treaty shot through with massive one-way loopholes.

This is because the United States has no SAMs with ABM capability or to which we can "give" ABM capability merely by tying them in with radars. The Soviet Union, on the other hand, as spelled out above, has already deployed "more than 1,000" and up to 9,000 SAMs that do not need to be "given" ABM capability because they already have it in their present capability to reach up and to reach out (altitude and range). All these missiles purport to have the *primary* purpose of shooting down aircraft, and that is probably true of the 8,000 SA-2s. The primary purpose of the SA-5s (which are physically ABM-capable) has always been ambiguous. Only a few in the Soviet hierarchy know for certain, and they are not telling. Even the SA-2s have high altitude capability now, and they have been nuclear capable since 1967.

Thus, all that is needed for the most massive and successful treaty circumvention in history is a tie-in with ABM-capable radar of these thousands of existing missile launchers (all of which are reported by reliable authorities to have reload capability that, after all, is logical for purported antiaircraft missiles). As usual, the one-way loopholes will permit the Soviets to circumvent in a number of ways, and to do so either by the strict technical-interpretation route or by the clandestine-and-uninspectable-undetectable route.

If they want to observe the letter of the treaty and still circumvent its spirit, they can lay all the necessary network of cable needed to connect radar nets and missile systems, but leave the last 10 feet or 10 inches unconnected. Then, at the end of the initial five-year period of the SALT I Interim Agreement, if we say we will give notice to terminate the treaty because they haven't agreed to a more comprehensive offensive weapons limitation agreement, the Soviets can have a nationwide "heavy" ABM network operational within a matter of hours. Or, the Soviets themselves could give the six-months notice of termination that the treaty requires, and have operational within six months a nationwide "heavy" ABM network the like of which would take us six to eight years to equal—even if they then stood still.

It is clear that the U.S. delegation recognized the hopelessness of attempting to prevent the Soviets from connecting their powerful radars that supposedly are not for ABM-connected use. In a Unilateral Statement that reeks of frustration and is almost pleading in tone, our delegates said:

> Since Henhouse radars [purportedly used for securing early warning of ballistic missile attack] can detect and track ballistic missile warheads at great distances, they have a significant ABM potential. Accordingly, the U.S. would regard any increase in the defenses of such radars by surface-to-air missiles as inconsistent with an agreement.

In other words, the U.S. delegation acknowledged that we really can do nothing to prevent the tie-in of the entire Soviet ABM network with other radars that the Soviets claim are non-ABM; and also that, if these radars were defended by additional missiles that purported to be SAMs, these missiles, too, would have ABM capability and could shoot down our missiles targeted at the Henhouse radar.

This point of specific frustration is a case where the U.S. delegation was unable to find a way to close a substantial loophole, but at least did not make it worse for our side.

4. *Legalization of MRVs.* Sometimes the U.S. delegation did make it worse for our side. Agreed Interpretation F presents an interesting problem. There is no way of knowing whether it originated with the Soviets or with the U.S. delegation, but it is more consonant with the techniques of our diplomats than with theirs. It states:

> The parties understand that Article V of the treaty includes obligations not to develop, test, or deploy ABM interceptor missiles for the delivery by each ABM interceptor missile of more than one independently guided warhead.

This accomplishes the specific purpose of making MIRVed ABM warheads illegal; but in doing that, it permits the invocation of a rule of legal construction that would recognize that MRVed ABM warheads are permitted.

The MIRVing of ABM interceptor missile warheads—that is, giving them multiple warheads with independent guidance—would seem far beyond the current state of technology; but MRVing them, or giving them multiple warheads that spread in a preset pattern, is not. Both sides have this technology, but the Soviets specialize in it. They have no real need for independent guidance features because they have such large numbers of "heavy" warheads.

This legalizing of MRVed ABM warheads gives a major potential advantage to the side that has an ongoing momentum in the production of missiles with the greatest throw-weight. The Soviet SS-9, which they have in "serial" or mass production, has a throw-weight of 15,000 pounds. (The SS-18 may have 30,000 pounds.) The U.S. Minuteman has less than 2,000 pounds. Multiple individual warheads for ABM missiles can be much lighter per megaton of explosive power than offensive missiles because they require no reentry shields (they will not be coming back from space into the atmosphere). A U.S. Poseidon 50-kiloton MIRVed warhead is authoritatively estimated to weigh no more than 300 pounds, complete with reentry shield.

Thus, an ABM warhead of the same total weight, but with shield-weight translated into the weight of additional explosive material, and with the Soviets' better yield/weight ratio, could be more than 100 kilotons. The SS-9 missile converted to an ABM mission could carry 50 or more of them. Because it does not require rocket fuel for intercontinental reach, it might carry far more.

Nothing in the ABM Treaty, or in any of its official interpretations, seeks to limit the size of ABM launchers or interceptor missiles. The effect of Agreed Interpretation F is to make MIRVed ABM interceptor missiles illegal under Article V, Paragraph 2, but to legalize MRVed interceptor missiles. This would provide the Soviets with a way of legally converting their total of 100 ABM missiles allowed under the Protocol into a 5,000 ABM warhead capability. Granted, the warheads would not be individually targetable, but they could create a massive barrage effect and, with improvements in technology, could be very effective against incoming U.S. missile warheads, especially if the U.S. missiles were MIRVs or missiles fired in a salvo.

If we tried to do the same thing, the Soviets would have an advantage of at least 10-to-1 against us. We have no ongoing land-based missile production programs for missiles of any sort with 15,000-pound throw-weight capability.

If that particular method of circumventing the ABM Treaty is not practical, there would be other methods for the Soviets to exploit their massive advantage in missiles that have more than 10 times the throw-weight of ours. It would seem that a limitation on the *size* of the missiles, and on the *number* of MRV as well as MIRV warheads in a single missile, would be a *sine qua non* of any treaty seeking to control the ABM race.

Entering into *any* antidefense treaty in the nuclear-space age can be explained only as a compulsion of MAD-ness, even if it were equitably and prudently drafted and if it established true mutuality. But analysis has demonstrated that this particular SALT I ABM Treaty is especially dangerous to the United States and concedes massive advantages to the Soviets in the present timeframe. The dangers to our national survival inherent in the present operation of the treaty, however, are vastly exceeded by the vital disadvantages stacked against us in the future operation of the treaty.

Any consideration of antimissile defense systems must be segregated into the three separate timeframes in which they have or will have their existence. These are (1) ABM systems in-being, defined in the treaty as consisting of ABM interceptor missiles, ABM launchers, and ABM radars (and frequently identified as current-state-of-the-art ABMs); (2) ABM systems consisting of current-state-of-the-art components but which differ from the in-being systems by reason of being sea-based, air-based, space-based, or mobile land-based, or which launch more than one ABM interceptor missile at a time from each launcher, or which have automatic or semiautomatic rapid reloading capabilities (and which might be called near-term future systems; and (3) "exotic" missile defense systems, which are based on physical principles other than and beyond the current-state-of-the-art systems and have components capable of substituting for ABM interceptor missiles, launchers, and radars (and which might be called midterm and far-future systems).

We have already discussed the first of these three ABM systems. A discussion of the second or near-term future ABM systems necessarily raises questions about the motivation and intelligence of the leadership of the U.S.S.R. as well as of the United States. The SALT I ABM Treaty expressly prohibits the development, testing, or deploying of any of these systems or their components. Why would both sides want to foreclose future developments which would make possible a better defense of their own populations against death by nuclear incineration? Why would they prefer instead to perpetuate their power to mass-murder scores of millions of helpless hostages offered up by the other side?

Article V of the SALT I Treaty raises these questions, but provides no clues as to the answers. Here is how it reads:

> 1. Each party undertakes not to *develop*, test, or deploy ABM systems or components which are sea-based, air-based, space-based, or mobile land-based.
>
> 2. Each party undertakes not to *develop*, test, or deploy ABM launchers for launching more than one ABM interceptor missile at a time from each launcher, nor to modify deployed launchers to provide them with such a capability, nor to *develop*, test, or deploy automatic or semiautomatic or other similar systems for rapid reload of ABM launchers.

None of these four systems prohibited by Section 1 of Article V is in the realm of far-out science fiction. Three of them are within the presently realized state of our technology, and the fourth may be no more than five years beyond. The United States has already done substantial work developing sea-based and space-based systems. The space-based system (designated BAMBI—Ballistic Missile Boost Intercept System) offers favorable prospects if equipped with nuclear warheads and most probably would be indispensable to effective use of laser-type destruction of missile warheads. In addition, all the improvements to present ABM systems that are prohibited by Article V, Section 2 have revolutionary potentials for providing a truly effective defense against even "heavy" missile attacks in the near future.

Thus, if the terms of Article V offer the Soviets even one major one-way loophole through which they can attain a substantial headstart over the United States *toward* deployment of any such new system or revolutionary improvement in any of the five prohibited areas, they could obtain a decisive strategic advantage over us. When Sections 1 and 2 included the term "develop" in the action prohibited under the treaty, this gave the Soviets just such an advantage.

When the United States solemnly undertakes by treaty not to "develop" specified new types of ABM systems, and not to "develop" specified types of improvements for existing systems, the Soviets know that they need have no concern for "verifying" the fact that we are not doing so. The Soviets know that we are bound by a quadruple guarantee: by our open society, by our congressional system of authorizations and appropriations, by our antidefense lobby, and by the ideological attitudes of our scientific and intellectual elite.

On the other hand, the U.S. "national technical means of verification" would have no realistic chance of detecting the Soviets engaging in any of the prohibited "developments" or, indeed, in all of them at once. They would be carried out routinely and as a matter of common sense, in protected areas impenetrable to U.S. satellite reconnaissance or electronic surveillance. What would they stand to gain by engaging in such secret development? Probably from three to five years on us in progress toward actual deployment—in areas so vital that even a year's advantage could be decisive.

The typical timeframe from research to deployment-in-force of a new strategic weapons system is 10 years. The research and development segments usually consume at least half the time span. Testing begins before development ends, of course, but there are many methods of concealing the actual purposes of tests, and of spoofing attempts to interpret the tests even if they are observed. Then there is the pivotal fact that, in interpreting the adversary's tests of exotic new weapons systems, especially those representing a scientific breakthrough, if we have not been working along similar lines in development the tests can remain a mystery to us even if we observe them.

This is another reason why the U.S. delegation should never have agreed to include "development" among the prohibitions of Article V. If we could proceed with development, we would have a far better chance of securing a meaningful interpretation of their tests. Even rigorous on-site inspections would be futile against deliberately concealed "development" of new types of ABM systems or revolutionary improvements.

Agreeing to depend on "national technical means of verification" in such vital areas appears to have been another irresponsible abdication of responsibility on the part of the U.S. delegation. It is a typical Kissinger concession to appease the men in the Kremlin, to demonstrate our full trust in them, and to appeal to their good will. For his trust in the Politburo, we may have to pay with our freedom or our lives. These uninspectable, unenforceable provisions can enable the Soviet Union to build up irreversible lead-times against us in their strategic defensive power. When coupled with the additional buildup of offensive power allowed them under the Interim Agreement, which they have been pursuing since May 1972 with programs of "staggering size and depth," they soon will be able to confront the United States with the stark options of the nuclear age: abject surrender or total destruction.

The relatively new SS-16 solid-fuel missile provides a spectacular demonstration of how the Soviets could avoid violation of all the prohibitions of Article V of the SALT I ABM Treaty, yet still provide themselves with a nationwide missile defense system of any degree of "thickness" they would be willing to pay for. U.S. authorities concede that it is uniquely suited to land-mobile launchers. Since it was first exhibited in 1973, it was undoubtedly "developed" prior to the effective date of the treaty in May 1972. It probably has ABM capability; Western military attachés thought it was an ABM interceptor missile when they first saw it displayed. The Soviets already have five types of ICBMs that cover all their offensive missile requirements and are highly advanced, extraordinarily powerful, and have accurate inertial guidance and on-board digital computers. So why would they spend the money on another ICBM when what they really need is an advanced ABM interceptor missile?

Let us see how the provisions of Article V apply to the SS-16. It was *developed* before the prohibition on development took effect. The producing of such mobile land-based ABM interceptor missiles is *not* prohibited, so the Soviets could *produce* SS-16s in any number they desire. It can be assumed that, although the Soviets want it as an ABM, it also has ICBM capabilities. Since the Interim Agreement does not prohibit the *deployment* of land-mobile ICBMs, they can be deployed at any time without violating SALT. The only remaining requirement to make the SS-16s into a heavy nationwide missile defense system would be to tie them into radar nets; and the Soviets have in-being 25 times more radars than we do. They need not *complete* the tie-in to the existing radar nets until they want the SS-16 system to go operational as ABM interceptors. Until they complete this tie-in, they would not be in technical violation of the treaty. The only close question would be the Article I provision "not to provide a base" for an area defense—but that expression is nowhere defined in a manner which would prohibit the deployment of SS-16s in the guise of ICBMs.

This is just one example of how the Soviets can take advantage of one-way loopholes in the SALT I ABM Treaty to provide a nationwide heavy missile defense. They undoubtedly have several others planned.

Although it was shocking that U.S. leadership would deprive the American people of all defense against nuclear incineration, it was not surprising after Robert McNamara had so effectively blocked our missile defenses for seven years against a unanimous Joint Chiefs of Staff and a near-unanimous Congress. It was initially surprising that the Kremlin leadership apparently would deprive the population of the Soviet Union of all defense against nuclear incineration; they might not love their people, but they do value disciplined slaves. The answer to this mystery is now solved. The Soviets did not leave their people defenseless; they provided escape hatches in the SALT I ABM Treaty.

18

Banning exotic future defensive systems was an enormous contribution. It was also an achievement. Governments sometimes but not often renounce weapons that do not exist.[1]

John Newhouse's *Cold Dawn: The Story of SALT* is not about what is in the SALT I Agreements, or their effect on the strategic balance, or their relationship to whatever chance the United States may still have of surviving in freedom—although, of some 302 pages, several paragraphs do deal, if somewhat obliquely, with the provisions of the SALT I Agreements, such as the above quotation purporting to interpret the ABM Treaty. Of the several books published on SALT I during the two years following the signing of the agreements in Moscow in 1972, Newhouse's was the only one that published the text of the agreements without the additional half-dozen pages of official "Agreed Interpretations" and "Unilateral Statements." Without them, no one, not even Henry Kissinger, could even make a fair pretense of understanding what the ABM Treaty and the Interim Agreement actually mean.

Newhouse does not appear to understand the SALT Agreements, but nevertheless his book may turn out to be one of the most important publications in history. It is seldom that a book can accurately be described as potentially devastating, but his certainly is. If it is read by the right people in Western Europe and England, it can destroy the NATO alliance. If it is read with understanding by enough people in the United States, it can destroy Henry Kissinger. In relating the negotiations leading up to the Moscow Summit of May 1972, Newhouse did not intend to provide any such destructive potential. But anyone who reveals, in wholesale quantities, the contents of Top Secret documents that relate to secret negotiations involving the life or death of the nation assumes the risk that someone will put those jigsawed pieces together with other intelligence and come up with the big picture of the whole truth.

The Newhouse extract given above accurately represents the interpretation placed on the SALT I ABM Treaty by the U.S. SALT delegation, the White House, the Defense Department, the State Department, and ACDA. In its official interpretation, State repeated that position three times. Newhouse must have worked closely with members of the U.S. negotiating staff for many months to have pried loose from them, or somehow persuaded them to reveal, all the Top Secret material he exposed in his book. It is clear from his references that they considered this alleged "ban on exotic future defensive systems" to be one of their crowning achievements. For confirmation, we have an identical interpretation of the same aspect of the treaty by a real strategic expert. Donald Brennan, in his testimony before the Senate Foreign Relations Committee that we quoted earlier in this book, authoritatively asserted that he was familiar with the U.S. positions on SALT; and he confirms the Newhouse statement of the U.S. interpretation as to the ABM Treaty ban on exotics. In his important *National Review* article of June 23, 1972, "When SALT Hit the Fan," Dr. Brennan stated:

> Even if it were agreed that currently achievable defense is too ineffective to be useful against even a suitably reduced offensive threat (a position that few informed persons would take), *it makes little sense to preclude the possibility of a more effective defense being found in the future.*
>
> *The proposed treaty does exactly that.*[2]

Before the Senate committee, Brennan testified flatly: "All future systems are prohibited by the treaty." So the official interpretation is that the ABM Treaty bans exotics.

An interpretation contrary to the administration's official interpretation, however, is asserted just as unequivocally by two recognized experts on nuclear strategy, Dr. William Kintner and Robert L. Pfaltzgraff, Jr.:

> The treaty applies only to the current state of the art ABM, namely, phased-array radars and short-range and long-range interception. Innovations in missile defense, for example, those based on a new principle such as the laser, are not proscribed.[3]

What difference does it make whether the ABM Treaty bans exotic defenses against missile attack since, by definition, no such defensive systems are in-being or, so far as we know from information available to the public, have even been designed?

The difference is the vast gulf between life and death, between freedom and slavery, and whether Communists will control the entire world. If the Soviet Union should be the first to develop an exotic system that would provide a total or near-total defense against enemy missiles—instead of the best defense now possible with a thick area-defense system of ABM launchers—what would happen? The Soviets would be invulnerable to U.S. retaliatory attack and would be entirely free to engage in nuclear blackmail, or even to launch a genocidal missile attack against the United States and get off scot-free because their exotic defense would cancel out our retaliation. It would automatically give them a fully credible, "splendid," preclusive, first-strike capability against the United States.

If the Soviets were only, say, six months ahead of us in attaining the capability of deploying such a system, they could preempt; that is, they could deploy theirs and then deliver a warning ultimatum to us that, if we did not immediately desist from attempting to deploy our own exotic defense system, they would launch a missile attack against us. We would be unable to retaliate because their exotic defense would be already in-being.

Such a development probably could not take place until the 1980s. But we have a good chance of reaching the 1980s as a free and independent nation only if, *before* 1977, we have reversed the Kissinger defense policies in time to rebuild our strategic deterrent. Do not misunderstand: lead-times are so long that *1977 will be too late to start* to reverse the Kissinger grand strategy of U.S. unilateral strategic disarmament; by that time the Soviets will have passed the preemption point in their strategic buildup that SALT I was supposed to terminate but did not even slow down.

But if the deployment of an exotic system for defense against nuclear missiles is not remotely probable until the 1980s, why worry now about the interpretation of the SALT I ABM Treaty? Because, if we are to prevent the Soviets from gaining that six-months' or even a five-years' lead-time advantage over us in building a near-total defense, we must start now with investment of substantial resources in a research program focused on exotic ABM defenses. In tandem with the research program should be an equally substantial development program for the actual system.

Does the SALT I ABM Treaty prevent us from immediately pursuing such a research and development program? *The shocking, frustrating answer is that nobody knows.* Nobody in this country. The danger is that Kissinger and his staff, and what is known as the U.S. SALT bureaucracy, *think* that they know. As we have seen, they *think* that it does "ban exotic future defense systems"; that is, that it bans development of the more effective future defense systems.

But the Soviets, because the relevant provisions of the ABM Treaty were drawn to their order, as were *all* other substantive provisions of *both* SALT I Agreements, know that it cannot be convincingly *proved* that exotic defense systems are banned by the existing treaty. They drafted a masterpiece of legalistic ambiguity exactly for this purpose. In their game of trick-in-the-treaty, their favorite device is the one-way loophole: a provision that, on its face, applies to both sides, but which in actual practice is an escape hatch open only to their side. The loophole about exotic ABM defenses is paralleled in the Interim Agreement, purportedly restricting offensive missile launchers, by their absolute refusal to specify how many missile launchers they had or even claimed to have; and by their refusal to define the term "heavy missile." These were the two absolutely critical elements of the agreement, and the Soviets got away with agreeing to absolutely nothing in these key areas. They knew they could get away with such contemptuous treatment of U.S. representatives because they had a secret weapon: Henry Kissinger. The Politburo members knew in advance that Henry Kissinger would provide the rationalization for, and sell to the U.S. President, any provision the Soviets insisted on.

This was demonstrated in the case of the imbalance in allowances of nuclear-propelled missile-launching submarines. The Soviets flatly demanded 62 to 44 for the United States. They did not try to justify this demand; 62 was the number they had projected as the total level of the force they were building; 62 was the number they had determined they needed for their strategy. They would not accept a limit of even one less. This large a number, so large a discrepancy, could not be justified under any theory heretofore advanced in the negotiations. It was a far greater number than they had deployed, plus even the number they could claim they had under construction. So Kissinger provided the rationalization: he created a fictitious number he estimated the Soviets *could* build in the future *if* they continued building at full capacity and did not stop at their preplanned total number. The Soviets not only knew that Dr. Kissinger *could* rationalize 62 submarines for them; they knew he *would* rationalize them, and then put it over on President Nixon. The Soviets knew this because they knew— as Kissinger admitted later—that the *obtaining* of an agreement was more important to him than what was *in* the agreement.

Thus it was that, on the horrendously critical matter of application of the SALT I Anti-Defense Treaty to exotic defenses possible in the future, Kissinger went along with language that *never even mentioned* any defense systems other than the *current* system. Under Article I, "each party undertakes not to deploy ABM systems" except as expressly permitted in Article III of the treaty, which would appear clearly to prohibit exotic systems. But Article II defines an ABM system, for the purposes of the treaty, as a system to counter strategic ballistic missiles or their elements in flight trajectory, currently consisting of:

(a) ABM interceptor missiles. . .

(b) ABM launchers. . .

(c) ABM radars. . .

Without the word "currently," the definition clearly would *not* include exotic systems. *With* the word "currently," it may or may not include "future" systems. So, the treaty itself is totally ambiguous.

Agreed Interpretation E, which was initialed by both sides, does deal with exotics, but without using that term. It is worth considering as a masterpiece in compounding ambiguity:

> In order to insure fulfillment of the obligation not to deploy ABM systems and their components except as provided in Article III of the treaty, the parties agree that in the event ABM systems based on other physical principles and including components capable of substituting for ABM interceptor missiles, ABM launchers, or ABM radars are created in the future, specific limitations on such systems and their components would be subject to discussion in accordance with Article XIII and agreement in accordance with Article XIV of the treaty.

If such exotic systems would, after their creation, require "discussion" as to specific limitation, and would be subjected to such specific limitations only after future agreement through the mechanisms set up by the treaty, then quite obviously they are *not* subject to the broad general prohibition against *any* deployment of "ABM systems" except as provided in Article III. If you have a broad general prohibition, specific limitations are unnecessary. Thus in the treaty, which contains a broad general prohibition in Article III, there are no "specific limitations"—only specific exceptions to the broad general prohibition.

The State Department bases its contention that deployment of exotic or future systems is banned on the argument that Article III prohibits the deployment of "any" ABM systems except as provided therein, and that it provides only for deployment of systems with ABM launchers, ABM interceptor missiles, and ABM radars. But the introduction of the word "any" before ABM systems is the State Department's own unilateral creation. The prohibition against deployment does refer to "ABM systems," but a system is not an "ABM system" within the meaning of the treaty, and hence is not prohibited and therefore needs no express exception to the ban against deployment, *unless* it meets the definition of Article II of the treaty. To meet that definition the ABM system must "currently" consist of ABM launchers, interceptors, and radars. The State Department cites Agreed Interpretation E as confirming its argument. But the fact that there *is* an Agreed Interpretation E is a recognition that ambiguity was present and needed resolution. So why didn't the U.S. delegation insist on a clear statement that exotic systems, as therein defined, were banned or were not banned? And if so, at what stage would the ban operate: at the research stage, at the development stage, at the testing stage, at the production stage, or only at the deployment stage?

The question of whether all future systems for defense against nuclear missiles will be prohibited for the treaty's term of "unlimited duration" is certainly sufficiently vital to be settled in the treaty itself, and not left to an ex post facto Agreed Interpretation that, in itself, only compounds the ambiguity.

The ones who actually exercised control of the drafting of the treaty knew *exactly* how to go about prohibiting a future system, and how to do it with no ifs, buts, or whereases. A prime example of this is Article V of the treaty, which provides:

> 1. Each party undertakes not to develop, test, or deploy ABM systems or components which are sea-based, air-based, space-based, or mobile land-based.

If it had been intended to prohibit future or exotic ABM systems, all that was needed was to add:

> or which are based on other physical principles and include components capable of substituting for ABM interceptor missiles, ABM launchers, or ABM radars.

It is a universally accepted principle of legal interpretation of documents that, where certain things are prohibited and the draftsmen of the document demonstrated that they knew how to accomplish that result if it were desired, the failure of express inclusion must be interpreted as an intent to exclude that prohibition. Note that the prohibitions of Article V are cognate (similar) to the systems in question. All the expressly prohibited systems of Article V are, in effect, "future" systems: the systems in question are future systems, and the distinction is solely on their being "based on other physical principles" from the present systems employing ABM interceptor missiles, launchers, and radars.

Suppose the U.S. delegation had requested such clarifying action in the treaty itself or, if not in the treaty, at least in Agreed Interpretation E—and suppose the Soviets had refused. In that case, those purporting to act in the interest of the United States could at least have appended an official Unilateral Statement that, because the Soviets refused to make it clear that the treaty prohibited "exotics," the United States had no alternative other than to proceed as if it were clear that the treaty did *not* prohibit them. But no one said a word for the interests of the United States.

The tragic result—the totally unnecessary result—has been that the Soviets are free to interpret the treaty in the sense most favorable to them; that is, in the sense most favorable to their development of a first-strike capability and a near-total defense against both the United States and the People's Republic of China. The Soviets demonstrated conclusively their compulsion to take advantage of even the most technical interpretations of agreements in the UN Treaty banning the orbiting of weapons of mass destruction in outer space. They went right ahead with the development and multiple testing of such weapons systems, and smirked at us when our State Department naively questioned their conduct. Robert McNamara rushed to their support and announced that such Soviet conduct was in no way prohibited by that agreement.

The Soviets know us from our past performances, including that same UN Outer Space Treaty. U.S. representatives will take the interpretation most unfavorable to development of U.S. strategic power, and will strain to comply with some supposed "spirit" of any agreement with the Kremlin. It was thus that we meekly turned over to the Soviet Union a total and unchallenged monopoly of weapons systems for employment from space: not only the Fractional Orbital Bombardment Systems (FOBS), but also the Multiple Orbital Bombardment Systems (MOBS).

Even before the SALT I Agreements were signed, we had a perceptive warning from a U.S strategic expert who has written brilliantly on the insanity of the Kissinger-U.S. positions in the SALT negotiations and agreements. William R. Van Cleave is a Professor of Strategic and Defense Studies at the University of Southern California, a consultant to RAND and Stanford Research Institute, a former Special Assistant to Secretary of Defense Melvin R. Laird, and has gained painful but practical experience about U.S. negotiating fads as an adviser to the U.S. delegation on SALT. The following is an excerpt from a paper he presented at the Fifth International Arms Control Symposium in Pittsburgh in October 1971. Since his paper was presented some seven months before the SALT I Agreements were signed, his warning sets a high level in prophecy:

> If there is a strategic arms limitation agreement, there will be a tendency to euphoria in the United States, which might well result in a paralysis of strategic force programs well beyond the actual terms of the agreement.
>
> *Similarly, one should expect there to be a disproportionate conformity to the "spirit" of the agreement, as contrasted to its literal provisions.* For specific example, if there is an agreement banning or limiting ABM to low levels, but not prohibiting R&D and/or modernization, we must expect that the Soviet R&D program will continue vigorously, while our own will suffer. A zero ABM agreement would probably mean zero over the long term for the United States but not for the Soviet Union—not only because, given the Soviet radar and interceptor base, it is difficult to

conceive a true zero for the Soviet Union, but also because strong Soviet air defense and ABM programs would likely continue. As a general proposition, it will be very difficult to get money for R&D in the United States for any system banned or limited by a strategic arms limitation agreement.

One other difference in decision-making concerning strategic forces relevant to the SALT is that the concepts generally held in the United States concerning stability influence U.S. decisions. The United States government has held a *mutual assured destruction view* in making its strategic force decisions, and, further, has tended to base them on an *action-reaction view* of arms competition. Such concepts have been included in our decisions and probably will continue to be. There is no evidence that this is true for the Soviet Union.[4]

Note that the two U.S. Government "views" cited by Dr. Van Cleave as influencing our decision-making are Pugwash-McNamara-Kissinger views that have split off U.S. strategic defense policies from reality ever since 1961, and which, over the 11-year period to the signing of the SALT I Agreements, have served to decimate U.S. strategic power. As Dr. Donald Brennan has noted, the MAD "posture as a goal is almost literally mad," and the "treaty itself contains evidence that the theory is little more than a fashion." As to the "action-reaction" view of the so-called arms race, that is simply a myth created by the Pugwash conferees and other elitist unilateral-disarmament pressure groups to rationalize U.S. strategic disarmament on the theory (now totally disproved by SALT I statistics) that, if the United States engaged in self-imposed "restraint," the Soviets would reciprocate and follow our unilateral example. This dressed-up lie is squarely contrary to the evidence of Soviet strategic programs since they developed the world's first ICBM in 1957. Remember the excerpt from Edward Luttwak's book on SALT:

> . . . studies of Russian strategic deployments since the Second World War show quite conclusively that the "action-reaction" phenomena can explain only *some* of their moves. More important is the question of incentives.[5]

As a survey demonstrating the falsity of the action-reaction theory of the arms race, Luttwak cites "Missile Defense, the Soviet Union, and the Arms Race," published in *Why ABM?*, edited by Johan J. Holst and William Schneider, Jr.[6]

Thus, with the philosophy underlying U.S. negotiations for SALT Agreements based on a blend of insanity and fraud, it would be somewhat optimistic to expect results beneficial to the United States. But the slick sellout of America's future so cunningly incorporated in the SALT Treaty's ban on ABM systems goes far beyond not securing us any benefits. The eight-months-pregnant ambiguity as to whether

Articles I, II, and III, and Agreed Interpretation E operate to prohibit all future systems for defense against missiles, or merely recognize future or exotic systems as a subject for future "discussions" and future possible agreements on "specific limitations," simply must be a deliberate trap. The very fact that there is an Agreed Interpretation E indicates that both parties recognized the existence of ambiguity. Yet Henry Kissinger, who was in total control for the United States, not only accepted this critical gap in the treaty's meaning, but sold it to the President of the United States.

Why?

Because the Pugwash conferees and other unilateral-disarmament elites have always—at least ever since the dawn of Henry Kissinger's imaginary missile gap *circa* 1960—met any attempt to protect the American people from nuclear incineration with shrill and near-hysterical opposition. At first, before the development of ABM systems, they campaigned against any reasonable passive or civil defense programs. They denounced blast and fallout shelters as "warmongering." In that period they frankly explained their reasoning: if the American people should ever get the idea that they might be able to survive a nuclear attack, they might not pressure the government to "go that last mile" in negotiations. Translated into reality, this means not pressure the government to surrender.

In the early 1960s the Pugwash conferees threw all their academic, political, and scientific influence into opposing the development of an *active* defense against missiles, that is, against ABM systems. At first they contended that it would be "destabilizing" if either side should deploy ABMs. By 1965, however, it became clear that the Soviets were seriously engaged in deploying an extensive ABM system; so then the Pugwash crowd rationalized that by saying the Russians were so inferior in offensive nuclear weapons they *had* to build ABM systems to equalize and stabilize the strategic equation. Then the Pugwashers opposed any attempt to build defenses for the *American* people, and dropped any mention of Soviet systems.

Henry Kissinger's SALT I ABM Treaty crowned more than a decade of dedicated efforts to keep the American people subject at all times to a Soviet genocidal nuclear attack. It is difficult to believe, but the U.S. SALT delegation *rejoiced* that they had ensured that the American people could be killed by the scores of millions. John Newhouse, in *Cold Dawn: The Story of SALT,* describes their feeling of accomplishment in the first phase of SALT I:

> ... Moscow had come more than halfway toward accepting the favorite apothegm of Washington's assured destruction school of strategy:
> "Offense is defense, defense is offense.
> "Killing people is good, killing weapons is bad."[7]

So help us God, despite their coy manner, they are serious. They really believe that they converted the Soviet SALT delegates to the same immoral insanity. Donald Brennan, in his *National Review* article previously cited, challenges that belief. He is convinced that the Russians have too close a grasp of reality to be carried away by enthusiasm for the genocide of Russians. He offers testimony, from Kosygin down to Soviet Army colonels, that they support ABM programs because they are designed to "prevent the death of people." He makes it clear that, if these Russians have *really* been converted to the U.S. Pugwash credo that "killing people is good," the change has come about only since 1970; and that, actually, they may instead have "decided to make us *think* they had changed their views." [Emphasis in the original.] It has been immutable doctrine in the Soviet Union since the time of Lenin to give the highest priority to saving people.

If the Pugwash-CFR-Kissinger elites are so dedicated to keeping the American people totally vulnerable to nuclear incineration, why didn't they come right out in the SALT I ABM Treaty and say in so many words that, in addition to banning current systems, all future or exotic missile defense systems—such as laser or particle generators—are also within the ban for the treaty's term of "unlimited duration"?

The decisive reason is that the Soviets, through their secret deals with Henry Kissinger, had the final say as to the drafting of the treaty. They did not *want* clear language and would *not* accept it. They wanted for themselves a free hand in developing, testing, and deploying future systems or "exotic" systems. Every time the Red Chinese deploy more IRBMs or test ICBMs, the Soviets become even more anxious to develop a near-total defense as soon as possible. As we will see, they are making huge investments in R&D in these areas. Although they are intent on developing exotic defense systems for themselves, they don't want the United States to create any. A U.S. defense system would cancel out the scores of billions of rubles they have invested in counterforce weapons systems such as the SS-9, SS-18, SS-17, SS-19, and SS-N-8. For us to have a near-total defense system on an exotic base would destroy their chance of ever attaining a preclusive first-strike capability against us. So, they resorted to brilliant ambiguity in the language of the treaty. That ambiguity simply cannot be conclusively resolved—at least not without the agreement of both parties, and there has been no such agreement. Our State Department's interpretation is unilateral only; and when State repeats it three times, it is whistling in the dark.

We do have an escape hatch from the treaty—and we should use it. Despite the treaty's express provision that it will "be of unlimited duration," each party is given the right to withdraw

> if it decides that extraordinary events related to the subject matter of this treaty have jeopardized its supreme interests.

Fortunately, we have the right to decide *unilaterally* if our supreme interests have been jeopardized. We do not have to wait until the 1980s, when the Soviets may be expected to deploy a new type of missile defense system. If we wait so long, we would have conceded them not a critical six months of lead time, but a decade of it; and our situation would be hopeless. But our "supreme interests" are in jeopardy right *now,* because of the treaty-induced imbalance in the respective research efforts of the U.S. and U.S.S.R. in the area of exotic defense systems. As we pointed out, and found confirmation in Professor Van Cleave's symposium paper, it will be difficult at best, and virtually impossible as a practical matter, to secure funding from Congress for R&D for a system that the U.S. Government regards as banned by the SALT I Anti-Defense Treaty.

Even without the psychological blocking of the ABM Treaty, we are coming out a very poor second to the Soviets in the general area of R&D. In the year 1972 the Soviets invested in scientific and techno-logical activities some 4.4 billion more rubles than in 1969, which was an increase of 44 percent in three years. Each year, the antidefense lobby in Congress cuts ours further. The magnitude of the Soviet effort is conveyed with some impact by a single paragraph in the foreword written by Ambassador Foy D. Kohler to a study entitled "Science and Technology as an Instrument of Soviet Policy":

> An idea of the magnitude of an expenditure for science and technology at the 14.4 billion (rubles) level for a single year can be grasped if it is considered that in terms of dollar equivalence (i.e., actual buying power as distinct from official exchange rate) this sum, according to conserva-tive estimates, amounts to something over $30 billion. Thus, and without having to take into account the added expenditures of a direct military category, *the Soviet Union will be spending more on science in the year 1972 than the total cost to the U.S. of the Apollo moon-landing program from its inception in 1961 to the present.*[8]

This proves, as Henry Kissinger has reminded us, that the Soviet leaders are "serious" men. They are especially serious about laser-re-lated R&D. We cannot know how much of that $30-billion-increasing-annually-by-more-than-10-percent goes for research on lasers, particle generators, and other research related to missile defense systems, but we do know that they give those areas high priority. The Soviets are traditionally defense-minded. In the nuclear-space age nothing makes such good sense as defense. They have been especially successful in laser developments. Their P. N. Lebedev Institute in Moscow is a world-leading laser-research agency staffed by such renowned experts as Nobel Laureate Nikolai Basov. In 1968 he became the first to dem-onstrate that a laser could induce the fusion reaction in a pellet of fuel.

Can we afford to meet and beat a competition willing to spend $30 billion a year on R&D?

An Israeli officer was once asked how his countrymen are able to build sufficient strength to survive against Arabs sworn to liquidate them and who outnumber the Israelis by 100-to-1. More precisely, the odds are 100 million to 3 million. He replied, "We have a secret weapon: *we have no choice.*"

That is our situation, too. But instead of admitting to ourselves that we have no choice but to meet and beat the Soviet competition, we seek escapes. In the world of reality we have no choice; so we opt out of reality into an imaginary and very temporary detente. In reality we have one trillion three hundred billion dollars a year in resources to meet and beat our competition. We have more than twice the industrial and technological resources of the Soviets. We could match that $30 billion Soviet annual bet on R&D, and still have some one thousand, two hundred seventy billion dollars left over each year for other essentials.

The greatest nation the world has ever known has everything except leadership. During the entire 20th century our continuing crisis has been in leadership. Now, fate has given us a man with many of the qualities that make a leader truly great but has endowed him with a character twist that compels him to lead in the wrong direction. We have been going 180 degrees wrong—toward national oblivion instead of national greatness. Henry Kissinger's title should be Secretary of Surrender.

19

The official title of the SALT I Interim Agreement signed in Moscow in 1972 is "Certain Measures With Respect to the Limitation of Strategic Offensive Arms." The title is honest in not claiming that the agreement actually does limit offensive arms. The title is also sufficiently ambiguous to permit gross misrepresentations of the meaning and effect of substantive provisions by the highest U.S. officials, with apparent good faith.

To determine the true meaning and effect of the Interim Agreement, it is necessary to examine the verbatim text. Paraphrasing for the sake of brevity will not do justice to the official language. Here are the operative Articles. The relevant paragraph of the "Protocol," which is an integral part of the Interim Agreement, is quoted immediately after Article III.

Article I
The parties undertake not to start construction of additional fixed land-based intercontinental ballistic missile (ICBM) launchers after July 1, 1972.

Article II
The parties undertake not to convert land-based launchers for light ICBMs, or for ICBMs of older types deployed prior to 1964, into land-based launchers for heavy ICBMs of types deployed after that time.

Article III
The parties undertake to limit submarine-launched ballistic missile (SLBM) launchers and modern ballistic missile submarines to the num-

bers operational and under construction on the date of signature of this Interim Agreement, and in addition launchers and submarines constructed under procedures established by the parties as replacements for an equal number of ICBM launchers of older types deployed prior to 1964 or for launchers on older submarines.

Protocol

The parties understand that, under Article III of the Interim Agreement, for the period during which that Agreement remains in force:

The U.S. may have no more than 710 ballistic missile launchers on submarines (SLBMs) and no more than 44 modern ballistic missile submarines. The Soviet Union may have no more than 950 ballistic missile launchers on submarines and no more than 62 modern ballistic missile submarines. . . .

The deployment of modern SLBMs on any submarine, regardless of type, will be counted against the total level of SLBMs permitted for the U.S. and the U.S.S.R.

Article IV

Subject to the provisions of this Interim Agreement, modernization and replacement of strategic offensive ballistic missiles and launchers covered by this Interim Agreement may be undertaken.

There is no provision for on-site inspection. The two sides are restricted to using "national technical means of verification." They agree not to interfere with each other's "technical means," and not to use "deliberate concealment measures." However, the Interim Agreement includes the same joker clause that was used in the ABM Treaty: "This obligation shall not require changes in current construction, assembly, conversion, or overhaul practices." That sentence means that the side that has been engaging in practices that involve deliberate concealment may continue such measures, but the side that has not been engaging in deliberate concealment may not begin such action.

The stated term of the Interim Agreement is five years. There is a provision that each side has the right to withdraw if it decides that "extraordinary events related to the subject matter of this Interim Agreement have jeopardized its supreme interests," and if it gives six-months' prior notice stating what it regards as these "extraordinary events" justifying withdrawal.

The most noteworthy feature of the entire Interim Agreement is how it does *not* limit strategic offensive arms. It does not even purport to put a limit on the *numbers of ICBMs* of any type each side may possess. It does not purport to limit the *manufacture or production of missiles* for either land-based or submarine launchers. It does not limit the *manufacture or production of missile launcher tubes,* equipment, or associated electronics. Regarding land-based weapons, all it does limit is "*start*[ing] *construction* of additional fixed land-based intercontinental ballistic missile (ICBM) launchers." This obviously means the "construction" of silos; *i.e.*, digging holes, lining the holes with concrete and steel, and installing the launcher tubes or other equipment inside the holes. It could also bar the construction of launching pads and the installation of launchers on them.

Anyone who is willing to count can spot massive imbalances in both numbers and types of strategic offensive arms not merely permitted, but promoted, by the Agreement. Substantially all expert and objective authorities who have written about the SALT I Agreements since they were signed, or who have testified concerning them before congressional committees, confirm the conclusions of knowledgeable laymen on these points. Quotation of one outstanding summary of these effects of the Interim Agreement on offensive weapons will provide adequate background for an examination of the major loopholes. Senator James Buckley, in the part of his testimony before the Senate Foreign Relations Committee on June 29, 1972, relating to offensive arms limitation, summed up the effect of the SALT I Interim Agreement:

> In the Interim Agreement, the United States has accepted a position of significant quantitative inferiority in every area of offensive strength which is subject to its control. Depending on how the parties choose to exercise their options under the agreement, the Soviet Union will be able to deploy, in round figures, between 1,400 and 1,600 intercontinental ballistic missiles to our 1,000, and up to 1,000 submarine-launched ballistic missiles to our 700. She will be able to expand her fleet of modern "Y-Class" nuclear-powered submarines to 62 while retaining 22 diesel-powered "G-Class" submarines, for a total force of 84 missile-launching submarines, in comparison with the fleet of 44 which we will be allowed to maintain.
>
> Most significantly, because of the enormous size of Russia's heavy missiles, the ceilings placed on intercontinental and submarine-launched ballistic missiles will provide the Soviets with a more than four times advantage over the United States in the payload capacity or "throw-weight" of these weapons systems. This means that the Russians will be guaranteed the *capability*, during the term of the agreement, to deploy with these weapons more than four times as many warheads as the United States should they achieve parity with us in warhead design.
>
> Because such parity has not yet been achieved, it is argued that the United States is likely to retain its existing two-to-one advantage in deliverable warheads during the life of the agreement. This argument is based on U.S. superiority in manned heavy bombers, in multiple warhead technology, and in forward-based systems. I believe, however, that it is important to emphasize the fragile and transitory character of this "advantage."
>
> First, with regard to the U.S. superiority in manned bombers, this advantage quickly disappears when one includes the medium bomber forces available to both sides. While the United States has about 75 medium-range FB-111 bombers in the Strategic Air Command which can

operate from forward bases as part of our retaliatory force, the Soviets have approximately 550 TU-16 Badgers and approximately 150 TU-22 Blinder medium bombers which are refuelable and quite capable of reaching the United States and then landing in airfields in Cuba or Mexico.

Second, while a combination of skillful warhead miniaturization and relatively accurate guidance systems provides the United States with a formidable present advantage in multiple warhead technology, we have little reason to be complacent. It should be noted that the United States developed its multiple warhead hardware in approximately three years, from 1966 through 1969. Discussions of the engineering characteristics of our multiple warhead missiles have been widely disseminated in trade journals and congressional hearings. It would be imprudent, at best, to presume that the Soviets are so technologically retarded that they would be incapable of developing and deploying significant numbers of multiple warheads within the five-year term of the Interim Agreement.

It has been argued that our intelligence estimates give the Soviet Union only a limited capability to develop multiple warhead technology. I would point out that these intelligence analysts are the ones who have consistently underestimated Soviet nuclear force objectives. It is these same intelligence analysts who advised Secretary of Defense Robert S. McNamara in the mid-1960s that the Soviet Union had permanently accepted the status of strategic inferiority.

It is these same intelligence analysts who concluded in 1964 that the Chinese Communists would detonate a primitive nuclear device made of plutonium rather than the uranium device actually detonated which required a huge gaseous diffusion plant for the manufacture of nuclear material.

With respect to these and other advantages which the United States may currently possess in noncontrolled strategic offensive weapons, it should be noted that there is nothing in the SALT accords to prevent the Soviet Union from overtaking us in every category, while these accords prohibit us from overtaking the Soviet Union in those areas where they have been assured substantial margins of superiority.

Senator Buckley's short analysis in no way exaggerates the fantastic faults of the SALT I Agreements, or the potentially fatal disadvantages they impose on the United States. No Senator would have the time to make the detailed analysis that would be required to demonstrate that the SALT I Agreements are actually far worse than he pictured them. But suppose that no further analysis had been made, and that the SALT I Agreements were "only" as bad as Senator Buckley conclusively demonstrated. He certainly made the points that they were suicidal for the United States, were unfair and inequitable, and that, instead of demonstrating good will on the part of the Soviets, they demonstrated malevolence and a desire to push us into the nuclear inferno.

Why, then, would the Senate consent to the SALT I Agreements with only three nay votes? There are about 30 Senators (the so-called anti-defense lobby) who will support *any* agreement that will disadvantage the United States and advantage Communists of any ilk—Soviet, Chinese, or Vietnamese. But that leaves something like 50 votes unexplained.

Those familiar with jury verdicts in civil cases in the law courts know from experience that, all too often, juries, being human, decide not in favor of the litigant who has the stronger case, but in favor of the one who has the more likable lawyer. To put the SALT I Agreements over, the Administration relied practically 100 percent on Henry Kissinger. No one paid any attention to Secretary of State Rogers. The near-unanimous Senate vote was really a vote of confidence—of overconfidence, rather—in Henry Kissinger, instead of an approval of the SALT I Agreements.

Regarding Soviet MIRVing, at the time of the signing of the SALT I accords we did not know and *could not know* positively that the Soviets did not then possess technological capability at least equal to ours. All that Kissinger professed to know was based on intelligence estimates based in turn on observation of Soviet tests. Such tests can be spoofed. A warhead packed with MIRVed miniatures can be designed to test only one of them. MIRV tests can be disguised as MRV tests. Our Defense Department has been reporting Soviet tests of multiple warheads since 1969. As long ago as early 1969, Dr. John S. Foster, Director of Defense, Research and Engineering, gave this illuminating testimony before a House Foreign Affairs subcommittee:

> ... the guidance and control systems employed in the SS-9 tests have capabilities much greater than that required to implement a simple MRV. The things we do know about this mechanism are completely compatible with MIRV, even though they do not prove MIRV capability.[1]

In 1971 Secretary of Defense Laird estimated that the Soviet lag behind the U.S. in MIRV technology was not more than two years. On June 20, 1972, he gave the Senate Armed Services Committee this key testimony that relates not only to Soviet multiple warhead technology but to the importance of all the major loopholes in the Interim Agreement:

> The President reported last week that Mr. Brezhnev and his colleagues in Moscow had made it absolutely clear that they intended to go forward with defense programs in the offensive area not limited by these agreements. [MIRVing is, of course, not limited by these agreements.] It should be no surprise when I report to you that this is precisely what they are doing.
>
> During the past several weeks the Soviet Union has been conducting *a series of tests involving new ballistic missile programs including multiple warhead technology.* In addition, continued testing of existing systems is moving ahead.

In connection with the massive potential advantage in MIRVs which the Interim Agreement grants to the Soviet Union, it must be remembered that at the time of Kissinger's 1972 SALT-selling activities he knew of two additional factors in the Soviets' favor. It was generally accepted that the Soviet advantage over us in total throw-weight, at the time of the SALT I signing, stood at a factor of four. Few computations, however, had taken into account the increase in this factor which will result if the Soviets decide to "modernize" their entire ICBM force by converting to their new supermissiles which had been developed but not yet exhibited. The Interim Agreement permitted the Soviets to do this; such modernization did not constitute conversion of "light" missiles into "heavy" missiles because Kissinger had failed to secure from the Soviets any definition whatsoever of a "heavy missile." And he revealed in his June 15, 1972, White House briefing for the five congressional committees that "undoubtedly they are planning to modernize within the existing framework some of the weapons they now possess."

The second factor is the Soviets' greater warhead-explosive power that is derived from their superior yield/weight ratio in the high-yield (tens of megatons) range. Prior to the unilateral-reciprocal nuclear test ban instituted in 1958 and terminated by the Soviets' surprise abrogation in September 1961 (after they had completed nearly three years of clandestine test preparations), the United States had a 2-to-1 advantage in yield/weight ratio for hydrogen warheads. By two massive series of tests in 1961 and 1962, the Soviets more than reversed our prior advantage in warhead technology. We then obliged them by freezing their advantage in the Moscow Test Ban Treaty of 1963. The gain the Soviets made in those tests—and which (under the influence of the Pugwash scientists) we enshrined for them in that treaty—has never been revealed to the American people. Contemporaneous testimony of the Joint Chiefs of Staff, however, conceded the Soviets' substantial superiority, and confirmed that we could never overtake this lead without atmospheric testing, which the treaty banned.[2]

The Soviet advantage in high-yield warhead technology is now reliably estimated at 2½-to-1 to 5-to-1 against us. Missile throw-weight or payload is rated in *pounds* of weight. Missile warhead explosive power is rated in megatons (the explosive equivalent of millions of tons of TNT). Thus, the Soviet 4-to-1 advantage in throw-weight will translate into a missile-force total megatonnage advantage of 10-to-1 to 19-to-1 against us. Significantly, this advantage would also carry over into MIRVs. Their four-times-as-many potential MIRV warheads could thus have 10 times as much explosive power. This Soviet advantage will be perpetuated by the Moscow Summit of '74 Threshold Test Ban Treaty.

In testifying before the Senate Armed Services Committee about the Interim Agreement, then-Defense Secretary Melvin Laird made this combination concession and contention:

> There are loopholes you might drive one or two 10- to 25-megaton weapons through, but it [sic] is not a serious loophole because our verification procedures are almost exact.

Unfortunately, the Secretary's estimate of the number of weapons that could be "driven through" SALT I loopholes is low by a factor of thousands; and his contention that the loopholes are not serious because of the exactitude of our verification procedures is largely irrelevant. All we could "verify," in the case of the most serious loopholes, would be that the Soviets were exercising their legal rights under the agreement.

It might be further contended that, even if the actions of the Soviets were legal, we could still exercise our right to terminate the agreement after six-months' notice. It is true that this would be our legal right. Unfortunately, there are loopholes in the agreement that would enable the Soviets legally and clandestinely to build up and stockpile such a reserve of rapidly deployable missiles that we would be foolhardy to attempt to resort to the escape hatch if the Soviets "advised" us not to. Here is a summary of the major loopholes:

1. *Land-mobile launchers and missiles.* The Interim Agreement accords to the Soviets the legal and moral right to continue to produce and deploy land-mobile launchers and missiles in any numbers, in any type, and in any size they choose. The "Unilateral Declaration" by the U.S. delegation that the United States will consider the deployment of such launchers as "inconsistent with the objectives of the agreement" has no legal force or effect whatsoever. It cannot make illegal the Soviet exercise of a right accorded them by the agreement itself and that they specifically refused to give up. The Soviets have the capability of producing 1,000 to 2,000 land-mobile launchers and missiles during the five-year term of the agreement. Added to their present offensive force, this would give them a full first-strike capability.

2. *Mobile SS-9s.* The most probable way that the Soviets would exploit the loophole created in the agreement when land-mobile launchers were excluded from coverage, would be by the production and deployment of large numbers of SS-16s in the ICBM mode. The same basic SS-16 missile probably has ABM interceptor missile capability.

There is, however, another grave danger inherent in the Soviets' option to resort to the mobility concept to circumvent the agreement's prohibition against construction of additional *fixed* land-based ICBM launchers. There have been repeated statements by Defense

Department experts and officials that, if the Soviets can build up their SS-9 force to slightly more than 400, they will be able to destroy substantially our entire Minuteman missile force, leaving us with no land-based deterrent. For example, Dr. John S. Foster stated that when the Soviets have "a little over 400 SS-9s" they can knock out "all but a small fraction" of our Minuteman missiles.[3] In 1969 Secretary Laird reported that 420 SS-9s could destroy 95 percent of our Minuteman force if they were armed with three 5-megaton warheads with a CEP of ¼ mile.

One of the great claims about benefits that SALT is supposed to provide for U.S. security is that the Interim Agreement blocks the building of additional SS-9s, now estimated to number 313. If, however, the Soviets can develop an SS-9 launcher that is sufficiently "mobile" to escape the definition of "fixed," they can add the extra 100+ they need to complete their first-strike capability. To be "mobile," the launcher need not be capable of moving across the country; it need only be capable of some movement. By one of the "Common Understandings" affixed to the SALT I Agreements, the United States and the Soviets agreed to define "mobile" ABM launchers as any launchers that are "not permanent fixed types."

In any event, conferring "mobility" on SS-9 launchers is far from impossible. There are many pictures of this type of missile being moved through the streets of Moscow on trucks. Although an SS-9 stands 115 feet tall, it is only 10 feet in diameter; its throw-weight is about 15,000 pounds.

Although it would be *legal* for the Soviets to *deploy* mobile launchers for SS-9s, they might prefer to produce both the missiles and their "mobile" launchers under such cover that the buildup would not be detected by "U.S. national means of verification." Their mobility would permit rapid deployment when the Soviets were ready to disclose them. The enormous counterforce destructive power of these additional SS-9s would give the Soviets a full first-strike capability.

3. Conversion of SS-9s to SS-18s, and of SS-11s to SS-17s and SS-19s. It is not clear whether the U.S. delegation even sought any provisions to prohibit this magnification of Soviet counterforce capability. If they did, they failed. There is absolutely nothing in the Interim Agreement to prevent the Soviet Union from "modernizing" its entire SS-9 force (estimated at 313 launchers) into launchers twice as powerful. Dr. Kissinger explained this accurately in a White House press conference held in Kiev, Soviet Russia, on May 29, 1972. His statement is also highly significant in that it constitutes a most explicit admission by the administration of (1) Soviet capability of building missiles more powerful than the SS-9 and their probable intent to do so, and (2) the threat posed by the SS-9s to our retaliatory force. The question was put by a press correspondent:

Q: You know, Senator Jackson has said that the Russians now have a 50-megaton missile, and he questions whether the SALT Agreement will really give us protection. Can you tell us, first of all, whether he is correct that they have this supermissile; and secondly, whether this agreement cuts off the SS-9s at a safe level?

Dr. Kissinger: I wouldn't go into a discussion of the megatonnage of individual Soviet weapons, but it is clear that the Soviets have weapons of substantial explosive power and that they are probably building some that are even more powerful than the ones we have seen.

I would maintain that the argument you have mentioned to us confuses two separate issues: One, the size of the explosive power on warheads of existing weapons; and two, the growth of the arsenal of these weapons. This agreement does nothing about the size of the warheads. This will have to be done, if at all, in a follow-on agreement. It does do something about the number of launchers on which these warheads can be built.

Therefore, the SS-9 is frozen at its current level of 313, but in this category nothing will prevent the Soviet Union from putting larger warheads on those weapons that they have. The argument that some critics are making that therefore, the agreement is dangerous, is fallacious because we would face the problem of these larger warheads, plus additional missiles, without the agreement. That is the argument.

We admit we have insisted at a time when most of our critics were denying it that—and we have always said it—the SS-9 is a threat to our retaliatory force, and it remains a threat to our retaliatory force. What this agreement does is to freeze the number of launchers. It does not affect the size of the warhead. On the other hand, if there were no agreement, there would be more launchers and more warheads, and therefore, we have reduced the danger by the margin of the number of weapons that would be built were it not for this agreement.

Dr. Kissinger's statement that "this agreement" does not attempt to impose any limit on the increased size of warheads that may be accomplished under the specific authorization of Article IV is accurate as to the agreement itself, but requires some amplification in view of several subsequent gambits by the U.S. delegation in attempting ex post facto to impose some limits on launcher enlargement by means of "modernization." Apparently the U.S. delegates hoped this would have the effect of limiting warhead size. Thus, they managed to secure from the Soviets "Agreed Interpretation J," which states that:

in the process of modernization and replacement, the dimensions of land-based ICBM silo launchers will not be significantly increased.

The U.S. delegation next secured from the Soviets "Common Understanding A," which states that:

The term "significantly increased" means that an increase will not be greater than 10-15 percent of the present dimensions of land-based ICBM silo launchers.

Apparently the U.S. delegation hoped that this would prevent the "modernization" or "replacement" of the 25-megaton SS-9s by the new SS-18s rated at 50+ megatons. The U.S. delegation probably chose the 15-percent limit because the new holes that the Soviets had already dug had a diameter 30 percent larger than SS-9 silos. The attempt was ineffectual, however, because the Soviets had already developed new pop-up cold-launch techniques that permit the retrofitting of their "new big ones"—the SS-18s—into SS-9 silos. The same cold-launch techniques permit upgrading of the SS-11 force of nearly 1,000 launchers to SS-17s and SS-19s (with throw-weights of from three to five times those of the early SS-11s).

It is only logical that the Soviets would protect their weapons construction by the necessary language because they were under no obligation to agree to a dimension limitation that would ruin a program on which they had spent scores of billions of rubles. They have every legal right to stand on the terms of the agreement itself. If the Soviets exploit this loophole, the more-than-double explosive power and MIRV capability that they can add to their present SS-9 force will give them a first-strike capability. So also as to their replacement of hundreds of SS-11s with SS-17s and SS-19s capable of carrying from four to six MIRVs each.

If the Soviets do retrofit the SS-9 silos with SS-18s, they could use 100 of the displaced SS-9 missiles as loads for the "mobile" SS-9 launchers, as described in Loophole 2 above, and use the remaining 200 SS-9s as suggested in Loophole 4 below, thus saving, quite literally, billions of rubles. The Soviets never scrap any instruments of strategic power. Because they saved their first and second generation ICBMs, the SS-7s and SS-8s (while McNamara threw ours away), the Soviets are able to "trade" them under the SALT I Agreement either for a significant SLBM advantage or for more SS-9s.

4. *Conversion of "light" or "older" ICBM launchers into SS-9 launchers.* The loophole that would permit this conversion is one of the most cleverly and intricately constructed and concealed in the entire Interim Agreement. The Kremlin's crafty draftsmen worked out a legal masterpiece. The segments of this one-way loophole must be fitted together like pieces in a jigsaw puzzle. The totality of the deception they put over on the U.S. delegation is well illustrated by this excerpt concerning "conversion" from Secretary of State William P. Rogers' official letter of explanation transmitting the SALT pacts to Congress:

B. Heavy ICBM Launchers

Article II provides that the parties shall not convert land-based launchers for light, or older heavy, ICBMs into land-based launchers for modern heavy ICBMs, such as the Soviet SS-9. All currently operational ICBMs other than the SS-9 are either "light" (the United States Minuteman and the Soviet SS-11 and SS-13) or "older" ICBM launchers of types first deployed prior to 1964 (the United States Titan and the Soviet SS-7 and SS-8).

Article II would thus prohibit the conversion of a launcher for an SS-7, SS-8, SS-11 or SS-13 into a launcher for an SS-9 or any new modern heavy ICBM, and would similarly prohibit the conversion of a launcher for a Minuteman or a Titan into a launcher for a modern heavy ICBM.

A quick reference back to the verbatim text of Article II will immediately establish that it does no such thing. Mr. Rogers and every other U.S. official read Article II *as if the last six words of the last line of the Article simply did not exist.* They read Article II *as if* it said:

The parties undertake not to convert land-based launchers for light ICBMs, or for ICBMs of older types deployed prior to 1964, into land-based launchers for heavy ICBMs . . .

But, in the text of the Interim Agreement, these six key words follow "heavy ICBMs":

of types deployed after that time.

An established rule of interpretation of even ordinary business contracts or agreements requires that effect be given, if at all possible, to *all* the words used. Especially is this true in an agreement of historic importance. U.S. officials have no legal basis, nor any basis in common sense, for reading the phrase "for launchers of heavy ICBMs of types deployed after that time" *as if* it said only "for launchers of heavy ICBMs."

The difference is critical. Only by omitting those six words could Secretary Rogers arrive at the interpretation that he officially gave Congress. He says that the Article prohibits the conversion of "launchers for light, or older heavy, ICBMs into launchers for *modern* heavy ICBMs, *such as the Soviet SS-9.*" Note that, in the emphasized words, he has substituted his own language for the explicit and unambiguous language of the agreement. International law could not possibly support such unilateral changes after certain express wording had been agreed to and signed by both sides.

Secretary Rogers' use of the "Soviet SS-9" as an illustration is most probably the exact contrary of the actual meaning of the words that the Soviets succeeded in getting into the agreement. To understand what the Soviets accomplished in this article, it is necessary to isolate the antecedent of the last two words in the phrase that Secretary Rogers pretends are not there: "that time." The expression "that time" can only refer back to "1964." As no specific date in 1964 is expressed, the Soviets are entirely within their legal rights in contending that "after that time" means *after December 31, 1964.*

Can it be considered a coincidence that it was early in 1964 that U.S. intelligence first noted the deployment of a new heavy Soviet land-based ICBM? It had not yet been given a NATO designation, but it was recognized as "at least twice as powerful" as Soviet ICBMs deployed prior to that time. The new missile was soon estimated to be of about 20 megatons in explosive power and was given the designation SS-9.[4]

The clinching item of evidence that Article II constitutes an artfully concealed, deliberate, and preplanned Soviet trap for the United States is the absolute and repeated refusal of the Soviet delegation to include in the agreement, or in any interpretation or addendum that could be binding on them, any additional definition of the term "heavy missile."

The reason for the Soviet refusal was, of course, a mystery to the U.S. SALT delegates, who would never suspect the Soviets of setting a trap, least of all in the most critical article of the agreement. Our delegates were apparently so naive that they did not even worry over such a mystery. Instead of worrying, they merely expressed this solemn "regret" in "Unilateral Statement D":

> The U.S. delegation made the following statement on May 26, 1972: "The U.S. delegation regrets that the Soviet delegation has not been willing to agree on a common definition of a heavy missile. Under these circumstances, the U.S. delegation believes it necessary to state the following: The United States would consider any ICBM having a volume significantly greater than that of the largest light ICBM now operational on either side to be a heavy ICBM. The U.S. proceeds on the premise that the Soviet side will give due account to this consideration."

As a matter of law and of common sense, the Soviets are entirely right in not agreeing on a common definition of the expression "heavy missile"; and the definition that the U.S. delegation sought to impose unilaterally is irrelevant. The *only* time the word "heavy" is used in the agreement is as part of the expression, "heavy ICBMs of types deployed after that time [1964]."

Often the only way to make complex problems of nuclear strategy come alive is by a scenario. Let us say the year is 1975. U.S. reconnaissance satellites have revealed that the Soviets are replacing 100 of their SS-7s and SS-8s with SS-9s. (Some 200 to 250 of these missile launchers are on soft pads, not in silos, so "Agreed Interpretation J" and "Common Understanding A" against increasing "the present dimensions of land-based ICBM silo launchers" more than 10-15 percent do not apply. Let us say also that the Soviets have exercised their option of digging new silos or modernizing or replacing the existing pads.)

The U.S. Representative on the SALT "Standing Consultative Commission" objects to this buildup of the SS-9 force and contends that the SS-9 type is covered by the U.S. definition of "heavy ICBM" as set out in "Unilateral Statement D."

The Soviet Representative rejoins: "We agree that the SS-9 does meet your definition of 'heavy ICBM'; and we do not object to your using that definition even though it is not binding on us.

"Even if the SS-9 is considered a 'heavy ICBM,' however, it is most certainly not a 'heavy ICBM of types deployed after that time,' that is, the time specified in the Interim Agreement, which is '1964.'

"The SS-9 type was deployed during, not after, 1964. Your intelligence records will verify this deployment date. Why else do you think we would have been so careful to choose the year 1964 and not tie it down to a specific day and month in that year? The express language of Article II makes the SS-9 a permissible replacement for either light ICBMs or 'ICBMs of older types deployed prior to 1964,' a definition that clearly includes the SS-7 and SS-8 types.

"The only Soviet 'heavy ICBM' that the Interim Agreement forbids us to use to replace light ICBMs or older ICBMs is the one you referred to as the 'new big one' at the time the agreement was signed. That is the only heavy ICBM type we deployed after 1964."

The U.S. Representative, pale from shock, finally speaks up: "If the Soviet Union continues to replace old model and/or light ICBMs with SS-9s, the United States will be forced reluctantly to consider giving six-months' notice of withdrawal from both the Interim Agreement and the ABM Treaty."

The Soviet Representative coolly replies: "I would suggest that if you do recommend that to your government, you also recommend that it be considered with all the relevant factors in mind. In the first place, what 'extraordinary event' within the meaning of the agreement could you cite to justify termination? The Soviet Union is not violating the agreement in any way. The plain language was there to read—even in your official English language version. How can you explain to your people and the press and the Congress that you were stupid enough to pretend that six key words of Article II were not there? Why do you think we chose the year 1964 as controlling? Why do you think we refused to agree on any other definition of what types of replacements were forbidden?

"It is certainly not an 'extraordinary event' for one side to act in accordance with the express and specific terms of a solemn agreement. How could you allege that the deployment of these old SS-9s could 'jeopardize the supreme interests of the United States'? Don't you realize that the United States and the Soviet Union are now peacefully coexisting in an era of negotiation instead of confrontation?

"There is also this further consideration. As you have no legal or moral reason for terminating the treaty and the Interim Agreement, the Soviet Union may have to treat your attempt to give notice of termination as an unfriendly act.

"I must warn you that we will have these additional 100 SS-9s operational long before the six months are up. I should also inform you of other actions the Soviet Union has taken, all entirely within the terms of the agreement. As you well know, the agreement in no way limits the *production* of missiles or missile launching tubes and equipment, nor does it prohibit the deployment of land-mobile ICBMs.

"We have produced and have in live storage, ready for immediate deployment, 500 land-mobile SS-16-type launchers. Since we had developed such great momentum on our production of SS-11 missiles, we kept the lines in operation and merely switched over to the SS-16 type. We now have 1,000 of them in storage. Of these, 500 will load the land-mobile self-propelled launchers. The other 500 we hold in reserve for rapid deployment on railroad cars, on trucks, and on prefabricated launching pads, all of which can be operational well within six months.

"So, would you really want to recommend U.S. action that would terminate our period of peaceful coexistence, and turn away from negotiation to confrontation, in the face of this massive but entirely legally acquired strategic power of the Soviet Union? Remember, this is no mere 'marginal' addition to our already vastly superior power. It gives us a completely credible first-strike capability. It makes detente, on Soviet terms, irreversible."

The U.S. Representative makes no answer. He is thinking: "The B-1 strategic bombers and the Trident submarines will be operational in the early 1980s—but this is 1975. Will there be a United States in the early 1980s?"

5. *Modernization of IRBM and MRBM launchers to provide intercontinental range.* The Soviets have in place and targeted on Western Europe from 700 to 1,000 intermediate-range and medium-range ballistic missile launchers. Prior to 1967 this missile force was needed to hold the NATO nations in Europe hostage during the years when the balance of intercontinental delivery vehicles was massively in favor of the United States.

The Soviets no longer need the larger part of this force because the U.S. strategic deterrent is no longer credible as a protection of Western Europe. Also, if the United States is neutralized as a nuclear power or is destroyed, Western Europe will have no rational alternative to a preemptive surrender. Furthermore, the Soviets have 700 medium bombers that can deliver strategic warheads on Western Europe, plus quite literally thousands of first-class fighter-bomber aircraft that can deliver relatively powerful tactical warheads in that area.

Many of these IRBMs and MRBMs are SS-4 and SS-5 types. Large numbers of them, however, have already been replaced with the "variable range" model of the SS-11, supposedly with only two propulsion stages that give them only intermediate range. As the Interim Agreement does not even cover launchers of less than intercontinental range, all these launchers could be "modernized" to take the SS-11 type, or even the SS-17 and SS-19 types that use cold-launch techniques. The SS-11s could be upgraded to intercontinental range at the same time merely by adding the third propulsion stage that this missile is already designed to accept. In any view possible to a U.S. reconnaissance satellite, it would be most difficult to prove that upgrading to ICBM capability had taken place.

Of the 10 major loopholes considered in this chapter, this is the only one that would involve the Soviet Union in an actual violation of the Interim Agreement. The other nine can be exploited legally. This loophole is presented only because the Soviet modernization program already in progress can so easily produce 700 to 1,000 additional missile launchers with ICBM capability. Also, they could dig new silos, purportedly for IRBMs, but designed for speedy enlargement to take the ICBM version of the variable-range SS-11 that is only slightly taller, or the SS-17 and SS-19, with three to five times the early SS-11 payload.

6. On-site reloads could be provided at all launcher sites. The Interim Agreement does not prohibit the production of ICBMs or even their deployment. As to land-based missiles, it prohibits only *starting* construction of additional fixed *launchers*. It contains no prohibition against adding reload missiles at launch sites. In view of the fact that the ABM Treaty contains an express prohibition of reload missiles at launch sites, this omission in the Interim Agreement as to offensive missiles must be considered intentional. This assumed new and critical importance with the development of the cold-launch pop-up technique for the SS-17, SS-18, and SS-19. All these launchers can now take reloads within short periods after an initial launch. Formerly, the tremendous heat of a blast-off damaged the launch tubes and required extensive repairs before reloading.

Then-Secretary of Defense Robert McNamara conceded as far back as his 1966 Report to Congress that some Soviet ICBMs had reload capability. It is undoubtedly still somewhat more difficult to provide reload capability for silo-launched missiles than for pad-launched missiles, but it is neither impossible or even impracticable; and it is certainly inexpensive compared to building more silos. Such reload missiles could even be stored on-site in a horizontal position and hardened to some extent; but with more than 1,000 missiles, including all their SS-9s, in hardened silos, the Soviets do not really need their additional missiles protected. They need not fear destruction of reloads even if they are "soft," because the United States has no counterforce capability that could rationally be used in a first strike.

7. Production and stockpiling of ICBMs under cover, in preparation for a crash program of deployment. The momentum of the actual production of the missiles themselves, their launching tubes, and associated electronic equipment requires protracted preparations and great expense to start, and cannot readily be resumed after a lengthy interruption. On the other hand, it does not take long to construct a pad type of launcher, as we learned at the time of the Cuban missile crisis in 1962.

Without any violation of the agreement, the Soviets can continue the mass production of missiles and launching tubes, and stockpile them under cover, ready for a crash deployment program. Undoubtedly, also, some sort of prefabricated pad could be developed, produced in quantity, and stored under cover. They had such prefabricated parts for IRBM launching pads in Cuba in 1962. The possession of a substantial number—say, 500 to 1,000—of stockpiled missiles could be quite an ace in the hole for the Soviets in case the United States should ever give notice of termination of the agreement, or start a rebuilding program in any strategic area.

8. Production of ICBMs and deployment on ships or barges. Nothing in the Agreement prohibits this, and the U.S. delegation did not register a unilateral advance warning of righteous indignation on our part if the Soviets should do it. This is not a far-out imaginary project. At the time of the Henry Kissinger-John Kennedy phony missile-gap alarm in 1960, the United States was seriously planning to mount ballistic missiles on cruisers and merchant ships, plus placing dummies on other merchant ships to provide a diversion to protect the real ones. It might be a good idea for us now that we have a real gap that will widen even more under SALT I.

9. Production and deployment of FOBS and MOBS launchers. Nowhere in the Interim Agreement is there any prohibition against the development, production, or deployment of launchers for Fractional Orbital Bombardment System rockets or launchers for Multiple Orbital Bombardment System rockets. Known as FOBS and MOBS respectively, these two systems constitute the major segments of the space weapons systems that we know the Soviets have produced, successfully tested over a period of years, and have ready for operational deployment.

The United States has no similar systems because Secretary McNamara and the State Department took the strained position that it would be contrary to the "spirit" of the United Nations Outer Space Treaty to develop or produce such weapons systems, although there was no provision in the treaty banning anything other than actually putting them into orbit. On the other hand, Secretary McNamara carefully pointed out that the Soviet FOBS was perfectly legal under the Space Treaty because, being "fractional," it did not make a complete orbit before hitting its target. Meanwhile, the Soviets boastfully pointed out the failure of the Space Treaty to ban development, production, or testing, and announced that they had done all these. The Soviets use their SS-9-type launchers for launching FOBS and MOBS rockets, and use the SS-9 propulsion system for putting these warheads into orbit or fractional orbit.

Although the Interim Agreement provisions about land-based weapons deal only with "intercontinental ballistic missile (ICBM) launchers," Secretary of State Rogers, in his official explanation to Congress of the provisions and effect of the two SALT I Agreements, asserted that "launchers for fractional orbital bombardment systems are considered to be ICBM launchers." Unfortunately, the Secretary did not indicate *who* "considers" them to be ICBM launchers. The agreement itself is totally silent on this subject. Neither the "Agreed Interpretations" nor the "Common Understandings," which might be considered to bind the Soviet Union, touch the subject at all. Even the "Unilateral Statements" contain no support whatsoever for Secretary Rogers' assertion.

10. Deployment of intermediate- and medium-range ballistic missiles to Cuba. This is one of the most shocking and obvious loopholes in the Interim Agreement. It is not merely a theoretical threat or a hypothetical case. The Soviets did it before—at a time when the strategic balance was 8-to-1 against them. Now the odds are reversed, and other aspects of the strategic balance are also much more opportune for such a move by the Soviets.

Back in 1962 they had to build their launching pads from scratch, install electronic equipment, and erect storage facilities. Now they have operational and in serial production very fine self-propelled land-mobile launchers for the two-stage intermediate-range version of the SS-11, which has three stages in the ICBM version. They have produced more than 100 of these, and their experience in deploying them in ways best calculated to conceal them from U.S. discovery dates from 1969.

The missiles themselves and the launchers could be shipped separately to Cuba, possibly even in sections, although they do not appear to be too big for shipment as a unit. In available photographs, the missile in its launching tube is carried by a motor vehicle that appears to be only about four times as long as a military jeep. As for *discovering* deployment of these mobile launchers, the Soviets claim that even their ICBM-size mobile launchers can be concealed effectively.

Unfortunately, even if our intelligence did detect them deployed in Cuba, such deployment is in no way a violation of the Interim Agreement, either in letter or in spirit. The SALT I Agreement simply does not deal at all with missiles of less-than-ICBM range. The most that we could do would be to protest that it is in violation of the so-called Kennedy-Khrushchev Agreement—which has never been revealed to the public, and which may or may not even exist in written form signed by authorized representatives.

In any event, both the principals have long since passed from the picture, and the Soviets have already tested our response to their offensive missiles in Cuba by building elaborate facilities for Soviet submarines in Cienfuegos. U.S. reaction was strong enough that they made a change: instead of calling them "Soviet" facilities, they changed and call them "Cuban" facilities. However, these "Cuban" facilities have substantial capabilities for servicing and supplying Soviet missile submarines.

This listing does not exhaust the loopholes in the SALT I Interim Agreement, but the others can be discussed more briefly elsewhere in this book.

In sharp contrast to the 10 major loopholes open to the Soviet Union under the provisions of the Interim Agreement pertaining to land-based offensive weapons, the opportunities left open to the United States to rebuild our strategic deterrent up to reasonable credibility are very limited. Even so, they represent our only chance for national survival other than depending entirely upon the grace and good will of the Soviets. What the United States *can* do under the strictures of the SALT I Agreements is presented later in this book as a specific program for national survival.

20

Dr. Kissinger's exquisitely artificial fig leaves, strategically patched on by him to adorn and conceal the major indecencies of the SALT I Agreements, began to come unfastened about the time of the Senate Foreign Relations Committee hearings on his confirmation as Secretary of State. Some of the laminar covers were suddenly blown—in the sense that term is used in counterintelligence stories. Others simply wore so thin as to become transparent. One way or the other, they all fell with surprising simultaneity and thus revealed the raw ugly truth about the sellout at the Moscow Summit of '72.

The fig-leaf covers crafted by Kissinger to hide from the public some private parts of the agreements had effectively concealed the tragic facts from all save a few experts or specialists. When the Kissinger rationalizations fell away in late 1973, SALT I was exposed as naked strategic surrender. All who cared enough about America could now see what had been done to our country.

How would one go about convicting as the deliberate architect of U.S. surrender a newly appointed Secretary of State who had just won resounding confirmation by the Senate? There would be no way. Some 99 and 44/100 percent of the American people were oblivious to the intricacies of SALT, let alone its duplicities; and they intended to stay that way. It was much more comfortable to trust the glamorously confident image of Henry Kissinger and to grant his passionate plea that we accept the 1972 Moscow Summit Agreements with "faith and fortitude." Not even the magnitude of the great grain robbery of

1972 shattered the wishful illusion, although it had cost us a billion dollars in taxes for subsidies and loans, and more than $3 billion in artificially inflated consumer prices of grain and meat.

Kissinger's charmed career appeared to be invulnerable, his influence overwhelming and invincible. He simply could not be convicted as the architect of the surrender of the United States. At the very high point of the acclaim tendered to him from pols and pundits alike, Henry Kissinger convicted himself. For reasons imponderable and buried deeply in his brain and personality, he in effect "signed" a confession. It was a "constructive" confession, but completely convincing and totally damning. It could not have been recognized as a confession that he was the architect of the surrender of the United States *unless and until* it was first established that a surrender had in fact been negotiated. This, in turn, could be demonstrated only by examining the SALT I Agreements without their many-splendored fig-leaf covers. If the American people had cared enough to look, they would have recognized the Kissinger constructive confession as a staggering admission of guilt.

The falling fig leaf that revealed the most about SALT to most Americans was the long-overdue admission by the administration that the Soviets had made in-flight tests of MIRVed warheads on at least three types of their ICBMs, including the heavy counterforce SS-18s and their new medium-heavy SS-17s and SS-19s. Henry Kissinger had used his "we-have-MIRVs-and-they-don't" argument as the principal reason for granting advantages to the Soviets ranging from substantial to overwhelming—in numbers of missiles (3 to 2), in throw-weight (5 to 1), and in missile-deliverable megatonnage (between 10 and 19 to 1).

One of Dr. Kissinger's most extreme claims in this area was in his Moscow press conference on May 27, 1972, in which he asserted:

In the assessment we now have it is about 2½ times as many warheads, and we expect at the end of the freeze period we will have about three times as many warheads.

In his comprehensive briefing to the five congressional committees at the White House on June 15, 1972, he revised the ratio:

... with our MIRVs we have a 2-to-1 lead today in numbers of warheads and this lead will be maintained during the period of the agreement even if the Soviets develop and deploy MIRVs of their own.

Analysis reveals that both claims are either wildly irresponsible or deliberately deceptive. If the Soviets had attained by 1972 the technology the United States had attained in 1969—and the evidence indicates that they had surpassed this—they can have, long before what Kissinger calls the end of the "period" (May, 1977, unless extended by SALT II), five times as many warheads as we will or can have. MIRVing a missile is like cutting a pie: the larger the pie, the more slices you can get, or the bigger the individual pieces can be, or both. The advantage goes with the advantage in throw-weight.

As of the signing of SALT I, all authorities (including Henry Kissinger) conceded that the Soviets had a 4-to-1 advantage in this area. But with the 3-to-5-times upgrade in throw-weight of the SS-11 replacements, the SS-17 and SS-19, and of the SS-9 (which, prior to development of the SS-18, was their heaviest missile), their total ICBM force throw-weight or payload advantage must have reached at least 6-to-1, and probably much more. The Defense Department concedes to the SS-18 only 30 megatons of explosive power (suggesting a 20-percent increase in payload), but this is probably a calculated understatement; it is inconsistent with the increase in volume of the new missile, and inconsistent also with Senator Henry Jackson's long-held (since 1972) estimate of 50+ megatons. His is more likely to be accurate, because he is not subject to censorship by Henry Kissinger, as is the Defense Department and especially Secretary James R. Schlesinger. It is logically untenable to credit the Soviets with only a 20-percent increase in megatonnage after so long a time for development and so much in the way of resources devoted to the SS-9/SS-18 series. Their predictable improvement in yield/weight ratio of the warheads would suggest more than that, even without allowing for an increase in the size of the missile, and that increase in the envelope has been already definitely established.

Because we are dealing with the most crucial issue concerning the SALT I Interim Agreement imbalances against the United States, we do not want this analysis to be subject to challenges of our estimate of the SS-18 throw-weight. Although our best computations and evidence credit the SS-18 with a throw-weight sufficient to deliver (because of their high yield/weight ratio) a 100-megaton warhead, we will base this MIRV-capability analysis on the Defense Department's rather obvious underestimate of 30 megatons.

A Poseidon launcher has the capability of launching a missile with a throw-weight of about 3,000 pounds, or probably less. A Poseidon missile has either 10 or 14 MIRVs mounted in the mother warhead. If 10 MIRVs are used per missile, each one can weigh no more than 300 pounds, and is reported at a power of 50 kilotons; if 14 MIRVs are used, each one cannot weigh more than about 214 pounds, and is reported at a power of 17 kilotons. This illustrates one great disadvantage of MIRVs from an operation-functional point of view: a single-warhead Poseidon could carry four megatons of explosive power; but when divided into 10 MIRVs of 50 kilotons each, the total is only 1/2 megaton. We throw away 3½ megatons of explosive power to gain the separate targeting capability; but the separate targeting capability will mean nothing if the yield of the individual warhead is too small to destroy its target, considering our current accuracy of guidance. By MIRVing too much, we may have thrown away the whole Poseidon, and certainly we have degraded its warhead reliability some 50 percent. Robert McNamara understood this all too well when he ordered that design for the Poseidon. Poseidon missiles a la McNamara would neither worry the Russians nor help us.

Now take the SS-18. The Defense Department estimate of 30 megatons would suggest a throw-weight of about 15,000 pounds. The Poseidon's throw-weight is 3,000 pounds. If the Poseidon can carry 10 MIRVs, the Soviet SS-18 can carry 50 similar MIRVs, but probably with more explosive power because of their better yield/weight ratio. Even the old nonupgraded SS-9s can carry 40 MIRVs to our Poseidon's 10. The Soviet advantage obtains also as to land-based ICBMs. Our latest, the Minuteman III, carries three MIRVs rated at 170 kilotons (0.17 megatons) each, but usually referred to as a round 200 kilotons each. The upgraded Soviet SS-17 probably carries two MIRVs of two megatons each, or three MIRVs of from one to two megatons each. If they were willing to accept the lower one megaton yield, they could have at least five of them on each SS-17; and the SS-19 can carry six MIRVs of one to two megatons each.

There is no question that, under the SALT I Interim Agreement, we are not only subjected to the 3-to-2 Soviet advantage in numbers of missiles, a 6-to-1 Soviet advantage in throw-weight or payload, and something between a 10-to-1 and 19-to-1 Soviet advantage in missile-deliverable megatonnage (depending on the force loading they choose)—but we are also subjected to a potential 6-to-1 Soviet advantage in MIRVed warhead numbers. This is quite different from the 2-to-1 to 3-to-1 U.S. advantage that Henry Kissinger promised us before SALT I was approved by Congrèss, and which he asserted would last beyond the five-year term of the Interim Agreement.

Of course the administration could not permit the public to know these facts. It was no longer possible to suppress the news that the Soviets had achieved successful in-flight tests of three types of MIRVs, but Kissinger's reputation had to be saved and it was necessary to head off questions as to the effect of Soviet MIRVs on the U.S. strategic position under the SALT Agreements.

So Secretary of Defense James Schlesinger came up with a set of the usual half-misleading truths and half-outright lies. The Soviets could, he pontificated, catch up with the United States in total warheads by 1979.[1] Part of that statement is true but, without proper qualification, it is materially misleading and must have been calculated to be so. The Soviets could, indeed, catch up with the United

States in total warheads by 1979 *if* all they wanted to do was catch up and *if* they did not want to reach that number before then. By 1979 they could, if they wanted to, have six times as many warheads—but by the end of 1976 they could have as many as the U.S. total and also retain their massive advantage in megatonnage.

To lend support to Schlesinger's wild implication that the Soviets could not equal the U.S. total until 1979, the Defense Department passed out this "not-directly-attributable" background information:

> They still must do considerable testing, especially for accuracy. U.S. experts estimate the elapsed time between the *first tests* and the beginning of deployment to be around two years. By this reckoning, the U.S.S.R. could *begin* placing MIRVs on missiles in 1975.

By this technique newsmen were led to assume that the Soviet MIRV tests had begun only a few weeks prior to Schlesinger's press conference on August 17, 1973, and on at least two types of missiles and possibly four. However, back in 1970 there was a great debate in the U.S. intelligence community as to whether the Soviets were conducting flight tests of MIRVs even then. All segments of U.S. intelligence agreed that they were at least "going forward with the development and testing of MIRV technology."[2] The only split was as to whether the tests included in-flight tests of MIRVs. It is unchallenged that the Soviets *could* have been conducting such tests without our being able to detect them—let alone obtain the "conclusive proof" that Kissinger requires. The Soviets could simply launch a five-MIRV warhead carrying five miniatures, but schedule only one to detach while the others remain on board to impact. In any event, on December 5, 1971, Dr. John S. Foster, Director of Research and Engineering for the Defense Department, stated on ABC's network program *Issues and Answers:*

> *My personal opinion is that they have demonstrated a MIRV.* I don't know whether or not they have demonstrated *sufficient accuracy* so there is a high probability of being able to kill three Minutemen with one of their SS-9 missiles. I simply don't know that. It may in fact exist and with high reliability, and it may not.

Dr. Foster is a brilliant scientist and an honest man, and his statement that the Soviet MIRVs may have attained high accuracy and high reliability without our knowledge must be taken at face value.

The Schlesinger implication at his August 17, 1973, press conference that the "first" Soviet MIRV tests had just taken place, should be compared with the following dispatch from Washington which appeared on page 1 of the *New York Times* on June 9, 1972:

> Secretary of Defense Melvin R. Laird, in secret testimony before the Senate Armed Services Committee, has disclosed that the Soviet Union

is *flight testing* a missile that can fire several warheads at individual targets. Thus far, such missiles have remained an American monopoly.

The disclosure that the Russians have begun testing what is known as the MIRV—or multiple independently targeted reentry vehicle—was made by Mr. Laird in answer to a Senator's question on the Soviet advances in this field. His remarks were made known by a Senate source and confirmed by Jerry W. Friedheim, the Pentagon spokesman.

The Soviets began testing MRVs no later than mid-1968, and their tests soon demonstrated suspicious sophistication for mere (non-independently-targeted) MRVs. The best evidence indicates that the Soviets began testing MIRVs as well as MIRV technology no later than 1970. We began deploying MIRVs in 1969-70, and we have it from Henry Kissinger himself that:

> I think it is safe to say that the Soviet Union has been engaged in the first step toward MIRV at a time when we have not yet deployed MIRV.[3]

When Laird told the truth about Soviet MIRV tests in June 1972, it had to be hushed up immediately. Laird's statement was relatively easy to suppress because it was made in secret testimony.

Add it all up and we know that James R. Schlesinger lied to the American public about Soviet MIRV capability by a period of at least a year, and probably two years. The statements implying that the "first tests" of Soviet MIRVs were in August 1973, coupled with the phony estimate of another two years before the Soviets would be ready to *begin* deployment of MIRVs, were deliberately misleading. Schlesinger must know very well that those were not "first" tests. He simply could not help but know it from the evidence we have reviewed above. He must know, therefore, that the 1973 tests were tests of *operational production* MIRVs, not experimental tests related to development. Nor could he or any of his "experts" know that the Soviets "still must do considerable testing, especially for accuracy." We have Dr. John Foster's word for what is not challenged by any objective specialist; namely, that if the Soviets are deliberately concealing their accuracy from us in their tests, we cannot reliably ascertain their maximum accuracy but only what they are willing to let us observe.

The MIRV fig leaf has thus been the prime instrument for deceiving the American people, the Congress, and our NATO allies. The only ones who could *not* be fooled are the masters of the Kremlin.

The deliberate and deceptive *understatement* of the Soviets' capability of MIRVing is only one segment of the net of deception that Dr. Kissinger's department of misinformation has woven around us. Equally dishonest is the calculated *overstatement* of the Soviets' *requirement* for MIRVing. The inescapable implication of the Schlesinger statement that the Soviets could catch up with the United States in total warheads by 1979, and *then* have "a very formidable force

427

structure" by the early or mid-1980s, is that, *until* they do catch up in total number of warheads, they have neither attained parity nor a very formidable force structure. This is completely untrue.

Secretary Schlesinger implies that the Soviets need to MIRV a couple of thousand missiles and that this will take them six years or more. Not so. In no circumstances under SALT could the Soviets have a critical requirement for MIRVs on more than 265 to 300 of their SS-9/SS-18 force. That would give them a sufficient number, coupled with the accuracy of guidance they can attain by 1975, to kill 99 percent of our Minuteman force. There are simply not enough other targets in the United States or Red China to require the Soviets to MIRV their already massive missile force. The United States is restrained by the 1974 Moscow Summit Protocol to the SALT I Anti-Defense Treaty from defending more than one city (Washington, D.C.) or one missile site (Grand Forks) with ABMs. MIRVs could be required to penetrate a heavy ABM defense, but we will not have one. Therefore the Soviets simply do not need additional MIRVs. Other than penetrating an ABM defense, anything a MIRVed warhead can do, a single-war-headed missile can do far better and more reliably—if, that is, the attacking country has enough numbers of missiles. And the Soviets do.

If a country MIRVs when it doesn't need to, it throws away explosive power and destructive power; more especially, it throws away reliability (plus lots of money). When we MIRV a Poseidon, as we have seen, if we assume the single warhead at a conservative three megatons (probably it is four), we get ten 50-kiloton (0.05 megaton) MIRVs, making a total of 1/2 megaton in the missile that single-headedly carried six times that much total explosive power. If we go to 14 MIRVs of 17 kilotons each (0.017 megaton), we get a total missile loading of 238 kilotons (0.238 megaton), or less than 1/4 a megaton. That is, we are throwing away, respectively, 5/6 or 11/12 of our explosive power. No wonder McNamara wanted MIRVs! In addition, there was a McNamara bonus: extreme miniaturization made our Poseidon MIRVed warheads less than 50 percent reliable, as of the end of 1973. We will probably improve our reliability, but it will require years to recoup a large percentage of the reliability that the un-MIRVed Poseidons could have possessed. Of course the Soviets have their other and permanent advantages in their much larger throw-weights and massively more powerful warheads. If they MIRV a 25-megaton SS-9 into three five-megaton warheads, they throw away only 2/5 of their single warhead explosive power, and probably get higher reliability.

In order to escape having to admit serious and probably decisive inferiority under SALT I, Kissinger's department of misinformation had to convince the American people that the Soviets desperately *need* MIRVs. Any admission that the Soviets don't need MIRVs might stimulate the awkward question: why do *we* need MIRVs? The tragic answer is that the United States doesn't need them nearly so badly as we need more missiles, more megatonnage, and better guidance—but McNamara and Kissinger needed MIRVs in order to play the "numbers game" against the American people. A warhead is a warhead is a warhead, is what McNamara, in effect, claimed, and Kissinger has echoed this ad nauseam. President Nixon's own Blue Ribbon Defense Panel Supplemental Statement, dated September 1, 1970, gave this warning to the Kissinger-beguiled President and to the unlistening nation:

> This simplistic type of comparison creates the illusion of abundant security if not U.S. overkill capacity.
> It would be difficult to conceive of a better way to mislead the public than to present—without precise definition and analysis—comparative figures of this kind. Those who present such distortions contribute to the confusion rather than enlightenment of our people.

Because the Blue Ribbon Defense Panel members who wrote this were absolutely correct, Henry Kissinger continued with the original McNamara deception. MIRVs have, indeed, contributed "to the confusion rather than enlightenment of our people" on the matter of how dangerously much Kissinger gave away to the Soviets in the SALT I Agreements.

In attempting to justify the vast imbalance in missile-launching nuclear-propelled submarines he granted the Soviets in the SALT I Interim Agreement—62 for them to 44 for us—Henry Kissinger, in presenting his grand rationale of SALT on June 15, 1972, at the White House for the five congressional committees, tossed in this gem:

> Then there are such factors as deployment characteristics. For example, because of the difference in geography and basing, it has been estimated that the Soviet Union requires three submarines for two of ours to be able to keep an equal number on station.

In that declaration Dr. Kissinger simply put his imprimatur on a Soviet argument. It could not have been true even then, so long as there is a submarine base in Cuba—and there is a submarine base there, at Cienfuegos. To ease Kissinger and Nixon out of the somewhat embarrassing situation because of the publicity about this base, it was decided to refer to it as a *Cuban* submarine base, not as a Soviet submarine base. However, Kissinger tripped himself up by a Freudian slip at his news conference in Moscow on May 29, 1972. In explaining to a reporter how the Moscow Declaration of Principles would work between the U.S. and the U.S.S.R., Kissinger said:

> Now again, Max, no one can be so naive as to say that if they build *another*

submarine base in Cuba, that the most telling argument will be the third principle of this declaration.

His department of misinformation, however, kept peddling the line about the terrible disadvantage the poor Soviets suffer in their deployment of submarines. The following leak was arranged to appear in one of our better news magazines dated September 24, 1973:

Western intelligence officials assessing relative U.S.-Soviet strategic power make this point: Russia is able to maintain "on station" only five of its 34 missile-launching submarines, whereas well over half of America's 41 missile subs are kept on their prescribed stations.

In the first place, the Soviets had 42 such submarines, not 34. In the second place, the United States only has 41 missile-firing submarines *less* the number being converted to Poseidons—an alleged "rebuilding" job that admittedly requires at least a 60-percent new-construction job and keeps them in the yard for some two years each. The number out of commission is usually seven. So the realistic number for the United States is 34. The "well over half" formula for U.S. submarines on station is somewhat exaggerated; 6/10 is the greatest claim that can be made.

The newsman who was suckered by that leak had overlooked one of the really big stories of 1973. The Soviets had deployed a new class of missile-launching submarines known as the Delta class—and it carries, not the former SLBMs, but what must be accurately described as SLICBMs, that is, Submarine-Launched Intercontinental Ballistic Missiles. That constitutes a substantial revolution in this area of strategic power. For the Soviets, it is pretty close to the ultimate weapon in the 1975-1995 timeframe. And they have it now. It is far and away the most nearly invulnerable weapon system—incomparably more so than our Poseidon force. The Delta submarine with its new long-range missiles is tremendously versatile. Because of the inertial guidance of the missiles—probably stellar-assisted—it can be a counterforce weapon. Because of its survivability, it is a deterrent to both a preemptive strike and preventive strike, and it is also the most effective weapon system for backing up a counterforce first-strike with a counterpopulation blackmail threat.

The Soviet Delta is, therefore, an ideal first-strike weapon—and should serve as a conclusive item of evidence as to Soviet intentions and the reason for the entire strategic buildup.

Most important, a Soviet Delta missile-launching submarine *is on station at all times*—not .16 of the time as is claimed in the U.S. underestimates about the Soviet Yankee-class submarines, nor .6 of the time as the administration claims about Poseidons, but all the time. The reason they can be considered on station at all times was stated, perhaps inadvertently, by the Chief of Naval Operations, Admiral

Elmo Zumwalt, in his testimony on the FY 1974 military posture before the House Defense Appropriations Subcommittee:

> . . . the Soviet Delta submarine with extended-range strategic missiles [is] *capable of reaching our population centers from their home ports* and in many respects [is] comparable to our planned Trident submarine.

To reach our population centers from their home ports, Soviet submarines must be deployed with missiles of more than the minimum ICBM range: that is, something more than 5,000 nautical miles. This is the range first attributed by published intelligence reports to the new Soviet SS-N-8. But when it was apparent that we could claim a range of no more than 4,500 nautical miles for our *planned* Trident missiles—planned for *circa* 1980—the figures on the Delta range given out by the Defense Department were cut to 4,400. Actually, the more than 5,000-mile-range Delta SS-N-8 *missiles* had successfully undergone several years of tests before we discovered the Delta *submarine* types. Our intelligence kept reporting that the Soviets were testing a new extended-range SLBM for which they had no known launching vehicle.

The versatility and potential of the Delta, with its extended-range missile and inertial guidance, is staggering. So far as invulnerability is concerned, the range of its missiles gives the Delta submarine an increase in operating area by a factor of more than 10 over a U.S. Poseidon, the missiles of which have less than half the Delta missiles' range. It is easy to visualize this with a globe of the world and a flexible plastic ruler or even a piece of string. First, swing a 5,000-mile radius centered on New York. You will see that the ocean depths for nearly half the globe are available to hide Soviet Delta missile submarines prowling within range of U.S. targets. No present or prospective anti-submarine warfare techniques could cope with a force of submarines with such a vast on-station area, especially when those areas include the waters of Soviet home ports.

Unlike the Soviet Y-class with shorter-range missiles, Delta submarines will not have to sneak out of their ports, make their way through narrow passages where we might detect them, and then travel thousands of miles to get within range of U.S. cities or missile sites. Delta submarines are already within range, as Admiral Zumwalt pointed out, even in their home ports. Even in the midst of changing crews, they could launch their missiles. As Admiral Hyman Rickover has testified, "in effect, the Russians already have their equivalent of our Trident." Because of the Soviets' geographical advantage of far-inland location of their principal cities, we will not be able to reach Soviet cities from our home ports until we get Trident II with a 6,000-mile range.

Next, on the globe of the world, take a 2,800-mile radius and swing

431

it around from Moscow, or from a missile-site location east of the Urals. You will see that, because of the extensive land areas covered by the first segment of the radius—which now represents the last segment of the flight path of a U.S. missile targeted on a large Soviet city—the ocean-operating areas of our Poseidon submarines are strictly limited and subject to Soviet antisubmarine surveillance, in addition to being thousands of miles from U.S. ports. Their present on-station duration periods are strictly dependent on foreign bases, such as in England and Spain. These may become unavailable when the British and Spanish see what SALT I and Kissinger have done to U.S. strategic power.

Employed as a first-strike weapon, the Soviet Delta submarines could double the number of missiles each submarine could launch at the United States. They could launch missiles from near their home ports, then return to superhardened submarine pens for reloading. The inertial guidance of their missiles ensures the accuracy required for their first launch to destroy our hardened missiles. Reloads could be held for threats against our population to secure our surrender and to preclude any retaliation by U.S. Poseidon submarines. This fast-reload capability is theirs alone until we get Trident II missiles on Trident submarines. Our Poseidons must travel days before reaching a home port for reloading because they have to go so far to get within range of Soviet cities.

This knowledge of the capabilities of Soviet Delta submarines tears away another vital fig leaf from the Kissinger coverup of what we gave away in SALT I. He argued, as we have seen, that the Soviets required three submarines to two of ours in order to keep an equal number on station. Now it is clear that the situation will be reversed as they multiply deployment of Deltas. As of late 1973 U.S. intelligence admits the deployment or under-construction status of 19 Deltas. At other times we have underestimated the number of Soviet submarines deployed by seven or eight, according to Soviet claims in the SALT negotiations that Kissinger honored. It is conceded that they can add eight or nine a year. All these can be on station all the time, at least for seven or eight years, until they require major overhaul. Indeed, they might even be able to launch their missiles at U.S. targets while undergoing overhaul. As for the Soviet Y-class submarines, 33 have been completed and can be kept on station for extended periods of time if the Cuban facilities available to the Soviets merely permit the changing of crews and resupply of consumable supplies. There is little question that the Cienfuegos base is available for extensive services and supplies.

The point is that although a nonexpert reporter on a news magazine can be excused for failing to understand the strategic significance of the new Soviet submarine and SLICBM developments Henry Kissinger cannot. He knew at the time he accepted the Soviet arguments based on their alleged disadvantage in keeping numbers of submarines on station that they had already developed and successfully tested the new SS-N-8 missile. In the press conference he frequently referred to the Soviet submarine type that carried only 12 missiles. That could only mean the Delta. (The Extended-Delta carries 16.) So Kissinger not only gave away a tremendous advantage to the Soviets in allowing them 62 missile-launching submarines to our 44; he did far more than that. He deliberately deceived the President and the Congress and the American people by endorsing a Soviet argument that he knew would be obsolete within a couple of years.

The Soviet development of the first intercontinental-range submarine-launched ballistic missile also solves another of the many mysteries of SALT: it explains why the Soviets insisted on holding open the greatest and most obvious loophole in the SALT I Interim Agreement, which purportedly limits offensive strategic weapons.

One of the three prime U.S. objectives throughout the entire 2½ years of the SALT negotiations was to freeze the number of Soviet ICBMs. They were building them so fast (they added nearly 1,000 while the negotiations were dragging out) that additional numbers would soon give them a preclusive first-strike capability against the United States. The only restraint the Soviets would agree to was on fixed land-based ICBM launchers and on SLBM launchers on modern submarines. This left all types of land-mobile and sea-surface mobile launchers absolutely unlimited. Without violating SALT I, the Soviets could legally build and deploy 1,000, or even 10,000, land-mobile ICBM launchers. Or put that many on surface ships that could cruise within Soviet coastal waters, under protection of the massive Soviet air-defense system of 10,000 SAMs and 3,000 fighter-interceptor aircraft. The Soviets would never need a fraction that many additional missile launchers, but that is how ineffective SALT I is as far as protecting the United States or inhibiting the Soviets.

Kissinger realized that if a single Senator were coached by an expert to analyze the effect of failing to restrict land-mobile missile launchers, the whole rigmarole of SALT I would be exposed as a fraud on the American people and Congress. The only type of land-based missile launcher that the agreement covered was the fixed-base type—a class of missile launcher that all experts knew would soon be obsolete because of the inexorably increasing accuracy of missile guidance. There was already enough experience available to "trend" the degree and pace of guidance improvement: roughly, a factor of two every three or four years. So, when the Soviets completed the extra 99 silos they had under construction, they would have completed their fixed-base program. Before the end of the five-year term of the SALT I Agreement, all fixed-base launchers would be vulnerable even to warheads as relatively weak as the Minuteman MIRVs (if the United States also availed itself of improved guidance technology). Henry Kissinger did not want to have to return to the United States and take the chance of defending a deal with the Kremlin in which he had sacrificed the highly sophisticated and successful U.S. ABM program, and made the American people helpless hostages to a Soviet missile force that was, for all practical purposes, not restrained at all by the SALT I Agreement.

Henry Kissinger, master of deals and diplomacy, was unable to budge the Soviet leaders an inch toward including land-mobile missile launchers in the prohibitions of the SALT I Agreement. What he may have offered them to do so, God only knows. If you were Henry Kissinger in Moscow in May 1972, and there were only three days left in which to secure a summit arms-limitation agreement, and President Nixon desperately needed such an agreement in time to make a television spectacular in order to exploit it in his current election campaign, and Brezhnev and his Politburo pals were refusing to close a gap in the draft agreement—a gap so massive as to make the agreement an obvious burlesque to knowledgeable people—what would you do? Well, Kissinger got President Nixon himself to make a personal impassioned plea to Leonid Brezhnev. On May 23, just three days before the signature ceremonies were scheduled in time to make the Friday evening television newscasts and the Sunday newspapers, the President himself made his own plea to Brezhnev. This was reluctantly revealed by Kissinger himself in one of his Moscow press conferences at the Intourist Hotel on May 27, 1972:

> Q: What were the two issues that the President settled with the Soviet leaders Tuesday night? Did they concern the submarine issue as well?
> Dr. Kissinger: No. One of them had to do with the ABM systems. I don't want to go into it in any more detail.
> Q: What is the other one?
> Dr. Kissinger: The other one involved the discussion of mobile missiles.

The way the President "settled" the land-mobile missile launcher issue was exactly the same way Kissinger had settled all other major issues with the Soviets on the SALT I Agreements: he surrendered to the Soviet demands. Kissinger tried hard to cover up his failure to get some sort of an agreement on mobile missile launchers, and to cover up the Nixon surrender under pressure. Kissinger included in the official addenda to the Interim Agreement the following Unilateral Statement:

B. Land-Mobile ICBM Launchers

. . . in the interest of concluding the Interim Agreement the U.S. delegation now withdraws its proposal that Article I or an agreed statement explicitly prohibit the deployment of mobile land-based ICBM launchers.

I have been instructed to inform you that, while agreeing to defer the question of limitation of operational land-mobile launchers to subsequent negotiations on more complete limitations on strategic arms, the U.S. would consider the deployment of operational land-mobile ICBM launchers during the period of the Interim Agreement as inconsistent with the *objectives* of that agreement.

Neither any member of the Soviet delegation, nor anyone speaking for Brezhnev, ever accepted the validity of that U.S. Unilateral Statement; and they specifically and explicitly refused to include a land-mobile prohibition in either Article I or an Agreed Interpretation. This left the Soviets free, after reducing the highly successful ongoing U.S. ABM program to shambles, and claiming the entire population of America as hostages, to build hundreds or even thousands of land-mobile ICBM launchers *and to deploy them*. Note that the U.S. Unilateral Statement—which is in no way binding on the Soviets—did *not* assert that such deployment would be inconsistent with the agreement, but only with "*the objectives of*" the Agreement. The "objectives" may also be a unilateral, subjective judgment, not at all binding on the other party. Those two words, "objectives of," are all-important, and no one knows that better than Henry Kissinger. So it is rather strange that, in his official, formal briefing at the White House for the five congressional committees specially concerned with the SALT I Agreements, he made this statement:

In the more important Unilateral Declarations we made clear to the Soviets that the introduction of land-mobile ICBMs would be inconsistent with the agreement.

A slip of the tongue? An inadvertent omission of only two words? Hardly. This was not an off-the-cuff or extemporaneous statement. It was a written document, carefully prepared in advance, by Kissinger himself. He has a genius for changing meanings by the manipulation of a word or two. By omitting those two little words, he accomplished two important objectives: (1) he pictured the agreement to his audience, and through them to the entire Congress and the American people, as entirely different on a most substantial matter from what it really was; and (2) he cut the guts out of the admission in the official U.S. Unilateral Statement that the deployment of land-mobile launchers was *not* prohibited by (a) the agreement itself, or (b) any "agreed interpretation" to which the Soviets were a party.

Why wouldn't the Soviets agree to the prohibition of land-mobile ICBM launchers? If they had given a little, it would have made the Kissinger-Nixon team look so much better to Congress and the informed members of the American public. There must have been an important reason why. Brezhnev knows full well, as does any official who has had expert strategic advice, that the advanced strategic offensive-weapons systems of the future *must* all be mobile: whether land-based, submarine-launched, launched from surface ships, or even launched from aircraft. Long-range missiles must have a movable platform launcher that cannot be pinpointed by the upcoming superaccurate missile-killing missiles.

History, acting through geography, has given the U.S.S.R. the greatest advantage in this world for the deployment of land-mobile missiles. The Soviets have some 9 million square miles of area in which to deploy mobile missiles, to disperse and conceal them, and even to garage them in mountain fastnesses. We have only 3 million square miles.

Always seeking to work in tandem with history, Soviet leadership, Soviet scientists, Soviet technologists, and Soviet industry have matched the incalculable advantage of their geography with a triumph of nuclear weapons technology: an offensive strategic missile with intercontinental range, inertial stellar-assisted guidance, *and* advanced pop-up launching, thus providing the best capability for mobility ever engineered into any long-range ICBM.

This is the same missile that we have already seen as revolutionizing the missile-launching submarine as a strategic weapons system, by making it at once the most survivable and the most flexible intercontinental-range, counterforce-accurate, offensive-weapons system. It also has the potential for revolutionizing the other types of mobile missile-launching systems—all of which are not covered by any SALT I limitations; that is, sea-surface platforms that can be either self-propelled or barge type; dromedary-type aircraft-launcher platforms; and land-mobile automotive- or locomotive-propelled types.

The key to the unprecedented versatility of the new Soviet missiles is the new, advanced, pop-up feature. Moving pictures of ICBMs blasting out of their silo launching tubes have been shown on television. This down-thrust of an inferno of flames and rocket power is very impressive. Those who haven't seen a missile blast-off on their television screens have probably seen telecasts of the blast-off of an Apollo rocket from Cape Kennedy on its way to the moon. The launching of a Polaris or Poseidon missile from a submarine is quite a contrast. No explosive, roaring flame is discharged into the launcher tube or submarine. It simply pops up into the air and the rocket blast then lifts it up, up and away into outer space. This would greatly simplify the problem of launching a mobile missile from a railway car, a truck, a surface vessel, or especially an aircraft. Even our ICBMs originally designed for mobile launching platforms, such as the Minuteman, were of the fiery-furnace blast-off type. Truck and railroad car platforms can be much simplified and need embody no blast shield. They would be far more easily disguised as something else, such as a tank car or tank truck. Of course, under SALT I, the Soviets have no need to camouflage their mobile missile launchers, but they might want to surprise us in order to back up an ultimatum of surrender or to launch a disarming first-strike against us. Their primary protection against destruction by enemy missiles is, of course, their mobility; nine million square miles provide plenty of that, but cover and disguise also help.

The new revolutionary Soviet pop-up missile has another bonus in that it can add much greater destructive power to silo-launched ICBMs without enlarging the silo. An Agreed Interpretation appended to the SALT I Agreement permits the Soviets to increase the size of their land-based silo launchers by not more than 15 percent of their "present dimensions." Such increases in silo dimensions, however, are very expensive and time-consuming. But the pop-up ICBM seems to be the solution to this problem: more clearance is required between the missile body and the silo-launcher tube walls for a blast-off/lift-off than for a pop-up/then-ignite launch. A much heavier missile, therefore, can be launched from the unaltered silo launchers. Apparently this is just what they have done with their 1,000 SS-11s in upgrading them into the far more powerful new SS-17s and SS-19s. All this exposes the SALT I restrictions on increase in silo dimensions as a macabre joke played by the Soviets on trusting and naive Americans.

This is the solution to one of the many mysteries revolving around the absolutely firm refusal of the Soviets to agree to a definition of a "heavy missile." If they had agreed, for example, to the unilateral U.S. definition, the SS-11 would probably have been classified as a "light" missile, but the new SS-17 and SS-19 would have to be classed as "heavy" missiles because the Soviets have increased the early SS-11 throw-weight by a factor of three to five—a physical impossibility without a "significant" increase in volume over the SS-11. So our naive representatives would then have thought that Article II of the Interim Agreement would prohibit the conversion of a "light" missile launcher into a "heavy" missile launcher. Actually, it would not, as we explain elsewhere, because Article II is stacked with jokers.

The most important features of the SALT I Agreements, so far as the possible survival of the United States is concerned, are the many imbalances and loopholes. Their very existence raises two major questions. First, did the Soviets deliberately demand imbalances, and boobytrap the SALT I Agreements with loopholes? If so, they must have had some plan to exploit the advantages that these traps would provide; and, if so, they were not negotiating in good faith and they must not have been sincere in pretending to go along with Kissinger's "broad new relationship" between the two superpowers that is supposed to create a "structure of peace."

Even more important is the second question. Henry Kissinger accepted for the United States all these imbalances and loopholes, provided rationalizations for them, persuaded President Nixon to accept them, and then "sold" them to Congress, to the press, and to the American people. In doing all this was he acting wittingly or half-wittedly? To be serious about a matter that is very serious indeed, did Henry Kissinger realize that these imbalances would seriously degrade the U.S. strategic deterrent to the point at which we might have no rational alternative to tendering a surrender to a Soviet ultimatum? Did he recognize that the loopholes were deliberately and cunningly crafted to permit the Soviets to continue their strategic buildup to the point of a preclusive first-strike capability against the United States?

An analysis of the falling fig leaves has given us the answer supported by much highly persuasive evidence and by some conclusive evidence. We have seen that when he justified accepting the massive imbalance against us in numbers of missiles, in throw-weight of missiles, and in megatonnage of missiles, on the basis of our alleged 2-to-1 advantage in numbers of warheads, he knew that the claim was misleading and, from an operational viewpoint, irrelevant. When he claimed that, at the end of the five-year duration of the Interim Agreement, we would still have a 2-to-1 or even a 3-to-1 advantage in number of warheads, he either had secret information from the Soviets that they did not want more MIRVs than we have, or he was misleading the President, Congress, and the media. He knew that in any MIRV race the Soviets could out-MIRV us by a factor of 4-to-1 or 5-to-1 because of their superior throw-weight—if they wanted to. When his docile Secretary of Defense finally had to admit, a year or two late, that the Soviets had been conducting in-flight tests of MIRV warheads on at least two and possibly four types of long-range missiles, that fig leaf had to fall. The ridiculous, insulting attempts of Secretary Schlesinger to mislead the public into believing that the Soviets would not have a "very formidable force structure" until the early or mid-1980s incriminated Kissinger just as much as if he had uttered them himself. He is the czar of all U.S. intelligence and national security policies; Schlesinger would not have dared to promulgate such false intelligence without Kissinger's approval.

The next fig leaf to fall was the one that concealed the indecencies growing out of Kissinger's accepting the 62-to-44 Soviet imbalance in modern missile-launching submarines (with the secret agreement restricting the United States to 41 instead of the public 44). In accepting U.S. inferiority, he elaborately rationalized not only the number of submarines the Soviets had operational and under construction, but he even fabricated a fictional number they could have built if they continued building submarines past their planned force level of 62, beyond any possible purpose and at a cost on the order of a quarter-billion dollars each. Kissinger argued that, because the Soviets could build 90, we should give them 62—nearly 1/3 more than we would be allowed to build. He supported giving the Soviets this massive advantage in the SALT I Agreement by adopting and endorsing their false argument about theoretical U.S. advantages in submarine time-on-station. He did this at a time when, as czar of U.S. intelligence, he knew that the Soviets had developed and successfully tested, and were about to deploy, a new and revolutionary submarine that would reverse any advantage we might theoretically have in on-station time.

We analyzed evidence that, when the Soviets demanded exclusion from the SALT I Agreement of any restriction at all on land-mobile missiles, they already had in hand the technology to exploit this major gap and build thousands of additional missile launchers, if they should ever want that many. We saw also that, when the Soviets absolutely refused even to consider agreeing on a definition of a "heavy" missile, they had an advance reason for that loophole too.

With all this evidence in mind, plus that forced upon us by analysis of other aspects of the SALT I Agreements, there simply is no avoiding the conclusion that all the imbalances and the 14 major loopholes of SALT were deliberately and malevolently planned by the Soviets; and that Kissinger not only accepted Soviet dictation of all the key provisions of the agreements, but sold them to President Nixon and the nation by providing rationalizations he knew were misleading. That is to say, he was working with the Soviets and against the United States of America.

He was deliberately and elaborately deceiving the American people, Congress, and probably the President with his cunning charade staged to make the SALT I Agreements appear as if they were the product of 2½ years of good-faith negotiations "hammered out" by the Soviet and U.S. delegations, respectively, in "give-and-take" bargaining. We have produced and considered much independent evidence that all the substantive provisions of both SALT I Agreements were in fact dictated by the Kremlin and secretly accepted by Henry Kissinger without the participation of the U.S. SALT delegation.

After all that independent evidence had been developed, full confirmation of Dr. Kissinger's secret negotiations with the Kremlin without the knowledge of the U.S. delegation, appeared in a source as totally unexpected as it is totally authoritative. Fred C. Iklé had been chosen by Dr. Kissinger to succeed Ambassador Gerard C. Smith as director of the U.S. Arms Control and Disarmament Agency when Kissinger fired the Ambassador for daring to warn Congress of the dangers to U.S. supreme interests in the SALT I Interim Agreement. Smith had been the head of the U.S. SALT negotiating delegation as well as director of ACDA, but Kissinger did not allow Iklé to serve as chief negotiator for the SALT II sessions.

When Iklé took office as director of ACDA on July 10, 1973, he was interviewed by *New York Times* Washington reporter Bernard Gwertzman. The interviewer intimated that both the ACDA and its new director were being downgraded in importance, and that this was indicated by the failure to appoint Iklé as head of the SALT negotiating team, as his predecessor, Ambassador Smith, had been. Apparently stung by this attack on the influence of ACDA and his own prestige as director, Iklé blurted out the truth as to why being head negotiator for the U.S. SALT negotiating team was not at all an important assignment. As reported by the *New York Times* on July 11, 1973,

> Mr. Iklé noted that the most recent stage of the strategic arms talks was negotiated secretly by Mr. Kissinger and Soviet officials in Washington and Moscow, therefore, the American negotiator at the talks was not responsible for "essential parts" of the agreement, anyway.

Precisely *why* did Henry Kissinger set up such an expensive charade to deceive the Congress and the American people?

So, we are again brought hard up against that nagging question: Is Henry Kissinger "some kind of a nut, or something"? Such elaborate structures of deception are simply not compatible with the behavior of a nut. Is not the evidence beginning to cumulate on the side of his being "something" more than a well-intentioned "nut"?

21

SALT is spiced with Soviet malevolence. The ruling members of the Politburo revenged themselves in SALT for their humiliation in the Cuban missile crisis 10 years before. Always arrogant, even in relative weakness, their high confidence in the now supererogatory power of their nuclear arsenal enabled them to phrase the SALT I Interim Agreement in a rather obvious mood of the present vindictive. Dedicated cadre Communists never forgive or forget, and the Cuban stratagem had been a very personal thing for first-among-equals Brezhnev and the not-quite-so-equal Number 8 Kosygin. Together with Nikita Khrushchev, they had been the only three Presidium-level creators and top-secret planners of the entire Cuban expedition.

Enormous amounts of scarce Soviet resources had been devoured by the crash production of IRBMs and MRBMs, with associated electronics equipment and multiple SAM batteries to protect the strategic weapons. Their clandestine shipment across Russia and over the ocean to Cuba added to the magnitude of the project. Yet, the only *public* result had been the blow to Soviet prestige resulting from the forced pullback of the missiles.

The 1962 state of the strategic balance had allowed the Soviets no alternative to accepting national humiliation before all the world. Having reversed that balance by 1972, Mr. Brezhnev and his colleagues (as Richard Nixon referred to them) felt an all-too-human inclination to reverse the roles of humiliator and humiliatee. They gave full and exuberant vent to this feeling in their demands as to the phrasing of the SALT I Interim Agreement. Mountainous and pervasive imbalances and advantages favoring the Soviets give notice to all the world (except only the President of the United States and the 210 million Americans who have not read it and wouldn't believe it if they did) that the new state of the strategic balance left the United States with no alternative (so long as Kissinger remains in power) to accepting a vastly more humiliating backdown than was negotiated with the Kremlin in the Cuban crisis.

The SALT I Interim Agreement was a strategic-military document. Members of the Politburo are predominantly political and ideologically oriented. They also desired a *political* document that would impose unequivocal humiliation on the United States—and knew they could get it from Kissinger and Nixon. It was revenge, indeed. But it also met another and more practical ideological requirement: notification to the cadre Communists throughout the entire world that their half-century of patient working and waiting was at last reaping its reward; that the United States had been forced to take the first giant step in formalized capitulation to the political policies of the Soviet Union—policies expressly designed to liquidate imperialism and bring about the total victory of communism throughout the world.

The political document takes the form of a Joint Declaration signed in Moscow on May 29, 1972, by President Nixon and the General Secretary of the Central Committee, Communist Party of the Soviet Union, Leonid I. Brezhnev, entitled "Basic Principles of Relations Between the United States of America and the Union of Soviet Socialist Republics." Less formally, representatives of our NATO allies have tagged it the "Decalogue of the Double-Cross" because it recites 10 major principles and sells out to the Soviets not only the United States but also our principal allies.

The true historical significance of the document is that it marks the first time that the second most powerful nation in the world—prior to its ultimate defeat by the most powerful nation in the world—has signed a formal agreement to conduct its relationships with that most powerful nation on the basis of *a strategy expressly designed to bring about the ultimate defeat and destruction of that second most powerful nation.* To put it bluntly, although we have not yet been defeated militarily by the Soviet Union, we formally conceded that we have no alternative but to submit to and participate in the execution of a Soviet strategy designed to bring about our own demise as a power and as a nation.

In the language of the first official U.S. warnings of the Japanese attack on Pearl Harbor, still incredulous after the bombs had been falling for nearly half an hour, "this is no drill *repeat* this is no drill." It is, in the words of the ubiquitous singing commercial, "the real thing." Although not a present political surrender, the joint U.S.-

U.S.S.R. document is unambiguously a declaration of intent *not* to resist conquest—not, that is, if resisting Soviet conquest would "serve to increase international tensions" or impede "detente."

The actual shocking meaning of the document will be analyzed and proved later. To provide just an interim solution to the question of how Kissinger could have gotten away with having Nixon sign a document committing us *not* to resist Soviet conquest of the world, there are two explanations: (1) Communist Aesopian code language is used to provide a light cover for the meaning of key provisions; and (2) the 12 principles (10 major, two minor), that require the space of less than one page in a news magazine,[1] are larded with no less than 41 words or expressions that have been built up over some 50 years by Soviet propaganda to serve as Pavlovian triggers for salivation in anticipation of an era of world "peace" on Communist terms. As explained in a Comintern resolution as far back as 1928, a "peace policy" is pursued as "merely another and—under given conditions—a more advantageous form of fighting capitalism." A half-century of brainwashing has paid off handsomely, and now a single one of these loaded terms will abruptly terminate our thinking process and shift us into emotional euphoria. If one such expression so influences Americans, consider what 41 will do!

Those not completely snowed by the use of so many "good" words may regard them as indicating that the entire document is only innocuous, assembled for propaganda purposes, and therefore unimportant as constituting an agreement between the United States and the Soviet Union. But the clever planners of the Politburo simply do not operate that way. The document is about as innocuous as a rattlesnake. If we analyze it realistically, it can serve as the warning rattle before the fatal strike.

For the Kremlin, the Declaration of Principles serves a threefold purpose. Besides embodying Soviet revenge for the humiliation of the Cuban missile crisis, and constituting a declaration of intent by the United States to cooperate in a Soviet strategy designed to bring about the ultimate liquidation of what the Soviets call capitalistic imperialism, it constitutes the formal and final termination of the Cold War by virtue of the capitulation of the United States. Thus, the 1972 Moscow Summit Declaration gives notice to all the nations of the world that there is now only one superpower, the Soviet Union; and further, it warns NATO nations and neutrals to make their deal with the Kremlin while they can still deal at all.

As Leonid Brezhnev explained to Castro just one month after the signing of the SALT I Agreements and the declaration, these documents "reflect the real state of affairs in the world . . . the thing to be done now is to put these major agreements into practice." So saying, he hung around Castro's neck, with appropriate kisses, the Soviet

Union's highest civilian decoration, the Order of Lenin. Brezhnev added that the award was in recognition of Castro's "outstanding services in the struggle against imperialism" (that is, against America).

As a reflection of the real state of affairs in the world, the Moscow Declaration is not merely an ideological triumph for the Kremlin and a capitulation by the United States. It is also a brilliant instrument of psychological warfare. During the entire period of the Cold War, from the end of World War II until 1972, there were two forces that enabled NATO effectively to resist the expansion of Soviet control over all the nations of Western Europe. The first of these forces was the strategic nuclear umbrella provided by the United States to deter a Soviet nuclear attack or invasion. The purpose of this deterrent was most dramatically declared by President Kennedy in his famous "I am a Berliner" speech at the Wall. "We will risk our cities," he assured the West Germans, "to save your cities."

Despite the hyperbolic ring of those brave words spoken to cheering thousands in Berlin, they really represented no more than our long-established commitment to our NATO partners. The U.S. strategic deterrent, thus committed to defend Western Europe, became the "shield" of NATO. Without it, as Winston Churchill stated, there would not have been a single free man left alive in Europe.

The second force opposing Soviet expansion was the NATO "sword" —the joint organization of conventional military power, plus tactical nuclear weapons furnished by the United States. With the Soviets deterred from using their strategic nuclear weapons against Western Europe by the commitment of the U.S. strategic force, the NATO conventional armies, air forces, and navies, backed by the potential of U.S. tactical "nukes," were supposed to be able to meet a conventional invasion by the Soviets.

The beauty of the NATO organization was that it worked for a quarter of a century. Because it did work, the dismemberment of NATO became a prime Soviet objective. It required some 25 years of patient and crafty planning and intensive effort, but the Kremlin finally attained this objective at the Moscow Summit of '72. Both the twin pillars of NATO were destroyed by the Summit Agreements: the shield has collapsed and the sword is shattered, as was made clear in the aftermath of the Yom Kippur war of 1973.

The commitment of U.S. strategic forces to defend NATO was effective as a deterrent only so long as that commitment was credible. The state of the strategic balance, U.S. vs. U.S.S.R., as revealed by the SALT I statistics, plus the additional buildup of imbalance favoring the Soviets under the SALT I Interim Agreement, plus the Kissinger-Nixon commitment to add no additional U.S. strategic power during the five-year term of that agreement, has destroyed the last shred of credibility of our strategic commitment to defend Western Europe.

The realistic interpretation of what we have done in SALT I to ourselves and to our NATO partners was presented to the Military Committee of the North Atlantic Assembly on November 20, 1972, by Senator Henry M. Jackson. Denouncing what he characterized as "an extreme concept of minimum deterrence" in SALT I, he laid the stark facts on the line:

> The strategic balance which is increasingly adverse to the United States leaves little room for an alternative American strategic posture.
>
> The last thing I would read into the ABM Treaty is the otherwise unsupported notion that the Soviets have accepted the doctrine of minimum deterrence.
>
> Minimum deterrence for the United States could easily be understood to mean *no deterrence at all for our allies*.[2]

What does this mean in the real world? Consider this scenario. The Kremlin calls Helmut Schmidt on the Bonn Hot Line and gives him this instruction:

> We have every German city, every industry, every railroad yard, every port, every communications center, every airport, targeted by intermediate-range strategic missiles, including 300 new SS-11 variable-range missiles.
>
> Tomorrow, we will move into West Germany with an invasion force patterned after the one we practiced on in Czechoslovakia in 1968, only three times as large.
>
> We demand a pledge of full cooperation and no military resistance whatsoever—just as we had in Czechoslovakia—and your surrender.
>
> If that pledge of cooperation and no resistance is not received in the Kremlin within four hours, we will start taking out your major cities, one each hour, until we receive the pledge and notification of your unconditional surrender.
>
> Ground all aircraft immediately upon receipt of this ultimatum. Be prepared to disarm all U.S. troops and units within your territory at the same time you dispatch your surrender to us.

What would the United States do? What *could* the United States do? Just suppose that Kissinger were not surrender-prone, and that he decided to execute President Kennedy's dramatic pledge to the West Germans. He sends the President to the Hot Line with this message to Leonid Brezhnev:

> Reference your ultimatum to Helmut Schmidt, withdraw it immediately. For every West German city you take out, we will take out two cities of the Soviet Union; and we will do it in each instance within 30 minutes of the time your missiles impact.
>
> Also, we will file a firm protest with the United Nations.
>
> The President of the United States

The Kremlin would probably respond with something like this:

Leonid sends. Dear Mr. President. You need a new Adviser on National Security Affairs. Because of some of the agreements he signed with us, we knew he must be insane, but we did not think he was stupid.

You are lucky—and so are the other 210 million Americans—that we are firmly convinced you would not attempt such a thing. If we did believe that you would attempt to carry out that ridiculous bluff, I would have launched a strike against the United States which would have taken out almost all your retaliatory weapons and absolutely all your cities—not in installments, but in one huge salvo. I would have given the launch order instead of sending this message, and our missiles would already be impacting. All the populated areas of the United States would be smoking masses of nuclear rubble, and retaliation against us would be substantially impossible and absolutely irrational.

Your young German adviser could have taken lessons in facing reality from that old unreconstructed German revanchist, Konrad Adenauer. He made the point as far back as 1963 that the United States could not deter the Soviet Union "by threatening to commit suicide."

That is exactly what your bluff amounts to: a threat that the United States will commit national suicide in an attempt to save German cities—and by actions that could not possibly save any German cities even if you attempted to carry out your threat.

We did believe John Kennedy when he made his pledge to the Federal Republic of Germany. His threat, when he made it, was credible. He did not say he would *sacrifice* U.S. cities to save German cities. He said he would *risk* them. The risk then, in 1963, was not great because the strategic nuclear odds at that time were 8-to-1 in his favor; but now they are 10-to-1 against you.

So we do not believe that *you* would do such a stupid thing. But we cannot afford to take chances with your Prince Metternich-Svengali of the West Wing, as some of his critics characterize him.

Sometimes he seems to be arranging a sophisticated covert surrender to us. But, as one of your South Vietnamese running dogs observed, Kissinger seems intent on creating a legend of Kissinger—and he just might decide that the legend would be better climaxed by going out with a bang instead of a whimper.

We have for years been stimulating what some of your writers have called "The Suicide of the West"—but we cannot tolerate a "Suicide of the West Wing" if there is the slightest danger in it of a U.S. strike at the Soviet Union with an undamaged strategic force—even such a weak force as you now possess.

We must demand, therefore, that you withdraw your Hot Line message of this date, and that you do so within one hour. We must get on with our occupation of West Germany, which we now declare is within the Brezhnev Doctrine which I declared in 1968, and which the United States approved in signing the Moscow Declaration of Principles in May 1972.

Within an hour, the Hot Line receiver in the Kremlin tapes out:

446

The President of the United States sends. Reference earlier message which had been dictated but not read: Cancel *repeat* cancel all but last 10 words.

The function of the Kissinger-Nixon-Brezhnev Moscow Summit Declaration of Principles of 1972 as an instrument of psychological warfare began to surface in 1973 in the workings of the conferences being held preliminary to and as preparations for the main bouts: the European Security Conference and the Conference on Mutual and Balanced Force Reductions. The Kremlin has pushed this slick-trick idea of an all-European security pact since at least 1954, but it was so obviously designed to kill NATO that the West rejected it with the diplomatic equivalent of derision. But the Soviets never give up, although they did relegate it to the deep-freeze after each crisis: the Hungarian bloodbath engineered by Khrushchev in 1956, the Cuban missile crisis in 1962, the Six Day War between the Israelis and the Arabs in 1967, and the Brezhnev invasion of Czechoslovakia in 1968.

The most effective and accurate explanation of the effect of "mutual" force reductions in Europe was presented in a single cartoon in 1967. Uncle Sam and the prototype of a Soviet dictator were pictured in an eyeball-to-eyeball confrontation on a plateau with level land stretching off in one direction, and a vertical cliff falling off into the ocean on the other. Uncle Sam had his back to the cliff, and the Soviet character had his back to the unending expanse of the plateau. The caption showed the Russian proposing: "Now let's each take three steps backward."

When the United States withdraws forces, we take them back across the ocean. The Soviets merely move back a few hundred miles or less into the European heartland, from whence they can be returned with speed and certainty on scores of thousands of mechanized troop carriers manufactured in their new truck plant, fully equipped with U.S. machinery financed by us or our allies.

If we tried an emergency return by aircraft, we would find every landing field in Western Europe either destroyed or under threat of immediate destruction as our first C-5 transport attempted to land. The Soviets could do this with either their IRBMs or their 700 strategic medium bombers. If we attempted to bring back our troops by ship, the Soviets' unequaled fleet of some 400 submarines would sink them.

The provisions of these two Soviet-sponsored international agreements, respectively governing "European Security" and "Mutual and Balanced Force Reductions," will control the fate of all the still-free nations of Europe. The short-term fate, that is. Unless the United States rebuilds the credibility of our strategic deterrent, there is no question about the ultimate longterm fate. The Soviets can and will take over all NATO nations, all the unaligned nations, and tighten their grip on their present slave states. Their takeover will by no means be along the pattern of "Finlandization," of which it has been fashionable to speak for several years. Without the U.S. nuclear umbrella, the destruction of which was memorialized in the SALT I Agreements, no European nation has any rational alternative to unconditional surrender whenever the Soviets so demand it.

Why, then, do we care about the terms of the two agreements on "European Security" and "Mutual and Balanced Force Reductions"? Nothing they could possibly provide could protect the United States against the Kremlin's completing its buildup to a splendid, full first-strike capability against us, or against the Soviets' actually using this capability to back an ultimatum for our surrender, or against their launching a massive surprise attack against us.

True enough. *But they can*—if the terms do not go too far too fast against the West—*buy us time.* Soviet grand strategy calls for *the take-over of Western Europe as a going concern.* This means not only that they do not want to destroy the industrial plant and cities and labor force, but also that they want to be prepared for a successful administration of these nations—which have a greater GNP than the Soviet Union and a massively larger foreign trade.

The more "peacefully" the Kremlin can bring these Western nations under their full and absolute control, the more successful and efficient will be their administrative effort, and, vitally important to them, the less disruptive this effort will be on their continued tight control of the huge non-Russian minorities within the U.S.S.R. itself. The time-span for the Kremlin to set up the transition will depend both on the terms of these two agreements and on the manner in which they are implemented. How this big picture will develop was foreshadowed by the smashing success of the Kremlin's crisis management of the "October War" of 1973, and should begin to emerge in painful detail for the NATO nations and the United States by the end of 1974.

So, it does matter to us 210 million Americans that, in influencing Nixon to sign the Moscow Summit Declaration of Principles, Dr. Kissinger has provided the Soviets with the lever they have actively sought for some 18 years: the lever that will enable them to split NATO unity in regard to the terms and implementation of the "European Security" and the "Reduction of Forces" agreements. So long as NATO continues to exist with any semblance of unified power, the Soviets would have to delay their plans to take over Western Europe "peacefully" enough to preserve its going-concern value.

Just as Kissinger talked Nixon into agreeing to the malevolent SALT I strategic *military* documents that destroyed the last shred of credibility of the U.S. strategic deterrent, he also talked him into signing the Politburo's *political* document that is the instrument to destroy the unity of—and hence the military effectiveness of—NATO's conventional and tactical-nuclear forces.

That the other NATO nations—unlike the American people—understand how Kissinger is undercutting them began to surface within weeks after the SALT I signing in indignant leaks from members of the North Atlantic Council. "It's Kissinger all over," said one European NATO council delegate; "I wouldn't be surprised if the State Department itself were unaware of the preparations for the Declaration." What had happened was that Kissinger had slipped across a double double-cross. The Moscow Summit Declaration took NATO completely by surprise, not through inadvertence but because it was planned that way. Here is how a *New York Times* dispatch described it on July 26, 1972:

> Inflaming the injury, NATO members read in the newspapers, which provided the first knowledge of the declaration, that Henry A. Kissinger said at a news conference that it had been worked out over several months of negotiation.
>
> They were aghast to realize that the United States had been drawing up the statement with the Russians at the same time that it was taking part in the NATO effort to produce a joint alliance declaration, without letting its NATO right hand know what its superpower left hand was doing.
>
> During the NATO discussions, the United States took different positions from the ones embodied in the Moscow agreement. . . .
>
> One chief allied delegate called it "a deception." Another said the Moscow Declaration was "a typical example" of current American disregard for the North Atlantic Treaty Organization.

The feeling of the NATO members that they had again been tricked by Kissinger "baffled and embittered" them, especially because they had sought assurances from (then) officially-higher-ranking U.S. sources against just such a contingency. One European ambassador, during the course of pre-SALT briefings for NATO members, directly asked Secretary of State William P. Rogers, "Will you talk about things that directly concern all of us?" He received an unequivocal "No." The same question was put to the Assistant Secretary of State for European Affairs (later Ambassador to Germany), and he gave the same assurance. He added that the only agreements planned for Moscow were the SALT I Agreements plus the window-dressing bilateral agreements on cooperation in space, health, science, technology, maritime incidents, and trade.

There was an additional exacerbation of the NATO feeling of having been sold out by Kissinger at the Moscow Summit. The experienced experts of the NATO alliance recognized immediately upon publication of the U.S.-U.S.S.R. declaration text that the United States had, by inescapable implication, capitulated to the Brezhnev Doctrine. This resulted from the supine acquiescence by Kissinger in the Soviet-drafted language forcing us to concede that we have "no alternative" to conducting our relations with the U.S.S.R. on the basis of "peaceful coexistence." In the context that can mean nothing else than our joining, as a junior partner, in implementation of the long-standing

Soviet strategy for control of the entire world by the Politburo. Just as the NATO experts knew this, so also did Henry Kissinger, as we will see when we attempt to understand just *why* he so enthusiastically sells Soviet traps to the United States.

In any event, by so capitulating to the Kremlin, Kissinger also pulled the rug out from under the NATO effort to secure the only substantive gains possible to the free nations of Europe (and to the captive nations, too) from the European Security Conference: a strong declaration of the rights of countries to self-determination, to change social systems, and to conduct independent foreign policies; and an equally strong declaration of the "right of free movement of people and ideas."

After an initial stunned silence and a long slow burn from June to November 1972 while they pondered on the cynical scorn with which they had been double-crossed by Kissinger in his deals with the Kremlin, the European members finally, in late November, broke through the thin diplomatic veneer of unity with the United States. The North Atlantic Assembly held a meeting just prior to the 34-nation talks in Helsinki in preparation for the European Security Conference. Setting the keynote for the NATO Assembly, Secretary General Joseph Luns made a remarkable speech. Without once mentioning Kissinger by name, he managed to denounce everything the Cowboy from Harvard had done at the Moscow Summit to undercut NATO solidarity. Luns described the Kissinger-Nixon approval of the Moscow Summit Declaration's legalization of the Brezhnev Doctrine as one of the many "traps" the Kremlin had laid in preparation for the European Security Conference. The implication was clear that Kissinger had led the United States directly into all of them.

Disavowing any intention by the European members of NATO of following Kissinger's lead into those traps, Secretary General Luns said:

> We are not prepared to subscribe to any principles which consecrate the Brezhnev Doctrine, that is, the Soviet attempt to apply a different set of principles to relations between the Communist states.

When it came to the final and formal action, the entire North Atlantic Assembly backed Luns' strong repudiation of Kissingerism. As reported by United Press out of Bonn on November 24, 1972:

> The North Atlantic Assembly urged the United States yesterday to stop dealing privately with Moscow and get in step with its European allies for vital East-West talks ahead.
>
> It approved resolutions designed to rescue the North Atlantic NATO Alliance from "grave stresses and strains" the assembly said was caused in part by President Nixon's [read Henry Kissinger's] private bargaining with Moscow.
>
> Later in the day, the annual assembly of 200 legislators from 14 NATO nations approved its first "advisory" to the Alliance partners. It said:

450

"Divisive political effects . . . may arise if Western policies are not harmonized before the conference with the Soviet bloc on European security. . . .

"There are possible dangers for Western solidarity in the growth of strictly bilateral diplomacy between the United States and the Soviet Union, if there is not adequate consultation."

Complaints about U.S.-Soviet bargaining were a recurrent theme in the speeches of the assembly delegates. The resolution was based upon a committee report that said America's European allies were offended by it.

The resolution urged the United States and its NATO allies to "start a high-level dialogue" to harmonize foreign policies.

Realists representing the European NATO members had hoped to do considerably more bargaining with the Soviets before agreeing to the Kremlin's 18-year objective of a European Security Conference. Again, however, Kissinger undercut NATO by agreeing to include in the communique on the Moscow Summit a commitment to participate in "multilateral consultations . . . looking toward" the Soviets' proposed Security Conference.

Why should the European NATO members seek to secure some concessions from the Kremlin as a quid pro quo for agreeing to a conference on European Security? Are they not also interested in an agreement establishing European security? The answer is that they understand—as Kissinger pretends not to—the underlying and ulterior purpose of the Soviet Communists in this stratagem. And it is a stratagem—not merely a tactic or a gambit. At the Helsinki 34-nation pre-conference conference, it became clear that the Kremlin was trying its favorite technique of setting up a "popular front" or "coalition government" type of organization to administer "European security." This would be the first trial of it on a supranational or continental scale, but the operative practices are the same as taking over a single nation by the first step of a coalition government or administrative body. For more than half a century this Communist technique has allowed a disciplined minority—backed by as much force or threat of force as necessary—to take over from a majority. It worked for the Bolshevik minority in Russia; it worked in Czechoslovakia; Averéll Harriman helped set it up in Yugoslavia and in Laos; and it worked along similar lines in Chile.

The Soviet threat to Europe will not be "occupation, Polish style." Once the SALT I provisions plus the Henry Kissinger defense policies have totally destroyed the credibility and effectiveness of the U.S. strategic deterrent, and the Soviet full first-strike capability can no longer be challenged; and once the European membership of NATO has been fragmented and the supranational unity of their conventional defense forces destroyed; then the Soviet occupation of Western Eu-

451

rope will be of a nature unprecedented thus far in any captive nation—not immediately upon the initial takeover, of course, but soon and inexorably.

That is because, thus far in their 57 years of power, the Soviets have never had a fully free hand in dealing with subjugated populations, either their own or those of captive nations. There has always been an alternative. If the police-state pressures on the peoples were made too harsh, there was always the risk of a simultaneous rebellion sweeping all the slave states at once, even if the prospects of success were nearly hopeless. People tyrannized beyond hope might feel they had nothing to lose. Such a rebellion might have spread to the huge national minorities in the U.S.S.R. The Russian language is the native tongue of only 55 percent of the population of the Soviet Union. There are nearly 50 million Ukrainians, and there are 13 other minorities with populations ranging between two and 10 million each.

As massive as this problem of potential rebellion has been ever since the workers fought Soviet tanks in the streets of East Berlin in June 1953, the Kremlin has had another pervasive restraint on intensifying their oppression of the captive peoples: the more deprived, the more degraded, the more hopeless life would appear under Soviet domination, the more effort the still-free nations of the West would be willing to expend on staying free. Adequate defense budgets would be popularly supported and appeasement-prone politicians would be thrown out of power. Even more critical to the men in the Politburo, the elite groups of scientists and internationalists might lose their enthusiasm for socialism, Kremlin style. The Pugwash scientists would become more difficult to brainwash; and they and their close allies, the unilateral-disarmament intellectuals of the Nitze-Gilpatric-McNamara type, might choose to risk being strong rather than choosing to be Red.

These people could explain away to themselves—or simply refuse to believe the evidence—of Stalin's having liquidated some 20 million people in the U.S.S.R. But if he had continued the Great Terror and exterminated, say, 100 million, they might have been unable to hide the harsh reality of the human costs of communism. They might have ceased their acts of betrayal of the United States and terminated their programs for our unilateral disarmament.

All these risks for the Kremlin will terminate once there is no alternative anywhere in the world to Communist rule. There will be no need for mine fields, machine gun posts, or barbed-wire borders. The Berlin Wall can at last be dismembered. There will be nowhere to flee to freedom because freedom will nowhere exist.

This brings up exactly the point that neither elitist power groups nor commonsense patriotic Americans have yet faced up to: Communist systems, Communist governments simply cannot live with

452

competition from other social and economic systems or systems of government. Take some practical examples. Why was North Vietnam *compelled* to invade South Vietnam? Why do those Communists have to fight on, year after year, at the cost of millions of lives, to destroy the system and government of South Vietnam? Why did they not accept the near-unconditional surrender of the United States *until* they and Kissinger were able to set up political arrangements conditioning a cease-fire that would enable them ultimately to take over the South Vietnamese government? Why did the Kremlin and Mao grant them billions of dollars in war supplies and weapons during those long years?

The answer to these questions is that the South Vietnamese, under their relatively free government, were making great economic, social, and political progress. The great surge of progress began there in the late 1950s. Life for farmers and fishermen and peasants of all kinds became much better in the South than in the North. Religion was allowed, as well as self-government to the extent the people were qualified. As the 1960s began, the Communist masters in the North recognized that the system in the South *must* be destroyed. They knew they would receive all the help they needed from the Soviet Union and Red China because those Communist governments also recognized that communism cannot live with competition.

Take the case of China. China had everything to gain, whereas the United States would gain nothing, by accepting the Kissinger-Nixon offers of credit, trade, industrial plants, technology, farm equipment and machinery, aircraft, and tourists. Yet the Chinese conditioned their acceptance of all these desperately needed resources from us upon a Kissinger sellout of the free Chinese government on Taiwan. Why? With the Red Chinese population of 800 million, why did they need to add the 15 million on Taiwan? With an area of more than 3 million square miles, why did the Red Chinese need to add Taiwan's insignificant area of 13,885 square miles?

It is the universal story. Red China cannot stand the competition. Taiwan's exports amounted to $7 billion in 1973—about the level of Mainland China with 50 times more people. Real economic growth in Taiwan has for years been the highest in the world: more than 11 percent a year. Per capita income is about $500 a year, something like four times that of the Red Chinese. Also, there has been no "Cultural Revolution," no Red Guard purge of millions of helpless people, no old people beaten to death.

The people are of substantially the same stock. The difference is the social and economic system and the system of government. Free enterprise and foreign investment are encouraged in Taiwan, and political freedom is allowed to the greatest extent possible, considering the immediate proximity of a mortal enemy that is the most populous nation in the world, a burgeoning nuclear power, and determined to destroy Free China.

It is because of this built-in and inexorable inability to live with competitive systems that the Kremlin *had* to build the Iron Curtain and the Berlin Wall, and is forced to attempt the conquest of all Europe and ultimately of the world. Even if the Soviets did not seek to exploit the industrial plant, the technology, the resources, and the skilled and energetic labor force of Western Europe, they would still be compelled to attempt to conquer these countries. To the Soviet planners, it is a matter of self-preservation. Only within the Communist system can they continue to hold their power. The Communist system, in turn, cannot live in competition with systems that permit political freedom, personal freedom, religious freedom, freedom of speech and the press, free enterprise, free trade, and private ownership of property.

All nations that permit such freedoms *must* be conquered. After conquest, they must be either (1) totally controlled and successfully administered, or (2) destroyed. Communist leadership—and especially Soviet Communist leadership—makes no secret of these ultimate objectives. Two major points of Communist doctrine, which have not changed in 57 years of power, reaffirm these compulsions. The first point is that world peace can never be established unless and until *all* resistance to communism has been destroyed. Lenin, Stalin, Khrushchev, and Brezhnev all put it the same way: "So long as imperialism exists, the danger of war will exist."

All those who believe that Kissingerism has converted the Kremlin to partnership with the United States must explain away a statement by Leonid Brezhnev at the June 1969 International Meeting of Communist and Workers' Parties. He even reaffirmed it in his post-SALT State Banquet for Castro at the Great Kremlin Palace on June 27, 1972:

> We think it would be an enormous mistake to underestimate the danger of war that is created by imperialism, and above all by the main force of world reaction, U.S. imperialism.

He stresses that systems competing with communism must and will be replaced, worldwide, and that the worldwide victory of communism is very close now:

> *As the possibilities of the anti-imperialist struggle increase,* the role of the Communist parties and their work with the masses grows accordingly. World development in the final third of the 20th century will depend to a large extent on the activity of the Communists.
>
> One cannot help but see that at present the ripening not only of the material but also the social and political preconditions for the *revolutionary replacement of capitalism by a new social system and for Socialist revolutions is intensifying.*

In rallying the militant ranks of staunch revolutionaries, carrying Marxist-Leninist ideology to the masses of workers and uniting allies of the working class around that class, *the Communists are fulfilling their historic mission in the struggle against imperialism and for the victory of socialism.*

It is interesting that General Secretary of the Central Committee of the Communist Party of the Soviet Union Brezhnev does not shilly-shally with words about *how* capitalism is going to be replaced, about *how* our social system is to be replaced, and about *how* the struggle against imperialism and the victory of socialism is going to be won: by revolution, that's how. He promises that there will be nothing peaceful about it; it will *not* be brought about by negotiation.

At the Moscow Summit in May 1972, Kissinger secured President Nixon's signature on the Kremlin-drafted document entitled "Basic Principles of Relations between the U.S. and the U.S.S.R." In it, the United States is bound to conduct future relationships with the Soviets on the basis of "peaceful coexistence" *in the Soviet meaning of that term.* The very first basic principle—and its "spirit" is pervasive throughout the entire document—recites that the parties

will proceed from the common determination that in the nuclear age there is no alternative to conducting their mutual relations on the basis of *peaceful coexistence.*

This does not in any way mean what the American public understands by that utopian-sounding term: existing together in peace on a live-and-let-live basis. It is a Soviet Aesopian-language expression describing a long-run strategy for Soviet-Communist control of the world; it means a form of intense class struggle designed to facilitate *victory* over all non-Communist societies.

The average American cannot be expected to know the true meaning of "peaceful coexistence," but Kissinger is not average and he *must* know. In his 1965 book, *The Troubled Partnership,* he asserted:

Peaceful coexistence is never advocated for its own sake. It is justified primarily as a tactical device to overthrow the West at minimum risk.

The leading study of the meaning of the term "peaceful coexistence" was conducted by one of the original members of his own White House staff. In 1963 the American Bar Association commissioned Richard V. Allen, chairman of the Study Program on Communism at the Center for Strategic and International Studies, Georgetown University, to do a documentary study of "the Communist strategy of peaceful coexistence." The study was published by the ABA in August 1964 under the title *Peaceful Coexistence: A Communist Blueprint for Victory.* The demand for the study in the American Bar Association alone ran to 40,000 copies in three printings. Its documentation proved conclusively, even to lawyers, that the term did indeed cover a Communist strategy for world domination. Although 124 pages of proof were presented in the 1964 edition, the ABA study was brought up to date in 1966 and expanded to 233 pages with additional documentation demonstrating the Communist meaning of "peaceful coexistence." The new edition was retitled: *Peace or Peaceful Coexistence?*

The learned Dr. Kissinger, expert in international relations and in dealing with the Communists, could hardly be ignorant of this definitive study. When he moved into the White House in January 1969, he apparently felt he needed one prominent conservative-in-residence to avert criticism of the obvious hyperliberal slant of the majority of his personal staff, so he appointed Richard V. Allen. Mr. Allen did not last long. Perhaps Kissinger read his study on "peaceful coexistence." In any event, Kissinger made his choice in Moscow in May 1972 between peace *or* "peaceful coexistence."

The most significant clue to the purpose of the Politburo planners in forcing us to pledge ourselves to peaceful coexistence is found in the Main Document of the 1969 International Meeting of Communist Parties:

> The defense of peace is inseparably linked up with the struggle to *compel* the imperialists to accept peaceful coexistence of states with different social systems. The policy of peaceful coexistence does not contradict the right of any oppressed people to fight for its liberation by any means it considers necessary—armed or peaceful. This policy in no way signifies the support of reactionary regimes.
>
> The attempts of imperialism to overcome its internal contradiction by building up international tension and creating hotbeds of war are hampered by the policy of peaceful coexistence.
>
> This policy does not imply either the preservation of the sociopolitical status quo or a weakening of the ideological struggle. It helps to promote the class struggle against imperialism on a national and worldwide scale. ... Mass action against imperialism is a condition for implementing the policy of peaceful existence.

To this, first-among-equals Comrade Brezhnev added emphasis on one key point:

> Peaceful coexistence does not extend to the struggle of ideologies, and this must be given decisive emphasis.

Note that the Soviets expressly deny that it means what we in the West understand it to mean: "preservation of the sociopolitical status quo." We tend to think it means a live-and-let-live arrangement; that it *does* mean that tranquility will prevail, and that the status quo will be preserved; that we will not attempt to change or destroy their system, and they will not attempt to change or destroy ours.

The entire policy of "peaceful coexistence" is directed against "reactionary regimes," and Brezhnev identifies the United States as "the main force of world reaction." It is, the Soviets explain, inseparably linked with the struggle for peace and the defense of peace; and, as we have seen, "peace" means a state in which all opposition to communism has been eliminated and all competing systems have been destroyed. It is clear that, by subscribing to "peaceful coexistence" as the first principle of our relationship with the Soviet Union, we are bound to help "promote the class struggle against imperialism [that is, ourselves] on a national and worldwide scale," and that we are obligated to join in the mass action against imperialism (ourselves and our system). *We are doing exactly this in our "trade" and technology programs* with the Kremlin and the other Communist states.

Thus Antony Sutton, the distinguished research fellow at Stanford University's Hoover Institution, did not exaggerate in entitling his recent book *National Suicide: Military Aid to the Soviet Union.*[3] His book documents massively and conclusively—precisely and across the board—how U.S. participation in Henry Kissinger's "detente" partnership with the Kremlin actually works to bring about our destruction as a nation.

Another interpretation of "peaceful" as used in the expression "peaceful coexistence"—also squarely contrary to *our* understanding—is that it permits the *Communist* side to fight against us "by any means it considers necessary, *armed* or peaceful."

It is fashionable in the West to disregard what the highest authorities in the Soviet Communist hierarchy say "peaceful coexistence" means, on the theory that *that* was merely an old and now-abandoned "hard line" appropriate to the Cold War, now ended, and that such definitions are no longer valid in the new era of Henry Kissinger's "broad spectrum of agreements."

To this it must be answered that all the language quoted above was reaffirmed expressly and specifically by Leonid Brezhnev, the signer of SALT, in a post-SALT declaration at his State Banquet for Fidel Castro on June 27, 1972. Also, in a post-SALT declaration, Mikhail Suslov, the chief theoretician of the Politburo and of the Communist Party of the Soviet Union, made this significant interpretation:

> The struggle has sharpened in the field of ideology, where there is not and cannot be peaceful coexistence between socialism and capitalism.

In evaluating Henry Kissinger's motivation in inducing President Nixon to bind the United States to conform to the Soviet concept of "peaceful coexistence," he cannot be excused on the theory that he was confronted in Moscow by the use of an expression that at worst is innocuous, and at best could even be called good. The use of the expression to embody a malevolent anti-U.S. strategy goes back specifically to Stalin, and the basic concept was practiced by Lenin as long ago as in the Brest-Litovsk Treaty with Germany in 1918.

The specific strategy of "peaceful coexistence" with which Brezhnev and his colleagues entrapped the United States in the Moscow Summit of '72 was ordained by Stalin almost exactly 20 years earlier. On October 18, 1952, in what turned out to be one of the last important declarations of his life, he explained that it would be good—"even very good"—if the Communist-instigated peace movement should succeed in preventing or postponing a given war or in preserving a given peace. This, Stalin suggested, could be achieved by bringing about the ousting of "belligerent governments" and replacing them with governments "ready to preserve peace for the time being." Nevertheless, he added, this would still be "insufficient," because imperialism would still remain in power. Consequently, he concluded,

> the inevitability of wars also remains. In order to eliminate the inevitability of wars, imperialism must be destroyed.

Thus he laid down the ultimate purpose of the strategy of peaceful coexistence, namely, the destruction of the United States as the greatest imperialist power; of, as Brezhnev later described us, "U.S. imperialism—main force of world reaction."

This was their strategy of "peaceful coexistence" 20 years ago, and this is their strategy for the 1972-77 post-SALT I era. Admiral Arleigh Burke has an intriguing update of it in a quotation in his SALT I article entitled, "Will America Be the Author of Its Own Weakness and Thus of Soviet Opportunity," published by the *Los Angeles Times*, August 13, 1972:

> For the past 10 years the Soviets have devoted their maximum effort to increasing their nuclear capability and developing a powerful navy. It is likely that they will continue to do so.
> Their words confirm that these are exactly their intentions. Mikhail A. Suslov very carefully explained to the Soviet Znanye Society that regardless of the SALT Agreement, the U.S. remains the enemy. Suslov justified the SALT Agreement in terms of the Soviets' needing an easing of tensions to develop still greater strength for the long and fierce battles ahead.

Average Americans (as distinguished from high officials whose responsibility demands that they have expert knowledge of Soviet strategy and tactics) can be excused for reading into the expression "peaceful coexistence" the meaning that we normally attach to those words. Actually, the terms were chosen exactly because the customary content and the comfortable connotations they conjure up are what the people in the West and the Free World generally most desire—and hence are most anxious to believe in. Soviet leadership has often taken extreme measures to capitalize on the term "peaceful coexistence" as their second most powerful verbal weapon of psychological warfare. (Their most powerful is, of course, "rather Red than dead.")

U.S. Kremlinologists and Soviet apologists have generally assisted Politburo leaders in deceiving the American public into believing that the Soviets are sincere in their desire for "peaceful coexistence." These apologists seized with enthusiasm and delight on Khrushchev's farewell address to the American people at the end of his visit here in 1959. It was carried by nationwide television networks on September 27 of that year, and here is his powerful conclusion:

> There can be no stability or tranquility in the world so long as the two strongest powers are not on good terms with each other. . . .
>
> Even in the Soviet Union, everyone is in favor of living in peace, everyone is in favor of peaceful coexistence.

Soviet sycophants in the United States, immediately echoed by certain segments of the mass media, overreacted into irrational euphoria, as the Soviet dictator's actions—as distinguished from his conciliatory words—would soon demonstrate. His shrewd television sales pitch to the American public for the Kremlin's "peaceful coexistence" stratagem set the stage for a one-two-three sequence of major strategic moves that were to follow at intervals of less than a year each. Together, they constitute a trilogy of real-life dramas never remotely equaled in all history.

Hannibal, Alexander, Julius Caesar, Attila, Constantine, Charlemagne, Napoleon, Bismarck—none of them ever approached that stolid-looking peasant Nikita Sergeevich Khrushchev in the scope of the changes he wrought on the course of history, in the quantum of military and political power he wielded, or in the brilliance, boldness, and innovative skill of his strategic concepts.

Opportunism played only a minor part in Khrushchev's incredible achievements. If the term is applied to him at all, it should be linked with the adjective "creative." If an opportunity did not exist, he would create one. Colonel Oleg Penkovskiy called him a devil, and his impassioned indictment was based on personal observation as well as on objective evidence. Diabolical genius the peasant dictator may have been, but genius he unquestionably was. His evil stemmed from his dedication to communism. The inherent evil of communism corrupts all who serve it, but, unfortunately, does not degrade the effectiveness or brilliance of its leaders.

Consider the situation of the Soviet Union vis-a-vis the United States as it was at the end of 1959 when Khrushchev made his television pitch to the American people for "peaceful coexistence." U.S. strategic military power exceeded that of the U.S.S.R. by a factor of five, and U.S. production of weapons systems was fast attaining that massive momentum that would carry it to an 8-to-1 supremacy by October 1962. Equally serious was the Soviet lag in the technology of strategic nuclear warheads. Although the wily Khrushchev—with the help of the U.S. Pugwash scientists—had conned President Eisenhower

459

into the 1958 nuclear test-ban arrangement, and thus had arrested U.S. technological progress in the strategic nuclear area, he desperately needed to gain two elements: time and secrecy. He needed these for protracted preparations to accomplish his incredible coup of overtaking the U.S. technological advantage of 2-to-1 in yield/weight ratio, and then more than reversing it.

Whenever Soviet Communist leadership needs to buy time, it has a sudden burst of enthusiasm for "peaceful coexistence." As chief theoretician Suslov explained, it provides a tension-easing period that they need in order to develop still greater strength for the long and fierce battles ahead. Khrushchev secured the time he required by assuming the guise of good old Grandfather Khrushchev on U.S. television screens.

The beaming and benevolent elder statesman, who had been preaching peaceful coexistence with every appearance of sincere friendship and camaradarie in the fall of 1959, totally transformed himself in May of 1960 into a ranting, screaming, hysterical, vengeance-swearing, uncouth enemy. Or so he made it appear. Actually, it was all a brilliantly contrived act. It was a single-character melodrama, staged by a master actor, to shake the world. Certainly he shook Eisenhower, who had so recently hosted, with generous and genial goodwill, the now-venomous dictator. The crafty Khrushchev characteristically exploited the latest technological advances for his purposes. He preempted the first truly worldwide television audience for his show. There were no "satellite-live" transoceanic transmissions in 1960 but that year, for the first time, the Winter Olympics were televised live from Squaw Valley, California, and the Summer Olympics were seen in the United States within a few hours after the events by means of videotape flown from Rome by commercial jets.

Thus, when Khrushchev staged a dramatic press conference to torpedo the Paris Summit of 1960 by announcing that he had shot down an American U-2 plane over the U.S.S.R., a contemporary news account reported that "viewers had to wait only a few hours to witness every gesture, every threat, every insult." The Soviet Premier, enjoying his own performance, denounced the President of the United States in terms so viciously insulting that they would have signaled a break in diplomatic relations in prenuclear times. Never before—other than in time of overt war—had the leader of one great nation addressed such insulting language to the head of another great nation.

Khrushchev's tantrum tremendously impressed hundreds of millions throughout the world. Americans were just beginning to be willing to believe the liberal propaganda picturing the worst about America. Our pseudointellectuals reasoned that if we had made the "peace-loving" premier of the Soviet Union so angry, we must have done something terrible indeed. Khrushchev demanded that the United

States tender a formal apology for having "violated Soviet air space." A young Senator took the floor of the U.S. Senate and demanded that the President of the United States make that apology. His advisers were carried away by the opportunity to humiliate President Eisenhower, a political opponent, and did not realize that they were laying a basis for grievous humiliations of their own man as President only a short time later.

Khrushchev's tantrum in aborting the Summit of 1960 marked one of the most significant and least noticed watersheds in the history of nations and ideologies. From then on the path of the power of the United States has been ever downward, from the highest peak attained by the greatest country, to potential oblivion and the brink of disaster, as represented by the slickly covered surrenders in the SALT Summit of '72.

Why did Khrushchev put on that sensational act? What did he seek to accomplish? And why did he choose that particular time? His immediate purpose was quite clear from the three demands he served on Dwight Eisenhower: (1) apologize for the spy flight, (2) promise never again to "violate" Soviet air space, and (3) punish those "guilty of such actions."

What baffled Eisenhower was that American U-2 photographic-reconnaissance aircraft had been overflying the Soviet Union with sustained frequency *for some four years*—and Khrushchev knew it, and Eisenhower knew that Khrushchev knew it, and Khrushchev knew that Eisenhower knew that Khrushchev knew it. So, why the sudden outburst?

The whole episode may have been planned by agents of the Politburo. The timing was just too, too convenient for Khrushchev's purposes, ulterior as well as overt. The Summit was scheduled for May 16, 1960. On May 1, Francis Gary Powers flew his U-2 into one of the then very few areas in which the Soviets could make even a credible claim to have shot down the plane from full altitude. And the Soviets did, indeed, claim that they had shot down the U-2 from its full altitude with a surface-to-air missile. But 1960 SAMs simply did not have all that reach, either up or slant. In all those four years of U.S. overflights the Soviets had never before been able to reach a single U-2.

Khrushchev's contrived rantings and vituperation so disturbed Secretary of State Christian Herter that on May 9 he was stunned into making this stark, truthful statement telling exactly *why* those reconnaissance flights were essential to our national self-preservation:

> The threat of surprise attack . . . presents a constant danger. It is unacceptable that the Soviet political system should be given the opportunity to make secret preparations to face the Free World with the choice of abject surrender or nuclear destruction.

461

President Eisenhower confirmed this reason, declaring that "it is a distasteful but vital necessity" because the safety of the whole Free World depends upon guarding against another surprise attack such as Pearl Harbor.

Khrushchev, the then-greatest living and the only practicing nuclear strategist, wanted to take advantage of his 9 million square miles of area in which to conceal his new and powerful missiles. The shrewd Khrushchev was thoroughly familiar with the then-realized state of technology in satellite reconnaissance, and he foresaw a potential three- to four-year gap if he could get the U-2s down before we could get the satellites up with high-resolution capability and operational reliability and regularity.

Lacking the *military* power to accomplish it, he outsmarted us by psychology and the cheap melodramatic act that torpedoed the 1960 Paris Summit. A logical and courageous U.S. reaction to his tantrum tactics would have been something like this:

> Well, Nikita Sergeevich Khrushchev, why didn't you start this screaming back in June 1956, when we first started our U-2 flights? You knew about them then.
>
> We consider these flights to be essential to the national security of the United States. Their purpose is to deny you the opportunity of secret preparations to confront us with the choice of abject surrender or nuclear destruction.
>
> International law has not yet developed as to sovereignty over air space more than 12 miles up. Even the Soviet Union does not claim sovereignty over the high seas more than 12 miles out. We contend that 12 miles is the limit of national air space. At least, we contend that such air space is free until the subjacent nation is able to exercise effective control over it. You have not been able to do this. In four years, you have not been able even to disable a single one of our U-2s. We are not impressed with the so-called shoot-down of Pilot Powers. We are not really sure whether he was working for us or for you on that particular flight. We think that *if you could* shoot down U-2s on a regular basis, you would do so rather than stage tantrums to pressure us to stop them.
>
> We will not object if you overfly the United States with unarmed observation aircraft at U-2 altitudes. The first law of international law is self-preservation. We will continue the U-2 flights. Shoot them down when and if you can.

Instead, U.S. leadership gave in to the newly effective pressures of the Pugwash scientists and surrender-prone intellectuals. For the first time in the nuclear age we surrendered the right to use our technological and scientific resources to protect America against secret preparations by an enemy to get into a position to destroy us. This was a failure of will, of courage, of common sense, and of dedication. We did not have to surrender. Our power was vastly superior in every aspect: militarily, technologically, and industrially.

The Pugwash and internationalist elitists, unwilling to entertain even the thought that the Soviets might be so malevolent as to contemplate an attack on the United States, ignored the official and responsible explanations of the purpose of the U-2 flights. They popularized the explanation that Khrushchev needed this "pretext" to break up the Paris Summit Conference. This was ridiculous since Khrushchev himself had been promoting the Paris Summit for at least a year.

Khrushchev never concealed the true purpose of his tantrum. He freely and openly stated that his true immediate and priority objective was to get the U-2s out of the air over the Soviet Union. He used the propaganda potential of sabotaging the summit to create a psychological weapon to shoot down all future U-2 flights. Not for another three years would Soviet SAMs have the capability of reaching a 100,000-foot altitude; and he wanted those U-2 flights stopped immediately! The sacrifice of a summit meeting with an outgoing U.S. President was peanuts compared to what he accomplished by his psychological attack on the United States.

The reason for his wanting to frighten the American leadership into canceling aircraft overflights of the U.S.S.R. is found in the then-realized state of aerospace technology. What was happening in communications and television tells us also what was available for photographic reconnaissance. Khrushchev could get a worldwide audience for his tantrum, but he could not reach it "live." Nevertheless, he could reach viewers throughout the world in only a few hours. This is because, in May 1960, the space age was less than three years old. The Soviets had orbited the world's first artificial satellite in 1957, but satellite technology was still primitive. But not so with aircraft; they were so technologically advanced that television tapes could be flown across oceans in a very few hours.

It was the same with photographic reconnaissance. The U-2s were doing a superb job with their photographs and also with electronic devices. They pinpointed missile sites, air bases, submarine-production facilities, and antiaircraft emplacements. Although reconnaissance satellites were on their way in *development,* and had even made some experimental flights in 1960, they would not be available *operationally* for several more years. It was not just a question of the satellite systems themselves: high-resolution photography needed further refinements, too. U-2s take their photos from 60,000 to 75,000 feet; satellites from 90 to 300 miles, with the additional problem of recovering the pictures from space.

What could Khrushchev have done if we had continued U-2 flights? Nothing at all. What could he do when we surrendered our right to take action in behalf of national self-preservation—action that was totally peaceful, conducted by unarmed reconnaissance aircraft? Plenty. He knew that if he could terminate all U.S. U-2 flights over the

Soviet Union as of May 1960 he could create a prolonged reconnaissance gap. Such a gap would give him something like three years of near-total secrecy for the protracted preparations essential to carrying out his plans. He did have critical plans, all of which required the element of surprise for their success.

U.S. satellite reconnaissance in the mid-1970s may be more effective than U-2 reconnaissance when Khrushchev bluffed us into a reconnaissance blackout in 1960. Certainly cameras, film, and related equipment are vastly better; but they surely would have to be, to make up for the 85- to 285-mile differential in distance from which the pictures are taken. At the time of Khrushchev's contrived blackout they certainly were not good enough for high resolution at such a distance.

There was general astonishment when President Eisenhower showed U-2 photographs taken from 13 miles up that revealed four-inch painted stripes in a parking lot of a San Diego air base. He made this exhibition in 1960 shortly after the Francis Gary Powers plane incident in order to show the American people the value of aerial reconnaissance. As of that time, photo interpreters could read-out U-2 pictures of the ace of spades at eight miles, or a newspaper banner headline at 12 miles. Satellite photography, however, was in the first phases of comprehensive experimentation at that time.

In mid-November 1962, the New York Times published an article by C. L. Sulzberger entitled "The U-2, Once Villain, Became Hero in Cuba." This excerpt is still of vital interest because of SALT:

> U-2 cameras can discern 12-inch objects from a height of 13 miles. Within two years [of 1962] orbiting satellites may provide equally accurate pictures.

Satellite photography technologists didn't make good this prediction: it actually required some 10 years. On November 30, 1964, U.S. News & World Report carried an authoritative planted leak concerning satellite capabilities that included this:

> One "starlight camera" that has been in development can take detailed photos of the Kremlin roof in Moscow from as high as 300 miles. Daytime cameras over Russia can photograph objects as small as an automobile.

Thus, satellites were discerning 20-foot objects three or four years later than U-2s were identifying 12-inch objects. Also in 1964, Khrushchev showed a suspicious preference for having the United States employ satellites instead of U-2s. The relevant quotation is from The Craft of Intelligence, by Allen Dulles,[4] Director of CIA from 1953 to 1961:

> The question whether the piloted U-2 can be superseded by pilotless satellites orbiting the globe at much higher altitudes came up in May

1964, when Premier Khrushchev declared that the United States could avoid international tensions by desisting from further flights of the U-2 over Cuba.

The space satellites, said Khrushchev, can do the same job, and he offered to show our President photographs of American military bases taken by Soviet "sky spies." I doubt that we would agree wholly with Khrushchev that space vehicles should supersede the manned plane for all reconnaissance purposes.

This bald attempt to pressure the U.S. President, by threats of increased international tension, into giving up the protection of the exact type of reconnaissance, over the same area, that had so lately saved us from the disaster of Soviet surprise attack with strategic nuclear weapons cannot realistically be attributed to a tender concern for Castro's face or feelings. Khrushchev always considered these subordinate to Soviet interests. His effort appears rather as persuasive evidence that he felt that the execution of secret Soviet plans in Cuba, such as construction of concealed missile-submarine bases or Soviet air bases, would be safer if the United States could be boxed in to rely exclusively on satellite reconnaissance for photographic evidence.

Even our earliest experience in Vietnam confirmed the need for all types of photo-reconnaissance. To target Soviet SAM sites in North Vietnam, hundreds of reconnaissance flights were made monthly by several types of the most modern specialized aircraft. Even so, it was difficult to pinpoint the missile sites.

A news dispatch from Saigon to the *Los Angeles Times* in July 1965 quoted Major General Gilbert I. Meyers, Vice Commander of the U.S. Air Force in Vietnam, as saying that even good photo-reconnaissance can only show up the earthworks and construction that "tend to mark" prepared missile positions, that "emplaced missiles are harder to detect," and that the first positive knowledge that the U.S. Command obtained that the Soviet SAMs were ready for action was by the actual shooting down of a U.S. jet fighter. Obviously, unless satellite photography left vital gaps in photographic intelligence, we would not have risked so many valuable reconnaissance aircraft, skilled pilots, and crewmen in Vietnam.

This discussion is in no way intended to denigrate satellite reconnaissance. It is, generally, incredibly good and getting better all the time. By 1972 the cameras were discerning 12-inch objects. Also, the already near-perfection of multispectrum systems is impressive. A comparison of observations made simultaneously in several portions of the spectrum yields far more information about the ground situation than any single sensor could. The visible-light camera gives high resolution of even small objects, and the other sensors, which do not have so high a degree of resolution, complement this by revealing the thermal emission, reflectivity, and color characteristics of the subjects.

Equally incredible are the capabilities of electronic-sensor satellites and other types of ELINT and COMINT equipment—earth-based (such as radars the size of the large phased-array ABM radars), airborne, and space-based. A U.S. ECM (electronic countermeasures) aircraft actually beat the U-2s to establishing the presence of Soviet missiles in Cuba in 1962. It picked up and taped strange signals that, when checked out, proved to be identical with those emanating from Soviet missile equipment never before then known to be located outside of Russia.

But these great systems for gathering intelligence cannot cover the most vital areas of possible Soviet surprise developments in strategic weaponry, offensive or defensive. These "national means of verification" are all we are permitted to use in order to check potential Soviet violations of the "spirit" or even the letter of the SALT I Agreements. Incredibly, Dr. Kissinger and President Nixon gave in to Leonid Brezhnev's demand, in the Washington Summit of 1973, that in the SALT II negotiations we would not ask for more reliable means.

Photographs may reveal the *existence* of research facilities, factories, shipyards, arsenals, and missile sites under construction, but they cannot reveal directly what is being researched, developed, manufactured, assembled, or stored *under roof* in any structure, under certain types of camouflage cover, or in caves. Nor can they even reveal what is being moved over the roads or in railroads on days when there is substantial cloud cover.

Cloud cover imposes a very substantial limit on satellite intelligence. Usually, some 60 percent of the earth is covered by clouds. Darkness also presents complications, although penetration is not as difficult as with heavy cloud cover. A satellite can see the sunlit surface of a given point on the earth's surface only about 20 percent of the time. The Soviet Union has more than its share of cloud protection. Satellite observation is not usually attempted when cloud cover conceals more than 50 percent of the area targeted. For example, there is only one chance in 20 that less than 3/4 of the noon sky over Moscow will be covered by clouds.

Summing up the accomplishments of Nikita Khrushchev's brilliant psychological-warfare gambit in May 1960 when he destroyed the will of U.S. leadership to continue U-2 reconnaissance over the Soviet Union, we have two absolutes and one imponderable. We know absolutely that his bluff-down of the U-2s assisted him in attaining technological supremacy over the United States in the critical area of strategic nuclear warheads, and in knowledge of nuclear weapons' effects and ABM warhead technology. The secrecy he attained for his massive and protracted preparations for the two ban-breaking series of tests was an essential precondition of success in that great venture. That technological superiority, enshrined by the 1963 Moscow Test Ban Treaty, was, in turn, an essential precondition of the operational superiority and the counterforce capability of their weapons—especially the SS-9, SS-18, SS-17, and SS-19—that they enshrined in the second treaty of Moscow, known as the SALT I Interim Agreement.

We also know absolutely that Khrushchev's 1960-63 blackout of U.S. reconnaissance enabled him to secure secrecy for the Soviet sector of his preparations for deploying the missiles to Cuba. This was also a precondition for the growing Soviet strategic supremacy of the SALT era, because this required the knocking down and holding down of U.S. strategic capabilities. In the Cuban adventure it was Khrushchev's demonstration of the will to use nuclear weapons that moved the U.S. elitist groups of Pugwash scientists and pseudo-intellectuals to go into *action* to secure the unilateral nuclear disarmament of the United States.

Now for the imponderable. In June 1956 the U-2 made its first Russian flight, flying directly over Moscow. Yet it provoked only secret diplomatic protests. Why no temper tantrums purportedly directed against "violation" of sacred Soviet airspace? Because the Soviets didn't have anything in that timeframe that required secret deployment or transportation or preparations which could be recorded from above. Only a handful of ICBMs had been deployed prior to 1960 (18 are estimated)—and for a highly practical reason. The pre-1960 Soviet ICBMs were not a very effective type. Known as the SS-6 (NATO designation "Sapwood"), it had a liquid-fuel motor, but the fuel could not be stored in the missile itself and had to be fed into the launcher as it stood on the pad. Together with other preparations, fueling is reported to have required up to 12 hours; and the nuclear warheads were reputedly stored something like 50 miles away from the missile launchers to guard against unauthorized or accidental launch of armed missiles.

But the Soviets had started intensive research and development on intercontinental range missiles as early as 1945, some nine years before the United States. At the end of World War II Stalin had ordered his scientists, industrialists, and generals to produce a rocket that could hit New York; and they immediately began testing and modifying the German V-2. By 1949 they were designing their own models and getting vastly longer range. They gambled that by the time they would have an effective ICBM booster and guidance system, a sufficiently powerful warhead would have been developed within the weight limitations of the rockets. Their gamble paid off.

The only post-World War II U.S. ballistic-missile project prior to Atlas was canceled in 1947. The United States was *not* willing to gamble on the availability of warheads within the then or projected rocket throw-weight capabilities. The best we could do in reducing the weight of thermonuclear warheads, which had enough explosive power to make them worthwhile at intercontinental ranges with the guidance then envisioned, was 9,000 pounds. A breakthrough in 1953, however, cut this to 3,000 pounds. So we started our Atlas project in 1954—at *least five years after the Soviets*. This, of course, gives the lie to the Pugwash-spawned propaganda that the so-called nuclear "arms race" has been an action-reaction spiral, with each upward thrust triggered by an aggressive U.S. move that the peace-loving Soviet Union was reluctantly compelled to counter. The Soviet headstart in ICBMs paid off handsomely: first in Sputnik I, then in the world's first ICBM in September 1957, and, finally, in 1973 in the world's first submarine-launched ICBM, known as the SS-N-8, with a range of 5,000+ nautical miles and carried by the Soviet Delta-class submarine.

By 1960 the Soviets had a whole new generation of ICBMs ready for serial production. Known as the SS-7, the booster for this type was the first ICBM rocket to have storable fuel and hence the capability for hardening and concealment in silos underground. It could also, of course, be launched from simple reinforced concrete pads. The Soviets did not have the warheads available as early as the missiles themselves—but this time the gamble that they would be available and would be effective was not so great. They knew from preliminary calculations available in 1960 that the ban-breaking test series of 1961 would perfect the essential warheads.

So it was that, in the early summer of 1960, timing had become critical for Khrushchev's plans. The so-called unilateral-reciprocal nuclear test ban had been in effect since October 31, 1958. In preparation for his surprise abrogation of the ban, Khrushchev's scientists had gone about as far as they could in their laboratories under roof and in minor cheating by underground tests. Two massive series of atmospheric tests had been planned for 1961, and protracted additional preparations were necessary. These included set-ups in proving grounds for nuclear explosions and also in missile-test launch sites. They planned many weapons-effect experiments that the United States has not matched to this day, including the firing of nuclear warheads through the explosion areas of antimissile nuclear warheads.

These types of preparations could have been detected by U-2 photographic and electronic reconnaissance, so Khrushchev needed to close the skies over Russia to U.S. aircraft. Fixed land-based missile launchers are highly vulnerable to discovery by aerial or satellite reconnaissance *during the process of deployment*. If they can be deployed and their pads or silos constructed without discovery, then they can be concealed from later discovery. Khrushchev's tantrum gambit secured for him a reconnaissance gap in which he was able to deploy the entire series of SS-7 missiles, and an unknown number of the next generation designated SS-8 and also conservatively rated at 5 megatons.

When U.S. satellite photography developed to the point of reasonable accuracy *circa* 1964, U.S. intelligence estimated that the Soviets had deployed about 220 SS-7s and SS-8s. (Some estimates gave them 200 of each.) We cannot really know because the tantrum-induced gap provided years in which the Soviets could cover them with simulated structures and other types of camouflage. This may be one explanation of why the Soviets refused—through the entire 2½ years of the SALT I negotiations—to reveal the numbers of fixed land-based missile launchers they had deployed, or even to confirm or deny the accuracy of U.S. estimates. If, instead of a mere 220 of these types, they had actually deployed, say, 600, they are entitled under SALT I to "modernize" them all, or replace them with new-type missiles. As explained elsewhere in relation to the SALT I loopholes, they could use the SS-9, its upgraded version the SS-18, or the upgrades of the SS-11 that are known as the SS-17 and SS-19. These will have up to five times the payload of the original missiles they replace. This would end all credibility for the U.S. land-based deterrent force.

To those who have the common sense, the patience, and an interest in the survival of the United States required to put together the jigsaw pieces of the history of the last decade or so, the far-reaching results of Khrushchev's staged tantrum are clear. Success in both his predetermined purposes has been total. The secrecy resulting from the reconnaissance gap between the U-2 and satellite coverage enabled the Soviets to conduct the protracted, comprehensive, and complex preparations required to make their massive nuclear test series of 1961 and 1962. These were by far the most creatively productive of the nuclear age. They more than reversed the preexisting U.S. technological lead in high-yield warheads. They developed antimissile warheads and gained knowledge of weapons' effects that are still a mystery to us. This technological advantage was, of course, a necessary precondition to the Soviet buildup of the substantial superiority in strategic forces that they held at the time of the signing of the SALT I Agreements, and will also be an essential ingredient in their climb to decisive supremacy during the period of the SALT I Interim Agreement. This they will surely accomplish—*if* Henry Kissinger still controls U.S. defense and foreign policies through the mid-seventies.

The more immediate results of Khrushchev's tantrum are also clear. The yield/weight ratio that the Soviets secured from their 1961 nuclear tests provided the warhead capability that was a precondition for Khrushchev in making his apparently incredibly risky decision to attempt a 15-year shortcut in accomplishing the destruction or securing the surrender of the United States by deploying strategic missiles to Cuba in 1962. In this adventure he had the benefit of two additional and unpremeditated advantages stemming from his creation of the reconnaissance gap stretching from the last U-2 flight over the Soviet Union in 1960 to the first effective satellite coverage about 1963-64. The first advantage was in preserving secrecy in the assembly and transportation of the missile launchers, missiles, and associated electronic equipment within the U.S.S.R., and their loading onto ships for transoceanic movement. With so much unusual activity, U-2 reconnaissance would surely have spotted some of it, especially since it was a rush project that made effective "cover" difficult.

The second advantage was that Khrushchev's tantrum had so impressed the Kennedy palace guard that they actually blocked early U-2 flights over Cuba during the missile crisis—and they almost succeeded in blocking the critical flights that took the first pictures of the Soviet missiles in the last nick of time. As we have seen, it was Khrushchev's demonstration of the *will to use* nuclear weapons to defeat the United States—even with the odds 8-to-1 against him, if he could secure the advantage of a surprise first-strike—that converted the Pugwash group of U.S. scientists and similar elitist cliques of great influence *from* unilateral-disarmament theoreticians *to* activists working to disarm the United States. The Cuban shock Khrushchev administered was also a necessary antecedent in the Soviets' acquiring that full first-strike capability that SALT I, plus SALT II negotiations, plus Kissinger policy, will soon hand them.

Both the Secretary of State and the President had solemnly and officially declared that the U-2 reconnaissance flights were essential to the United States. The accuracy of their declarations has been doubly demonstrated by history. As soon as the U-2 flights were canceled, the Soviets went ahead with secret preparations to betray the nuclear test ban, overturn our technological superiority, and build up the nuclear power to threaten our destruction or demand our surrender. Only one year later, the absence of U-2 flights gave them the opportunity to make elaborate preparations for the clandestine deployment of their missiles to Cuba. U.S. satellites were not yet advanced enough to detect these preparations—and the proof of this is that they did not do so. Here again, the Kremlin's intent and purpose was to confront the United States with the choice of abject surrender or nuclear destruction.

Khrushchev's Cuban adventure was no drill or gambit. He successfully created a massive and imminent threat to more than 9/10 of U.S. strategic forces. In 1962 our SAC strategic bombers represented more than 95 percent of our strategic delivery capability; and Khrushchev had 42 of the U.S. bases (all except two in the northwest) within range of his Cuban missiles. All major U.S. cities were also within their range. At that time of discovery he had only 42 missiles in place; but more were already in transit, and he let slip that he had intended a force of more than 142 IRBMs and MRBMs in Cuba. As we found out through Colonel Penkovskiy's revelations, a substantial number was required in Cuba because the Soviets had fewer ICBMs in the Soviet Union than our intelligence was estimating at that time. He probably had no more than 75 ICBMs in Russia. Yet that was enough, with the 42 MRBMs and IRBMs Khrushchev sneaked into Cuba, to scare hell out of our elite groups. Now, 10 years later, with a Soviet minimum force of 1,618 ICBMs established by the SALT I statistics, plus the full momentum maintained by the Soviets since the signing of SALT I in May 1972, these same elitists tell us we are in no danger and that we should be happy and honored that Dr. Kissinger has guaranteed a "free ride" against us to these thousands of Soviet missiles.

An especially notable feature of the missiles deployed to Cuba was stressed by Khrushchev in a contemporaneous communication to President Kennedy during the crisis: "You and I both know, Mr. President," he ominously threatened, "what kind of missiles these are." What he meant was that they were "soft" unprotected weapons; they had to be launched with the advantage of surprise, or at least "first"— or they could serve no purpose. Even conventional bombs could destroy them and thus ruin Khrushchev's billion-dollar investment in first-strike-only weapons placed within the U.S. warning net.

The part Khrushchev's brilliantly contrived reconnaissance gap played in all this is pictured by a contemporaneous description of what the Soviets got away with in concealing their preparations:

> . . . the Russians could hardly have devoted less than a year to their missile project. The missiles themselves were probably manufactured behind the Urals, moved by land and sea halfway around the world, unloaded only a few miles away from Florida, transported across Cuban highways, and then put in place—all without rippling official Washington's serene confidence that Nikita Khrushchev would never do such a thing.[5]

Ironically, the aftereffects of Khrushchev's psychological shoot-down of U-2 flights over the Soviet Union in 1960—which prevented detection of the clandestine deployment of the SS-7 and SS-8 intercontinental missiles within Russia—prevented detection two years later of the transportation across Russia of the IRBMs and MRBMs, their loading on ships for Cuba, and their off-loading, transportation, and emplacement in Cuba. The Kennedy palace guard, especially the Pugwash contingent, was still frightened by Khrushchev's staged tantrum. They dreaded to face a repetition and went all out to avoid "another U-2 incident." Their yellow streaks spread from their backs over their faces when, on September 9, 1962, a U-2 was shot down over Red China. Evidence that the Soviets were deploying strategic missiles in Cuba, however, was piling up to such an extent that they could no longer block the resumption of U-2 flights over Cuba. The need for aerial reconnaissance was too obvious and too urgent to be suppressed any longer.

At that point a typical Pugwash-inspired solution was adopted: U-2 flights would be permitted over Cuba, but *not in areas in which the Soviets had emplaced antiaircraft missiles!* Insane, yes; or a deliberate betrayal. Unless the Soviets were installing SAM air-defense complexes just for the hell of it, they were deploying them to protect something worth protecting. Tons of evidence demonstrated that the Soviets were deploying strategic missiles. What could be in more vital need of protection than "soft" nuclear missiles zeroed in on U.S. SAC bases and major American cities? If you were looking for strategic missile sites in Cuba, where would you look?

Well, the palace guard did not permit the U-2s to look in the areas guarded by antiaircraft missiles. Not surprisingly, therefore, the Cuban area photographed during these reluctantly permitted and carefully restricted flights was shown to be reassuringly free from any strategic weapons emplacements. Fortunately for 50 million Americans, however, in the period following the Red China incident, Navy photo-reconnaissance aircraft discovered some sensational evidence. They identified, on Soviet ships inbound for Cuba, crates that had been tailor-made for Ilyushin-28 Beagle jet bombers, known to have nuclear capability. Even with this evidence that the Soviets were building up a nuclear capability in Cuba, the U-2s were not allowed to extend their reconnaissance to Soviet SAM-protected areas until October 14, 1962. On that date the flights brought back the undeniable hard evidence of the strategic missile deployment.

Either the cowardice, naivete, and near-insanity of the palace guard, or the secret and still-undiscovered defection of one or more key U.S. officials, or both, had thus created—some 2½ years after Khrushchev's May 1960 tour de force—a reconnaissance gap in miniature. Yet, even in a time span from only September 9 to October 14, 1962, it vividly illustrates the horrendous potential of such gaps. Once the original U-2 photos of the two missions flown by SAC pilots on October 14 had been interpreted, unlimited additional flights were authorized. Low-level reconnaissance aircraft were added to the teams to bring back closeup pictures of suspicious areas that had been pinpointed by the U-2s or by the ground intelligence that had been so long ignored. Some 2,000 photo missions were carried out in the days following October 16. On October 27 one of the two SAC pilots who had flown the critical "first hard evidence" missions was shot down by Soviet SAM IIs and killed: Major Rudolph Anderson, Jr., one of our country's least publicized heroes.

Here is proof of one of the two great dangers of permitting a gap to be created. When these 2,000 reconnaissance missions were flown, they knew exactly what they were looking for and where to look. A single U-2, flying at an altitude of 14 miles, records a path up to 125 miles wide and up to 3,000 miles long. Developed pictures of this strip, if placed side-by-side, would themselves cover an area 20 feet wide and 10 miles long.

Yet all our efforts uncovered only 30 Soviet strategic missiles in Cuba. Khrushchev admitted to 42 and displayed these on decks of outgoing ships for "inspection" by our aircraft reconnaissance. Castro never permitted the on-site inspection promised by the Soviets at the UN, so there may have been many more concealed in the hundreds of caves or caverns that abound in Cuba. What we do know is that, at a minimum, a 33-day aerial reconnaissance gap was long enough to permit the effective concealment, in limited areas on a small island, of enough strategic missile launchers to cause our most intensive and urgent intelligence estimates, supported by more than 2,000 photographic missions, to miss by 40 percent on the low side. And these missions included low-level, closeup, specifically guided assignments.

Ironically, the minigap in 1962 that extended only from September 9 through October 14 might turn out to have been equally, or perhaps more, dangerous to our continued national existence in freedom. Our Pugwash scientists and other elitist power cliques trembled at the remembrance of Khrushchev's mighty wrath—even though Cuba was involved rather than Russia, and even though the Monroe Doctrine might have been considered still operative. (Khrushchev had not yet demanded that it "be buried, as every dead body is, so that it does not poison the air by its decay."[6]) This time Khrushchev did not need to stage any tantrums or simulate any wrath. The palace guard and the disarmament crowd quaked in their boots even without the stimulation of a Kremlin tantrum.

As the climactic point in the Cuban missile buildup neared, a standdown in U.S. U-2 flights was ordered on September 9 because of the shoot-down of one of our reconnaissance aircraft over Red China. When pressure from the critical state of affairs in Cuba ended this stand-down about September 15, the White House staff and CIA alibied for several days with the excuse of excessive cloud cover. Then came the mysterious "solution" of reinstating the U-2 flights, but restricting them to areas not protected by Soviet SAMs. Then came the Navy reconnaissance pictures of the nuclear-capable Soviet bombers being shipped in, plus the arrival of some six Soviet ships with no deck cargo, but outsized hatches capable of loading missiles as long as 70 feet. These ships docked at night under conditions of absolute secrecy.

A decision was forced on October 3 to assign U-2s to photograph the critical areas that were protected by Soviet SAMs. Mysteriously, however, this decision was not executed during the next 11 days that were critical. The ex-post-facto explanation, which was promoted by high-level White House spokesmen and saturated throughout the media, was that the weather intervened. We were told that Hurricane Ella delayed flights for a week and then cloud cover blocked high-altitude reconnaissance.

Evidence developed later that *Hurricane Ella had not covered the areas in question in the critical time period*. Ella did not assume the force of a tropical storm until October 15, or reach hurricane proportions until October 16; on October 14 she was more than 1,000 miles away from Cuba. Picture-taking weather prevailed over the areas in question from October 5 through 14, except for shower activity in the afternoons. But Hurricane Ella did provide such excellent "cover" for the administration's incredible failure to order U-2s over the critical areas that even the Senate Preparedness Investigating Subcommittee accepted it as an excuse.[7]

Richard Nixon referred to his 1972 visit to Red China as the "week that changed the world." Not likely. But those 33 days back in September and October 1962 actually did provide the Politburo Troika (Khrushchev, Brezhnev, and Kosygin) who had planned the Cuba adventure with the opportunity to change the history of the world. They exploited this opportunity ruthlessly and brilliantly—and almost too effectively for it to have been accomplished without cooperation from within the U.S. Government.

Is it all that important to us, in the mid-seventies, that palace-guard cowardice and lack of common sense—or else a deliberate betrayal of the United States by a person or persons not yet even suspected—are the only alternative explanations for the failure of U-2 coverage in the critical areas of Cuba during the entire period of September 9 through October 14, 1962? Was it really earthshaking that the administration caved in to the fear that risking "another U-2 incident" was also risking another terrible tantrum by Khrushchev? Could a mere 33 additional days of secrecy have really had a decisive effect on the outcome of the entire Cuban confrontation?

In all of America, the first few weeks after the Cuban missile crisis in 1962 were spent in a spree of euphoria. The delusion was so intense that the American people plunged happily into what a former Air Force Chief of Staff called "a national orgy of self-congratulation." Our glamorous young President had bested that stupid Russian bully in a *contest of wills* and had forced him to back down and remove his missiles in utter humiliation. Kennedy had looked eyeball-to-eyeball with Khrushchev and forced him to blink. So most Americans wanted to believe and were led to believe.

Even more than a decade later, most Americans still do not understand how the beautiful dream of victory dissolved into the degradation of surrender.

The Cuban confrontation did indeed start out as a contest of wills between the political leaders of the U.S.S.R. and the United States. During those climactic 13 days in October, however, it became a contest between power elites within the U.S. Government for control of the President of the United States. Although the young President was considering some six principal options in response to the imminent Soviet threat, he had only two real choices within his own government. The need for making the choice was urgent and inexorable. The choice, once made, would rapidly become irreversible—as Henry Kissinger is now demonstrating.

An initial majority of President Kennedy's advisers favored supporting peace *and* freedom through strength. They recognized the threat of nuclear incineration of scores of millions of Americans as being so immediate that it called for equally immediate action—not merely words. They advocated the *only option* that could degrade the Kremlin's capability of destroying scores of millions of American lives. This was a surprise air attack that would eliminate the Soviet missiles. Any other course of action, or inaction, would leave the Kremlin with the power to decide—*in extremis* or in a tantrum—to launch or threaten to launch their strategic nuclear missiles at 25 or 30 of the largest cities in the United States, which were absolutely defenseless then (as they remain today under Kissinger's policies) against nuclear missiles, and which, in missile travel-time were less than 300 seconds away from the Cuban launching pads.

All the professionals urged this course on the President. These included the Air Force Chief of Staff, General Curtis LeMay, who, as early as September 26, had ordered the Tactical Air Command to be combat-ready by October 20; the Chief of Naval Operations, Admiral George W. Anderson; the Army Chief of Staff; and even the dovish flexible-response advocate JCS Chairman Maxwell Taylor. The only professional intelligence expert on the so-called "Executive Committee" advising the President was the Director of the Central Intelligence Agency, John McCone, who also voted with the professional military in favor of an air strike to disarm the Soviet missile sites in Cuba before they could be employed to incinerate millions of Americans. The only professional statesman possibly worthy of that characterization on the so-called "Executive Committee" was former Secretary of State Dean Acheson. This commonsense and responsible side of the argument not only represented a monopoly of strategic-military-diplomatic expertise, but also an initial majority of the advisory group.

The arrogant amateurs, the apostles of appeasement, opposed *any* U.S. defensive action at all—even a disarming strike limited to tar-

475

geting only Soviet strategic missiles deployed in Cuba. Influence with the President for this side was furnished by his brother Robert Kennedy. The cunning was supplied by that slick master of deception Robert Strange McNamara. At first he openly advocated doing nothing in response to the imminent Soviet missile threat. Kennedy himself, however, soon made it clear that this would not be acceptable. "The most dangerous course of all," he asserted, "would be to do nothing." A congressional election was coming up within a couple of weeks, and it was not clear whether he was concerned about political or strategic danger. In any event, this presidential decision compelled McNamara to conceive, as his fallback position, one of the most monstrous charades in all history: a methodology for doing *nothing* under cover of the most massive display of conventional and nuclear power the world had ever seen.

McNamara's proposal was to place an embargo on military shipments to Cuba, support the embargo by an intensive and extensive naval and air blockade conducted under the euphemistic label of a "quarantine," and request Khrushchev to remove his offensive missiles. This stratagem of quarantine would have been great if it had been adopted and executed six or eight months earlier (when the American Security Council proposed it) *before* the Soviets had begun the movement of SAMs and offensive strategic missiles into Cuba. But because it was adopted at a time when the strategic missiles and their nuclear warheads were already in Cuba, it was an obvious case of locking the barn door after the horse was stolen. So far as lifting the danger of incineration hanging by a thread over millions of Americans, it did not amount even to a half-measure.

The weakness of this plan and, indeed, the weakness of the entire case against the one rational course (namely, an air strike to disarm the missiles zeroed-in on U.S. targets) was exposed by the totally ridiculous character of the argument against the air strike that is reported to have been decisive. Robert Kennedy is authoritatively quoted as having "passionately" declared: "My brother is not going to be the Tojo of the 1960s!"

Of course he was young at the time; but even the youngest Attorney General of the United States might be expected to understand the fundamental moral and legal difference between premeditated murder and justifiable homicide in self-defense. At the time of the Pearl Harbor attack the United States was not directly or imminently threatening Japan militarily. Indeed, to help cover the sneak attack, the Japanese had a simultaneous "peace mission" in Washington. The proposed U.S. air strike in the Cuban crisis was for the purpose of removing—the only sure way—the threat of death carried by the missiles Khrushchev had sneaked into Cuba and which were within *seconds of so many millions of Americans.*

The only way a true analogy to the Pearl Harbor attack could be drawn would be to *suppose* that U.S. submarine and air forces had been alert at the time and had attacked the Japanese aircraft carriers just minutes before they were to launch their bomber and torpedo aircraft in the murderous surprise attack that assassinated more than 2,000 helpless American sailors and airmen. Such an exclusively *defensive* move would certainly have been justified in employing an element of surprise so far as possible. Such a disarming strike would have been even more clearly justified in the Cuban missile case because the Soviet threat then was primarily against millions of defenseless civilians.

An additional pivotal distinction also existed. Dean Acheson challenged Robert Kennedy's Pearl Harbor analogy with it: a disarming air strike at the Cuban missile sites could not possibly constitute a sneak surprise attack, or even an attack without warning, because President Kennedy had served on the Soviets two specific warnings that the United States would not tolerate an offensive buildup in Cuba —once in a public statement on September 4, 1962, and again on September 13. A number of the missiles were brought in after those dates.

Why, then, with all the experts, all the professionals, all the responsible military advisers advocating an air strike to disarm the missiles, did President Kennedy choose the other course? Why did he choose the course advocated only by amateurs and the proponents of peace-at-any-price-including-a-concealed-surrender?

One single factor appears to have been decisive with the President: the advantage that accrued to the Soviets because of the U-2 reconnaissance gap from September 9 through October 14. This apparently minor concession, made in the fear of another U-2 incident triggering another Khrushchev tantrum, turned out to be critical in shaping the future course of history. It provided the Kremlin plotters with just enough time to accomplish two essentials: (1) the effective concealment of at least 12 missile launchers, and (2) the bringing to operational status of substantially all the medium-range missiles that had not been concealed.

President Kennedy was still smarting from his humiliating betrayal of the Cuban freedom fighters at the Bay of Pigs. Under the influence of his palace guard, plus UN Delegate Adlai Stevenson, he had abandoned to slaughter, disaster, and capture, more than 1,000 U.S.-trained anti-Communist Cubans. A single squadron of U.S. aircraft could have saved them and made the anti-Castro invasion a success. This would have prevented the later sneaking of Soviet missiles into Cuba to threaten millions of Americans with nuclear incineration. Kennedy would have preferred to erase that humiliation, if possible. Also, the upcoming congressional election was almost at hand and the public was highly restive. The intuition of a free people was warning them that their freedom and their existence faced serious threats. As Kennedy hit the hustings on the campaign trail that fall, he was confronted by pertinent placards inscribed with such captions as "Less Profile, More Courage" and "More Vigor about Cuber."

Kennedy *wanted* to do the right thing by his country and for his own place in history. He *wanted* to order that disarming air strike against Soviet missiles. Although on Thursday, October 18, he had tentatively approved the McNamara-Robert Kennedy plan to do-nothing-under-cover-of-much-ado, he held the final decision open for his determination alone, all the way through Sunday, October 21, even though his speech announcing the "quarantine" had been written for delivery on Monday evening.

What the young President desperately sought was assurance that, if he did order the air strike, it would in fact disarm *all* the Soviet missile-launching sites before they could launch a single missile at the United States. According to contemporaneous reports later confirmed, he had sought a guarantee from the Commander of the U.S. Air Force Tactical Air Command (TAC), General Walter C. Sweeney, Jr., that our bombing attack could be so swift and totally effective that *no* nuclear warheads would get off the ground.

At that point in time, the General had available in Florida at the highest state of alert about 1,000 fighter-bomber and attack aircraft. He was sure of one thing: *anything that could be seen from the air* could be destroyed by his TAC force—and could be destroyed before any missiles could be launched. Flight time from Florida was something like five to 10 minutes, and warning time far less. But General Sweeney was hypercautious as well as truthful. When asked by the President if he could destroy *all* the missiles before any was launched, he gave this answer: "Yes—unless some missiles have been moved back into the bush." The President, as well as the General, knew that the Soviet MRBMs were sufficiently mobile so that some of them could have been moved in the interval since they were first spotted by the U-2 flights of October 14.

We know now that at least 12 missile launchers had been effectively concealed. Our most intensive reconnaissance—thousands of flights—located only 30; yet we know that 42 were supposedly shipped out later. So far as Kennedy or Sweeney knew at that time, however, the number concealed could have been 20 or 30 or zero. If General Sweeney's TAC forces had made their disarming strike, and did in fact destroy all missile sites that could be located, and missed only the few effectively concealed, those "few" could possibly still be launched against U.S. cities and could *possibly* kill a "few" million Americans.

Actually, however, the possibility of those few missiles hidden in the bush did not pose anything like the horrendous danger young John F. Kennedy attributed to them. A greater or lesser man than

General Sweeney could better have served his country and Western civilization by giving his President more information—or less. In the first place, no matter how many unlocated missiles might be hidden in the bush or elsewhere, they could constitute no threat whatsoever to millions of American lives unless they were *operationally* deployed and the cover had been superimposed over a deployment that would have enabled them to go into action immediately. Merely *hiding* missiles and related equipment from aerial reconnaissance is no real problem in Cuba, where caves abound by the hundreds. But deploying them for action and then covering the entire complex is something else. Contemporaneous pictures show, for a single complex of four launchers of medium-range missiles, up to 37 large vehicles, including prime movers, fuel trailers, oxidizer tank trailers, plus shelter tents, numerous tracked areas, and, of course, the missile erectors themselves.

This does not mean that an operational complex cannot be effectively concealed. It can; but it takes more time than the Soviets had had up to that time in Cuba. So the missing 12 missiles were most probably in caves, awaiting deployment. But even if there were two or three operational complexes sufficiently concealed, early enough, to escape destruction by U.S. aircraft in the proposed surprise strike, there are other reasons why they most probably would not have been actually used to launch warheads against the United States. The U.S. surprise disarming attack should have been launched within a day or so of the initial discovery, to maximize the advantage and to ensure against any weapons being fired. At that time substantially all the Soviet missiles would have been targeted on U.S. SAC bases, which they would have expected to destroy by surprise with all their strategic bomber aircraft caught on the ground.

Once the U-2 pictures of October 14 had been interpreted, however, and SAC Commander-in-Chief Thomas S. Power had mounted his great airborne and sling-shot alert, and had dispersed the B-47 strategic bombers, this targeting—which could not have been rapidly changed with the equipment available in 1962—assured that any surviving remnants of the Soviet missiles in Cuba would not seriously threaten any substantial number of American lives, much less the survival of the United States.

But in the nuclear age it is not the *real* threat that is decisive but the threat *as perceived* by the decisionmakers. When President Kennedy was unable to obtain iron-clad assurance that, if he ordered a disarming strike at the Soviet missiles in Cuba, they could *all* be destroyed before a single warhead could be launched at a U.S. city, his fear of what *might* happen subjected him to control by the pro-surrender faction of his palace guard. His paralysis of fear enabled Robert McNamara to snatch defeat from the jaws of victory.

A covert surrender was sold to the young President under the guise of a gesture of statesmanlike restraint to avert a nuclear holocaust. One of the terms of the surrender was not covert: the scrapping of all U.S. Thor and Jupiter strategic nuclear missiles in Turkey, Italy, and England. For public consumption, McNamara prepared a cover story that these powerful missiles, able to reach targets in the U.S.S.R. within minutes, were "obsolete" and were being "replaced" by missiles on Polaris submarines. But none of the Thor and Jupiter missiles was more than a few months old, and they had cost us scores of millions of dollars. The McNamara lie stood substantially unchallenged for nearly 11 years and was never officially refuted. A United Press story datelined Washington, December 10, 1973, in connection with the release of six of the 10 Cuban missile crisis letters between Khrushchev and Kennedy, finally revealed to the public what had long been known to those on the inside in Washington:

> It is now generally accepted that those intermediate-range missiles [Thor and Jupiter] were removed under the terms of a *private addendum* to the agreement [as contained in the Khrushchev-Kennedy letters], although it was not formally acknowledged in any of the correspondence.

Vastly more secret than any "private addendum" in writing, however, was McNamara's unilateral strategic disarmament of the United States while the Soviets carried on their buildup of strategic weapons.

Not until the strategic-balance statistics were released to Congress in connection with the SALT I Agreements in May 1973 did the magnitude of the Cuban missile crisis surrender settlement become publicly apparent. Not until the Middle East crisis of 1973, triggered by the Arabs' launching of the Yom Kippur War against the Israelis, did the international political effect of the reversal of the strategic nuclear balance become publicly apparent. With the shift from the 8-to-1 U.S. superiority at the time of the Cuban missile crisis to a 19-to-1 Soviet superiority in missile deliverable megatonnage in 1973, control of the world had been handed over to the Kremlin. So long as the Soviets maintain such superiority, whenever Leonid Brezhnev wants the United States to change its policy, he merely need summon Kissinger to Moscow and give him his orders.

Still concealed from the American people, however, are the solutions to the two major mysteries of the climactic confrontation in Cuba in 1962: (1) why did Khrushchev—with the strategic odds 8-to-1 against him—decide to risk the near-certain, near-total destruction of the Soviet Union by sneaking strategic nuclear missiles into Cuba?; (2) why did the Kennedy Administration—with such tremendous odds favoring us—ever permit the Soviets to move those missiles into Cuba and bring them to a point of operational readiness so that they could threaten the lives of millions of Americans from inside our defense perimeters with near-zero warning?

As Dr. Kissinger noted in his September 16, 1970, press background briefing, "our strategic supremacy was overwhelming" in 1962. No rational leader would challenge such odds in strategic nuclear power, especially when the instruments of such power included a massive counterforce capability sufficient for a full disarming strike, as well as destruction of the population, cities, industry, and transportation. No Communist leader, especially, would risk such cataclysmic destruction of the base of Communist power. Even if he got away with it, as Khrushchev did, he would be ousted from power as a dangerous "adventurist." The magnitude of the risk *appeared* to be far too great for a gamble.

Yet Khrushchev *appeared* to take that gamble. He was neither insane nor a fool; indeed, he was a brilliant and knowledgeable nuclear strategist. Not only Khrushchev was involved: Leonid Brezhnev and Alexei Kosygin were in on all the planning for deployment of missiles to Cuba. Although Khrushchev held the political power, Brezhnev even then had enough pivotal influence with the Soviet military so that he could have vetoed the "adventure" if it were anything nearly so dangerous to the Soviets as it appeared to be.

Logically, there must have been some very good reason why Soviet leadership considered that they had a reliable lid to hold down that risk. The United States had then the capability of actually *delivering* more than 40 billion tons of explosive power on the Soviet Union. We had thousands of strategic and tactical bombers that could have totally saturated Soviet air defenses. If there had appeared to the three top Politburo planners any substantial risk that the United States would use this destructive power in defense of the millions of Americans threatened at near-point-blank range by the Soviet missiles in Cuba, Khrushchev, Brezhnev, and Kosygin would not have dared to make the aggressive move.

What gave the Kremlin Three such high confidence that the United States would not actually use its massive, decisive, horrendous nuclear power against the Soviets—even against their weapons zeroed-in on us in Cuba?

We have suggested from time to time that one basis for Khrushchev's confidence was his opinion that U.S. leadership was "too liberal to fight, even in defense of their own vital interests." This was undoubtedly part of it—but Soviet Communist leaders would not risk the lives of their valuable and disciplined population on such a psychological gamble against a people who had nuclear odds of 8-to-1 to bolster their courage. The odds were so great in our favor that all we had to do was to impose a peaceful embargo or declaration to make the Soviets desist.

It simply will not do to say that our leaders permitted the Soviets to move their missiles into Cuba during 1962 because they did not know what was happening. Some officials, it is true, because of their ideological blocking and belief that the Soviet Communists were "mellowing," did not believe the mountains of evidence. But those who had the real power and influence were not so naive as to believe that the Soviets would not move against us.

There must have been a still-unknown factor to influence the Kremlin's decision. Was it the same factor that caused U.S. leadership to permit the Kremlin to move those nuclear missiles into Cuba?

It remains to relate the effect of the 1960-63 reconnaissance blackout on U.S. vulnerability under the SALT I Agreements. We saw from the Cuban experience that a U-2 gap of only a month was sufficient to permit the deployment of 42 missiles. We spotted 30 but missed the other 12 that were effectively concealed. Thus they had 40 percent more than we had located and identified—this on a small island, despite the most intensive reconnaissance efforts in history and despite low-level close-ups aided by ground intelligence.

Cuba has an area of 44,217 square miles. The Soviet Union has at least 8,647,249 square miles; some computations put it at 9,200,000. From satellite distance—at least 90 miles up—missiles do, indeed, look like needles. Would you prefer—if your life depended on it—to have to find them in a 44,217-square-mile haystack, or a 9-million-square-mile haystack?

This is intensely relevant to our situation under SALT I. Yet it has been ignored—pushed under the rug of public indifference and smothered by official incompetence or perhaps deliberate deceit. The SALT I Agreements, and even Dr. Kissinger's explanation and rationale of them, makes it clear that we rely absolutely upon intelligence techniques and interpretations that have, year after year after year, been absolutely wrong.

The most illuminating exposé on this point resulted from a question by Senator Jackson in the question-and-answer session of the Kissinger White House briefing for the five congressional committees on June 15, 1972:

> Senator Jackson: . . . I think we all should agree that if we are going to have an agreement, it should be one that will stabilize and not destabilize. When you have a number of ambiguities such as we have in the present arrangement, I think it is fraught with some trouble. . . .
>
> There are a lot of them . . . there is no specific limitation other than our unilateral statement as to the number of land-based missiles, intercontinental, that are permitted.
>
> Would you comment? The same is true of "what is a heavy missile?"
>
> Dr. Kissinger: With respect to the numbers of missiles actually being deployed, the Soviet Union has been extremely reluctant to specify precise numbers, that is true. We have operated with a number of 1,618.

There is absolutely no question that if our intelligence should reveal that the Soviet numbers significantly exceed that figure that the whole premise of the agreement will be in question.

In the 9 million square miles of Soviet territory we have identified—according to our SALT figures—1,618 emplaced missiles. If we have missed another 40 percent, that would give the Soviets an *additional* 647 missile launchers that *would be entirely legal under the SALT I Interim Agreement.* Their total number of fixed land-based ICBMs would then be 2,265, or more than twice our 1,054. When the number of missiles is more than double, the chances are that such massive superiority represents a full first-strike capability—or at least a very close approach to it. This would be especially so when the new numbers would bring their throw-weight advantage to something like 8-to-1, and their missile megatonnage delivery capability to at least 19-to-1, and more probably 28+-to-1.

An additional 647 undiscovered Soviet ICBM fixed-base launchers is not a high probability—but it is a definite possibility. Our intelligence estimates indicate that only 220 ICBMs of the SS-7 and SS-8 types were deployed during the years 1961-63. Could the Soviets have *produced* many more than those 220 in that time interval? About 1,700 more—according to widely leaked contemporaneous authoritative intelligence reports. They were estimated to have the *capability* of deploying 100 by 1959 and 2,000 by 1963. Granted that they *could have* produced so many hundreds more than the 220 we credit them with having had, could they have *deployed* them without discovery then, and kept them concealed until now? Perhaps not the entire additional 1,700; but the hypothesized 647 does not appear to be at all incredible.

If the Khrushchev-created 1960-63 blackout had been effective enough to blind us to the massive preparations for the 1961-62 Soviet nuclear test series, and to blind us to the protracted and very substantial preparations for deployment of missiles to Cuba in 1961, it could certainly have served to conceal some 600 missile launchers in 9 million square miles of Soviet territory. Before that surveillance gap was closed by the regular operational status of the high-resolution satellites of the U.S. "program 622A" toward the end of 1963, those launchers could have been given the appearance of farm silos, warehouses, railroad service building, schoolhouses, oil rigs, or virgin forests. In addition to those deployed during the years of the gap, others may have been successfully deployed and concealed during periods of extraheavy and prevalent cloud cover. Others simply may not look like our idea of missile launchers.

In any event, the very possibility of such additional numbers of Soviet ICBM launchers being deployed, as of the time of the SALT I signing, demonstrates the wild irresponsibility of Henry Kissinger in agreeing to a freeze on numbers of fixed land-based ICBM launchers in the face of the *flat and unexplained* refusal by the Soviets to verify what numbers were to be frozen. Accepting such contumelious treatment from the Kremlin was, however, entirely in his character.

Why did the Soviets refuse to verify the numbers of their deployed fixed land-based ICBM launchers? It cannot be denied that their reason must have been that they preferred to negotiate on the basis of U.S. intelligence estimates. But why? Obviously they were convinced that they would secure a more advantageous SALT agreement on the basis of the U.S. estimates than on the actual numbers, and that they would receive, in addition, all the goodies that Kissinger packaged for them in his "broad spectrum of agreements." They needed this U.S. largess, especially the wheat, almost desperately.

On the other hand, the Soviets must have anticipated that, if they revealed true numbers substantially in excess of the U.S. estimates, they would get no U.S. agreement to their slickly drafted SALT I Agreements and no "golden egg"-type benefits in trade, technology, and credits. This is confirmed by additional statements by Dr. Kissinger when he admitted to Senator Jackson in the White House briefing of June 15, 1972, quoted above, that, if it were revealed that the Soviet numbers significantly exceed U.S. estimates, "the whole premise of the agreement will be in question." His further explanation carries far-reaching significance as to the Soviet refusal:

> But beyond that [the SALT pacts] . . . the two countries have a unique opportunity right now to move into an entirely different relationship of building additional trust. . . .
>
> If it should turn out that those numbers are being challenged in any significant way at all, then this would cast a doubt. It would not only threaten disagreement [on SALT], but it would threaten the whole basis of this new relationship which I have described.

It seems unfortunate that, in this new relationship of asserted "trust," the Soviets were unwilling to trust us with knowledge of *their* numbers. We gave them ours; and we also gave them our estimates of their numbers. The only rational explanation of their refusal to give the true numbers of fixed Soviet ICBM launchers should be obvious to anyone with common sense: U.S. intelligence estimates of Soviet strategic forces are now—as they have always been since 1962—substantial underestimates. The Soviet leaders, including the signer of the SALT I Agreements, have for years taken great glee in the naivete of these underestimates by the tremendously expensive U.S. intelligence community.

In mid-summer of 1965 McNamara's Pentagon came up with a report on Soviet ICBMs that downgraded them in numbers to between 270 and 300. The Master of the Kremlin felt he could afford a little derisive understatement in confiding to the graduating classes of the Soviet military academies in Moscow:

We hate to boast, and we do not wish to threaten anyone, however, it is necessary to note that the figures and calculations quoted in the West about the rocket and nuclear power of the Soviet Union do no credit at all to the intelligence services of the imperialist states.

Looking back from the mid-seventies, we can now see how long a shadow was cast on our future national security by our craven and unnecessary surrender to Khrushchev's bold psychological stroke back in May 1960. Just as the wicked flee when none pursueth, cowards cringe when no threat confronts them. So it is that the artificially created gap in U.S. aerospace reconnaissance, which lasted for some three years, in turn created a very real triple threat to the survival of the United States. In the inspired words of Aleksandr Solzhenitsyn, "the cost of cowardice is always evil."

22

An old backwoods story is told about a hunter who inadvertently stumbled onto a huge bear, angering the animal. Since the bear was obviously moving toward confrontation rather than negotiation, the hunter ran to escape, gasping out a prayer, "Lord, help me."

Several minutes later, he took a quick look back and saw that the space between him and the bear was remaining exactly constant. Thinking this over, the hunter composed a more modest prayer: "Oh Lord, if you won't help me, please don't help that bear."

Richard J. Whalen considers that the book *Kissinger: Portrait of a Mind* by Professor Stephen Graubard has, by synopsizing everything his subject has written over the past two decades, demonstrated

> that the brilliant refugee remains an unassimilated outsider—a European by heritage and cultural choice, a cosmopolitan by circumstance, an American by deliberate (and hazardous) calculation.

As to the Kissinger accomplishments, Whalen is even more accurate and eloquent:

> The Nixon-Kissinger foreign policy is the kinkiest since Franklin Roosevelt and Harry Hopkins redrew the map of the world upstairs at the White House. . . . Nixon and Kissinger, the coolly professional technicians, are bumblers on a far grander scale.
>
> They have conceived and executed in deepest secrecy a policy avowedly based on enduring national interest, yet characterized by sudden and sometimes ruthlessly unpredictable spasms of unilateral whim. They have detached themselves from the American public, the Congress, the foreign policy establishment, and many of our allies, and have behaved in a man-

ner more appropriate to a totalitarian state than a democratic republic at the heart of a worldwide security and economic system. . . .

What is lacking, in the architects and their handiwork alike, is a foundation in the country they purport to represent. What they will leave behind, predictably, is weakness and peril compounded.[1]

Whalen's use of the term "kinkiest" is artfully apt. In British usage, it means far-out or offbeat—but it is even more appropriate in the American mod-slang sense, in which its connotation is "somewhat perverted," which, in turn, is not too far from the dictionary meaning of "twisted."

These Whalen quotations pinpoint the major questions pondered in this book: Can what Henry Kissinger has done to the defense and foreign policies of the United States be justified on the theory that he is doing the best he can "under the political circumstances" that presently obtain in the nation? Or are they "kinky"? Or do they represent a deliberate betrayal of the United States for some unfathomable motive? These questions are, after all, a paraphrase of the question we have been pursuing throughout this book: Is Henry Kissinger "some kind of a nut, or something?"

William F. Buckley, Jr., asserts that, even if Kissinger subscribed to the foreign policy of General Curtis LeMay, Kissinger could not do any more than political reality (as represented by an increasingly anti-defense-minded Congress) would permit. The Buckley argument is that there is a "possibility" that "this country is far gone in flatulence, and will not, for the time being, respond," and that "Kissinger may be the man shrewd enough to recognize it."

This is a defense of defeatism; and defeatism is what got us into the position where some now call it "shrewd" to recognize that our position is hopeless, at least for the time being. We do not in any way concede that our situation is hopeless, or that "this country" is "so far gone in flatulence" that it will not respond. The crisis is in leadership. This country is the American people; and the reason they appear so far gone in flatulence is that they have been deliberately deceived for some 13 years.

For the moment let us accept the Buckley defense of Kissinger to explain what Kissinger is doing and not doing. As Buckley enunciates this defense, it would cover Kissinger for failure to act *affirmatively*. It would excuse *nonaction* of his obvious and priority duty, namely, to propose and advocate programs to rebuild the U.S. strategic deterrent so that the Soviets will not be able to demand our surrender or to force us by nuclear blackmail of even the subtlest sort into a concealed installment surrender.

The Buckley defense, however, will not in any way exonerate or justify Henry Kissinger if he has been acting *against* the United States. Even if every Senator and every Representative were a "Member of

Congress for Peace Through Law," Kissinger still would not be justified in taking a single action against (in the language of the SALT I Agreements) the "supreme interests" of the United States.

The United States Constitution, Article III, Section 3, states:

> Treason against the United States shall consist only in levying war against them, or in adhering to their enemies, giving them aid and comfort.

Is the Constitution of the United States adequate for the defense of the American people against mass incineration in the nuclear-space age? The way our Founding Fathers wrote it, that "most wonderful work ever struck off at a given time by the brain and purpose of man" was adequate. But Henry Kissinger, Leonid Brezhnev, and the U.S. Senate have changed that. Their SALT I ABM Treaty made it unconstitutional to provide any defense for the American people against the most horrendous threat in all history, a nuclear missile attack (except for the ½ of one percent of our population living in the Washington, D.C., area, and this is only an illusory option based on first destroying our only existing missile defense site in Grand Forks, North Dakota, in accordance with the 1974 Moscow Summit Protocol to the 1972 SALT I Treaty).

Other than that, however, the Constitution is brilliantly adaptable to a future known only to God. The key word in the definition of "treason" is "enemies." "Their enemies" means enemies of the United "States." Although, at the time the Constitution was written, "enemies" were usually visualized as "invaders" or potential invaders (as in the last sentence of Article I, Section 10), fortunately no definition was attempted. From the language of Article III, Section 3, quoted above, it is clear that the term is not restricted to those levying war against the United States.

Since the Constitution itself did not define who are our enemies, can that term now be defined to meet the needs of the nuclear space age? That it can; the Constitution is adequate. Article II, Section 8, in enumerating the specifically granted powers of Congress, includes the power "to declare war." By declaring war against a nation, Congress automatically defines that nation and its nationals as "enemies." Thus, defining *who are our enemies* is a constitutional power of Congress. The power to declare war is a greater power since it invokes the total might of the nation and sets the legal stage for initiation of hostilities. The power to define "enemies" of the United States is a lesser power included in the war power.

There is no doubt that Congress can define our "enemies" without declaring war. Declaring "war" instantaneously creates and defines "enemies"; but defining "enemies" does *not* amount to a declaration of war. The clear purpose of the framers of the Constitution in conferring on Congress the extraordinary powers usually referred to as the "war powers" was to enable Congress to meet a threat to national survival. The Constitution expressly recognizes the possibility of a situation in which it would be unreasonable and suicidal to await a formal declaration of war by the Congress. Thus, although the individual States are under a general prohibition "in time of peace" against engaging in war, they are granted an exception for self-preservation if "actually invaded" or "in such imminent danger as will not admit of delay." The power of national self-preservation is an inherent right of every sovereign nation, and the Constitution specifically delegates to Congress the exercise of this right.

Why should we care about how we can define our "enemies" in the nuclear age? Recognizing in advance of a massive nuclear attack exactly who are our "enemies" might be the only effective way to avert a nuclear strike. All our lives may well depend on this; certainly, our freedom and the continued independence of the United States will so depend. We need an authoritative definition so that effective legal action can be taken to defend ourselves against our "enemies" before it is too late. Under our legal system and the vast body of court-created constitutional law, the resources of our great nation simply cannot—short of a formal declaration of war—be marshaled against our enemies. This means, in effect, that they get a free shot at us—or many free shots. In the nuclear age, even one such free shot may be too many.

One of the most ancient, and certainly one of the wisest, aphorisms of war is "know your enemy." How can you know your enemy—whether nation or individual—if you have not precisely defined who is your "enemy"? Fighting against an unknown enemy is always frustrating and often futile.

Still another reason for defining the term "enemy" is that we do not want to repeat the mistake made by the Carthaginians. They permitted their leaders to disarm their nation-state and keep it disarmed in the face of Rome's growing military might. When the people saw that it was too late to reconstitute their own military power and that they would all be put to death as a result of their helplessness brought about by disarmament, they turned on their leaders and tore them limb from limb. Deterrence would have been better than such revenge; and the way we can establish deterrence is to secure an accurate definition of "enemies" that will make it legally punishable "treason" to give them aid and comfort. Americans could once more dare to call treason by its right name.

The final reason why we need a definition of "enemies" of the United States in the nuclear age is to answer the question: Has Henry Kissinger been helping that bear? Let's phrase it more formally—remembering, however, that the question is wholly hypothetical. We are not, anywhere in this book, accusing anyone of being a traitor or of being guilty of treason. If the *reader* feels that the evidence makes a case for *de facto* treason, that is his conclusion; but it cannot be *de jure* treason in the absence of a declaration of war or that essential congressional definition of "enemies."

The question can be formally phrased like this: Has a hypothetical U.S. official been giving aid and comfort to enemies of the United States?

We need a definition of "enemies" in order to pursue this inquiry, and we know that Congress has the *legal* power to make the definition. But does Congress have the necessary *understanding* of the fundamentals of strategic military power?

While our Constitution is adequate for survival of the nation in the nuclear age, Congress has not so proved itself—yet. Both the Senate and the House flunked their crucial tests in understanding the requirements for national survival in the era of nuclear missiles. By their near-unanimous approval of the SALT I ABM Treaty and Interim Agreement they demonstrated an irresponsible ignorance of what those agreements would do to the United States. It is obvious that the members of Congress had not read the texts of the agreements or, if they had read them, they had not taken the trouble to understand them. Not more than eight of them asked any of the right questions or made any of the appropriate analyses.

An Act

To define the term "Enemies of the United States" as used in the Constitution of the United States, Article III, Section 3.

Section 1. Any Foreign Power building an arsenal of weapons capable of subjecting the people of the United States to the will of the leaders of that Foreign Power is hereby declared to be an "Enemy of the United States" within the meaning of Article III, Section 3, of the Constitution of the United States.

Section 2. Any person who degrades the strategic nuclear deterrent so as to make the United States vulnerable to attack by an Enemy of the United States as defined in Section 1 hereof, or who knowingly contributes to the degradation of that deterrent, is guilty of giving aid and comfort to an Enemy of the United States, within the meaning of Article III, Section 3, of the Constitution of the United States.

That would do it. It has the irresistible power of self-evident truth. A foreign power engaged in such a malevolent undertaking sure as hell isn't any friend. Nor is any American who assists the foreign power in attaining such a coercive position against these United States. This draft statute makes clear the respective supplementary functions of our foreign and domestic enemies. The foreign power builds up its nuclear arsenal so that it can destroy us without suffering substantial retaliation. Our domestic enemies drag down our strategic retaliatory power, to degrade both its physical capability of inflicting damage against our foreign enemy and its credibility in our own eyes as well as those of the enemy, so that we would have no rational alternative remaining—no option save surrender.

What Section 1 of the draft statute means, of course, is that any foreign power attempting to build a first-strike capability against us is an enemy. But it is phrased in the nontechnical terms of what an enemy first-strike capability against us means to us and to the nation. The United States will have lost its sovereignty and its independence immediately upon a foreign power's attaining the power of life and death over the American people. At such a point the Constitution will have lost its power to protect our freedom and our individual rights, or even our lives. The restraints it imposes on the powers our own elected rulers may exercise over us will not operate at all against the Politburo of the Communist Party of the Soviet Union. We will, as implied by Section 1 of the proposed Act to define our enemies, be at the mercy of the leaders of a foreign power.

What will the quality of that mercy be? Can we realistically expect them to treat us better than they treated their own people under the Great Terror? Leonid Brezhnev served the CPSU well in the liquidation of 7 million Ukrainian men, women, and children by deliberately imposed starvation. Brezhnev carried out his assignment so well that he finished this genocidal mission with four "Order of Lenin" medals. Later he participated in other wholesale liquidations in the period 1945-50. From 1965 through 1973, under his personal dictatorship, Brezhnev's puppet government has conducted a campaign against Ukrainian intellectuals in which the most prominent are condemned to insane asylums and the less notable to slave labor camps, where they join some 3 million other U.S.S.R. citizens.

These are just a few reasons why we should not want the Soviets to attain a first-strike capability against us, and why we need the draft federal statute proposed above. The "aid-and-comfort-to-the-enemy" group defined in Section 2 has been on the offensive against the people of the United States at least since 1960. This draft federal statute would be our first means of striking back effectively at the contemporary domestic enemies of the Constitution of the United States.

But suppose we should perform the near-miracle of starting to turn the tide against the strategic surrender lobby. Then we would face the problem of proving that a foreign power, the Soviet Union, is, indeed, as Secretary of Defense Melvin Laird testified in 1969, "going for a first-strike capability. There is no question about that."

Unless we can prove that, we will have no legal case against U.S. citizens who are deliberately seeking to degrade our strategic deterrent, and who are accomplishing their task so efficiently that there is very little time left before it will be (in the words of Winston Churchill) gone forever. Already 141 Senators and Congressmen, calling themselves "Members of Congress for Peace Through Law," have signed a commitment to work for "general and complete disarmament." To cash in on federal funding, these prosurrender Congressmen are promoting a new antidefense instrument called the Office of Technology Assessment (OTA). It is clear that the Pugwash group will dominate both the congressional overseers and the OTA staff. If antisurrender Americans do not devise an instrument with which to fight back, they will lose ground even more swiftly than in the past.

How can we prove that the Soviets are "going for a first-strike capability" when the Pugwash conferees and their allied MAD elites insist that such a capability is impossible to attain?

Henry Kissinger has successfully obfuscated the meaning of his own declarations about the attainability of a first-strike capability. As he so often does, his *words* seem to espouse both positions. In his White House briefing for the five congressional committees on June 15, 1972, he adverted to

> . . . a more-or-less simultaneous and continuous process of technological advance, which opens more and more temptations for seeking decisive advantage.
>
> *A premium is put on striking first and on creating a defense to blunt the other side's retaliatory capability.* In other words, marginal additions of power cannot be decisive. Potentially decisive additions are extremely dangerous, and the quest for them very destabilizing.

At this point it seems he has conceded the possibility of a nuclear superpower attaining a first-strike capability, and that the temptations to seek it are great. He then implies, however, that, by creating for the Soviet leaders a chance to "move away from confrontation through carefully prepared negotiations," and by creating for the Soviets through SALT and its accompanying benefits of trade and technology "a vested interest in mutual restraint," he has averted a Soviet move toward first-strike capability.

To provide a sophisticated rationalization of his "subtle triangular" negotiations with Red China and the Soviet Union, however, he felt compelled to assert that the two Communist giants and the United States had come to a recognition of the fact that their differences are "nonessential" and overshadowed by common national interests, and that "we are bound together by one basic fact: none of us can survive a nuclear war."[2]

This Kissinger statement is an outright denial of the possibility that any of the three *could* attain a first-strike capability against any of the others. If a nation attains a first-strike capability, by definition it not only survives a nuclear war; it *wins* it. And that nation wins it *without* suffering unacceptable damage from the attacked nation's attempt, if any, at retaliation.

We must, therefore, face head-on the question of whether it is possible for the Soviet Union to attain a first-strike capability against the United States. Otherwise, it would not be profitable to marshal the evidence that the Soviet Union is seeking to attain such a capability; or to marshal, review, summarize, and analyze the evidence that all Henry Kissinger's policies tend to promote and accelerate the Soviets' progress toward a first-strike capability against us, and that their overall effect is to degrade the U.S. strategic deterrent.

As we mentioned earlier in this book, it took us many years to appreciate the *partial* truth in the Pugwash doctrine that, as between the U.S. and the U.S.S.R., a first-strike capability is impossible to attain, and we *suggested* that, as a practical matter, it would be impossible for the Soviets to attain such a capability versus America *unless* this nation were being betrayed by leaders in control of national security policies and grand strategy. We did not, however, explain at that point how this works. One fascinating aspect of it is that we discovered the clue in a Nixon enunciation of a strategic truism. Apparently somewhat fed up with Kissinger's writing every Administration foreign policy document (such as the annual *State of the World Report*), President Nixon, before embarking on his historic mission to Peking, began preparing his own analysis of foreign policy. On his return he worked it over, and completed his final version just after his return from the Moscow-SALT Summit. He signed it on June 11, 1972, and it was published over his own signature in *U.S. News* dated June 16, 1972. Here is the pertinent excerpt:

> The choice for both sides has really been whether to limit arms, or to have a runaway nuclear arms race—and in such a race there would be no winners, only losers.
>
> *Neither the United States nor the Soviet Union would, over the long run, allow a situation to develop in which either could confront the other with the sort of overwhelming nuclear advantage which the United States held at the time of the 1962 Cuban missile crisis.*
>
> To continue the nuclear arms spiral unchecked would set up a contest in which neither side could win, because *neither would feel it could afford to let the other win.*

In attempting to reason out for himself this climactic issue of nuclear strategy, Richard Nixon revealed a great deal about himself and about the hypnosis Kissinger had imposed on him. His approach was that of Richard Everyman—except that he had the disadvantage of being Pugwashed with Kissinger's untested assumptions. Nixon was not sufficiently confident of his own intellect when matched against Kissinger's to test the assumptions with a challenge; instead, he attempted to *support* them with his own common sense. Thus, the first sentence in the excerpt embodies two key Pugwash-Kissinger tenets: (1) the choice between "a runaway nuclear arms race" and "arms limitation" is an *either/or* choice; and (2) in such an arms race, there would be "no winners, only losers."

In the very next sentence in the excerpt, however, Nixon cited an example of a time in which the United States had *won* an arms race upon which no limits had been imposed. At the time of the Cuban missile crisis of 1962, there were "winners" as well as "losers." It is clear in the context that Nixon thinks of a "winner" in the arms race as the power that has attained a first-strike capability against its enemy; and this is an accurate concept. At the time of the Cuban missile crisis, the United States had—according to Nixon's own estimate—an 8-to-1 strategic superiority over the U.S.S.R. Equally important, we had a disarming capability. As one student of the strategic balance put it:

> In October 1962, Khrushchev and his associates were no doubt aware of the consequences of attacking the United States (e.g., in retaliation for an attack on Cuban MRBM sites); Russian bombers and ICBMs could have killed many Americans but could not have destroyed many strategic weapons.
>
> The Russian leaders must also have realized that, if *pushed over the brink, the Americans could destroy almost the entire Russian strategic arsenal in a first attack, while retaining an adequate second-strike force.* Khrushchev and his associates must have been highly conscious of the fact that strategic superiority opened a move to the Americans which was denied to the Russians.[3]

Thus, although our first-strike capability may not have attained the proportions of a "splendid" capability, nor quite that of a totally "preclusive" first-strike capability, it was, for all practical purposes, a first-strike capability. We attained it because the United States has an industrial and technological capacity more than twice that of the Soviet Union, and because the Pugwash-CFR-unilateral-disarmament elites had not yet attained control of our national security policies.

Nixon's attempt, by means of commonsense reasoning, to support the Pugwash concept that in an unlimited arms race there can be no "winners" (that is, neither side can attain a first-strike capability) is fascinating: "neither would feel that it could *afford* to let the other win," therefore neither "would allow" the other side to attain an "overwhelming nuclear advantage." On a second reading of the Nixon excerpt one cannot escape the commonsense and logic of his proposition *if it is considered in the inverse:* one side *could* win, but only if the other side *lets* it. Thus, the *only* way one superpower can attain a first-strike capability against the other is *if* the defender is being be-

494

trayed by its leadership. Otherwise its leaders would never permit a foreign power to attain the power of national life or death—through genocidal attack or nuclear blackmail—over the people who had trusted them.

Not since 1962, when McNamara defaulted the United States in the "arms race," has there really been an arms race. *If we had been racing, we would have won.* We had an 8-to-1 strategic superiority to start with, in addition to our industrial and technological advantages. Also, if we did not want an additional "upward spiral" in arms competition, we had sufficiently close to a preclusive first-strike capability to make a credible threat of preempting if the Soviets should embark upon a buildup calculated to bring them to a first-strike capability against us. We could have told them in 1965: "Knock off that SS-9 program, or we will do it for you." This would have been 90 percent bluff, but the Soviets could not then have afforded to take a 10 percent chance. But their continued buildup, coupled with McNamara's drag-down on us, soon thereafter deprived us of the capability, credibly, to threaten to preempt in order to cool down the "arms race."

With Richard Nixon's own explanation that a first-strike capability *is* possible unless the other side refuses to "allow" that development, we need now to consider how it can be determined and proved (1) that the Soviets are "going for a first-strike capability," and (2) that the person in actual control of U.S. defense policies is not merely "allowing" the Soviets to develop such a capability, but is affirmatively giving them aid and comfort in their development program.

Anyone who can draw an X on a sheet of graph paper can prove for himself both (1) and (2). The National Strategy Committee of the American Security Council did exactly that in 1967 in preparing a study for the House Armed Services Committee entitled *The Changing Strategic Military Balance: U.S.A. vs. U.S.S.R.* Since members of the House Committee and most of the members of the National Strategy Committee had access to classified information, they could not sign a study giving exact figures for Soviet and U.S. strategic forces at specific points in time. So they did an extensive analysis of hundreds of unclassified reports, and then drew a master graph with broad lines instead of single lines. The experts were willing and able to sign a report stating that the strategic capabilities fell within the area of the broad lines. Subsequent history has proved this graph, including its projection into future years, amazingly accurate.

The sharp angle of climb showing Soviet strategic-megatonnage-delivery capability made a first-strike capability predictable as early as 1965. Its continuation past parity in 1968, and past superiority in 1972, constitutes near-conclusive evidence of Soviet intentions.

The sharp angle of decline of U.S. strategic power makes it clear

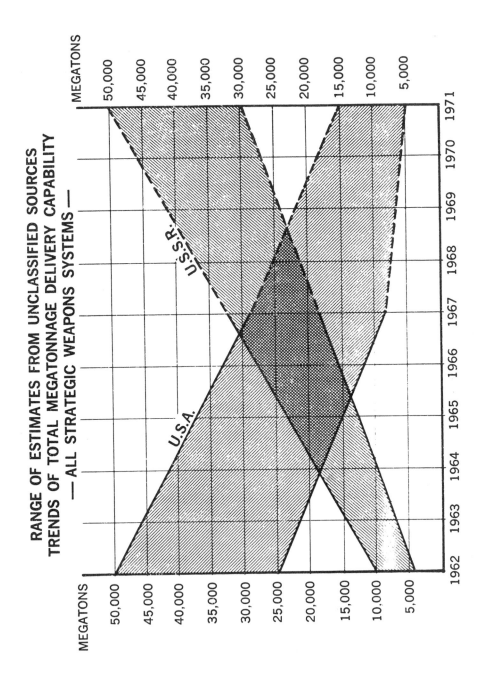

RANGE OF ESTIMATES FROM UNCLASSIFIED SOURCES
TRENDS OF TOTAL MEGATONNAGE DELIVERY CAPABILITY
— ALL STRATEGIC WEAPONS SYSTEMS —

that Robert McNamara was *deliberately* decimating the defense of the United States and helping the Soviets to attain a first-strike capability against the United States. The sharp angle of U.S. loss was just as essential to that objective as the Soviets' steeply climbing path.

When the data on the chart patterns into an X, the rational conclusion is that an architect planned it that way. The X proves that the United States is being betrayed. A new administration that takes over an "X" situation and does not correct it must be continuing the betrayal.

The official statistics published at the signing of the SALT I Agreements confirm the accuracy of the 1967 NSC-ASC chart. They also demonstrate that the Soviet buildup included hundreds of strategic weapons expressly and expensively designed to kill U.S. retaliatory weapons, plus other weapons designed to cut to near-zero the warning time of a surprise strike against us.

There was sufficient evidence of this sort to convince Secretary of Defense Melvin Laird in early March 1969 that "the Soviets are going for a first-strike capability. There is no question about that." If there was *no question then,* consider how horrendously *certain* it is *now.* In the interval between Laird's testimony and the signing of the SALT I Agreements, the Soviets more than doubled the power and numbers of their offensive missiles. If any additional evidence could possibly be more convincing, it would be the unprecedented dynamism of their entire post-SALT I strategic program.

At the time of the SALT I Agreements, the official statistics gave the Soviets a 4-to-1 superiority in throw-weight. All objective experts agree that the single most significant parameter for characterizing the potential of a missile force is throw-weight. In the year-and-a-half between the SALT I signing in Moscow and the end of 1973, the Soviets increased this advantage: their upgraded missiles and new pop-up silo-launching techniques have allowed them to more than double the throw-weight and megatonnage of some of their most important missile types. For example, their older SS-9s were rated at 25 megatons for a single warhead, whereas the new SS-18 is rated by the most reliable authorities at 50+ megatons. The SS-19 is five times greater in throw-weight than early models of the SS-11 which it will replace.

If, therefore, we had secured the enactment of the draft federal statute defining enemies of the United States in the nuclear age, it would be established that the Soviet Union is within the definition. The chart, plus a mountain of other evidence, would show that Robert McNamara meets the definition of having given aid and comfort to a foreign power as defined in the proposed statute.

Is there evidence that Henry Kissinger has knowingly contributed to the degradation of the U.S. strategic deterrent, either as to its physical sufficiency or its psychological credibility?

In the face of the massive momentum of the Soviet strategic nuclear threat against the United States, Henry Kissinger has done nothing to help us. He has thrown away the last five-year period in which the United States could have reconstituted our strategic deterrent without running perilously close to the point at which the Kremlin might rationally decide to preempt. In that period, in which we could have added, quite literally, thousands of strategic missile launchers to our retaliatory force, he added not a single launcher. Time is on the side of the nation that uses it: in that same climactic period, the Soviets more than doubled their offensive missile force up to the signing of SALT I in May 1972, and now are on the verge of redoubling the power of that force.

In focusing on the crucial question of whether Kissinger is helping the bear, no useful purpose would be served in reviewing the evidence unless you are prepared to *believe* the evidence. The best preparation for this is to consider whether there could be any motive that, operating within the complex Kissinger personality, would be sufficient to explain an otherwise incredible course of conduct.

Every American who can read, or even who only looks at pictures, knows exactly what a potential dictator will look like in this country. The image has been etched on our minds by unceasing repetition over a quarter of a century: the mythical man on horseback will be a character out of *Seven Days in May,* garbed in military uniform, like a Herblock cartoon of General Curtis LeMay—that is, demented, sadistic, gross, overbearing, stupid, and cunning. Likewise, we "know" what a power-mad dictator will *not* look like. In the bright lexicon of liberalism, there are no words to describe an *intellectual* on horseback; the mass-media cartoonists do not depict intellectuals as power-obsessed figures.

This is why John Roche's analysis of Henry Kissinger shines out as a flash of brilliant perception. His focus on Kissinger over a period of years reached a climactic point with this column of September 13, 1973:

> . . . But, as the Greeks said, character is fate, and Kissinger's behavior indicates to me that he has been having a passionate affair with "power."
>
> Obviously, his relationship with President Nixon was his fundamental base, but at the same time he appreciated (far more than the advertising honchos who dominated the pre-Watergate White House) the power of the press. I have long watched the Washington "power" game with a close and skeptical eye, and I would match Kissinger with Bill Moyers as a grand master of split-level backgrounding.

To put it less politely, Kissinger, like Moyers, always managed to turn up on both sides of the street whenever a really controversial issue arose. There is a way of tipping the wink, of saying "I work for the President and, of course, I share his views," which indicates to the sophisticated reporter that one has deep reservations.

Thus, somehow or other, the word permeated the Washington underground that Kissinger was opposed to the Cambodia invasion and later to the mining of Haiphong. He naturally denied both rumors, suggesting that they were invented by characters trying to destroy his relationship with the President, but nonetheless he managed to get a considerable amount of credit as the "inside opponent."

An extraordinarily charming and persuasive man—when he chooses to be—he developed the elite press corps as his line of defense against the slings and arrows of outraged Haldemans, who found his definition of "loyalty" a bit open-ended.

Over the years I have opposed a number of Kissinger's foreign policy initiatives, though I have always respected his judgment. Regrettably, I now find myself increasingly convinced that he is playing the game for its own sake, that—like President Nixon—he has no fixed ideological bearings. . . .

And then there was Kissinger's testimony on Sakharov (and by implication other Soviet dissidents). He said he was "very moved" but "painful as I find the Sakharov document, emotionally connected though I feel myself to him; I feel nevertheless that we must proceed" with the extension of trade concessions to Moscow.

This comment literally stunned me. Indeed, it flung me back through time about 35 years when it was standard justification for doing business with Nazi Germany, despite Hitler's vicious anti-Semitism.

Americans were "deeply moved," but did nothing. The Jews were exterminated. Is this a scenario that Kissinger, a German-Jewish refugee, can dispassionately contemplate for Sakharov, Solzhenitsyn and their courageous supporters?

Is this the price that Kissinger is prepared to pay for "power"?

If so, may God have mercy on his soul.

In selecting a passage from the Kissinger testimony relating to the Soviet dissidents, John Roche did him no injustice. Kissinger revealed the same attitude several times. Here is another typical example he gave in answer to a question by Senator McGovern at the confirmation hearings:

We cannot be indifferent to the denial of human liberty, but we cannot, at the same time, so insist on transformation in the domestic structure of the Soviet system as to give up the general evolution that we are hopefully starting.

It remained for Willy Brandt of Bonn to reveal the logical imperative of the Kissinger policy. At a press conference on September 12, 1973,

Brandt read aloud the Kissinger statement abjuring attempts to change internal Soviet policies, declared that he agreed with it, and added:

> I would still be for a lessening of tensions between East and West in the interest of securing peace even if Stalin were still the first man in the Soviet Union.

Willy Brandt's surprisingly frank words meant exactly the same thing as Henry Kissinger's skillfully equivocal words. If the Politburo of the Communist Party of the Soviet Union decided to conduct a Great Terror and liquidate 10 million of the 240 million people who are totally subject to the 16-member Politburo, even that—under the Kissinger-Brandt logic—would not justify withholding U.S. credits, technology, and machine tools to give those mass murderers the world's largest truck plant. Kissinger has now made it perfectly clear that he will not be moved from his policy of "hopefully" pursuing detente to the absolute exclusion of courageously encouraging freedom by even the most peaceful means. If they want to torture their intellectual dissidents to a slow death in insane asylums, it is within their *power* to do so.

Preferring such power over principle is as stupid as it is brutal. To put it first on the level of lowest pragmatism, it defaults the United States in all relationships with the Soviets in which common sense would have dictated our engaging in old-fashioned horse trading. James Burnham, philosophical historian for *National Review*, put the extreme case in the magazine dated August 31, 1973:

> In a public ceremony in July, two East German border guards were awarded decorations of valor in defense of the Fatherland. They had thwarted an attempt to escape across the Berlin Wall by five young East Germans. The guards had shot four of the group, killing two of them.
>
> No public protest of the killing or of the award was made, officially or unofficially, by any spokesman of the U.S. Government.

James Burnham then rehearses in brief but pungent summary the increasing intransigence of Soviet leaders since the Nixon Moscow Summit meeting in May 1972 that inaugurated Kissinger's "broad new relationship" with the Soviet Union: the persecution of the dissidents, the brutal redeclaration of the Brezhnev Doctrine at the Conference on European Security and Cooperation in Helsinki, the continued jamming of even the bland Voice of America broadcasts, and the surprise cancellation of advance-approved U.S. travel programs for tours of Moscow and Leningrad. He continued:

> What is the meaning of this detente that is presented to us as the crowning achievement of 20th-century diplomacy? Is its purpose, as the record so far suggests, merely to induce us to underwrite, politically, economi-

cally, and morally, this unabashed, unrepentant totalitarian regime? So far, this is all the detente has amounted to.

Even if we are ready and willing to pay that price . . . what do we get in return? Two things, we are told: Peace and profitable trade. . . . The products and technology we send will, like the grain, fill holes in the faltering totalitarian economy. A few businessmen will make a lot of money, some already have. But profit for the nation, for the national economy as a whole? It doesn't look so promising.

That peace too seems a distant affair . . . it doesn't seem to have interfered with the arrival of the new Soviet missile with a warhead even larger than that of the SS-9, which can carry a load a dozen times more powerful than our Minuteman. . . .

By the silence of our representatives and leaders, *we Americans have become the accomplices of those who man the Berlin Wall, who shut those who differ with them in madhouses run by the secret police, who lock their citizens inside their borders, who black out communication with their fellow man.*

As fact and as symbol the Berlin Wall sums up the essence of totalitarianism.

Can we not forget our bungling realpolitik long enough to make destruction of the Wall a precondition to diplomatic relations with East Germany?

The answer is, of course, no. We will never attach to the goodies we lavish on the Soviet Union and the People's Republic of China any preconditions that would benefit either the American people or any free people anywhere in the world; especially we would not attach any preconditions that would benefit the people in the Captive Nations or in the U.S.S.R. itself. Never. Never so long as Henry Kissinger's policies remain in control. His entire theory of a new world order, based upon "subtle triangular negotiations" and a "pentagonal equilibrium," depends on the Kremlin and Peking going along with it, at least in appearances. The price they exacted from Henry Kissinger for letting him appear as engineer and creator of that detente which is presented to us as "the crowning achievement of 20th-century diplomacy" is a commitment by the United States *not* to oppose Communist ideology and *not* to oppose expansion of communism. This is not speculation or hypothesis. It is embodied in the Declaration of Principles that Henry Kissinger talked Richard Nixon into signing at the Moscow Summit of '72.

James Burnham described the great Kissinger detente as the flowering of "bungling realpolitik," a description surpassed only by one of the incredibly courageous Soviet dissidents, Vladimir Y. Maksimov. On August 10, 1973, that distinguished writer denounced the Willy Brandt version of detente as creating a 1938 Munich in 1973, stating:

> Only the Almighty can know what price in blood we are going to pay for the diabolical games of the blockheads of modern diplomacy.

We have examined John Roche's conclusion that Kissinger's behavior indicates that "he has been having a passionate affair with
'power,' " and we have extended it to include evidence of what price
he willing to pay for power. Now we can focus more precisely on the
question: Does the price Kissinger is prepared to pay include *affirmative action* calculated to degrade the U.S. strategic deterrent and
accelerate acquisition by the Soviet Union of a first-strike capability
against the United States?

People who lie about particulars do not participate in the immunities
that cover people who lie in generalities.[4]

We will now consider the evidence to determine whether Henry
Kissinger lied about particulars, as well as lied in generalities, in a
campaign of affirmative action calculated to degrade the U.S. strategic
deterrent; whether he accomplished this by deceiving the President,
Congress, and the American people into believing that the United
States was powerless to add any additional strategic weapons to our
land or sea forces in the five-year period covered by the SALT I Interim
Agreement; and then whether, on the basis of this false representation, he persuaded them to accept imbalances and gaps in the SALT I
Agreement that would enable the Soviet Union to continue its massive
buildup to a preclusive first-strike capability against the United States.

Immediately after the SALT I Agreements were signed in Moscow
on May 26, 1972, Dr. Kissinger held a press conference. The following
excerpts from his statement about the documents that had just been
signed are relevant:

In assessing the significance of the freeze [of offensive weapons], it is
not useful to analyze whether the freeze reflects a gap between the forces
that are being frozen.

In the two categories which are being frozen, that is to say ICBMs and
submarine-launched ballistic missiles, the facts are these: The Soviet
Union has more intercontinental ballistic missiles than the United States.

The Soviet Union has been building intercontinental ballistic missiles;
the United States has not and has no such program at the moment.

The Soviet Union has been building submarine-launched ballistic
missiles at the rate of eight submarines a year. The United States has at
this moment no submarines under construction.

Therefore, the question to ask in assessing the freeze is not what
situation it perpetuates, but what situation it prevents. The question is
where we would be without the freeze. And if you project the existing
programs of the Soviet Union into the future, as against the absence of
[U.S.] building programs over the period of the freeze in either of the
categories that are being frozen, you will get a more correct clue to why
we believe that there is a good agreement and why we believe it has made
a significant contribution to reducing the arms race.

The weapons are frozen, as we pointed out, in categories in which we have no ongoing programs. Now, having said this, however, I am not implying that we gained a unilateral advantage because it is perhaps true that in the ABM field we had the more dynamic program which is being arrested as a result of these developments.[5]

In making an evaluation of the evidence as to whether Kissinger is acting affirmatively to help the bear, it is important to consider those points that relate to whether such statements as the above were merely hasty improvisations—the ad-libbed eloquence of the sophisticate who loves the sound of his own words—or were essential parts of a calculated deception of overriding importance. Thus, repetition, refinement, and elaboration are relevant factors. On the day after the press conference quoted above, Kissinger held a follow-up press conference at the Intourist Hotel in Moscow where he said, *inter alia:*

The Soviet Union has been building missiles at the rate of something like 250 a year. If I get arrested here for espionage, gentlemen, we will know who is to blame.

Question: What kind of missiles? Do you mean intercontinental?

Dr. Kissinger: I am talking about intercontinental and it has been building submarine missiles at the rate of 128 a year. So this is the backdrop against which you have to assess the Agreement.

Therefore, on any day you would have picked over the last year, over the last two years, and on any day you are going to pick in the future, you will be able to demonstrate a Soviet numerical advantage. Moreover, it was a numerical advantage that was growing, because *in the ICBM field, we have, as you know, no ongoing program.*

In the submarine field, as the question indicated, to which I responded earlier, *we also have no programs for missiles which will be operational. In the submarine field, we have now no submarine under construction. The first submarine that we have that would become operational would do so early in 1979 or late in 1978.*

Therefore, any time over the next five years we were confronting a numerical margin that was growing, and *a margin, moreover, which we could do nothing to reverse in that five-year period. . . .*

Question: . . . the idea that the United States got stuck with a submarine deal—

Dr. Kissinger: That is an absurdity. It is a total absurdity. It was the United States which insisted that submarines be included.

The United States was in a rather complex position to recommend a submarine deal since *we were not building any and the Soviets were building eight or nine a year, which isn't the most brilliant bargaining position I would recommend people to find themselves in.*[6]

This repetition of the basic Kissinger assertion that the Soviets had dynamic ongoing programs for the production of ICBMs, SLBMs, and submarines, whereas the United States had no such ongoing programs and could not, therefore, produce any within the five-year period of the SALT I Interim Agreement is highly significant. It is persuasive both in establishing deliberate intent in factual deception and in exposing the calculated campaign to convince knowledgeable critics of SALT I that his bargaining position was so weak vis-a-vis the Soviets that the Interim Agreement was not only the best bargain that could have been obtained, but was even favorable to the United States in preventing a further widening of the existing missile gap favoring the Soviets. His perfected and finalized version of the SALT-selling argument, based on this claim that the United States was helpless to narrow the gap, was expressed in his June 15, 1972, White House briefing of the five congressional committees. There he posed to himself the key question, "Does the Agreement perpetuate a U.S. strategic disadvantage?" and answered:

> The Interim Agreement perpetuates nothing which did not already exist in fact and which could only have gotten worse without an agreement.

Tragically for U.S. national security, the Kissinger argument worked. It worked even against the more intelligent, dedicated, and knowledgeable critics of SALT. As Kissinger had foreseen, his assumption (stated in the guise of a "fact") that the United States was helpless to close or even narrow the missile gap was not challenged. This was the successful sophisticated argument that beat down the realistic, commonsense criticisms that could have exposed the national-suicidal nature of the SALT Interim Agreement, such as the warning given at the time by Senator Henry M. Jackson:

> The stark facts are these: The United States—a country with a 2-to-1 economic superiority over the U.S.S.R., a country with innovative and technological superiority over the U.S.S.R.—has accepted Agreements which guarantee the United States a 3-to-2 inferiority in crucial categories of strategic offensive systems.
>
> All Americans . . . desire the increased security that flows from a potential aggressor's knowledge that he simply can't execute a disarming strike against our deterrent forces.
>
> Unfortunately, I see nothing in the present agreements that lessens the threat to the security of these deterrent forces. On the contrary, far from placing us in a position of stable deterrence, the agreement permits the Soviet Union to continue its offensive build-up in a way and on a scale that could prove highly dangerous.
>
> Simply put, the agreement gives the Soviets more of everything; more light ICBMs, more heavy ICBMs, more submarine-launched missiles, more submarines, more payload, even more ABM radars.
>
> In no area covered by the agreement is the United States permitted to maintain parity with the Soviet Union. . . .
>
> The "understandings" attached to the SALT Agreements . . . raise as many questions as they answer. . . . I am disturbed, first, that the understandings fail to identify the permitted number of Soviet missiles. Soviet refusal to state clearly the number they feel obligated to respect raises

504

the most fundamental doubts about whether they have negotiated in good faith.

Let me state the numbers that the Moscow Agreement omits. The Soviets are granted numerical superiority in every area: land-based missiles (1,618 to 1,054), modern submarines (up to 62 for them and 44 for us), missile-delivery capability (4 to 5 times as much for them).

Second, the Soviets have refused to agree to a definition of the all-important term "heavy missile."

The Administration has had to resort to a weak and unilateral assertion as to what we understand a "heavy missile" to be, while the Soviets have chosen even to withhold comment on our definition.

The failure to resolve disagreement on this term raises doubt about the central claim that is being made for the agreement: that it will prevent the Soviets from deploying more SS-9-type missiles.[7]

Senator Jackson's timely objections to the SALT I Interim Agreement recall for us the now-long-forgotten cogency of the objections to the agreement that Henry Kissinger had to overcome in order to consummate the SALT sellout. The crooked lever that accomplished this was the slick argument that the Soviets had dynamic ongoing programs in both land-based ICBMs and in modern missile-launching submarines and SLBMs, but the United States, according to Kissinger, had no ongoing programs in "either of the categories that are being frozen."

Every U.S. President since Franklin Roosevelt has recognized that his highest-priority concern is maintaining the effectiveness and credibility of the strategic deterrent; in the words of Lyndon Johnson, that is the President's "first responsibility to our people." Similar recognition of the overriding importance of preserving the reliability of deterrence of nuclear attack is repeated in the Kissinger-drafted-Nixon-enunciated annual State of the World Report for 1971 and again in 1972.

When Kissinger turned him around from his career-long dedication to the concept of U.S. strategic superiority, Nixon then pinned his self-esteem as a patriot on a personally created concept (a last fallback position, so to speak) that might be called "noninferiority." Analysis of all his speeches and statements circa the Moscow signing of SALT I in May 1972, and extending through his 1973 State of the World Report, demonstrates that he would cling fanatically to the self-created conviction that he had not and never would accept for the United States a fallback position lower in the strategic-power scale than this "noninferiority." If it became clear that the Soviet momentum in arms buildup had carried our nation down below that point of extreme peril, he would still refuse to admit that reality—his self-delusion shaped, of course, by Kissinger-interpreted intelligence and Kissinger-evolved rationalizations.

Thus it was that, in reporting to a joint session of Congress on June

1, 1972, on the results of the Moscow Summit and the SALT I Agreements, Richard Nixon tendered to the nation an assurance tragic in its distortion of the true facts and pitiful in its frenetic flight from the awesome reality of what he had permitted to be done to America:

> My colleagues in the Congress, I have studied the strategic balance in great detail with my senior advisers for more than three years. I can assure you, the members of Congress, and the American people tonight that the present and planned strategic forces of the United States are without question sufficient for the maintenance of our security and the protection of our vital interests.
>
> *No power on earth is stronger than the United States of America today. And none will be stronger than the United States of America in the future.*
>
> This is the only national defense posture which can ever be acceptable to the United States. *This is the posture I ask the Senate and the Congress to protect by approving the arms limitation agreements* to which I have referred.

He really seemed to believe this—perhaps through the hypnotic effect of Kissinger-Svengali, perhaps through self-hypnosis and because he could not live with himself if he stopped believing. Also, he seemed confident that if he kept repeating it the repetition would make it so. Thus, in his personally authored essay on "A New Foreign Policy for a New World," formally entitled "The Real Road to Peace, by President Richard M. Nixon,"[8] he again asserted that "our military capacities are still second to none" and that the SALT I Agreements "maintain a situation in which United States defenses are fully sufficient and second to none in the world."

Dedicated to winning what he asserted is history's highest accolade, the title of "peacemaker," it is significant that several months after the SALT I signing in Moscow he attacked those who sought to make cuts in our defense budget and who claim that

> it doesn't really make any difference whether the United States has the second strongest Navy, the second strongest Army, the second strongest Air Force in the world.

Then President Nixon introduced his concept of maintaining the peace:

> Let me say that as far as this particular proposal is concerned, it is one of the clearest issues of this campaign, because I can assure you, based on the experience of the last four years and based on looking back over 25 years of examining the world scene and traveling all over the world, *the day the United States of America becomes the second strongest nation in the world, the danger of war will be enormously increased and the prospect of peace will be harmed.*[9]

If and when the U.S. strategic inferiority sinks so low that we are left with no rational alternative to surrender, and the men in the Kremlin have the option to decide whether Americans will be Red or dead, this background on Nixon's compulsive belief in U.S. noninferiority will be useful in determining who is the real culprit in bringing America to a position of powerlessness.

If history is given a chance, it may finally demonstrate that Nixon's greatest *de facto* crime and most horrendous error in judgment was to trust in the loyalty of his most brilliant assistant. Henry Kissinger had full understanding of Nixon's fanatic belief in the noninferiority of U.S. strategic power vis-a-vis the Soviet Union. Kissinger knew that Nixon considered that maintaining that quantum of power was his first duty to the nation that had trusted him with a 49-to-1 landslide election in 1972; and Kissinger knew that Nixon was convinced that world peace, the avoidance of a nuclear inferno, and Nixon's place in history, all depended on ensuring that "no power on earth is stronger than the United States." Because Kissinger knew these things so well, he knew exactly how to exploit them most effectively.

Here is the ultimate proof of how shockingly successful the persuasive and totally trusted presidential assistant was in convincing his boss that *the United States was powerless to produce any new strategic weapons at all* within the five-year period of the SALT I Interim Agreement, and that only by getting the Soviets to enter that agreement could we prevent the Soviets from massively widening the existing missile gap in their favor. In his SALT I report to Congress, cited above, Nixon gave Congress and the nation this assurance concerning the SALT accords:

> From the standpoint of the United States, when we consider what the strategic balance would have looked like later in the Seventies, if there had been no arms limitation, it is clear that the agreements forestall a major spiraling of the arms race—one which would have worked to our disadvantage, since we have no current building programs for the categories of weapons which have been frozen, and since no new building program could have produced any new weapons in those categories during the period of the freeze.

It is the first duty of the national security adviser to the President to inform him of *all* options open to him in the making of any vital or even substantially important decision concerning the survival of the United States and its people in freedom. Henry Kissinger, in convincing Nixon of the truth of the emphasized statements in the quotation above, engaged in a calculated double default of duty. These statements, as we have shown in the two excerpts from Kissinger's Moscow Summit press conferences, originated with him, and were employed by him to deceive the press, and through the press, the American people and Congress. But first, he employed them to convince the President that he had *no option* in meeting the crisis of the missile gap favoring the Soviets, and no course of action open that

507

would prevent the dangerous widening of that gap except by entering into the SALT I Interim Agreement.

In the absence of the Kissinger deception, even Richard Nixon could have seen that there are two methods of preventing a missile gap from widening: (1) Kissinger's method—rely on an agreement with the Russians that they will restrain themselves from opening it further, and (2) rely on ourselves to build enough missiles to keep the Russians from widening the gap, and even to narrow and ultimately to close it.

Was the second method really open to us? Was the United States capable of building enough missiles to compete with the Soviets? Remember the quotation from Senator Jackson's speech: we are "a country with a 2-to-1 economic *superiority* over the U.S.S.R., a country with innovative and technological superiority over the U.S.S.R." Of course, we could do it! We had done it once; in Henry Kissinger's words of September 16, 1970, we had outclassed them so far in numbers and quality that "our strategic superiority was overwhelming."

So, why didn't Richard Nixon recognize that we could do it again? Because Dr. Kissinger had convinced him—and Kissinger's own words bear repeating because they can help to establish whether he is "lying about particulars"—that:

> In the ICBM field, we have, as you know, no ongoing program. In the submarine field . . . we also have no programs for missiles which will be operational. . . . We have now no submarine under construction. The first submarine that we have that would become operational would do so early in 1979 or late in 1978.

The true and particular facts are that *we did at that time have dynamic ongoing programs* for the production of new Minuteman III ICBMs and for the production of the equally new Poseidon SLBMs. The new production of ICBMs was to total at least 550 missiles, plus spares and test missiles, which would put the land-based new-missile total at more than 600. The new production of Poseidon missiles was to total 496 for operational purposes, plus spares and test missiles. Thus, at the time Henry Kissinger made his statements, the United States had in *operation missile production lines* capable of turning out at a deliberately slow pace, timed to the availability of incremental funds each fiscal year, a total of more than 1,100 ICBMs and SLBMs.

These were advanced-model missiles: missiles of the fourth generation. All were MIRVed. The Minuteman missiles had three 200-kiloton independently targetable warheads; the Polaris were over-MIRVed, according to McNamara's orders, with ten 50-kiloton warheads or fourteen 17-kiloton warheads. The important aspect of the Poseidon missiles is that they had a throw-weight about three times that of the most modern Polaris missiles, or nearly six times that of the first model Polaris. The Minuteman III was also a new missile, far advanced over the Minuteman I and II models and capable of more throw-weight, but the exact amount of this increase has not been revealed to Americans.

Here is the vital point. Because we had *in actual operation* production lines capable of turning out more than 1,000 new missiles at a deliberately slow pace, production could have been stepped up to more than 2,000, and possibly 3,000, by having the production lines work three shifts. When production lines are in actual operation, it is no big thing for a nation with the industrial, technological, and management resources of the United States to add more production lines. Thus, in the five-year period in which Henry Kissinger asserted we could produce *no* new ICBMs, and as to which he had hypnotized Richard Nixon into believing and officially reporting to the nation that we could not "have produced *any* new weapons during the period of the freeze," we *could* have averted the opening of the missile gap. Even if the Soviets had continued racing to build additional numbers of missile launchers, we could have averted the gap by adoption of two commonsense programs: (1) allocate sufficient additional funds to expand the two ongoing U.S. ICBM and SLBM programs; and (2) cancel programs for the destruction of U.S. strategic weapons systems in-being.

Instead of doing both or either of these things, Dr. Kissinger persuaded the President to rely upon Soviet "restraint" instead of on American resources. The Soviets showed their "restraint" during the one year of preparations for SALT I negotiations, and during the 2½ years of actual negotiations, by adding more than 1,000 ICBMs and SLBMs to their forces. The second phase of Soviet "restraint"— which Kissinger assured would result from the signing of the SALT I Agreements—consisted of adding, within 15 months of that signing, a plethora of qualitative improvements to their strategic forces that they had fully developed prior to the SALT I signing but that they had successfully concealed from U.S. intelligence until Brezhnev and Kissinger got Richard Nixon's signature on the Interim Agreement and the ABM Treaty.

These qualitative improvements included such things as MIRVed warheads for three series of ICBMs, including the heavy SS-9s and superheavy SS-18s, and the new medium-heavy SS-17s and SS-19s. The least of these Soviet MIRVed warheads were five times more powerful than the most powerful of our MIRVs. A second revolutionary improvement was their new pop-up launch technique, which enabled them to multiply by a factor of five the throw-weight of their most numerous missile type, the SS-11, and thus expose as ridiculous the SALT I provisions that Kissinger had assured Congress would prevent such increases in missile throw-weight and explosive power. Also there was the Soviet development and deployment of the SS-N-8, the world's first intercontinental-range submarine-launched ballistic missile. These qualitative improvements would enable the Soviets to increase their missile-deliverable throw-weight by a minimum of 50 percent, and possibly up to 100 percent. Translated into terms of missile-deliverable explosive power, this would enable the Soviets to add to their forces the equivalent of something like 2,000 to 4,000 U.S. Minuteman ICBMs.

That is what Henry Kissinger's policy of relying on Soviet "restraint" got for us. But Dr. Kissinger asserted—and convinced President Nixon —that we had no alternative but to rely upon Soviet restraint and SALT I promises.

We are at this point considering whether there is evidence to establish that, in making such assertions, Dr. Kissinger was lying about particulars and deceiving President Nixon into making false material representations to the nation. To prove this, it is not at all necessary to go to the full length of demonstrating that we could have closed the Soviet-favoring missile gap in the five-year period from 1972 to 1977. The Kissinger assertion—repeated by the President—that we could not produce "any" new ICBMs or SLBMs can be proved false by evidence that "any" number of new SLBMs and ICBMs have been or can be produced by ongoing U.S. production lines in the 1972-77 timeframe. A production line for new SLBMs was in operation as of May 27, 1972, and had produced 128 new missiles, plus spares and test missiles; and every year through 1976 that production would produce an additional 96 new SLBMs plus spares and test missiles up to the planned total of more than 500. Similarly, the production line for the new Minuteman III missiles had just gone into operation and would produce about 200 missiles each year, completing the programmed 550, plus spares, before July 1, 1974.

This is difficult to believe—after Kissinger's repeated statements in press conferences and briefings that we have documented, plus President Nixon's unqualified official statement quoted above. But it is easy to prove. Secretary of Defense Robert McNamara requested funds for development of both the Poseidon and Minuteman III missiles in his official statement on posture and appropriations on January 23, 1967, pages 56 and 57. From then on, appropriations for continuing the program were included each year, as specified in the annual statements made by the Secretary of Defense. The testing of the warhead systems for both systems was completed in June 1970 and operational deployment was initiated in 1971.[10] The Military Balance: 1973-1974, published by the International Institute for Strategic Studies in London, gives the best summary of progress on deployment of both Poseidon missiles and Minuteman III missiles, as produced by the two ongoing production lines for the new missiles:

The year after the May 1972 Soviet-American [SALT] Interim Agreement . . . the U.S. has deployed 350 Minuteman III ICBM, each with three

MIRV, and is now moving towards completing that programme, involving 550 Minuteman III. . . . At sea, about 320 Poseidon SLBM, each with 10-14 MIRV, have been deployed in some 20 submarines. Conversion of another 11 submarines to Poseidon is in train, and will be complete by 1975-76, at which time only 10 submarines with Polaris A3 SLBM will remain in service.

A specific attestation of the continued operation of a production line for the new Minuteman III missiles appeared in a United Press dispatch datelined Washington, June 20, 1973:

> The Air Force asked Congress yesterday for $23.1 million *to keep Minuteman III production lines open* so the United States will have the ability to deploy more than the presently approved 550 multiple warhead missiles if a decision were made to do so in the future.
>
> Lt. General Otto J. Glasser, deputy Air Force Chief of Staff for research and development, told the Senate Appropriations Committee such a precaution was "vital." . . .
>
> Glasser said the Air Force budget request of $414.5 million for Minuteman III procurement in fiscal year 1974, which begins July 1, would buy 136 missiles and complete the Minuteman III procurement.
>
> But, he said, included in the $414.5 million was $23.1 million "to protect the option to continue production of the Minuteman III beyond fiscal year 1974."

Since the United States had in operation ongoing programs for the building of new ICBMs and SLBMs, and since the production lines were open for both at the very time Henry Kissinger made his repeated statements in May 1972, and were supported by appropriations each year, how did he dare to speak lies that could so easily be refuted?

Whatever else Henry Kissinger is, he is a brilliant wordsmith. By the subtle and highly sophisticated use of just one word, Dr. Kissinger has been able to cover his tracks and to pull off one of history's most far-reaching operations. At the time of his press conferences in Moscow in May 1972, Kissinger's statements that the United States had no ongoing programs for building ICBMs, SLBMs, or missile-launching submarines, were unequivocal and specific, as evidenced by the above excerpts from his press conferences of May 26 and 27. Those were made *before* President Nixon's report to the joint session of Congress on June 1, 1972, in which the President adopted the false and misleading statements that Kissinger had originated. *Having gotten Richard Nixon on the hook* for those easily disprovable statements ("*no* current building programs for the categories of weapons which have been frozen"; and "*no* new building program could have produced *any* new weapons in these categories during the period of the freeze"), *Kissinger moved to get himself off that hook.*

Thus, in his grand rationale of SALT I in his briefing of the five congressional committees at the White House on June 15, 1972, he inserted in appropriate places, the single word "additional." This one

511

word changed an easily disprovable lie to a claim that was technically accurate, although he managed to retain all the misleading effect on his listeners and readers. The pertinent passage from his briefing to the five congressional committees must be repeated here because it is crucial to the execution of one of the most brilliant and evil schemes of all time. Here is how Kissinger phrased it:

> For various reasons during the 1960s, the United States had, as you know, made the strategic decision to terminate its building programs in major offensive systems and to rely instead on qualitative improvements.
> By 1969, therefore, we had no active or planned programs for deploying *additional* ICBMs, submarine-launched ballistic missiles, or bombers.
> The Soviet Union, on the other hand, had dynamic and accelerated deployment programs in both land-based and sea-based missiles. You know, too, that the interval between conception and deployment of strategic weapons systems is generally five to ten years.

Thus, in his written document prepared for this briefing, Kissinger's wordsmanship covered his misleading claim with technical accuracy. At that very time the United States did have active programs for building and deploying *new* ICBMs and submarine-launched ballistic missiles, but we indeed had no active or planned programs for deploying *additional* ICBMs or submarine-launched ballistic missiles.

What is the difference between a "new" ICBM or SLBM and an "additional" ICBM or SLBM? The difference depends upon a factor within the total control of Henry Kissinger: you prevent a new missile from becoming an "additional" missile *by destroying one deployed missile-in-being for each new missile deployed.*

Kissinger has acquired the reputation of being a master, even a genius, in dealing with power. This would be an understatement—if destroying power is considered "dealing" with it. *He prevented 550 new Minuteman III missiles from becoming "additional" ICBMs by destroying 550 Minuteman I and Minuteman II missiles.*

He ordered the carrying out of the destruction of our 550 operational Minuteman ICBMs at a time when he acknowledged that the Soviets had opened a missile gap in numbers against us and were moving dynamically to widen it further every month, as evidenced by this statement from his May 27, 1972, press conference:

> . . . on any day you could have picked over the last year, over the last two years, and on any day you are going to pick in the future, you will be able to demonstrate a Soviet numerical advantage. Moreover, it was a numerical advantage that was growing, because in the ICBM field we have, as you know, no ongoing program.

This is Kissinger's personal admission that the numerical ICBM gap existed as early as May 1970. Actually, it had opened in 1969. The then Secretary of Defense Melvin Laird reported in his Defense Statement delivered to Congress on February 20, 1970:

> The Soviets now have more operational ICBM launchers, over 1,100, than the United States, 1,054. More than 275 of these Soviet launchers are for the large SS-9. It is projected that there will be over 1,250 operational ICBMs on launchers by mid-1970.

Defense Department statements delivered in February of one year usually give intelligence estimates prepared from data gathered at least two to four months earlier; so that puts the opening of the numerical gap of ICBM launchers in 1969.

It is intriguing to analyze one of Kissinger's presentations to discover how great a quantum of technical truth he can weave into the pattern of his statement and still convey the effect of a monstrous lie to his audience. In the same short excerpt from his June 15, 1972, White House briefing cited above, in which he grafted the word "additional" onto his previously provable lies, he masterfully managed to put across two other sophisticated deceptions without making technically false statements.

First, he recited that the strategic decision to terminate U.S. building programs in major offensive systems was made "during the 1960s." This gives the impression that McNamara was exclusively responsible for the strategic decision that put the United States in the disadvantageous position of having no ongoing programs for building additional ICBMs or SLBMs while the Soviet Union had dynamic and accelerated programs in both types of missiles. That impression was fostered by the widespread knowledge that McNamara had totally dominated U.S. defense programs from January 1961 through 1967, and that no changes were made in his policies during 1968 by his short-term successor in office, Clark Clifford. But the fact is that Kissinger took over full control of defense programs in January 1969—and the year 1969 was very much a critical part of "the 1960s."

Robert McNamara was indeed the culprit who crafted the policies that brought the United States down from its 8-to-1 superiority in strategic power to such a low point that the Soviets were able to attain parity in numbers of missiles in 1969. But the critical decisions that permitted the Soviets to open the numerical missile gap of the 1970s *were made by Dr. Kissinger in 1969.* At that time Kissinger was fully in a position to secure adoption of programs that would have prevented the Soviets from opening any substantial numerical gap in either land-based ICBMs or SLBMs and missile-launching submarines. It will not do to contend that the anti-defense lobby in Congress could have blocked the programs by refusing funds, because the additional funds required would have been relatively insignificant.

Substantially all Dr. Kissinger needed do was (1) *not to carry out the* destruction of 550 operational Minuteman ICBMs, and (2) not to carry out the destruction of 27 operational Polaris submarines (four Polaris submarines were already in the shipyards for scrapping in 1969).

In the same excerpt from his June 15, 1972, briefing to the five congressional committees, after impliedly charging McNamara with all the blame for the missile gap, Kissinger concluded with a technical truth that was irrelevant but contained a high potential for deception. His artistry with words made his irrelevancy sound sincere and even helpful:

> You know, too, that the interval between conception and deployment of strategic weapons systems is generally five to ten years.

And so it is. But there was no need to "conceive" new weapons systems, research them, develop them, test them, produce them, prooftest them, and then put them into serial production and finally deploy them. Both the Minuteman III and the Poseidon had been conceived and researched well prior to 1967; in that year, funds were appropirated and we were "committed" to full production and deployment.[11] Serial production would begin in 1970 and they would be ready for deployment in 1971. So Dr. Kissinger's pontifical reference to the 5-to-10-year gestation period for strategic weapons systems was irrelevant and grossly misleading. All he had to do when he came into power in 1969 was, first, to permit the two production programs to take their prescheduled course—which he did; and, second, not destroy the missiles and missile launchers that the newly produced weapons were scheduled to replace.

At this point, we must meet head-on the results achieved by Kissinger in covering the most shocking aspects of his operation. He took over a McNamara-devised distortion of the term "conversion" and used it with such skill that it had a hypnotic effect and provided impenetrable cover for two of the most massive and protracted betrayals any great nation has ever suffered.

In 1969, when Henry Kissinger took office as National Security Advisor to the President and gained sufficient influence over Nixon to reduce the influence of Secretary of Defense Melvin Laird to near-zero, the oldest of our 1,000 Minuteman missiles were seven years of age, and hundreds were less than four years old. Thus, they were in no critical need of radical modernization. With only minor updating of their guidance and electronics from time to time, they would all have endured into the 1980s as effective strategic weapons; that is, as a retaliatory force that the Soviets would have been forced to target with hundreds of their own missiles and more than 1,000 warheads before they could have confidence in a first-strike capability against the United States.

This is what refutes the unilateral-disarmament intellectuals' contention that "numbers of missiles are not important." Sheer numbers *can* pivotally enhance national security and provide insurance for national survival—against nuclear blackmail, against loss of national prestige in the world, against "underdog" status and devaluation of our currency, and against a cutoff of essential raw materials, including oil.

To prove this to yourself, consider what might be called an exaggerated case. General Thomas S. Power, the late great commander of the U.S. Strategic Air Command, was a dedicated advocate of deploying 10,000 Minuteman missiles—yes, 10,000 land-based ICBMs in hardened silos. Such a massive retaliatory force would have made it an industrial and economic impossibility for the Soviets to gain a first-strike capability against us. If they had attempted to "race" against such a U.S. buildup, they would have bankrupted themselves in short order. The United States could easily have afforded to build such a force. We did not, however, really need 10,000 ICBMs. General Power advocated that number because of two things: he realized better than nearly any American the terrors of strategic war, and he loved the United States and did not want us to take even the slightest risk of being subjected to nuclear attack.

The point here is that *any* additional number would proportionately increase our security. The 1,000 additional Minuteman missiles that were actually scheduled under the Eisenhower Administration, but which McNamara canceled, would have bought us another five years of survival beyond what we can count on now. So also as to the 500 *mobile* Minuteman missiles that were canceled by McNamara after millions had been invested in developing the concept of deploying them on railroad cars. They would not only have multiplied the number of targets that the Soviets would have been required to destroy in order to achieve a first-strike capability, but would have multiplied even more the complexity and difficulty of planning their destruction.

The two options available to Kissinger in 1969 were (1) *add* 550 new missiles to the already operational 1,000 Minuteman force, or (2) employ the 550 new missiles as an *excuse* for the scrapping of more than half our existing Minuteman force. Dr. Kissinger chose the second option. He approved the destruction, on a 1-to-1 basis, of an existing operational Minuteman I or II for each new Minuteman III deployed—all 550 of them.

The "cover" for the destruction of so many hundreds of million dollars worth of strategic missiles in-being was the McNamara-manufactured myth that this was a "conversion" process, that is, that the older Minuteman Is and IIs were being "converted" or "modernized."

It may be contended that the silos occupied by the 550 so-called "old" missiles were needed for the deployment of the new Minuteman III missiles, that there was no ongoing program for the production of launchers to match the ongoing program for the production of the new missiles, and "what good is a missile without a launcher?"

The Minuteman III missiles, of course, did require launchers; but *they did not need to occupy the same holes* that had been occupied by the original 550 Minuteman I and II missiles, because the holes in the ground were still the same. Minuteman III (technically designated LGM-30G) is such a radically new "bird" that it required a radically new launcher. It has a larger and much more powerful third stage on the rocket, and carries substantially more throw-weight over a longer range; it has an entirely new warhead system that carries three MIRVs of 200 kilotons each; it has more accurate and more sophisticated guidance, advanced electronics, and far more shielding against radiation and electromagnetic pulse. It costs on the order of twice as much: $4.5 million each. The paint is the same as on the earlier models, but that is about all. Because of these changes, the launcher tubes and other launching equipment within the holes in the ground required $440 million worth of *modifications* to make those old holes in the ground serve as launchers for the new Minuteman missiles. Some $800,000 each is a lot of money to spend on "modifying" holes.[12]

The gross cheat perpetrated on the American people (especially the taxpayers) by scrapping 550 Minuteman missiles under cover of "converting" them to Minuteman III missiles or "modernizing" them now becomes apparent. We spent billions of dollars to "replace" our already operational missiles *so that we would not gain a single "additional" missile launcher,* or add a single operational missile to our retaliatory force. We were investing at least $2.475 billion in the 550 new missiles, and that does not count R&D, test missiles, spares, or nuclear material. It is a reasonable assumption that constructing all-new silos and launching equipment for the new missiles would have cost about $1 million each; that is, about $200,000 more each than it cost to "modify" the existing holes at $800,000 each. With advanced earth-moving equipment, the digging of holes is quite cheap.

So, for a puny extra $110 million, we could have secured 550 *additional* operational ICBMs, complete with launchers. This would have been four percent of the cost of the 550 Minuteman IIIs in their "modified" silos. Command and control equipment would have been extra, but this is not a massive expense.

If the commonsense decision had been made *not* to scrap the 550 Minuteman I and II missiles, and *not* to "modify" their existing silos, but instead to retain them as operational missiles, then putting the 550 new Minuteman III missiles into new silos was only one of the options available to us. A far more intelligent decision would have been to *add* them to our strategic force as *mobile* missiles. As such, they would have been virtually invulnerable to destruction by the Soviet heavy-missile force of SS-9s and SS-18s. We could have provided launchers on railroad cars—as originally planned for Minuteman back in 1960—or on self-propelled vehicles as the Soviets do, or on barges on rivers or the Great Lakes, or on surface ships, or on modified C-5 transport aircraft, or even on jumbo commercial types such as the Boeing 747.

Were the "old" Minuteman Is and IIs worth retaining as part of our strategic force through the 1970s? Yes. This answer cannot be challenged—especially from the operational point of view, and that is the only point that should be decisive. For several purposes these "old" missiles would be more effective and reliable than their new "replacements." First, the "old" 550 could deliver on Soviet targets nearly twice the explosive power that the "new" 550 could deliver, that is, 550 megatons as against between 280 and 330 megatons for the "new" Minuteman IIIs. MIRVing is always a profligate expenditure of throw-weight, especially as to missiles with relatively low throw-weight capability. Minuteman IIs, with about half the throw-weight of the IIIs, deliver with their single warhead twice as much megatonnage as the IIIs, with three warheads each.

Given the same accuracy of guidance, a CEP of, say, 1,500 feet, the one-megaton warhead of an "old" Minuteman has a 75 percent single-shot chance of destroying a hardened target (Soviet missile silo, hardened to 300 psi), whereas one of the "new" Minuteman MIRVed warheads—estimated by some at only 170 kilotons, but taking the larger claim of 200 kilotons—has only a 40 percent chance. Of course, if the three MIRVs are equally reliable, the theory is that they will have a better percentage chance of destroying the hardened target. Thus, using the same guidance and hardening assumptions, 550 "old" Minuteman missiles are credited with the capability of destroying 412 silos, and the new ones 431. But to destroy those 431 silos with Minuteman IIIs will cost us more than $3 billion, or about $7 million each; whereas, if Henry Kissinger had not ordered their destruction, it would have cost us only $110 million—using our operational "old" missiles—to destroy 412 silos, or $267,000 each. (The $110 million represents the differential estimated between the cost of 550 new silos for the new Minuteman IIIs instead of "modifying" the Minuteman I and II silos at the cost of $440 million.)

Looking at the same analysis from a different angle, the force of 550 "old" Minuteman missiles would be as effective, operationally, as 526 new ones; so Dr. Kissinger destroyed the equivalent of 526 Minuteman III missiles. Far more important, however, is that if he had not destroyed them, they would have required exactly the same number of Soviet missiles and warheads for their destruction as the new ones; which, in turn, would have delayed Soviet attainment of a preclusive first-strike capability at least two years. Gaining two years of time to rebuild our strategic deterrent will be worth not only billions but trillions of dollars to the American people. So, our answer is yes: the 550 Minuteman Is and IIs that Kissinger destroyed were well worth saving.

The second objection that will be advanced against placing the responsibility on Kissinger for destruction of 550 operational Minuteman missiles is that it was a McNamara program adopted in 1966,[13] and was so far advanced by 1969 that it was too late to stop it by the time Kissinger took office as National Security Adviser.

Not so. There were two parts to the Minuteman III program planned by McNamara: (1) the open program for the development, testing, and production of the new missiles, and (2) the clandestine program for the destruction of the 550 Minuteman Is and IIs that were operational. At the time Kissinger came into power the first part of the plan was well advanced and the first segment of the procurement of the new missiles was scheduled for that year; more were scheduled for procurement in 1970 and 1971, but none was to be *deployed* until 1971. That means that the near-total scrapping of the launching tubes and equipment in the 550 existing silos was not scheduled until 1971. The second part of the project, therefore, was totally scheduled for execution during 1969 and 1970. Not even the first segment of the existing operational Minuteman missiles was scrapped until 1971.

Thus Kissinger had his initial opportunity to abandon the clandestine destruction part of the McNamara program in 1969, but had additional opportunities in 1970 and even in early 1971 to exercise the option before a single U.S. ICBM had been destroyed. In each of the years from 1969 there was every reason for him to have acted to preserve and rebuild U.S. strategic power. At the end of 1969 the strategic balance in ICBMs stood at a total of 1,054 for the U.S. and 1,200 for the U.S.S.R.[14] At that time, as Dr. Kissinger reported in his press conferences and briefings on SALT I in May and June of 1972, the Soviets were adding ICBMs at the rate of 250 a year.

Thus it cannot rationally be contended that it would have been inconsistent with the then-pending SALT I negotiations for Kissinger to permit the programmed Minuteman III missiles to become "additional" ICBMs for the United States at the scheduled rate of 200 per year, after the Soviets had already opened a numerical ICBM gap of 146 against us, and were known to be widening it by 250 each year. In addition to the gap in numbers of missiles, the Soviets had by then opened vastly greater gaps in throw-weight and deliverable megatonnage.

It is also relevant here to recall that the Kissinger-Nixon *State of the World Report* delivered February 25, 1971, recognized that the continuing Soviet buildup was so great that "by any standard . . . the number of strategic forces now exceeds the need for deterrence," and that there was a continued deployment of systems

> particularly the SS-9 ICBM with large multiple warheads—which if further improved and deployed in sufficient numbers, could be *uniquely suitable for a first-strike against our land-based deterrent forces.*

A table included in the text of the *State of the World Report* showed that, between the end of 1969 and the end of 1970, the Soviets added 331 ICBMs to their already superior force. Thus, the Kissinger-Nixon report reasoned, the Soviet strategic programs raised "profound questions," including

> does the Soviet Union seek forces which could attack and destroy vital elements of our retaliatory capability, thus requiring us to respond with additional programs of our own involving another round of arms competition?

Then, applying the benign interpretation that Kissinger always assigns to Soviet intentions, the report concluded that "the past year has not provided definitive answers."

Perhaps not. But to an objective analyst hoping that the United States can avert both nuclear war and surrender, the answers seem horrendously definitive. The very next year piled up more evidence that should have been conclusive to anyone other than a dedicated apologist for the Soviet Union. The Kissinger-Nixon *State of the World Report* for 1972, submitted to Congress on February 9, listed a half-dozen specific Soviet moves—each of which pointed toward the crash deployment of a first-strike capability against the United States. The report summarized them:

> In short, in virtually every category of strategic offensive and defensive weapons the Soviet Union has continued to improve its capability.
>
> These collective developments raise serious questions concerning Soviet objectives. The Soviet Union is continuing to create strategic capabilities beyond a level which by any reasonable standard seems sufficient. It is therefore inevitable that we ask whether the Soviet Union seeks the numbers and types of forces needed to attack and destroy vital elements of our own strategic forces.

The next paragraph embodies a beautiful example of a Kissinger-convoluted conclusion; despite his knowledge of the tremendous investment made by the Soviets in building this stupendous strategic arsenal—a massive sum wrung out of a relatively weak economy obviously for a purpose of overriding importance—he rationalized:

> . . . it seems unlikely that the Soviet Union would actually plan to use these forces in an *all-out manner,* their existence is a disturbing reality . . .

Might that contain an implication that it is *not* "unlikely" that the Kremlin might be planning to use these forces in a less than "all-out manner"?

To use them in an all-out manner would be to employ them in a massive combination counterforce-counterpopulation strike: an attack designed to destroy our retaliatory weapons and annihilate our population. The less-than-all-out manner of employing their strategic forces is represented in the following scenario, which a number of objective experts on nuclear strategy consider may be chillingly probable in the short term—that is, within the next three to five years:

On July 5, 1976, the Soviets launch a disarming strike against all U.S. ICBMs and strategic bombers. By employing 25 percent of their ICBMs (say, 318 SS-9s and SS-18s + 107 SS-19s) and 50 percent of their SLBMs, they destroy 95 percent of our land-based retaliatory forces.

This counterforce strike is carefully targeted to kill only the minimum number of people consonant with effective destruction of our weapons. The entire surviving population—more than 200 million—is then held as hostage, subject to mass incineration by another 25 percent of the Soviet missile force. Kissinger's SALT I ABM Treaty has guaranteed that the entire American people (less possibly the population of the Washington, D.C., area) will be totally defenseless against those missiles; in his own words, the Soviet missiles would be guaranteed a "free ride" to incinerate our population.

At that point, Kissinger would have to make a somewhat difficult decision. (We say Kissinger would have to make it because he operates as *de facto* commander-in-chief of U.S. strategic nuclear forces.)

Kissinger could give the command to retaliate against the people of the Soviet Union with the undestroyed remnant of our Minuteman force plus the missiles of the on-station part of our Polaris-Poseidon force. Meanwhile, the Soviets would have accomplished the strategic evacuation of their cities, or moved exposed people to the shelters of their massive civil defense system. If Kissinger gave the order, our residual forces might possibly kill six to 10 million Russian civilians who had nothing to do with ordering or carrying out the strike against the United States.

In reaching his decision, Kissinger would know that, if he did order a retaliatory strike against Soviet cities, the Soviets would retaliate with a missile force capable of wiping out 180 million Americans. The remainder would be "mopped up" by the Soviet bomber force. And, of course, the Soviets would be left with 50 percent of their strategic missile force unexpended and in reserve.

Would Kissinger order retaliation under such circumstances? Would any sane man give such an order?

In his article "Reflections on Nuclear Strategy," General Bruce K. Holloway, USAF, who retired as commander-in-chief of our Strategic

Air Command in 1972, asks the relevant questions as to ordering such retaliation to accomplish mass destruction:

> Who believes we would do it? What would it accomplish? Since when has the United States been obsessed with such revengefulness? Why should we indulge in such monstrous immorality?[15]

Even more important, and apparently unnoticed by most authorities on nuclear strategy, we have a declaration on this point by Kissinger himself:

> ... to consider the mass use of nuclear weapons in terms of the destruction of civilian population, one faces a political impossibility, not to speak of a moral impossibility.[16]

In that scenario, therefore, the only rational course left open to the United States would be unconditional surrender.

Accordingly, it is clear (1) that Kissinger absolutely did understand that the Soviets were building with breathtaking speed toward decisive strategic superiority, and (2) that he fully appreciated the inevitable and horrendous consequences that would follow from the U.S. accepting critical inferiority. Indeed, in the 1971 *State of the World Report* he had Richard Nixon explicitly recognize the nonacceptability of strategic inferiority:

> Our strategic forces must be numerous enough, efficient enough, and deployed in such a way that an aggressor will always know that the sure result of a nuclear attack against us is unacceptable damage from our retaliation.
>
> *That makes it imperative that our strategic power not be inferior to that of any other state.*

It cannot be denied, therefore, that Kissinger was fully cognizant of the consequences of permitting the United States to fall into a position of decisive inferiority. Nor can it be denied that all during those years of 1969, 1970, and 1971 (the 1972 *State of the World Report* reflects the developments of 1971), Kissinger knew that the Soviet buildup in ICBMs had passed the numbers of U.S. ICBMs by hundreds, and that they were continuing to widen the gap by additional hundreds each year. At any time during those years Kissinger could have stayed the execution of the destruct order condemning 550 of our existing operational Minuteman missiles—more than half of our total land-based retaliatory force.

Yet he supported the program for their destruction. If, instead, he had permitted the 550 Minuteman IIIs to become "additional" ICBMs for our force, this would have brought the United States up to almost exact parity with the Soviet Union in the number of fixed-based ICBMs frozen by the SALT I Interim Agreement. We had 1,054; the "additional" 550 would have brought us up to 1,604, as compared with the Soviet total of 1,618. Because he destroyed our existing ICBMs, we were frozen with a 50-percent inferiority.

Almost equally bad, our strategic inferiority was published to all the world. It was this Kissinger-created, SALT-frozen, NATO-perceived Soviet strategic superiority that provided the essential backup for the Arab employment of the "oil weapon" against the entire non-Communist industrialized world in the wake of the Soviet-planned and -supported Yom Kippur War of October 1973. The Arabs could have been effectively pressured by collective action of Western Europe plus Japan, by conventional military action if necessary. But knowing that the United States was strategically impotent against the Soviet Union, they not only did not dare to act against the Soviet client states, but they did not dare to support the United States in attempting to restore the balance of conventional weapons in the Mideast.

All this evidence is convincing that Kissinger was absolutely correct when he repeated time and again in his SALT-selling campaign in May and June of 1972 that the SALT I Interim Agreement did not create the missile gap. That is true: SALT did not create the gap—but Kissinger did.

There is one thing worse than allowing the Soviets a numbers gap in operational ICBMs and that is bringing about a situation that will enable the enemy—years earlier than otherwise, and with high confidence—to develop the capability of destroying substantially the entire U.S. land-based retaliatory force. Ever since early 1969 officials and experts have conceded that if the Soviets deployed 400 SS-9 missiles or their equivalent in destructive power they could destroy on the order of 95 percent of our 1,000 Minuteman missiles in a surprise disarming strike. Kissinger also knew, that as of the 1970 Defense Posture Statement, the Soviets not only had more ICBMs than the United States but that "more than 275 of these Soviet launchers are for the large SS-9."

Did Kissinger recognize the serious quality of this threat? We do not have any documentation originating in the year 1970 on this point, but we have a SALT-related statement that implies that he recognized the SS-9 threat at least as early as 1970. On May 29, 1972, in a news conference he held in Kiev, Kissinger responded to a reporter's question as to whether the SALT Agreement "cuts off the SS-9 at a safe level":

> We admit we have insisted at a time when most of our critics were denying it that—and we have always said it—the SS-9 is a threat to our retaliatory force, and it remains a threat to our retaliatory force.

Also, the annual State of the World Reports recognize that the SS-9 is such a threat. For example, the report delivered February 9, 1972, refers to the Soviets building additional silos for large modern missiles, such as the SS-9, which, because of their warhead size and potential accuracy, could directly threaten our land-based ICBMs.

The evidence appears conclusive that in early 1970, when no operational U.S. Minuteman missiles had yet been destroyed, the Soviets were rapidly developing a capability of destroying some 95 percent of the 1,000 U.S. Minutemen in their silos. With a newly established production line about to start producing 550 Minuteman III missiles, Kissinger had two options that could have delayed in great part, or perhaps permanently defeated, the rapidly maturing Soviet capability substantially to destroy the entire U.S. land-based deterrent: (1) he could have ordered new silos constructed for the additional 550, which would have given us a total of 1,550 Minuteman missiles (assuming that, if the Soviets could destroy 95 percent of our 1,000 ICBMs with 400 SS-9s, it would take 600 to destroy 1,550, and therefore would have required the Soviets to produce and deploy the equivalent of 200 additional SS-9s, about a two-year job); or (2) he could have stockpiled the new Minuteman missiles for perhaps two or even four years while mobile launchers would be produced and deployed for them.

Thus it was that the Kissinger decision in early 1970 to proceed with the scrapping of the 550 Minuteman I and II missiles produced a twofold effect. It made inevitable the SALT I-enshrined missile gap of 1,618 known Soviet ICBMs to our 1,054. Far worse than that peacetime inventory gap, it set up the Soviets with a capability of creating a wartime post-first-strike gap of about 1,000 unexpended Soviet ICBMs to 50 surviving ICBMs for the United States. This estimate is based on the Soviets' needing to expend less than 600 of their total of 1,618 ICBMs in a disarming strike. Such a situation gives the Soviets high confidence in their approaching preclusive first-strike capability. Every one of Kissinger's major strategic policies or programs has accelerated Soviet progress toward that capability.

If mystery attends the motivation of Dr. Kissinger in destroying 550 Minuteman missiles in-being when we needed them so desperately to close the ICBM gap of the 1970s, the part he played in the plot against Polaris and in the Poseidon adventure is even more sensational. McNamara's part was also more spectacular than in the massacre of the Minutemen. Even before eight of our last 31 Polaris submarines were launched, he activated plans for their destruction. He covered the real purpose of his action under a euphemistic expression that made it sound innocuous: "the Poseidon *retrofit* program." In his January 26, 1967, Defense Posture Statement, he reported:

I also believe it would be prudent at this time to commit the

Poseidon missile to production and deployment. You may recall that we took action last year to place ourselves in a position to deploy such a force if that should become desirable. It was for this reason that we accelerated the Poseidon development program. . . . We propose to spread the Poseidon retrofit program over a period of years tied to the regular overhaul cycle.

. . .The total incremental cost of developing Poseidon and producing and deploying the proposed force is estimated at $3.3 billion.[17]

At the time he took the accelerating action he referred to, there were still six Polaris to be deployed in 1966 and "the final two by September 1967."

Interestingly, most of the 31 Polaris that were to be substantially destroyed in the phony "conversion" to Poseidon had already been through a genuine conversion that enabled them to carry Polaris A3 missiles instead of the earlier A2 model. The A3 is a far more powerful missile, with a longer range, and was ultimately equipped with three MRV warheads. The retrofit process to enable submarines designed for A2 missiles to carry A3s did not involve the scrapping of any of the boats or any important parts or systems thereof. But the McNamara program for the "retrofit" or "conversion" of the 31 newest Polaris submarines to Poseidons amounted to the virtual scrapping of these submarines, and reusing some salvaged parts to build 31 Poseidon submarines that were for all practical purposes—especially cost—new-construction submarines. McNamara's unsubstantiated claim was that, although 60 percent of each Poseidon would be new construction, 40 percent of the preexisting Polaris would be salvaged for reuse. Thus, by his own admission, the Poseidon fleet was to be predominantly new construction; but, by every realistic criterion, they were near total new construction.

Take the cost, for example. *George Washington*, our first Polaris submarine, commissioned in 1959 (deployed in 1960), cost $100 million with 16 A1 missiles.[18] By 1970, when the last ones were being completed, the cost of each, with 16 A3 missiles, was $125 million. Deducting from those figures the cost of the respective missile complements (about $1 million for an A1 missile and $1.46 million for an A3 missile), we come up with $84 million per Polaris without missiles, before inflation and improvements set in, and $101.64 million each after 10 years of inflation, or an average of $92.82 million. This is a rough but reasonable estimate. To ensure that we are not underpricing, we will assume that the Polaris fleet cost an average of $100 million each, without missiles. But, *the cost of what McNamara termed a "conversion" of a Polaris to a Poseidon was $170 million each.*[19]

That certainly sounds more like new construction than "conversion." Also, if you take McNamara at his word, and assume that excluded from that cost figure was material worth 40 percent of the cost of a Polaris, or $40 million, we get a cost figure of $210 million each for his "conversions." That would make a so-called Poseidon "conversion" cost 210 percent of the new construction figure for an original Polaris.

The time element also should be critical in determining realistically whether we are dealing with virtually new construction involving the scrapping of an earlier model and some salvage of parts for reuse, or with "conversion" of an existing submarine. According to Melvin Laird's 1970 Defense Posture Statement,[20] the first two Polaris submarines to be given the Poseidon configuration were authorized for FY 1968; that is, they went into the construction yard no later than June 30, 1967. Two more were authorized for FY 1969, and four more for FY 1970. Secretary Laird's statement continued:

> All eight SSBNs [nuclear-propelled ballistic missile submarines] thus far authorized for conversion are now in the shipyards. The first Poseidon equipped SSBN is scheduled to be deployed in January 1971.

Assuming first in, first out, the "conversion" or construction of the first Poseidon to be deployed required at least 3½ years in the process, that is, at least six months in the calendar year 1967, plus the years of 1968, 1969, and 1970. Also, we know from one of Dr. Kissinger's May 1972 Moscow Summit press conferences[21] that as of that date only a total of eight Poseidons had been deployed—presumably the eight that succeeded to the numbers of the eight Polaris that went into the shipyards between July 1967 (the beginning of FY 1968) and June 30, 1969. Taking a median date, say calendar 1968 at midyear, this confirms the 3½ years of construction time we estimated for the first Poseidon.

Work in a shipyard—that can realistically be classed as a "conversion"—appears to involve a matter of months—not years. The new construction, from scratch, of Polaris submarines required about three years. However, the accurately classified conversion of A2 missile-carrying Polaris submarines to carry the A3 missiles took only months. Another interesting fact tending to establish that Poseidons are new construction, rather than "converted" Polaris, is the admitted blocking of additional new-construction submarines because the protracted period required for work on Poseidons in the shipyards preempts the required submarine construction capacity. Thus, John Newhouse, in his Cold Dawn: The Story of SALT, in explaining why the new U.S. missile submarine Trident (he uses the older terminology: ULMS) cannot be deployed "much before the end of the decade," makes this point:

> The United States cannot now build more submarines because the current capacity is exhausted by the program of shifting over from Polaris to Poseidon missiles.[22]

Were these 31 Polaris submarines really so far gone in the aging process, or so close to operational obsolescence, that it was economical to scrap them? On September 17, 1973, the Members of Congress for Peace Through Law—an organization that has opposed every measure designed to strengthen the U.S. strategic deterrent against a Soviet nuclear attack—made public a study dealing with U.S. missile-launching submarines. The thrust of the report (issued by Senator James Abourezk) was to oppose the development and production of the proposed Trident—even in the 1978-83 timeframe. As explained by a *Washington Post* dispatch datelined Washington, September 19, 1973:

> The Abourezk report contends, however, that the Polaris/Poseidon subs were designed for a hull life of 25-30 years, and that *even the oldest ones, built in 1960, should not need to be retired until the 1985-90 period.*

For once the Members of Congress for the Unilateral Disarmament of the United States (operating under the euphemistic title of Members of Congress for Peace Through Law) were absolutely right. The entire U.S. Polaris fleet of 41 submarines could have been a tremendously effective segment of the U.S. strategic deterrent all the way through the 1980s; and this is especially true of the 31 youngest members of the Polaris fleet.

So the 31 destroyed Polaris were not old, worn-out, or obsolescent. But were they vulnerable to destruction by the Soviets? Not really. Consider this estimate—which represents the most widely held expert military opinion on the issue—by then-Secretary of Defense Melvin Laird in his 1970 Defense Posture Statement:

> According to our best current estimates, we believe that our Polaris and Poseidon submarines at sea can be considered *virtually invulnerable today. With highly concentrated effort, the Soviet Navy today might be able to localize and destroy at sea one or two Polaris submarines.*

Only by highly concentrated effort could the Soviets destroy one or two Polaris submarines. But Henry Kissinger destroyed 27 out of 41 because McNamara had set it up years in advance. In McNamara's case, of two probable patterns of motivation, one could partially exculpate him; in Kissinger's case, however, it is practically impossible to hypothesize circumstances that could support any other motivation than to accomplish the one result inescapably foreseeable at the time he acted—substantial, decisive acceleration in the Soviet attainment of a highly credible first-strike capability against the United States.

To attempt to penetrate the McNamara motivation for the light it sheds on the Kissinger motivation, let's try a short scenario in which you, the reader, are the leading player. Though you may find this role distasteful, it should nevertheless afford enlightenment. As always, no one is making any accusation of treason, even the *de facto* variety.

You are the Secretary of Defense of the United States. You are also the man with the computer brain. It is now 1966 and, in the years since 1961, you have acquired total control of U.S. national security policies. In every contest with the military in which they sought to strengthen or even maintain the strategic power of the United States, you prevailed—even when the military high command was backed by Congress with full funding or even a "mandate." You had succeeded in scrapping 1,400 B-47 strategic bombers, even though such numbers were needed to saturate the Soviet air defense. You killed the mach-3 B-70 strategic bomber (after successful tests at more than 2,000 miles per hour) with the argument that B-52s with Skybolt air-to-surface missiles would do the job; then you scrapped the Skybolt missile just as it passed all critical tests and was about to go into production. You also blocked production of advanced weapons systems known as Pluto, Dynasoar, and Orion. For six years you had stalled production of a missile defense for our nation.

But there was one advanced weapons system you had not been able to block: the missile-launching submarine. Our development was 10 years ahead of the Soviets; the design had been finalized in 1957, the first one was deployed in 1960, and the final units of the total of 41 boats were to be deployed in 1967. Even worse from the standpoint of the Soviet Union, the genius teams of scientists, designers, technologists, and production engineers and managers who had produced the near-miracle of the Polaris system a decade ahead of the Soviets, had now come up with a great new design for an even-more-advanced nuclear-propelled missile-launching submarine. The most influential members of Congress had nothing but respect and admiration for U.S. submarine experts, and they enjoyed the confidence and support of the media and the nation. They could not be overridden and suppressed, as you had so successfully done in other areas of weapons development. You just couldn't keep dedicated Americans such as Admiral Hyman Rickover from talking, and you couldn't keep the most influential congressional committees from listening to him.

The march of technology, fully supported by Congress and the nation, was moving inexorably forward toward production and deployment of the new Poseidon-class submarine. For once, not even the craftiest of the whiz-kids had come up with a slick scheme to swindle America out of a powerful and near-invulnerable instrument of defense. For once, such razzle-dazzle as cunningly coached computer read-outs and pompous recitations of cost-effectiveness formulas could not stop the program. Not merely the military, but the people and the Congress, held a serious view of the Soviet strategic threat in that era. For two years the Joint Chiefs of Staff had unanimously urged the accelerated deployment of an anti-ballistic-missile defense system for the entire nation: people, cities, and industry as well as our retaliatory weapons; and Congress was backing the ABM program with appropriations and near-unanimous support.

Because of the then-existing political environment and national commitment, you judged that the Poseidon program could not be stopped. But if it were not, the United States would gain a totally reliable, fully credible strategic deterrent to nuclear attack that would guarantee against our being forced to surrender or knuckle under to nuclear blackmail. Through the mid-1970s this deterrent would grow in power each year; and there was every reason to believe that it would provide national life insurance through the 1980s and even into the 1990s. The United States would have a highly survivable force of 41 Polaris submarines, plus an equal number of the newer Poseidons: a total of 82 missile-launching submarines capable of surviving a Soviet first-strike and retaliating with a force of 1,312 missiles. More important, of course, with such a powerful and near-invulnerable retaliatory force opposing them, neither the Politburo in Moscow nor its equivalent in Peking would seriously consider launching an attack against the United States.

The creation of such a situation would cancel out your six years of brilliant and sophisticated scheming. What would it have gained to cancel out the second 1,000 Minuteman ICBMs long-programmed to strengthen our deterrent, or to have blocked the production of the planned 500 mobile Minuteman missiles whose survivability would be protected by being mounted on specially constructed railroad cars?

Soviet developments in antisubmarine warfare and in ballistic missile defenses might, in the period after the mid-1970s, counter the on-station segment of a 41-submarine force—but not a force of twice that number.

So, what do you do now? You can't stop the new Poseidon force from coming into existence. So you use its advent as a reason for scrapping the already existing force of Polaris; do it by developing a precisely purposed terminology. You play up the new Poseidon missile and play down its major changes. Speak of "retrofitting" the Poseidon missile into the Polaris force. Never, never permit anyone to speak of a Polaris as being "scrapped" in relation to the construction of a Poseidon submarine; say, instead, that the Polaris is being "converted" into a Poseidon. Influence the military, especially the Navy, to feel that if they are for Poseidon, they must be against Polaris. Especially, convince the military that, in order to obtain the potentially great Poseidon force, the cost must be cut by making it a "conversion" program rather than a "new construction" program.

So, you institute the Polaris-to-Poseidon "conversion" program that makes you look like an honest-but-stupid steward of the taxpayers' money, trying to stretch the defense dollar to the limit in buying effective weaponry. The Poseidon "conversion" program will not expose you as the Kremlin's man in the Pentagon—but it will throw away billions to save millions, as was so successfully accomplished with the TFX/F-111.

How much money, if any, was saved by making "conversion" the basis of the construction of the Poseidon fleet? The greatest money saving, per Polaris "converted" to Poseidon, that McNamara claimed would translate into $40 million. He generalized that 40 percent of the value of a Polaris would be usefully embodied in the Poseidon version. As we have seen, $100 million is a reasonable estimate of what a Polaris cost us, on the average. But McNamara's track record demonstrates that his estimates may be off by scores of millions or even billions of dollars, as in the TFX case. It is inherently improbable that 40 percent of the value of a Polaris could be economically embodied in a Poseidon. As a class, Poseidon was deployed 11 years later and the design stage has about the same differential. In that decade tremendous progress was made in the technology of nuclear propulsion for submarines, and these changes involved not only the reactor design and fabrication but also the highly complex and expensive equipment for transferring nuclear power from the reactor into propulsion power. Then the entire system of the submarine and its missiles involves a myriad of electronics; and there was more than a decade of progress in that too. The changes wrought by time affected the most expensive elements and parts of the missile submarine.

You may remember the story of the Edsel owner who, when his car was a little more than two years old, discovered that the car was falling apart. He took it to the repair shop and asked the master mechanic what could be done with the ailing Edsel. "Jack up the horn," the mechanic responded after an inspection, "and run a new automobile under it." McNamara's plan for "conversion" contemplated severing some hull sections from the complex or working parts of the Polaris boats, and building a substantially new and greatly advanced type of submarine fore and aft of those retained sections. The more expensive a part, the less chance there was that it could be adapted economically to the new submarine.

But let us accept McNamara's claim that a Poseidon is 40 percent Polaris. Credit the Polaris with a 25-year life, and depreciate that 40-percent value for 10 years of aging, which might give us $24 million. Then increase that value by 10 years of inflation at an average of 2½ percent, which would bring it up to $30 million—very generous, indeed, for the least expensive and least complex parts. We know that the out-of-pocket cost to the U.S. Government of a Poseidon submarine without missiles is $170 million. Add to that the $30 million in assumed value of Polaris parts, and we have a total cost of $200 million per Poseidon. Thus, the $30 million in value assumed to be contributed by the "conversion" of the Polaris amounts to only 15 percent of the total cost of the Poseidon submarine. If the United States could afford 85 percent of the cost of the Poseidon fleet—a tiny fraction of one year's GNP—we could afford the whole thing.

There is one point on this issue that might possibly exculpate McNamara: whether it was worthwhile to scrap a Polaris to save 15 percent of the cost of a Poseidon would depend entirely on whether the Polaris had a value to the United States as an operational weapons system in that timeframe. If we had no reasonable requirement for additional missile submarines above the number of 41, then it would have been reasonable to scrap the Polaris to save 10 percent or even 5 percent of the cost of the Poseidon boats.

What was the value of an additional operational Polaris at that time, and how can it be determined? The requirement for additional submarines above the force level of 41 has to be estimated in relation to the strategic environment in that timeframe. In this calculation, everything favors McNamara and tends to incriminate Kissinger. As of the time McNamara announced his decision to proceed with the Poseidon "conversion" program, he reported the strategic balance (using October 1, 1966, figures):

U.S. vs. SOVIET INTERCONTINENTAL
STRATEGIC NUCLEAR FORCES

	U.S.	U.S.S.R.
ICBMs	934	340
SLBMs	512	130
Total Intercontinental Ballistic Missiles	1446	470
Intercontinental Bombers	680	155

Thus, he could truthfully claim that

As of now, we have more than three times the number of intercontinental ballistic missiles (i.e., ICBMs and SLBMs) the Soviets have. Even by the early 1970s, we still expect to have a significant lead over the Soviet Union in terms of numbers. . . .[23]

Thus, at the time McNamara made the decision to scrap more than three-fourths of the then-operational Polaris fleet under the euphemistic label of "conversion," we still had a very substantial factor of strategic superiority over the Soviets. He had cut us down to 3-to-1 from our former overwhelming supremacy of 8-to-1, but this was still sufficient to make a reasonable case that we had no urgent requirement for a fleet of more than 41 modern missile-launching submarines. It was perhaps an uneconomic decision to scrap Polaris submarines merely for the scrap they could contribute to the construction of Poseidon boats. Although we accepted for analysis his maximum claim that 40 percent of the value of the Polaris would go into the Poseidon, a more realistic estimate would be that only from 15 to 20 percent was reusable, which would make the saving about 7½ percent of the total cost of the Poseidons (without missiles). Therefore, the 31 Polaris submarines McNamara scheduled for scrapping were not a suicidal sacrifice from a strategic point of view.

530

At the time McNamara firmed up his plans to scrap three-fourths of the then-practically-brand-new U.S. missile-launching nuclear-propelled submarine fleet, in order to prevent the new-production Poseidons from becoming "additional" operational weapons systems and bringing our total to 72 submarines, the Soviets did not have a single modern nuclear-propelled missile-launching submarine. As of the end of 1965 they had only 107 SLBM launchers, and they were all on old diesel-powered submarines and could not be fired from below the surface.[24] As of the date of the 1970 Defense Posture Statement, when Kissinger continued the McNamara program for the destruction of Polaris submarines under the guise of "converting" them into Poseidons, the Soviets had finally gotten into a massive production program for their Y-class nuclear-propelled ballistic-missile-launching submarines. This type was similar to U.S. Polaris boats, and by then they had an unknown number of them deployed, had at least 12 of them continuously under construction in two shipyards, were turning them out at a rate of at least eight per year, and, as of early 1970, U.S. experts recognized that

it is possible that the rate of output from these two facilities will increase significantly.[25]

More starkly relevant to Kissinger's decision to continue scrapping Polaris submarines to prevent the on-coming Poseidons from becoming "additional" power to the U.S. strategic deterrent, however, was this more specific estimate in the latter part of the same Defense Posture Statement:

In early 1969 it was projected that the Soviets could have some 35-50 of these [Y-class] ships, 560-800 SLBM launchers, in 1975-77. It is now [early 1970] projected that this "end strength" could be achieved in 1974-75.[26]

Those estimates were not imaginary horribles. They were confirmed 2½ years later when Kissinger, in his June 15, 1972, White House briefing for the five congressional committees, accepted the Soviets' "claimed current level, operational and under construction, of about 740 missiles, some of them on an older type nuclear submarine." That divides up into about 46 nuclear submarines, most of them Y-class, but some the new Delta class with missiles of intercontinental range.

In any event, it is clear that in February 1970 Kissinger knew that the Soviets could, and very probably would, open a modern-missile-launching-submarine gap against the United States by 1974—if he continued the program of destroying one Polaris submarine for each Poseidon to be produced. At that time only six Polaris submarines had been scrapped beyond recall to provide parts for the "conversion" program. If he had halted the scrapping program, and ordered new parts instead of salvaging Polaris parts for 7½ to 15 percent of each new

Poseidon, he could have built a U.S. missile-firing submarine force composed of 35 Polaris, 6 Polaris-Poseidons, and 25 all-Poseidons—a total of 66 nearly invulnerable strategic weapons systems to preserve the effectiveness and credibility of our deterrent through the 1980s.

In such a force, the "additional" elements would have been the 25 Polaris that were not destroyed. The "additional" cost for each would only have been a dollar amount equal to the value of the salvageable and economically useful parts of the original submarine that had been programmed to be incorporated into the new Poseidon. That, we estimated, would not be more than $30 million, and probably closer to $15 million. To give an idea of how little that sum will buy in military power in this era, a U.S. F-14 Tomcat fighter aircraft now costs about $13.8 million The price of each "additional" missile submarine, therefore, would be about the equivalent of one or two tactical fighter aircraft—which would be history's greatest bargain in terms of "cost-effectiveness." There is every reason to project (considering the accelerated momentum with which the Soviets are moving toward completion of a preclusive first-strike capability) that a force of 25 additional Polaris would be worth on the order of a trillion dollars to the United States in 1976. That much invulnerable retaliatory power could very well be the critical difference between the Kremlin's giving a go or no-go order for a disarming strike against the United States in that year or the next; and that, in turn, would be the difference between the destruction or surrender of our $20 trillion going-concern-value nation.

There is another reason why the Polaris-Poseidon "conversion" program might well provide the Soviets with a critical advantage at a climactic point in their planning. If Kissinger had terminated the destruction of Polaris in 1970, it would have added the survivable retaliatory power of 25 missile submarines to our deterrent. But that is an understatement, an undercalculation. The so-called "conversion" program has, at nearly all times since 1969, withdrawn six operational Polaris submarines from our ready retaliatory forces. This has been covered by a slick McNamara trick, continued by Kissinger, of asserting that the "conversions" have been synchronized with the "regular overhaul" of the submarines. This cover glosses over the fact that even major overhaul of such ships requires only a matter of months, whereas the "conversion" of a Polaris to a Poseidon requires three to 3½ years. Thus, the claim that our Polaris-Poseidon force consists of a total of 41 is substantially misleading: up through 1976 the actual total is 35. If, instead of scrapping Polaris submarines, we scrapped the current Kissinger program for destroying them, we would add six to our available total within one year. This number may be pivotal in the critical years in the very near future—for, as Kissinger personally explained:

> The difficulty of keeping up in the technological race is magnified by our adoption of the strategic defensive—a position dictated by our value system. For the side which is on the defensive must *constantly* be prepared. Any weakness, however temporary, may tempt attack. . . . The aggressor can afford to build toward a target date. . . . The defender, by contrast, can deter only if he is ready at every moment of time.[27]

The Kissinger-created submarine gap did not come at a time when we possessed superiority in numbers of land-based intercontinental missiles. It came after the Soviets had already opened up a very substantial numbers gap in ICBMs, and much greater gaps in missile throw-weight and missile-deliverable megatonnage. Also, Kissinger knew, as we have seen, that the growing force of Soviet heavy missiles constituted a "direct threat" to our 1,000 Minuteman missiles. Kissinger must have recognized that the growing Soviet heavy missile force instilled a tremendous importance to our adding every possible missile-launching submarine to our deterrent. He had to see that, within several years, our 1,000-missile land-based deterrent would be vulnerable, and that we could depend for survivability only upon our submarine force.

If we are to secure for our country even a fighting chance of survival in freedom past the climactic period of 1976-77, we must penetrate the intricate and highly sophisticated web of deception woven by Kissinger and his staff around the present state of the U.S. strategic nuclear deterrent vis-a-vis the Soviet Union. We will now lay bare for examination several specific and key elements of the subversive scheme. That evidence will enable you to assess the three basic contentions at issue that involve our national survival.

Two of these he has reported time after time, but they are contained in their most highly refined and carefully hedged phraseology in his White House briefing of June 15, 1972, for the five congressional committees:

> . . . as a result of decisions made in the 1960s, and not reversible within the timeframe of the projected agreement [the SALT I Interim Agreement], there would be a numerical gap against us in the two categories of land- and sea-based missile systems whether or not there was an agreement. Without an agreement, the gap would steadily widen.
>
> The agreement would not create the gap. It would prevent its enlargement to our disadvantage. . . .

Into that short excerpt, Henry Kissinger managed to crowd five assertions. One of them is incontestably true: the SALT I Agreement did "not create the gap." Indeed not; Henry Kissinger did.

Taking up the other four seriatim, the evidence in this chapter establishes these four points:

(1) The numerical gap against us in the two categories of land- and sea-based missiles *was not the "result" of "decisions made in the 1960s."* Those "decisions" of the 1960s were, in their most important aspects, no more than *executory* decisions. They had been formulated in the 1960s, true enough; but in essence they were no more than *plans*, the critical parts of which could not be executed in the 1960s (except the "conversion-scrapping" of the first six of the 31 Polaris included in the plan; although deplorable, this was not pivotal in the creation of the gap in SLBMs and submarines). Robert Strange McNamara did, indeed, plan to scrap 550 of our existing Minuteman missiles in order to prevent the 550 Minuteman IIIs from becoming "additional" missiles to strengthen the U.S. land-based deterrent. But although he instituted in the 1960s the programs out of which developed the production line for the new Minuteman missiles, the finished product did not begin coming out of that production line until 1970, a time when Kissinger had taken over full control of U.S. defense policies. So it was not McNamara but Kissinger, in 1970, who made the decision to execute McNamara's plan.

(2) The next assertion in the Kissinger excerpt—"and not reversible within the timeframe of the projected agreement"—appears, grammatically at least, to modify the word "decisions." But we have seen that the critical parts of the plans implemented by the decisions of the 1960s were still executory in 1970; and, in any event, any policy decisions made by one administration as to the production or deployment of weapons during another administration is certainly subject to reversal. Perhaps the phrase is intended to mean that the "result" of the decisions made in the 1960s could not be reversed. If so, we have already shown that, as to the scrapping of the 550 existing Minuteman missiles, the "result" of the scrapping order could have been totally reversed in 1970 because none had yet been destroyed; and as to the scrapping of the Polaris submarines, the result of the destruction order could have been reversed as far as 25/31 of the boats, because only six Polaris had as of that time been scrapped beyond recall and a 25/31 reversal would have been sufficient to avert the opening of a missile-submarine and SLBM gap against us.

A possibility still remains that Kissinger meant by that phrase that the missile gap he was erroneously attributing to decisions made in the 1960s could not be reversed within the timeframe of the agreement, beginning with the date of its signing, May 26, 1972. Wrong again. As of that date, only eight Polaris had been "converted" to Poseidons and deployed, and perhaps three more had been cut up beyond recall. That would still have left 20 that could have been retained and not scrapped—enough to avert the opening of a submarine/SLBM gap. Also, as of that date, we estimate that only about 100 Minuteman I missiles had been scrapped to provide holes for Minuteman IIIs and their new launching tubes, so that the result of the decision of the 1960s to destroy 550 Minuteman Is and IIs could even then have been reversed for 450/550 of the missiles.

(3) Kissinger's next assertion is that "without an agreement, the gap would steadily widen." As we have seen, without the 1970 decisions by Dr. Kissinger to scrap our then-operational weapons on a 1-to-1 basis as we produced new ones, no gap would have opened. As to widening the gap, what caused that was and would be Kissinger's continuance in 1971, 1972, 1973, and 1974 of the program for destroying our weapons in-being, and his refusal to utilize the new production programs, with their ongoing production lines, to *add* new ICBMs and SLBMs to our forces.

(4) Kissinger's statement that the agreement "would prevent its [the gap's] enlargement to our disadvantage" is palpably false, and its falsity can be demonstrated by a single fact: the SALT I Interim Agreement in no way limits either the production or deployment of land-mobile ICBMs. The Defense Department conceded in the fall of 1973 that the Soviets had been developing and producing mobile ICBMs. They have the capability of producing at least 375 strategic missiles a year; this is attested by U.S. official figures during the SALT I negotiations. Therefore the agreement does *not* prevent the gap's enlargement to our disadvantage. So far as the agreement is concerned, the Soviets could produce and deploy 1,000 or more SS-16 mobile ICBMs of their powerful new pop-up-launch type disclosed in 1973, or they could produce them, conceal them under roof, and, later at their own timing, make a surprise mass deployment of them.

It is not totally true, technically, to say that Henry Kissinger created the missile gap of the 1970s. In substance, however, it is true, and only part of it is even technically open to criticism. The numerical gap we have been considering involves three elements: (1) missile-launching nuclear-propelled submarines, (2) SLBMS, and (3) ICBMs. As to the first two, the statement is 100 percent accurate; that is, if Kissinger had discontinued the program of scrapping Polaris submarines at any time from the date he came into power in January 1969 through the SALT I signature date in May 1972, no submarine or SLBM gap in favor of the Soviets could ever have come into existence.

As to the ICBM gap, however, it will be contended that our own figures show that, as of February 1970, there was already a numerical advantage of 46 in favor of the Soviets, and their advantage would have grown in the remainder of 1970 and in 1971 even if Kissinger had not continued the program of scrapping the 550 operational Minuteman Is and IIs. That is true, but it is a technical criticism only; because the very temporary gap would have begun to close in late 1971 and would have been substantially closed by 1974, when all the new 550 Minuteman IIIs could have been operational as "additional" ICBMs and brought our total ICBM force to 1,604 to the Soviets 1,618. This assumes, of course, that upon deciding not to scrap the 550 operational Minuteman Is and IIs, and therefore not to reconstruct their silos with new launching tubes and equipment, a program would have been concurrently initiated to dig 550 new holes in the ground and to install the new launching equipment therein—a program that could have been completed well before 1974 if initiated in 1970; or else that in 1970 a production and deployment program would have been initiated for mobile launchers for the new Minuteman missiles.

All this evidence is equally relevant to the proposition that Kissinger acted affirmatively against U.S. interests by his repeated assertions that the Soviets had ongoing programs for the production of ICBMs, SLBMs, and missile-launching submarines, and that the United States had no such programs. By this affirmative action and deliberate deceit, he convinced first the President of the United States, and then Congress, the media, and ultimately the nation, that, as officially reported to the Congress by the President, SALT—despite all its imbalances and loopholes favoring the Soviets—would work to our advantage because

> we have no current building programs for the categories of weapons frozen, and . . . no new building program could have produced any new weapons in those categories during the period of the freeze.

The fact that Kissinger could convince so many important people of the alleged utter helplessness of the United States to produce any new weapons within five years is evidence of near-hypnotic influence. It was well and widely known, both inside the government and out, that the great United States was not that helpless. And five years is not an insignificant length of time, even for advanced strategic nuclear weapons systems, when the necessarily protracted period for research, development, and testing has been completed and the production lines are already set up and ready to start turning out new submarines, SLBMs, and ICBMs on a quantity basis. That was exactly the state of our Minuteman III and Poseidon submarine and missile programs in 1970. To understand this required neither the highest degree of expertise in scientific weaponry nor a massive intellect. Ambassador Gerard C. Smith, head of the U.S. SALT I negotiating delegation and director of the U.S. Arms Control and Disarmament Agency (until Kissinger fired him in early 1973), gave some surprising testimony to the Senate Foreign Relations Committee. Senator Claiborne Pell of Rhode Island asked Ambassador Smith about the post-SALT I programs of the U.S. and U.S.S.R. in the construction of strategic weapons:

> If the Kremlin and the Pentagon move ahead on the same basis, and expand as much as they can within the framework of the agreement, would that put us in the very inferior position after a few years?

After Ambassador Smith had responded that he was confident that would not happen, even if the SALT Agreement went its full term, which he hoped it would not, Senator Pell asked if it would be correct to say that

> both sides really told each other we are going to go full steam ahead within the terms of the agreement?

Ambassador Smith replied:

> I think "full steam ahead" is much too strong a term. *Certainly as far as any programs I know of, if we wanted, we could go much further and much faster.* For instance, in such programs as the MIRV programs, you could step that up if you wanted to. *There are a number of ways that the United States could produce more launchers rather quickly if it wanted to.* So I don't see this as a full steam ahead situation. . .[28]

Someone was lying. As we have seen from the evidence, it was not Ambassador Smith. Henry Kissinger, on the other hand, had to attempt to cover not only his own lies about particulars, but those he had planted on Richard Nixon. It would not do, therefore, to have an authoritative witness on SALT I around who would tell the truth. So Gerard C. Smith had to go. Although Ambassador Smith had gone along with a five-year term for the Interim Agreement, his testimony revealed his very real fear of its actually continuing long without a new agreement to protect U.S. interests against Soviet advances:

> People shorthandedly say this is a five-year agreement. *I hope it won't be.* It may be a one-year agreement; it may be a two-year agreement, depending upon when we succeed in the follow-on negotiations.

Within a year from the signing of the SALT I Agreements evidence could no longer be suppressed that showed that five years is far too risky a gamble with U.S. survival. The Soviets had not only developed and successfully proof-tested operational MIRVs for four series of ICBMs, but had combined this technology with other revolutionary advances to create five new nuclear missile systems of up to 500 percent more throw-weight than the systems they replace; and they had not only developed the world's first intercontinental-range submarine-launched ballistic missile, but had deployed an unknown number of new submarines carrying them. These developments were not known to Ambassador Smith, or even suspected by him, when he so reluctantly agreed to the five-year term for the SALT I Interim Agreement. They meant that the Soviets had successfully concealed scientific and technological advances that would enable them to compress the timeframe of revolutionary strategic-weapons-systems developments from more than five years to less than one year.

We initiated this chapter with a restatement of the major questions considered in this book: Can what Henry Kissinger has done to the defense and foreign policies of the United States be justified on the theory that he has done and is doing the best he can "under the political circumstances which presently obtain in the nation"? Or are they "kinky"? Or do they represent a deliberate betrayal of the United States for some unfathomable motive?

The evidence in this chapter relates specifically to whether Kissinger intended certain actions and policies to have the *effect* of injuring U.S. national security interests and helping the Soviets accelerate their progress toward a decisive strategic superiority; or whether they could have resulted from an incompetence so pervasive as to have been previously unsuspected in a man of Kissinger's reputation and background.

The evidence goes far to establish that the Kissinger actions were all integrated parts of a complex and sophisticated pattern brilliantly calculated to deceive the President, the Congress, the media, and the nation; and that the thrust of his deception was threefold: to deceive all into believing (1) that the United States was helpless to add any strategic weapons to our retaliatory forces within the five-year term of the SALT I Interim Agreement, so that, unless the momentum of the ongoing Soviet ICBM and SLBM programs was constrained, we would be faced with a disastrously massive missile gap "by 1977 without a freeze"; (2) that the SALT I Interim Agreement "will stop the Soviet Union from increasing the existing numerical gap in missile launchers"; and (3) that in the Interim Agreement the Soviet Union has accepted a freeze of its heavy ICBM launchers, the weapons most threatening to our strategic forces.

The evidence establishes time and time again that Kissinger lied as to particulars as well as to generalities. It conclusively proves that all three of his major contentions, as summarized above, were false. The conclusion from all this is that the United States was deceived into accepting the SALT I ABM Treaty and Interim Agreement; and, surely even more important, into accepting Kissinger's policies governing U.S. strategic posture and grand strategy. Certainly it cannot be denied that much of the potentially tragic faith of the American people in Kissinger's detente with the Kremlin is based upon his solemn assurance that the Soviets, in entering into the SALT I Interim

Agreement with us, granted us "a sound arrangement that makes a major contribution to our national security."

Hundreds of pages of objective evidence submitted in this book establish the falsity of that assurance. Because that assurance represents the technique of lying in generalities, and therefore requires vastly more evidence for disproof than a lie as to particulars, it has been essential to touch all bases.

Having accomplished that, however, we are now free to turn to the more exciting question. In affirmatively helping the bear, in deliberately blocking any rebuilding of the power of the U.S. strategic deterrent, what has been Henry Kissinger's motivation?

23

Three of the four people on that original list were appointed to the National Security Council staff by me over the strong objection of all of my associates. Two of them were appointed to the National Security staff by me over the strong objection of the security officers and I personally gave them a clearance.

This was Secretary of State Henry Kissinger's own confession at his press conference in Salzburg, Austria, on June 11, 1974.

In seeking to determine what Dr. Henry Kissinger is doing to these United States, let us designate his unknown objective as X. Because of his known intelligence it is reasonable to assume that he has selected his staff on the basis of special qualifications to assist him to achieve objective X. Thus one way to throw light on what Kissinger is up to would be to examine the character of the persons he has chosen to help him do it. If there is a pattern common to the more influential staff members, it will point to the content of X.

Kissinger's choice of his principal deputy and most influential adviser is almost a burlesque of the boss. He has all of Kissinger's abrasive qualities of ego and arrogance, and many of his dangerous capabilities, without any of the qualities that make Kissinger not only tolerable as a person but hypnotically attractive. Here is how *Newsweek* described him in a late roundup entitled "Henry's Little Kissingers":

The first person that Kissinger called to his side when he was appointed Secretary of State was one of the most controversial men in Washington: Helmut Sonnenfeldt. A top-ranking Kissinger deputy since the beginning of the Nixon Administration, Sonnenfeldt is a study in striking contrast. He is a registered Democrat and an unreconstructed conservative. He is an unflinching hawk who has been criticized by superhawks as "a grave security risk."

He is a brilliant theoretician and strategist—and, say those who have worked with him, a harsh and often irascible boss. "He was a very demanding taskmaster," one insider said of the 47-year-old, cigar-chewing "Hal" Sonnenfeldt, "and sometimes he ran roughshod. Like many brilliant people, he can't tolerate mediocrity."

Like Kissinger, Sonnenfeldt is a German Jew whose family fled Hitler's Reich. . . . Sonnenfeldt joined the State Department. . . . During both the Eisenhower and Kennedy administrations, he was accused of leaking documents to the press and to foreign governments. Every investigation proved him innocent, but he made some very tenacious enemies. This year they resurrected the charges. When Sonnenfeldt—after serving four years as Kissinger's principal aide for Soviet and Eastern European affairs—was tapped to be Undersecretary of the Treasury, conservatives on the Senate Finance Committee blocked the nomination for 5½ months.

Ironically, one of the principal reasons the committee eventually approved the nomination was that Sonnenfeldt, in all likelihood, will never take the Treasury job. The man whom White House colleagues dubbed "Papa Doc"—after the late Haitian dictator Francois Duvalier—is expected to leave the National Security Council and rejoin Kissinger at the State Department in the high ranking post of counselor. As one White House aide who served with the two men notes: "Henry can't live with Hal—nor can he live without him."[1]

There is, of course, no way an investigation can prove a man "innocent" of leaking secret documents to the press and to foreign governments. Anglo-American law for centuries has recognized that proving the negative of such a proposition is practically impossible. That is why a defendant does not have to prove himself innocent. As a matter of fact, a full-scale FBI investigation developed so much evidence against Sonnenfeldt that, despite his strong support by high-level officials in the State Department, his file was transmitted to then-Attorney General William Rogers with the recommendation that Sonnenfeldt be prosecuted for violating security. There was also evidence in the file that he had been leaking classified information to the New York Times and to one of the national television networks.

The Nixon nomination of CFR member Sonnenfeldt to be Undersecretary of the Treasury was made on the personal recommendation of Dr. Kissinger, and would have placed Sonnenfeldt in charge of all U.S. trade and financial dealings with Russia, Red China, and the Captive Nations of Eastern Europe. Not surprisingly, therefore, Kissinger enlisted the cooperation of then-Attorney General-designate Elliot Richardson in withholding the FBI files on Sonnenfeldt from Treasury Department security officials when his confirmation was brought into question.

During the dispute over Sonnenfeldt's confirmation, columnist Paul Scott reported the story of a former foreign service officer who had worked in the same areas with Sonnenfeldt for more than a decade, John D. Hemenway:

> Hemenway furnished the names of former government security officials, including Otto Otepka, who can back up his charges and furnish the Senators with details of Sonnenfeldt's security breach.
>
> *They are ready to testify that Sonnenfeldt consistently supported a policy of appeasing the Soviet Union.*
>
> The careers of Hemenway and Sonnenfeldt have crossed several times in policy-making sessions. . . . A graphic illustration of their records deals with their recommendations during the Cuban missile crisis. Hemenway forecast in advance that the Russians were planning to put missiles into Cuba.
>
> As head of the Soviet section of the State Department's intelligence division, Sonnenfeldt took the opposite position. *He reported that the Russians would never do this. He also eliminated from his division's report going to Secretary of State Rusk the warning from Hemenway.*
>
> At this turning point in history, the Sonnenfeldt career story is just the opposite of Hemenway. While Hemenway is out, *Sonnenfeldt is on his way up the government ladder despite his faulty assessments of Soviet intentions* and his major security breach.[2]

Sonnenfeldt's suppression of the warning of Soviet intentions to sneak nuclear missiles into Cuba may have been pivotal in averting any timely U.S. move to keep those missiles out.

Another matter of particular interest is that Helmut Sonnenfeldt is the only member of Kissinger's personal staff who often attends the Secretary of State's closed conferences with Soviet Ambassador Anatoly Dobrynin. Sonnenfeldt was the one working with Kissinger in Moscow in the final days of the May 1972 Summit to put over the last-minute concessions to the Soviets in the SALT I Agreements.

No one who lived through the trauma of tragedy and outrage in 1963 when Lee Harvey Oswald assassinated President John Kennedy will ever forget it. But how many have heard the name of the U.S. Government official most directly responsible for that disaster?

His name is Boris H. Klosson. He is now Henry Kissinger's highest-ranking representative for political intelligence on the SALT II negotiating team. In November 1973 reporter Paul Scott dug out the facts on Boris Klosson's background and published this scoop:

> According to the records of the Warren Commission, which investigated the Kennedy assassination, Klosson was U.S. counselor for political affairs in Moscow in 1961 when Oswald sought visas for himself and his Russian wife to return to the U.S. Oswald had gone to Russia in 1959.

FBI officials credit Klosson with clearing the way for Oswald's return by sending the State Department a three-page report, dated July 11, 1961, indicating the defector had undergone a major change of heart and was not considered to be dangerous.

Titled "Citizenship and passports—Lee Harvey Oswald," Foreign Service Dispatch No. 49 was signed by Klosson and stated in part as follows:

"Twenty months of the realities of life in the Soviet Union has clearly had a maturing effect on Oswald. He (Oswald) stated frankly that he had learned a hard lesson the hard way and that he had been completely relieved of his illusions about the Soviet Union at the same time that he acquired a new understanding and appreciation of the U.S. and meaning of freedom.

"Much of the arrogance and bravado which characterized him on his first visit to the embassy appears to have left him."

State Department and FBI records furnished the Warren Commission clearly show that Klosson's report misled government security officials into believing that Oswald was not dangerous and should be permitted to return to the U.S. The report also paved the way for the State Department to grant Oswald a loan to pay his return passage.

Klosson's misleading report on Oswald was blasted by FBI Director Hoover when he appeared before the Warren Commission. Because of the report, Hoover contended, the FBI made only routine checks on Oswald and his Soviet-born wife following their return to the U.S.

Had Oswald been described as still a "dangerous person," Hoover indicated, the FBI would have opposed his return. If that failed, the agency would have kept him under a much tighter surveillance.

Klosson's judgment on matters relating to the Soviet Union also has been questioned by a number of Foreign Service officers. His security file shows that several of his colleagues reported that he "presented strong pro-Soviet views on every question that came up in the USSR country committee" on which he served.

In a recent State Department appeal case, another Foreign Service officer told how Klosson blocked him from sending a report back to Washington on the KGB, the Soviet secret police and espionage organization, while both were employed in the U.S. Embassy in Moscow. The report dealt with KGB secret operations against Americans in Russia.

Klosson, 54, was born in Buffalo, New York, and has been in the State Department since 1945. He joined the Department after serving in the Office of Strategic Services (OSS) during World War II.

In the 1940s, the FBI conducted an extensive investigation of Klosson after his name and address were found in the contact book of a woman spy picked up by the Immigration Service when she tried to enter the country. No additional association was turned up by the FBI probe.

Klosson is a close associate of Helmut Sonnenfeldt, a top aide of Dr. Henry Kissinger. . . . Klosson and Sonnenfeldt are members of a highly influential innercircle power group which Kissinger has set up throughout the Nixon Administration to carry out his policies.[3]

Dr. Kissinger has urgent need of a pro-Soviet voice in the political-intelligence area of the U.S. SALT II negotiating delegation. How else could he sustain the illusion that the Soviet and U.S. negotiating teams are conducting a meaningful "dialogue" in Geneva when, some two years after the signing of the SALT I Agreements, the Soviets are unequivocally stalling any progress toward a new agreement on offensive weapons while they race ahead on six new super-missile programs? Someone must help in making up myths to explain away the Soviet purpose in adding 50 percent to their already 4-to-1 superiority over the United States in missile throw-weight capacity. Also urgently needed on the U.S. delegation is someone with enough experience in developing pro-Soviet positions to cover for the Soviet proposal in the SALT II negotiations about which the New York Times reported: "A wide variety of American officials describe the Soviet draft treaty as 'outrageous' or as the '21 Soviet demands.'"[4]

It is easy to develop ulterior motives for Kissinger's selection of Boris Klosson for such a sensitive and important position on the U.S. SALT II team. It is far more difficult to find a legitimate reason for his selection. Either Klosson was outrageously naive and incompetent in his evaluations of the Lee Harvey Oswald case, or he was deliberately assisting a KGB program. Oswald had defected from the United States and renounced his American citizenship. He had attended a KGB school for nearly two years and married a Russian woman. Then he appeared at the U.S. Embassy and put on an act before Boris Klosson. Even if Klosson could not see through Oswald's charade, he should have known that the KGB would not put up with a defector from the United States who has been embraced by the Soviets, then wants to defect from the U.S.S.R. back to the United States. If Oswald had been sincere in his second defection, he would probably have been quietly liquidated and never heard of again. If, by some inexplicable chance, the Soviets were moved with more compassion for a double-defecting American than they ever showed for one of their own, they still would never have permitted his Russian wife to accompany him—unless they wanted him back in the United States and had programmed him for a vital mission.

In any event, Klosson's action in the Oswald case was an essential precondition to the assassination of President Kennedy in at least three separate ways. Without Klosson's active help, Oswald could not have secured permission to reenter the United States. He could not have obtained U.S. taxpayers' funds to pay his passage. And, if the FBI had been unable to block his reentry, it would have instituted such tight surveillance that he would not have had an unobstructed opportunity to commit his premeditated murder.

If you were the U.S. Secretary of State and the Assistant to the President for National Security Affairs, and if you were selecting the staff for crucial disarmament negotiations that you had repeatedly asserted involved the very survival of the United States—would you hire such a character as Boris H. Klosson? Henry Kissinger did. One wonders whether, in so doing, he attributed Klosson's action in regard to Oswald as having been a blunder, a wildly irresponsible error of judgment, or as evidence of something else.

In *The Day Kennedy Was Shot*, Jim Bishop describes a telephone call made by Jacqueline Kennedy:

> She phoned her mother. "He didn't even have the satisfaction of being killed for civil rights," she said. "It had to be some silly little Communist."

That silly little Communist was in the United States, and free from tight FBI surveillance, only because of Boris Klosson. The assassination simply could not have been set up by Lee Harvey Oswald without Klosson's persuading the State Department to readmit Oswald to the country whose citizenship he had renounced in favor of the Soviet Union; and to pay his fare; and to mislead J. Edgar Hoover and the FBI into believing that Oswald was no longer dangerous.

These things may be only sidelights on history, but they shed direct light on the question of what Kissinger plans to do to our country. In the cases of Helmut Sonnenfeldt, his principal deputy and expert on European and Soviet affairs, and of Boris Klosson, selected for a critical position in the U.S. delegation for SALT II, the common denominator is easy to spot. It is an attitude of extreme accommodation and servility toward the Soviet Union that has been translated into significant action.

The most comfortable conclusion that can be drawn from the actions of these men is that they resulted from errors in judgment. But if only misjudgments were involved, they were of a magnitude seldom equaled in history. At the very least such gross bungling would qualify the perpetrators as fools. Yet, we meet the assertion time after time in press descriptions of Kissinger that he simply will not put up with fools. That has a probability of accuracy because a man as smart as Kissinger usually will not put up with fools, and a man as busy as he is cannot afford to.

If they were not fools, what other explanation is there for the conduct that favors the Soviet Union against U.S. interests?

We examined the significant common denominator among members of Henry Kissinger's personal staff and found it to be a dedication to detente with the Soviet Union at any price: an ideological, intellectual, and even emotional commitment to the pursuit of peace by concessions. The purpose of this analysis was to throw light on Kissinger's undisclosed objectives; that is, what he plans to do to the United States. This objective we identified as "X." Identifying it more specifically is complicated by the fact that an objective is, by definition, planned and purposefully sought after. It may be the same as the inevitable *result* of his policies; but then again, it may not. By reason of the overconfidence that Dr. Kissinger exudes, or simply failure to think through the consequences of his theories of nuclear strategy and foreign relations, it may be that the result of his policies will come to him as a chilling surprise.

So what will be the result of his policies—and is it the same as his objectives? The best short answer has been provided by an objective foreign policy analyst whose experience has been as extensive as his perception is keen. He predicted Hitler's rise and Hitler's fall. This columnist has always been noted for his courage in presenting reality, regardless of how unpopular. Here are some excerpts from Edgar Ansel Mowrer's column of January 1, 1974:

> Over a year ago, on September 15, 1972, I reached the conclusion: 1973 probably would be a crucial year in world history.
>
> By crucial, I meant that by the end of the latter year, the United States would be irrevocably committed to the gamble of "cooperation instead of confrontation" with the Soviet Union begun in 1972. . . .
>
> Obviously, 1973 has been a crucial year, as decisively demonstrated by President Nixon's nomination of Henry "the Traveling Salesman" as U.S. Secretary of State. For of Henry it can be said, as Germans once said of the Berliner, "He not only knows everything, but also knows it better."
>
> From now on, only one of three things can, it would seem, force the abandonment of that policy: (1) a democratic evolution of the Russian peoples; or (2) ever more intolerable demands on the White House by the Kremlin; or (3) finally, *refusal by the American people to be "suckered" into ultimate defeat.*
>
> The first is, I fear, utopian; the second unlikely as long as the West continues to make the Soviets stronger and richer; the third, ultimately possible if U.S. hawks continue to become indignant at our unnecessary decline.
>
> So far the doves are winning. . . . Happily, there are signs even in the American Congress that more and more Americans consider that "cooperation" with avowed enemies has gone too far.
>
> Yet, as a result of Nixon's excessively "dovish" policy, U.S. military, political and economic power is still diminishing. Kissinger to the contrary, our relations with our European allies and Japan are steadily weakening since they do not believe that they can count on our nuclear defense in case of need and *resent Kissinger's love affair with the Kremlin.* How blame them?
>
> What can citizens do to convince the American people that our national interest (safety!) requires an end to the pursuit of peace by concessions?
>
> First of all, in my judgment, keep in touch with like-minded individ-

uals, organizations and news media and wherever possible, emphasize the all-but-inevitable failure of "cooperation" with our ideological enemies.

Edgar Ansel Mowrer compressed an accurate description of the inevitable result of Kissinger's policies into four admirably non-turgid words: the American people will be " 'suckered' into ultimate defeat." That is what will inexorably happen. But does Kissinger *intend* for this to happen? Or is he, in turn, being suckered by Anatoly Dobrynin and Leonid Brezhnev?

A funny thing happened during the period of the most intensive secret negotiations on SALT I between Kissinger and Dobrynin in the spring of 1971. Dobrynin was promoted from candidate member to full member of the Central Committee of the Communist Party of the Soviet Union. Although the individual members are not so powerful as members of the smaller 16-member Politburo, the Central Committee is the one body in the CPSU organization that makes or breaks the General Secretary (that is, the dictator) of the Soviet Union. It was the Central Committee that ousted Khrushchev as General Secretary and elected Brezhnev in his place. It is highly unusual for a nonresident—especially one who has been away from the infighting and power politics of the Central Committee and the Politburo for more than 13 years—to be elected a full member of the Central Committee. Certainly he became the first Washington-based full member. Was this unprecedented promotion a reward for having "suckered" Henry Kissinger? Or was it—in the language of the KGB—a reward for having "coopted" him?

To delve further into the question of whether the American people are being suckered into surrender by Kissinger, or whether he himself is at least partially being suckered by the Kremlin, it will help to consider his most significant appointment. The nomination of James R. Schlesinger to be U.S. Secretary of Defense was one of the strangest in our nearly 200 years of independence. Without the unique diversion of Watergate to distract President Nixon, not even Henry Kissinger's unprecedented power could have accomplished this—because Schlesinger was a career-long protege of Daniel Ellsberg, all the way from Harvard to RAND.

If Richard Nixon really had a list of enemies, Daniel Ellsberg would surely have topped the list. Ellsberg was the spectral threat to national security conjured up by Kissinger to panic Nixon into setting up the "plumbers" operation. According to a *New York Times* report, Kissinger had convinced the President that Ellsberg might have been a Soviet agent and that he was capable of passing to the Kremlin specifics of the closely held nuclear targeting schedule: the highly classified Single Integrated Operations Plan (SIOP), to which Ellsberg had access when he worked for Secretary McNamara in the Kennedy-Johnson administrations. The leverage Kissinger was exerting on Nixon to reinforce his fears was the report from an FBI counterintelligence agent (said to operate in the Soviet Embassy) that the Soviets had received a full set of *The Pentagon Papers* long before their publication in the *New York Times*. Although Ellsberg was not identified as the source of the Kremlin's acquisition of *The Pentagon Papers*, Kissinger professed to be in fear of leaks through him, and Nixon was convinced. The CIA was prohibited by law from engaging in domestic intelligence operations, and J. Edgar Hoover would not permit the participation of the FBI. Hence the President felt the need to set up a new organization to plug the feared national-security leaks, and hence, the creation of the "plumbers," the source of Nixon's most excruciating troubles.

Except for Daniel Ellsberg's sponsorship and influence, James R. Schlesinger would probably still be teaching economics at the University of Virginia, a job he acquired a year after receiving his Ph.D. at Harvard in 1956. In 1962 he obtained a grant from the Social Science Research Council to finance some research he was doing on an article entitled "Quantitative Analysis and National Security." Pedantic in style, its substance, if any, appeared to be a gentle criticism of the then-Secretary of Defense Robert McNamara's "cost-effectiveness" formula. Schlesinger failed to understand that it was merely a pseudosophisticated technique for producing an impressive-appearing computerized rationalization for any particular step in McNamara's clandestine unilateral strategic disarmament of the United States. Instead of penetrating to this reality, Professor Schlesinger based his criticism on the theory that McNamara's process might lack accuracy because of the "incommensurability of objectives" involved.

Even in its finished form, and bolstered by repetition of that polysyllabic phrase, the article was definitely unexciting—but it must have been much worse before Daniel Ellsberg helped Schlesinger rewrite it. Either that, or Schlesinger's footnote of fulsome acknowledgement accorded incommensurate credit to his mentor. The article, Schlesinger asserted, "has been immeasurably improved by the comments of Daniel Ellsberg." So much so, apparently, that Dr. Kissinger included this article in a collection he published in 1965 entitled *Problems of National Strategy*.[5]

It was through Daniel Ellsberg's employment at the RAND "think tank" that he was able to obtain access to the Top Secret *Pentagon Papers*, steal them from the corporation's custody, clandestinely copy them, and in 1971 fence them to the *New York Times* and the

Washington Post. Years earlier, however, his influence at RAND had been sufficient to secure employment there for his protege, James R. Schlesinger. Overnight, about 1965, the pedestrian pedant somehow became an expert on grand strategy. By 1969 he had become the director of strategic studies at RAND; perhaps the competition there was not too keen then. Its prestige had been eroding ever since the departure of Herman Kahn; and by 1967 it had become somewhat of a haven for the anti-Vietnam War cliques who did not understand Kissinger's policy to postpone the surrender to Vietnam communism in order to cover the pending clandestine strategic surrender to Soviet communism.

The Ellsberg establishment of the RAND connection for Schlesinger was an essential precondition to setting the stage for Schlesinger's meteoric rise in the Nixon Administration under the aegis of a far more powerful mentor. Henry Kissinger soon fashioned Schlesinger into an effective instrument for attaining several objectives vital to Kissinger's buildup of unprecedented personal power.

Schlesinger's track record of actual accomplishments is minimal because he never really *did* anything—other than prepare papers—until he was appointed chairman of the U.S. Atomic Energy Commission in 1971. He went from his Harvard Ph.D. in 1956 to the economics department of the University of Virginia, wrote papers there for more than eight years (including a book, *The Political Economy of National Security*, that failed to generate even a ripple); then he prepared papers at RAND; and in 1969 he went into the Nixon Administration's Office of Management and Budget, where he continued to prepare papers until he was appointed to the Atomic Energy Commission, his first job involving either policy-making or important administration.

One of the reasons Kissinger is so much of a threat to the survival of the United States is that he exploits the vulnerabilities of the democratic system to build superdictatorial power for himself. His personal power is quite literally beyond that of the Soviet dictators because, once he has overcome the checks, balances, and safeguards of our constitutional system, there are no restraints left to come into play.

In the Soviet Union there are pragmatic, extralegal restraints that have developed to ensure the survival of the dictatorship. Strangely, the basic ingredient that makes their system of restraints effective is loyalty—not loyalty to Mother Russia, or to the U.S.S.R., or to the Russian People, but loyalty to the Communist Party of the Soviet Union, a sort of indivisible spirit, a God-substitute for members of the CPSU. Westerners cannot understand it and usually underrate it. During Stalin's "Great Terror," when hundreds of thousands of lifelong-loyal party members went to their deaths, they nevertheless did not criticize the party for ordering their own executions. If the party ordered it, it must be right; such was their loyalty to the death.

This is why no CPSU dictator could get away with appointing to key positions in the Soviet Government men who were not proven by their records to be both loyal to the party and capable of serving it effectively. Being realists and career-long practitioners of power politics in internal organization, all Party officials, and even mere rank-and-file members, would expect the General Secretary to appoint to all key positions men who had demonstrated loyalty to the party.

Thus neither Khrushchev, at the pinnacle of his power, nor Brezhnev, after his total consolidation of power, could have gotten away with the appointments accomplished by Kissinger: appointments he carried out without even a ripple of congressional interest or public concern. Neither Khrushchev nor Brezhnev could have promoted an inexperienced Army Colonel (such as Alexander Haig) to the rank of four-star general, and then appointed him Vice Chief of Staff of the Army over the heads of scores of far more experienced and proven general officers. Neither of the Soviet dictators could have gotten away with appointing the likes of a James R. Schlesinger, in a matter of a few months, to be successively, Director of the Atomic Energy Commission, Director of the Central Intelligence Agency, and then Secretary of Defense—all agencies vital to U.S. survival.

Why not? Because Schlesinger is not only not qualified to be U.S. Secretary of Defense, but his record demonstrates that he is supremely unqualified to hold and attempt to exercise power and responsibilities of that magnitude. The conclusive proof is in the national-suicidal character of the "new nuclear strategy" he proclaimed in late 1973 and early 1974.

The great break for pipe-smoking Ph.D. Schlesinger came in 1970 while he was working in the Nixon Administration's Office of Management and Budget. Kissinger selected him to do the paperwork, laying out the plans for a major reorganization of the entire U.S. intelligence community. The project, in Kissinger's favorite terms, was identified as a "restructuring study." The intelligence conglomerate subjected to this reorganization encompassed some 200,000 employees, a budget of $6 billion a year, and all the major agencies: the CIA, DIA, NSA, I&R (State Department), AEC (detection and monitoring functions), and (except internally) the FBI. The prime purpose of this "study" was to come up with new organization charts that would bring every line of authority, every flow-of-information line, through Henry Kissinger. It did. It added two key review panels: the National Security Council Intelligence Committee, with plenary power to make all assignments to the intelligence community and to "review" the results, and the Net Assessment Group, with monopoly power to make specific comparisons of power balances throughout the world; and both of the new panels are chaired by Kissinger.

We have already documented the strategy and tactics employed by Kissinger to make him the intelligence czar of the United States. Schlesinger proved such a useful tool in drafting and preparing the plans for "restructuring" our intelligence community that he was rewarded by appointment as chairman of the Atomic Energy Commission. Having learned that the quick way to power and fame was as author of "drastic reorganizations," he instituted one immediately upon assuming the AEC chairmanship. To gather authority unto himself, he instituted a cutback in the high-level staff of AEC. Schlesinger's spectacular actions impressed even *U.S. News & World Report*. Here is an excerpt published on April 2, 1973, after he moved from AEC to CIA:

> *Changing Atomic Policy.* Mr. Schlesinger ordered a drastic reorganization of the AEC, resulting in a cutback of the high level staff. But that wasn't his only impact on the agency.
>
> One new job he created was that of general manager for environmental and safety affairs. And he is credited with making the AEC more conscious of the interests of conservationists in its planning for new uses of atomic energy.

The headline "Changing Atomic Policy" contains the germ of the terrible truth of the changes Schlesinger wrought in AEC. When he took over, the Agency was dedicated primarily to developing atomic energy for both peacetime and military use, and to encouraging and assisting private industry and science to make more and more of this greatest of all energy sources available to support the prosperity, power, and survival of the United States. Within little more than a year Schlesinger was able to distort AEC's mandate and mission from creative development and production of atomic power to a bureaucratic regulatory agency, restricting the productive efforts of private industry and giving the highest priority to accommodating the hallucinations of the politically powerful ecology freaks. This opinion is shared not only by those who worked at AEC in formerly creative activities, but by columnists in the *Washington Post*:

> In 16 months as chairman of the Atomic Energy Commission he reorganized that agency and transformed it from a promoter of nuclear power to a regulator of the industry. And then, before he left, he persuaded President Nixon to pick another maverick, Dixy Lee Ray, as the new AEC chairman.[6]

To accomplish that changeover in the shortest possible time, Dr. Schlesinger took a leaf out of the Kissinger management manual, consolidated all power and authority in himself, and froze out all nonsubservient employees from policy positions. The prime result was that whereas, under former Chairman Glenn Seaborg, a nuclear power plant could be licensed in five years, Schlesinger stretched this out so that it takes up to 11 years to grope through the bureaucratic obstacle course to attain a license.

This does not merely cause frustration for the applicants seeking to build new plants needed to ease our energy crisis; it threatens potential disaster for important sectors of U.S. industry, business, and even private homes. Emergency and conservation methods might well bridge a five-year gap, but can never cover an 11-year abyss. There are now some 200 plants under consideration, which means that industry has tied up a commitment of $100 billion—and, thanks to the Schlesinger stretch-out, the time span of years before they can get into production has been doubled.

Even worse than the impounding of money because of this extravaganza of bureaucratic delay is the lockup of brainpower it requires. To license a nuclear power plant, there must be an initial preliminary study that takes two years and produces, literally, two tons of paperwork. This means that our most brilliant, most experienced, and most extensively and expensively trained scientists and technologists are condemned to devote their capabilities and their irreplaceable time to useless, noncreative "busy work."

All this came about during the Schlesinger tenure. Most of it he brought about in the administrative process. Some of it resulted from legislation enacted by Congress, but this does not exculpate him because he not only did not oppose the legislation effectively, he did not oppose it at all. He stood by and gave an open field to a coalition of antinuclear environmentalists and slick "public interest" lawyers who specialize in throwing legalistic roadblocks in the path of U.S. progress, and whose financing is obscure. The AEC scientists whom Schlesinger permitted to go to Capitol Hill to testify went unprepared to expose the artificial nature of the skillfully exaggerated "threats" to the environment paraded against them.

When Dr. Schlesinger was abruptly lifted by Dr. Kissinger from AEC and perched on the pinnacle of U.S. intelligence organizations, the two Harvard Ph.D.s jointly selected a superficially inexplicable successor as AEC chairman. Upon notification of her nomination, her immediate reaction seemed to be: Who, me? Dixy Lee Ray had been a commission member only six months, her only experience with atomic energy matters. By profession she was a marine biologist, on leave from the University of Washington. She is accompanied to her office each day by Jacques and Ghillie, her miniature poodle and Scottish deerhound.

When asked her opinion of the significance of her appointment as AEC chairman, her answer was probably an intuitive understanding of the motivation of the two powerful Ph.D.s who had chosen her. She regarded it, she said, as "one way of saying that the bomb's not so important—that there are other uses of nuclear energy more important than the military today."[7]

Although undoubtedly selected as the one least likely to bring the Atomic Energy Commission back to its prime national purpose, Dixy Lee Ray proved to be a surprise and disappointment to her sponsors. They thought she was "just a woman" who could be controlled. Instead, it turned out that the energy crisis brought home to her the vital importance to the United States of speeding (instead of uselessly delaying) the advent of plentiful atomic power. She was trying, as of 1973 and early 1974, to run the AEC her way—which was (to use one of Schlesinger's favorite words) immeasurably better than his way. If she succeeds in freeing our top atomic scientists from the freeze of endless paperwork, they can compress the time required for effective and safe breeder reactors and bring us to the era of fusion power, perhaps via laser developments. Unfortunately, even after moving from CIA to the Pentagon, Schlesinger still kept his lines open to agents he had planted in AEC in 1971 and 1972, and he even adds a new one from time to time.

What Schlesinger did to AEC, however, was just an elementary training exercise in comparison with his accomplishments at CIA. Any understanding Chief Executive would have declared it a disaster area after a couple of months. As early as April 1973, Keyes Beech, formerly with the *New York Times* and long blessed with inside-leak sources almost equal to those of Joseph and Stewart Alsop, gave this report:

> Morale of the U.S. Central Intelligence Agency, once the highest of any government agency operating in Southeast Asia, has sunk to an all-time low under the impact of a drastic reorganization under the new director, James R. Schlesinger. . . .
>
> According to reports . . . more than 1,000 employees have been lopped off the CIA payroll since Schlesinger took charge, February 2. One division received an 18 percent across-the-board cut.
>
> "The Halls of Langley (the sprawling CIA headquarters in Virginia) are running red with blood," said one recently returned CIA man. "For the most part it's the World War II types who are getting the ax—men in their late 40s and 50s. But some younger men in their 30s are also losing their jobs." . . .
>
> Some senior CIA officials are returning to Washington without knowing what their next job will be—if they have one. Some are slated for retire-

ment, even though they don't know it. Some CIA men are threatening to resign after more than two decades in the service.

The choice may not be theirs. . . .[8]

Or, as reported by *Newsweek:*

In his first weeks on the job, the deceptively tweedy new master spy relieved three of the agency's top deputies—and sent waves of anxiety rippling down through the ranks. "They have always moved bodies around here," said one CIA insider, "but never have so many been moved so fast—or with so much clatter."

. . . Schlesinger has no experience in the spying trade. But he won high marks as an administrator during a 17-month stint as chairman of the Atomic Energy Commission.

Significantly, he enjoys the unreserved backing of White House Chief of Staff H. R. Haldeman.[9]

Or, as reported by *U.S. News & World Report:*

The supersecret U.S. intelligence apparatus is being rocked from within on a scale never before so visible to the public. . . .

Many CIA professionals in top and middle ranks are unhappy about the reorganization. A comment typical of this viewpoint:

"What is happening is that those who seek to present intelligence as it is, rather than as the situation is seen by those supporting specific policies, are being plucked out."

Aides of Mr. Schlesinger deny that he has any intention of "politicizing" the agency. . . .

Within the Nixon Administration, dissatisfaction with the CIA has centered particularly in the National Security Council staff, which is under the direction of Mr. Kissinger. . . .

One revision put into effect by Mr. Schlesinger has to do with preparation of CIA reports requested by the President and other high officials.

Condensed Intelligence. Previously, such requests were answered with detailed studies—20, 30, or even 50 pages long. Now, the reports run no longer than three double-spaced pages. A CIA official explained:

"Instructions from Schlesinger are to answer the questions asked—and no more. No background. No historical discussion. . . ."[10]

How's that for arrogance? A new CIA director, with absolutely no experience in intelligence work before his appointment, in effect says to the President and other high officials, "take our word for it. Don't expect any reasons, or any facts, or any background. We know you are a busy man, so we don't want to confuse you with any facts—especially not with any facts which might lead you to disagree with our conclusions or assumptions."

The above excerpts are from articles dealing with the situation a few weeks after Schlesinger took over CIA. When he left, a top CIA official is reported to have quipped, "There wasn't a wet eye in the entire agency." *U.S. News & World Report* opened its article with this lead:

The Central Intelligence Agency again has one of its own in command—and insiders say its recent "air of uncertainty, gloom and sagging morale" is already disappearing. . . .

Mr. Colby [William E. Colby, new Director of CIA] . . . faces an internal morale problem brought on by a 10 percent cutback in personnel under former Director James R. Schlesinger, who was recently named Secretary of Defense.[11]

What did James R. Schlesinger accomplish during his short term as director of CIA? Well, for one thing, he either discharged or brought about the premature retirement of more than 1,000 experienced employees—primarily those who did not believe in the Kissinger version of detente, although this was expressed more euphemistically. Thus, as described in the *Washington Post:*

He complained to Congress that the CIA is overloaded with overage spies recruited during the Cold War who have trouble adjusting to today's more peaceful world.[12]

A second Schlesinger accomplishment was, of course, a cut in the amount of intelligence gathered and evaluated, proportionate to the 10-to-15 percent cut he imposed on personnel. This was strictly in accord with Kissinger's plan for across-the-board cuts in all intelligence agencies, especially the Defense Intelligence Agency. The smaller the volume of intelligence acquired, the less there is to suppress. But what about the accuracy of intelligence—especially that relating to national survival—after the drastic Schlesinger reorganization?

There was plenty of room for improvement. In 1970 Defense Secretary Melvin Laird testified that U.S. security was being endangered by the rapid buildup of the Soviet nuclear arsenal, which had "moved much more rapidly" than anticipated

in the intelligence projections of the past five years, including the estimates for 1970, in fact.

Intelligence projections for the numbers of both intercontinental ballistic missiles (ICBMs) and submarine-launched ballistic missiles have been revised upward in each of the past five years, as additional information on Soviet deployments became available. . . . They have now gone ahead of us in numbers of land-based missiles, as you know. In actual numbers—and they have gone ahead of us in total megatonnage that can be delivered.[13]

So, the U.S. intelligence estimates had underestimated the Soviet strategic weapons buildup in the years 1966, 1967, 1968, 1969, and 1970. The same underestimates obtained in 1971, 1972, and 1973 (as confirmed in the Nixon-Kissinger *State of the World Reports* for those years).

With an eight-year record like that to improve on, it would take a rather stupid administrator, given the plenary powers accorded to

Schlesinger, to fail to increase accuracy. What happened?

Well, Secretary Schlesinger testified before the Senate Armed Services Committee on February 5, 1974, that the "depth and breadth" of recent Soviet missile development has surprised the administration. He added that these surprising Soviet programs have moved forward despite encouraging efforts to negotiate an era of detente.[14]

How well did the Schlesinger-reorganized intelligence community and its czar, Henry Kissinger, predict the Soviet-inspired Arab attack on Israel on October 6, 1973? Here is a *New York Times* report, quoting Secretary Kissinger verbatim from his press conference on October 25, 1973:

> The intelligence at our disposal and all the intelligence given to us by foreign countries suggested that there was no possibility of the outbreak of a war.[15]

According to the *New York Times* article, the Kissinger assertion contrasts with the statement of "a Soviet diplomat" who contended that

> Moscow had repeatedly warned Washington from June until September that war was imminent in the Middle East.
>
> American officials acknowledged that Moscow had given such warnings to President Nixon and his adviser on national security, Henry A. Kissinger. . . .
>
> And the Soviet Ambassador, Anatoly F. Dobrynin, later made the same point to Mr. Kissinger on several occasions.

The sad part of this is that, as early as December 1972, nearly a year before the Arab attack, U.S. intelligence did pick up comprehensive information on the Soviet deployment of many types of offensive weapons to the Arab states, including the SAM-6s without which the Arab attack could not have achieved even initial successes. But with the Kissinger detente in effect, who would believe that the residuals of the Cold War could be so momentous? As the reports noted, Schlesinger had fired as many as possible of those in the intelligence community who had been "recruited during the Cold War (and) who have trouble adjusting to today's more peaceful world." The *in terrorem* effect of this purge has rendered U.S. intelligence useless as to advance warning of a Soviet threat.

Another point of the proof of Schlesinger's performance in reorganizing the CIA and the intelligence community is that they made no prediction at all of the Arabs' employment of the "oil weapon." This was despite the established fact that the Soviets had for months been urging the Arabs to use that weapon. Even news reporters knew of this, so couldn't we expect our $6-billion-a-year intelligence community to warn us? Here is an excerpt from a *Los Angeles Times* dispatch datelined Moscow, December 24, 1973, which shows how open had been the Soviet efforts to pressure the Arabs into using the "oil weapon" against us:

> The record is clear that the Russians have long encouraged all Arab states to use their "oil weapon" against the capitalist powers.
>
> In September, a little more than a month before the latest Middle East war started, *Pravda*, the Communist Party daily, noted that oil was increasing as an economic factor because of the "power crisis" in the capitalist world.
>
> "As a result, additional possibilities emerge for the Arab countries to use this important lever for political purposes to solve such international problems as the Middle East crisis," the paper said.
>
> During the actual fighting in October, Moscow radio reiterated in the Arabic language a message it had been transmitting for many weeks: "The Arabs are capable of taking effective retaliatory measures against the forces hostile to them even if they are situated thousands of miles away."

Schlesinger's latest charade, written, directed, and produced by Kissinger, first surfaced in conservative journals, but since then has been played up far more sensationally by the liberal media. Usually headlined as "Schlesinger vs. Kissinger," with pictures in juxtaposition, the ploy is phony.

The U.S. Constitution provides a defense in depth against such disasters to the national security as the appointment and assumption of power of a Schlesinger to the office of Secretary of Defense. Three separate safeguards are set up to operate successively: first, the appointive power of the President is normally a safeguard against a nonqualified or dangerous nominee; second, the Senate has the power to advise and consent, or, more specifically, to advise and not consent; and third, the free press and other media have a concomitant duty to inform the public.

If any one of the three safeguards had functioned in a normal manner, the nation would have been spared the disaster of such a bizarre appointment. But the President was enmeshed in Watergate, and the one member of his staff obliged to warn him, the Assistant to the President for National Security Affairs, Kissinger, was the puppetmaster moving Schlesinger into the job. Neither the Congress nor the press dug out the man's total lack of qualifications, nor did they mention the easily ascertainable fact that, in the only two jobs of his entire career that involved any responsibility for administration or policy-making, Schlesinger had atomized the agencies' morale and blasted them into disaster areas in terms of their capability to perform vital functions.

So far as Kissinger was concerned, however, Schlesinger had demonstrated superlative ability to accomplish the sort of things that were vital in destroying the existing order in the Free World, so that it could be replaced by the planned new world order. Anyone who could, in a few months, destroy the value to the United States of its $6-billion-per-year investment in providing warning against Soviet aggression through timely and accurate intelligence, should be qualified to destroy the effectiveness of the entire $80-billion-per-year defense establishment.

Because the primary mission of the U.S. Department of Defense is to protect the nation against the greatest of all threats—the Soviet strategic nuclear threat—Dr. Schlesinger has devoted most of his activity to the strategic area. His three-pronged degradation program strives first to deceive the American people as to the seriousness of the Soviet threat by at once minimizing its magnitude and giving false assurance that it cannot mature for some eight to 10 years in the vague future. Second, he exaggerates U.S. strategic weapons capabilities, and minimizes the need for any additional strategic power. Third (and he has demonstrated a devious mastery of this technique), he has initiated a Kissingerlike program for completely confusing the American people as to U.S. grand strategy and nuclear targeting by means of a razzle-dazzle amalgam of highly publicized "new strategies."

Apparently much impressed with the sensational successes of Kissinger's multiplicity of charades, Schlesinger has attempted to stage one of his own design. Fortunately for our chances of survival, Schlesinger is no more than a pallid synthetic version of Kissinger. His strategic theories cry out so loudly for commonsense analysis that they may arouse some public or congressional interest, which should logically then shift to focus on the Kissinger grand strategy.

The good news about Schlesinger is that he has undermined the nuclear strategy of Mutual Assured Destruction. MAD is the theoretical basis for Kissinger's Moscow Summit SALT I ABM Treaty, which amended our Constitution to prohibit any active defense of our population or homeland against enemy missile attack. It provides, in Kissinger's words, a "free ride" for Russian and Red Chinese missiles against 210 million helpless Americans.

But the MAD Treaty of Moscow did provide one protection against a decision by those men in the Kremlin to liquidate us hostages in the greatest mass-murder in the history of man. If they launched a nuclear missile attack against us, we could launch our surviving missiles against the Soviet population in retaliation, which is also supposed to be vulnerable to liquidation. Thus, the MAD Treaty is at least theoretically supposed to provide an *exchange* of hostages. Actually, for a number of reasons we have examined earlier in this book, it does not do so. Chief among these is that, whereas we do not have any realistic passive or civil defense against missile attack, the Soviets have a massive and extensive system for passive defense, so well built and organized that they claim (and our objective experts agree) that it would save all but 6 percent of their people in an all-out U.S. attack against them with an undamaged strategic force. The corresponding figure for us is, in the most optimistic view, 60 percent. That is, it would take you and nine additional members of your family to constitute an "exchange" for one resident of the U.S.S.R.

Theoretically, the prospect of losing even 6 percent of their highly disciplined population might deter a missile launch order against us by the Moscow Politburo. But this deterrence, like all other instances of attempted nuclear deterrence, depends on two essential but independent factors: the existence of sufficient destructive capability and the credibility of its use.

So, here is the bad news about Schlesinger's "new" strategy. He has replaced the MAD strategy of Mutual Assured Destruction with the suicidally insane policy of Unilateral Assured Destruction—and we are the ones whose destruction is assured. That is, he has assured the Soviet leaders in advance that, even if they launch a missile attack against us, we would not effectively retaliate against the Soviet population. This he has done by a combination of (1) degrading the physical element—the destruction capability—by changing the targeting of an undisclosed percentage of our Minuteman missiles away from Soviet cities; and (2) destroying the psychological element—the credibility of the use of our destruction capability against the Soviet population—by simply repeating that it is not credible that we would do such a thing.

Dr. Schlesinger denies that he has done these things. It must be admitted that, by shifting his theories and his explanations every five to 15 days, he has so confused the picture that it is difficult to demonstrate anything except that he has proved himself wildly irresponsible and incredibly incompetent to be entrusted with the awesome duties of U.S. Secretary of Defense. He has yet to learn that, once the Secretary of Defense has made a solemn and presumably considered statement that it is incredible that we would launch our missiles against Soviet cities, a mere self-contradiction cannot erase the effect of the original statement. Nor can he, as Secretary of Defense, realistically expect to get away with describing his "new" strategy one day as the greatest change in U.S. strategy in a decade, and then describing it as no big thing. But he has been trying to do this.

On January 5, 1974, Dr. Schlesinger announced that the United States was putting into effect a "change of targeting practices." He gave it so little buildup at that time that National Review observed that the possible strategic shift might have "a significance much more profound than Secretary Schlesinger's rather offhand remark suggested to the unversed citizen."[16]

This initial version of the "new" Schlesinger strategy is of vital importance in getting the full picture. Here is a summary of the interview in which the strategy was first enunciated, as put on the national wires by the *Washington Post* on January 4, 1974:

> Since the early 1960s, American nuclear strategy has been based on what is called "Mutual Assured Destruction," euphemistically known as MAD. It entails having the ability to destroy enough Soviet cities and industrial centers, even after absorbing a surprise first strike, to deter any such attack.
>
> But Schlesinger, and others now in office, maintain that MAD was never really a strategy, but rather a way to measure the size of the U.S. arsenal and how much damage it could do.
>
> In his view, if the Soviet missile force—through eventual addition of large and accurate multiple warheads to their current missiles—gets big enough to knock out a portion of the U.S. nuclear arsenal in less than an all-out attack, it is no good just to have the ability to hit Soviet cities in return. The United States would know that American cities would be destroyed in a second volley.
>
> *Schlesinger believes that such a U.S. strategy is not credible in Russian eyes, nor even for that matter to most West European leaders.*
>
> Unless the multiple-warhead race is curbed through negotiations, Schlesinger wants the United States to have the ability to respond at least "selectively" against Russian military targets—presumably such things as certain large missile silos, underground control centers, command posts, missile storage depots and field headquarters—in a tit-for-tat basis short of holocaust.

At this point Dr. Schlesinger apparently began to consider that he had hold of something big—that he had a solution to the all-too-obvious loss of credibility of the U.S. strategic deterrent since the SALT I Agreements, and that this would endear him to Kissinger, who was becoming somewhat embarrassed as it became impossible to keep suppressed the disastrous results of the Moscow Agreements Kissinger sold the nation. Although Schlesinger referred to the "eventual" addition of MIRVs to the existing Soviet missile force, and although he himself had asserted on November 30, 1973, that there was no immediate threat to the survivability of U.S. weapons against a Soviet surprise attack,[17] in the real world "eventual" had become now, and the "no" could no longer truthfully modify "immediate" in describing the Soviet strategic threat. The large and accurate multiple warheads he had referred to as an "eventual" addition to the Soviet force could be deployed as early as 1975 (in a crash program), or by 1976 at a normal pace of deployment.[18] By 1976, therefore, according to the estimates of scientists, nuclear strategists, and former Defense Secretary Melvin Laird, the Soviets would be able to knock out virtually the entire U.S. Minuteman force with about 400 to 425 of their very heavy missiles (SS-9s, SS-18s, and the upgraded SS-17s and SS-19s). Thus, they could take out 95 percent of our Minuteman missiles, and retain more than 1,200 of their other ICBMs to hold hostage our cities, population, and industry.

This point concerning the vulnerability of the Minuteman force bears directly on whether the United States can survive, and for how long, and whether in 1976 or 1977 we could resist a Soviet ultimatum for surrender. After Henry Kissinger had successively taken three inconsistent positions as to the vulnerability of our Minuteman force, he has finally recognized that, if he or the administration admits that his SALT I Agreements and related defense policies have rendered our Minutemen vulnerable, Kissinger himself will be vulnerable. It would then become impossible to suppress any longer the tragic fact that Kissinger has destroyed the effectiveness and credibility of our strategic deterrent. So, finally, after first admitting that the Soviet SS-9s were a threat to Minutemen, and later that vulnerability "could occur" but is "not likely until the late '70s and early '80s,"[19] Kissinger finally took an unequivocal (but totally divorced from reality) position:

Minuteman is not vulnerable today, and it will not be for the remainder of the decade.[20]

Wow! And that so-positive answer was not handed out extemporaneously. It was a written response by Kissinger to a question submitted by Senator Carl T. Curtis for the record, so there had been plenty of time for research and consideration. Thus, the master of sophisticated verbal sleight-of-hand was caught in a positive statement of great moment that could be demonstrated, with computer-like exactitude, to be wrong, false, and materially misleading. Already it is giving him trouble.

In an interview reported on February 1, 1974, Dr. Fred Iklé, Kissinger's own nominee as director of the U.S. Arms Control and Disarmament Agency, declared that land-based missiles of both superpowers would become "increasingly vulnerable" to attack from the other side as missile accuracy improves. Furthermore, he added:

The solution to this problem does not lie in prolonging the life of these dangerous forces through one expedient or another. Rather, it lies in getting rid of such obsolete weapons through negotiations and in our own force planning.

Iklé told the reporter he was speaking for himself in this controversial matter, but an unnamed State Department official commented that

Dr. Iklé "does not have a suicidal bent." By this he implied, as the reporter explained in a masterpiece of understatement, that Iklé's views "may be shared at least by his boss, Secretary of State Henry Kissinger." Indeed, Kissinger's compulsion toward swift and vindictive retribution against a subordinate's speaking out of line is so well known that the assumption spread throughout all the SALT-negotiating arenas in the bureaucracy that Kissinger was conceding the vulnerability of Minuteman and sending up a trial balloon for a proposal to the Soviets in the SALT II negotiations that both sides phase out all land-based missiles and keep only submarine-based weapons. This would mean a proposal that the Soviets throw away four times as much missile throw-weight capability as we would, and all their present first-strike counterforce capability, plus their plans for controlling the world within any near timeframe. It is easy to imagine Anatoly Dobrynin storming into Kissinger's State Department sanctum with a demand for immediate and express disavowal. At any rate, he got it. We know this because of an intriguing leak reported in Newsweek under an appropriate heading:

Kissinger Cracks The Whip

Secretary of State Henry Kissinger has had to disown his own government's arms-control chief, Dr. Fred Iklé. In a recent interview, the director of the Arms Control and Disarmament Agency proposed that the U.S. and Russia phase out all land-based missiles and keep only their submarine-based weapons. Kissinger cabled his negotiators at the Geneva SALT II nuclear disarmament talks to say that Iklé's comment did "not represent official established U.S. policy."[21]

In contrast with Dr. James Schlesinger's January 4, 1974, statement about his "new" strategy, which was low key but branded "city-bashing" as no longer a credible strategy for the United States, his speech on January 10, 1974, to the Overseas Writers Club in Washington was played up by both wire services as signaling a development of major importance. UPI reported that Schlesinger said his new targeting policy was probably the greatest change in U.S. nuclear missile strategy in a decade. The Associated Press characterized it as "a major strategy change." Both wire services indicated that Schlesinger had not specified either the types or numbers of the new targets, or how many U.S. missiles were involved in the change. UPI sought amplification later from unnamed Defense Department officials, and was told that the new targets "include such points as airfields, dams, oil fields, and railheads—targets that would damage a nation's ability to make war but not kill millions of civilians." Then UPI reported the statements that so disturbed Kissinger that he considered bringing

Paul Nitze back from the SALT II negotiations for appointment as Assistant Secretary of Defense to ride herd on the talkative Schlesinger:

> Schlesinger, referring to the former strategy of massive retaliation as "bashing cities of the other side," said, "It is our intention that this not be the only option *or the principal option.*"
>
> Schlesinger painted a picture of a confrontation in which the *Soviets might decide to knock out only the 1,000 Minuteman missiles* dotted over the American plains and not touch population centers.
>
> Under the massive retaliation strategy, the only option an American President had was "concentrating on their cities which carries in its wake the inevitable destruction of our cities by Russia's remaining missiles.
>
> "*That is not an option likely to be* implemented," Schlesinger said.[22]

By pontificating his synthetic strategic theories before the Overseas Writers Club, Dr. Schlesinger was not only stealing Kissinger's thunder but imperiling the entire structure of the Kissinger revolution in the grand strategy of the United States, as well as exposing the most powerful official in Washington as some kind of a nut or something. In his few ill-chosen words, Schlesinger (assuming he was speaking after due consideration—and it would be utterly irresponsible for a Secretary of Defense to speak otherwise) destroyed both the essential elements of effective deterrence: that is, (1) sufficient destructive power in-being—by his assertion that the Soviets might knock it out so that it would no longer be in-being when we need it, and (2) the credible will to employ this power—by his one-two knockout punch at credibility through asserting (a) that "bashing cities of the other side" has been abandoned as our "principal option," and (b) in any event, "is not an option likely to be implemented."

Even though it may be tedious to keep talking about these technical abstractions, it is essential to understand that Kissinger's machinations and Schlesinger's antics have degraded the power and killed the credibility of the U.S. strategic deterrent. On the power and credibility of that deterrent depend all our lives, our freedom, our possessions, and Western civilization. If we lose that deterrent—or, rather, if we are defrauded of it by a brilliant and hypnotic megalomaniac and his strange puppets, the very best sort of life we can look forward to is in a nation of Gulag Archipelagoes.

From Schlesinger's speech to the Overseas Writers luncheon, the Associated Press picked up one intriguing conundrum and a stunning contradiction of a major Kissinger-Nixon position. Schlesinger disclosed, the AP reported, that the new strategy had been put into effect, and he explained:

> "We have targeting options which are more selective and which do

not necessarily involve major mass destruction on the other side. The purpose of this is . . . to maintain the capability to deter any desire on the part of an opponent to inflict major damage on the United States or its allies."

Putting it more simply, another Pentagon official said, "we have to be able to deter them on a tit-for-tat basis."

Here, however, is the blockbuster that is at the heart of the "great debate" triggered by Schlesinger's enunciation and renunciations of his "new" strategy:

Schlesinger told the luncheon *the change in targeting does not require an increase in the number or size of U.S. missile warheads.* . . .
With the present accuracy of U.S. warheads, missilemen will reportedly concentrate extra firepower on selected targets to make sure they would be knocked out, even though dug in below ground and shielded by reinforced concrete.[23]

Before considering some of the insoluble confusions of that great debate, we need two or three additional Schlesingerisms. In sharp contrast to the "major strategy change" and the "greatest change in U.S. nuclear strategy in a decade" with which he regaled the press and writers on January 10, consider how he reversed his field in a letter to Senator Edward W. Brooke:

The targeting decisions which you and I discussed are to ensure selectivity and flexibility of *relatively* small-scale options across the spectrum of possible targets in order to enhance deterrence.[24]

This is a rather emphatic statement, in defense pseudointellectual jargon, that the change in targeting strategy is no big thing. His letter to Senator Brooke went on, however, to add that the United States remains opposed to seeking a "disarming first-strike capability" while continuing to rely upon a strategy of seeking to deter nuclear attack. Within that framework, Schlesinger said, "assured destruction" remains an option in our deterrent doctrine, but this has not been our sole option, nor have we in practice targeted only cities.

In his testimony before the Senate Armed Forces Committee from time to time between February 5 and 11, 1974, however, Dr. Schlesinger departed from minimizing the importance of his new strategy, and at times sounded as if he were claiming that, by inventing it, he had singlehandedly snatched the nation from a nuclear inferno. As reported in a Knight Newspapers dispatch:

Tough-talking, pipe-smoking James Schlesinger, 45, Nixon's new Defense Secretary, unfolded a new strategy against the Russians. Its key points:
- Bigger, more accurate U.S. nuclear bombs.
- Retargeting of some U.S. nuclear missiles against Soviet military targets, rather than cities.

Essentially, Schlesinger was making the case that the U.S. should develop an ability to fight "limited" nuclear wars—what some have called "clean" or "surgical" wars. . . .

Borrowing a phrase from the late President Kennedy, *he declared that previous U.S. policy left the government with a choice only between "suicide or surrender."*

What he meant is that the U.S. has permitted no middle road between conventional war and an all-out nuclear war.

If the Russians were to start a war by picking off just a few military targets in Europe, for example, the U.S. would have to respond with all-out attacks on Russian cities, killing millions, he said.

Schlesinger made the point that U.S. cities are in danger, too.

"At the present time," he said with considerable emotion, "the Soviet Union can target any city in the U.S. it desires . . ."[25]

Finally, here is one more statement by Dr. Schlesinger, as reported by *U.S. News & World Report:*

It is inevitable, or virtually inevitable, that the employment by one side of its forces against the cities of the other side in an all-out strike will immediately bring a counterstrike against its own cities. Consequently, the range of circumstances in which an all-out strike against an opponent's cities can be counted has narrowed considerably, *and one wishes to have alternatives* . . . other than what would be . . . a suicidal strike against the cities of the other side.[26]

With so much Schlesinger-spawned confusion and contradictions as a source, a nationwide discussion of his "new" strategy was bound to raise discouraging questions as to the capability of the American people to comprehend the strategic issues on which our survival depends. The *New York Times,* in an editorial, promptly called for a "national debate" on the changes in strategy, and asserted that the "new Nixon strategy" would "require enormous numbers of new, highly accurate warheads."[27] This interpretation was a far cry from anything Schlesinger had actually said or even suggested; it implied that he was seeking a buildup of powerful missiles with sufficient accuracy and explosive power to destroy large numbers of Soviet missiles in their hardened silos, with the ultimate purpose of building a first-strike capability against the Soviet Union. Even a month later, Joseph Kraft was still interpreting the Schlesinger press conference of January 10 as a "plea for more emphasis on a nuclear force capable of hitting Soviet missile sites rather than Soviet cities." Kraft, however, also recognized that Schlesinger was rather rapidly shifting claims for his "new" strategy:

He seemed to take a step backward in a news conference two weeks later, perhaps because Kissinger has misgivings about the impact of a counterforce strategy on his arms control negotiations with the Russians.[28]

Henry Kissinger has a unique talent for playing both sides of the street and winning plaudits from the respective residents of both sides. When really challenged, he sometimes creates a third side of the street in some sort of fourth dimension of his own imagination and successfully plays that side too. Schlesinger is nowhere near so skillful. When he tried playing two sides of his new strategic theory, he scared both the fluttering doves and the hang-tough hawks—the doves because they did not understand what he was doing, and the hawks because they did.

All any official, Congressman, or student of nuclear strategy has to do to activate the defense doves into a frenzy of fright is to mention the word "accuracy" in relation to U.S. strategic weapons. This triggers a deeply implanted Pavlovian response to which they have been conditioned over the years by the Pugwash penetration. "Killing people is good, killing weapons is bad," they intone in the frenzy of the established religion of the unilateral disarmers. They know that additional accuracy is not required for the "good" purpose of killing people by the millions, so they stop thinking and emote. It matters not how often Schlesinger repeats that his aim is merely to give added nuclear flexibility. It matters not that, beginning in 1970, Kissinger and Nixon, in their annual State of the World Report, repeatedly pledged to the Kremlin that we will never, never develop sufficient accuracy, numbers, or explosive power in our missile force to knock out any substantial number of siloed Soviet missiles. It matters not that, for years, the American taxpayers have been cheated by the deliberate holdback of accuracy and yield in our missiles in order to ensure absolutely that we do not have any counterforce-capable weapons. When all this is pointed out to the fearful doves, they finally rejoin: well, the Soviets might think we are going for a first-strike capability, and this would "start a new spiral in the arms race."

Predictably, therefore, immediately following Schlesinger's mention of his "new" strategy before the Senate Armed Forces Committee, 20 Senators introduced a resolution calling on the administration to seek absolute reductions of missile forces in the SALT II talks. The group was led by Senators Edward M. Kennedy, Mike Mansfield, and Charles Mathias. Senate sources said it was "relevant" to the current push by Schlesinger for more accuracy.[29]

On the other hand, the hawks and those who think of themselves as such, together with all serious students of the strategic situation, were horrified at such shocking sabotage of the credibility of the U.S. strategic deterrent by a U.S. Secretary of Defense. Newsweek conceded:

> Pentagon critics say that the Russians might well interpret a continued U.S. strategic shift as an effort to build up a nuclear knockout punch.

Even worse, they say, by openly declaring that its *second-strike capability is no longer a credible deterrent,* the Pentagon may be encouraging the Kremlin to try a nuclear test of wills.[30]

From the excerpts we have examined of media and congressional attempts to make sense of Schlesinger's strange strategic pronouncements, it is a reasonable conclusion that sense cannot be made of them because sense was not there in the first place. The most deceptive attempt at evaluation of the Schlesinger strategy was the educational television network program called *The Advocates.* Purportedly presenting "both sides" of the issue, it actually presented two versions of how best to appease the Soviets and assure them that, if they did launch a nuclear strike against the United States, we could make no effective retaliation and therefore would make none at all. The side of the debate that was supposedly defending the hardline, support-U.S.-strength argument (in this case, Schlesinger's assumed quest for greater missile accuracy) permitted the soft-line (any improvements in U.S. missiles will accelerate the arms race) side to introduce, without challenge, the three main malevolent myths spun out of deliberate Pugwash deceit.

First of these is, of course, that there *is* an arms race; whereas the fact is that there has not been one since 1962, when McNamara blocked weapons entering production lines. To attempt to meet the undeniable fact that we have added no missiles while the Soviets have raced ahead with hundreds of additional missiles each year, the myth of the mini-MIRVs was introduced. This argument equates U.S. 50-kiloton warheads with Soviet 50-megaton single warheads—a big-lie factor of 1,000 to one. The supposedly "hard-line side" of the debate let the "soft-line side" get away with this fraud and charge the United States with escalating the wicked "arms race." One of the "experts" unctuously pontificated that the United States now has some 5,000 warheads to only a little more than 2,400 for the Soviets, and that very soon we would have 10,000 to their probable 3,000. The third malignant myth they got away with was a fanciful blow-up of different aspects of "overkill," all based, of course, on our peacetime inventory.

The best treatment of the Schlesinger strategy was in *National Review.* In tackling the frustrating problem of what Schlesinger's uncertain enunciation *could* mean, this magazine concluded that it would have "profound significance" in one or more of three ways:

(1) Conceivably, this is primarily a bargaining maneuver in the SALT II negotiations. Since SALT I, the Soviet Union has been rapidly upgrading its nuclear force in power, versatility, and accuracy. By this present Pentagon publicity about missiles, we may be in effect threatening Moscow with an all-out weapons race if they persist.

(2) Conceivably, it marks the beginning of a U.S. attempt to get first-strike capability, or to make Moscow wonder whether we are making the attempt. Conceivably, Moscow might *believe* we are aiming at first strike capability even if we aren't, and Moscow might react on that supposition.

(3) It is even conceivable that no fully developed new strategy is involved, and that the President and the Pentagon simply want, as they say, to increase the available options: specifically, to program the sort of nuclear strikes that, because they would avoid huge loss of life, might make possible and "thinkable," if Moscow accepted the same sort of restriction, a limited nuclear exchange instead of a nuclear holocaust.[31]

National Review's Conceivability No. 1—the bargaining chip ploy—is the fruit of a Kissinger plant, via Pentagon sources, with influential segments of the press. It appeared with giveaway simultaneity in news magazines, columns, and editorials in late January 1974, and represents a typically brilliant machination by Kissinger to transform a personally potentially disastrous liability into a substantial advance asset. Discussion of the Schlesinger strategy in the Senate had triggered a demand by some Senators "for a fullscale review of U.S. nuclear policy."[32] Such a development could not have arisen at a more vulnerable time for Kissinger's entire grandiose plan for liquidation of the U.S. strategic deterrent and the replacement thereof with detente at any price. Despite his tight hold on all intelligence information as to Soviet strategic developments in the interval since the SALT I signings, some specifics were beginning to reach the public. Thus, Joseph Alsop (who has the record for the most reliable and important Top Secret information sources in the government) revealed a growing amazement in informed quarters that the administration has not denounced the SALT I Agreements. The Soviets have four new series of operational ICBMs, including one superheavy type with eight multimegaton MIRVed warheads (SS-18), a new light-heavy type with 2¼ times the throw-weight of the series it will replace (SS-17), a new medium-heavy type (SS-19), and the SS-16, the land-mobile type which can be built by the hundreds without even technically violating the SALT I Interim Agreement. They have developed and deployed in substantial numbers the Delta and Extended-Delta missile-launching submarines, carrying the world's first SLBMs with intercontinental range.

Kissinger needs to confuse or confound any informed "fullscale review of U.S. nuclear policy"—at least until his covert policies become irreversible. So, here is how Kissinger went about the dual mission of frustrating a congressional inquiry into U.S. strategic nuclear policies and setting the stage for the Moscow SALT II "no agreement" ploy of 1974. Here is the not-directly-attributable, Kissinger-dictated, Pentagon-disseminated "backgrounder" information, as it appeared in *U.S. News & World Report* (in interview form, but with no names supplied):

> How is the new [Schlesinger] targeting strategy by the U.S. going to change Russia's tack?
> No one is sure it will, but the move is regarded in Western Europe and the U.S. as a clear signal to the Kremlin.
> That signal: If SALT II fails to produce a satisfactory treaty setting a ceiling on offensive missiles, the U.S. is ready, willing, and able to launch a new, major buildup of strategic arms.
> Mr. Schlesinger, in the eyes of defense experts, is trying to make clear to Soviet leaders that the Nixon Administration is determined to prevent the Russians from gaining a potentially important strategic advantage while delaying in SALT II.[33]

Will it work? Not at all against the Soviets, as a lever, persuasion, or threat.

National Review's Conceivability No. 2—that the Schlesinger strategy marks the "beginning of a U.S. attempt to get a first-strike capability" or make the Russians wonder whether we are doing so—is just as phony.

One must weep for our country, for freedom and religion in the world, and for Western civilization, remembering the many many wasted years during which the United States *could* have so easily made a positive assurance to the Soviets that, if they wanted a nuclear arms race, they could have it—and we would win it decisively, and bankrupt the U.S.S.R. in the process. In 1962, with an overwhelming nuclear superiority of 8-to-1, with a 2½-to-1 advantage in industrial capacity and gross national product, with incalculably advanced science and technology, and with nuclear submarines and SLBMs that they could not have matched for another decade, we could have said:

> For every missile launcher, you build and deploy, whether land-based or submarine-launched, we will build and deploy 2½.
> For every increase in accuracy of guidance you develop, we will invest the resources necessary to double your improvement.
> For every ABM launcher you produce and deploy, we will deploy 2½ ABMs.
> And to make sure that you could never believe that you could attain a first-strike capability against us, we will build 100 missile-launching submarines, changing the series to include all new developments after every 33rd sub, but never, never, scrapping a single one of our submarines in-being.

If we had said that in 1962, there would have been no "nuclear arms race." The men in the Kremlin have not risen to their present position of power by being fools. Any attempt by them to win against us would have put them further and further behind.

We could still have said this with assurance as late as 1967, and could have outbuilt them by 2½ to 1. As late as 1969, when Kissinger took over, we could have preserved superiority even without crash programs. Finally, in mid-1972, at the time of the signing of the SALT I Agreements, we still could have started building programs to preserve the effectiveness of our strategic deterrent before (in Winston Churchill's words) we lost it forever.

But at this point in the strategic balance, to threaten the Soviets with an "all-out weapons race" is as ridiculous as it is tragic—especially when made by a subordinate, not very bright, not very influential, but brash-talking member of the Kissinger-Nixon Administration. Kissinger has boxed us in against making any credible threats to the Soviet Union of a strategic arms race.

Could Kissinger himself make a credible threat to the Soviets that the United States is prepared to go all-out in an arms race? Not without saying either (1) I was stupid and incompetent when I said, in selling the SALT I Agreements, that the United States *could not* successfully race in an arms buildup with the Soviet Union, or (2) I was deliberately lying when I said we had no ongoing production programs for ICBMs or SLBMs and missile submarines. We can assume with high confidence that Kissinger will neither admit that he was stupid and incompetent, or that he was deliberately lying, when he sold our nation the SALT I Agreements. If he did, he would be admitting to grounds for impeachment.

We are left with Conceivability No. 3 as to the purpose of the enunciation of the Schlesinger strategy: namely, "that no fully developed new strategy is involved, and that the President and the Pentagon simply want, as they say, to increase the available options." But does the "new" Schlesinger strategy increase the options available to the United States? Schlesinger's own claims have kept this point totally vague and nonspecific. For instance, try to deduce something concrete out of this:

> We have targeting options which are more selective and which do not necessarily involve major mass destruction on the other side.[34]

Although Joseph Kraft quoted Schlesinger as making a "plea . . . for a nuclear force capable of hitting Soviet *missile sites* rather than cities," we cannot find any authority or documentation for such a specification by Schlesinger, nor even in any of the several elaborations put out by unidentified "Pentagon officials" in response to attempts by reporters to find out what Schlesinger meant. All the examples from these sources speak of "key military targets," but they all turn out to be targets for a conventional war, not a nuclear exchange, except for two illustrations: "nuclear weapons storage bunkers," and either "certain" or "some" Soviet missile sites. The most often mentioned "new" targets are "airfields, dams, oil fields, and railheads." One of the more detailed "explanations" of how the new targeting would work was supplied in *U.S. News & World Report:*

> How will this change help to defend the U.S.?
>
> It gives more options to the President, who is the only official with authority to order the use of nuclear weapons.
>
> For example, if the Navy's big base at Norfolk, Va., were hit by Russian missiles, the new strategy would permit the President to retaliate by striking a similar military target in the Soviet Union, rather than to destroy Moscow or some other city.
>
> After an "exchange" of missiles on fairly small targets, the theory goes, the two superpowers would have a chance to negotiate before going all-out.[35]

This is a rather ridiculous scenario, so far as the initiating Soviet choice is concerned, but let's follow through on it to demonstrate what a crude fraud is being put over on the American people in the "new" Schlesinger strategy:

> A Soviet missile hits and destroys the U.S. Naval Base at Norfolk. BUT before launching this missile, Brezhnev came up on the Moscow-Washington Hot Line with this warning to the President:
>
> "If you have any cute Schlesinger-type ideas of a limited retaliation, by striking a similar military target in the Soviet Union, *don't.*
>
> "If you attempt that, we will strike New York, Chicago, and Los Angeles. Because of the SALT I ABM Treaty, you have no active defenses, and you have been too stupid to build any substantial passive defenses such as we and the People's Republic of China have. So, you will be condemning something like 25 million Americans to death if you order the taking out of one of our military bases in retaliation for our taking out the Naval Base at Norfolk.
>
> "Is it worth it? Would any American President do such a thing?
>
> "And if, in attempted retaliation against our taking out your three largest cities, you attempt to take out three of our cities—or even one of our cities—we will utterly destroy every American city and many towns. In such a case, we will liquidate on the order of 180 million Americans, and the remainder will die soon after. We may mop up with our bombers, since you have scrapped all bomber defenses; or we may just let them die from starvation."

If the U.S. President believed the General Secretary of the Communist Party of the Soviet Union, he certainly would *not* attempt a Schlesinger-type limited retaliation. And *the President would believe Brezhnev* because the Kissinger defense policies and his SALT I Agreements have conceded to the Soviet Union decisive "escalation dominance."

This means that, *at any level* of violence, *the Soviets can win any exchange decisively.* If a conventional-weapons war is started, they can win that without resorting even to tactical nuclear weapons, much less strategic nuclear weapons. They have 165 divisions to our 13 (most of which are not combat-ready); they have four million men on active military duty, to our less than two million; they have four times as many ready reserves, twice as many tanks, three times as many military aircraft, and 10,000 SAM launchers for air defense to our zero SAM launchers.

If we attempt to move up one level of violence to tactical nuclear weapons, again they have overwhelming dominance. They have more weapons, more powerful weapons, more delivery vehicles, and their equipment across the board for tactical nuclear war is far more modern. McNamara blocked our modernization of tactical warheads and delivery systems, just as he did the strategic weapons.

The next level up in violence is the one we are dealing with in relation to the Schlesinger strategy. One way of expressing what he is purportedly attempting to do is to develop a capability for the United States to fight limited strategic nuclear wars. A capability to fight such limited exchanges is purposed to establish "deterrence tit-for-tat." That is, he hopes we will believe that he has now deterred the Soviets from making limited strategic strikes against U.S. military targets, and probably also against a so-called "slow-motion nuclear war" in which the Soviets would take out our cities one by one until we surrendered.

We have shown in the scenario above that we cannot play games with the Soviets on a limited-exchange basis because Kissinger has handed them escalation dominance. But the tragic fact is that, even if we did develop the capability of fighting and winning limited nuclear exchanges—by, for example, improving the accuracy of our missiles, which is the only major move even considered by Schlesinger—actually we could not afford to use that capability against the Soviets, or even threaten to use it, because Kissinger has destroyed the credibility of our strategic nuclear deterrent and put us in the position of relying entirely on Soviet detente instead of on a military deterrent. The other side of this coin is that Kissinger has conceded to the Soviets a capability of *fighting and winning* an all-out nuclear war. *They have decisive escalation dominance at the highest step on the escalation ladder.*

This means that, if we did have the capability Schlesinger *talks about*, that is of engaging in limited exchanges with the Soviets, *we* would not dare to start a limited exchange, nor to win one if *they* started one, because they could credibly threaten us with escalating to the all-out-nuclear-war level.

572

The much-talked-about "new" Schlesinger strategy, therefore, does not give our President any additional options whatsoever. We have seen that the three "conceivabilities" predicated as possible purposes of the Schlesinger enunciations are all demonstrated to be frauds. What, then, is the real purpose of the "great debate" initiated by Schlesinger? It is a synthetic razzle-dazzle to confuse the American people and Congress so that they will not understand what Kissinger has done to our strategic deterrent. It has been becoming rather obvious that our existing strategy is, indeed, as Schlesinger characterized it, a "suicide or surrender" choice, and a strategy unlikely ever to be implemented; that is to say, we would surrender rather than trigger the destruction of the nation by retaliating against Soviet cities after the Soviets had taken out virtually our entire Minuteman missile force. He figured that anyone knowledgeable as to nuclear strategy might be easy to convince that any change would be for the better. The experts have long known of the suicide-surrender nature of the choice left to us under the Kissinger strategy.

The experts' view of the total loss of credibility of our strategy is summed up convincingly in these paragraphs:

> With Soviet MIRV capability now a technical reality, the time has come to rid ourselves, once and for all, of the absurd notion that massive numerical superiority in strategic nuclear weapons in the hands of a potential enemy will not invite nuclear blackmail or coercion, by reason of our possession of a few nuclear missiles . . . which presumably would be fired in a mindless spasm of vengeance at the Soviet people in retaliation for Soviet nuclear onslaught—real or threatened.
>
> This is the doctrine of "assured destruction" or "population hostages" (put forward by defense intellectuals at a time of U.S. nuclear superiority) and the announced rationale of the SALT accords. The degree to which such doctrinal nonsense is decoupled from responsibility for execution is evidenced by the statement of General Bruce K. Holloway, retired Commander in Chief, Strategic Air Command and so recently in charge of all U.S. ICBMs, who, in the Spring issue of *Strategic Review* wrote: "Who believes we would do it?"
>
> Such a nonmilitary, immoral response is not likely to take place in any event, nor be believable to an aggressor; least of all as an act of the United States, with thermonuclear annihilation guaranteed by superior Soviet nuclear force levels and greater U.S. population vulnerability.[36]

Dr. Schlesinger's own official figures on Soviet strategic power, as contained in his 1974 Military Posture report to Congress, admitted that the Soviets have been making "a truly massive effort" in missile development; and because of this increase in their strategic offensive power, before the end of the decade our entire force of 1,000 Minuteman missiles will be subject to this threat. The Soviet buildup, he further conceded, includes four new series of intercontinental ballistic missiles designed to carry between four and eight highly accurate warheads, each capable of being aimed at separate targets; and the new Soviet MIRVs are larger (between one and two megatons) and more destructive than U.S. warheads. Commenting on the Soviet advantage in throw-weight, Schlesinger presented this calculation:

> This throw-weight, combined with increased accuracy and MIRVs could give the Soviets on the order of *7,000 one-to-two-megaton warheads in their ICBM force alone.*[37]

This statement totally discredits the "new" Schlesinger strategy and its claim to establish what has been known since the beginning of the serious study of nuclear strategy in the late 1950s as "Type III Deterrence" or "Deterrence Tit-for-Tat." Using the Schlesinger figures (which are really a massive understatement), after we had exhausted our 2,154 tits, the Soviets would still hold in reserve some 4,846 tats. That is, our ICBM force will be able to deliver only a maximum (no degradation percentages applied) of 2,154 warheads as against the Soviets' 7,000 warheads.

Bad as that is in warhead numbers, it is absolutely shocking when translated into missile-deliverable megatonnage. According to Schlesinger's admission, they can deliver 10,500 (a median figure between 7,000 and 14,000, with no degradation percentages applied) megatons against our 1,050 megatons. So their missile-deliverable megatonnage exceeds ours by a factor of 10; or, in megatons, by 9,450. We are almost as badly off in the balance on the other two legs of the strategic triad. In SLBMs the Soviet advantage in numbers will be on the order of 50 percent in 1976; and in the long-range bomber class, by then they should have 400 (including about 200 supersonic Backfire types) that should be able to penetrate to targets in the United States, whereas we will have only about 200 B-52 G/H aircraft plus 80 patched-up old B-52 Ds, of which only a total of 20 could be expected to survive a Soviet strike and penetrate their air defenses.

The most important thing about the Schlesinger 1974 estimate is that it backs up his concession that the Soviets have a missile-deliverable counterforce capability sufficient to destroy virtually the entire Minuteman force before the end of the decade. An honest evaluation of "before" the end of the decade is at least three years before, and probably four years before. Schlesinger estimates that most of their older missile force will be replaced by 1980, but this is a rather absurd attempt to deceive the American people. If the Soviets did in fact want to MIRV most of their missile force, they could do this before the end of 1975 at the latest; but they have no reason whatsoever to

MIRV most of their force. Their object in MIRVing can be only to develop a capability of killing our 1,000 Minuteman missiles, and this they can do by MIRVing only 400 heavy missiles.

The Schlesinger statements are in fact gross understatements of Soviet strategic capability. He concedes only a deliverable megatonnage of between 7,000 and 14,000 to the entire Soviet ICBM force. Even at the time of the SALT I accords in May 1972, the expert consensus was that the then 313 Soviet heavies alone could deliver 8,450 megatons, which would leave more than 1,200 additional ICBMs for single warheads or MRV triplets.

Quite apart from the Schlesinger understatement of megatonnage, he is employing one of the oldest and slickest tricks of deception in the nuclear age by resorting to "peacetime inventory" figures. We do have 1,000 Minuteman missiles in peacetime; but the Soviets have an admitted preemptive strategy and, realistically, a first-strike strategy, whereas the United States has through many years forsworn a first-strike. Any U.S. President, in a nuclear crisis, if he considered our country to be in extremis, could change that policy, but he could not change the hard fact that we have no strategic force with a counterforce capability sufficient to make its use rational for purposes of a first-strike. To attempt a first-strike with our type of strategic offensive force would be to commit national suicide. Kissinger had President Nixon assure the Soviets each year, in his annual State of the World Report, that we do not have a disarming capability against them. The assertion in the 1972 Report is typical:

> . . . we have acted with great restraint. The number of missile launchers in the U.S. strategic force has not changed for five years. We have improved the retaliatory capability of each missile with added warheads, but we have not provided our missiles with the combined numbers, accuracy, and warhead yield necessary to threaten the Soviet forces with a disarming strike.
>
> The Soviets have the technical capability to develop similarly sophisticated systems but with greater warhead yields and consequently greater capability for a disarming strike.

It is notable that the Soviets have never given us such reassuring words, let alone actions.

Schlesinger gave away as a fraud his much-touted change in targeting on January 10, 1974, when he gave specific assurance that it would not require an increase in the number or size of U.S. warheads. If he actually did secure funding for a program to increase the accuracy of our missiles, and invested billions in it, then, under the most optimistic of assumptions, we could hope to destroy only between 800 and 900 Soviet ICBMs, or something like half their land-based force. We would then be in the desperate situation of having no ICBMs in reserve, whereas the Soviets would have more than 800 available for the land-based element of their retaliation; and the megatonnage they could deliver would be sufficient to destroy about 180 million Americans. That miniscenario is *if* we struck first and by surprise. Of course, we will not, because it would be national suicide.

Thus, the Schlesinger strategy is *not* giving the President an option to launch a disarming strike against the Soviets. So what else could it be good for? Not much. It sounds impressive to talk about retargeting "some" of our 1,000 Minuteman force. He never named a percentage, but let's assume 20 percent since he did specify that he was discussing "relatively small-scale options across the spectrum of targets." Twenty percent of our 1,000 Minutemen is 200; but, by employing his own estimates of the Soviet ICBM force, if they deliver a disarming strike in their first-strike option, then there would be remaining only something like 50 Minuteman missiles—and, on an average, only 10 of these would be the retargeted ones. Assume that the command, control, and communications facilities necessary to give a launch order had survived, together with a decisionmaker with authority and the code necessary to activate the launch. Would it be rational to do so? Quite obviously not; we would still be trapped in the dread alternatives he characterizes as "surrender or suicide."

Is there *any* realistic situation in which the Schlesinger targeting *could* deter the Soviets from doing anything they might actually desire to do with their missiles? The decisive strategic superiority that Schlesinger concedes to them in his 1974 Posture Statement demonstrates that they hold escalation dominance at all levels of violence in a limited-exchange situation, as well as in the all-out-nuclear-war situation. Their overwhelming superiority, plus their counterforce capability for disarming strikes, gives them the capability of *fighting* and *winning* all types of nuclear war. Since they hold such power, we cannot play limited "games" with them because, in poker parlance, they can always call any bet we make and raise us a couple of thousand warheads and megatons.

Might they be willing to play limited nuclear exchange anyway, as the unilateral-disarmers have long fancied? The answer is no; playing limited games with strategic nuclear weapons is contrary to all their strategic doctrine, as enunciated by both their military and political leaders. Once during McNamara's regime, John McNaughton, sometime General Counsel and later Assistant Secretary of Defense, attempted a "dialogue" on this subject and communicated a limited exchange proposal to the Soviets. The Kremlin's resounding response, via their military spokesman, was: if you launch just one missile at the Soviet Union, we will strike back and destroy your country totally.

The Soviets—as we all should—hold strategic nuclear weapons in great awe. Such weapons are not to play around with in fun and games, or to test faddish theories dreamed of by intellectuals who have lost touch with reality and construct models of what Country X should do with its nuclear weapons and how Country Y should respond. That is why hypothesizing a Soviet strike against the United States to take out a single naval base is a ridiculous scenario. Two basic elements form the foundation of the entire body of Soviet strategy: (1) Never, never take any chance of being hit by the *undamaged* nuclear force of the enemy; if there is any doubt, resolve the doubt by preempting—launch in time to insure that the enemy force is damaged, and damaged as near totally as possible. (2) Always strike with the advantage of surprise if at all possible, and always strike with a massive number of missiles of the greatest power. Intelligence expert Peter N. James, in his recent book *Soviet Conquest from Space*, condenses the doctrine very well:

> Military strategy of the Soviet Communist Party is predicated on the fact that the success of a nuclear confrontation with the enemy requires the delivery of a massive number of nuclear rocket strikes and the one-time application of its entire strategic forces at the very beginning of the war.[38]

This doctrine is affirmed in every authoritative statement of Soviet strategy from 1960 to the present.

Thus it is clear that the "new" Schlesinger strategy has no place in the real world and its application is strictly limited in the play world of games. We *cannot* play games based on his changed targeting with the Soviets because we simply do not have the quantum, quality, or character of strategic nuclear power that is absolutely required to stay in the bidding. The Soviets *will not* play games with us because their doctrine and common sense forbid it. So there is only one function left for the "new" Schlesinger strategy: it was designed for the purpose of playing games with the American people—to deceive us into *believing* that we have a new and effective strategic deterrent against nuclear war.

We have referred to the "new" Schlesinger strategy with quotes around the "new." Although he introduced it as "new," it is neither "new" nor even "Schlesinger." Like most of the cynical games played with or against the survival of American people, its origin is in a highly sophisticated aberration of Kissinger's massive mind. Writing for President Nixon in the *State of the World Report*, he said that the United States must retain sufficiently secure forces so that, if attacked first, we could retaliate against cities. He added, however:

> Our forces must also be capable of flexible application. A simple "assured destruction" doctrine does not meet our present requirements for

a flexible range of strategic options. No President *should be* left with only one course of strategic action, particularly that of ordering the mass destruction of enemy civilians and facilities. Given the range of possible political-military situations which could conceivably confront us, our strategic policy *should not* be based solely on a capability of inflicting urban and industrial damage presumed to be beyond the level an adversary would accept. We *must* be able to respond at levels appropriate to the situation. This problem will be the subject of continuing study.

Such slick equivocation is apparently beyond Schlesinger's capabilities. Note that Kissinger does not claim that the President *does* have more than one course of strategic action; nor that our strategic policy *is* based on a capability of inflicting an unacceptable level of urban and industrial damage; nor that we *are* able to respond at levels appropriate to different situations. Not at all. Kissinger, with exquisite finesse, merely asserts that no President "should be" left with only one course of strategic action, that our strategic policy "should not" be based solely on the capability of inflicting an unacceptable level of urban and industrial damage, and that we "must" be able to respond at appropriate levels.

The wily Kissinger knows full well that, if he asserted that the President *has* more than one course of strategic action, some reporter might inquire, "well, what *is* the other course of strategic action?" or ask him to *name one* alternative basis of our strategic policy. If he had positively asserted that we *are* able to respond at levels appropriate to the situation, someone might ask, "How?"

But fools rush in where satanic angels fear to sound off. So, two years after Kissinger's slick and carefully crafted wordmanship, Schlesinger claimed that, under his new targeting strategy, the United States *does* possess all those options that Kissinger said we *should* have.

Incidentally, a "study" was conducted about alternative strategies, as promised in the last line of the above excerpt from the 1972 *State of the World Report*. By no coincidence, Kissinger directed the study. Details of the study were leaked to *New York Times* correspondent William Beecher and published in a front-page story headed "Major War Plans Are Being Revised By White House."[39] The news story did not substantiate the headline, but it contained every specific of Schlesinger's targeting changes announced in late 1973 and early 1974 as "new."

On March 4, 1974, Defense Secretary Schlesinger's Annual Department of Defense Report, FY 1975, was released and dashed any hopes that his "new" strategy would enable us to strengthen our deterrence. Defining his proposals, Dr. Schlesinger wrote:

This adjustment in strategic policy does not imply major new strategic weapons systems and expenditures.[40]

Adding more selective, relatively-small-scale options is not necessarily synonymous with adding forces. . . .[41]

But here is the sentence that is the clincher in demonstrating that the "new" Schlesinger strategy is just a razzle-dazzle game of words to deceive the American people:

It is . . . assured capability to retaliate decisively against Soviet cities after absorbing the full weight of a Soviet nuclear attack that offers the best hope of deterring attack and thus protecting our cities. . . .[42]

And when he summarizes the "principal features" of his proposed strategic posture, he includes:

the avoidance of any combination of forces that could be taken as an effort to acquire the ability to execute a first-strike disarming attack against the U.S.S.R.[43]

Schlesinger attempts to play both sides of the street. To the strong prodefense Senator he holds out a promise of additional options— "the selectivity and flexibility to respond to aggression in an appropriate manner." This is followed immediately by a Kissingerlike equivocation:

We do not *intend* that the Soviet Union *should have* a wider range of option than we do.

Note how slickly this conveys assurance without actually affirming anything at all. Schlesinger doesn't say that the Soviets do *not* have a wider range of options than we do. Such wordmanship is carefully chosen to assure the unilateral-disarmers that all his strong-sounding sentiments are merely words, and that he has no intention of initiating programs that would produce strategic power for the United States or permit funds to be spent for that purpose.

In his FY 1975 DOD Report, Dr. Schlesinger proclaims:

For a period of time prior to 1960 the United States had a virtual nuclear monopoly. By 1960 it was perceived that our monopoly advantage would ebb; and, in fact it not only began to ebb, but *by 1966-67 the Soviet Union had a very substantial counterdeterrent.* . . .

If anything, the need for options other than suicide or surrender, and other than escalation to all-out nuclear war, is more important for us today than it was in 1960, because of the growth of the capabilities possessed by other powers. These additional options do not include the option of a disarming first-strike.

Neither the U.S.S.R. nor the United States has, or can hope to have, a capability to launch a disarming first strike against the other, since each possesses, and will possess for the foreseeable future, a devastating second-strike capability against the other.

This *almost* certainly will deter the deliberate initiation of a nuclear attack against cities, for it would bring inevitable retaliatory destruction to the initiator. *Thus the basic deterrent remains intact.*[44]

Note that the effectiveness of Schlesinger's "basic deterrent" depends on our blocking the U.S.S.R. from obtaining a disarming first-strike capability. We are supposed to have guaranteed this for the foreseeable future by a combination of (1) our possessing a "devastating second-strike capability" and (2) somehow making "inevitable" the *actual employment* of that devastating second-strike capability in retaliation against an enemy strike against our cities. Implicit in his theory of basic deterrence are the twin assumptions (a) that our retaliation will be automatic and (b) that the aggressor will find credible the "inevitability" of our automatic retaliation.

How does Schlesinger figure that we have a devastating second-strike capability for the foreseeable future? It must be based on our Polaris-Poseidon submarine force, because he concedes that the Soviets' additional throw-weight in their three new series of missiles, plus their improved accuracy and MIRVs, will give them "a major one-sided counterforce capability against the United States ICBM force."[45] He even provides specifics as to the Soviet counterforce capability:

> Given the warhead yield and CEP currently estimated for the MIRVed version of the SS-X-18, and looking at the fixed land-based portion of our strategic Triad in isolation from other elements, a force of about 300 of these missiles (permitted under the Interim Agreement) could pose a threat to our ICBMs in their silos, even after those silos are upgraded. Moreover, it is more than likely that the MIRVed follow-on to the SS-11, whether it be the SS-X-17 or SS-X-19, will also achieve a respectable hard-target kill capability during the early part of the next decade.[46]

The SALT I Agreement permits the Soviets more than 300 very heavy ICBMs of the SS-9/SS-18 types. The number shown in the FY 1975 Posture Statement by Admiral Thomas H. Moorer, USN, Chairman of the Joint Chiefs of Staff, is 338 SS-9/SS-18 types.[47] Anyone who reads the fine print and loopholes in SALT I will find that the Soviets could claim an additional 66 by virtue of the fact that the restriction against enlarging silo dimensions by more than 15 percent does not apply to silos *under construction* (as distinguished from silos "in the process of modernization and replacement,"[48]) and there are at least 66 new silos under construction as of 1974. There are at least two additional loopholes in SALT I that would permit them legitimately to add more than these 66 very-heavies but, as Schlesinger points out above, the new medium-heavies (SS-17s and SS-19s) will have a "respectable" (that is, very effective) hard-kill capability, so they would not need additional SS-18s. To deceive the American people, he inescapably implies that this hard-kill capability for the

SS-17s and SS-19s will not be attained until the early 1980s. Again, either Dr. Schlesinger or Admiral Moorer is lying, because the latter reports:

> Both systems have on-board computers and have been tested with MIRV warheads. We estimate that one or both of these systems [SS-17 and SS-19] *could be deployed in 1975.*[49]

Thus it is clear that Dr. Schlesinger cannot hope to hold out our land-based ICBM force as an element of the "devastating second-strike capability." He must be counting on our Polaris-Poseidon force to supply the invulnerable "devastating second-strike capability" that is necessary to block the Soviets from attaining a first-strike capability. At one point in his rambling discussion of his "new" flexible targeting strategy, he asserts specifically that neither side is in a position to acquire a disarming first-strike capability "since each side has large numbers of strategic offensive systems that remain *untargetable* by the other." In this connection, he can only mean missile-launching submarines. There are any number of other "untargetable strategic offensive systems," such as land-mobile ICBMs, air-mobile ICBMs, surface ships carrying ICBMs, and even airborne-alert old-fashioned strategic bombers. But we have none of these.

Thus it is that Dr. Schlesinger brings us to confrontation with one of the most dangerous myths of the nuclear-space age: the assertion that our Polaris-Poseidon submarine force is entirely adequate as an invulnerable, devastating second-strike force to constitute an effective and *entirely credible strategic deterrent against a massive Soviet missile strike* against the United States. This myth was probably created by the Pugwash/Harvard-MIT Axis unilateral-disarmament elites, but it has been adopted, sponsored, and promulgated by all unilateralists and finite-deterrence advocates. The way they usually phrase it is that

> Even the Pentagon admits that if the entire Minuteman force is destroyed, together with all of our strategic bombers, our Polaris-Poseidon force can deliver on targets in the Soviet Union, more than 5,000 nuclear warheads.

Other more circumspect unilateral-disarmers merely claim capability for the delivery of "thousands" of nuclear warheads by our missile-launching submarines.

This so-hopeful but totally illusory belief that our SLBM force is all we need is a major source of the apathy in the American people that is permitting America's betrayers to set us up for abject surrender or nuclear destruction. All apathy degrades military power, but absolute apathy destroys it absolutely. We must destroy our submarine-based apathy before it destroys both us and our country.

Dr. Schlesinger's flat statement that "by 1966-67, the Soviet Union had a very substantial counterdeterrent" should be compared with the fact that, in 1966, the Soviets had deployed 300 ICBMs in silos. By 1973 they had more than *quintupled* the number of such ICBMs. In 1966 the Soviet missile throw-weight capacity was 70 percent of ours; in 1972 (at the time of the SALT I signing) they had multiplied it to 400 percent of U.S. missile throw-weight capacity; and in 1974 they were well on their way to 800 percent. As late as 1968 the Soviets had no modern nuclear-propelled submarines for launching missiles; as of 1974 Schlesinger credits them with 52, carrying "at least 744 launchers." The United States has not added a single strategic missile launcher, either land-based or submarine-launched, since 1967.

Why did the Soviets invest so many scores of billions of rubles in building an offensive nuclear-strike capability beyond a "very substantial" deterrent? Why did they stall the SALT I negotiations 2 1/2 years to give them time to add more than 1,000 ICBMs and SLBMs to their forces that "by any standard" exceed "the level needed for deterrence"? Why did they load the SALT I Interim Agreement with 10 major loopholes and with massive imbalances disadvantaging the United States in strategic offensive forces? Why did they insist on gaps leaving them free to produce and even deploy land-mobile missiles in any numbers up to the thousands, and why did they insist on being totally free to make their own definition of "light" and "heavy" ICBMs?

Since Dr. Kissinger could not deny the factors of strategic superiority conceded to the Soviets by SALT I, he instead denied the *importance* of strategic power. He went back to the Pugwash theory that strategic nuclear power is not "usable" power. Short of the decisive superiority required for a preclusive first-strike capability, he classified all advantages that could be attained by one superpower over the other as "marginal," and claimed that both the United States and the Soviet Union are not capable of turning "marginal" advantages to political gain. His grand rationale for SALT I, as enunciated in his White House briefing for the five congressional committees on June 15, 1972, is pervaded with this theory. Actually, he even contended that this great and mutual discovery by the United States and the U.S.S.R. was the pivotal factor inducing them to enter into the SALT I Agreements. Purporting to speak for both countries, Kissinger said:

> Both we and the Soviet Union have begun to find that each increment of power does not necessarily represent an increment of usable political strength. . . .
> Marginal additions of power *cannot be decisive.*

Of course, "marginal" additions of power cannot be "decisive." The words are mutually exclusive. If an addition of power were of sufficient magnitude to qualify as "decisive," then by definition it could not be merely "marginal." Some of the followers of the Pugwash penetration put the proposition like this: it's a waste of money for the United States to rebuild strategic nuclear power. Thus McGeorge Bundy, one of Kissinger's predecessors as Assistant to the President for National Security Affairs, stated flatly:

Strategic nuclear weapons, certainly as between the superpowers, are good for nothing except mutual deterrence.[50]

One of the sensational consequences of this Kissinger-Bundy-Pugwash theory is that it denies the validity of a "nuclear umbrella" being employed by either superpower to protect its client states. This is demonstrably false. The U.S. strategic nuclear umbrella protected Western Europe and all our allies, and even neutrals, for almost 30 years from the end of World War II until publication of SALT I accords in May 1972. However, we must now recognize that by the time of the Middle East October War in 1973 the plenary power and effectiveness of the Soviet strategic umbrella had been established. Its credibility was so high that *not a single nation in the Free World dared utter even an unkind word* in relation to the Soviet-instigated and -protected economic warfare so arrogantly launched by the Arab states.

Quite obviously a nuclear umbrella could not be effective unless the superpower extending protection over its client states could make —implicitly or explicitly—a credible threat of actually *using* its nuclear power in behalf of its clients. The U.S. umbrella was credible from World War II to SALT I because of the vast superiorities we held over the Soviets in numbers and deliverable throw-weight of our strategic weapons systems. Although these superiorities began to melt away by 1968, our umbrella retained a residual credibility deriving from a lag in international perception that the strategic balance was swinging to the Soviet side. Publication of the strategic balance statistics as of May 1972 destroyed the last vestiges of the credibility of the U.S. strategic umbrella. The massive Soviet superiorities became the *sine qua non* of the effective employment of the "oil weapon" by the Arabs against the great oil-consuming nations of the world—whose conventional military power overshadowed that of the Arabs by a factor on the order of 1,000-to-1.

Thus, the so-called "good for nothing" strategic weapons, when possessed by a superpower with the obvious will to use them if challenged, can provide the power to restructure the political and economic organization of the entire world; and mere possession, in sufficiently superior numbers and power, renders impotent all other forms of power that could otherwise be used for political purposes, including overwhelming conventional military power, massive industrial power, financial power, technological power, population power, and even food power. All those types are canceled out by the mere possession of decisive strategic nuclear superiority by one superpower.

Will the mere possession of nuclear-powered missile-launching submarines by one major nuclear power destroy the credibility or effectiveness of the nuclear umbrella held for protection of client states by the rival nuclear power that possesses an overwhelming over-all strategic nuclear superiority? The practical experience of the Middle East War of October 1973, with its use of the oil weapon, demonstrated that possession by the United States of its Polaris-Poseidon submarine force was irrelevant and in no way served to discredit the Soviet strategic umbrella protecting the Arabs from military or even economic retaliation by the nations of Western Europe or Japan.

Also, the Arab Oil Producing Countries Resolution of October 17, 1973, singled out the United States as the target for contemptuously insulting language and discriminatory action to an extent that—were it not for the Soviet strategic supremacy—could have been the cause for serious retaliation. Instead, Dr. Kissinger meekly knuckled under for more than five months and indulged in the most humiliating bribes ever tendered by a great nation, such as committing the U.S. Navy to sweep mines and bombs from the Suez Canal at the cost of tens of millions of dollars, a move that would greatly advantage the Soviet Navy and disastrously disadvantage the U.S. Navy.

Let us test Dr. Schlesinger's precise assertion that the U.S. possession of the Polaris-Poseidon submarine force will prevent the Soviets from attaining a first-strike capability against us and render impossible a preemptive strike. Using Schlesinger's own figures, as quoted above, here is a simplified scenario staged in 1976:

The Soviets launch 300 of their very-heavy SS-9/SS-18 missiles against the U.S. land-based missile force and destroy about 950 of our 1,000 Minutemen and about 50 of our 54 Titan IIs. Concurrently, two Extended-Delta Soviet missile-launching submarines on station outside the range of U.S. satellite and OTH warning nets launch 34 MIRVed SLBMs against our strategic bomber force and strategic tanker aircraft. With some 170 two-megaton warheads involved in this no-warning attack, more than 90 percent of our strategic bomber force is destroyed on the ground. Since we had only 200 B-52 G/Hs, 80 patched-up B-52 Ds, and 72 FB-111s, only about 35 bomber aircraft survive.

Moscow then comes up on the Hot Line to the White House with this warning:

Mr. President, you have remaining in your land-based retaliatory force less than 60 ICBMs and 40 old bombers.

We have nearly 1,300 land-based ICBMs unexpended, plus a number of reloads which have become practicable because of the pop-up cold-launch techniques of our SS-16s, SS-17s, SS-18s and SS-19s, so that launching does not burn the launching tubes within the silos. Also, we have a number of land-mobile SS-16s which we have produced and stockpiled under cover, but which can be deployed in a matter of hours.

If you attempt to send the remnants of your bomber force against us, they will face 10,000 of our SAMs, many of them equipped with small, clean nuclear warheads. Out of our force of more than 3,000 interceptor-fighter aircraft, we can send about 100 against each of your surviving bombers, if they reach our territory.

If you attempt to launch your handful of surviving ICBMs, you may or may not have the surviving communications, command, and control facilities required to dispatch them and target them. The chances are that you will not have the required capability. Even if you could launch them, you should not do so for reasons we will now make clear in relation to your Polaris-Poseidon force.

Our Pugwash-trained unilateral-disarmament lobby in the United States has convinced the American people, and perhaps even you, Mr. President, that your submarine force can deliver "thousands" of warheads on the Soviet Union, and therefore constitutes an effective deterrent against our attempting a preemptive strike. Well, by now, your intelligence has informed you of the results of our preemptive strike against your land-based retaliatory forces.

Here is why we were not deterred by the prospect of a retaliatory strike against us by your SLBMs. Your full complement in the Polaris-Poseidon force is 41. You have concealed from your people the fact that you have never had within six of that number since 1968, when the McNamara program for scrapping Polaris submarines to provide a few salvaged parts for new Poseidon submarines went into effect. Right now, eight Polaris submarines which have been scrapped for cannibalization have not yet been replaced by new Poseidons. So your full force now numbers only 33. Your on-station percentage is sometimes as low as 60, but we will be generous in our computation and credit you with 70 percent on-station and 30 percent in transit, in training, in the yards for minor repairs or minor overhaul, or changing crews, or on shakedown cruises.

You have on station, therefore, about 23 missile-launching submarines: probably about 18 Poseidons, and five old Polaris. The five Polaris subs should be able to launch 16 missiles each, and each missile may have three MIRV warheads of probably 2/10 megaton of explosive power.

Mr. President, you may or may not know about the deficiencies in the Poseidon missiles. Back in 1973 when operational tests were conducted, a shocking 58 percent failed to function properly. For that we have to thank Secretary McNamara. As revealed by your writer John Newhouse in Cold Dawn: The Story of SALT, McNamara deliberately degraded the Poseidon by burdening it with 10 to 14 small MIRVs instead of using the practical design of three much larger MIRVs. He claimed he was doing this in the interest of "stability," but actually he was doing it to please us in the Politburo.

McNamara achieved his desired result. The mounting of so many small warheads on the Poseidon missiles required excessive miniaturization of all components and imposed impossible tasks of complexity in design. As a final result, you were forced to seek funding in 1975 for a "Poseidon Modification Program" costing more than $126 million. The vitally important aspect now, however, is that the retrofitting of the corrected version of the Poseidon missile into the first 20 Poseidon submarines was scheduled to require some three years from 1975.[51] So now, only one-third of your Poseidon submarines have been fitted with the more reliable missile, and operational tests of these have not been completed.

The result is that, of the 18 Poseidons you have on station now, you cannot count on a missile-reliability percentage of more than 60. Assume that each launched its full complement of 16 missiles, that would be a total of 288 missiles launched, carrying a total of 2,880 warheads. If 60 percent were reliable, they would deliver only 1,728 warheads. Thanks to McNamara, these Poseidon MIRVs have only 50/1,000 of one megaton of explosive power each, or a total of 86.4 megatons, which you could hope to deliver by Poseidon missiles. Your five old Polaris on-station might possibly deliver as much as 80 megatons, or as little as 48 megatons.

Summing up, if you should decide to try to retaliate, you could hope to deliver on us 30 megatons from your surviving Minuteman missiles, 20 megatons from your surviving Titan IIs, 86.4 megatons from your Poseidons on station, and 80 megatons from your Polaris on station. This gives a pitiful total of 216.4 megatons of missile-deliverable explosive power. That is the most you could realistically count on because your 35 surviving strategic bomber aircraft could not possibly penetrate our 10,000-SAM air defense, backed by 3,000 fighter-interceptor aircraft.

216.4 megatons will not go far against a nation with 9 million square miles of area; it would be about one megaton for each 41,000 square miles. Also, 216.4 megatons will not accomplish much against a nation with such extensive passive defense systems as we have, and with a highly disciplined population trained for more than 15 years in strategic evacuation. Our passive defenses are so effective that, even if you had launched your entire undamaged strategic force against us, we calculate that you could not have destroyed more than 6 percent of our population, or less than we lost in World War II. As it is, with your more-than-decimated remnants of land-based ICBMs, and the negligible explosive power of your submarine-launched mini-MIRV's we calculate that we are risking no more than a million people out of our 250 million. Of course, the 14 million Communist Party members are already in safe shelters.

In addition, we have our active ABM defenses, which we have been able to render highly effective despite the SALT I ABM Treaty. Also, we have assigned at least four of our very effective attack submarines to each of your 23 Polaris-Poseidon submarines on station in order to shadow them and close in for the kill when ordered.

So much for what you could attempt to do to us in retaliation for our destruction of your Minuteman force and bombers. But now, here is why you will make no such attempt. Thanks to our massive efforts for some 20 years in building a huge counterforce capability as well as a counterpopulation capability into our strategic missile forces, and thanks equally to the unilateral strategic disarmament accomplished by McNamara and Kissinger, the Soviet Union has broken out of the "balance of terror."

There is no longer any such thing as "mutual assured destruction" or *mutual* terror. What sort of "balance" is it when we can deliver on your cities 20,000 megatons of explosive power to your 216.4? Our superiority factor, now that we have destroyed virtually your entire land-based retaliatory force, is almost 100 to one.

You can now see, from the smoking ruins of your great missile force, that your so-called "untargetable" Polaris-Poseidon force did not deter us from launching a disarming strike. To launch them now against us would, of course, be irrational. They were good only for deterrence, and your deterrence has failed.

If you attempt retaliation, you can do only minor damage. Because of our great active and passive defenses of Moscow, you cannot devastate that area, and it is our technological and scientific center as well as our greatest city and the strong hub of all our party and governmental activity. Any other cities are expendable, or can be repaired. Their populations have been safely evacuated and are protected by shelter. In any event, we will now take over all the great cities of Western Europe and eventually of the world.

If you make any attempt to launch missiles at the U.S.S.R—and this includes the type of minor military installations mentioned a couple of years ago by your then-Secretary of Defense—we will utterly destroy your population and your entire nation. That is, if you attempt to destroy a million Soviet citizens, we will then strike back with our more than 1,300 land-based ICBMs, plus our nearly 1,000 SLBMs, and exterminate some 210 million Americans. Your attempt at retaliation would be not merely irrational, but wildly insane, not to mention immoral and stupid.

We now deliver to you an ultimatum to order all your submarine force to surface, radio in their position, and await Soviet escort into Soviet ports under control of boarding parties. For each Polaris or Poseidon which fails to surface and report within 12 hours, we will take out one American city. As you already know, failure to surface would serve no useful purpose because the chances are that our shadowing attack submarines would sink any holdout. We are reasonably sure that the civilian leaders of the United States would not attempt retaliation because we have always recognized that the purpose of the McNamara "pause" and the Kissinger-announced refusal to adopt a launch-on-warning strategy was to enable you to tender a surrender—a covered surrender, if possible, but an unconditional surrender if we would give you no other terms.

Also, because we are about to take over Western Europe, we demand that you turn over to Soviet occupation forces all the tactical nuclear weapons you have in Europe. The same applies also, of course, to tactical nuclear weapons in the United States. Later, we will transmit our instructions for occupation of the United States.

The above scenario illustrates the fallacy of the theory that the mere possession of a submarine missile-launching force renders "impossible" a Soviet first-strike or preemptive disarming strike against us. It should also dispose of the Kissinger myth that strategic superiority in missile numbers, payload, and explosive power does not provide "usable" political power.

Actually, of course, Henry Kissinger has always known this. In the annual *State of the World Reports*, he has repeated time and again the substance of this assertion:

> In its broader political sense, sufficiency means the maintenance of forces adequate to prevent us and our allies from being coerced. . . . Sufficiency requires *forces that are adequate in quantity* and have the qualitative characteristics *to maintain a stable strategic balance despite technological change.*
>
> *The Soviet Union cannot be permitted, however, to establish a significant numerical advantage in overall offensive and defensive forces.*
>
> Our forces must be maintained at a level sufficient to make it clear that even an all-out surprise attack on the United States by the U.S.S.R. *would not cripple our capability to retaliate.*

On the very next page after these words in the 1972 *State of the World Report*, Kissinger put into the mouth of President Nixon the solemn pledge that has proved so cynically illusory:

> But under no circumstances will I permit further erosion in the strategic balance with the U.S.S.R. I am confident that the Congress shares these sentiments. . . . If the Soviet Union continues to expand strategic forces, compensating U.S. programs will be mandatory.

In every single month since then, further erosion in the strategic balance has been permitted. In every month, the Soviet Union has continued to accelerate the massive momentum of expansion of their already 20-times-more-than-"sufficient" strategic forces. Not a single U.S. compensating program has been initiated to produce strategic weapons in a timeframe relevant to the Soviet buildup.

What about the B-1 and the Trident submarine? In his FY 1975 DOD report, Secretary Schlesinger describes several "adjustments" in the B-1. Slippages would be a more accurate word. He recites the "rescheduling" of the "planned production decision date from July 1975 to May 1976." Then he enumerates a few more delays and states:

> Under the current proposed program plan, this [production] decision could be made in November 1976.[52]

Note the usual equivocation. Schlesinger does not state that the production decision *will* be made in November 1976, only that it *could* be. A far more accurate estimate as to the B-1 program appears in the FY 1975 Military Posture Report by JCS Chairman Admiral Thomas H. Moorer:

The B-1 will begin flight tests [with the first prototype] late this year. A production decision will be made, after detailed evaluation of the four RDT&E aircraft—*probably late in 1977.* Under current planning, the B-1 force *could be operational in the early 1980s.* . . .

Since the B-1 is not expected to enter the US force until the 1980s, the US intercontinental bomber force will continue to be composed of B-52s and FB-111s through the rest of this decade.[53]

Because no "production decision" has been made on it and probably will not be made before a year later than Schlesinger leads us to believe, that is in late 1977, the B-1 program is merely a development program to open in 1977 an "option" to go into a bomber production program. This means that the B-1 could not be deployed in force until some five years later. That five-year differential between 1977 and "the early 1980s" (which we reasonably interpret as no earlier than 1982) might well be pivotal. The question so vital to U.S. national survival in freedom is whether we can survive the 1970s. Beginning no later than mid-1976 we become increasingly vulnerable to a Soviet ultimatum or an actual Soviet first-strike. If a substantial number of B-1s were to be deployed in 1977, they just might add enough power and credibility to the U.S. strategic deterrent to avert a Soviet preemption of an attempt to rebuild our ICBM and SLBM forces. If B-1s are only delivered in the early 1980s, they may have to be turned over to the Soviet occupation forces.

The Schlesinger B-1 program is only one example of the fraudulent nature of his program. *Not a single segment of the Schlesinger program is relevant to the critical timeframe of the Soviet strategic threat.*

Take the Trident missile and submarine program, described by some as "accelerated" under the Schlesinger budget. Here is the Schlesinger-style "acceleration":

Accordingly, after starting the first Trident submarine in FY 1974, we now propose to build the nine remaining Trident submarines . . . at the rate of two a year (instead of three a year) beginning in FY 1975.

It takes a rather slick operator to slow a program 33 1/3 percent (from three to two a year) and get credit for "accelerating" the program.

If nothing goes wrong, if there are no slippages, if all necessary appropriations are secured despite the aggressive opposition of the 141 Members of Congress for Peace Through Law, the first Trident may become operational in the second quarter of FY 1979, and the first of the Trident I missiles may be available for fitting into the submarine at that time. Thus, under the most optimistic assumptions, we will have one Trident submarine operational in the calendar year 1979. After that Schlesinger's slowdown on production will begin to take effect. In calendar 1980, two more should be operational, for a grand total of three. In 1981, there should be five operational; in 1982, seven; in 1983, nine; and all the ten planned Tridents should be operational before the end of 1984.

It is enlightening to compare this timeframe with that of the Soviet Delta and Extended-Delta class. Back in August 1973, Admiral Hyman Rickover testified that, in their Delta missile-launching submarine,

> ... in effect, the Russians already have their equivalent of our Trident.[54]

The Soviet Delta's SS-8 missiles are rated by Schlesinger's people as having a range of 4,200 nautical miles, by the International Institute of Strategic Studies at 4,600 nautical miles, and by former Chief of Naval Operations Elmo Zumwalt at 5,000 nautical miles.

How many Deltas will the Soviets have? Schlesinger's FY 1975 DOD Report concedes that, by the end of 1973, "18 or 19 D-class [Delta-class or Extended-Delta-class] had been launched or were being assembled," that all the Soviet missile-launching submarine construction has been shifted to this D-class, and that

> At the current rate of production, 6-8 per year, the Soviet Union could have in operation 62 "modern ballistic missile submarines" by mid-1977.[55]

At that time, we will have 41 (if all the Poseidons have been completed by that date); none of ours will be very "modern," and none will have a range of more than about half that of the Soviet Deltas. Analysis of the Schlesinger figures shows that, as of the end of 1974, the Soviets will have more than twice the number of Deltas as we will have of Tridents at the end of 1984; and that before the end of 1976 the Soviets could well have 29 Deltas compared to the total of 10 Tridents that we hope to have eight years later.

Schlesinger's reason for slowing down production of the Trident program by 33 1/3 percent is very revealing. He said he is trying to avoid what happened in the case of the missiles designed for our 31 Poseidon submarines:

> While failures encountered in the Poseidon operation tests *have no direct relation* to the Trident missile program, they do remind us once again of the monetary risks involved in moving rapidly into large-scale production of any new major weapon system. . . . But by holding initial production to a reasonably low rate, we can reduce the costs of correcting those inevitable deficiencies which are not discovered until the system is operationally tested. This is particularly true in the case of such technically advanced and costly weapon systems as the Trident submarine.[56]

In late 1972 and early 1973, operational tests of Poseidon missiles showed that 58 percent were unreliable, and the tests were suspended. The principal reason they were unreliable was the extreme miniaturization imposed on the system by McNamara, which resulted not only in a throw-away of warhead explosive power, but a drastic cut in reliability. How he did it, as explained by his admirer, John Newhouse, in *Cold Dawn: The Story of SALT*, bears repeating:

> McNamara also struck a blow for stability by deciding to outfit Poseidon with 10 to 14 small MIRVs; in doing so, he chose to reject another version of the system that, using just three much bigger ones, would have packed a wallop so enormous as to inspire Soviet fears of a first-strike weapon.

With single warheads on its missiles, the Poseidon force of 31 submarines could launch against Soviet targets some 1,984 megatons of explosive power (31 boats x 16 missiles each x 4 megatons each missile). After each missile was divided into 10 MIRVs of 50/1,000 of a megaton, the megatonnage deliverability of the 31 subs is cut down to 248 megatons (31 boats x 16 missiles x 10 MIRVs x 50/1,000 of a megaton), or a throw-away of 1,736 megatons. McNamara's masterpiece of mini-MIRVing is the 14-MIRV nest on a single Poseidon missile. Those MIRVs are estimated authoritatively at 17/1,000 of a megaton each. This cuts down the delivery capability of the entire force of 31 Poseidon submarines to 118.05 megatons (31 x 16 x 14 x .017), for a throw-away of 1,865.95 megatons over the single warhead version.

The reliability of warheads with three MRVs had been established by the Polaris A-3 missile. The idea of mounting 14 or even 10 MIRVs on a single missile with the throw-weight of a Poseidon missile is ridiculous. The tremendous complexity required by the miniaturization guaranteed that years and years of experiments and refinements would be required to attain a minimally acceptable reliability quotient.

The mendacity of McNamara's motivation is attested by the Soviet policies in MIRVing. Authoritative leaks concede that they have not tested any MIRVs of less than a 1-to-2 megaton range, and the available evidence indicates that their average MIRV would be far more powerful. The largest number of MIRVs they have put on any single missile is five to eight, and that is on their huge SS-18 that has the single-warhead capability (at a minimum estimate) of 32 megatons and is credited by many authorities with up to 50 megatons. A reasonable estimate of the explosive power of each MIRV of a 5-MIRV Soviet SS-18 missile would be five megatons, so each one would be 100 times more powerful than a 50-kiloton Poseidon MIRV, or about 300 times more powerful than a 17-kiloton Poseidon MIRV.

What difference does that much margin in explosive power make, as a practical matter? Presumably, when you make a tremendous investment of national resources in acquiring missiles, their warheads ought to be able to *do something*. The function of a warhead is to destroy a target (or at least damage it so it is inoperable). Let's compare our 50-kiloton MIRV with a Soviet 5-megaton MIRV, and credit each with the same CEP (an accuracy of 1,500 feet, for practical purposes). The single-shot probability of destroying an ICBM silo hardened to 300 psi will be 17 percent for the 50-kiloton Poseidon MIRV, and 99 percent for the 5-megaton Soviet MIRV.[57] The probability of destroying a hardened silo with a 17-kiloton Poseidon MIRV is so ridiculously low that no figures are available on it in unclassified sources.

Thus, by burdening our Poseidon missiles with an insupportable multiplicity of warheads of minimum explosive power, McNamara delayed reliability for something like 10 years. Schlesinger's report stated that the "Poseidon Modification Program" will not be completed until 1977.[58]

Secretary Schlesinger has not proposed or requested authority to make *any improvements whatsoever* in our strategic forces. His talk of "keeping open the options" is merely a resort to the old McNamara placebo employed so effectively to stall new weapons systems. Here is how Schlesinger explains this:

> The principal impact of the new emphasis on "other strategic options" [other than "city-bashing"], as far as the FY 1975 budget is concerned, is on the Minuteman program. . . .
> Even without any additional R&D funding, we believe that the CEP of the Minuteman III will *gradually improve* with continued testing.
> Beyond that point, further improvements in the counter-military capabilities of our ICBM force would require deployment of more than the currently planned 550 Minuteman III missiles, large yield warheads, an improved new guidance system for Minuteman III, terminally guided maneuvering RVs (MaRVs) or the development and deployment of an entirely new ICBM.
> *In view of the ongoing SALT talks, we propose in the FY 1975 budget to take only those first few steps which are necessary to keep open these options; no decisions have been made to deploy any of these improved systems.*[59]

He is keeping open his "options" instead of building any improved systems, despite the fact that he is forced to concede that the Soviets are aggressively and arrogantly exploiting the gross imbalances, gaps, and loopholes with which Kissinger advantaged them in the SALT I accords. Here is Schlesinger's admission:

> Whether the Soviets believe that with the shift in these indicators [of strategic superiority from the U.S. to the U.S.S.R.] they have achieved any meaningful, exploitable advantage is not clear. However, they have

not been reticent in stressing to a variety of audiences their superiority over the United States in numbers of ICBMs and other strategic capabilities. Their words, at least, have suggested that they see these asymmetries as giving them diplomatic if not military leverage.

As far as we can judge, moreover, *the Soviets now seem determined to exploit the asymmetries in ICBMs, SLBMs, and payload we conceded them at Moscow.* Apparently, they are considering the deployment of large numbers of heavy and possibly very accurate MIRVs. As I have already indicated, this kind of deployment could in time come to threaten both our bombers and our ICBMs.[60]

Despite Schlesinger's absolute knowledge of what the Soviets are doing, all he is doing for the United States is talk about taking "only those first few steps which are necessary to keep open these options."

There is one small item in the Schlesinger budget that sounds as if it might mean improved guidance for U.S. missiles. Close analysis reveals, however, that this $32-million item is also illusory. Although allocated to Minuteman, the sum is restricted to developing "the *option* for some additional *refinements* in the *existing* Minuteman guidance system, mostly in the software program." This must be read together with his express disavowal (in the quotation cited above) of any program for development of "an improved or new guidance system for Minuteman." Thus, he proposes merely a minimum appropriation for minor research which may open an *option* to decide upon *developing* in some *future* time when no SALT talks are pending, some very minor "refinements" in Minuteman guidance. Even the size of the appropriation requested confirms the fact that no serious improvement is even contemplated. Substantial research for improvements in guidance would run into hundreds of millions, and the kind of guidance program we need for national survival insurance would cost billions.

Similarly, the vaunted Schlesinger cruise-missile program is merely a technology program designed to open some "options" for us in the far distant future. We are years away even from a decision to produce either the Air Launched Cruise Missile (ALCM) or the Ship Launched Cruise Missile (SLCM). Quoting Schlesinger, "it would be premature to make a production decision at this time." At a miserly $80 million for the ALCM and $45 million for the SLCM, we quite obviously do not have even a "development" program going. Even when the research program has—in, say, five years—ripened into a development program, the air-launched cruise missile will be a much less effective weapon than the Skybolt that McNamara killed back in 1965. The ship-launched version will be a much less effective system than the Navy's Regulus II cruise missile that had been fully and successfully developed for nuclear submarine launch in the late 1950s and was killed for lack of funds.

Much has been made of an alleged intensification of development of MaRV in the Schlesinger budget. It is described as a "maneuverable warhead that can be guided to its target." This implies a greatly improved accuracy, or smaller CEP; but this is not necessarily so. As Schlesinger explains, the MK 500 MaRV is "not terminally guided, since its maneuvering capability is intended to help it evade an ABM interceptor, rather than to increase its accuracy." It is not to be ready until FY 1979. It is so far into the future that advanced development has not yet even been initiated.

Finally, what about the "new" Minuteman missiles with a new higher-yield warhead, which some credit as a Schlesinger development? This is apparently a mid-1980s project. In FY 1975 only the "first increment" of $25 million was requested for research and development and tooling costs. The claimed "higher yield" in the "new higher-yield warhead" must, unfortunately, be rather modest, since the additional space and weight will come only from the saving effected in miniaturizing the arming and fusing mechanism.

The so-called "entirely new" ICBM mentioned in the Schlesinger program—the project that has heartened some Americans—is not even described as "opening an option" in the present timeframe. Schlesinger says only that it is to "ensure a realistic *option* to modernize our ICBM forces in the 1980s." To ensure that it cannot be ready before some remote time in the 1980s, the FY 1975 request is for only $37 million—and that is not for developing a new ICBM but is strictly limited to investment in developing "advanced technology *leading to the development of an entirely new ICBM."

We have now considered the entire Schlesinger package. His own official report establishes that *there is no element in it that will add strategic power to U.S. forces in a timeframe relevant to the massive Soviet buildup* that will give them overwhelming and clearly decisive strategic supremacy by 1977. If the Kissinger-Schlesinger policies are continued until then, the Soviets will be capable of delivering an ultimatum demanding our surrender, or actually delivering a strike. *We cannot reach the 1980s unless we first reach 1978.*

For the United States, the years 1976, 1977, 1978, 1979, and 1980 will represent a period of high vulnerability. The futility of the Kissinger-Schlesinger strategic programs is best exposed by referring again to Kissinger's 1961 words that are even more obviously applicable today:

> The aggressor can afford to build toward a target date. . . . The defender, by contrast, can deter only if he is ready at every moment of time. Here long-range planning produces *instant* readiness. The aggressor can risk a temporary weakness, for the choice of opening hostilities depends on him. For the defender any unbalance, however temporary in design,

may prove fatal. A stress on balance, on stretching out procurement, on awaiting new technological developments at the cost of present readiness, can be disastrous.

The excuse Schlesinger gives for his slowdown in production of the Trident submarine is a desire to avert the "monetary risks" that might be involved in "moving rapidly into large-scale production," as we encountered in the Poseidon tests. The B-1 bomber program is being delayed a matter of years for financial-risk reasons that are also totally trivial in relation to the risk to national survival. As Schlesinger explains:

> In consonance with our *fly-before-buy policy*, the B-1 is expected to undergo about *two years of flight testing* and achieve the essential critical milestones before a production decision is made.

Toleration of such delays—which Kissinger warned us can be fatal and disastrous—for such pipsqueak reasons must appear as either wildly irresponsible or cynical betrayal of U.S. national security. This is especially true because the Soviets already have their version of the Trident and soon will have 25 to 29 of them operational; and their new strategic supersonic bomber has been in full serial production since 1973 and is being produced in numbers to supply probably two 25-aircraft squadrons per year. Their Backfire bomber is 2½ times heavier than our FB-111, and is about 4/5 as large as our proposed B-1 concerning which Schlesinger *may* make a production decision "late in 1977" and which "could be" operational in the "early 1980s."[61]

Americans tend to believe that a Secretary of Defense must be doing the best he can. Many will contend further that Schlesinger could not have done more to rebuild U.S. strategic power because of Kissinger's overriding policy of relying on detente instead of on a strategic deterrent, and because of the political power of the anti-defense lobby in Congress.

Even if we grant that assumption, analysis demonstrates that Schlesinger has acted affirmatively and cynically to increase the danger to our national survival. He has fraudulently held out his program as adequate to meet the constantly growing Soviet threat. He gives false reassurance to the Congress and the American people that the strategic balance is far more favorable to us than it actually is. For example, he asserts:

> "With the rise of Soviet nuclear power, which has brought about an approximate parity in U.S.-Soviet nuclear capabilities . . . "[62]

He repeatedly talks about "essential equivalence" in a way designed to deceive readers into believing that such a balance actually does exist, and that the SALT I Agreements preserved this balance.

Here is the Schlesinger statement, however, that has served as his greatest current deception:

The United States is prepared to reduce, stay level, or if need be, increase our level of strategic arms, but in any case, that level will be fixed by the actions of the Soviet Union. *If the Soviet Union insists on moving ahead with a new set of strategic capabilities, we will be forced to match them.*[63]

In the last sentence in this key policy statement, Schlesinger is pledging to the American people two affirmative courses of action: (1) if the Soviets insist on an arms race, there will be an arms race; and (2) the United States can and will "match them." *U.S. News & World Report* and numerous columnists who were privy to official "background" information put out by Schlesinger or his staff interpreted Schlesinger as saying that his game plan demonstrates "that the U.S. is willing and able to match—and perhaps outrun—the Soviets if the Kremlin opts for a new arms race rather than an arms limitation treaty."

The Schlesinger assertion that we can and will match the Soviets can be demonstrated to be a slick and dangerous deception when linked with the inescapable inference that his programs will enable us to match the Soviets. He cannot help but know that they are totally inadequate and cannot operate in the relevant timeframe; therefore, coming from him, the assertion is a lie. The purpose of the Schlesinger program is to lull the American people into permitting a delay in the initiation of rearmament until the Soviets have built a strategic supremacy so overwhelming that they can preempt. Schlesinger is not deploying any advanced strategic systems. He is merely offering to *talk* about deploying systems in the 1980s [except for "scheduling" one Trident submarine by 1979].

The SALT II talks in which we seek an equitable agreement are ongoing in 1974-75. How much pressure will it bring against the tough-minded CPSU Politburo to threaten them with the statement that we might deploy some B-1 bombers in "the early 1980s" *if* we are able to make a decision in 1977 to produce B-1 bombers? How much pressure can we put on 1974 negotiations by threatening to deploy three Trident submarines by 1981? Especially when, according to Schlesinger's own figures,[64] the Soviets will have 62 modern missile-launching submarines to our 41, and 29 of theirs will probably be the Delta or Extended-Delta type.

If an armed man broke into your house tonight, do you think you could effectively deter him from robbing you and raping your wife by threatening him that you had ordered a handgun and that it would be delivered, hopefully, in six years? Or even the next day? This is why Senator James Buckley warns that "failure to deploy these [advanced] systems" will have the reverse effect and give the Soviets no incentive to negotiate responsibly.

It is clear from analysis based on his own statistics that the Schlesinger programs are totally illusory so far as putting "pressure" on the Soviets to give us a SALT agreement providing the "essential equivalence" he talks about. He won't fool the Soviet strategic experts, but he is doing a good job of fooling the American people.

What about the second prong of his argument: that his programs ensure that the United States "is ready to plunge into a new arms race" if the Soviets do not give us an equitable agreement on strategic arms control; and his pledge that if the Soviets move ahead with their new programs we are ready to race and "match" them? This assertion demonstrates that either Schlesinger is a liar, or Kissinger is a liar, or both are liars.

In his Defense Department Report, FY 1975, Schlesinger stated:

> As far as we can judge, moreover, the Soviets now seem *determined to exploit* the asymmetries in ICBMs, SLBMs, and payloads *we conceded* to them at Moscow [in the SALT I Agreements].

Kissinger, on the other hand, asserted time after time that we made *no* concessions to the Soviets in SALT I, that the imbalances embodied in the Interim Agreement merely recognized the fact of existing Soviet superiorities, and that the only way we could prevent the existing missile gap from widening was to cap their momentum by an agreement. SALT I was the only way, he repeated, because "without an agreement the gap would steadily widen."[65] Why would the gap widen without SALT I? Because, Kissinger asserted, we could not race the Soviets in strategic arms production because of "decisions made in the 1960s and not reversible within the timeframe of the SALT Agreement." He claimed we could not match the Soviets and would fall further and further behind.

The specific reason Kissinger identified for our not being able to match the Soviets if we attempted a race was that they had dynamic ongoing production programs "in both ICBMs and submarine-launched ballistic missiles," and the United States "had no active or planned programs for deploying additional ICBMs, submarine-launched ballistic missiles, or bombers." He specifically credited the Soviets with the capability of building 90 modern missile submarines by the end of 1977, and asserted that we could not produce an additional one "until 1978 at the earliest." He also said that we could not produce additional ICBMs within the five-year period.

Two years later, we are in exactly the same status: we still have no ongoing programs for producing "additional" ICBMs, SLBMs, or missile-launching submarines. (The 10 Trident submarines are scheduled by Kissinger to *replace* the last 10 Polaris which are not being replaced by Poseidons.) And Kissinger had President Nixon state we could not produce additional strategic weapons within five years.

Now Dr. Schlesinger pledges that if the Soviets move ahead with their programs we will race and "match" them!

If Schlesinger is telling the truth, then Kissinger was guilty of either deliberate deceit or gross incompetence in securing approval of the gross imbalances of SALT I by claiming that we are helpless to produce additional strategic weapons within five years, and that if we attempt to race we would lose. In either case, he should be dismissed.

If Kissinger was telling the truth, then Schlesinger is now lying to us by assuring us that we can successfully race against the Soviets and match them, and that we can do so on the basis of his FY 1975 programs (which are stated officially to cover all the years from FY 1975 through 1979). If Schlesinger is lying, he is lulling the American people and Congress into the belief that no new strategic power is needed and that his programs will ensure either that we get an agreement from the Soviets granting us "essential equivalence" or else that we can and will match them by plunging into a new arms race.

Because their statements are contradictory by no means eliminates the possibility that *both* Kissinger and Schlesinger are lying. We fully demonstrated and documented in the preceding chapter the mendacity of the Kissinger assertion. But what about Schlesinger? Will his programs allow us to race and catch up with ("match") the Soviets in strategic power? Fortunately, he has specified the Soviet force levels we would have to match:

> If all three new and heavier missiles are deployed, Soviet throw-weight in their ICBM force will increase from the *current 6-7 million pounds to an impressive 10-12 million pounds.*
>
> This throw-weight, combined with increased accuracy and MIRVs *could give the Soviets on the order of 7,000 one-to-two megaton warheads in their ICBM force alone.* They would then *possess a major one-sided counterforce capability against the U.S. ICBM force. This is impermissible from our point of view.*
>
> There must be essential equivalence between the strategic forces of the United States and the USSR—an equivalence perceived not only by ourselves, but by the Soviet Union and third audiences as well. This was the essence of the SALT I Agreements.[66]

We have already disposed of any hope that the United States—under Kissinger-Schlesinger programs—can attain anything like "equivalence" with the Soviets in SLBM forces, even by the mid-1980s. As for strategic bombers, we will be even more out of balance. The Soviets have nearly 800 to our about 450 if medium bombers on both sides are counted (and they must be, for theirs have more of an intercontinental capability than our 72 FB-111s). The Soviets have the world's most massive and modern bomber defenses, and we have none. They have 10,000+ SAMS and 3,000+ interceptor-fighter aircraft, some of them flying at mach 3; we have fewer than 300 interceptor aircraft and zero SAMs.

For us to attain "essential equivalence" in the third leg of the triad, we would have to attain the same counterforce capability as the Soviets. This would mean not merely matching the Soviet force of 7,000 warheads of from one-to-two megatons mentioned in the above Schlesinger excerpt. Elsewhere he points out that a force of "about 300" of the Soviet very-heavy SS-18-type missiles, which carry from five to eight MIRVed warheads each, "could pose a very serious threat to our ICBMs in their silos, even after those silos had been up-graded." That would leave them about 1,300 of their SALT I-permitted 1,618 fixed land-based missiles; plus however many SS-16 land-mobile missiles they care to produce and deploy (and this could be hundreds under SALT I); plus reloads, which are now practicable since the new-series Soviet ICBMs all employ the pop-up cold-launch techniques that do not burn the launch tubes in the silos.

To make it easier to compute the possibility of fulfilling Schle-singer's pledge of "matching" the Soviets, we will disregard the pos-sible land-mobile SS-16s and the reloads. To get the counterforce capability against *their* 1,618 ICBMs, that they have contra *our* 1,054 ICBMs (300 SS-18s x 8 MIRVs x 1-to-2 megatons), we would need 3,840 warheads of 1-to-2 megatons against their ICBM force. Because we have no ICBM MIRVs of more than 200 kilotons (1/5 of one megaton) either now or in prospect within the next five years, we would have to deploy and assign 3,840 Minuteman missiles with single improved warheads even to come close to the SS-18 MIRV explosive power. (We are using Schlesinger's 1-to-2 megaton estimate, but we esti-mate that the SS-18 MIRVs are more nearly in the 3-to-5 megaton range). Then, to match their reserve of 1,300 additional ICBMs not required for the counterforce attack against ICBMs, we would need 6,500 warheads of a 1-to-2 megaton range (1,300 x 5 MIRVs x 1-to-2 megatons). Again we would have to use single-warhead Minute-man missiles. This would require a total of some 10,340 Minuteman missiles. This assumes equivalent accuracy in missile guidance, which is a required realistic assumption because three of the new Soviet ICBM series carry on-board digital computers.[67]

A second way of checking out the number of U.S. Minuteman ICBMs required to provide dynamic equivalence to the Soviet of-fensive ICBM power is by throw-weight. Schlesinger estimates the improved Soviet force, when deployed, will have a throw-weight capacity of up to 12 million pounds. We consider that estimate low, but will accept it for the present purpose. He did not give the U.S. ICBM throw-weight capability. Highly authoritative leaks, however, put this at 2 million pounds. So if we were to attempt to attain throw-weight equivalence, we would need six times as many Minuteman missiles as we now possess. Throw-weight is considered the most meaningful parameter for equating missile power, and Schlesinger himself is reported to have urged a throw-weight criterion in negotiating with the Soviets for a SALT II agreement on MIRVs.[68]

So, to attain "essential equivalence" or to "match" the Soviets, in accordance with Schlesinger's pledge, would require the production and deployment of between 5,000 and 9,000 additional Minuteman missiles. None of them could be MIRVed, because the lower megatonnage would render them (in a favorite Schlesinger word) incommensurables compared with the 5-to-10 times more powerful 1-to-2 megaton Soviet warheads.

This is not an impossible task for the United States. We have a production line ongoing for Minuteman IIIs, and all that would be required would be to switch to a single warhead instead of the present three MIRVs of 170 to 200 kilotons. We could run three shifts on the existing production line and add two additional lines. All we would need would be the allocation of enough resources.

However, the Schlesinger programs do not help us even one percent toward attaining "essential equivalence." The vast overbalancing of the strategic equation in favor of the Soviets shows how obvious it is that the U.S. strategic umbrella can no longer protect any of the Free World nations. The Soviet strategic umbrella affords total protection for its clients, such as the Arab states, to engage in economic warfare and use the "oil weapon" to disrupt and even to destroy the economy of the Free World nations.

The task of the United States in rebuilding our strategic deterrent is far from hopeless—unless we permit such slick deception as presented in the Schlesinger programs to lull us into believing that he is doing all that is necessary for national survival. On the contrary, his entire performance is calculated to keep us in happy, but stupid, apathy until the Soviet strategic superiority becomes decisive and hence irreversible. The search for such irreversibility of the new U.S.-U.S.S.R. relationship was openly declared by Kissinger and Brezhnev during their March 1974 presummit conferences. Secretary of State Kissinger told Soviet officials during a luncheon toast:

> Our greatest goal over the next three years is that we can make the relationship that has grown up between our two peoples and our leaders irreversible.[69]

In Soviet Communist doctrine, the fundamental relationship between nations is the "relation of forces." The realistic relation of forces between the U.S. and the U.S.S.R. is most dramatically demonstrated in the massive imbalance of strategic power shown all too starkly in the figures set out above from the official Defense Department reports.

Schlesinger's frivolous conduct in preempting a Kissinger program, and then butchering it by claiming that we *have* alternative strategies instead of merely *wishing* we had them, finally backed Kissinger into a corner in which he had to leak a denial that he disagreed with what was his original creation. Thus, *U.S. News & World Report* carried this "Washington Whisper" on February 25, 1974:

Associates of Secretary of State Henry Kissinger label as "all wrong" the rumors that he disagrees with Defense Secretary James R. Schlesinger's strategic plan for retargeting nuclear weapons against Soviet military facilities as well as population centers. Aides say Mr. Kissinger has always advocated the option of being able to strike military targets, not just cities.

What could Kissinger do about his protege, whose brief taste of the power of spending $80 billion a year had given him a taste for the megalomanic machinations that, in this timeframe and in this administration, are a monopoly of the great Doctor himself? There were alarming indications that the Schlesinger ego-enlargement might evoke even more sensational symptoms. His rhetoric suddenly became turgid and pseudobiblical. In presenting the military budget to the Senate Armed Services Committee in February 1974, he abandoned the SECDEF tradition of sticking largely to a prepared annual statement of 200 to 300 pages and instead embarked on an extemporaneous speech that ran for some 70 minutes, and which he introduced by invoking the words of King Solomon telling us that "where there is no vision, the people perish." Then he abjured the Senators not to pin their hopes on a vision of utopia, because:

We must continue to build our peace structure on the hard facts of the international environment rather than the gossamer hopes for the imminent perfectibility of mankind.

Suppose the Senators should take his high-flown rhetoric seriously. Might they not begin to wonder whether Kissinger's detente with the Soviets was based on the hard facts of the international environment or upon gossamer hopes for the imminent perfectibility of mankind as represented by the Kremlin's Politburo?

Even more dangerous to Kissinger's myths that the U.S. strategic nuclear forces are or ever will be "sufficient" in the balance with the Soviet Union, Schlesinger was becoming careless in defining the timeframe of the imminence of the Soviet threat. A *New York Times* dispatch points this up:

He expressed concern that the Soviet Union, with the larger ballistic missiles it is developing, *could by 1980 acquire a 5-to-1 advantage over the United States* in the "throw-weight" *capability of their missile arsenal.* This, he warned, could upset the nuclear balance if the United States did not take offsetting steps.

At the same time, he declared that "for the *foreseeable future*, we have an appropriate balance of strategic forces."

. . . Adm. Thomas H. Moorer, the chairman of the Joint Chiefs of Staff, followed with a "posture statement" saying that the Soviet Union was embarked on "aggressive modernization programs that could place the United States in a position of strategic inferiority in the *foreseeable years ahead.*"[70]

Unless we interpret Schlesinger as meaning that having the United States in a position of strategic inferiority is an "appropriate balance of strategic forces," then either he or Admiral Moorer is quite obviously lying. Kissinger should indeed be worried by Schlesinger's having created a situation in which interested Senators or Representatives or newsmen might dig a little to see who is the liar. They might find out because Kissinger, in his own testimony before the Senate Foreign Relations Committee, conceded that, at the time of the SALT I signing in May 1972, the Soviets already had attained a 4-to-1 advantage over us in missile throw-weight capability. Indeed, he made this particular specific statement in writing, in commenting on a State Department news release at the request of Senator Symington. Here is the critical sentence:

> The Soviet advantages in the number of strategic missile launchers and *their 4-to-1 lead in throw-weight are balanced* against U.S. advantages in MIRV, heavy bombers, and the quality of our systems.[71]

Immediately after the signing of the SALT I Agreements the Soviets began testing four new improved series of ICBMs, and by May 1974 had had two years in which to upgrade their older missiles with the improvements. Each of their new missile series incorporated a substantial increase in throw-weight over the predecessor type, but the SS-17, which is one of the two upgrades of the SS-11, represents a 140-percent increase over the SS-11 throw-weight, which was 2,500 pounds. The second upgrade of the SS-11, the SS-19, has (according to Schlesinger's FY 1975 DOD Report) an increase of between 300 and 500 percent over its predecessor type, the SS-11. The throw-weight advantage of the Soviet missile force, therefore, had most probably exceeded 5-to-1 over us at the very time that Schlesinger predicted the possibility that it could reach that level by 1980; and certainly no realistic intelligence estimate could delay a 6-to-1 advantage beyond 1975.

In the spring of 1974, therefore, Schlesinger began to appear as an ambitious rival seeking to cut in on the Kissinger monopoly of superstarring in defense and foreign policy. He loomed as a danger to the elaborate Kissinger plan to hold down public and political pressure from demanding the rebuilding of the U.S. strategic deterrent in time to short-circuit the Soviet buildup to a first-strike capability against us. The entire program that had been initiated by McNamara back in 1961 was in danger of being jeopardized in the last critical months before it would become finally irreversible under Kissinger.

But Kissinger had already ousted one Secretary of Defense, and Schlesinger was his own nominee. So Kissinger tried a flank movement rather than a frontal assault in order to keep Schlesinger in line. Kissinger had the perfect appointee available for that delicate and vital assignment: Paul H. Nitze. Kissinger had known him ever since they lectured together in CFR programs back in 1957, and Nitze had worked with McNamara in the brilliant execution of the plan to reduce U.S. strategic power to the level at which we would have no rational alternative to surrender when ultimately confronted by the Soviet demand. Nitze had been the first to enunciate publicly the theory that we could *not win* a strategic arms race with the great Soviet Union and that, therefore, it would be safer to bring our power down to a *very weak second place*. When Nixon and Kissinger came to power in January 1969, Nitze was moved from his post as Number Two man in the Pentagon to principal delegate at the SALT negotiations. Kissinger knew that no one would work with greater zeal to enshrine by treaty with the Soviets the U.S. position of strategic inferiority that had required so many years of effort by McNamara and Nitze for its creation.

So Kissinger schemed to bring Nitze back into the Defense Department in exactly the same position to which President Kennedy had appointed him in 1961: Assistant Secretary of Defense for International Security Affairs. This is the one position that would give Nitze authoritative and official cognizance over the two areas in the Pentagon of special interest to Kissinger: foreign policy and strategic arms control.

Kissinger's plan to install Nitze in the Defense Department to guide and supervise Schlesinger ran into an unexpected phenomenon: one U.S. Senator with a memory, the conscience of a conservative, and courage. A single one of these qualities would, in the current climate, make a Senator outstanding; the combination of all three makes him Barry Goldwater. The sheer insulting effrontery of the attempt to nominate Paul Nitze to be Assistant Secretary of Defense, in a Republican administration that owed the pivotal segment of its support to Americans dedicated to the survival of the United States in freedom, so outraged Senator Goldwater that he flatly stated he was "unalterably opposed" to Nitze, whom he identified with "a group interested in bringing about our unilateral disarmament." For once, the Kissinger plan foundered in the Senate on the rocks of what the *New York Times* called "the bargaining power of the conservatives."[72]

24

Our country is in jeopardy. . . . If long continued, inflation at anything like the present rate would threaten the very foundation of our society.[1]
— *Arthur F. Burns, Federal Reserve Board Chairman*

Inflation in the Free World became so spectacular by the end of March 1974 that all three U.S. newsmagazines gave it priority treatment, even over Watergate. Both *Time* and *Newsweek* gave it the cover story for April 8. *Time* was so excited that the cover was a foldout. Like centerfolds, it presented figures; but these were "percent change" figures picturing the skyrocketing costs of food, fuel oil, coal, gasoline, and all consumer prices. The banner-size boldface headline proclaimed "Inflation: Up the Escalator." None of three newsmagazines could give a specific cause or solution, but *Time* had a number of clues:

> The ultimate threat is that inflation will eventually weaken confidence in democratic governments and institutions and prepare the way for sharp, violent shifts to the radical right or left. . . .
>
> Compounding the alarm—and further weakening faith in governments— is the uncomfortable feeling that no one quite knows what to do about inflation. The experts themselves are not immune from this despair. . . .
>
> That fear is not without justification: *the present world inflation is unlike any before it.* Runaway price boosts might wipe out savings, pauperize individuals, bring down governments—but *usually in only one or a few countries at any specific time, and for what seemed fairly clear reasons.* In the industrialized world, the worst inflations generally ac-

604

companied wars or revolutions, or struck countries that had tried to live beyond their means. . . .

Now inflation is running amok everywhere—and at a time of general peace.

The clues are in the emphasized words. The present world inflation is, indeed, unlike any before. The reasons for it are not clear to economists because the prime cause does not lie in economics. This inflation is peculiar to the nuclear-space age.

This is the first world inflation caused by one superpower's overwhelming the preexisting strategic balance and destroying the basis of the "peace of mutual terror"—a "peace" that had preserved stability and freedom and the opportunities for industrial and agricultural prosperity in the Free World since the end of World War II.

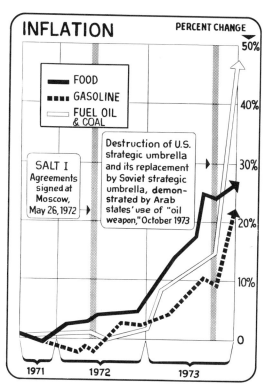

The above chart shows the critical dates of SALT I and the spiral of uncontrolled inflation. The April 1974 statistics of the Paris-based Organization for Economic Cooperation (OECD), to which all major Western industrialized nations belong, showed that all but seven of the 24 major member nations suffered inflation rates of 10 percent or more during the 12-month period ending in February 1974.

Chancellor Helmut Schmidt seemed to have some prescient understanding of it. He was quoted as observing: "I have only to go to the years 1931 and 1933 to say that the meaning of stability is not limited to prices." He is so right. The SALT I destruction of the credibility of the U.S. nuclear umbrella destroyed the foundations of all types of stability in Western Europe. The U.S. nuclear umbrella had been the basis for the stability of relationships in the international area (including the Atlantic alliance), for trade relationships and agreements, for the stability of the flow of raw materials in and finished products out, and for the availability of oil and other sources of energy at reasonable prices.

The logic of the Soviet Union's now-overwhelming strategic superiority predominates throughout the entire spectrum of conflict, which, as the Kremlin wages it, includes economics, national currencies, and political organization. Recognizing this, we can see that Henry Kissinger and his SALT-related defense policies give the Soviets the lever to destroy the stability of the several structures in the Free World upon which the stability of currencies, of prices, of trade relationships, and of governments depend. Every one of these pre-existing stabilities was based upon protection by a credible strategic nuclear deterrent. By agreeing to the imbalances favoring the Soviet Union in SALT I, by acknowledging publicly and officially the Soviet strategic superiorities, and by imposing on the United States a restraint that allows no challenge to the overwhelming Soviet advantages, Kissinger destroyed the credibility of the U.S. strategic umbrella upon which all of Western Europe totally depended.

The relationship of the strategic balance to the runaway inflation in the Free World is shown by the following chart. It shows that commodity prices had held steady for some four years, and even dipped slightly in 1971. But shortly after the SALT I accords were signed in Moscow in May 1972, the index shot up from its comfortable 500 (based on 1931 prices) to nearly 1,500.

Similarly, shortly after the meaning of SALT I sank in, the price of gold—the best indicator of inflation of currencies—began to climb and jumped in the free market from $60 in late 1972 to $127 in mid-1973. It dropped for a while until the October War in the Middle East demonstrated what it means for Soviet client states to have the protection of a credible nuclear umbrella (instead of Western industrial nations having the protection of a credible U.S. nuclear umbrella). Since October 18, 1973, gold has skyrocketed to undreamed-of highs ranging above $150 per ounce.

The great works on nuclear strategy were published in 1961 or earlier—before the Pugwash scientists and ideologically allied elitist groups had "made a captive of public policy" (as President Eisenhower's farewell address had warned) and established a monopoly of prestigious positions in government, foundations, and think-tanks. Herman

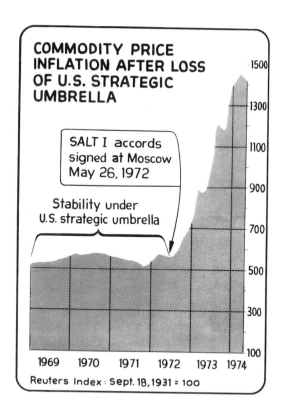

COMMODITY PRICE INFLATION AFTER LOSS OF U.S. STRATEGIC UMBRELLA

SALT I accords signed at Moscow May 26, 1972

Stability under U.S. strategic umbrella

1969　1970　1971　1972　1973　1974

Reuters Index: Sept. 18, 1931 = 100

Kahn published his opus *On Thermonuclear War* in 1960, and in 1961 *A Forward Strategy for America* was published by Robert Strausz-Hupe, William R. Kintner and Stefan T. Possony. The list of advisers and consultants to whom these three leading strategists gave acknowledgements sounds like a who's who in scholarly and intellectual circles. It included Fritz G. A. Kraemer, first discoverer of Henry Kissinger. The perceptive analysis made by the three scholars on the influence of strategic nuclear weapons on international relations is still unequalled, and now stands confirmed by subsequent history. The relevant point is contained in these lines:

The horrendous prospects of large-scale nuclear warfare have had an almost paralyzing effect on the thinking of even the most seasoned military professionals and civilian military experts. The *net result has been an irrational aberration from the traditional purpose of military power.* [Emphasis in original text] Thus far the U.S. has failed to discover a rational formula for integrating nuclear weapons and other technological paraphernalia into a constructive strategy. The Soviets appear to have accomplished this task almost simultaneously with their technological-military achievements.

Therefore a realistic consideration of American policies and their attendant strategies must begin with the clarification of the new dimensions which global-range nuclear weapons have introduced in the measurement of the international power balance.

For the first time in history there exist weapons permitting a technologically armed superpower to conquer the entire world.

Total nuclear war is more than just the most massive among the individual instruments of protracted conflict. Potentially, it could be the climax of the over-all conflict. *Even if a total nuclear war will never be fought, the necessities and risks of total nuclear war influence and, in many instances, determine alternative policies and strategies.*

The logic of total nuclear war predominates throughout the entire conflict spectrum in the same manner as the law of gravity influences physical events. . . .[2]

In 1974 Doctors Strausz-Hupe and Kintner were, respectively, U.S. ambassadors to Sweden and Thailand and could no longer be expected to write anything critical of the Secretary of State.

There is a legend about an ancient Greek king who was reputed to have more gold in his treasure vaults than any other king in the world. One day he showed his golden hoard to a traveling philosopher. Afterwards, the philosopher thanked the king, but without superlatives, and was preparing to take his leave. The king remarked that the philosopher did not seem very impressed with the greatest golden treasure in the world. The philospher replied that it was indeed impressive, but that the king should not rely too much upon it. "As soon as another king comes along with better iron," the philosopher warned him, "he will take all of your gold away from you."

What might be called physical military power has always rated first in the pecking order of power. The "better iron," of course, referred to the swords, spears, and shields of that era. The great and enormously wealthy Roman Empire fell into the dark ages after its own military power disintegrated and the Vandals and the Visigoths brought their crude but effective military power to bear. The classic highwayman of the 18th century summed it up in five words: "your money or your life." Regardless of how much gold you might have and how little he had, if he had a gun and you didn't, he could take both and the option was entirely his. The ancient aphorism "to the victor belongs the spoils" originated not in party politics but in contests of military power.

After World War II the United States demobilized the most powerful military force the world had ever known. We had enough power in-being to have overrun the U.S.S.R. and conquered the world. But, urged by subtle but powerful Soviet propaganda pressuring our government to "bring the boys home," we self-destructed our military power with irresponsible haste and waste. Shortly afterwards we abandoned the nations of Eastern Europe to the Soviets. (Stalin's forces were equipped, of course, largely by the United States, and were able to move only because of the U.S. gift of a million prime-mover automobile trucks.)

608

All of Western Europe would have fallen, too, because the wily Stalin had not demobilized the massive Soviet forces. But there was then in existence a new form of military power—nuclear power. By the grace of God, we had it, and the Soviets did not. It was then 1,000 times more powerful than conventional weapons. By 1952, with the invention of the hydrogen bomb (primarily by Dr. Edward Teller), nuclear power became a million times more powerful than conventional weapons. Now, Soviet warheads are up to 100-million times more powerful than conventional weapons.

The point, as made by Doctors Strausz-Hupe, Kintner, and Possony, is that, for the first time in history, there is a power so great as to permit a technologically armed superpower to conquer the entire world. After World War II the only thing that permitted the establishment of a world order in which free nations could exist and prosper was the God-given fact that the United States possessed this new type of military power. It was ours alone until 1949, when the Soviets, with the help of spies and sympathizers in the United States, broke our monopoly. Later, because we developed the world's first great long-range strategic bomber force, we maintained a decisive strategic superiority over the Soviets. Our massive margin of superiority in deliverable nuclear explosive power provided us and our allies, and even neutrals, with a nuclear deterrent against Soviet aggression conducted either with other nuclear weapons or with their massively superior conventional military forces.

This became known as the U.S. nuclear umbrella. Without it there would not have been a single free nation in Europe. Together with the NATO alliance, which reached its 25th anniversary in April 1974, it formed the foundation of stability for the structures—political, economic, and national-and-international financial—that permitted the highly civilized nations of Western Europe to retain their political freedom and develop remarkable prosperity, despite the Soviet Union's commitment to expansion and its superior conventional military capability.

As of the time of the Cuban missile crisis in 1962, the United States still held an 8-to-1 nuclear superiority over the Soviet Union. Defense Secretary Robert McNamara, assisted by Paul Nitze and Roswell Gilpatric, then began the process of the clandestine unilateral strategic disarmament of the United States. Our margin of superiority was so great, however, that despite their multiplicitous efforts to cut it down, the Soviets were not able to attain parity with us until 1968. By 1970 the Soviets had opened a missile gap in their favor, but our *reputation* for superior nuclear power had such a momentum of its own that our deterrent remained believable—and, therefore, effective with friends, enemies, and neutrals—until May 1972.

That date, of the Moscow SALT I Summit, was the watershed—the

609

end of the era in which stability was supported by the U.S. strategic nuclear umbrella. That was the time when Henry Kissinger poured SALT, so to speak, into the gasoline tank of the Free World. The explicit imbalances favoring the Soviets in the SALT Agreements themselves, and the statistics on the strategic balance publicly released at the time, killed as of that date the credibility of our strategic deterrent.

The result was to leave the nations of Western Europe vulnerable to conquest by any one, or a combination, of the three types of military power held in such massive superiority by the Soviets: conventional military forces, tactical nuclear forces, or strategic nuclear forces. Their escalation dominance is no longer subject to challenge at any level of military force. But to employ these forces in actual combat against the highly industrialized nations of Western Europe would at least dislocate and most probably disastrously damage their industrial and agricultural productive capacities. Employment of actual force—even if it threw the productive machinery out of kilter for only two years—would result in a gross-product loss of some two trillion dollars (2,000-billion dollars; $2,000,000,000,000).

If, however, the remaining political unity and conventional military capability still embodied in the shell of the NATO alliance could be destroyed or fragmented, the Soviet takeover of the industrialized nations of the West could be achieved without *actual employment* of force. Indeed, if the economies and unity of these countries could be sufficiently degraded, they might voluntarily seek inclusion in the Soviet bloc for the sake of stability. Without it, their populations might starve.

The psychotic criminal with a compulsion to plant evidence calculated to ensure his apprehension and conviction is a common type in both fiction and serious nonfiction. As we have seen, Henry Kissinger does some things so otherwise inexplicable that at times they seem to suggest a similar compulsion. We have seen how he gratuitously included in his testimony under oath before the Senate Foreign Relations Committee an unlimited endorsement of the accuracy and integrity of *Cold Dawn: The Story of Salt* and its author, for whom he expressed "enormous respect." We saw that he did this despite the fact that the book, if analyzed in relation to the SALT I accords, would go far toward proving that Kissinger was guilty of "high crimes and misdemeanors" within the meaning of the constitutional provision for impeachment (at least as interpreted by the House Judiciary Committee staff in 1974 in the case of Richard Nixon).

We have also seen how he blurted out admissions that the most meticulously protected secrets of the SALT negotiations—substantially all of which are classified Top Secret—were the results of private deals with Soviet Ambassador Anatoly Dobrynin; and that, if the Soviets should build a new submarine base in Cuba, it would constitute "another" Soviet submarine base there; and that he (Kissinger) should get the credit for the major breakthrough in the SALT I negotiations on May 20, 1972—a purported tour de force that he had repeatedly attributed specifically and directly to Richard Nixon, and that Nixon had repeatedly claimed for himself.

All these mea culpas were eclipsed in inexplicability, however, by his virtuoso performance before a group of congressional members' wives at the State Department on March 11, 1974. *National Review* characterized the Kissinger assertion as an "astonishing faux pas." Astonishing, yes. Faux pas? The evidence is piling up against it because that expression means a blunder, and to blunder is usually understood to mean to make a mistake through stupidity, ignorance, confusion, or carelessness. None of these dictionary definitions seems to be in character with the brilliant and sophisticated Dr. Kissinger. It is even more out of character for him to make a mistake at all. No Secretary of State *inadvertently* calls the leaders of his country's principal allies political bastards; at least not publicly. That sort of thing isn't done in the highest echelons of diplomacy. Secretary of State Kissinger didn't use that specific term; but what he did say was:

> The deepest problem in Europe today which we still see is that there have been, very rarely, *fully legitimate* governments in any European country since World War I.[3]

National Review's reporting on reaction to the incident was accurate:

> The notion that Chamberlain, Churchill, Eden, Macmillan, Wilson, Heath, Attlee, Adenauer, de Gaulle, Pompidou, and many others presided over semilegitimate governments has been received in Europe with surprise and outrage.[4]

An apology was called for, and it came in typical Kissinger phraseology:

> I want to make clear to the extent that the remarks lend themselves to the interpretation that was given, I regret them and I feel they made no great contribution to the Atlantic dialogue. . . .[5]

Nevertheless, the remarks could have made a vital contribution to an ulterior objective.

Most of the media, liberal and conservative alike, have assumed that the damage Kissinger has done or is doing to the NATO alliance and other powerful industrial nations of the Free World, and to U.S. allies such as Japan, has been inadvertent, unintentional, unpremeditated, and hence unplanned. However, from Kissinger's other performances we know he is a dedicated planner, even a compulsive schemer. To assume that a protracted sequence of actions by such a person is inadvertent or unplanned, rather than being purposeful, is very risky, especially if all the actions fall into a tight pattern. Thus, a leading British newspaper, *The Guardian,* editorialized:

> Singlehanded, in the space of a year, he has done as much to poison trans-atlantic relations and exacerbate the divisions within the European Community as General de Gaulle achieved in 10 years.[6]

The analysis in *U.S. News & World Report* on April 1, 1974, presented an interesting slant:

> But it is inside his own State Department . . . that the most sweeping and bitter criticism of the Secretary of State is to be found right now. A typical comment comes from a high-ranking official outside the team of intimates surrounding Mr. Kissinger:
> "I know that Henry is brilliant—but in some ways he is proving to be an unmitigated disaster as Secretary of State. He is arrogant and egocentric, with no apparent understanding of alliance diplomacy, and surprisingly little understanding of what makes Europeans tick."

In reporting the effect in Europe of the Kissinger-Nixon campaign in March 1974 to force a showdown with the Europeans on the issue of their future relationship with the United States, the analysis continued:

> The single-word description most widely used by headline writers in West Germany to describe the reaction is shock. Generals and unofficial military experts are in agreement that a further cut in military manpower would bring the U.S. below the credibility level.
> The Paris bureau [of *U.S. News*] cabled: "The French feel the Nixon threat is blackmail. . . ."
> The reaction in London, as expressed privately by a British diplomat: "I'm completely bewildered. This apocalyptic approach, with its threats of cataclysmic events to come, is playing with fire."
> A prominent analyst of European strategy complains: "It all seems so unnecessary. But every time Kissinger gets into an airplane with a group of journalists, he can't resist the temptation to say something indiscreet and offensive that does damage."

West German headline writers did a good job in isolating the single word that best encapsules Kissinger's totally consistent campaign against the NATO allies: the administration of "shocks." It cannot be viewed as coincidence that the Japanese press coined a new expression—"shockus"—to describe what Kissinger was doing to Japan by going behind the back of the pro-U.S. government to deal with Communist China and to devalue the dollar. What are shocks good for? Shocks can destroy foundations; and if you destroy foundations, you in turn destroy structures. Structures disintegrate and fall when their foundations are knocked out from under them by a series of well-planned shocks.

Under Henry Kissinger the campaign to destroy the political structure of the Free World alliance by demoralizing, discrediting, insulting, and abusing the NATO governments and leadership is reaching fruition. The series of shocks he has administered are emerging as deliberately planned. For years his apologists have insisted that his insults and bullying of NATO leadership were inadvertent; but, not even a stupid Secretary of State inadvertently calls the leaders of allied nations demibastards occupying doubtful offices under semilegitimate governments. Henry Kissinger may be many things to many people, but no intelligent observer calls him stupid.

Even columnists for the *New York Times* and the *Washington Post* are beginning to see that the Kissinger damage to NATO is deliberate. Thus, Leslie H. Gelb observed in April 1974:

> The Nixon Administration, instead of directing its main effort toward the *political union of Western Europe*—a stated objective of American policy for 25 years—has been trying to bolster relations with European nations individually. And it has been trying to check the French drive for leadership in Europe by telling the other European nations that they must choose between Washington and Paris. . . .
>
> The European governments, the officials explained, *had to be shocked* into seeing that they could not move together at the expense of American interests. . . .
>
> "Several weeks ago, the President and Henry," another White House official related, "talked about what the President would say in his press conference, and Henry's *statements—the calculated and the less calculated ones—were part of it.*"[7]

The Kissinger-Nixon talk referred to furnished the opportunity for Dr. Kissinger to plant on the President the idiotic threat to NATO that he enunciated in his March 15 speech in Chicago that they could not have "cooperation on the security front and then proceed to have confrontation and even hostility on the economic and political front."

Thus it is that Henry Kissinger went about deliberately destroying the political structure of the Free World alliance—the fruit of a quarter-century of patient statesmanship. It is quite obvious what power will fill the power vacuum in Western Europe created by the planned fragmentation of NATO; and that has been the priority long-range objective in the European area of Stalin, Khrushchev, and Brezhnev. We have seen earlier how Kissinger pulled the rug out from under our allies at the Moscow Summit in May 1972 by making concessions to Brezhnev on the Soviet-promoted Conference on European Security, and on the agenda for the conference on what had always been called "mutual and balanced" force reductions (until Kissinger capitulated by abandoning the "balanced").

As explained by Chalmers M. Roberts in the *Washington Post*, the Kissinger-Nixon move from confrontation to negotiation with the Soviets, and away from hostility to China,

> . . . to a large degree has been responsible for removing that "cement of fear" that was the chief bind between Western Europe and the United States.
>
> The NATO treaty, a quarter of a century old on April 4, was the irreducible minimum tie. . . .
>
> The Atlantic relationship was the centerpiece of American foreign policy.
>
> Messrs. Nixon and Kissinger have changed all that. By their opening of the dialogues with Moscow and Peking, and their playing off of one against the other, *Western Europe has been moved to a second and lower level of policy status.*
>
> One reason this has come about is that the nuclear relationship between Washington and Moscow *changed from one of American superiority, vast in Dulles' day, to something like rough parity.* If for no other reason, it was imperative to break the cold war heritage and try to negotiate with the Kremlin.[8]

Joseph Alsop has accurately denounced all such assertions of "parity" between the United States and the U.S.S.R. as "garbage."

The shocks that have destroyed the *political* structure of NATO could not have come into action until the preexisting vast American nuclear superiority was first destroyed. We can now recognize that the destruction of the credibility of the U.S. nuclear umbrella has permitted the Kremlin to destroy the *economic* structure of the Free World as well as the political structure. Henry Kissinger has played the climactic role in the economic as well as the political arena. The primary weapon used to destroy the Free World economic structure is runaway inflation. This inflation had to be staged in an unprecedented manner by the simultaneous degradation of the paper currency of *all* major industrial nations not yet controlled by communism.

Paper currency merely amounts to a promise to pay by the issuing government. Once a government loses control over its own national destiny, how valuable is its promise to pay? In this nuclear-space age a nation loses control over its national destiny by becoming vulnerable to control by a nuclear superpower through actual military attack or, more probably, by blackmail based on the threat, express or implied, of such an attack. From the end of World War II to the signing of the SALT I Agreements in Moscow in May 1972, it was only the combination of NATO political-military unity and the U.S. strategic umbrella that preserved for the free nations of Western Europe the credible capability of controlling their own destiny—and consequently, of making good on the promises of their paper currencies.

We have seen that Kissinger, as architect of SALT I and czar of U.S. defense policies, conceded massive strategic superiority to the Soviets. Similarly we have seen that for some five years Kissinger has been appeasing enemies and shocking allies, but doing this to our friends under the guise of inadvertence until the spring of 1974, when the explanation shifted to claim the "necessity" of winning NATO cooperation by administering shocks to our former friends. Thus Kissinger has simultaneously been attacking both pillars of a free and prosperous Western Europe. The Finlandization of Western Europe has long been recognized as a major interim objective of the Kremlin. It has become increasingly difficult to fail to see that Kissinger is setting up that objective.

To accelerate NATO's fragmenting, however, the Soviets coordinated attacks in the economic sector. The trillion-dollar-a-year industrial, trade, and agricultural machinery of the Common Market members is one of the most complex and vulnerable structures in world history. By inciting and supporting Arab use of the "oil weapon" in late 1973 and through early spring of 1974, the Soviets arrested and reversed the spectacular economic growth of the free nations. Severe cuts in production brought about by the embargo were accompanied by near-panic conditions brought on by the trebling of crude oil prices by the Arabs, which threatened to change the multi-billion-dollar trade surpluses of the nine nations to deficits.

Thus the major shock was that backward nations, with mostly nomadic primitive populations, could reduce the 257 million highly civilized inhabitants of free Europe to bankruptcy—provided only that the backward nations had the forward support of the only credible strategic umbrella remaining in the world.

How do the Soviets go about replacing the political, military, and economic structure of the Free World that they have destroyed? They have worked it all out, and even tested it, in advance, based on invoking the Brezhnev Doctrine. They held a full-dress rehearsal in Czechoslovakia in 1968 and demonstrated that it works. When President Nixon signed the Moscow "Declaration of Principles" in May 1972, the United States undertook to submit, without objection, to the Soviet program of conquest of the world under the strategy the Kremlin has code-named "peaceful coexistence."

Probably the first of the major nations to go under Communist control in Western Europe will be France or Italy. The loss of confidence in their governmental structures brought about by the Soviet-promoted fuel crisis in 1973-74, the deflation of their currency, and the runaway inflation that followed the SALT I accords and the Middle East War of October 1973, threw all the NATO nations, especially those two, open to political capture by popular fronts of Socialists and open Communists. Once a "popular front" government is voted in, the Brezhnev Doctrine will dominate Western Europe. The Soviets not only have on active duty in their armed forces some four million men (compared to less than two million for the United States), but they have four million ready reserves (to our at most one million). The Soviets have available reserves numbering some 20 million in their ground forces alone.[9] These are the occupation troops. Backed by more than twice as many modern tanks as the U.S. and NATO forces together have available in Europe, and by more than 1,700 more aircraft (and more modern and faster aircraft), they are ready to carry out the mandate of the Brezhnev Doctrine that, once the Communists attain governmental status in any country, the Soviets will intervene with armed forces to sustain the Communists against any attack.

The 1973-74 employment of the "oil weapon" was just the beginning of the harassment of the free industrial nations under cover of the Soviet nuclear umbrella. Soviet Foreign Minister Gromyko, addressing the sixth special session of the UN General Assembly during the debate on raw materials and development, called the oil crisis a failure of the capitalist system and not a real shortage; and he boasted that "the Socialist world has not practically experienced it."

The Soviets are backing the nationalization and monopoly control of all the raw materials of the so-called Third World states, all of which saw how the Kremlin was able to protect the weak Arab states from military attack and even from criticism. Third World states are all potential Soviet clients, all ready and willing to serve as Soviet Communist tools to destroy the economic structure of the West. The governmental structures of the NATO nations will fall, too, as their currencies become worthless, as they become bankrupt, and as their populations begin to starve. And starve they will, those 257 million West Europeans, once their economic and political structures collapse, unless new structures replace the old. So some of these now-sovereign states will call on the only power with the capability of restoring the order upon which complex industrial nations depend. They depend on trade in raw materials and finished products; they require a stable medium of exchange and stable relationships in the international sector.

The non-Communist governments that have been helpless to protect the national industrial systems will be replaced with coalition, or at least "popular front," governments. Then the Brezhnev Doctrine will be applied. All Europe will go under Soviet control. Once again raw materials and oil will flow to the great industrial plant, but no longer will the output be for the benefit of free peoples. The Soviets will take over a going concern—and their accomplishment will have depended on a Soviet buildup in strategic weapons.

As a result of what the shocks have done to Europe, we will be isolated, cut off from both raw materials and equally essential markets. Our own economy will stagnate and inflation will run wild. That much we would suffer even without the Kremlin's applying any strategic military power directly against us, or even making threats based on it.

It is a cardinal tenet of Communist conflict doctrine to strike for the jugular of the political structure. The United States is "the enemy society." Should we not expect to have received even more elaborate and cunningly schemed shocks than the other Western nations?

Vietnam was the most elaborate of the shocks we have already received. We have seen earlier that the fantastic dragging out of the Vietnam War was a McNamara machination. Below is a chart that the then-Secretary of Defense Melvin Laird included in his FY 1973 Defense Department Report submitted to the Senate and House Armed Services Committees on February 17, 1972.

This chart proves Laird's repeated assertion that the Vietnam War served as a gigantic diversion, committing scores of billions of dollars to the no-win strategy in Vietnam, and preventing the modernization of U.S. strategic forces to keep the Soviets from pulling decisively ahead of us. At a cost to them of never more than one billion dollars a year, they were able to take advantage of the up-to-$24-billion we were throwing away in Southeast Asia every year. Summing up, Laird said:

> This difference has had a significant and adverse impact on the military posture of the United States relative to that of the Soviet Union.[10]

RELATIVE IMPACT OF SOUTHEAST ASIA CONFLICT ON US vs. USSR

(IN FY 70 DEFENSE DOLLARS)

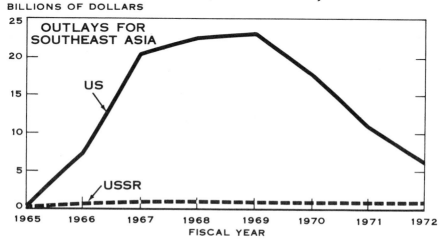

BILLIONS OF DOLLARS

OUTLAYS FOR SOUTHEAST ASIA

US

USSR

FISCAL YEAR

Thus, the prolongation of the Vietnam War, with its no-win strategy imposed by McNamara and his clique, served to create a massive advantage for the Soviets over the United States.

The Vietnam War dealt other shocks to our system. It caused more divisiveness in the United States and did more to demoralize and discredit the government than any previous event in our history. It alienated huge segments of American youth from a former devotion to our country and American institutions. According to *The Pentagon Papers*, in May 1967 John T. McNaughton, Assistant Secretary of Defense, wrote this note to McNamara:

> A feeling is widely held that "the Establishment" is out of its mind.
> The feeling is that we are trying to impose some U.S. image on distant peoples we cannot understand (any more than we can the younger generation here at home), and that we are carrying the thing to absurd lengths. Related to this feeling is the increased polarization that is taking place in the United States with *seeds of the worst split in our people in more than a century.*

After thinking over McNaughton's note for a month, McNamara made his decision in late June 1967 to commission *The Pentagon Papers*. This McNamara-initiated and -directed study, with its 3,000 pages of narrative history and 4,000 pages of appended documents, was carefully designed for its divisive results. Both right and left were provided with ammunition to use against each other in placing the blame for the tragic sacrifice of scores of thousands of American lives and billions of American dollars. As the *New York Times* foreword explained:

> The writers appear to have stood at the political and bureaucratic center of the period, directing their criticisms toward both right and left.
> In one section, Senator Eugene McCarthy, the antiwar candidate for the 1968 Democratic Presidential nomination, is characterized as "impudent and dovish" and as an "upstart challenger." At another point in the same section, the demands of Admiral U.S. Grant Sharp, commander of Pacific forces, for all-out bombing of North Vietnam, are characterized as "fulminations."

The first flowering of the drive to destroy our governmental structure was the destruction of the political career of Lyndon Johnson and his forced abdication from the presidential race in 1968. In Communist terminology, the Vietnam War was used by the "progressive" elements in our society to attack the "ruling classes." It was used to demonstrate that the President of the United States can be brought down by a sufficiently massive attack through the mass media.

When Henry Kissinger, in early 1974, attempted to bring Paul Nitze back into the Pentagon as Assistant Secretary of Defense for International Security Affairs this triggered appropriate outrage in Senator Goldwater. The Associated Press reported on March 1, 1974:

> "I have heard it said that I am only mildly opposed to Mr. Nitze's appointment," said Goldwater, a member of the Senate Armed Services Committee.
>
> "That is not true," he said. "I am opposed to this appointment just as strongly as it is possible for one who believes in this nation's maintaining an adequate defense to oppose a man who was formerly identified with a group interested in bringing about our unilateral disarmament. . . ."
>
> Goldwater, in a prepared statement, referred to Nitze as "a member of the old McNamara defense team which came very close to destroying this country's military capability."

How close is very close? Close enough for Kissinger to finish the job. In an interview in *U.S. News & World Report* of February 11, 1974, Senator Goldwater spelled out what he called "our worsening position in world power." Here is a fair summary of that interview:

(1) There is a "group interested in bringing about our unilateral disarmament."

(2) This group included "the old McNamara defense team," of which Paul Hilken Nitze was a leading member.

(3) This group came "very close" to destroying the military capability of the United States.

(4) This group brought us so low that, with the Nixon Administration's (that is, Henry Kissinger's) "perpetuation" of the "mistake," which was "started back in the Kennedy days" (that is, by McNamara and Nitze), we are now "second to the Soviets in every category of military strength. . . . The Soviets are now superior to us in every category of military equipment."

(5) The Moscow Test Ban Treaty (into which McNamara dragged us) and SALT I and now SALT II (into which Kissinger dragged us) are "designed to work the United States into a position of weakness from which we can't operate."

(6) The McNamara-Nitze defense team's put-down of U.S. strategic power—as enshrined and embellished by Kissinger and his SALT policies—has made us such a weak Number Two to the Soviets that we will soon be passed by Red China, thus eventually becoming Number Three.

(7) Once the SALT I and II Agreements with the Soviets work us down into a position of weakness from which we can't operate, we will be "slowly sucked once again" into a major world war—"World War III."

(8) The remedy is "to rebuild our military posture. . . . If it's going to take . . . 100 billion, let's spend it until we have built ourselves up into a stronger nation."

A group acting to accomplish the unilateral disarmament of the United States could not possibly come so very close to accomplishing its purpose without advance planning. As soon as members of the group started this planning, they became conspirators. Their planning was secret; that is, McNamara and Kissinger conducted their programs of clandestine unilateral strategic disarmament of the United States under various "covers"; e.g., McNamara used his famous "cost-effectiveness" formulas to kill off most advanced strategic weapons development projects; he ordered "studies" to determine "military requirements" that stalled projects until they died; under the guise of "modernization," he scrapped at least 1,400 strategic bombers that would have been effective for another 20 years; by asserting that we had attained a "technological plateau," he initiated a campaign of "technological obsolescence" under which research and development of advanced systems were degraded as useless and unnecessary; and, to cover the Soviet advance-past-parity toward decisive superiority, he played the numbers games with the American people by ordering U.S. missiles equipped with miniaturized warheads, good for nothing but to cut down the destructive power of our strategic forces, to make our warheads unreliable, and to deceive the American people and Congress.

The House Armed Services Committee did its best to expose McNamara back in 1966. House Report 1536 of May 16, 1966, adopted unanimously by the House Armed Services Committee, in effect indicted McNamara on the equivalent of charges that he had: (1) deliberately attempted to deceive Congress and the American people; (2) usurped Congress' constitutional authority; (3) sought to obstruct committees of Congress in the performance of their duties; (4) deliberately altered official testimony of the Joint Chiefs of Staff; and (5) abused his powers of classification to protect his own position from being exposed as contrary to that of the Joint Chiefs. Congress repudiated McNamara's blocking of the ABM program unanimously recommended by the Joint Chiefs of Staff. The vote against McNamara's policies ran as high as 356-to-2 in the House and 81-to-1 in the Senate.

Henry Kissinger covered his unilateral disarmament programs under the diverse excuses that it was impossible for the United States to produce additional numbers of missile launchers, and that the only way to prevent the missile gap in favor of the Soviets from continuing to widen drastically was to enter into the SALT I Interim Agreement that actually prescribed a freeze on U.S. weapons, but put no effective limits on Soviet buildups—in practical effect, therefore, more unilateral disarmament.

It is therefore established that McNamara, Nitze, and Kissinger are all conspirators who secretly plotted to disarm the United States unilaterally; and who were so ruthless and dishonest that they brought the United States down from what Henry Kissinger admitted was "overwhelming" strategic superiority in 1962, to a Kissinger-admitted Soviet advantage in missile throw-weight of 4-to-1 against us, which translates into a 10-to-1 to 20-to-1 superiority over us in missile-deliverable explosive power.

When McNamara, Nitze, and Kissinger planned to accomplish the unilateral disarmament of the United States and to make us inferior to the Soviets in strategic military power, they clearly betrayed their oaths of office under which which they pledged to "support and defend the Constitution of the United States against all enemies, foreign and domestic."

Although we could prove by conclusive circumstantial evidence that Henry Kissinger was carrying out the same policies of unilateral disarmament that McNamara initiated and carried on for seven years with the brilliant assistance of Paul Nitze, we could not conclusively establish the linkage with the original plotters themselves. But Kissinger himself established the linkage by attempting to name Paul Nitze as Assistant Secretary of Defense. There was no question that, if Kissinger had had President Nixon nominate Nitze, the Senate would have consented, and probably by a large majority. But hearings by the Senate Armed Services Committee would have brought to light the plot in which Paul Hilken Nitze was such a successful leader, and which Henry Kissinger has taken over and perpetuated. So, when Kissinger failed to put forth his best efforts to overcome Goldwater's opposition to Nitze, Nitze's ego erupted in a tantrum-like resignation from the SALT delegation.

The plot could have been exposed if the Senate Committee staff had prepared a parallel-column comparison of the proposals made by Paul Nitze at the National Strategy Seminar at Asilomar, California, on April 29, 1960, side by side with the updating of the Nitze program published by Roswell Gilpatric in the April 1964 issue of Foreign Affairs, and, in a third column, the actual strategic programs and policies carried out by the McNamara-Nitze-Gilpatric team as extended and embellished by Kissinger. The way that all three columns mesh is mechanically perfect and conclusive. Nitze was the architect of the master plan for the clandestine unilateral strategic disarmament of the United States, and the gut elements of his plan have been carried out to the letter.

Such a massive change simply cannot have "just happened." Common sense and logic tell us that it could not have been brought about without a master plan, any more than the United States could have rocketed men to the moon and brought them safely back to earth without a plan. The Apollo moon project involved about $30 billion. The reversal of the U.S. overwhelming strategic superiority involved hundreds of billions of dollars of investment in strategic weapons systems.

It will be claimed that prominent Americans in Nitze's walk of life do not betray our country. Yet, Paul Hilken Nitze's maternal uncle, who enjoyed a similar station in life and similar family and financial connections, did. Paul Hilken of Roland Park, Maryland, served as paymaster for German saboteurs in America during World War I. Hilken's confession was given by him in person to representatives of the Mixed Claims Commission on German Sabotage in World War I.[11]

Paul Hilken Nitze did not invent the *idea* of unilaterally disarming the United States under cover of the professed hope that Communist Russia would cooperatively follow suit. He did not originate the methodology of disarming the United States through a series of "unilateral initiatives" put into effect by the executive department without a treaty, thereby avoiding and short-circuiting the U.S. constitutional safeguards of Senate debate and consent. Nor was Nitze the first to provide a persuasive argument for the pervasive thesis that, in an eyeball-to-eyeball nuclear confrontation with the Soviets, it is safer to be weak than to be strong.

Paul Nitze's contribution, however, was creative, imaginative, pragmatic, and unprecedented. Never before had the idea, the method, the philosophical and strategic basis, and the essential specifics been so brilliantly blended in a single plan. Equally important, the Nitze proposal contained the semantic cover for the true purpose of the unilateral-disarmament and psychological-surrender features. This cover is absolutely essential to secure public and congressional acceptance of the parts of the program that surface in appropriations acts, Defense Department programs, and defense contracts. The cover worked so well that, 14 years later, Henry Kissinger is able to continue to implement the plan in the same way McNamara, Nitze, and Gilpatric did in the 1960s.

The Nitze semantic cover has worked so well, indeed, that it has earned the right to be known as the "fool-safe" feature of the unilateral disarmament plan. We could not have been reduced to our present low estate in strategic power unless the American people and the Congress had been fooled. The very existence of such a program has been kept safe from prying eyes, almost to the point of no-return. This semantic cover has worked in two ways: first, nuclear strategy is so complex that Nitze's skilled use of sophisticated terminology has rendered his program incomprehensible to non-experts; and second, when any good American does penetrate the meaning, he cannot believe that Nitze really meant what he said.

The semantic cover passed its acid test in November 1963 when the Senate Armed Services Committee voted 11 to 3 to approve

Nitze's appointment as Secretary of the Navy. Those who voted "no" were Senators Barry Goldwater, Strom Thurmond, and Harry Flood Byrd. The 11 in favor simply could not understand the true meaning of Nitze's proposals or could not believe that an American would seriously propose such shocking things. After proposing at the Asilomar Seminar that we scrap all counterforce-capable strategic weapons and retain only systems capable of retaliation, Nitze added:

> (3) that we multilateralize the command of our retaliatory systems by making SAC [the U.S. Strategic Air Command] a NATO command, and (4) that we inform the United Nations that NATO will turn over ultimate power of decision on the use of these systems to the General Assembly of the United Nations. . . .[12]

Nitze did not make these proposals just because he is an internationalist and a lifelong member of the Council on Foreign Relations. His purpose was to ensure that the United States *would never make any actual use of its retaliatory strategic force.* He explained, in highly sophisticated terms, that once a nation had stripped itself down to retaliation weapons only, such weapons could not support any *rational* strategy. A nation builds a retaliatory force only to create strategic deterrence. If the enemy nation actually launches a strategic nuclear strike against the would-be deterrent nation, deterrence has failed. As Nitze put it:

> If deterrence fails, the only reaction open to us is retaliation in support of a purpose that no longer exists—the purpose of deterring the enemy from taking the action that they have already taken.

He asked, rhetorically, if we are capable of making such an irrational response to a Soviet nuclear attack, and concluded that the Russians might well conclude that we are. Thus the purpose of his proposal that we turn over command of our strategic forces to NATO is simply to get as many fingers on the safety catch as possible (through multilateralized command), and the proposal to turn ultimate control over the U.S. retaliatory force to the UN is to ensure that that (Soviet- and so-called Third World-controlled) organization will veto any U.S. proposal to use our own weapons in retaliation against an attack on us.

Why in the world would any American want to do such a thing to the United States? Nitze explained in his 1960 Asilomar speech. He explained by analogy that he does not want to do anything that will result in our getting "clobbered" by a Soviet nuclear strike:

> In a poker game with several players, what is the most dangerous hand? Not the worst hand, but the second best hand. With the second best hand, one is tempted to follow up the betting, but if one does, one gets clobbered.[13]

Nitze's entire purpose in scrapping all U.S. strategic weapons that have what he calls a "Class A" or counterforce capability is to let the Soviets know that *they do not need to deliver a preemptive strike against us* because we have no weapons capable of rational use in a disarming strike against them. That part of his program has been executed by the successive policies of McNamara-Nitze and then Kissinger. But all that would be wasted if the Soviets *think* that we would ever use our weapons (or what remained of them) in a retaliatory strike against the Soviet Union. The Soviets would then feel they had to strike to take out our retaliatory force.

The Nitze program is designed to convince the Soviets that they do not need to strike to eliminate the danger that we might retaliate. Hence his somewhat elaborate proposals for NATO command and UN control of U.S. strategic forces. Even though the Soviets might believe that the Americans might be capable of such an irrational act as launching a retaliatory strike after deterrence had failed, they would know that at least some of our NATO allies would not withdraw their fingers from the multilevered safety catch; or, even if they did, that the UN would never consent to the use of strategic nuclear weapons against the Soviet Union—whose revenge could be expected to be terrible indeed against any small nation that could have prevented a nuclear strike against the U.S.S.R. but did not.

Although Nitze and McNamara at least attempted the NATO step of the Nitze plan, they could not get it accepted by either Congress or NATO. From the first the French were suspicious of the McNamara-Nitze proposals for a "multilateral force" and referred to it as a "multilateral farce." They got the point about the large number of fingers on the safety catch; and they also figured it was a McNamara ploy to forestall any national nuclear deterrents.

Thus, although the Nitze-Kissinger group succeeded so well in scrapping all existing U.S. counterforce capability, and in blocking development of any advanced systems capable of disarming strikes at Soviet missiles, the Nitze-Kissinger group still has to assure the Soviets that we will never actually use our retaliatory capability against the Soviets, no matter what they do to us first. This is why Dr. Kissinger has publicly expressed his conviction that, both morally and politically, retaliation against the enemy's population centers is "impossible."

This brings us at long last to the climactic point of the analysis of what Kissinger—under cover of all his charades and sideshows—is doing to the United States. The Nitze program for NATO command and UN control over U.S. strategic forces would (in Kissinger terminology) have "institutionalized" a procedure that would have *guaranteed to the Kremlin that no U.S. strategic nuclear weapons would ever be launched against the U.S.S.R.* The strategic-surrender elites have been unable as yet to achieve any substitute method of institutionalizing this "no-go" guarantee. Therefore, their only practicable course is to provide the Kremlin with another type of guarantee. We know that Kissinger has publicly declared that he himself would not consider it possible, either morally or politically, to give a launch order for U.S. strategic weapons, even in retaliation against a Soviet strike. But to make that guarantee effective, the Soviets would have to have high-confidence assurance that Henry Kissinger has seized de facto command of U.S. strategic forces; that is, that Henry Kissinger has usurped the power of the President over nuclear weapons.

But has he? And how important is that power? The answer to that is revealed by an analysis of the mystery of the Kissinger Strategic Alert Crisis of October 24-25, 1973.

The power of the President of the United States to unleash or hold-in-leash our strategic nuclear forces has never been more eloquently pictured than by John Fitzgerald Kennedy in a television and radio address in 1962:

> For of all the awesome responsibilities entrusted to this office, none is more somber to contemplate than the special statutory authority to employ nuclear arms in defense of our people and freedom.
>
> But until mankind has banished both war and the instruments of destruction, the United States must maintain an effective quantity and quality of nuclear weapons, so deployed and protected as to be capable of surviving any surprise attack, and devastating the attacker. Only through such strength can we be certain of deterring a nuclear strike, or an overwhelming ground attack upon our forces and allies.
>
> Only through such strength can we, in the Free World—should that deterrent fail—face the tragedy of another war with any hope of survival.[14]

To make more real just how awesome and somber that very special presidential power actually is, ponder what was described as a "matter of fact" remark by President Richard Nixon. Addressing a group of 35 southern Democratic Congressmen just prior to the Thanksgiving recess in November 1973, he said:

> I can go into my office and make a telephone call and, within 25 minutes, 70 million people will be dead.

After that direct quotation, the news report continued:

> The President said also that he believed Communist Party Secretary Leonid I. Brezhnev had the same power. The President is believed to have made a similar remark to other congressional groups.[15]

It is easy to visualize the awesome genocidal results of a nuclear strike against an unprotected population, as Nixon pictured it in that short scenario. It is far more difficult to foresee that the result of *not* possessing the resolute and unchallengeable will to launch a massive nuclear strike invites consequences more apocalyptic and cataclysmic (certainly as to 210 million Americans) than the irrational launch of such a strike by an aggressor. The disarmament elitists have always envisioned the horrendous danger that some madman—a Hitler or a Stalin—might make an "insane" decision to issue a launch order. Yet the real danger is not the insane *employment* of nuclear weapons by an aggressor, but the more radically insane *destruction* of the defender's nuclear weapons by an apparently sane McNamara or Kissinger. Not content with decimating our strategic power, they have destroyed, also deliberately, the credibility of our will to employ it for defense and deterrence. By so doing, they have rendered all American families vulnerable to nuclear incineration.

How real is that danger? One of the best analyses was presented by a then-36-year-old Harvard professor named Henry A. Kissinger:

> Deterrence . . . ultimately depends upon on an intangible quality: the state of mind of the potential aggressor. From the point of view of deterrence a seeming weakness will have the same consequences as an actual one. *A gesture intended as a bluff but taken seriously is more useful than a bona fide threat interpreted as a bluff.*
>
> Deterrence requires a combination of power, the will to use it, and the assessment of these by the potential aggressor.
>
> Moreover, *deterrence is the product of these factors and not a sum.* If any one of them is zero, deterrence fails. Strength, no matter how overwhelming, is useless without the willingness to resort to it. Power *combined with willingness to use it will be ineffective if the aggressor does not believe in it* or if the risks of war do not appear sufficiently unattractive to him. . . .
>
> There can be no gap in deterrence. Deterrence is either effective or it is not. There is no margin for error. Mistakes are likely to be irremediable. If the gains of aggression appear to outweigh the penalties even once, deterrence will fail. [16]

When we combine the Kennedy assertion that our hope of survival depends on maintaining adequate numbers and quality of nuclear weapons, with the Kissinger cliche that it depends also on the *will* to use such nuclear power times the potential aggressor's *belief in that will,* we see how terribly dangerous it would be to have in command of our awesome nuclear arsenal a person whom the enemy might believe lacked the will to use it if need be. The enemy might reach such a belief because they evaluated him as irresolute or, according to the Khrushchev formula we considered earlier, paralyzed by fear of nuclear war.

But consider how much worse off we would be if our man at the nuclear console, the man with his finger next to the nuclear "go" button, were seeking *deliberately* to convince the potential aggressor that he considers retaliation irrational, and would never, never give the launch order for U.S. nuclear weapons. Unless the American people are already resigned to suicide or surrender, this possibility must be considered in the light of the evidence that has already been developed.

The disarmament elitists are right in believing that there is a danger of the irrational first use of the weapons in our strategic arsenal. In fact, there is a double danger: if use should actually materialize, it would bring genocidal retaliation; if the Soviets worry enough about this possibility, it may bring preemption. At this point, it may appear that it might even be desirable to have a liberal ideologue at the nuclear console, on the theory that such a one would be the least likely to use our awesome power. But this is not so, as James Burnham has explained so convincingly:

> There are . . . specific features of liberal doctrine and habit that explain, in each case, *liberalism's demonstrated inability to meet the primary challenges to Western survival.* The deficiency can also be related . . . to a more general trait: to the fact that liberalism cannot come to terms with power, in particular with force, the most direct expression of power. It is not that liberals when they enter the governing class . . . never make use of force; unavoidably they do, sometimes to excess. But because of their ideology they are not reconciled intellectually and morally to force. They therefore tend to use it ineptly, at the wrong times and places, against the wrong targets, in the wrong amounts.
>
> . . . in the case of Cuba, United States policy was the product of liberal ideologues. . . . The force used in Vietnam is considerably greater, but no less unsurely and inconsistently applied. It is enough to keep the country in a turmoil and make sure that a good many people, among them Americans, get killed; but not enough, and not used properly, to defeat the Communists.
>
> It should not be inferred from examples such as these that liberals never turn to the all-out use of force; merely that they seldom turn to the right amount of force at the right time. It was the liberals who were the loudest in demanding war against Hitler, and who invented both the idea and the slogan of "unconditional surrender"; and it was a liberal, though he numbered Communists among his advisers, who called for the pastoralization of Germany.
>
> *And it is not inconceivable that a liberal, in a state of panic that cuts through his ideological cover, may press the button that begins a nuclear exchange.*[17]

Something quite close to just that may have happened to us on October 24, 1973. Late that night Henry Kissinger ordered a worldwide alert of U.S. strategic and conventional forces. This was purportedly in response to some action or threat by the Soviet Union. President Nixon, in a press conference the following night, called it the "most difficult" crisis since the 1962 Cuban missile crisis. He denied emphatically that it was a "blown up exercise" staged to divert public attention from Watergate. "I wish it had been that," he commented; "it was a real crisis."[18]

Henry Kissinger, too, insisted that it was a real crisis, and he publicly promised to reveal within a week or two exactly what had triggered the crisis. But he reneged on his pledge to tell all. Week after week, month after month, he continued to suppress the facts. This was so vital and notorious a suppression of material vital to national survival that, some six months after the U.S. Secretary of State made this solemn promise, Time magazine, in a cover story entitled "How Henry Does it," brought up the subject as an example of his sometimes "devious" dealings with the press. The article, treating primarily of his achievements toward "peace" reached a new far-out point in estimating Dr. Kissinger's importance; although the article was laden with fulsome praise and called Kissinger "the world's indispensable man," it nevertheless conceded:

Despite promises to the contrary, he has yet to reveal the reasons he says required a worldwide U.S. alert during the latest Middle East War.[19]

The press reported this because it involved suppression of news, but no one advanced the slightest suggestion of the true importance to national survival of Kissinger's handling of his strategic alert crisis of October 24-25, 1973. There are only two possible solutions to the mystery, and either one would provide a basis for Kissinger's dismissal or impeachment. Consequently he is successfully blocking the American people from access to any solution.

Shockingly, the House of Representatives backed him up in this arrogant conduct. The same House whose Judiciary Committee that same week had voted 33 to 3 to subpoena from President Nixon the tapes of 40 conversations between him and subordinates on minor matters, by voice vote killed a resolution demanding information on Kissinger's strategic alert. The resolution would have required Kissinger to turn over the text of all messages between Nixon and Soviet officials, and a list and chronology of all the orders and action taken during the crisis of October 24-25.

The Foreign Affairs Committee disapproved the measure on the asserted grounds that most of the information was sensitive and, in the national interest, should not be released now. Of course, that information is sensitive! If it revealed that the Kremlin had made a threat against the United States so horrendous as to justify Kissinger's ordering a worldwide strategic alert with all the risks this entailed, then the American people are entitled to know just how serious the threat was, so that they can demand a rebuilding of U.S. strategic power to defend against future threats. If it instead revealed that the Soviet threat or action was *not* against our vital national interests, then it would expose Kissinger as too wildly irresponsible and incompetent to bear the responsibilities entrusted to him, let alone those he has usurped.

Consideration of Kissinger's own account of what happened that night is valuable for the light it throws on his integrity, as well as on his competency, judgment, and courage. The real Henry Kissinger shines through in this performance; this time the charade was unrehearsed, not meticulously planned. He must have been rather sleepy, too, because he gave his version of the crisis decision at a press conference at noon on October 25, 1973, and he said the alert was ordered at 3:00 A.M. on that same date. Here are the highlights of the conference, pieced together from contemporaneous news accounts:

> The question of President Nixon's ability to lead a doubting nation in an international crisis was raised on the public record yesterday, as the United States and the Soviet Union appeared briefly to be on a confrontation course in the Middle East.
>
> The question came up four times in its most dramatic way at Secretary of State Henry Kissinger's news conference. ... Kissinger was asked ... whether the President had made a "totally rational decision" and whether the American decision was based on a "handful of smoke" or on "solid" facts.
>
> One of the first questions was whether the American alert might have been prompted by domestic considerations.
>
> Kissinger replied that "it is a symptom of what is happening to our country that it could even be suggested that the United States would alert its forces for domestic reasons." When the record is published, he added, it will be seen that "the President had no other choice."
>
> Later another reporter asked whether Kissinger supported the decision, whether the President initiated the alert, and "do you feel [it was] a totally rational decision?"

Now, here comes the clincher: something to remember when we discover who really ordered the alert:

> Kissinger said that because of the "particular implications of your remark, I may say that all of the President's senior advisers, all members of the National Security Council, were unanimous in their recommendations."
>
> The advisers reached their conclusions before Nixon joined the deliberations, Kissinger emphasized.
>
> When, finally, a reporter asked Kissinger why a "badly shaken" electorate should believe him, the Secretary replied with considerable feeling: "We are attempting to preserve the peace in very difficult circumstances. . . ."
>
> In a week or so, he added, the facts will be put on the record. "But there has to be a minimum of confidence that the senior officials of the American government are not playing games with the lives of the American people," he said.[20]

Of the quite literally hundreds of stories on Kissinger's crisis, the following one from the *Washington Star-News* is outstanding in revealing intriguing specifics:

> Except for the chill and tremor of it, the crisis between the United States and the Soviet Union over the Middle East was a vastly different situation than the 1962 missile crisis.
>
> When Nikita Khrushchev was detected installing ballistic missiles in Cuba 11 years ago, the public was shown U-2 photos that proved the magnitude of the threat. . . . This time, only a handful of high-ranking Washington officials knew what it was the Russians were doing in the Middle East. More than 200 million Americans awoke yesterday to be told that the nation faced a threat that could be met only by a "level 3" military alert.
>
> It soon became known that the Strategic Air Command B-52s were on airborne alert; that missiles and nuclear submarines were at the ready; that such quick-reaction forces as the 82nd Airborne Division and the 2nd Marine Division were on war footing.
>
> But few Americans were in a position to judge whether the Administration had adequate cause for playing a perilous game of brinkmanship because Washington disclosed no more than the bare outlines of the threat by Russia to send troops to the Middle East. . . .
>
> There was hope, or perhaps fear, that Secretary of State Henry A. Kissinger would disclose the magnitude of the threat at his news conference yesterday [Thursday, October 25, 1973].
>
> The world knew that the United States and the Soviet Union were eyeball-to-eyeball again, but almost no one knew why. Today [Friday, October 26, 1973], that is still very much the case.
>
> Kissinger was, to put it mildly, cryptic. . . . Kissinger refused to discuss the information or the diplomatic exchanges that had prompted the decision of the President and the National Security Council to order U.S. armed forces around the world on what was called a "precautionary alert." . . .
>
> Left with this vacuum of information, *Americans were left to wonder why they could not be entrusted with knowing what the Soviet Union presumably already knew.* The speculation ran the gamut from those who believed the worst to those who suspected the crisis was synthetic. . . .
>
> *Was a Russian threat to unilaterally move in troops to enforce the cease-fire enough to cause Kissinger to mention nuclear calamity six times during his news conference?*[21]

Exactly what was the Soviet threat? Kissinger's sustained refusal to divulge what triggered his decision to order the strategic alert led to multiple efforts by the press to find out. *Time* claimed that one of the two Brezhnev notes on October 24

> threatened the "destruction of the state of Israel" by Soviet forces if Israel did not stop violating the cease-fire order.[22]

No other media sources were able to confirm the *Time* report, but several publications did uncover wide discrepancies between Kissinger's press conference version and what really happened. All sources agree that Dr. Kissinger, in his October 25 press conference, specifically asserted that the President called a "special meeting of the National Security Council" at 3:00 A.M. of that same day. Attempting to check this out. Laurence Stern of the *Washington Post* examined the White House records and interviewed the staff of the National Security Council. He reported:

> Now the White House contends that there was no meeting of the NSC on that night of international peril when the word flashed to U.S. air, ground and sea forces to go into a high state of readiness.
>
> "That meeting is not in our formal listing of National Security Council meetings," said NSC staff secretary Jeanne W. Davis. This was corroborated by the White House press office. . . .
>
> Kissinger said the NSC meeting took place at 3 A.M. on the 25th. Schlesinger timed it at 11 P.M. on the 24th. The President said it was he who ordered the precautionary alert shortly after midnight on the 25th. . . .
>
> Schlesinger . . . said it was he who initiated the alert after a meeting of the "abbreviated National Security Council," though he added that "the President was in complete command at all times during the course of the evening."[23]

The *New York Times* had a somewhat intensive investigation conducted into the events of the night of October 24 and 25 and concluded:

> President Nixon remained in charge throughout, his aides say, but he was also remote, staying in his White House apartment and receiving the telephone messages of Mr. Kissinger and Mr. Schlesinger. Mr. Nixon empowered them to manage the crisis on their own, a Cabinet official said, leaving them to conceive and carry out the various moves.[24]

The remainder of the *New York Times* article recounted the events like this. Kissinger and Schlesinger met in the Situation Room in the basement of the White House at about 11:00 P.M. They were the only members of the National Security Council present. They swiftly agreed to the alert. CIA Director William Colby "had been called in belatedly," but there is no indication that he was ever physically present. Neither the chairman nor any member of the Joint Chiefs of Staff was present at the Kissinger-Schlesinger meeting. Schlesinger told the technical truth in saying that he "initiated" the alert, but there is no indication that he made the decision other than jointly with Dr. Kissinger. Schlesinger, not the Joint Chiefs, actually put the alert order into the military communications channels at about 11:30 P.M. The Joint Chiefs had had knowledge of movements of Soviet military units, but neither Kissinger nor Schlesinger informed them of the diplomatic messages. These messages so surprised the JCS that they "sent an aide to the CIA and the State Department to seek further word on Soviet intentions; he apparently returned empty-handed."

At about 1:00 A.M. Dr. Kissinger informed the British Ambassador, the Earl of Cromer. The Defense Department advised the NATO Council in Brussels at about 2:00 A.M., but the news went out to alliance capitals much later because of a "foul-up in the Brussels communication machinery."

Kissinger associates later acknowledged that the crisis managers "botched" the job of promptly informing U.S. allies of the night's actions. At around 2.00 A.M., Kissinger drafted a reply to the last Brezhnev note, saying that the United States would not tolerate a unilateral action by the Soviet Union, and calling for joint action in the United Nations.

At about 3:00 A.M. on October 25, "three and a half hours after the alert had been called," a very weary Henry Kissinger "walked upstairs and reported to President Nixon and obtained his 'ratification' of the moves." The New York Times article concluded:

> At his news conference at noon, the Secretary publicly reminded Moscow that both the Soviet Union and the United States had nuclear arsenals "capable of annihilating humanity" but that they also had "a special duty to see to it that confrontations are kept within bounds."
>
> An hour or so later, both countries joined in the 14-to-0 vote by which the United Nations Security Council decided to establish a United Nations peace-keeping force excluding the major powers—a move that in effect brought the American-Soviet exchanges to an end.
>
> And in those exchanges, officials noted, the Hot Line teletype machine that connects Moscow and Washington was never used.

In analyzing what really happened, the simplest issue relates to Kissinger's integrity and honesty in matters directly affecting U.S. national security. He specifically stated that the President called a "special meeting of the National Security Council," and that it was called at 3:00 A.M. on October 25. Yet all the evidence indicates that the worldwide strategic alert of U.S. forces went out at 11:30 P.M. on October 24. Also, there was no official meeting of the National Security Council at any time on those dates: and no other "advisers" or members of NSC were in on the decision.

Thus, it was highly misleading for Kissinger to inform the press at his conference on October 25 that "all of the President's senior advisers" and "all" NSC members were "unanimous" in their recommendations. The terms "all" and "unanimous" are not appropriate to describe the actions of two persons. Furthermore, the Joint Chiefs of Staff are certainly included, both by tradition and by law, among the President's "senior advisers" on military matters. Not only were they not present, but Kissinger did not permit them access to the relevant and vital information necessary to form an advisory opinion.

In fact, the whole decision-making process during those two critical days was so closely controlled by Kissinger that he did not permit even General Alexander Haig to participate in the policy determinations. As the *New York Times* report describes this:

> General Haig functioned more as a go-between [with the Defense Department and the JCS] than as a member of the decision-making group, aides said.

One major conclusion is absolutely certain. Kissinger distorted the truth concerning how and by whom the strategic alert was ordered. Neither Kissinger nor Schlesinger asked the President's specific approval before ordering the worldwide strategic alert, nor did they inform the President that an alert had been ordered until hours too late for him to reverse it if he had disapproved.

The second point is vital. For more than six months after making his solemn official promise to publish all the facts supporting the strategic alert order, Kissinger was still welching on that pledge. As one liberal newspaper editorialized:

> Especially compared to many other Nixon aides, Kissinger deservedly retains considerable esteem. By reversing himself on explaining the alert, he has not destroyed his credibility. But he has blemished it—and for a nation desperately searching for leaders to believe in, that is quite depressing.
>
> Full alerts in a nuclear world are extremely serious business. This one was either justified or not. Secretary Kissinger should share the record and the rationale with the American people, whose lives were on the line.[25]

What a time to worry about Kissinger's blemished credibility! His panic performance and wildly amateurish and irresponsible judgment could have precipitated the incineration of scores of millions of Americans. The editorial writer's conclusions, however, are accurate and make truly significant points: (1) either this alert was justified or it was not; and (2) our lives were, indeed, on the line.

Our lives were just as surely on the line if the strategic alert were *not* justified as if it were. If the alert were justified, the Soviet threat that triggered it must have related to the national survival of the United States; a lesser threat would not have justified the strategic alert—because ordering the alert itself risked our survival. Even if the calling of the alert did temporarily avert a serious threat, it could not eliminate either the attitude or motivation or weapons capability on which the threat was based.

If no such serious threat against the supreme interests of the United States had been made, then Kissinger was wildly irresponsible in ordering a worldwide strategic alert. He would indeed have been guilty of what he implicity denied (in what may have been a Freudian thought-association)—"playing games with the lives of the American people."

By ordering a strategic alert, he took a risk of triggering a massive strategic nuclear attack by the Soviet Union against the United States. The Soviets have one basic and overriding doctrine governing nuclear weapons: NEVER, NEVER take a risk of getting hit by the undamaged strategic force of a rival nuclear superpower. As we have seen earlier, even the most naive Soviet apologists—those who shrilly deny that the Soviets would ever launch a preventive strike at us—all concede that the Kremlin would certainly preempt if they believed that the United States were about to launch a strike at them. The Soviet doctrine is rigid and imperative; and it is firmly founded on common sense and a compassion for the Russian people. It *demands* a disarming strike launched "in good time" to destroy enemy missiles *before* they can be launched at the Soviet Union.

A worldwide strategic alert of U.S. forces means that we have put our weapons in a state of readiness that will permit a near-immediate launch of our total strategic forces. As described in the *Washington Star-News* excerpt above, our Strategic Air Command B-52 heavy bombers were on airborne alert; our missiles and nuclear submarines were ready. The somber strategists in the Soviet Politburo would know that—if some atomic maniac with access to the U.S. nuclear console should decide to go ahead—there would be little time left in which to order the launch of a preemptive strike against America.

Of course the Kremlin would know exactly the state of our strategic alert. As the *New York Times* article quoted above reported it:

Asked if the Soviet Union had been notified of the alert, a United States official said:

"No, the alert itself was a signal which we knew they would get through their own electronic intelligence."[26]

Because the Soviets would know about the worldwide alert, and that strategic forces were included, the most chilling feature is that the realists in the Kremlin would have to appraise the chances that a person in command of U.S nuclear forces who would risk ordering such an alert, in such a situation, might easily be panicked sufficiently to go even further.

Because of Kissinger's effective and prolonged suppression of the facts, we cannot determine whether or not his strategic alert was justified. But either way, his conduct during the crisis (which may even have been of his own creation) presents adequate grounds for impeachment. If the Soviet threat was not of such magnitude or imminence as to threaten the supreme national interests of the

United States, he demonstrated both shocking incompetence and wanton irresponsibility in ordering the alert. He thereby subjected the American people to the massive risks of nuclear incineration. If, instead, the Soviet threat was sufficient to justify the calling of the alert, Kissinger is covering for the Kremlin and in doing so deliberately withholding from the American people information vital to the continued survival of the United States. That in itself should be sufficient grounds for his impeachment, especially since the Soviets already have the information Kissinger is denying to the American people.

By far the most important warning that Americans can derive from an analysis of Kissinger's conduct during the critical hours of October 24 and 25 is that he achieved full control over the strategic nuclear forces of the United States. He has usurped what President Kennedy so accurately characterized as the most awesome power conferred by law especially and exclusively on the U.S. President. It is easy to believe that this is exactly the type of presidential responsibility that led the prudent drafters of the Constitution—by some sort of inspired foresight—to impose natural citizenship as an absolute requirement for holding the highest office in the nation.

The Founding Fathers could not, of course, have foreseen the like of Henry Kissinger. In the naivete of their age, they expected statesmen to be distinguished by wisdom rather than sophistication; by faith in God and country rather than megalomania. Kissinger is both fascinating and flabbergasting. All his earlier virtuoso performances were eclipsed, however, by the consummate and easy skill with which he took over the decision-making process that governs the cataclysmic command for the launch or no-launch of U.S. strategic nuclear weapons.

Take the first step: Kissinger's assertion that the President had called a special meeting of the National Security Council. Absolutely no one is in a position to challenge that. This is ensured by the Kissinger monopoly of access to the President in all areas relating to matters of foreign policy, national security, and intelligence. In this specific instance Kissinger did foul up his claim a little by picking a time for the alleged meeting that was some four hours later—3:00 A.M. on October 25—than the only time any meeting was actually convened in the White House on the crisis, which other witnesses all placed as around 11:00 P.M. on October 24. But, let's assume that the President really did call the meeting of the NSC in the Situation Room in the White House basement.

The impressive chairs at the table are for the President and the five additional statutory members of the Council. At 11:15 P.M. on October 24, however, only two of those chairs were occupied. Yet three statutory members are present-because Dr. Kissinger is not one, but two. He attends both in the capacity of Secretary of State and as Assistant to the President for National Security Affairs. In addition, Kissinger is entitled to chair the meeting from the seat the President would occupy if he were not asleep upstairs, because the Secretary of State is the senior member of the President's Cabinet.

The two other statutory chairs represent double blanks. Not only were their lawful occupants not present; they were not even in existence. Spiro T. Agnew's resignation had created a hiatus in the office of the Vice Presidency, and the retirement of George A. Lincoln as Director of Emergency Preparedness, more than a year earlier, had created an additional vacancy.

Thus, there was a legal quorum present; three out of the possible four entitled members. In such a situation, Kissinger holds in himself, not subject to legal challenge, and not merely by proxy, a majority vote on any question before the National Security Council. From this we have established that the ordering of the worldwide strategic alert was Kissinger's decision. This fixes the responsibility, and disposes of the later statement by Schlesinger that he "initiated" the alert. Those two days in October demonstrated conclusively that Henry Kissinger has usurped total control of the U.S. nuclear console.

Why did Henry Kissinger order a worldwide strategic alert of U.S. forces on October 24, 1973? Was it a bluff, a bona fide threat, or a typical Kissinger charade *arranged in advance by a deal with the Kremlin?*

Newspapers across the nation carried screaming banner headlines the next day, such as "Russia Backs Off in Crisis With U.S. Troops on Alert." A typical lead story said:

> The Soviet delegation to the United Nations backed down today from its agreement that Russian troops be part of a UN peacekeeping force in the Middle East after the United States placed its armed forces on a worldwide alert against the possibility of Russian involvement. . . . The decision was announced shortly after Secretary of State Henry Kissinger warned the Russians that sending in troops could bring a confrontation that would threaten all mankind.
> Russian threats to send troops to Syria and Egypt brought a midnight meeting of the U.S. National Security Council. . . .[27]

In a press conference the next day, on October 26, President Nixon said that he had ordered the alert of U.S. armed forces because the United States had reason to believe that the Soviet Union was planning to send "a very substantial force into the Mideast, a military force." He described the crisis over this issue as the "most difficult" since the Cuban missile crisis of 1962.

Early the following day in Moscow, Tass, the official Soviet news agency, took issue with the official U.S. explanation. Referring to the U.S. strategic alert, it reported:

> This step of the United States, that does not by any means promote detente, was taken obviously in an attempt to intimidate the Soviet Union. But those who are behind this step should be told they have the wrong address.[28]

Surprisingly, segments of the U.S. high military command agreed with the Tass estimate. A four-star U.S. commander said in an off-the-record conversation that Kissinger had threatened the Soviet Union and had won out. This assessment of what Kissinger was trying to do assumes that the Soviets had, indeed, made a definite threat to move large military forces into the Middle East battleground. But this is nothing more than an assumption. Just as Kissinger withheld all the intelligence relating to Kremlin notes and messages from the Joint Chiefs of Staff, and did not even notify them of the alert until it was being actually mounted on Schlesinger's communicated orders, no one in the military knew whether the Soviets had made any threat at all, or if they had, what was threatened.

Media representatives soon began to realize that none of them had been able to discover whether the Soviets had made a threat; and if so, was it such as to justify Kissinger's ordering of the alert. The harsh questions that had first emerged at the Kissinger news conference on October 25 were amplified and multiplied as newsmen could find no reasonable basis for the alert. Time published a one-page article entitled "Was the Alert Scare Necessary?,"[29] tearing apart Schlesinger's attempt at explanation:

> Even Schlesinger's evidence of Soviet military preparations left some intelligence experts unconvinced. They described it as "flimsy," "inconclusive," and "not materially different from what was going on throughout the crisis." For example, they said that the Soviet airborne units had been on and off alert ever since the end of the war's first week and that they had always had their own aircraft for transport.
>
> The puzzle of Kissinger's somber press conference also remained. He described the U.S.-Russian confrontation as one that could still go either way. Yet Nixon in his press conference left the impression that he and Brezhnev had solved the crisis the night before Kissinger's appearance. In fact, soon after Kissinger had finished outlining the reasons for the U.S. alert, the Soviets approved a Security Council resolution for a UN force to police the cease-fire.
>
> Thus Kissinger could be accused of being unduly alarmist in his televised appearance [news conference at noon on October 25, 1973], if indeed he knew by then that the Russians had agreed to back down.

William F. Buckley, Jr., in one of his syndicated columns, really penetrated to the crunch and suggested that the Senate Foreign Relations Committee should call in the Joint Chiefs of Staff and ask them the question:

> If the Soviet Union had called our bluff, *what would we have done about it?*[30]

Actually, since the threat implicit in the ordering of the strategic alert was not made by the Joint Chiefs, and they were neither consulted nor even informed in advance, that question should be put to Dr. Kissinger.

Regardless of how many sophisticated words he used to answer, the substance of it would be "nothing." Kissinger policies and SALT I have combined to give the Soviets escalation dominance on all rungs of the ladder over any type of military power Kissinger might invoke—conventional or nuclear, theater or central. Kissinger could not get away with a bluff, and he knew he could not get away with a bluff, and the Soviets knew he knew he could not get away with a bluff. A rational leader simply does not attempt a bluff when he knows positively that he cannot get away with it. In this case, for example, if the Soviets *had* made a threat, they could simply execute it and then point out to the world that Kissinger's strategic alert had been an empty and stupid bluff. U.S. prestige and credibility would be destroyed, and Kissinger might have been deposed. By ordering the alert as a bluff, then, Kissinger would have nothing to gain and everything to lose, and he would know this in advance.

Next, let us examine the view taken by some of the U.S. military that Kissinger made a bona fide threat to coerce the Soviets into backing down from a military action they had supposedly threatened. It is critical that this was a *strategic* alert: all U.S. nuclear forces went to a high state of alert. Even the B-52 bombers stationed on Guam were recalled on an emergency basis to continental United States where they would be more quickly available to launch against targets in the Soviet Union.

It is a cardinal point in Dr. Kissinger's strategic theory that nuclear power is not *usable* power; that it cannot be employed for political advantage, even if the power attempting to employ it has substantial strategic nuclear superiority. This is his basic rationale for giving away such obvious margins of superiority to the Soviets in the SALT I Interim Agreement. According to this theory, even the superior nuclear power could gain nothing by a bona fide threat to use it as a lever. And if the *superior* nuclear power could not effectively employ the threat, using its greater power, how much less chance would the substantially *inferior* nuclear power have?

The answer is none—unless the person controlling the use of the strategic forces of the inferior nuclear power were estimated to be irrational; or, to put it another way, had lost touch with reality; or, was scared out of his wits; or, to put it bluntly, was some kind of a nut. This analysis of the enemy leader in charge of his nation's nuclear console sounds far-out; but it is not, really. In fact, ever since the early years of study of nuclear strategy it has been much discussed, frequently under the Herman Kahn terminology of "the rationality of irrationality." There is quite a premium in convincing the opponents that you, as a master of the nuclear console, *can* be expected to act in an irrational manner. Thus, Kissinger in his 1961 book cited above, quoted President Eisenhower with respect to Berlin as having declared that "only a madman would start a nuclear war," and that "a great deal of Mr. Khrushchev's violence during the General Assembly of 1960 may have been designed as a warning of his capacity for irrationality if thwarted."[31]

Assuming that the Kremlin had no advance deal with Kissinger on the Middle East crisis, upon picking up their electronic intelligence of the U.S. worldwide strategic alert on the night of October 24 and the early morning of October 25, the first question the Politburo's strategic experts would have to analyze for Brezhnev and his colleagues would be the same one we have been pursuing: is Henry Kissinger some kind of a nut, or something?

We must analyze this same question, but we have an additional element to consider. The Politburo members *know* whether Henry Kissinger had made an advance secret deal with the Kremlin permitting the alert, but we do not. The ordering of the strategic alert could have been an entirely rational action for Kissinger—one that he might even consider brilliant—if it had been included in an advance secret deal with the Kremlin. There is much evidence to support this explanation, although most of it is necessarily circumstantial.

However, in the exchanges between Moscow and Washington during the October 1973 crisis, the *New York Times* and all other reports of an inquiring nature revealed that *the Hot Line teletype machine that connects Moscow and Washington was never used.* One explanation would be that neither party to a secret deal wanted to participate in creating documentary evidence of what was in the deal. A teletype machine would self-document the whole story. If the Congress had been one-millionth as interested in the survival of the United States as in exposing Watergate-related incidents, the Harrington-Stark resolution demanding information from Kissinger would have been passed by Congress and would then have caught the teletype print-out in its net.

If a secret deal were not arranged via the Hot Line, then how? Brezhnev hastily and imperiously summoned Kissinger to Moscow immediately after Kosygin returned to Moscow on October 19 with the news that the Egyptian III Corps, on the east bank of the Suez

Canal, was being encircled by the Israelis, and that the tide of the war had turned drastically against the Soviet Arab client states. Kissinger and the General Secretary of the Communist Party of the Soviet Union conferred together for many hours on October 20 and 21. Here is an item that bears on the peculiar type of secrecy with which meetings between these two are conducted. This is the text of a letter addressed to Secretary Kissinger on March 22, 1974, by Congressman Ben B. Blackburn:

Dear Mr. Secretary:

I have been advised, that on your last trip to the Soviet Union, you followed certain procedures which are causing me concern.

Specifically, with regard to your last trip to Moscow: I have been informed that, aside from being greeted by protocol personnel from our United States Embassy, you spent the remainder of your time generally incommunicado from U.S. Embassy personnel, and that you utilized the Soviet communications system for transmitting messages back to the United States.

I have been informed, further, that this was not a unique practice with you. Rather, that even in Washington, you use the Soviet Embassy communications system with Moscow rather than our own.

I am most anxious for your explanation at the earliest possible moment.

Sincerely,

Ben B. Blackburn, M.C.

The denial sent to Congressman Blackburn by a State Department employee raises the question as to why Secretary Kissinger chose to avoid replying himself. We have not been able to secure an independent check on Kissinger's use of Soviet communications, but we have verified that, for matters he considers of real importance, he does not use State Department communications, but instead uses the very secure and closely held CIA communications. The very existence of these channels is supposed to be Top Secret. Also, we have verified that Kissinger, in his conferences with Brezhnev and other Politburo members, often uses only the Soviet interpreter and does not permit a U.S. interpreter to be present; and he extended this practice to include Nixon conferences also.

Furthermore, Kissinger always has Anatoly Dobrynin close to him for the most secret type of communications. On that critical night of October 24, 1973, Anatoly Dobrynin personally delivered to Kissinger the second Brezhnev note of that date. There is no record of what Dobrynin said to Kissinger at that time, which was 10:40 P.M. It was at 11:30 P.M. that Kissinger ordered Schlesinger to initiate the worldwide strategic alert.

If the Kremlin had actually and seriously threatened physically to destroy Israel, as was widely reported, then the secret deal is not at all persuasive. In that case, both sides were probably attempting to play the nuclear-graveyard game of "chicken," and the Kissinger strategic alert was at least semiseriously intended. If so, Brezhnev probably backed down because (1) the Politburo experts estimated that Kissinger might really be irrational enough to attempt to threaten the massively superior Soviets and thus risk suicide for 210 million Americans; and (2) an advance of more than two years in the Kremlin's plan to deliver an ultimatum or strike at the United States was more than could be advantageously tolerated. Their four new series ICBMs of vastly greater destructive power are not expected to be deployed in substantial numbers until late 1975.

In any event, a Kremlin threat physically to destroy Israel was highly improbable. If the Soviets executed such a threat, their Arab clients would no longer have an absolute need for Soviet military assistance, and the Kremlin would risk losing this lever that secures Soviet presence in the Mideast for the next several years. Also, the shock of such a brutal action would stir the Americans to realize that we would be next, and that perhaps we should seek more reliable survival insurance than detente on Soviet terms. It would activate the ace-in-the-hole capability of the United States to invest huge sums of money, with great speed, in rebuilding our strategic power. We can, therefore, definitely rule out an alleged threat against the continued existence of Israel.

If any really brutal threat of physical destruction were made by the Politburo, it must have been a threat to destroy the United States by strategic weapons. If it were made, it was undoubtedly conveyed by Anatoly Dobrynin by word of mouth to Dr. Kissinger at 10:40 P.M. on October 24. This is one of the few persuasive explanations of why Kissinger ordered a worldwide strategic alert only 50 minutes later. It is also the only threat that would adequately explain Kissinger's extraordinary response to the reporters' challenge to the strategic alert at his noon press conference on October 25:

> I am absolutely confident that it will be seen that the President had no other choice as a responsible national leader.

Such a direct threat against the United States would also explain his referring, in that same press conference, six times to a "nuclear calamity."

To any threat other than a nuclear strike against continental United States, a relevant response would have been a conventional forces alert, worldwide, or in the Mediterranean theater. To put *strategic* nuclear forces on a high state of alert would have been (in bureaucratic jargon) "overreacting." Also, it would have been stupid; and Kissinger certainly is not stupid.

But if it were a direct nuclear threat against the United States, then a worldwide strategic alert would indeed have been the *only* relevant response, the *only* possibly effective reaction. In the face of an overt, explicit Soviet strategic threat, the only possibly credible deterrent we have left is to order our entire land-based ICBM force to a high state of alert, with orders to launch on receipt of verified warning that the Soviets have actually launched a salvo of missiles at us. Also, if that actually were the Soviet action that triggered the Kissinger strategic alert, the alert may have worked, and we all would owe him for averting a horrendous risk of nuclear incineration.

But, if the Soviets did make such a malevolent threat, then Kissinger owes it to the nation to make it known to the American people so we can take steps to defend ourselves against a repetition of the threat. If such information was suppressed in the interest of detente, then he should be impeached forthwith.

On an overall basis, however, the probability that the Soviets made a direct and explicit nuclear threat against the United States, although of vital importance, is not high. Certainly it is not high when weighed against the probability that the whole thing was a Kissinger-written-and-directed charade. We have seen that there was ample opportunity for Kissinger and Dobrynin, or even Kissinger and Brezhnev, to work out the details. As to motivation, the Soviets had nothing to lose as a result of the alert declaration because they had not made any public threats against either Israel or the United States, and the Soviets' denial, which we have quoted, was far more convincing than the vague assertions by Kissinger and Nixon. The Soviets did not lose face or prestige; they did not back down, having nothing overt to back down from.

But the Kremlin did benefit greatly by Kissinger's alert. As of the time of the alert, a crucial summit meeting had been scheduled for Moscow in June 1974 to complete a SALT II agreement supposedly to limit "further" strategic offensive nuclear weapons. As of October 1973, the Soviets had been stalling the SALT II negotiations for more than a year. It was clear that the Kremlin was going to continue its hard-line demands; but it was also clear that, for two new reasons that had developed since the SALT I signing, it was going to be difficult to sell another one-sided arms agreement to Congress and the American people. First, there was a fear that, because of his snowballing domestic weaknesses growing out of Watergate and related matters, Nixon would be so eager to get some sort of a treaty signed in Moscow that he would give dangerous concessions. Second, the rapidly increasing strategic inferiority of the United States vis-a-vis the Soviet Union was becoming more and more difficult to conceal. Anyone competent to read and understand the official reports of the Secretary of Defense and the Chairman of the Joint Chiefs of Staff for FY 1975 could hardly miss our critical weaknesses and the lack of programs to rebuild our deterrent in the relevant timeframe. There was a growing fear that we could no longer stand up against the growing power of the Soviet Union.

So, the Kissinger charade of the strategic alert may have been a typically brilliant Kissinger maneuver. With such an advance theatrical in favor of any SALT II agreement that might come out of a Moscow summit, the media would be prepared to sell the nation the views (1) that our strategic forces are still obviously "sufficient" to deter the Soviet Union even from attacking one of our client states, and therefore also sufficient to deter the U.S.S.R. from attempting to coerce the United States directly, and (2) that Kissinger had faced down the Soviet leadership in a crisis and could be expected to get the better of any arms-control agreement with those dull Kremlin characters. The Kremlin stood to get a double benefit from the charade: assurance that, despite the weakened U.S. domestic position, the incumbent President could, with Kissinger's great influence even more powerful because of the "success" of his crisis moves, secure acceptance of a SALT II deadlock in negotiations that would covertly but decisively favor the Soviet Union. And this is exactly what happened at the Moscow Summit of 1974.

It all worked out so beautifully that Kissinger started out for Moscow on March 23, 1974, in a euphoric mood. All he would ask of the Kremlin leaders would be their agreement to a SALT II pact not too obviously one-sided. Thus it was that:

> Kissinger left for the Soviet Union exuding optimism. Behind the scenes there seemed good reason for a few up-beat riffs. Kissinger took his children, Elizabeth, 14, and David, 13, as well as Soviet Ambassador Anatoly Dobrynin, who had assured him that a SALT breakthrough was achievable.[32]

When Kissinger arrived in Moscow on Sunday night, March 24, his expectations had so inflated that he went out on a limb in a statement to the press. What he expected to achieve in the SALT II meetings with Brezhnev was "a conceptual breakthrough" on major issues. He then drove off, we are told, to a magnificent official residence tucked away behind Florentine-yellow walls high on the Lenin Hills overlooking Moscow.

But next morning the official climate had changed. A special meeting of the CPSU Politburo rejected out of hand the American MIRV proposal that had been hammered out at an extraordinary session of the U.S. National Security Council over which President Nixon himself had presided two weeks earlier. The Kremlin-engineered deadlock was not broken during Kissinger's visit. The only agreement to come out of the visit should be ominous to all who understand what the Soviets mean by detente—it was an agreement that the parties should make the course of detente "irreversible." Just before General

643

Secretary Brezhnev opened the conference with Secretary Kissinger, he bluntly stated: "The alternative is war—there is no other alternative." Thus, the result of Kissinger's charade and his friendly negotiations with the Soviets was to elicit this thinly veiled ultimatum from the Politburo.

A painstaking review of the hour-by-hour developments of the worldwide strategic alert of U.S. forces ordered on October 24, 1973, has revealed much about Kissinger and his character. Far more important, however, it has revealed that Kissinger has usurped the most awesome powers of the President of the United States and has assumed the responsibilities of the Commander-in-Chief. The nuclear console controlling the strategic forces of the United States is in Kissinger's hands, with no effective restrictions. We know that he takes no advice from the military, and that he does not even keep the Joint Chiefs of Staff informed of the most critical developments.

The New York Times summed up his unprecedented power in a front-page article on April 21, 1974:

> Mr. Kissinger is treated by legislators, diplomats and journalists as if he had the last word. He is widely regarded as "president for foreign affairs."

The Times article described how Kissinger "has transformed most of Washington into a cheering section for his foreign policies." This includes getting Congressmen to treat him with "fawning gratitude," persuading journalists to swallow "a lot of theology" because he gives them wide access to "his sole possession of vital information," and cleverly eliciting the support of divergent groups by "telling those on opposing sides of an issue what each wants to hear" and conveying the feeling that "he is on the side of each." It all adds up to what the Times reporter called "an aura of indispensability."

We have seen from his repeated declarations in official reports[33] that he has definitely rejected the strategy that represents our only chance of national survival unless and until we rebuild the power of our strategic deterrent: the policy of ordering a launch-on-warning of our Minuteman missiles in retaliation for a verified Soviet nuclear launch against us. That is the only way the U.S. land-based retaliatory force can be saved from destruction by Soviet supermissiles, and hence be retained as a credible deterrent.

The resignation of Richard Nixon and the succession of Gerald Ford as President did not cause even a ripple in Kissinger's illegally seized monopoly of power over the presidential responsibility for employment of U.S. nuclear weapons. President Ford's first official act upon his inauguration on August 9, 1974, was to retain Kissinger. It would even appear that any of the possible Democratic candidates for President in 1976, except Henry Jackson and George Wallace, would retain Kissinger. CBS commentator Murray Kempton put it this way on June 4, 1974: "He is no longer just a man but, all by himself, a Foreign Office very like those that served the transient governments of the nineteenth century in Europe, being permanent where kings are temporary."

So long as Kissinger is continued in power, he will exercise, in ultimate effect, the same monopoly over the U.S. nuclear console that he managed under Richard Nixon. This is because of his total control over both the entire intelligence community and the National Security Council. If, for example, the Soviets launch an ICBM strike against our Minuteman missiles, Kissinger will get immediate warning from our new satellite intelligence system. All he would have to do is stall for 15 to 20 minutes, and a launch order would come too late to save our 1,000 Minuteman ICBMs from destruction.

In any event, the evidence that Kissinger does exercise such decisive and exclusive control over our national life or death, should force an examination of his record of dealing with the Kremlin. Such an examination must be far more specific that any attempted thus far, and must also force an analysis of his character. What do we really know about this man and his true loyalties? What do we really know about his mental stability?

When Henry Kissinger first entered office in 1969, he was talking, supposedly humorously, about his megalomania. Five years later, on his return trip from the shock Brezhnev administered by brutally rejecting all the Kissinger initiatives on SALT II, he stopped over in London and held a press conference. Here is the opening question and his answer:

> Question: Would you say, Mr. Secretary, that your relations with the new British government will be better than your relations with the former British government?
> Secretary Kissinger: Of course, my megalomania has reached a point where I was not aware of the fact that my relations with the old British government were bad. . . .[34]

As we suggested earlier, perhaps the reason that term is so often in his mind is that the dictionary definition is so incredibly apt: "a mania for great or grandiose performance; infantile feelings of omnipotence, especially when retained in later life."

Is it not worth considering that his megalomania may mean our megadeaths? Do we really want as the man in charge of our defense policy, our foreign policy, and our intelligence, a person whose "closest friend in Washington" is Soviet Ambassador Anatoly Dobrynin—the man who participated in attempting to deceive President Kennedy during the Cuban missile crisis? And do we want the hand on

645

our nuclear console to have severely bitten fingernails? As reported by the *London Observer*, Kissinger's

> fingernails are bitten severely. He can lose his temper. Most people who know him regard him as a complex man, with a giant ego yet peculiar insecurities.

The *New York Post* carried a series of articles in June 1974 by Ralph Blumenfeld and a team of 13 investigative reporters who spent five months interviewing some 400 people who personally knew Kissinger. The *Post* quotes an associate of Kissinger at Harvard during his undergraduate days as giving this rare view of Kissinger's psychic intensity:

> He sat in that overstuffed chair—the kind Harvard's rooms are full of—studying from morning till night and biting his nails to the quick, till there was blood.

And so the *New York Post* series concludes:

> Dr. Kissinger bites his fingernails. That has been a fact of life in Washington for five years now. That he bites them bloody, however, would lend another dimension to it.

25

The question which intrigues many Americans is, why is it that nobody else with a knowledge of our defense situation has spoken out and said the things in this book? Don't the members of the Joint Chiefs of Staff and others have access to enough information to figure out how desperate our situation is?

One reason why JCS members and other high defense officials do not speak out is that they are afraid the Russians will believe them, and they are sure that Americans will not.

To give the launch order for a massive strategic nuclear strike involves a decision which is awesome, indeed. Just suppose that the Soviets have a preventive strategy; and that their intelligence has given them high confidence that the time of maximum opportunity and minimum risk is at hand, but they still have a few shadowy doubts. They speculate, would it be even less risky if they delayed another year?

Now assume that, while the Soviets have this under consideration, a member of the U.S. Joint Chiefs, or recent Secretary of Defense, makes a public and specific statement of how desperate our situation is. Such a statement might trigger a Politburo decision to launch immediately. There would be two reasons for such a Soviet decision. Not only would their lingering doubts about U.S. weakness be resolved; but such a sensational statement by a high U.S. official with access to so much information might well penetrate the apathy of the American people so that they would demand the rebuilding of U.S. strategic power on a crash basis. Such a statement might also persuade enough influential people to pressure the President to shift immediately to a launch-on-warning strategy, which is the last thing the Politburo can stand.

No loyal American official wants to risk triggering a nuclear strike which would incinerate scores of millions of his fellow countrymen. The most a retiring chairman or member of JCS or high civilian official feels he can afford to say is, "We are all right *now*, but if we don't rebuild our strength, we will soon fall behind." Many officials have adhered to this formula. And, of course, this was literally true up through 1968, although it has been clear since 1967 at the latest that the Soviets are moving toward a first-strike capability.

There are many additional reasons why those on active duty cannot speak out. Not the least of these is the fact that, if a member of JCS were to assert that the President's military budget and programs were not fully adequate to prevent the Soviets from attaining a first-strike capability against us, he would in effect be accusing the Commander-in-Chief of failing to perform his first duty to the nation, as both John Kennedy and Lyndon Johnson defined it.

Americans are inclined to disbelieve anyone who speaks out bluntly as to how desperate our defense situation is. In the first place, it is very difficult to believe something you have neither heard nor read. If someone does speak out, the administration makes massive efforts to suppress the material and smear the one who spoke out. Most of the mass media will ignore it, if possible, and if not, will degrade or discredit it, and smear the one who speaks out. Finally, the American people, especially the patriotic ones, simply do not want to hear or believe any such bad news about their country. They have an emotional and ideological blocking which tells them that America is not only the greatest but the most powerful nation on earth, and that anyone who says otherwise must be a liar attempting to downgrade our country. Solzhenitsyn put his finger on the problem when he commented: "No, it is not any difficulties of perception that the West is suffering, but a desire not to know, an emotional preference for the pleasant over the unpleasant."

The truth is that many distinguished experts and authorities have spoken out, but one must search the fine print of official government documents and the little items on the back pages of the newspapers to find what they said. As William F. Buckley, Jr., aptly noted:

> The scandal of creeping American arms inferiority is easily the best kept secret in the world, notwithstanding that the facts are widely available and have been remarked by the Chiefs of Staff and the *Reader's Digest*, who between them cover just about everybody.[1]

In the same column, Buckley wrote that he "counted seven times" that Henry Kissinger defended the freezing of our inferiority on the ground that "we negotiated from inferiority." Yet the press still speaks of SALT I as having frozen a situation of "parity."

Even those with long experience in strategic military matters tend to lose confidence in their own judgment when they feel so alone. Senator Barry Goldwater, in a *U.S. News & World Report* interview on February 11, 1972, confessed:

> The Soviets are now superior to us in every category of military equipment. For a while I thought I was wrong, but now I'm more convinced than ever that they are.

Why should Goldwater, a longtime member of the Senate Armed Services Committee, with many years of access to classified information, think he was wrong? The clue is in another interview he gave four months earlier to the same magazine:

> There is not one responsible person in this government today that says we are weaker than the Soviet Union.[2]

After studying additional information for himself about the great gains the Soviets were making, he concluded that nevertheless our position was "worsening" so that we are now "second to the Soviets in every category of military strength except experience," and that it was no longer a question of "if" Red China passes us, but "when," and "that's not too far off."

That sort of assertion by Senator Barry Goldwater should have been at least as newsworthy as his statements about Watergate. The wire services should have picked it up. Newspapers should have printed banner headlines proclaiming: GOLDWATER SAYS U.S. NO LONGER NUMBER ONE; ALREADY NUMBER TWO, SOON TO FALL BEHIND CHINA. But there were no such headlines; not even *U.S. News* commented on its own news scoop.

A plan to bring the United States down from a factor of 8-to-1 superiority over the Soviets to the same factor of inferiority had to be very sophisticated, and it had to have a protective "cover" of appropriate sophistication.

Classification is one of the most viciously employed elements of this "cover." The system of classification is designed to protect the secrets of the United States and our allies. Instead, the disarmament elitists use it to protect Communist secrets from the American people and even from the American military. For example, no American officer or civilian official has ever been able to speak out bluntly on the magnitude of the McNamara swindle called the Nuclear Test Ban Treaty of 1963. The treaty froze the advantages the Soviets had gained over us by betraying the first nuclear test ban arrangement. Both the importance and the suppression of the facts about the Nuclear Test Ban Treaty of 1963 were set forth by the then-senior Republican

Senator on the Armed Services Committee, Margaret Chase Smith, in the *Reader's Digest* of March 1972:

Now, after nine years of reflection, my only regret is that the American people still have not been told the whole story about how the treaty worked to the Russians' tremendous advantage and to our own vast detriment. . . .

Having advanced their nuclear technology well beyond ours [by protracted secret preparations and betrayal of the 1958 nuclear test ban], the Soviets were naturally anxious to freeze their advantage.

To our great peril, they succeeded. Their tests enabled them to develop the kinds of monster warheads that they have since installed on their giant SS-9 ICBMs. And they learned how the electromagnetic radiations of high-yield nuclear detonations might affect our retaliatory ICBMs. Never having fired such high-yield shots, we could not know what these weapons' effects might be, and the treaty prohibits us from learning so that we can move to counter them.

All this should have been clearly explained at the time to the American people.

But President Kennedy and Secretary McNamara classified the information secret, prohibiting us from presenting it to the people.

The treaty was then rammed through and hailed as a great peace breakthrough. In reality it was a disaster for the American people and a great victory for the Russians who, with their superior nuclear technology, were soon embarked on a military buildup that has no parallel.

Now, nearly a decade later we are again involved in arms control negotiations with the Soviets. . . . Although, since the SALT talks began in 1969, the Russians have continued to arm at a quickening pace, the United States has virtually been standing still. . . .

President Nixon will risk his political life if he embarks on any new weapons-development program requiring major expenditures. But if he *fails* to do so for much longer, he will gravely risk our national future!

The key to security is public information. There is no doubt whatever in my mind about the will and determination of the American people to safeguard their freedom and the future security of their children.

But it is essential that we understand what has happened and is happening: that the Soviets have demonstrated that *they have no intention of settling for parity with us,* but are hell-bent on achieving across-the-board superiority. And we need only to recall the Soviet slaughter in Hungary in 1956, Russia's brazen attempt to place nuclear missiles in Cuba in 1962, and its ruthless suppression of Czechoslovakia in 1968 to imagine what kind of world it will be if we allow a dominance of Russian arms.

Classification was also invoked by Secretary McNamara to withhold from Americans the Soviet Top Secret strategic war doctrine which was passed to the West by Colonel Oleg Penkovskiy. The Defense Department still will not remove the classification.

Classification is a tremendously effective tool to conceal the unilateral disarmament program because American military personnel will not reveal classified information, even when they know that the classification is improper. The traditions of a life-long career and discipline simply cannot be broken. Even retired officers are subject to court martial and to prosecution for speaking with contempt of the Secretary of Defense.

Complexity is the next barrier in the way of patriots speaking out bluntly to inform the nation of the magnitude and imminence of the threat we face. Nuclear strategies and the postures required to support them are complex. Like the "scrambling" stage of a secret coding machine, the disarmament elitists' machinations fragment and mishmash actions taken in pursuit of their unilateral disarmament program so that they appear only as nonsignificant pieces of a gigantic jig-saw puzzle. Even if a prominent individual does speak out, he can give no more than a fragment or two of the big picture. To give a meaningful revelation would require scores of thousands of words—but few will listen so long.

The third curtain of concealment is fear of loss of *credibility*. This explains the troubled but deep silence of many military experts who are also patriotic Americans, some military and some civilian. Even if they are willing to face the inevitable smear campaigns, the pressures generated by the federal government, by government contractors, by universities and research institutions, and by think-tanks, even if they can resist the temptation of an appointment as ambassador or other rewards of money, power and prestige, none so far has been willing to sacrifice his "credibility" by stating publicly the shocking substance of the truth about McNamara's program to disarm the United States unilaterally, or about how it has been continued by the Kissinger-Schlesinger programs.

In private conversations, many of these men (both military and civilian, active and retired) are pathetically eager to give assurance that they, too, recognize that these tragic programs have brought us to the point of inferiority. But they explain that *if* they attempt to reveal the full truth publicly, they will lose all their hard-earned influence, along with their "credibility." They rationalize that they can be more "effective" and better serve the nation by preserving their credibility and by speaking only a little of the truth at a time, in small and presumably "credible" installments. As a result, the force of any criticism they make is frittered away. They appear to have no grand charges, only petulant assertions of peccadillos.

Centuries of experience in the administration of justice teach us that the more incredible the truth upon which your case depends, the more substantial and specific must be the foundation you lay for it before presenting the decisive evidence to the court. That is the purpose

651

of this book: to lay exactly such a foundation for the presentation of the case against Henry Kissinger and the strategic surrender elites who are his constituency. When the scrambled pieces are fitted together to show the big picture, whether Kissinger is negotiating the surrender of U.S. rights to control the Panama Canal, or spending $250,000,000 to clear the Suez Canal, or negotiating SALT agreements in Moscow, or making covert deals with Anatoly Dobrynin in Washington, the net result is always to degrade the power of the United States and promote the power of the Politburo in Moscow. From the simple giveaway of our wheat to the complex intricacies of the clandestine handing over of U.S. advantages in computer technology, to the euphoric "joint ventures" with the Soviets in space (which have brought hordes of Soviet "technicians" swarming through our secret space-science laboratories)—all Dr. Kissinger's major programs result in a loss for the United States and a gain for the Soviet Union.

To present any big picture requires a large canvas. The timeframe for this one stretches back at least to April 1960, when Paul Nitze presented his proposals for the unilateral strategic disarmament of the United States, and forward to the year 1976, which will be either the beginning of the third century of the independence of the United States or the end of our nationhood—depending on whether Dr. Kissinger is able to advance the Nitze program beyond the point of no return. This book has had to be exhaustive because of the sheer scope of the subject.

But there is another reason. When a James Schlesinger makes the seven-word assertion, "We have essential equivalence with the Russians," it takes an extended explanation to show that Schlesinger is equating warheads of 50 thousand tons of explosive power with warheads of 50 million tons of explosive power. It takes much evidence because it is so inherently incredible that all those thousands of mini-MIRVs, for which the American people have been taxed billions of dollars, are not at all to defend your life and freedom against Soviet Communists, but to deceive you into believing that we have such a defense.

These are a few of the reasons why more officials with authoritative knowledge of our desperate defense situation have not spoken out bluntly. Short statements will serve no useful purpose, and they do not want to volunteer to self-destruct their precious credibility. Only when the situation is changed to assure them a hearing instead of a smearing can we expect many to bear witness to the awesome truth.

There are, indeed, some stalwart souls who, despite all the difficulties detailed above, have spoken out about the state of our present peril. The fate they met, however, is not one to encourage others to do likewise.

Any individual who attempts to arouse the nation as to the desperate character of our national security becomes a "smearable" or a "suppressible." In the 1964 campaign, Senator Barry Goldwater was given the former treatment. He bluntly told the truth to the American people during that campaign that

> Under our present defense leadership, with its utter disregard for new weapons, our deliverable nuclear capacity may be cut down by 90 percent in the next decade.[3]

What Senator Goldwater said was absolutely true then, and has been proved true by the history of the decade following 1964. Yet McNamara's Defense Department called him a liar in an official statement which read:

> Even on its own misleading terms, Senator Goldwater's assertion is false. . . . Senator Goldwater's percentage is wrong as of today and still further wrong as applied to the future.[4]

Then, the smearmongers followed up with the television spots of the little girl picking daisies who disappeared in a mushroom cloud, and they peddled the vicious lie that Goldwater's election would bring on nuclear war, whereas Lyndon Johnson was a man of peace.

As an example of the "suppressibles," take the distinguished seven men on President Nixon's Blue Ribbon Defense Panel who wrote the Supplemental Statement. Here is the way Congressman John M. Ashbrook told the story in his landmark speech entitled "How the U.S. Lost Military Superiority," given in the House on February 1, 1972, four months before the SALT signing:

> Shortly after his election, President Nixon appointed a Blue Ribbon Defense Panel to study the workings of the Defense Department. Seven members of that panel became so alarmed about the loss of U.S. superiority that they wrote a Supplemental Statement called "The Shifting Balance of Military Power."
>
> This report was signed by seven of the most distinguished business and professional men in the country, including the new Supreme Court Justice Lewis Powell, Jr., who is reported to have been the principal author.
>
> This Blue Ribbon statement deplored "the abandonment by the United States of its former policy of maintaining strategic superiority," and concluded that "in the seventies neither the vital interests of the United States nor the lives and freedom of its citizens will be secure." The statement warned that: "The world of the future will bear a Soviet trademark, with all the peoples upon whom it is imprinted suffering Communist repression."
>
> The Blue Ribbon statement concluded that, if we want to avoid this fate, "The only viable national strategy is to regain and retain a clearly

*superior strategic capability. . . .*The road to peace has never been through appeasement, unilateral disarmament or negotiation from weakness. The entire history of mankind is precisely to the contrary. *Among the great nations, only the strong survive.*"

The other six men (in addition to Justice Powell) who signed the statement were George Champion, president of the Economic Development Council in New York and former president of the Chase Manhattan Bank; William P. Clements, Jr., president of the Southeastern Drilling Company in Dallas; John M. Fluke, president of the John M. Fluke Manufacturing Company in Seattle; Hobart D. Lewis, president of the Reader's Digest Association in Pleasantville, N.Y.; and Wilfred J. McNeil, director of Fairchild Hiller Corporation.

This Blue Ribbon Supplemental Statement was submitted to the President on September 30, 1970, whereupon *it was suppressed by the Nixon Administration for nearly six months. It was finally quietly released on March 12, 1971, without any comment, explanation, or refutation.*

A nine-page statement written December 29, 1971, on the letterhead of the Secretary of Defense [signed by William J. Baroody, Jr., Assistant to the Secretary and the Deputy Secretary] is the first attempt by the Nixon Administration to answer the Blue Ribbon Supplemental Statement or other criticisms of the Nixon defense policies. *This Defense Department statement proves that the Blue Ribbon Defense Panel members were wholly justified in their alarm* about the state of U.S. defense and our inability to defend ourselves against Soviet nuclear power.

It seems to be human nature, when charged with responsibility for a disaster, to rely upon one of two excuses: First, it is not true; or, second, it is someone else's fault. The Defense Department statement falls into a hopeless trap by making the mistake of trying to use both excuses. It says, in effect, first, it is not true that our strategic defenses are in bad shape; and second, the reason our defenses are in such bad shape is that Congress has cut so much from Nixon's budget requests.

The obvious conclusion is: why blame Congress for cutting budget requests when the Nixon Administration says, in effect, do not worry, our defenses are OK? The Defense Department statement is shot through with attempts to place all the blame on Congress for cutting the budget: yet the letter paints a rosy picture of our defenses which would entice almost any Congressman to slash spending.

In the course of his presentation, Congressman Ashbrook quoted a number of other individuals who have spoken out bluntly on the desperate state of our defenses, including a speech by General Bruce K. Holloway, former commander-in-chief of our Strategic Air Command, made to the Commonwealth Club of California on August 27, 1971:

The U.S.S.R. exceeds us in every offensive and defensive strategic weapon system, except missile submarines.

The points made by the Blue Ribbon Defense Panel Supplemental

Statement were highly newsworthy. The fact that the Nixon Administration suppressed the statement for nearly six months should have made them even more newsworthy. Yet, only a few Americans have ever even heard of it. It is only 35 printed pages long, but nearly every sentence in it is vital to our survival as a nation. Here are a few excerpts to show its corroboration of the material presented in this book:

A Second-Rate Power. If these observable trends continue, the U.S. will become a second-rate power incapable of assuring the future security and freedom of its people. . . .

A Soviet World Order. Since World War II a degree of world order has been maintained by the dominance of U.S. strategic military strength. This American-preserved world order is now disintegrating, as doubts arise as to our will and strength to preserve it. There is reason to believe that the Soviet Union envisions a new era which it will dominate, employing long-cherished political, economic, and even military objectives.

A Challenging Soviet Navy. The Soviet navy, modern and rapidly expanding, is now challenging U.S. naval superiority in every category except aircraft carriers. This Soviet naval buildup is a major element in the shifting balance of military power.

Retreat from the Threat of the 70s. The situation which our country faces is without precedent. As we enter the 70s, the strategy of American superiority has given way to the concept of deterrence by maintaining an assured retaliatory capability. But there is no longer any certainty that our nuclear deterrent will remain credible to the Soviet Union which apparently seeks a preemptive strike capability. . . .

Threat to Technological Superiority. U.S. qualitative superiority in weapons, due to its advanced technology, has afforded a decisive advantage over the past years. This advantage is now being eroded away, as the U.S. falls behind the Soviet Union in the support of R&D . . . There is an ever present risk of disastrous technological surprise in major weaponry where an open society is in competition with a closed Communist society. We are neglecting, by inadequate support and planning, to minimize this risk.

Negotiations—Trap or Opportunity? . . . hopes are now high for the success of the current SALT [I] talks. But the total experience of negotiating with Communist nations suggests the utmost caution and the need for the most critical analysis of the possible consequences of any proposed terms. Not only is the security of this country at stake, but it is possible that a limitations agreement as to strategic weapons could neutralize the U.S. as a strategic power, leaving the Soviet Union and Red China relatively free to employ their superior tactical capabilities wherever this seems advantageous.

The Consequences of Second-Rate Status. Communist dogma contemplates the employment—over such time span as may be necessary—of the entire arsenal of pressure against the United States as the strongest democratic power. . . . Throughout the past quarter of a century, when the Soviet Union was relatively weak strategically, it precipitated or supported crisis upon crisis. . . It is irrational to think, with the balance of military power shifting in its favor, that the policies of the Soviet Union will be less hostile, disruptive, and imperialistic.

The consequences of being second-rate, even if national survival is not threatened, could be seriouly detrimental to the most vital diplomatic and economic interests of this country.

The silence which attended the Blue Ribbon Defense Panel Supplemental Statement was just one example of why the American people are uninformed about the threat of our nation's survival. About a year later, there was the case of the 91 concerned Congressmen. On April 4, 1972, these Congressmen took almost an entire day delivering speeches on the seriousness of our defense situation. They included the chairman of the House Armed Services Committee and a substantial number of the committee. Their statements added up to a solemn warning to the nation which filled more than one hundred pages of the small type in the *Congressional Record*. All the material they presented was authentic, relevant, and important. Yet, this unique demonstration by more than a fifth of the House membership was almost totally ignored by the press. When reprimanded by some Congressmen for this neglect, a couple of newspapers responded by pleading that much of the material presented was not new. It is true that much of it had been said before; the point was that it had not been *reported* before. Only an informed people can remain a free people.

It is a strange anomaly of our time that the Russian heroes Aleksandr Solzhenitsyn and Andrei Sakharov risked persecution, torture, and death to attempt to win for the Russian people what we in the United States already enjoy, but which our unilateral-strategic-surrender elitist groups seek to throw away. If the United States surrenders to the Communist Party of the Soviet Union, or is destroyed by a nuclear holocaust *circa* 1977, all hope for freedom in the world will be destroyed for generations. We will then be in that pitiful position so eloquently described by Solzhenitsyn in a letter to the Kremlin masters written in 1973, but published in Paris on March 2, 1974:

Tear from our backs this "Marxist shirt," sweaty and filthy, already so bloody, which does not let the living body of our nation breathe, and this blood is that of 66 million men.

In 1969, four great scientists of national and international reputation—Nobel prize winners Willard F. Libby and Eugene P. Wigner, developer of over-the-horizon radar William J. Thaler, and Dr. Harold M. Agnew, head of the Atomic Energy Commission's Weapons Division at Los Alamos Laboratory—joined to produce the first authoritative warning that the U.S.S.R. had overtaken and substantially passed the United States in strategic military power. The study, published by the American Security Council, was entitled *The ABM and the Changed Strategic Military Balance*. Scientists and military experts who have won such international renown would only have risked their reputations by participating in and signing such a study if it were fully documented and logically demonstrable. Here are a few excerpts from their own summary:

It is no longer necessary to suppose . . . that the Soviets *will* aim for strategic military superiority. Reality now conforms to theory. We now *know* that the Soviets' military objective is strategic superiority because *they have passed "parity"* and are still building.

The combined total of ICBMs, IR/MRBMs (intermediate and medium range missiles) and SLMs (sea-launched missiles) is now estimated as 2,750 for the U.S.S.R. to 1,710 for the U.S.A.

Although the Gross National Product of the United States runs almost twice that of the gross in the U.S.S.R., the U.S.S.R. is investing two to three times more in strategic forces annually.

The U.S.S.R may invest at least $50 billion to $100 billion more in strategic forces between now and 1975, than the United States, unless the relative trends change substantially. . . .

The U.S.S.R. now has whole new families of military and naval weapons systems that the United States does not have in its inventory.

The U.S.S.R. has adopted . . . "innovative policies" to take advantage of both offensive and defensive opportunities. For example—the Soviets:

—presently enjoy a clear lead in space orbital weapons . . . properly deployed, a significant number, let us say 100, could be in a position to attack the United States in a matter of seconds after the button was pushed in the Kremlin. . .

—have an estimated 1,000 intermediate and medium range missiles which are primarily aimed at Europe and now completely pin Europe down . . .

—have very large . . . 50-100 megaton nuclear weapons which were tested in 1961-62 . . . adapted for missile delivery.

—have the Bear Bomber. It is the world's longest-range, highest endurance bomber . . .

In connection with their missile defense program, the Soviets are developing a comprehensive civil defense program . . . spending about 10 times as much effort as the United States in providing the Soviet society with an adequate civil defense. Moreover, civil defense in the Soviet Union is related directly to overall Soviet military strategy.

These findings become more significant when considered against the background of announced Soviet objectives and the continuing assertions of Soviet leaders that they are preparing for any eventuality that might trigger a nuclear war in their determination to achieve long-stated Communist goals, worldwide.

In both word and deed, the Soviets have shown that they regard the world struggle as a fight to the finish between two diametrically opposed social systems. Moreover, it is a fight the Soviets intend to win.

With special reference to the JCS position on the SALT I accords, Dr. Donald G. Brennan observed:

> A decade ago, it would have been absolutely inconceivable that, for instance, the Joint Chiefs of Staff would have approved either of these agreements, much less both of them. Their approval would have been almost as unthinkable five years ago. Within the past three years, however, and especially within the past two, a very noticeable loss of morale has been detectable within the Department [of Defense]. In the face of buffeting from Congress, from the President's own Bureau of the Budget, and from the general public, the military staffs have been looking to SALT to help "save" their situation. Even today, however, it is implausible that the Joint Chiefs could regard these agreements with enthusiasm; more likely, they faced a set of unpleasant alternatives, and judged these agreements to be the least unpleasant.[5]

Dr. Brennan's diagnosis is accurate. In effect, the JCS were told by their civilian superiors: Go along with SALT and we will help you get the B-1 and Trident. If you oppose SALT, it will be approved anyhow, and you will not get either B-1 or Trident.

There are others who have been speaking out. Two recently retired former chairmen of the Joint Chiefs of Staff are, together with two retired U.S. ambassadors, actively heading up an "Operation Alert" with the specific purpose of warning the American people how dangerously we are falling behind in strategic military power. This operation is being conducted by the American Security Council, and the four men are General Earle G. Wheeler, General Lyman L. Lemnitzer, Ambassador Elbridge Durbrow, and Ambassador Loy W. Henderson. The operation is explained as a "Massive Crusade for Survival: We must saturate the media with grim facts—because, tragically, nobody else is doing so."

Two other former JCS chairmen are members of the National Strategy Committee of the American Security Council, which is dedicated to informing the American people of the facts relating to our national security: General Nathan F. Twining, USAF (Ret.), and General Maxwell D. Taylor, USA (Ret.). Two former commanders-in-chief, U.S. Strategic Air Command, the late great General Thomas S. Power and General Bruce K. Holloway, USAF (Ret.), were or are members, as are General Bernard A. Schriever, USAF (Ret.), former Commanding General, Air Force Systems Command, who built the U.S. Minuteman force in five years less than the time estimated, and Admiral H. D. Felt, USN (Ret.), former Commander-in-chief in the Pacific. At least a dozen other distinguished retired general and flag officers are members of the American Security Council's National Strategy Committee.

All these men have spoken out on the weakness in our defenses and given serious warnings. The newsworthy point is that the scientists, military experts, and civilian strategic authorities of the American Security Council have never been wrong about a single major strategic development involving the U.S.S.R. and the United States, whereas the U.S. intelligence community has never been right.

It is axiomatic in military science that no realistic solution to a military threat can be formulated without first making an accurate "estimate of the situation." This is only common sense: you can't tell where you need to go next until you find out where you are now.

In the case of this book, however, there is an additional requirement for an estimate of the situation. If enough people can be brought to believe in the solution presented in this book, it is entirely possible that the United States can be saved from the alternatives of (1) strategic surrender or (2) nuclear destruction. At present, as a result of Kissinger's and Brezhnev's policies, those are the only courses open to us. Only on the basis of an accurate and persuasive picture of how desperate the situation is can we demonstrate our equally desperate need to get out, and the fact that *there is a way to get out*. Both Brezhnev and Kissinger are trying to convince us that our situation is hopeless by the old and effective ploy of the false alternatives.

A simple play on words, incorporating a distortion of logic, has been the primary weapon in bringing down the nation which has been not only the most powerful and prosperous the world has ever known, but also the one which enjoyed the greatest civilization. In the arsenal of the political-warfare geniuses in the Kremlin, the pen that wrote "rather Red than dead" was, indeed, mightier than the swords of scores of thousands of megatons of nuclear weapons. This slogan served as the rationale for the creation of the Nitze unilateral surrender plan, for the McNamara implementation of that plan, and for the Kissinger follow-on programs. It explains why so many Americans in places of high trust went along with the unilateral disarmament programs. They accepted the Nitze aphorism that it is safer to be weak than to be strong. They fell for his self-fulfilling prophecy that we could not compete with the Soviet Union and come out Number One in strategic power, and therefore, that it would be horrendously dangerous to come out a strong second, "stay in the bidding" (not surrender on demand), and therefore "get clobbered."

The tragedy of this mass betrayal of the United States is that we did not expect or require that these men take the position that they would rather be dead than Red. All that was needed was that they have the faith and courage to take some *risks* of being dead. For the first six years of their sellout program, the risk would have been small indeed. Any intelligent coward would have chosen to incur it. The falsity of the "Red or dead" alternatives lies in the fact that the *third alternative* is to risk being strong enough so that the enemy cannot make you Red by demanding your surrender, nor make you dead by an attack.

The set of false alternatives into which Kissinger and Brezhnev are presently attempting to trap us is merely the same old ploy phrased in slightly different words. Kissinger is saying that our only alternatives are detente or nuclear war. When Kissinger uses the word detente in that context, he means detente on Kremlin terms. Brezhnev is saying that the only alternatives the United States has are strategic surrender or nuclear war. In March 1974 he assured reporters that neither side has much choice in coming up with some kind of SALT agreement. "The alternative," he added bluntly, "is war—there is no other alternative."[6] The comprehensive proposal advanced by the Kremlin was so obviously the equivalent of a demand for the strategic surrender of the United States that even the most liberal and disarmament-minded U.S. officials concerned with the SALT II negotiations joined in referring to it as "the 21 outrageous demands."[7] The Soviets flatly refused any cut in their SALT I-established numerical superiority in missiles, and refused to accept any limit on their vastly greater megatonnage delivery capability. In short, they will accept no SALT II restrictions which would block completion of their buildup to a first-strike capability, at which point we would have no rational alternative to a strategic surrender.

Concerning Kissinger's statement of the detente-or-nuclear-war alternative, both politicians and columnists have spotted the fact that he is using the gambit of false alternatives. Thus, Senator Henry Jackson asserts that Kissinger has

> posed a false choice between avoiding nuclear war and keeping faith with traditional values of human decency and individual liberty.[8]

George F. Will, Washington editor of *National Review,* offered an eloquently outraged comment. He introduced it by referring to a star on the children's television program *Sesame Street* who is a cookie monster obsessed with cookies to the exclusion of other elements in a balanced diet, and who, regardless of the situation, cries out "Cookies! Cookies!"

> Have you noticed? Regardless of the situation, Henry Kissinger's resonant voice cries, "Detente! Detente!" He drags his obsession into public view on occasions that only demonstrate that he is indeed obsessed. How else explain citing detente as a reason for remaining mute about the heroism of Alexander Solzhenitsyn?
>
> At a recent press conference Kissinger was invited to express admira-

tion for Solzhenitsyn. Kissinger gagged like a man biting a bad oyster. Evidently he thinks candid acknowledgement of Soviet viciousness could destroy the detente that he has built on the myth of Soviet mellowness.

When he spoke he sounded like the cookie monster with his mouth gorged with chocolate chip cookies. The incredible message of his stammering:

We can use our influence on behalf of human rights, or we can avoid nuclear war through detente.

Kissinger, wrapped up in the fallacy of the false alternatives, is no worse than his boss. President Nixon never uttered a syllable on behalf of Solzhenitsyn.[9]

Dr. Kissinger's own most succinct obfuscation on detente reads like this:

Our concern for detente does not reflect approbation of internal Soviet policy but the *necessity of detente is produced by the unacceptability of general nuclear war* under present circumstances.[10]

This is very close to saying that our only alternatives are detente (on Soviet terms) or nuclear war. One of his most intriguing declarations on this subject came in his testimony on the then-pending trade bill before the Senate Finance Committee. He said that if Congress wrote restrictions against Russia in it, he would "think very seriously about recommending a veto" and

Let us remember that we seek detente with the Soviet Union for one overwhelming reason: both countries have the capability to destroy each other, and most of the world in the process.[11]

This is Henry Kissinger in his least attractive stance—arrogantly assuming that the American people are stupid. He is trying to frighten us into giving the Soviets trade advantages by threatening us with nuclear war if we don't; yet, the threat he states hypothesizes the classic "balance of terror." This concept has, since the beginning of nuclear strategy, been considered to represent a condition of stability and mutual assured deterrence. Winston Churchill used to call it the "peace of mutual terror," and predicted that it could support a long-term peace provided only that the terror was kept "mutual." If Kissinger were telling the truth about our alleged mutual capability of destroying each other, this book would not be necessary.

The next excerpt from his same testimony establishes that he has no confidence in our strategic deterrent, and that he does not believe in our capability to destroy the Soviet Union:

The issue is not whether we condone what the U.S.S.R. does internally;

it is whether and to what extent we can risk other objectives, and especially the building of a structure for peace, for these domestic changes.

I believe that we cannot and that to do so would obscure, and in the long run defeat, *what must remain our overriding objective—the prevention of nuclear war.*

Our deterrent, not detente, is what is supposed to prevent nuclear war.

There is an additional point to consider. Once you declare that your overriding objective is the prevention of nuclear war, you are well on your way to surrender. Once you set up a priority which puts peace before freedom, you have given notice that, if necessary to prevent nuclear war, you will surrender freedom. Indeed, Kissinger, in all his pronouncements relating to the detente-or-nuclear-war alternative, has either fallen or deliberately jumped into one of the better recognized traps of nuclear strategy, namely, to accept nuclear war as one of only two alternatives. Once you do that, you have surrendered, because no other alternative is that bad. So, if the only way to avert nuclear war is to choose the other of the two alternatives, you will take it. You will take it whether it is surrender, overt or covert, unconditional or on the installment plan. This, of course, is why we must demand a credible and effective strategic deterrent: it provides the third alternative to surrender on the one hand (euphemistically called detente) or nuclear war on the other hand.

Henry Kissinger knows all this. Despite Schlesinger's stylized minuet in the areas of flexible and selective retaliation, here is a direct quote:

> It is assured capability to retaliate decisively against Soviet cities even after absorbing the full weight of a Soviet nuclear attack that offers the best hope of deterring attack and thus protecting our cities. . . .[12]

That means we still rely on massive retaliation. Keeping this in mind, read this excerpt from Dr. Kissinger's 1961 book:

> . . . the threat of mutual destruction can be made plausible only by convincing the aggressor that the response to aggression will be nearly automatic; that at some point we will lose control over events.
>
> A country relying upon the doctrine of massive retaliation can resist blackmail only by maneuvering deliberately to demonstrate that *on some issues the question of whether they are worth a cataclysm will not be asked.*[13]

Yet, Kissinger shuttles back and forth across the world crying that our only alternatives are detente or nuclear war. Suppose they are right. Suppose Leonid Brezhnev and Henry Kissinger are telling the exact truth when they say that, for the United States, the only alternatives are detente (on Soviet terms) or nuclear war. If they are right, then our rational course would be to go along with Kissinger and let him continue to negotiate our strategic surrender. But surrendering to the Politburo of the Communist Party of the Soviet Union is a serious decision to make. Once made, it will be—as Kissinger and Brezhnev say of their detente—irreversible. The option will then be exclusively theirs as to whether they want us Red or dead. And if dead, how many? All 210 million Americans will be within their power after our strategic surrender; or, they could kill on a selective basis, as they did in the U.S.S.R. After all, they only liquidated 66 million of their own people to establish the Communist system there, according to Solzhenitsyn's figures. Robert Conquest's figures are more conservative. In his book *The Great Terror,* he estimates 30 million, but he does say that this is a minimum estimate.

If the Kremlin should decide against total genocide of the American people, and instead execute a selective liquidation of, say, from 10 to 20 percent (roughly, 20 to 40 million), you and your family might be among those spared. But you could not count on it. The best you can count on is being administered like the Soviet Union, by a Gulag Archipelago type of slave labor camps and prisons to keep you in line. Going along with their system is no guarantee of safety, either; in Stalin's Great Terror, thousands of loyal members of the Communist Party were executed or tortured to death. They all went to their deaths asking why.

It is important to decide whether we do have a viable third alternative to surrender (of some sort) to the Kremlin, on the one hand, or to nuclear war, on the other. The answer will depend on what estimates of the situation show about how close the Soviets are to attaining first-strike capability against us. More specifically, what we need to know is whether we can reconstitute our strategic deterrent in time to block the Soviets not only from attaining a "splendid" first-strike capability, but also to "cut them off at the pass," so to speak, before they attain high confidence that a preemptive strike would pay off. Answers to these questions depend also on how close the Soviets are to reaching their first-strike capability.

The seven members of President Nixon's Blue Ribbon Defense Panel who prepared the report called *The Shifting Balance of Military Power* gave comprehensive consideration to this problem. Unfortunately, the report itself speaks as of September 30, 1970, and the intelligence estimates upon which it is based are probably of mid-1970. Still, it remains the latest authoritative and objective consideration of the problem, and is the firmest foundation for an updated current estimate. Here is the official summary:

A Soviet First-strike Capability. Our planners in the 60s assumed that if both superpowers had an adequate retaliatory capability neither would prepare for or risk a first-strike. The *evidence is now reasonably conclusive that the Soviet Union*, rejecting this assumption, *is deploying strategic weapons systems designed for a first-strike capability.*

This evidence includes: (i) the continued Soviet production and deployment of ICBMs *after* having attained a clear numerical and megatonnage advantage; (ii) the emphasis on SS-9s, designed as counterforce weapons capable of destroying U.S. hardened missile silos; (iii) the development of MRV with warheads also designed as counterforce weapons, and of MIRV by 1971-72; (iv) the development of a fractional orbital missile which significantly minimizes warning time; (v) the construction of a Y-class atomic-powered submarine SLBM launching fleet capable, with no effective warning, of destroying our national command centers and much of our B-52 bomber force; and (vi) the continued Soviet emphasis on strategic defense systems against both missiles and bombers—an emphasis without parallel in this country.

The characteristics of these offensive weapons systems, which the Soviets continue to expand, are consistent only with a preemptive strike capability. Such a weapons mix and volume are not required for effective retaliation.

The structure of both their offensive and defensive forces strongly indicates that they have planned—and are moving to achieve—a first-strike capability of destroying our urban centers *and* neutralizing our retaliatory weapons except such Polaris submarines as happen to be on station.

(Footnote: Senator Jackson recently informed the Senate that "there is no doubt that their [the Soviets'] program, if continued, will produce a first-strike capability unless the U.S. takes appropriate counter measures." Senate speech, August 5, 1970.)

If the evidence of Soviet deployment of weapons for a first-strike was "reasonably conclusive" in 1970, it is totally conclusive now. In fact, that is the understatement of the nuclear age. In that four-year period, the Soviets have moved ahead in their strategic weapons buildup with swiftly accelerating momentum. Sheer numbers of additional weapons, all of them "past parity," should alone be conclusive. In the two years from mid-1970 to the SALT I signing in mid-1972, they added some 300 ICBMs, of which 100 were heavies of the SS-9 type. In submarine-launched ballistic missiles, their progress was fantastic. From about 10 modern Y-type missile-launching submarines in 1970, they more than quadrupled, to 46 operational or under construction.[14] By the end of 1973, according to Secretary Schlesinger's FY 1975 DOD Report, this number had reached 51 or 52; and projecting their building rate, at the end of 1974 should reach 60 deployed or under construction. Allowing 16 launchers for each submarine, except for four Delta I's which each have 12, would give them about 930 launchers. This means that they have added more than 700 SLBM launcher tubes since the Blue Ribbon estimate date which, plus the ICBMs, means that they have added more than 1,000 launchers of missiles capable of reaching the United States. At the Blue Ribbon date, they were already past parity; this will be 1,000 past that. As of late 1974, the Soviets will just about have reached their SALT I totals of 1,618 ICBMs in silos or on pads, and 740 SLBMs on modern submarines, for a grand total of 2,358 against our 1,710. (When they add additional SLBMs up to 950, they are *supposed* to scrap equivalent "old" ICBMs.)

One might think that those redundant numbers alone would be sufficient evidence of Soviet intentions. But not to Senator Edward Kennedy. During his spring 1974 trip to the Soviet Union, he delivered an address to the Soviet Institute of U.S. Studies, a think-tank which advises the Politburo about America. His audience was composed of mature, trained experts in the strategic area. Imagine their surprise, therefore, when Senator Kennedy, as reported by UPI, "called on the Kremlin to clarify whether it intended to use the missiles for war or for research." It probably had not occurred to them, or to anyone else, that any government could have such a panting interest in pure science that it would run the nation on a war footing for 15 years to wring enough hundreds of billions of rubles out of a tight economy in order to research, develop, produce and deploy 2,358 hydrogen-warheaded missiles to use them "for research."

Ever since Melvin Laird warned the nation in 1969 that the Soviets were going for a first-strike capability against us, he and his Director of Defense Research and Engineering, Dr. John S. Foster, warned also that the Soviets were so massively outspending us in research and development that we would have to expect substantial "technological surprises." In his FY 1973 DOD Report, dated February 17, 1972, Laird gave a short, sad history of what had happened and was happening:

> The 1957 Sputnik success shocked this country, and led to a flurry of remedial action which culminated in our successful moon landings. In that instance, fortunately, we were dealing with a peaceful competition; yet it took us more than 10 years to accomplish the job despite our significant technological lead.
>
> Beginning in 1965, at the same time we were devoting so much effort and technology to Vietnam, the Soviet Union was stepping up its research and development efforts and was beginning to produce many of the weapons systems we note today.
>
> The *U.S.S.R. has now reached a position where—unless we take appropriate action—there could be new surprises* and new "sputniks." But they

are less likely to be in areas such as the peaceful exploration of space; rather, they are more likely to be part of a major new Soviet military capability.

Several weeks later, in that same year, Secretary Laird gave an additional reason for extending our efforts on technology. It sounds even more chilling now than it did in 1972:

> The Soviet Union has already moved ahead quantitatively in land-based missiles. . . . Their land-based missiles are bigger than ours and therefore have a greater "throw-weight" than ours. By that I mean their bigger boosters give them a greater capability to deliver more and bigger warheads with their existing missiles than we have in our existing forces.
>
> Given their technological capabilities, I'm sure they can match our technology [in MIRVs] within two or three years.
>
> That is why *it is absolutely essential that we maintain technological superiority over the Soviet Union.* . . .[15]

Well, we didn't maintain our technological superiority. As the Blue Ribbon Panel Supplemental Statement warned us two years before the Laird statement, the resulting technological surprise could be "disastrous."

"Seeing the real facts was like seeing straight into hell," Joseph Alsop quotes one of the authors of the Gaither Report upon seeing an imaginary missile gap of 150 ICBMs favoring the Soviets in 1957.[16] The missile-gap hell into which those men of little faith stared in 1957 was at most a 750-megaton gap (150 ICBMs x 5 MT per ICBM =750 MT). The real one we must now face—before 1977— is a minimum of 20,000 megatons, is most probably on the order of 50,000 megatons, and could be even higher if the Soviets decide to maximize megatonnage delivery capability. As a practical matter, what they probably will do will be to develop and deploy alternative forces, *each* capable of a disarming strike against the U.S. Minuteman force. Their technological breakthrough in developing a method of multiplying missile throw-weight by 500 percent will enable them to develop four such forces; but even the hyperconservative redundancy-loving Soviet military will probably settle for two disarming-strike forces: one for primary reliance and a second for back-up.

To get an idea of the practical meaning of the Soviet achievement in multiplying by five the throw-weight of its formerly "light" missiles, while still using the same silos and launching tubes with only internal adjustments, let us imagine a transport aircraft about like a Boeing 747, and having a passenger-plus-baggage capacity for 500. Then suppose a competitor came out with a similar transport aircraft, somewhat but not dramatically greater in volume, which could use the same runways and loading ramps; but this new model had a

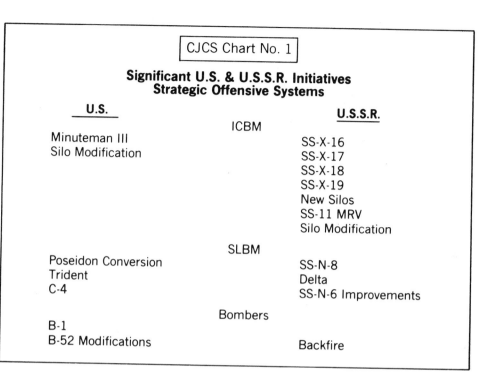

CJCS Chart No. 1

Significant U.S. & U.S.S.R. Initiatives
Strategic Offensive Systems

U.S.		U.S.S.R.
	ICBM	
Minuteman III		SS-X-16
Silo Modification		SS-X-17
		SS-X-18
		SS-X-19
		New Silos
		SS-11 MRV
		Silo Modification
	SLBM	
Poseidon Conversion		SS-N-8
Trident		Delta
C-4		SS-N-6 Improvements
	Bombers	
B-1		
B-52 Modifications		Backfire

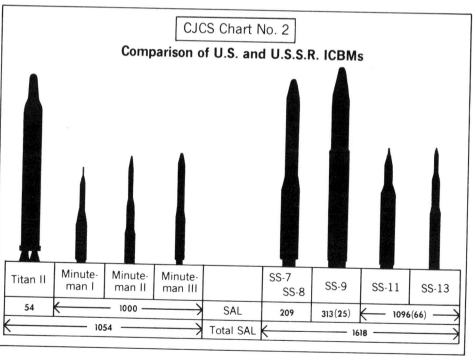

CJCS Chart No. 2

Comparison of U.S. and U.S.S.R. ICBMs

Titan II	Minute-man I	Minute-man II	Minute-man III		SS-7 SS-8	SS-9	SS-11	SS-13
54	←———— 1000 ————→			SAL	209	313(25)	←—— 1096(66) ——→	
←——————— 1054 ———————→				Total SAL	←——————— 1618 ———————→			

CJCS Chart No. 3			
New U.S.S.R. ICBMs			
SS-X-16	**SS-X-17**	**SS-X-18**	**SS-X-19**
Follow-on SS-13	SS-11	SS-9	SS-11
Range (NM) Over 5000	Over 5500	Over 5500	Over 5500
MIRV Warhead Probable	Yes	Yes	Yes
Estimated Number of MIRVs ?	4	5-8	4-6
Digital Computer Yes	Yes	Yes	Yes
IOC 1975	1975	1975	1975

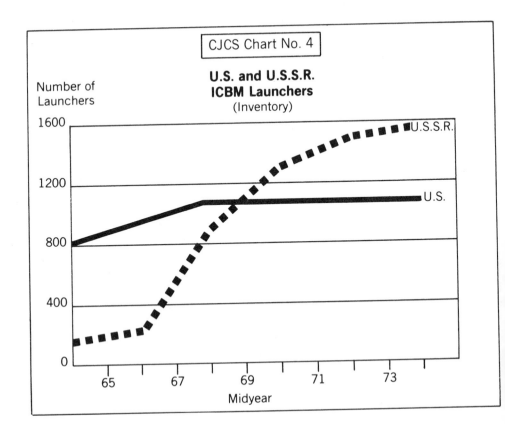

CJCS Chart No. 4

Number of Launchers

U.S. and U.S.S.R. ICBM Launchers
(Inventory)

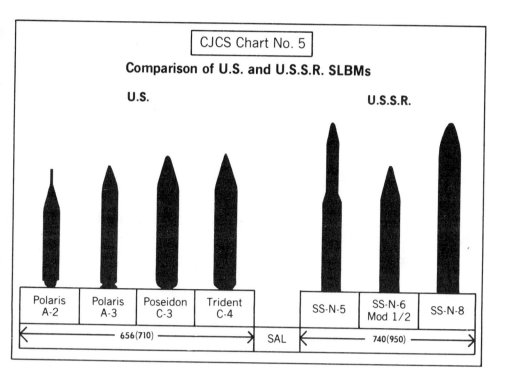

Comparison of U.S. and U.S.S.R. SLBMs

U.S.   U.S.S.R.

| Polaris A-2 | Polaris A-3 | Poseidon C-3 | Trident C-4 | | SS-N-5 | SS-N-6 Mod 1/2 | SS-N-8 |

← 656(710) → SAL ← 740(950) →

passenger-plus-baggage capacity of 2,500. Probably there would be no use for a commercial aircraft carrying 2,500 passengers in this time-frame, but it would certainly be handy for transporting freight. And, of course, it is freight which ICBMs carry. The greater the throw-weight, the larger the number of MIRVed warheads that can be carried, and the more explosive power each MIRV can carry.

The new Soviet SS-17 and SS-19 ICBMs are replacements for the SS-11s, of which the Soviets have more than 1,000. Since the SS-17s and SS-19s can also legally replace the earlier SS-7s and SS-8s, the Soviets could replace 1,300 existing ICBMs in silos or pads (SALT I allowance of 1,618 silos, minus 318 SS-9s or SS-18s). The throw-weight of the early SS-11 has been reliably leaked at 2,500 pounds.[17] In their high-yield weapons, the Soviets get about two megatons of explosive power for each 1,000 pounds of weight, but the yield/weight ratio is not that good in the lower ranges. Thus, the old SS-9 was assigned a throw-weight of either 12,000 or 13,000 pounds (Alsop and Brennan, respectively), and a yield of 25 megatons. If we allow 1-1/3 megatons per 1,000 pounds of throw-weight for the SS-11, it would give a yield of about three megatons; but, of course, it could go as high as five megatons. Every year of underground testing enables the Soviets to improve on their yield/weight ratio, which since their great tests of

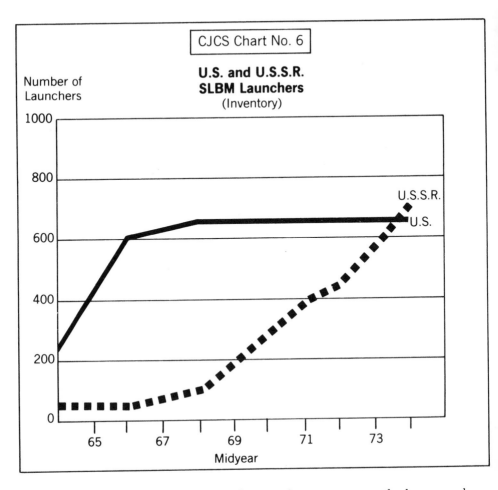

CJCS Chart No. 6

U.S. and U.S.S.R.
SLBM Launchers
(Inventory)

Number of Launchers

U.S.S.R.

U.S.

Midyear

1961-62 has been substantially better than ours; exactly how much better is classified to keep Americans from discovering what the Russians already know.

Let's take the lower figure, three megatons, and multiply by the number of missiles which can be replaced by the SS-17s or SS-19s; that is, 1,300 missiles at 3 MT each equals 3,900 megatons; then multiply that by the factor of five, which resulted from their technological breakthrough, and we get 19,500 megatons as the new force loading. This means that they will be able to *add* to their present ICBM force, if they decide to do so and employ principally single warheads, a delivery capability of 15,600 megatons. In terms of U.S. ICBMs, therefore, the Soviet technological surprise enables them to add to their existing substantially superior force the equivalent in explosive power of 15,600 one-megaton Minuteman missiles.

If, instead of maximizing their megatonnage delivery capability,

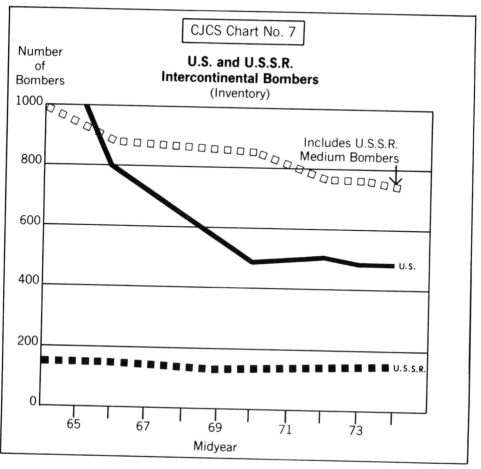

U.S. and U.S.S.R.
Intercontinental Bombers
(Inventory)

Number
of
Bombers

1000

800

600

400

200

0

Includes U.S.S.R.
Medium Bombers

U.S.

U.S.S.R.

65   67   69   71   73

Midyear

they decide to obtain the maximum number of warheads, they could get some 6,800 MIRVs out of an SS-19 force, or 5,200 out of an SS-17 force. On numbers of warheads alone, this doesn't sound too impressive, because our Minuteman force will have a total of 2,100 MIRVs; but it becomes tremendously impressive when we remember that our MIRVed warheads in the Minuteman force are at most two-tenths of a megaton, whereas the Soviet MIRVs are two megatons each. The single-shot hardened-silo kill probability of the 2-megaton warhead is twice as good at a CEP of 1,500 feet (80 percent vs. 40 percent).

We have been comparing the *total* U.S. ICBM force against only the "light" Soviet ICBM force and their new replacements. The same techniques which permitted the Soviets to put missiles with five times more throw-weight into the preexisting "light" ICBM silos work also with the very heavy ICBMs, the SS-9 type, only not so dramatically. An increase of 33 percent in throw-weight is officially ad-

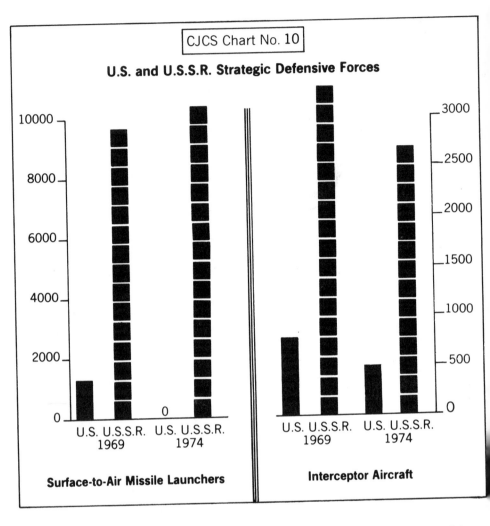

U.S. and U.S.S.R. Strategic Defensive Forces

U.S. U.S.S.R.   U.S. U.S.S.R.
1969   1974

Surface-to-Air Missile Launchers

U.S. U.S.S.R.   U.S. U.S.S.R.
1969   1974

Interceptor Aircraft

mitted. Unofficial leaks, however, are far more persuasive on this point. Senator Henry Jackson has been contending for three years that the SS-18 carries a single warhead with a yield of 50 megatons. Actually, this is entirely possible with only a 33 percent increase in throw-weight, considering the increased efficiency of very-high yield warheads, and the fact that the SS-9 has been rated at 25 megatons for nearly 10 years. The Soviets must have made some improvements in their burning techniques and improved their yield/weight ratio in that period. So the SS-18 should be rated at 50 megatons.

Three hundred and eighteen SS-18s would give a force loading, in single warheads, of 15,900 megatons. Add that to the 19,500 megatons of the maximized megatonnage once "light" but now definitely "heavy" SS-17s and SS-19s, and the Soviets could have, if they wished, before 1977, a missile-deliverable megatonnage capacity in their land-based force of ICBMs of 35,400 megatons. If, instead of maximizing megatons, the Russians want warheads, then they can get 318 x 8 out of the SS-18s, or 2,544. Add that to the 6,800 they could get out of an SS-19 force, and they will have a total of 9,344 MIRVs that are relatively huge compared to U.S. MIRVed warheads. Senator James L. Buckley managed to extract from James R. Schlesinger an interesting comparison in this MIRV area:

> In the most important single measure of the capability of a strategic force—missile "throw-weight"—the Soviets have taken a commanding lead. To gain an idea of the significance of this disparity, if the Soviets used the Poseidon type 50 kiloton warhead (more than 2½ times the size of the Hiroshima bomb) on their missile force, Secretary of Defense James R. Schlesinger recently noted, they could deploy about 23,000 warheads while we would have less than one-fourth that number.[18]

That sounds fairly truthful for Schlesinger; but we checked it out, and the number for the Soviets—in the land-based force alone—is far closer to 70,000. The throw-weight of an SS-11 is 2,500 pounds, and the SS-19s can quintuple this; therefore, 2,500 pounds per missile x 5 x 1,300 missiles equals 16,250,000 pounds throw-weight for the total SS-19 force. The throw-weight of an SS-18 is 16,500 pounds; therefore, 16,500 pounds per missile x 318 missiles equals 5,247,000 pounds throw-weight for the total SS-18 force. Thus the grand total throw-weight of the SS-19 and SS-18 forces is 21,497,000 pounds. Dividing that by 300 pounds per warhead (the generally accepted throw-weight of a Poseidon 50-kiloton MIRV) gives 71,657 warheads. So Schlesinger told one-third of the truth.

Actually, to do Schlesinger justice on his figuring, he is computing the number of Poseidon 50-kiloton MIRV-sized warheads the Soviets could deploy on their old SS-11 and SS-9 ICBM force. That old force belongs to the past, however; the CJCS FY 1975 Military Posture report cited above estimates that other than the relatively few old (SS-7 and SS-8) ICBMs which may be turned in on additional new SLBMs, "we believe the remaining ICBMs will be modernized by replacing them with the new systems already described."

When will the replacements be made? By March 1974, it was already under way. Here is a key sentence on that from the Posture Statement:

> This Soviet throw-weight advantage is a key element because it facilitates the *large-scale MIRV development, already under way at a rapid rate.*

As will be seen from the CJCS charts below, all four new Soviet ICBM systems are to go operational in 1975.

The charts presented in the report of the Chairman of the Joint

Chiefs of Staff entitled "U.S. Military Posture for FY 1975" include some of the most revealing that have been published in 20 years. A look at several of them is essential to making an intelligent estimate of what has been referred to as the "desperate state of our defenses" and which we sometimes describe as the Soviet breakout of the "balance of terror."

Charts #2 and #5 are the best place to start because they show our two types of ballistic missile forces. Chart #2 compares U.S.S.R. and U.S. ICBMs, and Chart #5 compares SLBMs. These two charts give the SALT I allowances (identified in the charts as "SAL," omitting the "T" which merely stands for "Talks"), which also happen to be almost exactly the current forces of both sides, except for SLBMs for the Soviets which will reach their total SALT I force levels by mid-1977. Thus, the imbalances in numbers of missiles favoring the Soviets are clearly shown. The massive imbalances favoring the Soviets in throw-weight and megatonnage are not shown, but they are hinted at. The second purpose of these two charts is to provide physical comparisons of the missiles. Looking at the silhouettes, an apparently very small advantage in volume means vastly greater throw-weight—because the scale, although accurate, is minute; also, the SS-11, which appears only slightly greater in volume than the U.S. Minuteman models, is liquid-fueled, which means greater throw-weight capability. But these are the most authoritative charts available in unclassified form which give helpful clues as to the strategic balance. For example, in Chart #5, the Soviet SS-N-8, which has been operational on Delta and Delta II submarines for two years, is revealed as of greater volume than the U.S. Trident C-4, which we only hope to have operational on one Trident submarine in 1979; and the SS-N-8 already has greater range than the Trident C-4 will have in 1979.

The first of the exciting charts is #3, "New U.S.S.R. ICBMs." We already know from Dr. Schlesinger's FY 1975 DOD Report about the revolutionary factor-of-five increase in throw-weight of the SS-17 and SS-19 over the SS-11 (he used the figure "3-5"; but with the factor of five available, it is inconsistent with Soviet doctrine to develop less than the maximum factor); but the chart answers the question, how about accuracy of guidance? Sadly, this too has been increased dramatically, thanks to the computer technology we have given the Soviets in trade programs. This was the sole substantial technological advantage we still retained over them as late as 1971; but they have it now. This paragraph from Schlesinger's FY 1975 DOD Report should be read along with Chart #3:

The breadth and depth of this Soviet ICBM program is further manifested by the wide variety of techniques and technology employed in the new systems. *All four of these systems have computers aboard the post boost vehicles.* New guidance concepts, two different types of post boost vehicle propulsion, and *two different types of launch techniques are employed.*

The on-board computer is what dramatically increases accuracy and decreases the CEP of missiles. So far as we can discover, this quotation on types of launch techniques is the only mention of this crucial subject in recent official reports. One reason, perhaps, is that the Soviets' new pop-up cold-launch technique makes that SALT I Interim Agreement look even more ridiculous than it does on its face. Although Henry Kissinger in his contemporaneous briefings and official statements on SALT asserted repeatedly that it imposed a ceiling on or restricted the number of missiles, and he even had the President report formally to Congress that the SALT I Interim Agreement "limits the overall level of strategic offensive missile forces," there is actually no limit whatsoever on numbers of *missiles*—only on certain limited types of missile *launchers*. With the old ICBM silo-launch techniques which we are still using—the blast-off is an inferno of flames within the launch tube within the silo—reloads within any reasonable time period were impractical or impossible. The tubes would require extensive repairs and adjustments. With the new Soviet techniques, however, reloads are just as practicable as they always have been on missile-launching submarines since that first U.S. Polaris in the late 1950s. Thus, a nation with a first-strike or even a positive preemptive strategy, and therefore in control of the timetable of a nuclear "exchange," could prepare for reloading of any number of launchers it might decide to invest in. This is another one-way advantage to the Soviets in SALT I.

Continuing with the CJCS charts, Chart #1 gives a harrowing preview of the future of our nation if Kissinger's policies continue to control our defense. It contrasts U.S. and U.S.S.R. initiatives in strategic offense systems—what might be called "ongoing" programs designed to produce power within the next several years. The Chairman of the Joint Chiefs of Staff, who is subordinate to the civilian control of Secretary Schlesinger and the President (and the de facto president for foreign relations and national security, Henry Kissinger), could not appropriately list, on the U.S. side, either "nothing" or "zero.' But that's what our side really means. It tells us also that all Dr. Schlesinger's talk about "hedges" for the future is merely talk. There is nothing on the U.S. side of the chart which will add any power to our strategic forces prior to our getting the first Trident submarine operational in 1979. The B-1, as we have seen, will not be operational, even *if* a decision to produce it is made in 1977, until the 1980s. The Minuteman III program was ordered in 1967, so it is hardly a new initiative and merely means mini-MIRVing the 550 Minuteman missiles. The C-4 is the SLBM for the Trident submarine. The B-52 modifications are a patchup program for the older worn-out B-52s to keep them from falling apart, and to enable them to be loaded with mini bombs so Dr. Schlesinger can play the numbers game.

A similar chart was presented by Senator James L. Buckley in the article cited earlier. In addition to the Backfire strategic bomber listed by CJCS, which flies at mach 2.0, the Senator adds one significant development to the Soviet side: "a mach 3.2 bomber designed by the Sukhoi design bureau" which he says is in development. In regard to strategic bombers, the best short statement is found in a footnote to Edward Luttwak's *The Strategic Balance 1972*:

> At a June 30, 1972, press conference, President Nixon addressed this point, saying, "As far as the Soviet Union is concerned, the fact that *they are not developing bombers* does not mean that they do not respect ours, and I would say too that *had we not had our present advantage in bombers, we could not then stand by and allow the Soviets to have a 1,600-to-1,000 advantage in terms of missiles that are land-based.*" Presidential adviser Henry Kissinger made the same point at considerable length when briefing members of Congress at the White House, June 15, 1972.[19]

Kissinger used "our present advantage in bombers" as a sales argument for SALT to the press and to congressional committees. The intelligence furnished to the President that the Soviets were "not developing bombers" was totally wrong. Compare the President's statement as of June 30, 1972, with a statement from the FY 1975 U.S. Military Posture Report of the Chairman of the JCS, delivered in March 1974:

> In each of my past three Military Posture statements, I have reported to you on the *progressive development of a new* variable-geometry wing, supersonic bomber by the Soviet Union. . . .It weighs 2½ times as much as an FB-111 and is about four-fifths as large as the B-1. We estimate that the Backfire will be deployed operationally in 1974. . . .When deployed with a compatible tanker force. Backfire constitutes a potential threat to the continental United States.

This means that the Soviet bomber development had been officially and publicly reported in each of two years *before* the President made his statement. Who was responsible for making sure that the President received and understood this intelligence?

CJCS Chart #7 compares strategic bomber forces. The significant curve for the U.S.S.R. is the upper one, which includes medium bombers. Their medium bombers have always been considered part of the strategic bomber force by all authorities except McNamara. The International Institute for Strategic Studies of London has always counted them, and so have the American Security Council and all other sources which make an objective and meaningful comparison. As the JCS Chairman explained, they could be used "on two-way missions against targets in Canada and Alaska and on one-way missions against other parts of the United States" (with landings provided in Cuba, for example). In any event, they have a longer range and greater payload than the U.S. FB-111s, which are counted in the U.S. force as strategic.

Chart #7 ends at the beginning of 1974, so it does not reflect the Backfire as part of the Soviet force; and the Backfire is by far the most modern, most effective, fastest strategic bomber aircraft in the world—more than twice as fast as the U.S. B-52. The Soviets could have the Backfire operational by the hundreds before 1977; they probably have more than four squadrons of 25 already deployed.

In the face of this Soviet bomber threat, Defense Secretary James Schlesinger ordered the scrapping of all our remaining bomber defenses. This means that, if the Soviets give the Cubans 17 old bomber aircraft and 17 one-megaton bombs, the Cubans could attack 17 U.S. cities with a total population of more than 50 million people—and not encounter any antiaircraft missile opposition. Or, that the Soviets, without firing a single ICBM or SLBM at us, could employ their bomber force against the continental United States and probably kill more than 150 million Americans.

Chart #10 shows how solicitous Kissinger and Schlesinger are to protect the American people compared to how much more the Kremlin leaders value the people of the U.S.S.R. As of 1975, the only SAM antiaircraft batteries we will have left in the United States are a few old ones for training. In the interceptor aircraft chart, although the United States is shown to have 500, these are old and slow, whereas more than 50 percent of the Soviet interceptor force of nearly 3,000 is composed of new or nearly new interceptor types, including the Foxbat (MIG-25), the fastest military aircraft in the world. Also, the 500 so-called U.S. interceptor aircraft are substantially useless because of scrapping or obsolescence of the aircraft warning system. Thousands of miles of our borders are unguarded and open.

Two of the CJCS charts graphically present strategic weapon system gaps for which the defense policies of Henry Kissinger are totally or substantially responsible. Chart #6 compares SLBM launchers. Notice the massive gap in favor of the United States and against the Soviet Union at the time Kissinger came to power in January 1969; we had 656 against the Soviets' less than 200. As we have shown earlier, if Kissinger, instead of falsely asserting that we had no ongoing programs for the production of SLBMs and missile-launching submarines, and were helpless to compete against the Soviet Union in producing them, had merely stopped scrapping operational Polaris submarines and continued the program of building Poseidons but without salvaged parts from scrapped Polaris, there never would have been an SLBM gap, and we could have had at least 62 missile-launching submarines by 1977, instead of only 41 to the Soviets' 62. Because Chart #6 ends at the beginning of 1974, it does not show the massive gap which will open up. As the Schlesinger figures demonstrate, the Soviets will have 950 launchers on 62 modern submarines by 1977 to our 656 launchers on 41 submarines.

In determining how close the Soviets are to a first-strike capability, we are not talking about the theoreticians' dream of a "splendid" or "full" or "preclusive" first-strike capability. That would require everything the Soviets will have in strategic offensive systems by 1977, plus a very effective antiballistic missile defense. What we are looking for here is simply whether the Soviets will soon attain the capability of destroying our Minuteman force, while retaining such a huge reserve of missiles for blackmail or annihilation of our population that we would have no rational alternative to surrender. That is, our entire land-based retaliatory force would have been disarmed so that we could threaten retaliation with only such of our submarine-launched missile force as happened to be on station and undamaged by antisubmarine warfare efforts or sabotage. The Soviet threat to coerce us into abandoning all attempts at retaliation would be the total destruction of our nation and the incineration of substantially our total population by a counterpopulation, countervalue strike of more than 1,000 ICBMs and a submarine-launched missile force half again more numerous than ours.

This question in itself demonstrates the incalculable value of the "balance of terror" to the preservation of nuclear peace. Churchill accurately called the period of peace after World War II the peace of mutual terror; but, he conditioned the duration of this peace on the duration of the *mutuality* of the terror. Similarly, the doctrinal basis of the SALT I Agreements was *"Mutual* Assured Destruction." If the Soviets are able to overturn the actual strategic balance of power so that the only assured destruction is the unilateral destruction of the United States, then our only rational course will be surrender on demand; or even the Nitze-McNamara ploy of tendering a preemptive surrender in advance in order to avert a Soviet counterforce-countervalue-counterpopulation strike being launched by surprise, with no opportunity for surrender.

The ultimate answer to this horrendous question of whether the United States is to be or not to be will be found in the Great Gap of 1977: the ICBM throw-weight gap. A throw-weight advantage can be converted into either a megatonnage delivery advantage, or a warhead advantage, or a combination of both. We are considering this as a projected gap, one which does not exist now, but which the Soviets can create before 1977 if they want to; and the evidence thus far indicates that they have made an irreversible decision to go for it.

We estimate the 1977 throw-weight capabilities to be 2,000,000 pounds for the United States and 21,500,000 pounds for the U.S.S.R. The Schlesinger estimate for the United States is not publicly stated; his estimate for the U.S.S.R. is 10,000,000 to 12,000,000 pounds. The 2,000,000 pounds for the United States, however, is rather generally accepted. The Minuteman in all models has less volume and yield than an old Soviet SS-11, which is usually rated at 2,500 pounds. So, allowing 2,000 pounds each for 1,000 missiles produces the 2,000,000 (the 54 Titan IIs usually are ignored, or lumped in with the Minuteman total). As for the Schlesinger estimate of 10-12 million pounds for the Soviets, our own computations suggest that it is low, and so does a computation based on the most reliable intelligence leaks. Joseph Alsop has been reliable on these matters for nearly two decades, and we have never found an exaggeration by him in estimating Soviet power. In his December 12, 1973, column, he gives this discussion of throw-weight:

> Throw-weight, of course, is the total weight of warhead and warhead-attached apparatus that a missile can throw. This in turn goes far to define the killing power of the missile, in just the way the caliber of a cannon largely defines a cannon's killing power.
>
> In SALT I, on the excuse that we had other technological leads besides MIRV, we already conceded the Soviets a large lead in throw-weight. The Soviets in fact had total allowed land-based throw-weight of eight million pounds against two million for the United States. The United States also had two million pounds of sea-based throw-weight, then balanced by only half that for the Soviets. But the agreement allowed continued Soviet submarine construction, permitting future superior Soviet throw-weight at sea as well as on land.
>
> These far from cheering figures are now to be most radically changed in the wrong direction by the new Soviet missiles. For example, the SS-9 has a throw-weight of 13,000 pounds as against 16,500 for its replacement, the SS-X-18.
>
> Worse still, the SS-11 missile has a throw-weight of only 2,500 pounds as against 6,000 pounds for the SS-X-17. Our land-based throw-weight disadvantage will thus end by being two million pounds as against at least 12 million pounds-plus.
>
> This amounts to placing a six-to-one handicap on our American scientists—an insurmountable handicap. Putting it another way, it amounts to accepting fatal Soviet strategic superiority!

At the time, obviously, Alsop had not heard of the SS-X-19, but both that and the SS-X-17 are potential competitors for replacement of the SS-11. But notice that he accepted a figure of less than 2½ for the SS-X-

17 increase in throw-weight over the SS-11. Schlesinger officially reported the SS-19 as "from three to five times" the SS-11 throw-weight. Having discovered by experience that, when a Schlesinger report gives alternative figures for Soviet advances, the higher one is nearer the truth, we accept his figure of five—and this is twice the figure used by Alsop in his computation. Since some 1,300 missiles are involved, this would put the figure up to our own computation.

Thus, the projected throw-weight gap in favor of the Soviets by 1977 is between 10 million and 19½ million pounds. This is vastly more than enough of an advantage to permit the Soviets to develop several forces of ICBMs, each of which could *independently* destroy the U.S. Minuteman force. James Schlesinger has admitted that a force "of about 300 SS-18s" could do it. His figure seems high, especially if the Soviets go for the 8-MIRV warhead configuration with each warhead at least two megatons. With a CEP of 1,000 feet, 200 SS-18s should do it, including suppression of the 100 U.S. ABMs at the Grand Forks site. If the Soviets want to employ the SS-18 force for some alternative mission, they could do the job with either 300 SS-17s or 300 SS-19s, given that same CEP. However, when the Soviets want to have high confidence in a mission's result, they employ redundant power to ensure that the mission is accomplished. So, let's figure, as Schlesinger does, 300 SS-18s to "seriously threaten" (that is, destroy 95 percent of) our Minuteman force; or, 400 SS-17s or SS-19s.

Thus we have established that the Soviets can kill our Minuteman force and have some 1,200 to 1,300 ICBMs in reserve, plus (also in reserve on land) whatever number of reloads they desire, and as many SS-X-16 land-mobile missiles as they construct between now and then. Is it dangerous to U.S. survival to permit the Soviets to attain such an advantage? As of February 9, 1972, the Kissinger-Nixon *State of the World Report* made these pledges:

> The Soviet Union . . . cannot be permitted to establish a significant numerical advantage in overall offensive or defensive forces. . . .
>
> But under no circumstances will I permit the further erosion of the strategic balance with the U.S.S.R.

Even more relevant, the Kissinger-Nixon doctrine of "strategic sufficiency," which they substituted for "clear superiority," includes among the "sufficiency criteria" the following:

> Preventing the Soviet Union from gaining the ability to cause considerably greater urban/industrial destruction than the United States could inflict on the Soviets in a nuclear war.[20]

If the Soviet Union could destroy substantially all our 1,000 Minuteman missiles with 300 of their ICBMs, and still have left 1,300 additional land-based missiles, plus half again more submarine-launched missiles than we have, then they would indeed have "gained the ability to cause considerably greater urban/industrial destruction than the United States could inflict on the Soviets in a nuclear war." They would have been permitted to establish a "significant numerical advantage in offensive forces." The Kissinger-Nixon policies would indeed have permitted "further erosion of the strategic balance with the U.S.S.R."

Dr. Henry Kissinger thus set up minimum criteria for sufficiency in the strategic power essential to deter a nuclear attack against the United States; and then he violated each and every one of his own criteria. Among these minimum criteria for sufficiency in strategic power essential to deter a nuclear attack against the United States, the Kissinger-Nixon *State of the World Report* said:

> For there is an absolute point below which our security forces must never be allowed to go. That is the level of sufficiency. Above or at that level, our defense forces protect national security adequately.
> *Below that level is one vast undifferentiated area of no security at all.* For it serves no purpose in conflicts between nations to have been almost strong enough.

If the Soviets are allowed to attain the capability of destroying our entire Minuteman ICBM force and still retain more than 1,000 additional land-based ICBMs in reserve, we will have descended to that "area of no security at all." We will have no rational alternative to surrender, and we will be subject to annihilation at the option of the men in the Kremlin.

After McNamara threw away eight years of lead-time for rebuilding U.S. strategic power, and Kissinger threw away another five years, *is it too late to ensure the survival of the United States?*

By no means. What is essential is that we make our Minuteman force invulnerable to destruction by the Soviet supermissiles—and we can do that. We can make our Minuteman force invulnerable not merely to 300 Soviet SS-18s, or 300 SS-18s plus 400 SS-19s, or even the entire Soviet offensive land-based missile force with all its 21,500,000 pounds of throw-weight, 35,000 megatons of explosive power, and 10,000 two-megaton MIRVs.

Despite all that Soviet power, we can make our Minuteman missiles invulnerable to destruction overnight. If we do it, we will buy time to rebuild our deterrent strong enough to reestablish security and structural stability in the Free World. As a fringe benefit, we will reestablish the stability of our dollar and block the spiral of inflation.

By exploiting certain technological breakthroughs, the Soviets are moving into a position to *destroy* our strategic deterrent. By exploiting other technological breakthroughs, we can make our land-based strategic deterrent *invulnerable*.

The Soviets have been exploiting breakthroughs which favor the strategic offensive. We have been ignoring the technological breakthroughs which favor the defense—breakthroughs which demand a fundamental change in our grand strategy.

Ever since the Kennedy Administration, the grand nuclear strategy of the United States has been based on a pledge never to strike first with nuclear weapons. But the elitists who control our defense policies have added an unnecessary and unrelated appendage to the no-strike-first doctrine, namely, "we will ride out any nuclear attack, and *then* strike back and devastate the aggressor."

At one point in the realized technology of strategic nuclear weaponry, this non sequitur was justified. The warning of a nuclear strike directed against us simply could not have been obtained soon enough, or reliably enough, to justify a launch of our missiles on warning. Also, the missiles themselves required a protracted countdown for preparation to launch. If the warning were mistaken the missiles could not be called back; and no one wanted to start a nuclear war by mistake. But as Kissinger explained in his 1961 book:

> The psychological aspect of deterrence becomes especially acute when technology is volatile. For then the truths of one year become the perils of another. Policies which were adequate at the time of their conception become obstacles to clear understanding when new conditions arise.[21]

In 1959, for example, the advance warning of a missile attack was a maximum of 15 minutes, of which at least three were required for making computations from the early warning radars. Furthermore, the danger of false interpretations was simply too high to risk a launch order from the radar pick-up. Kissinger quotes the late SAC Commander-in-Chief Thomas Power on this point in that timeframe:

> But in this time period we will also have a button whereby I can send the ICBMs on their way. I can press that button and send the missiles on their way.
>
> Do I want to do it, assuming I had authority to do so? . . . (The radars have picked up 1,000 objects. The computer says they are ballistic missiles, and they will impact the United States.)
>
> Because as sure as shooting, in another two or three minutes, this lad will say, "I am sorry, but those blips have disappeared off the scope." They were sputniks, interference, or something like that. Therefore I say, the missiles will have to ride out the attack.[22]

Thus, the only early warning was by unreliable radar, and it could not provide more than 13 minutes' effective warning.

Now we have a technological breakthrough in defense. New satellite warning systems can provide instantaneous and reliable warning upon the launching of an enemy missile. The warning period has extended to the full travel time of an ICBM between the U.S.S.R. and the United States, which is close to 30 minutes. Our new satellites give twice the warning time, and nearly infinitely more reliability. Our new satellite early warning system cannot make the mistake of confusing harmless space objects with ICBMs; its sensors can report only *missile* launches in their firing-booster stage.

There are other developments which also aid defense. The great advance provided by Over the Horizon (OTH) radar gives warning verification almost immediately after the satellite warning. A third verification is provided by the older type but now upgraded BMEWS radars mentioned in the General Power scenario above.

It is the satellite warning which revolutionizes the situation. There need no longer be any worry about starting a nuclear war by accident. It probably requires a 10-minute procedure to launch a Minuteman after the decision has been made. The countdown procedure would begin instantly upon the first satellite warning, and would be aborted if a second warning or verification were not received.

In the 1959-to-say-1967 timeframe, our ICBM force *could* "ride out an attack" with some reasonable chance of survival. This is no longer possible. The advance in guidance technology in the Soviet ICBM programs has made survival of any substantial portion of our land-based deterrent a physical impossibility. As we have noted, all the new Soviet series ICBMs have PBVs with on-board digital computers. That, combined with their now-more-than-adequate numbers of missiles and warheads and explosive power, has changed the former picture entirely and demands a revolutionary shift in our strategy.

We must change over immediately to a "launch on verification of warning" strategy. This will immediately render our 1,000 Minuteman force invulnerable and make it safe against a preemptive strike by the Soviets, or even a preventive strike. This will open up new, cheaper, and speedier methods of rebuilding our strategic force to the point of restoring a true balance. Instead of spending billions of dollars digging and constructing hardened silos for additional missiles, they will be just as invulnerable on inexpensive, easily constructed launching pads. Since the Minuteman III production lines are still open, we have ongoing production lines for the missiles.

Contrary to the alarmist cries of the disarmament elites, this change will not detract from but add to what they call "crisis stability." The actual effect of the new strategy will be to avert the causes of nuclear crises. An additional benefit of incalculable value, when dealing with the Soviets who have adhered to a preemptive strategy, is that it removes all temptation to preempt, because it will make preemption impossible.

> When you deal with the issue of *nuclear strategy* you are dealing with the *survival of the United States* and the survival of many other countries that depend on us.[23]

With this revelation from Secretary of State Kissinger on April 26, 1974, no one could quarrel. Our national survival depends on our nuclear strategy. So, how good is it?

Back in 1961, Doctors Strausz-Hupe, Kintner, and Possony characterized U.S. nuclear strategy as "an irrational aberration." More than a decade later, Dr. Donald Brennan denounced the current version as "MAD"—literally as well as acronymically. Our comprehensive analysis of the Kissinger-Schlesinger-Nixon strategy indicates that it is not merely "irrational" and "mad," but stupid and suicidal. It is a continuing crime against the American people which, unless terminated in time, will result in the genocide of the U.S. population. The word "crime" is not an exaggeration. Thus, President Dwight Eisenhower summed up the defense policies of his administration in these words now inscribed on the keel of the nuclear aircraft carrier which bears his name:

> Until war is eliminated from international relations, unpreparedness for it is well nigh as *criminal* as war itself.

The grand strategy of a great nation could not go so far wrong unless the vice were in the very foundation of the policies, in their philosophical and ideological basis. Our so-called strategy, which in essence is a mishmash of Pugwash elite theories, is exquisitely structured to implement the compulsion to surrender to communism so eloquently pictured by James Burnham in *Suicide of the West*.

The most fundamental feature of the Kissinger strategy, to use his own words, is that it is "defensive in its essence." It is, of course, a never-strike-first, retaliation-only strategy, as enunciated by Paul Nitze at Asilomar in April 1960. Even worse, it not only does not allow us strategic weapons capable of a disarming strike against Soviet weapons, but it bars us from having any weapons which the Soviets might *think* had such a counterforce capability. As Kissinger explained in the 1971 *State of the World Report*:

> Sufficiency also means numbers, characteristics, and deployment of our forces which the Soviet Union cannot reasonably interpret as being intended to threaten a disarming attack.

Our policy is to guarantee to the Soviets that our ICBMs will be home when theirs come to call. Having ensured to Soviet missiles in the SALT I ABM Treaty that they would have a "free ride" to all U.S. targets (except for 150 ICBMs at Grand Forks), the fatal urge to national suicide compelled Kissinger to go one further step in assisting a Soviet disarming strike—he assures the Soviets that our missiles will remain passively in their silos, awaiting their own destruction when the Soviet SS-18 force impacts.

The disarmament intellectuals are quite willing to spend hundreds of billions of dollars digging silo holes, reinforcing them with massive concrete and steel, and with shock-absorbing launch tubes—*if they are sure the protection will not work.* James Schlesinger has conceded that 300 Soviet SS-18s can threaten all our Minuteman missiles, even in their superhardened silos; and, years earlier, Secretary Melvin Laird and Dr. John Foster said the same thing about 400 SS-9s.

But the disarmament intellectuals will not tolerate the one and only effective method of protecting our Minuteman force from destruction in a Soviet disarming strike. They will not permit launching the Minuteman force, even after receiving totally reliable warning, twice verified, that the Soviets have launched a strike at us. The Kissinger strategy refuses to permit launch until *after impact* of the Soviet missile-killing ICBMs.

In the days before the advanced development of the satellite early warning system, when the warning period was only 13 to 15 minutes instead of 30, the rule-of-thumb computation was that, by not launching on warning and thereby subjecting our missiles in their silos to "riding out" the attack, we would risk destruction of 50 percent of our ICBM force. General Thomas Power affirmed this in his explanation that, by permitting the enemy to strike first in any event, you gave him a 50-percent advantage in available strategic weapons. We simply could not rely upon the then-crude radars of the Ballistic Missile Early Warning System (BMEWS) because of fear of starting a nuclear war by mistake.

Equally important, however, was that, until the Soviets passed "parity" with us in numbers of ICBMs, we could *afford* to risk losing the number of Minuteman missiles which they were capable of killing. After the strike, we would still have ICBM superiority and, hence, a credible deterrent. In 1967, we had 1,054 ICBMs and the Soviets had only 460. Even on a one-to-one exchange basis, if they launched their entire force at ours, they would have no reserve, and we would have more than 500 surviving ICBMs.

By 1977, the situation will have changed dramatically. The 300 Soviet SS-18s could destroy 95 percent of our Minuteman missiles, leaving us with 50 to the Soviets' reserve of 1,300 ICBMs. Our credibility, and hence the effectiveness of our deterrent, will be destroyed as soon as the Soviets have high confidence that they can destroy 950 of our 1,000 Minuteman missiles.

We are now in a position to see how highly accurate is Dr. Kissinger's statement that, when you deal with nuclear strategy, you are dealing with the survival of the United States. Under the Kissinger strategy of no-launch-of-retaliatory-missiles-until-after-impact-of-enemy-missiles, the land-based portion of our retaliatory threat is only 50 Minuteman missiles whose communications, command, and control facilities may or may not function. Under the launch-on-verification-of-warning strategy, the land-based portion of our retaliatory threat would be 1,000 undamaged Minuteman missiles, the launch of which would be controlled by an entirely undamaged command and control system. That is the difference between the two strategies in our capability to deter the Soviets from launching a disarming strike.

Would it make sense to try to deter the Soviets with 50 ICBMs, when, with the alternative strategy, we could deter them with 1,000 ICBMs? If you were in charge for the Russians, which strategy would be the more likely to deter you from giving the "go" command to launch a strike at the United States?

Why, then, would Kissinger and Schlesinger and their disarmament intellectuals insist on maintaining a strategy of suicide, when they could instead choose a strategy of survival? They give two "cover" or phony reasons for rejecting the launch-on-verification-of-warning strategy. First, they utter shrill cries of anguish supposedly based on the allegedly horrendous danger of accidental nuclear war, or the dangers of a false alarm. They have been able to keep hidden from public attention the new reliability and redundant verifications available in our warning systems. Here is the best and most authoritative description available in unclassified form, taken from Schlesinger's FY 1975 DOD Report:

> For surveillance and early warning of ballistic missile attack, we now depend upon a variety of systems. The most important of these is the satellite warning system. We now maintain on station one satellite over the Eastern hemisphere and two over the Western hemisphere.
>
> The eastern hemisphere satellite would provide the first warning of a Soviet (or PRC) ICBM launch. This warning would be verified first by the forward scatter Over-the-Horizon (OTH) system and then by the Ballistic Missile Early Warning System (BMEWS). The capability to correlate data from BMEWS, satellite, and other sources will provide highly credible warning of ICBM attack.[24]

It is clear from the variety of systems now available, and the twice-repeated verification opportunity, each by a different system, that the possibility of a false alarm is minute, and the probability of it near-zero. Nevertheless, as soon as possible on an urgent crash basis after adopting the new launch strategy, the satellite systems should be doubled for additional reliability, and as a hedge against the Soviets shooting down individual satellites.

The second argument of the unilateral-disarmament intellectuals masquerades under the jargon-tag of "crisis stability." By this they mean that we should make no response whatsoever to a Soviet nuclear attack until we "pause" and attempt negotiations. This is supposed to give the Soviets time to consider what a "serious" step they have taken by launching a nuclear attack—as if the compulsive planners of the Politburo in the Kremlin ever do anything without serious and protracted consideration. This doctrine of the "pause" was publicly applied by McNamara to the nuclear strategy of the tactical defense of NATO, and it so outraged de Gaulle that he pulled France out of NATO. According to McNamara, tactical nuclear weapons would not be employed—immediately or even promptly—against even a massive conventional invasion of Western Europe by the Russians. The "pause" must first be established to permit the Soviets to consider the seriousness of their action, even if the NATO conventional forces were about to be overwhelmed.

McNamara cliques have never publicized the "pause" doctrine in relation to the defense of the United States proper, probably because they realized that Americans would feel as de Gaulle did. But it is the heart of the Nitze-McNamara-Kissinger planning, as clearly revealed by Schlesinger's description of what he most wants in our posture:

This review . . . should indicate the principal features that we propose to maintain and improve in our strategic posture. They are:

—a capability sufficiently large, diversified, and survivable so that it will provide us at all times with high confidence of *riding out* even a massive surprise attack and of penetrating enemy defenses, and *with the ability to withhold an assured destruction reserve for an extended period of time.*

—. . . command-control capabilities required by our National Command Authorities *to direct the employment of the strategic forces in a controlled, selective and restrained fashion.*

—the avoidance of any combination of forces that could be taken as an effort to acquire the ability to execute a first-strike disarming attack against the U.S.S.R.[25]

It would be difficult for a U.S. Secretary of Defense to use any language better calculated to assure the Soviets that they can execute a massive disarming strike against the United States without triggering a retaliatory strike against Russia. *Our defense chief is assuring the enemy that we have the ability to* withhold *for an* extended period of time *any and all retaliation*, in other words, the "pause." The next most important feature he desires is a command-control capability to impose a tight control over the military to ensure that any attempt by U.S. forces to retaliate against a Soviet attack could be "restrained." Every single feature he stresses as desirable and as planned by him for our strategic posture, degrades the credibility of our strategic deterrent by negating the will of U.S. defense leaders to use our surviving forces for retaliation. The need for a pause for such an "extended period" is to provide time for negotiation of the surrender of the United States.

It is quite clear that Schlesinger has no stomach for launching a retaliatory strike against the Soviets. The more U.S. ICBMs which are held in their silos for destruction by the Soviet disarming strike, the less will be his responsibility to order a retaliatory strike, and the less explanation he would have to give to the nation for *not* employing our power against the enemy. Small wonder, then, that he and Kissinger and their followers so bitterly resent even the suggestion of a launch-on-verification-of-warning strategy. It is equally clear that he wants to signal the Kremlin his assurance that he will block for an "extended period" any U.S. attempt at launching a retaliatory strike.

Also included in the Schlesinger quotation above is his abject and servile pledge to avoid any combination of forces "that could be taken" as "an effort" to "acquire the ability" to execute a disarming first-strike.

Kissinger has given repeated abject assurances each year in the *State of the World Reports* that we abjured all thought of actually retaliating against a Soviet nuclear attack. He and the disarmament intellectuals consider it politically and morally impossible, as well as an irrational act. But even if it is irrational actually to launch a retaliatory strike after a Soviet attack has hit the United States, this is no excuse for any U.S. official to give the Russians *advance* assurance, either explicit or implied, that retaliation will not be ordered! Henry Kissinger himself explained that deterrence is equal to the physical capability to accomplish destruction *times* the will to employ that capability *times* the belief of the enemy in those first two factors. So, even by Kissinger's own definition, if any one of those three factors is zero, so is our deterrent.

The shift to the launch-on-verification-of-warning strategy will give us—for the first time since Nitze, McNamara and Gilpatric scrapped our counterforce-disarming capability and reduced us to a retaliation-only capability—a truly rational strategy. This in turn means that the credibility of our will to employ our retaliatory force can be reconstituted. Two of the additional advantages of the new strategy are of enormous world-stabilizing import. The sheer existence of the technological advances in early warning of a missile attack means that—if exploited by both superpowers—for the first time in more than a quarter century of the nuclear-space age, we can have *a world free from fear of a nuclear surprise attack.*

The next revolutionary potential advantage is that, if we exploit the new strategy which is now open to us with iron will and noble dedication, we can have a United States *free from realistic fear of nuclear attack or blackmail.* This latter advantage is quite an advance beyond freedom from fear of surprise attack. The momentum of the Soviet buildup in strategic offensive power will, in the 1977-80 timeframe, open to them many "win" strategies other than those relying upon surprise attack, plus many blackmail-pressure opportunities.

The best way to understand the blessings of this new strategy is to analyze how it overcomes specific spectres of the nuclear age.

The fear of surprise attack has been pervasive since the strategic bomber forces were developed in the early and mid-1950s. Although it infected laymen as well as experts in the nuclear field, the experts had a very special concern with it because the fear itself threatened to trigger nuclear war. As Herman Kahn explained it (with his customary generous attribution to the creative source):

> There is the problem that Thomas Schelling of Harvard (and RAND) has called the "reciprocal fear of surprise attack," where each side imputes to the other aggressive intentions and reads purely defensive preparations as being offensive. There are unfortunately many postures possible in which a disastrous train of self-confirming actions and counteractions could be set in motion.[26]

As Henry Kissinger expressed it in *The Necessity for Choice:*

> Short of an extraordinary technological breakthrough, *victory in an all-out war can be achieved only through surprise attack.*

Thus, if you suspect that your enemy is planning to *win* a nuclear war, you automatically suspect that he is preparing a surprise attack; and he feels the same way about you. Kissinger explains further about surprise attack capability and feasibility:

> In order to launch a surprise attack an aggressor requires preponderant strength and a high degree of assurance of success. No country will run the risk of annihilation if there is only a slight probability of victory. *Surprise attack is thus deterred when the aggressor must calculate that, regardless of the scale of his attack, he will suffer unacceptable damage in retaliation.*
>
> It is important to remember, however, that the criterion of unacceptability is the aggressor's and not the defender's. A level of damage which may seem unacceptable to us may prove bearable to the Soviet Union and even more so the Communist Chinese.[27]

One of the requisites of a surprise attack is surprise. It is interesting, looking back, to see that Kissinger was convinced in 1961 that a technological plateau had been reached as to warning; and he not only saw no chance of improvement, but could not visualize any way in which improved warning would be useful:

> Even if warning were obtained, it is far from clear to what use it could be put as the missile age develops. When solid-fuel missiles become op-

erational, the maximum warning available is likely to be less than 15 minutes—during which time information must be obtained, transmitted, evaluated and acted upon. This is hardly an interval making for sober calculation. And in the missile age, the penalty for acting upon the basis of incorrect information is enormous. . . . The decision to launch a missile is irrevocable. The danger of accident is therefore high.

Yet the effort to reduce this risk may increase vulnerability. The more carefully and strictly a warning is interpreted the less useful it may be. A country whose retaliatory force depends for its security on the ability to obtain warning will be torn between the Scylla of being too cautious and the Charybdis of being too trigger-happy.

In short, in the missile age a retaliatory force cannot gear its security to the expectation of warning. It must be sufficiently invulnerable so that it can ride out the attack and still inflict unacceptable losses on the aggressor.[28]

That view, which was generally held and which was supported by the realized state of technology until full development of the satellite early warning system, demonstrates why it is a major breakthrough to be able to obtain instantaneous warning of missile launch plus double verification within 15 minutes. Also, the capability to correlate data from these three sources is now nearly instantaneous and also enhances accuracy. Another technological development of near-breakthrough magnitude in its own right is the Command Data Buffer system, now being installed, which permits the rapid remote-retargeting of the entire Minuteman III force.

Although the dictionary defines breakthrough as a sudden advance in knowledge or technique, for functional purposes in this area of strategy it should meet the additional requirement of permitting or demanding a major change in offensive or defensive nuclear strategy. Tie together the three types of warning now available for ICBMs with the Command Data Buffer System, plus the new SLBM Phased Array Warning Radars, and the definition of a strategic breakthrough is certainly fulfilled.

The Soviet offensive breakthrough in launch and design techniques which enables them to multiply the throw-weight of their most numerous missiles by a factor of three to five, while still retaining the volume and configuration necessary to use the same silo launchers with no substantial increase in dimensions, absolutely *demands* a change in the defensive strategy of the United States—the change which is made possible by the breakthrough in early warning systems.

The defensive breakthrough in warning systems has thus eliminated one type of "win" strategy by a nuclear superpower aggressor: *it strikes the surprise from the surprise attack.*

The surprise-attack strategy, however, can be replaced by a new type of "win" strategy based upon sheer overwhelming deliverable destructive power in the Soviet offensive missile force. As Schlesinger recognizes, the Soviets have no use for 33,000 warheads on their ICBMs, but they are going for "7,000 to 8,000 one-to-two megaton weapons" aboard their potential force.[29] And only 2,400 of those (from the SS-18 force) would be required (according to Schlesinger's very generous computation discussed above) to destroy the substance of our Minuteman force. That would leave them with a reserve for other purposes of 4,600 to 5,600 warheads, each up to 40 times the explosive power of a U.S. Poseidon MIRV warhead. Once our Minuteman force is actually hit by such an attack, the United States will have no rational alternative to surrender. Note that, under this calculated "win" strategy, surprise is not essential to Soviet success. The only essentials are (1) their plenitude of destructive power, (2) their will to employ it, and (3) our holding our Minuteman missiles static in their silos awaiting destruction.

The new launch-on-verification-of-warning strategy would avert this threat. Our missiles would be one-third to one-half of the distance on their way to the Soviet Union. This new U.S. strategy gives realistic effect to another Kissinger-declared principle:

Pronouncements which seek to relate deterrence to the total numbers of missiles and airplanes are highly misleading. For the side on the defensive the numbers prior to attack are essentially irrelevant. The only figure that matters is the number which can survive a sudden blow.[30]

The beauty of the new U.S. launch strategy is that our entire peacetime inventory inevitably survives any attack. Even if the Soviet Union launched its entire ICBM force of 8,000 two-megaton warheads at our 1,000 Minuteman missiles (and relied for reserve on reloads and its large SLBM force), they still could not destroy a single one of our missiles which was successfully launched on verification of the instantaneous satellite warning. This new strategy will frustrate a Soviet calculated "win" strategy based on overwhelming destructive power as well as the one based upon surprise.

It has additional critical advantages. Just as it will defeat the calculated "win" strategies based on a Soviet preventive war policy, so also it will defeat a Soviet preemptive strike strategy. It will remove the primary and pivotal temptation to preempt. As explained by Kissinger in his 1961 book:

The smaller the gap between a country's first- and second-strike capability, the lower will be the opponent's incentive to launch a preemptive blow.[31]

Now, 13 years later, he purports to be tremendously worried about the potential danger of a great gap between those capabilities:

The overwhelming issue, as we see it, is the issue of multiple independent warheads whose deployment on the Soviet side is imminent.
Once these multiple warheads are fully deployed on both sides, and one
has then warheads upwards of 10,000 on both sides, or any number that
technology can make possible, then we face a situation of unprecedented nuclear plenty and *a potentially enormous gap between first-
and second-strike capabilities.*

This is what we are attempting to reduce in these [SALT II] negotiations.[32]

Let's pass over the Kissinger numbers-game obfuscations in which
he includes Poseidon 50-kiloton warheads as equivalents of Soviet
2-megaton ICBM warheads (each 40 times more powerful). U.S.
SLBMs are irrelevant to this discussion because they have neither the
power nor the accuracy of guidance essential to first-strike capability.
Here we are concerned with the number of Minuteman warheads
available for a first-strike, and the number which would survive a
Soviet disarming strike and be available for a second-strike. We assume the Soviets would employ against our Minuteman force either
300 SS-18s (the Schlesinger assumption) or 400 SS-9s (the Laird-Foster
assumption), which would kill 95 percent of our Minuteman missiles. As for Minuteman warheads, the maximum programmed
number is 2,000, and the maximum possible number (prior to 1979)
is 3,000 (three mark-12 MIRVs on each of 1,000 Minuteman ICBMs).

	Kissinger Strategy: Launch After Enemy Impact	Launch-on- Verification-of- Warning Strategy
Warheads Available for First-Strike	3,000	3,000
Warheads Available for Second-Strike	150	3,000
Warhead Gap	2,850	000

Thus, it is demonstrated that the Kissinger strategy of refusing to
launch until *after* the enemy disarming strike actually impacts (and
probably even until after a "pause" for "an extended period of time,"
according to the Schlesinger formula) provides the Soviets with maximum incentive to launch either a preventive or a preemptive
strike. (The preemptive angle would come in on the theory that, because of the near-total vulnerability of the U.S. land-based retaliatory
force, the Soviets might think that we would be tempted to preempt,
that is, to strike first in order to take advantage of a 3,000-warhead
striking force instead of risking being degraded to a 150-warhead

striking force.) Under the launch-on-verification-of-warning strategy, on the other hand, the Soviets would gain nothing by attempting either a preventive or a preemptive disarming strike; and they would see that the United States had no incentive for launching a preemptive strike.

Kissinger and all the disarmament elites, especially the Pugwash group, all purport to worship "stability." Yet, they will all come out screaming against any type of launch-on-warning strategy, despite the fact that this version of it will obviously foster maximum stability, whereas the Kissinger strategy will have the maximum destabilizing effect.

Their opposition to the launch-on-verification-of-warning strategy will also strip the hypocrisy from the disarmament intellectuals' devotion to the Mutual Assured Destruction "religion" (as John Newhouse characterizes it—and properly so, because it demands 210 million human sacrifices). Changeover to the new strategy will be absolutely the only way the United States can "assure" that the destruction in a nuclear exchange will be "mutual." If we adhere to the strategy of holding our Minutemen in their silos to be destroyed, the "destruction" will inexorably and assuredly be unilateral—that is, only Americans will be destroyed (unless we surrender).

This will expose the fact that the entire mythology of the MAD theory upon which both the SALT I Agreements are based was, so far as the Kissinger group was concerned, a fraud *ab initio*. They never intended that the threat of destruction would be *mutual*. They planned that it would be unilateral. And why would they do a thing like that? So the American people will have no rational alternative to surrender—and preferably, no alternative to a preemptive surrender, in accordance with the Paul Hilken Nitze Asilomar proposal.

A second-strike strategic force designed to support deterrence by retaliation only, can serve no rational purpose after deterrence has failed. Ordering launch of a retaliatory strike *after* a Soviet attack has destroyed the majority of our population, or a majority of our land-based retaliatory weapons, or both, would merely be an act of irrational revenge, an attempt to inflict punishment. It would not even punish the men in the Politburo who had ordered the strike at us, but merely (at most) several million Russian people who had had nothing to do with the strike order.

It's as simple as this: we would be acting too late with too little. If we seek to deter the Soviets by *threatening* to strike back *after we ride out the attack*, the threat is not credible because (1) to carry it out would not support deterrence, deterrence having already failed; (2) it cannot disarm the Soviets, because even our undamaged forces did not have that capability, and our damaged forces will have only a fraction of what was always too little; and (3) it will be too late to help the scores of millions of Americans already killed, but it will trigger a second Soviet salvo which will annihilate the U.S. survivors of the original Soviet strike.

The time of making the decision to retaliate is the essence of our new launch-on-verification-of-warning strategy. By making the decision in advance, and committing our forces to it irreversibly, we will avoid the too-lateness and the too-littleness of the Kissinger-Schlesinger strategy. This in turn will solve the crisis in our credibility raised by the irrationality of a too-late-with-too-little retaliatory strike. A decision made in advance is both highly rational and highly credible.

It is rational to believe that the enemy will be deterred from launching an attack against us—any type of attack—if he is highly persuaded that he will, without fail, be hit in retaliation by 1,000 ICBMs carrying 2,000 warheads. Because the only alternatives of not adopting this new strategy are nuclear destruction or abject surrender, it would be irrational and suicidal of us to fail to make this change in time.

This change, however, will be resisted by Henry Kissinger, James Schlesinger, and whoever is President if he retains those appointees and their elitist constituencies. We, therefore, propose the installation of computerized control of Minuteman launch. It will be programmed: (1) to go into a reflex-ready state of alert on the first warning by the satellite system of an ICBM launch from the Soviet Union; and (2) to withhold execution of launch until confirmation by at least two additional warning systems (ordinarily OTH radar and BMEWS warning systems).

A number of additional specifics of the new strategy will have to be considered. The first of these is how to handle the launch order when a launch from a missile-launching submarine is the first development. This would involve deployment of additional warning facilities, the funding for which has been mysteriously blocked in Congress. Next, the launch of the Minuteman force would have to be made "pin-down-proof," so that Soviet missile submarines close to our coasts, with short travel time for their SLBMs, could not hold the Minuteman missiles in their silos until the ICBMs from Russia completed their 30-minute voyage and impacted. There are several methods by which we could block this tactic. This is just one example of the probable Soviet attempt to end-run or short-circuit our new strategy.

These problems can all be met, but let us consider here the attacks on the "morality" of the new strategy which will be launched by Kissinger and all the forces which have devoted so many years to promoting unilateral strategic disarmament of the United States so that we would have no rational alternative to strategic surrender to the Soviet Union. This is our opportunity to turn the finely-spun theories of the unilateral disarmament intellectuals back on themselves.

If Kissinger or any of the leading SALT-sellers seeks to criticize the launch-on-verification-of-warning strategy, we should ask him, "Do you support the SALT ABM Treaty?" If the answer is yes, than he cannot oppose the new survival strategy without exposing the fact that, by supporting the SALT ABM Treaty, he is supporting a scheme to insure the *unilateral* destruction of the American people. The SALT I ABM Treaty is known to the more intelligent nuclear strategists as a "homicide pact." The theory of the Treaty is that it will strengthen deterrence by making the failure of deterrence result in *mutual* homicide. Kissinger explained that it ensures a "free ride" for enemy missiles against populations. As Donald Brennan explained it, the ABM Treaty provides the highest possible level of hostages. Even Senator William Fulbright conceded that this was a mutual hostage arrangement.

The immorality and stupidity of the SALT ABM Treaty lies in the fact that, if the SALT I Interim Agreement permits the Soviet Union to attain a first-strike capability or its practical equivalent, the combination of the two SALT I accords sets up the American people for mass murder. As soon as the Soviet offensive buildup is sufficiently overwhelming to permit a disarming strike which would destroy the major part of our deterrent, the 210 million American hostages will be totally at the mercy of the Kremlin. The SALT ABM Treaty will have deprived us of all effective defense, and the SALT I Interim Agreement, combined with the Kissinger policies and strategic theories, will have deprived us of our strategic deterrent.

The only way we can preserve our strategic deterrent and keep it credible, despite the massive momentum of the Soviet offensive buildup since SALT I, is by our launch-on-verification-of-warning strategy.

If the elitists who have enshrined Mutual Assured Destruction as a "religion" really love the mutual homicide pact purportedly set up by the SALT I Treaty, they must accept the only strategy which will keep it "mutual." If they do not, they will be conceding that they want no interference with their scheme to set up the American people for unilateral destruction, that is, mass murder by nuclear incineration.

The new U.S. survival strategy is also a refutation to Soviet criticism, which will rush to incite "world opinion" against us and try to brand us as "atomic maniacs" (as their chief theoretician, Suslov, has always called us). But by pushing for the SALT I ABM Treaty, the Soviets at least purportedly acquiesced in the philosophy of the "mutual homicide pact" and cannot logically object to the new machinery for keeping it "mutual" and therefore effective. We can assure them that we have no objection to their making the same arrangements for a retaliatory launch of their ICBMs. This would in no way endanger us because we have no weapons with sufficient counterforce capability to launch a disarming strike at the Soviet land-based force. To launch a first-strike at their population without also killing the substance of their ICBM force would be national suicide, so we obviously have no intention of launching such a strike.

We can point out to the Soviets and to the world that the *only* way the Soviets could get hit by the 1,000 Minuteman force would be if they first launched a missile strike at the United States. They, not we, would be the only ones who could trigger the launch of our Minuteman missiles. Coincidentally, by removing any doubt about the will of U.S. leaders to order a strike in retaliation, we would remove the weakest point of the credibility of our deterrent. The more credible our deterrent, the less the reason for the world or the Russian people to fear a nuclear war.

The remote possibility that there might be an unauthorized or accidental launch by either side, which would in turn precipitate an accidental war, can be easily taken care of. We could agree that the computer programming would permit up to four, but no more than four, missiles to be launched without activating our launch process. Considering that nuclear missiles have been around for more than 15 years, and there has never been a single accidental launch of a single missile, the launch of more than four would be conclusive evidence that it was more than an accident; and certainly it would be more than we should tolerate if we wish to survive.

The argument may be made that the Schlesinger strategy of "flexible response" is more desirable because it will permit keeping a limited nuclear war limited, and provide opportunities for calling the whole thing off before escalation into Armageddon. Such a strategy could be realistic only if two conditions coexist: (1) the U.S. retaliatory force would have to be *invulnerable* to a Soviet disarming attack, and (2) our strategic offensive and defensive capabilities would have to be *realistically equal.* Even under the late 1974 state of the strategic balance, and emphatically under the probable balance in 1976, it would be irrational and stupid for Soviet leadership to accept *any* damage by U.S. strategic nuclear weapons for the simple reason that *they do not have to.* They can deter us from attempting any so-called "limited" strike at them merely by informing us in advance that their response will be *unlimited.*

One of the Schlesinger scenarios has the Soviets taking out our naval base at Norfolk, Virginia; and then we respond by launching a missile to take out a similar base in the Soviet Union. If the Soviets accepted that, it would have two results unfavorable to them: (1) they would lose a valuable base; and (2) they would have set a precedent under which U.S. leadership would consider that the Soviets would tolerate our launching nuclear missiles at the U.S.S.R. Logic, common sense, and the most elementary strategic analysis would impel them to disarm our *entire* force, once they had acquired the capability of doing that. That would be the only way they could be sure they would not suffer retaliation. Suppose, for example, that Brezhnev ordered an attack to destroy 200 of our 1,000 Minuteman missiles. We might just ride out that attack and strike back with our remaining 800 on the theory that, if we did not use them while we could, the Soviets would get them on the next salvo. Those 800 Minuteman missiles could do considerable damage to the Soviet Union and its capability of taking over Western Europe. How would you like to be the Soviet dictator who had to explain to his colleagues that he *could* have ordered the destruction of the entire U.S. Minuteman force, but he didn't think the United States would order a retaliatory strike?

Soviet strategic doctrine has—as we have seen—one basic tenet: *never* risk getting hit with the *undamaged* nuclear force of the enemy. The Soviets will never risk a retaliatory strike by any enemy strategic weapons which they could destroy in advance of launch. The logic of the conclusion reached by Doctors Strausz-Hupe, Possony, and Kintner in their *Forward Strategy for America* in 1961 still stands:

> The Communists can not stop short, in prudence, of the total emasculation of American power. Here the fight between Rome and Carthage provides the apposite historic model: the struggle ends only with the total destruction of the weapons of one or the other contestant.[33]

The only claim made for the so-called "new" Schlesinger strategy is as a deterrent to *limited* nuclear attack, which, as we have seen, the Soviets would never launch. No claim is made that it will serve as a deterrent against an all-out nuclear attack on the United States, nor can any such claim be made because the Soviets have escalation dominance, and therefore can double and redouble and quadruple us on every "limited" response we might attempt. The Schlesinger strategy is, therefore, useless even as a deterrent against limited attacks. Its sole purpose is to confuse and comfort the American people into thinking we have sufficient strategic power to deter the Soviets from at least something. By adopting the launch-on-verification-of-warning strategy for our entire Minuteman force and abandoning the "new" Schlesinger strategy, therefore, we do not lose anything.

The launch-on-verification-of-warning strategy can also serve us as a bargaining chip, if we assume that Kissinger is seriously bargaining with the Kremlin instead of tendering covered capitulations. He could offer to call off the new launch strategy if the Soviets would liquidate their disarming capability against the U.S. Minuteman force.

The typical intelligent, nonexpert American will see no practical change in our strategy when we shift to launch-on-verification-of-warning. The typical American has always reacted to news of the Soviet weapons buildup with the response: "I'm glad they are wasting so much money on those terrible weapons which will never be used. They would never dare to use them against us because they know that if they did, we would strike back and destroy them." In other words, the average American has always assumed that we have what amounts to a launch-on-verification-of-warning strategy. To adopt it now will be merely putting into effect what the average American thinks has always been our strategy. He will not worry about the "morality" of the strategy; he has been for this all the time.

We can anticipate, of course, that the main opposition to a shift to the launch-on-verification-of-warning strategy will come from Henry Kissinger and his constituencies because it will upset their plans for leaving us naked to Soviet attack with no rational alternative to surrender. To refute Henry Kissinger *circa* 1974, let us again call upon Henry Kissinger *circa* 1961. Parenthetically, we might explain that there are three reasons why we so often quote Henry Kissinger to prove a point. One is that substantially none of the principles he enunciates is his own creation. In his early career and up until the time he ascended to power in the White House, he absorbed and reenunciated as his own the strategic theories created by his contemporaries. In that early period, there were some great creative minds at work in the strategic area, led by Herman Kahn and the Strausz-Hupe-Possony-Kintner group. Kissinger absorbed their ideas like a sponge, just as later he absorbed the insanities of the Kremlin-influenced Pugwash elite. A second reason for quoting Kissinger is that this book deals primarily with Kissinger, so a quotation from his works has added relevancy. Thirdly, almost every time we quote Kissinger's words prior to 1969, it is to refute Kissinger's pontifications made after that date.

In his 1961 book *The Necessity for Choice*, Kissinger introduces a scenario closely analogous to what the Soviets can accomplish prior to 1977, except that the percentage of damage to U.S. retaliatory forces would be much higher than he postulates, and the Soviet reserve forces to be held for use against our population would be almost immeasurably more powerful:

> This becomes clear if we consider a "rational" United States reaction to a blow against our retaliatory forces. Suppose that such an attack reduced our retaliatory force by 50 percent but held civilian casualties to a minimum. Assume also that coincident with the attack the Soviet Am-

bassador presented an ultimatum to the President somewhat to this effect:

"We have just destroyed x percent of your retaliatory force while sparing your cities. If you retaliate against our civilian population, we will respond in kind and our ability to inflict damage is superior to yours at least by the factor of destruction inflicted on your retaliatory force. We offer peace negotiations on certain specified conditions."

Considered purely rationally, there would be little sense in American retaliation. If our retaliatory forces were designed according to the maxims of finite deterrence—as a small counter-city force (which it has been, in accordance with the Nitze-McNamara-Kissinger policies)—there would be no point in retaliation whatsoever. A blow against the Soviet cities would devastate that Communist homeland. At the same time it would guarantee even more appalling destruction in the United States, because our population is more concentrated and because—by hypothesis— our retaliatory force will have been considerably disrupted by the initial Soviet attack. In these circumstances the harrowing possibility exists that the Communist leaders might come to believe that if they could induce *any* delay in our response they might escape unscathed from even a nuclear attack.

Conversely, if they refrain from such a course it will be because they are convinced that an attack on the United States would elicit reactions transcending any rational calculations. In short, *deterrence would result from the impression not that the President would order a counterblow but that he would not be able to prevent it.*

Indeed, if our retaliatory forces were designed exclusively for an attack against the aggressor's civilian population—and so understood by the opponent—*we might be able to prevent a war of attrition only by making our response nearly automatic.*

The aggressor would have to believe that our retaliatory force was so designed that an attack of a certain scale would trigger a counterblow almost mechanically.

In that eventuality, blackmail could not be effective because once a surprise attack were launched, the President would no longer *control* the decision to react. *By launching a surprise attack, the Soviet leaders would guarantee their own destruction.*[34]

Kissinger thus gives an analytically supported admission not only that a deterrent based upon our proposed strategy of automatic response to a Soviet attack on our retaliatory force would work, but that it might be the *only* way to deter a nuclear war. Much of this Kissinger material appears to have originated in Herman Kahn's earlier lectures (which became the basis of Kahn's book published in 1960); but in any event, Kahn does have by far the best discussion and the most convincing analysis of the "rationality of irrationality." He demonstrates conclusively that, although it might be irrational *after* an enemy attack has impacted to make a decision to launch a retaliatory strike, if the decision is made *in advance* of the attack and embodied in a "committal" strategy (such as the launch-on-verification-of-warning strategy we urge), it becomes entirely rational.

A nuclear war is worth preventing. In our present predicament, the only way we can prevent the Soviets from preempting if we attempt to rebuild our strategic deterrent is by changing from a ride-out-the-attack-and-then-strike-back-with-what-we-have-left strategy to a launch-on-verification-of-warning strategy. It will buy us time—say three years—and the United States can work miracles in three years if we have a leadership distinguished by intelligence, integrity, and courage.

The first thing we must do with this time is to prepare warning systems against a type of attack which, so far as we can determine, has been totally ignored by Kissinger and Schlesinger. The new Soviet Delta submarine's SS-N-8 missile represents a real technological breakthrough. It is not only the world's first intercontinental-range submarine-launched ballistic missile, but it has inertial guidance, an on-board computer, and stellar assistance. Such accuracy is hardly needed if it were merely designed for city-busting or to pin-down our ICBMs. As explained in Schlesinger's FY 1975 DOD Report, the SS-N-8's very long range allows deployment of the Delta submarines *in ocean areas not covered by both our Western Hemisphere satellites,* and in some cases there may be *temporary outages of coverage* by a single satellite caused by solar activity. Our existing "dish" warning radars (474N), which are supposed to complement the satellite warnings of SLBM launches, "have limitations against Soviet SLBMs, particularly the new longer range SS-N-8."

To provide full coverage of "the expanded SLBM threat area," the Defense Department proposed in the FY 1974 DOD Report to replace the old ineffective SLBM warning radars with two new SLBM Phased Array Warning Radars, one for each coast. They would cost only an estimated $50 million each and, together with the satellite systems, "would provide highly credible warning of a Soviet SLBM launch against the United States." This would enable our proposed strategy of launch-on-verification-of-warning to work against SLBM launches as well as ICBM launches from Russia. This warning system is also necessary to make our strategy viable against Soviet ICBMs, because we must make our Minuteman missiles "pin-down-proof." But we need the new phased array radars for a puny $50 million each.

Here is how the Chairman of the Joint Chiefs of Staff related the sad story of his 1973 request for the SLBM warning radar:

> Funds . . . were rejected by the Congress last year because of a belief that "our present warning systems are adequate."
> A study of these systems has been initiated by the House Appropria-

tions Committee "in order to adequately evaluate future requests of this nature from all of the Services." I welcome this study because I have been convinced by several JCS/DOD studies and reviews that *our SLBM warning systems are not adequate, particularly in the light of the deployment of the Soviet 4,200 nm SS-N-8 SLBM.*[35]

The Soviets have been testing satellite-killing satellites on and off and on since 1967. Their tests have demonstrated an in-hand capability of shooting down our early warning satellites. The United States has already taken steps to develop "survivable" communications satellites, and these techniques for protection must be extended to warning satellites; but we need more. For every satellite required to make the warning system effective, we must maintain two alternates as back-up measures. If the Soviets start shooting down our satellites, and we have verification of this, we must be prepared to launch the Minuteman force, and we must assure the Soviets of this in advance. Satellites can be equipped to communicate that they have been damaged by enemy action. The only reason the Soviets could have for shooting down our warning satellites would be to render us helpless against a Soviet massive missile attack.

A final reason for investing in the very best and most advanced early warning systems of all three existing types (satellite, OTH radar, and phased array radar) is that the Soviet Delta submarines appear more and more to constitute an advanced counterforce-disarming-strike echelon of their offensive systems. Their elaborate guidance should alert us that this SLBM is a missile-killer. Despite their now-demonstrated versatile MIRVing capability, the SS-N-8 has not yet been tested with MRVs, much less MIRVs—at least so far as U.S. intelligence has been able to discover (according to Schlesinger's FY 1974 DOD Report and the CJCS U.S. Posture Statement, FY 1975). On the other hand, in 1973 the Soviets carried out an intensive test program for a "new multiple RV version of the SS-N-6. These are MRVs rather than MIRVs, i.e., they are not individually targetable."[36]

This suggests that MRVs on the SS-N-6 will be very useful for the pin-down mission. But the retention of a single warhead on the far more advanced SS-N-8 shows that the Soviets stress a very high explosive power for their Delta weapons, as well as a small CEP. This means that, if they can defeat U.S. early warning systems and short-circuit a launch-on-verification-of-warning strategy, they can destroy our Minuteman force in one sure step instead of a two-step process—and thereby save hundreds of missiles.

For the United States to change over from the Kissinger-Schlesinger strategy to the survival strategy of launch-on-verification-of-warning won't cost us a dollar because it can be done by a stroke of the presidential pen. The improvements in our warning systems are essential regardless. It will actually save us $16 billion, which is our investment in our Minuteman missile force (the initial investment, plus the MIRVing program and silo modification). The shift in strategy, however, will buy us time which we could not buy with any amount of money. It will buy us about three years in which we can rebuild the power of the U.S. strategic deterrent. It will delay the fatal date on which the Soviets would reach the preemption point—after which our deterrent would be irreversibly lost.

How should we use those three years? Priority should be given to those programs which can produce the greatest number of strategic offensive weapons in the shortest time. Our present Minuteman force, to be launched with our new strategy and with some vital changes in targeting, can be an impressive deterrent, when coupled with our Polaris-Poseidon force and our old strategic bomber force, rejuvenated by some commonsense measures.

We will be working against time and high probability that the Soviets will soon demonstrate one or more breakthroughs in missile defense. Even worse, they may make breakthroughs and hold them secret. We must expect this because they have traditionally developed defensive systems along with their offensive systems. Thus, they began to deploy their early SS-9s and SS-11s in 1964 (our intelligence did not fully identify them until 1965), and they began to deploy their first-generation ABM systems in the same timeframe. Historically, the Soviets have since then deployed a new surface-to-air missile roughly every year and a half. About half are air defense, and the other half have antimissile capability or are exclusively ABMs.[37] Even in their air defense SAMs, they are years ahead of us technologically, as demonstrated by the effectiveness of their SAM-6s in the Middle East War of October 1973. It is highly improbable that they could make such extensive breakthroughs in offensive missiles without developing technology appropriate also to defensive missiles.

Our best bet appears to be to keep the ongoing production line for Minuteman III going, to run it on three shifts instead of one sloweddown shift, and to use it as the nucleus for two additional production lines. Our objective should be the production of 1,400 to 1,500 missiles with launching equipment within two years. We are just completing the production of 550 (with spares and test missiles) within several years. In a crash program, backed by ample resources, we could easily produce that number.

Heretofore, the digging of silos, their construction, hardening, shockproofing, and equipping, would have been time-consuming and expensive. But our new survival strategy will solve that problem. A fixed-based ICBM in the hardest silo is vulnerable to Soviet counterforce missiles under the old Kissinger-Schlesinger ride-out-the-attack-and-then-pause-before-launch strategy. But under our new survival strategy, *an ICBM on the softest launching pad is invulnerable to destruction prior to launch.*

The ideal way to deploy this new force of 1,500 Minuteman missiles would be on their own tracked land-mobile launchers and on railroad cars. Although the plans for these were developed years ago at the cost of scores of millions of dollars, McNamara canceled their production. Now, they could be reordered on a crash basis. If these permanent-type mobile mounts could not be ready in time, makeshift temporary expedients could be swiftly and inexpensively improvised. To be legal under SALT I (which merely prohibits starting construction of "additional *fixed* land-based ICBM launchers after July 1, 1972") our new-production Minuteman IIIs need not be highly mobile; if they are just barely movable, that is sufficient. Any type of launcher "not permanently fixed" to the ground can qualify as mobile. And we do not require true or speedy mobility to attain invulnerability or survivability. The timing of the launch before the disarming Soviet missiles impact supplies the survivability.

To save money and also the time required to set up additional communication, command, and control facilities, these slightly-mobile-but-not-permanently-fixed ICBMs could be deployed in existing Minuteman silo areas, and tied in with existing facilities. When the permanent mobile launchers become available, the added survivability not dependent on pre-impact launch would serve as a hedge against the Soviets' developing a method of frustrating our early warning system or launch procedures.

The added 1,500 Minuteman missiles would serve two major purposes essential to ensure U.S. survival: (1) they would hedge against a Soviet breakthrough in antimissile defense—in which case we would urgently need the additional 4,500 Minuteman MIRVed warheads (three per missile) to penetrate the Soviet defense; and (2) they would help to restore the "perceived" strategic balance between the United States and the U.S.S.R., without which stability cannot be restored to the political, economic, and social structures of the NATO alliance and the Free World. And without that, runaway double-digit inflation will ruin the United States and the Free World.

It goes without saying that we should not permit any further scrapping of existing Minuteman I and II missiles or their launching equipment. Kissinger has already permitted the destruction of some 550 of these expensive ICBMs, which would have been good for another 15 years. We have 450 remaining; and these should be retained in their existing silos. Our new production should be *added* to our strategic power in-being—not used as an excuse for destroying valuable weapons. We know a crash program to build additional Minuteman IIIs can be successful in time, because Schlesinger has permitted the funding and procurement of long-lead-time items for the additional 450 Minuteman IIIs (which he plans to *replace,* instead of add to, our existing models).

To make our additional force of 1,500 Minuteman IIIs more effective as a strategic deterrent, we should parallel their production with programs to improve the accuracy of their guidance and increase the power of their warheads. Fortunately, much study has already gone into developing these programs, but the parsimonious funding has deliberately slowed them down so that they could not produce results for about four or five years. Reasonable funding can vastly accelerate these essential developments. All the measures which we should be pursuing on an urgent-highest-national-priority basis are now being held back, as Schlesinger admits repeatedly, "in view of the ongoing SAL talks." Instead of moving ahead on these guidance and yield programs, he is using the old McNamara stall of "keeping open his options."

Similarly, Schlesinger is holding up all items grouped under the heading of "Advanced ICBM Technology." He admits that the Soviets have already developed an ICBM which can be deployed as a land-mobile missile, their SS-16. Theirs is in-being—now. To compete with it, we will need several new technological developments, which he admits. He is deliberately holding us back, proceeding so slowly that, unless accelerated, these programs will not produce until the 1980s. As he explains:

> We intend to pursue this new development at a very deliberate pace, pending the outcome of the current SALT negotiations.[38]

Until we build those additional Minuteman ICBMs and deploy them in some fashion, preferably mobile, but in any event as speedily as possible, we can beef up the deterrent effect of the 1,000 Minuteman missiles we already have in silos by two primary methods. One is by a series of "quick-fixes" designed to add additional destructive power to our deterrent, or to make more reliably deliverable against Soviet targets the weapons we already have. Here are some of the possible quick-fixes.

The greatest nonmissile addition to our deliverable strategic destructive power would be to improve the chances of our strategic bombers' surviving to deliver their bomb loads on target. They purportedly are loaded with some 2,000 warheads. These bombers are highly vulnerable to destruction on the ground before take-off. They could be hit by Soviet SLBMs of either normal ballistic flight or depressed trajectory; they could be destroyed by Soviet FOBS or MOBS. McNamara cancelled the airborne alert which would have rendered survivable whatever number might be on that stage of alert. For the next several critical years, the airborne alert should be restored. Also, a substantial number of B-52s should be put on 10-minute alert, and the remainder on 20-minute alert. Of course they should be dispersed at additional airfields, as far removed from both coasts as possible. Under present practices, expert estimates accord these bombers a maximum survival expectancy of 20 percent in their bases.

After the bombers take off safely from their U.S. bases, they have to face another tremendous threat. The Soviets have some 10,000 SAMs for antiaircraft defense, and they have advanced models to cover all altitudes, including the new SAM-6s for low levels. Then they have 3,000 fighter-interceptor aircraft. If McNamara had not scrapped our 1,400 B-47s, which would have been effective into the 1980s, we could have saturated even such massive defenses and suppressed them. Now, we must expect to lose 80 percent of those which survived take-off from the United States. So, something must be done to suppress the Soviet air defenses. The best way to get a quick-fix on this is to restore the Navy aircraft carriers to the strategic alert forces. McNamara took them off this essential mission on the pretext that they must always be available to fight no-win diversionary conventional wars with Soviet puppets such as North Vietnam. The Navy had some excellent so-called "attack" aircraft: A-6s and A-7s. These can carry one to four one-megaton bombs. Equally important, they have terrain-avoiding radar control, which permits them to make their attack runs at tree-top level, thus evading both enemy radar and SAMs.

If all our carriers were deployed on the strategic mission, they could carry 200 to 300 attack aircraft. It might be worthwhile to experiment with FB-111s on the three large nuclear-propelled carriers. They, too, have terrain-avoiding radar, and carry a heavier bomb load than either the A-6s or A-7s. The Navy high command would object that the FB-111 is too heavy for carrier duty, but it would be worth trying. With such a force of carrier aircraft fighting its way into Soviet targets, and suppressing SAMs and attracting the Soviet interceptors, our B-52 force should have a far greater survival percentage and be able to deliver many hundreds of nuclear weapons. Also, in case the Soviet SAMs have ABM capability—which they probably will have—this suppression of SAMs might mean the success of our Minuteman attack. In any event, this would greatly complicate Soviet defense problems and make our strategic deterrent more credible. In a somewhat more extended period—what might be called a medium-quick-fix category—we could mount Minuteman missiles on ships and barges in the Great Lakes, and Polaris or Poseidon missiles on surface ships on the ocean. Also, we could develop an air-launched version of Minuteman or Poseidon and load them on Air Force C-5s or modified civilian jumbo jets, such as the Boeing 747. One purpose of merely listing these possibilities of adding to our strategic offensive power is to show how misleading are Kissinger's assertions of helplessness to accomplish anything within five years.

In addition to these measures to add to the destructive power of our deterrent forces, we should resort to additional ways to worry the

Kremlin leadership considering an attack, or threats to attack, or demands for our surrender. As Kissinger said so long ago:

> Deterrence seeks to prevent a given course by making it seem less attractive than all possible alternatives.[39]

We should seek ways to deprive them of their most valued prize, the takeover of Western Europe as a going industrial and agricultural concern, and threaten them with what they fear the most. We can do this by smart-targeting of the 1,000 Minuteman missiles which our new strategy ensures will strike back at them if they strike at us, plus our SLBM force. The prime U.S. targeting for deterrence—as we have documented from Schlesinger's statement—is still Soviet cities, with the prime purpose of killing people. Our offensive weapons, however, are not really very effective for that purpose; they simply cannot deliver enough megatonnage. Melvin Laird in 1969 estimated that it would take 1,200 U.S. one-megaton warheads to destroy 45 percent of the Soviet population. But that was without considering their capability for strategic evacuation and civil defense. With these effectively employed, we would need 10 times as many warheads.

We should concentrate on only the largest cities in the U.S.S.R. for counterpopulation targeting, and devote the remainder of our offensive weapons to degrading and destroying on a massive scale the Soviet military forces and equipment essential to (1) their invasion and administration of Western Europe, and (2) their defense against the massive armies of the People's Republic of China. The Soviets have positioned some 50 divisions of troops (about one million men) on their border with China. Deployed with them are all sorts of mechanized equipment, hundreds and perhaps 2,000 aircraft, and food storage depots and military supply dumps. All this is supported (until Kissinger opened the Suez Canal at U.S. expense, with U.S. Navy equipment and personnel) by a single highly vulnerable railroad. Although the number of troops is about even on both sides, the Soviets are in command of the situation because of their massive numbers of tactical nuclear weapons and delivery systems.

Knowledge that a heavy attack on these forces and facilities by U.S. strategic nuclear weapons would result automatically from the launch of Soviet strategic weapons at the United States should have a considerable deterrent effect. The Kremlin has an almost psychotic fear of what they call the "hordes of yellow Chinese."

The ultimate and overriding objective of Soviet communism is, and has been for more than 55 years, control of the entire world. But the first step is to take over the industrial plant and skilled labor force of Western Europe, and the plan requires that it be taken over as a going concern, not as a mass of atomized ruins. To accomplish this requires masses of occupation troops and the largest conventional armed forces the world has ever known. Our smart-targeting should include every adjunct of military power, with special emphasis on all types of transportation, railroad yards, truck concentrations, and fuel storage. Actually, we already have detailed targeting plans for such a strike prepared in the pre-McNamara years when we could have saturated Soviet air defenses and delivered 40,000 megatons of nuclear explosive power distributed over every worthwhile target in the nine million square miles of the Soviet Union.

At the very least, we could drive the masters of the Kremlin to make the agonizing decision of whether they want the United States dead more than they want Western Europe Red. They might realize that the targeting we planned would leave them with a huge reserve of intercontinental ballistic strategic missiles for which they would have no profitable use, but with no transportation for the, say, 20 million troops it would require to conquer and administer Western Europe. With a little luck, we might also get several thousands of their battle tanks and masses of mechanized equipment for their ground forces. We cannot credibly threaten any substantial number of the Soviets' strategic nuclear forces, because ICBMs can be buried in silos and hardened with concrete and steel; but massive amounts of arms, ammunition, vehicles, and other mechanized equipment of conventional forces simply cannot be buried underground and protected by massive concrete and steel structures.

This type of targeting is not to be confused with the Schlesinger "selective" and "limited" targeting. We must commit every available strategic weapon to our automatic reaction to a Soviet strategic attack against the United States. We do not want to *fight* a nuclear war against the enormously superior forces of the Soviet Union. We would be overwhelmed by their superiority in throw-weight and megatonnage delivery capability. What we want to accomplish—and the only thing we can realistically hope to accomplish—is to *deter* a nuclear war, and to deter nuclear blackmail which would ultimately bring us to surrender. We can do this only by informing the American people of the disaster which will inexorably befall all of us and the United States if we do not immediately demand a reversal of the Kissinger policies which subject us to destruction by the Soviet Union.

Do the American people have the courage to face up to a realistic estimate of the situation, and the ingenuity and the dedication to take the action required to avert nuclear war and enable our nation to survive in peace and freedom? Dr. Edward Teller gave the answer to this question—an answer based on faith in America and a courageous evaluation of both the threat confronting us and the tremendous resources of the United States. He said that, when the American people understand the "ominous import" of the SALT I Agreements:

We shall have a thorough and lasting incentive to work for our survival and for the survival of freedom everywhere.

I believe that freedom is indivisible. I also believe that *the ingenuity and the dedication of free people can work miracles.*[40]

26

In late spring 1974, commentators speculated on the possibility that President Nixon might be so anxious to divert public attention away from his Watergate-related troubles that he might make serious concessions to secure a SALT II agreement during his forthcoming Moscow trip. Their worry was wasted, however, because the preliminary sell-out of the United States in SALT II was signed, sealed, and delivered a year earlier at the Washington Summit on June 21, 1973; and the climactic trap for the United States in the Moscow Summit of 1974 was to be in the far more subtle form of "no agreement" instead of an obviously bad agreement.

The 1973 sell-out was embodied in a declaration signed by the U.S. President and the General Secretary of the Communist Party of the Soviet Union committing both sides to make serious efforts to reach a permanent agreement on "more complete measures" limiting strategic offensive arms. Six additional principles were included in the declaration, and they successfully diverted attention from the climactic provision. Modernization and replacement of offensive arms were to be allowed—subject to limitations to be set out in the permanent agreement—and these limitations "can apply both to their quantitative aspects as well as their qualitative improvement."

Then came the key provision: "*The limitations must be subject to adequate verification by national technical means.*" Never in history have so few words with such a reassuring sound so degraded the defense of the lives and liberty of free people.

Let us examine what those twelve words mean, since they constitute the price Brezhnev extracted from Nixon and Kissinger for the promise of a Moscow SALT II agreement. Here is a pertinent statement by Dr. Edward Teller during his testimony on SALT I before the Senate Foreign Relations Committee:

> I raise only one little point that worries me. There is the question of the so-called national means of verification which undoubtedly we will discuss with the Russians. These national means of verification are secret. Reliance on the treaty depends on acts carried out in secrecy. We shall discuss these secrets with the Russians. We are not going to discuss them as it now appears, with our allies, with the American people or even with the Senate. This is highly improper.
>
> Since the national means of verification are the basis of reliance on the treaty, these national means of verification should be opened up, displayed, at least to our allies, at least to the Congress; I hope also to the people of the United States.[1]

Distrust of the American people is the basis for Kissinger's obsession with secrecy. Keeping this Soviet-shared secret from the American people is one of Kissinger's primary instruments for keeping them from discovering what he is doing to their national security.

This secrecy concept is a euphemistic formula to cover the Soviet refusal to *permit* any inspection or verification whatsoever. We are relegated to whatever we can do without their permission, and without their help or cooperation, such as satellite photography and electronic surveillance by satellite or aircraft over international areas, or huge array radars, or communications intelligence. The Russians agreed not to shoot down our satellites; but they retained the capability of doing exactly that, whenever it would be worth more to them than maintaining a semblance of detente.

Another way of explaining "verification by national technical means" is that its use in an arms-control agreement signifies that the Soviets have adhered to their 55-year-old formula of refusing to permit any on-site inspection. To admit that they have flatly rejected any method of inspection which would require admission of foreigners to Soviet territory, or any type of cooperation by the Soviet authorities, would cast doubt on Kissinger's assurance to Congress that we have "an entirely different relationship of building additional trust."

Before evaluating the significance of this U.S.-U.S.S.R. agreement in relation to SALT II agreements—whether temporary, fragmentary, or permanent—its legal implications must be made clear. The "limitations" imposed by any SALT II agreement "*must*" be subject to "adequate verification" by "national technical means." By all rules of legal interpretation of agreements, this excludes any other type of verification. Additionally, the very inclusion of one agreed type of inspection would *exclude* the use of any other type of verification. Furthermore, use of the expression "adequate verification," in relation to the national technical means, constitutes an agreement on the part of the United States that we consider that type of inspection as "adequate." No court or international tribunal, called upon to interpret that agreement, would listen to any attempt by us to claim that verification by national technical means could not be "adequate"; nor would we be permitted to present experts to testify as to the inadequacy of national technical means.

This is how the United States was sold out in SALT II a year before even a tentative temporary agreement was scheduled to be signed. At the Washington Summit in 1973, Kissinger, Nixon, and Brezhnev all knew very well that the publicized essence of any SALT II agreement would be a limitation on MIRVs. That was made evident by the specific inclusion in the Nixon-Brezhnev Declaration of Principles of June 21, 1973, that "modernization and replacement" of offensive arms would be allowed under SALT II agreements, subject only to such limitations as might be agreed upon by the parties, and that those agreed limitations on modernization and improvement could apply both to "quantitative" aspects and to "qualitative improvements."

The broad term "qualitative improvement" would cover any technological improvements, such as improved accuracy of guidance, reliability, yield of warheads, the MaRVing of warheads, and (by far the most important for the 1974-76 timeframe) the MIRVing of missiles.

So Dr. Kissinger—our great intelligence expert and czar of all U.S. intelligence—agreed to SALT II limitations on MIRVs with inspection solely and exclusively by "national technical means." But *national technical means of verification are useless in relation to MIRV limitations*—totally useless.

Here is some testimony from several career-long prodisarmament experts who would favor any disarmament measure, especially one so vital as a limitation on MIRVs. Robert R. Bowie, Director of the Center for International Affairs, Harvard University, gives a good basis for our understanding of this question:

> . . . in judging any limitation, each side must consider consequences not only if carried out, but also if violated by the other side. In case of violation, the risks will depend upon (1) whether it can be detected and how quickly, and (2) how long it will take to negate it or compensate for it.
>
> Inevitably, therefore, the reliability of inspection to verify compliance or detect violation directly affects the extent and kinds of limitations that will be acceptable. Thus the Soviet rejection of any on-site inspection as an improper intrusion sets drastic constraints on possible limitations. Artificial satellites and other national means now make it feasi-

ble to verify some kinds of limitations without on-site inspection. They can reveal what is being done physically on the observed territory and can therefore verify limitations based on counting or monitoring installations, or objects, or activities such as flight testing. *But such unilateral methods are not adequate to police restraints on qualitative changes or on research and development. Only actual on-site inspection could determine for certain whether the warhead of a missile contains MIRVs.*[2]

In the same article, Professor Bowie deals specifically with the threat of the Soviet SS-9 force and the possibility of agreed limitations:

> . . . it is probable that the "offensive" limitation will apply to the SS-9s in some way. But since restriction *of installation of MIRVs would require on-site inspection,* restricting numbers beyond the existing three hundred would have only limited significance in protecting the Minuteman missiles.[3]

That is, Professor Bowie assumes that, because a limitation on MIRVs simply cannot be verified by national technical means and absolutely requires on-site inspection, the United States would not enter into any agreement because the Soviets will not agree to on-site inspection. This is rather amusing because Professor Bowie was director of the Center for International Affairs at Harvard University when Henry Kissinger was a very junior associate there. Kissinger's 1961 book was published under the auspices of this center, and Robert Bowie was accorded the first acknowledgement of assistance by Kissinger in his preface to *The Necessity for Choice.*

Wynfred Joshua, senior political scientist and assistant director at the Strategic Studies Center of the Stanford Research Institute, Washington, D.C., discusses verification in SALT:

> Verification involves a wide spectrum of problems, but it appears reasonable to suggest that *national means of verification are best suited to monitoring agreements that call for quantitative rather than qualitative limitations.*
>
> *To illustrate, satellite surveillance* can detect and count silos and can indicate the size of the missile inside the silo, but it *cannot discover the number of warheads* or the degree of missile accuracy.[4]

As we have not encountered a single expert who contends that national means can adequately verify a limitation on MIRVs, we will not add cumulative testimony on this point. We can move on to the eponym of equivocality, Dr. Kissinger. At his White House briefing for the five congressional committees on SALT I on June 15, 1972, which embodied his grand rationale of SALT, he was asked this question by Congressman Clement J. Zablocki of Wisconsin: "Why didn't we pursue with greater determination the inclusion of MIRVs in the Interim Agreement?" Here is Kissinger's reply:

> Now, with respect to MIRV, MIRV is a complex issue for this reason: you can count numbers with national means of verification, but it is much more difficult to determine how many warheads are confined in the master warhead.
>
> Now, you have some indications but it is not very easy. Therefore, with respect to the deployment of MIRV, the inspection requirements have to be a little bit more rigid than would be otherwise the case.
>
> Now, we have made two proposals, two linked proposals, one is a ban on the testing of MIRV, this we are prepared to monitor by national means of inspection, and second, *a ban on the deployment of MIRV for which we asked for spot-checks on on-site inspection.* Now we considered the test ban absolutely crucial because we could have been somewhat more lenient on the frequency of on-site inspection if there had been a test ban on MIRVs because without testing, by definition, it is not easy to deploy them. It is, in fact, impossible to deploy them.
>
> The Soviet Union, for not ununderstandable reasons, because they are behind in MIRV technology, refused a test ban. They also refused a deployment ban, as such. What they proposed was a production ban but without inspection. A ban on production is totally unverifiable in the Soviet Union while they could verify ours through budget and other methods through which our industrial production generally becomes known.
>
> So, the Soviet counter-proposal for a production ban without a test ban was generally unacceptable to us and when we reached that stalemate, we could not proceed any further. This was the obstacle to proceeding on the MIRVs.

So there we have it from Dr. Kissinger himself. A ban on deployment of MIRVs, even if backed up by a ban on testing MIRVs before the Soviets had (to our knowledge) tested any, *could not be verified without "spot-checks on on-site inspection."* One year after making those statements, there had been no developments in national technical means of verification which would have permitted inspection of a MIRV deployment limitation. On the other hand, the Soviets were proceeding with multiple independently guided warhead testing. It had to be clear to our intelligence by June 1974 that the Soviets had substantially completed their MIRV testing for their four new series of advanced ICBMs. Therefore, by the time of the Moscow Summit, which would be the first chance to sign an agreement on MIRVs, it would be *too late for a MIRV test ban to be effective in limiting deployment of MIRVs.* The need for "spot-checks on on-site inspection," therefore, was vastly increased.

Yet, at the Washington Summit on June 21, 1973, Kissinger sold us out to the Soviets. The price he committed the United States to pay was perfectly clear and absolutely specific: *no effective inspection of* the limitations on the Soviet Union. We would have to accept Soviet compliance on the basis of trust, and nothing more.

Kissinger exacted no defined or definable price from Brezhnev—nothing at all except a totally illusory promise to make serious efforts to reach a permanent agreement on "more complete measures" limiting strategic offensive arms, with an "objective" of signing in 1974. The Soviets could claim full compliance by tendering a draft agreement limiting U.S. ICBM and SLBM launchers to zero and Soviet ICBM and SLBM launchers to 10,000 each. Although they could have gone that far, they actually didn't; instead they came up with "21 outrageous demands." The American people have not been trusted with a knowledge of what those 21 demands were. But the point is that the Soviets promised nothing of value in exchange for Kissinger's promise to abandon inspection, and so were within their rights at the Summit of '74 in refusing to agree to any additional limitation on offensive strategic weapons.

Thus it is that any MIRV limitation agreement which comes out of subsequent negotiations will embody a death trap for U.S. strategic power. This will be true regardless of whether the SALT II agreement purports to be temporary or partial or permanent; or whether the basis of the limitation is related to the numbers of MIRVs allowed, or the throw-weight of MIRVs allowed, or the types of ICBMs or SLBMs on which they are allowed. No agreement limiting MIRVs can be effectively verified by "national technical means of verification." It's as simple as that. Yet Henry Kissinger continued to tout such an agreement, even after the brutal rebuff in Moscow in June 1974.

In order to divert attention from the vital issue of verification and focus on some issue, real or artificial, Kissinger has staged a charade in the form of a controversy. As the scheduled Moscow SALT II Summit drew near, we began to hear about a "dispute within the U.S. defense establishment." According to the press, the big split was between Secretary of Defense James Schlesinger and Secretary of Detente Henry Kissinger. According to this media mythology, Schlesinger advocated a U.S. bargaining position based on seeking to obtain "equality" in throw-weight of missiles and MIRVs; and Kissinger, out of deference to detente, advocated accepting equality in numbers of MIRVs, ignoring the harsh reality that this might end up with the Soviets having a six-to-one advantage in MIRV-deliverable megatonnage, or a differential favoring the Soviets of 1,950,000 tons of TNT equivalent explosive power for each MIRV.

Discussion in the press turned on which of the "opposing" views would prevail and become the official U.S. position. Newsweek devoted nearly a full page to a discussion entitled "Throw-Weight and Warheads," but no space at all to the matter of verification.

Is there any chance that Brezhnev and Grechko will release Kissinger from his Washington Summit commitment *not* to request any form of verification of MIRV limitations other than by "national technical means"? Here is a clue furnished by Brezhnev himself during his May 1973 Bonn Summit with Willy Brandt. A West German interviewer asked him whether Moscow would accept the principle of Western German representation of West Berlin in the United Nations:

> I will not consider this question as to content, Brezhnev replied.
>
> But I shall tell you something of my character. I do not like to revert to questions that have already been solved.[5]

Defense Secretary James Schlesinger, in his FY 1975 Annual DOD Report, submitted to Congress on March 4, 1974, declared the overall U.S. policy relating to the Soviet strategic threat. His statement was given national publicity supposedly marking him as a courageous realist, a "hard-liner" who was willing to face up to the Soviet threat and would never be faced down by it. Commenting on the fact that the Soviets would soon deploy "on the order of 7,000 one-to-two megaton warheads in their ICBM force alone," which would give them "a major one-sided counterforce capability against the United States ICBM force," he asserted that "this is impermissible from our point of view." Then he set out exactly what the Kissinger-Schlesinger Administration proposed to do about it:

> With these things in mind, we are seeking in SALT II to ensure that the principle of essential equivalence is upheld. We are also proposing in the FY 1975 budget several strategic *R&D programs* conducted within the SALT I agreements *as hedges against the unknown outcome of SALT II and the uncertain actions of the U.S.S.R.*
>
> The United States is prepared to reduce, stay level, or if need be increase the level of our strategic arms, but *in any case that level will be fixed by the actions of the Soviet Union.* If the Soviet Union insists on moving ahead with a new set of strategic capabilities, *we will be forced to match them.*

On its face, the Schlesinger statement sounds reasonable. Why not wait (1) for the result of the SALT II negotiations, and (2) to ascertain what the uncertain actions of the Soviets concerning the buildup of their strategic forces will actually be?

But *every year since 1969,* those same two criteria have been advanced in DOD policy statements as excuses for failing to act to preserve the effectiveness of the U.S. strategic deterrent. In every one of those five years, the Soviets massively increased their strategic forces and either continued to stall the SALT negotiations, or refused in agreements to include any provisions which would restrain their planned and ongoing buildup. In the two and a half years of SALT I stalling, the Soviets added more than 1,000 strategic missile launchers. In the two years of SALT II negotiations, they began rapid deployment of massive technological improvement programs which would add the destructive-power equivalent of thousands of additional ICBMs.

In early 1969, Defense Secretary Melvin Laird warned and documented the fact that the Soviets were building their strategic forces up to attain a "first-strike capability against the United States." He warned that the Soviets had the capability of achieving by the mid-1970s "a superiority over the presently authorized and programmed forces of the United States in *all* areas—offensive strategic forces, defensive strategic forces, and conventional forces."[6]

In Kissinger's 1970 *State of the World Report,* he said that developments in Soviet strategic forces and in SALT "will largely determine whether we will be forced into increased deployments to offset the Soviet threat to the sufficiency of our deterrent. . ."

In his 1971 *State of the World Report,* he noted that "the level of Soviet strategic forces now exceeds the level needed for deterrence," and that those forces "could be uniquely suitable for a first-strike against our land-based deterrent forces." He noted also that over "the past year, the U.S.S.R. has continued to add significantly to its capabilities," but he stressed:

> In the light of the negotiations on strategic arms, we are acting with great restraint in introducing changes in our strategic posture,

and he added that we had not increased the number of our missiles and bombers, but instead

> we have deliberately adopted measures designed to demonstrate our defensive intent.

In the next year's *State of the World Report,* he noted that the Soviets were continuing to build "beyond a level which by any reasonable standard seems sufficient," noted the obvious first-strike capability they were developing, and then reenunciated the same old criteria:

> If the Soviet Union continues to expand strategic forces, compensating U.S. programs will be mandatory. The preferable alternative would be a combination of mutual restraint and an agreement in SALT. But under no circumstances will I permit the further erosion of the strategic balance with the USSR.

This clearly pledges to the American people that—SALT or no SALT—he will not permit further erosion in the strategic balance. Yet since he made that pledge, further erosion has resulted every month, culminating in the situations described in the Schlesinger FY 1975 DOD Report, which we have considered.

716

In the 1973 *State of the World Report*, the same criteria are again enumerated: "Soviet strategic developments, arms limitation . . . "; and, again, U.S. "restraint":

Our forces . . . are not designed to provide a capability for a disarming first-strike. Moreover, our programs are not so substantial that our objectives could be misunderstood, conceivably spurring a Soviet building cycle.

In 1974, the Secretary of Defense again spooned out the same criteria to a trusting American people, and again abandoned them.

With that background, the 1974 Schlesinger statement about "the uncertain actions of the U.S.S.R." and the United States being "forced to match them" appears no longer to be merely giving Soviet actions and SALT II negotiations a reasonable period of proof. Instead it is exposed as the *fifth* repetition of the same old lie by which the American people have been lulled into a totally false sense of security, while the Kissinger-Nixon Administration deliberately sacrificed another year of lead-time essential to the rebuilding of our strategic deterrent in time to save the United States from the stark alternatives of surrender or nuclear destruction.

If they can get away with these same lies just twice more, and thus throw away two more years of lead-time for rebuilding our deterrent, they will attain the objective jointly declared with Leonid Brezhnev in Moscow during Kissinger's April 1974 trip: to make detente, on Soviet terms, irreversible.

Some concerned Americans who know a little of the magnitude and imminence of the Soviet strategic threat have placed their hopes on SALT II and the promises of "hard-liner" Schlesinger. The background of the previous six years shows the illusory character of the Schlesinger promises that we are holding back the development of additional strategic power only to give SALT II and Soviet restraint a chance to prove themselves. But his promises are deceptive also in their own context. Whether we reduce, stay level, or increase our level of strategic arms, Schlesinger says, will be determined "by the actions of the Soviet Union," and, if they "insist on moving ahead" we will "be forced to match them."

Yet, substantially every paragraph in his own FY 1975 DOD Report paints a convincing picture of the Soviets' moving ahead massively and swiftly with building many new sets of strategic capabilities. His report does not show that they *may in the future* move ahead with such programs—it shows that they are doing it *now*.

In addition to the actions we have already reviewed from the text of his FY 1975 Report, he gave some even more convincing testimony before a closed session of a Senate Foreign Relations Subcommittee on March 4, 1974, which was released on April 3, 1974. The Soviet ongoing program "turned out to be staggering in its size and depth," and he made the astounding statement that the SS-19 has a throw-weight of two to three times that of the *latest modification* of the SS-11 now deployed. This confirms the statement he made in his FY 1975 DOD Report that the SS-X-17 and SS-X-19 had "three to five times the throw-weight of the early model SS-11." Thus 5 x early model SS-11 throw-weight = 3 x latest model SS-11 throw-weight; or 5 x 2,500 pounds = 3 x 4,166.6 = SS-19 throw-weight, 12,500 pounds; which sounds reasonable for a missile which can carry six MIRVs of one to two megatons.

The above several paragraphs prove conclusively that James Schlesinger does indeed realize that the "Soviets *are* moving ahead with a new set of strategic capabilities" which are "staggering in size and depth." Yet while repeating time after time that *if* they do that, "we will be forced to match them," Schlesinger proposes no improvements in quantity, not even in his favorite timeframe of the 1980s. As to quality, his own FY 1975 DOD Report states specifically:

In view of the ongoing SAL talks, we propose in the FY 1975 budget to take only those first few steps which are necessary to keep open these options; no decisions have been made to deploy any of these improved systems.[7]

Schlesinger says he will await "the *outcome* of current SALT negotiations"; that is, he will not be moved by what the Soviets are doing while they negotiate. Henry Kissinger started saying that in 1970. *National Review*, under the caption "Bitter SALT," summed it up like this:

The U.S. not only has no developed hardware to counterbalance these Soviet developments, but *has no serious* program beyond early research stages. . . .

It has been clear for some time that the interim strategic arms agreement reached by the U.S. and the Soviet Union in SALT I was, from the U.S. standpoint, a mistake. It now looks more and more like a disaster. . . .

The U.S. estimate of both Soviet capabilities and Soviet intentions was altogether incorrect. . . . The newly developed cold launch technique allows Moscow to replace their 1,000 single warhead SS-11 missiles and 300 SS-9s with the new MIRVed missiles without violating SALT I rules concerning silos.

These developments wipe out the qualitative superiority on which the U.S. relied and enable the Soviet Union to achieve in the relatively near future a vast superiority in warhead power and number. The new generation of SALT-sprung Soviet missiles could launch about four times as many warheads as the U.S. missiles, with a total weight of more than 10 million pounds as against a U.S. two million. . . .[8]

Robert Hotz, editor-in-chief of the authoritative technical journ *Aviation Week & Space Technology*, stated about SALT I and II:

. . . Held up now in the harsh light of Soviet performance, these pieces of paper are as full of holes as a Swiss cheese. . . .

Although U.S. officials are still lamely professing that SALT I was a "good" agreement because it could lead to something better, much of the fervor has gone out of this litany recently.

It is apparent to a growing audience that the U.S. was so badly outmaneuvered at SALT I that *it will be impossible to achieve any of its real objectives at SALT II or beyond.*

There is something both sad and dangerous in the way the U.S. gives away its best tangible assets to the U.S.S.R. in exchange for nebulous and transitory intangibles in these type negotiations. Most U.S. participants in SALT I agree that the Soviets were frantically anxious to achieve a halt to ballistic missile defense deployment. *The U.S. superiority in this field, which eventually would eliminate any possibility of a Soviet first-strike capability,* was a very tangible asset that this country gave up in SALT I. Meanwhile, the U.S.S.R. is pushing its own advanced missile site defense technology at a rapid pace to make up this disparity as soon as possible. It is already testing new ABM missiles and radars but has a large deficiency in computer technology.

Now there are whispers that, in a supposedly commercial deal, the U.S. is officially offering the Soviets the Control Data Corp. 7600 high-speed digital computer that is the heart of the U.S. ABM site defense system.

Now that they have eliminated the deployment threat of a U.S. ICBM site defense system by treaty, established their own prerogatives for a numerical superiority in ICBM launchers by agreement, and developed the technology to force a multiplication of that superiority into strategic significance, the Soviets are getting tougher in their demands for SALT II and even more nebulous in what they offer in return. The Soviets now believe that they are operating from growing technological strength against a growing U.S. political weakness caused by Watergate and no realistic understanding of the game being played. . . .

Too much of the SALT negotiations and their peripheral maneuvering have been conducted under the table in deep secrecy, with their significance only dimly perceived by many of the key participants. It is time that the American public and the Congress demanded more SALT on top of the table where they can see how much of their safety and future is being bartered away by glossy diplomats who do not really understand what they are doing.[9]

Robert Hotz thus gives the answer to *why* the Soviets were so desperately anxious to halt U.S. ABM development. While Kissinger studiously avoided giving any reason, Robert Hotz explains it. Once we had our missile defensive system, it "would eliminate any possibility of a Soviet first-strike capability."

While Robert Hotz is correct in his conclusion that SALT I was so shockingly bad for the United States that it will be impossible for us to achieve any of our "real objectives at SALT II or beyond," there are two major theories being advanced to persuade the American people to hope that SALT II will save us. Unless they are exposed as merely illusory, they will carry us past the point of no return and seduce us into throwing away those last essential two or three years of lead-time.

The first hope is based on the congressional resolution approving the SALT I Interim Agreement. It contained hopeful language urging the President to seek equal, not inferior, strategic forces for the United States in any permanent arms limitation agreement. But this congressional suggestion cannot bind Kissinger, the President, or the Kremlin. Worse, it just might give Kissinger an inspiration for a truly brilliant gambit. He knows that he cannot agree to the Kremlin demand that, as a condition of further SALT agreements, the United States should kill the B-1 and Trident programs (especially since the Soviets already have their Backfire supersonic bomber in operational squadrons and serial production, and have 19 of their Delta and Extended-Delta-class submarines already operational or under construction).

But he could suggest to the Soviets—in one of his secret conferences at which only Russian interpreters are present—that they come up with a declaration of solidarity with the U.S. congressional resolution on equality. The Soviets could pledge to work with sincerity to establish perfect equality in the SALT II permanent offensive arms limitation treaty. After such a Soviet declaration, the 141 Members of Congress for World Peace Through Law could pick up enough support to kill both the B-1 and the Trident the next time an appropriation comes up for a vote. It would be claimed that the sincerity of Soviet detente and good will is demonstrated by the Kremlin's promise to accord us perfect equality in the SALT II treaty, and that, therefore, further spending on weapons of destruction would be a waste of billions of dollars urgently needed to expand school busing or other domestic projects. Such a supposedly generous and conciliatory gesture would give the Soviets a perfect setup for conning us into abandoning attempts to amend the inequities of the SALT I Interim Agreement, which in turn would allow them to stall for another two and a half years in negotiating the specifics of the new Kissinger brainstorm—a "temporary" agreement to run until 1985.

The kicker, of course, is that by 1976 the Soviets will have in-being, or under construction and near completion, the strategic weapon force levels preplanned to give them a splendid first-strike capability.

Because their weapons would be in-being, the only thing the "equality" provisions would do for us would be to permit us to start building toward attaining in, say, 1981, the quantum and quality of strategic offensive power that the Soviets would have attained in 1975 under the cover of SALT I. The fatal danger to U.S. national survival in this situation was exquisitely expressed, as we stated before, by Dr. Kissinger before he became a SALT seller: "The defender can deter only if he is ready at every moment of time."

No piece of paper coming out of SALT II negotiations, therefore, which provides for a new and more equitable balance between U.S. and U.S.S.R. strategic weapons can save us—unless it also provides for the creation in time of sufficient additional U.S. weapons to achieve that balance. This could be actually accomplished only by the President proposing and the Congress approving and funding the programs which, as we have seen, would be even the more improbable if the Soviets were generous enough in the treaty to "permit" us to attain equality.

There is a second theory of how SALT II can save us that has also developed surprising support. Under this theory, SALT II could save us if it provided for the destruction of sufficient Soviet offensive weapons and U.S. weapons to bring us both down to a lower level of equality. Here is this proposal, persuasively explained by Senator Henry M. Jackson in a speech before the Overseas Press Club in New York in April 1974:

> In the current SALT II negotiations, the Soviets . . . are insisting on a SALT II arrangement that would widen and deepen their strategic margin still further. . . .
>
> In their desire to preserve the impression of momentum in the SALT negotiations, the Administration has abandoned its previous conviction that the essential purpose of a follow-on agreement should be to rectify the imbalance of SALT I. In their haste to meet an arbitrary and politically-expedient self-imposed June deadline, the Administration has now begun to entertain Soviet proposals which are inimical to the national security of the United States and to prospects of a SALT II Treaty based on U.S.-Soviet equality.
>
> Kept on such a course, SALT II is doomed to fail in the supreme mission of reducing the risk of mutual destruction. Indeed, instead of putting a damper on the arms race, such a failure would add fuel to the fire.
>
> Given this situation, I am persuaded the time is ripe for the United States to put forward a bold and imaginative proposal for serious disarmament—a proposal that will test uncertain Soviet intentions by inviting them to join with us in concluding a far-reaching agreement to bring about a measure of stability in the nuclear balance at sharply reduced levels of strategic forces.
>
> Instead of arms limitations agreements that do not limit, it is time for serious arms reductions by both sides—a stabilizing disarmament.
>
> I believe that strategic forces on both sides are larger than they need to be, providing that we can negotiate with the Soviets toward a common ceiling at a sharply lower level. Therefore I propose that we invite the Soviets to consider a SALT II agreement in which each side would be limited to 800 ICBMs and to no more than 560 submarine-launched missiles,

equivalent to 35 missile-firing submarines of the Poseidon type. Long-range strategic bombers, which were not included in the Interim Agreement, would also be limited to 400 on each side. Because the throw-weight of the Soviet missile force is so much greater than that of our own, the two SALT delegations would be instructed to negotiate a formula for varying these basic numbers so as to bring the basic throw-weight of the two intercontinental strategic forces into approximate equality.

The numbers resulting from the negotiating process need not be precisely the numbers outlined here . . . so long as the aggregate total of intercontinental launchers was 1,760 or less. Reduction to a level of equality would be carried out, in phases, over a period of time to be negotiated. . . .[10]

If Senator Jackson's proposal embodied a foolproof system of comprehensive inspection and a fail-safe system of enforcement, it would be all we ever wanted in an arms control agreement. Because it presents the dream of a secure world, it has attracted enthusiastic support.

"Ploy" is defined as: "1. escapade, frolic; 2. a tactic intended to embarrass or frustrate an opponent."[11] That's what Senator Jackson's SARP (Strategic Arms Reduction Proposal) is—a ploy, a tactic intended to embarrass or frustrate not just one but two opponents. No politician can survive for long if he is being smeared as an enemy of "disarmament." Because Senator Jackson was one of only three or four Senators who criticized the evil imbalances and slick loopholes in the SALT I agreements, he came under continuous attack from the unilateralists as an enemy of disarmament, and hence of detente, and hence of peace. When he proposed a little horse-trading with the Soviets in the humanitarian interest of Soviet dissidents and would-be emigrants, the attacks on him reached a screaming crescendo. So he launched his counterattack: strike the "limitation" from SALT; knock the "L" out of it. He would show his critics exactly *who* was for *real* disarmament—a reduction in existing inventories. Boldly and imaginatively, he made his proposal to cut existing stocks in half, save hundreds of billions of dollars, reduce tensions, end the fear of a first-strike by either superpower against the other, and establish stability at a low level of strategic forces. He stole the thunder from the right and the left.

Americans have a national susceptibility to utopian solutions, and Jackson's SARP is certainly a utopian solution. It sounds so logical and desirable that many Americans immediately assume that (1) it is possible and (2) it is attainable. The Senator knows that it is not possible, except in the most technical sense of that term, and he knows also that it is unattainable (that is, so long as Communists remain Communists). Since the Senator also knows that most Americans cannot be expected to understand these things, his proposal was probably made as a ploy—a tactic to embarrass two sets of opponents: (1) the SALT-at-any-price unilateral-disarmament elites who were criticizing him for attaching reservations to SALT I, and (2) the Soviets, who were criticizing him for obstructing detente (in their definition of that word). His ploy demonstrated that he is for true disarmament (reduction instead of a mere freeze), and that his proposal would go much farther toward establishing a real detente. To that extent, his strategic arms reduction proposal was a serious proposal. It was also sincere to the extent that he would be happy indeed if the Soviets would accept it. But he could not have seriously believed that it would ever be acceptable to the Soviets. He suggested this himself by asserting that it "would test uncertain Soviet intentions."

Senator Jackson knows that, if the Soviets agreed to his reduction in strategic armaments proposal, they would be giving up forever their objective of attaining a first-strike capability against the United States and, through that, control of the entire world. Such an agreement would be acceptable only to a status quo power which had given up all ambition of expanding its political influence. Stability rather than superiority would have to be its overriding objective in relation to the strategic nuclear balance. The unmistakable test for such a national attitude is whether a nation stops building up mountains of strategic arms when "parity" is reached. The Soviets did not. They continued to pile up added increments of superiority in strategic arms ever since 1968. They are now some six years and probably $300 billion past parity, and they are still building so strenuously that Schlesinger estimates it will cost the Soviets about $30 billion to replace the entire SS-11 force with SS-19 missiles, plus another $12 to $15 billion to replace the SS-9s with SS-18s.[12]

Let's look specifically at what the Jackson SARP would ask the Soviets to do to their program, compared to the United States:

	Soviet ICBMs	U.S. ICBMs
SALT I & 1976 Deployed levels:	1,618	1,054
Jackson's proposed reductions to:	800	800
Numbers required to be scrapped:	818	254

That looks as if the Soviets would be taking a massively greater cut, but those are just the proposed numbers. The two SALT delegations could be instructed to negotiate a formula for "varying these basic numbers so as to bring the basic throw-weight of the two intercontinental strategic forces into approximate equality." So the Soviets would not be allowed to retain 800 ICBMs, or anything like that number. Instead they could have only 800 minus the number necessary to be subtracted to bring them down to the U.S. throw-weight, which is generally agreed to be 2,000 pounds per Minuteman, or 1.6 million pounds total for the Jackson-reduced force level of 800.

Thus, if the Soviets decided to retain SS-18s, they would be limited to 97, because the most conservative estimate of the SS-18 throw-weight is 16,500 pounds. If the Soviets made this choice, it would be incredibly generous of them because our 800 Minuteman ICBMs would give us a high-confidence disarming capability against their 97 SS-18s, and we would have hundreds left in reserve. This would mean a total reversal of the present strategic balance. Of course, the Soviets would not decide to retain SS-18s if they were forced to make such a choice; they would retain old model SS-11s in order to obtain the maximum number of missiles within the allowed total throw-weight of 1.6 million pounds, and so could probably keep about 640. This would be much better for them because we would no longer have a disarming strike capability against their ICBM force, with a substantial number in reserve.

But if they made this best of all possible choices for them under the Jackson proposal, they would have to scrap all their SS-9s, all their SS-18s, all their SS-17s, and all their SS-19s. If they had actually upgraded all their old SS-11s and SS-9s to new missiles by the time the Jackson proposal took effect (after years of negotiation, of course) they would have wasted, according to the Schlesinger estimates, some $42 to $45 billion dollars on those new missiles, and would have to go to the additional expense of replacing the 640 old SS-11s. If they did not do that, the total Jackson throw-weight limitation would allow them only about 128 SS-19s.

Thus, the Soviets would be giving up all the fruits of their technological breakthrough in offensive missile developments, and thereby throwing away R&D expenditures running into scores of billions of dollar equivalents. Would they do that? What do you think?

Any argument that they would must be based on the assumption that the Soviets are a status quo power, have no desire for expansion, and prefer stability to superiority in the area of strategic power. Those arguments simply cannot stand in the face of the inescapable fact that the Soviets must have planned a use for those strategic offensive weapons which the Jackson proposal would require them to scrap.

One of the fundamental but suicidal tenets of the ideology of the U.S. unilateral-disarmament intellectuals is that the Soviets engage in the most massive strategic programs without any plans for their use, or any analysis of why they need them, or what kind of weapons and how many. The perverted religion of unilateral disarmament is built on a foundation of assumptions which are never questioned. One of their key assumptions is that the Soviets have no strategic military doctrine. Thus, John Newhouse puts it this way:

> The buildup of Soviet forces has not been accompanied by a formal strategic doctrine. There had been no Soviet equivalent of assured destruction, as such, even though Malenkov, as early as 1954, had observed that

possession by both sides of nuclear weapons and the means for delivering them would create a kind of mutual deterrence. Khrushchev, after attacking Malenkov's moderate tendencies, emulated his example. . . .

The Brezhnev-Kosygin leadership sustained Khrushchev's avowed policy of preventing nuclear war through deterrence, but, again, nothing like a rigorous strategic doctrine was laid down. . . .

Neither in 1968, nor again in 1969, did Washington really know why Moscow had opted for SALT. . . .[13]

The assumption that the Soviets have no strategic doctrine is essential to the arguments for the strategic disarmament of the United States. If you admit that the Soviets do have a strategy, then it is next to impossible to ignore the conclusive evidence of exactly what that strategy is, which has been cumulating since they created the first ICBM in 1957. We have seen that, just as Kissinger's strategy is *detente first at all costs*, the essence of Soviet strategy is *strike first at all costs*. The totally clinching evidence is in the highly specialized and fantastically expensive capabilities of the new types of ICBMs which the Soviets have deployed since the signing of SALT I in May 1972.

If the Soviets sincerely agreed to Senator Jackson's proposal for a SALT II agreement which would bind them to reducing their strategic forces to a numerical and throw-weight parity with a reduced U.S. strategic force, they would be scrapping not only nuclear weapons which cost them scores of billions of rubles, but their plans for the world of the future. The probability of the Kremlin's agreeing to the Jackson reduction proposal, therefore, can be judged by the intensity of their dedication to the strategy which their weapons have been designed to implement. In turn, the intensity of their dedication can be judged by the magnitude of the investment they have made in acquiring those weapons, and by the sacrifices they have made in other areas so they could make that massive investment.

Consider what it would mean, therefore, if we discover that the Soviets have been investing in military power each year a stunning 40 to 50 percent of their Gross National Product—compared with a U.S. expenditure of 5.8 percent of our GNP. Also, only 30 percent of Soviet military expenditures are personnel-related, whereas 55.7 percent of ours goes into pay and allowances for personnel. If a nation is spending from 40 to 50 percent of its GNP on military power, it is at war—all-out war, even if it is not actually launching any missiles. At the height of World War II spending, when we had nearly 15 million men under arms, and the largest Army, Navy, and Air Force the world had ever known, we were spending only 43 to 48 percent of our GNP on military power. And we had to ship all ammunition, supplies, food, arms and equipment overseas. That gives us an idea of the magnitude, measured in military power, of what can be produced by devoting anything like half of a great nation's GNP to military power.

For obvious reasons, the Soviets keep secret both the absolute expenditures and the percentage of GNP they devote to military power, and especially to strategic power. To make their secrecy even more difficult to penetrate, they put out cover figures of admitted military expenditures. The International Institute for Strategic Studies (a prestigious pro-arms-control, pro-SALT organization) offers its own guesstimate. Working through a complex formula in which the lack of certainty is equalled by the excess of obfuscation, it comes up with a range of from $87.2 to $90.6 billion. This is not exactly a piddling sum for a nation with a mere $550 billion GNP for 1972.[14] Actually, however, estimating the Soviet GNP requires dealing with so many factors suppressed by the Kremlin that the IISS and other agencies with a reputation to protect refuse to attempt it, and deal instead with NMT (Net Material Product), which also involves hundreds of enigmas.

The unilateral-disarmament intellectual community in the United States protects Soviet secrecy as if it were vital to U.S. national security. Every detail gathered by U.S. intelligence which would assist pro-Americans to figure out what the Kremlin is spending on its massive buildup of weapons is classified Top Secret. After all, their purposes merge. Both the Politburo in Moscow and the unilateralists in the United States are acting in concert to conceal from the American people information which would reveal the magnitude of the Soviet threat to U.S. survival. Dr. Edward Teller gave an eloquent denunciation of the U.S. government's policy of "keeping Russian secrets" before the Senate Foreign Relations Committee at its SALT I Hearings:

Now let me come to the last point and that is the role of research. It is research, it is technology, it is excellence in these fields which made of the United States the strongest country in the world. Today research on defense subjects is considered a dirty word on our university campuses. Research on any technical subject is looked down upon. Even respect for pure science is declining in our institutions of higher learning.

By contrast, the Russians have established a splendid institution, in Siberia, in Novosibersk, Academegorodok, the academic city which has been written up by Newsweek in the last issue. It is a place where people of privilege live in Russia, and this privilege includes an unheard-of privilege, for Russians, some free speech.

It is the greatest research and educational institution in the world. But it is only one of the tips of the Russian research iceberg whose mass is somewhere between the outskirts of Moscow and the Altai mountains. Again it is secrecy, the keeping of Russian secrets, which happens to be imposed on me by the United States government, which prevents me from describing to you this tremendous Russian research effort which *outstrips us and which is apt to insure Russian domination or at best a "Russian peace" for the world.*

I would like to become a little more specific about research because unless I do so I do not think you will fully understand what I am talking about. At the same time, *secrecy unfortunately prohibits me from giving you real details.*[15]

Dr. Teller's courageous attempt to warn us of the magnitude of the Soviet R&D program and the prestige of science in the U.S.S.R., coupled with its enormous budgets, meshes with the documentation we have considered earlier to the effect that (in terms of dollar equivalents, as distinct from artificial exchange rates) Soviet expenditures for "science" amounted to "something over $30 billion" in 1972, and are expanding at the rate of about 8.8 percent annually. Ambassador Foy D. Kohler stated:

Thus, and without taking into account the added expenditures of a direct military category, the Soviet Union will be spending more on "science" in the year 1972 than the total cost to the U.S. of the Apollo moon-landing program from its inception in 1961 to the present.[16]

Ambassador Kohler explains further that, separated from the "science" budget, there are additional expenditures "for military scientific research establishments," and therefore the open allocation to "science" can by no means be considered a "civilian" allocation "since much of it is directly related to military R&D and most of the remainder contributes to the development of the overall industrial power base of the country."

With their established 8.8 percent annual increase, it would appear that the Soviets will spend on the order of $38 billion during 1974, plus inestimable additions which go directly into military R&D. On our side, we have requested for FY 1975 some $8.4 billion, but $500 million of that is admittedly for inflation, from which the Soviets do not suffer. It is small wonder that they come up with technological breakthroughs which enable them to increase the throw-weight of their advanced ICBMs by a factor of up to five. So far as we can discover, the United States is not even attempting to duplicate that technological accomplishment.

With this information about the efforts of the unilateral-disarmament intellectuals—acting through the U.S. government—to hide from the American people the magnitude of Soviet expenditures on science and military R&D, we can make a reasonable estimate of the degree of secrecy they impose on the size of the Soviet military budget as a whole. General Creighton W. Abrams, Army Chief of Staff, made an almost bold attempt to reveal some of the truth. His exposé had to be subtle because of his official position, but it is highly suggestive:

The Soviet government claims to be spending about nine percent of their state budget on defense. But that figure is one of those artificial numbers that comes from a controlled economy and a currency of no clearly established value. *The actual cost to the people could well be up to three or even five times that.* We are not exactly sure, and we don't need to worry about precision. All we need to know is, if they see a requirement for more military spending, they spend—and the people pay....

The Soviet Army is equipped with weapons and systems which have sophisticated capabilities, the best that their modern technology can provide. I can tell you with confidence that *when they build a new piece of equipment, their cost-effectiveness analysis starts and ends with effectiveness.* They are not simply turning out a high volume of cheap equipment. Conclusions I have read recently about "proliferation over sophistication" in the recent Mideast war have been based on uninformed observations.

It is not proliferation *over* sophistication but proliferation *and* sophistication that the Soviet Union is bringing to bear.[17]

General Abrams also estimated that the Soviets, in stating the amounts they spend on military aid, understated their real cost by a factor of three. He observed that the Communist Party of the Soviet Union exerts direct influence on the government, and that "the party has traditionally been oriented toward military strength"; and that when the party declares that a military need exists, the government responds and

The people pay the cost. And that cost is *horrendous* in relation to what we pay for military strength. [Emphasis in original.]

Concerning Soviet power, General Abrams observes:

The threat is not gossamer—it is steel. Look at the hard facts: the Soviet Union within the past decade has increased its force to more than 165 divisions, an increase of about 10 percent. That's a *fact.* The number of men in their ground forces is greater by about 20 percent than a decade ago. *That's* a fact, too.

From all aspects, therefore, it becomes evident that Soviet spending on military power must be massively greater than that of the United States, on conventional as well as strategic nuclear power—notwithstanding the fact that our annual GNP exceeds theirs by $680 billion (U.S. = $1.2 trillion; U.S.S.R. = $550 billion).[18]

Thus, the magnitude of national effort which the Soviets have been assigning to military power makes it inherently improbable that the Kremlin would sincerely negotiate a massive reduction of strategic offensive weapons to bring them down to parity with the United States (which is the essence of the Jackson proposal), or that Kissinger can secure from the Soviets in the SALT II negotiations anything other than a demand for the strategic surrender of the United States. If they have been devoting anything like 40 percent of their GNP to attaining decisive superiority in both nuclear and conventional military power, they have been running a wartime economy.

McNamara and his cohorts could hardly have gotten away with decimating the in-being strategic power of the United States and blocking all new systems from development if the American people had realized that the Communist Party of the Soviet Union was preempting 40 to 50 percent of the Soviet GNP to attain strategic supremacy, and hence a first-strike capability, against the United States. Therefore, it was essential to keep the American people fooled. If the true facts had not been so successfully suppressed, apathy about our national survival would long since have departed. It would have been so easy to hold the first place in the technological competition. All we needed to do was *not* to default. All along, the Soviets have been tottering on the thin edge of national bankruptcy. All we needed to do was to give them a slight push, say, with an additional five percent of our own GNP, and the real arms race would have buried them.

Control over U.S. intelligence dealing with Soviet military budgets was so pervasive and successful in this country that the big breakthrough came from some of the heroic dissidents in Russia. Datelined out of Moscow on April 21, 1973, by the *Washington Post* Service, the news story preserved the anonymity of the two Leningrad economists who had prepared a 28-page study on Soviet defense spending, but revealed their conclusions and much of the methodology used in their analysis. The real defense expenditures for 1968 were not, they reasoned, the official figures of 17.9 billion rubles (which had been released for five consecutive years), but 80 billion rubles, or between 40 and 50 percent of the Gross National Product. According to the realistic evaluation rate used in the study cited above by the Center for Advanced International Studies, the actual buying power in the Soviet Union of one ruble, in the area of technology and defense, is slightly more than $2. (They equate 14.4 billion rubles with something over $30 billion.) On this basis, the Soviets are spending on the order of $160 billion on defense.

Looking at it from another angle, the officially admitted expenditures in 1969 amounted to 17.9 billion rubles, which equals about $24 billion at the official exchange rate. The two dissident economists, however, concluded that the actual defense spending amounted to four or five times that much. The figure of 80 billion rubles did not include capital investment in the defense industry; and in that year, 31 billion rubles were invested in heavy industry. Nor did it include the segments of the open appropriations or "science" directly related to R&D. Official Western estimates put the Soviet GNP at around $500 billion a year then, but the dissident critics contended that the actual figure was only half that much.

Corroborating this underground study was the figure of 40 percent used by Andrei Sakharov in an open letter to Brezhnev in 1972. Sakharov, the great nuclear physicist and father of the Soviet H-bomb, had occupied high and confidential positions in the Soviet defense hierarchy before he became a political dissenter. Here is a combination excerpt-summary of a syndicated column by Joseph Alsop which identifies the authors of the originally anonymous underground study and succinctly tells how long Americans have been deceived on this vital matter:

Meanwhile, there is growing worry in the inner corridors of power in the government, for another reason strongly bearing on the U.S. defense problem. In brief, it seems more and more likely that we have been fooling ourselves blind, and for years on end, about the scope, intensity, and general success of the Soviet defense effort.

This is a most explosive subject, simply because the U.S. government has perfect regiments of analysts, all engaged in measuring the Soviet defense effort. These are the people who have mastered the game irreverently known, inside the intelligence community, as "how many rubles can dance on the head of a pin?" *They have a strong vested interest in not being proved dead wrong.*

The current official theory, for instance, is that Soviet defense investment annually consumes about nine percent of the Soviet Gross National Product. *If this theory is true, of course, the Soviet-American balance of power cannot be changing radically;* and there is not much to worry about. The only trouble is that evidence has been steadily accumulating that *this comforting official theory is quite untrue.*

Yet there is this already-noted vested interest of the analysts who devised the theory, which makes the real truth mighty hard to come by. The vested interest was dramatically, almost comically, demonstrated some time ago, when two Leningrad economists, Alexander Gol'tsov and Sergei Ozerov, produced a "Samizdat" [underground-dissent] study entitled "Distribution of the National Income of the U.S.S.R."

This underground document showed that the Soviet defense spending in the year 1971 had consumed between 41 and 51 percent of the total national income. It was therefore violently at variance with the results obtained by the U.S. official analysts. You might have supposed that such a Soviet study would have caused the most laborious, cold-blooded reexamination of the prevailing view here.

After all, if Gol'tsov and Ozerov were right, this would provide an instant answer to an otherwise inexplicable, really monstrous mystery. The mystery, of course, is the miserable condition of the Soviet civilian economy, despite the known size of the Soviet GNP. If military costs eat up 40 to 50 percent of all you produce—or in this case, of your national income—the civilian side of the economy is bound to suffer from acute starvation.

In addition, the brave academician, Andrei Sakharov, himself lived in the corridors of Soviet power before he became a dissident. He has publicly explained the lamentable state of the Soviet civilian economy on just the lines above-given. He has further used the figure of 40 percent of GNP for annual Soviet direct, indirect and hidden outlays of military power.

Yet what happened when the Gol'tsov-Ozerov paper was carried out of Russia and academician Sakharov broadly confirmed that paper? On all sides the "methodology" of the Soviet economists was denounced. The confirmation offered by Sakharov was brushed aside. The U.S. government analysts in sum fought hard and successfully to defend the U.S. official figures for which they were responsible.[19]

All the purported "mistakes" made by our intelligence community have supported the Kissinger theories. The less the Soviets were estimated to be spending on the buildup of massive offensive strategic forces, the more we could trust them in SALT negotiations and agreements. One such intelligence "mistake" leads to others. If the analysts underestimate Soviet defense spending by a factor of five, then quite naturally they underestimate also the magnitude of Soviet weapons programs. Thus, naturally, Schlesinger viewed the Soviet programs for advanced ICBMs and SLBMs to be "far more comprehensive [at the time of his FY 1975 DOD Report] *than estimated even a year ago.*"[20]

Highly authoritative scholarly confirmation of the consistency of U.S. official underestimation of Soviet deployment of strategic weapons systems surfaced in May 1974 in the journal *Foreign Policy,* in an article by Albert Wohlstetter of the University of Chicago, a recognized leader in the nuclear strategy field since the late 1950s. Using newly declassified figures, he blasted the fraudulent assertion (by unilateral-disarmament-minded critics of the Defense Department) that the Pentagon systematically inflates estimates of Soviet programs to get approval for new weapons of its own. To the contrary, Wohlstetter demonstrates that even the highest Pentagon figures were too low in 42 of 51 cases. According to a *Los Angeles Times* Service article by Rudy Abramson, "Wohlstetter said that during the 1960s the United States' highest estimates were too low 9 of 11 times on ICBMs, 12 of 15 times on submarine-launched missiles, 12 of 14 times on heavy bombers, and 9 of 11 times on medium bombers."[21]

Many hitherto baffling mysteries are solved by finally learning the truth about Soviet defense expenditures. Why should a great power with nine million square miles of territory and 250 million people, plus tremendous natural resources, have to seek a $100 million credit from Japan, which has 142,812 square miles of territory, a population of 100 million, and very few natural resources? Why should the Soviets so desperately need a loan from the U.S. Export-Import Bank to finance a giant fertilizer plant, complete with facilities, railroad tank cars, and a 1,200-mile pipeline? Why did the Soviets need to be so crafty about negotiating a $750 million loan for grain and be so secretive about placing orders for grain at bargain prices? They need to pick up credits in $100 million increments, or whatever they can get, because they are spending their financial resources on military power to attain a first-strike capability.

Why would the U.S. Export-Import Bank lend the Soviets money (at half the interest rates ordinary Americans must pay) in order to facilitate the Soviets' spending $42 billion to modernize their already fabulously expensive ICBM force, or $30 billion to replace all their SS-11s with SS-19s, or $12 to $15 billion to replace their SS-9s with SS-18s? Because Richard Nixon ordered the Export-Import Bank to do exactly that. In a letter to Bank Chairman William J. Casey on May 20, 1974, President Nixon explained that the $180 million fertilizer loan

> makes exactly the kind of contribution to the national interest which I had envisioned when I made the determination on October 18, 1972, that it is in the national interest for the Export-Import bank to finance U.S. exports to the Soviet Union.[22]

The desperate Soviet need for credits, food, trade, and civilian technology from the West, as well as the exhausted state of their own civilian economy, testifies to the magnitude of their investment in military power. It is also significant that, so far as military power is concerned, the Soviets are doing everything at once: strategic nuclear and conventional; land, sea, and air. In every area, it is a case of proliferation *and* sophistication. They maintain 165 divisions to our 13-1/3. They have 10,000 air defense SAM launchers to our zero. They have 3,000 fighter-interceptor aircraft to our 500 obsolete types. They are building eight Extended-Delta-type missile-launching submarines a year, complete with super-intercontinental-range SLBMs. They are adding powerful new naval vessels to a fleet that already outstrips ours. They build battle tanks by the thousand, all more modern than our production of about 300 a year. They are developing two new types of ABM launchers and interceptor missiles. For their ICBM force of more than 1,600, they are presently deploying new warheads with five to eight MIRVs of from one to two megatons each.

Having exhausted their industry and agriculture in order to spend 40 to 50 percent of their GNP on military power, is it rational to expect that they will sincerely negotiate to throw it all away in SALT II?

It is highly possible that Senator Jackson made his "bold and imaginative" arms reduction proposal just to demonstrate how little chance there is of sincere negotiations by the Soviets to scrap half of their so-dearly-bought strategic power to come down to our level.

But although the Jackson proposal may not be dangerous in his hands, it could be nationally suicidal in Kissinger's hands. It sounds so eminently desirable that Americans of all shades of opinion would demand it. It would be quite clever of Kissinger and Brezhnev to pick up Jackson's bold and imaginative ball and run with it. They know that it would be neither inspectable nor enforceable, but it could keep the negotiations riding on American euphoria for years—until the end of the United States as a free nation. No matter what formula is devised for SALT II, we cannot expect the Soviets to give up the fruits of their so-costly strategic superiority.

If Kissinger had been consciously and deliberately acting on behalf of the Soviet Union, could he have promoted the Kremlin's interests any more effectively? Could he have weakened our strategic defense capability any more effectively? Have his SALT I agreements and related unilateral U.S. disarmament commitments made the United States vulnerable to a Soviet demand for our strategic surrender? Have his SALT I agreements and related policies destroyed the basis for the security and stability of the free world?

Although it is impossible to prove conclusively *why* Henry Kissinger has done the things he has, exactly what he has done can be established as facts, supported by evidence, and authoritatively documented. Our strategic surrender is being tendered now, and the Kremlin is already acting on it. Every additional month frittered away in SALT II negotiations brings us perilously closer to the point of no return. Kissinger has thrown away six years of lead-time in which the power of our strategic deterrent could have been rebuilt. The essential lead-time will have run against us irreversibly by 1977.

As late as his press conference on April 26, 1974, in the International Conference Room at the State Department, Henry Kissinger was still asserting that there were no concessions in SALT I, and that the SALT I agreements were and are highly advantageous to the United States. But, as we have seen, Defense Secretary James Schlesinger has conceded that there were concessions to the Soviets in SALT I, and that the Soviets are indeed exploiting them. He put it this way:

> As far as we can judge, moreover, the Soviets now seem determined to exploit the asymmetries in ICBMs, SLBMs, and payload *we conceded to them at Moscow*.[23]

Two additional aspects of Kissinger's character and performance begin to emerge, and each bears critically on whether the United States and Henry Kissinger can coexist, or whether the former will fall from power unless the latter is removed from power. The first is Kissinger's willingness to cover up Soviet actions which threaten U.S. survival, and the second is his use of a brilliantly contrived technique for carrying along members of the SALT delegation and staff.

Kissinger sold Congress the SALT I Interim Agreement by assuring them that the most critical U.S. objective—a safeguard against the further buildup of Soviet Minuteman-killing capabilities by the sub-

733

stitution of additional heavy missiles in the course of "modernizing" existing light missiles—had been achieved. At Dr. Kissinger's White House briefing for the five congressional committees on June 15, 1972, he made this flat statement:

> The agreement specifically permits the modernization of weapons. There are, however, a number of safeguards. First, there is the safeguard that *no missile larger than the heaviest light missile that now exists can be substituted.*

If there is such a safeguard in the agreement, then the Soviet Union is in open and notorious violation by their deployment of their new SS-17s and SS-19s. Both these series of new Soviet ICBMs have three to five times the throw-weight of the SS-11, which was the heaviest light missile existing at the time of the SALT I agreement in May 1972. It would, therefore, be impossible for them not to be "larger" than the SS-11.

But we have heard nothing from Kissinger about the Soviets' violating the SALT I agreement. He counts, of course, on the public's and Congress' forgetting that he claimed there is a safeguard against substitution of heavies for lights in the agreement.

However, he is correct in not accusing the Soviets of violating the agreement, because there is no such provision either in the agreement or in any of the bilateral Agreed Interpretations or Common Understandings which can be considered authoritative interpretations of the Interim Agreement. The fact is that Kissinger was lying about it, and deliberately assuring the congressional committees that there was no danger, when there is. We say *deliberately* because, so far as the United States is concerned, he was the architect of SALT I, and all the major decisions were his alone.

How could Kissinger have persuaded the U.S. SALT delegation and staff members to go along with such an arrangement when the agreement specifically permits the Soviets to modernize and replace both missiles and launchers, and when the Soviets expressly and continuously refused to agree to a definition of a heavy missile? They all know that, in negotiating an agreement on which "national survival depends,"[24] they had a duty to their country to insist on adequate safeguards against substitution of new heavy Soviet missiles for existing light ones. But Kissinger was able to conjure up a gambit to salve their consciences. Only a few hours before the signing of the SALT I agreements, he had this exquisitely slick document drawn up:

> The following Noteworthy Unilateral Statements were made during the negotiations by the United States Delegation:
> ... D. "Heavy" ICBMs
> The U.S. Delegation made the following statement on May 26, 1972: "The U.S. Delegation regrets that the Soviet Delegation has not been

willing to agree on a common definition of a heavy missile. Under these circumstances, the U.S. Delegation believes it necessary to state the following: *The United States would consider any ICBM having a volume significantly greater than that of the largest light ICBM now operational on either side to be a heavy ICBM. The U.S. proceeds on the premise that the Soviet side will give due account to this consideration.*

Of course, all U.S. staff members know that a "unilateral statement," regardless of how "noteworthy" it might be considered by the side making it, is not legally binding on the other side. But they convinced themselves that this would constitute a solemn warning to the Soviets that, if they violate our definition, the United States might denounce both the ABM Treaty and the Interim Agreement, and, in addition, the Soviets might lose the benefits of trade and technology, of wheat and credits, and of access to U.S. space secrets that are in the SALT I package. The U.S. representatives and staff members were given assurance that such a "violation" of our unilateral statement by the Soviets would result in a U.S. withdrawal from the SALT I agreements. Here is the evidence of this assurance from the Kissinger-endorsed account in John Newhouse's *Cold Dawn:*

> The Americans fared little better [than in the issue of no restrictions on mobile missiles] in dealing with missile size, an issue that contained two persistent difficulties: silo modification and the famous sublimit on very large missiles. The Soviets did agree to embellish the restriction on "significantly increasing" silo dimensions by specifying that any such increase would not exceed 10 to 15 percent. They were not conceding much. A missile of far greater power than any other could be placed in SS-9 silos increased by 15 percent.
>
> As for the sublimit, language worked out in Helsinki *probably* assures adequate protection against any increase in missiles of the SS-9 class; but it is nevertheless a bit vague and incomplete, *lacking, for example, a definition of what constitutes a heavy missile.* The Soviets were determined to keep it that way. And they did.
>
> *Still, any violation of the spirit of this language, let alone the letter, would probably oblige the United States to withdraw from the agreements.* Moscow understands that.[25]

So now what happens when the Soviets begin to "violate" the U.S. Noteworthy Unilateral Statement? Kissinger acts as if nothing has happened to disturb the new relationship of great trust with the Soviets and he insisted on continuing the SALT II negotiations and taking President Nixon to Moscow for the June 1974 Summit. Kissinger has shifted his position from claiming that the heavy missile definition was in the Noteworthy Unilateral Statement. Another explanation of the seriousness of the Soviet "violation" of our unilateral definition of heavy missile was presented by Dr. Kissinger's closest American friend in Washington, Joseph Alsop:

. . . the United States unilaterally but formally registered the fact that this country would regard any large increase in missile weight in the Soviet silos as *a serious breach of the spirit of the SALT agreement.*

That breach of SALT has now occurred. The new generation of Soviet missiles, including no less than four types of intercontinental missiles of wholly novel design, have vastly greater throw-weight than the existing missiles now in the silos. By no accident, the new missiles were carefully designed to provide this large added weight—and therefore added power—while fitting into the old silos after certain interior silo modifications.

In addition, we have now lost the main advantage that was supposed to compensate for the huge superiority in silo numbers allowed the Soviets in SALT. This advantage was the American MIRV. The new generation of Soviet missiles are all MIRVed—but the Soviet multiple warheads are in the megaton range whereas our multiple warheads are only in the kiloton range.

It is not surprising then, that a recent meeting of the so-called SALT Verification Panel produced a near-confession of policy bankruptcy. Secretary of State Henry Kissinger asked, in effect, "Where do we go from here in the new SALT negotiations?" No answer at all came from any of the others present. . . .

Meanwhile, it is worth examining the real nature of the huge advantage the Soviets stand to gain by just that step which we warned we should consider a violation of the spirit of SALT. Sen. Henry M. Jackson of Washington, in a most able speech on the subject, has defined the nature of this new Soviet advantage as a "spectacularly increased throw-weight demonstrated in their recent tests."

Throw-weight, of course, is the total weight of warhead and warhead-attached apparatus that a missile can throw. This in turn goes far to define the killing power of the missile, in just the way that the caliber of a cannon largely defines a cannon's killing power.[26]

In the face of all this, Kissinger came out with this remark on April 26, 1974:

Therefore, it is not helpful to us to talk ourselves into a state of mind in which we are strategically inferior.[27]

In the light of all the evidence, we should indeed worry about the state of the mind—and conscience—of the one who does not recognize the reality of the nearly decisive strategic inferiority imposed on the United States and frozen with SALT.

Why are the members of the SALT delegation and U.S. staff so reluctant to tell the American people what has happened? They all realized they should never have gone along with a SALT I agreement purportedly restraining offensive weapons without a positive safeguard against a Soviet buildup of 95-percent-kill capability against the U.S. Minuteman force—and they all know that an agreed specific definition of "heavy missile" was essential to such a safeguard. But having accepted Kissinger's gambit of the Noteworthy Unilateral Statement, they have permitted Kissinger to involve them as co-betrayers of U.S. national security; and that involvement keeps them silent. They are in no position to attack their own actions. Many of them would not have gone along with the totally illusory nature of the critical SALT I concession on "heavies" except for the promise that the United States would withdraw; but, when the promise was not honored, they were too deeply implicated in SALT, so they were dragged along with Kissinger's coverup for the Soviets and his determination to proceed with SALT II negotiations as though everything were according to plan.

Schlesinger invented his own technique for contributing to the coverup for the Soviets. According to the SALT I agreements and the Noteworthy Unilateral Statement, there are only two classes of ICBMs: light and heavy. Any ICBM having a volume significantly greater than that of the largest existing light ICBM operational, as of the SALT I signing, is a "heavy ICBM." Under SALT I, the parties agreed that anything more than 10 to 15 percent greater is "significantly greater." We know that the SS-17s and SS-19s have throw-weight 300 to 500 percent greater than the existing SS-11 light ICBMs. So, by the U.S. definition, the SS-17s and SS-19s are "heavy ICBMs." But James Schlesinger tries to invent a new category of missile, a classification wholly inconsistent with the official U.S. definition of ICBMs. In his DOD Report he describes "the SS-X-17 and the SS-X-19, two *medium liquid-fueled missiles with three to five times the throw-weight of the early model SS-11.*"[28]

In addition to such attempts to deceive the American people about Soviet weapons advances, Defense Secretary Schlesinger has also demonstrated considerable talent for sending surrender signals to the Kremlin. One spectacular example of this was revealed in his FY 1975 Defense Department Report:

—*Development of plans for relocation of the population in a crisis. As a first step in crisis relocation planning we are developing allocation schemes to permit the population from some 250 of our urbanized areas to be assigned to appropriate host areas. The primary end product of this first step is expected to be the publication of information materials for distribution to the public in periods of severe crisis. These publications would advise the public "where to go and what to do" should relocation be implemented. . . .*[29]

One could imagine the 50 million inhabitants of our 10 largest metropolitan areas being advised to go to Australia by the first available Boeing 747 and to stay until termination of the crisis. As a practical matter, they would have as much realistic chance of getting to Australia as they would of getting to "appropriate host areas"—which would have to be cities or towns smaller than the smallest of our 250 largest urban areas. The largest city ranking below those is Great Falls, Montana, with a population of 81,804; so we may assume it would be assigned as "host area" for the 10 million people from the New York metropolitan area. There are only 13 other smaller towns that are large enough to rate classification as Standard Metropolitan Statistical Areas (SMSAs) in the U.S. Census, and they drop very rapidly in population down to 55,000.

Another way of demonstrating the utterly ridiculous character of the Schlesinger-proposed "relocation schemes" is that about 120 million Americans live in those first 250 cities, and only about 10 million live in the next 250 cities. But the absolute giveaway of the Schlesinger scheme is that it is estimated to cost only a fraction of an appropriation of $37 million. This means that there could be no effective preparation made for transporting, feeding, sheltering, providing water and sanitary facilities for those 120 million urban Americans. Adequate advance preparations and food stockpiling, shelters, and living facilities would cost, according to Russian and Chinese experience, scores of billions.

Because the Communist leaders have far more regard for their slave-populations, their ultimate power bases, both Russia and China have elaborate, effective, and highly expensive civil defense systems to permit the strategic evacuation of all their large cities, and many of moderate size. To establish these evacuation systems required years of time, and scores of billions of dollars in value of labor, materials, and construction equipment. An effective system simply cannot be established on the cheap or on the quick. Therefore, the Schlesinger scheme is not at all for the same purposes as the two Communist systems. What, then, is its real purpose?

The clue is found in Herman Kahn's great work *On Thermonuclear War*, which is such a gold mine of expertise to expose the frauds of the unilateral-disarmament intellectuals.

> Any power that can evacuate a high percentage of its urban population to protection is in a much better position to bargain than one which cannot do this. There is an enormous difference in the bargaining ability of a country which can, for example, put its people in a place of safety in 24 to 48 hours, and one which cannot. If it is hard for the reader to visualize this, just let him imagine a situation where the Soviets have done exactly that and we have not. Then let him ask himself how he thinks we would come out at a subsequent bargaining table. . . . The Soviets seem to be preparing a program of civil defense which will enable them to complete such an evacuation. They have not only had extensive training programs, but they seem to have the physical capability, in terms of roads and truck transportation to evacuate almost all of their cities in about eight hours or so. . . .
>
> There is a possibility, of course, that rather than make people bolder, the evacuation may so frighten everybody that enormous pressure will be brought to bear to preserve the peace at any price. The last-minute (and obviously unplanned) preparations in London and Paris during the Munich Conference of 1938 seem to have had this effect. . . .[30]

738

In the Schlesinger scheme, actual preparations are not to be made, nor are masses of people to be trained. Printed material is to be stockpiled for convenient distribution to the public "in periods of severe crisis." The only public reaction to be expected is mass panic in fear of a nuclear attack and mass pressure on the government, in Kahn's words, "to preserve the peace at any price"; that is, for the United States to surrender to the Soviet Union on demand.

This, of course, is the exact culmination of the unilateral disarmament plan which has been clandestinely carried out against the American people by the Nitze-McNamara-Gilpatric-Kissinger cabal since 1961. It signals loud and clear to the Kremlin that U.S. surrender will be tendered with certainty and in good time.

Schlesinger's plan for panicking American cities did not exhaust his schemes for sending surrender signals to the Politburo in Moscow, or for setting up the U.S. urban population as helpless hostages to the Russians or even the Communist Cubans. Here is how he put it in his 'FY 1975 DOD Report:

> Since we cannot defend our cities against strategic missiles, there is nothing to be gained by trying to defend them against a relatively small force of Soviet bombers. . . .
>
> Accordingly we now propose to phase out all of the strategic Nike-Hercules batteries (which are located around nine urban areas) and eventually reduce the interceptor force to 12 squadrons—six active and six Air National Guard (ANG). The Nike-Hercules batteries and the fire coordination centers will be phased out by the end of FY 1975. Also in FY 1975, the active interceptor force will be reduced to six F-106 squadrons, and two F-106 squadrons will be added to the Air National Guard, for a total of six F-106 ANG squadrons. . . .
>
> A continental U.S. air defense system structured primarily for peacetime surveillance would not require an AWACS force, the principal purpose of which is to provide a survivable means of control of aircraft in a nuclear war environment.[31]

Unfortunately, when this statement was presented by Defense Secretary Schlesinger to congressional committees, no one asked the questions which would have exposed this particular Schlesinger scheme, such as:

> Dr. Schlesinger, is not the Soviet Union bound by the same SALT I ABM Treaty which precludes us from defending our cities against strategic missiles, so that they can defend only Moscow against U.S. missiles?
>
> Do the Soviets take the same position that you do—that "there is nothing to be gained from attempting to defend" their cities against bombers? Or is it not a fact that they go to the great expense of providing some 10,000 strategic air defense missile launchers (SAM launchers) instead of the zero you are providing for the American people, and some 3,000 fighter-interceptor aircraft, many of which are mach 3, instead of the fewer than 500 active interceptors (none of which is mach 3) that you are providing for the American people?

What's the answer, Dr. Schlesinger? Are the Russians insane to be spending so many billions of rubles on worthless defense items, or are you deliberately supporting a position which will leave the American people vulnerable to incineration by even the smallest modern bomber force?

As a practical matter, the Schlesinger no-defense-against-bombers posture offers us up to the Soviets as human sacrifices by the scores of millions. Without launching a single nuclear missile, a force of 200 Soviet Backfire bombers could with high confidence destroy the 100 largest U.S. cities including 50 percent of our population. If Moscow gave Havana as few as 20 Backfire bombers with only one H-bomb each, that force of insignificant numbers could with high confidence destroy the 10 largest U.S. cities and about 50 million Americans. They would not be met by any air defense missiles, and there would be insufficient warning and control to vector our six active-duty interceptor squadrons against Backfire bombers—and they could not catch them anyway.

Aside from the possibilities of actual destruction of millions of Americans that the Schlesinger no-defense scheme opens up, it will give the Soviets an intriguing and dramatic option whereby they could obtain our surrender not only without launching a single nuclear missile, but also without dropping a single nuclear bomb. The Kremlin could send a flight of 200 Backfire bombers to overfly New York, Boston, Newark, Philadelphia, Baltimore, Washington, Pittsburgh, Chicago, Detroit, Cleveland, St. Louis, Atlanta, Minneapolis-St. Paul, Richmond, and any other cities convenient to a plan of concentrating on areas of dense population. The flight would be timed to arrive over the largest centers during late-afternoon rush hours. No bombs would be dropped, but the Backfires would have them on board, and the Moscow Hot Line would warn the White House that, if any attempt were made to interfere with the Soviet overflight, several cities would be hit as an example. The Backfire bombers are large and impressive, and they fly at mach 2.5.

The force of 200 would be broken up into flights of 10, and they would sweep in low over our great cities at, say, 10-minute intervals; each flight would make two sweeps over each city. Sonic booms would break windows by the thousands. Motorists on the freeways and streets would abandon their cars, attempting to find shelter from what they would be convinced was a bombing attack. The overall result would be panic. No wheels would be moving because of the massive traffic jams everywhere. Telephone systems would be jammed by the volume of calls from frightened people trying to find out where to go and what to do. Of course, no one could go anywhere or do anything—except to pressure the government to surrender.

Then, the Kremlin could come up on the Hot Line to the White House with the demand to surrender. The threatened consequences of non-compliance would be a return of the Backfire bombers, this time to drop their 50-megaton bombs on our 100 largest cities. The bomber threat would be backed up by a missile threat, of course—that is, a combined disarming strike against our Minuteman missiles and our population. The bombers could refuel in Cuba, protected from a U.S. attack by the threat to unleash Soviet missiles from the U.S.S.R. and from submarines close in to our coasts.

This is just one way the Soviets could exploit our zero-air-defense posture. The Schlesinger zero-air-defense program bears the Kissinger indicia in the unilateralist tradition of Robert McNamara and the preemptive-surrender program of Paul Nitze. Since Kissinger took over the National Security Council in January 1969, all his major programs relating to the strategic posture of the United States have had this major feature in common: the advancement of acquisition by the Soviet Union of a first-strike capability against the United States. This is true even with the matter of no defense against bombers.

Soviet strategists have a compulsion toward redundancy of forces in setting up a mission. In planning an attack against U.S. Minuteman missiles, the Soviets might want to retain a thousand ICBMs in reserve —to back up the initial disarming strike in case destruction were not total enough, to threaten U.S. cities in a process of poststrike nuclear blackmail, or to have reserve against the Red Chinese attempting to cash in on a U.S.S.R.-U.S. exchange. Those 1,000 reserve missiles would no longer be required, however, with the Kissinger-Schlesinger-guaranteed free ride for their bomber force. The Kissinger-Schlesinger zero-air-defense may thus advance the Soviet timetable by the months or even a couple of years that it would take to produce the missiles they have scheduled for reserve.

The zero-air-defense free ride for Soviet bombers also gives them other strategic advantages of major importance. It drastically degrades the credibility and effectiveness of the Kissinger-Schlesinger strategy of the U.S. "pause" after a Soviet nuclear attack. This strategy calls for the "withholding" of surviving U.S. Minuteman missiles "for an extended period of time" to serve as "an assured destruction reserve."[32] Under the Kissinger-Schlesinger strategy of "pausing" for negotiations after a Soviet strike, we would have nothing left to bargain with if our "withheld strategic missile forces" can be destroyed; so our surrender would have to be unconditional.

In order to destroy our withheld ICBMs, the Soviets would need additional missiles and a reserve of missiles as a backup if their first attempts fail. If we guarantee Soviet bombers a free ride, we free their ICBMs from this requirement and give the Kremlin strategists high confidence that their risks will not be substantial if they give that fateful launch order. After a launch at the 1,000 Minuteman missiles, the Soviets do not have any method of knowing which survived and which were destroyed. The classic method is a second salvo, targeting again all the original silo locations. But if 950 were actually destroyed by the first wave of missiles, then at least 950 warheads would be wasted on empty holes in attempting to destroy the survivors. Bombers, however, unopposed by air defense, can take a look-see at the missile fields and determine exactly which ones survived. They waste no warheads and can make repeated attacks in the same area, if necessary. Thus, the new-generation Soviet strategic bombers can do a much more effective job in destroying a U.S. reserve of withheld ICBMs than could even their superpowerful multi-MIRVed missiles.

All in all, the Kissinger-Schlesinger strategy of not defending at all against bombers (because we cannot defend against missiles on account of SALT) is making Soviet bombers such a valuable strategic asset that it will stimulate them to produce additional hundreds of Backfire mach 2+ aircraft, and to go into production of their new mach 3.2 Sukhoi type, which Senator James Buckley warns is already in development.[33]

So it is that even the very latest of the programs worked out under Henry Kissinger's czarship are just like his earliest ones six years before. They all advance the attainment by the Soviets of a first-strike capability against the United States. Each year, on the average, he has presided over the scrapping of five Polaris submarines, 80 Polaris SLBMs, and 100 Minuteman I and II ICBMs. By his SALT I ABM Treaty of May 1972 plus the Moscow Summit of '74 Protocol, he deprived the American people of all active defense against missiles. In 1974 he is depriving us of all defense against enemy bombers by destroying and dismantling what we had in the way of air defense and air warning and control systems, and by refusing to ask for new and advanced systems. He has been consistent over all his years of power in destroying the strategic offensive capabilities of the United States.

27

Buried in two sentences in President Gerald Ford's first message to Congress on August 12, 1974, was a Kissinger "plant," identified by his inimitable indicia. To the American people it merely sounded typical of what we have been led to accept as the innocuous grandiloquence of a presidential pronouncement. To the Politburo in Moscow, however, it carried a convincing answer to the question the Kremlin must have been pondering: "Can Kissinger capture Ford as totally as he captured Nixon?" Here is Kissinger's answer in President Ford's address, with its veracity attested by its staggering brashness:

> To the Soviet Union, I pledge a continuity in our commitment to the course of the past three years. To our two peoples and to all mankind, we owe a continued effort to live and, where possible, to work together in peace—for in a thermonuclear age there can be no alternative to a positive and peaceful relationship between our nations.

The official voice was that of President Ford. The words are Henry Kissinger's, and they commit the new President to adopt and continue the Kissinger-Kremlin policies. This commitment extends not only to the policies which have been allowed to surface to public knowledge, but also to the mass of policies kept submerged and secret from the American people (such as the arrogant and brutal demands by the Soviets in the SALT II negotiations that we are allowed to learn only through fragmentary "leaks").

Those Kissinger policies in operation for the "past three years" have brought the United States down to the penultimate point of strategic surrender and to the brink of the ultimate political surrender which will inexorably follow. They subject the United States to detente on Soviet terms. Their continuance until 1977—as pledged in President Ford's address—will accomplish the jointly declared Kissinger-Brezhnev objective of making that detente irreversible, and thus rendering irreversible also the progressing U.S. strategic surrender. As these policies progressively degrade the credibility of the U.S. strategic deterrent, they will also continue the degradation of the credibility of the U.S. dollar and thus feed the fires of double-digit runaway inflation in America and throughout the Free World.

Henry Kissinger has even furnished the Kremlin with realistic assurances that Ford's captivity will endure. First, Kissinger revealed in language the Soviets will understand that his psychological campaign to paralyze Ford with a fear of thermonuclear war is succeeding. Second, Kissinger has trapped Ford in an artificial world so far divorced from reality that it has expunged from his memory more than 20 years of history through which Ford himself has lived. Third, he has involved Ford—without Ford's realizing it—in a campaign to lead the American people into that same artificial world past the point of no return.

Henry Kissinger has accomplished all this by having Gerald Ford affirm, in the passage from his address quoted above, a monstrous lie masquerading as an immutable truism:

—for in a thermonuclear age there can be no alternative to a positive and peaceful relationship between our nations.

This is no mere gambit of historical revisionism. It is a projected lobotomy on our national consciousness, using as a scalpel the soul-searing dread of nuclear incineration. It seeks to blank out nearly a quarter century of evidence in the lives of all those who were born before World War II. It is a campaign of psychological warfare with the American people as targets. Most especially, it was directed against the new President in order to bind his mind and spirit with a paralysis of fear. Those few words activate the cunning and deadly trap called the "false alternatives."

It simply would not do to have the new President of the United States pledge a continuance of the Kissinger-Brezhnev policy of detente-on-Kremlin-terms on the stated ground that our only alternatives are to be "Red or dead." It would have been almost equally shocking to have had Gerald Ford invoke this slogan's more sophisticated paraphrase, that is, "the choice is between detente or nuclear war." But what Gerald Ford said does assert precisely the same thing—more subtly, but just as positively, with the same dire threat of those same false alternatives.

Why can there be "no alternative"? Because we are "in a thermonuclear age." What is the predominant threat of the thermonuclear age? Obviously, it is thermonuclear war. So our minds are driven to the compulsive conclusion that there is indeed an alternative—nuclear war; but that alternative is so horrendous that it cannot be identified in explicit terms. The only other allowed alternative is "a positive and peaceful relationship" with the Soviet Union. The kicker is that, whereas it takes only one nation to launch a nuclear attack, it requires the full cooperation of *both* nations to maintain "a positive and peaceful relationship."

In the SALT II negotiations, the Politburo imposed a price on extending Soviet cooperation. The price demanded by the Kremlin for such a relationship (usually referred to as detente) was set out in the Soviets' "21 outrageous demands" served on the U.S. delegation early in the SALT II negotiations. The most authoritative version of the Soviet demands was leaked by Paul Nitze, and they are so drastic that acceding even to any substantial part of them would amount to the strategic surrender of the United States. The Kremlin's refusal to back off from these demands gave notice to the United States that we would be granted no new substantive agreement even purporting to remedy the obvious imbalances of the SALT I Interim Agreements. This is what created the so-called "deadlock" at the Moscow Summit of '74: a deadlock deliberately contrived by the Soviets because no agreement at all would serve them better than any new agreement that they could anticipate having approved by Congress at the present time. If the United States continues "the course of the past three years," the Soviets will soon attain a first-strike capability against us.

When and if the Soviets do attain such a capability against us, but not before then, the Soviets will be able to *demand* that we sign an agreement on their terms: a SALT II or SALT III agreement that will embody the strategic surrender of the United States. At that time— and not before—our only alternative will indeed be to subject ourselves to a nuclear attack if we refuse to surrender. But Henry Kissinger, by planting those two key sentences in Gerald Ford's first message to Congress, has committed him to the proposition that *even now* our only alternatives are nuclear war *or* purchasing detente from the Soviets at whatever price they demand.

It may indeed be true that in the nuclear age there is no rational alternative to peace. But peace does not have to be *bought* from a threatening aggressor. Peace can be *enforced* against aggression by strength—that is, by military power. The honest answer to the "Red or dead" assertion is that, if we are strong enough, no power can make us either Red or dead. With U.S. strategic retaliatory capability, we can preserve both peace and freedom by deterring the aggressor from attempting to make us surrender under threat of destruction. But Kissinger seeks to deny us this alternative by pretending it does not now exist and that we are *already* down to a choice of detente on Soviet terms or nuclear war.

But this time Henry Kissinger went too far in extending the time-frame of his false alternative to the entire thermonuclear age. The nuclear age opened in 1945 with the explosion of the first atomic bomb, and the thermonuclear age opened in 1951 with the explosion of the first hydrogen bomb. Not until the SALT I Agreements were signed under Kissinger's auspices in Moscow in May 1972 did the United States have what could be described as a "positive and peaceful" relationship with the Soviet Union.

So the history of 1951 to 1972 proved—and millions of us are witnesses to it—that there *is* an alternative other than nuclear war or detente on Soviet terms. History also proves that this alternative can work successfully because it did preserve the nuclear peace for some 27 years of the nuclear age and 21 years of the thermonuclear age. Peace between the great powers was preserved by the credibility of the U.S. strategic nuclear deterrent and, as demonstrated in this book, it was also the sine qua non for the preservation of freedom, prosperity, and industrial and agricultural development. It preserved the stability of Free World governments, their currencies, and trade relationships.

Henry Kissinger's destruction of and refusal to buy strategic nuclear power cost the American people, up to 1975, perhaps on the order of a thousand billion dollars. If his policies are continued, they will probably cost us our $26 trillion country (capital value estimated at 20 times the estimated 1974 GNP), not to mention our freedom, our sacred honor, and our lives (on a selective or total genocidal basis, at the Kremlin's option). On the day Gerald Ford took office, the U.S. wholesale price index recorded "a staggering 3.7 percent rise in July—44 percent on an annual basis . . . industrial commodities also leaped higher than expected—2.7 percent."[1] Other sources equated the July rise of 3.7 in the wholesale price index "to a compound annual rate of 54.6 percent."[2] The Dow Jones industrials index, which had stood at more than 1050 three years before, plunged down below 700 within ten days of the Ford address to Congress. Fear of continued runaway double-digit inflation was universally recognized as the reason for the stunning losses in stock values. Three years earlier, before the Kissinger-Kremlin policies took effect, the U.S. Gross National Product was growing at the rate of more than seven percent a year. After three years of these policies (in the first half of 1974), the total U.S. output was, at annual rates, down 4.1 percent. Instead of growing, it was shrinking.

The net change in growth rate of our GNP, therefore, approximates 11 percent. So as not to exaggerate, round it off to an even 10 percent. In 1973 our GNP was running at the rate of $1.3 trillion. At the growth rates before the Kissinger policies took effect, we would have gained $130 billion in real wealth in 1973. American investors lost roughly $300 billion in the stock market decline during those three years. So the Kissinger policies—if a causal relationship to those losses can be established—have cost the American people on the order of $430 billion, not including the halving in real value of a trillion dollars in insurance policies and savings accounts. And a causal relationship does indeed exist.

In the South, children of the second generation after the War Between the States in impoverished households had a unique toy for consolation. Instead of play money, they had quite literally scores of thousands of dollars in genuine American currency. Thousands of southern patriots had turned in their gold for this currency in order to purchase food and war materials from abroad. The first postwar generation still treasured this paper, hoping that some day it might be redeemed. They finally learned the lesson that the monetary promises of a government which is militarily defeated and destroyed will never again be honored. When the Confederate currency was first issued, it was accepted at face value in the South. As soon as it began to appear that the industrial North was building toward a substantial military superiority, the credibility of the Confederate Government's promise to pay began to deteriorate. After several years of military buildup by the North, it became widely perceived that the North's power would soon become overwhelming, and then decisive. So Confederate currency began its slide down to nothingness. It took a wheelbarrow load to buy the grain for a loaf of bread.

The same thing is now happening to the U.S. dollar. The Kissinger-Nixon-Schlesinger policies, and now the Kissinger-Ford-Schlesinger policies, have handed to the Soviet Union a strategic military superiority which is building toward decisive power with a staggering momentum, month by month. When an enemy superpower—which for more than half a century has openly declared that its historic mission is to destroy the economic, social, and political systems of our own government—finally approaches attainment of the military power actually to fulfill its mission, a massive loss of confidence cannot be far behind. Thus it happened that in August 1974, the financial pages of metropolitan newspapers began to spread predictions of possible breakdowns in our banking system and even the collapse of our entire economic system.[3] The U.S. balance of trade dipped into the red by a massive $783 million for the month of July 1974—and this was "traced directly to last fall's four-fold increase in oil prices,"[4] which in turn can be traced directly to Kissinger's having stripped the U.S. strategic deterrent of its credibility so that the newly credible Soviet strategic umbrella could protect the Arab states in their oil blackmail of the industrial West.

Those three years of Kissinger policies (now pledged by President Ford to be continued) have wrought equal disaster for our allies in the Free World. Destruction of the credibility of the U.S. nuclear umbrella made them vulnerable to the Soviet-sponsored Arab oil embargo and fantastic price increases, and brought their currencies to a crisis of confidence, their economies to a state of near-panic, and their political systems to the verge of collapse, with France and Italy narrowly escaping Communist coalition governments.

Kissinger's capture of Gerald Ford wasn't really the overnight accomplishment it appeared to be when he planted his cataclysmic capitulation to the Kremlin in Ford's first message to Congress. Kissinger had been persistently cultivating Gerald Ford. As a 1973 account put it, Kissinger had been "making an intensive effort to educate Ford in the nuances of superpower diplomacy," and the intensive effort was stepped up "as Watergate pressures on Nixon mounted." An anonymous Kissinger aide was quoted by a national newsmagazine as saying, "Ford was getting a seminar on foreign affairs."[5] "Pugwashed" rather than "educated" would have been a more precise description of the process. Time, in its special issue on the inauguration, included this enlightening incident in describing the Ford attitude toward foreign policy shortly before he became President:

> Ford . . . also approved Nixon's overtures to Peking, but concedes that he would not have made them had he been President then.
>
> "Not with my record of 23 years' opposition to communism," he told a reporter. "But I approve of the policy, and I would hope that when the time came, I would have been flexible enough to listen to reasons advanced by a person such as Kissinger."[6]

Gerald Ford's self-styled "square" qualities have maximized his susceptibility to Kissinger's highly sophisticated obfuscation and domination. The press unanimously assured us at the time of his inauguration that the new President possessed honesty, simplicity, openness, candor, lack of guile, trustworthiness, fairness, straightforwardness, loyalty, integrity, and patriotism. He was pictured as "an unabashed lowbrow," "an extrovert" with only a "minor ego," relaxed and self-confident; a "team player," not very different from your neighbor next door; and "Mr. Clean of the Middle Class." One metropolitan daily asserted the ultimate: "Gerald Ford is Middle America."

For President Ford to keep his inaugural pledge to the nation—"God helping me, I will not let you down"—he will have to force Henry Kissinger to step down. Yet Kissinger has tremendously more going for him now than when he first captured Richard Nixon. Then, Kissinger was relatively unknown outside the Council on Foreign Relations, Pugwash, and unilateral-disarmament elites. Now he has a worldwide reputation, the mass media in hypnotized adulation, and a very special relationship with the new President. To attain power back in January 1969, Kissinger needed Nixon. Now Ford needs Kissinger—as Ford made embarrassingly clear even before he took office as President. After being personally informed by Richard Nixon of the decision to resign, the first thing Gerald Ford did was to telephone Kissinger and ask for a meeting to talk about his staying on. The meeting that afternoon lasted two hours at which, according to *Time*'s account, Ford, in his characteristically simple and direct way, told Kissinger, "I need you."[7]

It appears that Kissinger will wield much more power in the Ford Administration than he did in the Nixon Administration—incommensurably more, as James Schlesinger might phrase it. In January 1969, Kissinger was substantially alone except for a few top members of his personal staff who were more notorious for their security-risk records than distinguished for any power-base connections. His title, Assistant to the President for National Security Affairs, was an office which had generated no world-shaking powers in the past. He was outranked by Cabinet officers and his spheres of influence were circumscribed by the Secretaries of State and Defense and their massive bureaucracies. The Secretary of State, William P. Rogers, was a longtime personal and political associate of the President, and Secretary of Defense Melvin R. Laird had political power bases of his own. The CIA Director was an expert of established reputation. The most influential Assistants to the President, John D. Ehrlichman and H. R. Haldeman, were Kissinger's rivals for power and tended also to be his personal enemies.

By stunning contrast, in August 1974 when Gerald Ford took office as President, all Kissinger's rivals and all his obstacles to power had been eliminated. He had his own men in all relevant key positions; they all "owe" him. Defense Secretary Schlesinger owes Kissinger for successive appointments as AEC Chairman, CIA Director, and Secretary of Defense. Kissinger himself is not only Secretary of State but he also is the National Security Council, chairing all its committees except the one which is ex officio chaired by his subordinate. Kissinger possesses two votes in his own right in the National Security Council, plus the votes of the Secretary of Defense and the Vice President. The Central Intelligence Agency Director is William E. Colby, a Kissinger nominee in the Nixon Administration and now beholden to

Kissinger for retention in the Ford Administration; and he acts like it. Whenever the most minute proposal is made to strengthen the U.S. position in any part of the world (such as the Diego Garcia communications base in the Indian Ocean), he rushes over to the cognizant congressional committee and warns in a voice of doom that, if we do *anything*, it will "compel" the Russians to follow suit. He says the same thing about any effort to add desperately needed power to the U.S. Navy: if we do it, it will "trigger" a Soviet reaction, although the Soviets have been outbuilding us in modern combatant vessels for more than ten years and have never waited for any "triggering" action on our part.

With all these levers and leverages that Kissinger has established in the areas of foreign and defense policies, plus the structures he has created in the intelligence community that are capable of controlling *any* incumbent President, never in the history of our nation has any one man exercised such vast and pervasive power, uncheckable by constitutional balances. It is no surprise that, interviewed on West German television in July 1974, Kissinger admitted to "a sort of erotic relationship with power."[8]

During Gerald Ford's eight months as Vice President, Kissinger patiently nurtured a relationship for him with Soviet Ambassador Anatoly Dobrynin. When Nixon photographs were stripped from the walls of the White House on the morning of August 9, 1974, one of the large replacements showed Vice President Gerald Ford in conference with Dobrynin. Then on August 15, UPI, in a report on the Cyprus crisis, placed on the nationwide wires a picture of a cozy huddle of Dobrynin, Kissinger, and Ford. It was reproduced by *Newsweek* on August 26 and should have been entitled "the most powerful man in Washington, the most powerful American in Washington, and the President of the United States." Describing the resulting crisis management as "something less than a triumph" for the United States, *Newsweek* recounted it this way:

> . . . when the Cyprus crisis struck, Kissinger essentially took over. . . . While Kissinger cleared each move with the new President, Ford's essential reaction was to listen and say, "That's a good tack, Henry." . . . As one Administration aide noted, "The President went along with Kissinger this time. Henry just better make darn sure it doesn't go awry."

Of course, it didn't go awry from the standpoint of either Dobrynin or Kissinger. The Kissinger "tilt" toward Turkey drove Greece out of active military participation in NATO, and will probably deprive U.S. naval forces of the continued use of Greek ports. It will also destroy NATO's eastern flank and add nearly 1,000 miles to the distances U.S. naval vessels will have to travel to reach vital trouble spots in the strategic Middle Eastern oil producing areas. Kissinger's other accomplishment in advantaging the Soviet Navy was to put our naval forces and facilities to work to clear the Suez Canal, to pledge scores of millions of U.S. tax dollars to finance the job, and ultimately produce the result of reducing by 5/6, or some 9,000 miles each way, the travel required of Soviet naval vessels to reach the critical Gulf of Aden. If this were just an isolated instance of Kissinger damaging NATO, it might be different—but it fits perfectly the pattern of his destroy-NATO tactics documented earlier in this book.

On the afternoon Gerald Ford took office as President, he attended meetings with diplomats from some 57 different countries. To the Soviet chargé d'affaires, he marveled over the twelve-year ambassadorship of Anatoly Dobrynin in Washington. "He seems to go on and on," Ford remarked.[9]

Gerald Ford's powers of observation were working fine—much better than his powers of deduction. Apparently no warning bell in his subconscious alerted him to the fact that he had stumbled on a vitally important Soviet stratagem. It is no accident that Anatoly Dobrynin "goes on and on." Each year he becomes more valuable to the Politburo—as attested by his recent elevation to become the only nonresident member of the powerful Central Committee of the Communist Party of the Soviet Union. He not only gets to know more and more key U.S. officials better each year, but he gets to know more and more *about* each of them, and about the American people. He is ex officio head of the KGB in the United States and has at his command quite literally hundreds of its best agents. It would be naive to assume that once in a while they do not turn up an official especially vulnerable to blackmail, or who can be bought by money or women. Also, we know from the Kissinger-endorsed John Newhouse book *Cold Dawn: The Story of SALT* that Dobrynin conducted an elaborate propaganda campaign with Congress, the media, and academic circles, to bring them around to the Soviet views on the SALT negotiations. The same apparatus could serve any other Soviet plans.

Dobrynin simply is too close to Henry Kissinger personally, and has too much influence with him, for the best interests of the United States. But would Dobrynin deceive a high U.S. official? Isn't he too eager to build the structure of U.S.-U.S.S.R. peaceful relations to risk fracturing it by a deception? Consider his record. In October 1962 he participated with Soviet Foreign Minister Andrei A. Gromyko in giving a direct lie to President John F. Kennedy in their attempt to convince him that the Soviets had no strategic nuclear missiles in Cuba.

President Kennedy had the U-2 photographs in his desk drawer at the time the Dobrynin-Gromyko pair was attempting to deceive him. In his famous October 23, 1962, television and radio address to the nation warning of the Soviet nuclear missiles zeroed in on the United States from Cuba, he publicly denounced the Gromyko assurance as "false." That should have made his partner-in-lies Dobrynin persona non grata right then. Ambassadors are not supposed to participate personally in direct lies to the head of state; that just isn't done. But Dobrynin must have had the same sort of close relationship with high U.S. officials then as he has now. Despite being caught in the act of lying to the U.S. President, he was allowed "to go on and on." When President Ford begins to inquire into the matter of Dobrynin's unprecedented tenure, it should signal some thinking independent of Kissinger coaching.

On June 14, 1974, just before the opening of the Moscow Summit, Paul Hilken Nitze abruptly resigned as senior delegate on the U.S. SALT negotiating delegation. His first surprise move after his apparent démarche was to provide Senator Henry Jackson with some secret material alleging that Kissinger had entered into secret agreements covering up a 70-missile loophole in the SALT I Protocol. The question, however, was so complex that neither Senator Jackson and Nitze on the one side, nor Kissinger on the other, in a series of press conferences, could explain to media representatives what they were talking about. Probably the most concrete result was that Kissinger—initially describing the Nitze-Jackson interpretation as "absurd," "ridiculous," and "esoteric"—finally lost his cool and characterized their view as based on a "shyster interpretation." In any event, it was much ado about nearly nothing. What's a 70-missile loophole in an Interim Agreement with demonstrable loopholes for thousands of additional missiles, such as land-mobile ICBMs, and the equivalent of additional thousands by converting light missile launchers to heavy missile launchers because Kissinger allowed the Soviets to get away with their refusal to agree to a definition of a heavy missile?

Paul Nitze's second move carried real impact. In February 1974, Vice President Gerald Ford had asserted that "Secretary Kissinger is a superb negotiator."[10] (This suggests that Mr. Ford had never read the SALT I pacts or heard about the Soviet grain deal of 1972.) On July 2, 1974, Nitze presented testimony to the House Subcommittee on Arms Control and Disarmament which, if carefully read and thoroughly understood, presents a strong case for the dismissal of Henry Kissinger on the ground that as a negotiator he is incompetent, irresponsible, and downright stupid. Unfortunately, the Nitze material (the substance of which was contained in his prepared opening statement, subsequently put into the Congressional Record of July 2, 1974, by Congressman Charles H. Wilson, Subcommittee Chairman) is beyond the understanding of nonexperts in the jargon of the unilateral-disarmament intellectuals, of which Nitze has been Number One Theoretician and Number Three Activist since 1960. Only an expert in interpreting their highly stylized and obfuscatory understatement can penetrate the true thrust of the Nitze testimony.

For example, Nitze, having revealed that the Soviets have never during two years of SALT II negotiations receded substantially from their 21 outrageous demands (which he characterizes as "heavily one-sided in the Soviet favor"), explains how they expect an agreement finally to be reached:

> Soviet officials have indicated the view that what they call "the correlation of forces," which in Communist terminology includes the aggregate of forces bearing on the situation, including psychological, political, economic, and military factors, is moving in their favor and that, even though we may today believe that their proposals are one-sided and inequitable, eventually realism will bring us to accept at least the substance of them.

Translated into nonintellectual American language, Nitze's explanation might sound like this:

> Those arrogant Soviet Communist bastards do not even bother to deny that their demands are outrageous and amount to the strategic surrender of the United States. Instead, they warn us that the strategic nuclear balance has swung so far in their favor, carrying with it inexorable psychological, political, and economic factors, that we must soon face the reality of the situation, which is that we have no rational alternative but to surrender to their decisively superior power.

Since the Soviets' "21 outrageous demands" are really tantamount to a U.S. strategic surrender, Henry Kissinger classified them Top Secret to preserve the illusion of detente and to cover the fact that prolonged negotiations are continuing to throw away valuable lead-time required to rebuild U.S. strategic power before it is too late. Paul Nitze gives the first authoritative summary of their substance. Here is his description of the position the Soviets maintained throughout the negotiations.

> The position taken by the Soviets was heavily one-sided in the Soviet favor. It would carry over into a permanent agreement [which was supposed to replace the SALT I Interim Agreement] the approximately 40 percent Soviet superiority in the number of offensive nuclear missile launchers and preserve the Soviet advantage in missile launcher dimensions provided by the Interim Agreement. It would negate U.S. offsetting advantages in MIRV and heavy bomber capabilities.
>
> Furthermore, it called for the withdrawal of nuclear capable systems deployed in defense of U.S. allies and capable of striking Soviet territory and the liquidation of associated bases. It would ban the deployment of new U.S. systems such as Trident and B-1, but would not ban the deployment of the new family of Soviet offense systems now under active development or deployment. Reductions would be put off until the indefinite future.

This translates unequivocally into a demand for our strategic surrender. The "new family of Soviet offense systems" includes *at least* four new and up-to-five-times more powerful ICBM types, two new types of heavy supersonic bombers, and the Extended-Delta-type missile-launching submarine with its intercontinental-range SLBMs. Earlier in this book we also established that the deployment of these systems would give the Soviets, for all practical purposes, a first-strike capability against the United States.

Putting together only these two items from the Nitze material (and there are others equally important), they give the lie to the Kissinger assertions that strategic superiority is useless and cannot be employed for either political or military purposes, and that he successfully educated the Soviets into recognizing these theories. They are employing their rapidly approaching decisive strategic superiority to back up their demand that we sign an agreement tantamount to strategic surrender, which they can follow up at any time with a demand for our political surrender.

The Nitze material generally exposes the fact that Kissinger is being suckered by the wily Soviet negotiating techniques, that he simply does not understand Soviet intentions or policies, that he especially does not understand the Soviet concepts of detente or peaceful co-existence, and that he is not up to date on the latest authoritative evaluations of Soviet objectives in relation to world conquest. Any one of these weaknesses would, of course, constitute a sufficient and urgent basis for removing Kissinger from a position in which he could wreak potentially fatal damage upon U.S. interests and our chances of survival in freedom. Put all these weaknesses together and he is exposed as a disaster so far as America is concerned, although from the standpoint of the Politburo he may indeed be a "superb negotiator."

Paul Nitze gives two outstanding specifics to support his charges which can be understood in their full significance only if it is remembered that extreme understatement is traditional and mandatory among the unilateralists, and that Nitze is not, of course, in any position to indict the Secretary of State by name. The first of these examples relates to how Kissinger is being taken in by Soviet negotiating tactics, and the second deals with Kissinger's failure to understand Soviet intentions:

> . . . I believe the Soviet strategy is to deal with each segment of the problem piecemeal, nailing down one piece after another, in a manner favorable to Soviet interests and using all effective measures—diplomatic, propaganda, and *through increased strategic capabilities*—to bring pressure on the United States to achieve agreement.
>
> Among the issues they consider already settled are the inequalities already provided by the Interim Agreement. Their current interest in *a threshold nuclear test ban and an agreement to forgo a second ABM site*

754

is consistent with such a strategy and with inhibiting a U.S. response to the imminent deployment of the Soviet Union's new and much more effective family of offensive strategic weapons.

(Nitze made the above statements on July 2, 1974, the day prior to termination of the Moscow Summit of '74; and he was correct in his predictions. Kissinger did indeed fall into both the Soviet traps of which Nitze warned.)

I believe the significance of the impending increases in Soviet capability are generally recognized. Not generally recognized [Nitze here means not recognized by Henry Kissinger], however, are the indications of Soviet strategic policies which can be gleaned from what members of the Soviet hierarchy say to each other in open Russian language articles and speeches. Ambassador Foy Kohler's recent monograph entitled "The Role of Nuclear Forces in Current Soviet Strategy," bears on this question. *It brings out the distinction between the Western concept of detente and the Soviet concept of "peaceful coexistence" with its implications of a continuing struggle ending with "the complete and final victory of communism on a world scale."* It further notes Soviet emphasis upon deterrence through a war-winning capability, with its implications of military superiority, preemption, and counterforce.

Translating this into plain English, Nitze is telling us that Kissinger is either so stupid that he has been deceived into relying on the Western concept of detente to protect us, or else he is deliberately deceiving us into believing that he really believes in the sincerity of Soviet detente, whereas the Soviets are actually using it as a stratagem in their campaign for the "final victory of communism on a world scale." Nitze also points out that Kissinger has missed—or would have us believe he has missed—the fact that the Soviets plan on using "military superiority" to give them capabilities in a war against us, to preempt if it will be to their advantage, and to employ their counterforce capability to disarm us. Kissinger's theories deny each of these three concepts. Here is one concluding excerpt from Nitze's testimony which brilliantly understates a warning of our impending defeat:

There is a tendency in certain [read Kissinger-favored] American studies of arms control to look upon the action and reacting strategic relationships between the sides in a way which leans over backwards in its objectivity. Albert Wohlstetter's recent analysis, however, demonstrates that contrary to widely held views, the United States has for many years underestimated future Soviet offensive deployments, decreased its constant dollar expenditures on strategic forces, and decreased both the megatonnage and the equivalent megatonnage of its strategic nuclear arsenal. While doing so it has *increased the number of its offensive warheads while greatly reducing their size.* . .The question is whether we can continue to follow such a course, in the face of the imminent Soviet increases in offensive capability, without danger to the security of the United States and its allies.

So far as it goes, Nitze's recent testimony is accurate, strategically sound, inherently probable, is confirmed by a number of earlier leaks on the SALT II negotiations, and would have been contradicted by someone on behalf of Kissinger if that could have been safely done. But what Nitze revealed is probably less than one percent of the case he could have made against Kissinger *if* Nitze had not been equally motivated to keep the American people in continued ignorance of the dangers of the SALT I pacts and the Kissinger defense policies.

One cogent clue to Paul H. Nitze's motivation is found in a *National Review* evaluation of Senator Henry Jackson's recommendations on Red China. *National Review* finds it easy to understand why Jackson goes along with the Kissinger-Nixon rationale about relations with China, "viewing China in a geopolitical context," but puzzles why he went one large step beyond Nixon and Kissinger by urging that we "put our embassy in Peking and our liaison office in Taipei." After considering a few possible minor motivations for Senator Jackson's deserting his "moral" and "civil libertarian" concepts on this issue, the analysis concludes, "But, closer to the nub, he is also running flat out for the Democratic nomination," and the proposal, "whether or not it represents a serious projection of foreign policy, is perhaps at least as much an attempt to achieve detente with his leftist opponents within the Democratic Party."[11]

Whereas Senator Jackson is running flat out for the Democratic nomination for President, Paul Hilken Nitze is running flat out to win appointment as successor to Henry Kissinger, that is, to become the next Democratic President's Secretary of State, Assistant on National Security Affairs, and negotiator-in-chief of the arms control agreements. Nitze has a great deal going for him in seeking such an appointment, especially with Jackson. Nitze's publicized attacks on Kissinger as a negotiator mark an effective attempt by Nitze to achieve a sort of detente with conservative defense-minded leaders in both the Democratic and Republican Parties (who are searching so desperately for a champion of U.S. strategic power to refute the Kissinger policies). Nitze obviously needs no additional accreditation with the liberals on either side of the aisle because his record since 1960 speaks for itself much more convincingly than any self-serving words.

Nitze may even be speculating that he will not have to await the next Presidential election in 1976 to become a new "Henry Kissinger." Even though the Nitze testimony before a congressional subcommittee represents only one percent of the case he *could* have made against Kissinger, a serious investigation based on that one percent would require President Ford to get rid of Kissinger for political if not patriotic reasons. Even an influential group of liberal Democratic pro-disarmers is challenging Kissinger's fundamental claims. Headed by Eugene V. Rostow, this newly assembled task force includes 17 prominent liberals such as George W. Ball, former Under Secretary of State, Henry H. Fowler, former Secretary of the Treasury, and John P. Roche of the Fletcher School of Law and Diplomacy. They denounced Kissinger's vaunted "detente" as a "myth" and called upon the American people not to be deceived by this false concept. More important, they challenge Kissinger's contentions that a nuclear first-strike capability is impossible to attain and that the Kremlin has abandoned its attempts to gain military advantages over the United States. Here is how the Rostow group puts it:

> The official Nixon-Brezhnev proclamation of detente was disregarded by the Soviets in the two main theaters of world conflict from the moment it was signed [the Middle East and Indochina] and they [the Soviets] have not slowed down their headlong drive for first-strike capability in both nuclear and conventional arms.[12]

Nitze understands nuclear strategy far better than Kissinger and fully realizes that Kissinger has been skating on very thin ice in pontificating totally contradictory strategic theories to justify his policies and concessions to the Soviets. Any informed debate or investigation by a congressional committee could destroy the entire structure of Kissinger's house of card tricks. Whenever that happens, Nitze will be waiting in the wings to take over stage-management of future charades in negotiations with the Kremlin. Such an opportunity just might come to pass even during the Ford-Rockefeller Administration. An administration that would consider appointing Senator William Fulbright as ambassador to Great Britain might even consider Paul Nitze as a replacement for Henry Kissinger.

Other than the fact that he lacks Kissinger's hypnotic personality and worldwide reputation, Nitze would be just as dangerous to U.S. survival. There is a Jack Kennedy anecdote that is supposed to be apocryphal, but the reason it is funny is that it is so close to the truth. As he told it during one of his final campaign swings across the country in 1960, he received this telegram from his multimillionaire father, Joseph Kennedy:

> JACK THIS BIG SPENDING MUST STOP DO NOT BUY A SINGLE VOTE MORE THAN NECESSARY TO WIN THE ELECTION STOP I WILL NOT PAY FOR A LANDSLIDE STOP.

Paul Nitze's motivation in his congressional testimony is exposed by the fact that he did not reveal a single thing more than was necessary to discredit Kissinger as a negotiator and to build a new image of

Nitze as a "concerned American patriot" risking controversy in order to support U.S. military strength. He did not reveal any of the horrendous dangers to U.S. survival posed by the SALT I accords. (He had to admit, of course, that he had supported congressional approval of the SALT I Interim Agreement in June 1972.)

All through his statement, Nitze pretends that the concept of "essential equivalence" is a valid and honest objective for the United States, whereas he knows very well that it is merely a verbal placebo to drug the American people further into apathy. As an expert on nuclear strategy, Nitze knows that any such "equivalence" between the Soviet strategic force with its massive counterforce capability and the U.S. force with no disarming capability is a deceptive myth. Although he mentions minor disadvantages to the United States in the 1974 Moscow Summit treaties on a threshold nuclear test ban and on limiting ABM defenses to one site, he does not expose the truly critical traps which they contain. In discussing MIRV deployment and test limitations, he totally ignores the fact that verification by national technical means only, to which Kissinger had already bound the United States in the 1973 Washington Summit agreement, is totally inadequate to protect U.S. interests.

Finally, there is always the possibility that Paul H. Nitze's now-burning desire to replace Kissinger as Unilateral Disarmer-in-Chief of the United States is because Nitze originated the unilateral program, created its theoretical basis and rationalization through sophisticated manipulation of the "it's safer to be weak than strong" concept, and worked in tandem with Defense Secretary McNamara in executing the program for some eight years before Kissinger took it over.

Liberal commentators tended to rate the result of the Moscow Summit of 1974 as a "scoreless tie," whereas conservative analysts seemed to consider it almost a U.S. victory because we did not sign another lopsided agreement such as the SALT I pacts that came out of the 1972 Moscow Summit. The actual result was unmitigated disaster. The dimensions of the disaster are still unsuspected by the American people and by most members of Congress. As always, when the United States is represented by Henry Kissinger, the Soviets came out with *all* they wanted, and *exactly* what they wanted. In 1974 they fully attained their objective: a completely unconstrained opportunity to continue at full speed the "staggering" momentum of their massive buildup of strategic offensive nuclear weapons systems to the force levels required to attain a first-strike capability against the United States. Coupled with this, they obtained guarantees that the United States would take no compensating action against the Soviet buildup, and would make no response whatsoever in the timeframe relevant to the Soviet threat.

The U.S. commitment to make no response to the Soviets' onrushing deployment of all their major new strategic offensive systems is contained in a complex and esoteric structure consisting of one treaty, one new treaty-protocol, an "invisible" agreement, a "no-agreement," and a web of U.S. defense policy declarations directed by Henry Kissinger and enunciated by Secretary of Defense James Schlesinger.

No *agreement* which could have come out of the Moscow Summit of 1974 could possibly have been so advantageous to the Soviets and so disastrous to the United States as the "no-agreement" which did come out. The preplanned deadlock in the negotiations was a brilliant Soviet ploy to make an end-run around U.S. congressional evaluation and public understanding. There was wide apprehension that a politically crippled Nixon-Kissinger team (with an impeachment report imminent) might attempt a grandstand play in foreign policy by securing some sort of agreement to replace SALT I with any agreement, no matter how strategically disadvantageous. The real danger all along was the *unamended continuation* of the SALT I Interim Agreement with its U.S.-no-response posture.

Under the American system, there are specific safeguards which govern international agreements, ranging from the advice and consent of the Senate required by the Constitution for treaties, down to formal or informal congressional review, plus exposure to the media and public opinion. No similar safeguards can possibly apply, however, to a no-agreement plus protracted negotiations toward a still hoped-for agreement held out as continuing bait.

The SALT I Interim Agreement gave the Soviets everything they could possibly need to advantage them and disadvantage us. Otherwise, by exploiting Kissinger's delusions of grandeur and Nixon's political needs, they would not have signed it until it was changed to meet their every requirement. The Soviets were completely in control of the negotiations which produced SALT I in 1972. So in 1974 they not only had no need of a *new* lopsided agreement, they wanted *no* agreement. They wanted to continue the 1972 SALT I Interim Agreement for its stated maximum term, that is, until June 1977.

Even that five-year term itself had been a brilliant Soviet stratagem. The hope and expectation of the U.S. SALT delegation was that it would be replaced by a more nearly equitable agreement in one or two years or, in any event, before the Soviets could accomplish any significant breakout of the strategic balance which existed when SALT I was signed. On June 19, 1972, in the Senate Foreign Relations Committee hearings on SALT, a Senator asked Ambassador Gerard C. Smith, chairman of the SALT delegation, if the Kremlin should expand as much as they can within the framework of the SALT I agreements, "would that put us in the very inferior position after a few years?" Here is Ambassador Smith's reply:

I think one of the keys to the answer to your question is in your last few words, "after a few years." Now, one cannot tell how long this interim freeze will last. People shorthandedly say this is a five-year agreement. I hope it won't be. It may be a one-year agreement; it may be a two-year agreement, depending on when we succeed in the follow-on negotiations.

Now, it is our calculation that nothing the Soviets can do even if it went the full term of five years could upset the strategic balance. . . . It is our confident calculation that the strategic balance will remain firm during that period.[13]

This statement was in addition to Noteworthy Unilateral Statement A, discussed earlier, which warned that, if a "more complete" strategic offensive arms agreement that would constrain and reduce "threats to the survivability" of our retaliatory force were not reached within five years, "U.S. supreme interests could be jeopardized," and this would constitute a basis for withdrawal from the ABM Treaty.

Note that the assumption upon which the United States agreed to a maximum term of five years for the Interim Agreement was our "calculation" that the Soviets could not possibly upset the balance within that time. Unilateral Statement A should be read to mean that our supreme interests would be jeopardized if a new agreement were not reached within five years *or in any shorter time within which the Soviets could upset the strategic balance.* An escape hatch of six months' notice for withdrawal from the Interim Agreement was provided to take care of such an "extraordinary event."

Evidence of such an unexpected development surfaced within a very few days after the signing of the Interim Agreement in May 1972. The Soviets began testing new types of ICBMs vastly more powerful than the types they had previously deployed. By the summer of 1973, there was so much evidence of the Soviets' having tested four new types of powerful ICBMs and MIRVed warheads with inertial guidance packages that the developments could no longer be suppressed. Nor could it be credibly denied that, if the Soviets proceeded with deployment programs for their new supermissiles and MIRVs, they could and would upset the balance, and could provide a massive, near-total threat to the survivability of U.S. strategic land-based retaliatory forces.

But it was not politically expedient for President Nixon to denounce the Interim Agreement, and it became clear in early 1974 that there were only two other courses open to the United States to head off the

Soviets from attaining the capability of destroying substantially our entire ICBM retaliatory force: (1) we would have to obtain no later than the July 1974 Moscow Summit a new agreement (to replace the Interim Agreement) that would restrain Soviet deployment of their new powerful offensive systems; or (2) we would have to embark on massive crash programs to produce enough additional weapons of our own to meet the new Soviet threat.

So what did Henry Kissinger do at the Moscow Summit of 1974? Suppose he had signed an *agreement* permitting the Soviets to continue their "staggering" momentum of deployment of their new offensive systems, but restraining us not only from adopting new programs now to add additional strategic weapons to our forces, but restraining us also from accelerating *research* programs permitting us to institute *development* some five years into the future. Such an agreement would not have been approved by Congress. It would have been denounced by most of the media and stimulated pressures for Kissinger's departure.

What Henry Kissinger actually did at the 1974 Moscow Summit accomplished the same thing for the Soviets. First, he accepted the Soviets' "deadlock" under which no agreement was to be permitted to replace the SALT I Interim Agreement unless the United States accepted the substance of the "21 outrageous demands" that were tantamount to U.S. strategic surrender. Second, he did not break off negotiations, which would have been the rational response to the Soviets' arrogance and threats. Third, he did not even put the Soviets on notice that, if they continued their massive deployment programs, we would immediately start responsive programs of our own on a crash basis.

Fourth, in the official Joint U.S.-Soviet Communique, he included a commitment by the United States to the Soviet Union. Although it was not officially designated as an "agreement," for all practical purposes it amounted to an "invisible" agreement. In international law it would be treated as an agreement because of the substantive promises it contained. It bound the United States to continue negotiations for a new agreement "to cover the period until 1985," and the Soviets agreed that such an agreement "should be *completed* at the earliest possible date, before the expiration of the Interim Agreement." But the Soviets drew a sharp distinction between when the new agreement should be "completed," and when it should *take effect* and thus supersede the Interim Agreement. Henry Kissinger agreed that the new agreement, regardless of how soon "completed," would not interrupt or terminate the Interim Agreement, but instead would "follow" it. Here is the operative language from the Communique dated at Moscow on July 3, 1974, and signed by Richard Nixon, as President of the United States, and L. Brezhnev, acting in his capacity as General Secretary of the Central Committee, CPSU:

II. *Further Limitation of Strategic Arms* and
Other Disarmament Issues

... In the course of the talks, the two sides ... concluded that the Interim Agreement on offensive strategic weapons *should be followed by a new agreement* between the United States and the Soviet Union on the limitation of strategic arms. *They agreed* that such an agreement should cover the period until 1985 and deal with both quantitative and qualitative limitations. *They agreed* that such an agreement should be completed at the earliest possible date, before the expiration of the Interim Agreement.

In any sort of reasonable legal interpretation, the parties here are differentiating between two different time factors: (1) the time for completing a new agreement, which is stated to be "at the earliest possible date, before the expiration of the Interim Agreement," and (2) the time when that new agreement, regardless of when completed, will go into effect, that is, it will "follow" the Interim Agreement (upon expiration thereof according to its terms, which will be in June 1977). So, even if a new agreement is "completed," signed, and ratified by both sides, it could not take *effect* (according to the 1974 agreement, as spelled out in the Joint Communique) until the *expiration* of the SALT I Interim Agreement (three years after the date of the Communique).

This three-year term before any new agreement could take effect (unless we are smart enough to repudiate the agreement contained in the Joint Communique) is vital. Even Henry Kissinger himself has recognized that, if we allow a year and a half to elapse, it will be too late to catch the pace of deployment of the new Soviet weapons and their powerful MIRVs. He announced in a press conference in Brussels on June 26, 1974, that he would seek a limit on Soviet deployment of MIRVs,

But I would say we have about a year and a half altogether before the decisions [of the Soviets on deployment rate of MIRVs] will be irrevocable, but it becomes harder with every passing six-month period.

At his next press conference, this time in Moscow on July 3, 1974, just following completion of the Summit conference and agreements, he twice reaffirmed his estimate that

we have about 18 months to gain control of multiple warheads, control not in the nature of eliminating it, but by introducing some stability into the rate and nature of their deployment.

Gerald Ford and the American people must decide if we want to prevent the Soviets from attaining such decisive superiority over us that they will have the option of demanding our surrender or destroying us. We cannot accomplish this by an agreement; our only hope is to introduce crash programs to strengthen our own strategic forces. But Henry Kissinger has eliminated that possibility—at least so long as he stays in power over U.S. defense programs. This was revealed in a press conference held jointly by Defense Secretary James Schlesinger and ACDA Director Fred Iklé on July 3, 1974, almost immediately after Kissinger's announcement in Moscow of the results of the Moscow Summit of '74. That joint press conference was extremely revealing about the shoddy charade of the alleged "Schlesinger-Kissinger feud." The reporters present kept asking if the press conference was held "at the suggestion of White House officials" for the purpose of expressing support of what was done or not done at the Moscow Summit. The answers to these questions given by both Schlesinger and Iklé were so equivocal that one reporter finally put it this way:

Q. I think what we are trying to get at is, flatly and in plain English, did somebody above you tell you to hold the news conference?

Dr. Schlesinger: (Inaudible) in contact with them, and we decided that this would be an appropriate approach to take.

Q. They did not decide for you?

Dr. Schlesinger: That is correct.

However, both Schlesinger and Iklé repeatedly announced that they supported "the President's" decisions in Moscow. Neither one, however, was able to give any plausible defense for the disadvantages imposed on the United States by the 1974 Threshold Test Ban Treaty or the 1974 ABM Protocol, but Iklé said, "These are important agreements . . . [and I am] delighted to support them." Schlesinger said he was "enthusiastic" about the possibilities of the Moscow Summit of '74 agreements, adding, "I fully endorse what has taken place in Moscow and I regard it as significant."

Yes, Sir, Dr. Kissinger; yes, Sir! Other than shooting fish in a barrel, cracking the whip is the favorite sport of certain types of megalomaniacs. Schlesinger's attitude is exactly what might be expected when the most vulnerable member of a Cabinet about to acquire a new President is given a "suggestion" by the only invulnerable member. After all, following through on a "suggestion" would be a small price to pay in order to retain the post of U.S. Secretary of Defense— a position which includes the power to supervise (under the policy directives of the Assistant to the President for National Security Affairs) expenditures on the order of $80 billion a year; to preside over a personal office force of some 2,000 employees and a million more under the DOD; and a salary of $60,000 a year, which would not be inconsequential to a 45-year-old Ph.D. whose only positions in civilian life were those of professor of economics and a theoretician at the RAND think tank.

It is hardly necessary to ask who was the actual architect for the United States of the Moscow '74 Summit agreements that James Schlesinger "fully supported" and is so "enthusiastic" about. Richard Nixon was not merely a political lame duck, he was potentially a dead duck living on borrowed time. Back in early April 1974, Gerald Ford had given an impetuous interview with the *New Republic*'s White House correspondent, John Osborne, in which Ford designated his proposed Cabinet. As authoritatively summarized, Ford said that

as President, he would certainly keep Secretary of State Kissinger and probably fire Secretary of Defense Schlesinger.

The transparent sycophancy of James Schlesinger's conduct at this very special press conference, coupled with his obsequious praise of a set of agreements that subject the United States to potential disaster, should dispel the last illusions of those who have been relying on "hard-liner" Schlesinger to combat Kissinger's pro-surrender-to-the-Kremlin policies. Schlesinger is supporting the Kissinger sellout at the Summit of '74, whose shocking character is revealed by analysis of the product which came out of Moscow, together with the policies declared by Schlesinger during the remote-controlled press conference.

Equally important with the substance of what Kissinger did to the United States at Moscow in 1974 is the evidence of how he is deceiving Gerald Ford and involving him in deceptive pledges to the American people—pledges which Kissinger himself has rendered impossible of fulfillment. Here is what Kissinger pledged—for himself and expressly for the President—in his address to the American Legion National Convention in Miami on August 20, 1974:

Just as we must insure a balance of conventional forces, so we must also assure a nuclear balance. *We are determined never to fall behind in nuclear arms. We will never accept the strategic preponderance of another power.* We will maintain our strategic weapons program at whatever level is needed to achieve this end. . . .

. . . President Ford, an ardent advocate of national defense, as one of his first acts as President has invited the Soviet leaders to join with us in an intensified effort to negotiate an effective and equitable limitation on strategic arms. We will be guided by two basic principles:

—First, *until further arms limits are negotiated, we will maintain American strategic strength whatever the cost.* Our power will not falter through lack of resolve or sacrifice.

—Second, we will pursue the strategic arms limitations talks with an energy and conviction equal to the challenge before us. We are determined to become the masters of our own technology, not its slave.

The President has asked me to emphasize his view that the choice is clear. *We will maintain the nuclear balance by unilateral actions if we must and by negotiations if at all possible.* I can assure you that these negotiations will not fail for lack of good will and readiness to explore new solutions on our part.

To expose this latest achievement of sophisticated obscurantism to the light of reality, three elements must be considered: Is it "at all possible" that the nuclear balance can be maintained (1) by the fruit of past negotiations, i.e., the SALT I Interim Agreement, or (2) by hoped-for future negotiations, or (3) by U.S. unilateral actions?

(1) During the course of the Kissinger-directed, Schlesinger/Iklé-conducted press conference immediately following the Moscow Summit of '74, this colloquy took place:

> Q. When you were talking to us on the eve of these negotiations, you alerted us to the danger that the Russians were on the verge of deploying this new family of increased missiles, the more powerful missiles armed with MIRVs. Do you see them going forward with that now?
> Dr. Schlesinger. Indeed, they are unconstrained at the present time. We hope, through the course of negotiations that lie ahead of us, to persuade them that restraint on their side will be matched by restraint on our side and that both sides would benefit from such restraint.

Yet in a press conference about two weeks earlier, on June 17, 1974, in answer to a question as to whether there had been any indication of a unilateral slowdown by the Soviets in deploying their new and more powerful missile systems, Dr. Schlesinger responded:

> I think not. I think the Soviet program is moving forward in accordance with the original pace that was desired by the Soviet Government.

Schlesinger had already described that "pace" by saying that the Soviet momentum and programs were far greater than anticipated even a year earlier and were "staggering." In his June 17, 1974, press conference, he also stated that none of the Soviet programs in deployment of the SS-17, SS-18, or SS-19 was "a violation" of the agreement. So the conclusion has to be that no fruit of past negotiations, no existing SALT agreement, can serve to prevent an upset of the nuclear balance by the Soviets, nor constrain in any way their ongoing deployment programs.

(2) It will not be "at all possible" for future negotiations to constrain the further upset of the nuclear balance for the reasons considered above in relation to the official U.S.-Soviet Joint Communique issued at the Moscow Summit of '74. Both sides recognized that the "completion" of a new agreement may not come until just before expiration of the SALT I Interim Agreement and that, regardless of when a new agreement might be "completed," it will only "follow" the SALT I Interim Agreement rather than interrupt or replace it prior to its agreed expiration date in 1977. We have already noted Dr. Kissinger's admission that by then it will be too late. Also, we have the Nitze

testimony considered above that the Soviets are not receding substantially from their original negotiating demands (the "21 outrageous demands") and are threatening us with their increasingly superior military power to coerce us into signing an agreement that will not constrain them but will block our Trident and B-1 programs.

[3] How are we fixed to "maintain the nuclear balance by *unilateral actions* if we must," as pledged by Henry Kissinger for himself and expressly for President Gerald Ford?

As discussed earlier in this book, Kissinger's basic explanation for subjecting the United States to the open and notorious imbalances in the SALT I Interim Agreement was his repeated claim that the United States could not by unilateral action possibly prevent the Soviets from overturning the nuclear balance. The Soviets had dynamic ongoing programs in both ICBMs and SLBMs, he claimed, and we did not; if we attempted to rely on unilateral action, the gap would open wider; we could not produce additional strategic systems within the five-year period; in effect, he claimed, we were helpless to help ourselves and, therefore, even with its imbalances favoring the Soviets, the SALT I Interim Agreement made a "major contribution to our national security." During the interval between the SALT I Interim Agreement's signature in 1972 and the Moscow Summit of 1974, no new programs to add strategic missile launchers for either SLBMs or ICBMs were started. The Trident and B-1 programs will not begin to produce strategic power in-being until 1979, even if fully funded and not further slowed down by Schlesinger.

So, if we could have helped ourselves by unilateral action beginning back in 1972, Kissinger was lying then and he sold the SALT I Interim Agreement to the United States on the basis of that lie. If he was not lying then, and we actually were unable to maintain the nuclear balance by resorting to unilateral action, it would be equally impossible now, and therefore he must be lying now in pledging that "we will" maintain it by unilateral action "if we must." And he also must be deliberately implicating President Ford in that pledge which he knows will be impossible to keep.

There are even several additional methods by which Kissinger, through the Moscow 1974 Summit agreements and no-agreements, made it impossible for us to maintain (restore would be the more accurate term) the nuclear balance in the face of the momentum of the new Soviet offensive weapons programs. For example, take the Moscow Threshold Test Ban Treaty of 1974 (referred to as TTB). If ratified, it will ban the testing of nuclear weapons with a yield of more than 150 kilotons (1/6 of one megaton) after March 31, 1976. After that time, it will theoretically ban both sides from testing any megaton-range warheads. But its practical result will be to enshrine forever the Soviet monopoly in reliable MIRV warheads in the megaton range. The Soviet Union has substantially completed (according to Schlesinger's admission in his July 3, 1974, press conference and his official FY 1975 DOD Report) their testing of MIRVed warheads for the SS-17, SS-18, and SS-19. By official reports, all the Soviet MIRV warheads on their new series are in the megaton range; they admit a 1-to-2 megaton yield, but the probabilities are that the SS-18 MIRVs have been tested up to a yield of five megatons. As long as four years before, they had tested five-megaton MRV warheads for the older model SS-9s. The heaviest U.S. MIRV warheads we have tested for operational use are the Minuteman III MIRVs which run from 170 to 200 kilotons in explosive power. We have no ongoing programs for MIRVs of any greater explosive power.

If we ever recover from the Kissinger-Schlesinger suicidal policies of relying on such low-powered MIRV warheads and design new ones comparable to the Soviet two-megaton MIRVs, we would be precluded from testing them by the 1974 TTB Treaty. Obviously, we could not develop such operational warheads in the interim 21-month period without going into crash programs, so we are effectively precluded from testing them. We could not take the terrible gamble of replacing existing tested warheads with untested warheads, even of much greater power. Could we test in miniature? Henry Kissinger was asked that question in his Moscow press conference on July 3, 1974, and here is his answer:

> It is my understanding that miniature testing is rarely done, never done with operational weapons, and the concern that has been expressed to us, as we were discussing this within our government, was precisely the necessity of full-scale tests of those categories of weapons of principal significance.

The Soviets' new series of ICBMs—all of which have been tested in operational versions—are "next generation" weapons. The United States has no "next generation" weapons whatsoever, not even on the drawing board, not even in advanced research states; and Schlesinger has no programs for production or even development of new weapons. All he offers is preplanning programs designed to open "options" for new programs in the 1980s.

The obvious question is, why did the United States agree to a Threshold Nuclear Test Ban that will hold us forever inferior to the Soviets in the explosive power of MIRVs? What good is TTB? It cannot be argued that it will prevent pollution of the atmosphere: the tests concerned would all be underground, and there has been no claim that there has been any substantial escape of radiation from underground tests by either side. The only possible excuse for the TTB Treaty is that Henry Kissinger was trying to buy some good will from the Soviets. Knee-jerk unilateral disarmers will claim that it is worthwhile as a step toward outlawing *all* nuclear tests—but it cannot be claimed as a necessary step, or even as a step which will inevitably lead to a total test ban. So long as we lag behind the Soviets in warhead power, all test bans are bad, and a total ban would be totally bad—for our chances of survival.

In any event, by the TTB Treaty, Henry Kissinger has invalidated in advance his pledge to the American Legion convention that "We are determined never to fall behind in nuclear arms. We will never accept the strategic preponderance of another power." The Soviets *are* ahead of us in the vital area of megaton-range MIRVed warheads. That will give them strategic preponderance when coupled with their massively greater number of launchers and their acknowledged 4-to-1 1972-advantage in throw-weight that is now rapidly growing into a 6-to-1 advantage. Their most numerous MIRVs (on SS-19s replacing most of their older SS-11s) will average two megatons each—or 12 times more powerful than our Minuteman III MIRVs. Their guidance accuracy is at least as good as ours and improving at a more rapid rate, because they suffer from no restrictions based either on policy (they never worry about what the United States will think) or on monetary limitations.

The other agreement signed at the 1974 Moscow Summit was a protocol to the 1972 Moscow SALT I anti-defense treaty which reduced the number of ABM sites allowed each side from two to one, and cut the number of allowed ABM interceptor launchers from 100 at each of two sites to 100 at the single site. It is also supposed to permit the United States to decide, within five years, whether to relocate its single missile defense site in Washington, D.C., instead of in Grand Forks, North Dakota, at the cost of scrapping the hundreds of millions of dollars worth of ABM equipment already built there.

As a practical matter, this 1974 ABM Protocol substantially favors the Soviets. It leaves them with their single ABM site already operational in the Moscow area. The ABM launchers allowed them there will defend a population of more than seven million, 300 ICBM silos, the largest industrial-scientific-technological concentration in the U.S.S.R., the headquarters of the Communist Party of the Soviet Union, and their strategic-military National Command Center. In contrast the single U.S. ABM site protects almost zero population, no industrial or scientific facilities, and only 150 ICBM silos. More important, the new protocol allows us no protection whatsoever for our National Command Center because it would be politically unrealistic to expect a decision to scrap the hundreds of millions of dollars' worth of in-being missile defense equipment and facilities which could not be practicably moved from North Dakota to Washington, D.C.

The primary reason the Soviets wanted to bind the United States by the 1974 single-site protocol is to degrade the credibility of the U.S. strategic deterrent by depriving the National Command Center at Washington of any ballistic missile defense. The probability of an authoritative and effective decision to retaliate against a Soviet nuclear attack would be greatly enhanced if there were assurance that the President, the Joint Chiefs of Staff, the Secretary of Defense, and other high officials concerned with national security, had a reasonable probability of surviving at least the first ICBM salvos of enemy attack.

Theoretically, if the National Command Center and all the highest ranking officials are wiped out, an Air Force general officer in an airborne emergency Command Center (known by the code name "Looking Glass" aircraft) has the authority to order a retaliatory launch. As a practical matter, the uncertainty involved degrades the credibility of retaliation. It would be more important to protect the credibility of retaliation by our total strategic forces than to defend 150 out of our 1,054 ICBMs. Both the Kremlin war-planners and the U.S. strategic-surrender-promoting elitists take the realistic view that the chances of a preemptive surrender are enhanced by denying the National Command Center personnel all protection against nuclear attack.

The way Kissinger has imposed additional restrictive policies against any effective U.S. unilateral action to restore the nuclear balance was revealed, surprisingly, by James Schlesinger in his July 3, 1974, news conference. His statements must be evaluated in the light of his knowledge that the Soviets had refused at the Moscow Summit of '74 to agree to any constraints on the deployment at a "staggering" momentum of their new families of vastly more powerful offensive weapons, that the continuing negotiations might not produce any "completed" agreement until just before termination of the Interim Agreement in 1977, and that regardless of when any new agreement might be reached it would not take effect in time to slow down or stop any new Soviet offensive programs, but it would or could block the U.S. Trident and B-1 programs. Here is the stunning answer that (supposedly "hard-line") James Schlesinger gave to a very perceptive question:

Q: Mr. Secretary, will you recommend—you recall that in your Defense budget you recommended certain bargaining chips, such as improving the accuracy and power of our warheads, there was a whole family of things in there that you wanted done, *put in the research and development stage*—will you now as a result of failure to reach an agreement in Moscow, *will you recommend that these go into production and be deployed?*

Dr. Schlesinger: No sir, not as yet. [After that clearcut reply, Secretary Schlesinger proceeded with his customary obfuscation.] We are developing these capabilities. With regard to accuracy improvements, as I have indicated before, such improvements contribute to although are not essential to the new targeting doctrine with emphasis on selectivity and flexibility.

Q: On the other hand, to follow it up, Mr. Secretary, as a result of what came out of this Third Summit, do you feel it will be possible to slow the pace of some of these development options that you included in your FY '75 budget request and if not, would you anticipate in '76 that you'll be asking to accelerate these, or slow them?

Dr. Schlesinger: I would not anticipate accelerating them in 1976; I see no reason to slow them. Most of the hardware developments are what we might deploy—might deploy—in the event the Soviets take certain steps. I would hope that in the course of negotiations the Soviets will be persuaded to refrain from taking certain steps and consequently that we can similarly avoid taking the steps necessary to match their developments; therefore, it is a difficult thing to predict. The growth of our strategic capabilities will be based upon Soviet development.

Q: Mr. Secretary, not basing it on the development of the future, but on the now and present possibility of the Soviet development, how soon can they get to our coast and shoot at our cities and how close do we get to their coast? I think the American people want to know this.

Dr. Schlesinger: With the new SS-N-8 missile, the Soviets have a range of approximately 4,000 miles. So that, in effect, if you are talking about submarines, which I assume was the reference, they can fire at the United States virtually upon exit from port. When we have completed our Trident development, we will have the same type of range available in our SLBMs.

Q: By about what year will that be?

Dr. Schlesinger: That should be about 1978.

Q: Can you tell us whether you consider what has just happened in Moscow really very significant and, in fact, do you endorse what has taken place there?

Dr. Schlesinger: I fully endorse what has taken place in Moscow and I regard it as significant. . . . They are useful steps in and of themselves. I think that they must be endorsed enthusiastically by the entire American people.

The Kissinger policies, as enunciated by Schlesinger in relation to the 1974 Moscow Summit agreements and no-agreements, gave the Kremlin assurance that, regardless of how fast they move ahead with deployments of their new and more powerful offensive weapons, the United States will make no response in the relevant timeframe. Here is another colloquy from the Schlesinger press conference of July 3, 1974:

Q: If the Russians continue their weapons program at the current rate, at what point in time will the U.S.—would you be forced to recommend a break in the specific numbers set in the '72 agreement and also the intent of that agreement?

Dr. Schlesinger: I think that the agreement runs till 1977 and we would anticipate making no recommendation for a unilateral break in the agree-

ment. The pace of the Soviet program will be such that until 1977 there will continue to be an adequate balance between the two sides.

Thus, Defense Secretary Schlesinger gave the Soviets positive assurance that we will not invoke the right of national self-preservation in order to use the six months' notice escape hatch designed to guard against jeopardy of supreme national interests—*no matter* what the Soviets do in their buildup toward a first-strike capability against us. He is boxing in the new President and ensuring that Gerald Ford will not be able to make good the pledge given in his name by Kissinger at the American Legion convention that "we will maintain the nuclear balance by unilateral action if we must."

The contempt which Schlesinger and Kissinger have for the intelligence of the American people shines with dazzling arrogance through the mendacious assertion about the pace of the Soviet program. Schlesinger is speaking about a period which runs only one month and one week less than three years: from July 3, 1974, to May 26, 1977. Just how does Schlesinger have the arrogance to expect us to believe that he knows what the pace of the Soviet program will be that far in the future? Does he think that not even one American will remember that in his FY 1975 DOD Report he admitted that

the scope of the Soviet [offensive weapons] program as it has now emerged is *far more comprehensive than estimated even a year ago.*[14]

Does he think that no American will remember his admission that, within six months after SALT I was signed, the Soviet program had attained a momentum which he described to Congress as "staggering in size and depth"?[15] Does he think we have all forgotten the result of the highly expert study by Albert Wohlstetter that U.S. intelligence estimates of Soviet ICBMs were too low 9 out of 11 times, and on SLBMs were too low 12 out of 15 times, and that we have stupidly believed that the Soviets sought nothing more than numerical equality?[16] Does he believe that none of us remembers that only two weeks earlier he admitted that there had been no slowdown by the Soviets, and that "the Soviet program is moving forward in accordance with the original pace"?[17] Does he think that none of us can remember that the Chairman of the Joint Chiefs of Staff reported in the FY 1975 Posture Statement that all four of the new series of Soviet ICBMs are estimated for deployment during 1975? And Schlesinger himself admitted that

the SS-19 is probably close to being ready for deployment; the SS-18 is not quite there yet; the SS-17 and SS-16 are probably a little bit further back.[18]

And has he forgotten that his own official statistics from the FY 1975 DOD Report give the lie to his bald-faced assertion that until 1977 "there will continue to be an adequate balance between the two sides"? Under the Schlesinger programs, the U.S. throw-weight for our ICBM force will remain at two million pounds in 1977, but Schlesinger reported that,

> if all three of the new and heavier missiles are deployed [he excludes the SS-16], throw-weight in the Soviet ICBM force will increase from the current 6-7 million pounds to an impressive 10-12 million pounds. This throw-weight, combined with increased accuracy and MIRVs, could give the Soviets on the order of 7,000 one-to-two megaton warheads in their ICBM force alone.[19]

The good news, however, is that the American people, who are thus treated with such cynical contempt by Schlesinger and Kissinger, are vastly more intelligent and (pardon the Schlesingerism) incommensurably more dedicated to our country and more courageous than the elitist unilateral disarmers. Each year beginning in 1972 the American Security Council has employed an independent nationally recognized scientific-survey agency, the Opinion Research Corporation, to conduct polls on "national security issues." The 1974 results show that 67 percent of Americans of voting age favor U.S. military superiority over the Soviet Union. Here is the conclusion:

> The results of our 1973 and 1974 National Security Issues Polls continue to show that national defense policies are seldom in keeping with public opinion, and that in some cases, those policies are in striking defiance of the public's views. The reason for this is that the policy-makers in Washington from both political parties follow the newspapers and news magazines closely and watch the daily news reports on television. They also listen—of necessity—to noisy demonstrations of dissident elements who collect outside their offices and to anti-defense activists who flood the Congress with mail and pester the members with visits.
>
> This exposure to one basic point of view leads our policy-makers in time to believe that public opinion is represented by the New York Times-Washington Post-TV Network Axis and by the anti-defense lobby.
>
> How else can it be when they hear so little from the pro-defense majority?
>
> The lack of correlation between public opinion and national security policy is strikingly exemplified in the responses to question No. 3, which reads: "Should the United States have military strength greater than that of the Soviet Union?" Overwhelmingly, American Security Council members voted in favor of superior military strength for the U.S.: 91% Yes; only 3% No. At the height of the SALT negotiations in 1972, with all the talk of detente and parity, 94% of ASC's members voted along the same lines when they expressed approval of a "policy of military superiority."
>
> Moreover, the Opinion Research Corporation survey in 1972 showed the general public in favor of a policy of military superiority by almost a three to one majority, 68% FOR and 23% AGAINST. This year's Opinion

772

Research Corporation finding on military superiority was 67% in favor of greater military strength for the U.S. and 25% opposed.[20]

The poll result that should encourage the President the most is that, when asked if they would support spending $20 billion more each year to regain U.S. strategic superiority, a resounding 91 percent of American Security Council members and a surprising 65 percent of the scientific national sample voted yes. And 93 percent and 85 percent, respectively, want the United States to have an anti-missile defense.

Henry Kissinger's outburst at Salzburg, Austria, on June 11, 1974, had to be the trigger of a career crisis. It was not at all based on the many massive wrongs he had done his adopted country, nor on the many sophisticated lies with which he had covered them. He was trapped by a totally unnecessary and useless coverup operation, a tissue of partial truths designed to mislead, but not explicit enough for a perjury charge.

The issue Kissinger had hoped to resolve by his megalomanic threat to resign was the extent of his involvement in the wiretapping of 13 Government officials and four newsmen between May 1969 and February 1971. When he appeared before the Senate Foreign Relations Committee for the hearings on his confirmation as Secretary of State, the first question put to him by Chairman J. William Fulbright focused on the "electronic surveillance" of the 17:

Did you or anyone else acting in your name, or on your authority, first propose any of these wiretaps?

Kissinger was under oath and he had no intention whatsoever of giving a direct answer to Fulbright's question. It was not like his SALT I briefing when he had so carefully avoided being placed under oath. Instead, here is how Kissinger waffled his reply:

Mr. Chairman, I think it would be helpful if I explained the circumstances of this particular event, and I think that will contain the answer to your question. . . .

With that evasive introduction, Kissinger proceeded to talk for two pages of testimony in vague generalities without ever answering yes or no. He gave the impression that the President and the Attorney General were the ones who had taken the initiative:

At that time, I had been in the government for four months, and I must say that it did not occur to me to question the judgment of these two officials.

Another typical answer was:

After wiretaps were placed on certain individuals, *I was not necessarily informed* of the fact that a wiretap had been placed.

To Kissinger, it must have been frustrating indeed that the reporters did not recognize a genius at evasion. Thus it was that, in what was to have been a triumphant press conference in the crowded State Department auditorium on June 6, 1974, celebrating his having wrapped up his historic Middle East peace agreement, he was subjected by reporters to what he angrily denounced as "a cross-examination." Leaks from the House Judiciary Committee for the previous several weeks had indicated that Kissinger had played a far more active part in the wiretapping than he had conceded in public and private statements. One reporter came up with the question which Kissinger later made clear was the one which "had particularly got to him."[21] Have you, the reporter asked, "consulted and retained counsel in preparation for a defense against a possible perjury indictment?" According to *Newsweek,* Kissinger

was furious. Hunching over the podium, he replied: "I have not retained counsel, and I am not conducting my office as if it were a conspiracy. . . . I will answer no further questions on this topic."[22]

Authorizing the wiretaps on the 17 was legal to protect national security against repeated leaks of vital information. Some of these men had access to highly sensitive classified material such as the Single Integrated Operations Plan (SIOP). Kissinger would have been home free if only, in testifying under oath on September 7, 1973, he had not made his implicit denials.

Far more relevant to his having exclusive control of our nuclear console and foreign and defense policies is his conduct in calling that strange press conference in Salzburg and the grotesque content of his statements. It is so revealing of the Kissinger values, as well as of his emotional and mental instability, that—even standing alone—it would warrant a serious study of whether he is "some kind of a nut, or something."

Kissinger said he had informed the President in advance of his sudden calling of a special news conference, but did not tell him what he would say. Reporters described White House officials as "appearing stunned as they listened to Kissinger, his voice cracking with emotion and anger, lash out at the 'impugning of my honor.' " He asserted, "his voice quavering with emotion," that his reputation was being defamed by reports cropping up in the news media back home. He denounced these "leaks and innuendos" and then delivered his megalomanic ultimatum:

I do not believe it is possible to conduct the foreign policy of the United States under these circumstances. If it is not cleared up, I will resign.[23]

White House press secretary Ronald Ziegler issued a statement for a surprised President, concluding that "the Secretary's honor needs no defense." Actually, the Secretary's defense merited little honor. The gist of it was: don't blame me—blame the President. Twice within a few paragraphs, he attempted to shift the responsibility to Richard Nixon. Kissinger read to the news conference a letter he had written to Chairman Fulbright in which he recalled that he had testified under oath the previous September that the wiretaps "were ordered by the President and carried out by the FBI under the authority of the Attorney General." He said that in 1969 he was ordered to give the names of subordinates who had access to materials which had been leaked or who could have been suspected of leaking them, and "I understand the order came from the President." This blatant disloyalty to the man who had given him unprecedented power, honor, and prestige, received no comment from the media. There was comment, however, that Kissinger's timing could not have been worse for Nixon. A typical example was this column in the *Los Angeles Times*:

> What puzzled Washington—more than his request that the Senate Foreign Relations Committee return to the questions it asked him last fall and settle them once for all—was his choice of timing. Why would he force such an issue at the very moment Nixon is going to accept tribute for the Administration's role in peacemaking?[24]

There was wide speculation on why he did it at all. Some said Kissinger's new wife had become especially distraught over the wiretap charges, and that he in turn worried about her concern. Others suggested that his "emotional press conference in Austria" had been triggered by exhaustion from his Middle East negotiations. Some were unkind enough to suggest that Kissinger was "putting distance between himself and the embattled Administration."

More than 50 Senators, including most members of the Senate Foreign Relations Committee, rushed to express support for Kissinger. Even Hubert Humphrey said,

> We obviously do not want him to resign. I want to say to him as a friend, "stay with it—cool it."

But the warning to cool it came too late. Kissinger's action was already making people wonder whether a man who would lose his cool so easily possesses the emotional stability and maturity of character necessary for the nation's number one diplomat and czar of our defense policies.

There are dozens of valid and sufficient reasons why Henry Kissinger should be dismissed or impeached or stripped of all power, de facto as well as de jure, to control the destiny of the United States. But the dismissal or departure of Henry Kissinger for any reason other than his unilateral disarmament of the United States would be tragic—because his policies would linger on to destroy us.

We will never regain stability or true prosperity again until we rebuild our strategic superiority. Strategic nuclear power is not only the greatest power—by a factor of 100 million—that the world has ever known. It also is the greatest bargain in power. Since we lost our superiority and Dr. Kissinger announced it to the world in his SALT I statistics in 1972, we have lost in the diminished growth factor of our GNP more than enough to have paid for strategic forces twice more powerful than those of the Soviet Union. Double-digit inflation is robbing our people of their earnings and entire life savings. Insurance, bank savings accounts, bonds, and pensions, all have lost value more swiftly every year since we lost strategic superiority. In 1974, the rate of inflation climbed to 12 percent. At that rate, how much will your insurance, bonds, and savings accounts be worth in eight years? These personal losses of wealth should be charged up to the unilateral-disarmament intellectuals who deprived our nation of defense, and our dollar of its worth. No other remedy for inflation will work.

The great prosperity built by our free enterprise system is why we can easily afford to rebuild our strategic deterrent and surpass the Soviets in strategic power. To build and maintain military power, the Kremlin has been holding the Russian people down to a wartime living standard and preempting 40 to 50 percent of national production. The Soviets have been racing unilaterally as fast as they can without actually starving their population.

Exactly what Kissinger has done to the military power of the United States—both strategic nuclear and conventional—has been established by conclusive evidence. He has never wavered from his consistent course of unilateral disarmament. It has been established that he made to the Soviets in the SALT I agreements concessions which may be fatal to our national survival, and that the Soviets are exploiting these concessions. It has also been proved that Kissinger has covered up for himself and for the Soviet exploitations. All that is left is to answer the question, why did he do it?

This brings us back again to his character, especially as revealed at his Salzburg press conference. The mystifying point is that only when he was engulfed in charges of a Watergate-related type did he suddenly become concerned with his honor. He worried not at all about his honor or what the American people thought when, in the SALT I ABM Treaty, he set us up as helpless hostages to the Kremlin, and then made concessions in the SALT I Interim Agreement which permitted the Soviets to destroy our deterrent. Kissinger has long been especially sensitive to Watergate and its related tentacles. Nearly a year earlier, Shana Alexander wrote in *Newsweek*:

> That evening, I met Henry Kissinger, a sorrowful and bitter figure now forced to watch his own historical monument dissolving in Watergate's acid rain. "The American people don't yet realize how gravely wounded the country is," he said. "This is Dunkirk."[25]

Of course, both the columnist and Kissinger were overly pessimistic. As Nixon grew weaker, Kissinger attained added stature. But his long-standing concern suggests that he may believe himself more vulnerable than anyone has yet suggested. Kissinger's defeatism and tendency to panic are further confirmed by Marvin and Bernard Kalb in their 1974 book entitled *Kissinger*. The authors quote Kissinger as saying in response to the killings at Kent State:

> I'm dead. Every war has its casualties. I am a casualty of this one.

Of course, Kissinger wasn't even seriously affected by the Kent State repercussions, but his immediate reaction was panic, and his pervasive emotion was fear.

This pessimistic strain in his complex character is one of the few clues to why he conceded to the Soviets such massive advantages in the SALT I accords and negotiations, and why he has destroyed so much of the in-being strategic power of the United States and for six years has blocked the buildup of additional strength.

Kissinger not only feels a deep fear of the Soviets, but he imposed it on Richard Nixon (who, in his pre-Kissinger years, was rather famous for standing up to the Russians and demanding U.S. strategic superiority). There is no question as to the originator of the language used by the President in his June 5, 1974, address to U.S. Naval Academy graduates:

> Eloquent appeals are now being made for the United States, through its foreign policy, to transform the internal as well as the international behavior of other countries, especially that of the Soviet Union. . . .
>
> We cannot gear our foreign policy to transformation of other societies. *In the nuclear age, our first responsibility must be the prevention of a war that could destroy all societies.*[26]

Kissinger, in his White House briefing on June 15, 1972, speaking of the awesome nuclear forces created by the United States and the U.S.S.R., pontificated:

> Each of us has thus come into possession of power singlehandedly capable of exterminating the human race. . . . We are compelled to coexist.

Despite the fact that this statement is a scientific monstrosity and highly misleading, he has repeated it ad nauseam ever since. By the time of his speech to the American Legion National Convention in Miami on August 20, 1974, his hypothesized hydrogen holocaust had escalated from exterminating the "human race" to "life itself." Presumably not a creature would be left stirring, not even a mouse or an amoeba, let alone a tree or a blade of grass. Although few see beneath Kissinger's public image, here is an excerpt from a perceptive article by David Binder of the *New York Times* in April 1974:

> I, fresh from a long sojourn in Europe, confess that Kissinger struck me as a man obsessed. But, aside from the show-business of American politics, obsessed with what? Not until his repetition of the leitmotif of "nuclear holocaust" and "structure of world peace" had become familiar did I begin to sense what he was talking about.
>
> Then on November 21 [1973], at a press conference, in reference to the West European stance during the Mideast war, he remarked: "One cannot avoid the perhaps melancholy conclusions that some of our European allies saw their interests so different from those of the United States that they were prepared to break ranks with the United States on a matter of very grave international consequence. . . ."
>
> Melancholy is a European, an un-American, attitude, if you will. The United States does not have a society geared for despondency. Americans fight gloom the way they fight body odor. Kissinger, the American, fights his European melancholy with equal fervor, seeking "charters," "agreements," and "treaties" to exorcise the feeling of despair.
>
> In the back of his mind are visions of Auschwitz and Hiroshima and Nagasaki. His is an apocalyptic vision, and those who do not share it with him make him melancholic.[27]

In that analysis, Auschwitz symbolizes the inhuman and (to both victims and potential victims) the invincible power of dictatorships; and Hiroshima is the symbol of the soul-as-well-as-body-searing holocaust threatened by the mere existence of nuclear weapons. David Binder intuitively identified both of the awesome and awful fears which impregnate Kissinger's character with defeatism. These twin obsessions laid the ineradicable basis for his subconscious conviction that people are helpless to defend either human dignity or life against the amoral power of totalitarianism; and that all humanity is subject to atomic doom.

Binder's judgment that Kissinger's defeatist attitude toward dictatorship actually originated as far back as his early experience under Hitler was confirmed by intriguing evidence unearthed in one of the most comprehensive projects of investigative reporting of the 1970s: a series of articles originating with the *New York Post* and nationally syndicated over the byline of Ralph Blumenfeld during the latter part of June 1974. An introductory note to the series explained:

Henry A. Kissinger, the U.S. Secretary of State, is one of the most widely known men in the world. But Kissinger the private man remains almost a mystery. To penetrate this mystery a newspaper team of 13 reporters conducted an exhaustive five-month investigation into Kissinger the man.

The series, entitled "Kissinger: Man and Statesman," is highly informative and objective. One of the "more than 400" investigative interviews was with Fritz Kraemer, Kissinger's first discoverer, and dealt with whether the Hitler persecution permanently scarred Kissinger's character. Kraemer explains:

What the Nazis did to these people is unspeakable. You can do damage to the soul of a man and never touch his body. For five years, the most formative years (10 to 15), Henry had to undergo this horror. And the real horror is the breakdown of the world. Imagine what it means when your father, who is your authority, the father you admire . . . is suddenly transformed into a frightened little mouse.

The *Post* article then summarizes the remainder of the Kraemer evaluation and continues:

Kraemer, who is still a close friend, says the experience was so traumatic that Kissinger literally can't talk about it. For any outsider, Kissinger's silence can be measured only when it is broken. And only twice since he rose to world prominence has Kissinger vented any feelings about the holocaust.

Once was last December [1973] on a cold, rainy tour of Yad Vashem, the memorial to Nazi victims near Jerusalem, when a reporter pestered Kissinger to describe his emotions, he turned on her, livid with rage. He said that this was a private visit, and that he expected there would be no more questions about it.

And when Kissinger was on an official visit to Bonn some years ago, the press office there announced that he would visit his relatives while in Germany, Kissinger said: "What the hell are they putting out? My relatives are soap."

The *New York Post* account then flashes back to Kissinger's pre-World War II struggle as a refugee in New York, trying to make a living and obtain an education:

So now the future Secretary of State began, at $11 a week, a job squeezing moisture from new bristles for a shaving-brush manufacturer. . . . His duties also included sweeping floors and packing crates. . . .

At City College Kissinger was preparing for "what was then the height of my ambition: becoming an accountant." But soon the warring world reached out again for Henry and his refugee friends.

One friend was Kurt Silbermann from Munich. . . . "One thing I remember," Silbermann said, "is the night of Pearl Harbor, December 7, 1941. We had a meeting that night, our group. We discussed how it would affect our lives." They were 18 or 19 years old, and to all the boys in the group, Pearl Harbor represented a kind of double jeopardy. They had eluded Hitler once, but. . . .

"We were prepared to die in the war, either by war action or as a result of the war. Because we expected Hitler to win," said Henry Gitterman, a civil engineer in Teaneck, N.J., who knew Kissinger in Fuerth and Washington Heights.

"We thought we would lose the war because we remembered times in Germany when we couldn't cross the street for six days, there were so many tanks rolling by. Not until I got to the Philippines as an infantryman, where I could see the [U.S.] fleet arrayed as far as the eye could see, could I believe that we would win the war."

In 1942, Kissinger's future was cloudy. . . . And then it was interrupted by a letter from Henry's draft board. On March 5, Pvt. Kissinger reported for active duty with the U.S. Army. It was a difficult time for any emotional commitment, and many of their friends doubt that Henry committed himself to Ann [Anneliese Fleischer, who became, some seven years later, Kissinger's first wife]. They can't be certain, but they doubt it. *They know that Henry, too, expected Hitler to win.*

So there we have it. Impressed on his psyche by the traumatic experience of having his world destroyed and his father cowed by Hitler's persecution during the five formative years of his life was his apocalyptic vision of Auschwitz, carrying with it a lifelong tendency to melancholia, and an ineradicable conviction of the invincibility of dictatorships and the omnipotence of dictators. Just as he was compulsively convinced in 1941 that Hitler would win over the United States, in 1961 he was just as convinced that Khrushchev would win out over the United States in the contest for strategic nuclear power and that Americans would be helpless to close the missile gap he imagined then existed.

But the most alarming manifestation of his apocalyptic vision—and his defeatism at the very thought of confrontation with a dictatorship vastly more powerful than Hitler's—surfaced during his October 25, 1973, press conference during the strategic alert crisis, in which Henry Kissinger mentioned nuclear calamity six times. We have quoted before his criticism of our people from the first page of his 1961 book, *The Necessity for Choice:*

> Nothing is more difficult for Americans to understand than the possibility of tragedy. Yet nothing should concern us more. For all the good will, for all the effort, we can go the way of other nations which to their citizens probably seemed just as invulnerable and eternal.

The picture which emerges is that of a man who lacks the courage to stand up to the Soviet Union with its massive nuclear power, a man who has repeatedly refused to criticize Soviet police-state methods and totalitarianism on the ground that our only alternatives are detente or nuclear war, a man obsessed with nuclear holocaust. A psyche sick with such pervasive fears is most apt to produce the vulnerability described by Khrushchev: a fear of nuclear war so intense as to paralyze the will, betray that fear to the enemy, and thus make nuclear attack "inevitable." As Khruschchev's warning made clear:

> I have always been against war, but at the same time I've always realized full well that the fear of nuclear war in a country's leader can paralyze that country's defenses. And if a country's defenses are paralyzed, then war really is inevitable: the enemy is sure to sense your fright and try to take advantage of it.[28]

This, then is the final and fatal flaw in the leadership qualities of Henry Kissinger: *an obsessive, pervasive fear of nuclear war.* The United States could coexist with a megalomaniac, with a man of delicately balanced emotions and a thrower of temper tantrums, and with a man lacking in personal loyalty to the President. But the United States cannot survive in freedom if our foreign and defense policies are under the one-man control of a dictatorial leader possessed by fear of nuclear war. In the nuclear environment of the mid-1970s, fear of nuclear war between the sole nuclear superpower and the sole sub-superpower is irrational. Neither power is preparing for nuclear war. The United States has no weapons capable of rational use in launching and fighting a nuclear war. If we should start such a war, it would be deliberate national suicide.

Nor do the Soviets want a nuclear war. They fear the damage which a nuclear war might do to their power base. They have not been building up their weapons to fight a nuclear war. The Kremlin dictators have been holding the entire U.S.S.R. on the austere basis of a wartime economy, sacrificing agriculture, civilian industry, technology, housing, mechanization, and civilian technology, in order to build the armaments essential *to avert* a nuclear war.

Thus it is that Henry Kissinger and all those who have advocated U.S. unilateral disarmament have been right on one point: the United States and the U.S.S.R. have a mutual interest in averting nuclear war. Tragically, however, the masters of the Kremlin have no mutual interest with us in averting the unilateral nuclear destruction of the United States. Why should they? If they eliminate the United States, or totally neutralize our strategic power, then the world and all its goods will belong to the Communist Party of the Soviet Union.

This explains why the Soviets have continued to build up strategic weapons past parity, past sufficiency, and even past substantial superiority. Their objective is not to deter nuclear war, but to accomplish our nuclear destruction on a unilateral basis.

Those leaders who fear nuclear war threaten the very survival of this nation by their policies because *everything they do in an attempt to avert nuclear war makes our unilateral nuclear destruction more probable and more imminent.* The more we disarm unilaterally, and the more we concede to the Soviet Union, the faster we will bring them to the completion of a first-strike capability against us. This is true whether our disarmament leaders are deliberately plotting to bring U.S. strategic power down so low that we will have no rational alternative to surrender to a Soviet ultimatum, or whether they are stupid enough to believe that unilateral disarmament is a means to peace.

Chilling new confirmation of the imminence of the Soviet threat was given by Admiral Elmo Zumwalt while he was still on active duty in 1974 as Chief of Naval Operations and member of the Joint Chiefs of Staff:

> At this moment, I consider that the Soviets have a possible first-strike capability, whereas we do not.[29]

The nearest parallel history provides to the fate our unilateral disarmers are selling us into is that of the Jewish people who were powerless to resist being marched into the gas ovens of Auschwitz and the other Hitlerian genocide factories. But the difference is that the Jews did not have the *power* to resist going to their death. The parallel between them and us would be close only if they had had the power— say, a military organization and ample modern arms to resist—and their leaders had persuaded them to disarm themselves and trust instead in a spirit of detente with the Hitler organization. Or, to make the parallel exact, let us hypothesize that the Jewish people had had sufficient military power to resist Hitler's forces successfully, but their own Jewish leaders had clandestinely destroyed nine-tenths of the instruments of their power while continuously assuring them that a "sufficiency" of arms was being retained.

Fortunately, the Israelis learned the lesson well. To survive in freedom, a nation must have both the military power and the will to use it.

Our leaders disarmed us because of a paralyzing *fear of nuclear war*—a fear which is irrational because the only realistic threat against us is the threat of unilateral nuclear destruction. Since the dawn of the nuclear age, and certainly since the Soviets attained the H-bomb and the world's first ICBM to deliver it, the fear of nuclear war has been exploited against us. By clever use of the false alternatives "Red or dead," the psychological warfare experts in the Kremlin subverted U.S. elite leadership groups who control our defense policies. Just as strategic nuclear power is the greatest power the world has ever known in a physical sense, *fear* of nuclear war is the greatest power the world has ever known in a psychological sense. The Communists were smart enough to exploit it against us.

But we can be smart enough to exploit it against them! If we can convince them that any attempt by them to accomplish the unilateral destruction of the United States will result in nuclear war—that is, in a bilateral nuclear exchange—then they will not attempt our unilateral destruction. They do not want a bilateral nuclear war. They have spent hundreds of millions of dollar equivalents just to insure their power base against nuclear destruction.

The technology is now available to avert the threat of a Soviet first-strike capability. The new satellite early warning system and computerized control systems, backed by U.S. leadership with courage and dedication, can turn the threat of nuclear war into insurance for our peace and freedom. Fortunately, the program for the development of the new satellite early warning system came up during Melvin Laird's Defense Secretaryship. McNamara would never have permitted it because it would have eliminated his "pause" to negotiate our surrender after a Soviet attack. Here is a tribute to it by Elliot L. Richardson during his short tenure as Defense Secretary:

> The maturing of satellite-based sensor technology has permitted the successful development and deployment of the early warning satellite system.
>
> This system now provides high confidence, virtually immediate warning of ballistic missile launch from current ballistic missile submarine launch areas, as well as ICBM and FOBS launch areas.
>
> The satellites are deployed in synchronous equatorial orbits. Data obtained by the satellites is transmitted to ground stations, processed, and sent to SAC, NORAD, NMCS and other users. Additional satellites will be launched as required to keep this system fully operational.[30]

Thus the technology required to buy for us a three-year stay of execution is in hand. If we buy that time, we can use it to reconstruct our strategic superiority and our nuclear umbrella, and to restore stability and prosperity and control inflation in the United States and the Free World. Also, it will give us time to develop an advanced defense system against Soviet supermissiles. Only such a defense can give us a national policy of "assured survival" instead of the immoral Kissinger policy of assured unilateral destruction.

Kissinger's Salzburg outburst of June 1974 provided hard evidence that his megalomania affects his judgment and his mental and emotional balance in a manner which degrades the rationality of his decisions. Even one of his greatest admirers, James Reston of the *New York Times*, commented:

> Henry Kissinger's threat to resign is the silliest thing he had done since he came into the government, and is not really to be taken seriously. . . .
> Even the most intelligent of men do strange things and the Kissinger

press conference is stranger than most. There was no great issue about him in the public mind. He was the one practical man, dealing successfully with intractable questions, but now he has made a big issue out of his credibility in the wiretapping matter and the Congress will have to sort it out.[31]

Bearing even more directly on Kissinger's admitted megalomania is this excerpt from a column entitled "Kissinger's Agony," by Marilyn Berger:

Kissinger's friends agree that the criticism, in the words of one, "has hurt him very deeply." There is the sense that Kissinger feels—although he had never expressed it—that he had done so much for the nation, and now is being treated so shabbily, that he is becoming the victim of a kind of witch-hunt.[32]

Henry Kissinger has indeed become a victim, but not of a witch hunt or any other force external to his own character. He has become the victim of his own megalomania. The compulsion for grandiose performances and glittering charades which swept him up so high, so fast, and for so long, finally brought him down. As he stood in Salzburg before shocked newsmen, "his voice faltering, his hands shaking, his eyes glistening with tears," his all-too-obvious lack of emotional stability and maturity of mind opened wide cracks in his public image which he had so long and so successfully projected and preserved. "After Salzburg," concluded Newsweek, "Henry Kissinger was marked as mortal."[33]

The commentators and the news analysts never came close to answering the question they posed, "Why did Henry Kissinger do it?" The question "why" assumes that there must be a reason. There was not. When Kissinger made that fateful decision to call the Salzburg press conference, he was not (in those so descriptive words of Herman Kahn) being "smart in a reasoned way." Kissinger was driven by megalomanic compulsions based on his own delusions of grandeur— a grandeur so massive, as he saw it, that the United States would quail before his threat of resignation. If his assumption had been true, it would have been a smart course of action. But since it was an illusion, he was being smart in an illusioned way; and, according to Kahn's analysis, "if you're smart in an illusioned way, you're smart and crazy." That is, some kind of a nut, or something.

The Salzburg outburst also demonstrated Kissinger's total inability to understand or appreciate what might be called typical American values. Out of all the deals he has made, all the secret actions he has taken, all the lies he has told, the only issue which he felt so deeply concerned his "honor" that he had to make a national and international dramatization of it, was the "accusation" that he had "initiated" the 17 wiretaps. The average American couldn't care less. Why not "initiate" wiretaps after there had been open and notorious leaks of vital national security information? But Henry Kissinger's values are based on one-world structure-of-peace utopian theories, and his point of view is that of the ultraliberal European intellectuals. Kissinger just can't understand that the American national honor is more critically involved in never selling out our people or our allies (especially small allies who are totally powerless against Communist aggression) than in wiretapping possible security risks.

Perhaps his most important miscalculation is his assumption that the American people may be willing to surrender to the Soviet Communists—especially without resorting to our residual power and the great material and spiritual assets of the United States. It is Henry Kissinger's too easy acceptance of the inevitability of tragedy, and his too often demonstrated defeatism in relation to the Soviet Union, which have linked him with the Nitze-McNamara-Gilpatric group and policies. Kissinger is carrying out all segments of their program for unilateral disarmament and a preemptive surrender to the Soviets.

There are those who reassure themselves that Henry Kissinger will never surrender the United States because it is his only power base. Unfortunately, however, he has never had much faith in our capability of surviving; and if one's power base is destined to disaster, why should the Secretary go down with a sinking Ship of State? After all, to a self-anointed architect of a new world order, it may appear that patriotism is an ignoble parochialism, and that the only meaningful loyalties are supranational or egocentric.

"Henry," say some who know him well, "has no God." Does he have a country?

Appendix

The SALT I Agreements
Signed in Moscow, May 26, 1972

Treaty Between the United States of America and the Union of Soviet Socialist Republics on the Limitation of Anti-Ballistic Missile Systems

The United States of America and the Union of Soviet Socialist Republics, hereinafter referred to as the Parties,

Proceeding from the premise that nuclear war would have devastating consequences for all mankind,

Considering that effective measures to limit anti-ballistic missile systems would be a substantial factor in curbing the race in strategic offensive arms and would lead to a decrease in the risk of outbreak of war involving nuclear weapons,

Proceeding from the premise that the limitation of anti-ballistic missile systems, as well as certain agreed measures with respect to the limitation of strategic offensive arms, would contribute to the creation of more favorable conditions for further negotiations on limiting strategic arms,

Mindful of their obligations under Article VI of the Treaty on the Non-Proliferation of Nuclear Weapons,

Declaring their intention to achieve at the earliest possible date the cessation of the nuclear arms race and to take effective measures toward reductions in strategic arms, nuclear disarmament, and general and complete disarmament,

Desiring to contribute to the relaxation of international tension and the strengthening of trust between States,

Have agreed as follows:

ARTICLE I

1. Each Party undertakes to limit anti-ballistic missile (ABM) systems and to adopt other measures in accordance with the provisions of this Treaty.

2. Each Party undertakes not to deploy ABM systems for a defense of the territory of its country and not to provide a base for such a defense, and not to deploy ABM systems for defense of an individual region except as provided for in Article III of this Treaty.

ARTICLE II

1. For the purposes of this Treaty an ABM system is a system to counter strategic ballistic missiles or their elements in flight trajectory, currently consisting of:

(a) ABM interceptor missiles, which are interceptor missiles constructed and deployed for an ABM role, or of a type tested in an ABM mode;

(b) ABM launchers, which are launchers constructed and deployed for launching ABM interceptor missiles; and

(c) ABM radars, which are radars constructed and deployed for an ABM role, or of a type tested in an ABM mode.

2. The ABM system components listed in paragraph 1 of this Article include those which are:

(a) operational;

(b) under construction;

(c) undergoing testing;

(d) undergoing overhaul, repair or conversion; or

(e) mothballed.

ARTICLE III

Each Party undertakes not to deploy ABM systems or their components except that:

(a) within one ABM system deployment area having a radius of one hundred and fifty kilometers and centered on the Party's national capital, a Party may deploy: (1) no more than one hundred ABM launchers and no more than one hundred ABM interceptor missiles at launch sites, and (2) ABM radars within no more than six ABM radar complexes, the area of each complex being circular and having a diameter of no more than three kilometers; and

(b) within one ABM system deployment area having a radius of one hundred and fifty kilometers and containing ICBM silo launchers, a Party may deploy: (1) no more than one hundred ABM launchers and no more than one hundred ABM interceptor missiles at launch sites, (2) two large phased-array ABM radars comparable in potential to corresponding ABM radars operational or under construction on the date of signature of the Treaty in an ABM system deployment area containing ICBM silo launchers, and (3) no more than eighteen ABM radars each having a potential less than the potential of the smaller of the above-mentioned two large phased-array ABM radars.

ARTICLE IV

The limitations provided for in Article III shall not apply to ABM systems or their components used for development or testing, and located within current or additionally agreed test ranges. Each Party may have no more than a total of fifteen ABM launchers at test ranges.

ARTICLE V

1. Each Party undertakes not to develop, test, or deploy ABM systems or components which are sea-based, air-based, space-based, or mobile land-based.

2. Each Party undertakes not to develop, test, or deploy ABM launchers for launching more than one ABM interceptor missile at a time from each launcher, nor to modify deployed launchers to provide them with such a capability, nor to develop, test, or deploy automatic or semi-automatic or other similar systems for rapid reload of ABM launchers.

ARTICLE VI

To enhance assurance of the effectiveness of the limitations on ABM systems and their components provided by this Treaty each Party undertakes:

(a) not to give missiles, launchers, or radars, other than ABM interceptor missiles, ABM launchers, or ABM radars, capabilities to counter strategic ballistic missiles or their elements in flight trajectory, and not to test them in an ABM mode; and

(b) not to deploy in the future radars for early warning of strategic ballistic missile attack except at locations along the periphery of its national territory and oriented outward.

ARTICLE VII

Subject to the provisions of this Treaty, modernization and replacement of ABM systems or their components may be carried out.

ARTICLE VIII

ABM systems or their components in excess of the numbers or outside the areas specified in this Treaty, as well as ABM systems or their components prohibited by this Treaty, shall be destroyed or dismantled under agreed procedures within the shortest possible agreed period of time.

ARTICLE IX

To assure the viability and effectiveness of this Treaty, each Party undertakes not to transfer to other States, and not to deploy outside its national territory, ABM systems or their components limited by this Treaty.

ARTICLE X

Each Party undertakes not to assume any international obligations which would conflict with this Treaty.

ARTICLE XI

The Parties undertake to continue active negotiations for limitations on strategic offensive arms.

ARTICLE XII

1. For the purpose of providing assurance of compliance with the provisions of this Treaty, each Party shall use national technical means of verification at its disposal in a manner consistent with generally recognized principles of international law.

2. Each Party undertakes not to interfere with the national technical means of verification of the other Party operating in accordance with paragraph 1 of this Article.

3. Each Party undertakes not to use deliberate concealment measures which impede verification by national technical means of compliance with the provisions of this Treaty. This obligation shall not require changes in current construction, assembly, conversion, or overhaul practices.

ARTICLE XIII

1. To promote the objectives and implementation of the provisions of this Treaty, the Parties shall establish promptly a Standing Consultative Commission, within the framework of which they will:

(a) consider questions concerning compliance with the obligations assumed and related situations which may be considered ambiguous;

(b) provide on a voluntary basis such information as either Party considers necessary to assure confidence in compliance with the obligations assumed;

(c) consider questions involving unintended interference with national technical means of verification;

(d) consider possible changes in the strategic situation which have a bearing on the provisions of this Treaty;

(e) agree upon procedures and dates for destruction or dismantling of ABM systems or their components in cases provided for by the provisions of this Treaty;

(f) consider, as appropriate, possible proposals for further increasing the viability of this Treaty, including proposals for amendments in accordance with the provisions of this Treaty;

(g) consider, as appropriate, proposals for further measures aimed at limiting strategic arms.

2. The Parties through consultation shall establish, and may amend as appropriate, Regulations for the Standing Consultative Commission governing procedures, composition and other relevant matters.

ARTICLE XIV

1. Each Party may propose amendments to this Treaty. Agreed amendments shall enter into force in accordance with the procedures governing the entry into force of this Treaty.

2. Five years after entry into force of this Treaty, and at five year intervals thereafter, the Parties shall together conduct a review of this Treaty.

ARTICLE XV

1. This Treaty shall be of unlimited duration.

2. Each Party shall, in exercising its national sovereignty, have the right to withdraw from this Treaty if it decides that extraordinary events related to the subject matter of this Treaty have jeopardized its supreme interests. It shall give notice of its decision to the other Party six months prior to withdrawal from the Treaty. Such notice shall include a statement of the extraordinary events the notifying Party regards as having jeopardized its supreme interests.

ARTICLE XVI

1. This Treaty shall be subject to ratification in accordance with the constitutional procedures of each Party. The Treaty shall enter into force on the day of the exchange of instruments of ratification.

2. This Treaty shall be registered pursuant to Article 102 of the Charter of the United Nations.

Done at Moscow on May 26, 1972, in two copies, each in the English and Russian languages, both texts being equally authentic.

For the United States of America:

RICHARD NIXON,
President of the United States of America.

For the Union of Soviet Socialist Republics:

L. I. BREZHNEV,
General Secretary of the Central Committee of the CPSU.

Interim Agreement Between the United States of America and the Union of Soviet Socialist Republics on Certain Measures With Respect to the Limitation of Strategic Offensive Arms

The United States of America and the Union of Soviet Socialist Republics, hereinafter referred to as the Parties,

Convinced that the Treaty on the Limitation of Anti-Ballistic Missile Systems and this Interim Agreement on Certain Measures with Respect to the Limitation of Strategic Offensive Arms will contribute to the creation of more favorable conditions for active negotiations on limiting strategic arms as well as to the relaxation of international tension and the strengthening of trust between States,

Taking into account the relationship between strategic offensive and defensive arms,

Mindful of their obligations under Article VI of the Treaty on the Non-Proliferation of Nuclear Weapons,

Have agreed as follows:

ARTICLE I

The Parties undertake not to start construction of additional fixed land-based intercontinental ballistic missile (ICBM) launchers after July 1, 1972.

ARTICLE II

The Parties undertake not to convert land-based launchers for light ICBMs, or for ICBMs of older types deployed prior to 1964, into land-based launchers for heavy ICBMs of types deployed after that time.

ARTICLE III

The Parties undertake to limit submarine-launched ballistic missile (SLBM) launchers and modern ballistic missile submarines to the numbers operational and under construction on the date of signature of this Interim Agreement, and in addition to launchers and submarines constructed under procedures established by the Parties as replacements for an equal number of ICBM launchers of older types deployed prior to 1964 or for launchers on older submarines.

ARTICLE IV

Subject to the provisions of this Interim Agreement, modernization and replacement of strategic offensive ballistic missiles and launchers covered by this Interim Agreement may be undertaken.

ARTICLE V

1. For the purpose of providing assurance of compliance with the provisions of this Interim Agreement, each Party shall use national technical means of verification at its disposal in a manner consistent with generally recognized principles of international law.

2. Each Party undertakes not to interfere with the national technical means of verification of the other Party operating in accordance with paragraph 1 of this Article.

3. Each Party undertakes not to use deliberate concealment measures which impede verification by national technical means of compliance with the provisions of this Interim Agreement. This obligation shall not require changes in current construction, assembly, conversion, or overhaul practices.

ARTICLE VI

To promote the objectives and implementation of the provisions of this Interim Agreement, the Parties shall use the Standing Consultative Commission established under Article XIII of the Treaty on the Limitation of Anti-Ballistic Missile Systems in accordance with the provisions of that Article.

ARTICLE VII

The Parties undertake to continue active negotiations for limitations on strategic offensive arms. The obligations provided for in this Interim Agreement shall not prejudice the scope or terms of the limitations on strategic offensive arms which may be worked out in the course of further negotiations.

ARTICLE VIII

1. This Interim Agreement shall enter into force upon exchange of written notices of acceptance by each Party, which exchange shall take place simultaneously with the exchange of instruments of ratification of the Treaty on the Limitation of Anti-Ballistic Missile Systems.

2. This Interim Agreement shall remain in force for a period of five years unless replaced earlier by an agreement on more complete measures limiting strategic offensive arms. It is the objective of the Parties to conduct active follow-on negotiations with the aim of concluding such an agreement as soon as possible.

3. Each Party shall, in exercising its national sovereignty, have the right to withdraw from this Interim Agreement if it decides that extraordinary events related to the subject matter of this Interim Agreement have jeopardized its supreme interests. It shall give notice of its decision to the other Party six months prior to withdrawal from this Interim Agreement. Such notice shall include a statement of the extraordinary events the notifying Party regards as having jeopardized its supreme interests.

Done at Moscow on May 26, 1972, in two copies, each in the English and Russian languages, both texts being equally authentic.

For the United States of America:

RICHARD NIXON,
President of the United States of America.
For the Union of Soviet Socialist Republics:

L. I. BREZHNEV,
General Secretary of the Central Committee of the CPSU.

Protocol to the Interim Agreement Between the United States of America and the Union of Soviet Socialist Republics on Certain Measures With Respect to the Limitation of Strategic Offensive Arms

The United States of America and the Union of Soviet Socialist Republics, hereinafter referred to as the Parties,

Having agreed on certain limitations relating to submarine-launched ballistic missile launchers and modern ballistic missile submarines, and to replacement procedures, in the Interim Agreement,

Have agreed as follows:

The Parties understand that, under Article III of the Interim Agreement, for the period during which that Agreement remains in force:

The U.S. may have no more than 710 ballistic missile launchers on submarines (SLBMs) and no more than 44 modern ballistic missile submarines. The Soviet Union may have no more than 950 ballistic missile launchers on submarines and no more than 62 modern ballistic missile submarines.

Additional ballistic missile launchers on submarines up to the above-mentioned levels, in the U.S.—over 656 ballistic missile launchers on nuclear-powered submarines, and in the U.S.S.R.—over 740 ballistic missile launchers on nuclear-powered submarines, operational and under construction, may become operational as replacements for equal numbers of ballistic missile launchers of older types deployed prior to 1964 or of ballistic missile launchers on older submarines.

The deployment of modern SLBMs on any submarine, regardless of type, will be counted against the total level of SLBMs permitted for the U.S. and the U.S.S.R.

This Protocol shall be considered an integral part of the Interim Agreement.

Done at Moscow this 26th day of May, 1972.

For the United States of America:

RICHARD NIXON,
President of the United States of America.

For the Union of Soviet Socialist Republics:

L. I. BREZHNEV,
General Secretary of the Central Committee of the CPSU.

Agreed Interpretations

(a) INITIALED STATEMENTS.

The texts of the statements set out below were agreed upon and initialed by the Heads of the Delegations on May 26, 1972.

ABM Treaty

[A]

The Parties understand that, in addition to the ABM radars which may be deployed in accordance with subparagraph (a) of Article III of the Treaty, those non-phased-array ABM radars operational on the date of signature of the Treaty within the ABM system deployment area for defense of the national capital may be retained.

[B]

The Parties understand that the potential (the product of mean emitted power in watts and antenna area in square meters) of the smaller of the two large phased-array ABM radars referred to in subparagraph (b) of Article III of the Treaty is considered for purposes of the Treaty to be three million.

[C]

The Parties understand that the center of the ABM system deployment area centered on the national capital and the center of the ABM system deployment area containing ICBM silo launchers for each Party shall be separated by no less than thirteen hundred kilometers.

[D]

The Parties agree not to deploy phased-array radars having a potential (the product of mean emitted power in watts and antenna area in square meters) exceeding three million, except as provided for in Articles III, IV, and VI of the Treaty, or except for the purposes of tracking objects in outer space or for use as national technical means of verification.

[E]

In order to insure fulfillment of the obligation not to deploy ABM systems and their components except as provided in Article III of the Treaty, the Parties agree that in the event ABM systems based on other physical principles and including components capable of substituting for ABM interceptor missiles, ABM launchers, or ABM radars are created in the future, specific limitations on such systems and their components would be subject to discussion in accordance with Article XIII and agreement in accordance with Article XIV of the Treaty.

[F]

The Parties understand that Article V of the Treaty includes obligations not to develop, test or deploy ABM interceptor missiles for the delivery by each ABM interceptor missile of more than one independently guided warhead.

[G]

The Parties understand that Article IX of the Treaty includes the obligation of the U.S. and the U.S.S.R. not to provide to other States technical descriptions or blueprints specially worked out for the construction of ABM systems and their components limited by the Treaty.

Interim Agreement

[H]

The Parties understand that land-based ICBM launchers referred to in the Interim Agreement are understood to be launchers for strategic ballistic missiles capable of ranges in excess of the shortest distance between the northeastern border of the continental U.S. and the northwestern border of the continental U.S.S.R.

[I]

The Parties understand that fixed land-based ICBM launchers under active construction as of the date of signature of the Interim Agreement may be completed.

[J]

The Parties understand that in the process of modernization and replacement the dimensions of land-based ICBM silo launchers will not be significantly increased.

[K]

The Parties understand that dismantling or destruction of ICBM launchers of older types deployed prior to 1964 and ballistic missile launchers on older submarines being replaced by new SLBM launchers on modern submarines will be initiated at the time of the beginning of sea trials of a replacement submarine, and will be completed in the shortest possible agreed period of time. Such dismantling or destruction, and timely notification thereof, will be accomplished under procedures to be agreed in the Standing Consultative Commission.

[L]

The Parties understand that during the period of the Interim Agreement there shall be no significant increase in the number of ICBM or SLBM test and training launchers, or in the number of such launchers for modern land-based heavy ICBMs. The Parties further understand that construction or conversion of ICBM launchers at test ranges shall be undertaken only for purposes of testing and training.

(b) COMMON UNDERSTANDINGS.

Common understanding of the Parties on the following matters was reached during the negotiations:

A. *Increase in ICBM Silo Dimensions.*—Ambassador Smith made the following statement on May 26, 1972: "The Parties agree that the term 'significantly increased' means that an increase will not be greater than 10-15 percent of the present dimensions of land-based ICBM silo launchers."

Minister Semenov replied that this statement corresponded to the Soviet understanding.

B. *Location of ICBM Defenses.*—The U.S. Delegation made the following statement on May 26, 1972: "Article III of the ABM Treaty provides for each side one ABM system deployment area centered on its national capital and one ABM system deployment area containing ICBM silo launchers. The two sides have registered agreement on the following statement: 'The Parties understand that the center of the ABM system deployment area centered on the national capital and the center of the ABM system deployment area containing ICBM silo launchers for each Party shall be separated by no less than thirteen hundred kilometers.' In this connection, the U.S. side notes that its ABM system deployment area for defense of ICBM silo launchers, located west of the Mississippi River, will be centered in the Grand Forks ICBM silo launcher deployment area." (See Initialed Statement [C].)

C. *ABM Test Ranges.*—The U.S. Delegation made the following statement on April 26, 1972: "Article IV of the ABM Treaty provides that 'the limitations provided for in Article III shall not apply to ABM systems or their components used for development or testing, and located within current or additionally agreed test ranges.' We believe it would be useful to assure that there is no misunderstanding as to current ABM test ranges. It is our understanding that ABM test ranges encompass the area within which ABM components are located for test purposes. The current U.S. ABM test ranges are at White Sands, New Mexico, and at Kwajalein Atoll, and the current Soviet ABM test range is near Sary Shagan in Kazakhstan. We consider that non-phased-array radars of types used for range safety or instrumentation purposes may be located outside of ABM test ranges. We interpret the reference in Article IV to 'additionally agreed test ranges' to mean that ABM components will not be located at any other test ranges without prior agreement between our Governments that there will be such additional ABM test ranges."

On May 5, 1972, the Soviet Delegation stated that there was a common understanding on what ABM test ranges were, that the use of the types of non-ABM radars for range safety or instrumentation was not limited under the Treaty, that the reference in Article IV to "additionally agreed" test ranges was sufficiently clear, and that national means permitted identifying current test ranges.

D. *Mobile ABM Systems.*—On January 28, 1972, the U.S. Delegation made the following statement: "Article V (1) of the Joint Draft Text of the ABM Treaty includes an undertaking not to develop, test, or deploy mobile land-based ABM systems and their components. On May 5, 1971, the U.S. side indicated that, in its view, a prohibition on deployment of mobile ABM systems and components would rule out the deployment of ABM launchers and radars which were not permanent fixed types. At that time, we asked for the Soviet view of this interpretation. Does the Soviet side agree with the U.S. side's interpretation put forward on May 5, 1971?"

On April 13, 1972, the Soviet Delegation said there is a general common understanding on this matter.

E. *Standing Consultative Commission.*—Ambassador Smith made the following statement on May 23, 1972: "The United States proposes that the sides agree that, with regard to initial implementation of the ABM Treaty's Article XIII on the Standing Consultative Commission (SCC) and of the consultation Articles to the Interim Agreement on offensive arms and the Accidents Agreement,* agreement establishing the SCC will be worked out early in the follow-on SALT negotiations; until that is completed, the following arrangements will prevail: when SALT is in session, any consultation desired by either side under these Articles can be carried out by the two SALT Delegations; when SALT is not in session, *ad hoc* arrangements for any desired consultations under these Articles may be made through diplomatic channels."

Minister Semenov replied that, on an *ad referendum* basis, he could agree that the U.S. statement corresponded to the Soviet understanding.

F. *Standstill.*—On May 6, 1972, Minister Semenov made the following statement: "In an effort to accommodate the wishes of the U.S. side, the Soviet Delegation is prepared to proceed on the basis that the two sides will in fact observe the obligations of both the Interim Agreement and the ABM Treaty beginning from the date of signature of these two documents."

In reply, the U.S. Delegation made the following statement on May 20, 1972: "The U.S. agrees in principle with the Soviet statement made on May 6 concerning observance of obligations beginning from date of signature but we would like to make clear our understanding that this means that, pending ratification and acceptance, neither side would take any action prohibited by the agreements after they had entered into force. This understanding would continue to apply in the absence of notification by either signatory of its intention not to proceed with ratification or approval."

The Soviet Delegation indicated agreement with the U.S. statement.

* See Article 7 of Agreement to Reduce the Risk of Outbreak of Nuclear War Between the United States of America and the Union of Soviet Socialist Republics, signed September 30, 1971.

Unilateral Statements

(a) The following noteworthy unilateral statements were made during the negotiations by the United States Delegation:—

A. Withdrawal from the ABM Treaty

On May 9, 1972, Ambassador Smith made the following statement: "The U.S. Delegation has stressed the importance the U.S. Government attaches to achieving agreement on more complete limitations on strategic offensive arms, following agreement on an ABM Treaty and on an Interim Agreement on certain measures with respect to the limitation of strategic offensive arms. The U.S. Delegation believes that an objective of the follow-on negotiations should be to constrain and reduce on a long-term basis threats to the survivability of our respective strategic retaliatory forces. The U.S.S.R. Delegation has also indicated that the objectives of SALT would remain unfulfilled without the achievement of an agreement providing for more complete limitations on strategic offensive arms. Both sides recognize that the initial agreements would be steps toward the achievement of more complete limitations on strategic arms. If an agreement providing for more complete strategic offensive arms limitations were not achieved within five years, U.S. supreme interests could be jeopardized. Should that occur, it would constitute a basis for withdrawal from the ABM Treaty. The U.S. does not wish to see such a situation occur, nor do we believe that the U.S.S.R. does. It is because we wish to prevent such a situation that we emphasize the importance the U.S. Government attaches to achievement of more complete limitations on strategic offensive arms. The U.S. Executive will inform the Congress, in connection with Congressional consideration of the ABM Treaty and the Interim Agreement, of this statement of the U.S. position."

B. Land-Mobile ICBM Launchers

The U.S. Delegation made the following statement on May 20, 1972: "In connection with the important subject of land-mobile ICBM launchers, in the interest of concluding the Interim Agreement the U.S. Delegation now withdraws its proposal that Article I or an agreed statement explicitly prohibit the deployment of mobile land-based ICBM launchers. I have been instructed to inform you that, while agreeing to defer the question of limitation of operational land-mobile ICBM launchers to the subsequent negotiations on more complete limitations on strategic offensive arms, the U.S. would consider the deployment of operational land-mobile ICBM launchers during the period of the Interim Agreement as inconsistent with the objectives of that Agreement."

C. Covered Facilities

The U.S. Delegation made the following statement on May 20, 1972: "I wish to emphasize the importance that the United States attaches to the provisions of Article V, including in particular their application to fitting out or berthing submarines."

D. "Heavy" ICBM's

The U.S. Delegation made the following statement on May 26, 1972: "The U.S. Delegation regrets that the Soviet Delegation has not been willing to agree on a common definition of a heavy missile. Under these circumstances, the U.S. Delegation believes it necessary to state the following: The United States would consider any ICBM having a volume significantly greater than that of the largest light ICBM now operational on either side to be a heavy ICBM. The U.S. proceeds on the premise that the Soviet side will give due account to this consideration."

E. Tested in ABM Mode

On April 7, 1972, the U.S. Delegation made the following statement: "Article II of the Joint Draft Text uses the term 'tested in an ABM mode,' in defining ABM components, and Article VI includes certain obligations concerning such testing. We believe that the side should have a common understanding of this phrase. First, we would note that the testing provisions of the ABM Treaty are intended to apply to testing which occurs after the date of signature of the Treaty, and not to any testing which may have occurred in the past. Next, we would amplify the remarks we have made on this subject during the previous Helsinki phase by setting forth the objectives which govern the U.S. view on the subject, namely, while prohibiting testing of non-ABM components for ABM purposes: not to prevent testing of ABM components, and not to prevent testing of non-ABM components for non-ABM purposes. To clarify our interpretation of 'tested in an ABM mode,' we note that we would consider a launcher, missile, or radar to be 'tested in an ABM mode' if, for example, any of the following events occur: (1) a launcher is used to launch an ABM interceptor missile, (2) an interceptor missile is flight tested against a target vehicle which has a flight trajectory with characteristics of a strategic ballistic missile flight trajectory, or is flight tested in conjunction with the test of an ABM interceptor missile or an ABM radar at the same test range, or is flight tested to an altitude inconsistent with interception of targets against which air defenses are deployed, (3) a radar makes measurements on a cooperative target vehicle of the kind referred to in item (2) above during the reentry portion of its trajectory or makes measurements in conjunction with the test of an ABM interceptor missile or an ABM radar at the same test range. Radars used for purposes such as range safety or instrumentation would be exempt from application of these criteria."

F. No-Transfer Article of ABM Treaty

On April 18, 1972, the U.S. Delegation made the following statement: "In regard to this Article [IX], I have a brief and I believe self-explanatory statement to make. The U.S. side wishes to make clear that the provisions of this Article do not set a precedent for whatever provision may be considered for a Treaty on Limiting Strategic Offensive Arms. The question of transfer of strategic offensive arms is a far more complex issue, which may require a different solution."

G. No Increase in Defense of Early Warning Radars

On July 28, 1970, the U.S. Delegation made the following statement: "Since Hen House radars [Soviet ballistic missile early warning radars] can detect and track ballistic missile warheads at great distances, they have a significant ABM potential. Accordingly, the U.S. would regard any increase in the defenses of such radars by surface-to-air missiles as inconsistent with an agreement."

(b) The following noteworthy unilateral statement was made by the Delegation of the U.S.S.R. and is shown here with the U.S. reply:

On May 17, 1972, Minister Semenov made the following unilateral "Statement of the Soviet Side:" "Taking into account that modern ballistic missile submarines are presently in the possession of not only the U.S., but also of its NATO allies, the Soviet Union agrees that for the period of effectiveness of the Interim 'Freeze' Agreement the U.S. and its NATO allies have up to 50 such submarines with a total of up to 800 ballistic missile launchers thereon (including 41 U.S. submarines with 656 ballistic missile launchers). However, if during the period of effectiveness of the Agreement U.S. allies in NATO should increase the number of their modern submarines to exceed the numbers of submarines they would have operational or under construction on the date of signature of the Agreement, the Soviet Union will have the right to a corresponding increase in the number of its submarines. In the opinion of the Soviet side, the solution of the question of modern ballistic missile submarines provided for in the Interim Agreement only partially compensates for the strategic imbalance in the deployment of the nuclear-powered missile submarines of the U.S.S.R. and the U.S. Therefore, the Soviet side believes that this whole question, and above all the questions of liquidating the American missile submarine bases outside the U.S., will be appropriately resolved in the course of follow-on negotiations."

On May 24, Ambassador Smith made the following reply to Minister Semenov: "The United States side has studied the 'statement made by the Soviet side' of May 17 concerning compensation for submarine basing and SLBM submarines belonging to third countries. The United States does not accept the validity of the considerations in that statement."

On May 26 Minister Semenov repeated the unilateral statement made on May 17. Ambassador Smith also repeated the U.S. rejection on May 26.

Joint U.S.-Soviet Communique
Moscow, July 3, 1974

In accordance with the agreement to hold regular U.S.-Soviet meetings at the highest level and at the invitation extended during the visit of General Secretary of the Central Committee of the Communist Party of the Soviet Union L. I. Brezhnev to the U.S.A. in June 1973, the President of the United States of America and Mrs. Richard Nixon paid an official visit to the Soviet Union from June 27 to July 3, 1974. . . .

Accompanying the President of the U.S.A. and participating in the talks was Dr. Henry A. Kissinger, U.S. Secretary of State and Assistant to the President for National Security Affairs. . . .

FURTHER LIMITATION OF STRATEGIC ARMS AND OTHER DISARMAMENT ISSUES

Both sides again carefully analyzed the entire range of their mutual relations connected with the prevention of nuclear war and limitation of strategic armaments. They arrived at the common view that the fundamental agreements concluded between them in this sphere continue to be effective instruments of the general improvement of U.S.-Soviet relations and the international situation as a whole. The U.S.A. and the U.S.S.R. will continue strictly to fulfill the obligations undertaken in those agreements.

In the course of the talks, the two sides had a thorough review of all aspects of the problem of limitation of strategic arms. They concluded that the Interim Agreement on offensive strategic weapons should be followed by a new agreement between the United States and the Soviet Union on the limitation of strategic arms. They agreed that such an agreement should cover the period until 1985 and deal with both quantitative and qualitative limitations. They agreed that such an agreement should be completed at the earliest possible date, before the expiration of the Interim Agreement.

They hold the common view that such a new agreement would serve not only the interests of the United States and the Soviet Union but also those of a further relaxation of international tensions and of world peace.

Their delegations will reconvene in Geneva in the immediate future on the basis of instructions growing out of the Summit.

Taking into consideration the interrelationship between the development of offensive and defensive types of strategic arms and noting the successful implementation of the Treaty on the Limitation of Anti-ballistic Missile Systems concluded between them in May 1972, both sides considered it desirable to adopt additional limitations on the deployment of such systems. To that end they concluded a protocol providing for the limitation of each side to a single deployment area for ABM systems instead of two such areas as permitted to each side by the treaty.

At the same time, two protocols were signed entitled "Procedures Governing Replacement, Dismantling or Destruction and Notification thereof, for Strategic Offensive Arms" and "Procedures Governing Replacement, Dismantling or Destruction, and Notification thereof for ABM Systems and Their Components." These protocols were worked out by the Standing Consultative Commission which was established to promote the objectives and implementation of the provisions of the Treaty and the Interim Agreement signed on May 26, 1972.

The two sides emphasized the serious importance which the U.S. and U.S.S.R. also attach to the realization of other possible measures—both on a bilateral and on a multilateral basis—in the field of arms limitation and disarmament.

Having noted the historic significance of the Treaty Banning Nuclear Weapon Tests in the Atmosphere, in Outer Space and Under Water, concluded in Moscow in 1963, to which the United States and the Soviet Union are parties, both sides expressed themselves in favor of making the cessation of nuclear weapon tests comprehensive. Desiring to contribute to the achievement of this goal the U.S.A. and the U.S.S.R. concluded, as an important step in this direction, the Treaty on the Limitation of Underground Nuclear Weapon Tests providing for the complete cessation, starting from March 31, 1976, of the tests of such weapons above an appropriate yield threshold, and for confining other underground tests to a minimum. . . .

NOTES

Chapter 1 (pages 11-40)

1. New York Times Service, serialized Dec. 9 to 14, 1972.
2. Springfield, Mass.: G. & C. Merriam Co., 7th Collegiate edition, 1971.
3. Henry A. Kissinger, *The Necessity for Choice* (New York: Harper & Brothers, 1961).
4. Henry A. Kissinger, background briefing given in Chicago, Sept. 16, 1970.
5. Kissinger book, 1961, *op. cit.*
6. Kissinger briefing, 1970, *op. cit.*
7. Henry A. Kissinger, White House briefing for five congressional committees, June 15, 1972. Reprinted in *Weekly Compilation of Presidential Documents*, June 19, 1972, and also in U.S. Senate Foreign Relations Committee, *Hearings on SALT Agreements*, June 19 to July 20, 1972, pp. 393 ff.
8. Henry A. Kissinger, news conference at the Intourist Hotel, Moscow, May 27, 1972. Reprinted in *Weekly Compilation of Presidential Documents*, June 5, 1972.
9. Edward Luttwak, *The Strategic Balance 1972*, published under the auspices of the Center for Strategic and International Studies, Georgetown University, as No. 3 of a series entitled *The Washington Papers* (New York: Library Press, 1972).
10. Melvin R. Laird, *A House Divided: America's Strategy Gap* (Chicago: Henry Regnery Co., 1962).
11. Nikita S. Khrushchev, "For New Victories for the World Communist Movement," Jan. 6, 1961.
12. Robert Strausz-Hupe, William R. Kintner, and Stefan T. Possony, *A Forward Strategy for America* (New York: Harper & Brothers, 1961).
13. Henry A. Kissinger, news conference, Moscow, May 29, 1972.
14. "State of the Union Message," Jan. 7, 1959.
15. White House briefing, *op. cit.*, June 15, 1972.
16. James Nathan Miller, "The Unthinkable Thoughts of Herman Kahn," *Reader's Digest*, April 1973.
17. White House briefing, *op. cit.*, June 15, 1972.
18. U.S. Senate Foreign Relations Committee, *Hearings on SALT Agreements*, June 19 to July 20, 1972, p. 264.
19. FY 1971 Defense Program and Budget, Feb. 20, 1970, p. 45.

Chapter 2 (pages 41-62)

1. FY 1973 Defense Budget and FY 1973-77 Program, Feb. 17, 1972.
2. FY 1975 Posture Report.
3. Joseph Alsop column, datelined Peking, China, Dec. 4, 1972.
4. *Ibid.*

Chapter 5 (pages 89-121)

1. Henry A. Kissinger, background briefing given in Chicago, Sept. 16, 1970.
2. John W. Finney, "Zumwalt: Russia Has Edge at Sea," New York Times Service, May 15, 1974.
3. Edward Luttwak, The Strategic Balance 1972, published under the auspices of the Center for Strategic and International Studies, Georgetown University, as No. 3 of a series entitled The Washington Papers (New York: Library Press, 1972), p. 75.
4. Blue Ribbon Defense Panel Supplemental Statement, The Shifting Balance of Military Power, submitted to the President and the Secretary of Defense by seven members of the presidentially appointed Blue Ribbon Defense Panel, Sept. 30, 1970.
5. Henry A. Kissinger, White House briefing for five congressional committees, June 15, 1972.
6. Luttwak, op. cit.
7. New York: Holt, Rinehart & Winston, 1973.
8. Agence France press dispatch, datelined Tokyo, Jan. 19, 1973.
9. Fred Charles Iklé, "Nuclear Deterrence," Foreign Affairs, Jan. 1973.
10. Kosta Tsipis (Executive Secretary, U.S. Pugwash Group), "Strategic Stability with SALT," MIT Technology Review, Oct./Nov. 1972.
11. Iklé, op. cit.

Chapter 6 (pages 122-133)

1. Robert G. L. Waite, in the "Afterword" of The Mind of Adolph Hitler, by Walter C. Langer (New York: Basic Books, 1972).

Chapter 7 (pages 134-152)

1. Henry A. Kissinger, The Necessity for Choice (New York: Harper & Brothers, 1961), p. xi.
2. Newsweek, Oct. 2, 1972, p. 40.
3. Henry A. Kissinger, Nuclear Weapons and Foreign Policy (New York: Harper & Brothers, 1957).
4. Stephen R. Graubard, Kissinger: Portrait of a Mind (New York, W. W. Norton & Co., 1973).

Chapter 9 (pages 168-210)

1. Even prominent fellow-members of the CFR were moved to speak out against Kissinger's crude and brutal treatment of our friends. Former Ambassador to Japan Edwin O. Reischauer asserted: "I'll attack my colleague Henry Kissinger quite directly because I think he's as much to blame for this [shocking treatment of Japan] as anybody. . . . [The Kissinger-Nixon policies] have been disastrous on . . . the relationships with our friends." Former Under Secretary of State George Ball commented: "The Administration has been unilateralist in dealing with problems affecting American-European and American-Japanese relations." Zbigniew Brzezinski, Columbia University's Sovietologist, declared: "By allowing Japan to feel insulted by neglect, Kissinger has struck a raw nerve." Newsweek, July 30, 1973.
2. UPI dispatch, Washington, Jan. 4, 1973.
3. Copley News Service, Nov. 24, 1972.
4. Sir John Harrington, 1561-1612.
5. President Richard Nixon, "Immediate Report to Congress on the Results of the Moscow Summit," June 1, 1972.
6. Henry A. Kissinger, White House briefing for five congressional committees, June 15, 1972.
7. Ibid.
8. U.S. News & World Report, Aug. 6, 1973.
9. International Institute for Strategic Studies, London, Adelphi Paper No. 89: "Military Technology and the European Balance," August 1972.
10. Los Angeles Times Service, datelined Vienna, Feb. 5, 1973.
11. Military Posture Report, FY 1975, of Chairman of Joint Chiefs of Staff to Congress, March 1974.
12. Address by General Creighton W. Abrams, U.S. Army Chief of Staff, to Association of the Army, Fort Dix, N.J., Mar. 8, 1974: "We have seen a growth in real sophistication in Soviet weaponry and equipment in recent years—expensive sophistication. For instance, their tanks are very effective, very modern, and very expensive weapons systems. Among other features, they all have an underwater fording capability built right in—even in the tanks they exported to the Mideast. For us to provide our tank fleet with this capability would cost in the neighborhood of $150 million—just for that single capability. Their tanks have auxiliary, automatic and backup features that ours do not have. We call it gold plating; they call it a military requirement. For us to provide even part of these capabilities—without changing the existing fighting character-

istics of the tank—we would have to spend thousands of dollars more per tank. In fact, one estimate of what it would cost to add all the extra Soviet tank features onto the U.S. tank fleet—in effect to make them equivalent in all features—is $2 billion. That is what the add-on cost would be for us for our smaller tank force. We see this sophistication elsewhere, too. A few years ago the Soviets paraded a new infantry fighting vehicle. Ours is still under development. But from everything we learn, their infantry fighting vehicle is the last word in technology. It has many features we would call 'gold plating' in our terms, but which are 'requirements' in their terms. And the same is true of their trucks, their ammunition, and so on. They spend very heavily to gain even a small advantage, to incorporate nice-to-have features which we forgo, because of the cost."

13. Melvin R. Laird, *A House Divided: America's Strategy Gap* (Chicago: Henry Regnery Co., 1962), p. 51.

14. *Ibid.*, p. 75.

Chapter 10 (pages 211-246)

1. *Chicago Tribune*, Nov. 11, 1973.
2. James Daniel and John G. Hubbell, *Strike in the West: The Complete Story of the Cuban Crisis* (Chicago: Holt, Rinehart & Winston, 1963), p. 42.
3. May 7, 1973.
4. Final Report to the Congress, Jan. 8, 1973.
5. Nov. 22, 1971, p. 31.
6. George C. Wilson, *Washington Post*, Nov. 29, 1972.

Chapter 11 (pages 247-260)

1. Dr. Donald G. Brennan, "When SALT Hit the Fan," *National Review*, June 23, 1972, p. 689.
2. U.S. Senate Foreign Relations Committee, *Hearings on SALT Agreements*, June 19 to July 20, 1972, p. 188.
3. U.S. Senate Foreign Relations Committee, *Hearings on Nomination of Henry A. Kissinger to be Secretary of State*, Sept. 10, 1973, p. 79.
4. Allen Drury, *Advise and Consent* (New York: Doubleday & Co., 1959), p.34.

Chapter 12 (pages 261-281)

1. Frances FitzGerald, "For the President's Adviser on Foreign Policy, Business as Usual," review of *Kissinger, Portrait of a Mind* by Stephen R. Graubard, in the *New York Times Book Review*, July 15, 1973, p. 3.
2. Emmet John Hughes, *Newsweek*, August 20, 1973, p. 13.
3. *Ibid.*
4. *Ibid.*
5. FitzGerald, *op. cit.*
6. *Ibid.*
7. Henry A. Kissinger, White House briefing for five congressional committees, June 15, 1972.
8. Los Angeles Times Service, Nov. 8, 1973.
9. Edward Luttwak, *The Strategic Balance 1972*, published under the auspices of the Center for Strategic and International Studies, Georgetown University, as No. 3 of a series entitled *The Washington Papers* (New York: Library Press, 1972).

Chapter 13 (pages 282-310)

1. Sept. 1972.
2. Press conference, Intourist Hotel, Moscow, May 27, 1972.
3. U.S. Senate Foreign Relations Committee, *Hearings on SALT Agreements*, June 19 to July 20, 1972, p. 264.
4. St. Matthew 25:14-30.
5. Press conference statement, Aug. 17, 1973, *U.S. News & World Report*, Sept. 3, 1973, p. 60.

Chapter 14 (pages 311-321)

1. John Newhouse, *Cold Dawn: The Story of SALT* (New York: Holt, Rinehart & Winston, 1973), p. 77.
2. *Ibid.*, p. 77.

3. *Ibid.*, p. 83.
4. *Ibid.*, pp. 84, 85, 86, 87.
5. *Ibid.*, p. 88.
6. *Ibid.*, p. 88.
7. *Ibid.*, p. 89.
8. White House briefing for five congressional committees, June 15, 1972.
9. Newhouse, *op. cit.*, p. 91, note 1.
10. *Ibid.*, p. 94.
11. *Ibid.*, p. 111.
12. *Ibid.*, p. 129.
13. *Ibid.*, p. 132.
14. *Ibid.*, pp. 135, 136.
15. Documented and discussed in Chapter 15 of this book.
16. U.S. Senate Foreign Relations Committee, *Hearings on Nomination of Henry A. Kissinger to be Secretary of State*, Sept. 11, 1973, pp. 109-110.

Chapter 15 (pages 322-347)

1. John Newhouse, *Cold Dawn: The Story of SALT* (New York: Holt, Rinehart & Winston, 1973).
2. Washington Post Service, June 8, 1973.
3. Newhouse, *op. cit.*, p. 168.
4. *Ibid.*, p. 177.
5. *Washington Post* dispatch from Moscow, Sept. 19, 1973, quoting Brezhnev speech delivered in Bulgaria on Sept. 18, 1973.
6. In his White House briefing to the five congressional committees on June 15, 1972.
7. Newhouse, *op. cit.*, p. 147.
8. *Ibid.*, p. 146.
9. *Ibid.*, p. 7.
10. *Ibid.*, p. 162.
11. *Ibid.*, p. 171.
12. *National Review*, Sept. 14, 1973.
13. Newhouse, *op. cit.*, p. 203.
14. *Ibid.*, p. 192.
15. *Ibid.*, p. 193.
16. *Ibid.*, p. 193.
17. *Ibid.*, p. 212.
18. AP dispatch, March 29, 1963.
19. NANA dispatch, Paris, Dec. 27, 1964.
20. UPI dispatch, Paris, May 31, 1965.
21. Edward Luttwak, *The Strategic Balance 1972*, published under the auspices of the Center for Strategic and International Studies, Georgetown University, as No. 3 of a series entitled *The Washington Papers* (New York: Library Press, 1972).
22. Arms Control and Disarmament Agency, *Documents on Disarmament*, 1969, p. 255.
23. Nov. 12, 1973, p. 60.
24. Newhouse, *op. cit.*, p. 234.

Chapter 16 (pages 348-371)

1. Statement by Marshal Kiril Moskalento, former Commander-in-Chief of Soviet Strategic Rocket Troops, now Soviet Deputy Minister of Defense, quoted in *The ABM and the Changed Strategic Military Balance*, by the American Security Council, May 1969.
2. Henry A. Kissinger, *The Necessity for Choice* (New York: Harper & Brothers, 1961). pp. 178-179.
3. *Ibid.*, p. 209.
4. Henry A. Kissinger, *The Troubled Partnership: A Re-Appraisal of the Western Alliance* (New York: McGraw-Hill, 1965), p. 198.
5. *The Necessity for Choice, op. cit.*, p. 42.
6. Henry A. Kissinger, White House briefing for five congressional committees, June 15, 1972.
7. *The Troubled Partnership, op. cit.*, p. 18.
8. *Ibid.*, p. 18.
9. Henry A. Kissinger, *A World Restored: Castlereagh, Metternich & Restoration of Peace, 1812-1822* (Boston: Houghton-Mifflin, 1957).

Chapter 17 (pages 372-391)

1. "When SALT Hit the Fan," *National Review*, June 23, 1972.
2. See the diagram prepared for the series of five technical articles published in *Aviation Week & Space Technology* beginning on October 4, 1971, entitled "The Growing Threat—New Soviet Weapons Technology."

Chapter 18 (pages 392-403)

1. John Newhouse, *Cold Dawn: The Story of SALT* (New York: Holt, Rinehart & Winston, 1973), p. 268.
2. The parenthetical phrase is in the original. Dr. Brennan refers to the ABM Treaty as a "proposed" treaty because it had not yet been ratified by the Senate at the time he published his article.
3. William R. Kintner (former Director of the Foreign Policy Research Institute and now Ambassador to Thailand) and Robert L. Pfaltzgraff, Jr., *SALT: Implications For Arms Control in the 1970s* (Pittsburgh, Pa.: University of Pittsburgh Press, 1973), p. 386.
4. William R. Van Cleave, "Implications of Success or Failure of SALT," included in *SALT: Implications for Arms Control in the 1970s*, edited by William R. Kintner and Robert L. Pfaltzgraff, Jr. (Pittsburgh, Pa.: University of Pittsburgh Press, 1973).
5. Edward Luttwak, *The Strategic Balance 1972*, published under the auspices of the Center for Strategic and International Studies, Georgetown University, as No. 3 of a series entitled *The Washington Papers* (New York: Library Press, 1972), p. 79.
6. New York: Pergamon Press, 1969, pp. 161-169.
7. Newhouse, *op. cit.*, p. 176.
8. Mose L. Harvey, Leon Goure, and Vladimir Prokofieff, *Science and Technology as an Instrument of Soviet Policy*, Monographs in International Affairs (Miami, Fla.: University of Miami: Center for Advanced International Studies, 1972).

Chapter 19 (pages 404-421)

1. U.S. Subcommittee on National Security Policy and Scientific Developments, House Foreign Affairs Committee, *Hearings*, 1969, p. 244.
2. The Joint Chiefs of Staff told the Senate Foreign Relations Committee: "The U.S.S.R. is ahead of the United States in the high-yield (tens of megatons) technology, in weapons-effect knowledge derived from high-yield explosives, and in the yield/weight ratios of high-yield devices." *Hearings on the Nuclear Test Ban Treaty*, Aug. 15, 1963, p. 273.
3. *U.S. News & World Report*, Nov. 30, 1970.
4. Rear Admiral Chester Ward, "The 'New Myths' and 'Old Realities' of Nuclear War," *Orbis*: University of Pennsylvania Foreign Policy Research Institute Quarterly, Summer Issue, 1964, p. 279.

Chapter 20 (pages 422-440)

1. *U.S. News & World Report*, Sept. 3, 1973.
2. Laird testimony, U.S. Senate Foreign Relations Committee, *Hearings on SALT Agreements*, June 19 to July 20, 1972, p. 104.
3. Press conference, Intourist Hotel, Moscow, May 27, 1972.

Chapter 21 (pages 441-485)

1. *U.S. News & World Report*, June 12, 1972, p. 80.
2. Los Angeles Times Service, dispatch from Bonn, Nov. 20, 1972.
3. New Rochelle, N.Y.: Arlington House, 1973.
4. New York: Harper & Row, 1963.
5. James Daniel and John G. Hubbell, *Strike in the West* (Chicago: Holt, Rinehart & Winston, 1963).
6. *Time*, Sept. 21, 1962, p. 17.
7. Report made public May 9, 1963.

Chapter 22 (pages 486-539)

1. "A Foreign Policy Without a Country," *National Review*, Sept. 14, 1973. p. 1005.

2. Henry Kissinger in a CBS interview with Marvin Kalb, excerpted in *Newsweek*, Feb. 12, 1973, p. 19.
3. Edward Luttwak, *The Strategic Balance 1972*, published under the auspices of the Center for Strategic and International Studies, Georgetown University, as No. 3 of a series entitled *The Washington Papers* (New York: Library Press, 1972).
4. William F. Buckley, Jr., *National Review*, June 22, 1973.
5. Henry A. Kissinger, press conference in Moscow, May 26, 1972; reprinted in *Weekly Compilation of Presidential Documents*, June 5, 1972.
6. Henry A. Kissinger, Intourist Hotel, Moscow, May 27, 1974.
7. Senator Henry M. Jackson's address on June 16, 1972, and a statement issued by him on June 14, 1972, reprinted in *U.S. News & World Report*, July 3, 1972.
8. Exclusive to *U.S. News & World Report*, June 26, 1972.
9. *U.S. News & World Report*, Oct. 16, 1972.
10. International Institute for Strategic Studies, *Strategic Survey*, 1969.
11. Defense Posture Statement, Jan. 23, 1967.
12. U.S. Senate Armed Services Committee, *Hearings on Authorization for Military Procurement, R&D, FY 1972*, 1971, Part 2, p. 1317.
13. Defense Posture Statement, Jan. 23, 1967, p. 56, under heading "Minuteman."
14. These totals are presented with a specific breakdown into types in the International Institute for Strategic Studies *Strategic Survey*, 1969, p. 27.
15. *Strategic Review*, Spring 1973, p. 10.
16. Henry A. Kissinger, Intourist Hotel, Moscow, May 27, 1972.
17. Pp. 56-57.
18. Washington Post Service, Dec. 31, 1959, p. 1.
19. *Military Review*, August 1971; Defense Posture Statement, 1970.
20. Feb. 20, 1970, p. 114.
21. Intourist Hotel, May 27, 1972.
22. P. 25.
23. Defense Posture Statement, Jan. 23, 1967.
24. *State of the World Report*, Feb. 25, 1971.
25. Defense Posture Statement, 1970, p. 36.
26. *Ibid.*, p. 105.
27. Henry A. Kissinger, *The Necessity for Choice* (New York: Harper & Brothers, 1961), p. 26.
28. U.S. Senate Foreign Relations Committee, *Hearings on SALT Agreements*, June 19 to July 20, 1972, p. 23.

Chapter 23 (pages 540-603)

1. Dec. 10, 1973, p. 63.
2. Paul Scott column, Apr. 20, 1973.
3. Paul Scott column, Nov. 22, 1973.
4. Leslie H. Gelb dispatch, Dec. 8, 1973.
5. New York: Frederick A. Praeger, 1965.
   Apr. 2, 1973. p. 57.
6. Stuart Auerbach column, Washington Post Service, May 20, 1973.
7. *Newsweek*, Feb. 19, 1973, p. 55.
8. *Chicago Daily News*, Apr. 16, 1973.
9. Mar. 19, 1973.
10. May 7, 1973, p. 78.
11. Aug. 13, 1973.
12. Stuart Auerbach column, Washington Post Service, May 20, 1973.
13. *U.S. News & World Report*, May 11, 1970, p. 64.
14. Los Angeles Times Service, Feb. 6, 1974.
15. Leslie H. Gelb, "Russian Says U.S. was Warned of Mideast War," *New York Times*, Dec. 21, 1973.
16. Feb. 15, 1974, p. 182.
17. Washington Post Service report of Schlesinger press conference, Nov. 30, 1973.
18. *U.S. News & World Report*, interview with Gen. George S. Brown, Air Force Chief of Staff, Feb. 25, 1974, p. 63.
19. U.S. Senate Foreign Relations Committee, *Hearings on Nomination of Henry A. Kissinger to be Secretary of State*, Sept. 14, 1973, p. 127.
20. *Ibid.*, p. 230.
21. Feb. 25, 1974.
22. UPI dispatch, Washington, Jan. 11, 1974.
23. AP dispatch, Washington, Jan. 11, 1974.
24. AP dispatch, Washington, Feb. 11, 1974.

25. Feb. 11, 1974.
26. Jan. 28, 1974.
27. Jan. 15, 1974.
28. Column of Feb. 10, 1974.
29. UPI dispatch, Washington, Feb. 8, 1974.
30. Feb. 4, 1974, p. 23.
31. Feb. 15, 1974.
32. *Newsweek*, Feb. 4, 1974, p. 23.
33. Jan. 28, 1974, p. 30.
34. Statement at the Overseas Writers Club luncheon, Feb. 10, 1974.
35. Jan. 28, 1974, p. 30.
36. Editorial: "Decline of the West," U.S. Strategic Institute, *Strategic Review*, Summer 1973, p. 4.
37. AP dispatch, Washington, Mar. 4, 1974.
38. New Rochelle, N.Y.: Arlington House, 1974, p. 169.
39. Aug. 5, 1972.
40. Department of Defense Report, FY 1975, Mar. 4, 1974, p. 5.
41. *Ibid.*, p. 39.
42. *Ibid.*, p. 67.
43. *Ibid.*, p. 45.
44. *Ibid.*, p. 4.
45. *Ibid.*, p. 5.
46. *Ibid.*, p. 46.
47. Military Posture Report, FY 1975, by Chairman of Joint Chiefs of Staff, Chart No. 2, p. 10.
48. See Agreed Interpretation J.
49. Military Posture Report, FY 1975, by Chairman of Joint Chiefs of Staff, p. 16.
50. "Prospects for the 1970s," 20th Stevenson Memorial Lecture, published in *The World Today*, 28 (2) Feb. 1972, p. 52.
51. Department of Defense Report, FY 1975, Mar. 5, 1974, p. 58.
52. *Ibid.*, pp. 62 and 64.
53. Posture Report, FY 1975, p. 25.
54. Washington Post Service, Sept. 18, 1973.
55. Department of Defense Report, FY 1975, p. 47.
56. *Ibid.*, p. 59.
57. Edward Luttwak, *The Strategic Balance*, published under the auspices of the Center for Strategic and International Studies, Georgetown University, as No. 3 of a series entitled *The Washington Papers* (New York: Library Press, 1972).
58. Department of Defense Report, FY 1975, p. 58.
59. *Ibid.*, p. 51.
60. *Ibid.*, p. 43.
61. Statistics from the Military Posture Report, FY 1975, by Chairman of the Joint Chiefs of Staff.
62. Department of Defense Report, FY 1975, p. 81.
63. *Ibid.*, p. 6.
64. *Ibid.*, p. 47.
65. White House briefing for five congressional committees, June 15, 1972.
66. Department of Defense Report, FY 1975, p. 6.
67. Military Posture Report, FY 1975, by Chairman of the Joint Chiefs of Staff, p. 15.
68. *Newsweek*, Apr. 8, 1974, p. 32.
69. UPI dispatch, Moscow, Mar. 26, 1974.
70. John W. Finney, "Defense in Perspective," New York Times Service, Feb. 6, 1974.
71. U.S. Senate Foreign Relations Committee, *Hearings on Nomination of Henry A. Kissinger to be Secretary of State*, Sept. 7-14, 1973, p. 127.
72. Mar. 22, 1974.

Chapter 24 (pages 604-646)

1. Arthur F. Burns, Chairman of the Federal Reserve Board, Commencement Address, Jacksonville, Ill., May 26, 1974.
2. Robert Strausz-Hupe, William R. Kintner and Stefan T. Possony, *A Forward Strategy for America* (New York: Harper & Brothers), 1961.
3. Reported by all the major wire services, March 11, 1974. See also the New York Times Service, April 9, 1974.
4. March 29, 1974, p. 360.
5. UPI dispatch, Washington, March 14, 1974.
6. Reported in *U.S. News & World Report*, April 1, 1974, p. 18.
7. New York Times Service, Apr. 9, 1974.
8. Washington Post Service, Apr. 10, 1974.

9. Military Posture Statement, FY 1975, by Chairman of the Joint Chiefs of Staff, Mar. 1974.

10. Department of Defense Report, FY 1972, p. 33.

11. Records of the Mixed Claims Commission on German Sabotage in World War I, U.S. Archives, Washington, D.C.; cited by Rose L. Martin in *The Selling of America* (Santa Monica, Ca.: Fidelis Publishers, 1973), p. 46.

12. *Power and Policy Problems in the Defense of the West*, Proceedings of the Asilomar National Strategy Seminar, U.S. Army, Apr. 28, 1960.

13. *Ibid.*, p. 6.

14. Television and radio address by President John F. Kennedy, Mar. 2, 1962, as quoted in *Problems of National Strategy*, edited by Henry A. Kissinger (New York: Frederick A. Praeger, 1965).

15. Marquis W. Childs, *St. Louis Post-Dispatch*, Dec. 14, 1973.

16. Henry A. Kissinger, *The Necessity for Choice* (New York; Harper & Brothers, 1961), p. 12.

17. *Suicide of the West* (New York: John Day Co., 1964), pp. 292-296.

18. Washington Post Service, Oct. 27, 1973.

19. Apr. 1, 1974, p. 31.

20. Carroll Kilpatric, "Domestic Motivation in Nixon Alert Denied," Washington Post Service, Oct. 26, 1973.

21. Jeremiah O'Leary, "Kissinger Leaves Lots of Questions," *Washington Star-News*, Oct. 26, 1973.

22. Nov. 5, 1973, p. 15.

23. "Anyone See the NSC?," Washington Post Service, Nov. 28, 1973.

24. David Binder, "An Implied Soviet Threat Spurred U.S. Forces' Alert," *New York Times*, Nov. 21, 1973.

25. *Honolulu Advertiser*, Dec. 13, 1973.

26. Nov. 21, 1973, pp. 1, 17.

27. *Honolulu Star Bulletin*, Oct. 25, 1973, p. 1.

28. AP dispatch, Moscow, Oct, 27, 1973.

29. Nov. 5, 1974, p. 15.

30. Nov. 4, 1974.

31. Pp. 46-47.

32. *Newsweek*, Mar. 24, 1974.

33. The annual *State of the World* and other U.S. foreign policy reports.

34. State Department news release, Mar. 28, 1974.

Chapter 25 (pages 647-708)

1. *National Review*, Sept. 29, 1972, p. 1083.

2. Oct. 15, 1973, p. 78.

3. *Newsweek*, Aug. 24, 1964, p. 21.

4. *New York Times*, Aug. 21, 1964, pp. 1, 4.

5. "When SALT Hit the Fan," *National Review*, June 23, 1972, p. 689. The Brennan conclusion about the "alternatives" is confirmed in John Newhouse, *Cold Dawn: The Story of SALT* (New York: Holt, Rinehart & Winston, 1973), p. 246: "Moorer [CJCS] wanted White House support for speeding up the Trident submarine program. Trident, in a sense, was bait."

6. *Newsweek*, Apr. 8, 1974, p. 32.

7. "A wide variety of American officials," according to the *New York Times*, Dec. 9, 1973.

8. Stephen S. Rosenfeld, "Solzhenitsyn, Detente, and Moral Values," *Washington Post*, Feb. 26, 1974.

9. "Amoral Detente," syndicated column, Feb. 22, 1974.

10. UPI dispatch, Feb. 13, 1974.

11. UPI dispatch, Mar. 7, 1974.

12. Department of Defense Report, FY 1975, Mar. 4, 1974, p. 67.

13. *The Necessity for Choice* (New York: Harper & Brothers, 1961), p. 46.

14. From Kissinger's briefing to the five congressional committees on SALT I.

15. Melvin Laird interview, *U.S. News & World Report*, Mar. 27, 1972, p. 42.

16. "Awesome Missile Gap Confronting America," Dec. 4, 1973.

17. Joseph Alsop column, Dec. 12, 1973.

18. "The Perilous Posture of Our National Defense," *Human Events*, Apr. 27, 1974, p. 47.

19. Center for Strategic and International Studies, Georgetown University (New York: Library Press, 1972), p. 75.

20. Department of Defense Report, FY 1973, by Melvin Laird, Feb. 17, 1972.

21. *The Necessity for Choice, op. cit.*, p. 13.

22. House Appropriations Subcommittee Hearings, 86th Congress, 1st Session, Defense Department Appropriations for 1960, Part 2, Financial Statements, Field Commanders, 1959, pp. 378-379.

23. Henry Kissinger, press conference, State Department news release, Apr. 26, 1974.
24. Department of Defense Report, FY 1975, Mar. 4, 1974, p. 72.
25. Ibid., pp. 44-45.
26. On Thermonuclear War (Princeton, N.J.: Princeton University Press, 1960).
27. The Necessity for Choice, op. cit., p. 17.
28. Ibid., p. 22.
29. Aviation Week & Space Technology, Apr. 8, 1974, p. 21.
30. The Necessity for Choice, op. cit., p. 19.
31. Ibid., p. 18.
32. Department of State News Release, Apr. 26, 1974.
33. P. 16.
34. Pp. 44-45.
35. U.S. Military Posture Report, FY 1975, p. 31.
36. Department of Defense Report, FY 1975, Mar. 4, 1974, p. 47.
37. The ABM and the Changed Strategic Military Balance, American Security Council, May 1969.
38. Department of Defense Report, FY 1975, Mar. 4, 1974, pp. 52 and 56.
39. The Necessity for Choice, op. cit., p. 12.
40. National Review, July 7, 1972, pp. 744-5.

Chapter 26 (pages 709-742)

1. U.S. Senate Foreign Relations Committee, Hearings on SALT Agreements, June 26, 1972, p. 222.
2. "The Bargaining Aspects of Arms Control: The SALT Experience," published in SALT: Implications For Arms Control in the 1970s, edited by William R. Kintner and Robert L. Pfaltzgraff, Jr. (Pittsburgh, Pa.: University of Pittsburgh Press, 1973), p. 129.
3. Ibid., p. 135.
4. "SALT and the Middle East," published in SALT: Implications For Arms Control in the 1970s, op. cit., p. 241.
5. AP dispatch, June 4, 1973.
6. Speech to Florida Press Association, Apr. 1960.
7. P. 52.
8. May 10, 1974, p. 16.
9. "More SALT on the Table," Aviation Week & Space Technology, Apr. 29, 1974, p. 11.
10. Excerpted from text published in Aviation Week & Space Technology, May 6, 1974, p. 7.
11. Webster's Seventh New Collegiate Dictionary (Springfield, Mass: C. & G. Merriam Co., 1971).
12. "Throw Weight Seen Critical in SALT II," Aviation Week & Space Technology, Apr. 8, 1974, p. 21.
13. Cold Dawn: The Story of SALT (New York: Holt, Rinehart & Winston, 1973), pp. 104-105.
14. Expressed in 1973 dollars. Source: U.S. Agency for International Development, reported in U.S. News & World Report, June 10, 1974, p. 33.
15. U.S. Senate Foreign Relations Committee, Hearings on SALT Agreements, June 28, 1972, p. 223.
16. Foreword by Ambassador Foy D. Kohler to "Science and Technology as an Instrument of Soviet Policy" by Mose L. Harvey, Leon Goure, and Vladimir Prokofieff, Monographs in International Affairs (Miami, Fla.: Center for Advanced International Studies, University of Miami, 1972).
17. Address to the Association of the U.S. Army at Fort Dix, New Jersey, Mar. 8, 1974.
18. 1972 outputs expressed in 1973 dollars. U.S. Agency for International Development, reported in U.S. News & World Report, June 10, 1974.
19. Joseph Alsop, syndicated column, Jan. 8, 1974.
20. Department of Defense Report, FY 1975, p. 45.
21. May 28, 1974.
22. Washington Post Service, May 21, 1974.
23. Department of Defense Report, FY 1975, Mar. 4, 1974, p. 43.
24. Henry A. Kissinger, White House briefing for the five congressional committees, June 15, 1972.
25. John Newhouse, Cold Dawn: The Story of SALT, op. cit., p. 252.
26. Syndicated column, Dec. 12, 1973.
27. Press conference, International Conference Room Department of State, Apr. 26, 1974.
28. Department of Defense Report, FY 1975, p. 45. A funny thing happened at the joint news briefing held by Dr. James Schlesinger and Dr. Fred C. Iklé on July 3, 1974. Asked by a reporter if U.S. officials had any particular concern about the Soviet "large missiles," Schlesinger observed:
   . . . There are the SS-17 and 19 which have a very substantial throw-weight and as a consequence they can no longer be treated as light missiles.
   Q: Mr. Secretary, if the 17 and 19 can no longer be treated as light missiles, are you saying the Russians will break the agreement if they deploy them?
   Schlesinger: No, sir, no, sir. . .

813

Q: Do you count them as heavy missiles against that 333 limit?

Schlesinger: No, sir. . .

Q: They can't replace these light missiles with heavy missiles or anything . . .

Schlesinger: These are what might be called medium-weight missiles.

Q: You're backing away from calling them heavy missiles?

Schlesinger: The modern large ballistic missile has a specific definition—Jerry, will you get the precise definition?

And Jerry did—but not in time for the inquiring reporter to use it to tie down Dr. Schlesinger on his evasion of the definition of heavy ICBM. Here it is, as furnished in a footnote to the official transcript of the press conference: "The U.S. definition of a heavy ICBM is any ICBM with a total volume significantly greater than the largest light ICBM operational on either side at the time of the SALT I Agreement." Since Schlesinger's own official reports show that the SS-17 and SS-19 have throw-weights three to five times the SS-11 (the largest operational light ICBM at the time of the SALT I Agreement), his "backing away from calling them heavy missiles" is exposed by the official U.S. definition as a deliberate deception.

29. *Ibid.*, p. 79.
30. Herman Kahn, *On Thermonuclear War* (Princeton, N.J.: Princeton University Press, 1960), pp. 213-214.
31. Department of Defense Report, FY 1975, pp. 68-69.
32. This is Schlesinger's language from his description of the "improved" U.S. strategic posture he has programmed in his FY 1975 Department of Defense Report, p. 44.
33. James L. Buckley, "On SALT II," *National Review*, Mar. 15, 1974.

Chapter 27 (pages 743-785)

1. *Newsweek*, August 19, 1974, p. 65.
2. *Time*, August 19, 1974, p. 76.
3. *U.S. News & World Report*, August 19, 1974, p. 30. Hobart Rowan, writing for the Washington Post Service (August 25, 1974), noted that the inflation rate for the third quarter of 1974 was continuing close to the double-digit rate of 12 percent, and then observed: "There are some highly-placed and serious people in this town who think that, if the combination of inflation and stagnation is not checked soon, there could be *a breakdown in the whole system*, leading not only to economic woes but to social disturbance." Nicholas von Hoffman wrote in a perceptive syndicated column on August 25, 1974, that "the banking system is probably insolvent." He quotes expert Tom Holt who was recently retained by General Electric as a consultant: "In terms of damage done to most non-blue chips, the ongoing market decline is already as bad as in 1929. Thousands of individual issues have already lost more than 50 percent of their value. It's just that the current collapse, unlike the 1929 debacle, has been stretched out by persistent institutional support of the large capitalization issues." And James Barton, a regional manager of a large brokerage firm, commenting on the significance of the decline in the Dow Jones Industrial Average to "a new low point in a disastrous year," concluded that "the magnitude of these recent declines would seem to indicate either *the anticipated collapse of the U.S. economic system* or an approaching market bottom." (*Honolulu Star-Bulletin & Advertiser*, August 25, 1974.)
4. UPI dispatch, Washington, August 27, 1974.
5. *Newsweek*, August 19, 1974, p. 62.
6. *Time*, August 19, 1974, p. 33.
7. *Time*, August 19, 1974, p. 13A.
8. UPI dispatch, Munich, July 8, 1974.
9. *Newsweek*, August 19, 1974, p. 23.
10. Barry Schweid, AP dispatch, Washington, August 9, 1974.
11. *National Review*, August 16, 1974, p. 908.
12. Bernard Gwertzman in the *New York Times*, July 31, 1974, and Murrey Marder in the *Washington Post*, July 31, 1974.
13. U.S. Senate Foreign Relations Committee, *Hearings on SALT Agreements*, June 19 to July 20, 1972, p. 23.
14. P. 45.
15. *Aviation Week & Space Technology*, April 22, 1974, p. 7.
16. *Foreign Policy*, May 1974.
17. Press conference at the Pentagon, June 17, 1974.
18. *Ibid.*
19. Department of Defense Report, FY 1975, March 4, 1974, p. 46.
20. American Security Council, *Washington Report*, July 1974.
21. Gannett News Service dispatch, Salzburg, June 12, 1974.
22. June 17, 1974, p. 29.

23. AP dispatch, Salzburg, June 11, 1974, and UPI dispatch, Salzburg, June 12, 1974.
24. Column by Rudy Abramson and John Aerill, June 12, 1974.
25. *Newsweek*, Aug. 6, 1973.
26. AP dispatch, Annapolis, Md., June 5, 1974.
27. David Binder, "Recent US-EC Differences are Part of Changing International 'Club' Life," *European Community*, May 1974, p. 15.
28. *Khrushchev Remembers* (New York: Little, Brown and Company, 1970), p. 569.
29. *National Review*, June 7, 1974, p. 633.
30. Department of Defense Report, FY 1974, Apr. 10, 1973, p. 63.
31. James Reston, New York Times Service, June 13, 1974, amusingly headlined in the *Honolulu Advertiser* (which serves an area in which pidgin English is widely used) "Cool Head Main T'ing, Henry."
32. Washington Post Service, June 12, 1974.
33. *Newsweek*, June 24, 1974, p. 24.

Glossary

A-7A	U.S. Navy carrier-based strike aircraft; range 3,400 miles; speed mach 0.9; weapon load 15,000 pounds; nuclear-capable, up to four 1-MT bombs.
ABM	Anti-Ballistic Missile: a missile designed to intercept an enemy missile in flight and destroy it by a nuclear explosion.
ACDA	Arms Control and Disarmament Agency, located in the State Department Building, Washington, D.C.; the director is Fred C. Iklé.
AEC	Atomic Energy Commission; it has cognizance over all U.S. atomic energy programs for both weapons and peaceful purposes; the chairman is Dixy Lee Ray.
ALCM	Air-Launched Cruise Missile: an aircraft-launched air-breathing flying missile that cannot leave the atmosphere and does not follow a ballistic path, but is guided.
AMSA	Advanced Manned Strategic Aircraft: U.S. strategic heavy bomber designed to replace the B-70 bomber which was killed by McNamara; AMSA was never built.
active defenses	Anti-ballistic missile systems; antiaircraft systems.
Apollo	Name assigned by NASA to the U.S. program to put men on the moon and return them to earth.
B-1	Proposed new U.S. strategic bomber to replace the B-52; supersonic speed; 144 feet long; production decision scheduled for 1977.
B-47	U.S. strategic medium bomber; jet-propelled; probably mach 0.9; capable of heavy load of 10 MT H-bombs; intercontinental range with refueling.

B-52	U.S. strategic long-range heavy bomber; range 12,500 miles; mach 0.95; weapons load 75,000 pounds; formerly carried two 24-MT H-bombs (pre-McNamara).
B-70	U.S. strategic long-range heavy bomber; world's first supersonic aircraft of its size; successfully flew at mach 3 in 1964; killed by McNamara.
BAMBI	Projected space-based ABM system designed to intercept hostile missiles in the booster stage, that is, within five minutes of launch; would kill the bus and all MIRVs at once.
BMEWS	Ballistic Missile Early Warning System; the old-style U.S. radar warning.
Backfire	Soviet heavy strategic bomber first deployed in 1971; mach 2+; world's most advanced bomber.
Blue Ribbon Defense Panel	Appointed by President Nixon in 1969; seven members of this panel in 1970 issued the Supplemental Statement called "The Shifting Balance of Military Power."
Bluestreak	Projected British rocket-propelled strategic missile to be launched from bomber aircraft; never built.
Brezhnev Doctrine	The doctrine that the Soviet Union will "protect" any "Socialist" government from being overthrown; it is the ex post facto doctrinal rationalization for the 1968 Soviet invasion of Czechoslovakia.
C-5	The largest U.S. cargo aircraft; a payload of 75+ tons (more than twice that of the C-141 at 27 tons); 79 in total force.
CEP	Circular Error Probability: the radius of a circle in which 50 percent of the warheads will fall; the measure of the accuracy of an offensive missile's warhead package.
CFR	Council on Foreign Relations: a private elitist organization whose members control U.S. foreign and defense policies and key personnel.
CIA	Central Intelligence Agency; charged with the conduct of U.S. foreign intelligence operations outside the United States.
COMINT	Communications Intelligence; includes intelligence acquired through highly classified electronic techniques and equipment.
CPSU	Communist Party of the Soviet Union; of 250 million people in the U.S.S.R., 14 million are members; the Central Committee of the CPSU elects the 16-man Politburo.
CSCE	Conference on Security and Cooperation in Europe; see European Security Conference.
civil defense	See passive defenses.
cold-launch	A new secret Soviet technique for launching ICBMs by "popping" them up out of their silos before ig-

niting the booster rockets; it is a "cold launch" because the launcher tube is not subjected to the intense heat of the rocket engines and is therefore available for reload.

Command Data Buffer System
An advanced computer system for the almost instantaneous targeting and retargeting of U.S. Minuteman missiles from a remote command center.

conventional
Descriptive of nonnuclear weapons; explosive power measured in pounds of TNT.

counterforce
Descriptive of weapons aimed at the enemy's strategic weapons before they are launched; missiles or bombers which have a "kill" capability against the enemy's strategic weapons; weapons designed to "counter" the "force" the enemy plans to use against you.

counterforce capability
Possession of offensive strategic weapons in sufficient numbers, with enough explosive power and accuracy, to destroy the enemy's strategic offensive forces.

counterpopulation
Descriptive of weapons or an attack designed primarily to kill people.

countervalue
Descriptive of an attack designed to destroy assets of the enemy which are "valued" by him; e.g., people, cities, industrial plant, facilities.

cruise missile
See ALCM and SLCM.

Cuban missile crisis
The nuclear confrontation between the U.S. and the U.S.S.R. resulting from the Soviets' clandestine deployment of strategic nuclear missiles into Cuba in 1962.

DIA
Defense Intelligence Agency; created by mergers of intelligence personnel of Army, Navy, and Air Force, under the direction of SECDEF.

Delta submarine
The great new Soviet missile-launching submarine; carries the new 5,000-nautical-mile-range SLBM with inertial guidance.

dish warning radars
Radar installations laid out in the shape of a huge dish.

Doghouse
The secondary Soviet ABM radars which take over tracking incoming missiles from the long-range Henhouse radars (which acquire the incoming offensive missiles first).

Dynosoar
A prototype U.S. aerospace weapons system with the potential of a powerful strategic system; never built because it was killed by McNamara.

ECM
Electronic Counter Measures: equipment and techniques for countering the enemy's electronic systems; generally highly classified.

ELINT
A very highly classified type of intelligence involving electronics.

electromagnetic pulse	One effect of a large nuclear explosion by which, if it is close enough to a silo or missile in flight, it can disable enemy missiles or their guidance systems without having to score a direct hit; the Soviets discovered this in their 1962 nuclear tests; the U.S. knows little about it.
envelope	Generally construed to mean the "silo envelope," including all its dimensions, not merely diameter.
essential equivalence	A verbal placebo with no ascertainable definition; devised by Kissinger and Schlesinger to replace the earlier term "nuclear sufficiency," which had to be abandoned because Kissinger had enunciated four criteria for it and then abandoned them all in SALT I. Both terms were designed to conceal the fact that U.S. strategic nuclear power has been brought down from overwhelming superiority, through parity, and is heading toward decisive inferiority.
European Security Conference	A conference the Soviets have been seeking for 12 years in order to legitimatize by international agreement their seizure of the East European satellites and East Germany.
exotics	Ballistic missile defense systems based on technology not yet in hand but expected in the future, such as lasers.
F-15	The newest U.S. fighter-interceptor aircraft.
F-111	The Air Force fighter version of the TFX; McNamara estimated the cost at $4 million each; the cost is now up to $14 million.
F-111B	Proposed Navy version of the TFX; never accepted by the Navy because of excessive weight, substandard performance, and poor maneuverability.
FB-111	The fighter-bomber version of TFX; range of 3,800 miles (only one-third of the B-52); weapons load 37,500 pounds (less than half of the B-52).
FOBS	Fractional Orbital Bombardment System; a heavy ICBM modified to follow an orbital path instead of a ballistic path, and to impact before completing orbit.
FY	Fiscal year; for the U.S. Government, FY 1975 would be the year from July 1, 1974, through June 30, 1975.
Finlandization	An expected technique for Soviet takeover of Western European nations without overt control, like Finland.
first-strike capability	Having sufficient numbers, power, and accuracy in offensive strategic weapons to destroy a major part of the enemy's offensive weapons before launch, and thereby reduce retaliatory damage to a level that is an "acceptable" risk.
footprint	The pattern in which MRV warheads will impact on targets.

Foxbat	Soviet fighter-interceptor aircraft; MIG-25; reputed to be the world's fastest: mach 3+.
fractional orbit	Less than one full orbit; a strategic nuclear bombardment system which complies with the letter (but not the spirit) of the UN treaty banning orbital weapons.
fractional orbital bombardment system	See FOBS.
free ride	A guarantee to incoming enemy missiles that their targets will not be defended; what the SALT I ABM Treaty guarantees to Soviet and Red Chinese nuclear missiles.
full or preclusive first-strike	Capability of destroying substantially all an opponent's ICBMs, bombers, and SLBMs, before launch, so that the defender nation is "precluded" from retaliating effectively.
G-class submarine	Older type Soviet submarine, propelled by diesel-electric motors; not counted under SALT I Interim Agreement Protocol as "modern" missile-launching submarines (which are nuclear-propelled).
GNP	Gross National Product: the sum total of all products (agricultural as well as industrial) and services produced by a nation in one year.
GRU	The Chief Intelligence Directorate of the Soviet General Staff; the military branch of the Soviet intelligence services.
Galosh	See SA-7.
Ganef	See SA-4.
grand strategy	The master plan for employing the political, economic, psychological, and military forces of the nation to accomplish the paramount national purpose; Communist powers also employ trade, cultural exchanges, and research.
Griffon	See SA-5.
Harvard-MIT Axis	A self-styled elitist group of professors and officials of Harvard and MIT with a common interest in unilateral disarmament; no formal organization.
heavy ICBM	Unilaterally defined by the U.S. as any missile having a volume significantly greater than the largest light missile operational at the time of the SALT I signing.
heavy launcher	A launcher capable of launching a heavy missile.
Henhouse	The huge Soviet radar used for early warning or for perimeter acquisition of incoming ICBMs; part of the Soviet ABM system.
Hot Line	A secure teletype system linking the Kremlin and the White House for urgent confidential communications between highest level officials.
ICBM	Inter-Continental Ballistic Missile: a missile with a strategic nuclear warhead or warhead package with a range of more than 4,000 nautical miles.

IOC	Initial Operational Capability: the date of deployment (ready for operational missions) of a significant number of a new weapons system, but short of deployment of the full force.
IRBM	Intermediate-Range Ballistic Missile: a strategic missile with a range of 1,500 to 4,000 nautical miles.
Ilyushin-28 Beagle	Soviet medium jet bomber; range 2,500 miles; mach 0.81; weapons load 4,850 pounds.
inertial guidance	The basic guidance system for ballistic missiles, consisting of an encased gyroscopic mechanism which detects and corrects deviation from planned trajectory and velocity.
intermediate-range ballistic missile	See IRBM.
JCS	The Joint Chiefs of Staff of the United States; membership consists of the Chairman, the Chief of Staff of the Army, the Chief of Staff of the Air Force, and the Chief of Naval Operations.
Jupiter	U.S. early-model first-generation IRBM with nuclear warhead; liquid-fueled.
KGB	Soviet intelligence service formally entitled the Committee of State Security; larger, more pervasive, and more powerful than the military GRU.
Kennedy-Khrushchev Agreement	The secret agreement between President John Kennedy and Nikita Khrushchev for settlement of the Cuban missile crisis of 1962.
kilometer	1,000 meters; 0.62 U.S. statute miles.
kiloton	1,000 tons: nuclear explosive power equivalent to the explosive power of 1,000 tons of conventional explosive material, usually TNT.
LGM-30B	Minuteman I.
LGM-30F	Minuteman II.
LGM-30G	Minuteman III.
laser	Acronym for Light Amplification by Stimulated Emission of Radiation; light energy is compressed into a needle-thin beam which travels with the speed of light (186,000 miles per second); present military use is for guidance of "smart" bombs and missiles; future use expected in exotic missile-defense systems of mid-1980s and beyond.
lead-time	The time required for the gestation of a new weapons system, or component thereof, from the date the new concept is developed by research, through development of the technology required to produce it, through testing and actual production of the hardware to operational deployment.
light ICBM	An ICBM which has relatively less throw-weight (than a heavy ICBM), such as the U.S. Minuteman with about 2,000 pounds, and the Soviet SS-11 with about 2,500 pounds.

light launcher	A launcher capable of launching a light missile.
M-60	U.S. medium tank; more than 10 years old but still our most modern.
M-70	Proposed new U.S. main battle tank whose program was terminated by Congress in 1971.
MAD	Mutual Assured Destruction; name given by unilateral-disarmament intellectuals to an arms control arrangement purportedly making the populations of each nation hostage to each other.
MaRV	Maneuverable Reentry Vehicle for ICBMs and SLBMs; can be maneuvered to evade enemy ABMs or for terminal guidance.
MBFR	Mutual and Balanced Forces Reduction; negotiations between NATO and Warsaw Pact powers to bring about reductions in conventional weapons.
MBT	Main Battle Tank.
MIRV	Multiple Independently-targeted Reentry Vehicle: reentry vehicles included in an ICBM or SLBM package which can be individually targeted; ICBMs and SLBMs pass through outer space, and their warheads must be capable of *reentering* the earth's atmosphere.
Mk500 MaRV	A reentry vehicle under early research and development for the Minuteman; will not be more accurate than present MIRVs because its maneuverability is to evade ABM interceptors, not for terminal guidance.
MOBS	Multiple Orbital Bombardment System.
MRBM	Medium-Range Ballistic Missile: a strategic missile with a range of 500 to 1,500 miles.
MRV	Multiple Reentry Vehicles; reentry vehicles included in an ICBM or SLBM warhead package which fall in a pattern, but cannot be individually targeted.
MT	Megaton.
Mya-4 Bison	Soviet heavy long-range strategic bomber; range 6,050 miles; mach 0.87; weapons load 20,000 pounds.
mach	The ratio of the speed (of an aircraft) to the speed of sound.
megaton	The energy of a nuclear explosion having a yield equivalent to one million tons of TNT; equivalent to 1,000 kilotons.
megatonnage delivery capability	The number of megatons of nuclear explosives which can be delivered on target by a particular delivery system.
Members of Congress for Peace Through Law	The 141 Members of Congress organized under that name who oppose funds for weapons and support unilateral disarmament.
Minuteman I	The first U.S. solid-fuel ICBM; range 7,500 statute miles; estimated yield 1 MT.
Minuteman II	U.S. ICBM; range 8,000 statute miles; yield 1+ MT.

Minuteman III	U.S. ICBM; range 8,000 statute miles; yield, three MIRVed warheads estimated at 170 to 200 kilotons (0.2 MT).
Moscow Declaration of Principles	Political agreement signed at Moscow Summit meeting in May 1972 by Nixon and Brezhnev.
Moscow Test Ban Treaty	The 1963 treaty between the U.S. and the U.S.S.R. banning tests of nuclear weapons in the earth's atmosphere or in outer space; in effect, it limits nuclear tests to underground tests.
Moscow Threshold Test Ban Treaty	The 1974 treaty between the U.S. and the U.S.S.R. banning underground tests in excess of 150 kilotons; effective date delayed until March 31, 1976.
NASA	National Aeronautics and Space Administration.
NATO	North Atlantic Treaty Organization; a primarily military, quasi-political defensive alliance comprising the major nations of Western Europe plus the United States.
NCA	National Command Authority.
NSC	See National Security Council.
NSDM	National Security Decision Memorandum: a classified (usually Top Secret) Executive Order embodying a presidential decision on a matter of national security; drafts of NSDMs can originate only in the NSC staff, under direction of Dr. Kissinger, and are approved personally by him before submission to the President.
NSSM	National Security Study Memorandum: a directive signed by the President or Dr. Kissinger, as Assistant to the President for National Security Affairs, assigning the subject of a study to be conducted on a matter relating to national security, and designating which U.S. agencies must conduct it.
National Command Authority	The highest civilian and military officials having the legal authority and military power to conduct the defense of the United States.
National Security Council	A statutory body whose function is to make policy on national security; it is composed by law of the President, the Vice President, the Secretary of State, the Assistant to the President for National Security Affairs, the Secretary of Defense, and the Director of the Office of Emergency Preparedness.
Nike-X	Earliest U.S. ABM system; predecessor of the Sentinel and the Safeguard; never deployed.
net	To integrate into a network like a TV network; the purpose is to make radar systems work together to give wide coverage of incoming ICBMs and direct ABM interceptors against them.
nm	Nautical mile: 6,076 feet; approximately 800 feet longer than a statutory or land mile.

nuclear console	Figure of speech representing the mechanism or control panel for exercising command of strategic nuclear weapons.
nuclear umbrella	Figure of speech describing the protection or shelter accorded allied or neutral nations by the deterrent of a nation with strategic nuclear superiority; effective only if it is credible.
nukes	Any offensive nuclear weapons, strategic or tactical.
OSS	Office of Strategic Services: the U.S. World War II intelligence and clandestine-operations agency which later developed into the CIA.
OTA	Office of Technology Assessment: an evaluation group to conduct studies on military projects and programs and advise Congress.
OTH	Over the Horizon: a newer type of radar which permits scanning beyond the line-of-sight horizon; picks up incoming enemy missiles thousands of miles further out than conventional radar warning systems.
PBV	Post Boost Vehicle; usually refers to a ballistic missile bus-type dispensing system for MIRV warheads; *i.e.*, the package containing guidance mechanism and warheads; called "post boost" because it carries on after the boost rocket is dropped.
POL	Storage, transportation, and distribution facilities for petroleum products (gasoline, jet fuel, fuel oil, etc.), oil, and lubricants.
PRC	People's Republic of China; Red China.
Paris Summit (1960)	The scheduled summit meeting between President Eisenhower and Khrushchev, which Khrushchev cancelled.
parity	Strategic nuclear parity is a relationship wherein opposing forces are roughly equal (measured in numbers of launchers, total deliverable megatonnage, throw-weight, and warheads with sufficient reliability, explosive power, and accuracy of guidance) and neither side has a substantial counterforce capability.
particle generator	A potential far-future exotic system for defense against missiles; classified Top Secret.
passive defenses	Protection against nuclear attack by blast and fallout shelters, by evacuation of cities, and by locating industrial plants underground and weapons in hardened silos.
payload	The weight the rockets of a missile are required to lift; this includes the weight of the reentry vehicle with its warhead package, plus the weight of the booster stage of the missile.
peaceful coexistence	Soviet Communist code name for a strategy designed to lull the West into apathy while the Soviets build the strategic power to conquer the world.

Peking Summit	The meeting in Peking between President Nixon, Dr. Kissinger, Mao Tse-tung, and Chou En-lai in February 1972; sometimes referred to as "the week that changed the world."
phased-array radars	Radars in which the beam is steered electronically, which enables handling many targets at once.
pin-down	A technique designed to prevent the launch of silo-based ICBMs by a continuing barrage of nuclear warhead explosions over the area.
Ploughshare	A program for development of peaceful uses of nuclear explosions; name taken by AEC from "beating swords into ploughshares."
Pluto	A U.S. low-altitude supersonic nuclear-propelled missile called "the most powerful weapon conceived by man"; cancelled by McNamara.
Polaris A1	U.S. SLBM; first generation submarine-launched missile; range about 1,200 nm; single-warhead yield 500 to 700 kilotons; carried by the Polaris submarine.
Polaris A2	U.S. SLBM; technical designation UGM-27B; range 1,750 nm; single-warhead yield 800 kilotons.
Polaris A3	U.S. SLBM; technical designation UGM-27C; range 2,880 nm; yield, single warhead 1 MT or three MRVs of 200 kilotons each.
pop-up	Description of the "cold launch" technique for a ballistic missile in which power external to the missile "pops" the missile up out of the launcher silo or tube before ignition of the missile's rocket engines; this technique has permitted the Soviets to multiply the throw-weight of their ICBMs by a factor of up to five.
Poseidon	The latest operational U.S. missile-launching submarine and the SLBM it launches; technical designation UGM-73A; range 2,880 nm; yield ten 50-kiloton MIRVs to each missile.
Posture Report	A report outlining the dimensions of Soviet strategic and conventional forces and U.S. capabilities in weapons systems and personnel to counter the threat; usually an annual report presented to Congress by the JCS Chairman.
preemption point	Point in time at which the aggressor nation has so far developed a practical first-strike capability that it can credibly threaten a strike to preempt the defender nation's attempt to build additional strategic power.
preemptive attack	A first-strike targeted to destroy enemy weapons, military facilities, cities, or industry, in anticipation of and to prevent an enemy strike believed to be imminent.
preventive attack	Same as preemptive attack, but delivered before an enemy strike is considered imminent in order to

psi	Pounds per square inch; a measure of overpressure caused by nuclear explosions; ICBM silos are usually assumed to be hardened to withstand 300 psi over-pressure without damage.
Pugwash	The name of the series of international scientific conferences that started in Pugwash, Nova Scotia; fully described in Chapter 9.
R&D	Research and Development: the scientific research on and technological development of advanced systems, usually weapons systems.
RAND	A research organization or "think-tank" originally sponsored by the U.S. Air Force; the name is a composite of R and D, meaning Research and Development.
RV	Reentry Vehicles; usually means multiple warheads launched from a single missile such as MRVs, MIRVs, and MaRVs.
reentry shields	The shielding of a warhead or any other object which must reenter the earth's atmosphere from outer space; necessary to keep it from burning up.
Regulus II	A submarine-launched cruise missile developed by the U.S. Navy in the late 1950s, but killed because of lack of funding.
reload capability	ICBMs, SLBMs and ABMs are launched from launcher tubes; if, after launching one missile, the launcher tube can be reloaded with another, it has reload capability.
reprogramming	Giving the missile's computer a new and different set of directions as to what target to hit.
retrofitting	The process of adapting an existing system to take and employ new components; e.g., Polaris submarines carrying A-2 missiles were adapted to take A-3 missiles; the A-3s were retrofitted.
SA-2	Soviet surface-to-air missile; NATO code name, Guideline; slant range 25 miles; effective at altitude of 1,000 to 80,000 feet.
SA-4	Soviet surface-to-air missile; twin-mounted on tracked carrier; long-range, air-transportable; solid-fuel booster with ram-jet sustainers; NATO code name, Ganef.
SA-5	Soviet two-stage-boosted antiaircraft missile; slant range 50+ miles; capability against air-to-surface missiles and possibly against ABMs; NATO code name, Griffon.
SA-6	Soviet surface-to-air missile; NATO code name, Gainful; triple-mounted on tracked vehicle; low-level missile.

The opening line above the glossary continues: "forestall an enemy buildup for a future war considered to be inevitable or highly probable."

SA-7	Soviet surface-to-air ABM interceptor missile; range 200+ miles; nuclear warheads in the megaton range; perimeter acquisition by phased-array Henhouse radars; target acquisition by phased-array Doghouse; 64 deployed around Moscow; NATO code name, Galosh.
SAC	U.S. Strategic Air Command; commands all U.S. ICBMs as well as bombers.
SALT	Strategic Arms Limitation Talks between the U.S. and the U.S.S.R.; sometimes written SAL Talks to avoid redundancy; SALT I talks extended from 1969 through May 1972; SALT II talks began after May 1972.
SALT I agreements	Consist of the SALT I Treaty, Interim Agreement, and Protocol; signed at Moscow, May 26, 1972; also referred to as the SALT I pacts or SALT I accords.
SALT I Interim Agreement	A five-year agreement between the U.S. and the U.S.S.R. which limits construction of some types of offensive missile launchers; includes the Protocol which limits the number of SLBM launchers on modern missile-launching submarines; also referred to as the SALT I Agreement.
SALT I Treaty	A treaty "of unlimited duration" between the U.S. and U.S.S.R. limiting deployment of ABMs and ABM radars; also referred to as the SALT I ABM Treaty, and as the SALT I Anti-Defense Treaty (because its function is to limit defense); amended by a Protocol signed at Moscow, July 3, 1974.
SAM	Surface-to-air missile; a missile fired from the ground against a target in the air.
SECDEF	The U.S. Secretary of Defense.
SLBM	Submarine-Launched Ballistic Missile; follows a ballistic trajectory.
SLCM	Submarine-Launched Cruise Missile: a submarine-launched air-breathing flying missile that cannot leave the atmosphere and does not follow a ballistic path, but is guided.
SLICBM	Submarine-Launched Inter-Continental Ballistic Missile, such as the Soviet SS-N-8, with a range in excess of 4,000 nm (U.S. Polaris and Poseidon SLBMs have a range of 2,880, which is more than 1,000 miles short of ICBM range).
SRAM	Short-Range Attack Missile; air-to-surface; carried by B-52 bombers and possibly by FB-111s.
SS-4	Soviet MRBM; range 1,200 miles; yield 1 MT; number deployed 500.
SS-5	Soviet IRBM; range 2,300 miles; yield 1 MT; number deployed 100+.
SS-6	The first Soviet and the world's first ICBM; tested in August 1957; same booster and launcher used for

	the first satellite, *Sputnik;* now obsolete and probably no longer in inventory.
SS-7	Soviet ICBM "Saddler"; range 6,900 nm; yield 5 MT; number deployed, together with SS-8s, 209.
SS-8	Soviet ICBM "Sasin"; range 6,900 nm; yield 5 MT.
SS-9	Soviet heavy ICBM "Scarp"; range 7,500 nm; yield, single warhead 25MT or three MRVs of 5MT each; 313 deployed, beginning in 1964; also used for FOBS launchers.
SS-11	Soviet ICBM; range 6,500 nm; yield 2 to 5 MT; about 1,000 deployed.
SS-13	Soviet ICBM "Savage"; solid-fuel; range 5,000 nm; yield 1 to 2 MT; 60 deployed.
SS-16	Soviet ICBM; solid-fuel with dual capability as fixed-base or land-mobile; range estimated 6,000+ nm; yield estimated 5+ MT.
SS-17	New Soviet ICBM; range estimated 7,000+ nm; yield, single warhead 15+ MT or five MIRVs of 1-2 MT each; a replacement (along with the SS-19) for the SS-11 series.
SS-18	New Soviet super-ICBM; range 7,500 nm; yield, single warhead estimated 33 to 50 megatons, or up to ten MIRVs of 2+ MT each.
SS-19	Late-model Soviet ICBM with five times the throw-weight of the early SS-11; yield, up to six MIRVs of up to 2 MT each.
SS-N-8	Newest Soviet SLBM; world's first ICBM/SLBM of intercontinental range; range, 4,200 nm by official estimates, 5,000+ nm by unofficial estimates; has inertial guidance and on-board digital computer.
SSX-17	Same as SS-17 (see above); X designates it as an experimental model.
SSX-18	Same as SS-18 (see above); X designates it as an experimental model.
Saturn V	U.S. largest space-program rocket; used to launch the Apollo spacecraft for lunar landings and return.
Scamp	NATO designation for a Soviet intermediate-range ballistic missile.
Scrooge	Soviet land-mobile missile, believed to be IRBM, but an added rocket stage could give it ICBM capability; tracked vehicle, self-propelled.
shield-weight	The weight added to a reentry vehicle by the shielding required to prevent its burning up when reentering the earth's atmosphere.
Six Day War	The Arab-Israeli War of June 1967 in which Israel astonished the world by defeating the Arab nations in six days; the conquest expanded Israeli-controlled territory by 200 percent.
Skybolt	A revolutionary U.S.-developed long-range air-to-

surface missile with inertial guidance; it passed all its tests but was killed by McNamara.

Spartan	The U.S. anti-missile which can intercept an incoming enemy missile before it reenters the earth's atmosphere; yield 5 MT.
Sprint	The U.S. anti-missile which can intercept an incoming enemy missile after it reenters the earth's atmosphere.
stellar-assisted guidance	A mechanism to conduct in-flight star tracking, and adjust powered flight accordingly, in order to reduce the slight errors in the inertial guidance of ballistic missiles.
strategic	Planned, designed, or trained to strike an enemy at the sources of his military, economic, and political power.
strategic doctrine	The basic, central doctrines of a nation's grand strategy; theories for effective application of a nation's total power to win against enemies.
strategic surrender	Permitting an enemy to attain a practical first-strike capability. This permits the enemy to deliver at any time an ultimatum (backed up by a credible threat of a nuclear attack) demanding total military and political surrender, and also permits the enemy to preempt any attempt by the defender nation to rebuild its strategic forces.
strategic weapons	Nuclear weapons designed to conduct a central war against a nation's war-making capabilities rather than to win battles; distinguished from "tactical" nuclear weapons which are classified as "battlefield" weapons; strategic weapons are generally longer range (more than 500 miles), and generally 1 MT or more.
superiority	Strategic nuclear superiority is the possession by one nation of an overall advantage in nuclear weaponry, ranging from substantial to decisive, measured in deliverable megatonnage, numbers of launchers, throw-weight, target-killing warheads, and counterforce capability.
T-62 tank	Soviet medium battle tank; in inventory by the thousands; more elaborately equipped than U.S. tanks; most have amphibious crossing capability for rivers and streams and carry infra-red night-fighting equipment.
TAC	U.S. Tactical Air Command.
TFX	Tactical-Fighter-Experimental aircraft; operational designations, F-111 for Air Force version; F-111B for Navy version (cancelled as a total failure); FB-111 for fighter-bomber version.
TTB	See Moscow Threshold Test Ban Treaty.
TU-16 Badger	Soviet strategic bomber; range 4,000 miles; mach 0.8; weapons load 20,000 pounds.

TU-22 Blinder	Soviet medium bomber; range 1,400; mach 1.5; weapons load 12,000 pounds.
TU-95 Bear	Soviet strategic heavy long-range bomber; range 7,800 miles; mach 0.78; weapons load 40,000 pounds.
tactical weapons	Nuclear weapons designed for battlefield employment; usually short-range (less than 500 miles); yield usually less than 1 MT (although the Soviets have a nuclear weapon they classify as "tactical" that has a yield of 1+ MT; NATO designation "Scaleboard").
Tallinn line	Soviet defensive system of surface-to-air missiles; stretches from Tallinn, Estonia, across the U.S.S.R.; its 10,000 SAM launchers probably have substantial ABM capability, even though some elements of U.S. intelligence rate them as having only anti-aircraft capability.
30-meter miss	The hypothesized ultimate in accuracy of guidance of an ICBM: a CEP of 30 meters; that is, half the warheads would impact within a circle around the target, the circle having a radius of 30 meters, or roughly 100 feet; considered possible with the expected technology of the next six to eight years and an expenditure of $30 billion.
Thor	U.S. MRBM deployed in Turkey and Italy, but scrapped as part of the "secret addendum" to the deal with the Kremlin for withdrawal of its missiles from Cuba in 1962.
throw-weight	The weight of a missile's reentry vehicle with its warhead package; the weight of the booster stage of the missile is not included in the throw-weight (as it is in the payload).
Titan I	A first-generation U.S. liquid-fueled ICBM; scrapped in the prime of life by McNamara.
Titan II	Second-generation U.S. liquid-fueled ICBM; by far the most powerful U.S. ICBM; rated at 5 to 10 MT; we have 54 deployed.
Triad	The U.S. combination of three types of strategic offensive nuclear weapons systems: (1) land-based Minuteman and Titan ICBMs; (2) land-based strategic bombers; and (3) Polaris and Poseidon missile-launching submarines.
Trident I	The SLBM to be carried by the Trident submarine; proposed to be deployed beginning in 1979; range 4,000 nm.
Trident II	An improved proposed model of the SLBM to be carried by the Trident submarine; a claimed range of 6,000 nm; hoped for in the 1980s.
U-2	A U.S. extremely-high-altitude, quiet reconnaissance aircraft designed to overfly enemy countries without detection.

UN Outer Space Treaty	A treaty banning the orbiting in space of weapons of mass destruction, to which the U.S. and U.S.S.R. are signatory; sponsored by the United Nations.
unilateral-disarmament intellectuals	The pseudointellectuals who would rather be Red than risk being dead, and who purport to believe that it is safer to be weak than strong; they often style themselves as "defense intellectuals," but are actually against defense and for unilateral disarmament; also called unilateral disarmers or unilateralists.
verification	Inspection techniques and procedures to ascertain whether the terms of a treaty are being complied with, especially the SALT I Agreements.
Vulcan II	A British strategic medium bomber; six squadrons deployed.
warhead	The explosive charge, nuclear or conventional, with its detonating mechanism; delivered by a missile or other delivery system.
win/strike-first	Possession of sufficient strategic nuclear weapons to "win" a nuclear conflict against an enemy by destroying its war-making capability.
win/strike-second	Possession of sufficient survivable nuclear weapons to "win" a conflict after the enemy strikes first.
XM-1	A proposed new U.S. main battle tank to replace the former proposed M-70; now under prototype development.
Y-class submarine	Soviet first-generation modern missile-launching nuclear-propelled submarine; copied after the U.S. Polaris from plans stolen by Soviet spies.
yield/weight ratio	The formula for computing the efficiency of a nuclear explosive technique: the total yield (expressed in kilotons or megatons) over explosive material weight.
Yom Kippur War	The October 1973 War initiated by Arab surprise attack against Israel on Jewish religious holiday of that name.

Index

750; Kissinger's deals with, 611; and October '73 strategic alert, 640-41, 642, 643

Donovan, Hedley, 148

Donovan, William J. ("Wild Bill"), 125

Douglas, William O., 180

Dow Jones industrials index, 746

Drummond, Roscoe, 148

Drury, Allen, 259

Dulles, Allen W., 147, 248; *The Craft of Intelligence,* 464-65

Dulles, John Foster, 20, 149, 248

Durbrow, Elbridge, 658

Eaton, Cyrus, 174, 177; importance of, to Pugwash movement, 187

Ehrlichman, John D., 217, 218, 221, 222, 268, 269, 749

Eisenhower, Dwight D., 20, 27-28, 248, 249; defense policy of, 684; and Pugwash movement, 187; and U-2 incident, 460-70

Eisenhower, John S. D., 131

elitism, 232, 249; and CFR, 259; Kissinger's relation to, 134-52; and U-2 incident, 463

Elliot, William Yandell, 135

Ellsberg, Daniel, 146, 158, 160-61, 162, 164, 166, 235, 548; naive belief of, about *Pentagon Papers,* 159, 163; role of, in Kissinger strategy, 547-48

Emelyanov, Vasily S., 177

enemies, definition of: need for, 488-90; proposed act regarding, 490

"essential equivalence," 595, 598, 600

European Security Conference, 1973, 33, 447, 448, 450

exotics, 393-401; banned by SALT I ABM Treaty, 393

Export-Import Bank, U.S., 731-32

Extended-Delta submarine, 357, 590, 732

fallout-shelter program: failure of, 99

FBI: and Lee Harvey Oswald case, 543, 544, 545

FB-111, 589, 598, 676, 677

Feld, B. T., 188

Felt, H. D., 658

Finlandization, 169, 447-48, 615

first-strike, 168, 176, 298, 491-97, 582, 692; primary targeting of, 108; Soviet capability for, 124, 130, 143, 154, 170, 211, 213, 281, 288, 299, 300-301

Fisher, Adrian S., 276

Fitzgerald, Frances, 264, 269, 270

Fluke, John M., 654

FOBS. *See* Fractional Orbital Bombardment System

Ford Foundation, 285

Ford, Gerald, 644, 743-58, 762, 764, 771

Ford-Rockefeller Administration, 757

Foreign Affairs, 114, 137, 151, 621; 50th anniversary of, 144; revolutionary influence of, 136; on Soviet invasion of Czechoslovakia, 152

Foreign Relations Committee, Senate, 37, 251

Fortas, Abe, 180

Fortune, 282

40 Committee, 238, 242

Forward Strategy for America, A (Strausz-Hupe; Kintner; Possony), 25, 607-8, 697

Foster, John S., 277, 408, 411, 665; on Soviet MIRV capability, 426, 427

Founding Fathers, 259, 635

Fowler, Henry H., 757

Foxbat (MIG-25), 677

Fractional Orbital Bombardment System (FOBS), 359, 398, 419-20, 704

Frank, Jerome D., 188, 191

Frankfurter, Felix, 18

free ride, 111, 115, 124, 213, 255, 558; ensured by SALT Agreements, 281, 368, 373

Free World, 151, 301; inflation in, 604-18

Friedheim, Jerry W., 427

Frisch, David, 185

Fulbright, J. William, 36, 163, 250, 305, 373, 379, 695, 757, 773

MAD. See Mutual Assured Destruction

Maginnes, Nancy, 127

Magruder (Jeb), 221

Maksimov, Vladimir Y., 501

manpower comparison, 199-201

Mansfield, Mike, 566

Mao Tse-tung, 34, 45

Marchetti, Victor, 180

massive retaliation, 515; John Foster Dulles' doctrine of, 91

Mathias, Charles, 566

MBTs. See tanks, main battle

media, 11, 156-57, 208, 538; CFR influence on, 147-48; foreign, and Kissinger, 611-13; reaction of, to defense crisis, 656

medium-range ballistic missiles. See MRBMs

megalomania, 13, 292, 645-46

Members of Congress for Peace Through Law, 492, 526, 589, 720

Meselson, Mathew, 188

Metternich, Prince, 137, 261, 368

Meyers, Gilbert I., 465

MI. See Mission Impossible

Middle Americans, 163, 268; suckered by Kissinger, 101-2

Military Balance: 1973-1974, The (International Institute for Strategic Studies), 510-11

military spending: Soviet, 725-33

Milton, John, 290

minimum deterrence, 445

Minuteman, 17, 103-4, 286, 309, 599, 666, 669-71; compared, 667, 679; scrapped, 512, 514-18, 521-22. See also Minuteman III

Minuteman III, 104, 425, 508-9, 510-11, 514, 667, 675-76, 683, 702-4

MIRVs, 110, 314-15, 387-88, 408-9, 424-29, 591-93, 599-600, 767; numbers game regarding, 101-3, 429; and SALT II, 711-15; Soviet testing of, 426-27; technology, 102, 408

"missile gap," 14, 18-19, 228-29

Mission Impossible (MI), 214-18, 222, 228

Mitchell, John, 13

mobile missiles, 355-56

MOBs. See Multiple Orbital Bombardment System

Monroe Doctrine, 473

Moorer, Thomas H., 304, 580, 581, 602

Moscow Summit, 1972, 26, 27, 32, 123, 155, 346, 500

Moscow Summit, 1974, 735, 755, 758-73

Moscow Summit Protocol, 1974, 385, 428

Moscow Test Ban Treaty, 1963, 51, 107, 307, 409, 649

Moscow Threshold Test Ban Treaty. See Threshold Test Ban Treaty

Mowrer, Edgar Ansel, 546-47

Moyers, Bill, 148, 498-99

MRBMs, 417-18

MRVs, 427, 767; legalization of, 387-88

multicentrism, 151, 152

multiple independently targeted re-entry vehicles. See MIRVs

Multiple Orbital Bombardment System (MOBS), 359, 398, 419-20, 704

multiple reentry vehicles. See MRVs

Murphy, Charles, 282

Mutual and Balanced Force Reductions, Conference on, 447, 448

Mutual Assured Destruction (MAD), 255-56, 300-301, 693; danger of, 374-76; doctrinal basis of, 678; undermined by James Schlesinger, 558-60

National Command Authority, 309

National Command Center. See National Command Authority

National Review, 611, 756; "Bitter SALT," 718-19; on Schlesinger strategy, 567-68, 569

National Security Council, 60, 66, 126, 185, 223, 237, 238; Kissinger's use of, 252-54; and October '73 strategic alert, 631, 632, 635-36

National Security Decision Memorandum (NSDM), 242, 243, 251

National Security Study Memorandum (NSSM), 251-52, 254

National Suicide: Military Aid to the Soviet Union (Sutton), 457

NATO, 199, 200; reaction of, to 1972 Joint Declaration of Principles, 448-51; response of, to Soviet invasion of Czechoslovakia, 152; sabotaged by Kissinger, 124, 344-47, 448-51, 611-16; weakened by McNamara, 342-44

Necessity for Choice, The (Kissinger), 21, 33-34, 134, 361, 362, 689, 698, 780

Nedzi, Lucien N., 36-37

Net Assessment Group, 237, 238, 551

New Republic, The, 320

new world order, 291-92

New York Post, 778-80

New York Times, 346, 541, 565; on October '73 strategic alert, 631-32, 633, 644; and The Pentagon Papers, 160

New York Times Magazine, 56

Newhouse, John, 110, 245, 315-21, 400, 525, 724-25; Cold Dawn: The Story of SALT, 110, 314, 322-41, 735; Kissinger's "debt" to, 336-37

Newsweek, 230, 232, 234-35, 243, 346, 566-67, 750, 774; on Helmut Sonnenfeldt, 540-41

Niemeyer, Gerhart, 25

Nitze, Paul Hilken, 57, 132, 133, 146, 147, 160, 161, 164, 259, 271, 285, 741; Kissinger's plan for, 603, 618-19; nuclear paralysis of, 272; surprise moves of, 752-58; and unilateral disarmament, 609, 620-24

Nixon Administration, 130, 157; and communism, 267; Kissinger takeover in, 334-36

Nixon Doctrine, 90, 91, 92

Nixon, Richard M., 14, 16, 39, 250, 251, 252-53; artificial world of, 218-22; on fertilizer loan, 732; on foreign policy, 141; handled by Kissinger, 261, 507; Kissinger's assessment of, 139; Kissinger's influence on, 22-23, 40, 169, 211-14; and October '73 strategic alert, 627-44; "The Real Road to Peace," 365, 370, 506; Red China visit of, 474; on strategic balance,

506; and Vietnam War, 153-58; and Watergate, 125

North Atlantic Treaty Organization. See NATO

NSDM. See National Security Decision Memorandum

NSSM. See National Security Study Memorandum

nuclear blackmail, 90, 95, 204, 207, 227, 291, 515, 688-89

nuclear deterrence, 99, 207; Churchill on, 296-97, 301; U.S. strategic, 97, 98, 204, 281. See also strategic deterrence

nuclear umbrella, 90, 113, 448; effectiveness of, 583-84

Nuclear Weapons and Foreign Policy (Kissinger), 21, 137, 138, 139, 149

October War. See Yom Kippur War

O'Donnell, Kenneth, 266

Office of Strategic Services (OSS), 125, 181, 236

Ogarkov, Nikolai, 283, 340-41

oil weapon, 12, 96

On the Beach (Shute), 109

On Thermonuclear War (Kahn), 47, 607, 738

one-world government, 129, 136; and Wall Street international bankers, 139

Opinion Research Corporation, 772-73

Oppenheimer, J. Robert, 150

"Order of Lenin," 491

Organization for Economic Cooperation, 605

Osborne, John, 764

Oswald, Lee Harvey, 542-43

Otepka, Otto, 542

"overkill," 190, 295, 567

Over-the-Horizon radar, 683, 686, 694, 701

Ozerov, Sergei, 730, 731

Paris Summit, 1960: torpedoed by Khrushchev, 460, 461, 462

parity, 162, 169, 191, 271, 614

passive defenses, 99, 100, 103; lack of,

Rockefeller, Nelson A., 21, 127, 149, 749; opposed by conservatives, 266; relationship of, to Kissinger, 139, 212

Rogers, William P., 250, 273, 449, 749; confused by Kissinger, 326; letter of, on SALT pacts, 413-14, 415

Roman Empire, 608

Romney, George, 265

Roosevelt, Franklin, 163, 220, 233, 486

Rope Dancer, The (Marchetti), 180

Rosin, Axel G., 148

Rostow, Eugene V., 161, 757

Rostow, Walt W., 144, 161, 179, 182, 217

Ruina, J. P., 184, 185

Rusk, Dean, 161, 162, 164, 167, 320

Russell, Bertrand, 173

Russell, Richard, 316

SAC. See Strategic Air Command

Safeguard (ABM system), 35, 38, 262, 277

Sakharov, Andrei, 499, 656, 730-31

SALT I ABM Treaty, 31, 36, 114, 255, 348, 372-91, 799-803; analysis of, 378-91; appraised by Brennan, 377; official interpretation of, 393

SALT I ABM Treaty Protocol, 1974, 768-69

SALT I Agreed Interpretations, 392, 396, 397, 400, 412, 415, 420, 435, 437, 734, 807-10

Salt I Agreements, 12, 25, 26, 29, 31, 36, 98, 107, 192-93, 226-27, 799-806; importance of, 348; inequities of, 349-71, 437-40. See also SALT I ABM Treaty; SALT I Interim Agreement; SALT I negotiations

SALT I Common Understandings, 411, 412-13, 415, 420, 734

SALT I Interim Agreement, 31, 144, 348, 358, 597, 804-5; examination of, 404-21; limitations of, 354, 355; loopholes in, 410-21, 480; and 1974 Moscow Summit, 760-73; U.S. capitulation in, 442

SALT I Interim Agreement Protocol, 358, 806

SALT I negotiations, 319-21, 349, 733-42; hoax of, 282-310; and inflation, 605-10; start of, 311-21

SALT I pacts. See SALT I Agreements

SALT I Unilateral Statements, 392, 415, 416, 420, 434-35, 734-35, 811-13

SALT II negotiations, 466, 544, 545, 568, 569, 709-33; sell-out in, 709-15

Salzburg outburst, 773, 774-75, 783-84

SAMs, 275-76, 382-84, 385; launchers for, 54, 672, 732

satellite photography, 231-32, 463-66, 468-70

satellite surveillance, 223, 280, 465-66, 685-90, 701; technology advances in, 682-83

Saturday Review, 180

Schelling, Thomas C., 109, 689

Schlesinger, Arthur, Jr., 136

Schlesinger, James R., 81, 141, 147, 236, 298, 547-603, 673, 714, 715, 716-18; accomplishments of, as CIA director, 555; admission of, 286, 303; background of, 548-49; downgrades strategic weapons, 581-602; Ellsberg protege, 235, 246, 547; and "feud" with Kissinger, 763-65; July 3, 1974, press conference of, 769-71; Kissinger's most significant appointment, 547; misrepresentations of, 425-26, 427, 428; "new" strategy of, 562-65, 566-78, 696-97; and 1974 Moscow Summit, 764-65; overhauls CIA, 553-58; "Quantitative Analysis and National Security," 548; reorganizes AEC, 551-53; role of, in October '73 strategic alert, 631, 633, 636, 637; as Secretary of Defense, 558-603; slowdown of Trident by, 589-90, 595; surrender signals of, 737-42; undermines MAD, 558-60

Schmidt, Helmut, 445, 606

Schneider, William, 383, 399

844